ŚRĪLA PRABHUPĀDA LĪLĀMṚTA

ŚRĪLA PRABHUPĀDA LĪLĀMṚTA

VOLUME ONE

A Biography of

His Divine Grace
A. C. Bhaktivedanta Swami Prabhupāda
Founder-*Ācārya* of the International Society for Krishna Consciousness

Second and enlarged edition

SATSVARŪPA DĀSA GOSWAMI

THE BHAKTIVEDANTA BOOK TRUST

Readers interested in the subject matter of this book are invited to correspond with the publisher at one of the following addresses:

The Bhaktivedanta Book Trust
P.O. Box 34074
Los Angeles, CA 90034
USA
Phone: +1-800-927-4152
Fax: +1-310-837-1056
E-mail: bbt.usa@krishna.com

The Bhaktivedanta Book Trust
Korsnäs Gård
14792 Grödinge
Sweden
Phone: +46-8-53029800
Fax: +46-8-53025062
E-mail: bbt.se@krishna.com

The Bhaktivedanta Book Trust
P.O. Box 262
Botany, NSW 2019
Australia
Phone: +61-2-96666466
Fax: +61-2-96663060
E-mail: bbt.au@krishna.com

The Bhaktivedanta Book Trust
Hare Krishna Land, Juhu
Mumbai 400 049
India
Phone: +91-22-6206860
Fax: +91-22-6205214
E-mail: bbt.in@krishna.com

www.krishna.com

Set in Times, Birch and Trajan

ISBN 0-89213-355-4 (*volume 1*)
ISBN 0-89213-356-2 (*volume 2*)
ISBN 0-89213-357-0 (*set, two volumes*)

Printed in Germany

Contents

Preface

After the disappearance of His Divine Grace A. C. Bhaktivedanta Swami Prabhupāda from this mortal world on November 14, 1977, many of his disciples saw a need for an authorized biography of Śrīla Prabhupāda. The responsibility of commissioning such a work rested with the Governing Body Commission of the International Society for Krishna Consciousness. At their annual meeting in 1978, the GBC resolved that a biography of Śrīla Prabhupāda should be written and that I would be the author.

According to the Vaiṣṇava tradition, if one aspires to write transcendental literature, he must first take permission from his spiritual master and Kṛṣṇa. A good example of this is Kṛṣṇadāsa Kavirāja Gosvāmī, the author of Lord Caitanya Mahāprabhu's authorized biography, *Śrī Caitanya-caritāmṛta.* As Kṛṣṇadāsa Kavirāja has explained:

> In Vṛndāvana there were also many other great devotees, all of whom desired to hear the last pastimes of Lord Caitanya.
>
> By their mercy, all these devotees ordered me to write of the last pastimes of Śrī Caitanya Mahāprabhu. Because of their order only, although I am shameless, I have attempted to write this *Caitanya-caritāmṛta.*
>
> Having received the order of the Vaiṣṇavas, but being anxious within my heart, I went back to the temple of Madana-mohana in Vṛndāvana to ask His permission also.

So to say the *Śrīla Prabhupāda-līlāmṛta* is an authorized biography does not mean that it is a flattering portrait commissioned by an official body, but that it is an authorized literature presented by one who is serving the order of Kṛṣṇa and *guru* through the disciplic succession. As such, *Śrīla Prabhupāda-līlāmṛta* is not written from the mundane or speculative viewpoint, nor can ordinary biographers comprehend the significance and meaning of the life of a pure devotee of God. Were such persons to objectively study the life of Śrīla Prabhupāda, the esoteric meanings would evade them. Were they to charitably try to praise Śrīla Prabhupāda, they would not know how. But because *Śrīla Prabhupāda-līlāmṛta* is authorized through the transcendental process, it can transparently present the careful reader with a true picture of Śrīla Prabhupāda.

Another important aspect of the authenticity of *Śrīla Prabhupāda-līlāmṛta* is the vast amount of carefully researched information that I am able to focus into each volume. The leading devotees of the Kṛṣṇa consciousness movement, in addition to giving me permission to render this work, have also invited the world community of ISKCON devotees to help me in gathering detailed information about the life and person of Śrīla Prabhupāda. The Bhaktivedanta Book Trust, Prabhupāda's publishing house, has given me his collection of letters, totaling over seven thousand; and scores of Prabhupāda's disciples have granted interviews and submitted diaries and memoirs of their association with Śrīla Prabhupāda. Aside from his disciples, we have interviewed many persons in various walks of life who met Śrīla Prabhupāda over the years. The result is that we have a rich, composite view of Śrīla Prabhupāda, drawn from many persons who knew him in many different situations and stages of his life. The Acknowledgments section in this book lists the persons who cooperated to bring about *Śrīla Prabhupāda-līlāmṛta*.

Despite the authorized nature of this book and despite the support of my many well-wishers, I must confess that in attempting to describe the glories of our spiritual master, His Divine Grace A. C. Bhaktivedanta Swami Prabhupāda, I am like a small bird trying to empty the ocean by carrying drops of water to the land. The picture I have given of Śrīla Prabhupāda is only a glimpse into his unlimited mercy, and that glimpse has only been possible by the grace of *guru* and Kṛṣṇa.

Satsvarūpa dāsa Goswami

Acknowledgments

I would like to acknowledge the many persons who cooperated to make this biography of Śrīla Prabhupāda possible. Notable among them are:

Ācārya-devī dāsī
Agrāhya dāsa
Arundhatī-devī dāsī
Aṣṭa-sakhī-devī dāsī
Baladeva Vidyābhūṣaṇa dāsa
Balāi-devī dāsī
Baradrāja dāsa
Bhakti-caru Swami
Bhakti-mārga-devī dāsī
Bimala-devī dāsī
Brahma-sampradāya-devī dāsī
Bṛhad-mṛdaṅga dāsa
Dāsyarasa-devī dāsī
Dhṛṣṭaketu dāsa
Dhṛti-devī dāsī
Dīrgha-devī dāsī
Duḥkhahantrī-devī dāsī
Ekanātha dāsa
Gaura-pūrṇimā dāsa
Gopīparāṇadhana dāsa
Jadurāṇī-devī dāsī
Jagadīśvarī-devī dāsī
Jagat-kāraṇa-devī dāsī
Jayādvaita Swami
Jayapatāka Swami
Jita-śakti-devī dāsī
Kīrtana-rasa dāsa
Kṣamā-devī dāsī
Kṛṣṇa Gopāla dāsa
Kṛṣṇa-sneha dāsa
Kuṇḍalī dāsa
Kuśakratha dāsa
Mamatā-devī dāsī
Maṇḍaleśvara dāsa
Mukunda Goswami
Nāgarāja dāsa

Nārada-ṛṣi dāsa
Nārāyaṇī-devī dāsī
Nitya-tṛptā-devī dāsī
Parama-rūpa dāsa
Parīkṣit dāsa
Patita-pāvana dāsa
Prāṇadā-devī dāsī
Pūrṇacandra-devī dāsī
Rādhāvallabha dāsa
Rājendranātha dāsa
Rāmadāsa Abhirāma dāsa
Rāmeśvara dāsa
Ṛkṣarāja dāsa
Rukmiṇī-devī dāsī
Sādhana-siddhi dāsa
Santoṣa dāsa
Sarvabhāvana dāsa
Śeṣa dāsa
Siṁheśvara dāsa
Sītā-devī dāsī
Śrīkānta dāsa
Subhadrā-devī dāsī
Sureśvara dāsa
Tejās dāsa
Vidyānanda dāsa
Viśākhā-devī dāsī
Yadubara dāsa
Yamarāja dāsa

Introduction

From childhood, Śrīla Prabhupāda worshiped Lord Kṛṣṇa, understanding Him to be the Supreme Personality of Godhead, the source of all existence. And beginning at age twenty-two, after his first meeting with his spiritual master, Śrīla Bhaktisiddhānta Sarasvatī Ṭhākura, Śrīla Prabhupāda became more and more active in spreading the teachings of Lord Kṛṣṇa.

In *Śrīla Prabhupāda-līlāmṛta Volume 1,* we see Śrīla Prabhupāda struggling alone to publish *Back to Godhead* magazine, personally typing, editing, visiting the printer, and then distributing the copies on the streets of New Delhi. Working alone in Jhansi, India, Prabhupāda gathered a few part-time followers to create the League of Devotees, an early attempt to enact his vision of introducing people from all nations, races, and levels of society to Kṛṣṇa, the Supreme Personality of Godhead.

Śrīla Prabhupāda was still alone as he arrived in America in 1965. But he was filled with faith in Kṛṣṇa and determination to establish Kṛṣṇa consciousness in the West and thus fulfill the desire of his spiritual master and the prediction of the scriptures and previous saints. Young men and women on New York's Lower East Side joined, attracted not so much to Vedic culture as to "Swamiji" and his chanting of Hare Kṛṣṇa. Thus, beginning from a small storefront, Śrīla Prabhupāda introduced the Hare Kṛṣṇa movement to America.

We follow Śrīla Prabhupāda to San Francisco's Haight-Ashbury during the hippie heyday of 1967, as he establishes his Kṛṣṇa consciousness movement there, just as he had done in New York City. Then in May of '67 he appeared to suffer a heart attack and retired to India to recuperate. It became even clearer that the Kṛṣṇa consciousness movement—its life and its growth—depended entirely upon him. Although a few dozen sincere workers were dedicated to his service, they felt helpless and incompetent to do any missionary work—or even to maintain their own spiritual vows to abstain from illicit sex, meat-eating, intoxication, and gambling—unless he were personally present to lead them. In December 1967 Śrīla Prabhupāda returned to America and his young spiritual family.

As Śrīla Prabhupāda would comment several years later, his movement didn't really begin until this return to America in December 1967. His time was limited, he knew—the heart attack had proven that. Now, in whatever time was left, he had to accomplish his mission. And as his International Society for Krishna Consciousness began to grow, it gradually spread beyond its simple and sometimes humorous beginnings to become a spiritual institution considered noteworthy even among world religions.

In the present volume we follow Śrīla Prabhupāda through the years of his greatest active participation in ISKCON, the International Society for Krishna Consciousness, as its sole leader. In 1968 Śrīla Prabhupāda has approximately fifty disciples and six ISKCON centers. Although his followers have increased their numbers, most of them are no more than sincere neophytes. Prabhupāda is personally available to each of his disciples, and he continues to manage and maintain each ISKCON center. Then in July of 1970 Śrīla Prabhupāda forms his Governing Body Commission and begins to turn over ISKCON's management to his board of G.B.C. secretaries. Yet we find Prabhupāda still actively guiding the activities of his society, expanded by 1971 to six hundred disciples and sixty-five centers.

Although the teachings of Kṛṣṇa consciousness have existed since time immemorial within India's Sanskrit Vedic literatures and are the origin and essence of all religious expression, until Śrīla Prabhupāda began his preaching, Kṛṣṇa consciousness in its original purity had never been widely spread. In the most popular and basic Vedic text, *Bhagavad-gītā,* Lord Kṛṣṇa teaches that He is the Supreme Personality of Godhead and that real religion, real knowledge, and real endeavor can be understood only when one dedicates his life to the loving service of the Lord. Only full surrender to the Supreme can bring one freedom from the laws of karma and the cycle of repeated birth and death.

Śrīla Prabhupāda was convinced that devotional service to Lord Kṛṣṇa is life's goal and that to engage others in devotional service is the highest welfare activity. And these convictions drove him in his traveling and preaching on behalf of his spiritual master and Kṛṣṇa.

Śrīla Prabhupāda's success in spreading Kṛṣṇa consciousness was due to his being directly empowered by the Supreme Personality of Godhead. *Caitanya-caritāmṛta* states, *kali-kālera dharma-kṛṣṇa-nāma-saṅkīrtana/ kṛṣṇa-śakti vinā nahe tāra pravartana:* "The fundamental religious system in the age of Kali is the chanting of the holy name of Kṛṣṇa. Unless empowered by Kṛṣṇa, one cannot propagate the *saṅkīrtana* movement." Yet although Śrīle Prabhupāda was empowered, his life's story is not one in which success comes neatly and automatically, everything being miraculously enacted by God. Rather, Śrīla Prabhupāda's story is one of constant attempts on behalf of his spiritual master. Successes come, but only after great endeavor and faith.

Prabhupāda encountered difficulties in trying to spread love of God in a godless world. He sometimes met opposition from governments, the media, and religionists, including those in India; and even within his own society he met difficulties caused when his neophyte disciples fell to the allurements of the material world. Yet through all difficulties Śrīla Prabhupāda persevered with the sublime tolerance, kindness, and unflinching determination of a pure devotee of Lord Kṛṣṇa.

By material standards it is extraordinary that a person of Śrīla Prabhupāda's age could constantly travel, confront problems and opposition, and simultaneously produce volume after volume of translated Vedic literatures. But material vision cannot comprehend Śrīla Prabhupāda's activities. He was truly a *mahātmā,* as described by Kṛṣṇa in *Bhagavad-gītā:* "The *mahātmās* are always working under the direction of My internal energy." In spreading Kṛṣṇa consciousness, Śrīla Prabhupāda was far from merely a religious zealot trying to increase a sect; his writing, traveling, and preaching were done in pure devotion to Lord Kṛṣṇa and were therefore transcendental. It was Kṛṣṇa Himself, Śrīla Prabhupāda saw, who was bringing the results.

Lord Caitanya's has stated,

pṛthivīte āche yata nagarādi grāma
sarvatra pracāra haibe mora nāma

"In every town and village the chanting of My name will be heard." These words, directly spoken by Lord Caitanya, are certainly true; the Lord's prediction must come to pass. Many Gauḍīya Vaiṣṇavas, however, even as recently as the disciples of Bhaktisiddhānta Sarasvatī, considered the Lord's prediction problematic. The name of Lord Caitanya in every town and village? Should this be taken allegorically? Certainly the Americans, the Europeans, the Africans, the Polynesians, the Mongolians—the uncultured *mlecchas* outside of India—could never become Vaiṣṇavas. Thus Lord Caitanya's words had seemed an enigmatic topic for speculation.

Śrīla Prabhupāda, however, was under orders from his spiritual master, Śrīla Bhaktisiddhānta Sarasvatī, to preach Kṛṣṇa consciousness beyond India. And alone, in 1965, he took the great step and left India, crossed the Atlantic, and began the International Society for Krishna Consciousness in New York City.

Although some of Prabhupāda's Godbrothers had gone to England some thirty years before, they had failed to establish anything and had even concluded that to give Kṛṣṇa consciousness to the Western people was not possible. But Śrīla Prabhupāda, fulfilling Lord Caitanya's prediction, traveled and employed his disciples in traveling, to open centers in New York City, San Francisco, Los Angeles, Boston, Montreal, Buffalo, Seattle. He also sent his disciples abroad, to London and other countries, they succeeded where Prabhupāda's Godbrothers had failed.

As the present volume explains, Śrīla Prabhupāda traveled not only to enlist new devotees and establish Kṛṣṇa consciousness in new places around the world, but also to maintain what he had already begun. Had he not continued to travel to each temple, instructing his disciples, observing their progress, correcting their mistakes, raising the standard of their Kṛṣṇa consciousness, the devotees would not have been able to continue. Repeatedly, Prabhupāda had to go around the world.

Śrīla Prabhupāda, by his faith in Kṛṣṇa, by his selfless dedication to the order of his spiritual master, and by the blessings of Lord Caitanya, did what no one else could have done. As *Caitanya-caritāmṛta* states, *kṛṣṇa-śakti vinā nahe tāra pravartana:* "Only one empowered by Lord Kṛṣṇa can actually spread the chanting of Hare Kṛṣṇa around the world."

This volume is an account of years of struggle and ultimate fulfillment in Śrīla Prabhupāda's life, and I invite the reader to relish them. Here is the "rags to riches" story of one who started alone with nothing but whose movement, writing, and personal life created an astounding and permanent impression on the world. By following Śrīla Prabhupāda through these times, we gain an understanding of his exalted and humble life.

I am unable to describe Śrīla Prabhupāda fully. I have therefore composed an invocation, praying that I be permitted to tell this story purely from the transcendental viewpoint—otherwise it would be ruined and incomprehensible. When properly told, the life of the pure devotee brings the greatest joy and benefit to the hearers.

Invocation

According to Kṛṣṇdāsa Kavirāja, an invocation involves offering obeisances, defining the objective, and bestowing benedictions.

I offer my respectful obeisances to my eternal spiritual master, His Divine Grace A. C. Bhaktivedanta Swami Prabhupāda, whose service is my life and soul. It is for his pleasure that I offer *Śrīla Prabhupāda-līlāmṛta* as an act of devotional service. He has blessed the entire world with Kṛṣṇa consciousness, and he is therefore the best friend of all people and all living entities. He is the most powerful *ācārya,* delivering pure love of God, and he is delivering the message of Lord Caitanya strictly in disciplic succession. No one else has ever spread Kṛṣṇa consciousness as widely as he. I am praying that he will allow me to surmount the difficulties involved in presenting his biography and that he will be pleased with the results. I am convinced that by his good wishes this work can be successful and that if he is not pleased, I am powerless to write anything of merit.

By offering obeisances to my spiritual master, I am offering respects to all other *ācāryas* in the disciplic succession—to Śrīla Prabhupāda's *guru,* Bhaktisiddhānta Sarasvatī Ṭhākura, to his *guru,* and so on, to the six Gosvāmīs, Lord Caitanya, and Lord Kṛṣṇa Himself. Only by the grace of Śrīla Prabhupāda can I bow down in the temple, prostrate at the lotus feet of Gaura-Nitāi, Kṛṣṇa-Balarāma, and Rādhā-Śyāmasundara and have access to Their mercy.

One objective of *Śrīla Prabhupāda-līlāmṛta* is to present the life and teachings of Śrīla Prabhupāda in the transcendental perspective, never portraying Śrīla Prabhupāda as an ordinary man, subject to the modes of nature. Śrīla Prabhupāda was a divinely empowered pure devotee. He was sent to this world by the Supreme Lord just to spread the Kṛṣṇa consciousness movement to people of all nations, races, classes, and creeds and thus to offer everyone the opportunity to become a pure devotee and go back to Godhead.

Another objective of this work is to attract the leaders and influential members of society to appreciate and love Śrīla Prabhupāda. This biography must be honest, factual, and correct in transcendental knowledge, and it must captivate and please the reader. *Śrīla Prabhupāda-līlāmṛta* must enlighten and please and also move the reader to inquire into the writings of Śrīla Prabhupāda. My ultimate objective is that the reader be further moved to take up service to His Divine Grace Śrīla Prabhupāda.

Although it is appropriate while writing an invocation to offer a benediction to the reader, I am fallen and cannot offer any benedictions. Yet I can confidently assure my readers that by reading the life and teachings of Śrīla Prabhupāda they will gain quick access to the mercy of Kṛṣṇa, because it is only by the mercy of a great devotee that anyone gets the mercy of Kṛṣṇa. By reading *Śrīla Prabhupāda-līlāmṛta,* those who associated with and served Śrīla Prabhupāda will refresh their remembrance of him and thus derive ecstasy and rededication to his service. Those who never knew Śrīla Prabhupāda will also be blessed, because according to the Vedic literatures, even a moment's association with the pure devotee can make one's life perfect. To read *Śrīla Prabhupāda-līlāmṛta* is to associate with Śrīla Prabhupāda through the transcendental process of hearing. Therefore, although I myself cannot award any benediction to my readers, this work can do so, as it attracts everyone to Śrīla Prabhupāda.

Thus having made the invocation to this work—offering obeisances, describing my objectives, and offering benedictions—I remain fallen and dumb, begging at the lotus feet of my Guru Mahārāja and waiting for his mercy, which alone can allow this poor writer and poor devotee to speak well.

My dear Śrīla Prabhupāda, my dear Lord Kṛṣṇa, if you think I can be trusted to write correctly, then please allow me to do so. There is a great need for this transcendental literature, as the human beings of Kali-yuga are in a deplorable state of spiritual blindness, with no knowledge of the relief to be gained by service to the pure devotee. The devotees of the Lord and the many sincere followers of Śrīla Prabhupāda are eagerly receiving this work. They want to hear more and more of Śrīla Prabhupāda's activities and instructions, and they want to see them presented expertly so that others may also become attracted to join us in loving, dedicated service to *guru* and Gaurāṅga.

My dear Śrīla Prabhupāda, I know I have to work hard to produce this literature, and I promise to do so. But my efforts will be only a spinning of concocted, empty words unless you become present in these words and bring them to life with transcendental potency.

Satsvarūpa dāsa Goswami

CHAPTER ONE

Childhood

We would be sleeping, and father would be doing ārati. *Ding ding ding—we would hear the bell and wake up and see him bowing down before Kṛṣṇa.*

—Śrīla Prabhupāda

IT WAS JANMĀṢṬAMĪ, the annual celebration of the advent of Lord Kṛṣṇa some five thousand years before. Residents of Calcutta, mostly Bengalis and other Indians, but also many Muslims and even some British, were observing the festive day, moving here and there through the city's streets to visit the temples of Lord Kṛṣṇa. Devout Vaiṣṇavas, fasting until midnight, chanted Hare Kṛṣṇa and heard about the birth and activities of Lord Kṛṣṇa from *Śrīmad-Bhāgavatam*. They continued fasting, chanting, and worshiping throughout the night.

The next day (September 1, 1896), in a little house in the Tollygunge suburb of Calcutta, a male child was born. Since he was born on Nandotsava, the day Kṛṣṇa's father, Nanda Mahārāja, had observed a festival in honor of Kṛṣṇa's birth, the boy's uncle called him Nandulal. But his father, Gour Mohan De, and his mother, Rajani, named him Abhay Charan, "one who is fearless, having taken shelter at Lord Kṛṣṇa's lotus feet." In accordance with Bengali tradition, the mother had gone to the home of her parents for the delivery, and so it was that on the bank of the Ādi Gaṅgā, a few miles from his father's home, in a small two-room, mud-walled house with a tiled roof, underneath a jackfruit tree, Abhay Charan was born. A few days later, Abhay returned with his parents to their home at 151 Harrison Road.

An astrologer did a horoscope for the child, and the family was made jubilant by the auspicious reading. The astrologer made a specific prediction: When this child reached the age of seventy, he would cross the ocean, become a great exponent of religion, and open 108 temples.

* * *

Abhay Charan De was born into an India dominated by Victorian imperialism. Calcutta was the capital of India, the seat of the viceroy, the Earl of Elgin and Kincardine, and the "second city" of the British Empire. Europeans and Indians lived separately, although in business and education they intermingled. The British lived mostly in central Calcutta, amidst their own theaters, racetracks, cricket fields, and fine European buildings. The Indians lived more in north Calcutta. Here the men dressed in *dhotīs* and the women in *sārīs* and, while remaining loyal to the British Crown, followed their traditional religion and culture.

Abhay's home at 151 Harrison Road was in the Indian section of north Calcutta. Abhay's father, Gour Mohan De, was a cloth merchant of moderate income and belonged to the aristocratic *suvarṇa-vaṇik* merchant community. He was related, however, to the wealthy Mullik family, which for hundreds of years had traded in gold and salt with the British. Originally the Mulliks had been members of the De family, a *gotra* (lineage) that traces back to the ancient sage Gautama; but during the Mogul period of pre-British India a Muslim ruler had conferred the title Mullik ("lord") on a wealthy, influential branch of the Des. Then, several generations later, a daughter of the Des had married into the Mullik family, and the two families had remained close ever since.

An entire block of properties on either side of Harrison Road belonged to Lokanath Mullik, and Gour Mohan and his family lived in a few rooms of a three-story building within the Mullik properties. Across the street from the Des' residence was a Rādhā-Govinda temple where for the past 150 years the Mulliks had maintained worship of the Deity of Rādhā and Kṛṣṇa. Various shops on the Mullik properties provided income for the Deity and for the priests conducting the worship. Every morning before breakfast, the Mullik family members would visit the temple to see the Deity of Rādhā-Govinda. They would offer cooked rice, *kacaurīs,* and vegetables on a large platter and would then distribute the *prasādam* to the Deities' morning visitors from the neighborhood.

Among the daily visitors was Abhay Charan, accompanying his mother, father, or servant.

Śrīla Prabhupāda: *I used to ride on the same perambulator with Siddhesvar Mullik. He used to call me Moti ("pearl"), and his nickname was Subidhi. And the servant pushed us together. If one day this friend did not see me, he would become mad. He would not go in the perambulator without me. We would not separate even for a moment.*

* * *

As the servant pushed the baby carriage into the wide expanse of Harrison Road, timing his crossing between the bicycles and horse-drawn hackneys, the two children in the pram gazed up at the fair sky and tall trees across the road. Sounds and sights of the hackneys, with their large wheels spinning over the road, caught the fascinated attention of the two children. The servant steered the carriage towards the arched gateway within the red sandstone wall bordering the Rādhā-Govinda Mandira, and as Abhay and his friend rode underneath the ornate metal arch and into the courtyard, they saw high above them two stone lions, the heralds and protectors of the temple compound, their right paws extended.

In the courtyard was a circular drive, and on the oval lawn were lampposts with gaslights, and a statue of a young woman in robes. Sharply chirping sparrows flitted in the shrubs and trees or hopped across the grass, pausing to peck the ground, while choruses of pigeons cooed, sometimes abruptly flapping their wings overhead, sailing off to another perch or descending to the courtyard. Voices chattered as Bengalis moved to and fro, dressed in simple cotton *sārīs* and white *dhotīs.* Someone paused by the carriage to amuse the golden-skinned boys, with their shining dark eyes, but mostly people were passing by quickly, going into the temple.

The heavy double doors leading into the inner courtyard were open, and the servant eased the carriage wheels down a foot-deep step and proceeded through the foyer, then down another step and into the bright sunlight of the main courtyard. There they faced a stone statue of Garuḍa, perched on a four-foot column. This carrier of Viṣṇu, Garuḍa, half man and half bird, kneeled on one knee, his hands folded prayerfully, his eagle's beak strong, and his wings poised behind him. The carriage moved ahead past two servants sweeping and washing the stone courtyard. It was just a few paces across the courtyard to the temple.

The temple area itself, open like a pavilion, was a raised platform with a stone roof supported by stout pillars fifteen feet tall. At the left end of the temple pavilion stood a crowd of worshipers, viewing the Deities on the altar. The servant pushed the carriage closer, lifted the two boys out, and then, holding their hands, escorted them reverentially before the Deities.

Śrīla Prabhupāda: *I can remember standing at the doorway of Rādhā-Govinda temple saying prayers to Rādhā-Govinda* mūrti. *I would watch for hours together. The Deity was so beautiful, with His slanted eyes.*

Rādhā and Govinda, freshly bathed and dressed, now stood on Their silver throne amidst vases of fragrant flowers. Govinda was about eighteen inches high, and Rādhārāṇī, standing to His left, was slightly smaller. Both were golden. Rādhā and Govinda both stood in the same gracefully curved dancing pose, right leg bent at the knee and right foot placed in front of the left. Rādhārāṇī, dressed in a lustrous silk *sārī*, held up Her reddish right palm in benediction, and Kṛṣṇa, in His silk jacket and *dhotī*, played on a golden flute.

At Govinda's lotus feet were green *tulasī* leaves with pulp of sandalwood. Hanging around Their Lordships' necks and reaching down almost to Their lotus feet were several garlands of fragrant night-blooming jasmines, delicate, trumpetlike blossoms resting lightly on Rādhā and Govinda's divine forms. Their necklaces of gold, pearls, and diamonds shimmered. Rādhārāṇī's bracelets were of gold, and both She and Kṛṣṇa wore gold-embroidered silk *cādaras* about Their shoulders. The flowers in Their hands and hair were small and delicate, and the silver crowns on Their heads were bedecked with jewels. Rādhā and Kṛṣṇa were slightly smiling.

Beautifully dressed, dancing on Their silver throne beneath a silver canopy and surrounded by flowers, to Abhay They appeared most attractive. Life outside, on Harrison Road and beyond, was forgotten. In the courtyard the birds went on chirping, and visitors came and went, but Abhay stood silently, absorbed in seeing the beautiful forms of Kṛṣṇa and Rādhārāṇī, the Supreme Lord and His eternal consort.

Then the *kīrtana* began, devotees chanting and playing on drums and *karatālas.* Abhay and his friend kept watching as the *pūjārīs* offered incense, its curling smoke hanging in the air, then a flaming lamp, a conchshell, a handkerchief, flowers, a whisk, and a peacock fan. Finally the *pūjārī* blew the conchshell loudly, and the *ārati* ceremony was over.

*   *   *

When Abhay was one-and-a-half years old, he fell ill with typhoid. The family physician, Dr. Bose, prescribed chicken broth.

"No," Gour Mohan protested, "I cannot allow it."

"Yes, otherwise he will die."

"But we are not meat-eaters," Gour Mohan pleaded. "We cannot prepare chicken in our kitchen."

"Don't mind," Dr. Bose said. "I shall prepare it at my house and bring it in a jar, and you simply ..."

Gour Mohan assented. "If it is necessary for my son to live." So the doctor came with his chicken broth and offered it to Abhay, who immediately began to vomit.

"All right," the doctor admitted. "Never mind, this is no good." Gour Mohan then threw the chicken broth away, and Abhay gradually recovered from the typhoid without having to eat meat.

On the roof of Abhay's maternal grandmother's house was a little garden with flowers, greenery, and trees. Along with the other grandchildren, two-year-old Abhay took pleasure in watering the plants with a sprinkling can. But his particular tendency was to sit alone amongst the plants. He would find a nice bush and make a sitting place.

One day when Abhay was three, he narrowly escaped a fatal burning. He was playing with matches in front of his house when he caught his cloth on fire. Suddenly a man appeared and put the fire out. Abhay was saved, although he retained a small scar on his leg.

In 1900, when Abhay was four, a vehement plague hit Calcutta. Dozens of people died every day, and thousands evacuated the city. When there seemed no way to check the plague, an old *bābājī* organized Hare Kṛṣṇa *saṅkīrtana* all over Calcutta. Regardless of religion, Hindu, Muslim, Christian, and Parsi all joined, and a large party of chanters traveled from street to street, door to door, chanting the names Hare Kṛṣṇa, Hare Kṛṣṇa, Kṛṣṇa Kṛṣṇa, Hare Hare/ Hare Rāma, Hare Rāma, Rāma Rāma, Hare Hare. The group arrived at Gour Mohan's house at 151 Harrison Road, and Gour Mohan eagerly received them. Although Abhay was a little child, his head reaching only up to the knees of the chanters, he also joined in the dancing. Shortly after this, the plague subsided.

* * *

Gour Mohan was a pure Vaiṣṇava, and he raised his son to be Kṛṣṇa conscious. Since his own parents had also been Vaiṣṇavas, Gour Mohan had never touched meat, fish, eggs, tea, or coffee. His complexion was fair and his disposition reserved. At night he would lock up his cloth shop, set a bowl of rice in the middle of the floor to satisfy the rats so that they would not chew the cloth in their hunger, and return home. There he would read from *Caitanya-caritāmṛta* and *Śrīmad-Bhāgavatam,* the main scriptures of Bengali Vaiṣṇavas, chant on his *japa* beads, and worship the Deity of Lord Kṛṣṇa. He was gentle and affectionate and would never punish Abhay. Even when obliged to correct him, Gour Mohan would first apologize: "You are my son, so now I must correct you. It is my duty. Even Caitanya Mahāprabhu's father would chastise Him, so don't mind."

Śrīla Prabhupāda: *My father's income was no more than 250 rupees, but there was no question of need. In the mango season when we were children, we would run through the house playing, and we would grab mangoes as we were running through. And all through the day we would eat mangoes. We wouldn't have to think, "Can I have a mango?" My father always provided food—mangoes were one rupee a dozen.*

Life was simple, but there was always plenty. We were middle class but receiving four or five guests daily. My father gave four daughters in marriage, and there was no difficulty for him. Maybe it was not a very luxurious life, but there was no scarcity of food or shelter or cloth. Daily he purchased two and a half kilograms of milk. He did not like to purchase retail but would purchase a year's supply of coal by the cartload.

We were happy—not that because we did not purchase a motorcar we were unhappy. My father used to say, "God has ten hands. If He wants to take away from you, with two hands how much can you protect? And when He wants to give to you with ten hands, then with your two hands how much can you take?"

My father would rise a little late, around seven or eight. Then, after taking bath, he would go purchasing. Then, from ten o'clock to one in the afternoon, he was engaged in pūjā. *Then he would take his lunch and go to business. And in the business shop he would take a little rest for one hour. He would come home from business at ten o'clock at night, and then again he would do* pūjā. *Actually, his real business was* pūjā. *For livelihood he did some business, but* pūjā *was his main business. We would be sleeping, and father would be doing* ārati. *Ding ding ding—we would hear the bell and wake up and see him bowing down before Kṛṣṇa.*

Gour Mohan wanted Vaiṣṇava goals for his son; he wanted Abhay to become a servant of Rādhārāṇī, to become a preacher of the *Bhāgavatam,* and to learn the devotional art of playing *mṛdaṅga.* He regularly received *sādhus* in his home, and he would always ask them, "Please bless my son so that Śrīmatī Rādhārāṇī may be pleased with him and grant him Her blessings."

Enjoying each other's company, father and son used to walk as far as ten miles, saving the five-paisa tram fare. On the beach they used to see a *yogī* who for years had sat in one spot without moving. One day the *yogī's* son was sitting there, and people had gathered around; the son was taking over his father's sitting place. Gour Mohan gave the *yogīs* a donation and asked their blessings for his son.

When Abhay's mother said she wanted him to become a British lawyer when he grew up (which meant he would have to go to London to study), one of the Mullik "uncles" thought it was a good idea. But Gour Mohan would not hear of it; if Abhay went to England he would be influenced by European dress and manners. "He will learn drinking and women-hunting," Gour Mohan objected. "I do not want his money."

From the beginning of Abhay's life, Gour Mohan had introduced his plan. He had hired a professional *mṛdaṅga* player to teach Abhay the standard rhythms for accompanying *kīrtana.* Rajani had been skeptical: "What is the purpose of teaching such a young child to play the *mṛdaṅga*? It is not important." But Gour Mohan had his dream of a son who would grow up singing *bhajanas,* playing *mṛdaṅga,* and speaking on *Śrīmad-Bhāgavatam.*

When Abhay sat to play the *mṛdaṅga,* even with his left and right arms extended as far as he could, his small hands would barely reach the drumheads at the opposite ends of the drum. With his right wrist he would flick his hand just as his teacher instructed, and his fingers would make a high-pitched sound—*tee nee tee nee taw*—and then he would strike the left drumhead with his open left hand—*boom boom.* With practice and age he was gradually learning the basic rhythms, and Gour Mohan looked on with pleasure.

Abhay was an acknowledged pet child of both his parents. In addition to his childhood names Moti, Nandulal, Nandu, and Kocha, his grandmother called him Kacaurī-mukhī because of his fondness for *kacaurīs* (spicy, vegetable-stuffed fried pastries, popular in Bengal). Both his grandmother and mother would give him *kacaurīs,* which he kept in the many pockets of his little vest. He liked to watch the vendors cooking on the busy roadside and accept *kacaurīs* from them and from the neighbors, until all the inside and outside pockets of his vest were filled.

Sometimes when Abhay demanded that his mother make him *kacaurīs,* she would refuse. Once she even sent him to bed. When Gour Mohan came home and asked, "Where is Abhay?" Rajani explained how he had been too demanding and she had sent him to bed without *kacaurīs.* "No, we should make them for him," his father replied, and he woke Abhay and personally cooked *purīs* and *kacaurīs* for him. Gour Mohan was always lenient with Abhay and careful to see that his son got whatever he wanted. When Gour Mohan returned home at night, it was his practice to take a little puffed rice, and Abhay would also sometimes sit with his father, eating puffed rice.

Once, at a cost of six rupees, Gour Mohan bought Abhay a pair of shoes imported from England. And each year, through a friend who traveled back and forth from Kashmir, Gour Mohan would present his son a Kashmiri shawl with a fancy, hand-sewn border.

One day in the market, Abhay saw a toy gun he wanted. His father said no, and Abhay started to cry. "All right, all right," Gour Mohan said, and he bought the gun. Then Abhay wanted another gun. "You already have one," his father said. "Why do you want another one?"

"One for each hand," Abhay cried, and he lay down in the street, kicking his feet. When Gour Mohan agreed to get the second gun, Abhay was pacified.

Abhay's mother, Rajani, was thirty years old when he was born. Like her husband, she came from a long-established Gauḍīya Vaiṣṇava family. She was darker-skinned than her husband, and whereas his disposition was cool, hers tended to be fiery. Abhay saw his mother and father living together peacefully; no deep marital conflict or complicated dissatisfaction ever threatened home. Rajani was chaste and religious-minded, a model housewife in the traditional Vedic sense, dedicated to caring for her husband and children. Abhay observed his mother's simple and touching attempts to insure, by prayers, by vows, and even by rituals, that he continue to live. Whenever he was to go out even to play, his mother, after dressing him, would put a drop of saliva on her finger and touch it to his forehead. Abhay never knew the significance of this act, but because she was his mother he stood submissively "like a dog with its master" while she did it.

Like Gour Mohan, Rajani treated Abhay as the pet child; but whereas her husband expressed his love through leniency and plans for his son's spiritual success, she expressed hers through attempts to safeguard Abhay from all danger, disease, and death. She once offered blood from her breast to one of the demigods with the supplication that Abhay be protected on all sides from danger.

At Abhay's birth, she had made a vow to eat with her left hand until the day her son would notice and ask her why she was eating with the wrong hand. One day, when little Abhay actually asked, she immediately stopped. It had been just another prescription for his survival, for she thought that by the strength of her vow he would continue to grow, at least until he asked her about the vow. Had he not asked, she would never again have eaten with her right hand, and according to her superstition he would have gone on living, protected by her vow.

For his protection she also put an iron bangle around his leg. His playmates asked him what it was, and Abhay self-consciously went to his mother and demanded, "Open this bangle!" When she said, "I will do it later," he began to cry, "No, now!" Once Abhay swallowed a watermelon seed, and his friends told him it would grow in his stomach into a watermelon. He ran to his mother, who assured him he didn't have to worry; she would say a *mantra* to protect him.

Śrīla Prabhupāda: *Mother Yaśodā would chant* mantras *in the morning to protect Kṛṣṇa from all dangers throughout the day. When Kṛṣṇa killed some demon she thought it was due to her chanting. My mother would do a similar thing with me.*

His mother would often take him to the Ganges and personally bathe him. She also gave him a food supplement known as Horlicks. When he got dysentery, she cured it with hot *purīs* and fried eggplant with salt, though sometimes when he was ill Abhay would show his obstinacy by refusing to take any medicine. But just as he was stubborn, his mother was determined, and she would forcibly administer medicine into his mouth, though sometimes it took three assistants to hold him down.

Śrīla Prabhupāda: *I was very naughty when I was a boy. I would break anything. When I was angry, I would break the glass hookah pipes, which my father kept to offer to guests. Once my mother was trying to bathe me, and I refused and knocked my head on the ground, and blood came out. They came running and said, "What are you doing? You shall kill the child."*

Abhay was present when his mother observed the ceremony of Sādhahotra during the seventh and ninth months of her pregnancies. Freshly bathed, she would appear in new clothing along with her children and enjoy a feast of whatever foods she desired, while her husband gave goods in charity to the local *brāhmaṇas,* who chanted *mantras* for the purification of the mother and the coming child.

Abhay was completely dependent on his mother. Sometimes she would put his shirt on backwards, and he would simply accept it without mentioning it. Although he was sometimes stubborn, he felt dependent on the guidance and reassurance of his mother. When he had to go to the privy, he would jump up and down beside her, holding her *sārī* and saying, "Urine, mother, urine."

"Who is stopping you?" she would ask. "Yes, you can go." Only then, with her permission, would he go.

Sometimes, in the intimacy of dependence, his mother became his foil. When he lost a baby tooth and on her advice placed it under a pillow that night, the tooth vanished, and some money appeared. Abhay gave the money to his mother for safekeeping, but later, when in their constant association she opposed him, he demanded, "I want my money back! I will go away from home. Now you give me my money back!"

When Rajani wanted her hair braided, she would regularly ask her daughters. But if Abhay were present he would insist on braiding it himself and would create such a disturbance that they would give in to him. Once he painted the bottoms of his feet red, imitating the custom of women who painted their feet on festive occasions. His mother tried to dissuade him, saying it was not for children, but he insisted, "No, I must do it, also!"

Abhay was unwilling to go to school. "Why should I go?" he thought. "I will play all day." When his mother complained to Gour Mohan, Abhay, sure that his father would be affectionate, said, "No, I shall go tomorrow."

"All right, he will go tomorrow," said Gour Mohan. "That's all right." But the next morning Abhay complained that he was sick, and his father indulged him.

Rajani became upset because the boy would not go to school, and she hired a man for four rupees to escort him there. The man, whose name was Damodara, would tie Abhay about the waist with a rope—a customary treatment—take him to school, and present him before his teacher. When Abhay would try to run away, Damodara would pick him up and carry him in his arms. After being taken a few times by force, Abhay began to go on his own.

Abhay proved an attentive, well-behaved student, though sometimes he was naughty. Once when the teacher pulled his ear, Abhay threw a kerosene lantern to the floor, accidentally starting a fire.

In those days any common villager, even if illiterate, could recite from the *Rāmāyaṇa, Mahābhārata,* or *Bhāgavatam*. Especially in the villages, everyone would assemble in the evening to hear from these scriptures. It was for this purpose that Abhay's family would sometimes go in the evening to his maternal uncle's house, about ten miles away, where they would assemble and hear about the Lord's transcendental pastimes. They would return home discussing and remembering them and then go to bed and dream *Rāmāyaṇa, Mahābhārata,* and *Bhāgavatam.*

After his afternoon rest and bath, Abhay would often go to a neighbor's house and look at the black-and-white pictures in *Mahābhārata.* His grandmother asked him daily to read *Mahābhārata* from a vernacular edition. Thus by looking at pictures and reading with his grandmother, Abhay imbibed *Mahābhārata.*

In Abhay's childhood play, his younger sister Bhavatarini was often his assistant. Together they would go to see the Rādhā-Govinda Deities in the Mulliks' temple. In their play, whenever they encountered obstacles, they would pray to God for help. "Please, Kṛṣṇa, help us fly this kite," they would call as they ran along trying to put their kite into flight.

Abhay's toys included two guns, a wind-up car, a cow that jumped when Abhay squeezed the rubber bulb attached, and a dog with a mechanism that made it dance. The toy dog was from Dr. Bose, the family physician, who gave it to him when treating a minor wound on Abhay's side. Abhay sometimes liked to pretend that he was a doctor, and to his friends he would administer "medicine," which was nothing more than dust.

* * *

Abhay was enamored with the Ratha-yātrā festivals of Lord Jagannātha, held yearly in Calcutta. The biggest Calcutta Ratha-yātrā was the Mulliks', with three separate carts bearing the deities of Jagannātha, Baladeva, and Subhadrā. Beginning from the Rādhā-Govinda temple, the carts would proceed down Harrison Road for a short distance and then return. The Mulliks would distribute large quantities of Lord Jagannātha's *prasādam* to the public on this day.

Ratha-yātrā was held in cities all over India, but the original, gigantic Ratha-yātrā, attended each year by millions of pilgrims, took place three hundred miles south of Calcutta at Jagannātha Purī. For centuries at Purī, three wooden carts forty-five feet high had been towed by the crowds along the two-mile parade route, in commemoration of one of Lord Kṛṣṇa's eternal pastimes. Abhay had heard how Lord Caitanya Himself, four hundred years before, had danced and led ecstatic chanting of Hare Kṛṣṇa at the Purī Ratha-yātrā festival. Abhay would sometimes look at the railway timetable or ask about the fare to Vṛndāvana and Purī, thinking about how he would collect the money and go there.

Abhay wanted to have his own cart and to perform his own Ratha-yātrā, and naturally he turned to his father for help. Gour Mohan agreed, but there were difficulties. When he took his son to several carpenter shops, he found that he could not afford to have a cart made. On their way home, Abhay began crying, and an old Bengali woman approached and asked him what the matter was. Gour Mohan explained that the boy wanted a Ratha-yātrā cart but they couldn't afford to have one made. "Oh, I have a cart," the woman said, and she invited Gour Mohan and Abhay to her place and showed them the cart. It looked old, but it was still operable, and it was just the right size, about three feet high. Gour Mohan purchased it and helped to restore and decorate it. Father and son together constructed sixteen supporting columns and placed a canopy on top, resembling as closely as possible the ones on the big carts at Purī. They also attached the traditional wooden horse and driver to the front of the cart. Abhay insisted that it must look authentic. Gour Mohan bought paints, and Abhay personally painted the cart, copying the Purī originals. His enthusiasm was great, and he became an insistent organizer of various aspects of the festival. But when he tried making fireworks for the occasion from a book that gave illustrated descriptions of the process, Rajani intervened.

Abhay engaged his playmates in helping him, especially his sister Bhavatarini, and he became their natural leader. Responding to his entreaties, amused mothers in the neighborhood agreed to cook special preparations so that he could distribute the *prasādam* at his Ratha-yātrā festival.

Like the festival at Purī, Abhay's Ratha-yātrā ran for eight consecutive days. His family members gathered, and the neighborhood children joined in a procession, pulling the cart, playing drums and *karatālas,* and chanting. Wearing a *dhotī* and no shirt in the heat of summer, Abhay led the children in chanting Hare Kṛṣṇa and in singing the appropriate Bengali *bhajana, Ki kara rāi kamalinī.*

> What are You doing, Śrīmatī Rādhārāṇī?
> Please come out and see.
> They are stealing Your dearmost treasure—
> Kṛṣṇa, the black gem.

If the young girl only knew!
The young boy Kṛṣṇa,
Treasure of Her heart,
Is now forsaking Her.

Abhay copied whatever he had seen at adult religious functions, including dressing the deities, offering the deities food, offering *ārati* with a ghee lamp and incense, and making prostrated obeisances. From Harrison Road the procession entered the circular road inside the courtyard of the Rādhā-Govinda temple and stood awhile before the Deities. Seeing the fun, Gour Mohan's friends approached him: "Why haven't you invited us? You are holding a big ceremony, and you don't invite us? What is this?"

"They are just children playing," his father replied.

"Oh, children playing?" the men joked. "You are depriving us by saying that this is only for children?"

While Abhay was ecstatically absorbed in the Ratha-yātrā processions, Gour Mohan spent money for eight consecutive days, and Rajani cooked various dishes to offer, along with flowers, to Lord Jagannātha. Although everything Abhay did was imitation, his inspiration and steady drive for holding the festival were genuine. His spontaneous spirit sustained the eight-day children's festival, and each successive year brought a new festival, which Abhay would observe in the same way.

* * *

When Abhay was about six years old, he asked his father for a Deity of his own to worship. Since infancy he had watched his father doing *pūjā* at home and had been regularly seeing the worship of Rādhā-Govinda and thinking, "When will I be able to worship Kṛṣṇa like this?" On Abhay's request, his father purchased a pair of little Rādhā-Kṛṣṇa Deities and gave Them to him. From then on, whatever Abhay ate he would first offer to Rādhā and Kṛṣṇa, and imitating his father and the priests of Rādhā-Govinda, he would offer his Deities a ghee lamp and put Them to rest at night.

Abhay and his sister Bhavatarini became dedicated worshipers of the little Rādhā-Kṛṣṇa Deities, spending much of their time dressing and worshiping Them and sometimes singing *bhajanas*. Their brothers and sisters laughed, teasing Abhay and Bhavatarini by saying that because they were more interested in the Deity than in their education they would not live long. But Abhay replied that they didn't care.

Once a neighbor asked Abhay's mother, "How old is your little son?"

"He's seven," she said, as Abhay listened with interest. He had never heard anyone discuss his age before; but now he understood for the first time: "I am seven."

In addition to the education Abhay received at the kindergarten to which he had at first been forcibly dragged, he also received private tutoring at home from his fifth year to his eighth. He learned to read Bengali and began learning Sanskrit. Then in 1904, when he was eight years old, Abhay entered the nearby Mutty Lall Seal Free School, on the corner of Harrison and Central roads.

Mutty Lall was a boys' school founded in 1842 by a wealthy *suvarṇa-vaṇik* Vaiṣṇava. The building was stone, two stories, and surrounded by a stone wall. The teachers were Indian, and the students were Bengalis from local *suvarṇa-vaṇik* families. Dressed in their *dhotīs* and *kurtās,* the boys would leave their mothers and fathers in the morning and walk together in little groups, each boy carrying a few books and his *tiffin.* Inside the school compound, they would talk together and play until the clanging bell called them to their classes. The boys would enter the building, skipping through the halls, running up and down the stairs, coming out to the wide front veranda on the second floor, until their teachers gathered them all before their wooden desks and benches for lessons in math, science, history, geography, and their own Vaiṣṇava religion and culture.

Classes were disciplined and formal. Each long bench held four boys, who shared a common desk, with four inkwells. If a boy were naughty his teacher would order him to "stand up on the bench." A Bengali reader the boys studied was the well-known *Folk Tales of Bengal,* a collection of traditional Bengali folk tales, stories a grandmother would tell local children—tales of witches, ghosts, Tantric spirits, talking animals, saintly *brāhmaṇas* (or sometimes wicked ones), heroic warriors, thieves, princes, princesses, spiritual renunciation, and virtuous marriage.

In their daily walks to and from school, Abhay and his friends came to recognize, at least from their childish viewpoint, all the people who regularly appeared in the Calcutta streets; their British superiors traveling about, usually in horse-drawn carriages; the hackney drivers; the *bhaṅgīs,* who cleaned the streets with straw brooms; and even the local pickpockets and prostitutes who stood on the street corners.

Abhay turned ten the same year the rails were laid for the electric tram on Harrison Road. He watched the workers lay the tracks, and when he first saw the trolley car's rod touching the overhead wire, it amazed him. He daydreamed of getting a stick, touching the wire himself, and running along by electricity. Although electric power was new in Calcutta and not widespread (only the wealthy could afford it in their homes), along with the electric tram came new electric streetlights—carbon-arc lamps—replacing the old gaslights. Abhay and his friends used to go down the street looking on the ground for the old, used carbon tips, which the maintenance man would leave behind. When Abhay saw his first gramophone box, he thought an electric man or a ghost was inside the box singing.

Abhay liked to ride his bicycle down the busy Calcutta streets. Although when the soccer club had been formed at school he had requested the position of goalie so that he wouldn't have to run, he was an avid cyclist. A favorite ride was to go south towards Dalhousie Square, with its large fountains spraying water into the air. That was near Raj Bhavan, the viceroy's mansion, which Abhay could glimpse through the gates. Riding further south, he would pass through the open arches of the Maidan, Calcutta's main public park, with its beautiful green flat land spanning out towards Chowranghee and the stately buildings and trees of the British quarter. The park also had exciting places to cycle past: the racetrack, Fort William, the stadium. The Maidan bordered the Ganges (known locally as the Hooghly), and sometimes Abhay would cycle home along its shores. Here he saw numerous bathing *ghāṭas,* with stone steps leading down into the Ganges and often with temples at the top of the steps. There was the burning *ghāṭa,* where bodies were cremated, and, close to his home, a pontoon bridge that crossed the river into the city of Howrah.

At age twelve, though it made no deep impression on him, Abhay was initiated by a professional *guru.* The *guru* told him about his own master, a great *yogī,* who had once asked him, "What do you want to eat?"

Abhay's family *guru* had replied, "Fresh pomegranates from Afghanistan."

"All right," the *yogī* had replied. "Go into the next room." And there he had found a branch of pomegranates, ripe as if freshly taken from the tree. A *yogī* who came to see Abhay's father said that he had once sat down with his own master and touched him and had then been transported within moments to the city of Dvārakā by yogic power.

Gour Mohan did not have a high opinion of Bengal's growing number of so-called *sādhus*—the nondevotional impersonalist philosophers, the demigod worshipers, the *gāñjā* smokers, the beggars—but he was so charitable that he would invite the charlatans into his home. Every day Abhay saw many so-called *sādhus,* as well as some who were genuine, coming to eat in his home as guests of his father, and from their words and activities Abhay became aware of many things, including the existence of yogic powers. At a circus he and his father once saw a *yogī* tied up hand and foot and put into a bag. The bag was sealed and put into a box, which was then locked and sealed, but still the man came out. Abhay, however, did not give these things much importance compared with the devotional activities his father had taught him, his worship of Rādhā-Kṛṣṇa, and his observance of Ratha-yātrā.

* * *

Hindus and Muslims lived peacefully together in Calcutta, and it was not unusual for them to attend one another's social and religious functions. They had their differences, but there had always been harmony. So when trouble started, Abhay's family understood it to be due to political agitation by the British. Abhay was about thirteen years old when the first Hindu-Muslim riot broke out. He did not understand exactly what it was, but somehow he found himself in the middle of it.

Śrīla Prabhupāda: *All around our neighborhood on Harrison Road were Muhammadans. The Mullik house and our house were respectable; otherwise, it was surrounded by what is called* kasbā *and* bastī. *So the riot was there, and I had gone to play. I did not know that the riot had taken place in Market Square. I was coming home, and one of my class friends said, "Don't go to your house. That side is rioting now."*

We lived in the Muhammadan quarter, and the fighting between the two parties was going on. But I thought maybe it was something like two guṇḍās *[hoodlums] fighting. I had seen one* guṇḍā *once stabbing another* guṇḍā, *and I had seen pickpockets. They were our neighbor-men. So I thought it was like that: this is going on.*

But when I came to the crossing of Harrison Road and Holliday Street I saw one shop being plundered. I was only a child, a boy. I thought, "What is this happening?" In the meantime, my family, my father and mother, were at home frightened, thinking, "The child has not come." They became so disturbed they came out of the home expecting, "Wherefrom the child will come?"

So what could I do? When I saw the rioting I began to run towards our house, and one Muhammadan, he wanted to kill me. He took his knife and actually ran after me. But I passed somehow or other. I was saved. So as I came running before our gate, my parents got back their life.

So without speaking anything I went to the bedroom, and it was in the winter. So without saying anything, I laid down, wrapped myself with a quilt. Then later I was rising from bed, questioning, "Is it ended? The riot has ended?"

* * *

When Abhay was fifteen he was afflicted with beriberi, and his mother, who was also stricken regularly had to rub a powder of calcium chloride on his legs to reduce the swelling. Abhay soon recovered, and his mother, who had never stopped any of her duties, also recovered.

But only a year later, at the age of forty-six, his mother suddenly died. Her passing away was an abrupt lowering of the curtain, ending the scenes of his tender childhood: his mother's affectionate care, her prayers and *mantras* for his protection, her feeding and grooming him, her dutifully scolding him. Her passing affected his sisters even more than him, though it certainly turned him more towards the affectionate care of his father. He was already sixteen, but now he was forced to grow up and prepare to enter on his own into worldly responsibilities.

His father gave him solace. He instructed Abhay that there was nothing for which to lament: the soul is eternal, and everything happens by the will of Kṛṣṇa, so he should have faith and depend upon Kṛṣṇa. Abhay listened and understood.

CHAPTER TWO

College, Marriage, and Gandhi's Movement

I joined Gandhi's movement in 1920 and gave up my education. Although I had passed my final examination—B.A.—I gave it up and did not appear.

—Śrīla Prabhupāda

IN 1914 THE WAR came, and many Indians enlisted in the fight on behalf of their ruler, Great Britain. Abhay saw British airplanes landing on the racetrack in Maidan Park, and the newspaper told him of the war, but he was not directly affected. In 1916 he began college.

There were two prestigious colleges in Calcutta: Presidency and Scottish Churches'. Abhay entered Scottish Churches' College. It was a Christian school but well reputed amongst the Bengalis, and many Vaiṣṇava families sent their sons there. The professors, most of whom were priests in the Church of Scotland, were known as sober, moral men, and the students received a good education. It was a proper and respectable institution, and since it was in north Calcutta and not far from Harrison Road, Gour Mohan could keep Abhay at home.

Gour Mohan had long ago decided that he would not allow Abhay to go to London and in the name of education become exposed to the corruption of the West. He wanted Abhay to be a pure devotee of Śrīmatī Rādhārāṇī and Lord Kṛṣṇa. Yet on the other hand, Gour Mohan didn't want to give up his son to become the *brahmacārī* disciple of a *guru.* Where was such a qualified *guru* to be found? His experience of *yogīs* and swamis had not inspired such confidence. He wanted his son to keep all the principles of spiritual life, yet he also knew that Abhay would have to marry and earn a livelihood. Under the circumstances, enrolling Abhay in Scottish Churches' College was the most protection Gour Mohan knew to give his son.

The college had been founded by the Reverend Alexander Duff, a Christian missionary who had gone to Calcutta in 1830. A pioneer in getting Indians to appreciate European civilization, the Reverend A. Duff had first founded the General Assembly Institution, for "propagation of the gospel through education, at once liberal and religious, on Western principles and with English as the medium of instruction in the higher classes." Later he had founded the College of the Church of Scotland and in 1908 had amalgamated both institutions as Scottish Churches' College.

Śrīla Prabhupāda: *We respected our professors as our fathers. The relationship between the students and the professors was very good. The vice-chancellor, Professor W. S. Urquhart, was a perfect and kindhearted gentleman, with whom we sometimes joked.*

In my first year I studied English and Sanskrit, in my second year Sanskrit and philosophy. Then philosophy and economics. Another professor was J. C. Scrimgeour. He was professor of English literature. While teaching English literature he would give parallel passages from Bankim Chandra Chatterji. "Yes, yes," he would say, "your Bankim Bābū says like this." He had studied Bankim's literatures, and he compared Bankim Chandra Chatterji to Walter Scott. In those days, Dickens and Sir Walter Scott were two very great English literary men. So he taught us those novelists, and the relationship was very nice.

Abhay became a member of the English Society and would recite Keats, Shelley, and other poets to his classmates. As a member of the Sanskrit Society, he recited the *Gītā,* and some of his fellow students especially noted how eloquently he recited the Eleventh Chapter, describing the universal form of Kṛṣṇa. He also played soccer and took part in theatrics.

Amritlal Bose, a famous organizer and director of theater in Bengal, rehearsed Abhay and a group of his classmates in a drama from the life of Lord Caitanya. Since *caitanya-līlā* was available in the public theater for half a rupee, Mr. Bose argued, what was the need for an amateur production? And his answer was, "They should appreciate your performance of Lord Caitanya so much that after seeing it they will agree never to sin."

The eminent director was volunteering his service and training these boys, but on one condition: they would not perform publicly unless he said the production was perfect. For more than a year, Abhay and the others rehearsed the Caitanya play, until finally their director allowed them to stage a public performance. Abhay, playing the part of Advaita Ācārya, noticed that many people in the audience were crying. At first he could not understand why, but then he realized that because the players had been well trained and because they were sincere, the audience was moved. That was Abhay's first and last dramatic performance.

Abhay's psychology teacher, Professor Urquhart, gave evidence that woman's brain weighed less than man's. His economics professor lectured on Marshall's theory that family affection is the impetus for economic development. In Sanskrit Abhay used a text by Rowe and Webb that described Sanskrit as the mother of all languages.

While studying Kālīdāsa's *Kumāra-sambhava* in Sanskrit, Abhay was impressed by Kālīdāsa's explanation of the word *dhīra,* which means "undisturbed," or "self-controlled." According to Kālīdāsa, once long ago Lord Śiva was sitting in deep meditation. Because the demigods were at war with the demons, they wanted a commander in chief born from the semen of Lord Śiva, so the demigods sent a beautiful young girl, Pārvatī, to interrupt his meditation. Although Pārvatī worshiped Lord Śiva and even touched his genitals, he was not disturbed. His resistance to temptation was the perfect example of being *dhīra.*

As at other British-run schools in India, all the European teachers at Scottish Churches' had to learn the local language. Once Professor Urquhart walked past Abhay and a group of students as they were eating some peanuts and talking together. One of the students, speaking in Bengali, made a joke at Professor Urquhart's expense. To their surprise, Professor Urquhart immediately turned to the jokester and answered in Bengali, and Abhay and the others felt ashamed.

Bible study was compulsory. The Bible Society had issued each student a beautifully bound Bible, and each morning everyone gathered for scripture reading, prayers, and hymns.

One of the professors criticized the Vedic teachings of *karma* and transmigration of the soul. In a court of law one cannot be prosecuted for a crime unless there is a witness. Similarly, he argued, although according to Hindus the soul suffers in his present life for the misdeeds of his past life, where is the witness to these misdeeds? Abhay was displeased to hear this criticism, and he knew how to refute it, but being only a student he had remained silent. Socially he was inferior, and a student had little scope to challenge a professor. But he knew that the professor's argument against *karma* was insubstantial; he knew there was a witness.

Some of the students, having come to Calcutta from small villages, viewed the big city and the presence of so many Europeans with bewilderment and timidity. But to Abhay, Calcutta and the British were not alarming, and he even held a certain fondness for his Scottish teachers. Although he looked up to them with a mixture of awe, distance, and some tension, he admired their moral uprightness and their gentlemanly, courteous behavior with the boys. They seemed to him kindhearted.

The governor of Bengal, who was Scottish, once came to Scottish Churches' College, visiting all the classrooms. The rooms were large, holding 150 students, but Abhay had a front-row seat and got a close look at the famous governor, the Marquis of Zetland.

The school operated on the principle of strict social distance between Europeans and Indians. Even the Bengali faculty members, being of a supposedly inferior race, had to use a faculty lounge separate from that of the European professors. Part of the college syllabus was *England's Work in India,* by M. Ghosh, an Indian. The book elaborately explained how India had been primitive before the British rule. Abhay's economics professor would sometimes shout at his class when he became frustrated with their slowness. Addressing them as representatives of the whole Indian nation, he would say, "You should never expect independence! You cannot rule! You can only work like asses, that's all!"

College life was demanding. No longer was Abhay free to spend hours before the Deities of Rādhā and Govinda early in the morning. That had been a boyhood luxury, when he would daily pass hours in the Mulliks' temple before the golden forms of Rādhā-Govinda, watching the *pūjārīs* as they worshiped the Deities with incense, flowers, lamps, musical *kīrtana,* and opulent *prasādam.* As a child he had played within the grassy compound of the temple or watched the men cooking *kacaurīs* on the roadside or bicycled or flown his kite with Bhavatarini. His life had always centered on his home at Harrison Road, his mother's talks, his father's worshiping Kṛṣṇa. These scenes were now past.

Now he spent his days within the compound of Scottish Churches' College. Here there was also a lawn and a garden with birds and even a small banyan tree. But instead of worship, there was study. The atmosphere at Scottish Churches' was academic, and even the casual conversation among the students as they gathered before the notice boards at the main entrance or passed in groups in and out of the main gates was usually about class assignments or collegiate activities.

When Abhay was not actually sitting side by side with his fellow students, sharing a classroom bench before one of the long desks that stood row after row in the lecture hall, when he was not looking attentively forward during the lecture of one of his professors — usually a reverend dressed in a European suit, speaking a Scottish brogue and pronouncing words like *duty* as "*juty*" — when he was not actually in the classroom hearing their lectures on Western logic or chemistry or psychology, then he was at his homework assignments, sitting at a table amidst the bookshelves in the college library, reading from an open book or writing notes while the electric fans overhead rippled the pages, or he was at home with his father, sisters, and brothers, but reading his lessons or writing a paper for the reverend in the lecture hall. He had had to abandon worshiping the Kṛṣṇa Deity he had demanded his father give him years before; he had retired his Deities to a closed box.

Gour Mohan was undisturbed that his pet son could no longer attend to all the devotional activities of his childhood. He saw that Abhay was remaining pure in all his habits, that he was not adopting Western ideas or challenging his own culture, and that as a student at Scottish Churches' College he would not likely be exposed to immoral behavior. Gour Mohan was satisfied to see Abhay getting a good education to prepare for a career after graduation. He would be a responsible Vaiṣṇava; he would soon marry and get a job.

One of Abhay's classmates and close companions was Rupendranatha Mitra. Abhay and Rupen would study together and sit side by side in the assembly hall during Bible class, uttering the compulsory prayers. Rupen noticed that although Abhay was a serious student, he was never enamored of Western education or ambitious for scholastic achievements.

Abhay would confide to Rupen, "I don't like these things," and sometimes he spoke of moving away. "What are you thinking?" Rupen would ask, and Abhay would reveal his mind. Rupen found that Abhay was always thinking about "something religious, something philosophical or devotional about God."

Abhay studied the Western philosophers and scientists, yet they held no fascination for him. After all, they were only speculating, and their conclusions were not in the devotional mood and spirit of the Vaiṣṇava training he had received from his father and the Vedic scriptures. The sudden access to the wealth of Western knowledge, which created in some an appetite to study deeply and in others a desire to get ahead in the world through good grades and career, left Abhay untouched. Certainly within his heart he was always thinking of "something religious, something philosophical or devotional about God," and yet, as a Scottish Churches' College man, he gave his time and attention to academic life.

One night, after his first year of college, Abhay had an unusual dream. The Deity of Kṛṣṇa his father had given him appeared to Abhay complaining, "Why have you put Me away in this box? You should take Me out and worship Me again." Abhay felt sorry that he had neglected his Deity, and he resumed his worship of Rādhā and Kṛṣṇa at home, despite his assignments.

* * *

In the class one year ahead of Abhay was a very spirited nationalist, Subhas Chandra Bose. He had been a student at Presidency College but had been expelled for organizing a student strike against a British professor who had repeatedly abused Indian students. At Scottish Churches', Bose appeared to be a serious student; he was secretary of the Philosophy Club and was working cooperatively with Vice-Chancellor Urquhart. From Subhas Bose and others, Abhay heard talks of Indian independence. He heard the names well known in his native Bengal: Bipinchandra Pal, who had fought to repeal the Arms Act; Surendranatha Bannerjee, who startled the British with his agitation against the 1905 partition of Bengal; Lala Lajpat Rai; and, most notably, Mohandas K. Gandhi.

Scottish Churches' College was strict in forbidding antigovernment propaganda, but the students were sympathetic to the cause of home rule. Although there were no open signs of rebellion, students sometimes held nationalistic meetings in secret. When Subhas Chandra Bose urged the students to support the Indian independence movement, Abhay listened. He liked Bose's faith in spirituality, his enthusiasm and determination. Abhay wasn't interested in political activity, but the ideals of the independence movement appealed to him.

Many Bengali speakers and writers expressed India's drive for independence (*svarāj*) as a spiritual movement. For the nationalists, political emancipation was analogous to the soul's liberation from material bondage. Abhay was interested in devotional service to Lord Kṛṣṇa, the Absolute Truth, a conviction he had imbibed from his father and maintained since his childhood, whereas Indian independence was a temporary, relative truth. But some of the leaders of *svarāj,* while admitting that the Vedic scriptures were indeed absolute, asserted that the original glory of Indian culture could not shine forth for the world's benefit until India became free from the stigma of foreign rule. The foreigners, they pointed out, blasphemed and castigated the preeminence of India's culture.

Abhay had felt this also. In his assigned reading in M. Ghosh's *England's Work in India,* he had encountered the theory that the Vedic scriptures were impure, recent writings and that India's had been a spiritually backward culture before British rule and the spread of Christianity. There were many British insults against the *śāstras*—such as Abhay's professor's trying to discount the law of *karma.* But if India could gain national freedom, then everyone—not only Indians, but the entire world—could benefit from India's highly evolved Vedic culture.

The call to *svarāj,* although covert, attracted virtually all the students, and Abhay amongst them. He was especially interested in Gandhi. Gandhi always carried a *Bhagavad-gītā;* he daily read Lord Kṛṣṇa's holy words and spoke of being guided by the *Gītā* above all other books. Gandhi's personal habits were pure. He abstained from all intoxication, meat-eating, and illicit sex. He lived simply, like a *sādhu,* yet he seemed to have more integrity than the begging *sādhus* Abhay had seen so many times. Abhay read his speeches and followed his activities—maybe Gandhi could carry spirituality into the field of action. The *Gītā's* truth, Gandhi proclaimed, belonged in a most prominent place, where the *Gītā* not only could be read but could *work* for everyone's freedom. And the symbol of that freedom was *svarāj.*

Nationalist sympathies at Scottish Churches' College remained underground during Abhay's years as a student. It was a prestigious school.

A student had to study very seriously to obtain a degree there, and he could then look forward to a fine career. To speak openly against British rule and in favor of independence meant to risk being expelled. To lose education and career—only the most rebellious would dare. So the students met undercover and listened to the revolutionary leaders: "We want *svarāj*! We want independence! Our own government! Our own schools!"

* * *

Gour Mohan watched his son with concern. He saw Abhay not as one of the hundreds of millions of instruments meant to change India's political destiny, but as his pet son. His first concern was for Abhay's welfare. While world events moved across the stage of history, Gour Mohan concentrated on his son's future as he hoped it would be and as he had always prayed it would be. He was planning for Abhay to become a pure Vaiṣṇava, a devotee of Rādhārāṇī. He had taught Abhay to worship Kṛṣṇa and be pure in character and had arranged for his education. Now Gour Mohan thought of getting him married.

According to the Vedic system, a marriage should be carefully arranged by the parents, and it should take place before the girl reaches puberty. Gour Mohan had gotten his first daughter married in her ninth year, his second daughter at twelve years, and his third daughter at eleven. When his second daughter was going on twelve, Rajani had said, "I shall go to the river and commit suicide if you don't get her married at once." In the Vedic system there was no courtship, nor was the couple allowed to live together during the first years of their marriage. The young girl would begin serving her husband by cooking for him at her parents' house and coming before him to serve him his meal or by taking part in some other formal exchange. Then as the boy and girl grew to physical maturity, they would become so lovable to one another that they would be inseparable. The girl would naturally remain faithful to her husband since she would have no association with any other boy as she grew to puberty.

Gour Mohan had many friends in Calcutta with eligible young daughters, and for a long time he had been considering a suitable wife for Abhay. After careful consultation, he finally chose Radharani Datta, the daughter of a *suvarṇa-vaṇik* family associated with the Mulliks. Radharani was eleven years old. After the meeting between her father and Gour Mohan, both families agreed upon the marriage.

Although Abhay was a third-year college student with no income, it was not uncommon for a student to marry, and he would have no immediate financial responsibilities. Abhay didn't appreciate his father's choice of a wife—he had thought of marrying another girl—but in deference to his father he put aside his reluctance. For the time being, he was living with his family and she with hers; so his marital responsibilities of supporting a family would not be immediate. First he had to finish college.

During his fourth year at Scottish Churches', Abhay began to feel reluctant about accepting his degree. As a sympathizer to the nationalist cause, he preferred national schools and self-government over the British institutions, but he could see that as yet no such alternatives existed. Gandhi, however, was calling on Indian students to forsake their studies. The foreign-run schools, he said, instilled a slave mentality; they made one no more than a puppet in the hands of the British. Still, a college degree was the basis of a life's career. Abhay weighed the choices carefully.

Gour Mohan didn't want Abhay to do something he would later regret. He had always tried to plan the best for his son, but Abhay was twenty-three and would have to make this decision for himself. Gour Mohan thought of the future; the horoscope said his son would be a great religious preacher at age seventy, but Gour Mohan did not expect to live to see it. Still, he had every reason to accept the horoscope as accurate, and he wanted to prepare Abhay. He tried to plan things accordingly, but there was no way to guess what Kṛṣṇa would do. Everything depended on Kṛṣṇa, and Kṛṣṇa was above nationalism, above planning and the laws of astrology, and above the desires of a modest cloth merchant aspiring to make his son a pure devotee of Śrīmatī Rādhārāṇī and a preacher of *Śrīmad-Bhāgavatam.* Although Gour Mohan had always allowed Abhay to do what he wanted, he had also carefully guided him always on the path he knew was best. Now, without interfering with Abhay's decision about college, Gour Mohan set about to arrange good employment for him, regardless of what else might happen.

In 1920 Abhay completed his fourth year of college and took the B.A. exam. Afterwards, with the ordeal of final examinations behind him, he took a short vacation. To fulfill a long-cherished desire, he traveled alone a day's journey by train to Jagannātha Purī.

Śrīla Prabhupāda: *Every day of my boyhood I used to think, "How to go to Jagannātha Purī?", and "How to go to Vṛndāvana?" At that time the fare was, for Vṛndāvana, four or five rupees, and similarly for Jagannātha Purī. So I was thinking, "When shall I go?" I took the first opportunity to go to Jagannātha Purī.*

* * *

He walked along the same broad street where for thousands of years the Ratha-yātrā procession had passed. In the market, shops displayed small carved and painted wooden *mūrtis* of Lord Jagannātha. Although it was not Ratha-yātrā season, tourists were purchasing souvenirs, and in the temple they purchased Jagannātha *prasādam*. In the Jagannātha temple, fifty-six gigantic offerings of cooked rice and vegetables were presented daily in worship before the deities of Jagannātha, Balarāma, and Subhadrā.

Abhay entered the temple and saw the deities. On a side altar stood the *mūrti* of Lord Caitanya in His six-armed form, manifesting Himself simultaneously as Kṛṣṇa, Rāma, and the *sannyāsī* Lord Caitanya. Lord Caitanya was famous in Purī, where He had spent the last eighteen years of His life, conducting Hare Kṛṣṇa *kīrtana* with His followers and dancing ecstatically at the yearly Ratha-yātrā as the carts were wheeled along the main road, surrounded by thousands of devotees. Lord Caitanya had danced and swooned in the ecstasy of His intense love in separation from Lord Kṛṣṇa.

Passing over the parade route, Abhay recalled his own childhood pastimes—singing and dancing in the street, the miniature cart, the procession, Jagannātha smiling, his father and mother, Rādhā-Govinda. Somehow the fame of Lord Jagannātha had inspired him as a child, and it had remained within him all these years: "When shall I go to Jagannātha Purī?" His childhood dreaming of Purī and Vṛndāvana and his compulsively studying the train tables, scheming since the age of five to travel here, were based on more than just a desire to tour Purī's marketplace, and he was not satisfied by once seeing the Deity in the noisy, crowded temple. He had been impelled to come to Purī as a pilgrim, and his motive was his devotion to Kṛṣṇa.

Now nationalism was strongly influencing his life, and he had recently married and was facing the decisions of graduation and career. Yet here he was, hardly more than a boy, walking alone in Purī, where Lord Caitanya had lived and where Lord Kṛṣṇa's Jagannātha still resided. Abhay relished his break from the pressure of duties in Calcutta. He didn't know how the love he felt for Kṛṣṇa and Kṛṣṇa's pilgrimage place would fit into his life. He knew that Kṛṣṇa was more important than anything else—He was God, the supreme controller, and everyone's inner guide. But there was so much token, superficial service to God. Even the nationalist speakers, although they carried the *Gītā* on their person, were more intent on nationalism than on Kṛṣṇa. Only those who were sincere devotees knew the importance and attraction of Kṛṣṇa—people like his father.

An odd incident occurred at Purī. Gour Mohan had given Abhay a letter of introduction to an acquaintance who lived in Jagannātha Purī. Abhay went to see him and was well received. When the man was offering him lunch, however, Abhay noticed a small lump within one of the cooking pots. He questioned his host, who replied, "Oh, it is meat."

Abhay was unable to restrain his shock: "No! What is this! I have never taken meat." Abhay looked at his host in astonishment: "I never expected this at Jagannātha Purī."

Ashamed, his host said, "I did not know. I thought this was the best." Abhay pacified the man, but he put his food aside and took no more meals there. After that, Abhay ate only the Jagannātha *prasādam* from the temple.

Abhay stayed in Purī for three or four days, wandering around the holy places and visiting the famous Purī seaside, with its sparkling beach and strongly pounding surf. Several times he recognized some of the priests from the Jagannātha temple as they smoked cigarettes, and he heard of other unsavory activities of the *sādhus* connected with the temple. What kind of *sādhus* were these who ate fish with their Jagannātha *prasādam* and smoked? In this respect, he found Jagannātha Purī disappointing.

*　　*　　*

When Abhay returned home, he found his young wife crying. Then he heard how her friends had told her, "Your husband is not coming back." He told her not to worry, there was no truth in the story; he had only gone for a few days and was now back.

Although his marriage had only recently begun, Abhay was dissatisfied. Radharani Datta was an attractive young girl, but Abhay had never really liked her. He was thinking maybe a different wife would be better, a second wife besides this one. In India it was socially acceptable to marry a second wife, so Abhay decided to take the matter into his own hands; he made arrangements to approach the parents of another girl. But when his father heard about it, he called Abhay and said, "My dear boy, you are eager to take a second wife, but I would advise you not to. It is Kṛṣṇa's grace that your present wife is not to your liking. Take it as a great fortune. If you do not become too attached to your wife and family, that will help you in your future advancement in spiritual life." Abhay accepted his father's advice; he wanted to obey his father, and he appreciated the saintly viewpoint. But he remained thoughtful, a bit awed by his father's forethought, and he wondered how one day in the future he would be advancing in spiritual life and be grateful that his father had done this. "Your future advancement in spiritual life"—Abhay liked the idea. He reconciled himself to the wife he had been given.

* * *

Abhay Charan De's name was included on the posted list of students who had passed the B.A. exams and who were invited to appear for their diploma. But Abhay had decided he didn't want a diploma from Scottish Churches' College. Although as a graduate he would have a promising career, it would be a British-tainted career. If Gandhi succeeded, India would soon be rid of the British. Abhay had made his decision, and when graduation day arrived, the college authorities learned of his rejecting his diploma. In this way, Abhay registered his protest and signaled his response to Gandhi's call.

Gandhi's protest had increased its pitch in recent months. During the war, Indians had remained loyal to the Crown in hopes of generating British sympathy towards the cause of independence. But in 1919 England had passed the Rowlatt Act to repress the move for Indian freedom.

Gandhi had then called on all Indians to observe a *hartāl,* a day in which people all over the country had stayed home from work and school in protest. Although it had been a nonviolent protest, one week later in Amritsar in the public square known as Jallianwalla Bagh, British soldiers shot to death hundreds of unarmed, defenseless Indians who had gathered for a peaceful meeting. Gandhi then lost all faith in the intentions of the empire towards India. Calling for complete noncooperation, he ordered a boycott of everything British—commodities, schools, courts, military honors. And Abhay, in refusing his degree, was moving to align himself more closely with Gandhi's independence movement.

But his heart was not in it. Just as he had never given his heart to college studies, to earning a degree, to his wife, so he was reserved about becoming a full-fledged nationalist. Abhay had become inclined towards the cause, but never really convinced. Now, out of school, out of work, caring little for his career, education, or wife, he remained at home. He tried his hand at writing poetry for the occasion of a friend's wedding. He read *Śrīmad-Bhāgavatam* and the latest speeches of Gandhi. He had no immediate plans.

* * *

Gour Mohan had his plans for Abhay, and the college degree had been an integral part of those plans. But Kṛṣṇa, it seemed, had other plans. The political protest of refusing the Bachelor of Arts degree was more a mark of honor than a social stigma, and Gour Mohan did not reproach his son for it. But Abhay still needed to take up some kind of work. Gour Mohan approached his friend Kartick Bose and asked him to employ Abhay.

Dr. Kartick Chandra Bose, an intimate friend, had been the family doctor since Abhay's childhood. He was a distinguished surgeon, a medical scholar, and a chemical industrialist. He had his own establishment, Bose's Laboratory, in Calcutta, where he manufactured drugs, soaps, and other products for the pharmaceutical industry. Dr. Bose was well known throughout India as the first Indian to manufacture pharmaceutical preparations that had formerly been monopolized by European firms. He agreed to accept Abhay as a department manager at his laboratory.

Although Abhay knew little of the pharmaceutical industry or of management, he felt confident that by reading a few related books he could learn what he needed to know. But when this new young man was suddenly given the post of department manager, several workers became dissatisfied. Some of them were elderly and had been forty years with the firm. They voiced their dissatisfaction amongst themselves and finally confronted Dr. Bose: Why had this young man been put in charge? Dr. Bose replied, "Oh, for that position I needed someone I could trust like my own son. He is signing checks for forty thousand rupees. I could only entrust the personal handling of my accounts in that department to him. His father and I are very close, and this young man is known to me practically as my son."

Gour Mohan felt he had done his best. His prayer was that the principles of pure Vaiṣṇavism he had taught his son would stay with him and guide him throughout his life. Gandhi and the cause of *svarāj* had disrupted Abhay's college career, and Abhay was still inclined towards nationalism, but not so much for a political motive as for a spiritual vision. So Gour Mohan was content. He knew the marriage arrangement was not pleasing to Abhay, but Abhay had accepted his explanation that detachment from wife and family affairs would be good for spiritual advancement. And Abhay was showing an inherent disinterest in materialistic affairs. This also did not displease Gour Mohan, to whom business had always been subservient to his worship of Lord Kṛṣṇa. He had expected this. Now Abhay had a promising job and would be making the best of his marriage. Gour Mohan had done what he could, and he depended on Kṛṣṇa for the ultimate result.

* * *

Gandhi, bolstered by his emergence as a leader among the Congress Party, now openly attacked the empire's exploitative cloth trade with India. England was purchasing raw cotton from India at the lowest prices, manufacturing it into cloth in the Lancashire mills in England, and then selling the monopolized cloth at high prices to the Indian millions. Gandhi's propaganda was that India should return to making her own cloth, using simple spinning wheels and handlooms, thus completely boycotting the British-made cloth and attacking an economic base of Britain's power over India. Traveling by train throughout the country, Gandhi repeatedly appealed to his countrymen to reject all foreign cloth and wear only the simple coarse *khādī* produced from India's own cottage industry. Before the British rule, India had spun and woven her own cloth. Gandhi argued that by breaking the cottage industries, the British were sinking the Indian masses into semistarvation and lifelessness.

To set the example, Gandhi himself worked daily at a primitive spinning wheel and wore only a simple, coarse loincloth and shawl. He would hold meetings and ask people to come forth and reject their imported cloth. On the spot, people would throw down heaps of cloth, and he would set it ablaze. Gandhi's wife complained that the *khādī* was too thick and not convenient to wear while cooking; she asked if while cooking she could wear the light, British-made cloth. "Yes, you're free to cook with your mill cloth on," Gandhi had told her, "but I must exercise a similar freedom by not taking the meal so prepared."

The cause of cottage industry appealed to Abhay. He, too, was not enamored with the modern industrial advances the British had introduced in India. Not only was simple living good for the long-term national economy of hundreds of millions of Indians, as Gandhi was emphasizing, but to Abhay it was also the way of life most conducive to spiritual culture. Abhay put aside his mill-manufactured cloth and took to wearing *khādī*. Now his dress revealed him to whomever he met, British and Indian alike. He was a nationalist, a sympathizer of revolution. To wear *khādī* in India in the early 1920s was not a mere clothing fad; it was a political statement. It meant he was a Gandhian.

CHAPTER THREE

"A Very Nice Saintly Person"

There has not been, there will not be, such benefactors of the highest merit as [Chaitanya] Mahaprabhu and His devotees have been. The offer of other benefits is only a deception; it is rather a great harm, whereas the benefit done by Him and His followers is the truest and greatest eternal benefit. This benefit is not for one particular country, causing mischief to another; but it benefits the whole universe.

—Śrīla Bhaktisiddhānta Sarasvatī

ABHAY'S FRIEND NARENDRANATH Mullik was insistent. He wanted Abhay to see a *sādhu* from Māyāpur. Naren and some of his friends had already met the *sādhu* at his nearby *āśrama* on Ultadanga Junction Road, and now they wanted Abhay's opinion. Everyone within their circle of friends considered Abhay the leader, so if Naren could tell the others that Abhay also had a high regard for the *sādhu,* then that would confirm their own estimations. Abhay was reluctant to go, but Naren pressed him.

They stood talking amidst the passersby on the crowded early-evening street, as the traffic of horse-drawn hackneys, oxcarts, and occasional auto taxis and motor buses moved noisily on the road. Naren put his hand firmly around his friend's arm, trying to drag him forward, while

Abhay smiled but stubbornly pulled the other way. Naren argued that since they were only a few blocks away, they should at least pay a short visit. Abhay laughed and asked to be excused. People could see that the two young men were friends, but it was a curious sight, the handsome young man dressed in white *khādī kurtā* and *dhotī* being pulled along by his friend.

Naren explained that the *sādhu,* Śrīla Bhaktisiddhānta Sarasvatī, was a Vaiṣṇava and a great devotee of Lord Caitanya Mahāprabhu. One of his disciples, a *sannyāsī,* had visited the Mullik house and had invited them to meet Śrīla Bhaktisiddhānta. A few of the Mulliks had gone to see him and had been very much impressed.

But Abhay remained skeptical. "Oh, no! I know all these *sādhus,*" he said. "I'm not going." Abhay had seen many *sādhus* in his childhood; every day his father had entertained at least three or four in his home. Some of them were no more than beggars, and some even smoked *gāñjā.* Gour Mohan had been very liberal in allowing anyone who wore the saffron robes of a *sannyāsī* to come. But did it mean that though a man was no more than a beggar or *gāñjā* smoker, he had to be considered saintly just because he dressed as a *sannyāsī* or was collecting funds in the name of building a monastery or could influence people with his speech?

No. By and large, they were a disappointing lot. Abhay had even seen a man in his neighborhood who was a beggar by occupation. In the morning, when others dressed in their work clothes and went to their jobs, this man would put on saffron cloth and go out to beg and in this way earn his livelihood. But was it fitting that such a so-called *sādhu* be paid a respectful visit, as if he were a *guru?*

Naren argued that he felt that this particular *sādhu* was a very learned scholar and that Abhay should at least meet him and judge for himself. Abhay wished that Naren would not behave this way, but finally he could no longer refuse his friend. Together they walked past the Parsnath Jain Temple to 1 Ultadanga, with its sign, Bhaktivinod Asana, announcing it to be the quarters of the Gaudiya Math.

When they inquired at the door, a young man recognized Mr. Mullik—Naren had previously given a donation—and immediately escorted them up to the roof of the second floor and into the presence of Śrīla Bhaktisiddhānta Sarasvatī, who was sitting and enjoying the early evening atmosphere with a few disciples and guests.

Sitting with his back very straight, Śrīla Bhaktisiddhānta Sarasvatī appeared tall. He was slender, his arms were long, and his complexion was fair and golden. He wore round bifocals with simple frames. His nose was sharp, his forehead broad, and his expression was very scholarly yet not at all timid. The vertical markings of Vaiṣṇava *tilaka* on his forehead were familiar to Abhay, as were the simple *sannyāsa* robes that draped over his right shoulder, leaving the other shoulder and half his chest bare. He wore *tulasī* neck beads, and the clay Vaiṣṇava markings of *tilaka* were visible at his throat, shoulder, and upper arms. A clean white brahminical thread was looped around his neck and draped across his chest. Abhay and Naren, having both been raised in Vaiṣṇava families, immediately offered prostrated obeisances at the sight of the revered *sannyāsī*.

While the two young men were still rising and preparing to sit, before any preliminary formalities of conversation had begun, Śrīla Bhaktisiddhānta immediately said to them, "You are educated young men. Why don't you preach Lord Caitanya Mahāprabhu's message throughout the whole world?"

Abhay could hardly believe what he had just heard. They had not even exchanged views, yet this *sādhu* was telling them what they should do. Sitting face to face with Śrīla Bhaktisiddhānta Sarasvatī, Abhay was gathering his wits and trying to gain a comprehensible impression, but this person had already told them to become preachers and go all over the world!

Abhay was immediately impressed, but he wasn't going to drop his intelligent skepticism. After all, there were assumptions in what the *sādhu* had said. Abhay had already announced himself by his dress to be a follower of Gandhi, and he felt the impulse to raise an argument. Yet as he continued to listen to Śrīla Bhaktisiddhānta speak, he also began to feel won over by the *sādhu's* strength of conviction. He could sense that Śrīla Bhaktisiddhānta didn't care for anything but Lord Caitanya and that this was what made him great. This was why followers had gathered around him and why Abhay himself felt drawn, inspired, and humbled and wanted to hear more. But he felt obliged to make an argument—to test the truth.

Drawn irresistibly into discussion, Abhay spoke up in answer to the words Śrīla Bhaktisiddhānta had so tersely spoken in the first seconds of their meeting. "Who will hear your Caitanya's message?" Abhay queried. "We are a dependent country. First India must become independent. How can we spread Indian culture if we are under British rule?"

Abhay had not asked haughtily, just to be provocative, yet his question was clearly a challenge. If he were to take this *sādhu's* remark to them as a serious one—and there was nothing in Śrīla Bhaktisiddhānta's demeanor to indicate that he had not been serious—Abhay felt compelled to question how he could propose such a thing while India was still dependent.

Śrīla Bhaktisiddhānta replied in a quiet, deep voice that Kṛṣṇa consciousness didn't have to wait for a change in Indian politics, nor was it dependent on who ruled. Kṛṣṇa consciousness was so important—so exclusively important—that it *could not wait.*

Abhay was struck by his boldness. How could he say such a thing? The whole world of India beyond this little Ultadanga rooftop was in turmoil and seemed to support what Abhay had said. Many famous leaders of Bengal, many saints, even Gandhi himself, men who were educated and spiritually minded, all might very well have asked this same question, challenging this *sādhu's* relevancy. And yet he was dismissing everything and everyone as if they were of no consequence.

Śrīla Bhaktisiddhānta continued: Whether one power or another ruled was a temporary situation; but the eternal reality is Kṛṣṇa consciousness, and the real self is the spirit soul. No man-made political system, therefore, could actually help humanity. This was the verdict of the Vedic scriptures and the line of spiritual masters. Although everyone is an eternal servant of God, when one takes himself to be the temporary body and regards the nation of his birth as worshipable, he comes under illusion. The leaders and followers of the world's political movements, including the movement for *svarāj,* were simply cultivating this illusion. Real welfare work, whether individual, social, or political, should help prepare a person for his next life and help him reestablish his eternal relationship with the Supreme.

Śrīla Bhaktisiddhānta Sarasvatī had articulated these ideas many times before in his writings:

> There has not been, there will not be, such benefactors of the highest merit as [Chaitanya] Mahaprabhu and His devotees have been. The offer of other benefits is only a deception; it is rather a great harm, whereas the benefit

> done by Him and His followers is the truest and greatest eternal benefit. ... This benefit is not for one particular country causing mischief to another; but it benefits the whole universe. ... The kindness that Shri Chaitanya Mahaprabhu has shown to jivas absolves them eternally from all wants, from all inconveniences and from all the distresses. ... That kindness does not produce any evil, and the jivas who have it will not be the victims of the evils of the world.

As Abhay listened attentively to the arguments of Śrīla Bhaktisiddhānta Sarasvatī, he recalled a Bengali poet who had written that even less advanced civilizations, like China and Japan, were independent and yet India labored under political oppression. Abhay knew well the philosophy of nationalism, which stressed that Indian independence had to come first. An oppressed people was a reality, the British slaughter of innocent citizens was a reality, and independence *would* benefit people. Spiritual life was a luxury that could be afforded only after independence. In the present times, the cause of national liberation from the British was the only relevant spiritual movement. The people's cause was in itself God.

Yet because Abhay had been raised a Vaiṣṇava, he appreciated what Śrīla Bhaktisiddhānta was saying. Abhay had already concluded that this was certainly not just another questionable *sādhu,* and he perceived the truth in what Śrīla Bhaktisiddhānta said. This *sādhu* wasn't concocting his own philosophy, and he wasn't simply proud or belligerent, even though he spoke in a way that kicked out practically every other philosophy. He was speaking the eternal teachings of the Vedic literature and the sages, and Abhay loved to hear it.

Śrīla Bhaktisiddhānta, speaking sometimes in English and sometimes in Bengali, and sometimes quoting the Sanskrit verses of the *Bhagavad-gītā,* spoke of Śrī Kṛṣṇa as the highest Vedic authority. In the *Bhagavad-gītā* Kṛṣṇa had declared that a person should give up whatever duty he considers religious and surrender unto Him, the Personality of Godhead (*sarva-dharmān parityajya mām ekaṁ śaraṇaṁ vraja*). And the *Śrīmad-Bhāgavatam* confirmed the same thing. *Dharmaḥ projjhita-kaitavo 'tra paramo nirmatsarāṇāṁ satām:* all other forms of religion are impure and should be thrown out, and only *bhāgavata-dharma,* performing one's duties to please the Supreme Lord, should remain. Śrīla Bhaktisiddhānta's presentation was so cogent that anyone who accepted the *śāstras* would have to accept his conclusion.

The people were now faithless, said Bhaktisiddhānta, and therefore they no longer believed that devotional service could remove all anomalies, even on the political scene. He went on to criticize anyone who was ignorant of the soul and yet claimed to be a leader. He even cited names of contemporary leaders and pointed out their failures, and he emphasized the urgent need to render the highest good to humanity by educating people about the eternal soul and the soul's relation to Kṛṣṇa and devotional service.

Abhay had never forgotten the worship of Lord Kṛṣṇa or His teachings in *Bhagavad-gītā*. And his family had always worshiped Lord Caitanya Mahāprabhu, whose mission Bhaktisiddhānta Sarasvatī was espousing. As these Gaudiya Math people worshiped Kṛṣṇa, he also had worshiped Kṛṣṇa throughout his life and had never forgotten Kṛṣṇa. But now he was astounded to hear the Vaiṣṇava philosophy presented so masterfully. Despite his involvement in college, marriage, the national movement, and other affairs, he had never forgotten Kṛṣṇa. But Bhaktisiddhānta Sarasvatī was now stirring up within him his original Kṛṣṇa consciousness, and by the words of this spiritual master not only was he remembering Kṛṣṇa, but he felt his Kṛṣṇa consciousness being enhanced a thousand times, a million times. What had been unspoken in Abhay's boyhood, what had been vague in Jagannātha Purī, what he had been distracted from at college, what he had been protected in by his father now surged forth within Abhay in responsive feelings. And he wanted to keep it.

He felt himself defeated. But he liked it. He suddenly realized that he had never before been defeated. But this defeat was not a loss. It was an immense gain.

Śrīla Prabhupāda: *I was from a Vaiṣṇava family, so I could appreciate what he was preaching. Of course, he was speaking to everyone, but he found something in me. And I was convinced about his argument and mode of presentation. I was so much struck with wonder. I could understand: Here is the proper person who can give a real religious idea.*

It was late. Abhay and Naren had been talking with him for more than two hours. One of the *brahmacārīs* gave them each a bit of *prasādam* in their open palms, and they rose gratefully and took their leave.

They walked down the stairs and onto the street. The night was dark. Here and there a light was burning, and there were some open shops. Abhay pondered in great satisfaction what he had just heard. Śrīla Bhaktisiddhānta's explanation of the independence movement as a temporary, incomplete cause had made a deep impression on him. He felt himself less a nationalist and more a follower of Śrīla Bhaktisiddhānta Sarasvatī. He also thought that it would have been better if he were not married. This great personality was asking him to preach. He could have immediately joined, but he was married; and to leave his family would be an injustice.

Walking away from the *āśrama,* Naren turned to his friend: "So, Abhay, what was your impression? What do you think of him?"

"He's wonderful!" replied Abhay. "The message of Lord Caitanya is in the hands of a very expert person."

Śrīla Prabhupāda: *I accepted him as my spiritual master immediately. Not officially, but in my heart. I was thinking that I had met a very nice saintly person.*

* * *

After his first meeting with Śrīla Bhaktisiddhānta Sarasvatī, Abhay began to associate more with the Gaudiya Math devotees. They gave him books and told him the history of their spiritual master.

Śrīla Bhaktisiddhānta Sarasvatī was one of ten children born to Bhaktivinoda Ṭhākura, a great Vaiṣṇava teacher in the disciplic line from Lord Caitanya Himself. Before the time of Bhaktivinoda, the teachings of Lord Caitanya had been obscured by teachers and sects falsely claiming to be followers of Lord Caitanya but deviating in various drastic ways from His pure teachings. The good reputation of Vaiṣṇavism had been compromised. Bhaktivinoda Ṭhākura, however, through his prolific writings and through his social position as a high government officer, reestablished the respectability of Vaiṣṇavism. He preached that the teachings of Lord Caitanya were the highest form of theism and were intended not for a particular sect or religion or nation but for all the people of the world. He prophesied that Lord Caitanya's teachings would go worldwide, and he yearned for it.

> The religion preached by [Chaitanya] Mahaprabhu is universal and not exclusive. ... The principle of kirtan as the future church of the world invites all classes of men, without distinction of caste or clan, to the highest cultivation of the spirit. This church, it appears, will extend all over the world and take the place of all sectarian churches, which exclude outsiders from the precincts of the mosque, church, or temple.

> Lord Chaitanya did not advent Himself to liberate only a few men of India. Rather, His main objective was to emancipate all living entities of all countries throughout the entire universe and preach the Eternal Religion. Lord Chaitanya says in the Chaitanya Bhagwat: "In every town, country, and village, My name will be sung." There is no doubt that this unquestionable order will come to pass. ... Although there is still no pure society of Vaishnavas to be had, yet Lord Chaitanya's prophetic words will in a few days come true, I am sure. Why not? Nothing is absolutely pure in the beginning. From imperfection, purity will come about.
>
> Oh, for that day when the fortunate English, French, Russian, German, and American people will take up banners, mridangas, and kartals and raise kirtan through their streets and towns. When will that day come?

As a prominent magistrate, Bhaktivinoda Ṭhākura was a responsible government officer. He served also as superintendent of the temple of Lord Jagannātha and was the father of ten children. Yet in spite of these responsibilities, he served the cause of Kṛṣṇa with prodigious energy. After coming home from his office in the evening, taking his meals, and going to bed, he would sleep from eight until midnight and then get up and write until morning. He wrote more than one hundred books during his life, many of them in English. One of his important contributions, with the cooperation of Jagannātha dāsa Bābājī and Gaurakiśora dāsa Bābājī, was to locate the exact birthplace of Lord Caitanya in Māyāpur, about sixty miles north of Calcutta.

While working to reform Gauḍīya Vaiṣṇavism in India, he prayed to Lord Caitanya, "Your teachings have been much depreciated. It is not in my power to restore them." And he prayed for a son to help him in his preaching. When, on February 6, 1874, Bhaktisiddhānta Sarasvatī was born to Bhaktivinoda Ṭhākura in Jagannātha Purī, the Vaiṣṇavas considered him the answer to his father's prayers. He was born with the umbilical cord wrapped around his neck and draped across his chest like the sacred thread worn by *brāhmaṇas.* His parents gave him the name Bimala Prasada.

When Bimala Prasada was six months old, the carts of the Jagannātha festival stopped at the gate of Bhaktivinoda's residence and for three days could not be moved. Bhaktivinoda Ṭhākura's wife brought the infant onto the cart and approached the Deity of Lord Jagannātha. Spontaneously, the infant extended his arms and touched the feet of Lord Jagannātha and was immediately blessed with a garland that fell from the body of the Lord. When Bhaktivinoda Ṭhākura learned that the Lord's garland had fallen onto his son, he realized that this was the son for whom he had prayed.

One day, when Bimala Prasada was still a child of no more than four years, his father mildly rebuked him for eating a mango not yet duly offered to Lord Kṛṣṇa. Bimala Prasada, although only a child, considered himself an offender to the Lord and vowed never to eat mangoes again. (This was a vow that he would follow throughout his life.) By the time Bimala Prasada was seven years old, he had memorized the entire *Bhagavad-gītā* and could even explain its verses. His father then began training him in proofreading and printing, in conjunction with the publishing of the Vaiṣṇava magazine *Sajjana-toṣaṇī*. With his father, he visited many holy places and heard discourses from the learned *paṇḍitas*.

As a student, Bimala Prasada preferred to read the books written by his father instead of the school texts. By the time he was twenty-five he had become well versed in Sanskrit, mathematics, and astronomy, and he had established himself as the author and publisher of many magazine articles and one book, *Sūrya-siddhānta*, for which he received the epithet Siddhānta Sarasvatī in recognition of his erudition. When he was twenty-six his father guided him to take initiation from a renounced Vaiṣṇava saint, Gaurakiśora dāsa Bābājī, who advised him "to preach the Absolute Truth and keep aside all other works." Receiving the blessings of Gaurakiśora dāsa Bābājī, Bimala Prasada (now Siddhānta Sarasvatī) resolved to dedicate his body, mind, and words to the service of Lord Kṛṣṇa.

In 1905 Siddhānta Sarasvatī took a vow to chant the Hare Kṛṣṇa *mantra* a billion times. Residing in Māyāpur in a grass hut near the birthplace of Lord Caitanya, he chanted the Hare Kṛṣṇa *mantra* day and night. He cooked rice once a day in an earthen pot and ate nothing more; he slept on the ground, and when the rainwater leaked through the grass ceiling, he sat beneath an umbrella, chanting.

In 1911, while his aging father was lying ill, Siddhānta Sarasvatī took up a challenge against pseudo Vaiṣṇavas who claimed that birth in their caste was the prerequisite for preaching Kṛṣṇa consciousness. The caste-conscious *brāhmaṇa* community had become incensed by Bhaktivinoda Ṭhākura's presentation of many scriptural proofs that anyone, regardless of birth, could become a *brāhmaṇa* Vaiṣṇava. These *smārta-brāhmaṇas,* out to prove the inferiority of the Vaiṣṇavas, arranged a discussion. On behalf of his indisposed father, young Siddhānta Sarasvatī wrote an essay, "The Conclusive Difference Between the Brāhmaṇa and the Vaiṣṇava," and submitted it before his father. Despite his poor health, Bhaktivinoda Ṭhākura was elated to hear the arguments that would soundly defeat the challenge of the *smārtas.*

Siddhānta Sarasvatī then traveled to Midnapore, where *paṇḍitas* from all over India had gathered for a three-day discussion. Some of the *smārta-paṇḍitas* who spoke first claimed that anyone born in a *śūdra* family, even though initiated by a spiritual master, could never become purified and perform the brahminical duties of worshiping the Deity or initiating disciples. Finally, Siddhānta Sarasvatī delivered his speech. He began quoting Vedic references glorifying the *brāhmaṇas,* and at this the *smārta* scholars became very much pleased. But when he began discussing the actual qualifications for becoming a *brāhmaṇa,* the qualities of the Vaiṣṇavas, the relationship between the two, and who, according to the Vedic literature, is qualified to become a spiritual master and initiate disciples, then the joy of the Vaiṣṇava-haters disappeared. Siddhānta Sarasvatī conclusively proved from the scriptures that if one is born as a *śūdra* but exhibits the qualities of a *brāhmaṇa,* then he should be honored as a *brāhmaṇa,* despite his birth. And if one is born in a *brāhmaṇa* family but acts like a *śūdra,* then he is not a *brāhmaṇa.* After his speech, Siddhānta Sarasvatī was congratulated by the president of the conference, and thousands thronged around him. It was a victory for Vaiṣṇavism.

With the passing away of his father in 1914 and his spiritual master in 1915, Siddhānta Sarasvatī continued the mission of Lord Caitanya. He assumed editorship of *Sajjana-toṣaṇī* and established the Bhagwat Press in Krishnanagar. Then in 1918, in Māyāpur, he sat down before a picture of Gaurakiśora dāsa Bābājī and initiated himself into the *sannyāsa* order. At this time he assumed the *sannyāsa* title Bhaktisiddhānta Sarasvatī Gosvāmī Mahārāja.

Bhaktisiddhānta Sarasvatī was dedicated to using the printing press as the best medium for large-scale distribution of Kṛṣṇa consciousness. He thought of the printing press as a *bṛhad-mṛdaṅga,* a big *mṛdaṅga.* Although the *mṛdaṅga* drum had traditionally been used to accompany *kīrtana,* even during the time of Lord Caitanya, and although Bhaktisiddhānta Sarasvatī himself led *kīrtana* parties and sent groups of devotees chanting in the streets and playing on the *mṛdaṅgas,* such *kīrtanas* could be heard only for a block or two. But with the *bṛhad-mṛdaṅga,* the big *mṛdaṅga* drum of the printing press, the message of Lord Caitanya could be spread all over the world.

Most of the literature Abhay began reading had been printed on the Bhagwat Press, which Bhaktisiddhānta Sarasvatī had established in 1915. The Bhagwat Press had printed the *Caitanya-caritāmṛta,* with commentary by Bhaktisiddhānta Sarasvatī, the *Bhagavad-gītā,* with commentary by Viśvanātha Cakravartī, and one after another, the works of Bhaktivinoda Ṭhākura. This literature was the spiritual heritage coming from Lord Caitanya Mahāprabhu, who had appeared almost five hundred years before.

Abhay had been a devotee of Lord Caitanya since childhood, and he was familiar with the life of Lord Caitanya through the well-known scriptures *Caitanya-caritāmṛta* and *Caitanya-bhāgavata.* He had learned of Lord Caitanya not only as the most ecstatic form of a pure devotee who had spread the chanting of the holy name to all parts of India, but also as the direct appearance of Śrī Kṛṣṇa Himself in the form of Rādhā and Kṛṣṇa combined. But now, for the first time, Abhay was in touch with the great wealth of literature compiled by the Lord's immediate associates and followers, passed down in disciplic succession, and expanded on by great authorities. Lord Caitanya's immediate followers—Śrīla Rūpa Gosvāmī, Śrīla Sanātana Gosvāmī, Śrīla Jīva Gosvāmī, and others—had compiled many volumes based on the Vedic scriptures and proving conclusively that Lord Caitanya's teachings were the essence of Vedic wisdom. There were many books not yet published, but Śrīla Bhaktisiddhānta Sarasvatī was intent on establishing many presses, just to release the sound of the *bṛhad-mṛdaṅga* for the benefit of all people.

Śrīla Bhaktisiddhānta Sarasvatī was teaching the conclusion of Lord Caitanya's teachings, that Lord Kṛṣṇa is the Supreme Personality of Godhead and that the chanting of His holy name should be stressed above all other religious practices. In former ages, other methods of attaining to God had been available, but in the present Age of Kali only the chanting of Hare Kṛṣṇa would be effective. On the authority of the scriptures such as the *Bṛhan-nāradīya Purāṇa* and the *Upaniṣads,* Bhaktivinoda Ṭhākura had specifically cited the *mahā-mantra:* Hare Kṛṣṇa, Hare Kṛṣṇa, Kṛṣṇa Kṛṣṇa, Hare Hare/ Hare Rāma, Hare Rāma, Rāma Rāma, Hare Hare. Lord Kṛṣṇa Himself had confirmed in *Bhagavad-gītā* that the only method of attaining Him was devotional service: "Abandon all varieties of religion and just surrender unto Me. I shall deliver you from all sinful reactions. Do not fear."

Abhay knew these verses, he knew the chanting, and he knew the conclusions of the *Gītā.* But now, as he eagerly read the writings of the great *ācāryas,* he had fresh realizations of the scope of Lord Caitanya's mission. Now he was discovering the depth of his own Vaiṣṇava heritage and its efficacy for bringing about the highest welfare for people in an age destined to be full of troubles.

* * *

Śrīla Bhaktisiddhānta was often traveling, and Abhay was busy with his family and business, so to arrange another meeting was not possible. Yet from their first encounter Abhay had considered Bhaktisiddhānta Sarasvatī his spiritual master, and Abhay began thinking of him always, "I have met such a nice saintly person." Whenever possible, Abhay would seek out Śrīla Bhaktisiddhānta's disciples, the members of the Gaudiya Math.

As for Gandhi's movement, Gandhi had suffered a bitter setback when his nonviolent followers had blundered and committed violence during a protest. The British had taken the opportunity to arrest Gandhi and sentence him to six years in jail. Although his followers still revered him, the nationalist movement had lost much of its impetus. But regardless of that, Abhay was no longer interested. Śrīla Bhaktisiddhānta Sarasvatī had defeated his idea that the nationalist cause was India's first priority. He had invoked Abhay's original Kṛṣṇa consciousness, and Abhay now felt confident that Bhaktisiddhānta's mission was the real priority. Śrīla Bhaktisiddhānta had invited him to preach, and from that moment Abhay had wanted to join the Gaudiya Math as one of Śrīla Bhaktisiddhānta Sarasvatī's disciples. But now, instead of his political inclinations, it was his family obligations that stood in the way. He was no longer thinking, "First let us become an independent nation, then preach about Lord Caitanya." Now he was thinking, "I cannot take part like the others. I have my family responsibilities."

And the family was growing. In 1921 Abhay and his wife had had their first child, a son. And there would be more children, and more income would be needed. Earning money meant sacrificing time and energy, and it meant, at least externally, being distracted from the mission of Bhaktisiddhānta Sarasvatī. Indian culture had the highest regard for the family institution, and divorce was unheard of. Even if a man was in great financial difficulty, he would remain with his wife and children. Although Abhay expressed regret at not being a *sannyāsī* disciple in the Gaudiya Math, he never seriously considered leaving his young wife so early in their marriage. Gour Mohan was pleased to hear of his son's attraction to a Vaiṣṇava *guru,* but he never expected Abhay to abandon responsibilities and enter the renounced order. A Vaiṣṇava could remain with wife and family, practice spiritual life at home, and even become active in preaching. Abhay would have to find ways to serve the mission of Bhaktisiddhānta Sarasvatī as a family man.

Abhay thought that if he were to become very successful in business, then he could spend money not only to support his family but also to help support Śrīla Bhaktisiddhānta Sarasvatī's mission of spreading Kṛṣṇa consciousness. An astrologer had even predicted that Abhay would become one of the wealthiest men in India. But with his present income he could do little more than provide for his family's needs. He thought he might do better by trying to develop a business on his own.

Abhay expressed his feelings to Dr. Bose, who listened like a sympathetic father and suggested that Abhay become his agent for all of northern India. Abhay could purchase medicines, liniments, rectified spirits, toothpastes, and other items wholesale from Dr. Bose's factory and travel widely throughout northern India, building up his own business. Also, Abhay had enough experience with Bose's Laboratory that he could try to make and market some of his own medicines and products. Dr. Bose and Abhay decided that the centrally located city of Allahabad would be a good place for Abhay to make his headquarters.

* * *

In 1923, Abhay and his wife and child moved to Allahabad, a twelve-hour train ride northwest from Calcutta. The British had once made Allahabad the capital of the United Provinces, and they had built many good buildings there, including buildings for a high court and a university. Europeans and affluent Indian families like the Nehrus lived in a modern, paved, well-lit section of town. There was also another, older section, with ancient narrow streets closely lined with buildings and shops. Many Bengalis resided there, and it was there that Abhay decided to settle his family.

He had chosen Allahabad, traditionally known as Prayāga, as a good location for business, but it was also one of India's most famous places of pilgrimage. Situated at the confluence of the three holiest rivers of India—the Ganges, the Yamunā, and the Sarasvatī—Allahabad was the site of two of India's most widely attended spiritual events, the annual Māgha-melā, and the Kumbha-melā, which took place every twelve years. And in search of spiritual purification, millions of pilgrims from all over India would converge here each year at the time of the full moon in the month of Māgha (January) and bathe at the junction of the three sacred rivers.

Abhay's home at 60 Badshahi Mundi consisted of a few rented rooms. For his business he rented a small shop in the commercial center of the city at Johnston Gung Road, where he opened his dispensary, Prayag Pharmacy, and began selling medicines, tinctures, syrups, and other products manufactured by Bose's Laboratory. He met an Allahabad physician, Dr. Ghosh, who was interested in a business partnership, so Abhay asked him to become his attending physician and move his office to Prayag Pharmacy. Dr. Ghosh consented and closed his own shop, Tropical Pharmacy.

At Prayag Pharmacy, Dr. Ghosh would diagnose patients and give medical prescriptions, which Abhay would fill. Dr. Ghosh would then receive a twenty-five-percent commission from the sale of the prescriptions. Abhay and Dr. Ghosh became friends; they would visit at each other's home, and they treated each other's children like their own family members. Often they discussed their aspirations for increasing profits.

Dr. Ghosh: *Abhay was a business-minded man. We were all God-fearing, of course. In every home we have a small temple, and we must have Deities. But he used to always talk about business and how to meet family expenses.*

Although at home Abhay wore a *kurtā* and *dhotī,* sometimes for business he would dress in shirt and pants. He was a good-looking, full-mustached, energetic young man in his late twenties. He and Radharani De now had two children—a daughter was born after they had been in Allahabad one year. Gour Mohan, who was now seventy-five, had come to live with him, as had Abhay's widowed sister, Rajesvari, and her son, Tulasi. Gour Mohan mostly stayed at home, chanted on his beads, and worshiped the *śālagrāma-śilā* Deity of Kṛṣṇa. He was satisfied that Abhay was doing right, and Abhay was satisfied to have his father living comfortably with him and freely worshiping Kṛṣṇa.

Abhay led a busy life. He was intent on building his business. By 8:00 A.M. he would go to his pharmacy, where he would meet Dr. Ghosh and begin his day's work. At noon he would come home, and then he would return to the pharmacy in the late afternoon. He had purchased a large Buick for eight thousand rupees, and although he never drove it himself, he let his nephew, a good driver, use it for his taxi business. Occasionally, Abhay would use the car on his own business excursions, and his nephew would then act as his chauffeur.

It so happened that both Motilal Nehru and his son Jawaharlal were customers at Prayag Pharmacy. Because Jawaharlal would always order Western medicines, Abhay thought he must have felt that Indian ways were inferior. Once, Jawaharlal approached Abhay for a political contribution, and Abhay donated, being a conscientious merchant. During the day Abhay would talk with his customers and other friends who would stop by, and they would tell him many things. A former military officer used to tell Abhay stories of World War I. He told how Marshal Foch in France had one day ordered the killing of thousands of Belgian refugees whose maintenance had become a burden to him on the battlefield. A Muhammadan gentleman, a member of a royal family in Afghanistan, would come daily with his son to sit and chat. Abhay would listen to his visitors and converse pleasantly and make up their prescriptions, but his thoughts kept returning to his meeting with Bhaktisiddhānta Sarasvatī. He went over it again and again in his mind—how he had looked, his mannerisms, what he had said.

At night Abhay would go home to his wife and children. Radharani was a chaste and faithful wife who spent her days cooking, cleaning, and caring for her two children. But she was not inclined to share her husband's interest in things spiritual. He could not convey to her his feelings about Bhaktisiddhānta Sarasvatī.

* * *

Abhay; his wife; their two children; Gour Mohan; Abhay's younger brother, Krishna Charan; Abhay's widowed sister, Rajesvari; and her son,

Tulasi das, all went together to an Allahabad studio for a family portrait. The photo shows Abhay in his late twenties. He is thin and dark, with a full mustache. His forehead is broad, his eyes dark and clear. He wears a white *kurtā* and *dhotī* and plain dark slippers. He sits in a chair, his wife standing behind him, an attractive young woman in a white *khādī sārī* with a line of color on the border. Her slim arm rests behind Abhay's head on the back of his chair, her small hand gripping the edge of the chair. Her left hand hangs by her side, gripped in a fist. She is barefoot. With his left hand, Abhay steadies his two-year-old boy, "Pacha" (Prayag Raj), a glaring infant, on his lap, the boy seeming to squirm, his baby legs and bare feet dangling by his mother's knee. Abhay seems a bit amused by the son on his lap. Abhay is a handsome Indian man, his wife an attractive woman, both young.

Also behind Abhay stands his nephew Tulasi and his brother, Krishna Charan. Sitting on the far right is Abhay's sister Rajesvari, dressed in a widow's white *sārī,* holding Sulakshmana, Abhay's daughter, on her lap. Sulakshmana is also squirming, her foot jutting towards the photographer. In the center sits Gour Mohan. His face is shriveled, and his whole body is emaciated with age. He is also wearing a white *kurtā* and *dhotī.* His hands seem to be moving actively on his lap, perhaps with palsy. He is short and small and old.

* * *

Abhay traveled frequently throughout northern India, intent on expanding his sales. It was not unusual for him to be gone a few days in a week, and sometimes a week or more at a time, as he traveled from one city to another. The pharmaceutical industry was just beginning in India, and doctors, hospitals, and pharmacies were eager to buy from the competent, gentlemanly agent who called on them from Bose's Laboratory of Calcutta.

He would travel by train and stay in hotels. He liked the feeling of freedom from home that traveling afforded, but the real drive was servicing accounts and getting new ones; that was his business. Riding in a third-class unreserved compartment was often uncomfortable; the only seats were benches, which were often dirty, and passengers were permitted to crowd on without reservations. But that is how Abhay traveled, hundreds of miles every week. As the train moved between towns, he would see the numberless small villages and then the country land that spread out before him on either side of the tracks. At every stop, he would hear the cries of the tea vendors as they walked alongside the train windows: "*Chāy*! *Chāy*!" Tea! The British had introduced it, and now millions of Indians were convinced that they could not get through the morning without their little glass of hot tea. As a strict Vaiṣṇava, Abhay never touched it, but his wife, much to his displeasure, was becoming a regular tea drinker.

Although Abhay was accustomed to dressing as a European businessman, he never compromised his strict Vaiṣṇava principles. Most of his fellow Bengalis had taken up fish-eating, but Abhay was always careful to avoid non-Vaiṣṇava foods, even at hotels. Once at a vegetarian hotel, the Empire Hindu Hotel in Bombay, he was served onions, and sometimes hotel people tried to serve him mushrooms, garlic, and even eggs, but all of these he carefully avoided. Keeping a small semblance of his home routine, he would take his bath early in the morning with cold water. He followed this routine year-round, and when, in Saharanpur, he did so during the bitter cold weather, the hotelkeeper was greatly surprised.

Abhay conversed with many people in his travels. A doctor in Dacca told him that on his way to the office he had passed a farmer talking to a friend and could tell by the sound of the farmer's cough that the farmer would die within a few hours. Another doctor told Abhay that he had just come from seeing a pneumonia patient who was defying nature and medical science by continuing to live. He met a Muhammadan doctor in Gayā who lamented that he had just lost a patient, although he had given the man the very best medicine. Such accounts from men of the medical profession confirmed Abhay's conviction that without God's sanction no one could be saved. Not that he ever thought of his medical sales as philanthropic work; Bhaktisiddhānta Sarasvatī had already convinced him that the only way to save a person was by giving him Kṛṣṇa consciousness. Abhay's medical products were strictly for business.

On one business trip—it was in 1925—he traveled through Agra, only forty miles south of Vṛndāvana. Taking the opportunity, he made his first visit to holy Vṛndāvana, fulfilling his childhood aspiration. He loved the sight of Vṛndāvana, but he could spend only a day or two; even a single day away from his sales work could be critical. As a reverent pilgrim, Abhay visited a few temples, especially the principal temples established by the followers of Lord Caitanya. But he had to move on.

There were also risks in traveling. Once he was sitting in a train compartment in Mathurā station when a monkey suddenly entered and took away his belongings. Early one morning before dawn, while he was on his way to Kanpur in a two-wheeled horse carriage, the horse was going at a fast trot when suddenly it hit a large heap of rubbish in the middle of the road. The carriage turned upside down, horse, driver, and carriage all landed in a heap, and Abhay was thrown into the air. But he landed unharmed, feeling as though he had just changed to another seat. Because Abhay sat but said nothing, the driver thought he had been knocked unconscious and became anxious. The passenger was all right, however, and the driver considered it a miracle, since the cart had so violently ejected him. Abhay took it that he had been saved by Kṛṣṇa, and he remembered similar incidents, starting with his childhood when his clothing had caught on fire. Kṛṣṇa had always protected him.

For five years Abhay traveled widely out of Allahabad, and when he was home he put in long hours at the dispensary. But he also spent time with his wife and played with his children.

Śrīla Prabhupāda: *When my son was about two years old, he was very naughty, always doing some mischief. My friends used to visit me and call my son, Pacha. "Pacha, if you sit down for one minute, silently, I will give you a gift." But the boy failed. He could not sit down, even for a minute. There was a table fan, and Pacha was wanting to touch it. I said, "No, no, don't touch." But again he tried to touch it, so my friend said, "Just lower the speed and let him touch it." So I unplugged the fan, and then he touched it. It did not harm him, but it hit his finger with a loud noise,* "Tunng!" *And then he would not touch again. I would ask him, "Touch again?" but he would not.*

As soon as his daughter, Sulakshmana, could speak, he began teaching her the Bengali translation of the prayer *Gurv-aṣṭakam,* which begins, "The spiritual master is receiving benedictions from the ocean of mercy. Just as a cloud pours water on a forest fire to extinguish it, the spiritual master extinguishes the blazing fire of material life, of repeated birth and death."

Except for his obligatory travels, Abhay stayed at home and satisfied his family. He tended diligently to his business, and it prospered.

* * *

It was Kumbha-melā, January 1928. Bhaktipradīpa Tīrtha Mahārāja of the Gaudiya Math had come to Allahabad with a few men. One day he walked unannounced into the Prayag Pharmacy, and all of a sudden Abhay was seeing them again, after so many years. "Oh, these are the people I saw before!" he thought. "Gaudiya Math. Yes, come in."

Bhaktipradīpa Tīrtha Swami was the same *sannyāsī* who had visited Narendranath Mullik in Calcutta, a visit that had led to Abhay's going to visit Bhaktisiddhānta Sarasvatī. Folding his palms in a humble gesture, standing before Abhay in simple saffron *khādī* robes, his shaven head, with a tuft of *śikhā* in the back, his forehead marked with Vaiṣṇava *tilaka,* Tīrtha Mahārāja said to Abhay, "We are new here. We are going to establish a temple in Allahabad. We have heard your name, so we have come to you. Please help us."

Abhay was joyful: "Yes, I will help you." He contributed what money he could and then introduced Tīrtha Mahārāja to Dr. Ghosh, who also contributed.

Abhay invited the Gaudiya Math devotees to come to his home and hold a *bhajana* and lecture; his wife would cook *prasādam.* They accepted, but when they arrived there was a misunderstanding. Gour Mohan, who was invalid, was staying in his room upstairs. "Please come down," Abhay called. "There's a meeting of the Gaudiya Math." Gour Mohan came downstairs, but when he saw the *sādhus* he mistook them for impersonalists from a nondevotional mission. He had not heard correctly what Abhay had said. Gour Mohan took his seat, but he observed the saffron-clothed men sullenly and even made a critical remark. Abhay, who was enlivened at the opportunity to associate with the Vaiṣṇavas and hear from them *kṛṣṇa-kathā,* could not understand his father's behavior. Then, as soon as Bhaktipradīpa Tīrtha Swami began his lecture, Gour Mohan understood. "Oh, they are Vaiṣṇavas!" he cried. Old and invalid as he was, he immediately fell down at their feet: "I misunderstood you, sir. I thought you were *sannyāsīs* from another mission. I am glad to meet you."

After Kumbha-melā, Pradīpa Tīrtha Swami left, but five or six *brahmacārī* disciples of Bhaktisiddhānta Sarasvatī stayed on in Allahabad, maintaining a small *maṭha* headquarters. They worshiped the Deity, held an evening program of *kīrtana* and lecture, and preached actively to the local people. The devotee in charge, Atulānanda Brahmacārī, would visit the homes of Allahabad citizens, trying to solicit subscriber members for the *maṭha;* for half a rupee per month, a person would receive a subscription to the Gaudiya Math magazine.

In the course of his door-to-door soliciting, Atulānanda knocked on the door of Abhay Charan De. Abhay received him very hospitably and offered him some rice and fruit. Abhay was very receptive to the philosophy and relished discussions with Atulānanda, who made it a point to visit Mr. De repeatedly and speak with him about Lord Caitanya and the *Bhagavad-gītā.* Abhay also inquired into the recent activities of Śrīla Bhaktisiddhānta Sarasvatī. By now, Śrīla Bhaktisiddhānta had established the Gaudiya Printing Works in Calcutta and had begun to publish the *Śrīmad-Bhāgavatam,* in several volumes with his own annotations. He had also published an edited version of *Śrī Caitanya-bhāgavata* from his center in Dacca. He had opened centers in Bhubaneswar, Madras, and Purī.

Abhay's interest was insatiable. Atulānanda told him how in 1925 Śrīla Bhaktisiddhānta Sarasvatī had led a big procession, circumambulating the holy land of Navadvīpa, with Deities riding on the backs of gorgeously decorated elephants, and with devotees from all parts of India attending. Envious professional priests who opposed Śrīla Bhaktisiddhānta's acceptance of disciples from all castes had employed a gang to help them hurl bricks and rocks on the procession. But Śrīla Bhaktisiddhānta had continued, undaunted. In 1926 he had toured throughout India, preaching the message of Lord Caitanya. He had also installed Deities in the large temple of Shri Chaitanya Math in Māyāpur. And a year ago he had begun publishing his magazine *Sajjana-toṣaṇī* in three languages, including an English edition called *The Harmonist.*

After several visits and hours of discussion on the activities and philosophy of Gauḍīya Vaiṣṇavism, Atulānanda brought Mr. De to the Allahabad *āśrama.* Shortly thereafter, the *maṭha* relocated to a rented house on South Mallaca Street near Ram Bagh, just a short walk from Abhay's house. Now it was possible for Abhay to visit every evening. After work, he would attend the *maṭha,* where he would play the *mṛdaṅga,* surprising the *brahmacārīs* with his already developed *mṛdaṅga*-playing skills. He sang *bhajanas* with them and sometimes took the lead part in the congregational singing. He would also bring important persons from Allahabad to visit the *maṭha.* For the *brahmacārīs,* Abhay seemed to give new life to their *āśrama,* and for Abhay new life had come to him in his reunion with the disciples of Bhaktisiddhānta Sarasvatī.

* * *

In 1930 Gour Mohan's health took a turn for the worse, and his family members gathered around him, thinking that his end had come. Abhay had been in Bombay on business, and it was late when he reached Allahabad and knocked on the door. Gour Mohan told his daughter Rajesvari, "Open the door. Abhay has come." She replied, "No, he is in Bombay." Gour Mohan repeated, "I tell you that he has come. You open the door!" It was about midnight. She went downstairs, opened the door, and found that her brother had indeed come. Abhay went to his father: "How are you?"

"I am all right," Gour Mohan replied. "You just take rest for the night."

The next morning Abhay called the doctor. "How your father is living we don't know," the doctor told him. "He has practically no pulse. He has been living without food for several months."

Abhay asked his father, "What is your wish? Tell me."

"Why are you asking?" his father replied. "Has the doctor told you anything?"

Abhay said, "No, I am asking because I am staying in Bombay and you are here. So if you have any wish, any intention, let me know. I am here. I am here for you." Gour Mohan told him to give their cow to the Allahabad Gaudiya Math. So Abhay took the cow, along with her calf, and donated them to the *maṭha.*

Then again he asked his father, "Have you got any other wish?"

And again his father asked, "Has the doctor told you anything?"

"No, no! I am simply asking because for my business I have to go."

Then Gour Mohan said, "Invite all the Gauḍīya Vaiṣṇavas of Allahabad, and other Vaiṣṇavas also. Let them chant *hari-nāma* in the evening, and you supply them with good food. That is my wish." Abhay arranged it, and in the evening the *hari-nāma* started. At eleven o'clock all of them took *prasādam* and left. That night, Gour Mohan passed away.

Abhay felt the loss of his father painfully. His father had given him everything he had ever wanted, had been careful to raise him as a pure

Vaiṣṇava, and had always worshiped Rādhā and Kṛṣṇa. Although Abhay was a competent young man, he felt lost without his dearmost protector and friend. More than anyone else, Gour Mohan was the one who had always guided Abhay and treated him as the most special person. Without his father, Abhay now felt hopeless. He suddenly felt the same dependency he had felt as a small boy—but now without his father. The one who had always treated him as a pet son deserving all loving attention, the one who had given him whatever he had wanted and who had literally prayed to every holy man he met that his son become a great devotee of Śrīmatī Rādhārāṇī—that best well-wisher was now gone.

On the day of *śrāddha,* thirteen days after Gour Mohan passed away, Abhay and his brother posed for a formal photograph. In accordance with the religious custom, the two sons had shaved their heads. The photograph shows Abhay and his brother sitting on either side of a formal portrait of their father. The portrait is on an elevated stand and is surrounded with dark cloth. The picture is nicely framed. Gour Mohan looks old but still thoughtful and intent—not so old as in the former portrait where he had looked emaciated, with eyes almost dimmed.

Abhay, with his head shaved, looks like a renounced monk, and his body is covered with the robes of a monk, simple drapes in broad folds covering the upper and lower parts of his body. He looks quite different than he had in the picture that was taken in the same place, with the same rough carpet on the floor, years before. In that picture, with his wife and children gathered around him, he was very much the young householder, surrounded by his responsibilities of family and looking like he knew how to conduct himself well and move energetically in the world. But in this photo, although his children are present, they are seated unattended on the floor. Abhay's left hand is on his knee, poised and yet at rest, whereas in the former picture, his left hand had been holding his restless son. Abhay's wife is not present.

In this picture, Abhay looks striking. One cannot tell that he usually has a head of hair and a mustache, which he has only recently shorn for the mournful observance of his father's passing away. Instead, this seems to be his natural appearance. There is a mysterious, spiritual air about him, as one might expect in a meditating saint. His look is neither agitated nor cheerful nor sorrowful. It is peaceful and knowing, as if he has suddenly become a *sādhu* on the day his father has passed away. He looks like the *sādhu* his father envisioned he would become. He looks as if he is and always was a *sādhu* and has suddenly been revealed as such on this day. Even by the most casual inspection of the photo, it appears that by shaving his head and dressing in robes, with no shirt or shoes, Abhay has become a *sādhu*.

CHAPTER FOUR

"How Shall I Serve You?"

I have every hope that you can turn yourself into a very good English preacher if you serve the mission to inculcate the novel impression of Lord Chaitanya's teachings to the people in general as well as philosophers and religionists.

—Śrīla Bhaktisiddhānta Sarasvatī
in a letter to Śrīla Prabhupāda,
December 1936

IN OCTOBER OF 1932, Śrīla Bhaktisiddhānta Sarasvatī led a group of hundreds of disciples and pilgrims on a month-long *parikrama,* or circumambulation, of the sacred places of Vṛndāvana. Vṛndāvana residents and visitors perform *parikrama* by following the old, dry bed of the Yamunā River and circumambulating the Vṛndāvana area, stopping at the places where Kṛṣṇa performed His pastimes when He roamed in Vṛndāvana five thousand years ago. Abhay had wanted to attend Śrīla Bhaktisiddhānta Sarasvatī's *parikrama* but couldn't because of his work. Nevertheless, on the twentieth day of the pilgrimage he traveled from Allahabad, intent on seeing Bhaktisiddhānta Sarasvatī again and hoping to join the *parikrama* party at Kosi, just outside Vṛndāvana, at least for a day.

The *parikrama* Śrīla Bhaktisiddhānta had organized was one of the biggest ever seen in Vṛndāvana. By engaging so many people, he was using the *parikrama* as a method of mass preaching. Even as early as 1918, when he had first begun his missionary work, Śrīla Bhaktisiddhānta's specific contribution had been his emphasis on preaching. Prior to his advent, the Vaiṣṇavas had generally avoided populated places, and they had performed their worship in holy, secluded places like Vṛndāvana. Even when they had traveled to preach, they would maintain the simple mode of the impoverished mendicant. The Gosvāmī followers during Lord Caitanya's time had lived in Vṛndāvana underneath trees; one night under one tree, the next night under another.

Śrīla Bhaktisiddhānta Sarasvatī, whose aim was on preaching worldwide, knew that the renunciation of the Gosvāmīs was not possible for Westerners; therefore he wanted to introduce the idea that devotees could even live in a big palatial temple. He had accepted a large donation from a wealthy Vaiṣṇava merchant and in 1930 had constructed a large marble temple in the Baghbazar section of Calcutta. In the same year, he had moved, along with many followers, from his small rented quarters at Ultadanga to the impressive new headquarters.

Śrīla Bhaktisiddhānta was demonstrating that although a devotee should not spend a cent for his own sense gratification, he could spend millions of rupees for the service of Kṛṣṇa. While previously Vaiṣṇavas would not have had anything to do with the mechanized contrivances introduced by the British, Śrīla Bhaktisiddhānta, on the authority of scripture, was demonstrating a higher understanding. It was Rūpa Gosvāmī, the great disciple of Lord Caitanya, who had written, "One is perfectly detached from all materialistic worldly entanglement not when one gives up everything but when one employs everything for the service of the Supreme Personality of Godhead, Kṛṣṇa. This is understood to be perfect renunciation in *yoga*." If everything is God's energy, then why should anything be given up? If God is good, then His energy is also good; material things should not be used for one's own sense enjoyment, but they could be and *should* be used for the service of Kṛṣṇa. So Śrīla Bhaktisiddhānta wanted to use the most modern printing presses. He wanted to invite worldly people to hear *kṛṣṇa-kathā* in gorgeously built temples. And, for their preaching, devotees should not hesitate to ride in the best conveyances, wear sewn cloth, or live amidst material opulence.

It was in this spirit that he had constructed the building at Baghbazar and there displayed a theistic exhibition, a series of dioramas assembled from finely finished, painted, and dressed clay dolls. Such dolls are a traditional art form in Bengal, but the staging of nearly one hundred elaborate displays depicting the Vaiṣṇava philosophy and the pastimes of Lord Kṛṣṇa had never before been seen. The theistic exhibition created a sensation, and thousands attended it daily.

In that same year, Śrīla Bhaktisiddhānta Sarasvatī had taken about forty disciples on a *parikrama* all over India, a tour featuring many public lectures and Śrīla Bhaktisiddhānta's meetings with important men. By 1932 he had three presses in different parts of India printing six journals in various Indian dialects.

In Calcutta a politician had asked Śrīla Bhaktisiddhānta Sarasvatī how he could possibly print his *Nadiyā Prakāśa* as a *daily* newspaper. Śrīla Bhaktisiddhānta Sarasvatī had replied that it was not so amazing if one considered that in Calcutta alone there were almost half a dozen ordinary daily newspapers, although Calcutta was but one city amongst all the cities of India, India was but one nation amongst many nations on the earth, the earth was but an insignificant planet amidst all the other planets in the universe, this universe was one amongst universes so numerous that each was like a single mustard seed in a big bag of mustard seeds, and the entire material creation was only one small fraction of the creation of God. *Nadiyā Prakāśa* was not printing the news of Calcutta or the earth but news from the unlimited spiritual sky, which is much greater than all the material worlds combined. So if the daily Calcutta newspapers could report limited earthly tidings, then small wonder that *Nadiyā Prakāśa* could appear daily. In fact, a newspaper about the spiritual world could be printed every moment, were there not a shortage of interested readers.

One of Śrīla Bhaktisiddhānta's publications was in English, *The Harmonist,* and it advertised the Vṛndāvana *parikrama* of 1932.

CIRCUMAMBULATION OF SHRI BRAJA MANDAL

His Divine Grace Paramahamsa Shri Shrimad Bhaktisiddhanta Sarasvati Goswami Maharaj, the spiritual head of the Madhva-Gaudiya Vaishnava community, following Shri Krishna Chaitanya Mahaprabhu, has been pleased to invite the co-operation of all persons of every nationality, irrespective of caste, creed, colour, age, or sex, in the devotional function of

> circumambulation of the holy sphere of Braja in the footsteps of the Supreme Lord Shri Krishna Chaitanya, Who exhibited the leela of performing the circumambulation of Shri Braja Mandal during the winter of 1514 A.D.

When Abhay had heard from the members of the Allahabad Gaudiya Math about the *parikrama,* he had been fully occupied with his local Prayag Pharmacy business and traveling to secure new accounts. But he had calculated how he could join at least for a day or two, and he had fixed his mind on again obtaining the *darśana* of Śrīla Bhaktisiddhānta Sarasvatī.

Śrīla Prabhupāda: *I was not initiated at the time of the* parikrama, *but I had very good admiration for these Gaudiya Math people. They were very kind to me, so I thought, "What are these people doing in this* parikrama? *Let me go." So I met them at Kosi.*

The *parikrama* party traveled with efficient organization. An advance group, bringing all the bedding and tents, would go ahead to the next day's location, where they would make camp and set up the kitchen. Meanwhile, the main party, bearing the Deity of Lord Caitanya Mahāprabhu and accompanied by *kīrtana* singers, would visit the places of Lord Kṛṣṇa's pastimes and in the evening arrive in camp.

The camp was divided into sections and arranged in a semicircle, and pilgrims were assigned to a particular section for the night. In the center were the quarters of Śrīla Bhaktisiddhānta and the Deity of Lord Caitanya, and close by, the tents of the *sannyāsīs.* There were separate camps for ladies and men—married couples did not stay together. There was also a volunteer corps of guards who stayed up all night, patrolling the area. At night the camp, with its hundreds of tents with gaslights and campfires, resembled a small town, and local people would come to see, astonished at the arrangements. In the evening, everyone would gather to hear a discourse by Śrīla Bhaktisiddhānta Sarasvatī.

The pilgrims would rise early each morning and chant Hare Kṛṣṇa together. Then, carrying the Deity of Lord Caitanya, they would set out in procession—*kīrtana* groups, the police band, the lead horse, the flag bearers, and all the pilgrims. They traveled to the holy places: the birthplace of Lord Kṛṣṇa, the place where Lord Kṛṣṇa slew Kaṁsa, the Ādi-keśava temple, Rādhā-kuṇḍa, Śyāma-kuṇḍa, and many others.

Śrīla Bhaktisiddhānta Sarasvatī's massive pilgrimage had been rolling on with great success when he met with serious opposition. The local temple proprietors in Vṛndāvana objected to Śrīla Bhaktisiddhānta's awarding the sacred brahminical thread to devotees not born in the families of *brāhmaṇas.* Śrīla Bhaktisiddhānta, throughout his lectures and writings, had repeatedly proven from the Vedic scriptures that one is a *brāhmaṇa* not by birth but by qualities. He often cited a verse from Sanātana Gosvāmī's *Hari-bhakti-vilāsa* stating that just as base metal when mixed with mercury can become gold, so an ordinary man can become a *brāhmaṇa* if initiated by a bona fide spiritual master. He also often cited a verse from *Śrīmad-Bhāgavatam* in which the great sage Nārada tells King Yudhiṣṭhira that if one is born in the family of a *śūdra* but acts as a *brāhmaṇa* he has to be accepted as a *brāhmaṇa,* and if one is born in the family of a *brāhmaṇa* but acts as a *śūdra* he is to be considered a *śūdra.* Because the prime method of spiritual advancement in the Age of Kali is the chanting of the holy name of God, any person who chants Hare Kṛṣṇa should be recognized as a saintly person.

When the local *paṇḍitas* approached Śrīla Bhaktisiddhānta Sarasvatī for discussion, they questioned his leniency in giving initiation and his awarding the brahminical thread and *sannyāsa* dress to persons of lower castes. Because of Bhaktisiddhānta Sarasvatī's scholarly, forceful presentation, the *paṇḍitas* seemed satisfied by the discussion, but when the *parikrama* party arrived at Vṛndāvana's seven main temples, which had been erected by the immediate followers of Lord Caitanya, the party found the doors closed. Vṛndāvana shopkeepers closed their businesses, and some people even threw stones at the passing pilgrims. But the *parikrama* party, led by Śrīla Bhaktisiddhānta Sarasvatī, continued in good spirits, despite the animosity, and on October 28 the party arrived at Kosi, the site of the treasury of Kṛṣṇa's father, King Nanda.

Abhay arrived in Mathurā by train from Allahabad and approached Kosi by ricksha. The countryside was full of charm for Abhay; instead of factories and large buildings there were mostly forests, and aside from the main paved road on which he traveled, there were only dirt roads and soft sandy lanes. As a Vaiṣṇava, Abhay felt sensations an ordinary man wouldn't. Now and then he sighted a peacock in the field, its exotic plumage proclaiming the glories of Vṛndāvana and Kṛṣṇa. Even a nondevotee, however, could appreciate the many varieties of birds, their interesting cries and songs filling the air. Occasionally a tree would be filled with madly chirping sparrows making their urgent twilight clamor before resting for the night. Even one unaware of the special significance of Vṛndāvana could feel a relief of mind in this simple countryside where people built fires from cow manure fuel and cooked their evening meals in the open, their fires adding rich, natural smells to the indefinable mixture which was the odor of the earth. There were many gnarled old trees and colorful stretches of flowers—bushes of bright violet camellia, trees abloom with delicate white *pārijāta* blossoms, and big yellow *kadamba* flowers, rarely seen outside Vṛndāvana.

On the road there was lively horse-drawn *ṭāṅgā* traffic. The month of Kārttika, October-November, was one of the several times of the year that drew many pilgrims to Vṛndāvana. The one-horse *ṭāṅgās* carried large families, some coming from hundreds of miles away. Larger bands of pilgrims, grouped by village, walked together, the women dressed in bright-colored *sārīs,* brown-skinned men and women sometimes singing *bhajanas,* carrying but a few simple possessions as they headed for the town of thousands of temples, Vṛndāvana. And there were businessmen like Abhay, dressed more formally, coming from a city, maybe to spend the weekend. Most of them had at least some semblance of a religious motive—to see Kṛṣṇa in the temple, to bathe in the holy Yamunā River, to visit the sites where Lord Kṛṣṇa had performed His pastimes such as the lifting of Govardhana Hill, the killing of the Keśī demon, or the dancing in the evening with the *gopīs.*

Abhay was sensitive to the atmosphere of Vṛndāvana, and he noted the activity along the road. But more than that, he cherished with anticipation the fulfillment of his journey—his meeting again, after a long separation, the saintly person he had always thought of within himself, Śrīla Bhaktisiddhānta Sarasvatī, who had spoken to him in Calcutta and had convinced him of Lord Caitanya's mission to preach Kṛṣṇa consciousness. Abhay would soon see him again, and this purpose filled his mind.

Upon reaching the lantern-illuminated camp of the Gaudiya Math and inquiring at the registration post, he was allowed to join the *parikrama* village. He was assigned to a tent of *gṛhastha* men and was offered *prasādam.* The people were friendly and in good spirits, and Abhay talked of his activities with the *maṭha* members in Calcutta and Allahabad. Then there was a gathering—a *sannyāsī* was making an announcement. This evening, he said, there would be a scheduled visit to a nearby temple to see the Deity of Śeṣaśāyī Viṣṇu. Some of the pilgrims cheered, "*Haribol*! Hare Kṛṣṇa!" The *sannyāsī* also announced that His Divine Grace Bhaktisiddhānta Sarasvatī Ṭhākura would speak that evening for the last time and would be leaving the *parikrama* party the next day. So there was a choice of going on the *parikrama* or staying for the lecture.

Śrīla Prabhupāda: *So I met them in Kosi, and Keśava Mahārāja was informing that Śrīla Bhaktisiddhānta is going to Mathurā tomorrow morning and he will speak* hari-kathā *this evening. Anyone who wants to may remain. Or otherwise they may go to see Śeṣaśāyī Viṣṇu. So at that time I think only ten or twelve men remained—Śrīdhara Mahārāja was one of them. And I thought it wise, "What can I see at this Śeṣaśāyī? Let me hear what Śrīla Bhaktisiddhānta Sarasvatī will speak. Let me hear."*

When Abhay arrived, Śrīla Bhaktisiddhānta was already speaking. He sat with his back erect, a shawl around his shoulders, not speaking like a professional lecturer giving a scheduled performance, but addressing a small gathering in his room. At last Abhay was in his presence again. Abhay marveled to see and hear him, this unique soul possessed of *kṛṣṇa-kathā*, speaking uninterruptedly about Kṛṣṇa in his deep, low voice, in ecstasy and deep knowledge. Abhay sat and heard with rapt attention.

Bhaktisiddhānta Sarasvatī had been speaking regularly about *sambandha, abhidheya,* and *prayojana. Sambandha* is the stage of devotional service in which awareness of God is awakened, *abhidheya* is rendering loving service to the Lord, and *prayojana* is the ultimate goal, pure love of God. He stressed that his explanations were in exact recapitulation of what had originally been spoken by Kṛṣṇa and passed down through disciplic succession. Bhaktisiddhānta Sarasvatī's particular utterance, mostly Bengali but sometimes English, with frequent quoting of Sanskrit from the *śāstras,* was deep with erudition. "It is Kṛṣṇa," said Bhaktisiddhānta Sarasvatī, "who is the only Superlord over the entire universe and, beyond it, of Vaikuṇṭha, the transcendental region. As such, no one can raise any obstacle against His enjoyment."

An hour went by, two hours ... . The already small gathering in Śrīla Bhaktisiddhānta's room gradually thinned. A few *sannyāsīs* left, excusing themselves to tend to duties connected with the *parikrama* camp. Only a few intimate leaders remained. Abhay was the only outsider. Of course, he was a devotee, not an outsider, but in the sense that he was not a *sannyāsī,* was not handling any duties, was not even initiated, and was not traveling with the *parikrama* but had joined only for a day—in that sense he was an outsider. The philosophy Śrīla Bhaktisiddhānta Sarasvatī was speaking, however, was democratically open to whoever would give an ardent hearing. And that Abhay was doing.

He was listening with wonder. Sometimes he would not even understand something, but he would go on listening intently, submissively, his intelligence drinking in the words. He felt Śrīla Bhaktisiddhānta Sarasvatī revealing to him the direct vision of the spiritual world, just as a person reveals something by opening a door or pushing aside a curtain. He was revealing the reality, and this reality was loving service to the lotus feet of Rādhā-Kṛṣṇa, the supremely worshipable Personality of Godhead. How masterfully he spoke! And with utter conviction and boldness!

It was with such awe that Abhay listened with fastened attention. Of course, all Vaiṣṇavas accepted Kṛṣṇa as their worshipable Lord, but how conclusively and with what sound logic was the faith of the Vaiṣṇavas established by this great teacher! After several hours, Śrīla Bhaktisiddhānta Sarasvatī stopped speaking. Abhay felt prepared to go on listening without cessation, and yet he had no puzzling doubts or queries to place forward. He wanted only to hear more. As Śrīla Bhaktisiddhānta made his exit, Abhay bowed, offering his obeisances, and then left the intimate circle of *sannyāsīs* in their row of tents and went to the outer circle of tents, his mind surcharged with the words of his spiritual master.

Now their relationship seemed more tangible. He still treasured his original impression of Śrīla Bhaktisiddhānta Sarasvatī, the saintly person who had spoken to him on the rooftop in Calcutta; but tonight that single impression that had sustained him for years in Allahabad had been enriched and filled with new life. His spiritual master and the impression of his words were as much a reality as the stars in the sky and the moon over Vṛndāvana. That impression of hearing from Śrīla Bhaktisiddhānta Sarasvatī was filling him with its reality, and all other reality was forming itself around the absolute reality of Śrīla Gurudeva, just as all the planets circle around the sun.

The next morning, Abhay was up with the others more than an hour before dawn, bathed, and chanting *mantras* in congregation. Later in the morning the tall, stately figure of Śrīla Bhaktisiddhānta Sarasvatī, dressed in plain saffron, got into the back seat of a car and rode away from the camp. Thoughtful and grave, he looked back and waved, accepting the loving farewell gestures of his followers. Abhay stood amongst them.

* * *

A little more than a month later, Abhay was again anticipating an imminent meeting with Śrīla Bhaktisiddhānta, this time at Allahabad. Abhay had only recently returned from Vṛndāvana to his work at Prayag Pharmacy when the devotees at the Allahabad Gaudiya Math informed him of the good news. They had secured land and funds for constructing a building, the Śrī Rūpa Gaudiya Math, and Śrīla Bhaktisiddhānta would be coming on November 21 to preside over the ceremony for the laying of the cornerstone. Sir William Malcolm Haily, governor of the United Provinces, would be the respected guest and, in a grand ceremony, would lay the foundation stone in the presence of Śrīla Bhaktisiddhānta. When Abhay learned that there would also be an initiation ceremony, he asked if he could be initiated. Atulānanda, the *maṭha's* president, assured Abhay that he would introduce him to Śrīla Bhaktisiddhānta Sarasvatī.

At home, Abhay discussed his initiation plans with his wife. She had no objection, but she did not want to take initiation herself. They were already worshiping the Deity at home and offering their food to the Deity. They believed in God and were living peacefully.

But for Abhay that was not enough. Although he would not force his wife, he knew that *he* must be initiated by a pure devotee. Avoiding sinful life, living piously—these things were necessary and good, but in themselves they did not constitute spiritual life and could not satisfy the yearning of the soul. Life's ultimate goal and the absolute necessity of the self was love of Kṛṣṇa. That love of Kṛṣṇa his father had already inculcated within him, and now he had to take the next step. His father would have been pleased to see him do it.

What he had learned from his father was now being solidified by someone capable of guiding all the fallen souls of the world to transcendental love of God. Abhay knew he should go forward and take complete shelter in the instructions of his spiritual master. And the scriptures enjoined, "He who is desirous of knowing the Absolute Truth must take shelter of a spiritual master who is in disciplic succession and who is fixed in Kṛṣṇa consciousness." Even Lord Caitanya, who was Kṛṣṇa Himself, had accepted a spiritual master, and only after initiation did He manifest the full symptoms of ecstatic love of Kṛṣṇa while chanting the holy name.

As for the ritual initiation he had received at age twelve from a family priest, Abhay had never taken it very seriously. It had been a religious formality. But a *guru* was not a mere officiating ritualistic priest; so Abhay had rejected the idea that he already had a *guru*. He had never received instructions from him in *bhakti*, and his family *guru* had not linked him, through disciplic succession, with Kṛṣṇa. But by taking initiation from Bhaktisiddhānta Sarasvatī he would be linked with Kṛṣṇa. Bhaktisiddhānta, son of Bhaktivinoda Ṭhākura and disciple of Gaurakiśora dāsa Bābājī, was the *guru* in the twelfth disciplic generation from Lord Caitanya. He was the foremost Vedic scholar of the age, the expert Vaiṣṇava who could guide one back to Godhead. He was empowered by his predecessors to work for the highest welfare by giving everyone Kṛṣṇa consciousness, the remedy for all sufferings. Abhay felt that he had already accepted Śrīla Bhaktisiddhānta as his spiritual master and that from their very first meeting he had already received his orders. Now if Śrīla Bhaktisiddhānta would accept him as his disciple, the relationship would be confirmed.

He was coming so soon after Abhay had seen and heard him in Vṛndāvana! That was how Kṛṣṇa acted, through His representative. It was as if his spiritual master, in coming to where Abhay had his family and business, was coming to draw him further into spiritual life. Without Abhay's having attempted to bring it about, his relationship with Śrīla Bhaktisiddhānta was deepening. Now Śrīla Bhaktisiddhānta was coming to him, as if by a higher arrangement.

On the day of the ceremony, Bhaktisiddhānta Sarasvatī met with his disciples at the Allahabad Gaudiya Math on South Mallaca Street. While he was speaking *hari-kathā* and taking questions, Atulānanda Brahmacārī took the opportunity to present several devotees, Abhay amongst them, as candidates for initiation. The Allahabad devotees were proud of Mr. De, who regularly attended the *maṭha* in the evening, and led *bhajanas,* listened to the teachings and spoke them himself, and often brought respectable guests. He had contributed money and had induced his business colleagues also to do so. With folded palms, Abhay looked up humbly at his spiritual master. He and Śrīla Bhaktisiddhānta were now face to face, and Śrīla Bhaktisiddhānta recognized him and was visibly pleased to see him. He already knew him. "Yes," he said, exchanging looks with Abhay, "he likes to hear. He does not go away. I have marked him. I will accept him as my disciple."

As the moment and the words became impressed into his being, Abhay was in ecstasy. Atulānanda was pleasantly surprised that his Gurudeva was already in approval of Mr. De. Other disciples in the room were also pleased to witness Śrīla Bhaktisiddhānta Sarasvatī's immediate acceptance of Mr. De as a good listener. Some of them wondered when or where Śrīla Bhaktisiddhānta had arrived at such an estimation of the young pharmacist.

At the initiation, Śrīla Bhaktisiddhānta Sarasvatī was seated on a *vyāsāsana,* and the room was filled with guests and members of the Gaudiya Math. Those to be initiated sat around a small mound of earth, where one of Śrīla Bhaktisiddhānta Sarasvatī's *sannyāsīs* prepared a fire and offered grains and fruits into the flames, while everyone chanted *mantras* for purification. Abhay's sister and brother were present, but not his wife.

Abhay basked in the presence of his Gurudeva. "Yes, he likes to hear"—the words of his spiritual master and his glance of recognition had remained with Abhay. Abhay would continue pleasing his spiritual master by hearing well. "Then," he thought, "I will be able to speak well." The Vedic literature described nine processes of devotional service, the first of which was *śravaṇam,* hearing about Kṛṣṇa; then came *kīrtanam,* chanting about and glorifying Him. By sitting patiently and hearing at Kosi, he had pleased Kṛṣṇa's representative, and when Kṛṣṇa's representative was pleased, Kṛṣṇa was pleased. Śrīla Bhaktisiddhānta Sarasvatī had not praised him for donating money to the *maṭha* and hadn't advised him to forsake his family and business and travel with him, nor had he asked Abhay to perform great austerities, like the *yogīs* who mortify their bodies with fasts and difficult vows. But "He likes to hear," he had said. "I have marked him." Abhay thought about it and, again, listened carefully as his spiritual master conducted the initiation.

Finally, Śrīla Bhaktisiddhānta called for Abhay to come forward and receive the *hari-nāma* initiation by accepting his beads. After offering prostrated obeisances, Abhay extended his right hand and accepted the strand of *japa* beads from the hand of his spiritual master. At the same time, he also received the sacred brahminical thread, signifying second initiation. Usually, Śrīla Bhaktisiddhānta gave the first initiation, *hari-nāma,* and only after some time, when he was satisfied with the progress of the disciple, would he give the second initiation. But he offered Abhay both initiations at the same time. Now Abhay was a full-fledged disciple, a *brāhmaṇa,* who could perform sacrifices, such as this fire *yajña* for initiation; he could worship the Deity in the temple and would be expected to discourse widely. Śrīla Bhaktisiddhānta added *aravinda,* "lotus," to his name; now he was Abhay Charanaravinda.

After Śrīla Bhaktisiddhānta Sarasvatī left Allahabad for Calcutta, Abhay keenly felt the responsibility of working on behalf of his spiritual master. At the initiation Śrīla Bhaktisiddhānta had instructed Abhay to study Rūpa Gosvāmī's *Bhakti-rasāmṛta-sindhu,* which outlined the loving exchanges between Kṛṣṇa and His devotees and explained how a devotee can advance in spiritual life. *Bhakti-rasāmṛta-sindhu* was a "lawbook" for devotional service, and Abhay would study it carefully. He was glad to increase his visits to the Allahabad center and to bring new people. Even at his first meeting with his spiritual master he had received the instruction to preach the mission of Lord Caitanya, and now he began steadily and carefully considering how to do so. Preaching was a responsibility at least as binding as that of home and business. Even in his home he wanted to engage as far as possible in preaching. He discussed with his wife about his plans for inviting people into their home, offering them *prasādam,* and holding discussions about Kṛṣṇa. She didn't share his enthusiasm.

Śrīla Prabhupāda: *My wife was a devotee of Kṛṣṇa, but she had some other idea. Her idea was just to worship the Deity at home and live peacefully. My idea was preaching.*

* * *

It was not possible for Abhay to travel with his spiritual master or even to see him often. His pharmaceutical business kept him busy, and he traveled frequently. Whenever possible, however, he tried to time a business trip to Calcutta when his spiritual master was also there. Thus over the next four years he managed to see his spiritual master perhaps a dozen times.

Whenever Abhay visited Calcutta, the assistant librarian at the Gaudiya Math, Nityānanda Brahmacārī, would meet him at Howrah train station with a two-horse carriage belonging to the *maṭha.* Nityānanda saw Abhay as an unusually humble and tolerant person. As they rode together to the *maṭha,* Abhay would inquire eagerly into the latest activities of Śrīla Bhaktisiddhānta: his traveling, his publishing, how many centers were currently open, how his disciples were doing. They wouldn't talk much about Abhay's business. Abhay would stay at the Gaudiya Math, usually for about five days. Sometimes he would visit one of his sisters who lived in Calcutta, but his main reason for coming was Śrīla Bhaktisiddhānta; and Abhay would take advantage of every opportunity to hear him.

Abhay didn't try to become a leader in the inner management of the Gaudiya Math. His spiritual master had initiated eighteen *sannyāsīs,* who carried out most of the preaching and leadership of the mission. Abhay was always the householder, occupied with his own business and family, never living within the *maṭha* except for brief visits. And yet he began to develop a close relationship with his spiritual master.

Sometimes Abhay would go to see him at the Chaitanya Math, at the birthplace of Lord Caitanya in Māyāpur. One day at the Chaitanya Math, Abhay was in the courtyard when a large poisonous snake crawled out in front of him. Abhay called out for his Godbrothers, but when they came everyone simply stood looking, uncertain what to do. Śrīla Bhaktisiddhānta came out on the veranda of the second floor, glanced down, saw the snake, and immediately ordered, "Kill it." A boy then took a large stick and killed the snake.

Śrīla Prabhupāda: *So I thought, "How is it that Guru Mahārāja ordered the snake to be killed?" I was a little surprised, but later on I saw this verse, and then I was very glad:* modeta sādhur api vṛścika-sarpa-hatyā, *"Even saintly persons take pleasure in the killing of a scorpion or a snake." It had remained a doubt, how Guru Mahārāja ordered the snake to be killed, but when I read this verse I was very much pleased that this creature or creatures like the snake should not be shown any mercy.*

Śrīla Bhaktisiddhānta was reputed to be so austere and so strong in argument against other philosophies that even his own disciples were cautious in approaching him if he were sitting alone or if they had no specific business with him. Yet even though Abhay's contact with him was quite limited, Śrīla Bhaktisiddhānta would always treat him kindly.

Śrīla Prabhupāda: *Whenever I met my Guru Mahārāja, he would always treat me very affectionately. Sometimes my Godbrothers would criticize because I would talk a little freely with him, and they would quote this*

English saying, "Fools rush in where angels fear to tread." But I would think, "Fool? Well, maybe, but that is the way I am." My Guru Mahārāja was always very, very affectionate to me. When I offered obeisances, he used to return, "Dāso 'smi": *"I am your servant."*

Sometimes as Śrīla Bhaktisiddhānta paced back and forth chanting the Hare Kṛṣṇa *mantra* aloud while fingering his beads, Abhay would enter the room and also chant, walking alongside his spiritual master. Once when Abhay entered Śrīla Bhaktisiddhānta's room, his spiritual master was sitting on a couch, and Abhay took his seat beside him on an equal level. But then he noticed that all the other disciples in the room were sitting on a lower level, at their spiritual master's feet. Abhay kept his seat, and Śrīla Bhaktisiddhānta Sarasvatī said nothing of it, but Abhay never again sat on an equal level with his spiritual master.

Once in a room with many disciples, Śrīla Bhaktisiddhānta Sarasvatī was speaking and Abhay listening when an old man beside Abhay motioned to him. As Abhay leaned over to hear what the man wanted, Śrīla Bhaktisiddhānta suddenly spoke out in annoyance at the two apparently inattentive students. "Bābū," he first addressed the old man beside Abhay, "do you think you have purchased me with your 150-rupees-per-month donation?" And then, turning to Abhay: "Why don't *you* come up here and speak instead of me?" Abhay was outwardly mortified, yet he treasured the rebuke.

It was in a private meeting that Śrīla Bhaktisiddhānta once told Abhay of the risks he took by preaching so boldly.

Śrīla Prabhupāda: *My Guru Mahārāja's contribution is that he defeated the caste* gosvāmīs. *He defeated this Brahmanism. He did it the same way as Caitanya Mahāprabhu did. As Caitanya Mahāprabhu said,* kibā vipra, kibā nyāsī, śūdra kene naya/ yei kṛṣṇa-tattva-vettā, sei 'guru' haya: *"There is no consideration whether one is a* sannyāsī, *a* brāhmaṇa, *a* śūdra, *or a* gṛhastha. *No. Anyone who knows the science of Kṛṣṇa, he is all right, he is* gosvāmī, *and he is* brāhmaṇa."

But no one else taught that since Lord Caitanya. This was my Guru Mahārāja's contribution. And for this reason, he had to face so many vehement protests from these brāhmaṇa-caste gosvāmīs.

Once they conspired to kill him—my Guru Mahārāja told me personally. By his grace, when we used to meet alone he used to talk about so many things. He was so kind that he used to talk with me, and he personally told me that these people, "They wanted to kill me."

They collected twenty-five thousand rupees and went to bribe the police officer in charge of the area, saying, "You take these twenty-five thousand rupees. We shall do something against Bhaktisiddhānta Sarasvatī, and you don't take any steps." He could understand that they wanted to kill him. So the police officer frankly came to Bhaktisiddhānta Sarasvatī: "Of course, we accept bribes, and we indulge in such things, but not for a sādhu, *not for a saintly person. I cannot dare." So, the police officer refused and said to my Guru Mahārāja, "You take care. This is the position." So vehemently they protested!*

But he liked boldness in his disciples. Abhay heard of an occasion when one of Śrīla Bhaktisiddhānta Sarasvatī's disciples had been very outspoken at a public meeting and had denounced a highly regarded Māyāvādī monk as "a foolish priest." The remark had caused a disruption at the meeting, and some of the disciples reported the incident to Śrīla Bhaktisiddhānta, thinking he would be displeased that his disciple had caused a disturbance. But Śrīla Bhaktisiddhānta was pleased and remarked, "He has done well." His displeasure occurred, rather, when he heard of someone's compromise.

Śrīla Prabhupāda: *When my Guru Mahārāja was present, even big, big scholars were afraid to talk with even his beginning students. My Guru Mahārāja was called "living encyclopedia." He could talk with anyone on any subject, he was so learned. And no compromise. So-called saints,* avatāras, yogīs—*everyone who was false was an enemy to my Guru Mahārāja. He never compromised. Some Godbrothers complained that this preaching was a "chopping technique" and it would not be successful. But those who criticized him fell down.*

Śrīla Bhaktisiddhānta was known as the *siṁha* ("lion") *guru.* On occasion, when he saw someone he knew to be a proponent of impersonalism, he would call that person over and challenge: "Why are you cheating the people with Māyāvādī philosophy?" He would often tell his disciples not to compromise. "Why should you go flatter?" he would say. "You should speak the plain truth, without any flattery. Money will come anyway."

Whenever Śrīla Bhaktisiddhānta wrote or spoke the Vaiṣṇava philosophy, he was uncompromising; the conclusion was according to the *śāstra,* and the logic strong. But sometimes Abhay would hear his spiritual master express the eternal teachings in a unique way that Abhay knew he would never forget. "Don't try to see God," Śrīla Bhaktisiddhānta would say, "but act in such a way that God sees you."

Śrīla Bhaktisiddhānta condemned temple proprietors who made a business of showing the Deity for a living. To be a sweeper in the street was more honorable, he said. He coined a Bengali phrase, *śālagrām-dvārā bādāṁ bhaṅga:* "The priests are taking the *śālagrāma* Deity as a stone for cracking nuts." In other words, if a person shows the *śālagrāma* form of the Lord (or any form of the Deity) simply with a view to make money, then he is seeing the Deity not as the Lord but as a stone, a means for earning his livelihood.

Abhay had the opportunity to see his spiritual master deal with the nationalist Subhas Chandra Bose, who had been Abhay's schoolmate at Scottish Churches' College. Bose had come in a somewhat critical mood, concerned about Śrīla Bhaktisiddhānta's recruiting young men into religious life.

Śrīla Prabhupāda: *Subhas Chandra Bose came to my Guru Mahārāja and said, "So many people you have captured. They are doing nothing for nationalism."*

My Guru Mahārāja replied, "Well, for your national propaganda you require very strong men, but these people are very weak. You can see, they are very skinny. So don't put your glance upon them. Let them eat something and chant Hare Kṛṣṇa." In this way he avoided him.

Śrīla Bhaktisiddhānta used to say that when the day came when high court judges were devotees of Kṛṣṇa with Vaiṣṇava *tilaka* on their foreheads, then he would know that the mission of spreading Kṛṣṇa consciousness was becoming successful.

He said that Jesus Christ was a *śaktyāveśa-avatāra,* an empowered incarnation of God. "How can it be otherwise?" he said. "He sacrificed everything for God."

In his scholarly language he declared, "The materialistic demeanor cannot possibly stretch to the transcendental autocrat." But sometimes in speech he phrased it in a more down-to-earth way: "The mundane scholars who are trying to understand the Supreme Lord by their senses and mental speculation are like a person trying to taste the honey in a bottle by licking the outside of the bottle." Philosophy without religion, he said, is dry speculation; and religion without philosophy is sentiment and sometimes fanaticism.

Śrīla Bhaktisiddhānta said that the whole world was simply a society of cheaters and cheated. He gave the example that loose women often visit certain holy places in India with the idea of seducing the *sādhus,* thinking that to have a child by a *sādhu* is prestigious. And immoral men dress themselves as *sādhus,* hoping to be seduced by the cheating women. His conclusion: a person should aspire to leave the material world and go back to Godhead, because "this material world is not a fit place for a gentleman."

Abhay saw that when disciples asked his spiritual master about something in the future, he never replied, "Yes, it is going to happen," or "Yes, we are going to do it." Rather, he would say, "Yes, if Kṛṣṇa desires, it may be." Although in his younger years he had been an astrologer and able to predict the future, he had given it up.

Śrīla Bhaktisiddhānta was a lifetime *brahmacārī* and was very strict about avoiding association with women. Once Abhay was sitting with his spiritual master when another disciple was present, along with his young wife. The wife asked Śrīla Bhaktisiddhānta if she might speak with him privately, but he replied, "No, whatever it is, you can ask here. I cannot see you in private." Abhay was impressed by this, since Śrīla Bhaktisiddhānta was in his sixties and the girl could have been his granddaughter; regardless, he would not speak with any woman alone.

Śrīla Bhaktisiddhānta liked to make his disciples into *sannyāsīs.* But one day one of his *sannyāsa* disciples was forcibly dragged away by his wife. In tears, Śrīla Bhaktisiddhānta lamented that he was unable to save that soul. Yet he did not speak disparagingly of Kṛṣṇa conscious family life: "I would have sex hundreds of times if I thought that I could raise Kṛṣṇa conscious children."

He would send his *brahmacārīs* out to sell the Gaudiya Math magazine and books, and even if a *brahmacārī* were able to sell only one or two, it would please him very much, and he would exclaim, "You are so nice." In considering whether essays were worthy for publication, he would count how many times the word *Kṛṣṇa* or *Caitanya* had been used; if these holy names had been quoted sufficiently, he would say, "That's all right. This can be used."

He would say in Bengali, *"Prāṇ āche yār, se hetu pracār:"* "A person must have life to be a preacher—a dead man cannot preach." When some of his preachers who had gone to chant and speak reported that no one had attended their meeting, Śrīla Bhaktisiddhānta replied, "That doesn't matter. The four walls will hear you. That is sufficient. Don't be disappointed. Go on chanting." And in commenting on the fact that some of his disciples had fallen away: "Some of the soldiers will die," he said.

But he did not want his disciples to lead an easygoing life—he once criticized a disciple as being "ease-loving"—nor should they attempt to practice austerities in seclusion. He would sing a song of his own composition, *Duṣṭa mana, tumi kisera vaiṣṇava?* "My dear mind, what kind of Vaiṣṇava are you? You are chanting Hare Kṛṣṇa in a solitary place, imitating the great saints Haridāsa Ṭhākura and Rūpa Gosvāmī, but your meditation is actually to think of women and money. Your mind is filled with such dirty things, so your *bhajana* is simply cheating." He taught that if a devotee gave up his preaching in the city in favor of solitary meditation, that was a method of cheating by imitating the great saints in hopes of getting cheap adoration from others. Therefore, Śrīla Bhaktisiddhānta never liked to open a branch of the Gaudiya Math in a place that was not very much populated.

Abhay went on listening to his spiritual master at every opportunity, but rarely did Abhay put a philosophical inquiry before him. He preferred simply to listen.

Śrīla Prabhupāda: *I never asked my spiritual master a question, except one: "How shall I serve you?"*

* * *

Abhay Charan De became prominent in the pharmaceutical business. He worked well for Bose's Laboratory, and other companies wanted him as their agent. He had hopes of becoming rich.

Śrīla Prabhupāda: *My Guru Mahārāja ordered me, "You do this." But I thought, "Let me first of all become a rich man. Then I shall do." In the beginning, I was thinking, "Now my Godbrothers have taken* sannyāsa. *They are begging from door to door. Why shall I beg? Let me earn money and start Kṛṣṇa consciousness."*

The biggest pharmaceutical company in India, Bengal Chemical, made him an offer, but when they did not fulfill all his conditions he turned them down—though later he regretted it. Still, there were good signs. The astrologer had predicted he could become one of India's richest men, and Dr. Kartick Bose had told his father-in-law, "He's a very intelligent man!"

But there were also other signs. As many accounts as he had secured by his wide travels, there were also that many bills to collect. Many of the accounts began to fall behind in their payments, and the accumulated debt began to grow, until he owed Bose's Laboratory a total of ten thousand rupees. And Abhay had enemies. The manager who had taken over Abhay's old position as office manager with Bose's Laboratory in Calcutta tried to turn Dr. Bose against Abhay, insinuating that he was too independent—they had heard of his negotiating with Bengal Chemical, and the new manager attributed the accumulating debt to Abhay's lack of loyalty to the home office. Kartick Bose remained favorably inclined towards Abhay, but when the debt became a financial strain he went to Allahabad to investigate. At Prayag Pharmacy he spoke with Dr. Ghosh, who told him, "He is a very honest man. It is no fault of his. In good faith he gave all these chemists drugs and credit. But he can't realize the money."

"All right," Dr. Bose said, "but I can't go on giving him money." Abhay went over the accounts with Dr. Kartick Bose, and they both agreed that the best way to settle the matter was for Dr. Bose to take over the Prayag Pharmacy and all of Abhay's accounts. Thus Abhay was absolved of debt but unemployed.

Atulānanda Brahmacārī approached him: "Why don't you come to the *maṭha*? Now you are free." Abhay began to visit more frequently the nearby Rupa Goswami Math, where the Gaudiya Math men, in their renounced *brahmacārī* spirit, suggested that he depend completely on Kṛṣṇa, give up the world, move in with them, and become a full-time preacher. But for Abhay there was no question of abandoning business. If he did, what would happen to his wife and children? He and Radharani now had a third child, a son, so the financial responsibility was increasing. The *brahmacārīs* were well intentioned in asking him to renounce the world, and it was fine for them to do so, but Abhay couldn't take it very seriously.

Without work he was in a critical situation; but he remained confident and eager to take on new employment. There were other companies that would like to have him as their agent. And some of his old customers wanted him to service them, even if he weren't Bose's man. Abhay thought about starting his own pharmaceutical laboratory. Finally he decided he would start his own factory, but in a much bigger city than Allahabad. He settled on Bombay.

He decided that his family should remain in Allahabad and he and his brother would travel to Bombay, take an apartment, and survey the prospects for starting a factory there. Although Radharani was used to her husband's traveling, it had never been as extended as this promised to be. Abhay talked with her, explaining that his recent business loss had been the arrangement of Kṛṣṇa. Now, again to provide for his family, he would have to start a large business, and that could best be done in a major city like Bombay. But family life in Allahabad would be temporarily disrupted. He set up a very small pharmaceutical manufacturing operation there in Allahabad, put his nephew Tulasi in charge, and left for Bombay with his brother.

In Bombay, Abhay rented an apartment on Grant Road and, applying the knowledge he had gained as manager of Bose's Laboratory, started his own pharmaceutical factory. Business was going well, when a large company, Smith Institute, wanted him as their sales agent. Abhay took the job, thinking that he could earn money as Smith's representative while at the same time developing his own business. He was confident of his ability to earn money in the pharmaceutical line.

While traveling around Bombay on business, Abhay met some members of the Gaudiya Math—Bhaktirakṣaka Śrīdhara Mahārāja and Bhakti-sāraṅga Gosvāmī, senior *sannyāsī* disciples of Bhaktisiddhānta Sarasvatī. Abhay recognized them as respected Godbrothers, well versed in the scriptures and Vaiṣṇava philosophy. It seemed he was destined to find his Godbrothers wherever he went. Both he and the *sannyāsīs* regarded their apparently odd meeting in the city as auspicious. Like the members of the Gaudiya Math he had met in Allahabad, these preachers had no permanent center, but they were trying to start one. On behalf of Bhakti-siddhānta Sarasvatī, they were going door to door soliciting supporters for a Bombay branch of the Gaudiya Math.

Abhay wanted to help. As a fellow Godbrother in the service of his spiritual master, he offered them his services. Although as *sannyāsīs* they were in a superior position, in their somewhat helpless condition they looked up to Abhay for help. They had been staying in a small place on Proctor Road and had found little opportunity to make important contacts. Now they formed a team, Abhay introducing the *sannyāsīs* to business acquaintances and the *sannyāsīs* taking donations for the new center. Abhay Charanaravinda was good at collecting funds, and he willingly gave his time. Again, his Godbrothers began pulling at him to participate fully in the Gaudiya Math preaching.

Śrīla Prabhupāda: *We made a party for collecting alms—Śrīdhara Mahārāja, Gosvāmī Mahārāja, and myself. I took them to some of my chemist and doctor friends, and in two days we collected five hundred rupees. Śrīdhara Mahārāja would speak, I would introduce, and Gosvāmī Mahārāja would canvass. So Gosvāmī Mahārāja very much appreciated, and he began to speak highly about me: "For a* bābū, *he is so expert. He has got so many friends, and he has collected so much. Why should he not be in charge of our* maṭha? *Why shouldn't he live with us? Why is he living separately?"*

Abhay visited the *maṭha* quarters on Proctor Road, where he joined the devotees in *kīrtana* and heard them speak from the *Bhāgavatam.* At the *sannyāsīs'* request, Abhay took on the responsibility of finding a more suitable place for the Bombay center. Wherever he went in the city, he looked for likely locations. Just as he had responsibilities for his wife and family in Allahabad, by dint of his initiation he was responsibly bound to assist his Godbrothers. He had to take part in the preaching, not simply struggle so that he might exist in the world of business competition. But he didn't think he could ever live like the *sannyāsīs*—no possessions, no business, sleeping on the bare floor, taking only simple meals.

February 25, 1935

It was the sixty-second birthday of Śrīla Bhaktisiddhānta Sarasvatī. At Jagannātha Purī, where Śrīla Bhaktisiddhānta Sarasvatī was residing, the devotees observed the day with ceremony. At the small Bombay center, the few disciples planned an evening observance and invited local people. For the occasion, Abhay wrote a poem.

Adore adore ye all
  The happy day,
Blessed than heaven,
  Sweeter than May,
When he appeared at Puri
  The holy place,
My Lord and Master
  His Divine Grace.

Oh! my Master
  The evangelic angel,
Give us Thy light,
  Light up Thy candle.
Struggle for existence
  A human race.
The only hope
  His Divine Grace.

Misled we are
All going astray.
Save us Lord
Our fervent pray.
Wonder Thy ways
To turn our face.
Adore Thy feet
Your Divine Grace.

Forgotten Krishna
We fallen souls,
Paying most heavy
The illusion's toll.
Darkness around
All untrace.
The only hope
His Divine Grace.

Message of service
Thou hast brought.
A healthful life
As Chaitanya wrought.
Unknown to all
It's full of brace.
That's your gift
Your Divine Grace.

Absolute is sentient
Thou hast proved,
Impersonal calamity
Thou hast moved.
This gives us a life
Anew and fresh.
Worship Thy feet
Your Divine Grace.

Had you not come
Who had told
The message of Krishna
Forceful and bold.
That's your right.
You have the mace.
Save me a fallen
Your Divine Grace.

The line of service
As drawn by you
Is pleasing and healthy
Like morning dew.
The oldest of all
But in new dress.
Miracle done
Your Divine Grace.

—Abhay Charan das

Abhay also composed a speech, which he read before the assembled guests and members of the Gaudiya Math. Although his first language was Bengali, his English was clear and natural.

Gentlemen, the offerings of such a homage as has been arranged this evening to the Acharyadeva is not a sectarian concern, because when we speak of the fundamental principle of Gurudeva or Acharyadeva, we speak of something that is of universal application. There does not arise any question of discriminating my Guru from that of yours or anyone else's. There is only one Guru who appears in an infinity of forms to teach you, me and all others. The Guru or Acharyadeva, as we learn from the bona fide scriptures, delivers the message of the absolute world, I mean the transcendental abode of the Absolute Personality where everything nondifferentially serves the Absolute Truth.

Like the poem, the speech was personal, but even more than the poem it was authoritative, philosophical *preaching*. The Godbrothers were impressed to hear Abhay presenting the Vaiṣṇava philosophy so expertly. How was it possible? Of course, it should not have come as a surprise; he had heard the Vaiṣṇava philosophy from Śrīla Bhaktisiddhānta Sarasvatī, just like his Godbrothers. Why should he not be able to enunciate the teachings of his spiritual master, having heard from him and having read *Gītā* and *Bhāgavatam* and *Bhakti-rasāmṛta-sindhu*? Was he not a devotee in the *paramparā*? But until now, no one knew he could preach in English so expertly.

> Therefore, if the Absolute Truth is one, about which we think there is no difference of opinion, the Guru also cannot be two. The Acharyadeva to whom we have assembled tonight to offer our humble homage is not the Guru of a sectarian institution or one out of many differing exponents of the truth. On the contrary, he is the Jagatguru, or the Guru of all of us, the only difference is that some obey him wholeheartedly, while others do not obey him directly.

The *guru* of whom Abhay spoke, of course, was Śrīla Bhaktisiddhānta Sarasvatī, the representative of the original compiler of the scriptures, Vyāsadeva. Abhay explained how Lord Kṛṣṇa had delivered transcendental knowledge to Brahmā, the creator of this particular universe. From Brahmā the knowledge had descended to Nārada, from Nārada to Vyāsa, from Vyāsa to Madhva ... . Because Śrīla Bhaktisiddhānta was presenting the Vedic knowledge as is, without any interpretation—in *paramparā*—he was the bona fide *ācārya* who could enlighten others with the revealed knowledge of the *Vedas*.

Abhay continued:

> Gentlemen, our knowledge is so poor, our senses are so imperfect and our sources are so limited that it is not possible for us to have even the slightest knowledge of the absolute region without surrendering ourselves at the lotus-feet of Sree Vyasadeva or His bona fide representative.

This transcendental knowledge, Abhay explained, had been known in India for thousands of years, and this knowledge—although presently obscured—was India's real gift to the world.

> We must conclude that the darkness of the present Age is not due to lack of material advancement, but that we have lost the clue to our spiritual

advancement which is the prime necessity of human life and the criterion of the highest type of civilisation. Throwing of bombs from aeroplanes is no advancement of civilisation from the primitive, uncivilised way of dropping big stones on the heads of the enemies from the tops of the hills. Improvement of the art of killing our neighbours by inventing machine guns and by means of poisonous gases is certainly no advancement from primitive barbarism priding itself on its art of killing by bows and arrows, nor does the development of a sense of pampered selfishness prove anything more than intellectual animalism. ...

Thus, while others were yet in the womb of historical oblivion, the sages of India had developed a different kind of civilisation which enables us to know ourselves. They had discovered that we are not at all material entities, but that we are all spiritual, permanent and non-destructible servants of the Absolute.

The speech continued, describing the horrible consequences of a misspent human life, the sufferings of repeated birth and death. Again and again, Abhay stressed the need to surrender to the spiritual master. He criticized empirical, mundane philosophers, godless politicians, and blind sense gratifiers. He repeatedly pointed to the soul's natural and sublime position as the servant of God and as the servant of the pure devotee of God. Abhay, an initiated disciple of his spiritual master for a little more than two years, referring to himself as a student, continued:

Gentlemen, although we are like ignorant children in the knowledge of the transcendence, still His Divine Grace, my Gurudeva, has kindled a small fire within us to dissipate the invincible darkness of the empirical knowledge, and we are so much so on the safe side that no amount of philosophical argument of the empiric schools of thought can deviate us an inch from the position of our eternal dependence on the lotus-feet of His Divine Grace—and we are prepared to challenge the most erudite scholars of the Mayavada school on this vital issue: that the Personality of Godhead and His transcendental sports in Goloka alone constitute the sublime information of the Vedas.

He then ended his speech with an eloquent prayer of submission.

Personally I have no hope to have any direct service for the coming crores of births of the sojourn of my life, but I am confident that some day or other I shall be delivered from this mire of delusion in which I am at present so deeply sunk. Therefore, let me with all my earnestness pray at the lotus-feet of my Divine Master to let me suffer the lot which I am destined to do for all my past misdoings, but to let me have this power of recollection that

> I am nothing but a tiny servant of the Almighty Absolute Godhead, realised through the unflinching mercy of my Divine Master. Let me, therefore, bow down at his lotus-feet with all the humility at my command.

He submitted both the poem and speech to *The Harmonist.* The poem, Abhay's first publication, announced him as a competent writer in English, and Swami Bhaktipradīpa Tīrtha, editor of *The Harmonist,* informally dubbed Abhay as *kavi,* "learned poet." Some of Abhay's Godbrothers also picked up on the name and began calling him *kavi.* Most of them, even the *sannyāsīs,* were not so proficient in English. But Abhay was not ordinary. They could appreciate that the poem was personal, written out of Abhay's genuine worship and his joy at having accepted a genuine spiritual master, but it was also written strictly in accord with the conclusions of the scriptures.

For Abhay, however, the glory of his "Sree Vyas Puja Homage" came when the poem reached Śrīla Bhaktisiddhānta Sarasvatī and it gave him pleasure. One stanza specifically made Śrīla Bhaktisiddhānta so happy that he made a point of showing it to all of his guests.

> Absolute is sentient
> Thou hast proved,
> Impersonal calamity
> Thou hast moved.

Somehow, in this simple couplet Abhay had captured the essence of his spiritual master's preaching against the Māyāvādīs, and Śrīla Bhaktisiddhānta took it as an indication of how well Abhay knew the mind of his Gurudeva. Abhay was delighted when he heard that the couplet was pleasing to his spiritual master. One of Abhay's Godbrothers compared this verse by Abhay to a verse in which Rūpa Gosvāmī had expressed the inner thinking of Caitanya Mahāprabhu and had thus moved Him to ecstasy.

Śrīla Bhaktisiddhānta Sarasvatī also found the essay pleasing, and he showed it to some of his confidential devotees. He instructed the editor of *The Harmonist,* "Whatever he writes, publish it."

* * *

Abhay thought it only natural that he should have many business enemies or competitors—it was a sign of success. But his Bombay competition caused him to lose another good chance to become wealthy. The "enemy" was the son of Abhay's supervisor at Smith Institute. Both son and father complained to the Smith Institute executives that Abhay Charan De was pushing goods from his own laboratory and not Smith's. By this intrigue, Abhay lost his position with Smith Institute, and his supervisor placed his own son as the new agent. Abhay was again on his own.

While continuing to help his *sannyāsī* Godbrothers in Bombay, he found a two-story building for rent at Gawlia Tank Road. Everyone agreed it would make a suitable center, and Abhay arranged for the rental and for initial repairs and helped the *sannyāsīs* move in. It seemed that his endeavors for spiritual things were always successful, whereas his business efforts were consistently failing. Of course, a few business enemies were no cause for discouragement—intrigues and losses were always part of the game, and he was still well known in the pharmaceutical business throughout India. But it wasn't so much the give and take of business that disturbed him as his own doubts about whether this was the best way for him to serve his spiritual master. Business was good only if it could go side by side with his spiritual life. Lord Caitanya had said that the chanting of Hare Kṛṣṇa should be spread to every town and village, and Abhay wanted to assist his spiritual master in fulfilling that prophecy, especially by contributing money and helping establish centers. His earnings should not go solely for his family.

Ideally, family life and spiritual life should progress side by side. But the difficulty was Abhay's wife. She was disturbed over the business losses and apathetic to the spiritual successes. She wanted to stay within the orbit of home and family, and despite Abhay's suggestions she refused to accept initiation from Śrīla Bhaktisiddhānta. It was his own wife who was his most formidable competitor. And she waged her opposition right in the home, where it was least welcome.

When Abhay occasionally visited his family in Allahabad, he tried to satisfy them with his good intentions. Business had not gone so well in Bombay, but he had new plans, and he assured his family that there was no need to worry. He planned to do more preaching in his home—the whole family could become more involved in spiritual activities. He wanted to invite guests, hold discussions on *Bhagavad-gītā* and *Śrīmad-Bhāgavatam*, perform *kīrtana*, distribute *prasādam*. He wanted to preach, just as his spiritual master and Godbrothers were preaching. Such a program wouldn't require that a *sannyāsī* or *brahmacārī* come and preside. Abhay could do it himself. This would be an example of the ideal household life. But Radharani was unsubmissive. Rather than coming to hear him speak, she stayed with the children in another room—taking tea.

In Bombay, Abhay associated with Śrīdhara Mahārāja and Bhaktisāraṅga Gosvāmī. Both *sannyāsīs* were highly literate scholars. Śrīdhara Mahārāja was respected for his erudition in the *śāstras,* and Bhaktisāraṅga Gosvāmī for his writing and preaching in English. Sometimes Abhay would discuss his realizations with them.

Abhay also studied the scriptures on his own—his spiritual master's commentary on the *Gītā* and *Śrīmad-Bhāgavatam* as well as commentaries by the previous *ācāryas.* While reading Viśvanātha Cakravartī Ṭhākura's commentary on *Bhagavad-gītā* (Second Chapter, forty-first verse), he read that the disciple should consider the order of the spiritual master to be his life and soul. These words produced a deep effect on Abhay, strengthening his desire to execute Śrīla Bhaktisiddhānta Sarasvatī's command. And in the Eighty-eighth Chapter of the Tenth Canto of *Śrīmad-Bhāgavatam,* he came upon a verse in which Lord Kṛṣṇa said something that startled him:

yasyāham anugṛhṇāmi
hariṣye tad-dhanaṁ śanaiḥ
tato 'dhanaṁ tyajanty asya
svajanā duḥkha-duḥkhitam

"When I feel especially mercifully disposed towards someone, I gradually take away all his material possessions. His friends and relatives then reject this poverty-stricken and most wretched fellow." Abhay shuddered as he read the verse. It seemed to speak directly to him. But what did it mean? "Does it mean," he thought, "that Kṛṣṇa will take away all my money?" Was that what was actually happening? Was that why his business plans were failing? He discussed the meaning of the verse with Śrīdhara Mahārāja. Yes, Śrīdhara Mahārāja confirmed, this might very well be what was happening between Lord Kṛṣṇa and Abhay.

* * *

In July 1935, Śrīla Bhaktisiddhānta Sarasvatī came to install the Deity of Lord Kṛṣṇa and to institute Deity worship at the Bombay center. He was pleased with what his disciples had done so far, and Bhaktisāraṅga Mahārāja admitted that much of the work was due to Abhay Bābū, who had collected funds and established the new center. "Why is Abhay living separately?" Bhaktisāraṅga asked. "He should be president of this Bombay center."

Bhaktisiddhānta Sarasvatī replied, "It is better that he is living outside your company. He will do. When the time comes, he will do everything himself. You don't have to recommend him."

Abhay had not been present when this was spoken, but his Godbrothers told him what Śrīla Bhaktisiddhānta had said. These words of his spiritual master, with their mysteriously prophetic air, were important to Abhay. He treasured the words within himself and meditated upon their meaning.

* * *

In November 1935 he was again with his spiritual master in Vṛndāvana. It was the Kārttika season, the ideal time to visit Vṛndāvana, and Śrīla Bhaktisiddhānta was staying for a month with his disciples at peaceful Rādhā-kuṇḍa, the sacred lake where Rādhā and Kṛṣṇa used to sport.

After leaving Bombay in July, Bhaktisiddhānta Sarasvatī had gone to Calcutta, where he had spoken on radio, delivered many public lectures, welcomed back the preachers he had sent to Europe, and finished publishing his *Śrīmad-Bhāgavatam* translation and commentary. Then in October he had come to Rādhā-kuṇḍa. Occupying the small one-story house Bhaktivinoda Ṭhākura had constructed, he had been reading and speaking to the assembled devotees on the *Upaniṣads, Caitanya-caritāmṛta,* and *Śrīmad-Bhāgavatam.* He had also installed Deities at Śrī Kuñjavihārī Math.

The banks of Rādhā-kuṇḍa were overhung with bright green foliage growing from the gnarled branches of ancient tamarind, *tamāla,* and *nim* trees. In the shallows of the water, cranes stood on stiltlike legs, while river terns skimmed across the lake, sometimes abruptly diving for fish. Sometimes a tortoise would poke its nose up from the water's depth, or a fish would jump. Green parrots, usually in pairs, flew in and out of the green trees, and sparrows chirped and hopped from place to place.

Peacocks were also there, mostly in nearby gardens, as were occasional rabbits and even deer.

The atmosphere was enriched with the history of *kṛṣṇa-līlā.* Five thousand years ago, Rādhā and Kṛṣṇa had engaged in transcendental pastimes here, and only five hundred years ago Lord Caitanya had rediscovered Rādhā-kuṇḍa. Lord Caitanya's great follower Raghunātha dāsa Gosvāmī had resided here for many years, constantly chanting Hare Kṛṣṇa and discussing the activities of Lord Caitanya Mahāprabhu. And here, in a small *bhajana-kuṭīra,* Kṛṣṇadāsa Kavirāja had written *Caitanya-caritāmṛta,* the narrative of the pastimes of Lord Caitanya that Bhaktisiddhānta Sarasvatī relished so much. Many of the inhabitants at Rādhā-kuṇḍa were *bābājīs,* living in small *bhajana-kuṭīras* and spending their time chanting Hare Kṛṣṇa.

Having heard of his spiritual master's stay here, Abhay, bringing his son with him, had traveled from Bombay, just to have *darśana* of his spiritual master. To see Śrīla Bhaktisiddhānta was always an occasion for jubilation, but to see him in Vṛndāvana was an added perfection. This meeting with his beloved guide and friend was different from the time in 1932 when Abhay had seen him on the Vṛndāvana *parikrama.* Now Abhay was no longer sitting anonymously in the back of a room. Now he was a bona fide disciple, recognized as the "*kavi,*" who had written the praiseworthy poem and essay, the young man who listened well, the devotee who had helped the Allahabad *maṭha* and who had established the *maṭha* in Bombay. Already on this visit Abhay had had occasion to be alone with his spiritual master, who had remembered Abhay's son and presented him with a small *bandhī* (jacket). And now, as they walked together alone on the bank of Rādhā-kuṇḍa, Śrīla Bhaktisiddhānta turned and spoke confidentially to Abhay.

There had been some quarreling amongst his leading disciples in Calcutta, he said, and this distressed him very much. Even now, in Vṛndāvana, it weighed heavily on his mind. Some of his disciples had been fighting over who would use various rooms and facilities at the Gaudiya Math headquarters in Calcutta. These devotees were all members of the same *maṭha,* and the building was for propagating Kṛṣṇa consciousness under the leadership of Bhaktisiddhānta Sarasvatī. Yet even in their spiritual master's presence they were quarreling. *Brāhmaṇas* and Vaiṣṇavas were supposed to be free from envy of any creature, what to speak of envy of one another. If they were to fight now, what would they do after their spiritual master passed away? Abhay had no part in these matters and did not even know the details or who was involved. But as he listened to his spiritual master, he also became distressed.

Deeply concerned, Śrīla Bhaktisiddhānta said to Abhay, "*Āgun jvalbe*": "There will be fire"—one day there would be fire in the Calcutta Gaudiya Math, and that fire of party interests would spread and destroy. Abhay heard but did not know what to make of it. Śrīla Bhaktisiddhānta had fought so long and boldly to establish that anyone of any birth could be elevated to become a *brāhmaṇa,* a *sannyāsī,* or a Vaiṣṇava. But if his followers became contaminated by a little wealth and the desire for prestige, thereby showing themselves to be still low-class men despite their training and purification, then his mission would be disrupted. If in the name of religion they became attached to ease, position, and prestige, it could only mean that they had failed to grasp the teachings of their spiritual master.

Śrīla Prabhupāda: *He was lamenting that these men are simply after the stones and bricks of the building. He condemned. He was very, very sorry.*

"When we were living in a rented house," Śrīla Bhaktisiddhānta said, "if we could collect two hundred or three hundred rupees we were living very nicely at Ultadanga. We were happier then. But since we have been given this marble palace in Baghbazar, there is friction between our men. Who will occupy this room? Who will occupy that room? Who will be the proprietor of this room? Everyone is planning in different ways. It would be better to take the marble from the walls and secure money. If I could do this and print books, that would be better."

Abhay felt his spiritual master speaking to him in urgency, as if asking him for help or warning him to avert a disaster. But what could he do?

Śrīla Bhaktisiddhānta then said directly to Abhay, "*Āmār icchā chila kichu bai karānā*": "I had a desire to print some books. If you ever get money, *print books.*" Standing by Rādhā-kuṇḍa and beholding his spiritual master, Abhay felt the words deeply enter his own life—"If you ever get money, *print books.*"

* * *

December 1936

Śrīla Bhaktisiddhānta was in poor health at Jagannātha Purī. Abhay was in Bombay, and he wanted to write his Guru Mahārāja a letter.

"He is a little kind upon me," Abhay thought. "He will understand my request." And he began to write:

> Dear Guru Mahārāja,
>
> Please accept my humble obeisances at your lotus feet. You have got many disciples, and I am one of them, but they are doing direct service to you. Some of them are brahmacharies, some of them are sannyasis, but I am a householder. I cannot. Sometimes I give monetary help, while I cannot give you direct service. Is there any particular service I can do?

Two weeks later, Abhay received a reply.

> I am fully confident that you can explain in English our thoughts and arguments to the people who are not conversant with the languages of the other members.
>
> This will do much good to yourself as well as your audience.
>
> I have every hope that you can turn yourself into a very good English preacher if you serve the mission to inculcate the novel impression of Lord Chaitanya's teachings in the people in general as well as philosophers and religionists.

Abhay at once recognized this to be the same instruction he had received at their first meeting, in 1922. He took it as a confirmation. There was now no doubt as to the purpose of his life. What his spiritual master had said in Calcutta in 1922 had not been a chance remark, nor had that been a chance meeting. The instruction was the same: "Turn yourself into a very good English preacher. This will do much good to yourself as well as your audience."

* * *

Śrīla Bhaktisiddhānta passed away from the mortal world on January 1, 1937. He had been spending his last days reading *Caitanya-caritāmṛta* and chanting on his beads. When a doctor had visited him, wanting to give him an injection, Śrīla Bhaktisiddhānta had protested, "Why are you disturbing me in this way? Simply chant Hare Kṛṣṇa, that's all." Amongst his last words to his disciples were,

> I advise all to preach the teachings of Rupa-Raghunatha [disciples of Lord Caitanya] with all energy and resources. Our ultimate goal shall be to become the dust of the lotus feet of Shri Shri Rupa and Raghunatha Gosvamis. You should all work conjointly under the guidance of your spiritual master

> with a view to serve the Absolute Knowledge, the Personality of Godhead. You should live somehow or other without any quarrel in this mortal world only for the service of Godhead. Do not, please, give up the service of Godhead, in spite of all dangers, all criticisms, and all discomforts. Do not be disappointed, for most people in the world do not serve the Personality of Godhead; do not give up your own service, which is your everything and all, neither reject the process of chanting and hearing of the transcendental holy name of Godhead. You should always chant the transcendental name of Godhead with patience and forbearance like a tree and humbleness like a straw. ... There are many amongst you who are well qualified and able workers. We have no other desire whatsoever.

In his last days he had remained fully conscious and had given instructions until the end. He had specifically and openly ordered that the affairs of his Gaudiya Math be maintained by a twelve-man governing body, which the devotees should select amongst themselves. Finally he had said, "Please accept my blessings to you all, present and absent. Please bear in mind that our sole duty and religion is to spread and propagate service to the Lord and of His devotees." At 5:30 A.M. on January 1 he breathed his last.

Word very soon reached Abhay in Bombay. His immediate response was to cry with grief—no more the joy of an anticipated meeting, no more trips to Calcutta or Vṛndāvana on the plea of business just to see the tall, commanding form of Śrīla Bhaktisiddhānta, the "evangelic angel." This sense of never meeting again was difficult to bear. Philosophically, Abhay knew that there was no reason to lament. Bhaktisiddhānta Sarasvatī had come into the world to execute the mission of Lord Caitanya, and now it was required that he leave this place and go to another, where he would again engage in the same activity. Yet even armed with this philosophy, Abhay felt all alone. His two great well-wishers were gone—his father and now his spiritual master. But he felt grateful that he had received a special mercy, a final instruction, just two weeks before his spiritual master's departure. Abhay read his letter again and again—there would not be another. The intimate talks and meetings were now gone, but by this letter especially, Abhay would live in the instructions of Bhaktisiddhānta Sarasvatī. The letter had come just in time. Now he knew for certain, no matter what anyone else said, how to please his spiritual master and stay linked with Kṛṣṇa. Following his order, he would conquer the feeling of loss at the disappearance of his most affectionate well-wisher.

CHAPTER FIVE

The War

Under the circumstances since 1936 up to now, I was simply speculating whether I shall venture this difficult task and that without any means and capacity; but as none have discouraged me, I have now taken courage to take up the work.

—Śrīla Prabhupāda,
Back to Godhead magazine

THE "FIRE IN the *maṭha*" broke out almost immediately. A senior disciple said that there should be one *ācārya* who would be the spiritual successor to Bhaktisiddhānta Sarasvatī and who would perform all initiations and settle all controversies. But Bhaktisiddhānta Sarasvatī had never said that. He had never called for one *ācārya*. Rather, he had instructed the members of the Gaudiya Math to form a governing body of twelve men and carry on a concerted effort. But that instruction was abandoned, and the suggestion that there be one leader took hold. A single person, instead of twelve, should take charge, and now it became a rush for *who*.

Two parties contested. Ananta Vāsudeva, one of Śrīla Bhaktisiddhānta's leading preachers, was ambitious, and he pressed his claim with a group of influential *sannyāsī* supporters. Another man, Kuñjavihārī, shrewdly went after the properties. He had been a leading administrator under Śrīla Bhaktisiddhānta, and now he claimed ownership of the palatial temple in Calcutta as well as all the other properties and assets of the India-wide Gaudiya Math. Although in his will Śrīla Bhaktisiddhānta had expressed his desire that his disciples select a governing board to manage all properties and funds of the Gaudiya Math, Kuñjavihārī contested the will's legitimacy. He and his supporters argued that since Śrīla Bhaktisiddhānta had received the properties on behalf of God, he was not their rightful owner and therefore could not determine their future ownership. Thus he and the others disputed over the legal and theological aspects of the former *ācārya's* position.

Shortly after Śrīla Bhaktisiddhānta's passing away, litigation had begun. Ananta Vāsudeva, supported by a majority of the members of the Gaudiya Math, had claimed that he, as the next *ācārya,* was the owner and director of the properties. But although Kuñjavihārī had only a few supporters, he defied the majority by pressing his claim through lawyers in court. Kuñjavihārī and his men had possession of the Chaitanya Math and the temples in Māyāpur. Vāsudeva's party captured other buildings. Quarreling and fistfights broke out. The preaching of the Gaudiya Math stopped.

Abhay's inability to take part in the activities of the Gaudiya Math was suddenly in his favor. He had always been more a visitor than a member at the *maṭha* and, at least externally, more the *gṛhastha* businessman than a missionary worker. This automatically put him at a distance from the fray. Of course, he was associated with the *maṭhas* in Bombay and Allahabad, but he had no managerial position, no claims to ownership, and no role in the litigation. Nor did he desire to take sides in the struggle for power. Like many of the other disciples, he was mortified to see that his spiritual master's instructions for cooperation had been disregarded and his mission thrown into a legal dispute. Abhay knew that Śrīla Bhaktisiddhānta had wanted the leaders to work cooperatively, and so he could not sympathize with the warring factions. Both parties were an insult to Śrīla Bhaktisiddhānta Sarasvatī.

But he wanted to preach. Although becoming "a very good English preacher" was something he was meditating on more than actively doing, the Gaudiya Math would logically have been the vehicle for his preaching. He had already contributed articles to the Gaudiya Math's publications and had been working with his Godbrothers at the Allahabad and Bombay centers. Naturally he thought of serving his spiritual master in terms of serving within his spiritual master's mission. But the Gaudiya

Math, which had always been known for pure, bold preaching of the message of Lord Caitanya, was now becoming known for embroiled factions. As the Gaudiya Math broke down, he was also affected. Under the present circumstances, how could he carry out his spiritual master's order to preach? Previously the main obstacle to his preaching had been family commitments, but now the obstacles were compounded. Now he had to wait helplessly for the outcome of this struggle. What would Kṛṣṇa bring about?

* * *

1938

His Bombay business diminishing, Abhay, now forty-two, moved back to Calcutta with his wife and family and rented a house at 6 Sita Kanta Banerjee Lane. The street was but a narrow lane, lined on either side with three-story houses. His office was on the first floor, facing the street; the family lived upstairs. He rented the adjoining building, number seven, and on the first floor operated a small chemical laboratory manufacturing distilled water, De's Pain Liniment, Vimal Tonic, Alpa (an injection for boils), and various other medicines. He also utilized a small outbuilding in the rear as part of his lab. Out front he hung a large signboard—Abhay Charan De and Sons—displaying a picture of a mustached Abhay Charan.

Sometimes he would employ two or three servants to assist him, but mostly he worked alone. And he would deliver his glass jugs of distilled water to agents, such as Bengal Company and Gluconet. He printed a brochure advertising De's Pain Liniment: "Good for relieving gout, rheumatism, and all pains." And if one wanted to be free of recurring diseases like rheumatism and gout, Abhay's brochure directed that in addition to using De's Pain Liniment one refrain from "alcohol and all sorts of drinking or intoxicating habits, and food and drink should be very simple and innocent such as vegetables and milk."

The new Calcutta business enjoyed an early success, but Abhay didn't have his heart in it. It was a duty—he had to do it to maintain his family. His new acquaintances in Calcutta found him to be a devotee of God at heart—a businessman, a family man, but more concerned with writing and preaching than with business and family.

Chandi Mukerjee (a neighbor from nearby Bihari Street): *He was interested only in devotional activities, and he did his business only to maintain the family. He didn't seem interested in the profit motive, in accumulating money or becoming a rich man.*

Charan Mukerjee (Abhay's next-door neighbor): *Abhay Charan De was always a very patient listener to every illogical argument that anybody, including myself, would bring to him. Not knowing philosophy, I would illogically present so many arguments, and Mr. De would always very patiently listen. Nothing agitated him. He was always very calm, and he taught me about God. He would speak only of Kṛṣṇa. He was translating the* Gītā *and was maintaining his business.*

Neighbors would often see him sitting on his cot in the front room. He would read his spiritual master's books and sometimes recite the Sanskrit *ślokas* out loud. He liked to discuss philosophy with anyone who came by. His family keeping mostly upstairs, Abhay would sit alone in the downstairs front room, dressed in *dhotī* and *kurtā,* or sometimes a *dhotī* and only a vest. Often he would be at his writing, while outside the door his children played with the children of the Ganguli family, who lived in the rear apartment of the same building.

The neighbors lived openly in a kind of joint neighborhood family, and Abhay talked freely with the other neighbors—but of Vaiṣṇava philosophy and only rarely of business. Mr. Ganguli found Abhay's speech "scholastic and always very philosophical." Abhay was absorbed in the philosophy of Kṛṣṇa consciousness, and even in brief conversations he would refer to Lord Kṛṣṇa and to *Bhagavad-gītā's* description of Lord Kṛṣṇa as the basis of both the material and spiritual worlds. While working in his laboratory, or receiving a delivery of empty bottles from the Muslim bottle merchant, or going out to sell his medicine, he would be talking or thinking about God.

In those days, for a person in Calcutta to be interested in God consciousness was not so unusual. Abhay found even a man like Abdullah, the Muslim bottle merchant, to be very religious. One day Abhay asked Abdullah, who had once been very poor but had become rich by his business, "Now you've got money. So how are you going to use your money?" The bottle merchant replied, "My dear sir, I have an intention to construct a mosque."

* * *

Meanwhile, the war of the Gaudiya Math raged on. Both factions were ill-motivated, and both deviated from the instructions of their spiritual master. The very act of trying to determine ownership of the properties through legal action meant that the Godbrothers were disobeying the express desire of their spiritual master, as stated in his will. The litigation continued year after year, but the legal wrangling could not bring them together or purify them. One court ruled in favor of Ananta Vāsudeva, but then a higher court awarded two thirds of the *maṭha's* properties to Kuñjavihārī and one third to Vāsudeva. Still, although Vāsudeva had fewer properties, he inspired more followers—he seemed to them more intent on reviving the preaching of the Gaudiya Math. But when Vāsudeva subsequently fell down from the principles of *sannyāsa* by going off with a woman, the groups broke further to pieces.

Most of the *sannyāsīs* continued to maintain their principles, but many now left the jurisdiction of the two contending factions in disgust. Individuals formed their own *āśramas:* Gaudiya Mission, Caitanya Gaudiya Math, and others. The unified entity of Gaudiya Math as an all-India mission consisting of many temples, several presses, and hundreds of devotees working cooperatively under one leadership ceased to exist. Godbrothers continued to uphold the teachings of Lord Caitanya Mahāprabhu as they had received them from Śrīla Bhaktisiddhānta Sarasvatī, but because they were meant to work together, they lacked their former united potency. Illusions of proprietorship and prestige had superseded the spiritual master's order, and Śrīla Bhaktisiddhānta's cause—a worldwide movement for propagating Lord Caitanya's teachings—collapsed.

*　　*　　*

Wherever Abhay went he seemed to attract the company of his Godbrothers. Some followers of Śrīdhara Mahārāja—the same Śrīdhara with whom he had worked in Bombay and whom he had always regarded as a good devotee and scholar—met Abhay at his place on Banerjee Lane and told this news to Śrīdhara Mahārāja, who was then living at his own *āśrama* in Māyāpur. Śrīdhara Mahārāja had disaffiliated himself from the factions of the Gaudiya Math, but as a *sannyāsī* he was still preaching and was interested in publishing Vaiṣṇava literature. He had wanted to maintain an *āśrama* in Calcutta, so for twenty rupees a month he rented from Abhay the four rooms on the second floor of number seven, above Abhay's chemical laboratory.

Now, whenever they came to Calcutta, Śrīdhara Mahārāja, Purī Mahārāja, and Bhaktisāraṅga Mahārāja based themselves there, staying in small separate rooms. It became a regular *āśrama* for *sannyāsīs* and *brahmacārīs,* and Śrīdhara Mahārāja put a sign out front: Devananda Sarasvati Math.

Śrīdhara Mahārāja's establishment of a *maṭha* in Māyāpur with a branch in Calcutta was his response to the Gaudiya Math's split. Like other *sannyāsīs,* he had been initiating disciples and preaching, not waiting for the outcome of the litigation, with its continued appeals and counterclaims. Abhay was glad to encourage Śrīdhara Mahārāja and the others who joined him at his little *āśrama.* Here Abhay and Śrīdhara Mahārāja and his followers could remain aloof from the warring factions and together pursue their plans for spreading Kṛṣṇa consciousness.

The *sannyāsīs* cooked in their separate kitchen, performed their *pūjā,* and held morning and evening *kīrtanas* and lectures. Abhay remained with his family, taking his own meals and performing his own *pūjā,* but he often went to discuss *Śrīmad-Bhāgavatam* with Śrīdhara Mahārāja. From his roof, Abhay could see the towering steeple of his spiritual master's building, the Gaudiya Math of Baghbazar, its ownership now contested by bitter factions.

Abhay would often accompany Śrīdhara Mahārāja and his assistants at preaching programs, where he would play the *mṛdaṅga.* And when Śrīdhara Mahārāja fell ill, Abhay led the other devotees on preaching engagements, performing *kīrtana,* playing *mṛdaṅga,* and giving lectures on the *Bhāgavatam.*

Śrīdhara Mahārāja: *We did not see Abhay as working very hard for making money, nor did he seem very rich or to have a lot of liquid funds. He was attracted more to the spiritual side of affairs than to his family affairs. He never discussed business prospects with me—whether the business was up or down, or whether he was planning to do this or that. Monetarily, he did not have sufficient funds for giving any to the mission.*

* * *

Abhay began to think seriously about writing Vaiṣṇava literature. His spiritual master had seemed very pleased and had told the editor of *The Harmonist,* "Whatever he writes, publish it." Business profits, if he could somehow expand them, could go for printing books in English, as his spiritual master had said. "If you ever get money, print books." Certainly the Gaudiya Math was not going to do it; Kuñjavihārī had sold Bhaktisiddhānta's printing presses to offset his legal expenses. No, Abhay would have to continue on his own, maintaining his business and simultaneously trying to write and publish. And that was also the prescription of Śrīla Bhaktisiddhānta: "It is better that he is living outside your company. When the time comes, he will do everything himself."

It was in 1939 that Abhay wrote "Introduction to Geetopanishad." It was a short piece, but it signaled his intention to take on the task of one day translating *Bhagavad-gītā* into English with commentary. Of course, there were already many commentaries in English, but most of them had been written by impersonalists or others who had not delivered the original spirit of the *Gītā,* the spirit of Arjuna on the Battlefield of Kurukṣetra hearing *Bhagavad-gītā* directly from Lord Kṛṣṇa. Abhay knew, however, that he could present *Bhagavad-gītā* in the proper spirit by writing an English commentary based on the teachings of Lord Caitanya and the disciplic succession. So he began. Whenever he could make time, he would write. Although a strict grammarian could find fault in his English composition, his meaning was always clear.

In his "Introduction," Abhay reflected on the time when as a young schoolboy he had attended a lecture, "Vidyā-ratna—The Jewel of Education." The theme of the lecture had been that God does not exist and could not exist. If there were God, He would certainly have appeared on earth to put an end to all religious rivalry; but since God had not obliged man in this way, we should banish all thought of His existence from our minds. The audience, Abhay explained, consisting only of so many young boys, did not delve deeply into the subject matter of the lecture, yet the majority, impressed by the arguments, "carried away lofty ideas of godlessness, and thus became agnostics at home."

Abhay had not been satisfied with the agnostic conclusion, "because

I had been trained by my father to be engaged in the worship of Śrī Śrī Rādhā-Govinda. But as a result of the Vidyā-ratna lecture, I was experiencing some mental conflict between agnosticism and the existence of Godhead." Later, having heard from his spiritual master, Śrīla Bhaktisiddhānta, Abhay understood that the Personality of Godhead exists in every sphere of activity. "But we do not have the eyes to see Him," Abhay wrote. "Even if the Lord personally manifests Himself on earth, the quarreling mundaners will not stop their fighting and look upon Godhead or His representative, due to ignorance. This is the birthright of the individual soul by the grace of God."

Bhagavad-gītā is the true "jewel of education." And in the *Gītā* Lord Kṛṣṇa "declares to the fighting people on earth, 'Here I am. Do not quarrel.'" The agnostic who had spoken of the "jewel of education" had been blinded by the jewel and therefore could not see and appreciate the Personality of Godhead. Thus he had gone on to convince others to become so-called jewels also.

Following his spiritual master, Abhay displayed an aggressive spirit for confronting all opponents of pure theism. In responding to his spiritual master's order to develop into an English preacher, Abhay was not simply making neutral scholarly presentations; he was willing and ready to fight—whether against modern agnostics or Vaiṣṇavism's old, traditional enemy, Māyāvāda impersonalism.

Although few scholars taught the way of surrender to Lord Kṛṣṇa, as espoused in *Bhagavad-gītā,* almost all respected *Bhagavad-gītā* as presenting the essence of all knowledge. The *Gītā,* therefore, was the perfect vehicle for confronting those who misrepresented God and religion. The *Gītā* was a "challenge to the agnostics, apotheosists, anthropomorphists, impersonalists, henotheists, pantheists, and absolute monists." Although there were already more than six hundred commentaries on *Bhagavad-gītā,* they had been written by persons with "an inner hatred for the Personality of Godhead," and therefore they were imperfect. "Such envious persons," Abhay wrote, "have no entrance into the real meaning of Bhagwat Geeta inasmuch as a fly cannot enter into the covered jar of honey."

Abhay described Indian culture as an almost impassable ocean, due to its depth of thought and apparent mixtures of conclusions. "But in this book," Abhay declared, "I will establish that Krishna is the Absolute

Personality of Godhead by referring to the available records of scriptures which are the recorded history of Indian culture and thought."

The *sannyāsīs* at 7 Banerjee Lane were impressed by the scope of Abhay's thought and intentions. As it was customary to award a title to an especially worthy Vaiṣṇava according to his qualities, Bhaktisāraṅga Gosvāmī wanted to confer upon Abhay the title Bhaktisiddhānta. Śrīdhara Mahārāja, however, thought it inappropriate to give Abhay the same title as their spiritual master, and he asked that Abhay's title be changed to Bhaktivedanta, *bhakti* meaning "devotion" and *vedānta* meaning "the end of knowledge." Abhay was grateful. The title combined the devotion of religion with the scholarship of the most rigorous philosophy, as passed down by the scholarly followers of Lord Caitanya. He appreciated the sincere gesture of his Godbrothers and accepted the title as a further commitment to his spiritual path of preaching Kṛṣṇa consciousness.

Abhay continued regularly associating with Śrīdhara Mahārāja and discussing with him *Śrīmad-Bhāgavatam.* Abhay encouraged him to preach widely, although Śrīdhara Mahārāja was admittedly more the scholar and rather shy about going out and preaching. On several occasions, Abhay tried to convince Śrīdhara Mahārāja to go with him and charge Gandhi and Nehru as to why they weren't following the principles of *Bhagavad-gītā.*

Another fruit of the spiritual association at 7 Banerjee Lane was a book called *Prapanna-jīvanāmṛta,* compiled by Śrīdhara Mahārāja. A collection of verses from various Vaiṣṇava scriptures, including excerpts from the works of Rūpa Gosvāmī, it was divided into six chapters, according to the six divisions of surrender. Abhay, along with the *sannyāsīs* of the Devananda Sarasvati Math, financed the publication. Thus it was published as a joint effort by friends.

* * *

September 3, 1939

Lord Linlithgow, viceroy of India, announced that India was at war with Germany. Thus England swept India into the war—without consulting any Indians. Although independence-minded India certainly resented such a show of foreign control, there were mixed feelings about the war. India wanted independence, yet she sympathized with the allied cause against fascism in the West and feared an invasion by imperial Japan in the East. "Since you dislike the British so violently," one author asked a typical New Delhi student of the day, "would you want Japan to invade and conquer India?" Student: "No, but we Indians pray that God may give the British enough strength to stand up under the blows they deserve."

Although at the outbreak of the war India had only 175,000 men in her armed forces, the British managed to increase the number of Indian soldiers to two million. There was no draft, but the British sent recruiting agents all over India, especially in the Punjab, where military service seemed an attractive offer to the local poor. The Punjabis proved good fighters, whereas Bengalis enlisted as officers, doctors, contractors, and clerks. Indian soldiers were dispatched to battlefields in Egypt, Iraq, Syria, Persia, Malaya, Burma, and Assam.

While the British were attempting to mobilize Indians for the war, the Indian nationalist movement, which had continued off and on for more than twenty years, became very active. Members of the Congress Party refused to cooperate with the war effort and demanded guaranteed independence for India. Some thought that since England had her hands full with Germany, the time was ripe to revolt and gain independence by force. Gandhi's position had been one of unconditional pacifism, and he had opposed the idea of Indians taking up arms, even to defend India. But by 1942 he had become more inimical and had reduced his policy towards the British to a simple, unequivocal "Quit India!" Thousands of Indians responded by chanting slogans in the street and even by tearing up the railway lines.

Abhay's militant former schoolmate Subhas Chandra Bose fought against the British in his own way. He had approached Hitler in Germany and gotten him to agree that when the Germans captured Indian soldiers, Germany would return them to Bose, who would maintain them in his nationalist army. With this army Bose planned to return to India and drive the British from Indian soil. But dissatisfied with his progress in Germany, Bose made a similar agreement with Tojo in Japan, and soon thousands of Gurkhas and Sikhs (the best fighters in the Indian army) had defected from the British army to join Bose's freedom fighters in Singapore. Bose began to prepare his army to invade India from the north.

Then in 1943 the British found that the Japanese, who had already taken Burma, were at the doors of India, approaching Bengal. By their tactic known as the "denial policy," the British sank many Indian boats carrying food and destroyed large rice crops, fearing that they would fall into the hands of the enemy. This left local Indians starving and without the boats they needed for trade. The famine that ensued was the worst that had hit Bengal in 150 years. The government removed all control of food costs, and those who could not afford to buy at the skyrocketing prices died in the streets of Calcutta.

Śrīla Prabhupāda: *I have got experience—the government created artificial famine. The war was going on, so Mr. Churchill's policy was to keep the people in scarcity so they will volunteer to become soldiers. So this policy was executed. Big men, they collected the rice. Rice was selling at six rupees per* mound. *All of a sudden it came to fifty rupees per* mound. *I was in the grocer shop purchasing, and all of a sudden the grocer said, "No, no. I am not going to sell any more!" At that moment the price was six rupees per* mound. *So suddenly he was not going to sell. A few hours later, I went back to purchase, and the rice had gone up to fifty rupees per* mound.

The government-appointed agents began to purchase the rice and other commodities which are daily necessities. They can offer any price, because the currency is in their hands. They can print so-called papers, a hundred dollars, and pay. A man becomes satisfied, thinking, "Oh, I have a hundred dollars." But it is a piece of paper. ...

That was the policy. "You have no money, no rice? So another avenue is open—yes, you become a soldier. You get so much money." People, out of poverty, would go there. I have seen it. No rice was available in the market. And people were hungry. They were dying.

Abhay managed to purchase just enough for his own family to survive. But he saw the beggar population increase by the hundreds. Month after month he saw the footpaths and open spaces congested with beggars, cooking their food on improvised stoves and sleeping in the open or beneath the trees. He saw starving children rummaging in the dustbins for a morsel of food. From there it was but a step to fighting with the dogs for a share of the garbage, and this also became a familiar sight in the Calcutta streets. The British had little time to spare from their war efforts, and they worked only to save those lives essential for the fight. For the common people the empire's prescription was uniform and simple—starvation.

Śrīla Prabhupāda: *One American gentleman was present at that time. He remarked, "People are starving in this way. In our country there would have been revolution." Yes, but the people of India are so trained that in spite of artificial famine they did not commit theft, stealing others' property. People were dying. Still they thought, "All right. God has given." That was the basic principle of Vedic civilization.*

Abhay knew that under the laws of nature there was no scarcity; by God's arrangement the earth could produce enough food. The trouble was man's greed. "There is no scarcity in the world," Śrīla Bhaktisiddhānta Sarasvatī had said. "The only scarcity is of Kṛṣṇa consciousness." And this was how Abhay saw the 1943 famine. Now more than ever, this spiritual vision was relevant—Kṛṣṇa consciousness was the prime necessity. How else could man be checked from his evil propensities to become greedy, hoard, make war, and thus create misery for millions?

He had seen the heinous activities of the British in India—their cutting off the thumbs of the weavers so that Indian-made cotton goods could not compete with the foreign-made cloth, their shooting down of unarmed, innocent citizens, their creating artificial famine, their propagating the myth that Indian civilization was primitive—still, he did not believe that an independent Indian government would necessarily be an improvement. Unless the leadership was Kṛṣṇa conscious—and neither Gandhi nor Subhas Chandra Bose was—then the government would be able to provide no real solutions, only stopgap measures. Without obedience to the laws of God, as expressed by the scriptures and sages, governments would only increase human suffering.

Then Calcutta was bombed, day after day. The bombing was concentrated in specific areas, such as the Kittapur port facility and Syama Bazaar in north Calcutta, very near Abhay's home at Sita Kanta Banerjee Lane. American planes had been leaving from airfields near Calcutta for targets in China and Japan, so the air raids on Calcutta seemed an inevitable retaliation. It was the Japanese striking back.

Or was it? Some said it was the forces of Subhas Chandra Bose, since the bombs fell mostly in the European quarter. But for the people of Calcutta it made little difference who was attacking. After the first bombing, people evacuated the city. Blackouts were imposed, and at night the entire city was dark.

Śrīla Prabhupāda: *The whole Calcutta became vacant. Perhaps only myself and a few others remained. I sent my sons to Navadvīpa—of course, my daughter was married. My wife refused to go out of Calcutta. She said, "I'll be bombed, but I will not go." So I had to remain in Calcutta. I have seen bombing in Calcutta all night. I was just eating when there was the siren. So, the arrangement was that ... in your house would be the shelter room. I was hungry, so I first finished eating. Then I went to the room, and the bombing began.* Chee—Kyam! *I was thinking that this was also Kṛṣṇa in another form. But that form was not very lovable.*

* * *

In the midst of these calamities, Abhay felt more than ever the need to propagate Kṛṣṇa consciousness. He had something to say to the war-weary citizens of the world, and he longed for a more effective forum—a publication of some kind, a way to present the world's crises through the eyes of scripture in the same bold style as had his spiritual master. There was no shortage of ideas, and he had been saving money from his business for this very purpose.

Yet how could he dare produce such a journal when even learned *sannyāsīs,* senior disciples of Śrīla Bhaktisiddhānta, were not. He never considered himself a great scholar among his Godbrothers. Although they called him *kavi* and now Bhaktivedanta, as a *gṛhastha* he wasn't expected to take the lead or publish his own journal.

But times had changed. The English journal *The Harmonist* had not been published since before Śrīla Bhaktisiddhānta's passing away. Now almost a decade had passed, and the Gaudiya Math had been too busy fighting in court to consider preaching. Long gone was the tireless spirit that for ten consecutive years had produced the daily *Nadiyā Prakāśa.* No longer were four separately located printing presses pumping out transcendental literature under the direction of Bhaktivinoda Ṭhākura's empowered son; the presses had been sold by Kuñjavihārī. Times *had* changed. The Gaudiya Math was only fighting, while the nondevotees were killing each other in a world war.

From his front room at 6 Sita Kanta Banerjee, Abhay conceived, wrote, edited, and typed the manuscript for a magazine. He designed a logo, a long rectangle across the top of the page. In the upper left-hand corner was a figure of Lord Caitanya, effulgent with rays of light like rays from the sun. In the lower right were silhouettes of a crowd of people, in darkness but groping to receive light from Lord Caitanya. And between Lord Caitanya and the people, the title unfurled like a banner—BACK TO GODHEAD. In the lower right corner was a picture of Śrīla Bhaktisiddhānta Sarasvatī seated at his writing, looking up thoughtfully as he composed. Above the logo ran the motto "Godhead is Light, Nescience is darkness. Where there is Godhead there is no Nescience." Below the logo were the following lines:

EDITED & FOUNDED
(Under the direct order of His Divine Grace
Sri Srimad Bhakti Siddhanta Saraswati Goswami Prabhupada)
By Mr. ABHAY CHARAN DE.

Abhay had already gained some printing experience in connection with his business, and after completing the manuscript he brought it to Saraswaty Press, the best printers in Bengal. He also hired an agent, Calcutta's prestigious booksellers Thacker, Spink and Company, who would take responsibility for distributing the journal to bookstores and libraries, including outlets in several foreign countries.

But when he went to buy paper, he met with government restrictions. Because of the war and the subsequent paper shortage, they wanted to assay what he had written in terms of the national needs; during this time of world crisis, an ordinary citizen's religious newspaper was hardly top priority.

Abhay's request for paper was perfunctorily denied, but he persisted. He appealed that using paper to print the teachings of the Personality of Godhead was not a waste and not untimely in the present troubled atmosphere. Finally he obtained permission to print his first edition of *Back to Godhead,* a forty-four page publication.

Abhay Charan greeted his readers by defining his motto: "Godhead is Light, Nescience is darkness." When man forgets that he is the son of

Godhead and identifies himself with the body, then he's in ignorance. He's like a man who's very concerned with the automobile's mechanism yet with no knowledge of the driver.

> The defect of the present day civilisation is just like that. This is actually the civilisation of Nescience or illusion and therefore civilisation has been turned into militarisation. Everyone is fully concerned with the comforts of the body and everything related with the body and no one is concerned with the Spirit that moves the body although even a boy can realise that the motor-car mechanism has little value if there is no driver of the car. This dangerous ignorance of humanity is a gross Nescience and has created a dangerous civilisation in the form of militarisation. This militarisation which, in softer language, is Nationalisation is an external barrier to understanding human relations. There is no meaning in a fight where the parties do fight only for the matter of different coloured dresses. There must be therefore an understanding of human relation without any consideration of the bodily designation or coloured dresses.
>
> "BACK TO GODHEAD" is a feeble attempt by the undersigned under the direction of His Divine Grace Sri Srimad Bhakti Siddhanta Saraswati Goswami Prabhupada, the celebrated founder and organiser of the Gaudiya Math activities—just to bring up a real relation of humanity with central relation of the Supreme Personality of Godhead.
>
> That there is a great and urgent need of a literature like this is keenly felt by the leaders of all countries and the following statements will help much in the procedure.

It was 1944, and Abhay specifically addressed the crisis of world war. The world's political leaders were expressing their disgust at their people's suffering and scarcity. After four years of fighting, costing millions of human lives, the second world war within twenty years was still scourging the earth. Although the end was in sight, leaders expressed not so much happiness and hope as weariness and uncertainty. Even if this war ended, would there be yet another war? Had man not yet grasped the vital lesson of how to live in peace?

Abhay quoted the Archbishop of India: "India guided by God can lead the world back to sanity." He quoted the President of the United States: "A programme, therefore, of moral re-armament for the world cannot fail to lessen the dangers of armed conflict. Such moral re-armament, to be most highly effective, must receive support on a world wide basis." He mentioned former President Herbert Hoover, who had affirmed that the world needs to return to moral and spiritual ideals, and he quoted a resolution by the British House of Commons affirming that spiritual principles are the common heritage of all people and that men and nations urgently need to acknowledge the sovereignty of God. He quoted Wendell Willkie, who, after his return from Russia, had reported millions of Russians killed, wounded, or missing in the war and millions more suffering from a winter of terrible scarcity and subjugation.

"What is true for the Russian people," Abhay wrote, "is also true for other people, and we Indians are feeling the same scarcity, the same want, and the same disgust." He quoted Britain's foreign secretary, Anthony Eden, who had been filled with lamentation and indignation at the miseries of war. He quoted the Archbishop of Canterbury:

> In every quarter of earth men long to be delivered from the curse of War and to find in a world which has regained its peace, respite from the harshness and bitterness of the world they have known till now. But so often they want the Kingdom of Heaven without its King. The kingdom of God without God. And they cannot have it.
>
> *OUR RESOLVE MUST BE BACK TO GOD.* We make plans for the future for peace amongst the nation and for civil security at home. That is quite right enough and it would be wrong to neglect it. But all our plans will *come to ship-wreck on the rock of human selfishness unless we turn to God. BACK TO GOD,* that is the chief need of England and of every nation.

He also quoted Sir Francis Younghusband of Britain: "Now that religion is everywhere attacked brutally, *we look to India, the very home of religion, for a sign.*" And finally he quoted Sir Sarvapalli Radhakrishnan:

> This war, when it would be won, would prove to be the breeding ground of other wars if the peace was not saved. It could happen only if powerful nations ceased to take pride and glory in their possessions which were based on labour and tribute of other weaker nations. This perhaps was what Sir Harcourt Butler meant when he said that the principles of Hinduism contained the essential elements for the saving of world civilisations.

And in another quote from Dr. Radhakrishnan, Abhay offered a statement he also used as one of the mottoes of the magazine:

> We have to defeat tyranny in the realm of thought and create a will for world peace. Instruments for training the mind and educating human nature should be used to develope a proper social outlook without which institutional machinery was of little use.

Abhay expressed his confidence that the spiritual resources of India could be used by everyone, not only to enhance the glory of India but to benefit the whole world.

Next he told how he had come to begin *Back to Godhead* magazine—how he had written a letter two weeks before the disappearance of Śrīla Bhaktisiddhānta Sarasvatī, and how his spiritual master had instructed him to preach in English.

> Under the circumstances since 1936 up to now, I was simply speculating whether I shall venture this difficult task and that without any means and capacity; but as none have discouraged me ... I have now taken courage to take up the work. ... But at the present moment my conscience is dictating me to take up the work although the difficulties are not over for the present situation arising out of War conditions.

Abhay stated that his paper would contain only the transcendental messages of the great sages of India, especially Lord Caitanya, and that his duty would be simply to repeat them, just like a translator. He would not manufacture anything, and so his words would descend as transcendental sound for guiding people back to Godhead. He admitted that the subject matters of *Back to Godhead,* being from a totally different sphere of consciousness, might seem dry to his readers, but he held that anyone who actually gave attention to his message would benefit.

> Sugar-candy is never sweet to those who are suffering from the disease of the bile. But still, sugar-candy is the medicine for bilious patients. The taste of sugar-candy will gradually be revived if the bilious patient goes on taking sugar-candy regularly for the cure of the disease. We recommend the same process to the readers of "Back to Godhead."

Abhay focused on presenting the timeless message of the *Vedas,* but in the context of current crises. In his essay "Godhead and His Potentialities," he presented Vedic evidence and logical arguments to explain the transcendental nature of Godhead and the individual souls, both being deathless, blissful, and full of knowledge. Because men have forgotten and neglected their vital connection with God, they can never be satisfied in the material world, which is temporary and beset with unavoidable miseries. As spiritual souls, everyone is eternal by nature, and therefore everyone tries to avoid the onslaught of distresses and dangers, which come one after another. But the material body is meant for suffering and ultimately for destruction.

> The exodus of the residents of Calcutta to other places out of fear of being raided by the Japanese bombs, is due to the same tendency of non-destructible existence. But those who are thus going away, do not remember that even after going away from Calcutta saved from the raids of the Japanese bombs, they are unable to protect their bodies as non-destructible in any part of the material universe, when the same bodies will be raided by the bombs of material nature in the form of threefold miseries.
>
> The Japanese also—who are threatening the Calcutta people with ruthless air-raids for increasing their own happiness by possession of lands—do not know that their happiness is also temporary and destructible as they have repeatedly experienced in their own fatherland. The living beings, on the other hand, who are designed to be killed, are by nature eternal, impenetrable, invisible, etc. So all those living entities who are threatened to be killed as well as those who are threatening to conquer are all alike in the grip of the "Maya" potency and are therefore in the darkness.

Abhay wrote that never by their own devices could men escape the conditions of destruction. So many world leaders were seeking relief from the war, but all were useless, because their attempts for peace were within the material conception of life. Their attempts were like attempts to alleviate darkness with darkness; but darkness can be removed only by light.

> Without light, any amount of speculation of the human mind (which is also a creation of the material nature) can never restore the living entities to permanent happiness. In that darkness any method of bringing peace in the world ... can bring only temporary relief or distress, as we can see from all creations of the External Potency. In the darkness non-violence is as much useless as violence, while in the light there is no need of violence or non-violence.

Abhay did not deal exclusively with the war. In "Theosophy Ends in Vaishnavism," he criticized the shortcomings of the fashionable ideas of Theosophy, which the followers of Madame Blavatsky had popularized in India.

In "Congregational Chanting," he upheld the scriptural prediction that the *saṅkīrtana* movement of Lord Caitanya would spread to every town and village on the surface of the earth.

> From this foretelling we can hope that the cult of Samkirtan will take very shortly *a universal form of religious movement*, and this universal religion—

> wherein there is no harm in chanting the Name of the Lord nor is there any question of quarrel—will continue for years, as we can know from the pages of authoritative scriptures.

The central theme of *Back to Godhead* was clearly the order of Bhaktisiddhānta Sarasvatī. In its cover with its picture of a thoughtful Śrīla Bhaktisiddhānta, in its "Dedication," in its statement of the magazine's purpose, in its handling of issues, its analysis of Theosophy, its prediction of the spread of *saṅkīrtana*—in its every aspect, the theme of *Back to Godhead* was the order of Śrīla Bhaktisiddhānta Sarasvatī.

There were also four shorter essays by other contributors, including Bhaktisāraṅga Gosvāmī.

An advertisement on the back cover highlighted

GEETOPANISHAD
BY
ABHAY CHARAN DE
Editor and Founder "Back to Godhead"
In Three Parts, 1,200 Pages, Royal Size
FIRST CLASS MOROCCO BINDING

An elaborate exposition of the world famous Hindu Philosophy—"The Bhagbat Geeta"—in its true, scientific, theistic interpretations by the chain of disciplic succession from Sree Krishna, Brahma, Narada, Vyasa, Madhva, Madhabendra Puri, Iswara, Lord Chaitanya, Rupa Goswami, Jiva Goswami, Krishnadas, Narottama, Biswanath, Valadeva, Jagannath, Thakur Bhakti Vinode, Gour Kishore, Thakur Siddhanta Saraswati down to the Author
With Numerous Illustrations in Colours and Plain from Many Authentic Scriptures

To be Published Shortly—Customers Booked in Advance
Price—India Rs. 18/-, Foreign £1 10s.

And a second major work: *Lord Chaitanya,* in two parts, totaling one thousand pages. Neither of these manuscripts was actually near completion, but Abhay was expressing his eagerness to undertake such large works on behalf of his spiritual master.

In attempting to print the second issue of *Back to Godhead,* Abhay encountered the same difficulty as before. Twice he requested permission to purchase newsprint, and twice the government denied his request.

Paper was restricted on account of the war. On July 10, 1944, Abhay wrote a third letter.

> With due respect, I beg to submit that under the instruction of His Divine Grace, Sri Srimad Bhakti Siddhanta Saraswati Maharaj, the spiritual head of the Gaudiya Vaishnavas, I had to start a paper under the caption, "Back to Godhead." The very name will suggest the intention of starting such a paper in the midst of heavy turmoil through which the world is now passing. A copy of the same booklet is sent herewith for your kind perusal. In that booklet you shall find strong world opinions, even by many reputed politicians all over the world, in favour of such a movement to bring back the world into sanity by training the mind and educating human nature for the unshaking spiritual plane, considered to be the supreme need of humankind. I hope you will kindly go through the paper by making some time and I may draw your attention specially to the introductory portion.

Abhay also remarked that the editorial board of *Back to Godhead* felt that there was not so much a scarcity of paper as a scarcity of education. Taking the opportunity to preach, Abhay explained that although the ultimate supplier was the Personality of Godhead, godless men consider themselves the proprietors of all things.

> Catastrophe that is now in vogue in the present war of supremacy, is guided by this false sense of proprietorship and therefore there is need of making propaganda amongst all human beings, in order to bring them back to the sense of the ultimate proprietorship of Godhead. ...

Abhay conceded that there might indeed be a paper shortage in India. But in ancient times, he wrote, enlightened Indians had regularly sacrificed tons of valuable ghee and grains in the fire during religious sacrifices, and in those times there had not been any scarcity. People now, however, having abandoned all sacrifices to the Supreme Lord, were producing only scarcity.

> Can we not therefore sacrifice a few reams of paper in the midst of many wastages, for the same purpose in order to derive greater benefit for the humankind? I request that the Government should take up this particular case in the light of spiritualism which is not within the material calculation. Even in Great Britain the Government has immensely supported a similar movement called The Moral Re-Armament Movement without consideration of the scarcity of paper which is more acute there than here.
>
> Let there be a page only if not more for the publication of "Back to Godhead" for which we do not mind but my earnest request is that the

> Government should at least let there be a ventilation of the atmosphere for which my paper "Back to Godhead" [is] meant. Kindly therefore give it a serious consideration and allow me to start even by one page every weekly or monthly as you think best without thinking it as ordinary waste of paper, for the sake of humanity and Godhead.

The letter was successful. Now, with veiled sarcasm, he headlined his second issue, "Thanks to the Government of India." He informed his readers, many of whom had been disappointed to learn that the government had curtailed his printing, that he would be able to continue his magazine every month. Abhay printed his letter to the government paper officer and also the reply granting him permission.

His articles were shorter, this time displaying the flair of a news columnist, as with philosophical criticism, verve, and a touch of ironic humor he commented on world leaders and crises. "Gandhi-Jinnah Talks," "Mr. Churchill's 'Humane World,'" "Mr. Bernard Shaw's Wishful Desire," and "Spontaneous Love of Godhead" comprised the issue.

"Gandhi-Jinnah Talks": "We are sorry to learn that Gandhi-Jinnah talks about unity of the Indian people have failed for the present." Abhay was not very optimistic about the results of such "occasional talks between several heads of communities." Even if they made a successful solution, it would break up and take the shape of another problem. They were looking for unity between Muslims and Hindus, but in Europe the fighting parties were Christians, and in Asia they were mostly Buddhists—but still they were fighting. "So fighting will go on between Hindu and Mohammedan, between Hindus and Hindus or between Mohammedan and Mohammedan, between Christians and Christians and between Buddhist and Buddhist till the day of annihilation." As long as there was the contaminated self-interest of sense gratification, there would be fighting between brother and brother, father and son, and nation and nation. Real unity would stand only on a plane of transcendental service to the Supreme. "Mahatma Gandhi," Abhay wrote, "is far above ordinary human being and we have all respects for him." But Abhay advised Gandhi to give up his activities on the material plane and rise to the transcendental plane of the spirit—then there could be talks about the unity of all people. Abhay cited *Bhagavad-gītā's* definition of a *mahātmā:* one who concentrates his attention on the service of the Supreme Lord, Śrī Kṛṣṇa. He requested Mahatma Gandhi to adhere to the teachings of *Bhagavad-gītā* and preach its message of surrender to the Supreme Personality of Godhead, Śrī Kṛṣṇa. In this way, Mahatma Gandhi, through his influential position in the world, could bring about universal relief, simply by preaching the message of *Bhagavad-gītā*.

"Mr. Churchill's 'Humane World'":

> We are pleased to find that leaders of world politics such as Mr. Churchill have nowadays begun to think of a humane world and trying to get rid of the terrible national frenzy of hate. The frenzy of hatred is another side of the frenzy of love. The frenzy of love of Hitler's own countrymen has produced the concomitant frenzy of hatred for others and the present war is the result of such dual side of a frenzy called love and hatred. So when we wish to get rid of the frenzy of hate, we must be prepared to get rid of the frenzy of so-called love. This position of equilibrium free from love and hatred is attained only when men are sufficiently educated.

Until men were educated to see the soul within the body, the dual frenzy of love and hate would continue, and a humane world would not be possible. "This introspection," Abhay concluded, "is ... easily attained by the service of Godhead. So Mr. Churchill's Humane World implies that we must go 'Back to Godhead.'"

"Mr. Bernard Shaw's Wishful Desire":

> Mr. Bernard Shaw has congratulated Mahatma Gandhi on the occasion of the latter's 76th birthday in the following words: "I can only wish this were Mr. Gandhi's 35th birthday instead of his 76th." We heartily join with Mr. Shaw in his attempt to subtract 41 years from the present age of Mahatma Gandhi.

But death does not respect our "wishful desire." Neither Mr. Shaw nor Mahatma Gandhi, nor any other great personality, had ever been able to solve the problem of death.

> The leaders of nations have ... opened many factories for manufacturing weapons for the art of killing, but none has opened a factory to manufacture weapons for protecting man from the cruel hands of death, although our wishful desire is always not to die.

Men were preoccupied with the problem of how to get bread, although this problem was actually solved by nature. Man should try to solve the problem of death.

Bhagavad-gītā tells that the problem of death can be solved. Although death is everywhere in the material world, "One who attains to Me," says

Kṛṣṇa, "never has to take his birth again in the material world." There is a spiritual world, nondestructible, and one who goes there does not come back to the region of death. Why should the leaders of nations cling to the planet of their birth, where death is inevitable? Abhay concluded, "We wish that in their ripe old age Mr. Shaw and Mahatma Gandhi will make combined effort to educate men to learn how to go back to home, back to Godhead."

After two issues of *Back to Godhead,* Abhay had to stop. Printing was costly. But he kept writing regularly, working at *Geetopanishad,* turning out new articles and philosophical purports on the scriptures—even in the same book in which he wrote his pharmaceutical formulas.

* * *

One night, Abhay had an unusual dream. Śrīla Bhaktisiddhānta appeared before him, beckoning. He was asking Abhay to leave home and take *sannyāsa.* Abhay awoke in an intensely emotional state. "How horrible!" he thought. He knew it was not an ordinary dream, yet the request seemed so difficult and unlikely. Take *sannyāsa*! At least it was not something he could do immediately. Now he had to improve the business, and with the profits he would print books. He went on with his duties, but remained shaken by the dream.

* * *

In 1945, the war over and India still in turmoil under British rule, Abhay saw a good opportunity to make his business more successful. In Lucknow, six hundred miles from Calcutta, he rented a building and opened his own factory, Abhay Charan De and Sons.

It was a major investment, requiring forty thousand rupees to start, and he began on a larger scale than ever before. Also, according to law, to insure that he was not dealing in the black market or misusing chemicals, he had to employ three government inspectors. Yet despite a high overhead he established a good market, and his products were in demand. He closed his small operation in Calcutta and concentrated on the Lucknow business.

Although the building was known locally to be haunted by ghosts, Abhay had not been deterred. But when he began his operations, some of the workers came to him frightened: "Bābū, Bābū, there is a ghost!" Abhay then went through the entire building chanting Hare Kṛṣṇa, and after that there were no more complaints of ghosts.

On November 13, Abhay wrote to his servant Gouranga, mentioning some of his difficulties in Lucknow and asking him to come there to help. In this letter, Abhay spoke bitterly of his wife, Radharani, and children.

> Gouranga Prabhu,
>
> Please accept my obeisances. I received your letter dated 7th. Due to lack of time I could not reply in time. I stay here alone with some servants. If I leave now, then I have to close everything down. Due to my leaving once and closing the business, I have lost about 10,000 rupees and the good will has also been affected and my enemies have increased. That is why I am fighting, practically staking my whole life. I am staying here all alone in the middle of so many difficulties not for nothing. That's why I was writing to you repeatedly to come here. As soon as you receive this letter show it to Dubra. Take at least ten rupees from him and come here. When you come here, I will make arrangements to send money to your home. What's the point in holding you back with an excuse that there is no servant or maid-servant? I tried to serve them enough by keeping servants, maidservants and cooks. But up until today they have not become attached to devotional service. So I am no more interested about those affairs. When you come here, then I will go to Calcutta. If I see that they are interested about devotional service, then only will I maintain my establishment there. Otherwise, I will not maintain them any more. Bring a quilt for me.
>
> Yours,
> Abhay

The two interests—family and preaching—were conflicting. Radharani had never shown any interest in *Back to Godhead.* She seemed to work against his enthusiasm, both for publishing and for earning. The business was called Abhay Charan De and Sons, and yet the sons were disinclined to help. And when he had called for his servant to join him in Lucknow, the family had objected, saying they needed Gouranga more there.

What was the use? The family was interested neither in backing him in his business nor in taking up the life of devotional service. And since his business was primarily an outcome of his family life, he resented that he had to give it so much of his energy. It was the old economic law by Marshall that he had learned in college: Without family affection, a man's economic impetus is weakened.

Of course, there could be a compatible balance between family service and devotional service. Bhaktivinoda Ṭhākura had described two simultaneous obligations: bodily and spiritual. Social status, mental development, cleanliness, nourishment, and the struggle for existence were all bodily obligations; the activities of devotional service to Kṛṣṇa were spiritual. And the two should parallel one another. In Bhaktivinoda Ṭhākura's life, his family was a source of spiritual encouragement, and he used his social position to advance his preaching.

But Abhay's experience had been different; the two paths seemed to be at war, each threatening the other's existence. He felt himself operating somewhat like the materialists he had criticized in his writings, absorbed in the struggle for existence with insufficient time for self-realization. Although his family made more and more demands of him, he was feeling less inclined to work for them and more inclined to preach Kṛṣṇa consciousness. It was a predicament. He could only push on diligently, support his family, expand his business, and hope for a great success so that he could revive his publishing.

But the Lucknow factory seemed almost beyond his means. He had purposely begun on a large scale with the aim of making a larger profit. But monthly expenses were high, he had fallen behind in his rent, and now he was involved in a court case with the landlord. Although he was visiting Calcutta regularly and shipping raw materials from Calcutta to Lucknow daily, he always found his family members in Calcutta uncooperative. His servant Gouranga was also reluctant to work as Abhay required and was thinking of going back to live with his family. Abhay again wrote to Gouranga on the twenty-third.

> Offering my humble obeisances at the feet of the Vaishnava. Gouranga Prabhu, I have received your postcard dated 18/11/45 and got all the informations. There is no need to come here just for a month after spending the money and then go back. For the present take 25 rupees from Dubra and go home. Write a letter to me after your arrival, then I will send the rest of your money in one or two installments by money order. Then from there you let me know when can you come here.
>
> I have started my work here in a fairly big scale. You have seen that with your own eyes. ... So if there is no income, who will spend [for a court]

interrogation? Everything is on my head. The brother and sons are just eating and sleeping like a bunch of females and breaking the axe on my head.

You go home as soon as you get the money and try to come back as soon as possible.

Yours,
Sri Abhay Charan De

CHAPTER SIX

An Unknown Friend

Let the sharp moralists accuse me of being illusioned; I do not mind. Experts in Vedic activities may slander me as being misled, friends and relatives may call me frustrated, my brothers may call me a fool, the wealthy mammonites may point me out as mad, and the learned philosophers may assert that I am much too proud. Still, my mind does not budge an inch from the determination to serve the lotus feet of Govinda, though I am unable to do it.

—Mādhavendra Purī

ASIDE FROM HIS difficulties with business and family, Abhay had to survive the cataclysms of Indian independence and partition. He was not active politically, but was one of hundreds of millions affected by the violent dawn of Indian independence.

While Gandhi and the Hindu-dominated Congress were demanding a united free India, the Muslim League, led by M. A. Jinnah, called for partition and their own Muslim nation—Pakistan. The conflict raged. In August 1946 the outgoing British government invited Jawaharlal Nehru, Congress Party president, to form an interim national government; but the League objected—the Muslim cause would be denied. Jinnah had already declared August 16 "Direct Action Day," which amounted to little in most parts of India but in Calcutta erupted in Hindu-Muslim rioting. In five days of violence, four thousand died, and thousands more were wounded. In the months that followed, Hindu-Muslim rioting repeatedly flared up throughout India.

Early in 1947, when the new viceroy, Lord Mountbatten, met with Indian political leaders to plan transfer of power, riots again broke out as Muslims demanded Pakistan. At the threat of civil war, Congress finally agreed on partition, and on July 18, the Indian independence bill passed without dissent. One month later India and Pakistan emerged as independent nations, with Jawaharlal Nehru as India's first prime minister.

Partition tore India, leaving five million Sikhs and Hindus in Pakistan and as many Muslims in India. And the great migration began. Refugees fleeing from Pakistan to India and from India to Pakistan clashed with each other and even with their own countrymen of the opposing faith, and the violence that erupted claimed hundreds of thousands of lives.

Śrīla Prabhupāda: *Our independence movement was started by Mahatma Gandhiji for uniting all the different sections of the people. But actually the result was that instead of being united, India was partitioned. And the partition became so poisonous that formerly there was only sporadic Hindu-Muslim riots in some places, but now there was organized fighting between Pakistan and Hindustan. So actually we were not being united, we were being separated.*

The Hindus would go to the mosque of the Muslim and break it, and the Muslim would go to the temples of the Hindus and break the idol. And they will think, "We have finished the Hindus' God." Just like the Hindus also think, "Oh, we have broken their God." They are all ignorant. God cannot be Hindu. God cannot be Muslim. God cannot be Christian. God is God.

We have seen in 1947—Hindu-Muslim fighting. One party was Hindu, the other party was Muslim. They fought, and so many died, and after death there was no distinction who was Hindu or who was Muslim—the municipal men gathered them together in piles to throw them somewhere. They fought, and in Baghbazar there were heaps of dead bodies. And when it is a dead body, nobody could understand who was Hindu and who was Muslim. Simply it was to be cleared from the road.

Abhay was not expecting Indian independence to bring any real solutions. Unless the leaders were God conscious, what change would there be? Now he saw that instead of suffering at the hand of a foreign rule, the people were free to suffer under their own countrymen. In fact, the fighting and suffering had increased.

Throughout the years of India's political struggles, Abhay had never lost his desire to propagate Kṛṣṇa consciousness. He had seen how promises of unity and independence had brought mostly higher prices and civic mismanagement. He had seen neighborhoods where Indians had lived peacefully for generations erupt in hatred and rioting, in the wake of British and Indian diplomatic manipulations. It was as Śrīla Bhaktisiddhānta Sarasvatī had described it:

> Persons who are strongly entrapped by the consciousness of enjoying material life, and who have therefore accepted as their leader or guru a similar blind man attached to external sense objects, cannot understand that the goal of life is to return home, back to Godhead, and engage in the service of Lord Vishnu. As blind men guided by another blind man miss the right path and fall into a ditch, materially attached men led by another materially attached man are bound by the ropes of fruitive labour, which are made of very strong cords, and they continue again and again in materialistic life, suffering the threefold miseries.

The Vaiṣṇava prays to his spiritual master, "who has opened my eyes with the torchlight of transcendental knowledge," and he feels obliged to help humanity by bearing the same torch. As a representative of the eternal Vaiṣṇava *paramparā,* Abhay wanted to shed the light of transcendental knowledge onto the field of current crises. That had been the purpose of *Back to Godhead,* although since 1944 he had been unable to print the magazine.

But even without the means to publish, Abhay continued writing. His most ambitious project was *Geetopanishad,* his translation and commentary of *Bhagavad-gītā.* Gandhi and others often spoke of the wisdom of *Bhagavad-gītā*—Indians never forgot their *Gītā*—but most proponents did not teach it as Kṛṣṇa had taught it. They would not recognize Lord Kṛṣṇa, the speaker of their *Gītā,* as the Supreme Personality of Godhead, but would extract His words as slogans to bolster their own philosophies. Whether political leaders, religious leaders, or scholars, they almost invariably made their own symbolic and allegorical interpretations. Abhay wanted to present *Bhagavad-gītā* as is. It was to be twelve-hundred pages—three illustrated, beautifully bound volumes. For Abhay the books were already a reality, from which he was separated only by time. Over the past two years he had accumulated hundreds of manuscript pages. He wrote in notebooks and on loose papers and then typed the numbered manuscript pages. He could never give the book his full time, but gradually it began to take shape.

He also preached Lord Caitanya's message through letters, writing to many leaders in the government, to respectable acquaintances, and to people whose articles he had read or whose activities had caught his eye in the newspaper. Presenting himself as a humble servant, he wrote to them of his ideas on how India's original Kṛṣṇa conscious culture could be applied as the successful solution to all manners of dilemmas. Sometimes his letters drew replies, and Abhay would respond, fanning the sparks of interest wherever he found them.

A well-known reformer, Mahendra Pratap Raja, was forming what he called the World Federation. Abhay had read a newssheet, which Mr. Pratap had published from Vṛndāvana, in which he addressed all nations and peoples of the world and called for a unity of mankind.

Abhay wrote to him suggesting that Lord Kṛṣṇa's teachings in *Bhagavad-gītā* provided a theistic science capable of uniting all religions. Mr. Pratap replied, in May 1947, "I admire your deep study of Shreemad Bhagwat Geeta. I myself am a great admirer of the great classic. I assure you that I am working strictly according to the book." Mr. Pratap mentioned his book, *Religion of Love,* and suggested that Abhay read it if he wanted to know the World Federation's view of religion. "In the meanwhile," Mr. Pratap wrote, "I do not agree to your suggestion of making the name of 'Krishna' or 'Govinda' as the basis of the Unity of Religions. This would amount to conversion and won't lead to unity of religions. I highly appreciate your efforts in the direction of 'Back to Godhead.'"

Abhay got the book, read it, and in July 1947, while he was visiting Kanpur, wrote a reply. He had traveled to Kanpur not as a spiritual teacher but as a pharmaceutical salesman. Yet a typewriter had been available, and out had come his preaching.

> In continuation of my last post card, I beg to inform you that I have finished the reading of your book Religion of Love. In my opinion the whole thesis is based on the philosophy of Pantheism and the approach is made by the services of mankind. Religion of Love is the true religious idea but if the

> approach is made through the service of mankind only, then the process is made imperfect, partial and unscientific.
>
> The true Religion of Love is perfectly inculcated in the Bhagwat Geeta. ... Besides you have not quoted any authority for all your statements. So it is more or less dogmatic. If different men put different dogmatic views about religion and its essentials, who is to be accepted and who is not to be? Therefore the approach shall be and must be authoritative, scientific and universal.

Abhay then gave a summary of the *Bhagavad-gītā* in ten points, concluding, "The highest service that can be rendered to Mankind is, therefore, to preach the philosophy and religion of Bhagwat Geeta for all time, all places and all people."

But extended philosophical dialogue was not usually the result of his letters. In 1947, when Abhay wrote to high government officers of the newly formed government of India suggesting a remedy for riots, they turned him away. When he asked to talk with the governor of West Bengal, the governor's secretary replied, "His Excellency regrets that he is unable to grant you an interview at present, owing to heavy pressure of work." When he wrote to the assistant secretary to the minister of education, an assistant to the assistant secretary replied, "The Government of India regret that they are unable to accede to your request."

Sometimes official interest took the form of a patronizing pat on the head: "I am sure your scheme for establishing peace will meet with response from our Prime Minister." And another: "He [the minister of education] is glad to see you are taking to route out communalism. He suggests that you get in touch with ..."

A local official asked not to be seen:

> I thank you for all that you have written and the fine sentiments which you have expressed. It is no use arguing the matter, as I do not think that I can serve any useful purpose by joining the organization which you wish to set up. And therefore you need not take the trouble of seeing me. I wish you, however, all success.

In October, after the Calcutta riots of 1947, Abhay wrote to the chairman of the rehabilitation committee, who replied:

> Regarding hari kirtan and prasadam, you may make any program of your own, but I am afraid I am not interested in the same. Nor my committee, and therefore there is no necessity of your meeting with me.

Abhay was fulfilling his role as a Vaiṣṇava preacher, and the secretaries of the various government offices were recognizing and addressing him as such. But they could not appreciate his applications of the philosophy of *Bhagavad-gītā* and his suggestions for *hari-kīrtana*. Occasionally, however, someone seemed interested. Mr. N. P. Asthana, high court advocate, replied:

> I am very much obliged to you for your letter re: your broad scheme about spiritual improvement. I thoroughly appreciate the fine feelings which have prompted you to write this letter and the kindness with which you have considered my query. I have been a student of Bhagwat Geeta and have also imbibed some of its teachings, but I still lack a good deal and will be glad to be guided by a person of your accomplishment. You may kindly, therefore, send your scheme to me, on receipt of which I will be able to express my views.

* * *

It was inevitable that Abhay would think of engaging Mahatma Gandhi in devotional service. Because of his lifetime of courageous, ascetic, and moral activities on behalf of his countrymen, Mahatma Gandhi had great power to influence the Indian masses. As with Mahendra Pratap of the World Federation, Mahatma Gandhi's idea of serving God was to try to bring happiness to man through politics and through his own invented methods. As one Englishman had said of Mahatma Gandhi, "He is either a saint amongst the politicians or a politician amongst the saints." But be that as it may, he was not as yet fully engaged in pure devotional service, and his activities were not those of a *mahātmā* as described in *Bhagavad-gītā*. The *Gītā* defines a *mahātmā* as one who fully engages in worshiping Lord Kṛṣṇa as the Supreme Personality of Godhead, always chanting His glories. The *mahātmā* encourages others to surrender to Kṛṣṇa.

But because as a young man Abhay had been a follower of Gandhi's, Abhay had a special feeling for him. Of course, Śrīla Bhaktisiddhānta Sarasvatī had later convinced him to engage exclusively in devotional service. But now Abhay felt his old friendship for Gandhi, even though Gandhi was a towering figure of worldwide fame and Abhay unknown both to Gandhi and to the world.

On December 7, 1947, Abhay wrote to Gandhi from Kanpur. Gandhi was living at the Birla Mansion in Delhi, where large military forces throughout the city discouraged Hindu-Muslim rioting. Gandhi's secretary, Pyarelal Nayar, described Gandhi at this time as "the saddest man one could picture." The men he had led in the struggle for Indian independence, Jawaharlal Nehru, Vallabhbhai Patel, and others, had taken the leadership of the nation. And Gandhi, with his doctrines of nonviolence, unity, and agrarianism, was now at odds with them in many ways. He feared he was becoming an anachronism. His former colleagues admired him but rejected his leadership. All his programs—Hindu-Muslim unity, nonviolence, upliftment for the poor—although praised throughout the world, were failures in the India of 1947. On a recent visit to a Muslim refugee camp, a crowd of Muslims who surrounded his car had cursed him, and at a public prayer meeting a Hindu crowd had shouted him down and ended his meeting when he had attempted to read from the *Koran.* At seventy-eight years, Gandhi was physically weak and melancholy.

In all likelihood, Abhay's letter would never reach him. Abhay knew it. Sending a letter to Gandhi would be like putting a note in a bottle and sending it to sea. It would arrive in the flood of mail, and Gandhi would be too busy to see it. But Abhay sent it nonetheless.

> Dear Friend Mahatmajee,
>
> Please accept my respectful Namaskar. I am your unknown friend but I had to write to you at times and again although you never cared to reply them. I sent you my papers "Back to Godhead" but your secretaries told me that you have very little time to read the letters and much less for reading the magazines. I asked for an interview with you but your busy secretaries never cared to reply this. Anyway, as I am your very old friend although unknown to you, I am writing to you in order to bring you to the rightful position deserved by you. As a sincere friend I must not deviate from my duty towards a friend like your good self.
>
> I tell you as a sincere friend that you must immediately retire from active politics if you do not desire to die an inglorious death. You have 125 years to live as you have desired to live but if you die an inglorious death it is no worth. The honour and prestige that you have obtained during the course of your present lifetime, were not possible to be obtained by anyone else within the living memory. But you must know that all these honours and prestiges were false in as much as they were created by the Illusory Energy of Godhead called the Maya. By this falsity I do not mean to say that your so many friends were false to you nor you were false to them. By this falsity I mean

> illusion or in other words the false friendship and honours obtained thereby were but creation of Maya and therefore they are always temporary or false as you may call it. But none of you neither your friends nor yourself know this truth.

A *sādhu* is not supposed to flatter but to cut. This is the basis of his friendship—that he cuts away the illusion of the materialistic person. Mahatma Gandhi, forsaken by his friends, bitterly disappointed at the outcome of the long, hard struggle for Indian independence, and apprehensive about the future, had been reduced to a position in which he might be able to realize that his friends and work were ultimately illusory. Thus it was the perfect time for him to comprehend Abhay's message.

> Now by the Grace of God that Illusion is going to be cleared and thus your faithful friends like Acharya Kripalini and others are accusing you for your inability at the present moment to give them any practical programme of work as you happened to give them during your glorious days of non-cooperation movement. So you are also in a plight to find out a proper solution for the present political tangle created by your opponents. You should therefore take a note of warning from your insignificant friend like me, that unless you retire timely from politics and engage yourself cent percent in the preaching work of Bhagwat Geeta, which is the real function of the Mahatmas, you shall have to meet with such inglorious deaths as Mussolini, Hitler, ... or Lloyd George met with.

For years Abhay had wanted to approach Mahatma Gandhi with this message. In fact, he had written before, although it had been of no avail. But now he was convinced that unless Gandhi got out of politics he would soon die "an inglorious death." That Gandhi was remaining active in politics rather than preaching devotional service put him in need of a warning. Abhay was writing to save a friend.

> You can easily understand as to how some of your political enemies in the garb of friends (both Indian and English) have deliberately cheated you and have broken your heart by doing the same mischief for which you have struggled so hard for so many years. You wanted chiefly Hindu-Moslem unity in India and they have tactfully managed to undo your work, by creation of the Pakistan and India separately. You wanted freedom for India but they have given permanent dependence of India. You wanted to do something for the upliftment of the position of the Bhangis but they are still rotting as Bhangis even though you are living in the Bhangi colony. They are all there-

fore illusions and when these things will be presented to you as they are, you must consider them as God-sent. God has favoured you by dissipating the illusion you were hovering in and by the same illusion you were nursing those ideas as Truth.

Abhay dutifully attempted to inform Gandhi that there was nothing absolute within this relative world. *Ahiṁsā,* or nonviolence, must always be followed by violence, just as light is followed by darkness. Nothing is absolute truth in the dual world. "You did not know this," wrote Abhay, "neither you ever cared to know this from the right sources and therefore all your attempts to create unity were followed by disunity and Ahimsa was followed by Himsa."

Abhay pointed out that Gandhi had never undergone the standard practice for spiritual advancement, namely, accepting a bona fide spiritual master. Although *Bhagavad-gītā* declares the necessity of accepting a *guru* in disciplic succession, Gandhi was well known for listening to his inner voice and for extracting ideas from various writers like Ruskin and Thoreau and mixing them with teachings from the New Testament and the *Gītā.* Had Gandhi approached a *guru,* said Abhay, he would not have become bewildered within the sphere of relative truth.

In the Katha Upanishad it is ordered that one must approach the bona fide Guru who is not only well versed in all the scriptures of the world but is also the realised soul in Brahman the Absolute—in order to learn the science of Absolute Truth. So also it is instructed in the Bhagwat Geeta as follows:

Tad Biddhi Pranipatena Pariprasnena Sebaya
Upadekshyanti Te Jnanam Jnanina Tatwadarshina
(4/34)

But I know that you never underwent such transcendental teaching except some severe penances which you invented for your purpose as you have invented so many things in the course of experimenting with the relative truths. You might have easily avoided them if you had approached the Guru as above mentioned.

Recognizing Mahatma Gandhi's godly qualities and austerities, Abhay requested him to employ his moral elevation for surrendering to the Absolute Truth. Abhay urged him to get out of politics immediately.

> But your sincere efforts to attain some Godly qualities by austerities, etc. surely have raised you to some higher platform which you can better utilise for the purpose of the Absolute Truth. If you, however, remain satisfied with such temporary position only and do not try to know the Absolute Truth, then surely you are to fall down from the artificially exalted position under the laws of Nature. But if you want really to approach the Absolute Truth and want to do some real good to the people in general all over the world, which shall include your ideas of unity, peace and non-violence, then you must give up the rotten politics immediately and rise up for the preaching work of the philosophy and religion of "Bhagwat Geeta" without offering unnecessary and dogmatic interpretation on them. I had occasionally discussed this subject in my paper "Back to Godhead" and a leaf from the same is enclosed herewith for your reference.
>
> I would only request you to retire from politics at least *for a month only* and let us have discussion on the Bhagwat Geeta. I am sure, thereby, that you shall get a new light from the result of such discussions not only for your benefit but for the benefit of the world at large—as I know that you are sincere, honest and a moralist.
>
> Awaiting your early reply with interest.
>
> Yours sincerely,
> Abhay Charan De

There was no reply. A month later, Gandhi announced that he would fast until death unless India made a payment of 550 million rupees to Pakistan, a previous condition of the partition agreement. At first Hindu refugees from Pakistan demonstrated outside Gandhi's darkened room, chanting, "Let Gandhi die!" But as he fasted, each day closer to death, he aroused the heartfelt concern of the nation, and the government leaders repaid the money to Pakistan. Then, great crowds approached him, chanting, "Let Gandhi live!" Meanwhile, Hindu-Muslim violence continued.

On January 30, the day after he had drafted a new constitution for the Congress Party, Gandhi took his evening meal, worked at his spinning wheel, then walked towards his evening prayer meeting and was shot three times in the chest. He died, crying out the name of God—"*He Rāma*!" Abhay's letter of the previous month suddenly read like a prophecy. But it had not been read by the person for whom it had been intended.

* * *

When the directors of the Mahatma Gandhi Memorial National Fund invited suggestions on how to commemorate Gandhi's life and work, Abhay wrote to them and simultaneously to Vallabhbhai Patel, India's deputy prime minister, proposing "the Gandhian way" to use the funds.

> Gandhi's whole life was dedicated to the service of humanity at large with special interest for raising the moral standard. His later activities showed that he was equal to everyone and all the people of the world knew him more as a spiritual leader than a mere politician. Devotion to Godhead was his ultimate aim and when I say that his sacred memory should be perpetrated not in the ordinary way but in the Gandhian way, I mean that fitting respects to his memory will be done in the following manner.

Abhay wrote of a Mahatma Gandhi rarely described: Gandhi as a Vaiṣṇava. Despite his pressing political activities, Gandhi had never missed his daily prayer meetings in the evenings. Even at the time of his assassination, he had been on his way to attend his daily *kīrtana*. Abhay stressed that it was because of Gandhi's regular participation in congregational prayer that he had been strong in his work to raise the moral standard of humanity. "Gandhiji minus his spiritual activities," Abhay wrote, "is an ordinary politician. But actually he was a saint amongst the statesmen. ..." Abhay wrote that it had been Lord Caitanya who had originated the congregational chanting of the names of Kṛṣṇa and Rāma, and His followers the six Gosvāmīs had left a wealth of literature for discussion and understanding. The Memorial Fund board should take this lesson from Mahatmaji's practical life and develop it on a large scale. Therefore, one fitting memorial to Mahatma Gandhi would be to institute daily congregational readings from the *Bhagavad-gītā*. When peoples' spiritual instincts were kindled by daily prayer meetings, then they would develop the highest qualities in their character.

Abhay had a second suggestion. Gandhi was known for his attempts to enable the lower classes to enter the temples, and in Noakhali he had installed the Deity of Rādhā and Kṛṣṇa for the ordinary man to worship. Although this was generally taken as a side issue of Gandhi's work, Abhay took it as the essence—that Gandhi's was a theistic movement. Abhay explained that although there were hundreds and thousands of temples in India, they were not being properly managed, and therefore educated citizens were neglecting them. In the original Vedic culture, the purpose of the temples had been to nurture spiritual culture. If the temples of India could be reorganized as vital spiritual centers, then the disturbed minds of the day could be trained for life's higher duties. "Such education and practice," Abhay wrote, "can help man in realising the existence of God, without whose sanction, according to Mahatma Gandhi, 'not a blade of grass moves.'"

He also referred to Gandhi's *harijan* movement, which most people saw as Gandhi's humanitarian effort to grant equal rights to untouchables, whom Gandhi had recognized as *harijan,* "people of God." Abhay stressed that this was also an essentially spiritual aspect of Gandhi's life. But rather than simply rubber-stamping an untouchable as *harijan,* Abhay argued, there must be a systematic program for elevating people of the lower classes. This program was taught in the *Bhagavad-gītā* and could best be applied under the guidance of a bona fide devotee of the Lord. Abhay volunteered to take up the work on behalf of the Memorial Board. If the board, in attempting to commemorate Gandhi's efforts and accomplishments, neglected the essential spiritual aspects of Gandhi's life, Abhay warned, "his memory will soon be dead, as has been the lot of other politicians."

Perhaps they saw Abhay as another opportunist seeking money or as a sectarian religionist. But Abhay saw himself as a lowly servant of Śrīla Bhaktisiddhānta Sarasvatī. Seeing certain Vaiṣṇava qualities in the character of Mahatma Gandhi, Abhay took the opportunity to introduce his spiritual master's message to the world. And by so doing, he paid tribute to Mahatma Gandhi, praising him as a great devotee interested in *kīrtana,* temple worship, and elevating unfortunates to become people of God.

* * *

While on business in Madurai, in South India, Abhay showed some of his writings to Muthuswamy Chetty, another medical salesman. Mr. Chetty was impressed and felt he could persuade his wealthy friend Dr. Allagappa, the famous "Birla of the South," to finance the printing. In April of 1948, Mr. Chetty wrote to Abhay, saying that he had been prompted to help Abhay "for something God has meant." He asked Abhay Charan to send him the complete *Geetopanishad* manuscript so that he could present it to Dr. Allagappa in Madras. Mr. Chetty had already written Dr. Allagappa about the "first-class work Geetopanishad, to cover 1,200 pages of royal size" and had urged him to publish it for the benefit of religious-minded people. He had also mentioned that Abhay had been trying to publish the book since 1946.

Dr. Allagappa soon replied to Mr. Chetty that he was interested, and Mr. Chetty wrote to Abhay, "So I am on my way to help you, and only God must help me." As for talking business with Dr. Allagappa, there would be no need, since "once he does it, it is for the sake of benevolence. ..." Anticipating success, Mr. Chetty invited Abhay to come to Madras to meet Dr. Allagappa. "There he will arrange for what God has meant for you to do in your religious duty." In Madras, Abhay would be able to check and correct the proofs of the manuscript and see the book through the various stages of printing. It was a big opportunity, and Abhay was not one to miss an opportunity. If the book could be published, it would be a great victory in his mission to fulfill the request of Śrīla Bhaktisiddhānta Sarasvatī.

But then the worst thing happened. The manuscript was stolen. It was the only copy, the one Abhay was keeping safely at home. He questioned his family and servants—no one knew what had happened. Abhay was baffled; so much work had been undone. He felt he had worked so many months for nothing. Although he couldn't prove anything, he suspected that his servant or even his son might have done it, with a motive for raising money. But it remained a mystery.

* * *

During 1949, Abhay wrote articles in Bengali and submitted them to his Godbrother B. P. Keśava Mahārāja, who published them in his *Gauḍīya Patrikā*. Abhay's format for addressing world problems was the same as his spiritual master's. Even at their first meeting, in 1922, Śrīla Bhaktisiddhānta Sarasvatī had countered Abhay's nationalistic arguments by stressing that the real crisis in the world was neither social nor political nor anything material, but was simply the dearth of transcendental knowledge. Abhay simply elaborated on this theme. He never advocated that the ordinary concerns of the world be disregarded, but he stressed that crises can be solved only when the leadership is God conscious. If Kṛṣṇa consciousness were put first, other concerns could be brought into line. But without Kṛṣṇa consciousness, so-called solutions were only folly.

Abhay began his first Bengali article by quoting an editorial from the Allahabad edition of the Calcutta newspaper *Amrita Bazar.* The editor had sorely lamented that India's worst troubles had not yet ended, despite national independence.

> The national week has begun. The memories of Jallianwalla Bagh and political serfdom no longer trouble us. But our trouble is far from being at an end. In the dispensation of Providence, mankind cannot have any rest. If one kind of trouble goes, another quickly follows. India, politically free, is faced with difficulties no less serious than those that troubled us under a foreign rule.

Abhay seized on this editorial reflection as proof of the basic defect of all worldly plans for amelioration. He pointed out that although India had been subjugated by foreign rulers since the time of Muhammad Ghori (A.D. 1050), India prior to that had never been subjugated. In those days, India had been a God conscious nation. It was when India's leaders had abandoned their spiritual heritage that India had fallen.

Thus, Indians should see that they were now being punished by the stringent laws of material nature. "The honorable editor of *Amrita Bazar Patrika,*" Abhay noted, "has written so sadly, 'If one trouble goes, another quickly follows,' but that was stated in the Bhagwat Geeta a long time previously." It was the same theme he had stated in his 1944 *Back to Godhead* articles and the theme of so many of his letters also: Man, due to his neglect of the Supreme Lord, is being punished by material nature, which is directly controlled by the Supreme Lord. Men may write newspaper articles, pass measures at meetings and conferences, and attempt to overcome nature by scientific research, yet they will remain unable to surmount nature's law. As they try to escape their punishments, the Supreme Lord will cast them deeper into illusion, and they will fail miserably. Abhay quoted an appropriate Bengali saying: "I was trying to make a statue of Shiva, but I ended up making a monkey."

> In order to rid the world of misery and bring about happiness, we have now created the atomic bomb. Seeing the all-pervading destruction, which could take place in the near future by atomic reactions, Western thinkers have become greatly disturbed. Some people try to give consolation, saying that we will only use this atomic energy to bring about happiness in the world. This is also another enigma of the illusory potency.

The problem, Abhay explained, was that the world was lacking Kṛṣṇa conscious devotees. Leaders under the influence of material nature could never solve the problems of the world. Materialistic illusion was especially prevalent in the Western countries, which Indians should not try to imitate. Abhay prophesied, however, that Kṛṣṇa consciousness would one day reach the West.

> In the Western countries there has never been any discussion of the relation between the atomic individual soul and the Supreme complete conscious Personality of Godhead. Neither their activities nor their state in ultimate perfection has been investigated. That is why, even though they have made so much material advancement, they are squirming in the burning poison of sensualism. ... We can be absolutely certain that India's real peace formula will one day reach their ears.

Abhay's articles began appearing regularly in the *Gauḍīya Patrikā*. His Godbrothers appreciated his writings; his denunciation of the materialistic mentality was reminiscent of Śrīla Bhaktisiddhānta Sarasvatī's. In Abhay's hands, the *Bhagavad-gītā's* concept of the *asura* (demon) was no longer merely a depiction of a mythological or legendary enemy; the *asuras* had come to life in the modern-day Hitler, Churchill, or even an Indian prime minister. But, as Abhay pointed out, his denunciation of the misleaders was not his own; he was only repeating the words of Kṛṣṇa.

* * *

During 1950–51 he continued his letter-writing, attempting to gain a hearing with various organizations and leaders. He wrote the World Pacifist Committee, the president of India, and the minister of education. He wrote to the Indian Congress for Cultural Freedom, which wrote back suggesting that Abhay had written them by mistake. He wrote to an official of the All-Religions Conference in Bombay, advising that because of their approach nothing practical would come out of their conference; "The practical solution is lying in the transcendental message of Sree Krishna, the Personality of Godhead, as given by Him in the Bhagwat Geeta."

On September 14, 1951, he corresponded with Daniel Bailey of the *American Reporter,* a magazine published by the American embassy in New Delhi. Abhay pointed out that the philosophy of understanding the Absolute Truth, as realized by the sages of India, was higher than attempts to combine East and West. Mr. Bailey replied that he was aware of Eastern philosophical and religious influence in the West and cited the progress of a *yoga* mission in New York City, which he said had some influence on the Protestants in America. But when Abhay asked if one of his articles could appear in the *American Reporter,* Mr. Bailey replied, "If we were to give considerable space in the *American Reporter* to, say, the *Gītā,* we in all fairness would have to give equal space to the other philosophies and our desire is not to endorse or condemn any of them, but simply to assist in a better understanding. ..." In a further reply, Abhay differed with Mr. Bailey's contention that people should be encouraged to make their own interpretation of religion: "Less intelligent men are always guided by those who are superior in knowledge in all spheres of life."

Abhay even wrote to the Ford Foundation in Detroit, and a staff assistant wrote back, "Regret to advise you that we are unable to pursue your suggestions concerning the establishment of an association of the intelligent class of people. The Ford Foundation has no program in which specific ideas such as you describe might be included."

Although most of his suggestions were rejected, occasionally he received words of appreciation. A certain Doctor Muhammad Sayyid, Ph.D., a professor at the University of Allahabad, wrote, "You seem to have assimilated the universal teaching of ancient India, which is ... really laudable." And the governor of Uttar Pradesh replied, "You are doing noble work, for nothing is nobler than to be God minded."

Not only was Abhay giving advice in his letters, but he was hinting that he could also give practical help. If he could obtain institutional backing, he was prepared to do many things: teach classes, manage temples, teach temple worship, and initiate devotees, as well as organize various kinds of field work to propagate the principles of *Bhagavad-gītā.* Usually he did not spell out exactly how things should be done, but he pointed to the philosophical defects in the present methods and the superiority of working in accord with the Vedic literature. By the grace of his spiritual master, he knew the science of applying *Bhagavad-gītā* to almost any situation; if someone would only show interest, he could teach that person the superiority of working according to *Bhagavad-gītā.*

After attending a meeting in which a prominent industrialist had stressed harmonious relationships between labor and management in his factory, Abhay wrote a long letter, suggesting the man consider the good effects the congregational chanting of Hare Kṛṣṇa could produce. Since the factory had a special employees' club and lounge, Abhay suggested that the workers assemble there and chant Hare Kṛṣṇa.

Abhay urged everyone to surrender to Kṛṣṇa, but most people had their own philosophies and took his spirit to be sectarian or proselytizing. But *Bhagavad-gītā* was universal, Abhay wrote, and God could not be omitted from any program, even in the name of a secular state. Kṛṣṇa, as the father of all living beings, had jurisdiction over all programs, organizations, and governments. Indians especially should appreciate the universal scope of *Bhagavad-gītā.*

Although Abhay always had a plan of action behind his suggestions, he first sought the interest of his correspondent. There wasn't much interest, and he was repeatedly turned down, but he never felt discouraged; he always anticipated finding a sympathizer. He kept copies of all his letters and their replies, a word of appreciation or a slight show of interest from a correspondent being sufficient to elicit from Abhay another thoughtful reply.

He had developed a keen sense of dedication to Lord Caitanya's mission, without expecting leadership from the Gaudiya Math. He still cherished the idea that his Godbrothers would soon come together and preach, but he didn't put any energy in the *maṭhas,* since to do so would mean to become involved in one of the factions. Staying clear of the Gaudiya Math's internal fray, Abhay continued his letter-writing campaign alone, introducing himself as a preacher of *Bhagavad-gītā* and editor of *Back to Godhead* magazine.

* * *

In 1948, Abhay closed his Lucknow factory. He had fallen behind in employees' salaries, and since 1946 he had been paying past rent in installments. But when sales dropped off, continuing the factory became impossible. He lost everything.

Śrīla Prabhupāda: *I started a big laboratory in Lucknow. Those were golden days. My business flourished like anything. Everyone in the chemical business knew. But then, gradually, everything dwindled.*

With the help of some acquaintances in Allahabad, he opened a small factory there, in the same city where his Prayag Pharmacy had failed fifteen years before. He moved to Allahabad with his son Brindaban and continued manufacturing medicines. While the rest of the family remained at Banerjee Lane in Calcutta, Abhay continued his traveling; but now he was often away for months at a time.

And then he had the dream a second time. Śrīla Bhaktisiddhānta Sarasvatī appeared before him; again he was beckoning, indicating that Abhay should take *sannyāsa.* And again Abhay had to put the dream aside. He was a householder with many responsibilities. To take *sannyāsa* would mean to give up everything. He had to earn money. He now had five children. "Why is Guru Mahārāja asking me to take *sannyāsa*?" he thought. It was not possible now.

The Allahabad business was unsuccessful. "At present, the condition of our business is not very good," he wrote his servant Gouranga, who had asked to rejoin him. "When the condition gets better and if you are free at that time I will call for you." He worked earnestly, but results were meager.

As with everything else, Abhay saw his present circumstances through the eyes of scripture. And he could not help but think of the verse from *Śrīmad-Bhāgavatam,*

yasyāham anugṛhṇāmi
hariṣye tad-dhanaṁ śanaiḥ
tato 'dhanaṁ tyajanty asya
sva-janā duḥkha-duḥkhitam

"When I feel especially merciful towards someone, I gradually take away all his material possessions. His friends and relatives then reject this poverty-stricken and most wretched fellow."

He had heard Śrīla Bhaktisiddhānta Sarasvatī quote the verse, and now he thought of it often. He took it that his present circumstances were controlled by Lord Kṛṣṇa, who was forcing him into a helpless position, freeing him for preaching Kṛṣṇa consciousness.

Śrīla Prabhupāda: *Somehow or other, my intention for preaching the message of Lord Caitanya Mahāprabhu increased, and the other side decreased. I was not disinclined, but Kṛṣṇa forced me: "You must give it up." The history is known—how it decreased, decreased, decreased.*

In *Śrīmad-Bhāgavatam,* Queen Kuntī had also prayed, "My dear Lord

Kṛṣṇa, Your Lordship can easily be approached, but only by those who are materially exhausted. One who is on the path of [material] progress, trying to improve himself with respectable parentage, great opulence, high education, and bodily beauty, cannot approach You with sincere feeling."

Śrīla Prabhupāda: *So in 1950 I retired, practically. Not retired, but a little in touch with business—whatever is going on. Then almost it became nil. Whatever was there, all right. You do whatever you like.*

Abhay's wife independently moved along with her sons back to her father's house at 72 Mahatma Gandhi Road. She had reasoned that her financial support was becoming precarious.

Abhay was spending most of his time away from home. He was gradually disassociating himself from the family. When after several months he would meet his wife and children, his father-in-law would criticize him: "You are always going outside. You are always worshiping God. You are not looking after my family." Whenever he could, Abhay would send his family some money.

Mr. Sudhir Kumar Dutta (Abhay's nephew): *I sometimes noticed how he was thinking so many things—about his family, about his writings, about making bigger and bigger in business. "What to do, what to do?" He was thinking seriously to earn more money from his business. But that means he has to give more time for his business. And his writing he'd never give up. He was writing more and more, and people sometimes abused him: "Hey, you are writing religious things. You are only thinking of God? Then who will maintain your family? What will you do for the family?" Sometimes he argued with them: "What has this family given me? Why should I forget about God? This is the real thing, what I am doing. You cannot realize what I am doing."*

On a visit to Calcutta, Abhay stayed at the home of his father-in-law, where he was given his own room. When his wife served him dinner, he noticed that everything had been purchased from the market. "How is this?" he asked.

"The cook is sick today," Radharani replied.

Abhay thought, "It is better that we not live here at the home of her father, or else she will be spoiled even more." So he moved his family to a new address on Chetla Street. Here he sometimes stayed with his family for a few months, writing articles and doing a minimal amount of business, but most of the time he stayed in Allahabad.

In Allahabad, Abhay, now fifty-four, lived like a *vānaprastha,* or one who has retired from family life. He was indifferent to the activities of family and business—activities a family man generally considers his prime objects of responsibility and happiness.

In his writings Abhay had several times discussed the four *āśramas,* or spiritual divisions of Vedic society: *brahmacārī, gṛhastha, vānaprastha,* and *sannyāsa.* In the first division, the *brahmacārī-āśrama,* a young boy's parents send him to the place of the *guru,* or *gurukula,* where he lives a simple life, studying the Vedic literature under the guidance of his *guru.* Thus in his childhood and youth he learns the principles of austerity and spiritual knowledge that form the basis for his entire life.

At age twenty-one the *brahmacārī* may take a wife and thus enter the next *āśrama,* the *gṛhastha-āśrama;* or, like Bhaktisiddhānta Sarasvatī, he may choose to remain a lifelong *brahmacārī.* In his boyhood, Abhay had remained celibate and had imbibed the principles of devotion to Kṛṣṇa from his father and mother. Although he had lived at home, his upbringing had been the equivalent of *brahmacārī* life. And by marriage at the age of twenty-one, he had entered the *gṛhastha-āśrama* at the appropriate age. Gour Mohan's example had shown Abhay how to remain a devotee of Kṛṣṇa, even in family life. And as Vaiṣṇavas, Abhay and his wife had avoided the excesses of materialistic household life.

At fifty a man is supposed to retire from his family activities, and this stage is called *vānaprastha.* In the *vānaprastha-āśrama,* both man and wife agree to abstain from further sexual contact; they may continue living together, but the emphasis is on spiritual partnership. As *vānaprasthas* they may travel together on pilgrimage to the holy places in India, preparing for their inevitable departure from the material world. Thus the Vedic *āśramas,* after allowing one to fulfill material life, enable one to end the cycle of repeated birth and death and attain the eternal spiritual world. A man of fifty should be able to see by his aging body that inevitable death is approaching, and he should have the good sense to prepare.

In the final division, the *sannyāsa-āśrama,* the man places his wife in the care of a grown son and fully dedicates himself to serving the Supreme Lord. Formerly the *sannyāsa-āśrama* meant a solitary life of penances in the Himalayas. But in the Gauḍīya Vaiṣṇava line, Śrīla Bhaktisiddhānta Sarasvatī had emphasized preaching.

Although Abhay had not formally defined his status within the four *āśramas,* he appeared to be living more as a *vānaprastha* than a *gṛhastha.* He saw his business failures and his distasteful family situation as Kṛṣṇa's blessings, freeing him from family responsibilities and turning him wholeheartedly towards executing Śrīla Bhaktisiddhānta Sarasvatī's order to preach.

* * *

In Allahabad, Abhay managed to save enough money to revive the printing of *Back to Godhead,* and in February 1952, from his editorial office (and home) at 57B Canning Road, the first issue in eight years appeared. As before, he did everything himself—all the writing, typing, editing, meeting with the printer, and finally distributing the copies by hand as well as mailing them to respectable leaders throughout India. *This,* he felt, was the real purpose of living in Allahabad, or anywhere; this was the best use of money, the purpose of human life: to engage fully in glorifying the Supreme Lord. Other things were temporary and would soon be lost.

When he visited his family in Calcutta, old friends would gather in his room, and he would preach and give classes on *Bhagavad-gītā.* Abhay invited his wife and family to take part in these discussions, but they would resolutely sit in an upstairs room, often taking tea, as if in defiance of his preaching. Abhay was supporting them, he was still associating with them, but he was bent on preaching, and they were not making it attractive for him to do so within the family. If there were to be family life for Abhay, then his wife and sons would have to recognize and rejoice in the fact that he was becoming a full-fledged preacher. They would have to understand that his life's concern was to serve his spiritual master's mission. They could not simply ignore his transformation. They could not insist that he was simply an ordinary man. Abhay continued to try to draw his wife in, hoping she would gradually follow him in the preacher's life. But she had not the slightest interest in her husband's preaching.

And why should he spend his days worrying about family, chemicals, and money? Let his relatives criticize, but *Back to Godhead* was the real service he could offer to the whole family of mankind. Mādhavendra Purī, a great spiritual preceptor and predecessor of Lord Caitanya, had written about the devotees' indifference to worldly criticism:

> O demigods and forefathers, please excuse me. I am unable to perform any more offerings for your pleasure. Now I have decided to free myself from all reactions to sins simply by remembering anywhere and everywhere the great descendant of Yadu and the great enemy of Kaṁsa [Lord Kṛṣṇa]. I think that this is sufficient for me. So what is the use of further endeavors?
>
> Let the sharp moralists accuse me of being illusioned; I do not mind. Experts in Vedic activities may slander me as being misled, friends and relatives may call me frustrated, my brothers may call me a fool, the wealthy mammonites may point me out as mad, and the learned philosophers may assert that I am much too proud; still my mind does not budge an inch from the determination to serve the lotus feet of Govinda, though I be unable to do it.

Why should he waste time with petty family problems when he held answers to the problems of India and the world? As a knower of *Bhagavad-gītā,* he felt that his first obligation was to offer solutions to the complex crises of war, hunger, immorality, crime—all symptoms of godlessness. And if dedicating himself to such work meant that other, lesser responsibilities suffered, then there was no loss.

* * *

In March 1952, Abhay published another issue of *Back to Godhead.* It was dedicated mostly to a biographical article Abhay had written about Śrīla Bhaktisiddhānta Sarasvatī and his father, Śrīla Bhaktivinoda Ṭhākura.

> He [Bhaktivinode Thakur] vehemently protested against the principles of those pseudo-transcendentalists now passed in the name of Lord Chaitanya. He initiated the reformatory movement by literary contributions while he still engaged as a high Government Officer. During his householder life and serving as a Magistrate, he wrote books of various descriptions in Bengali, English, Sanskrit & etc. to present an actual picture of pure devotional activities to Lord Chaitanya. Sreela Bhakti Siddhanta Saraswati Goswami Maharaj got inspiration from his very Childhood all about Sreela Thakur Bhaktivinode's movement. [He] worked as the private secretary of

> Sreela Bhaktivinode Thakur and as such Bhaktivinode Thakur gave Him (Sreela Saraswati Thakur) the transcendental Power of Attorney to espouse the cause of Lord Chaitanya. And so after Sreela Bhaktivinode Thakur's departure, Sreela Saraswati Thakur took up reins of that reformatory movement.

Absorbed in producing his monthly journal, Abhay went about his other activities only superficially. Sometimes he traveled on business or, taking the night train from Allahabad to Calcutta, visited his family. When his compartment was not crowded, he would turn on a light while others slept. Riding a night train provided a good opportunity to think or even write. Sometimes he would sleep for a few hours and then sit up again and look out the window to see only night and the reflected lights of the train compartment shining back at him, the windows reflecting his face.

Halfway through the twelve-hour journey, the sky would lighten, turning from gray to light blue, and the first white clouds would appear in the sky. He could see lights in the towns and hear the train horn warning. When the train slowed and stopped at a station, tea vendors would walk alongside the train windows yelling, "*Chāy*! *Chāy*! *Chāy*!" their loud singsong din filling the ears with "*Chāy*!" and *chāy* filling the air with its aroma, as hundreds of passengers sipped their morning tea.

During his more than twenty years of extensive train travel, Abhay had noticed more and more people smoking cigarettes and more and more women traveling alone. India was becoming Westernized. And the national leaders were paving the way—the blind leading the blind. They wanted the kingdom of God without God. They wanted a progressive, industrialized India, without Kṛṣṇa. From the windows he could see large fields being left uncultivated, and yet people were hungry.

Abhay would sometimes read a newspaper and cut out an article that seemed to warrant a reply in *Back to Godhead* or that sparked an idea for an essay. He would deliberate over how to approach people for assistance, whom to approach, and how to start a society of Kṛṣṇa conscious devotees. People not only in India but all over the world could take to Kṛṣṇa consciousness. The *Caitanya-bhāgavata* had predicted that the name of Lord Caitanya would one day be known in every town and village. Śrīla Bhaktisiddhānta had wanted that. He had sent preachers to England, but they had only gained a protocol visit with the royalty, stood in line, bowed before the Crown, and then come back to India without effecting any change in the Western people. Abhay thought about sending *Back to Godhead* abroad. His agents, Thacker, Spink and Company, had contacts in America and Europe. People read English all over the world, and some of them would surely appreciate the ideas from *Bhagavad-gītā* and *Śrīmad-Bhāgavatam.* This was what Śrīla Bhaktisiddhānta Sarasvatī had wanted. Kṛṣṇa consciousness was not for India alone. It was India's greatest gift, and it was for everyone.

CHAPTER SEVEN

Jhansi: The League of Devotees

"Wanted—candidates from any nationality to qualify themselves as real Brahmins for preaching the teachings of Bhagwat Geeta for all practical purposes throughout the whole world. Deserving candidates will be provided with free boarding and lodging. Apply: A. C. Bhaktivedanta, Founder and Secretary of the League of Devotees, Bharati Bhawan, P.O. Jhansi (U.P.)"

—Abhay Charan De

IT WAS ANOTHER twelve-hour ride with dozens of stops. The train's rattling and clattering and its rocking from side to side made writing difficult, but Abhay, crowded on the wooden bench with other third-class passengers, kept writing. Within the dingy compartment, passengers eyed one another complacently, and soot and dust blew in the open windows as the train sped along. Outside, past the monotonous embankment of loose stones, bright violet trumpet flowers bloomed on tall stalks in the shallow trackside ditches. Water buffalo and oxen grazed in the distance or sometimes pulled a plow before a solitary farmer.

Abhay was going to Jhansi—not for business, but for preaching. One month before, in October of 1952, when Abhay had visited Jhansi on business, Mr. Dubey, a customer and the owner of a Jhansi hospital, had invited him to lecture at the Gita Mandir. Many Jhansi people appreciated things religious or humanitarian, whether from Vaiṣṇavas, theosophists, Māyāvādīs, politicians, or whatever. They regarded almost any path as "*dharma*" as long as it showed some edifying piety or tended towards the public welfare. Mr. Dubey had read with interest several issues of *Back to Godhead* and had therefore requested Abhay to speak. Abhay had been eager. And he had found keen interest amongst the audience of more than a hundred people, many of them young medical students and graduates from the local Ayurvedic college.

Abhay was fifty-six, and his commanding presentation of Kṛṣṇa consciousness had impressed the young, religious-minded people of Jhansi. Twenty-five-year-old Prabhakar Misra, principal of the Vedanta Sanskrit College and head medical officer of the Jhansi Ayurvedic University, saw that Abhay was very forceful in his desire to spread Kṛṣṇa consciousness. Dr. Misra regarded him as a kind of *guru,* although dressed in white. "Here is a humble person," he thought, "a real *sādhu.*"

Short and stocky Dr. Sastri, just beginning his career in Ayurvedic medicine, was an active young man, fascinated by Abhay's purity and his vision of a world movement for distributing India's culture. Older men, like tall, suave Ramcharan Hayharan Mitra, a utensils shopkeeper who wrote poetry and wore a white Nehru cap, also wanted to learn more about Lord Caitanya from Abhay. Dr. Mullik, who was the Gita Mandir secretary, and Dr. Siddhi from the university, along with their wives, had sincerely approached Abhay after his talk and asked him please to visit Jhansi again.

Abhay had come to them not as a pharmaceutical salesman or as a man with family concerns, but purely as a devotee of Lord Caitanya Mahāprabhu. Although the specific applications of Kṛṣṇa consciousness as given by Śrīla Bhaktisiddhānta Sarasvatī were new to his audience, these teachings had interested them, and the more Abhay had expressed these teachings and spoken of his ambitions for spreading Kṛṣṇa's message, the more his hearers had encouraged him. Several of them had suggested he conduct his mission in Jhansi, and they had promised to help him. Dr. Sastri had even invited Abhay to come live with him; he would introduce Abhay to important citizens and arrange for lectures in the various meeting places of Jhansi.

After staying for ten days, Abhay had returned to Allahabad, but remembering Jhansi he had been unable to concentrate on his business.

Something more important was on his mind: the need for an association of devotees propagating the teachings and practices of Kṛṣṇa consciousness worldwide. With the Gaudiya Math now broken into permanent schisms—his Godbrothers conducting their own private *āśramas* in separate locales, apparently impervious to any reconciliations—something would have to be done if the overwhelming atmosphere of godlessness were to be corrected. There must emerge, as Śrīla Bhaktisiddhānta Sarasvatī had envisioned, a league of preachers with activities worldwide.

The nations of the world had sought unity through the League of Nations, and recently through the United Nations. The League had failed, and so would the United Nations, unless it recognized the true, spiritual unity and equality of all living beings in terms of their intimate relationship with the Supreme Personality of Godhead. Abhay did not expect any good to come of such organizations; though they wanted peace and unity, their attempts were simply another feature of godlessness. No, creating peace and unity was the duty of Vaiṣṇavas.

So Abhay had been thinking that perhaps a likely place to start an organization of devotees would be Jhansi. It wasn't a major city, but at least he had found concerned people. The students had listened and accepted and had said they would help. Abhay had sensed a certain lack of sincerity and depth in their appreciation and a sentimentality that made him doubt their seriousness—but if he could find a few or even one who was serious, then he would have a beginning. He wanted to preach—that was his mission. Besides, he was already getting older; if something were to begin, it should be now. So he would go to Jhansi again, to stay for an indefinite duration. Without much concern for his Allahabad affairs, Abhay left his pharmaceutical business with his son and nephew, informing them that he was going to Jhansi.

As the train pulled into the station, Abhay saw Dr. Sastri waving energetically. They rode together by *ṭāṅgā* to Dr. Sastri's dispensary, and the talkative, effusive doctor promised many preaching opportunities and interviews. Dr. Sastri also spoke of the lore of Jhansi: The site of the present city had formerly been a part of the forest in which Lord Rāmacandra had practiced austerities many thousands of years ago. The Pāṇḍavas had lived here during their exile, and since then many great

Vedic sages had had their hermitages in the area. Jhansi had also been the home of an Indian heroine, Lakshmi Bhai, who in the mid-nineteenth century had taken part in starting the Indian independence movement against the British regime. Statues and pictures of Lakshmi Bhai riding a horse and holding a sword in her upraised hand were displayed throughout the town. But the Jhansi of 1952 was a crowded, poor city with dirt streets and minimal technological amenities.

Dr. Sastri lived alone in a two-story rented building in Jhansi's Sipri Bazaar. On the first floor he had his clinic and upstairs his one-room residence, which he had offered to share with Abhay. The young but influential doctor was a good person to introduce Abhay to receptive citizens of Jhansi, and he was eager to do so. Outgoing and energetic, he moved easily amongst the people of his town. He was respectful towards Abhay, who was twice his age and whom he appreciated as being firmly fixed in the Vaiṣṇava philosophy and way of life. Dr. Sastri saw it as his duty to help Abhay, and he gladly introduced Abhay to others and arranged for lectures.

Abhay and Dr. Sastri would cook and eat together like family members. Abhay revealed his idea for a "League of Devotees," an organization with worldwide scope but based in Jhansi. The citizens of Jhansi, he said, should all take part in helping spread Lord Kṛṣṇa's mission. Lord Caitanya had said that Indians have a special responsibility to distribute God consciousness, both in India and around the world.

Dr. Sastri: *In his heart, always it was burning that the whole world was suffering in the materialistic view—everyone is busy in eat, drink, and be merry. So the whole day he was touring and preaching his mission that was prescribed by Caitanya Mahāprabhu and his Guru Mahārāja. He was having iron-will determination and self-confidence about his mission. He was not doubtful at all. He was* dṛḍha-vrata *[staunchly determined]. Actually, he was always preaching:* harer nāma harer nāma harer nāmaiva kevalam/ kalau nāsty eva nāsty eva nāsty eva gatir anyathā—*no other way except Hare Kṛṣṇa* nāma. *So, always discussing, sometimes the whole night he was discussing with me, and sometimes I was fed up. I was requesting, "Please don't disturb me. Please let me sleep." And he—the old man missionary worker—he was just like a young man. I was a young chap, and he was just like my friend, my elder brother. He was like my guide and teacher—because the preacher is a friend, philosopher, and guide.*

He was always trying to create a good atmosphere through Śrīmad-Bhāgavatam *and* Bhagavad-gītā. *The whole* Bhagavad-gītā *was his practical life. His mission was not a mission of preaching only, but of practical action. He was also trying to catch me for this mission, and I would try to slip away. I did not think that he would do any miracle for spiritual revolution of the world, although that is what he urged us.*

While Dr. Sastri tended his clinic, Abhay sat and spoke with patients, occasionally recommending medicines but mostly preaching. For now he was content to live and preach in Jhansi. Here was life—people receptive to his preaching, who responded to his urging them to chant Hare Kṛṣṇa. His desire and determination to leave everything else behind and preach day and night, depending on Kṛṣṇa for the result, were increasing.

He began regularly lecturing and chanting at various programs in the city, sometimes at several in one day. On Sundays he would lecture at the Sadhana Mandir, another day at the Gita Mandir, another day at the Theosophical Society, and regularly in people's homes.

Mr. Ram Mitra, the shopkeeper-poet, maintained a Śiva temple near his home, and Abhay began to perform *kīrtana* and lecture there. Sometimes Mr. Mitra would speak in Hindi on *Bhagavad-gītā* at the Sadhana Mandir, and Abhay would attend. Sometimes Abhay would visit Mr. Mitra at his utensils shop. The shop was in a crowded Jhansi bazaar and opened onto the busy street. Abhay would sit down like an ordinary customer, amidst stacks of stainless-steel buckets, plates, bowls, and *loṭās,* and speak to Mr. Mitra and friends about *Caitanya-caritāmṛta.* Or sometimes he would listen to Mr. Mitra tell about his published book of poetry and his literary reputation.

Mr. Mitra saw that Abhay's ambition was no less than to make the whole city of Jhansi alive with Kṛṣṇa consciousness. Abhay quoted *Caitanya-caritāmṛta:* "One who has received the great fortune of taking birth in India should make his life perfect and then do good for others by spreading Kṛṣṇa consciousness." "And," Abhay would add, "the whole world is waiting, Mr. Mitra, for our spiritual revolution." Mr. Mitra would nod, his handsome Nehru-like face forming a smile. But he saw that Abhay wanted people to do more than merely listen to him—he wanted them to *do* something.

Once Mr. Mitra offered Abhay a copy of his book, showing him the foreword by a famous man, and repeatedly mentioned that the great *sādhu* Vinoba Bhave had liked the poems very much. When Mr. Mitra learned that Abhay was a regular milk drinker, he began offering Abhay fresh milk daily from his cow, a black cow (and black cows, Mr. Mitra said, gave especially good milk). Abhay invited Mr. Mitra to accompany him on foot to nearby villages along with a *kīrtana* party for preaching. But Mr. Mitra declined, being unable to get anyone to tend the shop for him.

Another young Ayurvedic doctor was Dr. Siddhi, who immediately expressed interest in Abhay's enthusiastic plans for spreading Kṛṣṇa consciousness.

Dr. Siddhi: *He came several times to my place. I've got a* kīrtana *room on my roof, and he performed* kīrtana *there as well as at the Gita Mandir. We were also going daily to the Theosophical Society. There was an atmosphere, a very pious, sacred, and calm atmosphere, when the* kīrtana *and preaching and lectures were performed. He used to play harmonium. We accompanied him for meeting people and preaching his mission. The main thing was to perform* kīrtana *and give a lecture on the* Bhagavad-gītā *and the life of Kṛṣṇa. Caitanya Mahāprabhu was his Lord, and I also loved Him.*

Radhelal Mullik, secretary of the Gita Mandir and Sadhana Mandir, began meeting often with Abhay.

Radhelal Mullik: *I was very much influenced by him. I used to spend three or four hours every morning in his association. He had many, many big scriptures. He was mainly concerned about the books about Śrī Caitanya Mahāprabhu. He was also writing at that time. The president of the Gita Mandir and I both volunteered to cook for him.*

* * *

It was during a morning walk with Radhelal Mullik that Abhay first spotted the Bharati Bhavan, a picturesque temple complex across from the large Antiya pond. The neighborhood, known as Antiya Tal, was quiet and sparsely populated, but it was near Sipri Road, the main thoroughfare between downtown Jhansi and Sipri Bazaar. Abhay inquired from Mr. Mullik about the temple, and together they turned from the main road and walked down a sloping footpath that led through the main gates of the compound.

There they found several secluded acres, nestled within a grove of *nīm* and mango trees. The main structure was the Radha Memorial. It was small like a chapel, but its proportions were stout and bold. Sitting on an octagonal stone base, it rose on eight ornate pillars of red and white chipped marble, to a stone dome on top. Two elephants, bearing the goddess of fortune, Lakṣmī, on their upraised trunks, decorated the entrance. Concrete bunting and striped patterns of red, green, and blue added to the decorative yet massive effect. The entrance was marked with the words Rādhā-smarak carved in Hindi script, and above it the English translation: Radha Memorial.

When Abhay saw the Sanskrit inscription across the side of the stone temple—Hare Rāma, Hare Rāma, Rāma Rāma, Hare Hare—he turned to Radhelal Mullik and said strongly, "The Lord has built this building for my use." From that moment, Abhay was determined to have the building.

Mr. Mullik explained that the temple had been built in 1939 as a memorial to the wealthy Vaiṣṇava landowner Radha Bhai but at the present was not in use. Dr. Prabhakar Misra, whom Abhay had already met on several occasions, was occupying some of the rooms, but otherwise it was deserted. Mr. Mullik and Abhay sought Dr. Misra in his quarters in the main building, and when Dr. Misra saw Abhay's enthusiasm, he invited Abhay to stay there with him. Dr. Misra confirmed that except for his Sunday-morning *Gītā* class the facility was sitting idle, and he welcomed Abhay to carry on his writing and preaching there.

Abhay liked the idea. Immediately he began thinking of uses for the buildings, surveying the land with increasing interest. A second, larger building, also with stone pillars and facades, held a hall and five rooms. Abhay made mental plans for each room: in this room, *kīrtanas* and lectures with large gatherings; in this room, the Deity of Lord Caitanya Mahāprabhu; in these rooms, resident *brahmacārīs* and *sannyāsīs;* guests here; an office there; the printing press here. There was even land for grazing a cow. It was a self-contained unit. Hundreds of people could come here for *kīrtana, prasādam,* and discourses. Preachers could go out from here distributing *Back to Godhead* magazines; some could even go abroad with Lord Caitanya's message.

As Abhay and his companions walked through the compound, appreciating it as a suitable place to start an *āśrama,* his companions encouraged him, saying they were sure that Mr. Reva Sankar Bhayal, the agent who handled all the properties of Radha Bhai's descendants, would have no objection to Abhay's living there. Why couldn't the landlord *give* him the buildings? Abhay asked. They were simply going to waste. If it were actually to be a memorial to Rādhā, it should be used in Kṛṣṇa's service, since Kṛṣṇa is Rādhā's worshipable Lord.

Abhay was determined, and his friends agreed to help him. First they met with Ram Mitra, who said that he was such a close friend of Mr. Bhayal's that Mr. Bhayal would probably give the place simply at his request. Dr. Sastri said that he also wanted to go to impress upon Mr. Bhayal how much the people of Jhansi wanted Abhay to have this place.

When Reva Sankar Bhayal met with his friend Ram Mitra, also present were Abhay, Dr. Sastri, Radhelal Mullik, Prabhakar Misra, and Suryamukhi Sharma, a young, educated Jhansi woman. They presented the case from several angles, and Mr. Bhayal listened. He agreed that he wasn't using the place at present and this seemed to be a good cause. He agreed to let Abhay use the facilities for his League of Devotees for as long as he liked. And, at Abhay's request, he agreed to become a member of the League. They shook hands. On behalf of the estate, Mr. Bhayal presented the Bharati Bhavan properties in charity to Abhay Charan De and the League of Devotees.

* * *

During December and January, Abhay prepared a League of Devotees charter. He wanted to begin vigorous, extensive preaching, following the example of his spiritual master. Once he began to set his goals to paper, the project immediately began to expand—beyond Jhansi, beyond India. Of course, the League of Devotees was for the young people of Jhansi—they were already expressing great interest—but Abhay's charter described more than merely evening classes and *kīrtana.* It was a broad scheme, including a description of the four orders of society (*brāhmaṇa, kṣatriya, vaiśya,* and *śūdra*) and detailed plans to accommodate a worldwide religious movement. The charter set forth a probationary period for prospective members, it described spiritual initiation, it arranged for economic reciprocation between individual members and the League, it arranged to provide lodgings for preachers, and it defined prohibited activities: "illegitimate connection with women, intoxicating habit, diets [other than] regulated strictly on vegetable kingdom, gambling, [and] unnecessary sporting or recreation enterprises."

To establish his League with the registrar in Lucknow, Abhay required a "Memorandum of Association" signed by the League members. In this document, which was to list the objectives of the society, Abhay expressed his vision for the continuation of his spiritual master's mission. Like his Godbrothers who had created new *maṭhas* after the dissolution of the Gaudiya Math, Abhay was forming a new branch of the Gauḍīya *sampradāya,* to be called the "League of Devotees." He was not simply claiming proprietorship of a few buildings; he was establishing a Kṛṣṇa conscious society that would expand into a world movement. His intentions were clearly not insular, but were directed towards creating "centres for spiritual development all over the world... ." Abhay wrote: "... Lord Chaitanya ... revealed the transcendental process of approaching the ABSOLUTE GODHEAD, and in [His] teachings nothing appears to be absurd from the point of human reasoning and nothing against any religion as accepted by the human and civilised world." In enumerating the League's goals, he included the opening of centers in all parts of the world, thus establishing the League as "an International Organisation for spiritual developments through education, culture as also by recruiting members from all nations, creeds and castes." The League would publish literature in many languages and print a monthly magazine, *Back to Godhead.*

Abhay obtained the necessary signatures for his Memorandum of Association. He then took the train to Lucknow and, on February 4, paid the deposit of fifty rupees and filed his application. He returned to Jhansi.

* * *

In his room in the Radha Memorial, Abhay would rise daily at 4:00 A.M. and arouse his young neighbor, Prabhakar Misra. From four to five Abhay would write, at five he would walk in the Antiya Tal area, at five-thirty bathe, and then chant Hare Kṛṣṇa on his beads until seven, when he would hold a class on the *Caitanya-caritāmṛta* or *Śrīmad-Bhāgavatam* (although Prabhakar Misra was usually the only listener). At eight he would return to his literary work, typing until after ten, when he would begin to prepare a meal. In the afternoon he would often go around Jhansi, meeting people and preaching, looking for anyone willing to take part in the League of Devotees. In the early evening he would write until seven, when he would prepare for the *kīrtana* and lecture he would hold at one of various places in the city, depending on where he was invited.

Although Abhay had no money for continuing *Back to Godhead,* a well-established part of his preaching was to write essays, regardless of whether they were to be immediately published or not. He wrote a long essay, some twenty-four thousand words, entitled "Message of Godhead." He also wrote a series of chapters propounding the teachings of *Bhagavad-gītā,* especially as they applied to world problems, and *Science of Devotion,* a summary study of Rūpa Gosvāmī's *Bhakti-rasāmṛta-sindhu.*

* * *

On May 16, 1953, Abhay held a grand-opening celebration for the League of Devotees, with continuous readings, *kīrtana,* and *prasādam* distribution from early morning until night. The buildings were decorated with leaves, flowers, and many earthen waterpots. In the evening, when attendance was the greatest, Abhay lectured from the Ninth Chapter of *Bhagavad-gītā* on "*Rāja-guhya Yoga.*" Prabhakar Misra conducted a fire sacrifice, and several *brāhmaṇas* chanted *mantras* from *Brahma-saṁhitā.* Guests received a sixteen-page prospectus containing Abhay's essay on the need for the League and an excerpt from the charter explaining its goals. It was signed, "OM ... TAT ... SAT, Abhay Charanaravindo Bhaktivedanta, Founder and Secretary."

The opening was a pleasant, auspicious event for the people of Jhansi, and hundreds gathered in the evening for Abhay's lecture. Dr. Sharma, a charter member of the League and editor of the Jhansi daily newspaper, had already publicized the event and was planning a write-up for the following day. The *Gauḍīya Patrikā* also reported on the opening.

> The editor of the local Theosophical Society, Sri Laksminarayan Rajapali, was also present; although he holds different philosophical opinions from

> Bhaktivedanta Prabhu, he is very sympathetic with this movement. In the assembly there were many people worth mentioning. ... The inauguration and establishing of Deities will be done soon. The assembly will request Rajapati Sri K. M. Munshi to perform the inauguration ceremony. ... Their center has been registered by the Societies Registration Act. Sri Bharati Bhavan is the name of the League's building, in which they have a lecture hall and a temple that resembles a palace. The assembly has many activities at the center, and there are also facilities for members to live there.

Abhay felt confident that the Bharati Bhavan would now be established and recognized as the home of the League of Devotees. He was happy to see that the opening day was not merely his private affair but an event celebrated by the most important citizens of Jhansi.

* * *

His past life was seeming further and further behind him each day. But one day after he had been in Jhansi about six months, a telegram arrived, bringing a startling reminder of his past connections. His business in Allahabad had been burglarized. His servants had stolen all his money and medicine and anything else of value. It had been a loss of seven thousand rupees. Abhay read the news, laughed, and uttered the *Bhāgavatam* verse

yasyāham anugṛhṇāmi
  hariṣye tad-dhanaṁ śanaiḥ
tato 'dhanaṁ tyajanty asya
  sva-janā duḥkha-duḥkhitam

Prabhakar Misra advised Abhay to go back to Allahabad to recover what he could. "No," Abhay said, "this is good for me. I was sad, but now one great attachment has come to an end, and my life is fully surrendered and dedicated to Śrī Śrī Rādhā-Mādhava."

Abhay's son Brindaban soon arrived in Jhansi, requesting Abhay to come to Calcutta to revive the business, Abhay Charan De and Sons. As they sat together in Abhay's room at the Radha Memorial, Abhay explained that he could not go back. He requested Brindaban to stay and assist him by doing typewriting. But Brindaban returned to Calcutta.

* * *

From his first meeting with Prabhakar, Abhay had urged the younger, educated man to take part in the League of Devotees as a full-time assistant. Although as lecturer and medical officer Prabhakar had many duties at the university, he helped as much as he felt he could; he soon became Abhay's most active assistant. Abhay appointed him secretary to the League and, after several months, initiated him. Thus Abhay became Prabhakar's spiritual master, and Prabhakar became Abhay's first disciple. As a preacher, Abhay was duty-bound to accept disciples, giving them the Hare Kṛṣṇa *mantra* and the *paramparā* instructions as he had received them from his spiritual master. Prabhakar, however, not being a completely surrendered disciple, remained independent, more like an assistant than a disciple. As university principal, Sanskrit scholar, and medical doctor, he continued to pursue his own interests also.

Śrīla Prabhupāda: *That League of Devotees—I was alone. There were some students, but they were not so active. I was doing everything. I wanted to organize with Prabhakar Misra and others, but they were not interested to devote their whole time. If you asked him to do full-time work, that he'd not do. But he was initiated. They were all learned scholars in Sanskrit—medical men.*

Thus when the *Gauḍīya Patrikā* had reported the opening-day ceremonies, it had referred to Prabhakar in honorable terms, as Abhay's partner in the League of Devotees, although he was actually Śrīla Bhaktivedanta's initiated disciple.

> Bhaktivedanta Prabhu summoned the service of the Honourable Acarya Srimad Prabhakar Misra Sastri, kavya- (poetry), vyakarana- (grammar), vedanta- (philosophy) tirtha, BIS MSA—to perform the sacrifice. He is the principal of a college in which the Vedas and the Vedangas are taught and degrees are given. He is also the Assistant Manager of the League of Devotees.

According to time and circumstances, Abhay was engaging this young man in devotional service. Abhay was interested not in collecting disciples but in establishing the League of Devotees. And for that he needed assistants.

Prabhakar Misra: *When I first met Swamiji, he said to me, "You're a* brāhmaṇa *and a* prabhākar, *and you are eating in a restaurant? You come with me—I will feed you myself, and I shall cook." So we would prepare* prasādam, *and offering it to the Lord, we would take* bhagavat-prasādam *together. In this way, by his mercy, I got the chance to take* prasādam. *He also said to me, "You become* keśa-hīn *[shaven]." So I went with shaven head to the college where I taught, and everyone laughed at me. When I told Swamiji the situation, he said, "Since you are a medical officer, you can grow out your hair."*

When I took dīkṣā, *Swamiji gave me my name, Ācārya Prabhākar. My original name was Prabhakar Misra, so he said, "You don't write the Misra. You are Ācārya Prabhākar." He gave me the name and offered me a* tulasī-mālā *and put* tilaka *on my forehead and tied a* kaṇṭhī-mālā *around my neck. He had registered the foundation of the League of Devotees, and he appointed me as its secretary for preaching throughout the world. We used to go to the villages for* saṅkīrtana *and* Bhagavad-gītā kathā *continuously.*

* * *

Abhay started a *saṅkīrtana* movement in Jhansi. At first, accompanied only by Ācārya Prabhākar, he used to walk about the neighborhood of Naybhasti, chanting Hare Kṛṣṇa. As he continued this practice, his group gradually increased until fifty people were gathering regularly to go out on *parikrama,* chant together, and visit temples. Afterwards, they would gather at the Radha Memorial for an evening lecture.

When Abhay would go to preach in the nearby villages, he would usually be accompanied by whatever League members were free. Once he went with Ācārya Prabhākar on *pāda-yātrā* (traveling on foot and preaching) to Chirgoan, some twenty miles from Jhansi. In Chirgoan there lived a nationally known poet, Maithili Saran Gupta, who received Abhay and his disciple at his home for dinner. Abhay told his host that since he was an accomplished poet, he should write something glorifying Kṛṣṇa, and the poet agreed. After preaching in Chirgoan, Abhay and Prabhākar returned to Jhansi, spending one day in each of five villages along the way. At night the villagers would gather, and Abhay would lead *kīrtana.* He explained to Prabhākar that although most of these simple farmers were not scholars in *Bhagavad-gītā* or *Bhāgavatam,* they could achieve the highest spiritual benefit simply by *kīrtana.* Abhay was well received by the villagers, who begged him to return soon but to give them notice next time so that they could prepare a proper reception.

While preaching locally, Abhay was simultaneously working to give an international scope to his League of Devotees. He wrote to government agencies, asking them to help him expand his genuine educational project, and he also tried to recruit preachers from amongst his friends. He wrote to his old college classmate Rupen Mitra in Calcutta, inviting him to join in worldwide missionary activities.

> My mission desires to train up 40 trainees ... and I have asked help from the Government for this useful educational purpose. I want that you may be one of the trainees in this regard and you can ask Kartikdada to join us in this spirit. You will know from the papers sent to you how we live and what we do and thus you can make up your mind whether it is possible for you to join us. The first thing is that we want to train up some retired men in the Vanaprastha life and some young men in the Brahmacarya life. I have no inclination for the Sannyas life, which is rather a difficult job for the fallen people of this age. The so-called sannyasis in red garments have spoiled the good name of such order of life. [*Abhay also asked Rupen,*] Kindly let me know the charges of this advertisement in the English and vernacular papers of Calcutta.
>
> EDUCATIONAL
>
> "Wanted—candidates from any nationality to qualify themselves as real Brahmins for preaching the teachings of Bhagwat Geeta for all practical purposes throughout the whole world. Deserving candidates will be provided with free boarding and lodging. Apply: A. C. Bhaktivedanta, Founder and Secretary of the League of Devotees, Bharati Bhawan, P.O. Jhansi (U.P.)"

* * *

Abhay wanted a deed stating that the Bharati Bhavan belonged to the League of Devotees. So far he had only a promise. Thinking of Jhansi as a permanent headquarters, he wanted a written commitment. When he approached Reva Sankar Bhayal for "a deed of gift," Mr. Bhayal gave Abhay a form requesting him to pay five hundred rupees to register the buildings. But since Abhay had just suffered a loss of seven thousand rupees in Allahabad and had recently spent three thousand rupees in his preaching (much of it going towards the opening-day festival), he found himself unable to raise even five hundred rupees. Ācārya Prabhākar, despite his academic position, had very little money and was being subsidized by his parents with three rupees a day. Most of Abhay's congregation, especially the students, were in a similar position. Mr. Bhayal's request for five hundred rupees didn't seem urgent, nor did he say what would happen if Abhay couldn't pay. But he soon made another request: Mr. Abhay Charan De should buy the Bharati Bhavan for five thousand rupees.

It was disconcerting; the generous gift had turned into a purchase offer. The people in town were already referring to the property as Abhay Bhaktivedanta's *āśrama,* and "The League of Devotees" was printed in large letters across the wall of the compound. When pressed by Abhay's friends, Mr. Bhayal assured them that Abhay could go on living there. But ultimately he would have to buy. Mr. Bhayal said he would give the League of Devotees first consideration and a good price.

Abhay worried, not knowing what the landlord would do next. If the League could purchase the property, that would be best. But he had been unable to raise even five hundred rupees; five thousand seemed impossible. Abhay found no strong financial backing from his congregation; his League did not include even a single full-time worker.

He did know of one way to raise money: his pharmaceutical business. He still had a small operation being run by his son in Calcutta. Abhay had formerly been earning three thousand rupees a month. He considered approaching Godbrothers for help, but the prospects for earning the money himself seemed more likely. For thirty years he had earned money by his pharmaceutical business, and he could do it again—for the most worthy cause.

* * *

When he arrived in Calcutta in the spring of 1954 he was without money. He chose to live with his Godbrothers at the Gaudiya Sangha in Chetla, the same neighborhood his family lived in. Since he had no money, the head of the *āśrama* bore his expenses. Abhay gave daily discourses on *Śrīmad-Bhāgavatam,* which the Gaudiya Sangha *brahmacārīs* highly appreciated.

Kṛṣṇa Kumāra Brahmacārī: *Even after he left, his sweet, melodious voice would ring in my ears. He used to often express a desire to go abroad and preach.*

One of his sons was running a small business, Vimaltone Laboratory, and thus supporting the family. Abhay knew that his wife would not be interested in his work in Jhansi; his son had been there but had not been impressed. The family would see his preaching in Jhansi as a threat to their home life. Abhay, however, was sustaining himself by his vision—which was now taking practical shape—of a world reformed by Kṛṣṇa consciousness. He even thought of opening a branch of the League of Devotees in Calcutta.

But inevitably he was plunged again into family responsibilities: some of his children were still unmarried, rent and bills had to be paid. Even if he were to develop the Vimaltone Laboratory, the family would demand whatever he earned, and even if he were to accede to their demands, live at home, and give up preaching, the greatest difficulty would still remain: they weren't serious about devotional service. Nor could he change them. What was the use of conducting a business if they would not be devotees?

He visited his family, and the same, old scene occurred. Local friends came to visit, and Abhay began preaching, giving *Bhagavad-gītā* classes just as he had been doing in Jhansi. Meanwhile, his wife and the rest of the family would take tea in a separate room.

Śrīla Prabhupāda: *I wanted as much as possible to get her to work with me in spreading Kṛṣṇa consciousness, to get her help. But she was very determined. She wouldn't help me in spreading Kṛṣṇa consciousness. So finally, after many years, I could understand—she would not be any assistance to me.*

She was very attached to drinking tea. I was always telling her not to drink tea, because I wanted to have a nice Vaiṣṇava family. So although I was repeatedly telling her, this time I finally said, "You have to choose between me or tea. Either the tea goes or I go." In this way, I was even criticizing my own family. But because they were thinking I was the husband or father, they couldn't take my instruction seriously. So she replied, "Give up tea-drinking or give up my husband? Well, I will have to give up my husband, then." Of course, she thought I was joking.

One day, Radharani made a great mistake. There was a system of barter in which a customer would place on a scale an object a shopkeeper considered valuable and the shopkeeper would then balance it with an equal weight of merchandise. So while Abhay was out, his wife took his worshipable *Bhāgavatam* to the market and traded it for tea biscuits. When Abhay came home and looked for the book, she told him what had happened. She hadn't taken the matter as a very serious thing—she was out of tea biscuits—but Abhay was shocked. At first he felt depressed, but then a wave of absolute resolution passed over him: his family life was finished.

When he told them he was leaving, they didn't understand what he meant. He had been leaving for thirty years. He was always coming and going. When he walked out the door, they thought, "There he goes again. He's leaving." It was the usual routine. Everyone could see, even the neighbors—Mr. De was going again. He had been at home; now he was going. He would be back again. But Abhay knew he would never come back.

Śrīla Prabhupāda: *Before leaving my family, I wanted to get all my sons and daughters married, but some of them disagreed. But then ... the time is up. Never mind whether they are married or not. Let them see to their own business. Suppose I die immediately—who will take care of my daughter? At that time we say, "God will take care." Then why not now? God will take care. My Guru Mahārāja used to say [that renunciation of family life was] "civil suicide." If you commit suicide, that is criminal. But that [renunciation of family] is voluntarily committing suicide—"Now I am dead. Whatever you like, you do."*

Kṛṣṇa says, sarva-dharmān parityajya—*give up all religion. So family is* gṛha-dharma, *the religion of the family. But Kṛṣṇa says give that up. But that attachment is there. And if we say that feeling of attachment has to be given up gradually, then that we cannot do, because the attachment is there. But if God will take care of them if I die immediately, then why not now?*

His spiritual emotions were so turbulent that he wasn't thinking of going to Jhansi. He wanted to take a train to ... *anywhere.* Then he remembered some old Godbrother friends who were living in an *āśrama* in Jhargram, only a short train ride south of Calcutta. So he borrowed ten rupees from a friend and bought a ticket to Jhargram.

It was a small *maṭha.* When Abhay arrived, he was welcomed by Paramahaṁsa Mahārāja, Dāmodara Mahārāja, and others. Paramahaṁsa Mahārāja had been present when Abhay had first met Bhaktisiddhānta Sarasvatī, and he remembered Abhay as he had looked then, dressed in white *khādī,* looking like a Gandhian "anarchist." Abhay explained to him, "I couldn't fulfill my family's needs. So now let me preach the message of Lord Caitanya." Abhay told him how his business had failed and how he had willingly left his family and was now destitute.

Paramahaṁsa Mahārāja: *When Abhay arrived he appeared very poor, starving. He had no means. He came alone to the* maṭha, *and when he arrived he only chanted Hare Kṛṣṇa, nothing else.*

Abhay spent his time in Jhargram chanting the holy name and becoming settled in detachment from his family. For several days he chanted *japa* almost continuously. Paramahaṁsa Mahārāja would lecture in the evenings, and then Abhay would also speak on *Bhagavad-gītā.* But as time passed, his thoughts turned again to Jhansi, and he soon felt ready to go back to the League of Devotees. He had to secure the buildings and go on with the preaching.

But before returning he obtained a large Deity of Lord Caitanya that he planned to install at the Bharati Bhavan. Ironically, he had gone to Calcutta to do business and raise money, but now he had no money, no business, *and* no family responsibilities. He had been married thirty-six years, and now, at age fifty-eight, he had fully taken to the *vānaprastha* order. Now he could dedicate his life fully to preaching Kṛṣṇa consciousness.

* * *

Abhay did not adopt the saffron dress of a *vānaprastha,* but continued wearing a white *dhotī* and *kurtā.* The people of Jhansi had always known him as a preacher with no family, ever since he had first arrived, a year and a half before. Now he was returning to them with a Deity of Lord Caitanya and a determination to establish Lord Caitanya's temple in Jhansi. Abhay met with a warm welcome from Ācārya Prabhākar and others. But he also met with competition for possession of the Radha Memorial.

It began with a Sanskrit conference, the Bandelkand Sanskrit Sammelan, which brought to Jhansi the governor of the province, K. M. Munshi, and his wife, Lilavati. An active social organizer, Lilavati Munshi had opened several branches of the Mahila Samity Sangha, a society that aimed at socially uplifting women by teaching them secretarial skills and English. Two educated Jhansi ladies, Candramukhi and Suryamukhi, wanted such a women's social program for Jhansi, and they took the opportunity to approach Lilavati Munshi during her visit. She inspired them, and they began to talk about where in Jhansi they could open one of her social centers. Perhaps, suggested one of the ladies, the Bharati Bhavan could be used. Although Suryamukhi Sharma had been one of the sympathizers who had first approached Mr. Bhayal on behalf of Abhay Charan De and had asked that he be given the Bharati Bhavan for his League of Devotees, she felt that the ladies' cause was more important—and she knew that Abhay's ownership of the buildings was not settled. The women agreed that the buildings would be an excellent facility for a Mahila Samity Sangha branch and that their cause was more urgent than Abhay Charan's.

Suryamukhi, assured of support by the governor's wife, called on A. C. Bhaktivedanta. She explained that his league of worldwide Vaiṣṇavas would never take shape. He was a nice person, and she liked him, but she didn't think he could realize his extraordinary expectations. She suggested he vacate the Bharati Bhavan so that the governor's wife could organize a women's social center. "You can go here and there for the sake of building a temple," she told him. "You are free to travel anywhere. But these poor women in Jhansi have nothing, so they must be given these buildings for their use." She found him adamantly opposed.

"No," Abhay said, "find another building." Abhay argued that his work was not just for a section of people, but for all living beings. Suryamukhi left frustrated. Abhay was surprised that a member of the League of Devotees was now working against him. And the maneuver was being backed by the governor's wife!

Mrs. Munshi could work at a much more influential level, without having to confront Abhay directly and without his even knowing what she was doing. After she talked with Mr. Bhayal, word got around that Mr. Bhayal had been pressured to persuade Abhay Charan to relinquish his claim on the Bharati Bhavan. Mr. Bhayal owned a cinema house in Jhansi and there was talk that he could have a lot of difficulty with his operator's license unless Abhay Charan vacated the Radha Memorial.

In December 1954 Mrs. Munshi wrote Abhay in reference to his failure to raise the five thousand rupees. "Dear Bhaktivedantaji," she wrote, "You wanted to organize there, but you could not. But I have got this institution, Mahila Samity. Why not give it to me?" Abhay was of a mind to resist. He had lawyer friends who advised him that even though he was opposed by the governor's family, he had a good case that would stand up well in court; India's tradition of respect for religious buildings was on his side.

Abhay replied to Mrs. Munshi, introducing himself as the founder of the League of Devotees. He explained the goal of the League, enclosed a copy of his prospectus, and presented many statements by prominent people—Dr. Rajendra Prasad, Sri Sitaram, Raja Mahendra Pratap, and even her husband, Sri K. M. Munshi—praising the wonderful work of the League of Devotees. He also mentioned that the president of the League had recently received a one-hundred-rupee donation in Mathurā from His Excellency the Governor, Mr. Munshi himself. Abhay said that although work had been going on slowly but peacefully in Jhansi, his mind had now been bothered by Mrs. Munshi's negotiations. He requested her not to pressure anyone about his occupying the Bharati Bhavan, though he admitted, "If you or any one of your agents do try ... the pressure will be more weightful. ... I am a nonentity in that comparison."

Abhay hoped that by his presenting the details of his League, she would understand that his was a better cause than the Mahila Samity. He quoted the first three verses of the Fourth Chapter of *Bhagavad-gītā,* wherein Lord Kṛṣṇa describes how the ancient science of *bhakti-yoga* is received through *paramparā* (the order of succession from one teacher to the next) and how kings are responsible for seeing that Kṛṣṇa consciousness spreads for everyone's benefit. He also argued that since, according to *Bhagavad-gītā,* only a few amongst thousands and thousands of men endeavor for self-realization, and since the League of Devotees engaged its members in self-realization, he was providing an important and rare service. He offered to meet with Mrs. Munshi along with some fifteen *sannyāsīs* from the area and suggested that she work cooperatively with them and understand the importance of the League. The League of Devotees was benefiting all classes. As Śrī Kṛṣṇa had said in *Bhagavad-gītā,* "Even one of a low birth can attain the shelter of the Supreme Lord." But the Mahila Samity, Abhay pointed out, was based on bodily conceptions of caste, creed, color, and sex; therefore, it could not be as important a cause. Abhay closed by requesting Mrs. Munshi not to try to occupy the Radha Memorial, which was already being used for a noble and well-appreciated cause. He signed, "A. C. Bhaktivedanta, Founder and Secretary, League of Devotees."

Aware that he was involved in an intrigue, Abhay organized his thoughts and set down on paper a "Short History," outlining important events surrounding his possession of the Bharati Bhavan.

SHORT HISTORY

1. I came to Jhansi some time in October, 1952.
2. I delivered some lectures at Gita Mandir on Gandhi Jayanti Day, 1952.
3. Made acquaintance with Prabhakar Sastri.
4. My idea of League of Devotees implemented.
5. He took me to Reva Sankar for Bharati Bhavan.
6. Sri Reva Sankar agreed to hand over the Bharati Bhavan to League of Devotees and he agreed to become a member of it in the presence of Prabhakar, Mitraji, and myself.
7. I write letters from Allahabad to confirm.
8. He confirmed my letter on 10/12/52.
9. Prabhakar intimated the desire of Reva Sankar on 1/1/53.
10. I got the document needed for League of Devotees and came to Jhansi for signature of the members. Reva Sankar signed and agreed to become an executive member.
11. The document was submitted for registration on 4/2/53 at Lucknow. ... Returned on 10/10/53.
12. The League of Devotees ceremoniously started 16/5/53 and work began. So I am occupying the building since then and continuing my work.

Abhay went on to enumerate more than thirty points, including news publicity and congratulations he had received. He listed the story of how he "came here sacrificing my business and family. ... I received a telegram from Allahabad instructing the news of burglary by breaking lock. I could not attend the business for work here and it was closed subsequently at a loss of Rs. 7,000."

Abhay thought of turning to some of his *sannyāsī* Godbrothers for help. If he or they could purchase the buildings, his competitors would be silenced. He thought it worthwhile to interest his Godbrothers in purchasing the buildings as an adjunct to their own missions.

Vṛndāvana was not far away—a four-hour train ride to Mathurā and then a short *ṭāṅgā* ride. He had gone there on pilgrimage in October of 1953 and had even looked at an available room in a temple near

Keśī-ghāṭa, with the idea of staying there some day. He had also traveled there several other times since he had begun residing in Jhansi. This time, he went to the Imlītala temple to see his Godbrother Bhaktisāraṅga Gosvāmī and ask if he would like to take over the proprietorship of the Bharati Bhavan so that it might be used for preaching Kṛṣṇa consciousness according to the teachings of Śrīla Bhaktisiddhānta Sarasvatī. But Bhaktisāraṅga Gosvāmī was not interested. After approaching another Godbrother, Dāmodara Mahārāja, who was also not interested in Jhansi, Abhay took the short *ṭāṅgā* ride back to Mathurā to see another Godbrother, Keśava Mahārāja. Keśava Mahārāja was in Mathurā with a group of his disciples to establish a center, but he had not yet located a suitable place. So when Abhay told him about the buildings in Jhansi, he was interested. Abhay and Keśava Mahārāja composed a letter to Mr. Bhayal presenting their requests and the aims of their movement and then traveled to Jhansi in a group—Abhay and Keśava Mahārāja with his disciples.

Keśava Mahārāja and his party stayed for several days in Jhansi, holding *kīrtanas* and lectures. They had an appointment with Reva Sankar Bhayal, but Mr. Bhayal broke it, so they had to wait to see him on another day. Meanwhile, Keśava Mahārāja had time to form an opinion of Jhansi and discuss with Abhay the likelihood of making this his headquarters. He noted that the people were receptive but that the location was too remote. Even before meeting with Mr. Bhayal, Keśava Mahārāja felt reluctant to stake his whole mission in Jhansi. Abhay agreed, aware that Śrīla Bhaktisiddhānta Sarasvatī had said that a preacher should go into the big cities and not practice his *bhajana* in seclusion, and he admitted that after two years in Jhansi he had made no full-time followers.

When they finally met with Mr. Bhayal, Mr. Bhayal failed to present clear terms for purchasing the property. He said they were eligible to buy it, but he made their use of the buildings conditional: he wanted to have a say in the nature of the programs they would hold. Abhay knew that this was just a further sign of shady dealings, and he suspected that Mr. Bhayal was under mounting pressure to give the buildings over to the Mahila Samity. Keśava Mahārāja, having lost all interest, decided to go back to Mathurā, and he invited Abhay to join him.

But Abhay remained. Mr. Bhayal wanted him out, and he even returned Abhay's deposit of 210 rupees, claiming that Abhay now had no justification for residing at the Bharati Bhavan. Abhay noted down the latest events in his "Short History."

> 29. He has also give me a check for Rs. 210 in lieu of my deposit money with him, but he has no money in the bank. The bank has returned it with remark.
> 30. The money which was given to him ... was misappropriated by him for his own purpose and now he has given a false check with an arrangement with the bank.
> 31. It is plain cheating to me from the beginning to the end.
> 32. I must be compensated for all the money before I can leave the buildings.

But he saw it as the inscrutable will of Kṛṣṇa. Events and opinions were turning him against conducting a mission in Jhansi. It no longer seemed auspicious.

Śrīla Prabhupāda: *I wanted to start from there. It was a nice, big house. It was not given to me rightly, but I was using. So, somehow or other, she got imagination that this house is very nice. She was the governor's wife. Through collector and through government officials, she made pressure. So, of course, there were many lawyer friends. They advised me, "You do not give up." But I thought, "Who's going to litigate?" I thought that "I have left my home, and now should I take up litigation? No, I don't want this house."*

Abhay remembered how the Gaudiya Math preachers had expended their energy for years in the courts. Having terminated his long entanglement with family and business, he had no taste for a legal fight. He could have fought, but he remembered what Keśava Mahārāja had said about Jhansi's being out of the way. Of course, the whole thing had just sprung up here; otherwise Abhay would never have chosen to establish his worldwide League in such an obscure place. The educated young men and women wished him well, just as they had good wishes for the ladies' league, the Theosophy Society, the Arya Samaj, and many other causes. But their good intentions were certainly short of pure surrender and devotion: even his one disciple could offer him only part-time help. But these considerations had not been sufficient to force him out. The real thing was that he was being driven out.

Śrīla Prabhupāda: *If I did not leave, nobody could drive me, that was a fact. But I thought, Who is going to litigate these things? It is the governor's wife, and she is pressing through collector. The manager who is in charge, he had some cinema house. So they had to renew the license. And the collector pressed him that unless you arrange for this house, we are not going to renew your license. I thought, unnecessarily this man will be in trouble. I will have to pay many rupees, and she is the governor's wife.*

He decided to leave. He told his friends to carry on the League of Devotees in his absence. They were sad to see him go, and yet even some of his friends openly praised the work of the ladies' society and were glad to see it come. They had not been able to help him financially, although they knew he had been unable to purchase the buildings on his own.

His closer followers were more affected, but he assured them that their relationship would continue. He would write letters to them—Ācārya Prabhākar, Radhelal Mullik, Mr. Mitra, Dr. Sastri—and he gave them instructions on what they should do. Especially Ācārya Prabhākar—Abhay told him he would be calling for him and expected him to continue as secretary of the League of Devotees, even if they didn't make Jhansi their main residence. Yet it was obvious that this chapter of making ambitious plans for a world movement, going from house to house and village to village, performing *saṅkīrtana,* lecturing on the *Gītā,* distributing *prasādam*—this was ended. And it was not likely that he would return or that the residents of Jhansi could expect to see him again.

When Abhay left the Bharati Bhavan, with its six-foot-high lettering—"LEAGUE OF DEVOTEES"—painted across the outside wall, he felt sad. It had been a natural, spontaneous success for him. The young, educated people of Jhansi had looked up to him from the start, and had it not been for the intrigue, he would never have left. But he felt he had no real choice. He had come as a family man on business and was leaving as a homeless *vānaprastha,* forced to take shelter of Kṛṣṇa. His plans were uncertain, but his desire was strong and his health good. So he moved on to Mathurā, carrying with him the Deity of Lord Caitanya.

CHAPTER EIGHT

New Delhi—"Crying Alone in the Wilderness"

I have got the clue of going "Back to Godhead" just after leaving my present material body, and in order to take along with me all my contemporary men and women of the world, I have started my paper, "Back to Godhead," as one of the means to the way. Please don't think of me as ... something wonderful or a madman when I say that I shall go "Back to Godhead" after leaving my present material body! It is quite possible for everyone and all of us.

—From a letter to India's president,
Mr. Rajendra Prasad

WHEN ABHAY ARRIVED in Mathurā, he sought out Keśava Mahārāja, who was now establishing his *maṭha,* and presented him with the Deity of Lord Caitanya. At Keśava Mahārāja's request, Abhay agreed to stay there and edit the *Gauḍīya Patrikā.* Abhay was given a room, and for the first time (aside from brief visits) he lived in a *maṭha* with his Godbrothers. As a senior, experienced devotee, Abhay held classes and instructed the *brahmacārīs*—who were young, uneducated, and even illiterate—in the disciplines of devotional service and the philosophy of *Bhagavad-gītā.*

He had only recently begun his duties when Bhaktisāraṅga Gosvāmī, another *sannyāsī* Godbrother, asked Bhaktivedanta Prabhu to assist him in New Delhi at his *āśrama,* Gaudiya Sangha. Both Keśava Mahārāja and Bhaktisāraṅga Gosvāmī recognized Abhay as an accomplished writer and editor and wanted to work with him. It was accepted amongst Śrīla Bhaktisiddhānta's disciples that A. C. Bhaktivedanta Prabhu was an expert preacher and writer, whether in English, Hindi, or Bengali. Now Keśava Mahārāja wanted Abhay to stay and work on the *Gauḍīya Patrikā,* while Bhaktisāraṅga Mahārāja, who had to go to Bengal, was requesting him to come to Delhi to produce *The Harmonist* (known in Hindi as *Sajjana-toṣaṇī*). Abhay was agreeable to Bhaktisāraṅga Gosvāmī's proposition, and Keśava Mahārāja consented, on the condition that Abhay also continue to edit the *Gauḍīya Patrikā,* at least by mail.

As an editor Abhay was in his element, and he was happy to preach in cooperation with his Godbrothers. Although Abhay didn't consider himself an accomplished scholar or author, Śrīla Bhaktisiddhānta Sarasvatī had been pleased by his writings and had encouraged him to continue, and now these senior *sannyāsīs* of Bhaktisiddhānta Sarasvatī were turning to him for help. They were practically competing to see who would get the benefit of his services. Perhaps, Abhay thought, this should be his life's work: serving humbly under the direction of his Godbrothers.

His ejection from Jhansi had been a kind of setback; at least it had left him temporarily unsure of how Kṛṣṇa wanted to use him. But now his Godbrothers seemed to be answering the question. Living and working in an *āśrama* with *brahmacārīs* and *sannyāsīs* was a way of life Abhay had once considered too austere. And Bhaktisiddhānta Sarasvatī had remarked, "Better he live outside your company." But now he would either have to struggle alone, with nothing, or stay within the shelter of a friendly portion of the Gaudiya Math. Perhaps he could carry out his desires to preach Kṛṣṇa consciousness within the *āśramas* of his Godbrothers.

Since he would soon be the editor of *Sajjana-toṣaṇī,* he began thinking of how to expand it. It was a scholarly Vaiṣṇava journal, but cheaply produced and with a very limited circulation. He envisioned it surpassing India's slick *Illustrated Weekly;* it should be more popular than *Time* or *Life* magazines of America. And why not? Kṛṣṇa was no poor man. Abhay thought of how he could start an ambitious subscription program by approaching the many prominent and wealthy men of New Delhi.

Then, by Kṛṣṇa's grace, he would soon be able to print color photos and use high-quality paper for *Sajjana-toṣaṇī.* He would give it his best effort, depending on Kṛṣṇa. And while soliciting subscribers, he could take his book manuscripts and try to get them published. Dr. Allagappa in South India had wanted to publish his *Geetopanishad;* no doubt there were many men like him. Or perhaps Bhaktisāraṅga Gosvāmī would be willing to publish Abhay's works with funds from the Gaudiya Sangha.

Abhay soon received a letter from Bhaktisāraṅga Gosvāmī's assistant, carefully instructing him how to travel to Delhi at the least expense. He was to travel by train third class to Delhi and from there take a *ṭāṅgā.* Since *ṭāṅgās* at the station gate charged too much, Abhay should first walk about a hundred meters towards the right-hand side of the station, where he would find a cheaper one. Were he to ride alone, he should pay no more than one rupee and twelve annas, but he should try to share the *ṭāṅgā* with another passenger—that would be cheaper. "Keeping the crematorium to your left-hand side," the assistant instructed him, "if you look towards the right, then you will be able to see our red flag and the signboard written in Hindi and English. When you reach here, we will pay for the *ṭāṅgā.*"

At the Gaudiya Sangha, Abhay found a disconcerting state of affairs. In the absence of their *guru,* Bhaktisāraṅga Gosvāmī, the *brahmacārīs* were quarreling and shirking their duties, and as a result the preaching and donation-gathering were being neglected. Cleanliness, Deity worship, cooking, and even peace amongst the devotees were below standard. And like most of the *maṭhas* of his Godbrothers, the Gaudiya Sangha was poor. Abhay had come thinking he would be editing a magazine, but he found himself contending with a group of quarreling neophyte devotees. He learned that the *brahmacārī* responsible for giving public lectures had not done any preaching, the devotees who had previously been holding *kīrtanas* in people's homes were now negligent, and the errand boy refused to run because he had lost his bicycle. Then a *brahmacārī* handed Abhay a letter from Bhaktisāraṅga Gosvāmī requesting him to take up the general management of the *maṭha.*

> Inspire everyone to be engaged in service, otherwise, I do not know how we are going to print the English monthly magazine. ... Since we don't have much money in the fund and since the brahmacaris are quite careless,

> Akinchan Maharaj wrote that he is unable to take the responsibility of the management. It will be very nice if you could keep your eyes on these affairs.

And Abhay found other obstacles in trying to produce *Sajjana-toṣaṇī:* no typewriter, and bad relations with the printer.

In a few days, Abhay received another letter from Bhaktisāraṅga Gosvāmī, telling him what articles to print, cautioning him not to change essential elements in the magazine, and reminding him of his special duty:

> I have asked Akinchan Maharaj to hand over the keys of my room to you so that you may use my room only for your office work. As you are there, you should try to maintain peace in the asrama for giving necessary instructions to one and all.

Abhay saw that he could do no editorial work until the laxity and petty quarreling in the *āśrama* stopped. But when he tried to help as Bhaktisāraṅga Gosvāmī had directed, some of the devotees rebelled and even wrote to their spiritual master complaining.

It was against many obstacles that Abhay met the publisher's deadline for the August 1955 issue of *Sajjana-toṣaṇī.* Yet owing to the printer's delay, the magazine did not come out until September. When at last the first copies were delivered, Abhay sent several to Bhaktisāraṅga Gosvāmī in Calcutta, asking for his response.

Abhay never heard from his Godbrother directly, but received further instructions from Bhaktisāraṅga Gosvāmī's secretary, Rāmānanda, who pointed out various mistakes in the issue, without mentioning whether Bhaktisāraṅga had been pleased with it. The errors were mostly technical matters of style: Abhay had done the contents page in a different way and had not printed Bhaktisāraṅga Gosvāmī's name exactly as he had wanted it on all his articles. Regarding Abhay's request for a typewriter, Rāmānanda wrote that if "the matters are distinctly written there is no necessity of them being given to the printer in typewriting."

Abhay wrote to Bhaktisāraṅga Gosvāmī requesting him to return to Delhi and establish a peaceful atmosphere in the *maṭha.* Regarding *Sajjana-toṣaṇī,* Bhaktisāraṅga Gosvāmī had suggested that the paper for the cover be improved and that the whole magazine be done on nicer paper by an up-to-date press, and Abhay agreed. But improvements depended on money.

> The suggestion ... that the paper may be printed from Calcutta is alright. But my suggestion is that either in Calcutta or in Delhi we must have our own press with good equipments so that we may be able to broadcast the message of Shri Chaitanya Mahaprabhu in all the important languages specially in Hindi and in English. Hindi is meant for all India propaganda while English is meant for world-wide propaganda.

Abhay further reported that since it was almost impossible to expect a printer to work speedily from handwritten manuscripts, he had already rented a typewriter. He also mentioned his ideas for increasing the number of subscribers.

* * *

Abhay's son Brindaban came to live with him for a few months at the Gaudiya Sangha. There was no question of Abhay's returning to his family, and Brindaban simply associated with his father, following the routines of the *maṭha* and helping Abhay in his duties.

One day a prominent advocate, the president of the Hindu Mahasabha, paid an unexpected visit to the Gaudiya Sangha. The *maṭha* was mostly deserted, and there was no *prasādam* on hand, so Abhay and Brindaban received the prominent guest, cooking for him, offering him *prasādam,* and acquainting him with the activities of the Sangha.

* * *

When Abhay wasn't busy managing the disorganized *maṭha* and working on *Gauḍīya Patrikā* and *Sajjana-toṣaṇī,* he spent his time preparing a Hindi translation of *Caitanya-caritāmṛta.* Although he was more accustomed to writing in English and Bengali, he reasoned that as long as he was preaching in Hindi-speaking areas, such a book would be important.

Bhaktisāraṅga Gosvāmī wrote that he wanted to print only five hundred copies of *Sajjana-toṣaṇī* for the September issue. But Abhay wanted to print more. After making an agreement with the printer that the charges would be the same for one thousand copies as for five hundred, he wrote Bhaktisāraṅga Gosvāmī, informing him of the good news. Abhay also told him that he had recently secured a donation of printing paper and that he had arranged for a one-quarter reduction in the postal charges.

> So why for the matter of saving some papers we shall not print the full number. In my opinion we should print more than 1000 copies every month and distribute them in large scale.

But Bhaktisāraṅga replied through a brief postcard that they should print no more than five hundred.

Abhay continued his attempts to improve *Sajjana-toṣaṇī.* For him it was not a perfunctory duty but absorbing preaching. In a letter to Bhaktisāraṅga Gosvāmī, he expressed anxiety over waiting for him to send articles for the next issue. Funds were scarce—so scarce that Abhay had no decent *dhotī*—and yet he continued to envision a glorious future for *Sajjana-toṣaṇī.*

> I wish to see this paper just to the standard of "*Illustrated Weekly*" with numerous pictures in order to make it a very popular literature and for this I wish to move myself to secure subscribers as well as advertisers. I wish to visit good businessmen, insurance companies and Govt. officers in this connection. But I have no proper dress at all. I want two sets of good dresses in order to take up this responsibility and I shall be glad to have your decision on this matter. It is my heart's desire that this paper is improved to the highest elevation.

Abhay also requested that Bhaktisāraṅga Gosvāmī help him publish his Hindi *Caitanya-caritāmṛta.* Some "non-Bengalee gentlemen" were demanding the book and had assured Abhay that they would pay twenty-five rupees per volume. Abhay requested a loan of six hundred rupees, under any arrangement suitable to Bhaktisāraṅga Gosvāmī, for publishing the first part of this work. "If this part is sold out," Abhay wrote, "the other parts will automatically come out."

But just as life in the Gaudiya Sangha and work on the *Sajjana-toṣaṇī* under Bhaktisāraṅga Gosvāmī's hand produced strain for Abhay, Abhay's ambitions for increased circulation and his strong editorial opinions also created strain for Bhaktisāraṅga Gosvāmī. In response to Abhay's letter,

Bhaktisāraṅga Gosvāmī's secretary, Rāmānanda, wrote a letter full of flowery praises of Bhaktivedanta Prabhu, but with the intent of dismissing him from his position with the Gaudiya Sangha.

> With innumerable humble obeisances at the lotus feet of a Vaiṣṇava
>
> Srimat Bhaktivedanta Prabhu,
> We received your letter written to Sri Guru Mahārāja on the 5/10/55. Your project is very lofty, and you are a well wisher of our society; we got to know that also. ...
>
> Since the last two months, in spite of so many difficulties—the difficulties of prasadam and misunderstanding of the devotees there—and in spite of various other difficulties, the kind of enthusiasm that you have shown, that is possible only for an elevated Vaiṣṇava like yourself.
>
> You are a favorite Vaisnava of Srila Prabhupada and a friend of all the special associates of Srila Prabhupada. Most of the devotees in Gaudiya Sangha Asrama in Delhi are new and less respectful. They cannot give proper respect to an elevated personality like yourself. ... Especially the lofty speculations that you have. Our society, at the present circumstances, has a little ideas. We hope, with all your qualities, very soon you will become settled independently and fulfilling the desires of Srila Prabhupada, start preaching very widely.
>
> We are suspecting that it won't be possible for an able and respectable Vaisnava like yourself to stay there long adjusting with the illiterate and less educated devotees of the Gaudiya Sangha in Delhi. Moreover, you are the head of the editorial board of Srimat Kesava Maharaja's Vedanta Samiti's Gaudiya Patrika and Bhagavata Patrika, so if you spend much time in our asrama then he might become annoyed. With many devotees, he is setting out to circumambulate the land of Braja and we are sure that he will need your assistance in this parikrama. So, you consider all the pros and cons and if you do not neglect the duty as a leader of his organisation we will be pleased.
>
> Some articles have been sent for the October issue *Sajjana Toshani* and some more might be sent. We will be very much obliged if you would instruct Kesavananda Prabhu to publish the October issue. We hope that Sri Sri Guru Maharaja will be able to personally publish the November and December issues. We wish to transfer it to Calcutta from the month of January. Sri Sri Guru Maharaja has become old and most of the time he has to depend on us. We are happy to know that you are trying very hard to publish the *Caitanya*

Caritamrta in Hindi, but at the present circumstances, it won't be possible for us to invest 600 rupees from our fund in order to print that. Because Sri Sri Guru Maharaja has taken up many projects in different directions now and he has to spend a lot of money, so he can't take the responsibility of printing that book.

Kesavananda Prabhu wrote that your clothes are getting torn, so buy a pair of clothes from the fund of the temple and if the devotees commit offences at your lotus feet due to their shortsightedness, please forgive them.

(Signed) The servant of the servant of
the Vaisnava, Sri Ramananda Das

It was not a fact that Abhay was being called for leadership in Keśava Mahārāja's *parikrama,* although it was a good excuse for Rāmānanda's suggesting that Abhay leave the Gaudiya Sangha. So after living as a dutiful member in the *āśramas* of Keśava Mahārāja and Bhaktisāraṅga Mahārāja, Abhay was again on his own.

* * *

Without income or institutional shelter, Abhay began staying in various homes in Delhi, living from week to week wherever he received an invitation. In terms of food, clothing, and shelter, these were the most difficult times he had ever gone through. Since his childhood, there had always been plenty of food and good clothes and no question of where he would live. He had been the pet child of his father, and he had received special guidance and affection from Śrīla Bhaktisiddhānta Sarasvatī. But now Abhay sometimes felt alone.

Homeless, he moved around Delhi from one temporary residence to another — a Viṣṇu temple, a room at the Kapoor College of Commerce. But he was seeking donors, preaching from *Bhagavad-gītā,* writing. His goal wasn't to find a permanent residence but to print his transcendental literature and to establish (or join forces with) a pure, powerful movement for spreading Kṛṣṇa consciousness.

Abhay made a list of several books he wanted to publish.

1. SHRI CHAITANYA CHARITAMRITA (HINDI)	2,000	pages.
2. GEETOPANISHAD (ENGLISH)	1,200	"
3. SCIENCE OF DEVOTION (ENGLISH)	300	"

4. LORD CHAITANYA'S SAMKEERTAN MOVEMENT (ENGLISH)	300	"
5. MESSAGE OF GODHEAD (ENGLISH)	300	"
6. BHAGAVANER KATHA (BENGALI)	50	"

But to print he needed donors. He called on wealthy men in their offices and homes, presenting his manuscripts and explaining his mission. He had a list of donors, but few responded. And when he did receive a donation, it was usually only five or ten rupees. Occasionally he would receive a letter of appreciation or endorsement.

One appreciation came from Narain Dass Rai Bahadur, a retired executive engineer and secretary of the Birla Mandir Trust, who had attended a public reading Abhay had held in the presence of a popular *guru,* Mother Anandamoyee. Impressed by Abhay's reading from his Hindi *Caitanya-caritāmṛta,* Mother Anandamoyee had donated fifty rupees and suggested that Abhay also visit a well-known *sādhu,* Sri Hari Baba, who was lying ill in the hospital. Abhay, accompanied by Narain Dass, had then visited Hari Baba, who had claimed that Abhay's reading put him into ecstasy. Meanwhile, Narain Dass was becoming inclined to help, and in December he wrote a letter suggesting that everyone "extend their helping hand for the successful publication of Shri A. C. Bhaktivedanta's various writings in Hindi, English, and Bengali. I wish him all success in his noble attempt."

Abhay would show this and other such letters to prospective supporters. In Delhi it was not difficult to see government ministers, judges, lawyers, business executives, religious heads; there was always someone willing to hear seriously and, occasionally, to offer support. Thus Abhay, with the two *dhotīs* and *kurtās* the Gaudiya Sangha had supplied him, with his ability to preach and convince, but with little support and no fixed residence, continued his preaching, undaunted.

Writing and trying to publish was only half his effort; the other half was taking part in efforts for a world movement like the League of Devotees. Through Narain Dass, Abhay inquired whether there might be a way he could do his work under the auspices of the Birla Mandir (one of the largest and richest temples in Delhi). Abhay proposed that he be put in charge of propaganda in the English language, both within India and abroad. Since Narain Dass considered himself a follower of *sanātana-dharma,* Abhay wrote to him explaining how the teachings of

Bhagavad-gītā set forth the real *sanātana-dharma.* Abhay had many ideas about how *sanātana-dharma,* as the eternal religion for all living beings, could be expanded and practically applied—if Narain Dass would but help him.

> I want to train up 40 educated youths, to learn this science of transcendental knowledge and just prepare them for going to foreign countries for ... missionary work. ...
> To start immediately an English paper or to revive my paper 'Back to Godhead' in the style of Illustrated Weekly of India. ...
> To organize a Sankirtan party which shall not be only of good singers and musicians but must also be used to [practice] 'Sadhana' or self-realization. ...

Abhay promised that as soon as he had done some groundwork, he, along with men and equipment, could start for foreign countries to propagate this missionary work. But he admitted also that he was externally in dire straits: "Kindly do arrange for the above immediately and give me a proper place to live. I must remove from this temporary quarter by Monday next latest."

The directors of the Birla Mandir did not take Abhay up on his offer. But he thought of another way of engaging them: he would hold a public meeting at the Birla Mandir to help generate interest in the League of Devotees. He approached Shri R. N. Agarwal, president of the Delhi Municipal Committee, who, after hearing the names of several respectable people who would be attending, agreed to preside over the meeting. Abhay set the date for December 22 and printed five hundred announcements and two hundred invitation cards.

Striking a cosmopolitan note, he stated in his announcement, "By the grace of the Almighty, Delhi is becoming ... the centre of cultural association of the world." The leaders of both Russia and India had recently pointed to the need for cultural contact between all nations. But the highest culture, Abhay suggested, was scientific spiritual knowledge; therefore, the best cultural resources in the world existed in India. And these resources, Abhay stressed, should not be left to the unorganized *sādhus* and *sannyāsīs,* but should be taken up by important members of society in an organized way.

The December 22 *Hindustan Times* listed the meeting of the League of Devotees in the "Today's Engagements" column, along with announcements for meetings of the Rotary Club, the Tagore Society, the Indian

Council of World Affairs, Bharat Scouts, and the Indian Pharmaceutical Congress.

The League's meeting began with a *kīrtana* led by Professor H. Chand, and then A. C. Bhaktivedanta, founder and secretary of the League of Devotees, explained his movement's objectives. Then Narain Dass spoke and afterwards read a number of proposed resolutions from the founder-secretary attesting that the persons present supported the League of Devotees and that they recommended that the central government of India also support it as a movement for world peace based on Gandhian principles. After adoption of the resolutions, the meeting closed with another *kīrtana* and *prasādam*.

Abhay was convinced that if his well-wishers and fellow humanitarians would support him on a grand scale, he could create a movement for world peace, based on the principles of devotional service to Lord Kṛṣṇa. But his role was simply to present Kṛṣṇa consciousness to whomever he could. The results were up to Kṛṣṇa. Abhay was aware that the good intentions of most of the participants in his Birla Mandir meeting would not go past that one meeting. But he wasn't discouraged. Through all his tireless evangelism, he maintained a philosophic jollity. In one sense he was already fully satisfied; he was happy to be working on behalf of his spiritual master.

Although he was changing addresses so fast that his mail could hardly catch up to him, he wrote a newspaper ad for a home study course.

EDUCATIONAL

> Study the spiritual secret of "Bhagwat Geeta" at home by correspondence and be a strong man. Full course fee Rs. 50 only. The instruction is imparted not in the ordinary imaginative way of qualified interpretations, but in the "Parampara" system of preceptorial succession. All questions are properly solved. Apply A. C. Bhaktivedanta. Students of all communities and nationalities are welcome.

* * *

He had not published *Back to Godhead* in four years (since 1952), but he decided to revive it. *Back to Godhead* was a mission worthy of his full attention, and it took all his efforts—to collect the funds, compose the articles, see to the printing, and then distribute a thousand copies. The money he would raise by obtaining interviews and soliciting donations. One donor and friend was Justice Bipin Chandra Misra, a Supreme Court judge in New Delhi.

Justice Misra: *He used to come to me once a month. I gave him donations for his paper. It was only a four-page magazine, but it showed his study of the subject and his earnestness and his devotion to Lord Kṛṣṇa. He appeared to be a very simple man and modest, and it was pleasant to talk to him. He had a smiling demeanor. The main thing was his humility. He could talk with affection and confidence, and he knew we were discussing things near to God. So every talk with him would sublimate us.*

I was a rather important personality at that time in religious affairs. But he would not be expected to make any contribution to the main religious life of Delhi at that time because of the language difficulty, because his aim was to reach the English-educated persons, not the Hindi ones. And also, because his means and his popularity were not at all established, the magazine did not have a wide appeal among these people. Other religious leaders were all well established. The only thing that impressed one and was worth noticing at that time was the simplicity of his abiding faith in God's name and His mission.

Writing articles was no problem. By the grace of his spiritual master, he was neither short of ideas nor unable to set them down. Translating and commenting on the Vaiṣṇava scriptures, his pen flowed freely. He was inspired by the miracle of the press, the *bṛhad-mṛdaṅga*. The work of writing his message down and printing it a thousand times—with the awareness and urgency of speaking directly to everyone, not just people in Delhi or India, but *everyone*—put Abhay into an ecstatic meditation. He would contemplate how copies of *Back to Godhead* could reach thoughtful people who might read them gratefully.

Nor was maintenance a problem. In the *Śrīmad-Bhāgavatam*, Śukadeva Gosvāmī had declared that a devotee's problem was not food, clothing, or shelter. If one had no bed, he could always lie on the ground and use his arms for a pillow. For clothes he could always find some rejected garments in the street. For food he could live on fruits from the trees. And for lodging he could stay in the mountain caves. Nature supplies all necessities; a transcendentalist should not flatter materialists to maintain himself. Of course, Abhay wasn't living in the mountains or jungle but in the city of New Delhi, yet he had virtually adopted the renounced mode Śukadeva had suggested—not to punish his body or prove himself pure and uncompromising, but because he *had* to live in poverty if he wanted to regularly produce *Back to Godhead.*

For Abhay it was a great labor of love, and purchasing paper for printing became a priority even before eating. Neglecting his personal needs for preaching was a manifestation of his faith in Kṛṣṇa, of which Abhay suffered no scarcity. He had full faith that if he served Kṛṣṇa, he would be provided for. To work alone was not an insurmountable problem; it was pleasant and simple. It was better than having to manage the neophyte inmates of the Gaudiya Sangha. The ecstasy of working hard to serve his spiritual master was not a problem. The problem was the condition of the world.

According to the *śāstras,* the current age, Kali-yuga, would create continual degradation in society. And Abhay could see this evidenced every day in Delhi. Delhi, formerly known as Hastināpura, had been the ancient capital of King Yudhiṣṭhira, who, five thousand years before, under the patronage of Lord Kṛṣṇa had been the most opulent king in the world and whose citizens had been fully protected and provided for. Now, after a thousand years of foreign subjugation, India was again independent, and New Delhi was the capital.

Yet even in Abhay's relatively brief sixty years of experience, he had seen Indian culture—which in his childhood had retained much of the original purity of the Vedic age—degrade. Now he saw a society in which his countrymen were victimized by the propaganda that they could be happy in gross materialistic indulgence. The British had introduced tea, tobacco, meat, and factories; and now, even after independence, these were a part of India's new way of life. Having driven away the British, the Indians were imitating Western ways, and India's leaders were deliberately ignoring the Vedic principles of God consciousness, the very treasures India was meant to distribute to the whole world. Abhay had seen how India had abandoned her spiritual heritage and gone running after the modernization of the West—but now, where was that material advancement? Were Indians any happier in their independence than they had been in British days? To Abhay, the overpopulated city was a hell of ruffians and fools. Although thousands of poor people were employed in the burgeoning steel mills and tire factories, their living conditions had worsened.

Abhay voiced his concern about these conditions in his *Back to Godhead.* Could the poor eat the nuts and bolts produced in the factories? Could they be nourished by cinema, television, or sex songs on the radio? The leaders were unable to see that abandoning spiritual principles had led to the very ills they officially abhorred: a decadent, rebellious youth, corruption in every area of civic life, and even economic instability and scarcity. When Abhay had been a youth in Calcutta, there had been no cinema billboards advertising lurid sexual fantasies, but now India had developed the third largest movie industry in the world, and film advertisements were all over Delhi. Beef shops and liquor shops had sprung up. The newspapers regularly ran editorials deploring the degradation of young Indian boys who teased, insulted, and affronted women on the street. Women's leagues complained about increased juvenile promiscuity and the obscene treatment of women in films and advertisements. But there were no upright *brāhmaṇas* or saintly administrators to do anything about it.

Abhay saw the need for a respiritualization of society. But society was rushing headlong in the opposite direction. In February, even as Abhay was trying to publish his *Back to Godhead,* Prime Minister Nehru, while speaking with concern of India's "crisis of the spirit," simultaneously launched another Five-Year Plan for rapid industrialization. Everyone from the prime minister down to the common man was concerned about the symptomatic problems, but no one seemed to understand that the *real* problem was the lack of God consciousness.

Abhay had to deliver the medicine for the ills of Kali-yuga. He knew it was needed on a much larger scale than he could reach on his own, but even to administer one issue of *Back to Godhead* was almost beyond his means. Writing the articles, typing them, taking them to the printer, and distributing them should not have been the work of one lone, impoverished devotee, but in working with his Godbrothers he had met with their decided lack of organization and their lack of desire for vigorous preaching. Bhaktisāraṅga Gosvāmī had seemed determined to keep *Sajjana-toṣaṇī* small, and his *maṭha,* like so many others, had been ineffectual in attracting new members. *This* was the petty-mindedness that would cripple preaching. Therefore, he was now working alone on a small scale—happy in his spiritual welfare work, yet aware that his four-page newspaper was only a drop of water in the desert.

In February of 1956—while the U.S. was struggling with civil rights, while Khrushchev and Eisenhower were both openly deploring the arms race and were maneuvering in nuclear disarmament talks, and while the Shah of Iran was visiting New Delhi—Abhay was trying to print *Back to Godhead.* In winter's discomfort he walked through the early-morning streets of Delhi to visit Surendra Kumar Jain, the printer, to read the latest proofs. By walking he saved money. Only when he was delivering paper from the paper dealer to the printer would he rent a ricksha. He had no *cādara,* only a lightweight cotton jacket, and he wore rubber shoes. He also wore a cotton hat that covered his ears and tied beneath his chin, protecting him from the forty-degree wintery mornings and the sometimes gusty winds.

Kumar Jain: *My first impression was that he was a nice person and straightforward. I felt pity also because of the conditions under which he would come. I know he didn't have even twenty-five paisa. He would come all the way on foot and without any breakfast or anything. He would come in the morning to the press, and when I would ask him, "Swamiji, did you have anything to eat this morning?" he would say, "Oh, no, Mr. Jain. I just came because I had to see the proofs."*

"That's all right," I would say, "I will get breakfast for you." I would call for breakfast, and then he would sit and work.

He would do the proofreading himself. The printing was done by me, and most of the time he would like to be present when that final printing was being done. He would come in the morning around seven and stay until he had seen all the proofs. It was a regular thing that he would come without breakfast, I would arrange for breakfast, and we would sit across the table from one another for hours together. He was always talking on religious subjects only. But when we would be sitting, especially when waiting for the proofs to come, we would discuss many things. I felt that he knew quite a lot, because he was a well-read person. He was more a friend than just a person coming to get things printed. He was a very simple man, straightforward in his habits. But his mission at that time was particularly to further the movement of Back to Godhead.

His financial condition was very, very weak. Sometimes the printing would be difficult because he was not able to arrange for the paper. Many times I told him that if he was feeling difficulty, why was he continuing? But he said, "No, it is my mission, and I will always carry it on as far as possible." I tried to accommodate him to the maximum possible extent. But he was a real pauper.

I only did the printing, and he had to arrange for the paper. So sometimes it was delayed. Although my job was printing, sometimes I would say, "All right, you are so keen. I will give you the paper." But usually he would arrange for it himself, since we only did printing. He would bring it in a ricksha.

We were not uncomfortable together, but as business would have it, if the bills were standing for a long time, then I would ask him if he could do something about it. He would say, "Don't worry, you can be sure that your money is coming." I never asked him where his funds were coming from, because I felt that it was his personal matter. But it was embarrassing for him when he could not pay, so I never tried to embarrass him. He was concerned that if he didn't have money, how could he print the paper? And he definitely wanted to run that paper.

He wanted to preach the teachings of the Gītā. *He thought of it as a sort of movement, that it was the only way that people in the world could find peace. His conviction was very strong.*

After picking up the copies from the printer, Abhay would walk around the city selling them. He would take a seat at a tea stand, and when someone sat beside him Abhay would ask him please to take a copy of *Back to Godhead.* He also went to the homes and offices of people who had already donated or agreed to see him, and he sought out new contacts, sometimes on recommendation or sometimes by going uninvited wherever he could find a potential reader. When he delivered copies to regular donors, he would discuss the previous issue's philosophy with them and sometimes write articles on topics they requested: "Our esteemed friend, Sri Bishan Prasad Maheswari, one of the learned advocates of the Supreme Court, has requested us to write something on the principle of fruitive action with special reference to Vice and its potency." Often donors agreed to see him not so much out of genuine interest or affection as out of a sense of obligation; in their traditional Hindu piety, they felt obliged to see the *sādhu,* take his paper, and even think well of him—but not necessarily to read his newspaper. Once, when Abhay was approaching a well-to-do house, the owner came onto the second-floor veranda and shouted, "Go away! We don't want you here!"

Abhay, responding to the resistance (polite and impolite) that he met while selling *Back to Godhead,* wrote an article, "NO TIME, A Chronic Disease of the Common Man," for the March 16 edition.

> When we approach some gentleman and request him to become a reader of "Back to Godhead," sometimes we are replied with the words "NO TIME."
>
> They say that they are too busy in earning money for maintaining the body and soul together. But when we ask them what do they mean by the 'Soul,' they have nothing to reply.
>
> Dr. Meghnath Saha, a great scientist, was busily going to a meeting of the planning Commission. Unfortunately while going in his car on the road he died and could not ask Death to wait because he had **no time** at that moment.
>
> Dr. Ansari, the great Congress leader, while dying in a moving train, on his way to home, said that he was himself a medical man and almost all his family men were so, but Death is so cruel that he was dying without any medical treatment.
>
> Therefore, Death has been described in the Bhagwat as ... the **indefatigable.** Death is awaiting everyone although everybody thinks that he may not die. **There is life after death**. The busy man should try to know this also as to whither he is going. This life is but a spot in his longest sojourn and a sane person should not be busy with a spot only. Nobody says that the body should not be maintained—but everybody should know from "Bhagwat Geeta," that the body is the outward dress and the 'Soul' is the real person who puts on the dress. So if the dress is taken care of only, without any care of the real person—it is sheer foolishness and waste of time.

Abhay was an unusual newspaper vendor. He didn't loudly hawk his paper on the street or sell it from a newsstand; he approached individuals quietly as they sat to drink tea, or he would call on acquaintances in their offices or places of business. Taking a copy from the stack he carried underneath his arm, he would present what appeared to be an ordinary tabloid newspaper with bold black headlines across the front page. But what odd headlines—"The Lowest of the Mankind," "Philosophical Problems Within Social Awareness," "Sufferings of Humanity," "The Pure Consciousness of Nationalism." Anyone could tell at a glance that this was no ordinary newspaper. Abhay would say something to try to convince them to take it anyway—before they said, "No time."

On behalf of his spiritual master and the previous Vaiṣṇava authorities, he was playing a role, the newspaper salesman—a smiling demeanor, a gentlemanly invitation. No, it wasn't an ordinary newspaper, but they would find it interesting, and it cost only six paisa. Thus he was extending the mercy of Lord Caitanya, handing out the truths of the *Vedas* in the easy-to-take form of a newspaper.

Despite his desperate poverty and the urgency of his message, his writing was never shrill, strident, or fanatical. He wrote expecting to find his reader prepared to hear sound philosophy and always willing to accept the truth, especially when presented logically and relevantly and supported by the authoritative Vedic literature. Although experience on the streets of Delhi had shown him that people were shallow, distracted, and uninterested in self-realization, he knew that most people, at least at some time in their lives, pondered the crucial themes of philosophy: whether God exists, whether He is a person, why there is suffering. So Abhay appealed to their higher sentiments.

Spring of 1956 brought visits from U.S. Secretary of State Dulles and, a few days later, Lord Mountbatten, the former governor-general of India, who was greeted at the airport by thousands. Then came the celebration of the once-sacred day of Holi, when urchins spray all passersby with colored dyes. Prime Minister Nehru toured the Delhi slums expressing disgust at the prevailing conditions. He announced India's intention to develop atomic energy, stressing its peaceful uses. The weather warmed. A border clash began between India and Pakistan. Delhi railway workers went on strike. Meanwhile, Abhay continued to preach.

He somehow managed to meet the financial, editorial, and printing demands and published his sixth issue for the year of 1956, the May 20 edition of *Back to Godhead.* The front page carried a special notice:

> As a matter of Principle
>
> Please read 'Back to Godhead' and revive your deeper aspect of personality. There is nothing in it which is our ideology manufactured by imperfect sense perception but all that it contains are messages of our liberated sages. We are simply helping them to speak again to men and women in easy language for real life. Every responsible man and woman must therefore read it regularly at a cost of very insignificant sum of Rs. 2/4/-a year or As.-/3/- per month. Do not neglect it. It is for your interest. It will create a happy society of humanity.

In "How to Broadcast the Teachings of Bhagwat Geeta," he talked about the need for spiritual organization in society. A model community, which he named Gita-nagari ("the village where the Bhagwat Geeta is sung"), would live by the *Bhagavad-gītā* and preach its message to the world. Praising Mahatma Gandhi for his Vaiṣṇava qualities, Abhay suggested that Gandhi had also esteemed the Gita-nagari concept. It was the only way of relief from the sufferings caused by "demoniac-principled leaders" who were misguiding the present demoralized civilization.

He was calculating how to capture the restless popular imagination. He wanted to present Kṛṣṇa's teachings in a clear, straightforward way and distribute them widely; he felt that good arguments from authoritative scripture would appeal to sane, impartial, educated people, even though they claimed to be uninterested. He knew that somehow, without abandoning his gravity and his absolute conclusion, he must capture their interest. They were relegating religion to some book of scripture on the shelf that they never read, didn't understand, or couldn't believe; he brought it to them as a newspaper—yet it was as good as the scriptures. No, it wasn't what they expected in a newspaper, but they might read it.

> The chanting process of the Holy Name of God as conducted by the propaganda of "Back to Godhead" is not pleasing to the superficial pleasure-hunters describing men and women in indecent literatures in national news, but it is the means of relishing the transcendental eternal life.

In addition to selling *Back to Godhead* at tea stalls and delivering copies to donors, Abhay also mailed out free copies—both within India and abroad. For years, the vast audience of English-speaking readers outside India had concerned him, and he wanted to reach them. Having gathered addresses of libraries, universities, and cultural and governmental outlets outside India, he mailed as many *Back to Godhead*s as he could afford. He prepared a letter for his Western readers, suggesting that they should be even more receptive than his countrymen.

> Although the messages contained in ... BACK TO GODHEAD are all gifts of the ancient sages of India who actually realised the Absolute Truth, yet at the present moment the so-called leaders of India are too much enamoured by the western way of material advancement of knowledge. They are completely neglecting the treasure house of knowledge left by the sages.

> You gentlemen of the western countries have seen much about material science and yet peace is not within your control. In most cases you may be feeling the want of peace although you have enough [materially]. This basic defect of materialism remains undetected by the misleaders of India and therefore they are not serious about going BACK TO GODHEAD, the ultimate aim of life's journey.

On the home front, Abhay sent copies of his latest issues of *Back to Godhead* to the president of India, Dr. Rajendra Prasad, along with a letter warning of the perilous fate that awaits a society conducted by **asuras — "Please therefore save them** from the great fall down." Abhay's letter of November 21 was outspoken.

> I have got the clue of going "Back to Godhead" just after leaving my present material body, and in order to take along with me all my contemporary men and women of the world, I have started my paper, "Back to Godhead," as one of the means to the way. Please don't think of me as ... something wonderful or a madman when I say that I shall go "Back to Godhead" after leaving my present material body! It is quite possible for everyone and all of us.

Abhay requested His Excellency at least to glance over the headlines of the enclosed one dozen copies of *Back to Godhead* and consider granting the editor an interview. There was immense work to be done on behalf of India's spiritual heritage, and there should be a specific ministry of spiritual affairs for this purpose. "I am crying alone in the wilderness at the present moment," wrote Abhay. But His Excellency never replied.

In his *Back to Godhead,* Abhay was making propaganda against the atheistic view. In "Hope Against Hope," he frankly admitted that eighty percent of the people he met while selling *Back to Godhead* were atheists.

> Sometime we meet gentlemen of up-to-date taste and try to make them interested in the matter of "Back to Godhead." ... they say very frankly that they have not only no interest in such theistic subject but also they condemn the attempt to bring back people in general to the path of 'Back to Godhead.'
>
> According to these gentlemen, economic conditions of the Indian people deteriorated on account of their too much faith in God and the sooner they forget everything about Godhead, it is better for them. But we cannot agree

> with this atheistic conclusion of such up-to-date gentlemen devoid of the sense of Godhead.

Abhay argued that although independent India was now educating her citizens in godless materialism, her economic conditions were not improving. Many Indians did not even have the bare necessities of life. He cited that 120,000 were unemployed in Delhi.

> Some of the well posted Government servants or some of the fortunate businessmen may feel themselves happy but 90 per cent of their brother citizens do not know how to meet the both ends together and therefore the economic condition is definitely not satisfactory.

He quoted former United States President Harry S. Truman as saying that national independence means that the citizens should have a comfortable life. So if that were the case, said Abhay, where was India's independence? His point was that all attempts at happiness and prosperity are unlawful as long as they fail to recognize the proprietorship of the Supreme Lord. An atheistic civilization could never produce peace.

In "Progressive Ambition and Unsatiated Lust," Abhay wrote:

> There is no dearth of money but there is dearth of peace in the world. The whole human energy having been diverted to this money making business, it has certainly increased the cheap money making capacity of the total population but the result is that such unrestricted and unlawful inflation of money has created a bad economy and has enabled us to manufacture huge costly weapons for destroying the result of such cheap money making business. The authorities of big money making countries, instead of enjoying peace, are now engaged in making important plans as to how they can save themselves from the modern destructive weapons and as a matter of fact a huge sum of money is being thrown into the sea for making an experiment on such dreadful weapons. Such experiments are being carried out not only at huge costs but also at cost of many poor lives, binding thereby such nations in the laws of Karma.

Those who unlawfully accumulated money would find it snatched away by taxes for wars and other "agents of illusory nature in the shape of medical practitioners, lawyers, tax collectors, societies, constitutions, so-called Sadhus, famines, earthquake and many such calamities."

> A miser who hesitated to purchase a copy of 'Back to Godhead' by the dictation of illusory nature spent up Rs. 20,000/- for a week's ailments and died at the end. A similar thing happened when a man who refused to spend

a paisa for the service of the Lord spoiled Rs. 30,000/- in litigation affairs between members of the home. That is the law of nature.

A worker in a New Delhi post office, noticing the title of the magazines Abhay was sending abroad, took the opportunity to argue his atheistic opinions with Abhay.

Śrīla Prabhupāda: *The postmaster was an Arya Samaji, and he was talking to me about the paper,* Back to Godhead. *He raised the question, "If we do our duty nicely, then what is the use of worshiping God? If we become honest, if we become moral, if we do not do anything which is harmful to anyone, if we act in this way, then what is the need of this?" Because our paper's name was* Back to Godhead, *he was indirectly protesting, "What is the use of propagating this philosophy of Godhead if we act nicely?" That is the Arya Samajist's view—how to avoid God.*

So I replied that if one is not God conscious, he cannot be a moralist, he cannot be truthful, he cannot be honest—this is our point of view. You study the whole world just on these three points—morality, honesty, dutifulness—but if he is not God conscious, he cannot continue such things. To revive all these good qualities in society, you first have to invoke God consciousness.

A Delhi man, noticing Abhay distributing *Back to Godhead,* remarked "Where is Godhead? Can you show me God?" Abhay replied to the challenge, but he also pondered a deeper reply as he moved throughout the city during the day. On returning to his room, he began an article, "Where Is Godhead? Is It Possible to See Him?"

In the Secretariat Buildings in New Delhi there is an inscription on the stone that Liberty does not descend upon a people but it has to be earned before it can be enjoyed. Actually this is the fact and we have seen it that much sacrifice had to be rendered by the people of India before they could gain Swaraj. But in the matter of Godhead some irresponsible people ask, "Where is God?" "Can you show me?" "Have you seen God?" These are some of the questions put forward by some irresponsible men who want to have everything very cheap. If for attaining a temporary false sense of liberty in this material world so much labour and sacrifice have to be requisitioned, is it possible to see Godhead The Absolute Truth so cheaply? To see God means complete liberty from all conditions. But is Godhead an attending orderly so that He may be present at my command? The atheist however demands like that, as if Godhead is his paid servant, and he thinks that Godhead is an imaginary thing otherwise He would have appeared before us as soon as the demand to see Him is made.

One time, while he was walking on a secluded street, pursuing his *Back to Godhead* duties, a stray cow—the kind commonly seen wandering the streets of any Indian town or city—suddenly charged him, goring his side with her horn, and knocked him down. At first he couldn't get up, and no one came to help him. As he lay there, he wondered why it had happened.

Summer came, and the 110-degree heat made it almost intolerable to spend time out of doors. Hot, dust-laden winds blew in the city streets. Streetside hawkers closed their businesses during the day. In early May, during 112-degree heat, a man collapsed in the street and died of heatstroke. But Abhay ignored the heat and the ordinary limitations of the body.

One day while delivering *Back to Godhead* to various addresses in the city, Abhay suddenly began reeling, half unconscious, overcome by the heat. At that very moment, an acquaintance of his, a man he had approached during his preaching, happened to be passing by in his car, and he took Abhay to a doctor. The doctor diagnosed him as a victim of heatstroke and ordered him to rest.

On June 20, Abhay produced the eighth consecutive fortnightly edition of the year, its front-page article condemning both materialistic family life and false renunciation of family life. It had been almost two years exactly since he had left his home and taken to the *vānaprastha* order, and his comments on family life seemed autobiographical as well as scriptural. He quoted a statement by Prahlāda Mahārāja from *Śrīmad-Bhāgavatam.*

> Persons who are always disturbed in mind with cares and anxieties of household affairs may quit off the place which is the black hole temporary abode [family life] to kill one's self and take shelter unto the lotus feet of the Personality of Godhead by entering into the forest.

And he admitted, "The management of a family is more difficult than that of an empire."

But trying to avoid family life by living in the jungle without the real spirit of renunciation was "monkey renunciation." In the jungle there were many monkeys, who lived naked, ate fruits, and kept female companions.

> The real remedy lies in the act of accepting the service of the lotus feet of the Lord. That makes one free from all cares and anxieties of life. That makes one able to see Godhead always and everywhere.

Real renounced life, therefore, was possible without going into the forest. Even if one remained in the dress of a householder, he could be freed from cares and anxieties by engaging himself in devotional service.

On September 1, U.S. President Eisenhower condemned the Soviet's secret testing of a nuclear bomb equal to one million tons of TNT and scoffed at the Soviet's claims for peace. In the Mideast, Egypt's Nasser nationalized the operation of the Suez Canal, causing an international crisis. On September 20, eighty-one nations met at the U.N. to form a new international agency to help "tame" the atom for peaceful purposes. Abhay saw some of the headlines and heard talk of the latest news from gentlemen he visited. He frankly told them that without Kṛṣṇa consciousness the promises of cooperation by the politicians were all phantasmagoria.

Bhaktisiddhānta Sarasvatī had said that if only one soul could be turned into a pure devotee, his mission would be a success. Yet sometimes Abhay became overwhelmed when he thought of how small he was, how much work had to be done on behalf of Kṛṣṇa, and how difficult it was to convince even one conditioned soul.

CHAPTER NINE

A Resident of Vṛndāvana

I was sitting alone in Vṛndāvana, writing. My Godbrother insisted to me, "Bhaktivedanta Prabhu, you must do it. Without accepting the renounced order of life, nobody can become a preacher." So he insisted. Not he insisted; practically my spiritual master insisted. He wanted me to become a preacher, so he forced me through this Godbrother: "You accept." So, unwillingly I accepted.

—Śrīla Prabhupāda

THE PASSENGER CARS behind the locomotive moved forward almost silently. Thumping at a slow rhythm over the tracks, the train pulled out of the station—past freightyards, a neighborhood of run-down tenements, the old Delhi fort, the garbage dump at Nizamuddin with its hundreds of crows and vultures flying overhead, and then past a marble-domed red sandstone mosque. Seated in a third-class compartment, his luggage stored beneath his seat, Abhay could see factory workers walking near the tracks, carrying their lunches in metal *tiffins,* and then the factories, surrounded by huts of mud and straw. He passed the thatched roofs and tarpaulin tents, the cow-dung fires that smoked in the morning air. The tall stacks of the Indraprastha electrical powerhouse spewed out a different smoke, and sooty black clouds poured back from the locomotive. He saw red and violet wildflowers blooming from bramble bushes at trackside, and beyond he saw the road to Mathurā, with its border of fruitless *kīkar* trees.

It was the morning train to Agra, and there were few passengers. Abhay would be riding as far as Mathurā and then traveling by *ṭāṅgā* to Vṛndāvana. He had ridden widely the Indian railway, especially in the 1920s, '30s, and '40s, when he had traveled on business in Bengal, Punjab, Uttar Pradesh, Maharashtra, and Andhra Pradesh.

He had been to Vṛndāvana several times. In his childhood reveries over the train timetables, it had been the first place he had thought of visiting. His first visit, in 1925, had been but a brief pilgrimage while he had been in nearby Agra on business. Then in 1932 Śrīla Bhaktisiddhānta Sarasvatī had been in Vṛndāvana on *parikrama.* That had been a memorable visit; Abhay had heard him speak at Kosi, and Śrīla Bhaktisiddhānta had marked him—"He likes to hear." And then at Rādhā-kuṇḍa three years later he had been with his spiritual master again. But he had never gone like this—to live there. Dressed in a simple white *dhotī,* his hand in his bead bag, fingering his *japa* beads, he looked out the window, quietly chanting the holy name.

The train passed through the dense thickets of Faridabad and into the agricultural fields, with their interspersed patches of wheat, *dāl,* and sugarcane beginning at trackside and stretching for half a mile to the dry, uncultivated land that continued as far as the eye could see. The train sped faster. Rural villages drifted past the window. An hour out of Delhi, the land was mostly flat and open, dotted with small villages. Occasionally he would glimpse a striking old temple. But mostly it was the land—now barren, with a few palm trees, now cultivated with irrigated fields—under the expanse of blue sky and blazing sun.

For a long time Abhay had wanted to take shelter in Vṛndāvana, and now there was no obstacle. His purpose remained the same: he would write *Back to Godhead* and deliver it to the printer in Delhi fortnightly. As long as he could afford to travel, he would return to Delhi to distribute *Back to Godhead.* But he would live in the shelter of Vṛndāvana. He had in mind the room at the Vaṁśī-gopālajī temple near Keśī-ghāṭa, a rooftop room that commanded a view of almost all of Vṛndāvana. And since his 1953 visit from Jhansi, he had kept in touch with the temple manager.

In moving to Vṛndāvana, Abhay was following his predecessor spiritual masters. Śrīla Bhaktisiddhānta Sarasvatī and Bhaktivinoda Ṭhākura had had their house at Rādhā-kuṇḍa and had preached in Vṛndāvana. Gaurakiśora dāsa Bābājī, Jagannātha dāsa Bābājī, Viśvanātha Cakravartī, and Narottama dāsa Ṭhākura had lived either in Vṛndāvana or in Navadvīpa, near the birthplace of Lord Caitanya.

Lord Caitanya and His immediate followers had an especially intimate relationship with Vṛndāvana. Lord Caitanya had commissioned Rūpa Gosvāmī and Sanātana Gosvāmī to uncover the places of Kṛṣṇa's pastimes in Vṛndāvana that over the centuries had become lost. Rūpa and Sanātana had left their prestigious government posts and gone to live in Vṛndāvana. Dressed in simple loincloths, they had lived without fixed residence, staying each night under a different tree. They and Jīva Gosvāmī, Raghunātha dāsa Gosvāmī, Raghunātha Bhaṭṭa Gosvāmī, and Gopāla Bhaṭṭa Gosvāmī, known and worshiped as the six Gosvāmīs of Vṛndāvana, had compiled a voluminous literature on *kṛṣṇa-bhakti.* They had inspired wealthy Vaiṣṇava patrons to erect Vṛndāvana's great temples: Govindajī, Madana-mohana, Rādhā-Dāmodara, Rādhā-ramaṇa. At Rādhā-kuṇḍa, shortly after Lord Caitanya's departure from the world, Raghunātha dāsa Gosvāmī had chanted one hundred thousand names of Kṛṣṇa and discoursed for several hours daily on the pastimes of Lord Caitanya. There also, Kṛṣṇadāsa Kavirāja had compiled the *Caitanya-caritāmṛta,* describing the life and teachings of Lord Caitanya.

Even those Gauḍīya Vaiṣṇavas who did not live in Vṛndāvana kept Vṛndāvana always in their hearts and proclaimed its glories. The *Caitanya-caritāmṛta* describes the great ecstasy Lord Caitanya felt while traveling from Purī to Vṛndāvana: "Śrī Caitanya Mahāprabhu's mind was absorbed in ecstatic love at Jagannātha Purī, but when He passed along the road on the way to Vṛndāvana, that love increased a hundred times. The Lord's ecstatic love increased a thousand times when He visited Mathurā, but it increased a hundred thousand times when He wandered in the forests of Vṛndāvana. When Śrī Caitanya Mahāprabhu was elsewhere, the very name of Vṛndāvana was sufficient to increase His ecstatic love. Now when He was actually traveling in the Vṛndāvana forest, His mind was absorbed in great ecstatic love day and night. He ate and bathed simply out of habit."

Vṛndāvana is the earthly manifestation of Lord Kṛṣṇa's eternal spiritual abode, which the Lord Himself describes in *Bhagavad-gītā:* "There is another nature, which is eternal and is transcendental to manifested and unmanifested matter. It is never annihilated. It is the supreme destination. When one goes there, he never comes back. That is My supreme abode." Kṛṣṇa's activities of eternity, bliss, and knowledge and His abode, Goloka Vṛndāvana, are described in many Vedic literatures: "I worship Govinda, the primeval Lord, the first progenitor, who is tending the cows, yielding all desires, in abodes built with spiritual gems, where He is surrounded by millions of purpose trees and always served with great reverence and affection by hundreds and thousands of Lakṣmīs, or *gopīs*."

Although Lord Kṛṣṇa's abode, Goloka Vṛndāvana, is far beyond the material world, when Kṛṣṇa comes to earth He displays His eternal abode in the Vṛndāvana of India. That eighty-four-square-mile tract in north India is identical with the eternal world in the spiritual sky.

To live and die in Vṛndāvana guarantees the devotee's transfer to the eternal spiritual world. The residents of Vṛndāvana, even the animals, are exalted; at the end of life they will transfer to Goloka Vṛndāvana. Lord Brahmā, therefore, prayed that he might take birth as a clump of grass on the outskirts of Vṛndāvana so that these pure devotees would purify him with the dust from their feet. And Vaiṣṇava *śāstras* declare that even by only a brief visit to Vṛndāvana one can realize the Supreme Lord in his heart.

Caitanya-caritāmṛta states, "Like the transcendental body of Lord Kṛṣṇa, Gokula is all-pervading, infinite, and supreme. It expands both above and below, without any restriction. That abode is manifested within the material world by the will of Lord Kṛṣṇa. It is identical to that original Gokula; they are not two different bodies. The land there is touchstone [*cintāmaṇi*], and the forests abound with desire trees, although material eyes see it as an ordinary place. ... The ideal place to execute Kṛṣṇa consciousness is Vrajabhūmi, or Vṛndāvana, where people are naturally inclined to love Kṛṣṇa and Kṛṣṇa is naturally inclined to love them."

The train arrived at Mathurā. Abhay stepped down with his luggage and looked around, noting the recently constructed Mathurā Junction Building. Proceeding through the gate and out of the station, he found a *ṭāṅgā* driver, agreed on the fare, and started for Keśī-ghāṭa.

For half a mile the wobbling horse-drawn cart followed the road between the tracks and the railway yard. At the main road, they turned left, passed under a railroad bridge, and entered an open market. Piles of fruits, vegetables, and grains were displayed on the ground, their vendors sitting beside them, bartering and measuring while customers milled about. The women of Mathurā, dressed in brightly colored *sārīs*—yellows, greens, pinks, and purples—moved busily in the market. The vehicular traffic consisted mostly of bullock carts, the drivers often squatting on the wooden yokes between the shoulders of their animals, whipping alternately one ox and then the other with a length of rope joined to a wooden handle. Although this was the most populated area in the trip to Vṛndāvana, compared to Delhi it seemed simple and rural.

The sun was high, but the *ṭāṅgā's* top provided a partial shelter, and the summer's heat had passed. Beyond the bazaar the road curved to the right, and Abhay saw the nearby white domes of the massive sandstone mosque marking Kṛṣṇa-janmasthāna, the birthplace of Lord Kṛṣṇa. Centuries ago invading Muslims had destroyed the large Kṛṣṇa temple and created the mosque in its stead, and now directly in front of the mosque stood a newer, smaller Kṛṣṇa temple.

They approached the three-way junction: New Delhi, central Mathurā, Vṛndāvana. The driver struck the horse with his whip, and the *ṭāṅgā* proceeded along the Vṛndāvana road, edging through a herd of white cows, the herdsman walking amongst them, carrying his stick. The road was busy with *ṭāṅgās* and slow, creaking oxcarts, loaded with market commodities and pulled by squat, black water buffalo. A string of small, spindle-legged donkeys carried oversized loads of firewood and sandbags.

Although much had changed in Abhay's life since he had come here to see his spiritual master during the *parikrama* years ago, Vṛndāvana had remained the same. He felt he had done the best thing in coming here, leaving the heat, the traffic and fumes, the human passions of Delhi. It was a natural relief. Yet even as he felt transcendental emotions for Vṛndāvana, impressions of his months of preaching in Delhi lingered in his mind—the city streets, and himself, going from place to place with his *Back to Godheads*. Life in Delhi had been constant, vigorous preaching. Now he was more than sixty years old, but he was not coming to Vṛndāvana to retire. He had retired from household responsibilities, but not from his responsibilities of making *Back to Godhead* as popular and sophisticated as *Illustrated Weekly*. He would live in Vṛndāvana and commute to Delhi. But he would never stop preaching.

The sight of taller trees signaled the precincts of Vṛndāvana, as the thin horse trotted along, past the police station and water trough for animals. On either side appeared the garden courtyards of private estates and *āśramas.* Fragile white *mālatī* flowers, golden marigolds, frangipani trees, red hibiscus, "trees of sorrow," and many other flowers and trees, some known only in Vṛndāvana, bloomed forth in the brilliant sunlight. The Rādhā-Govinda temple loomed fortresslike on his left, and opposite, in the distance, the high-rising tower of the Raṅganātha temple. They entered narrow streets, tighter and busier places with markets and city dwellings, and then it became quieter again. At the end of a narrow street, by the Yamunā River, near the Keśī bathing *ghāṭa,* stood the small and beautifully ornate entrance of the Vaṁśī-gopālajī temple, a narrow, three-storied building with three domes and many decorated arches.

After stepping over the curbside drain and walking up three marble steps, Abhay entered the front door, the driver following him, carrying the luggage. Once inside, Abhay removed his shoes and entered the courtyard, which was open to the sky through a metal grate, on which a few birds sat two floors above. A column of sunlight lit one side of the courtyard, where a potted *tulasī* sat atop a pillar. The temple seemed cool and quiet. Adjacent to the courtyard was the Deity room, its doors locked shut. Overhead was a mezzanine with rooms whose entrances were visible from the courtyard; a few *sārīs* and strips of cloth hung on improvised clotheslines.

Mahant Gopal, the temple *pūjārī,* whom Abhay had known since 1954, greeted him cheerfully. He was about the same age as Abhay and had long gray hair and an unruly beard. Although Abhay's attire was modest, he appeared well dressed compared with Gopal, who wore only a coarse *dhotī.*

Gopal led Abhay upstairs. Coming out onto the roof, Abhay smiled to see again the wonderful vista. Barely a hundred yards away he could see the Yamunā, not only the immediate patch of water flowing before him, but to his left and right a broad curving sheet of river shimmering in the afternoon sun. There were sand deltas, herds of cows and buffalo grazing, the flat grassy banks of the Yamunā, and plains and trees as far as the eye could see. And in the opposite direction was the town of Vṛndāvana, marked by dozens of temple spires and domes.

Abhay's room, the only one on the roof, was small, with narrow double doors and barred windows. Sitting on the apartment's roof, monkeys with their tiny offspring sat watching, unalarmed. Just outside the door, a two-foot-high cement pyramid signified that the temple Deity was directly beneath. Abhay entered the room. Through the barred windows he could see the palace at Keśī-ghāṭa, the venerable tower of the Gopīnātha temple, and, beyond, the uninterrupted, flat river, the green banks, and the sky.

After acquainting Abhay with the details of the room — the small kerosene burner, the rope and bucket for drawing bathwater from the well to the roof — Gopal meticulously produced a government-stamped rental agreement. Abhay wrote a short paragraph, declaring himself a disciple of the late Śrī Śrīmad Bhaktisiddhānta Sarasvatī Prabhupāda and attesting to his renting the room at five rupees per month. Both parties signed.

After his bath, Abhay took *prasādam* and rested. When he heard the bells ringing in the temple below, he went down to see the Deities. Gopal, who had been the temple's *pūjārī* for many years and had seen its reconstruction in 1923, had told Abhay that the temple Deity, Vaṁśī-gopālajī, had been installed 350 years before by Mahant Prahlāda dāsa of the Nimbārka Vaiṣṇava-sampradāya. Gopal himself had installed the Deity of Rādhārāṇī. Vaṁśī-gopālajī, standing in a graceful threefold-bending form and holding His flute, was very appealing. He was three feet tall and of black marble; Rādhārāṇī, slightly shorter, was of brass. They were simply dressed in rough white cotton and illuminated by the dim glow of a kerosene lamp. Abhay could see that They were being cared for, but because of poverty there was no opulence.

He returned to the roof as the sun was setting over the town of Vṛndāvana. Having the entire roof's walkway to himself, Abhay walked and chanted *japa,* enjoying the cooling early-evening breeze from the Yamunā. Occasionally a solitary boat would pass on the calm waters of the Yamunā, and a devotee, somewhere unseen, could be heard chanting evening prayers at Keśī-ghāṭa. He felt pleased with this location in the heart of the pastimes of Lord Kṛṣṇa. He was not a newcomer spending his first day in a strange town; everything here was already familiar and dear. As Vṛndāvana was Kṛṣṇa's abode, Abhay was Kṛṣṇa's servant, the servant of the six Gosvāmīs, the servant of his spiritual master. He felt at home.

As day turned to twilight, temple bells rang throughout the town. Abhay walked to the western side of the roof and looked into the city of thousands of temples. The Govindajī temple, the Raṅganātha temple, and thousands of smaller temples were having their *sandhyā-ārati* and *kīrtana,* glorifying Lord Kṛṣṇa.

Abhay responded to the sights and sounds of Vṛndāvana as only a pure devotee could; his thoughts and emotions were full of appreciation and awareness of Kṛṣṇa, Kṛṣṇa's devotees, and Kṛṣṇa's land. Naturally he began to think of preaching, hankering for others to know the intimate peace and ecstasy of Vṛndāvana. Kṛṣṇa, the Supreme Personality of Godhead, was inviting all souls to join Him in His eternal abode; yet even in India, few understood. And outside India, people knew nothing of Vṛndāvana or of the Yamunā or of what it means to be free of material desires. Why shouldn't people all around the world have this? This was the abode of peace, yet no one knew anything of it, nor were people interested. But this is what they were actually hankering for.

Abhay thought of *Back to Godhead* and how, by Kṛṣṇa's grace, he might expand his preaching beyond India to the whole world. His Godbrothers ... it would have been better if they had all worked together in the Gaudiya Math, but many of them were at least keeping the regulative principles. None of them, however, seemed to be doing much beyond maintaining a temple here, an *āśrama* there, worshiping a Deity, eating and sleeping. But there was so much more to be done in broadcasting the glories of Vṛndāvana. Abhay chanted and thought of Kṛṣṇa. Gradually he turned to his task of producing the October issue of *Back to Godhead,* due to be printed shortly in Delhi. He had a deadline to keep.

The next morning, before sunrise, the residents of Vṛndāvana were astir, bathing in the Yamunā, performing *pūjā* to their Deities, reciting *mantras.* But Abhay was awake even before most, writing in stillness beneath the light in his rooftop room. As he wrote diligently in English, scriptural references appeared and took their place within convincing arguments. For hours he wrote, page after page in an exercise book, until gradually the chirping of awakening birds signaled the end of the dark night's stillness. Soon the sun would rise.

Keeping to his regular schedule, he put aside his writing and began chanting *japa,* staying in his room, uttering the Hare Kṛṣṇa *mantra* in a soft, deep voice. Even before the first traces of light in the sky, before the river was visible, a few *bābājīs* reciting prayers made their way through the streets, heading for the Yamunā. By 4:00 A.M., gongs and temple bells throughout the city heralded the *maṅgala-ārati* of the Deity. Abhay continued chanting alone for another hour. Then he prepared to bathe, lowering the bucket on its long rope and hauling water up to the rooftop.

It was light when he went out, his bead bag around his neck, a few copies of *Back to Godhead* in his hand. Turning right at the temple door, he walked the tight, crooked lane, past alleys, dirt paths, and cross lanes, which interlaced in a winding network. There were no shops in the area, only silent buildings, many of them hundreds of years old. The neighborhood was serene. Behind closed shutters, someone played on wooden clackers and sang Hare Kṛṣṇa softly. At a crossroads where dark women filled brass waterpots from a well, Abhay turned left onto a street lined with small, open porches. On either side he saw ornate temple architecture: one entrance marked by two stone lions, another by a carved elephant with teeth like a tiger's. A brick-and-mortar wall was crumbling with age.

Soon Abhay arrived at the Rādhā-ramaṇa temple, established almost five hundred years before by Gopāla Bhaṭṭa Gosvāmī, one of Lord Caitanya's chief followers. Here residents of Vṛndāvana were coming and going according to their vows, following a strict schedule that allowed not a moment's delay, making their daily visit to various temples. Abhay entered and stood amidst a group of worshipers, viewing the Deity of Kṛṣṇa, Rādhā-ramaṇa. The Deity, wearing a fresh garland of flowers, His enchanting black form adorned with bright silks and jewels, appeared very opulent.

Knowing the priests of Rādhā-ramaṇa to be respected, learned Sanskritists, some of whom also read English, Abhay had brought with him a few copies of *Back to Godhead.* He met Viśvambhara Gosvāmī, a young priest in his thirties who after the death of his father had left his law practice and taken over some of the temple management. The temple was run under a "caste *gosvāmī*" system, and thus for five hundred years Viśvambhara's ancestors had handed down charge of the temple. Although Viśvambhara had met many *sādhus,* he was immediately struck by Abhay's gentle and humble demeanor. He accepted the copies of *Back to Godhead* and sat and talked with Abhay.

Abhay then continued along Vṛndāvana's winding lanes to visit another temple, Rādhā-Dāmodara. He passed old *bābājīs* and women carrying water, a commercial shop beside an open porch where people worshiped a Śiva *liṅga.* Monkeys sitting atop a high concrete wall and ranging from roof to roof, ledge to ledge, chattered and gestured as Abhay walked beneath. As the morning progressed, barefoot children had begun to appear more frequently, playing within the open doorways. As he walked along chanting *japa,* his right hand in his bead bag, his lips moving softly, hardly anyone in Vṛndāvana knew him. But as an elderly, cultured Bengali gentleman, he did not seem an unusual sight; he was a religious *bābū* in a town devoted entirely to religion.

* * *

Abhay would regularly visit Vṛndāvana's important temples, and afterwards he would shop, returning to his room around eleven with vegetables for cooking. Using the kerosene burner and a three-tiered cooker, he would cook rice, potatoes, and sometimes *sabjī.* He would also cook *capātīs.* He would take only one meal a day, at noon, and in the evening a cup of milk. When he did not have time to cook, he would take the *prasādam* of the Deity. After lunch he would nap for fifteen minutes and then write. He rarely received visitors, but stayed alone, writing.

Just before sunset, he would again go out visiting temples. At Keśī-ghāṭa he would pass by *sādhus* sitting alone here and there, facing the Yamunā. The river itself was little trafficked, sometimes a boat or two slowly moving on the river's placidity. Sometimes a fish splashed in the water, or a bird winged along the river, watchful. Keśī-ghāṭa was quiet and beautiful, especially after the sun had relented for the day. *Sādhus* would hail Abhay on sight with Vṛndāvana's common greeting, "*Jaya* Rādhe!" and Abhay would return his "Hare Kṛṣṇa!"

When in the evening he walked through town, he would find himself amidst the vibrations of one *kīrtana* after another. In the temples of Kṛṣṇa, Rāma, Caitanya, Nṛsiṁha, or Śiva, in *āśrama* halls, in homes, even amongst groups walking on the streets, there would be *kīrtana:* Hare Kṛṣṇa, Hare Kṛṣṇa, Kṛṣṇa Kṛṣṇa, Hare Hare/ Hare Rāma, Hare Rāma, Rāma Rāma, Hare Hare. He would often see Bengali widows gathered together in a hall. Thousands of them lived in *āśramas* in Vṛndāvana, staying together with few wants, wearing dull white *sārīs,* keeping their hair cut short, never leaving Vṛndāvana even for Mathurā, wanting only to stay in Vṛndāvana, to die in Vṛndāvana chanting Hare Kṛṣṇa. A man would sit playing *mṛdaṅga* and leading a chant while a group of widows clapped their hands unevenly, responding in their childlike voices. The drum, the clapping, the singers—unpolished but earnest—made a sweet sound in the evening. As Abhay walked, no sooner would the sound of one *kīrtana* fade than another would rise loudly before him and then fade behind him as another rose to meet him, a temple bell ringing formidably, intermingling with the drums, cymbals, and chorus of another group or a single person passing nearby singing his own "Rādhe, Rādhe."

Even the greetings were *kīrtana:* "*Jaya* Rādhe!" "*Haribol*!" As faces passed, as carts clattered by, as men joked or made their last transaction of the day in the market, and as stray cows made their way home, their bells clanging around their necks, somehow everything was in connection with Kṛṣṇa. And as Abhay returned to the secluded Vaṁśīgopālajī temple, there also he would hear *kīrtanas,* only more private, perhaps only a husband and wife in their room, the man playing *mṛdaṅga* and singing one line of a *bhajana,* his wife singing in response. Vṛndāvana was not ordinary. Every singer sounded sweet, in his own way an expert melodist, and everyone sang of Kṛṣṇa. Kṛṣṇa was present in every occasion and event.

Śrīla Prabhupāda: *The glories of Kṛṣṇa nobody can understand. Similarly, Vṛndāvana. The land which is known as Vṛndāvana also has unlimited potency. When you go to Vṛndāvana, you will find unlimited potency of spiritual atmosphere, still. If you go to Vṛndāvana, you will see so many saints and sages—still they are worshiping Vṛndāvana-dhāma. As Lord Kṛṣṇa is worshipable, similarly His place, Vṛndāvana, is as good as Kṛṣṇa. It is also worshipable.*

* * *

Commuting became difficult. He would take the morning train into Delhi and, having nowhere to stay, return to Vṛndāvana the same night. That didn't give him much time in Delhi, and it was expensive. At first he had stayed with Mr. Gupta, a pious gentleman who studied the *Gītā* regularly and afforded *sādhus* a place to stay. Abhay had explained to Mr. Gupta about his *Back to Godhead* and his desires to preach in the West. It had been a good arrangement, and Abhay had kept to himself, writing. But in time another *sādhu* took the room.

Even with his minimal personal expenses, it was difficult to raise enough in donations to cover traveling, printing, and mailing. Giving copies of *Back to Godhead* away wasn't difficult, and he was doing that in Vṛndāvana. But working alone—writing, editing, selling, soliciting donations—was too much. The printer, Mr. Jain, was amazed, wondering why a person would put himself through such difficulties, printing a newspaper he couldn't afford.

Śrīla Prabhupāda: *I worked for* Back to Godhead *day and night. In the beginning, when I was a householder, I did not care if somebody paid or not paid. I used to distribute liberally. But when I left my household life and I was living alone, sometimes in Vṛndāvana and sometimes in Delhi, or sometimes traveling for pushing on BTG—they were very hard days.*

After his twelfth consecutive fortnightly edition, the issue for November 20, 1956, Abhay ran out of money. Mr. Jain had to throw up his hands, saying he couldn't print simply out of friendship. Abhay returned to Vṛndāvana, where he spent his time writing but with no plan for publication.

It was because people weren't interested in becoming Kṛṣṇa conscious—because they had "no time"—that *Back to Godhead* had failed financially. Certain *sādhus* in India were celebrated and influential, but Abhay was not amongst them. Of course, the uncompromising preaching he had learned from his spiritual master, the "chopping technique" in which he openly criticized revered politicians and holy men, was not likely to win him favor and patronage. "Don't flatter," Bhaktisiddhānta Sarasvatī had said. "Speak the truth. And if Kṛṣṇa is pleased, then you will come out successful. Money will come." And Abhay had firm faith in this.

That was his outstanding asset—his faith in his spiritual master. He was sure that by following Śrīla Bhaktisiddhānta Sarasvatī, he would receive his blessings and the blessings of Lord Caitanya. Although for the last two years he had followed any path that had opened as far as it had led, he had remained one-pointed, aimed at serving the order of Bhaktisiddhānta Sarasvatī. He was confident. Sooner or later he would obtain substantial backing, he would find a sympathetic audience, sincere workers would join him.

A letter came to Abhay in Vṛndāvana from his disciple, Ācārya Prabhākar Misra, and it gave Abhay an idea. Ācārya Prabhākar, who was in Bombay working as secretary of the Sanskrit Department at the Bharatiya Vidya Bhavan, invited Śrīla Bhaktivedanta Prabhu to join him there for preaching together, just as in the old days. The founder-director of the Bharatiya Vidya Bhavan was Governor K. M. Munshi (the same governor whose wife had pressured Abhay to give up the Radha Memorial in Jhansi). But Ācārya Prabhākar, having recently established a friendship with the governor, intimated to Abhay that the governor might be willing to help. Thus in January 1957, after assuring Mahant Gopal that he would return and that he would send five rupees a month for his room, Abhay traveled to Bombay.

Ācārya Prabhākar got Abhay quarters in the faculty residence and introduced him to various scholars and religionists. They then attended a lecture by Governor Munshi, "What Is Wrong With the World?" Afterwards, Abhay approached the governor, expressing his appreciation of the speech, but stressing that it would take a *spiritual* movement to avert the imminent global disasters. Without God consciousness, even Mr. Munshi's work in the Bharatiya Vidya Bhavan would be a waste of time. Abhay spoke of his interest in reviving the League of Devotees, and he suggested how he might work within the Bharatiya Vidya Bhavan to infuse the life of God consciousness into the governor's cultural projects. Governor Munshi responded by offering Abhay a post as Honorary Professor of *Bhagavad-gītā.* Abhay accepted and gave the governor some copies of *Back to Godhead,* requesting that he read them in his spare time.

As Honorary Professor of *Bhagavad-gītā,* Abhay began each class with Hare Kṛṣṇa *kīrtana* and then lectured on the *Gītā,* presenting Lord Kṛṣṇa as the Supreme Personality of Godhead, but he soon found his post confining. Within the Bharatiya Vidya Bhavan, he found little scope for reviving the League of Devotees.

Then, along with other members of the Bharatiya Vidya Bhavan, Abhay attended the fifth annual convention of the World Academy of Sanskrit at Kurukṣetra (where five thousand years before, Lord Kṛṣṇa had spoken *Bhagavad-gītā*). India's president, Dr. Rajendra Prasad; Governor Munshi; and many scholars and *paṇḍitas* from all over India participated in the discourses. But everyone there had his own thing to say, apart from the conclusions of Lord Kṛṣṇa, so Abhay considered the meeting a waste of time. Since he was not scheduled to speak, since the nondevotional discussions on the *Gītā* disturbed him, and since he saw that nothing practical would come of such a theoretical meeting, he left Kurukṣetra and returned to Vṛndāvana.

Ācārya Prabhākar soon joined Abhay. As they talked together in Abhay's room at Vaṁśī-gopālajī temple, Abhay spoke again of his desire to revive the League of Devotees. After having recently seen the watered-down cultural programs in Bombay and Kurukṣetra, he felt even more keenly the need for a society of pure devotees. There were already so many cultural and religious organizations; if he liked he could join one. But where was that organization with which he could affiliate himself wholeheartedly? Only the League of Devotees espoused the conclusions of Lord Caitanya and Bhaktisiddhānta Sarasvatī: vigorous, worldwide preaching of devotional service to Lord Kṛṣṇa, the Supreme Personality of Godhead.

Abhay drafted "An Appeal to the Generous Public, Modern Philosophers, Leaders, and Religionists" on behalf of the League of Devotees. The activities of the League, he stated, would be to publish *Back to Godhead* in English (with translations in many other languages), to educate young men and women for worldwide preaching, and to operate a press solely for printing transcendental literature. These programs would require an estimated three thousand rupees per month, and he appealed for help. Abhay concluded, "Vrindaban is the sacred place of topmost importance and the Headquarter of this League is therefore situated here." Using the impressive new titles, Honorary Professor of *Gītā,* Bharatiya Vidya Bhavan, and Honorary Ṣecretary of Hari Bhavan, Abhay, with the assistance of Ācārya Prabhākar, launched another attempt at rallying support for *Back to Godhead* and the League of Devotees.

Within a few days, Ācārya Prabhākar returned to his post in Bombay, and Abhay was again alone in Vṛndāvana. He loved Vṛndāvana, yet with no means to publish and preach, he was not content there. If he were to travel, he might be able to enlist members for the League. He thought of Kanpur, which was nearby, a city of more than one hundred big factories and many wealthy industrialists, some of whom he had met during his business travels. He decided to go. After printing some League of Devotee membership forms, he explained to Mahant Gopal that he would be away for a couple of months.

The Mahant was surprised. Although most elderly *sādhus* who came to Vṛndāvana stayed put and some even took vows never to leave, this quiet *bābū* was coming and going constantly.

* * *

Abhay preached actively in Kanpur, staying in various homes and canvassing for League members. As the guest of the Anandesvar Satsang Mandal, he lectured regularly at the popular Parmat bathing *ghāṭa* on the Ganges. He especially made acquaintances among industrialists and educators, often sitting and conversing with them for hours, and many were impressed by his dedication and his soft-spoken talks. But his collections were small. When he offered the wealthy magnates his "constitutional membership," they usually opted in favor of the two-rupees-a-year "subscriber membership." He collected a few letters of appreciation, but after two months he left.

After some months in Vṛndāvana, Abhay decided to go back to Bombay and preach. In Bombay, he quickly broke off his association with the stifling Bharatiya Vidya Bhavan and moved out of the faculty residence there. Staying a week at a time in the homes of various patrons, he tried to generate interest in his missionary activities. When a friend of Ācārya Prabhākar's arranged for Abhay to address Sunday-evening crowds at a Bombay beach, Abhay accepted. Following already established custom, he sat on a cushion, and the people gathered—from five hundred to a thousand, sitting and listening—as he loudly spoke the philosophy of *Bhagavad-gītā*. Abhay spoke for several nights. And there were other lecture opportunities also. One week he spoke several times at a Bombay Viṣṇu temple.

But Abhay wanted to do more than deliver occasional lectures to uncommitted audiences. The conviction was growing within him that he should preach outside India. The idea, of course, had been there for some time. He had expressed it in his prospectus for the League of Devotees, before gatherings at the Radha Memorial in Jhansi, during his meeting at the Birla Mandir in Delhi, and on many other occasions. Informally he had expressed it hundreds of times to acquaintances. And he had woven his dream throughout his writings.

He was ready to travel anywhere if he could fulfill Śrīla Bhaktisiddhānta Sarasvatī's order to preach in English. In India the English-speaking population was small, so Abhay continued to dream of going to the West. If he could travel to Bombay, Delhi, and Kanpur, why not to London or New York, where millions spoke English and had never heard the message of Lord Caitanya? Writing to Mr. Ved Prakash, a Kanpur industrialist, Abhay explained his idea.

> Lord Chaitanya said "praninam upakaraya"; i.e. to say, for the benefit of all living being concerned ... . While rendering first aid service in the battlefield the Red Cross men, although equally disposed to all the wounded soldiers, they give first preference to the hopeful ones. *The hopeless ones are sometimes neglected.* ...
>
> In India, even after the attainment of Swaraj, the mentality is predominent by "*Made in London*" ideas. It is a long story. But in nutshell the Leaders of India in the name of secular government they have engaged themselves in everything foreign. They have carefully set aside the treasure house of India's spiritual asset and they are imitating the western material way of life, constantly engaged in the acts of error of judgment, misgivings, imperfectness, and duplicity.
>
> India's Vedic knowledge is above all the conditional defects mentioned above. But we Indians at the present moment have neglected such wonderful Vedic knowledge. It is due to its improper handling. ...
>
> This Vedanta-sutra is [presented in India] by *unauthorized persons* of different camps and as such the people are being misguided. Newly sprung up national enthusiasm of the Indian leaders, industrialists, and planmakers, have no time nor the desire to understand the message of Vedanta-sutra or even the Bhagavad-Gita. You cannot do acts of humanity without proper guidance. ...
>
> So my idea of preaching in the foreign countries means that they are rather fed up with material advancement of knowledge. They're seeking the message guidance of the Vedanta-sutra or for the matter of the Bhagavad-Gita in an authentic way. And I am sure India will again go back to the spiritual life when the principle is accepted by the Europeans, Americans etc. because the Indian people are now in the habit of begging, after neglecting their own property. That was my view point. But all the same we must take only the opportunity of service.

One way of expanding his way of preaching was to mail copies of *Back to Godhead* outside India. And as an incentive for enlisting donors, he made it known that the donor's name would be printed on each copy. His ambition was to bring in large donations, run large printings, and send *Back to Godhead* to more than fifty countries. He assigned quotas: America would receive ten thousand copies, Argentina five hundred, Belgium five hundred, Brazil five hundred, Burma one thousand, Canada five hundred, Chile five hundred, China ten thousand, and so on, including ten thousand for Russia and ten thousand for England. But the donors and donations never appeared, and the plans for *Back to Godhead* were never realized.

Abhay found that while the people of India's educated, cultured class were rejecting their own spiritual culture, the religiously inclined masses were being baffled by an array of conflicting, unauthorized doctrines presented in the name of Hinduism. An alarming example of this came to his attention as he was preaching in Bombay during the summer of 1958. "Bhagwat Week" was being publicized by a group whose teachings conflicted with the pure *paramparā* presentation of the *Bhāgavata*. The *Bhāgavata, Śrīmad-Bhāgavatam,* was the devotional scripture par excellence, the literary incarnation of Kṛṣṇa, yet the organizers of Bhagwat Week were using *Śrīmad-Bhāgavatam* to teach impersonalism and minimize Lord Kṛṣṇa. Through friends, Abhay learned of the outrageous meetings, and finally, on July 28, 1958, he wrote to the Bhagwat Week leader, Sri Ratanshi, imploring him to stay away from *Śrīmad-Bhāgavatam.*

> I beg to inform you that I am in receipt of your invitation letter in the matter of observing Bhagwat week through the secretary of Bombay spiritual Centre. As I know what sort of Bhagwat week can be observed by the Mayavadins for misleading the innocent public and therefore I not only restrained myself from attending the function but also I advised many others not to attend, for the very reason that the recitation of the holy Bhagwat is being performed by men who have no access in this great scripture, in which only the liberated persons, who are freed from all pretentious religiousities, can take part. ... Some friends who attended your Bhagwat week have told me how the pastimes of Lord Krishna [were] being wrongly interpreted in your organisation on the pretext of saving Krishna from being an immoral personality. To save these foolish audiences in future, Maharaj Parikshit had already asked Sripad Sukhdeva Goswami to clear the Rasaleela activities of Lord Shri Krishna. The transcendental nature of Rasaleela does not require to be apologised by any Mayavadi or mundane moralist. The Leela is what it is.
>
> In the sloka No. 30 it is forbidden that a mundane person should indulge in hearing Rasaleela or ... should hear Rasaleela from a mundane person. In

> your organisation both the audience and the lecturer are mundane persons and their indulgence in the matter of Rasaleela out of sheer foolishness will result in imitating Rudra, who swallowed up an ocean of poison.

Abhay warned that legal action could be taken against such a religious fraud. But Bhagwat Week continued, and hundreds were cheated.

While the professed followers of Vedic culture were being baffled in their allegiance, modern Westernized Indians were rejecting Vedic culture as backwards and irrelevant. There was Prime Minister Nehru, who wasn't at all spiritually inclined; he was for modernization and for what Abhay called "Made in London" ideas. At least Mahatma Gandhi, although he had never responded to Abhay's letters, had been spiritually inclined. But not so his follower, Pandit Nehru. Still, out of concern for the way India's leaders were rejecting their country's spiritual heritage, Abhay decided to write Pandit Nehru.

Although in Bombay Abhay was practically homeless, in August of 1958 he boldly wrote the prime minister, expressing his conviction that India's spiritual culture must not only be revived at home, but also be distributed to the West. He reminded Pandit Nehru that from ancient Greece down to the atomic age the Western world had seen only materialism and had therefore never known peace. If Nehru were to continue following the path of materialism, the only results would be strife and war.

> Therefore, India may not waste her time in imitating the western way of life. You have admitted it that the position of Indian culture is of high order, but at the same time you want to bring in material prosperity by scientific advancement of knowledge. But what is that scientific knowledge? Spiritualism is also advanced scientific knowledge. Material advancement of scientific knowledge cannot give even material prosperity to the people in general. Do you think that horseless carriage, or telephonic or radio communication or any other such ephemeral facilities of life can bring in material prosperity? No it cannot. Material prosperity means the people must have sufficient to eat or to maintain the body very soundly. Do you think that your different plans have brought in that material prosperity or that modern western civilisation can bring in that prosperity? Even they are given that facility, the unrest will continue to go on till there is spiritual satisfaction of life. That is the secret of peace.

Even without having been to the West, Abhay expressed his conviction that the Americans and even the Russians were hankering for spiritual realization; they could not have become satisfied merely with material advancement. Pandit Nehru, therefore, should help his friends in the West by offering them spiritual knowledge from India.

> Poverty means poverty of knowledge. Prime Minister Chanakya used to live in a thatched cottage but he was the dictator of India during the time of Chandra Gupta. Mahatma Gandhi voluntarily accepted the way of living of the so-called poor man and was the dictator of Indian destiny. But was he poverty stricken? He was proud of his spiritual knowledge. Therefore spiritual knowledge makes a man really rich man and not the radio set or the motorcar etc.

Back in the 1930s the Nehru family had bought their medicines from Abhay's Prayag Pharmacy, and Abhay now appealed to Pandit Nehru as an old friend from Allahabad. Just as Abhay had requested Mahatma Gandhi, he requested Nehru to leave his political responsibilities "and as a popular gentleman of the world, engage the rest of your life in this organised spiritual movement to make a real adjustment of western material science combined with Indian way of spiritual realisation." As with his letter to Gandhi, his letter to Nehru went unanswered.

Among Abhay's former Bombay contacts was Mr. Harbanslal, a landlord who had once assured Abhay that he would provide him lodging whenever he needed. In the summer of 1958 Abhay went to call on Mr. Harbanslal, only to find that he had gone to the West. When Abhay learned that Mr. Harbanslal was traveling not only on business but on a cultural mission, his imagination seized on the idea of an Indian on a cultural mission in the West. He wrote to Mr. Harbanslal, asking for a place to stay, but also presenting his own cultural mission. Abhay knew that many Westerners respected Indian culture. He had heard from his German Godbrother that although Indians who went to the West, especially to Germany, were well received, they were sometimes tested on their knowledge of Indian culture. So Abhay advised Mr. Harbanslal to teach the real conclusion of Indian culture as he traveled.

> I think that people need this Indian message in this hour of necessity when the atomic bomb is hovering over the head of the human society.
>
> ... Please therefore begin the activities for the benefit of all people in the foreign countries since you have gone there.

Clearly, Abhay would have liked to have gone himself.

Abhay also reminded Mr. Harbanslal of his promise to provide him with an apartment: "... I am passing my days in Bombay in great inconvenience for want of a suitable residential place." But the letter never caught up with the touring Mr. Harbanslal.

Wanting to go to the West as soon as possible, Abhay visited one of his Godbrothers in Bombay, Kṛpāsindhu, and asked him to help.

Kṛpāsindhu: *He came to my house and asked me to help him in going to America. He gave me some* Back to Godheads *which he said I could show to people to ask for help on his behalf. I tried to do something in this regard. I introduced Abhay Bābū to one man, a big industrialist, Hemraj Khandelwala. I went also. The three of us sat down, and I told the man how Abhay wanted to go to the West and how he was a good devotee and was writing and doing so many things. But somehow or other the man did not help.*

Kṛpāsindhu told Abhay of how the Gaudiya Math in Bombay had sometimes been assisted by a pious business magnate, Mrs. Sumati Morarji, head of Scindia Steamship Lines. Abhay tried to see her but was unable. He did, however, see one of Mrs. Morarji's employees, a deputy manager for the Scindia Company, who heard him out and, to Abhay's surprise, responded generously. Considering Abhay a genuine *sādhu,* the Scindia agent offered him a fifty-percent concession on a voyage from India to the United States. He even put it in writing. Abhay immediately began arranging for his passport and visa. But he could not raise even the half fare.

Back in 1956 in Delhi he had been struggling and homeless. And now, as he considered his last two years of traveling out of Vṛndāvana, he felt that his position hadn't really improved; perhaps Kṛṣṇa didn't want him to succeed in this way. But one positive thing he had gained: determination to go to the West and preach. There he would surely meet with success.

* * *

Alone and poor, Abhay returned to Vṛndāvana. He was sixty-two, but he wasn't thinking of retiring. More than ever, his mood was reflective and renounced. Because few people knew him and because he wanted to write, he kept to himself.

He enjoyed deep peace as a resident of Vṛndāvana. Outside his window, the sacred Yamunā flowed by in a peaceful panorama for his private audience. The Keśī-ghāṭa neighborhood was quiet, though in the predawn he could hear a few devotees bathing and chanting. When the moon was full, the river seemed like a coolly resplendent jewel. And in the morning the sun would appear, like a red smudge, a fire burning through an opaque wall, at last bursting forth and clearing the entire sky, until in the hot blaze of noon, while the room would be in shadows, Abhay could see from his window a shimmering sun high in the sky and glittering across the silver sheet of the gentle river. Without so much as leaving his room, from his doorway he could see hundreds of temples clustered together for miles in the friendly town of Vṛndāvana. The various punctual *kīrtanas* and bell-ringings in the temples, the spontaneous songs to Lord Kṛṣṇa in numerous homes and in the streets rose and filled the air with devotion.

On the veranda Abhay could chant *japa,* and there would be no interruption. He enjoyed a simple, almost carefree life of minimized physical wants—a few hours of rest at night, a little *prasādam* at noon, the simplest clothing. And he did not have to flatter anyone, support anyone, or manage anyone's life. His mind and intelligence were free and dwelt constantly on his service to his spiritual master. He saw his present circumstances as a preparation for a greater task before him. Despite his advanced age, he felt that he had barely begun his work. Yet he felt confident. He had his vision of a world association of devotees. It was not an idle dream, although he was not certain how it would all come about. But he knew his duty. For the present he would go on describing his vision, the vision of his predecessor spiritual masters, in articles and books. But as soon as possible he should go to the West. Westerners, he had concluded, were not satisfied with a materially comfortable life devoid of spiritual understanding; more than his fellow Indians, they would be open to the message of the Absolute Truth. He knew he should go. And he would go—if Kṛṣṇa desired.

Abhay lived frugally in Vṛndāvana, keeping exact account of every expenditure and every receipt. He carefully kept a ledger, just as if he were running a substantial business, even though his purchases were only a little milk, a few vegetables, charcoal for cooking, bus rides, and his major expenditure, postage.

*   *   *

Abhay composed a Bengali poem, "Vṛndāvana-bhajana." Its opening stanzas were especially self-reflective and personal.

1

I am sitting alone in Vṛndāvana-dhāma.
In this mood I am getting many realizations.

I have my wife, sons, daughters, grandsons, everything,
But I have no money, so they are a fruitless glory.
Kṛṣṇa has shown me the naked form of material nature;
By His strength it has all become tasteless to me today.
Yasyāham anugṛhṇāmi hariṣye tad-dhanaṁ śanaiḥ:
"I gradually take away all the wealth of those upon whom I am merciful."
How was I able to understand this mercy of the all-merciful?

2

Everyone has abandoned me, seeing me penniless—
Wife, relatives, friends, brothers, everyone.
This is misery, but it gives me a laugh. I sit alone and laugh.
In this *māyā-saṁsāra,* whom do I really love?
Where have my loving father and mother gone now?
And where are all my elders, who were my own folk?
Who will give me news of them, tell me who?
All that is left of this family life is a list of names.

3

As the froth on the seawater mixes again in the sea,
Māyā-saṁsāra's play is just like that.
No one is mother or father, or personal relative;
Just like the sea foam, they remain but a short time.
Just as the froth on seawater mixes again in the sea,
The body made of five elements meets with destruction.
How many bodies does the embodied soul take in this way?
His relatives are all related merely to the temporal body.

4

But everyone is your relative, brother, on the spiritual platform.
This relationship is not tinged with the smell of Māyā.
The Supreme Lord is the soul of everyone.
In relation to Him, everyone in the universe is the same.

All your relatives, brother! All the billions of *jīvas.*
When seen in relation to Kṛṣṇa they are all in harmony.
Forgetting Kṛṣṇa, the *jīva* desires sense gratification,
And as a result he is firmly grasped by Māyā. ...

* * *

On an October visit to Delhi, Abhay received a donation from Kaviraj Baidya Nath Sircar, to be used for printing one thousand copies of *Back to Godhead.* Abhay promptly produced an October 20 issue of *Back to Godhead* with the donor's name on the front page. It was the first issue in two years. Another donor, Mr. Subodh Kumar Kapoor of Ramalal Kapoor and Sons, followed Mr. Sircar's example and donated one thousand copies for the November 20 issue.

The front-page article in the November issue was "Truth and Beauty." An editorial in *The Times of India,* speculating on whether truth and beauty were compatible, had opined that truth was not always beautiful but often ugly and unpleasant. Abhay disagreed: "Truth is so beautiful that many sages, saints, and devotees have left everything for the sake of Truth. ... but we are habituated to love untruth from time immemorial in the name of truth." Abhay agreed, however, that mundane truth and beauty were incompatible. Not only was mundane truth not beautiful; it was not truth. And mundane beauty was not real beauty. To explain, Abhay told a story.

Once a man fell in love with a beautiful girl, who tried to resist the man's advances. When he persisted, she requested that he wait for seven days, after which she would accept him. During the next seven days, the girl took a strong purgative and laxative and repeatedly passed stool and vomited. She stored the refuse in buckets. Thus "the so-called beautiful girl became lean, thin like a skeleton and turned blackish in complexion and the beautiful eye balls were pushed into the sockets of the skull."

> The man appeared on the scene well dressed and well behaved and asked the waiting girl, who was depressed in appearance, about the beautiful girl who called him there. The man could not recognise the waiting girl as the same beautiful girl whom he was asking for. The same girl however was in a pitiable condition and the foolish man in spite of repeated assertion could not recognise her. It was all due to the action of the medicine only.
>
> At last the girl told the powerful man all the story of her beauty and told him that she had separated the ingredients of her beauty and stored them up

> in the reservoirs. She also told him that he could enjoy the juices of beauty stored up in the reservoirs. The mundane poetic or the lunatic man agreed to see the juices of beauty and thus he was directed to the store of loose stool and liquid vomit which were emanating unbearable bad smell and thus the whole story of beauty liquid was disclosed to him.

Abhay went on to assert that literature which did not describe the ultimate truth and beauty of the Supreme Person was no better than stool and vomit, even though it be presented as poetry and philosophy.

In "Standard Morality," Abhay explained, "Morality is the standard of activity by which the Supreme Authority is satisfied." The scriptures contain moral codes prohibiting unholy sex relations, animal slaughter, intoxication, and gambling. Abhay attributed Mahatma Gandhi's success as a public leader to his observance of these moral principles. Abhay also praised the Vedic system of marriage: "after the attainment of puberty a woman wants a male, and if she is not married within that time and allowed to mix up with boys, ... it is quite natural that there is every chance of fall down either by the boy or the girl." Despite changing social conditions, Abhay argued, "You cannot indulge in unholy connection with the opposite sex [just] because the social conditions have changed. Because unholy connection with woman is the beginning of all immorality."

In "Scholars Deluded," Abhay presented a critical review of Dr. Radhakrishnan's edition of *Bhagavad-gītā,* citing specifically the thirty-fourth verse of the Ninth Chapter, wherein Lord Kṛṣṇa declares that one should always think of Him and become His devotee. Dr. Radhakrishnan had commented, "It is not the personal Krishna to whom we have to give ourselves up utterly, but the unborn, beginningless eternal who speaks through Krishna." Although the obvious meaning of *Bhagavad-gītā* was that one should surrender to Kṛṣṇa, the Supreme Person, impersonalists like Dr. Radhakrishnan obscured the direct meaning with their word jugglery.

* * *

On the disappearance day of Śrīla Bhaktisiddhānta Sarasvatī, Abhay keenly felt separation from his spiritual master. He perfectly understood that Śrīla Bhaktisiddhānta's instructions were more important than his physical presence and that, in fact, the spiritual master was present within his instructions; in this way, Abhay had always been with his spiritual master. Yet on this annual day, Abhay could not help feeling loss. He remembered how in 1932 he had been a *gṛhastha* and a new disciple. At that time he had not been free to do as much service as now. Yet it had been in those years that he had been able to see his spiritual master, offer obeisances before him, eat the remnants of his *prasādam,* walk beside him, hear his voice, receive his personal glance. Abhay thought of their meetings together.

How powerful had been Śrīla Bhaktisiddhānta's mission! His presses had been running day and night, printing magazines, books, the daily *Nadiyā Prakāśa.* And Europe had been a promising new preaching field. With Śrīla Bhaktisiddhānta Sarasvatī Ṭhākura at the helm, the Gaudiya Math had entered into battle against *māyā's* forces, and Śrīla Bhaktisiddhānta had made all his disciples unafraid. Abhay had always been eager to serve his spiritual master, to serve within the Gaudiya Math with its headquarters in Calcutta. But exactly how he would serve had never been clear to him until his last letter from Śrīla Bhaktisiddhānta Sarasvatī.

Abhay looked back on the more than twenty years since his spiritual master's disappearance. The Gaudiya Math had been undone by its leaders, and everyone else had scattered like leaves in a storm. It was an unspeakable loss. And it was an old story—how the big *sannyāsīs* had disregarded their spiritual master's instructions and had intrigued, disputed, litigated. Violent party factions, false leaders claiming to be world *ācārya*—and which party had been right? No, both had been wrong, all wrong, because the Gaudiya Math had disintegrated. Now there were dozens of little *maṭhas* and no preaching, no real preaching as before, when he, Siṁha-guru, had cast fear into the Māyāvādīs, had led an army of young, powerful preachers to march throughout India and the world. And the greatest sufferers of the Gaudiya Math's dissolution were the people, the nondevotees, who had little hope of being delivered from the batterings of *māyā.* Śrīla Bhaktisiddhānta Sarasvatī had begun a spiritual revolution, but that revolution had now been overthrown by *māyā.* The scattered particles of the Gaudiya Math had settled quietly into self-satisfied, insular, almost impotent units. And it was the people in general who suffered.

Abhay groped after memories of his spiritual master. He felt secure in that his own relationship with Śrīla Bhaktisiddhānta Sarasvatī was intact, continuing. Yet he felt helpless. He was diligently pursuing his spiritual master's order to preach in English, yet without his spiritual master's physical presence he felt small and very much alone. At times like this, he questioned the wisdom of having left his family and business.

Lamenting Śrīla Bhaktisiddhānta's absence and the fall of the Gaudiya Math, he composed a Bengali poem, "Viraha-aṣṭaka."

> Śrīla Prabhupāda, you are always compassionate towards the suffering *jīva* souls.
> On this occasion of your separation, I see only dejection.
>
> An unlimited ocean of mercy, cutting an illusion, Nityānanda distributed an ocean of flood of love of God.
>
> The *jāti-gosāi* stopped the stream,
> But coming yourself, Lord, you revealed this illusion.
>
> So once again everyone was immersed in the flood of love,
> Even one so fallen, insignificant, and sinful as I.
>
> On the strength of Lord Caitanya's order
> You sent all of your servants door to door as *gurus.*
>
> There was preaching everywhere, from the sea to the Himalayas.
> Now, in your absence, everything is darkness.
>
> O Śrīla Prabhupāda, you are always compassionate towards the suffering *jīva* souls.
> On this occasion of your separation, I see only dejection.
>
> In the same way that Advaita Prabhu brought Lord Gaura,
> so did Bhaktivinoda pray.
>
> His enthusiasm brought you; on the strength of his enthusiasm you came
> And made everyone understand that India is a holy land.
>
> One who takes his birth in the land of Bhārata
> Must make his life perfect and then preach to others.

This *mahā-mantra* message you preached everywhere.
Now in your absence, Lord, everything is darkness.

Your ocean of compassion has again been stopped.
This spear of great misery has cut through my heart.

Without Lord Caitanya's message, there is just confusion.
Seeing this, all the Vaiṣṇavas feel pangs of separation.

The conditioned souls are all in darkness once again.
They are searching for peace, but are dying in an ocean of anxiety.

O Śrīla Prabhupāda, you are always compassionate towards the suffering *jīva* souls.
On this occasion of your separation, I see only dejection. ...

Abhay's was a dark view. The golden era of preaching that had flourished in the days of Śrīla Bhaktisiddhānta Sarasvatī was no longer. "By the influence of *māyā*," Abhay wrote, "now everything is darkness ... All devotional instructions have been destroyed. ... now everything has been reversed." Meditating on that great personality possessed of the divine power to save the entire world, Abhay expressed his feelings of weakness and helplessness: "Because of those not fixed in devotional service, many branches have spread all over ... Your conclusive message did not touch the ear/ Where will I get the strength for the *saṅkīrtana* movement?" How could he, a tiny spiritual child, survive without his spiritual father? Now who could save the world, which was so much more oppressed than ever before?

Śrīla Bhaktisiddhānta had said that a dead man could not preach; only one with life could preach. As long as Abhay and others could deeply regret the Gaudiya Math's failure, there was still life and still hope: "If everyone obtained this right and went out and made disciples, / Then the suffering souls in the world could be saved." It was useless to cry over what his Godbrothers had done, yet in seeing and resenting it, Abhay found, within the pain of what might have been, a continuing spark of what still might be.

Abhay sent this poem and "Vṛndāvana-bhajana" to Keśava Mahārāja, who published them in the *Gauḍīya Patrikā*.

* * *

One night Abhay had a striking dream, the same dream he had had several times before, during his days as a householder. Śrīla Bhaktisiddhānta Sarasvatī appeared, just as Abhay had known him, the tall, scholarly *sannyāsī*, coming directly from the spiritual world, from Kṛṣṇa's personal entourage. He called to Abhay and indicated that he should follow. Repeatedly he called and motioned. He was asking Abhay to take *sannyāsa*. Come, he urged, become a *sannyāsī*.

Abhay awoke in a state of wonder. He thought of this instruction as another feature of the original instruction Śrīla Bhaktisiddhānta Sarasvatī had given him at their first meeting in Calcutta, the same instruction that his spiritual master had later solidified in a letter: become an English preacher and spread Kṛṣṇa consciousness throughout the Western world. *Sannyāsa* was for that end; otherwise, why would his spiritual master have asked him to accept it? Abhay reasoned that his spiritual master was saying, "Now take *sannyāsa* and you will actually be able to accomplish this mission. Formerly the time was not right."

Abhay deliberated cautiously. By accepting *sannyāsa,* a Vaiṣṇava dedicates his body, mind, and words totally to the service of the Supreme Personality of Godhead, renouncing all other engagements. He was doing that already. Śrīla Bhaktisiddhānta Sarasvatī had offered *sannyāsa* to his leading disciples so that they could continue his mission; they hadn't done it. Preaching in the West had proved perilous even for the Gaudiya Math's most recognized *sannyāsīs*. How could he, a mere householder, presume he could succeed where the others had failed? He was hesitant. The helpless, incapable feeling he had expressed in his "Viraha-aṣṭaka" was there. But now his spiritual master was beckoning him—over all other considerations, even over natural humility. Now, although he was elderly and alone, the desire to preach just as his spiritual master had preached remained within him, a fierce though sometimes quietly expressed determination.

The Vedic standard and the example set by the previous *ācāryas* was that if one wanted to lead a preaching movement, *sannyāsa* was required. Śrīla Bhaktisiddhānta had taken *sannyāsa* to facilitate his missionary work. Lord Caitanya had taken *sannyāsa* to further the *saṅkīrtana* movement. Of course, Lord Caitanya was the Supreme Personality of Godhead, but when His young students had been disrespectful towards Him, treating Him as an ordinary man, He had taken *sannyāsa*. Because a *sannyāsī* is automatically respected, Lord Caitanya's acceptance of *sannyāsa* was a calculated tactic; as soon as He began traveling throughout India as a *sannyāsī,* He immediately attracted thousands of followers to the *saṅkīrtana* movement.

Knowing that many cheaters would accept the saffron dress and abuse the respect given to *sannyāsīs,* Lord Caitanya had advised against accepting *sannyāsa* in the Age of Kali. He knew that cheaters, in the guise of *sādhus,* would act immorally, accumulate funds for their own sense gratification, and make many followers simply to enhance their own prestige. Posing as swamis, they would cheat the public. Because the people in Kali-yuga are unable to follow the rules and regulations of *sannyāsa,* Lord Caitanya had recommended that they simply chant Hare Kṛṣṇa. However, if a person could actually follow the rules, and especially if he had to spread the *saṅkīrtana* movement, *sannyāsa* was necessary.

Abhay first had to approach one of his Godbrothers for permission. He decided to turn to Bhaktivilāsa Tīrtha Mahārāja (formerly Kuñjavihārī), the leader of the Chaitanya Math in Calcutta. Abhay still thought of the Chaitanya Math as the headquarters of his spiritual master's mission. During the heated legal disputes, the Chaitanya Math had been the most prized acquisition, and since 1948 it had been under the legal ownership of Bhaktivilāsa Tīrtha Mahārāja. Now, although each *sannyāsī* had his own place or places, the Chaitanya Math and Bhaktivilāsa Tīrtha Mahārāja legally represented the Gaudiya Math entity. Abhay felt that if he were to take *sannyāsa* and go preach in America, he should give the Chaitanya Math the first opportunity to support his work. In April 1959, Abhay wrote to Tīrtha Mahārāja, inquiring about *sannyāsa* and the Chaitanya Math's printing some of his manuscripts. And since no one was going abroad, he volunteered to do so on behalf of the Chaitanya Math.

Bhaktivilāsa Tīrtha Mahārāja replied that Abhay should first join the Chaitanya Math. He mentioned the strife that still lingered: "Those who are acting against Chaitanya Math, they are motivated by their individual ambitions." Anyone who was against the Chaitanya Math, he said, was acting illogically and against the instructions of Bhaktisiddhānta Sarasvatī. So according to Tīrtha Mahārāja, the thing for Abhay to do, the thing he had neglected to do for so many years, was to join the Chaitanya Math and act under his direction. Tīrtha Mahārāja mentioned several members of the Chaitanya Math who had recently accepted the *sannyāsa* order, and he said that Abhay could also become one—in time. He invited Abhay to come reside at the Chaitanya Math: "The houses that we have, there are rooms that are airy and well lit. We will treat you exclusively. There won't be any difficulty. We will take care that no inconveniences are caused." But as for printing books:

> We are eagerly awaiting to print the books like Satsandarbha, Vedanta, based on devotional service, and many other rare books by the goswamis. First we will print them. Books written by you will be checked by the editorial staff, and if the funds can be raised, then they can be printed according to priority. The books will be printed only if they are favorable for the service of the Caitanya Math. Therefore, if the fund is raised, then there is a plan to go abroad as well.

Abhay was not encouraged. The main difficulty, he felt, was the Chaitanya Math's shortage of funds.

Śrīla Prabhupāda: *I was working with my broken typewriter. I went to our Tīrtha Mahārāja: "You give me a room and print my books. Give me some money. I will join you." I had thought, "This is Guru Mahārāja's institution." He did not say no, but the printing of books was a difficult task for him. He had no money. He was hardly collecting for maintaining. Printing of books is a big job, and there is no guarantee of sale.*

Without printing books and going to the West, *sannyāsa* did not have meaning for Abhay. And who knew when Tīrtha Mahārāja would sanction his taking *sannyāsa*? There was no point in going to Calcutta just to reside in an airy, well-lit room; that he had already in Vṛndāvana. Abhay wrote back to Tīrtha Mahārāja, mentioning his direct order from Śrīla Bhaktisiddhānta Sarasvatī to preach to the English-speaking people. He wanted to go to the West right away, and he had thought the Chaitanya Math would welcome his offer. Both Abhay and Tīrtha Mahārāja had their responsibilities, but perhaps they could work together to carry out the desire of their spiritual master. Abhay asked Tīrtha Mahārāja to reconsider. On May 7, 1959, Bhaktivilāsa Tīrtha Mahārāja wrote back.

> My suggestion is don't make any hasty decisions. For the time being you stay with us and engage yourself in the service of the society and then accept tridanda [*sannyāsa*]. The purpose of accepting tridanda is to serve the society.
>
> If that is your desire then Sri Caitanya Math will decide about your going to America to preach and make all the arrangements. It can never be the principle of the society to let one act according to his individual attempt or

> desire. The society will decide after consulting with the heads what is to be done by whom. This is what I want to say. First of all, it is necessary to identify oneself with the society.
>
> In order to preach in America or in other foreign countries, it is important to have a dignified organization in the background and secondly it is necessary to establish one's self in India before going to preach in the foreign countries.
>
> Now it is that there are no conferences or meetings in the West as before. Communication is done through the media of television.

Abhay could understand the needs and priorities of the Chaitanya Math, but he could not allow them to overrule what he considered the highest mandate: preaching as Śrīla Bhaktisiddhānta Sarasvatī had ordered. Abhay had offered his services to the leaders of the Chaitanya Math, thinking they might also see things his way. He thought that with the world's crying need for Kṛṣṇa consciousness staring them in the face, they might see that this Abhay Bābū was convinced and enthusiastic and so should be sent right away with whatever he required. But they had other priorities.

Abhay next turned to Keśava Mahārāja in Mathurā, and Keśava Mahārāja told Abhay to take *sannyāsa* immediately. After corresponding with Tīrtha Mahārāja, Abhay had felt some uncertainty about accepting *sannyāsa,* and now that he was being encouraged so strongly, he resisted. But Keśava Mahārāja was insistent.

Śrīla Prabhupāda: *I was sitting alone in Vṛndāvana, writing. My Godbrother insisted to me, "Bhaktivedanta Prabhu, you must do it. Without accepting the renounced order of life, nobody can become a preacher." So he insisted. Not* he *insisted; practically my spiritual master insisted. He wanted me to become a preacher, so he forced me through this Godbrother: "You accept." So, unwillingly I accepted.*

* * *

Keśavajī Gaudiya Math was located in the midst of one of Mathurā's downtown bazaars. Its main entrance, an arched doorway, led into a courtyard, open to the sky through a metal grating above. The architecture was similar to that of the Vaṁśī-gopālajī temple. The atmosphere was secluded, as in a monastery. Abhay was a familiar, welcomed figure here. He had lived here, written and studied in the library here, edited the *Gauḍīya Patrikā,* and donated the Deity of Lord Caitanya who stood on the altar beside the Deities of Rādhā and Kṛṣṇa (Śrī Śrī Rādhā Vinoda-vihārījī). But his visit during September of 1959 was not an ordinary one. He entered the *maṭha* dressed in white, Abhay Bābū, but he would soon be leaving dressed in saffron, a swami.

Abhay had been living as a renunciant for nine years; there was no need for him to observe a ceremony or to proclaim himself a *sādhu* by changing to saffron dress. But it was the *paramparā* system that a man take *tridaṇḍi-sannyāsa* at the end of his life. He was aware of the cheating *sannyāsīs;* even in Vṛndāvana he had seen so-called *sādhus* who did not preach but simply spent their days hunting for *capātīs.* Some "swamis" of Vṛndāvana even indulged illicitly in what they had supposedly come here to reject: sex life. Such persons were making a mockery of *sannyāsa.* And there were the caste *gosvāmīs* also, who lived like ordinary householders, running temples as a business to support their families and accepting honor and donations from the public on the false basis of birth. Abhay knew of these abuses of *sannyāsa,* but he also knew the real purpose of *sannyāsa. Sannyāsa* was for preaching.

On the morning of September 17, 1959, in the fifty-by-twenty-five-foot Deity room on the second floor of the Keśavajī Math, a group of devotees sat before the Deities of Rādhā-Kṛṣṇa and Lord Caitanya. The Deities were colorfully dressed in royal clothing and silver crowns. Rādhārāṇī's right hand faced palm-forward in benediction for the worshiper; at Her side, Her left hand held a flower for Kṛṣṇa. Kṛṣṇa stood like a dancer, placing His right leg in a casual tiptoe pose before His left, playing His long silver flute, which He held gracefully to His red lips. His long black hair reached down past His shoulders, and the garland of marigolds around His neck reached down to His knees. On His right stood the Deity of Lord Caitanya, His right arm raised, left arm at His side, His body straight, feet together. He was a soft golden color, and He had large eyes, a well-formed red mouth, and straight black hair down to His shoulders. One level below the Deities were pictures of the spiritual masters in disciplic succession: Jagannātha dāsa Bābājī, Bhaktivinoda Ṭhākura, Gaurakiśora dāsa Bābājī, Bhaktisiddhānta Sarasvatī, Bhaktiprajñāna Keśava Mahārāja.

Abhay sat on a mat of *kuśa* grass beside ninety-year-old Sanātana, also to receive *sannyāsa* that day. Sitting opposite the two candidates, Nārāyaṇa Mahārāja, Keśava Mahārāja's disciple, prepared to conduct the ceremony of *mantras* and offerings of grains and ghee into the fire.

Akiñcana Kṛṣṇadāsa Bābājī, Abhay's Godbrother, known for sweet singing, played *mṛdaṅga* and sang Vaiṣṇava *bhajanas.* Sitting on a raised *āsana,* His Holiness Keśava Mahārāja presided. Since there had been no notices or invitations, only the *maṭha's* few residents attended.

Nārāyaṇa Mahārāja chanted the required *mantras* and then sat back silently while Keśava Mahārāja lectured. Then, to everyone's surprise, Keśava Mahārāja asked Abhay to speak. Abhay had not expected this. As he looked around at the gathering of devotees, he understood that the common language was Hindi; only Keśava Mahārāja and a few others spoke English. Yet he knew he must speak in English.

After Abhay's speech, each initiate received his *sannyāsa-daṇḍa,* the traditional head-high staff made of four bamboo rods bound together and completely enwrapped in saffron cloth. They were given their *sannyāsa* garments: one piece of saffron cloth for a *dhotī,* one for a top piece, and two strips for underwear. They also received *tulasī* neck beads and the *sannyāsa-mantra.* Keśava Mahārāja said that Abhay would now be known as Bhaktivedanta Swami Mahārāja and that Sanātana would be Muni Mahārāja. After the ceremony, the two new *sannyāsīs* posed for a photo, standing on either side of their *sannyāsa-guru,* who sat in a chair.

Keśava Mahārāja didn't impose any strictures on Abhay; he simply encouraged him to go on preaching. Yet Abhay knew that to become A. C. Bhaktivedanta Swami did not mean merely that he was giving up family, home comforts, and business. That he had done five years ago. Changing from white cloth to saffron cloth, from Abhay Bābū to Bhaktivedanta Swami Mahārāja, had a special significance: it was the mandate he had required, the irrevocable commitment. Now it was only a matter of time before Bhaktivedanta Swami would travel to the West as Bhaktisiddhānta Sarasvatī had ordained. This was Bhaktivedanta Swami's realization of his new *sannyāsa* status.

The *Gauḍīya Patrikā's* account of the *sannyāsa* initiation included a biographical sketch of Śrī Śrīmad Bhaktivedanta Swami Mahārāja, listing the major events of his life. The article concluded:

> Seeing his enthusiasm and ability to write articles in Hindi, English, and Bengali, Bhaktisiddhanta Sarasvati Maharaja gave him the instruction to take *tridandi-sannyasa.* For nearly one year he had been ready to accept *sannyasa.* In the month of Bhadra, on the day on which Vishvarupa accepted *sannyasa,* Bhaktivedanta Swami at the Shri Keshavaji Gaudiya Math accepted *sannyasa* from the founder of the Vedanta Samiti, Bhaktiprajnana

Keshava Maharaja. Seeing him accept his *asrama* of renunciation, seeing this pastime for accepting the renounced order of life, we have attained great affection and enthusiasm.

CHAPTER TEN

"This Momentous Hour of Need"

Our capacity of presenting the matter in adequate language, specially a foreign language, will certainly fail and there may be so many literary discrepancies inspite of our honest attempt to present it in the proper way. But we are sure that with our all faults in this connection the seriousness of the subject matter will be taken into consideration and the leaders of the society will still accept this on account of its being an honest attempt for glorifying the Almighty Great so much now badly needed.

—from *Śrīmad-Bhāgavatam*,
Canto 1, Vol. 1

BHAKTIVEDANTA SWAMI, ACCOMPANIED by some of the Keśavajī Math's devotees, made a short preaching tour of Agra, Kanpur, Jhansi, and Delhi. But he was soon back in his own place at the Vaṁśī-gopālajī temple. No one called him Abhay Bābū any longer; even amongst friends it was Swamiji or Mahārāja. And people often addressed him as Swami Bhaktivedantajī, Swami Mahārāja, A. C. Bhaktivedanta Swami. People readily recognized him as a *sādhu* and offered respect. Yet his basic problems remained. He wanted to write and print, but he had no money. He wanted to broadcast the message of Godhead, but few were willing to listen. Such things hadn't been changed by his becoming a swami.

When a librarian advised Bhaktivedanta Swami to write books (they were permanent, whereas newspapers were read once and thrown away), he took it that his spiritual master was speaking through this person. Then an Indian Army officer who liked *Back to Godhead* suggested the same thing. Bhaktivedanta Swami took it as a revelation from his spiritual master. As a dependent servant constantly meditating on the desires of his transcendental master and seeking his guidance, Bhaktivedanta Swami felt his spiritual master's reciprocal blessings and personal presence. More and more he was feeling confidential contact with Śrīla Bhaktisiddhānta, and now he was feeling an inspiration to write books.

He considered *Śrīmad-Bhāgavatam,* because it was the most important and authoritative Vaiṣṇava scripture. Although *Bhagavad-gītā* was the essence of all Vedic knowledge, presented in a brief *ABC* fashion, *Śrīmad-Bhāgavatam* was elaborate. And Śrīla Bhaktisiddhānta Sarasvatī and Bhaktivinoda Ṭhākura had both written Bengali commentaries on the *Bhāgavatam.* In fact, most of the great Vaiṣṇava *ācāryas* of the past had commented on *Śrīmad-Bhāgavatam.* Lord Caitanya Himself had recommended *Śrīmad-Bhāgavatam* as the spotless Vedic literature. An English translation and commentary for this book could one day change the hearts of the entire world. And if he could publish even a few books, his preaching would be enhanced; he could go abroad with confidence and not appear empty-handed.

One day Gaurachand Goswami, proprietor of the Rādhā-Dāmodara temple, approached Bhaktivedanta Swami, inviting him to come live at the Rādhā-Dāmodara temple; being the eternal home of Jīva Gosvāmī and Rūpa Gosvāmī, it would be more suitable for his writing and translating. Bhaktivedanta Swami was interested. He had never stopped his regular visits there, and he always felt inspired in the presence of the *samādhi* tombs of the great leaders of Lord Caitanya's movement, Jīva Gosvāmī and Rūpa Gosvāmī. But when he went to look at the two available rooms, he found them in poor repair; they had not been maintained or lived in for many years. Not wanting to miss the opportunity, however, Bhaktivedanta Swami agreed to take the rooms, at five rupees per month. He estimated that for a little more than five hundred rupees he could have electricity installed and extensive repairs made; and when it was finished he could move in.

Bhaktivedanta Swami saw the invitation as auspicious, and living there would complement his new project of presenting *Śrīmad-Bhāgavatam* in English. Of all Vṛndāvana's temples, Rādhā-Dāmodara had the largest collection of original writings by the six Gosvāmīs and their followers—more than two thousand separate manuscripts, many of them three hundred, some even four hundred years old. Bhaktivedanta Swami looked forward to residing there some day and serving in the company of Śrīla Rūpa Gosvāmī and Śrīla Jīva Gosvāmī. For now he would remain at the Vaṁśī-gopālajī temple, and with whatever money he could collect he would gradually repair the rooms.

* * *

It was an important maxim of Bhaktisiddhānta Sarasvatī's that a preacher should go to the cities and not remain in the seclusion of a holy place. So in that spirit, Bhaktivedanta Swami continued commuting to Delhi, even though to him it was a hell and even though he had no fixed residence there. Often he was taken in by businessmen who felt obliged on the basis of Indian culture: a good man, if he wanted to be favored by God, should accommodate the *sādhus* and give them meals and a place to stay. But the vision of such pious men was a sentimental Hinduism, and their receptions were artificial; they could not really appreciate Bhaktivedanta Swami's work. And Bhaktivedanta Swami was not of a mind to impose himself upon such hosts.

Then he spoke with Mr. Hitsaran Sharma, manager of the Radha Press. In the past Mr. Sharma had printed flyers and stationery for the League of Devotees, and Bhaktivedanta Swami had stayed in Mr. Sharma's house on occasion. Mr. Sharma introduced Bhaktivedanta Swami to Pandit Shri Krishna Sharma, a caste *brāhmaṇa* and active religionist, secretary to the century-old Delhi religious society Shri Naval Prem Sabha. Out of sympathy for Bhaktivedanta Swami's literary labors, Krishna Pandit gave him a room in his Rādhā-Kṛṣṇa temple in the Chippiwada neighborhood of Old Delhi. Now Bhaktivedanta Swami would have a permanent office in Delhi.

The train from Mathurā would arrive at the Old Delhi station near Chandni Chowk, the broad avenue down which poured a river of workday traffic: rickshas, bicycle riders sometimes a dozen abreast, autos in lesser numbers, men running on foot pulling heavy carts, and beasts of burden—donkeys, oxen, an occasional camel or elephant, carrying heavy loads and being driven by men with whips in their hands.

From the intensely busy Chandni Chowk, Bhaktivedanta Swami would take the short walk to Chippiwada, past the Red Fort, keeping the Gaurī-Śaṅkara temple on his left, then proceeding along a side street past the large, imposing Jama Mosque. Near Chippiwada the streets would become narrow. Chippiwada had been a Muslim neighborhood until the India-Pakistan partition of 1947, when thousands of Punjabi Hindus had settled there. Chippiwada was part of a mixed Hindu-Muslim neighborhood so crowded with people that cars were not allowed to enter the streets; only oxcarts and rickshas could penetrate the narrow, crowded lanes, and in some areas the lanes were planted with iron posts to keep rickshas out. Even a bicycle rider would create havoc amongst the densely packed crowds of shoppers and workers who moved along the streets and lanes. Side streets led to other side streets—lanes so narrow that the second-floor balconies on opposite sides of the street were only inches apart, practically forming a roof over the street, so that a pedestrian could glimpse only the narrowest patch of sky. Private yards, shops, and alleys became almost indistinguishable from the public thoroughfares. Although most shops bore signs in Hindi with subheadings in English, some bore the curvy scripts of Arabic, and women dressed in black with veiled faces were a common sight. In the heart of this intense city life was the narrow entrance of Krishna Pandit's Rādhā-Kṛṣṇa temple, with a plaque of the demigod Gaṇeśa and a row of nesting pigeons just above its simple arched door.

The temple, with its resident families, retained some of the tenement atmosphere of the neighborhood. Although the temple room was dark, the Rādhā-Kṛṣṇa Deities on the altar were well illuminated. Rādhārāṇī was the color of cream, and Kṛṣṇa was black marble and stood about two feet tall. He was decorated with dots of fresh sandalwood pulp and a mask of yellow sandalwood on His forehead. Both Deities were dressed in silk garments. On the second floor, just above the Deity room, was a guest room, Bhaktivedanta Swami's room. Its cement walls and floor were completely bare. Protruding up from the floor was a three-foot high concrete pyramid with a spire, indicating that the Deities were directly beneath.

Bhaktivedanta Swami soon found that his room was not secluded but was side by side with other residential rooms. Outside the door, a metal grating smaller than in the Vaṁśī-gopālajī temple and Keśavajī Math revealed the small temple courtyard below. From the roof, hardly a single tree could be seen. The view was of tenement rooftops so tightly crowded together that it seemed one could walk from roof to roof all the way to the colossal Jama Masjid. The mosque's three large domes, surrounded by taller minarets, rose high above the ordinary buildings, attracting flocks of pigeons, which perched upon the domes or flew in wheeling patterns in the sky.

Krishna Pandit dressed in a black, lightweight cotton coat, the kind made internationally recognizable by Pandit Nehru, and he had the Nehru hat also. He spoke good English and was garrulous. He was well known and respected within the neighborhood. He saw Bhaktivedanta Swami as God-sent—a *sādhu* for him to take care of and thus prove once again the piety of Hindu culture. He found his new guest likable: a simple, gentle, gracious, and accomplished Vaiṣṇava scholar.

Krishna Pandit said he understood the importance of Bhaktivedanta Swami's *sanātana-dharma* mission and his need for a Delhi office, and he vowed to supply his guest with whatever he required. Although Bhaktivedanta Swami was reluctant to ask for anything for himself, Krishna Pandit brought in a sitting mat and a low table, placing them before the pyramid, and he also brought a mattress. He showed Bhaktivedanta Swami how to operate the room's single light, a bulb and metal shade that hung from a cord and could be raised or lowered by hand. He brought a picture of Rādhā and Kṛṣṇa that had been given to his *guru* by the Mahārāja of Jaipur and set it within a niche in the wall, relishing that Bhaktivedanta Swami could gaze upon it with the eyes of a true devotee.

Bhaktivedanta Swami had wanted a secure place for writing books before going to the West, and Lord Kṛṣṇa had provided it. Now he could work either in Vṛndāvana or in Delhi. Almost immediately he began *Back to Godhead* again, serializing book excerpts from his previous manuscripts, while at the same time beginning *Śrīmad-Bhāgavatam.*

When Krishna Pandit learned of his guest's lone struggles to produce *Back to Godhead,* he volunteered to help with some of the business aspects of the publication. Bhaktivedanta Swami was indeed gratified by Krishna Pandit's sincere help, and in appreciation he gave him an addition to his name: Hari-bhaktānudāsa, "one who serves the Lord's devotee." After six months in Chippiwada, Bhaktivedanta Swami wrote an appreciation in the temple's guest book.

> I am pleased to write herein that I have come to Delhi from my H.Q. 1/859, Keshi Ghat, Vrindaban (U.P.) purely on spiritual mission to propagate the cult of devotional service of the Lord. And I am more pleased to mention herewith that Sriman Sri Krishna Sharma, Haribhaktanudas, has provided me a suitable room for my literary activities. I am publishing an English fortnightly magazine of the name "Back to Godhead" from this place and the Nawal Prem Shabha of which Sri Krishnaji is the Hony. Secretary is arranging for my daily lectures on Srimad Bhagwat.
>
> Late Pandit Jyoti Prasad Sharma, father of Shri Krishnaji, was also known to me, and during his lifetime whenever I used to come to Delhi, Late Pandit Jyoti Prasadji would provide me with residential place. His good son is also following in the footprints of his noble father, and as secretary of the Nawal Prem Shabha, he is doing good service in propagating Rama Nama all over the city.

In neat English script, Bhaktivedanta Swami went on to write that, in his opinion, temples should be used solely for educating the public in spiritual values and that it was his personal mission to organize temples for that service.

> Temples are not meant for ordinary householders engaged simply in the matters of animal propensities. Those who are actually engaged in the service of the Lord Deity, the predominator of the temple, can only be allowed to remain in the temple, otherwise not.

Trying to compose *Śrīmad-Bhāgavatam* at Chippiwada while surrounded by sometimes noisy families with their nondevotional domestic habits had impressed upon him the importance of *not* using a temple as an apartment house.

* * *

Despite his plans to settle down and begin the monumental task of translating *Śrīmad-Bhāgavatam,* Bhaktivedanta Swami was ready to preach in other ways also. In October of 1959 he had encountered a news article in *The Times of India.* Two American scientists had received the Nobel prize in physics for discovering the antiproton. "According to one of the fundamental assumptions of the new theory," the article read, "there may exist another world or an anti-world built up of antimatter." The "other world" reminded Bhaktivedanta Swami of the eternal spiritual world described in *Bhagavad-gītā.* He was well aware that the scientists were not speaking of *antimaterial* in the sense of "eternal," or "spiritual" but he thought of using their scientific terms to capture the interest of scientific-minded people. He conceived of an essay presenting the theistic science of *Bhagavad-gītā* in terms of the antimaterial particle and the antimaterial world.

It was a time when the whole world was talking of space travel. Indian news media had reported the Russian Sputnik two years ago, and the race for space had begun. Seizing on the current interest in space travel, Bhaktivedanta Swami described how by *bhakti-yoga* the soul can travel past the farthest reaches of space to the eternal planets of the spiritual world, where life is blissful and full of knowledge. He gave his own fresh translations of *Bhagavad-gītā* verses, couched in the language of the new physics, with its antimaterial particle and antimaterial world. The complete work, *Easy Journey to Other Planets,* was a fifteen-thousand-word manuscript, and he showed it to Hitsaran Sharma of Radha Press. But he didn't have enough money to get the little book printed.

In February of 1960 Bhaktivedanta Swami decided to print it himself in two installments of *Back to Godhead.* The articles drew an immediate response from a physicist at the Gujarat University in Ahmedabad, Mr. Y. G. Naik, who received *Back to Godhead* through the mail. Dr. Naik thought Bhaktivedanta Swami's application of the antimaterial principle was "really a grand one. ... This is no doubt a classic essay. ..." Dr. Naik was interested in further discussion on physics and transcendental knowledge, and Bhaktivedanta Swami replied with equal enthusiasm, finally asking the physicist to join him in distributing the cultural heritage of India to the whole world.

Convinced that such an essay had great potential to interest educated English-speaking readers, Bhaktivedanta Swami worked hard to raise enough in donations to print *Easy Journey to Other Planets* as a paperback book. He finally did so in the fall of 1960. A foreword by Dr. N. K. Sidhanta, vice chancellor of the University of Delhi, arrived late but was included in the book as an insert.

> While everyone may gain from it, the student community in particular is recommended to read the book with care and practise Bhaktiyoga, which will help to strengthen the mind and build up character. I shall be glad to see this work read by the students and the teachers alike. ...

Several Indian scientists and scholars contributed reviews, noting the book's "scientific cum spiritual vision" and "the method of speeding over space not by mechanical acceleration of speed, but through psychological effort and spiritual emancipation." It was only thirty-eight pages, but it was his first publication aside from the one-page folded newspaper, *Back to Godhead.* He tried to distribute the little book effectively. He gave one copy to Dr. P. Bannerji of the National Museum of New Delhi.

Dr. Bannerji: *He used to come to the library and consult some books, and I met him there. He gave me a book called* Easy Journey to Other Planets. *He gave me some copies to distribute for a rupee or half a rupee each.*

I felt attracted to him. I thought he was a saintly person with pure devotion and without any outward glamor. He was not out to attract people just for name and fame. He had little support from anybody. He was living alone in a small room in Chippiwada. He was devoted to his studies. So I asked him, "Sir, if you have time and you don't mind coming to my house, could you kindly come on Sundays and recite the Bhāgavata *in my house? He readily agreed. He was a good scholar. He was learned in the scriptures, and he was fond of communicating his ideas to others. He was a good speaker and a good conversationalist. He was very polite.*

Whatever he said he said very distinctly. He spoke in Bengali and explained the essence of the verses. Sometimes he also referred to the commentaries, just to give me more information. The others were not very much interested in commentary or in difficult aspects, but because he knew that I had some studies in the field, he explained the commentaries for my sake and for the sake of one or two other gentlemen who were also very elderly and very scholarly.

The gatherings at my home would be attended by about twenty or thirty people, and he would continue his explanation for one or two hours. Then he would recite the Hare Kṛṣṇa mantra, *and we would also take part with the* karatālas *and harmonium. So it was a very enjoyable gathering, because he made the difficult things very easy and he explained everything to all of us according to our needs. He knew that this much is for this person, this much is intended for this man, this much for the others.*

After the meetings, he used to take a little rest in my house. I requested him to take meals in my house, but he said he did not take meals prepared by others. But when he met my wife and she said she would be happy to prepare the meals, he said, "All right, I will take," and she used to prepare meals on Sundays when he would come.

He sometimes asked me how to get more and more people attracted towards this field. But as a government worker, I could not persuade anyone very openly. Nor had I the time to organize anything on a big scale for him. But he was not satisfied with that. He asked me if I could organize on a bigger scale. He knew that the people who attended the meetings at my house were very old—seventy, eighty, one was ninety years of age—retired, educated persons.

It lasted for no less than a year. After that, he said he would be trying to go out to other places. He asked me to continue the gatherings, but I said, "I am not initiated." He said I could continue anyway, because I was born as a brāhmaṇa. *He gave me the authority to continue for some time. But I could not continue, because I used to go out. I lost all interest after he left. I was a government servant.*

*   *   *

Easy Journey to Other Planets had been like a warm-up for his real work of presenting *Śrīmad-Bhāgavatam.* But now he was even more convinced of the need for books. To preach, he would have to have books—especially if he were to go to the West. With books he could create a spiritual revolution. There was so much literature in the West, but Westerners had nothing like this, nothing to fill their spiritual vacuum.

Although he wanted to give as much time as possible to *Śrīmad-Bhāgavatam,* he decided to continue with *Back to Godhead* by using excerpts from already existing book manuscripts as articles. Occasionally, however, he would write and print a new article. In "Relevant Inquiries" he wrote:

> We are just trying to make an humble attempt to save the human being by propaganda of Back to Godhead. This propaganda is not fictitious. If there is any reality at all this propaganda of Back to Godhead is the beginning of that era-of-reality.

In "A Godless Civilization" Bhaktivedanta Swami referred to Prime Minister Nehru's complaints about the misuse of public funds in the name of religion. Bhaktivedanta Swami noted that although there were undoubtedly instances in which religious leaders were implicated in criminal offenses, if statistics were compared the religious cheaters would be outnumbered by the political cheaters. Although Pandit Nehru had been right in warning of religious fraud, the warning could not be effective without a thorough reform of spiritual institutions, and that reform could be accomplished only with the cooperation of government leaders. Bhaktivedanta Swami quoted from his letter in which he had asked Prime Minister Nehru to take up the study of *Bhagavad-gītā;* but, as he informed his *Back to Godhead* readers, Pandit Nehru had never replied. "Because of his lack of spiritual knowledge ... he thought that this institution [the League of Devotees] might be something like the so many mathas and temples which have become the source of headache for the Pandit."

Bhaktivedanta Swami charged that Pandit Nehru thought that any spiritual organization "is a dungeon for accumulating public funds and then misuse it for questionable purposes."

> He, however, approves of the so-called Sadhus who do social service and talk nonsense in the spiritual science. This is so because he has no depth of spiritual knowledge for himself although he is Brahmin and Pandit. Ignorance in spiritual knowledge is the qualification of the Sudras or the labouring class.

He requested Pandit Nehru not to be afraid of the word *God* or *Kṛṣṇa:* "but we can assure him that there is no such cause of fear, because Krishna is everyone's friend and ... able to render real help to everyone. ..." Bhaktivedanta Swami ended by suggesting that immoral practices were not confined only to the temples of India, but were common to materialistic civilizations all over the world. In particular he cited the disturbances amongst youth that were becoming rampant in the 1960s.

> The best thing will be for the physician to heal himself first. Because in Godless civilisation, while the occupants of the Mathas and temples have been the cause of headache for the Pandit, the same thing under a different

> label has become the cause of headache for other European and Asian statesmen. The unbridled youngsters of those countries under the name of "Teddy Boys" in England, the "Rebels without Cause" in America, and the "Half Strong" in Germany, the "Leather Jackets" in Sweden, the "Children of the Sun" in Japan, and the "Style Boys" in U.S.S.R. are some of the by-products of a Godless Civilisation. And that is the root cause of all headache. That requires a thorough treatment.

* * *

At Chippiwada, Bhaktivedanta Swami followed much the same daily schedule as at Keśī-ghāṭa, except that with Krishna Pandit doing some of the secretarial work for *Back to Godhead,* he was free to devote more hours to *Śrīmad-Bhāgavatam.*

Krishna Pandit: *He used to translate* Śrīmad-Bhāgavatam *before dawn, about 3:00* A.M. *In the beginning there was no typewriter, but then he arranged a portable typewriter. He would do his daily work and then cook his food himself. I arranged raw materials for his cooking. Sometimes he used to come to my family asking my wife to get some food. Sometimes he would also bathe at 5:00 or 6:00 in the afternoon.*

Every day he was typing. And he himself was reading some Bhāgavatam. *And he was going down in the temple for* darśana. *Then he was going outside, sometimes returning at 2:00 or 4:00 in the afternoon. Then he was typing and sending the proofs of* Back to Godhead *to a place and checking them. He was doing by hand all this type of work. His main activity was typing many hours a day.*

Bhaktivedanta Swami worked from a Sanskrit and Bengali *Bhāgavatam,* edited by Śrīla Bhaktisiddhānta Sarasvatī and a large book containing the original commentaries of twelve great *ācāryas.* He had a standard format: he made a roman transliteration of the Sanskrit *devanāgarī* script, then word-for-word English synonyms, an English prose translation, and finally his English purport on that verse. Before writing his own purport, however, he would consult the commentaries of the *ācāryas,* especially Śrīla Bhaktisiddhānta Sarasvatī, Viśvanātha Cakravartī, Jīva Gosvāmī, Vijayadhvaja Tīrtha, and Śrīdhara Svāmī.

He contemplated the size of the project he was attempting. The *Bhāgavatam* contained eighteen thousand verses. The First Canto's seventeen chapters would fill three volumes of four hundred pages each, and the Second Canto, with ten chapters, would take two volumes. Up through the Ninth Canto there would be maybe thirty volumes. The Tenth Canto, containing ninety chapters, would take twenty volumes. There were twelve cantos, and so the total would be at least sixty volumes. He thought he might be able to finish it in five to seven years: "If the Lord keeps me physically fit, then in the fulfillment of Śrīla Prabhupāda's will I could complete this work."

He decided to introduce the first volume with a biographical sketch of Lord Caitanya Mahāprabhu, "The Ideal Preacher of the *Bhāgavatam.*" The reader could best appreciate the *Bhāgavatam* by seeing its practical demonstration in the life of Lord Caitanya. The special feature of Lord Caitanya's presentation had been His desire that *Śrīmad-Bhāgavatam* "be preached in every nook and corner of the world by everyone who happens to take his birth in India." Lord Caitanya had called *Śrīmad-Bhāgavatam* the "spotless *Purāṇa*" and had considered the chanting and hearing of *Śrīmad-Bhāgavatam* along with the Hare Kṛṣṇa *mantra* to be a complete scientific process for developing pure love of God.

Working from Śrīla Bhaktisiddhānta Sarasvatī's commentary on *Caitanya-caritāmṛta* and *Caitanya-bhāgavata,* Bhaktivedanta Swami gave a fifty-page synopsis of Lord Caitanya's life and His *saṅkīrtana* movement. He described Lord Caitanya's divine ecstasies, His philosophical confrontations with leading scholars of the day, and His inauguration of the *saṅkīrtana* movement, the congregational chanting of the holy name. Bhaktivedanta Swami especially connected Lord Caitanya's life and teachings to what he saw as the present crucial time in history. Help for humanity in "this momentous hour of need" lay in the Vedic literature, and especially in *Śrīmad-Bhāgavatam.*

> We know that the foreign invaders of India could break down some of the monumental architectural work in India, but they were unable to break up the perfect ideals of human civilisation so far kept hidden within the Sanskrit language of Vedic wisdom.

The Sanskrit language had protected the secret for thousands of centuries, but now the secret had to be released to the world.

As he approached the first verses of *Śrīmad-Bhāgavatam,* Bhaktivedanta Swami became absorbed in the *Bhāgavatam's* purpose. The verses stressed that the *Bhāgavatam* alone could save society from the evil influences of the Age of Kali. *Śrīmad-Bhāgavatam's* recommendation for this age was simply to hear from the pure devotees about the Supreme Personality of Godhead, Kṛṣṇa.

The setting of the *Bhāgavatam* was a gathering of sages at Naimiṣāraṇya about five thousand years ago, at the dawn of the present Age of Kali. Foreseeing the degradation of humanity, the sages asked the senior member of the assembly, Sūta Gosvāmī, "Now that Lord Kṛṣṇa, the shelter of all religious principles, has returned to His spiritual abode, where are religious principles to be found?" Sūta's answer was that the epic *Śrīmad-Bhāgavatam,* "which is as brilliant as the sun," was a literary incarnation of God and would give direction to persons lost in the dense darkness of Kali-yuga.

In the beginning of *Śrīmad-Bhāgavatam,* Śrīla Vyāsadeva, under the instruction of his spiritual master, Nārada Muni, sat down and entered a deep meditation. In trance he saw the Supreme Personality of Godhead, His energies, and the suffering souls of Kali-yuga. He also saw that the remedy for their suffering was pure devotional service. With this vision and the instructions of his spiritual master as his inspiration, Vyāsadeva set about to compile *Śrīmad-Bhāgavatam* to give the highest benefit to the suffering souls of Kali-yuga.

In presenting the literary incarnation of God, *Śrīmad-Bhāgavatam,* for the benefit of the Western world, Bhaktivedanta Swami realized that he was performing an important task, following in the footsteps of Śrīla Vyāsadeva. As Śrīla Vyāsadeva had had a vision of Kṛṣṇa and had received direction from his spiritual master before beginning his literary mission, Bhaktivedanta Swami had his vision and had received instructions from his spiritual master. Bhaktivedanta Swami envisioned distributing in mass the book of Śrīla Vyāsadeva. He would not merely translate it; he would personally take it to the West, present it, and teach people in the West—through the book and in person—how to develop pure love of God.

Śrīla Prabhupāda: *The communist party has become popular simply by distributing their literatures. In Calcutta, the communist agents were inviting friends and reading their literature. The Russians never came to India, but by distributing literature in every language they got a pretty good number of followers. If it is possible for ordinary, third-class, mundane literature, why shouldn't transcendental literature create devotees all over the world? There is good potency for pushing on these literatures very vigorously from village to village. The* bhāgavata-dharma *is the original religion of the human society. Whatever else may be passing as religion has come from the Vedic literature. People are after these books. They are hankering for them. Lord Caitanya said that in every town and village on the surface of the world they will know the message of the* saṅkīrtana *movement. This means that in every village and town all over the world there are many candidates who are awaiting this message. It is transcendental literature. Nobody can challenge it. It is done so nicely, without any spot, the spotless* Purāṇa.

Bhaktivedanta Swami put his faith in *Śrīmad-Bhāgavatam,* giving up almost all other kinds of missionary activity. And this had been the advice and example of his spiritual master and of Lord Caitanya. They had not been interested in building costly temples or in creating many neophyte disciples. Śrīla Bhaktisiddhānta Sarasvatī had stressed preaching. Preaching meant books, and the best book was *Śrīmad-Bhāgavatam.* To write and publish the *Bhāgavatam* for the enlightenment of the general populace was real service to the Lord. That was Śrīla Bhaktisiddhānta Sarasvatī's opinion. He had preferred publishing books to establishing temples, and he had specifically told his disciples to write books. It was the business of advanced, empowered devotees to write books, publish them, and distribute them widely. A program to distribute transcendental literature everywhere (with even more expertise than the communists) would create a great positive effect on the people of Europe and America. And if Europeans and Americans turned to Kṛṣṇa consciousness, then the rest of the world would follow. Bhaktivedanta Swami continued working alone in his room at Chippiwada, absorbed in thoughts of spreading the news of Kṛṣṇa on a scale never before attempted.

He sometimes wondered how Westerners, who were so far removed from the Vedic culture, could adopt it. They were meat-eaters, *mlecchas.* When one of his Godbrothers had gone to England, the Marquis of Zetland, on hearing the four prohibitions against sinful life, had laughed scornfully, "Impossible!" But *Śrīmad-Bhāgavatam* spoke for itself.

"Sri Krishna the Personality of Godhead who is also the Paramatma in every one's heart and the benefactor of the truthful devotee, does cleanse the desire for material enjoyment in the heart of the devotee who has developed the urge for hearing His (Krishna's) messages which are themselves virtuous when properly heard and chanted."

Although he was known as an English preacher, Bhaktivedanta Swami knew there were always faults in his presentation in that foreign language; and there was no editor to correct them. But such technical faults would not keep him from printing *Śrīmad-Bhāgavatam.* This idea was also presented in the opening chapters of the *Bhāgavatam.* "The literature which is full with description of transcendental glories of the Name, Fame, Forms, Pastimes etc. of the Unlimited Supreme Lord, is a different creation of transcendental vocabulary all **meant for bringing about a revolution in the impious life of a misdirected civilization of the world.** Such transcendental literatures even though irregularly composed, is heard, sung and accepted by the purified men who are thoroughly honest."

Bhaktivedanta Swami wrote in his purport: "We know that in our honest attempt for presenting this great literature conveying transcendental message for reviving the God-consciousness of the people in general, as a matter of re-spiritualisation of the world atmosphere, is fret with many difficulties. ... our capacity of presenting the matter in adequate language, specially a foreign language, will certainly fail and there may be so many literary discrepancies inspite of our honest attempt to present it in the proper way. But we are sure that with our all faults in this connection the seriousness of the subject matter will be taken into consideration and the leaders of the society will still accept this on account of its being an honest attempt for glorifying the Almighty Great so much now badly needed. When there is fire in the house, the inmates of the house go out for help from the neighbours who may be foreigners to such inmates and yet without any adequate language the victims of the fire express themselves and the neighbours understand the need even though not expressed in adequate language. The same spirit of cooperation is needed in the matter of broadcasting this transcendental message of the Srimad Bhagwatam throughout the whole polluted atmosphere of the present day world situation. After all it is a technical science of spiritual values and as such we are concerned with the techniques and not with the language. If the techniques of this great literature are understood by the people of the world, there is the success."

Certainly Kali-yuga was such an emergency—the house was on fire. Honest men who could understand the need would welcome *Śrīmad-Bhāgavatam,* even though it was now being presented "with so many faulty and broken linguistic technicalities. ..." Bhaktivedanta Swami was presenting *Śrīmad-Bhāgavatam* unchanged, with the greatest respect for Śrīla Vyāsadeva. And that was his cardinal virtue. He was adding his own realizations, but not in a spirit of trying to surpass the previous spiritual masters. In the all-important matter of presenting the subject strictly in *paramparā,* Bhaktivedanta Swami suffered from no "faulty and broken technicalities." He knew that without the *paramparā* the *Bhāgavatam* purports would have no value. Day and night he typed at his desk beneath the small adjustable light that dangled from the ceiling on its cord. He sat on a thin mat, his back to the large pyramid that stood oddly upright within the bare room. Pages accumulated, and he kept them in place with stones. Food and sleep, although necessary, were only incidental. He was completely convinced that his *Śrīmad-Bhāgavatam* would create a revolution in a misdirected civilization. Thus he translated each word and gave each purport with exacting care and concentration. But it had to be done as quickly as possible.

* * *

In February of 1961, on Vyāsa-pūjā day, the anniversary of the appearance of Śrīla Bhaktisiddhānta Sarasvatī, Bhaktivedanta Swami was again in Vṛndāvana. In honor of their spiritual master, some of Śrīla Bhaktisiddhānta's disciples had gathered, offered flowers before his picture, and held congregational chanting in the temple. But Bhaktivedanta Swami thought that they should be doing much more than that; they should be planning and executing the worldwide preaching mission that Bhaktisiddhānta Sarasvatī had desired. Instead, they were a gathering of independent individuals, each with his own small idea, each maintaining a small center or living at a center, but with no world programs, not even a program for India. Most of them had no plans or vision beyond their own bodily maintenance. Bhaktisiddhānta Sarasvatī had asked for a governing body to conduct his movement, but there was no governing body, and practically there was no movement. Some who had fought bitterly were again on speaking terms and feared that any sudden organizational attempts now might simply stir up old animosities. At least they could gather together and make an offering to their spiritual master.

Amongst his Godbrothers, Bhaktivedanta Swami was a junior *sannyāsī.* Although a recognized writer and editor, he had no temple or followers.

Yet he knew he was trying to follow Bhaktisiddhānta Sarasvatī. He saw himself helpless and alone against the vast forces of *māyā.* His Godbrothers were not an army united against *māyā's* forces, but were more like apathetic monks, growing old, holding on to religious principles and rituals, devoid of life. How could they gather to worship their spiritual master without distressfully admitting their failure and, in the spirit of "better late than never," trying to rectify it?

Since the custom on Vyāsa-pūjā day was for each disciple to write an offering glorifying his spiritual master and to share it within the assembly of Godbrothers, Bhaktivedanta Swami wrote an offering—more like an explosion than a eulogy—and humbly placed it before his Godbrothers for their response.

> Even now, my Godbrothers, you return here on the order of our master, and together we engage in this *pūjā.*
>
> But simply a festival of flowers and fruits does not constitute worship. The one who serves the message of the *guru* really worships him. ...
>
> Oh, shame! My dear brothers, aren't you embarrassed? In the manner of businessmen you increase your disciples.
>
> Our master said to preach! Let the neophytes remain inside the temples and simply ring the bells. ...
>
> But just take a good look at the terrible situation that has arisen. Everyone has become a sense enjoyer and has given up preaching. ...
>
> From the seas, across the earth, penetrate the universal shell; come together and preach this Kṛṣṇa consciousness.
>
> Then our master's service will be in proper order. Make your promise today. Give up all your politics and diplomacy.

If the disciples of Bhaktisiddhānta Sarasvatī could join and preach together, there was every chance that they could create a spiritual revolution within the sinful world. That had been the hope of Śrīla Bhaktisiddhānta Sarasvatī, and Bhaktivedanta Swami expressed that hope in his Vyāsa-pūjā offering.

> When will that day come when a temple will be established in every house in every corner of the world?

> When will the high-court judge be a Gauḍīya Vaiṣṇava with *tilaka* beautifully decorating his forehead?
>
> When will a Vaiṣṇava winning votes be elected president of the land and preaching be spread everywhere?

As he read the poem, its truth exploding in the midst of the gathering of aging *sannyāsīs,* some approved, and some were incensed. Their meeting, however, took no new direction; they did not sit down together and plan as he had pleaded. Swami Mahārāja's poem was taken as another poetic expression or as an opinion. The Godbrothers were inclined to let the old wounds heal with the passing of time. To go back over the whole thing again and reconstruct the mission as it had been before, when Śrīla Bhaktisiddhānta Sarasvatī had been present, and to attempt all those ambitious programs—how was it possible? They were getting old. Some did not want to leave the shelter of Vṛndāvana. They would worship Bhaktisiddhānta Sarasvatī within the holy *dhāma.* If Bhaktivedanta Swami could do something more, let him go ahead and try.

Bhaktivedanta Swami returned to Keśī-ghāṭa, thoughtful. For many years he had been unable to take a leading part in the mission because of family commitments. In 1935, in Bombay, his Godbrothers had even asked him to be president of the *maṭha* there, but Bhaktisiddhānta Sarasvatī had said that it was not necessary that Abhay Charan join them; he would come in his own way. Now, by the grace of his spiritual master, he was ready to fulfill the meaning of *sannyāsa.* The Kṛṣṇa conscious world he had described in his poem was not a utopia, presented merely to incite his Godbrothers, a dreamer's talk of the impossible. It was possible. But in any case, he had to write and print Kṛṣṇa conscious books and preach abroad. It was what Śrīla Bhaktisiddhānta Sarasvatī wanted. If his Godbrothers would not do it jointly, then he would do it.

* * *

In January of 1961 one of Bhaktivedanta Swami's Delhi acquaintances had shown him an announcement for the Congress for Cultivating Human Spirit, a convention to be held in Tokyo, May 10–20. The theme was world peace through cultivating human spirit. International participants were invited. As soon as Bhaktivedanta Swami had seen it, he had wanted to go. Although his main interest had always been the

U.S., if Japan presented itself first, why not? And their invitation was in English. If they accepted his reservation, they would pay for his board and lodging at the convention hotel, although he would have to pay his own travel expenses.

Bhaktivedanta Swami wrote to the sponsors, the International Foundation for Cultural Harmony, and proposed a speech, "How Should One Cultivate Human Spirit?" The secretary general of the foundation, Mr. Toshihiro Nakano, wrote back to him at Keśī-ghāṭa, expressing his high regard both for Indian spiritual culture and for his proposed presentation. Mr. Nakano also enclosed an official certificate, as he had requested, stating that Bhaktivedanta Swami was a bona fide visitor to their convention whose expenses in Japan would be paid. They requested—"To Whom It May Concern"—that his passport and visa be granted in time for his May 10 arrival in Japan.

Bhaktivedanta Swami then conceived a special project for the convention. The Tenth Canto, Twentieth Chapter, of *Śrīmad-Bhāgavatam* presents a description of autumn in Vṛndāvana, and for each seasonal phenomenon the *Bhāgavatam* presents a parallel teaching from the *Vedas.* For example, it compares the dark, cloudy evening of the rainy autumn season to the present Age of Kali, when the bright stars of Vedic wisdom (the saints and scriptures) are temporarily obscured by a godless civilization. The chapter contains dozens of such examples, and Bhaktivedanta Swami proposed fifty commentaries to accompany fifty illustrations to be displayed at the convention. He began preparing the commentaries, which he entitled "The Light of Bhagwat." He wrote directions from which an artist could design a painting to go with each "Lesson from the Picture." Fifty pictures and commentaries, Bhaktivedanta Swami felt, would make an impressive display for visitors at the convention. The convention organizers liked the idea.

> As for your proposal to get pictures drawing by artists according to your suggestion, the institution department of the congress will immediately take people disposal for it under the full consideration of about some specimen idea of picture which will be given to us by you, so I should like to get them as soon as possible.

Bhaktivedanta Swami worked quickly to produce a twenty-thousand-word manuscript—fifty lessons for fifty illustrations. The pictures were to depict the forests, fields, and skies of Vṛndāvana during the rainy season, and the lessons were sometimes criticisms of godless governments, materialists, and false religionists, sometimes assertions of moral principles and God consciousness, and sometimes depictions of Lord Kṛṣṇa and His eternal associates in Vṛndāvana.

Everything went smoothly between Bhaktivedanta Swami and the sponsors in Japan. The problem was to raise the travel fare. He approached the likely sources, writing to the central government's Ministry for Scientific Research and Cultural Affairs; he presented his certificate from Mr. Nakano and explained his position as a *sannyāsī*. In late March the ministry sent him a form to complete and return. Time was getting short. On March 29 he wrote the vice president, Dr. Radhakrishnan, with whom he had a speaking acquaintance (as well as a philosophical difference).

> You know that I am a Sannyasi without any relation with Bank, neither I am attached with financing institution. But the Japanese organisers have liked my literatures and they want me to be present there.

He pleaded that since the great *ācāryas* of India had formerly presented their knowledge for the benefit of the world, the Indian government today should send representatives of the *ācāryas* "to deliver the message of Atma or the Human Spirit." He also wrote the deputy manager of Scindia Steam Navigation Company in Bombay, reminding him of his 1958 offer to give a fifty-percent concession on a ticket to the United States. After explaining his invitation from Mr. Nakano in Japan, Bhaktivedanta Swami pointed out that the full round-trip fare to Japan would be less than half the fare to the United States.

Trying all possibilities at once, and with less than a month and a half before the convention, he wrote to another potential donor, Mr. Brijratan S. Mohatta, who had once expressed his willingness to send Bhaktivedanta Swami to South America when an Indian sponsor there had written expressing interest. At that time, Bhaktivedanta Swami had been unable to get the proper certification from the Indian government. But here, he explained, was a new opportunity to present the message of the Vedic literature to an international gathering of interested people; and passage to Japan was less than to South America. On the same day he wrote to Mr. Mohatta he also mailed his completed form to the Ministry for Scientific Research. In answer to their question as to why he was asking for a donation and whether he had done so before, he replied:

> Before this I never asked the Ministry for any financial assistance as there was no need for it. As Sannyasi I can ask for financial help when there is absolute necessity. Our life is dedicated to render service to the humanity at large for reviving the dormant spiritual consciousness.

Meanwhile, his other arrangements proceeded with full cooperation from Japan. He had already sent Mr. Nakano the first twenty illustrative ideas from "The Light of Bhagwat." "Japan is famous for artistic work," he wrote, "and India is famous for spiritual culture. We should now combine... ." He suggested they also print the text and pictures as a book.

Mr. Nakano assured Bhaktivedanta Swami that they would be eager to meet him at Haneda airport; they would be readily recognizable, since they would be holding a flag. And if he liked, he could stay in Japan for an entire month and hold local meetings after the scheduled convention. Mr. Nakano also asked a favor of Bhaktivedanta Swami. To solidify relations with the mayors of three Japanese cities, he asked that Bhaktivedanta Swami send letters to the mayors, requesting their full support of the Human Spirit Congress. Bhaktivedanta Swami immediately complied.

By now it was April, and no money had come. Finally, after a personal interview in which he received a definite no from Dr. Radhakrishnan, Bhaktivedanta Swami turned to Mr. Nakano in disappointment. On April 18 he wrote:

> I am in due receipt of your letter of the 9th instant and I am grateful to you for all that you have said for me. I am a humble creature and I am just trying to do my bit in this connection because I was so ordered by my spiritual master, Shri Bhaktisiddhanta Saraswati Goswami Maharaj. ...
>
> While I am feeling too much ecstasy for the reception arrangement you are doing for me, I beg to inform you that my passage expenses which is near about Rs. 3500/- is not yet settled. I submitted one application to the Govt. of India for help and the copy of my application is also sent herewith. I also wrote a private letter to Dr. S. Radhakrishnan in this connection and the reply which I have received is also enclosed herewith.
>
> All these are not very encouraging for me. I therefore saw the Vice President today personally but he says the same thing as he has written in his letter. Although the matter is not yet hopeless altogether I am disturbed in my mind thinking what shall I do in case the Govt. denies to help. I am therefore seeking your good advice in this connection. Dr. S. Radhakrishnan said to me that you had also invited him to attend your congress and he opines that the passage expenses might have been paid by you.
>
> The hope and expectation of the congress is undoubtedly very great and I wish that I may fully utilise this opportunity for general welfare of the

> entire human society. I have fully explained my views authoritatively in my statements already sent to you for publication and the gist idea is expressed in the letter of the Mayors, the copy of which is also enclosed.
>
> As a Sannyasi, I have no personal purse for expenditure. Under the circumstances if the Government denies to help for the passage then I will have to ask for the same from you otherwise my going to the congress will end in dream only. I have very little faith in the dealings of the politicians and specially of the Indian politicians.
>
> From the conversation of Dr. S. Radhakrishnan, it appeared to me that the Govt. does not approve of such congress as are organised by private persons and as such they do not participate in such congress. I shall wait for the final decision for one week more when the matter will be clear, yes or no.

Replies from prospective donors in India were all negative. On April 20, he cabled Mr. Nakano.

> As you have developed a deep love for me, I dare to ask you to send me financial help to take me to Japan. I think you can immediately instruct your Embassy in Delhi to do the needful and dispatch me to Japan on your behalf. I am feeling too much to meet you and the congress so that we can build up a solid institute for spiritual cultivation. I shall await your instruction by cable to fix up my programme.

But Mr. Nakano could not help. And Bhaktivedanta Swami's effort ended in a dream only.

* * *

In July 1962 Bhaktivedanta Swami changed his Vṛndāvana residence from Vaṁśī-gopālajī temple to Rādhā-Dāmodara temple. For three years he had been paying the rent of five rupees per month for his Rādhā-Dāmodara rooms and paying for the extensive repairs. Now the main room had electric lighting and a fan, and the walls had been plastered and painted. The room was seven feet by fifteen feet, with smooth plaster walls and a floor of sandstone squares of uneven sizes, the same as the stone tiles cemented in front of the *samādhi* of Rūpa Gosvāmī. The room was furnished with a small, low desk, a *kuśa* mat, and a wooden cot with a rope-woven surface to lie on. The view was not the panorama he had enjoyed at Keśī-ghāṭa, and the neighborhood was not so secluded, but now, without even moving from his room, he could look into the temple and see a portion of the altar and the four-foot-high form of

Vṛndāvana-candra, the black marble Kṛṣṇa Deity Kṛṣṇadāsa Kavirāja had worshiped hundreds of years ago. The main room was connected to the kitchen by a ten-foot-long veranda, which faced the courtyard, and from his kitchen he could see the *samādhi* of Rūpa Gosvāmī. So the place was superior to his room at the Vaṁśī-gopālajī temple, because now he was living in the temple of Jīva Gosvāmī, where great souls like the Gosvāmīs Rūpa, Sanātana, Raghunātha, and Jīva had all gathered, taken *prasādam,* chanted, and discussed Kṛṣṇa and Lord Caitanya. It was the best place to work on *Śrīmad-Bhāgavatam.*

* * *

At 1:00 A.M., when no one else was up and it was very quiet, Bhaktivedanta Swami would wake and begin writing. Since electric failures were not uncommon in Vṛndāvana, he would often work by lantern light. But in any case, a beam of light would shine out from his room onto the veranda, while inside the room he worked under its brightness. While he wrote in stillness, sometimes a toad, as dry as the stone floor, would hop out of hiding and across the floor, exiting through the cement latticework of the opposite wall. Sometimes a tiny mouse would run out from behind a window shutter and hide in another place. Otherwise, the room was complete sanctified stillness, and the inspiration of being in the presence of the six Gosvāmīs was strong. Above the open courtyard, the sky would be full of clearly visible stars. As he worked, the only sounds would come from the town, perhaps of a dog barking in the distance.

At 4:00 A.M., the temple *pūjārī,* who slept under a shelter near the Deity doors, would awake, turn on an electric light and, with a long pole, clear the bats from the rafters. At 5:00 A.M., after waking the Deities, the *pūjārī* would open the doors before the altar and begin *maṅgala-ārati.* He would offer a flame while a few resident devotees gathered and chanted, playing instruments; usually someone would bang a gong while someone else rang a large bell.

Any sound from the courtyard carried immediately to Bhaktivedanta Swami's quarters, and the clanging bell and gong would suddenly reverberate against the walls of his small room. From his sitting place, he could see only Vṛndāvana-candra, on the left of the altar. Sometimes he would pause at his work and walk into the courtyard to see the Deities and Their *ārati.* The altar was filled with Deities of Rādhā and Kṛṣṇa who had been worshiped by Jīva Gosvāmī and other Vaiṣṇava *ācāryas* hundreds of years ago. After ten minutes, the *pūjārī,* having offered the flame and then a conchshell filled with water, would turn and sprinkle offered water on the heads of the devotees, and the ceremony would end.

After working a few hours on *Śrīmad-Bhāgavatam,* Bhaktivedanta Swami would sit in his room and chant *japa.* As the morning sky turned light blue, the stars would vanish, and residents of Vṛndāvana would arrive to visit the Deities and the *samādhis* of the Gosvāmīs. Old women would enter the temple, calling out "*Jaya* Rādhe!" in broken voices.

When Bhaktivedanta Swami opened the shutters, his room would fill with light. His windows faced a courtyard, but they were not so much windows as cement latticework in the wall; although passersby could not easily see into the room, the latticework allowed light to enter. In the morning light, the room was clearly revealed: the arched ceiling, the freshly painted walls with arched niches, the floor of inlaid stone. Bhaktivedanta Swami's thin *sannyāsa-daṇḍa,* wrapped in heavy saffron *khādī,* leaned against one corner of the room. On one shelf he had placed a picture of Bhaktisiddhānta Sarasvatī, on another a stack of books and manuscripts. The room's two doors appeared flimsy even when locked, and the whole room tilted slightly to the left. It was bare but peaceful.

Often, sitting on the veranda between the two rooms, he would view the courtyard, the altar, and the Deities. Rādhā-Dāmodara, Vṛndāvana-candra, and several other Rādhā-Kṛṣṇa Deities awaited Their visitors. During the morning, the Deity doors remained open as a regular file of visitors turned the temple into a bustling place of pilgrimage. No one stayed very long. Some had rigid schedules to visit many temples and hurried on. Poor people and also local businessmen, their wives in colorful *sārīs*—all devotees—headed towards the altar, calling, "*Jaya ho,*" "*Jaya* Rādhe!" After greeting the Deities, they would disappear through the door to the outdoor area of the temple compound to visit the *samādhis.*

Although in Vṛndāvana there were hundreds of small templelike tombs honoring past Vaiṣṇava *ācāryas,* Bhaktivedanta Swami regularly visited the chief *samādhis,* those of Śrī Jīva Gosvāmī, Śrīla Bhaktisiddhānta Sarasvatī, and Śrīla Kṛṣṇadāsa Kavirāja Gosvāmī. Within a separate area of the temple compound were the *bhajana-kuṭīra* and the *samādhi* of Rūpa Gosvāmī. Bhaktivedanta Swami often sat chanting *japa* before Rūpa Gosvāmī's *samādhi.* The line of pilgrims from the temple would continue entering the outdoor area of the compound, coming to offer *daṇḍavats* to Rūpa Gosvāmī. Most pilgrims considered this the most important feature of their visit to Rādhā-Dāmodara temple, and even if they offered respect nowhere else, they would stop before the *samādhi* of Rūpa Gosvāmī. They would stop with folded hands and bow, chanting "*Jaya* Rādhe!" or, with their hands in their bead bags, chant the Hare Kṛṣṇa *mantra,* circumambulating the *samādhi.*

Bhaktivedanta Swami would sit and chant even after the early-morning rush of visitors, or sometimes he would walk to the nearby temples of Rādhā-Śyāmasundara or Rādhā-Madana-mohana, always returning by eleven to cook his meal. As he cooked, and later as he sat to take his *prasādam,* he could see through the latticework the *samādhi* of Rūpa Gosvāmī. Feeling Rūpa Gosvāmī's presence, he would think of his own mission for his spiritual master.

The devotees of Lord Caitanya are known as *rūpānugas,* followers of Rūpa Gosvāmī; without following the teachings and example of Rūpa Gosvāmī, one cannot enter the path of pure devotion to Rādhā and Kṛṣṇa. Śrīla Bhaktisiddhānta Sarasvatī was especially known as a strict *rūpānuga,* as described in the Sanskrit prayers written in his honor: "I offer my respectful obeisances unto Śrīla Bhaktisiddhānta Sarasvatī, the personified energy of Śrī Caitanya's mercy, who delivers devotional service enriched with conjugal love of Rādhā and Kṛṣṇa, coming exactly in the line of revelation of Śrīla Rūpa Gosvāmī. I offer my respectful obeisances unto you, who are the personified teachings of Lord Caitanya. You are the deliverer of the fallen souls. You do not tolerate any statement that is against the teachings of devotional service enunciated by Śrīla Rūpa Gosvāmī."

Bhaktivedanta Swami's spiritual master and the previous spiritual masters in the disciplic succession had wanted the Kṛṣṇa consciousness movement to spread all over the world, and as Bhaktivedanta Swami daily gathered inspiration, sitting before Rūpa Gosvāmī's *samādhi,* he prayed to his spiritual predecessors for guidance. The intimate direction he received from them was an absolute dictation, and no government, no publisher, nor anyone else could shake or diminish it. Rūpa Gosvāmī wanted him to go to the West; Śrīla Bhaktisiddhānta Sarasvatī wanted him to go to the West; Kṛṣṇa had arranged that he be brought to Rādhā-Dāmodara temple to receive their blessings. At the Rādhā-Dāmodara temple, he felt he had entered an eternal residence known only to pure devotees of the Lord. Yet although they were allowing him to associate intimately with them in the place of their pastimes, they were ordering him to leave—to leave Rādhā-Dāmodara and Vṛndāvana and to deliver the message of the *ācāryas* to forgetful parts of the world.

* * *

In June the weather became intolerably hot, and one could not remain active through the afternoon. During the most oppressive hours, Bhaktivedanta Swami would shut his doors and shutters and run the overhead fan. By evening the heat would abate, again a flurry of visitors would arrive, and in the temple compound there would be evening *kīrtanas*. Sitting on his veranda, Bhaktivedanta Swami would sometimes talk with visitors, or sometimes they would come to his door and observe him as he worked at his typewriter. He was known in Vṛndāvana as a scholar and a sublime devotee. But he kept to himself as much as possible, especially in the summer of 1962, working on *Śrīmad-Bhāgavatam*.

That was his real purpose in coming here: to prepare the books he could distribute to the people of the West. Although as yet he had no means for traveling even as far as Japan, and no means for printing books, these were the goals for which he worked. He had not come to Vṛndāvana to die and return to Godhead. Rather, he had come because it was the ideal place to gain spiritual strength for his main life's work. The exact shape of his future mission Bhaktivedanta Swami did not know, but he did know that he must prepare himself for preaching *Śrīmad-Bhāgavatam* to the English-speaking Western world. He must become a perfectly equipped instrument of his masters. And if they desired, they would send him.

CHAPTER ELEVEN

The Dream Come True

I planned that I must go to America. Generally they go to London, but I did not want to go to London. I was simply thinking how to go to New York. I was scheming, "Whether I shall go this way, through Tokyo, Japan, or that way? Which way is cheaper?" That was my proposal. And I was targeting to New York always. Sometimes I was dreaming that I have come to New York.
—Śrīla Prabhupāda

WRITING WAS ONLY half the battle; the other half was publishing. Both Bhaktivedanta Swami and his spiritual master wanted to see *Śrīmad-Bhāgavatam* printed in English and distributed widely. According to the teachings of Bhaktisiddhānta Sarasvatī, the most modern methods of printing and distributing books should be used to spread Kṛṣṇa consciousness. Although many books of Vaiṣṇava wisdom had already been perfectly presented by Rūpa Gosvāmī, Sanātana Gosvāmī, and Jīva Gosvāmī, the manuscripts now sat deteriorating in the Rādhā-Dāmodara temple and other locations, and even the Gaudiya Math's printings of the Gosvāmīs' works were not being widely distributed. One of Bhaktivedanta Swami's Godbrothers asked him why he was spending so much time and effort trying to make a new commentary on the *Bhāgavatam,* since so many great *ācāryas* had already commented upon it. But in Bhaktivedanta Swami's mind there was no question; his spiritual master had given him an order.

Commercial publishers, however, were not interested in the sixty-volume *Bhāgavatam* series, and Bhaktivedanta Swami was not interested in anything less than a sixty-volume *paramparā* presentation of verses, synonyms, and purports based on the commentaries of the previous *ācāryas.* But to publish such books he would have to raise private donations and publish at his own expense. Rādhā-Dāmodara temple may have been the best place for writing *Śrīmad-Bhāgavatam,* but not for printing and publishing it. For that he would have to go to New Delhi.

Among his Delhi contacts, Bhaktivedanta Swami considered Hitsaran Sharma a likely helper. Although when he had stayed in Mr. Sharma's home Mr. Sharma had appreciated him more as a member of a genre than as an individual, at least Mr. Sharma was inclined to help *sādhus,* and he recognized Bhaktivedanta Swami as a genuinely religious person. Therefore, when Bhaktivedanta Swami approached him in his office, he was willing to help, considering it a religious duty to propagate *Śrīmad-Bhāgavatam.*

Hitsaran Sharma was qualified to help for two reasons: he was the secretary to J. D. Dalmia, a wealthy philanthropist, and he was the owner of a commercial printing works, Radha Press. According to Mr. Sharma, Mr. Dalmia would not directly give money to Bhaktivedanta Swami, even if his secretary suggested it. Mr. Sharma therefore advised Bhaktivedanta Swami to go to Gorakhpur and show his manuscript to Hanuman Prasad Poddar, a religious publisher. Accepting this as good advice, Bhaktivedanta Swami journeyed to Gorakhpur, some 475 miles from Delhi.

Even such a trip as this constituted a financial strain. Bhaktivedanta Swami's daily ledger showed a balance of one hundred and thirty rupees as of August 8, 1962, the day he started for Gorakhpur. By the time he reached Lucknow he was down to fifty-seven rupees. Travel from Lucknow to Gorakhpur cost another six rupees, and the ricksha to Mr. Poddar's home cost eighty paisa.

But the trip was well worth the cost. Bhaktivedanta Swami presented Mr. Poddar with his letter of introduction from Hitsaran Sharma and then showed him his manuscript. After briefly examining the manuscript, Mr. Poddar concluded it to be a highly developed work that should be supported. He agreed to send a donation of four thousand rupees to the

Dalmia Trust in Delhi, to be used towards the publication of Śrī A. C. Bhaktivedanta Swami's *Śrīmad-Bhāgavatam.*

Indian printers do not always require full payment before they begin a job, provided they receive a substantial advance payment. After the job is printed and bound, a customer who has not made the complete payment takes a portion of books commensurate to what he has paid, and after selling those books he uses his profit to buy more. Bhaktivedanta Swami estimated that printing one volume would cost seven thousand rupees. So he was three thousand short. He raised a few hundred rupees more by going door to door throughout Delhi. Then he went back to Radha Press and asked Hitsaran Sharma to begin. Mr. Sharma agreed.

Radha Press had already produced much of the first two chapters when Bhaktivedanta Swami objected that the type was not large enough. He wanted twelve-point type, but the Radha Press had only ten-point. So Mr. Sharma agreed to take the work to another printer, Mr. Gautam Sharma of O.K. Press.

In printing Bhaktivedanta Swami's Volume One of the First Canto of *Śrīmad-Bhāgavatam,* O.K. Press printed four book pages twice on a side of one sheet of paper twenty by twenty-six inches. But before running the full eleven hundred copies, they would print a proof, which Bhaktivedanta Swami would read. Then, following the corrected proofs, the printers would correct the hand-set type and run a second proof, which Bhaktivedanta would also read. Usually he would also find errors on the second proof; if so, they would print a third. If he found no errors on the third proof, they would then print the final pages. At this pace Bhaktivedanta Swami was able to order small quantities of paper as he could afford it—from six to ten reams at a time, ordered two weeks in advance.

Even as the volume was being printed, he was still writing the last chapters. When the proofs were ready at O.K. Press, he would pick up the proofs, return to his room at Chippiwada, correct the proofs, and then return them. Sometimes fourteen-year-old Kantvedi, who lived at the Chippiwada temple with his parents, would carry the proofs back and forth for the Swami. But in the last months of 1962, Bhaktivedanta Swami usually made a daily walk to O.K. Press.

His walk through the tight, crowded lanes of Chippiwada soon led him to a road close to the Jama Mosque, and that road led into the noisy, heavily trafficked Chawri Bazaar. The neighborhood was a busy paper district, where laborers with ropes strapped across their shoulders pulled stout wooden carts, heavily loaded with stacks of paper, on small iron wheels. For two blocks, paper dealers were the only businesses—Hari Ram Gupta and Company, Roop Chand and Sons, Bengal Paper Mill Company Limited, Universal Traders, Janta Paper Mart—one after another even down the side alleys.

The neighborhood storefronts were colorful and disorderly. Pedestrian traffic was so hectic that for a person to dally even for a moment would cause a disruption. Carts and rickshas carried paper and other goods back and forth through the streets. Sometimes a laborer would jog past with a hefty stack of pages on his head, the stack weighing down on either end. Traffic was swift, and an unmindful or slow-footed pedestrian risked being struck by a load protruding from the head of a bearer or from a passing cart. Occasionally a man would be squatting on the roadside, smashing chunks of coal into small pieces to sell. Tiny corner smoke shops drew small gatherings of customers for cigarettes or *pān*. The shopkeeper would rapidly spread the *pān* spices on a betel leaf, and the customer would walk off down the street chewing the *pān* and spitting out red-stained saliva.

Amidst this milieu, as the Chawri Bazaar commercial district blended into tenement life and children played in the hazardous streets, Bhaktivedanta Swami was a gentle-looking yet determined figure. As he walked past the tenements, the tile sellers, the grain sellers, the sweet shops, and the printers, overhead would be electric wires, pigeons, and the clotheslines from the tenement balconies. Finally he would come to O.K. Press, directly across from a small mosque. He would come, carrying the corrected proofs, to anxiously oversee the printing work.

After four months, when the whole book had been printed and the sheets were stacked on the floor of the press, Mr. Hitsaran Sharma arranged for the work to be moved to a bindery. The binding was done by an ancient operation, mostly by hand, and it took another month. Bhaktivedanta Swami would come and observe the workers. A row of men sat in a small room, surrounded by stacks of printed paper. The first man would take one of the large printed sheets, rapidly fold it twice, and pass it to the next man, who performed the next operation. The pages would be folded, stitched, and collated, then put into a vise and hammered together before being trimmed on three sides with a handsaw and glued. Bit by bit, the book would be prepared for the final hard cover.

In addition to his visits to O.K. Press and the bindery, Bhaktivedanta Swami would also occasionally travel by bus across the Yamunā River to Mr. Hitsaran Sharma's Radha Press. The Radha Press was printing one thousand dust jackets for the volume.

Hitsaran Sharma: *Swamiji was going hither and thither. He was getting whatever collections he could and depositing them. And he was always mixing with many persons, going hither and thither. With me he was very fond that I should do everything as soon as possible. He had a great haste. He used to say, "Time is going, time is going. Quick, do it!" He would be annoyed with me also, and he would have me do his work first. But I was in the service of Dalmia, and I would tell him, "Your work has to be secondary for me." But he would say, "Now you have wasted my two days. What is this, Sharmaji? I am coming here, I told you in the morning to do this, and you have not done it even now." But I would reply, "I have got no time during the day." Then he would say, "Then you have wasted my complete day." So he was very much pressing me. This was his temperament.*

The binding was reddish, the color of an earthen brick, and was inlaid with gold lettering. Bhaktivedanta Swami had designed the dust jacket himself, and he had commissioned a young Bengali artist named Salit to execute it. It was a wraparound picture of the entire spiritual and material manifestations. Dominating the front cover was a pink lotus, and within its whorl were Rādhā and Kṛṣṇa and Their pastimes in Vṛndāvana, along with Lord Caitanya chanting and dancing with His associates. From Kṛṣṇa's lotus planet emanated yellow rays of light, and in that effulgence were many spiritual planets, appearing like so many suns. Sitting within each planet was a different four-armed form of Nārāyaṇa, each with His name lettered beneath the planet: Trivikrama, Keśava, Puruṣottama, and so on. Within an oval at the bottom of the front cover, Mahā-Viṣṇu was exhaling the material universes. On the inside cover was Bhaktivedanta Swami's explanation of the cover illustration.

When the printing and binding were completed, there were eleven hundred copies. Bhaktivedanta Swami would receive one hundred copies, and the printer would keep the balance. From the sale of the one hundred copies, Bhaktivedanta Swami would continue to pay off his debt to the printer and binder; then he would receive another supply of books. This would continue until he had finished paying his debt. His plan was to then publish a second volume from the profits of the first, and a third volume from the profits of the second.

Kantvedi went to pick up the first one hundred copies. He hired a man who put the books in large baskets, placed them on his hand truck, and then hauled them through the streets to the Chippiwada temple, where Bhaktivedanta Swami stacked them in his room on a bench.

Bhaktivedanta Swami went out alone to sell his books and present them to important people. Dr. Radhakrishnan, who gave him a personal audience, agreed to read the book and write his opinion. Hanuman Prasad Poddar was the first to write a favorable review:

> It is a source of great pleasure for me that a long cherished dream has materialised and is going to be materialised with this and the would-be publications. I thank the Lord that due to His grace this publication could see the light.

Bhaktivedanta Swami went to the major libraries, universities, and schools in Delhi, where the librarians found him "calm and quiet," "noble," "polite," "scholarly," "with a specific glow in him." Traveling on foot, he visited school administration offices throughout Delhi and placed copies in more than forty schools in the Delhi area. The Ministry of Education (which had previously denied him assistance) placed an order for fifty copies for selected university and institutional libraries throughout India. The ministry paid him six hundred rupees plus packing and postage charges, and Bhaktivedanta Swami mailed the books to the designated libraries. The U.S. embassy purchased eighteen copies, to be distributed in America through the Library of Congress.

The institutional sales were brisk, but then sales slowed. As the only agent, Bhaktivedanta Swami was now spending hours just to sell a few copies. He was eager to print the second volume, yet until enough money came from the first, he could not print. In the meantime he continued translating and writing purports. Writing so many volumes was a huge task that would take many years. And at his present rate, with sales so slow, he would not be able to complete the work in his lifetime.

Although there were many who took part in the production of the book and still others who became customers, only Bhaktivedanta Swami deeply experienced the successes and failures of the venture. It was his project, and he was responsible. No one was eager to see him writing prolifically, and no one demanded that it be printed. Even when the sales slowed to a trickle, the managers of O.K. Press were not distressed; they would give him the balance of his books only when he paid for them. And since it was also he who had the burden of hiring O.K. Press to print a second volume, the pressure was on him to go out and sell as many copies of the first volume as possible. For Hanuman Prasad Poddar, the volume had been something to admire in passing; for Hitsaran Sharma, it had been something he had tended to *after* his day's work for Mr. Dalmia; for the boy who lived at Chippiwada, the book had meant a few errands; for the paper dealers it had meant a small order; for Dr. Radhakrishnan it had been but the slightest, soon-forgotten matter in a life crammed with national politics and Hindu philosophizing. But Bhaktivedanta Swami, by his full engagement in producing the *Bhāgavatam,* felt bliss and assurance that Kṛṣṇa was pleased. He did not, however, intend for the *Bhāgavatam* to be his private affair. It was the sorely needed medicine for the ills of Kali-yuga, and it was not possible for only one man to administer it. Yet he *was* alone, and he felt exclusive pleasure and satisfaction in serving his *guru* and Lord Kṛṣṇa. Thus his transcendental frustration and pleasure mingled, his will strengthened, and he continued alone.

His spiritual master, the previous spiritual masters, and the Vedic scriptures all assured him that he was right. If a person got a copy of the *Bhāgavatam* and read even one page, he might decide to take part in Lord Caitanya's movement. If a person seriously read the book, he would be convinced about spiritual life. The more this book could be distributed, the more the people could understand Kṛṣṇa consciousness. And if they understood Kṛṣṇa consciousness, they would become liberated from all problems. Bookselling was real preaching. Bhaktisiddhānta Sarasvatī had wanted it, even at the neglect of constructing temples or making followers. Who could preach as well as *Śrīmad-Bhāgavatam*? Certainly whoever spent sixteen rupees for a book would also take the time at least to look at it.

In the months that followed, Bhaktivedanta Swami received more favorable reviews. The prestigious *Adyar Library Bulletin* gave a full review, noting "the editor's vast and deep study of the subject" and concluding, "Further volumes of this publication are eagerly awaited."

His scholarly Godbrothers also wrote their appreciations. Swami Bon Mahārāja, rector of the Institute of Oriental Philosophy in Vṛndāvana, wrote:

> *I have nothing but admiration for your bold and practical venture.* If you should be able to complete the whole work, you will render *a very great service* to the cause of Prabhupada Sri Bhaktisiddhanta Saraswati Goswami Maharaj, Sri Chaitanya Mahaprabhu and the country also. *Do it and rest assured there will be no scarcity of resources.*

Bhaktisāraṅga Mahārāja wrote a full review in his *Sajjana-toṣaṇī.*

> We expect that this particular English version of Srimad Bhagwatam will be widely read and thereby spiritual poverty of people in general may be removed forever. At a time when we need it very greatly, Srimad Bhaktivedanta Swami has given us the right thing. We recommend this publication for everyone's serious study.

Shri Biswanath Das, governor of Uttar Pradesh, commended the volume to all thoughtful people. And *Economic Review* praised the author for attempting a tremendous task.

> At a time when not only the people of India but those of the West need the chastening quality of love and truth in the corrupting atmosphere of hate and hypocrisy, **a work like this will have uplifting and** corrective influence.

Dr. Zakir Hussain, vice president of India, wrote:

> I have read your book Srimad Bhagwatam with great interest and much profit. I thank you again for the kind thought which must have prompted you to present it to me.

The favorable reviews, although Bhaktivedanta Swami could not pay the printer with them, indicated a serious response; the book was valuable. And subsequent volumes would earn the series even more respect. By Kṛṣṇa's grace, Bhaktivedanta Swami had already completed many of the translations and purports for Volume Two. Even in the last weeks of printing the first volume, he had been writing day and night for the second volume. It was glorification of the Supreme Lord, Kṛṣṇa, and therefore it would require many, many volumes. He felt impelled to praise Kṛṣṇa and describe Him in more and more volumes. Śrīla Bhaktisiddhānta Sarasvatī had said that the presses of the world could not print fast enough the glories of Kṛṣṇa and the spiritual world that were being received at every moment by pure devotees.

Bhaktivedanta Swami decided to return to Vṛndāvana for several months of intensive writing on Volume Two. This was his real business at Rādhā-Dāmodara temple. Vṛndāvana was the best place for writing transcendental literature; that had already been demonstrated by the Vaiṣṇava *ācāryas* of the past. Living in simple ease, taking little rest and food, he continually translated the verses and composed his Bhaktivedanta purports for Volume Two. After a few months, after amassing enough manuscript pages, he would return to Delhi and once again enter the world of publishing.

In Volume One he had covered the first six-and-a-half chapters of the First Canto. The second volume began on page 365 with the eighth verse of the Seventh Chapter. Bhaktivedanta Swami wrote in his purport that the *Śrīmad-Bhāgavatam* was meant for *paramahaṁsas,* persons engaged purely in self-realization. "Yet," he wrote, "it works into the depth of the heart of those who may be worldly men. Worldly men are all engaged in the matter of sense gratification. But even such men also will find in this Vedic literature a remedial measure for their material diseases."

Bhaktivedanta Swami returned to Delhi to raise funds for printing Volume Two. When he visited a prospective donor, he would show the man Volume One and the growing collection of reviews, explaining that he was asking a donation not to support himself but to print this important literature. Although for the first volume he had received no donations equal to the four thousand rupees he had received from Mr. Poddar, an executive in the L & H Sugar factory gave a donation of five thousand rupees for Volume Two.

Bhaktivedanta Swami had been dissatisfied with Hitsaran Sharma as a production supervisor. Although supposedly an expert in the trade, Hitsaran had caused delays, and sometimes he had advised Gautam Sharma without consulting Bhaktivedanta Swami. The work on Volume One had slowed and even stopped when a job from a cash customer had come up, and Bhaktivedanta Swami had complained that it was Hitsaran's fault for not giving money to O.K. Press on time. For Volume Two, Bhaktivedanta Swami decided to deal directly with O.K. Press and supervise the printing himself. He spoke to Gautam Sharma and offered a partial payment. Although the majority of the copies of Volume One were still standing on their printing floor, Bhaktivedanta Swami wanted O.K. Press to begin Volume Two. Gautam Sharma accepted the job.

It was early in 1964 when Volume Two went to press, following the same steps as Volume One. But this time Bhaktivedanta Swami was more actively present, pushing. To avoid delays, he purchased the paper himself. At Siddho Mal and Sons Paper Merchants, in the heart of the paper district, he would choose and order his paper and then arrange to transport it to O.K. Press. If the order was a large one he would have it carried by cart; smaller orders he would send by ricksha or on the head of a bearer.

In his Preface to the second volume, Bhaktivedanta Swami expressed the apparent oddity of working in Delhi while living in Vṛndāvana.

"The path of fruitive activities *i.e.* to say **the path of earn money and enjoy life,** as it is going on generally, appears to have become also our profession although we have renounced the order of worldly life! They see that we are moving in the cities, in the Government offices, banks and other business places for promoting the publication of **Srimad Bhagwatam.** They also see that we are moving in the press, paper market and amongst the book binders also away from our residence at Vrindaban, and thus they conclude sometimes mistakenly that we are also doing the same business in the dress of a mendicant!

"But actually there is a gulf of difference between the two kinds of activities. This is not a business for maintaining an establishment of material enjoyment. On the contrary it is an humble attempt to broadcast the glories of the Lord at a time when the people need it very badly."

He went on to describe how in former days, even fifty years ago, well-to-do members of society had commissioned *paṇḍitas* to print or hand-write the *Bhāgavatam* and then distribute copies amongst the devotees and the general people. But times had changed. "At the present moment the time is so changed that we had to request one of the biggest industrialists of India, to purchase 100 (one hundred) copies and distribute them but the poor fellow expressed his inability. We wished that somebody may come forward to pay for the actual cost of publication of this Srimad Bhagwatam and let them be distributed free to all the leading gentlemen of the world. But nobody is so far prepared to do this social uplifting work."

After thanking the Ministry of Education and the director of education for distributing copies to institutions and libraries, Bhaktivedanta Swami again stated his predicament before his reading public. "The problem is that we must get some money for completing the work which is admittedly a mighty project. The sales proceeds are being employed in the promotional work and not in sense gratification. Herein lies the difference from the fruitive activities. And for all this we have to approach everyone concerned just like a businessman. There is no harm to become a businessman if it is done on account of the Lord as much as there was no harm to become a violent warrior like Arjuna or Hanumanji if such belligerent activities are executed to satisfy the desires of the Supreme Lord.

"So even though we are not in the Himalayas, even though we talk of business, even though we deal in rupees and paisa, still, simply because we are 100 per cent servants of the Lord and are engaged in the service of broadcasting the message of His glories, certainly we shall transcend and get through the invincible impasse of *Maya* and reach the effulgent kingdom of God to render Him face to face eternal service, in full bliss and knowledge. We are confident of this factual position and we may also assure to our numerous readers that they will also achieve the same result simply by hearing the glories of the Lord."

On receipt of the first copies of the second volume—another four-hundred-page, clothbound, brick-colored *Śrīmad-Bhāgavatam,* with the same dust jacket as Volume One—Bhaktivedanta Swami made the rounds of the institutions, scholars, politicians, and booksellers. One Delhi bookseller, Dr. Manoharlal Jain, had particular success in selling the volumes.

Manoharlal Jain: *He would come to me for selling his books. He would come often, and he used to chat with me for one or two hours. He had no other business except selling his books as much as possible. We would discuss the difficulties he was having and also many other things*—yoga, Vedānta, *and religious aspects of life. His problem was distributing his work, because it was a big publication. He had planned to publish it in many volumes. Naturally, I told him it was not possible for any individual bookseller or publisher here to publish it and invest money in it. So that was a little bit of a disappointment for him because he could not bring out more volumes.*

But my sales were good because this was the best translation—Sanskrit text with English translations. No other such edition was available. I sold about one hundred and fifty to two hundred copies in about two or three years. The price was very little, only sixteen rupees. He had published his reviews, and he had a good sell, a good market. The price was reasonable, and he was not interested in making money out of it. He was printing in English, for the foreigners. He had a good command of Sanskrit as well as English. When we met, we would speak in English, and his English was very impressive.

He wanted me to publish, but I didn't have any presses and no finances. I told him frankly I would not be able to publish it, because it was not one or two volumes but many. But he managed anyhow. I referred him to Atmaram and Sons. He also used to go there.

He was a great master, a philosopher, a great scholar. I used to enjoy the talks. He used to sit with me for one or two hours, as much as he could afford. Sometimes he would come in the morning, eleven or twelve, and then sometimes in the afternoon. He used to come in for money: "How many copies are sold?" So I would pay him. Practically, he was not doing very well with finances at that time. He only wanted that his books should be sold to every library and everywhere where the people are interested in it.

We used to publish a catalog every month, and I would advertise his book. Orders would be coming from all over the world. So, at least for me, the sales were picking up. If I sold one hundred copies of the first volume, then I figured the second volume would be sold in the same number, naturally. But definitely those who would take the first volume would also take Volume Two, because it was institutional and the institutions will always try to complete their set. He used to discuss with me how the volumes can be brought out and how many it would take to complete the Śrīmad-Bhāgavatam. *He was very much interested in bringing out the whole series.*

In January of 1964, Bhaktivedanta Swami was granted an interview with Indian vice president Zakir Hussain, who, although a Muslim, had written an appreciation of Bhaktivedanta Swami's *Śrīmad-Bhāgavatam.* As Dr. Hussain cordially received the author at the presidential palace, Bhaktivedanta Swami spoke of the importance of *Śrīmad-Bhāgavatam* in the cause of love of Godhead. But Dr. Hussain wanted to know how love of Godhead could help humanity. The question, put by ruler to *sādhu,* was filled with philosophical implications, but the vice president's busy schedule of meetings did not permit Bhaktivedanta Swami to answer fully. For the vice president the interview was a gesture of appreciation, recognizing the Swami for his work on behalf of India's Hindu cultural heritage. And Bhaktivedanta Swami humbly accepted the ritual.

Later, however, he wrote Dr. Hussain a long letter, answering the question he had not had time to answer during their brief meeting. "... Mussalmans [Muslims] also admit," he wrote, "that 'There is nothing greater than Allah.' The Christians also admit that 'God is Great.' ... *The human society must learn to obey the laws of God.*" He reminded Dr. Hussain of India's great cultural asset the Vedic literature; the Indian government could perform the best welfare work for humanity by disseminating Vedic knowledge in a systematic way. *Śrīmad-Bhāgavatam* was "produced in India"; it was the substantial contribution India could offer to the world.

* * *

In March of 1964, Krishna Pandit, Bhaktivedanta Swami's sponsor at the Rādhā-Kṛṣṇa temple in Chippiwada, arranged for him to reside for a few months at the Śrī Rādhāvallabhajī temple in the nearby Rosanpura Naisarak neighborhood. There he could continue his writing and publishing, but he would also be giving a series of lectures. Krishna Pandit provided Bhaktivedanta Swami about fifteen hundred rupees for his maintenance. On Bhaktivedanta Swami's arrival at Śrī Rādhā-vallabhajī temple, the manager distributed notices inviting people to "take full advantage of the presence of a Vaishnava Sadhu." As "resident *ācārya*," Bhaktivedanta Swami held morning and evening discourses at the temple, without reducing his activities of writing and printing.

* * *

In June, Bhaktivedanta Swami got the opportunity to meet Prime Minister Lal Bahadur Shastri. The meeting had been arranged by Doladram Khannah, a wealthy jeweler who was a trustee of the Chippiwada temple and had often met with Bhaktivedanta Swami there. An old friend of Prime Minister Shastri's since his youth, when they had attended the same *yoga* club, Mr. Khannah arranged the meeting as a favor to Bhaktivedanta Swami. Let the prime minister meet a genuine *sādhu,* Mr. Khannah thought.

It was a formal occasion in the gardens of the Parliament Building, and the prime minister was meeting a number of guests. Prime Minister Shastri, dressed in white *kurtā* and *dhotī* and a Nehru hat and surrounded by aides, received the elderly *sādhu.* Bhaktivedanta Swami, looking scholarly in his spectacles, stepped forward and introduced himself—and his book, *Śrīmad-Bhāgavatam.* As he handed the prime minister a copy of Volume One, a photographer snapped a photo of the author and the prime minister smiling over the book.

The next day, Bhaktivedanta Swami wrote to Prime Minister Shastri. He soon received a reply, personally signed by the prime minister:

> Dear Swamiji, Many thanks for your Letter. I am indeed grateful to you for Presenting a copy of "Srimad Bhagwatam" to me. I do realise that you are doing valuable work. It would be good idea if the libraries in the Government Institutions purchase copies of this book.

Bhaktivedanta Swami wrote back to the prime minister, requesting him to buy books for Indian institutions. Mr. R. K. Sharma of the Ministry of Education subsequently wrote back, confirming that they would take fifty copies of Volume Two, just as they had taken Volume One.

* * *

To concentrate on completing Volume Three, Bhaktivedanta Swami returned to the Rādhā-Dāmodara temple. These were the last chapters of the First Canto, dealing with the advent of the present Age of Kali. There were many verses foretelling society's degradation and narrating how the great King Parīkṣit had staved off Kali's influence by his strong Kṛṣṇa conscious rule. In his purports, Bhaktivedanta Swami wrote that government could not check corruption unless it rooted out the four basic principles of irreligion—meat-eating, illicit sex, intoxication, and gambling. "You cannot check all these evils of society simply by statutory acts of police vigilance but you have to cure the disease of mind by the proper medicine namely advocating the principles of Brahminical culture or the principles of austerity, cleanliness, mercy, and truthfulness. ... We must always remember that false pride ... undue attachment for woman or association with them and intoxicating habit of all ... description will cripple the human civilisation from the path of factual peace, however the people may go on clamouring for such peace of the world."

To raise funds for Volume Three, Bhaktivedanta Swami decided to try Bombay. He traveled there in July and stayed at the Premkutir Dharmshala, a free *āśrama.*

Śrīla Prabhupāda: *At Premkutir they received me very nicely. I was going to sell my books. Some of them were criticizing, "What kind of* sannyāsī? *He is making business bookselling." Not the authorities said this, but some of them. I was writing my book then also.*

Then I became a guest for fifteen days with a member of the Dalmia family. One of the brothers told me that he wanted to construct a little cottage at his house: "You can live here. I will give you a nice cottage." I thought, "No, it is not good to be fully dependent and patronized by a viṣayī *[materialist]." But I stayed for fifteen days, and he gave me exclusive use of a typewriter for writing my books.*

Bhaktivedanta Swami made his rounds of the institutions and booksellers in Bombay. He now had an advertisement showing himself with Prime Minister Shastri, and he also had the prime minister's letter and the Ministry of Education's purchase order for fifty volumes. Still, he was getting only small orders.

Then he decided to visit Sumati Morarji, head of the Scindia Steamship

Company. He had heard from his Godbrothers in Bombay that she was known for helping *sādhus* and had donated to the Bombay Gaudiya Math. He had never met her, but he well remembered the 1958 promise by one of her officers to arrange half-fare passage for him to America. Now he wanted her help for printing *Śrīmad-Bhāgavatam.*

But his first attempts to arrange a meeting were unsuccessful. Frustrated at being put off by Mrs. Morarji's officers, he sat down on the front steps of her office building, determined to catch her attention as she left for the day. The lone *sādhu* certainly caused some attention as he sat quietly chanting for five hours on the steps of the Scindia Steamship Company building. Finally, late that afternoon, Mrs. Morarji emerged in a flurry of business talk with her secretary, Mr. Choksi. Upon seeing Bhaktivedanta Swami, she stopped. "Who is this gentleman sitting here?" she asked Mr. Choksi.

"He's been here for five hours," the secretary said.

"All right, I'll come," she said and walked up to where Bhaktivedanta Swami was sitting. He smiled and stood, offering *namaskāras* with his folded palms. "Swamiji, what can I do for you?" she said.

Bhaktivedanta Swami told her briefly of his intentions to print the third volume of his *Śrīmad-Bhāgavatam.* "I want you to help me," he said.

"All right," Mrs. Morarji replied. "We can meet tomorrow, because it is getting late. Tomorrow you can come, and we will discuss."

The next day, Bhaktivedanta Swami met with Mrs. Morarji in her office, where she looked at the typed manuscript and the published volumes. "All right," she said, "if you want to print it, I will give you the aid. Whatever you want. You can get it printed."

With Mrs. Morarji's guarantee, Bhaktivedanta Swami was free to return to Vṛndāvana to finish writing the manuscript. As with the previous volumes, he set a demanding schedule for writing and publishing. The third volume would complete the First Canto. Then, with a supply of impressive literature, he would be ready to go to the West. Even with volumes One and Two he was getting a better reception in India. Already he had seen the vice president and prime minister. He had successfully approached a big business magnate of Bombay, and within a few minutes of presenting the book, he had received a large donation. The books were powerful preaching.

* * *

Janmāṣṭamī was drawing near, and Bhaktivedanta Swami was planning a celebration at the Rādhā-Dāmodara temple. He wanted to invite Biswanath Das, the governor of Uttar Pradesh, to preside over the ceremony honoring Lord Kṛṣṇa's appearance. Shri Biswanath had received a copy of *Śrīmad-Bhāgavatam* Volume One and had written a favorable review. Although a politician, he was known for his affection and respect for *sādhus.* He regularly invited recognized *sādhus* to his home, and once a year he would visit all the important temples of Mathurā and Vṛndāvana. Bhaktivedanta Swami asked Vṛndāvana's municipal president, Mangalal Sharma, to invite the governor to the Janmāṣṭamī celebration at Rādhā-Dāmodara temple. The governor readily accepted the invitation.

Bhaktivedanta Swami printed a flyer announcing:

On the Occasion of JANMASTAMI ceremony at
The Samadhi ground of Srila Rupa and Jeeva Goswami
SRI SRI RADHA DAMODAR TEMPLE
Sebakunj, Vrindaban.
Goudiya Kirtan Performances
In the Presence of
His Excellency Sri Biswanath Das
GOVERNOR OF UTTAR PRADESH
&
The chief Guest SRI G. D. SOMANI of Bombay
Trustee of Sri Ranganathji Temple, Vrindaban.
Dated at Vrindaban Sunday the 31st August, 1964 at 7-30 to
8-30 p.m.

The flyer contained an advertisement for the *Śrīmad-Bhāgavatam* series, to be completed in sixty volumes. *Bhajanas* to be sung on the occasion—"Śrī Kṛṣṇa Caitanya Prabhu," "Nitāi-pada-kamala," the "Prayers to the Six Gosvāmīs," and other favorite songs of the Gauḍīya Vaiṣṇavas—were printed in Bengali as a songbook.

The program was successful. A large crowd attended and sang songs to Lord Kṛṣṇa and took *prasādam.* Bhaktivedanta Swami lectured on a verse from *Śrīmad-Bhāgavatam* describing the Age of Kali as an ocean of faults that had but one saving quality: the chanting of Hare Kṛṣṇa. After leading Hare Kṛṣṇa *kīrtana,* Bhaktivedanta Swami presented a copy of his second volume of *Śrīmad-Bhāgavatam* to the governor and spoke of his plans to preach all over the world.

The day after Janmāṣṭamī was Bhaktivedanta Swami's sixty-ninth birthday. A few days later, Biswanath Das requested Swami Mahārāja to visit him at his mansion in Lucknow. It was a special occasion, and the governor had invited several *sādhus* and planned a *kīrtana* program. He had invited a professional musical group who toured India performing *kīrtanas* and giving recitals. One of the musicians, young Sisir Kumar Bhattacarya, was very impressed with Bhaktivedanta Swami.

Sisir Bhattacarya: *We were invited to perform* kīrtana *in the governor's house in Lucknow. We had about seven or eight in our group. This was the governor's house, a big home, and I was sitting on a dais. I saw the governor, Biswanath Das, and beside him was a* sādhu *who was old but I thought was really strong. When I saw the governor sitting there, I came down from the dais and bowed down. Then I asked which subject he wanted to listen to. He said, "Let's have something about Caitanya Mahāprabhu." Then I said, "I'm very glad you selected this." About one half hour we spent on Mahāprabhu's* kīrtana, *and then we had our dinner in the big banquet hall on all silver plates with the governor's symbols on each of them.*

We sat together, and I was sitting side by side with the same sādhu, *and he introduced himself as Bhaktivedanta Swami. We discussed, and then the Swami presented me with a book,* Śrīmad-Bhāgavatam. *Bhaktivedanta Swami said, "I am interested to propagate* kṛṣṇa-nāma *and Caitanya Mahāprabhu in the Western countries. I am trying to get some way to find some ticket. If I get, I will go, and I will propagate Mahāprabhu's teachings." And he uttered this verse from Mahāprabhu:* pṛthivīte āche yata nagarādi grāma/ sarvatra pracāra haibe mora nāma.* *But I did not think he would actually be able to do it, because he was very simple and poor.*

* * *

With the manuscript for Volume Three complete and with the money to print it, Bhaktivedanta Swami once again entered the printing world, purchasing paper, correcting proofs, and keeping the printer on schedule so that the book would be finished by January 1965. Thus, by his

---

* Caitanya Mahāprabhu had predicted, "One day My name will be known in every town and village in the world."

persistence, he who had almost no money of his own managed to publish his third large hardbound volume within a little more than two years.

At this rate, with his respect in the scholarly world increasing, he might soon become a recognized figure amongst his countrymen. But he had his vision set on the West. And with the third volume now printed, he felt he was at last prepared. He was sixty-nine and would have to go soon. It had been more than forty years since Śrīla Bhaktisiddhānta Sarasvatī had first asked a young householder in Calcutta to preach Kṛṣṇa consciousness in the West. At first it had seemed impossible to Abhay Charan, who had so recently entered family responsibilities. That obstacle, however, had long ago been removed, and for more than ten years he had been free to travel. But he had been penniless (and still was). And he had wanted first to publish some volumes of *Śrīmad-Bhāgavatam* to take with him; it had seemed necessary if he were to do something solid. Now, by Kṛṣṇa's grace, three volumes were on hand.

Śrīla Prabhupāda: *I planned that I must go to America. Generally they go to London, but I did not want to go to London. I was simply thinking how to go to New York. I was scheming, "Whether I shall go this way, through Tokyo, Japan, or that way? Which way is cheaper?" That was my proposal. And I was targeting to New York always. Sometimes I was dreaming that I have come to New York.*

Then Bhaktivedanta Swami met Mr. Agarwal, a Mathurā businessman, and mentioned to him in passing, as he did to almost everyone he met, that he wanted to go to the West. Although Mr. Agarwal had known Bhaktivedanta Swami for only a few minutes, he volunteered to try to get him a sponsor in America. It was something Mr. Agarwal had done a number of times; when he met a *sādhu* who mentioned something about going abroad to teach Hindu culture, he would ask his son Gopal, an engineer in Pennsylvania, to send back a sponsorship form. When Mr. Agarwal volunteered to help in this way, Bhaktivedanta Swami urged him please to do so.

Śrīla Prabhupāda: *I did not say anything seriously to Mr. Agarwal, but perhaps he took it very seriously. I asked him, "Well, why don't you ask your son Gopal to sponsor so that I can go there? I want to preach there."*

But Bhaktivedanta Swami knew he could not simply dream of going to the West; he needed money. In March 1965 he made another visit to Bombay, attempting to sell his books. Again he stayed at the free *dharmaśālā,* Premkutir. But finding customers was difficult. He met Paramananda Bhagwani, a librarian at Jai Hind College, who purchased books for the college library and then escorted Bhaktivedanta Swami to a few likely outlets.

Mr. Bhagwani: *I took him to the Popular Book Depot at Grant Road to help him in selling books, but they told us they couldn't stock the books because they don't have much sales on religion. Then we went to another shop nearby, and the owner also regretted his inability to sell the books. Then he went to Sadhuvela, near Mahalakshmi temple, and we met the head of the temple there. He, of course, welcomed us. They have a library of their own, and they stock religious books, so we approached them to please keep a set there in their library. They are a wealthy* āśrama, *and yet he also expressed his inability.*

Bhaktivedanta Swami returned to Delhi, pursuing the usual avenues of bookselling and looking for whatever opportunity might arise. And to his surprise, he was contacted by the Ministry of External Affairs and informed that his No Objection certificate for going to the U.S. was ready. Since he had not instigated any proceedings for leaving the country, Bhaktivedanta Swami had to inquire from the ministry about what had happened. They showed him the Statutory Declaration Form signed by Mr. Gopal Agarwal of Butler, Pennsylvania; Mr. Agarwal solemnly declared that he would bear the expenses of Bhaktivedanta Swami during his stay in the U.S.

Śrīla Prabhupāda: *Whatever the correspondence was there between the father and son, I did not know. I simply asked him, "Why don't you ask your son Gopal to sponsor?" And now, after three or four months, the No Objection certificate was sent from the Indian Consulate in New York to me. He had already sponsored my arrival there for one month, and all of a sudden I got the paper.*

At his father's request, Gopal Agarwal had done as he had done for several other *sādhus,* none of whom had ever gone to America. It was just a formality, something to satisfy his father. Gopal had requested a form from the Indian Consulate in New York, obtained a statement from his employer certifying his monthly salary, gotten a letter from his bank showing his balance as of April 1965, and had the form notarized.

It had been stamped and approved in New York and sent to Delhi. Now Bhaktivedanta Swami had a sponsor. But he still needed a passport, visa, P-form, and travel fare.

The passport was not very difficult to obtain. Krishna Pandit helped, and by June 10 he had his passport. Carefully, he penned in his address at the Rādhā-Kṛṣṇa temple in Chippiwada and wrote his father's name, Gour Mohan De. He asked Krishna Pandit also to pay for his going abroad, but Krishna Pandit refused, thinking it against Hindu principles for a *sādhu* to go abroad—and also very expensive.

With his passport and sponsorship papers, Bhaktivedanta Swami went to Bombay, not to sell books or raise funds for printing; he wanted a ticket for America. Again he tried approaching Sumati Morarji. He showed his sponsorship papers to her secretary, Mr. Choksi, who was impressed and who went to Mrs. Morarji on his behalf. "The Swami from Vṛndāvana is back," he told her. "He has published his book on your donation. He has a sponsor, and he wants to go to America. He wants you to send him on a Scindia ship." Mrs. Morarji said no, the Swamiji was too old to go to the United States and expect to accomplish anything. As Mr. Choksi conveyed to him Mrs. Morarji's words, Bhaktivedanta Swami listened disapprovingly. She wanted him to stay in India and complete the *Śrīmad-Bhāgavatam.* Why go to the States? Finish the job here.

But Bhaktivedanta Swami was fixed on going. He told Mr. Choksi that he should convince Mrs. Morarji. He coached Mr. Choksi on what he should say: "I find this gentleman very inspired to go to the States and preach something to the people there. ..." But when he told Mrs. Morarji, she again said no. The Swami was not healthy. It would be too cold there. He might not be able to come back, and she doubted whether he would be able to accomplish much there. People in America were not so cooperative, and they would probably not listen to him.

Exasperated with Mr. Choksi's ineffectiveness, Bhaktivedanta Swami demanded a personal interview. It was granted, and a gray-haired, determined Bhaktivedanta Swami presented his emphatic request: "Please give me one ticket."

Sumati Morarji was concerned. "Swamiji, you are so old—you are taking this responsibility. Do you think it is all right?"

"No," he reassured her, lifting his hand as if to reassure a doubting daughter, "it is all right."

"But do you know what my secretaries think? They say, 'Swamiji is going to die there.'"

Bhaktivedanta made a face as if to dismiss a foolish rumor. Again he insisted that she give him a ticket. "All right," she said. "Get your P-form, and I will make an arrangement to send you by our ship." Bhaktivedanta Swami smiled brilliantly and happily left her offices, past her amazed and skeptical clerks.

A "P-form"—another necessity for an Indian national who wants to leave the country—is a certificate given by the State Bank of India, certifying that the person has no excessive debts in India and is cleared by the banks. That would take a while to obtain. And he also did not yet have a U.S. visa. He needed to pursue these government permissions in Bombay, but he had no place to stay. So Mrs. Morarji agreed to let him reside at the Scindia Colony, a compound of apartments for employees of the Scindia Company.

He stayed in a small, unfurnished apartment with only his trunk and typewriter. The resident Scindia employees all knew that Mrs. Morarji was sending him to the West, and some of them became interested in his cause. They were impressed, for although he was so old, he was going abroad to preach. He was a special *sādhu,* a scholar. They heard from him how he was taking hundreds of copies of his books with him, but no money. He became a celebrity at the Scindia Colony. Various families brought him rice, *sabjī,* and fruit. They brought so much that he could not eat it all, and he mentioned this to Mr. Choksi. Just accept it and distribute it, Mr. Choksi advised. Bhaktivedanta Swami then began giving remnants of his food to the children. Some of the older residents gathered to hear him as he read and spoke from *Śrīmad-Bhāgavatam.* Mr. Vasavada, the chief cashier of Scindia, was particularly impressed and came regularly to learn from the *sādhu.* Mr. Vasavada obtained copies of Bhaktivedanta Swami's books and read them in his home.

Bhaktivedanta Swami's apartment shared a roofed-in veranda with Mr. Nagarajan, a Scindia office worker, and his wife.

Mrs. Nagarajan: *Every time when I passed that way, he used to be writing or chanting. I would ask him, "Swamiji, what are you writing?" He used to sit near the window and one after another was translating the Sanskrit. He gave me two books and said, "Child, if you read this book, you will understand." We would have discourses in the house, and four or five Gujarati ladies used to come. At one of these discourses he told one lady that those who wear their hair parted on the side—that is not a good idea. Every Indian lady should have her hair parted in the center. They were very fond of listening and very keen to hear his discourse.*

Every day he would go out trying to get his visa and P-form as quickly as possible, selling his books, and seeking contacts and supporters for his future *Śrīmad-Bhāgavatam* publishing. Mr. Nagarajan tried to help. Using the telephone directory, he made a list of wealthy business and professional men who were Vaiṣṇavas and might be inclined to assist. Bhaktivedanta Swami's neighbors at Scindia Colony observed him coming home dead tired in the evening. He would sit quietly, perhaps feeling morose, some neighbors thought, but after a while he would sit up, rejuvenated, and start writing.

Mrs. Nagarajan: *When he came home we used to give him courage, and we used to tell him, "Swamiji, one day you will achieve your target." He would say, "Time is still not right. Time is still not right. They are all* ajñānīs. *They don't understand. But still I must carry on."*

Sometimes I would go by, and his cādara *would be on the chair, but he would be sitting on the windowsill. I would ask him, "Swamiji, did you have any good contacts?" He would say, "Not much today. I didn't get much, and it is depressing. Tomorrow Kṛṣṇa will give me more details." And he would sit there quietly.*

After ten minutes, he would sit in his chair and start writing. I would wonder how Swamiji was so tired in one minute and in another minute ... Even if he was tired, he was not defeated. He would never speak discouragement. And we would always encourage him and say, "If today you don't get it, tomorrow you will definitely meet some people, and they will encourage you." And my friends used to come in the morning and in the evening for discourse, and they would give namaskāra *and fruits.*

Mr. Nagarajan: *His temperament was very adjustable and homely. Our friends would offer a few rupees. He would say, "All right. It will help." He used to walk from our colony to Andheri station. It is two kilometers, and he used to go there without taking a bus, because he had no money.*

Bhaktivedanta Swami had a page printed entitled "My Mission," and he would show it to influential men in his attempts to get further financing for *Śrīmad-Bhāgavatam.* The printed statement proposed that God consciousness was the only remedy for the evils of modern materialistic society. Despite scientific advancement and material comforts, there was no peace in the world; therefore, *Bhagavad-gītā* and *Śrīmad-Bhāgavatam,* the glory of India, must be spread all over the world.

Mrs. Morarji asked Bhaktivedanta Swami if he would read *Śrīmad-Bhāgavatam* to her in the evening. He agreed. She began sending her car for him at six o'clock each evening, and they would sit in her garden, where he would recite and comment on the *Bhāgavatam.*

Mrs. Morarji: *He used to come in the evening and sing the verses in rhythmic tunes, as is usually done with the* Bhāgavatam. *And certain points—when you sit and discuss, you raise so many points—he was commenting on certain points, but it was all from the* Bhāgavatam. *So he used to sit and explain to me and then go. He could give time, and I could hear him. That was for about ten or fifteen days.*

His backing by Scindia and his sponsorship in the U.S. were a strong presentation, and with the help of the people at Scindia he obtained his visa on July 28, 1965. But the P-form proceedings went slowly and even threatened to be a last, insurmountable obstacle.

Śrīla Prabhupāda: *Formerly there was no restriction for going outside. But for a* sannyāsī *like me, I had so much difficulty obtaining the government permission to go out. I had applied for the P-form sanction, but no sanction was coming. Then I went to the State Bank of India. The officer was Mr. Martarchari. He told me, "Swamiji, you are sponsored by a private man. So we cannot accept. If you were invited by some institution, then we could consider. But you are invited by a private man for one month. And after one month, if you are in difficulty, there will be so many obstacles." But I had already prepared everything to go. So I said, "What have you done?" He said, "I have decided not to sanction your P-form." I said, "No, no, don't do this. You better send me to your superior. It should not be like that."*

So he took my request, and he sent the file to the chief official of foreign exchange—something like that. So he was the supreme man in the State Bank of India. I went to see him. I asked his secretary, "Do you have such-and-such a file. You kindly put it to Mr. Rao. I want to see him." So the secretary agreed, and he put the file, and he put my name down to see him. I was waiting. So Mr. Rao came personally. He said, "Swamiji, I passed your case. Don't worry."

Following Mrs. Morarji's instruction, her secretary, Mr. Choksi, made final arrangements for Bhaktivedanta Swami. Since he had no warm clothes, Mr. Choksi took him to buy a wool jacket and other woolen clothes. Mr. Choksi spent about 250 rupees on new clothes, including some new *dhotīs*. At Bhaktivedanta Swami's request, Mr. Choksi printed five hundred copies of a small pamphlet containing the eight verses written by Lord Caitanya and an advertisement for *Śrīmad-Bhāgavatam,* in the context of an advertisement for the Scindia Steamship Company.

Mr. Choksi: *I asked him, "Why couldn't you go earlier? Why do you want to go now to the States, at this age?" He replied that, "I will be able to do something good, I am sure." His idea was that someone should be there who would be able to go near people who were lost in life and teach them and tell them what the correct thing is. I asked him so many times, "Why do you want to go to the States? Why don't you start something in Bombay or Delhi or Vṛndāvana?" I was teasing him also: "You are interested in seeing the States. Therefore, you want to go. All Swamijis want to go to the States, and you want to enjoy there." He said, "What I have got to see? I have finished my life."*

But sometimes he was hot-tempered. He used to get angry at me for the delays. "What is this nonsense?" he would say. Then I would understand: he is getting angry now. Sometimes he would say, "Oh, Mrs. Morarji has still not signed this paper? She says come back tomorrow, we will talk tomorrow! What is this? Why this daily going back?" He would get angry. Then I would say, "You can sit here." But he would say, "How long do I have to sit?" He would become impatient.

Finally Mrs. Morarji scheduled a place for him on one of her ships, the *Jaladuta,* which was sailing from Calcutta on August 13. She had made certain that he would travel on a ship whose captain understood the needs of a vegetarian and a *brāhmaṇa*. Mrs. Morarji told the *Jaladuta's* captain, Arun Pandia, to carry extra vegetables and fruits for the Swami. Mr. Choksi spent the last two days with Bhaktivedanta Swami in Bombay, picking up the pamphlets at the press, purchasing clothes, and driving him to the station to catch the train for Calcutta.

He arrived in Calcutta about two weeks before the *Jaladuta's* departure. Although he had lived much of his life in the city, he now had nowhere to stay. It was as he had written in his "Vṛndāvana-bhajana":

"I have my wife, sons, daughters, grandsons, everything,/ But I have no money, so they are a fruitless glory." Although in this city he had been so carefully nurtured as a child, those early days were also gone forever: "Where have my loving father and mother gone to now?/ And where are all my elders, who were my own folk?/ Who will give me news of them, tell me who?/ All that is left of this family life is a list of names."

Out of the hundreds of people in Calcutta whom Bhaktivedanta Swami knew, he chose to call on Mr. Sisir Bhattacarya, the flamboyant *kīrtana* singer he had met a year before at the governor's house in Lucknow. Mr. Bhattacarya was not a relative, not a disciple, nor even a close friend; but he was willing to help. Bhaktivedanta Swami called at his place and informed him that he would be leaving on a cargo ship in a few days; he needed a place to stay, and he would like to give some lectures. Mr. Bhattacarya immediately began to arrange a few private meetings at friends' homes, where he would sing and Bhaktivedanta Swami would then speak.

Mr. Bhattacarya thought the *sādhu's* leaving for America should make an important news story. He accompanied Bhaktivedanta Swami to all the newspapers in Calcutta—the *Hindustan Standard,* the *Amrita Bazar Patrika,* the *Jugantas,* the *Statesman,* and others. Bhaktivedanta Swami had only one photograph, a passport photo, and they made a few copies for the newspapers. Mr. Bhattacarya would try to explain what the Swami was going to do, and the news writers would listen. But none of them wrote anything. Finally they visited the *Dainik Basumati,* a local Bengali daily, which agreed to print a small article with Bhaktivedanta Swami's picture.

A week before his departure, on August 6, Bhaktivedanta Swami traveled to nearby Māyāpur to visit the *samādhi* of Śrīla Bhaktisiddhānta Sarasvatī. Then he returned to Calcutta, where Mr. Bhattacarya continued to assist him with his final business and speaking engagements.

Mr. Bhattacarya: *We just took a hired taxi to this place and that place. And he would go for preaching. I never talked to him during the preaching, but once when I was coming back from the preaching, I said, "You said this thing about this. But I tell you it is not this. It is this." I crossed him in something or argued. And he was furious. Whenever we argued and I said, "No, I think this is this," then he was shouting. He was very furious. He said, "You are always saying, 'I think, I think, I think.' What is the importance of what you think? Everything is what you think. But it doesn't matter. It matters what* śāstra *says. You must follow." I said, "I must do what I think, what I feel—that is important." He said, "No, you should forget this. You should forget your desire. You should change your habit. Better you depend on* śāstras. *You follow what* śāstra *wants you to do, and do it. I am not telling you what I think, but I am repeating what the* śāstra *says."*

As the day of his departure approached, Bhaktivedanta Swami took stock of his meager possessions. He had only a suitcase, an umbrella, and a supply of dry cereal. He did not know what he would find to eat in America; perhaps there would be only meat. If so, he was prepared to live on boiled potatoes and the cereal. His main baggage, several trunks of his books, was being handled separately by Scindia Cargo. Two hundred three-volume sets—the very thought of the books gave him confidence.

When the day came for him to leave, he needed that confidence. He was making a momentous break with his previous life, and he was dangerously old and not in strong health. And he was going to an unknown and probably unwelcoming country. To be poor and unknown in India was one thing. Even in these Kali-yuga days, when India's leaders were rejecting Vedic culture and imitating the West, it was still India; it was still the remains of Vedic civilization. He had been able to see millionaires, governors, the prime minister, simply by showing up at their doors and waiting. A *sannyāsī* was respected; the *Śrīmad-Bhāgavatam* was respected. But in America it would be different. He would be no one, a foreigner. And there was no tradition of *sādhus,* no temples, no free *āśramas.* But when he thought of the books he was bringing—transcendental knowledge in English—he became confident. When he met someone in America he would give him a flyer: "'Srimad Bhagwatam,' India's Message of Peace and Goodwill."

It was August 13, just a few days before Janmāṣṭamī, the appearance day anniversary of Lord Kṛṣṇa—the next day would be his own sixty-ninth birthday. During these last years, he had been in Vṛndāvana for Janmāṣṭamī. Many Vṛndāvana residents would never leave there; they were old and at peace in Vṛndāvana. Bhaktivedanta Swami was also concerned that he might die away from Vṛndāvana. That was why all the Vaiṣṇava *sādhus* and widows had taken vows not to leave, even for Mathurā—because to die in Vṛndāvana was the perfection of life. And the Hindu tradition was that a *sannyāsī* should not cross the ocean and go to the land of the *mlecchas.* But beyond all that was the desire of Śrīla Bhaktisiddhānta Sarasvatī, and his desire was nondifferent from that of Lord Kṛṣṇa. And Lord Caitanya Mahāprabhu had predicted that the chanting of Hare Kṛṣṇa would be known in every town and village of the world.

Bhaktivedanta Swami took a taxi down to the Calcutta port. A few friends and admirers, along with his son Vrindaban, accompanied him. He writes in his diary: "Today at 9 A.M. embarked on M.V. Jaladuta. Came with me Bhagwati, the Dwarwan of Scindia Sansir, Mr. Sen Gupta, Mr. Ali and Vrindaban." He was carrying a Bengali copy of *Caitanya-caritāmṛta,* which he intended to read during the crossing. Somehow he would be able to cook on board. Or if not, he could starve—whatever Kṛṣṇa desired. He checked his essentials: passenger ticket, passport, visa, P-form, sponsor's address. Finally it was happening.

Śrīla Prabhupāda: *With what great difficulty I got out of the country! Some way or other, by Kṛṣṇa's grace, I got out so I could spread the Kṛṣṇa consciousness movement all over the world. Otherwise, to remain in India—it was not possible. I wanted to start a movement in India, but I was not at all encouraged.*

The black cargo ship, small and weathered, was moored at dockside, a gangway leading from the dock to the ship's deck. Indian merchant sailors curiously eyed the elderly saffron-dressed *sādhu* as he spoke last words to his companions and then left them and walked determinedly toward the boat.

For thousands of years, *kṛṣṇa-bhakti* had been known only in India, not outside, except in twisted, faithless reports by foreigners. And the only swamis to have reached America had been nondevotees, Māyāvādī impersonalists. But now Kṛṣṇa was sending Bhaktivedanta Swami as His emissary.

CHAPTER TWELVE

The Journey to America

Today the ship is plying very smoothly. I feel today better. But I am feeling separation from Sri Vrindaban and my Lords Sri Govinda, Gopinath, Radha Damodar. My only solace is Sri Chaitanya Charitamrita in which I am tasting the nectarine of Lord Chaitanya's lila. I have left Bharatabhumi just to execute the order of Sri Bhakti-siddhanta Saraswati, in pursuance of Lord Chaitanya's order. I have no qualification, but have taken up the risk just to carry out the order of His Divine Grace. I depend fully on Their mercy, so far away from Vrindaban.

—*Jaladuta* diary
September 10, 1965

THE *JALADUTA* IS a regular cargo carrier of the Scindia Steam Navigation Company, but there is a passenger cabin aboard. During the voyage from Calcutta to New York in August and September of 1965, the cabin was occupied by "Sri Abhoy Charanaravinda Bhakti-vedanta Swami," whose age was listed as sixty-nine and who was taken on board bearing "a complimentary ticket with food."

The *Jaladuta,* under the command of Captain Arun Pandia, whose wife was also aboard, left at 9:00 A.M. on Friday, August 13. In his diary, Śrīla Prabhupāda noted: "The cabin is quite comfortable, thanks to Lord Sri Krishna for enlightening Sumati Morarji for all these arrangements.

I am quite comfortable." But on the fourteenth he reported: "Seasickness, dizziness, vomiting—Bay of Bengal. Heavy rains. More sickness."

On the nineteenth, when the ship arrived at Colombo, Ceylon (now Sri Lanka), Prabhupāda was able to get relief from his seasickness. The captain took him ashore, and he traveled around Colombo by car. Then the ship went on toward Cochin, on the west coast of India. Janmāṣṭamī, the appearance day of Lord Kṛṣṇa, fell on the twentieth of August that year. Prabhupāda took the opportunity to speak to the crew about the philosophy of Lord Kṛṣṇa, and he distributed *prasādam* he had cooked himself. August 21 was his sixty-ninth birthday, observed (without ceremony) at sea. That same day the ship arrived at Cochin, and Śrīla Prabhupāda's trunks of *Śrīmad-Bhāgavatam* volumes, which had been shipped from Bombay, were loaded on board.

By the twenty-third the ship had put out to the Red Sea, where Śrīla Prabhupāda encountered great difficulty. He noted in his diary: "Rain, seasickness, dizziness, headache, no appetite, vomiting." The symptoms persisted, but it was more than seasickness. The pains in his chest made him think he would die at any moment. In two days he suffered two heart attacks. He tolerated the difficulty, meditating on the purpose of his mission, but after two days of such violent attacks he thought that if another were to come he would certainly not survive.

On the night of the second day, Prabhupāda had a dream. Lord Kṛṣṇa, in His many forms, was rowing a boat, and He told Prabhupāda that he should not fear, but should come along. Prabhupāda felt assured of Lord Kṛṣṇa's protection, and the violent attacks did not recur.

The *Jaladuta* entered the Suez Canal on September 1 and stopped in Port Said on the second. Śrīla Prabhupāda visited the city with the captain and said that he liked it. By the sixth he had recovered a little from his illness and was eating regularly again for the first time in two weeks, having cooked his own *kicharī* and *purīs.* He reported in his diary that his strength renewed little by little.

Thursday, September 9

To 4:00 this afternoon, we have crossed over the Atlantic Ocean for twenty-four hours. The whole day was clear and almost smooth. I am taking my food regularly and have got some strength to struggle. There is also a slight tacking of the ship and I am feeling a slight headache also. But I am struggling and the nectarine of life is Sri Chaitanya Charitamrita, the source of all my vitality.

Friday, September 10
Today the ship is plying very smoothly. I feel today better. But I am feeling separation from Sri Vrindaban and my Lords Sri Govinda, Gopinath, Radha Damodar. The only solace is Sri Chaitanya Charitamrita in which I am tasting the nectarine of Lord Chaitanya's lila [pastimes]. I have left Bharatabhumi just to execute the order of Sri Bhaktisiddhanta Saraswati in pursuance of Lord Chaitanya's order. I have no qualification, but have taken up the risk just to carry out the order of His Divine Grace. I depend fully on Their mercy, so far away from Vrindaban.

During the voyage, Śrīla Prabhupāda sometimes stood on deck at the ship's rail, watching the ocean and the sky and thinking of *Caitanya-caritāmṛta,* Vṛndāvana-dhāma, and the order of his spiritual master to go preach in the West. Mrs. Pandia, the captain's wife, whom Śrīla Prabhupāda considered to be "an intelligent and learned lady," foretold Śrīla Prabhupāda's future. If he were to pass beyond this crisis in his health, she said, it would indicate the good will of Lord Kṛṣṇa.

The ocean voyage of 1965 was a calm one for the *Jaladuta.* The captain said that never in his entire career had he seen such a calm Atlantic crossing. Prabhupāda replied that the calmness was Lord Kṛṣṇa's mercy, and Mrs. Pandia asked Prabhupāda to come back with them so that they might have another such crossing. Śrīla Prabhupāda wrote in his diary, "If the Atlantic would have shown its usual face, perhaps I would have died. But Lord Krishna has taken charge of the ship."

On September 13, Prabhupāda noted in his diary: "Thirty-second day of journey. Cooked bati kichari. It appeared to be delicious, so I was able to take some food. Today I have disclosed my mind to my companion, Lord Shri Krishna. There is a Bengali poem made by me in this connection."

This poem was a prayer to Lord Kṛṣṇa, and it is filled with Prabhupāda's devotional confidence in the mission that he had undertaken on behalf of his spiritual master. An English translation of the opening stanzas follows:*

I emphatically say to you, O brothers, you will obtain your good fortune from the Supreme Lord Kṛṣṇa only when Śrīmatī Rādhārāṇī becomes pleased with you.

Śrī Śrīmad Bhaktisiddhānta Sarasvatī Ṭhākura, who is very dear to Lord Gaurāṅga [Lord Caitanya], the son of mother Śacī, is unparalleled in his

* See Appendix for the complete Bengali verses with English translation.

> service to the Supreme Lord Śrī Kṛṣṇa. He is that great, saintly spiritual master who bestows intense devotion to Kṛṣṇa at different places throughout the world.
>
> By his strong desire, the holy name of Lord Gaurāṅga will spread throughout all the countries of the Western world. In all the cities, towns, and villages on the earth, from all the oceans, seas, rivers, and streams, everyone will chant the holy name of Kṛṣṇa.
>
> As the vast mercy of Śrī Caitanya Mahāprabhu conquers all directions, a flood of transcendental ecstasy will certainly cover the land. When all the sinful, miserable living entities become happy, the Vaiṣṇavas' desire is then fulfilled.
>
> Although my Guru Mahārāja ordered me to accomplish this mission, I am not worthy or fit to do it. I am very fallen and insignificant. Therefore, O Lord, now I am begging for Your mercy so that I may become worthy, for You are the wisest and most experienced of all. …

The poem ends:

> Today that remembrance of You came to me in a very nice way. Because I have a great longing I called to You. I am Your eternal servant, and therefore I desire Your association so much. O Lord Kṛṣṇa, except for You there is no means of success.

In the same straightforward, factual manner in which he had noted the date, the weather, and his state of health, he now described his helpless dependence on his "companion, Lord Krishna," and his absorption in the ecstasy of separation from Kṛṣṇa. He described the relationship between the spiritual master and the disciple, and he praised his own spiritual master, Śrī Śrīmad Bhaktisiddhānta Sarasvatī, "by whose strong desire the holy name of Lord Gaurāṅga will spread throughout all the countries of the Western world." He plainly stated that his spiritual master had ordered him to accomplish this mission of worldwide Kṛṣṇa consciousness, and feeling unworthy he prayed to Lord Kṛṣṇa for strength. The last verses give an unexpected, confidential glimpse into Śrīla Prabhupāda's direct relationship with Lord Kṛṣṇa. Prabhupāda called on Kṛṣṇa as his "dear friend" and longed for the joy of again wandering the fields of Vraja. This memory of Kṛṣṇa, he wrote, came because of a great desire to serve the Lord. Externally, Śrīla Prabhupāda was experiencing great inconvenience; he had been aboard ship for a month and had suffered heart attacks and repeated seasickness. Moreover, even if he were to recover from these difficulties, his arrival in America would undoubtedly bring many more difficulties. But remembering the desire of his spiritual master, taking strength from his reading of *Caitanya-caritāmṛta,* and revealing his mind in his prayer to Lord Kṛṣṇa, Prabhupāda remained confident.

After a thirty-five-day journey from Calcutta, the *Jaladuta* reached Boston's Commonwealth Pier at 5:30 A.M. on September 17, 1965. The ship was to stop briefly in Boston before proceeding to New York City. Among the first things Śrīla Prabhupāda saw in America were the letters "A & P" painted on a pierfront warehouse. The gray waterfront dawn revealed the ships in the harbor, a conglomeration of lobster stands and drab buildings, and, rising in the distance, the Boston skyline.

Prabhupāda had to pass through U.S. Immigration and Customs in Boston. His visa allowed him a three-month stay, and an official stamped it to indicate his expected date of departure. Captain Pandia invited Prabhupāda to take a walk into Boston, where the captain intended to do some shopping. They walked across a footbridge into a busy commercial area with old churches, warehouses, office buildings, bars, tawdry bookshops, nightclubs, and restaurants. Prabhupāda briefly observed the city, but the most significant thing about his short stay in Boston, aside from the fact that he had now set foot in America, was that at Commonwealth Pier he wrote another Bengali poem, entitled "Mārkine Bhāgavata-dharma" ("Teaching Kṛṣṇa Consciousness in America"). Some of the verses he wrote on board the ship that day are as follows:*

> My dear Lord Kṛṣṇa, You are so kind upon this useless soul, but I do not know why You have brought me here. Now You can do whatever You like with me.
>
> But I guess You have some business here, otherwise why would You bring me to this terrible place?
>
> Most of the population here is covered by the material modes of ignorance and passion. Absorbed in material life they think themselves very happy and satisfied, and therefore they have no taste for the transcendental message of Vāsudeva [Kṛṣṇa]. I do not know how they will be able to understand it.
>
> But I know that Your causeless mercy can make everything possible, because You are the most expert mystic.
>
> How will they understand the mellows of devotional service? O Lord, I am simply praying for Your mercy so that I will be able to convince them about Your message.

---

* See Appendix for the complete Bengali verses with English translation.

All living entities have come under the control of the illusory energy by Your will, and therefore, if You like, by Your will they can also be released from the clutches of illusion.

I wish that You may deliver them. Therefore if You so desire their deliverance, then only will they be able to understand Your message. ...

How will I make them understand this message of Kṛṣṇa consciousness? I am very unfortunate, unqualified, and the most fallen. Therefore I am seeking Your benediction so that I can convince them, for I am powerless to do so on my own.

Somehow or other, O Lord, You have brought me here to speak about You. Now, my Lord, it is up to You to make me a success or failure, as You like.

O spiritual master of all the worlds! I can simply repeat Your message. So if You like You can make my power of speaking suitable for their understanding.

Only by Your causeless mercy will my words become pure. I am sure that when this transcendental message penetrates their hearts, they will certainly feel gladdened and thus become liberated from all unhappy conditions of life.

O Lord, I am just like a puppet in Your hands. So if You have brought me here to dance, then make me dance, make me dance, O Lord, make me dance as You like.

I have no devotion, nor do I have any knowledge, but I have strong faith in the holy name of Kṛṣṇa. I have been designated as Bhaktivedanta, and now, if You like, You can fulfill the real purport of Bhaktivedanta.

Signed—the most unfortunate, insignificant beggar,
A. C. Bhaktivedanta Swami,
On board the ship *Jaladuta,* Commonwealth Pier,
Boston, Massachusetts, U.S.A.
Dated 18th September 1965.

He was now in America. He was in a major American city, rich with billions, populated with millions, and determined to stay the way it was. Prabhupāda saw Boston from the viewpoint of a pure devotee of Kṛṣṇa. He saw the hellish city life, people dedicated to the illusion of material happiness. All his dedication and training moved him to give these people the transcendental knowledge and saving grace of Kṛṣṇa consciousness, yet he was feeling weak, lowly, and unable to help them on his own. He was but "an insignificant beggar" with no money. He had barely survived the two heart attacks at sea, he spoke a different language, he dressed strangely—yet he had come to tell people to give up meat-eating, illicit sex, intoxication, and gambling, and to teach them to worship Lord

Kṛṣṇa, who to them was a mythical Hindu god. What would he be able to accomplish?

Helplessly he spoke his heart directly to God: "I wish that You may deliver them. I am seeking Your benediction so that I can convince them." And for convincing them he would trust in the power of God's holy name and in the *Śrīmad-Bhāgavatam.* This transcendental sound would clean away desire for material enjoyment from their hearts and awaken loving service to Kṛṣṇa. On the streets of Boston, Prabhupāda was aware of the power of ignorance and passion that dominated the city; but he had faith in the transcendental process. He was tiny, but God was infinite, and God was Kṛṣṇa, his dear friend.

On the nineteenth of September the *Jaladuta* sailed into New York Harbor and docked at a Brooklyn pier, at Seventeenth Street. Śrīla Prabhupāda saw the awesome Manhattan skyline, the Empire State Building, and, like millions of visitors and immigrants in the past, the Statue of Liberty.

Śrīla Prabhupāda was dressed appropriately for a resident of Vṛndāvana. He wore *kaṇṭhī-mālā* (neck beads) and a simple cotton *dhotī,* and he carried *japa-mālā* (chanting beads) and an old *cādar,* or shawl. His complexion was golden, his head shaven, *śikhā* in the back, his forehead decorated with the whitish Vaiṣṇava *tilaka.* He wore pointed white rubber slippers, not uncommon for *sādhus* in India. But who in New York had ever seen or dreamed of anyone appearing like this Vaiṣṇava? He was possibly the first Vaiṣṇava *sannyāsī* to arrive in New York with uncompromised appearance. Of course, New Yorkers have an expertise in not giving much attention to any kind of strange new arrival.

Śrīla Prabhupāda was on his own. He had a sponsor, Mr. Agarwal, somewhere in Pennsylvania. Surely someone would be here to greet him. Although he had little idea of what to do as he walked off the ship onto the pier—"I did not know whether to turn left or right"—he passed through the dockside formalities and was met by a representative from Traveler's Aid, sent by the Agarwals in Pennsylvania, who offered to take him to the Scindia ticket office in Manhattan to book his return passage to India.

At the Scindia office, Prabhupāda spoke with the ticket agent, Joseph

Foerster, who was impressed by this unusual passenger's Vaiṣṇava appearance, his light luggage, and his apparent poverty. He regarded Prabhupāda as a priest. Most of Scindia's passengers were businessmen or families, so Mr. Foerster had never seen a passenger wearing the traditional Vaiṣṇava dress of India. He found Śrīla Prabhupāda to be "a pleasant gentleman" who spoke of "the nice accommodations and treatment he had received aboard the *Jaladuta*." Prabhupāda asked Mr. Foerster to hold space for him on a return ship to India. His plans were to leave in about two months, and he told Mr. Foerster that he would keep in touch. Carrying only forty rupees cash, which he himself called "a few hours' spending in New York," and an additional twenty dollars he had collected from selling three volumes of the *Bhāgavatam* to Captain Pandia, Śrīla Prabhupāda, with umbrella and suitcase in hand, and still escorted by the Traveler's Aid representative, set out for the Port Authority Bus Terminal to arrange for his trip to Butler.

CHAPTER THIRTEEN

Butler, Pennsylvania: The First Testing Ground

By the grace of Lord Krishna, the Americans are prosperous in every respect. They are not poverty stricken like the Indians. The people in general are satisfied so far as their material needs are concerned, and they are spiritually inclined. When I was in Butler, Pennsylvania, about five hundred miles from New York City, I saw there many churches, and they were attending regularly. This shows that they are spiritually inclined. I was also invited by some churches and church governed schools and colleges, and I spoke there, and they appreciated it and presented me some token rewards. When I was speaking to the students, they were very eager to hear about the principles of Srimad Bhagwatam. But the clergymen were cautious about allowing students to hear me so patiently. They feared that the students might be converted to Hindu ideas—as is quite natural for any religious sect. But they do not know that devotional service of the Lord Sri Krishna is the common religion for everyone, including even the aborigines and cannibals in the jungle.

—from a letter to Sumati Morarji

THE BUS CAME swinging out of the terminal into the daylight of mid-town Manhattan, riding along in the shadows of skyscrapers, through asphalt streets crowded with people, trucks, and automobiles and into the heavy traffic bound toward the Lincoln Tunnel. The bus entered the tunnel and emerged on the Jersey side of the Hudson River, continuing down the New Jersey Turnpike past fields of huge oil tanks and sprawling refineries. The Manhattan skyline was on the left, while three lanes of traffic sped sixty miles an hour in each direction. Newark Airport came up close by on the right, with jets visible on the ground. Electric power lines, spanning aloft between steel towers, stretched into the horizon.

Śrīla Prabhupāda had never before witnessed anything of such magnitude. He was now seeing for himself that American culture was based on passion for more and more sense gratification—and it was a scene of madness. For what important business were people rushing to and fro at breakneck speed? He could see their goals advertised on the billboards.

Of course, he had many times traveled the road from Delhi to Vṛndāvana, but it did not have many advertisements. A traveler would see mostly the land, roadside streams, temples, homes, farmers in their fields. Most people went on foot or traveled by oxcart or bicycle. And in Vṛndāvana even the ordinary passersby greeted each other by calling the names of God: "*Jaya* Rādhe!" "Hare Kṛṣṇa!" Now there were factories outside Delhi, but nothing like this. The cumulative effect did not pack nearly the materialistic punch of these fields of oil tanks, mammoth factories, and billboards alongside the crowded superhighway. Meat-eating, illicit sex, intoxication, and gambling—the very sins Śrīla Prabhupāda had come to preach against—were proudly glamorized on mile after mile of billboards. The signs promoted liquor and cigarettes, roadside restaurants offered slaughtered cows in the form of steaks and hamburgers, and no matter what the product, it was usually advertised by a lusty-looking woman. But Prabhupāda had come to teach the opposite: that happiness is not found in the passion for sense gratification, and that only when one becomes detached from the mode of passion, which leads to sinful acts, can one become eligible for the eternal happiness of Kṛṣṇa consciousness.

Prabhupāda felt compassion. The compassion of a Kṛṣṇa conscious saint had been explained in an age long ago by Prahlāda Mahārāja: "I see that there are many saintly persons indeed, but they are interested only in their own deliverance. Not caring for the big cities and towns, they go to the Himalayas or the forests to meditate with vows of silence. They are not interested in delivering others. As for me, however, I do not wish to be liberated alone, leaving aside all these poor fools and rascals. I know that without Kṛṣṇa consciousness, without taking shelter of Your lotus feet, one cannot be happy. Therefore I wish to bring them back to shelter at Your lotus feet."

The scenery gradually changed to the Pennsylvania countryside, and the bus sped through long tunnels in the mountains. Night came. And it was late—after eleven—when the bus entered the heavily industrialized Pittsburgh area on the shore of the Allegheny River. Śrīla Prabhupāda couldn't see the steel mills clearly, but he could see their lights and their industrial fires and smoking stacks. Millions of lights shone throughout the city's prevailing dinginess.

When the bus finally pulled into the terminal, it was past midnight. Gopal Agarwal was waiting with the family Volkswagen bus to drive Prabhupāda to Butler, about one hour north. He greeted Prabhupāda with folded palms and "Welcome, Swamiji," bowing from the waist several times.

This was not any of Gopal's doing. His father, a Mathurā businessman with a fondness for *sādhus* and religious causes, had requested him to host the Swamiji. This wasn't the first time his father had arranged for a *sādhu* acquaintance to come to America. Several times he had sent sponsorship papers for Gopal to sign, and Gopal had obediently done so—but nothing had ever come of them. So when the sponsorship letter for A. C. Bhaktivedanta Swami had come, Gopal had promptly signed and returned it, thinking that this would be the last they would hear of it. But then just a week ago a letter had come. Sally Agarwal had opened it and then, in alarm, called to her husband: "Honey, sit down. Listen to this: the Swami is coming." Śrīla Prabhupāda had enclosed his picture so that they would not mistake him. The Agarwals had looked curiously at the photograph. "There'll be no mistake *there,*" Gopal had said.

The unsuspecting Agarwals were "simple American people," according to Sally Agarwal, who had met her Indian husband while he was working as an engineer in Pennsylvania. What would they do with an Indian swami in their house? Prabhupāda was a shock for them. But there was no question of *not* accepting him; they were bound by the request of Gopal's father. Dutifully, Gopal had purchased Śrīla Prabhupāda's ticket from New York to Pittsburgh and had arranged for the agent from Traveler's Aid to meet him. And dutifully he had driven tonight to meet him. So it was with a mixture of embarrassment, disbelief, and wonder that

Gopal Agarwal helped his guest into the VW and drove back home to Butler.

* * *

September 20

"BUTLER, PENNSYLVANIA, HOME OF THE JEEP" read a granite plaque in the city park. Butler, famous as the town where the U.S. Army jeep was invented in 1940, was an industrial city of twenty thousand, settled amid the hills of an area rich in oil, coal, gas, and limestone. Its industry consisted mainly of factories for plate glass, railroad cars, refrigerators, oil equipment, and rubber goods. Ninety percent of the local laborers were native Americans. The nominal religion had always been Christian, mostly Protestant with some Catholic, and in later years a few synagogues had appeared. But there was no Hindu community at that time; Gopal Agarwal was the first Indian to move to Butler.

As the VW bus pulled into town, the predawn air was warm and humid. The morning edition of the *Butler Eagle* would soon be going to the newsstands—"Red Chinese Fire on India"; "Prime Minister Shastri Declares Chinese Communists Out to Dominate World"; "United Nations Council Demands Pakistan and India Cease-fire in 48 hours."

Śrīla Prabhupāda arrived at the Agarwals' home—Sterling Apartments—at 4:00 A.M., and Gopal invited him to sleep on the couch. Their place, a townhouse apartment, consisted of a small living room, a dining room, a kitchenette, two upstairs bedrooms, and a bath. Here they lived with their two young children. The Agarwals had lived in Butler for a few years now and felt themselves established in a good social circle. Since their apartment had so little space, they decided that it would be better if the Swami took a room at the YMCA and came to visit them during the day. Of course, living space wasn't the real difficulty—it was *him*. How would he fit into the Butler atmosphere? He was their guest, so they would have to *explain* him to their friends and neighbors.

Śrīla Prabhupāda was immediately a curiosity for whoever saw him. In anxiety, Mrs. Agarwal decided that instead of having people speculate about the strange man in orange robes living at her house, it would be better to let them know about him from the newspapers. She explained her plan to Prabhupāda, who laughed, understanding that he didn't fit in.

Sally hurried off to a Pittsburgh newspaper office, but the interviewer wasn't able to comprehend why this person should make an interesting story. Sally then took him to the local *Butler Eagle,* where his presence was accepted as indeed newsworthy.

September 22

A feature article appeared in the *Butler Eagle:* "In fluent English, Devotee of Hindu Cult Explains Commission to Visit the West." A photographer had come to the Agarwals' apartment and had taken a picture of Śrīla Prabhupāda standing in the living room holding an open volume of *Śrīmad-Bhāgavatam.* The caption read, "Ambassador of Bhakti-yoga."

The article began:

> A slight brown man in faded orange drapes and wearing white bathing shoes stepped out of a compact car yesterday and into the Butler YMCA to attend a meeting. He is A. C. Bhaktivedanta Swamiji, a messenger from India to the peoples of the West.

The article referred to *Śrīmad-Bhāgavatam* as "Biblical literature" and to Śrīla Prabhupāda as "the learned teacher." It continued:

> "My mission is to revive a people's God consciousness," says the Swamiji. "God is the Father of all living beings, in thousands of different forms," he explains. "Human life is a stage of perfection in evolution; if we miss the message, back we go through the process again," he believes. ... Bhaktivedanta lives as a monk, and permits no woman to touch his food. On a six-week ocean voyage and at the Agarwal apartment in Butler he prepares his meals in a brass pan with separate levels for steaming rice, vegetables, and making "bread" at the same time. He is a strict vegetarian, and is permitted to drink only milk, "the miracle food for babies and old men," he noted. ... If Americans would give more attention to their spiritual life, they would be much happier, he says.

The Agarwals had their own opinion as to why Prabhupāda had come to America: "to finance his books," and nothing more. They were sure that he was hoping only to meet someone who could help him with the publication of his *Śrīmad-Bhāgavatam,* and that he did not want any followers. At least they hoped he wouldn't do anything to attract attention; and they felt that this was his mentality also. "He didn't create waves," Sally Agarwal says. "He didn't want any crowd. He didn't want anything. He only wanted to finance his books." Perhaps Prabhupāda, seeing their nervousness, agreed to keep a low profile, out of consideration for his hosts.

At Prabhupāda's request, however, Mr. Agarwal held a kind of open house in his apartment every night from six to nine.

Sally: *It was quite an intellectual group that we were in, and they were fascinated by him. They hardly knew what to ask him. They didn't know enough. This was just like a dream out of a book. Who would expect to meet a swami in someone's living room in Butler, Pennsylvania? It was just really tremendous. In the middle of middle-class America. My parents came from quite a distance to see him. We knew a lot of people in Pittsburgh, and they came up. This was a very unusual thing, having him here. But the real interest shown in him was only as a curiosity.*

He had a typewriter, which was one of his few possessions, and an umbrella. That was one of the things that caused a sensation, that he always carried an umbrella. And it was a little chilly and he was balding, so he always wore this hat that someone had made for him, like a swimming cap. It was a kind of sensation. And he was so brilliant that when he saw someone twice, he knew who they were—he remembered. He was a brilliant man. Or if he met them in our apartment and saw them in a car, he would remember their name, and he would wave and say their name. He was a brilliant man. All the people liked him. They were amazed at how intelligent he was. The thing that got them was the way he remembered their name. And his humorous way. He looked so serious all the time, but he was a very humorous person. He was forbidding in his looks, but he was very charming.

He was the easiest guest I have had in my life, because when I couldn't spend time with him he chanted, and I knew he was perfectly happy. When I couldn't talk to him, he chanted. He was so easy, though, because I knew he was never bored. I never felt any pressure or tension about having him. He was so easy that when I had to take care of the children he would just chant. It was so great. When I had to do things, he would just be happy chanting. He was a very good guest. When the people would come, they were always smoking cigarettes, but he would say, "Pay no attention. Think nothing of it." That's what he said. "Think nothing of it." Because he knew we were different. I didn't smoke in front of him. I knew I wasn't supposed to smoke in front of Gopal's father, so I sort of considered him the same. He didn't make any problems for anybody.

One evening a guest asked Prabhupāda, "What do you think of Jesus Christ?" And Prabhupāda replied, "He is the Son of God." Then he added that he — the guest — was also a son of God. Everyone was interested to hear that the Swami accepted Jesus Christ as the Son of God.

Gopal: *His intent was not to have you change your way of life. He wasn't telling anybody they should be vegetarian or anything. All he wanted you to do was to follow what you are, but be better. He didn't stress that we should give up many things.*

Śrīla Prabhupāda followed a regulated daily schedule. Every morning he would walk the six or seven blocks from the YMCA to Sterling Apartments, arriving there about seven. When he had first landed in New York, he had in his luggage a large bundle of dried cereal, similar to rolled oats. This supply was enough for several weeks, and every morning at breakfast he would take some with milk. At seven forty-five Gopal would leave for work, and around nine-thirty Prabhupāda would start preparing his lunch in the kitchen. He made his *capātīs* by hand, without even a rolling pin. He worked alone for two hours, while Mrs. Agarwal did housework and took care of her children. At eleven-thirty he took *prasādam.*

Sally: *When he cooked he used only one burner. The bottom-level pot created the steam. He had the* dāl *on the bottom, and it created the steam to cook many other vegetables. So for about a week he was cooking this great big lunch, which was ready about eleven-thirty, and Gopal always came home for lunch about twelve. I used to serve Gopal a sandwich, and then he would go back to work. But it didn't take me long to realize that the food the Swami was cooking we'd enjoy too, so he started cooking that noon meal for all of us. Oh, and we enjoyed it so much.*

Our fun was to show him what we knew of America. And he had never seen such things. It was such fun to take him to the supermarket. He loved opening the package of okra or frozen beans, and he didn't have to clean them and cut them and do all those things. He opened the freezer every day and just chose his items. It was fun to watch him. He sat on the couch while I swept with the vacuum cleaner, and he was so interested in that, and we talked for a long time about that. He was so interesting.

So every day he'd have this big feast, and everything was great fun. We really enjoyed it. I would help him cut the things. He would spice it, and we would laugh. He was the most enjoyable man, most enjoyable man. I really felt like a sort of daughter to him, even in such a short time. Like he was my father-in-law. He was friend of my father-in-law, but I really felt very close to him. He enjoyed everything. I liked him. I thought he was tremendous.

After lunch, Prabhupāda would leave, about 1:00 P.M., and walk to the YMCA, where the Agarwals figured he must have worked at his writing until five. He would come back to their apartment about six in the evening, after they had taken their meal. They ate meat, so Mrs. Agarwal was careful to have it cleared away before he came. When one night he came early, she said, "Oh, Swamiji, we have just cooked meat, and the smell will be very disagreeable to you." But he said, "Oh, think nothing of it. Think nothing of it."

In the evening he would speak with guests. The guests would usually take coffee and other refreshments, but he would request a glass of warm milk at nine o'clock. He would stay, speaking until nine-thirty or ten, and then Mr. Agarwal would drive him back to the YMCA.

Prabhupāda would also do his own laundry every day. He washed his clothes in the Agarwals' bathroom and hung them to dry outside. He sometimes accompanied the Agarwals to the laundromat and was interested to see how Americans washed and dried their clothes. To Sally he seemed "very interested in the American ways and people."

Sally: *Our boy Brij was six or seven months old when the Swami came—and the Indians love boys. The Swami liked Brij. He was there when Brij first stood. The first time Brij made the attempt and actually succeeded, the Swami stood up and clapped. It was a celebration. Another time, our baby teethed on the Swami's shoes. I thought, "Oh, those shoes. They've been all over India, and my kid is chewing on them." You know how a mother would feel.*

Almost every night he used to sit in the next-door neighbor's backyard. We sat out there sometimes with him, or we stayed in the living room. One time something happened with our little girl, Pamela, who was only three years old. I used to take her to Sunday school, and she learned about Jesus in Sunday school. Then when she would see Swamiji with his robes on and everything, she called him Swami Jesus. And this one time when it first dawned on us what she was saying, she called him Swami Jesus, and Swami smiled and said, "And a little child shall lead them." It was so funny.

Prabhupāda spoke to various groups in the community. He spoke at the Lions Club in early October and received a formal document:

> Be it known that A. C. Bhaktivedanta Swami was a guest at the Lions Club of Butler, Pa., and as an expression of appreciation for services rendered, the Club tenders this acknowledgment.

He also gave a talk at the Y and at St. Fidelis Seminary College in Herman, Pennsylvania, and he spoke regularly to guests at the Agarwal home.

* * *

When Professor Larsen, the chairman of the philosophy department at Slippery Rock State College, read in the *Butler Eagle* of a visiting Indian swami and Vedic scholar, he phoned the Agarwals' home to invite Prabhupāda to lecture on campus.

Allen Larsen: *I called the number given in the newspaper article, but it turned out that the Swamiji was actually staying in a room at the YMCA. When I arrived, he was waiting on the street corner, and I picked him up. He seemed very much alone. When we were driving to Slippery Rock, I asked him to pronounce his name for me so I would have it right when I introduced him to my class. He said, "Swamiji Bhaktivedanta," and then he proceeded to tell me what that meant. Since I was not used to Indian names, he had to repeat it several times before I got it right. He showed no impatience with my slowness. Even at this early junction of our association, I was convinced that this man had an inner stability and strength that would be very difficult to shake, and this initial impression was further reinforced throughout the rather busy day.*

A hundred students from several classes had gathered to hear the lecture, as Prabhupāda, in his natural, unrehearsed manner, walked down the aisle, up the three wooden steps, and onto the plain wooden stage. He sat down, erect and cross-legged, and began softly singing Hare Kṛṣṇa, his eyes closed. Then he stood and spoke (without a lectern or microphone) and answered questions from the audience. The program lasted only fifty minutes and ended abruptly with a bell signaling the next class.

Allen Larsen: *After the first class, I had a short conversation with the Swamiji while sitting outside on a bench on the campus lawn. Most of the time when he was not directly engaged in conversation he would repeat a short prayer while moving prayer beads through his fingers. He was sitting up cross-legged, and we were speaking back and forth. He said that the trees around us were beautiful, and he asked, "What kind of trees are these?" I replied, "They're shade trees." Then he said that it was too bad they weren't fruit or nut trees to provide food and benefit people.*

At one o'clock Prabhupāda lectured again. Afterward, he accompanied Dr. Mohan Sharma, a member of the faculty who had attended the lecture, and his sixteen-year-old daughter, Mini, to Dr. Sharma's campus residence. Prabhupāda accepted warm milk and dried fruit, and at Dr. Sharma's request, blessed his home and touched the forehead of his daughter in a gesture of benediction. Around three o'clock, Professor Larsen drove him back to Butler.

Allen Larsen: *The Swamiji seemed to present himself as an Indian scholar who had come for a short time to do translation work. I never thought of him as a missionary. But during the course of the day there grew in me a warm affection for this man, because he was unmistakably a good man who had found his way to a stability and peace that is very rare.*

The lectures in Pennsylvania gave Prabhupāda his first readings of how his message would be received in America. At Commonwealth Pier in Boston he had stated in his poem: "I am sure that when this transcendental message penetrates their hearts, they will certainly feel gladdened and thus become liberated from all unhappy conditions of life." Now this principle was actually being tested in the field. Would they be able to understand? Were they interested? Would they surrender?

* * *

October 15

Śrīla Prabhupāda received a letter from Sumati Morarji in Bombay:

> Poojya Swami,
>
> I am in due receipt of your letter dated the 24th ultimo, and glad to know that you have safely reached the U.S.A. after suffering from seasickness. I thank you for your greetings and blessings. I know by now you must have recovered fully from the sickness and must be keeping good health. I was delighted to read that you have started your activities in the States and have already delivered some lectures. I pray to Lord Bala Krishna to give you enough strength to enable you to carry the message of Sri Bhagwatam. I feel that you should stay there until you fully recover from your illness and

return only after you have completed your mission.
Here everything is normal. With respects,

Yours sincerely,
Sumati Morarji

Prabhupāda regarded the last line of this letter as especially significant: his well-wisher was urging him to stay in America until he had completed his mission. He had told the immigration officials in New York that he would be staying in America for two months. "I have one month's sponsorship in Butler," he thought, "and then I have no support. So perhaps I can stay another month." So he had said two months. Sumati Morarji, however, was urging him to stay on. He saw that the prospects for preaching to the Americans were good, but he felt he would need support from India.

At any rate, he had spent long enough in Butler, and he now had one month left in America. So he decided to go to New York City and try to preach there, before his time was up. But first he wanted to visit Philadelphia, where he had arranged a meeting with a Sanskrit professor, Dr. Norman Brown, at the University of Pennsylvania.

Mrs. Agarwal was sorry to see him go.

Sally: *After a month I really loved the Swami. I felt protective in a way, and he wanted to go to Philadelphia. But I couldn't imagine—I told him—I could not imagine him going to Philadelphia for two days. He was going to speak there, and then to New York. But he knew no one in New York. If the thing didn't pan out in Philadelphia, he was just going to New York, and then there was no one. I just couldn't imagine. It made me sick.*

I remember the night he was leaving, about two in the morning. I remember sitting there as long as he could wait before Gopal took him to Pittsburgh to get on that bus. Gopal got a handful of change, and I remember telling him how to put the money in the slot so that he could take a bath at the bus station—because he was supposed to take a bath a few times a day. And Gopal told him how to do that, and told him about the automats in New York. He told him what he could eat and what he couldn't eat, and he gave him these coins in a sock, and that's all he left us with.

As a *sannyāsī,* Śrīla Prabhupāda was used to picking up and leaving one place for another. As a mendicant preacher, he had no remorse about leaving behind the quiet life of the Butler YMCA. And he had no attachment for the domestic habitat where he would cook and talk with Sally Agarwal about vacuum cleaners, frozen foods, and American ways.

But why had he gone to Butler? And why was he going to New York? He saw it as Kṛṣṇa's grace. As a pure devotee of Kṛṣṇa, he wanted to be an instrument for distributing Kṛṣṇa consciousness.

His stay in Butler had been helpful. He had gotten first-hand experience of American life, and he gained confidence that his health was strong and his message communicable. He was glad to see that America had the necessary ingredients for his Indian vegetarian diet, and that the people could understand his English. He had learned that casual onetime lectures here and there were of limited value, and that although there would be opposition from the established religions, people individually were very much interested in what he had to say.

On October 18, he left Butler, via Philadelphia, for New York City.

CHAPTER FOURTEEN

Struggling Alone

I used to sit in the back and listen to his meetings silently. He was speaking all impersonal nonsense, and I kept my silence. Then one day he asked if I would like to speak, and I spoke about Kṛṣṇa consciousness. I challenged that he was speaking manufactured philosophy and all nonsense from Śaṅkarācārya. He tried to back out and said he *was not speaking, Śaṅkarācārya was speaking. I said, "You are representing him. That is the same thing." He then said to me, "Swamiji, I like you very much, but you cannot speak here." But although our philosophies differed and he would not let me speak, he was kind, and I was nice to him.*

—Śrīla Prabhupāda in conversation

PRABHUPĀDA KNEW NO one in New York City, but he had a contact: Dr. Ramamurti Mishra. He had written Dr. Mishra from Butler, enclosing the letter of introduction Paramananda Mehra had given him in Bombay. He had also phoned Dr. Mishra, who welcomed Prabhupāda to join him in New York.

At the Port Authority Bus Terminal, a student of Dr. Mishra's met him as he arrived from Philadelphia and escorted him directly to an Indian festival in the city. There Prabhupāda met Dr. Mishra as well as Ravi Shankar and his brother, the dancer Udai Shankar. Prabhupāda then accompanied Dr. Mishra to his apartment at 33 Riverside Drive, beside the Hudson River. The apartment was on the fourteenth floor and had large windows overlooking the river. Dr. Mishra gave Prabhupāda a room to himself.

Dr. Mishra was a dramatic, showy personality, given to flashing glances and making expressive gestures with his hands. He regularly used words like "lovely" and "beautiful." Presenting an artfully polished image of what a *guru* should be, he was what some New Yorkers referred to as "an uptown swami." Before coming to America, Dr. Mishra had been a Sanskrit scholar and a *guru,* as well as a doctor. He had written a number of books, such as *The Textbook of Yoga Psychology* and *Self-Analysis and Self-Knowledge,* a work based on the teachings of the monistic philosopher Śaṅkara. After he came to the United States, he continued with his medical profession, but as he began taking disciples he gradually dropped his practice. Although a *sannyāsī,* he did not wear the traditional saffron *dhotī* and *kurtā,* but instead wore tailored Nehru jackets and white slacks. His complexion was dark, whereas Prabhupāda's was golden, and he had thick, black hair. At forty-four, he was young enough to be Prabhupāda's son. Dr. Mishra had been suffering from bad health when Śrīla Prabhupāda came into his life, and Prabhupāda's arrival seemed the perfect medicine.

Ramamurti Mishra: *His Holiness Prabhupāda Bhaktivedanta Goswamiji really knocked me down with love. He was really an incarnation of love. My body had become a skeleton, and he really brought me back to life—his cooking, and especially his love and his devotion to Lord Kṛṣṇa. I was very lazy in the matter of cooking, but he would get up and have ready.*

Dr. Mishra appreciated that Prabhupāda, cooking with the precision of a chemist, would prepare many dishes, and that he had a gusto for eating.

Ramamurti Mishra: *It was not bread he gave me—he gave me* prasādam. *This was life, and he saved my life. At that time I was not sure I would live, but his habit to eat on time, whether I was hungry or not—that I very much liked. He'd get up and say, "All right, this is* bhagavat-prasādam,*" and I would say, "All right."*

Joan Suval, an old student of Dr. Mishra's, often saw Śrīla Prabhupāda and her teacher together at the Riverside Drive apartment.

Joan Suval: *I have a memory of Swamiji as a child, in the sense of his being very innocent, a very simple person, very pure. The impression*

I have from Dr. Mishra is that he regarded Swamiji as a father figure who was kindly and good. But basically the words most often used referring to Swamiji were "like a child," meaning that he was simple in a classical, beautiful sense. Dr. Mishra mentioned to me when I was first introduced to Swamiji that he was a very holy man, very religious, rapt in God consciousness.

Swamiji was very sweet. I myself remember him as a very, very good man, even in the practical details of living in New York, which seemed to involve him very much, because he was a practical man and was looking for the best place to begin his work. I remember very well that he was always careful about washing his clothes out every night. I would come in and find a group of students in the living area of Dr. Mishra's apartment, and in the bathroom would be hung Swamiji's orange robes.

Śrīla Prabhupāda would sometimes discuss with Dr. Mishra the aim of his visit to America, expressing his spiritual master's vision of establishing Kṛṣṇa consciousness in the West. He requested Dr. Mishra to help him, but Dr. Mishra would always refer to his own teaching work, which kept him very busy, and to his plans for leaving the country soon. After a few weeks, when it became inconvenient to maintain Prabhupāda at the apartment, Dr. Mishra shifted him to his *haṭha-yoga* studio on the fifth floor of 100 West Seventy-second Street, near Central Park. The large studio was located in the center of the building and included an office and an adjoining private room, where Prabhupāda stayed. It had no windows.

Philosophically at complete odds with Prabhupāda, Dr. Mishra accepted the Absolute Truth in the impersonal feature (or Brahman) to be supreme. Prabhupāda stressed the supremacy of the personal feature (or Bhagavān), following the Vedic theistic philosophy that the most complete understanding of the Absolute Truth is personal. The *Bhagavad-gītā* says that the impersonal Brahman is subordinate to Bhagavān and is an emanation from Him, just as the sunshine is an emanation from the sun planet. This conclusion had been taught by the leading traditional *ācāryas* of ancient India, such as Rāmānuja and Madhva, and Śrīla Prabhupāda was in disciplic succession from Madhva. Dr. Mishra, on the other hand, followed Śaṅkara, who taught that the impersonal presence of the Absolute Truth is all in all and that the Personality of Godhead is ultimately an illusion. Whereas Prabhupāda's theistic philosophy accepted the individual spiritual self (*ātmā*) as an eternal servant of the supreme spiritual being (Bhagavān), Dr. Mishra's view accepted the spiritual self as not an individual. Rather, his idea was that since each person is identical with God, the Supreme Brahman, there is no need to worship God outside oneself. As Dr. Mishra would put it, "Everything is one."

Prabhupāda challenged: If each of us is actually the Supreme, then why is this "Supreme" suffering and struggling in the material world? Dr. Mishra would counter that the Supreme is only temporarily covered by illusion and that through *haṭha-yoga* and meditation one would become enlightened, understanding, "It is all the Supreme." Prabhupāda would again challenge: But if the Supreme could be covered by illusion, then illusion would be greater than God, greater than the Supreme.

Prabhupāda considered Dr. Mishra a "Māyāvādī" because of his inadvertent acceptance that *māyā,* illusion, is greater than the Absolute Truth. For Śrīla Prabhupāda, not only was the impersonal philosophy unpalatable, it was an insult to the Personality of Godhead. According to Kṛṣṇa in the *Bhagavad-gītā* (7.24, 9.11), "Unintelligent men, who know Me not, think that I have assumed this form and personality. Due to their small knowledge, they do not know My higher nature, which is changeless and supreme. ... Fools deride Me when I appear in this human form. They do not know My transcendental nature and My supreme dominion over all that be." Lord Caitanya had also strongly refuted the Māyāvāda philosophy: "Everything about the Supreme Personality of Godhead is spiritual, including His body, opulence, and paraphernalia. Māyāvāda philosophy, however, covers His spiritual opulence and advocates the theory of impersonalism."

Before coming to America, Śrīla Prabhupāda had written in his *Bhāgavatam* purports, "The ambitious Māyāvādī philosophers desire to merge into the existence of the Lord. This form of *mukti* (liberation) means denying one's individual existence. In other words, it is a kind of spiritual suicide. It is absolutely opposed to the philosophy of *bhakti-yoga. Bhakti-yoga* offers immortality to the individual conditioned soul. If one follows the Māyāvāda philosophy, he misses his opportunity to become immortal after giving up the material body." In the words of Lord Caitanya, *māyāvādī kṛṣṇa-aparādhī:* "Māyāvādī impersonalists are great offenders unto Lord Kṛṣṇa." Thus Lord Caitanya had concluded that if one even *hears* the commentary of Śaṅkara, one's entire spiritual life is spoiled. Dr. Mishra was content to align himself with the philosophy of Śaṅkara and allow Prabhupāda to stay with Lord Kṛṣṇa and the *Bhagavad-gītā.*

But Śrīla Prabhupāda pointed out that even Śaṅkara accepted that the Personality of Godhead, Kṛṣṇa, or Nārāyaṇa, exists eternally beyond the material world. Therefore, He is a transcendental person—*nārāyaṇaḥ paro 'vyaktāt.*

A mendicant, Prabhupāda was temporarily dependent on the good will of his Māyāvādī acquaintance, with whom he regularly ate and conversed and from whom he accepted shelter. But what a great inconvenience it was! He had come to America to speak purely and boldly about Kṛṣṇa, but he was being restricted. In Butler he had been confined by his hosts' middle-class sensibilities; now he was silenced in a different way. He was treated with kindness, but he was considered a threat. Dr. Mishra could not allow his students to hear the exclusive praise of Lord Kṛṣṇa as the Supreme Personality of Godhead.

Spending most of his time in his new room, Śrīla Prabhupāda kept at his typing and translating. But when Dr. Mishra held his *yoga* classes, Prabhupāda would sometimes come out and lead a *kīrtana* or lecture.

Robert Nelson (one of Prabhupāda's first young sympathizers in New York): *I went to Dr. Mishra's service, and Dr. Mishra talked. Swamiji was sitting on a bench, and then all of a sudden Dr. Mishra stops the service and he gets a big smile and says, "Swamiji will sing us a song." I think Dr. Mishra wouldn't let him speak. Somebody told me Dr. Mishra didn't want him to preach.*

Every morning, several hours before dawn, Prabhupāda would rise, take his bath, chant Hare Kṛṣṇa on his beads, and work at his translating, while outside his closed-in, windowless chamber, dawn came and the city awoke. He had no stove, so daily he had to walk the seven blocks to the Riverside Drive apartment to cook. It would be late morning when he would come out onto the busy street. He would walk north on Columbus Avenue amid the steady flow of pedestrians, pausing at each intersection in the sweeping breeze from the river. Instead of the small-town scenery of Butler, he passed through the rows of thirty-story office buildings on Columbus Avenue. At street level were shoe repair shops, candy stores, laundries, and continental restaurants. The upper stories held the professional suites of doctors, dentists, and lawyers. At Seventy-fifth Street, he would turn west and walk through a neighborhood of brownstone apartments and then across Amsterdam to Broadway, with its center-island park. The greenery here could more accurately be described as "blackery," since it was covered with soot and city grime. Broadway displayed its produce shops and butcher shops, with their stands extending onto the sidewalk, and old men sat on benches in the thin strip of park between the northbound and southbound traffic. The last block on Seventy-fifth before Riverside Drive held high-rise apartment buildings with doormen standing. Thirty-three Riverside Drive also had a doorman.

Sometimes Prabhupāda would walk in Riverside Park. Still careful for the condition of his heart, he liked the long stretches of flat walking area. Sometimes he would walk from Dr. Mishra's studio down Seventy-second Street to Amsterdam Avenue, to the West End Superette, where he would buy produce and spices for his cooking. Sometimes he would wander through Manhattan, without any fixed direction, and sometimes he would take buses to different areas of the city.

On weekends, Prabhupāda would accompany Dr. Mishra to his Ananda Ashram, one hour north of the city, in Monroe, New York. Joan Suval, who used to drive them, would overhear their animated conversations in the back seat of her car. Although they spoke in Hindi, she could hear their discussions turn into loud, shouting arguments; and afterward they would again become friends.

At Ananda Ashram Prabhupāda would usually hold *kīrtana,* with Dr. Mishra's students joining him in the chanting, and even in dancing. Dr. Mishra was particularly fond of Prabhupāda's chanting.

Ramamurti Mishra: *I have never seen or met any devotee who sang so much. And his* kīrtana *was just ambrosial. If you pay attention and become relaxed, that voice has very electrical vibrations on your heart. You cannot avoid it. Ninety-nine percent of the students, whether they liked it or not, got up and danced and chanted. And I felt very blessed to meet such a great soul.*

Harvey Cohen (a visitor to Ananda Ashram): *Everyone got up early and went to morning meditation. Dr. Mishra was dressed in a golden Indian-style jacket, and his students were already deeply into it when I entered the room. All the cushions were taken, so I picked a spot in the back of the room where I could lean against the wall to facilitate my meditation. Seated at one side was an older Indian man in saffron cloth and wrapped in a pinkish wool blanket. He seemed to be muttering to himself, and I later discovered that he was praying. It was Swami Bhaktivedanta. His forehead was painted with a white V-shaped sign, and his eyes were half shut. He seemed very serene.*

Harvey tried, but he couldn't do the *rāja-yoga.* He was new to Ananda Ashram and had only come up for a weekend retreat. During his morning meditation, he found himself more attracted to the green mists above the lake outside the window than to the circle on the wall he was supposed to be meditating on.

Harvey: *I went to my room. The rain was increasing and beating against the windows. It was peaceful, and I was glad to be alone. I read for a while. Suddenly I sensed someone standing in the doorway. Looking up, I saw it was the Swami. He was wrapped in his pink blanket, like a shawl. "Can I come in?" he asked. I nodded yes, and he asked if he could sit in the chair in the corner. "What are you reading?" He smiled. "Kafka's* Diaries," *I replied, feeling a little embarrassed. "Uh," he said, and I put the book down. He asked what I was doing at the* āśrama *and if I was interested in* yoga. *"What kind of* yoga *are you studying?" "I don't know much about it," I answered, "but I think I'd like to study* haṭha-yoga." *This didn't impress him. "There are better things than this," he explained. "There are higher, more direct forms of* yoga. Bhakti-yoga *is the highest—it is the science of devotion to God."*

As he spoke, I got the overpowering realization that he was right. He was speaking the truth. A creepy ecstatic sensation came over me that this man was my teacher. His words were so simple. And I kept looking at him all weekend. He would sit so calm and dignified with warmth. And he asked me to visit him when we got back to the city.

Dr. Mishra would give lectures carrying the impersonal interpretation of *Bhagavad-gītā* according to Śaṅkara, and Prabhupāda, when allowed to speak, would counter them. Once Prabhupāda asked Dr. Mishra to help him in spreading Lord Caitanya's movement, but Dr. Mishra sidestepped Prabhupāda by saying that he considered Prabhupāda an incarnation of Caitanya Mahāprabhu and therefore not in need of help. Prabhupāda replied that since "Mishra" was also the name of Lord Caitanya's father, Dr. Mishra should help spread Lord Caitanya's movement. Śrīla Prabhupāda offered to engage him in checking the Sanskrit to his translations of *Śrīmad-Bhāgavatam,* but Dr. Mishra declined—a decision he later regretted.

Hurta Lurch (a student at Ananda Ashram): *My direct encounter with him was in the kitchen. He was very particular and very definite that he would only eat what he cooked himself. He would come and say, "Get me a pot." So when I brought him a pot, he'd say, "No, bigger." So I brought a bigger pot, and he'd say, "No, smaller." Then he would say, "Get me potato," so I'd bring him a potato. He prepared food very, very quietly. He never spoke very much. He prepared potatoes and then some vegetables and then* capātīs. *After cooking, he would eat outside. He would usually cook enough to go around for Dr. Mishra and about five or six other people. Every day he would cook that much when he was there. I learned to make* capātīs *from him. He usually stayed only for the weekends and then went back to the city. I think he felt that was where his main work was to be done.*

* * *

That was certainly true, but what could he do there with no money or support? He was thinking of staying for only a few weeks and then going back to India. In the meantime, he was working on his *Śrīmad-Bhāgavatam* manuscripts, walking in Manhattan, and writing letters. He was studying a new culture, calculating practically and imagining hopefully how to introduce Kṛṣṇa consciousness to the Western world. He expressed his thoughts to Sumati Morarji:

October 27

> So far as I have studied, the American people are very much eager to learn about the Indian way of spiritual realization, and there are so many so-called yoga ashrams in America. Unfortunately, they are not very much adored by the government, and it is learned that such yoga ashrams have exploited the innocent people, as has been the case in India also. The only hope is that they are spiritually inclined, and immense benefit can be done to them if the cult of Srimad Bhagwatam is preached here. ...

Śrīla Prabhupāda noted that the Americans were also giving a good reception to Indian art and music. "Just to see the mode of reception," he attended the performance of a Madrasi dancer, Bala Saraswati.

> I went to see the dance with a friend, although for the last forty years I have never attended such dance ceremonies. The dancer was successful

> in her demonstration. The music was in Indian classical tune, mostly in Sanskrit language, and the American public appreciated them. So I was encouraged to see the favorable circumstances about my future preaching work.

He said the *Bhāgavatam* could also be preached through music and dance, but he had no means to introduce it. The Christian missions, backed by huge resources, were preaching all over the world, so why couldn't the devotees of Kṛṣṇa combine to preach the *Bhāgavatam* all over the world? He also noted that the Christian missions had not been effective in checking the spread of Communism, whereas a *Bhāgavatam* movement could be, because of its philosophical, scientific approach.

He was deliberately planting a seed of inspiration in the mind of the devoted, wealthy Sumati Morarji.

November 8

Prabhupāda wrote to his Godbrother Tīrtha Mahārāja, who had become president of the Gaudiya Math, to remind him that their spiritual master, Śrīla Bhaktisiddhānta Sarasvatī, had a strong desire to open preaching centers in the Western countries. Śrīla Bhaktisiddhānta had several times attempted to do this by sending *sannyāsīs* to England and other European countries, but, Prabhupāda noted, "without any tangible results."

> I have come to this country with the same purpose in view, and as far as I can see, here in America there is very good scope for preaching the cult of Lord Chaitanya. ...

Prabhupāda pointed out that there were certain Māyāvādī groups who had buildings but were not attracting many followers. But he had talked with Swami Nikhilananda of the Ramakrishna Mission, who had given the opinion that the Americans were suitable for *bhakti-yoga.*

> I am here and see a good field for work, but I am alone, without men and money. To start a center here, we must have our own buildings. ...

If the leaders of the Gaudiya Math would consider opening their own branch in New York, Śrīla Prabhupāda would be willing to manage it.

But without their own house, he reported, they could not conduct a mission in the city. Śrīla Prabhupāda wrote that they could open centers in many cities throughout the country if his Godbrothers would cooperate. He repeatedly made the point that although other groups did not have the genuine spiritual philosophy of India, they were buying many buildings. The Gaudiya Math, however, had nothing.

> If you agree to cooperate with me as I have suggested above, then I shall extend my visa period. My present visa period ends by the end of this November. But if I receive your confirmation immediately, then I shall extend my visa period. Otherwise, I shall return to India.

* * *

November 9
(6:00 P.M.)

While Prabhupāda sat alone in his fifth-floor room in Dr. Mishra's *yoga* studio, the lights suddenly went out. This was his experience of the first moments of the New York City blackout of 1965. In India, power failure occurred commonly, so Prabhupāda, while surprised to find the same thing in America, remained undisturbed. He began chanting the Hare Kṛṣṇa *mantra* on his beads. Meanwhile, outside his room, the entire New York metropolitan area had been plunged into darkness. The massive power failure had suddenly left the entire city without electricity, trapping 800,000 people in the subways and affecting more than 30,000,000 people in nine states and three Canadian provinces.

Two hours later, a man from Dr. Mishra's apartment arrived at the door with candles and some fruit. He found Prabhupāda in a pleasant mood, sitting there in the darkness chanting Hare Kṛṣṇa. The man informed him of the serious nature of such a blackout in New York City; Prabhupāda thanked him and returned again to his chanting. The blackout lasted until 7:00 the next morning.

Śrīla Prabhupāda received a reply to his letter of November 8 to Tīrtha Mahārāja in Calcutta. Prabhupāda had explained his hopes and plans for staying in America, but he had stressed that his Godbrothers would have to give him their vote of confidence as well as some tangible support. His Godbrothers had not been working cooperatively. Each leader was interested more in maintaining his own building than in working with the others to spread the teachings of Lord Caitanya around the world. So how would it be possible for them to share Śrīla Prabhupāda's vision of establishing a branch in New York City? They would see it as his separate attempt. Yet despite the unlikely odds, he appealed to their missionary spirit and reminded them of the desires of their spiritual master, Śrīla Bhaktisiddhānta Sarasvatī Ṭhākura. Their Guru Mahārāja wanted Kṛṣṇa consciousness to be spread in the West. But when Prabhupāda finally got Tīrtha Mahārāja's reply, he found it unfavorable. His Godbrother did not argue against his attempting something in New York, but he politely said that the Gaudiya Math funds could not be used for such a proposal.

Prabhupāda replied, "It is not very encouraging, still I'm not a man to be disappointed." In fact, he found a little hope in Tīrtha Mahārāja's reply, so he described to his Godbrother the property he had recently found for sale at 143 West Seventy-second Street. The building, only eighteen-and-a-half feet wide and one hundred feet deep, consisted of the first-floor store, a basement, and a mezzanine. Prabhupāda presented Tīrtha Mahārāja the price—$100,000 with a $20,000 cash down payment—and remarked that this building was twice the size of their Research Institute in Calcutta. Prabhupāda conceived of the basement as a kitchen and dining area, the first floor as a lecture hall, and the mezzanine as personal apartments, with a separate area for the Deity of Lord Kṛṣṇa.

Appropriately, Prabhupāda had described himself as "a man not to be disappointed." He was convinced that if there were a center where people could come hear from a pure devotee, the genuine God conscious culture of India could begin in America. Yet because he had made his plans dependent on obtaining an expensive building in Manhattan, his goal seemed unreachable. Still, he was persistently writing to prominent devotees in India, though they were not interested in his plans.

"Why should they not help?" he thought. After all, they were devotees of Kṛṣṇa. Shouldn't the devotees come forward to establish the first Kṛṣṇa temple in America? Certainly he was qualified and authorized to spread the message of Kṛṣṇa. As for the place, New York was perhaps the most cosmopolitan city in the world. He had found a building—not very expensive, a good location—and there was a great need for a Kṛṣṇa temple here to offset the propaganda of the Indian Māyāvādīs. The *kṛṣṇa-bhaktas* to whom he was writing understood Lord Kṛṣṇa to be not simply a Hindu Deity but the Supreme Lord, worshipable for the whole world. So they should be pleased to see Kṛṣṇa worshiped in New York. Kṛṣṇa Himself said in the *Bhagavad-gītā,* "Give up all other duties and surrender to Me." So if they were Kṛṣṇa's devotees, why would they not help? What kind of devotee was it who did not want to glorify the Lord?

But Śrīla Prabhupāda did not judge beforehand who would serve Kṛṣṇa's mission and who would not. He was fully surrendered and fully dependent on Kṛṣṇa, and in obedience to his spiritual master he would approach everyone, without discrimination, to ask for help.

There was Sumati Morarji. She had helped him in publishing the *Bhāgavatam,* and she had sent him to America. In a recent letter to her he had only given hints:

> I am just giving you the idea, and if you kindly think over the matter seriously and consult your beloved Lord Bala Krishna, surely you will be further enlightened in the matter. There is scope and there is certainly necessity also, and it is the duty of every Indian, especially the devotees of Lord Krishna, to take up the matter.

But he had received no reply. He had not heard from her since Butler, though her words to him had seemed prophetic. And they had stuck with him: "I feel that you should stay there until you fully recover from your illness and return only after you have completed your mission."

Now Sumati Morarji must do something big. He told her point-blank:

> I think therefore that *a temple of Bala Krishna in New York* may immediately be started for this purpose. And as a devotee of Lord Bala Krishna, you should execute this great and noble work. Till now there is no worshipable temple of the Hindus in New York, although in India there are so many American missionary establishments and churches. So I shall request you to do this noble act, and it will be recorded in the history of the world that the first Hindu temple is started by a pious Hindu lady *SRIMATI SUMATI MORARJI* who is not only a big business magnate in India, but a pious

> Hindu lady and great devotee of Lord Krishna. This task is for you, and glorious at the same time. ...

He assured her that he had no ambition to become the proprietor of a house or temple in America; but for preaching, a building would be absolutely required:

> They should have association of bona fide devotees of the Lord, they should join the kirtan glorifying the Lord, they should hear the teachings of Srimad Bhagwatam, they should have intimate touch with the temple or place of the Lord, and they should be given ample chance to worship the Lord in the temple. Under the guidance of the bona fide devotee, they can be given such facilities, and the way of the Srimad Bhagwatam is open for everyone. ...

He informed her that he had located a building "just suitable for this great missionary work." It was ideal, "as if it was built for this purpose only."

> ... and your simple willingness to do the act will complete everything smoothly.
>
> The house is practically three stories. Ground floor, basement, and two stories up, with all the suitable arrangements for gas, heat, etc. The ground floor may be utilized for preparation of prasadam of Bala Krishna, because the preaching center will not be for dry speculation but for actual gain—for delicious prasadam. I have already tested how the people here like the vegetable prasadam prepared by me. They will forget meat-eating and pay for the expenses. American people are not poor men like the Indians, and if they appreciate a thing, they are prepared to spend any amount on such hobby. They are being exploited simply by jugglery of words and bodily gymnastics, and still they are spending for that. But when they will have the actual commodity and feel pleasure by eating very delicious prasadam of Bala Krishna, I am sure a unique thing will be introduced in America.

Now, according to his plans, he had a week left in America.

> My term to stay in America will be finished by the 17th of November, 1965. But I am believing in your foretelling, "You should stay there until you fully recover your health, and return after you have completed your mission."

* * *

TAGORE SOCIETY OF NEW YORK Inc.
CORDIALLY INVITES YOU
to a lecture:
"GOD CONSCIOUSNESS"
by A. C. Bhaktivedanta Swami

Date: Sunday, November 28, 1965
Time: Lecture, 3:30 P.M. Tea, 4:30 P.M.
Place: New India House, 3 East 64th Street
A widely respected scholar and religious leader in India, Swami Bhaktivedanta is briefly visiting New York. He has been engaged in a monumental endeavor of translating the sixty-volume Srimad Bhagwatam from Sanskrit into English.

November 28

Daoud Haroon had never met Śrīla Prabhupāda. He was a musician living downtown, and he used to attend the meetings of the Tagore Society up on Sixty-fourth Street.

Daoud Haroon: *I went uptown and walked into the auditorium, and I noticed that the stage was empty and a few people were sitting toward the rear of the auditorium. I walked forward down the center aisle, because I usually like to sit up front. Then I saw an old gentleman sitting over to the right, and he sort of drew me over to him. So I went over and sat beside him, and then I noticed that he was saying his beads. Even though he had his beads in a bag, I could hear them, and I could see his body moving. And I felt very comfortable, because this was something I was used to.*

As I was sitting there looking around the auditorium, he just turned around and smiled at me very nicely. He nodded his head, and I nodded my head, and he smiled and turned around. Then he turned back to me again and softly asked me if I was from India. I said, "No, sir, I'm not from India. I am from here, the United States." He turned back, and he kept chanting with his beads. Then he turned around the next time and asked if I was a Hindu. I said, "No, sir, I'm not a Hindu. I'm a Muslim." And he said, "Oh, very good, very good. Yes, many times I hear the children in India reciting the Koran." And then he turned back around and his body was moving, rocking, and he was working with his beads.

Then there were a few more exchanges of pleasantries, sort of inter-

mittent. And then a lady came up on the stage and announced that the lecture was to begin and if the folks could give the speaker a round of applause they would welcome him to the stage. At that point, the man I was sitting next to put his hand on my shoulder and said, "Excuse me, sir, could you do me a favor?" And I said, "Yes, anything." He said, "Would you watch over my books?" I looked down on the floor, and he had several boxes of books and an umbrella and several other articles. I said yes I would watch over these. And he said, "Excuse me." He walked up the aisle, and surprisingly, he walked up on the stage. And it was the man I had come to hear—Swami Bhaktivedanta!

He walked up on the stage and introduced himself to the people and tried to get them to come forward. He said, "Come forward, come forward." A few of them came up to the front. There were mixed couples, many Indians, male and female, mostly middle-aged and some college-aged, a lot of professor-types and ladies were there.

Then he began his speech. He dove right into it. He just started exclaiming, proclaiming, the greatness of the Creator and that the most important thing is to remember the Creator and remember God. He began to expand on God consciousness, what God consciousness is and how God is everywhere and how it behooves us all to remember God—no matter what we call Him, what names we call Him by, but that we should call Him. He gave a demonstration which was very moving. He chanted Hare Kṛṣṇa, Hare Rāma and spoke about the power and saving grace in the mantra. *He took a little break about halfway through and had some water.*

The last thing he said as he was coming down from the podium was that he had copies of the Śrīmad-Bhāgavatam. *He explained that he had been working on them and that they came in three volumes and were sixteen dollars. Then he concluded and came down.*

A lot of people went over to him. Some were timid, some were enthusiastic. Some people shook his hand and were asking for books. At first there were about fifteen people gathered around him talking to him and asking questions. With so many people around, he came over to me and said, "Sir, would you do me one more favor? Will you kindly take over the selling of the books? People will be coming to you for the books, so you sell the books and put the money in this little box, and I will be with you in a minute." I said, "Fine."

So while he talked to the people, others came up to me. They must have thought I was somehow his secretary or his traveling companion, and people were coming over to me and asking me personal questions about him, which I couldn't really answer because I didn't know. Some people were buying the books or looking through them. So this went on, and I was trying to listen to him carry on his conversations with people and carry on the book-selling at the same time.

Some of the people were looking for a guru *and trying to find out what he was supposed to be. Some of them were really interrogating him. But he just smiled and answered all their questions simply. I remember he told them, "You will know. There's no pressure. You will know if I am your guru." He suggested that people go over and read the books.*

And then the group dwindled down to about half a dozen, and the few remaining were just looking at him, and some were too timid to approach him. He walked over to them and spoke to them, putting them at ease. Later he came over, and we counted the collection, and I helped him pack up his box and carry downstairs the boxes of books that were left. As we parted he thanked me very much, and I gave him my name and address and phone number and purchased a set of the Śrīmad-Bhāgavatams.

CHAPTER FIFTEEN

"It Will Not Be Possible to Assist You"

I have come here in this old age neither for sightseeing nor for any personal interest. It is for the interest of the entire humanity that I am trying to implement the science of Krishna which will actually make them happy. So it is the duty of every devotee of Lord Krishna to help me by all means.

—from a letter to Sumati Morarji

NOVEMBER PASSED AND December came, and Prabhupāda, having obtained an extension on his visa, stayed on. America seemed so opulent, yet many things were difficult to tolerate. The sirens and bells from fire engines and police cars seemed like they would crack his heart. Sometimes at night he would hear a person being attacked and crying for help. From his first days in the city, he had noted that the smell of dog stool was everywhere. And although it was such a rich city, he could rarely find a mango to purchase, and if he did, it was very expensive and usually had no taste. From his room he would sometimes hear the horns of ocean liners, and he would dream that some day he would sail around the world with a *saṅkīrtana* party, preaching in all the major cities of the world. The weather went below freezing, colder than he had ever experienced in India. Daily he had to walk toward the Hudson against a west wind that even on an ordinary winter's day would take your breath away and make your eyes water and your face grow numb. On a stormy day, the driving wind and sudden gusts could even knock a man down. Sometimes a cold rain would turn the streets slick with ice. The cold would become especially severe as one approached the shelterless, windswept area of West Side Drive, where occasional whirlwinds carried brown leaves and paper trash mysteriously high into the air.

Śrīla Prabhupāda wore a coat Dr. Mishra had given him, but he never gave up wearing his *dhotī,* despite the cold, windy walks. Swami Nikhilananda of the Ramakrishna Mission had advised Prabhupāda that if he wanted to stay in the West he should abandon his traditional Indian dress and strict vegetarianism. Meat-eating and liquor, as well as pants and coat, were almost a necessity in this climate, he had said. Before Prabhupāda had left India, one of his Godbrothers had demonstrated to him how he should eat in the West with a knife and fork. But Prabhupāda never considered taking on Western ways. His advisors cautioned him not to remain an alien but to get into the spirit of American life, even if it meant breaking vows he had held in India; almost all Indian immigrants compromised their old ways. But Prabhupāda's idea was different, and he could not be budged. The others may have had to compromise, he thought, but they had come to beg technological knowledge from the West. "I have not come to beg something," he said, "but to *give* something."

In his solitary wanderings, Śrīla Prabhupāda made acquaintances with a number of local people. There was Mr. Ruben, a Turkish Jew, who worked as a New York City subway conductor. Mr. Ruben met Prabhupāda on a park bench and, being a sociable fellow and a world traveler, sat and talked with the Indian holy man.

Mr. Ruben: *He seemed to know that he would have temples filled up with devotees. He would look out and say, "I am not a poor man, I am rich. There are temples and books, they are existing, they are there, but the time is separating us from them." He always mentioned "we" and spoke about the one who sent him, his spiritual master. He didn't know people at that time, but he said, "I am never alone." He always looked like a lonely man to me. That's what made me think of him like a holy man, Elijah, who always went out alone. I don't believe he had any followers.*

When the weather was not rainy or icy, Prabhupāda would catch the bus to Grand Central Station and visit the Central Library on Forty-second Street. His *Śrīmad-Bhāgavatams* were there—some of the same volumes he had sold to the U.S. embassy in New Delhi—and he took pleasure in seeing them listed in the card catalog and learning that they were being regularly checked out and read. He would sometimes walk through U.N. Plaza or walk up to New India House on Sixty-fourth Street, where he had met Mr. Malhotra, a consulate officer. It was through Mr. Malhotra that he had contacted the Tagore Society and had secured an invitation to lecture before one of their meetings back in November.

Riding the bus down Fifth Avenue, he would look out at the buildings and imagine that some day they could be used in Kṛṣṇa consciousness. He would take a special interest in certain buildings: one on Twenty-third Street and one with a dome on Fourteenth Street attracted his attention. He would think of how the materialists had constructed such elaborate buildings and had yet made no provisions for spiritual life. Despite all the great achievements of technology, the people felt empty and useless. They had built these great buildings, but the children were going to LSD.

December 2

New York Times headlines: "New York City Hospitals Report Marked Rise in LSD Cases Admitted for Care." "Protest Against U.S. Participation in Vietnam War Mounts."

The weather grew cold, but there was no snow in December. On Columbus Avenue shops were selling Christmas trees, and the continental restaurants were bright with holiday lighting. On Seventy-second the Retailers' Association erected tall red poles topped with green tinsel Christmas trees. The tops of the trees on both sides of the street sprouted tinsel garlands that spanned the street and joined in red tinsel stars surrounded by colored lights.

Although Śrīla Prabhupāda did no Christmas shopping, he visited many bookstores—Orientalia, Sam Weiser's, Doubleday, the Paragon, and others—trying to sell his *Śrīmad-Bhāgavatams.* Mrs. Ferber, the wife of the Paragon Book Gallery proprietor, considered Prabhupāda "a pleasant and extremely polite small gentleman." The first time he called she wasn't interested in his books, but he tried again, and she took several volumes. Prabhupāda used to stop by about once a week, and since his books were selling regularly, he would collect. Sometimes when he needed copies to sell personally, he would come by and pick them up from Mrs. Ferber, and sometimes he would phone to ask her how his books were selling.

Mrs. Ferber: *Every time he came he would ask for a glass of water. If a customer would make such a request, I would ordinarily say,* "There *is the water cooler." But because he was an old man, I couldn't tell him that, of course. He was very polite always, very modest, and a great scholar. So whenever he would ask, I would fetch him a cup of water personally.*

Once Prabhupāda was talking with Mrs. Ferber about Indian cuisine, and she mentioned that she especially liked *samosās.* The next time he paid her a visit, he brought a tray of *samosās,* which she enjoyed.

* * *

Harvey Cohen came often to room 501 to visit the swami who had so impressed him at Ananda Ashram.

Harvey: *The room he occupied was a tiny office in the back of the Yoga Society in uptown Manhattan. I began to go there regularly, and we sat facing each other on the floor in this little office with his typewriter and a new tape recorder on top of two suitcases. And there was a box of books he had brought from India and a color reproduction of dancing figures which he looked at often. I told Swami Bhaktivedanta that I was an artist, and he asked me to please paint the picture of the dancers, which he explained was of Lord Caitanya and His disciples. The painting was called "Saṅkīrtana." Whenever I came to visit him, Swami would always be happy to see me. I told him about myself, and we chanted Hare Kṛṣṇa together in his room many nights that winter. I would get the train uptown from my apartment to go see him.*

* * *

January 11, 1966

Prime Minister Lal Bahadur Shastri died of a heart attack while visiting Russia. The prime minister had been a personal acquaintance of Śrīla Prabhupāda's in India and an admirer of his *Śrīmad-Bhāgavatam* translation. He had been scheduled to visit America, and Prabhupāda had expected to obtain a personal sanction from him for the release of funds from India. His untimely death was a great upset in Śrīla Prabhupāda's plans to purchase the building at 143 West Seventy-second Street. The realtors had shown him the building, and he had already mentally designed the interior for Deity worship and distribution of *prasādam.* The money was to come from India, and Prime Minister Shastri was to give personal sanction for release of the funds. But suddenly that was all changed.

January 14

Prabhupāda decided to write to the owner of the building, Mr. A. M. Hartman. He explained how his plans had been upset, and he posed a new plan.

> Now the Prime Minister, Mr. Lal Bahadur Shastri, is suddenly dead, and I am greatly perplexed. ... As there is now great difficulty for getting money from India, I am requesting you to allow me to use the place for the International Institution for God Consciousness, at least for some time. The house is lying vacant for so many days without any use, and I learn it that you are paying the taxes, insurance, and other charges for the house, although you have no income from there. If you, however, allow this place for this public institution, you shall at least save the taxes and other charges which you are paying now for nothing.
>
> If I can start the institution immediately, certainly I shall be able to get sympathy locally, and in that case I may not be required to get money from India. I am also requesting that your honor become one of the Directors of this public institution, because you will give a place to start the institution.

A. M. Hartman wasn't interested.

On the same day he wrote Mr. Hartman, Prabhupāda received a letter from Sir Padampat Singhania, the director of the very large JK Organization in India. Prabhupāda had written Sir Padampatji for financial support, and his reply gave him hope. Not only was the Singhania family fabulously wealthy, but its members were devotees of Lord Kṛṣṇa.

> My dear Swamiji,
>
> I have gone through your letter. I am very glad to note your idea of

erecting a Shri Radha Krishna temple in New York. I think the proposal is a good one, but the following are the difficulties:

1. We have got to send foreign exchange for building the temple, for which Government sanction is required. Without the Government sanction, no money can be sent abroad. If the Government of India agrees, then one can think of erecting the temple in New York.
2. I doubt whether with this small amount of Rs. 7 lakhs [$110,000.00] a temple can be built in New York. I mean to carry out a nice Construction with Indian type of architecture. To get a temple completed in Indian type of architecture we have to send a man from India.

These are the two main difficulties, otherwise, your idea is very good.

Śrīla Prabhupāda and Mr. Singhania had a basic disagreement. A magnificent Indian temple in New York would cost many millions of dollars to construct. Prabhupāda knew, of course, that if Padampat Singhania wanted, he could provide millions of dollars. But then how would they get so much money out of India? Prabhupāda therefore again suggested that they spend only seven lakhs. "After purchasing the house," he wrote, "we can build another story upon it with a temple dome, *cakra,* etc." Prabhupāda had his own line of reasoning:

> Lord Dwarkadish exhibited His opulence at Dwarka with 16,000 queens, and it is understood that He built a palace for each and every queen. And the palaces were made with jewels and stones so that there was no necessity for artificial light in the palaces. So your conception of building a temple of Lord Krishna is in opulence. But we are residents of Vrindaban, and Vrindaban has no palaces like your Dwarka. Vrindaban is full of forests and cows on the bank of the Jamuna, and Lord Krishna in His childhood played the part of a cowherd boy without any royal opulence as you people, the inhabitants of Dwarka, are accustomed. So when the Dwarka walas meet the Vrindaban walas, there may be a via media.

With Sir Padampat's Dvārakā-like wealth and Śrīla Prabhupāda's Vṛndāvana-like devotion, Lord Kṛṣṇa, the Lord of both Vṛndāvana and Dvārakā, could be properly worshiped.

January 21

He received Bon Mahārāja's reply. Two weeks before, Prabhupāda had written to his Godbrother, the director of the Institute of Oriental Philosophy in Vṛndāvana, that he had found a place for a temple in

New York and that he wanted to install Deities of Rādhā and Kṛṣṇa. In his reply, Bon Mahārāja quoted price estimates for fourteen-inch brass Deities of Rādhā-Kṛṣṇa, but he also warned that to begin Deity worship would be a heavy responsibility. Śrīla Prabhupāda responded:

> I think that after the temple has started, some men, even from America, may be available, as I see they have at the Ramakrishna Mission as well as in so many yoga societies. So I am trying to open a temple here because Srila Prabhupad [Bhaktisiddhānta Sarasvatī] wanted it.

Prabhupāda also requested Bon Mahārāja's assistance in getting the government to sanction release of the money he felt Padampat Singhania would donate. He mentioned that he had carried on an extensive personal correspondence with the vice-president of India, Dr. Radhakrishnan, who was also known to Bon Mahārāja.

> Tell him that it is not an ordinary temple of worship but an international institution for God consciousness based on the Srimad Bhagwatam.

January 22

While Śrīla Prabhupāda prayed to receive Rādhā-Kṛṣṇa in New York, a snowstorm hit the city. That morning, Śrīla Prabhupāda, who had perhaps never before seen snow, woke and thought that someone had whitewashed the side of the building next door. Not until he went outside did he discover that it was snow. The temperature was ten degrees.

The city went into a state of emergency, but Prabhupāda continued his daily walks. Now he had to walk through heavy snow, only a thin *dhotī* beneath his overcoat, his head covered with his "swami hat." The main roads were cleared, but many sidewalks were covered with snow. Along the strip of park dividing Broadway, the gusting winds piled snowbanks to shoulder height and buried the benches. The Broadway kiosks, plastered with layers of posters and notices, were now plastered with additional layers of snow and ice. But despite the weather, New Yorkers still walked their dogs, the pets now wearing raincoats and mackinaws. Such pampering by American dog owners left Prabhupāda with a feeling of surprised amusement. As he approached West End Avenue, he found the doormen blowing whistles to signal taxis as usual, but also scattering salt to melt the ice and create safe sidewalks in front of the buildings.

In Riverside Park the benches, pathways, and trees were glazed with ice and gave off a shimmering reflection from the sky.

In the news, Selective Service officials announced the first substantial increase in the draft since the Korean war; a month-long peace ended with the U.S. Air Force bombing North Vietnam; the New York transit strike ended after three weeks, and the transit labor leader died in jail of a heart attack.

January 30

The East Coast was hit by severe blizzards. Seven inches of snow fell on the city, with winds up to fifty miles an hour. The City of New York offered warm rooms and meals for people living in tenements without heat. JFK Airport was closed, as were train lines and roadways into the city. For the second time within eight days, a state of emergency was declared because of snow.

As a lone individual, Śrīla Prabhupāda could not do anything about the snow emergency or the international warfare—he saw these as mere symptoms of the Age of Kali. Always there would be misery in the material world. But if he could bring Rādhā and Kṛṣṇa to a building in New York ... Nothing was impossible for the Supreme Lord. Even in the midst of Kali-yuga a golden age could appear, and people could get relief. If Americans could take to Kṛṣṇa consciousness, the whole world would follow. Seeing through the eyes of the scriptures, Śrīla Prabhupāda pushed on through the blizzard and pursued the thin trail for support of his Kṛṣṇa consciousness mission.

February 4

He wrote again to Tīrtha Mahārāja, who had agreed to try for the government sanction if he first received written confirmation from a responsible donor pledging the funds for a temple. Prabhupāda informed him that the donor would be Sir Padampat Singhania, and he enclosed Mr. Singhania's favorable letter of the fourteenth. Prabhupāda reminded his Godbrother:

> Srila Prabhupad Bhaktisiddhanta wanted such temples in foreign cities like New York, London, Tokyo, etc., and I had personal talks with him when

> I first met him at Ulta Danga in 1922. Now here is a chance for me to carry out his transcendental order. I am just seeking your favor and mercy in making this attempt successful.

February 5

Discouragement came to the plans Śrīla Prabhupāda had formed around the promise of support by Padampat Singhania. The Dvārakāvālā wrote to express his dissatisfaction with the Seventy-second Street building.

> I am afraid that I cannot agree with your suggestion that you should buy a small house and erect something on top of it. Unfortunately, such a kind of proposal will not suit me. The temple must be a small one, but it must be constructed properly. I quite agree that you cannot spend a lot of money at present, but within the amount the government may sanction, you should build something according to the architecture of Indian temples. Then only will we be able to create some impression on the American people. This is all I can write to you in this connection. I am very grateful for your taking the trouble of writing me.

Prabhupāda did not take this letter as final. He maintained hope that Sir Padampat Singhania would still give money for the temple, if only the transfer of money could be arranged. He continued writing his Godbrothers and other devotees, asking them to try to secure the government's sanction. He maintained his same aspirations, even though his sole prospective donor had rejected his scheme of a *cakra* and dome atop a conventional two-story building.

* * *

February 15

He moved from room 501 downstairs two floors to a room all his own.

> I have changed my room to Room 307, in the same building as above mentioned, for better air and light. It is on the roadside junction of two roads, the Columbus Avenue and 72nd Street.

According to Dr. Mishra, Prabhupāda moved in order to have his own place, independent of the Mishra Yoga Society.

* * *

February 16

Prabhupāda wrote to the proprietors of the Universal Book House of Bombay, giving some hints for selling his *Śrīmad-Bhāgavatam* in the Bombay area. He explained that he was trying to establish a Rādhā-Kṛṣṇa temple and that "a big industrialist of India has promised to pay for the cost." Since it seemed that he might stay in the United States "for many more days," he wanted the Book House to take increased charge of selling his books throughout India. They were his agent for selling his books in Maharashtra, but now he recommended they take the responsibility in *all* provinces and introduce his books in colleges and universities throughout India. He also requested that they credit his bank account there for the books sold so far.

February 26

Mr. A. P. Dharwadkar of the Universal Book House replied:

> I cannot give you very happy news on the progress of the sale of Srimad Bhagwatam, because the subject is religious and only a small section of society may personally be interested in the books. ... We tried to push them through some book sellers to Nagpur, Ahmedabad, Poona, etc., but regret to inform you that after some time these book sellers return the books for want of response. As such, we are not only unenthusiastic to agree to your proposal of taking up sales for all India, but we were just thinking of requesting you to nominate some other people in our place to represent your sale program in Maharashtra.

So far, they had sold only six sets of his books, for which they were about to transfer Rs. 172 to his account. This was hardly encouraging to the author. Again, India was not interested. Even in "the land of religion," religious subjects were only for "a small section of society."

March 4

Another reverse. On February 8, Śrīla Prabhupāda had written to India's new prime minister, Indira Gandhi, requesting her to sanction the release of money from India. A reply, dated February 25, New Delhi, came from the prime minister's official secretary, Mr. L. K. Gha.

Dear Swamiji,

The Prime Minister has seen your letter of February 8, 1966. She appreciates the spirit which prompted you to carry the spiritual message of Srimad Bhagwat Geeta and Srimad Bhagwatam to other countries. Owing to the critical foreign exchange situation which the country is facing, it is greatly regretted that it will not be possible to assist you from here in your plan to set up a Radha Krishna temple.

But Prabhupāda had other hopes. After writing to the prime minister, he had written again to Tīrtha Mahārāja, asking him to request Dr. Radhakrishnan to persuade the government to sanction the release of funds. He waited for one month. No answer.

Apparently his Godbrothers felt little obligation toward preaching in America; he had written that he needed encouragement from them to continue in America, because it was so expensive. He had explained that he was spending the equivalent of one thousand rupees a month. "As such, I am counting every day to receive your favorable replies." But there was no reply.

March 18

He wrote again to Sir Padampat Singhania, requesting him to send a man from India to supervise work on the temple in New York, as Mr. Singhania had previously suggested.

There is no record of any reply to this request.

Prabhupāda wrote again to Sumati Morarji, requesting her to please send him a *mṛdaṅga* to accompany his chanting of the Hare Kṛṣṇa *mantra*. He also requested her that in the future, when he would send many men from India, she oblige by giving them free passage on Scindia Steamship Lines.

No reply.

As his financial situation became more urgent and his hopes more strained, his support from India withdrew in silence. His unanswered correspondence was itself a kind of message, loud and clear: "We cannot help you."

Although no one encouraged him, Śrīla Prabhupāda trusted in the order of his spiritual master and the will of Kṛṣṇa. The word from the prime minister regarding government sanction had been a definite no. But he had received another extension of his visa. Now his last hope was Sir Padampat Singhania. Prabhupāda knew that he was so influential a man in India that if he wanted he could send the money. He was Prabhupāda's final hope.

April 2

Mr. Singhania did not reply personally. He had his secretary, Mr. Easwara Iyer, write to Prabhupāda, thoroughly discouraging his last hopes for purchasing a building in New York.

> I regret to write that Sir Padampatji is not interested in the scheme of building a Radha Krishna temple in New York at present. In regard to the inquiry contained in the last paragraph of your letter, Sir Padampatji duly received your books of Srimad Bhagwatam from your Delhi office. Yours faithfully.

* * *

Seeing him from a distance—a tiny figure walking Manhattan's streets and avenues among many other tiny figures, a foreigner whose visa had almost run out—we come upon only the external appearance of Śrīla Prabhupāda. These days of struggle were real enough and very difficult, but his transcendental consciousness was always predominant. He was not living in Manhattan consciousness, but was absorbed in dependence upon Kṛṣṇa, just as when on the *Jaladuta* he had suffered his heart attacks, his reading of *Caitanya-caritāmṛta* had supplied him "the nectarine of life."

He had already succeeded. Certainly he wanted to provide Rādhā and Kṛṣṇa a temple in New York, but his success was that he was remembering Kṛṣṇa, even in New York City in the winter of 1965–66, whether the world recognized him or not. Not a day went by when he did not work on Kṛṣṇa's book, *Śrīmad-Bhāgavatam.* And not a day went by when he did not offer food to Kṛṣṇa and speak on Kṛṣṇa's philosophy of *Bhagavad-gītā.*

Lord Kṛṣṇa says in *Bhagavad-gītā,* "For one who sees Me everywhere and sees everything in Me, I am never lost to him, and he is never lost to Me." And Kṛṣṇa assures His pure devotees that, "My devotee will never be vanquished." There was never any doubt about this for Prabhupāda.

The only question was whether Americans would take notice of the pure devotee in their midst. At this point it seemed that no one was going to take him seriously.

CHAPTER SIXTEEN

Free to Preach

Here I am now sitting in New York, the world's greatest city, such a magnificent city, but my heart is always hankering after that Vṛndāvana. I shall be very happy to return to my Vṛndāvana, that sacred place. But then, "Why are you here?" Now, because it is my duty. I have brought some message for you people. Because I have been ordered by my superior, my spiritual master: "Whatever you have learned, you should go to the Western countries, and you must distribute this knowledge." So in spite of all my difficulties, all my inconveniences, I am here. Because I am obligated by duty.

—from a lecture by Śrīla Prabhupāda

ROOM 307 WAS never meant for use as a residence or *āśrama* or lecture hall. It was only a small, narrow office without furniture or a telephone. Its door held a large pane of frosted glass, the kind common in old offices; above the door was a glass-paned transom. Prabhupāda placed his blankets on the floor before his metal footlocker, which now became a makeshift desk where he wrote. He slept on the floor. There were no facilities here for cooking or even for bathing, so daily he had to walk to Dr. Mishra's apartment.

When he had lived in room 501 at Dr. Mishra's *yoga-āśrama,* Dr. Mishra had financed his needs. But now Prabhupāda was on his own, and whatever he could raise by selling his books, he would have to use for his daily maintenance and for the monthly rent of seventy-two dollars. He noted that for a little powdered chili the West End Superette charged twenty-five cents, ten times what he would have paid in India. He had no guaranteed income, his expenses had increased, and his physical comforts had reduced. But at least he had his own place. Now he was free to preach as he liked.

He had come to America to speak about Kṛṣṇa, and even from the beginning he had found the opportunity to do so, whether at an informal get-together in the Agarwals' living room or before a formal gathering at the Butler Lions Club, Dr. Norman Brown's Sanskrit class, Dr. Mishra's Yoga Society, or the Tagore Society. But he did not attach much importance to lecturing where the people who gathered would hear him only once. This was the main reason he wanted his own building in New York: so that people could come *regularly,* chant Hare Kṛṣṇa, take *prasādam* in his company, and hear him speak from *Bhagavad-gītā* and *Śrīmad-Bhāgavatam.*

Moving out of the *yoga* studio into the small office downstairs gave Prabhupāda what he was looking for—his own place—but not even euphemistically could that place be called a temple. His name was on the door; anyone seeking him there could find him. But who would come there? By its opulence and beauty, a temple was supposed to attract people to Kṛṣṇa. But room 307 was just the opposite: it was bare poverty. Even a person interested in spiritual topics would find it uncomfortable to sit on the rugless floor of a room shaped like a narrow railroad car.

One of Dr. Mishra's students had donated a reel-to-reel tape recorder, and Prabhupāda recorded some of his solitary *bhajanas,* which he sang to his own accompaniment of hand cymbals. He also recorded a long philosophical essay, *Introduction to Gītopaniṣad.* "Even if no one attends," Śrīla Bhaktisiddhānta Sarasvatī had told him, "you can go on chanting to the four walls." But since he was now free to speak his message in the new situation God had provided, he decided to lecture three evenings a week (Monday, Wednesday, and Friday) to whoever would come.

His first audiences consisted mainly of people who had heard about him or met him at Dr. Mishra's *yoga* studio. And despite the poverty of his room, the meetings became a source of new life for him.

March 18

He expressed his optimism in a letter to Sumati Morarji:

> I was very much encouraged when you wrote to say, "I feel that you should stay there until you fully recover from your illness, and return only after you have completed your mission." I think these lines dictated by you are the words of Lord Bala Krishna expressed through your goodness.
>
> You will be pleased to know that I have improved my health back to normal, and my missionary work is nicely progressing. I hope my project to start a temple of Sri Sri Radha Krishna will also be realized by the grace of the Lord.
>
> Since I came to New York from Butler, Pennsylvania, I have rented the above room at seventy dollars per month, and am delivering lectures on the Bhagwat Geeta and Srimad Bhagwatam, accompanied by sankirtan, and the American ladies and gentlemen come to hear me. You will be surprised to know that they do not understand the language of sankirtan, yet they hear with attention. The movement which I have started here is completely new to them, because the Americans are generally acquainted with the Indian yoga gymnastics as performed by some Indian yogis here. They have never heard of the bhakti cult of the science of Krishna before, and still they are hearing me. This is a great success for me.

* * *

Outside the closed windows of room 307, the late winter night has fallen. Prabhupāda's words are punctuated with the muted sounds of car horns and occasional sirens from the street, and sometimes by the startling chords of a lonely foghorn on the Hudson. Although bare, the room is warm. Prabhupāda is speaking on the Second Chapter of *Bhagavad-gītā.*

Now Arjuna is perplexed. He is perplexed about whether to fight or not to fight. After seeing in front of him his relatives with whom he was to fight, he was perplexed. And there was some argument with Kṛṣṇa.

Now here is a point: Kṛṣṇa is the Supreme Personality of Godhead. ...

Prabhupāda's voice is earnest, persuading. Sometimes his speech becomes high-pitched and breaks with urgency. His cultured British diction bears a heavy Bengali accent.

Suddenly he pauses in his lecture and addresses someone in the room.

Prabhupāda: *What is that?*

Man: *What?*

Prabhupāda: *What is this book?*

Man: *Well, this is a translation of the* Bhagavad-gītā.

Prabhupāda is obviously displeased that while he is speaking someone is looking through a book. This is hardly like the respect offered to learned speakers described in the *Śrīmad-Bhāgavatam.*

Prabhupāda: *Well, no, you can hear me.*

Man: *I am hearing.*

Prabhupāda: *Yes, don't turn your attention. Just hear me.*

He is taking the role of a teacher correcting his student. Of course, there is no compelling reason why any of his casual guests should feel obliged to obey him. He simply begs for their attention, and yet demands it—"Just hear me"—as he attempts to convince them of Kṛṣṇa consciousness.

You have heard that one must accept the spiritual master after careful examination, just as one selects a bride or a bridegroom after careful examination. In India they are very careful. Because the marriage of boys and girls takes place under the guidance of the parents, so the parents very carefully see to it. Similarly, one has to accept the spiritual master. It is necessary. According to Vedic injunctions, everyone should have a spiritual master. Perhaps you have seen a sacred thread. We have got sacred thread. Mr. Cohen? You have seen? Sacred thread.

Prabhupāda pauses. His audience has not noted the thin, white cords he wears beneath his shirt across the upper part of his body. For thousands of years, *brāhmaṇas* in India have worn such threads, placed diagonally across the torso, looped over the left shoulder and down to the right waist. A *brāhmaṇa* holds his thread in his right hand while chanting the sacred Gāyatrī *mantra* three times a day. But this is all strange indeed to Americans. Prabhupāda himself is exotic to them. His gray *cādara* wrapped around his shoulders, he sits cross-legged and erect on a thin pillow, and they sit facing him on the other side of his trunk, which now serves as a desk and lectern. They are close together in the narrowness of the room. He is frail and small and foreign to them, yet somehow he is completely assured, in a way that has nothing to do with being a foreigner in New York. Visitors sense his strong presence. Two white lines of clay run neatly vertical on his forehead. His pale peach clothes are gathered in loose folds around his body. He pauses only a few seconds to inquire whether they have seen a sacred thread.

That sacred thread is a sign that a person has a spiritual master. Here, of course, there is no such distinction, but according to the Hindu system a married girl also has some sign so that people can understand that this girl is married. She wears a red mark so that others may know that she is married. And according to the division in the hair ... what is this line called?

Man: *Part.*

Prabhupāda: *Hmm?*

Man: *Part.*

Prabhupāda: *What is the spelling?*

Man: *Part.*

Prabhupāda: *Part. This parting also has some meaning.* (They know English, and he knows the *Gītā*. But he knows a good deal of English, whereas they know practically nothing of the *Gītā*, which he has to spoon-feed to them. But occasionally he asks their help in English vocabulary.) *When the part is in the middle, then the girl has her husband, and she is coming from a respectable family. And if the part is here, then she is a prostitute.* (With a slight gesture he raises his hand toward, but never really reaching, his head. Yet somehow the half-gesture clearly indicates a part on the side of the head.) *And then again when a girl is well dressed, it should be understood that she has her husband at home. And when she is not well dressed, it is to be understood that her husband is away from home. You see? And a widow's dress ... There are so many symptoms. So, similarly, the sacred thread is a sign that a person has accepted a spiritual master, just as the red mark symbolizes that a girl has a husband.*

Although his audience may be momentarily enamored by what appears to be a description of Indian social customs, a careful listener can grasp the greater context of Prabhupāda's speech: Everyone must accept a spiritual master. It's a heavy topic for a casual audience. What is the need of taking a spiritual master? Isn't this just for India? But he says, "Everyone should have a spiritual master." What is a spiritual master anyway? Maybe he means that accepting a spiritual master is just another cultural item from Hinduism, like the thread, or the part in a woman's hair, or the widow's dress. The audience can easily regard his discussion as a kind of cultural exposition, just as one comfortably watches a film about the living habits of people in a foreign land although one has no intention of adopting these habits as one's own. The Swami is wearing one of those threads on his body, but that's for Hindus, and it doesn't mean that Americans should wear them. But these Hindu beliefs are interesting.

Actually, Prabhupāda has no motive but to present the Absolute Truth as he has heard it in disciplic succession. But if anyone in that railroad-car-shaped room were to ask himself, "Should I surrender to a spiritual master?" he would be confronted by the existential presence of a genuine *guru*. One is free to regard his talk as one likes.

In every step of one's life, the spiritual master guides. Now, to give such guidance a spiritual master should also be a very perfect man. Otherwise how can he guide? Now, here Arjuna knows that Śrī Kṛṣṇa is the perfect person. So therefore he is accepting Him—śiṣyas te 'haṁ śādhi māṁ tvāṁ prapannam.

Sanskrit! No one knows a word of it! But there is never any question for Śrīla Prabhupāda—even if they don't understand it, the transcendental sound of *śāstra* will purify them. It is his authority, and he cannot omit it. And even at first impression, it presents an air of scholarly authority—the original, though foreign, words of the sages.

"I am just surrendering unto You, and You accept me as Your disciple," Arjuna says. Friendly talks cannot make a solution to perplexity. Friendly talks may be going on for years together, but no solution. So here, Arjuna accepts Kṛṣṇa as the spiritual master. This means that whatever Kṛṣṇa will dictate, he has to accept. One cannot deny the order of the spiritual master. Therefore, one has to select a spiritual master by whose orders one will not commit a mistake.

Suppose you accept the wrong person as spiritual master and he guides you wrongly. Then your whole life is spoiled. So one has to accept a spiritual master whose guidance will make one's life perfect. That is the relationship between spiritual master and disciple. It is not a formality. It is a great responsibility, both for the disciple and for the spiritual master. And ... Yes?

Student: *But if the disciple is in ignorance before ...*

Prabhupāda: *Yes.* (Prabhupāda acknowledges a serious question. It is for answering questions like this—from "disciples in ignorance"— that he has left retirement in India and come to America.)

Student: ... *how does he know which master to choose?—because he doesn't have the knowledge to make a wise decision.*

Prabhupāda: *Yes. So the first thing is that one should be searching after a spiritual master, just as you search after some school. You must at least have some preliminary knowledge of what a school is. You can't search for a school and go to a cloth shop. If you are so ignorant that you do not know what is a school and what is a cloth shop, then it is very difficult for you. You must know at least what a school is. So that knowledge is like this:*

tad-vijñānārthaṁ sa gurum evābhigacchet
samit-pāṇiḥ śrotriyaṁ brahma-niṣṭham

According to this verse, the spiritual master is required for a person who is inquisitive about transcendental knowledge. There's another verse in the Śrīmad-Bhāgavatam: tasmād guruṁ prapadyeta jijñāsuḥ śreya uttamam. *"One should search after a spiritual master if one is inquisitive about transcendental subject matters." Unless one is at least conversant with preliminary knowledge of transcendental matters, how can he inquire from the spiritual master?*

His questioner seems satisfied. The lecture is not a prepared speech on a specific subject. Though grave and thorough in scholarship, it ranges over several philosophical points. Yet he never pauses, groping for words. He knows exactly what he wants to say, and it is only a question of how much his audience can take.

But sometimes his mood is light, and he commiserates with his fellow New Yorkers, chuckling about the difficulties they share: "Suppose there is a heavy snowfall, the whole New York City is flooded with snow, and you are all put into inconvenience. That is a sort of suffering, but you have no control over it." Sometimes he praises Dr. Mishra's students for having learned so nicely from their teacher: "Now, what Dr. Mishra is teaching is very nice. He is teaching that first of all you must know, 'Who am I?' That is very good, but that 'Who am I?' can be known from *Bhagavad-gītā* also—'I am not this body.'" And sometimes a guest suddenly speaks out with an irrelevant question, and the Swami patiently tries to consider it.

Yet behind his tolerance, Prabhupāda's mood is always one of urgency. Sometimes he talks quickly and one senses his desire to establish Kṛṣṇa consciousness in the West as soon as possible. He has no followers, only a few books, no temples, and he openly states that he is racing against time: "I am an old man. I could leave at any time." So behind the formal delivery of Kṛṣṇa conscious philosophy is an anxiety, an almost desperate desire to convince at least one soul to take up Kṛṣṇa consciousness. Immediately.

Now the constrained situations of Butler and the Ananda Ashram and Dr. Mishra are behind him. He is free to speak about the Absolute Truth in full. Throughout his life he has prepared for this, yet he is still discovering the best ways to present Kṛṣṇa, exploring his Western audience, testing their reactions.

We should always remember that He is God. He is all-powerful. In strength, no one could conquer Him. In beauty—as far as beauty is concerned, when He was on the battlefield ... . Have any of you seen a picture of Kṛṣṇa? Have you seen? Have any of you ever seen Kṛṣṇa? Oh. ... No?

Prabhupāda's voice fades as he pauses, looking out at his audience. No one has ever seen Kṛṣṇa. None of them have the slightest previous knowledge of Lord Kṛṣṇa. In India, hundreds of millions worship Lord Kṛṣṇa daily as the eternal form of all beauty and truth and view His graceful form in sculpture, painting, and dance. His philosophical teachings in *Bhagavad-gītā* are all-famous, and Prabhupāda is His intimate emissary. Yet the ladies and gentlemen in room 307 look back at the Swami blankly.

Prabhupāda is discussing the real meaning of going to a sacred place in India.

One should go to a sacred place in order to find some intelligent scholar in spiritual knowledge living there and make association with him. Just like I ... my residence is at Vṛndāvana. So at Vṛndāvana there are many big scholars and saintly persons living. So one should go to such holy places, not simply to take bath in the water. One must be intelligent enough to find some spiritually advanced man living there and take instruction from him and be benefited by that. If a man has attachment for going to a place of pilgrimage to take a bath but has no attraction for hearing from learned people there, he is considered to be an ass. (He laughs.) Sa eva go-kharaḥ. Go *means "cow," and* khara *means "ass." So the whole civilization is moving like a civilization of cows and asses. Everyone is identifying with the body. ... Yes, you want to speak?*

Woman: *In the places known as secret places—*

Prabhupāda: *Sacred. Yes.*

Woman: *Is it "sacred" places?*

Prabhupāda: *Yes.*

Woman: *Isn't it also a fact that there is more magnetism because of the meeting of saints and more advanced people?*

Prabhupāda: *Oh, yes, certainly. Certainly. Therefore the place itself has got some magnetism.*

Woman: *Yes, and when—*

Prabhupāda: *Just like at Vṛndāvana—that is practical. Here I am now sitting in New York, the world's greatest city, such a magnificent city, but my heart is always hankering after that Vṛndāvana.*

Woman: *Yes.* (Laughs.)

Prabhupāda: *Yes. I am not happy here.*

Woman: *Yes, I know.*

Prabhupāda: *I shall be very happy to return to my Vṛndāvana, that sacred place. But then, "Why are you here?" Now, because it is my duty. I have brought some message for you people. Because I have been ordered by my superior, my spiritual master: "Whatever you have learned you should go to the Western countries, and you must distribute this knowledge." So in spite of all my difficulties, all my inconveniences, I am here. Because I am obligated by duty. If I go and sit down in Vṛndāvana, that will be good for my personal conveniences—I shall be very comfortable there, and I will have no anxiety, nothing of the sort. But I have taken all the risk in this old age because I am duty-bound. I am duty-bound. So I have to execute my duty, despite all my inconveniences.*

An outsider opens the door and hesitantly glances inside.

Prabhupāda (stopping his lecture): *Yes, yes, come in. You can come here.*

* * *

Robert Nelson was like a slow, simple country boy with a homespun manner, even though he had grown up in New York City. He was twenty years old. He wasn't part of the growing hippie movement, he didn't take marijuana or other drugs, and he didn't socialize much. He was a loner. He had gotten some technical education at Staten Island Community College and had tried his hand at the record manufacturing business, but without much success. He was interested in God and would attend various spiritual meetings around the city. So one night he wandered into the Yoga Society to hear Dr. Mishra's lecture, and there he saw Prabhupāda for the first time.

Robert: *Swami was sitting cross-legged on a bench. There was a meeting, and Dr. Mishra was standing up before a group of people—there were about fifty people coming there—and he talked on "I Am Consciousness." Dr. Mishra talked and then gave Swami a grand introduction with a big smile. "Swamiji is here," he said. And he swings around and waves his hand for a big introduction. It was beautiful. This was after Dr. Mishra spoke for about an hour. The Swami didn't speak. He sang a song.*

Afterward, I went up to him. He had a big smile, and he said that he likes young people to take to Kṛṣṇa consciousness. He was very serious about it. He wanted all young people. So I thought that was very nice. It made sense. So I wanted to help.

We stood there talking for about an hour. Mishra had a library in the back, and we looked at certain books—Arjuna, Kṛṣṇa, chariots, and things. And then we walked around. We looked at some of the pictures of swamis on the wall. By that time it was getting very late, and Prabhupāda said come back the next day at ten to his office downstairs.

The next day, when Robert Nelson went to room 307, Prabhupāda invited him in. The room was clearly not intended to serve as a living quarters—there was no toilet, shower, chair, bed, or telephone. The walls were painted "a dark, dismal color." Prabhupāda showed Robert the three-volume set of *Śrīmad-Bhāgavatam,* which Robert purchased for $16.50. Then Prabhupāda handed him a small piece of paper with the Hare Kṛṣṇa *mantra* printed on it.

Robert: *While Swamiji was handing it to me, he had this big smile on his face like he was handing me the world.*

We spent the whole day together. At one point he said, "We are going to take a sleep." So he lay down there by his little desk, and so I said, "I am tired too." So I lay down at the other end of the room, and we rested. I just lay on the floor. It was the only place to do it. But he didn't rest that long—an hour and a half, I think—and we spent the rest of the day together. He was talking about Lord Caitanya and the Lord's pastimes, and he showed me a small picture of Lord Caitanya. Then he started talking about the devotees of Lord Caitanya—Nityānanda and Advaita. He had a picture of the five of them and a picture of his spiritual master. He said some things in Sanskrit, and then he translated. It wasn't much of a room, though. You'd really be disappointed if you saw it.

Robert Nelson couldn't give Prabhupāda the kind of assistance he needed. Lord Caitanya states that a person has at his command four assets—his life, money, intelligence, and words—at least one of which he should give to the service of God. Robert Nelson did not seem able to give his whole life to Kṛṣṇa consciousness, and as for money, he had very little. His intelligence was also limited, and he spoke unimpressively, nor did he have a wide range of friends or contacts among whom to speak. But he was affectionate toward the Swami, and out of the eight million people in the city, he was practically the only one who showed personal interest in him and offered to help.

From his experience in the record business, Mr. Robert, as Swamiji called him, developed a scheme to produce a record of Swamiji's singing. People were always putting out albums with almost anything on them, he explained, and they would always make money, or at least break even. So it would be almost impossible to lose money. It was a way he thought he could help make the Swami known, and he tried to convince Prabhupāda of the idea. And Prabhupāda didn't discourage Mr. Robert, who seemed eager to render this service.

Robert: *Me and the Swami went around to this record company on Forty-sixth Street. We went there, and I started talking, and the man was all business. He was all business and mean—they go together. So we went in there with a tape, and we tried talking to the man. Swami was talking, but the man said he couldn't put the tape out. I think he listened to the tape, but he wouldn't put it out. So we felt discouraged. But he didn't say much about it.*

Prabhupāda had been in business in India, and he wasn't about to think that he could suddenly take up business in a foreign country on the advice of a young boy in New York City. Besides, he had come not to do business but to preach. Robert, however, was enthusiastically offering service. Perhaps he wouldn't become a regular *brahmacārī* student, but he had a desire to serve Kṛṣṇa. For Prabhupāda to refuse him would be perhaps to turn away an interested Western young person. Prabhupāda had come to speak about Kṛṣṇa, to present the chanting, and if Mr. Robert wanted to help by arranging for an American record album, then that was welcome.

Mr. Robert and the Swami made an odd combination. Prabhupāda was elderly and dignified, a deep scholar of the *Bhāgavatam* and the Sanskrit language, whereas Robert Nelson was artless, even in Western culture, and inept in worldly ways. Together they would walk—the Swami wearing his winter coat (with its imitation fur collar), his Indian *dhotī,* and white pointed shoes; Mr. Robert wearing old khaki pants and an old coat. Prabhupāda walked with rapid, determined strides, outpacing the lumbering, rambling, heavyset boy who had befriended him.

Mr. Robert was supposed to help Prabhupāda in making presentations to businessmen and real estate men, yet he himself was hardly a slick fellow. He was innocent.

Robert: *Once we went over to this big office building on Forty-second Street, and we went in there. The rent was thousands of dollars for a whole floor. So I was standing there talking to the man, but I didn't understand how all this money would come. The Swami wanted a big place, and I didn't know what to tell the man.*

Prabhupāda wanted a big place, and a big place meant a big price. He had no money, and Robert Nelson had only his unemployment checks. Still, Prabhupāda was interested. If he were to find a building, that would be a great step in his mission. And this was also another way of engaging Mr. Robert. Besides, Kṛṣṇa might do anything, give anything, or work in any way—ordinary or miraculous. So Prabhupāda had his reasoning, and Mr. Robert had his.

Robert: *The building was between Sixth and Broadway on Forty-second Street. Some place to open Kṛṣṇa's temple! We went in and up to the second floor and saw the renting agent, and then we left. I think it was five thousand a month or ten thousand a month. We got to a certain point, and the money was too much. And then we left. When he brought up the prices, I figured we had better not. We had to stop.*

On another occasion, Robert Nelson took Prabhupāda by bus to the Hotel Columbia, at 70 West Forty-sixth Street. The hotel had a suite that Prabhupāda looked at for possible use as a temple, but again it was very expensive. And there was no money.

Sometimes Robert would make purchases for Prabhupāda with the money from his unemployment checks. Once he bought orange-colored T-shirts. Once he went to Woolworth's and bought kitchen pots and pans and some picture frames for Prabhupāda's pictures of Lord Caitanya and his spiritual master.

Robert: *One time I wanted to know how to make* capātī *cakes, so Swami says, "A hundred dollars, please, for the recipe. A hundred dollars please." So I went and got some money, but I couldn't get a hundred dollars. But he showed me anyway. He taught me to cook and would always repeat, "Wash hands, wash hands," and "You should only eat with your right hand."*

And whoever met the Swami was almost always impressed. They would start smiling back to him, and sometimes they would say funny things to each other that were nice. The Swami's English was very technical always. I mean, he had a big vocabulary. But sometimes people had a little trouble understanding him, and you had to help sometimes.

* * *

The Paradox, at 64 East Seventh Street on the Lower East Side, was a restaurant dedicated to the philosophy of Georges Ohsawa and the macrobiotic diet. It was a storefront below street level with small dining tables placed around the candlelit room. The food was inexpensive and well reputed. Tea was served free, as much as you liked. More than just a restaurant, the Paradox was a center for spiritual and cultural interests, a meeting place reminiscent of the cafés of Greenwich Village or Paris in the 1920s. A person could spend the whole day at the Paradox without buying anything, and no one would complain. The crowd at the Paradox was a mystical congregation, interested in teachings from the East. When news of the new swami uptown at Dr. Mishra's reached the Paradox, the word spread quickly.

Harvey Cohen and Bill Epstein were friends. Harvey was a freelance artist, and Bill worked at the Paradox. After Harvey had been to Prabhupāda's place at Dr. Mishra's *yoga* studio a few times, he came by the Paradox and began to describe all about the new swami to Bill and other friends.

Bill: *I was working at the Paradox one night, when Harvey came to me and said, "I went to visit Mishra, and there's a new swami there, and he's really fantastic!" Well, I was involved in macrobiotics and Buddhism, so at first I couldn't care less. But Harvey was a winning and warm personality, and he seemed interested in this. He said, "Why don't you come uptown? I would like you to see this."*

So I went to one of the lectures on Seventy-second Street. I walked in there, and I could feel a certain presence from the Swami. He had a certain very concentrated, intense appearance. He looked pale and kind of weak. I guess he had just come here and he had been through a lot of things. He was sitting there chanting on his beads, which he carried in a little bead bag. One of Dr. Mishra's students was talking, and he finally got around to introducing the Swami. He said, "We are the moons to the Swami's sun." He introduced him in that way. The Swami got up and talked. I didn't know what to think about it. At that time, the only steps I had taken in regard to Indian teaching were through Ramakrishna, but this was the first time, to my knowledge, that bhakti *religion had come to America.*

Bill Epstein, quite in contrast to Robert Nelson, was a dashing, romantic person, with long, wavy dark hair and a beard. He was good-looking and effervescent and took upon himself a role of informing people at the restaurant of the city's spiritual news. Once he became interested in the new swami, he made the Swami an ongoing topic of conversation at the restaurant.

Bill: *I went in the back, and I asked Richard, the manager, "I'm going to take some food to the Swami. You don't mind, do you?" He said, "No. Take anything you want." So I took some brown rice and other stuff, and I brought it up there.*

I went upstairs, and I knocked on the door, and there was no answer. I knocked again, and I saw that the light was on—because it had a glass panel—and finally he answered. I was really scared, because I had never really accepted any teacher. He said, "Come in! Come in! Sit down." We started talking, and he said to me, "The first thing that people do when they meet is to show each other love. They exchange names, they exchange something to eat." So he gave me a slice of apple, and he showed me the tape recorder he had, probably for recording his chants. Then he said, "Have you ever chanted?" I said, "No, I haven't chanted before." So he played a chant, and then he spoke to me some more. He said, "You must come back." I said, "Well, if I come back I'll bring you some more food."

James Greene, a thirty-year-old carpentry teacher at Cooper Union, was delving into Eastern philosophy. He lived on the same block as the Paradox and began hearing about the Swami from Harvey Cohen and Bill Epstein while regularly taking his evening meal at the restaurant.

James: *It was really Harvey and Bill who got things going. I remember one evening at Mishra's in which Swamiji was only a presence but did not speak. Mishra's students seemed more into the bodily aspect of* yoga. *This seemed to be one of Swamiji's complaints.*

His room on Seventy-second Street was quite small. He was living in a fairly narrow room with a door on the one end. Swamiji would set himself up along one side, and we were rather closely packed. It may have been no more than eight feet wide, and it was rather dim. He sat on his thin mattress, and then we sat on the floor.

We wouldn't chant. We would just come, and he would lecture. There was no direction other than the lecture on the Bhagavad-gītā. *I had read a lot of literature, and in my own shy way I was looking for a master, I think. I have no aggression in me or go-getting quality. I was really just a listener, and this seemed right—hearing the* Bhagavad-gītā*—so I kept coming. It just seemed as if things would grow from there. More and more people began coming. Then it got crowded, and he had to find another place.*

The new group from the Paradox was young and hip, in contrast to the older, more conservative uptown people who had been attending Prabhupāda's classes. In those days, it was still unusual to see a person with long hair and a beard, and when such people started coming to the Swami's meetings on the West Side, some of the older people were alarmed. As one of them noted: "Swami Bhaktivedanta began to pick up another kind of people. He picked them up at the Bowery or some attics. And they came with funny hats and gray blankets wrapped around themselves, and they startled me."

David Allen, a twenty-one-year-old seeker who came up from the Paradox, had just moved to the city, optimistically attracted by what he had read about experimentation with drugs. He saw the old group as "a kind of fussbudgety group of older women on the West Side" listening to the Swami's lectures.

David: *We weren't known as hippies then. But it was strange for the people who had originally been attracted to him. It was different for them to relate to this new group. I think most of the teachers from India up to that time had older followers, and sometimes wealthy widows would provide a source of income. But Swamiji changed right away to the younger, poorer group of people. The next thing that happened was that Bill Epstein and others began talking about how it would be better for the Swami to come downtown to the Lower East Side. Things were really happening down there, and somehow they weren't happening uptown. People downtown really needed him. Downtown was right, and it was ripe. There was life down there. There was a lot of energy going around.*

CHAPTER SEVENTEEN

On the Bowery

I couldn't understand the difference between friends and enemies. My friend was shocked to hear that I was moving to the Bowery, but although I passed through many dangers, I never thought that "This is danger." Everywhere I thought, "This is my home."
—Śrīla Prabhupāda in conversation

April 1966

SOMEONE BROKE INTO room 307 while Śrīla Prabhupāda was out and stole his typewriter and tape recorder. When Prabhupāda returned to the building, the janitor informed him of the theft: an unknown burglar had broken the transom glass, climbed through, taken the valuables, and escaped. As Prabhupāda listened, he became convinced that the janitor himself was the culprit. Of course, he couldn't prove it, so he accepted the loss with disappointment. Some friends offered replacements for his old typewriter and tape recorder.

In a letter to India, he described the theft as a loss of more than one thousand rupees ($157.00).

> It is understood that such crime as has been committed in my room is very common in New York. This is the way of material nature. American people have everything in ample, and the worker gets about Rs. 100 as daily

wages. And still there are thieves for want of character. The social condition is not very good.

Prabhupāda had told Joseph Foerster, the Scindia ticket agent, that he would be returning to India in a couple of months. That was seven months ago. Now, for the first time since his arrival, Prabhupāda had returned to the Scindia ticket office in Brooklyn. He talked about the theft to Mr. Foerster, who responded with, "Welcome to the club," and told Prabhupāda about the recent theft of his own automobile. Such things, he explained, were not unusual for New York City. He told Prabhupāda of the dangers of the city and how to avoid thefts and muggings. Prabhupāda listened, shaking his head. He told Mr. Foerster that American young people were misguided and confused. He discussed his plans for returning to India and showed Mr. Foerster one of his *Bhāgavatams.*

Prabhupāda had lost his spirit for living in room 307. What would prevent the janitor from stealing again? Harvey Cohen and Bill Epstein had advised him to relocate downtown and had assured him of a more interested following among the young people there. It had been an attractive proposal, and he began to reconsider it. Then Harvey offered Prabhupāda his studio on the Bowery.

Harvey had been working as a commercial artist for a Madison Avenue advertising firm when a recently acquired inheritance had spurred him to move into a loft on the Bowery to pursue his own career as a painter. But he was becoming disillusioned with New York. A group of acquaintances addicted to heroin had been coming around and taking advantage of his generosity, and his loft had recently been burglarized. He decided to leave the city and go to California, but before leaving he offered his loft for Prabhupāda to share with David Allen.

David Allen had heard that Harvey Cohen was moving to San Francisco if he could sublet his A.I.R. loft. Harvey hadn't known David very long, but on the night before Harvey was supposed to leave, he coincidentally met David three different times in three different places on the Lower East Side. Harvey took this as a sign that he should rent the loft to David, but he specifically stipulated that the Swami should move in too.

As Prabhupāda was preparing to leave his Seventy-second Street address, an acquaintance, an electrician who worked in the building, came to warn him. The Bowery was no place for a gentleman, he protested. It was the most corrupt place in the world. Prabhupāda's things had been stolen from room 307, but moving to the Bowery was not the answer.

* * *

Śrīla Prabhupāda's new home, the Bowery, had a long history. In the early 1600s, when Manhattan was known as New Amsterdam and was controlled by the Dutch West India Company, Peter Minuit, the governor of New Netherland, staked out a north-south road that was called "the Bowery" because a number of *bouweries,* or farms, lay on either side. It was a dusty country road, lined with quaint Dutch cottages and bordered by the peach orchards growing in the estate of Peter Stuyvesant. It became part of the high road to Boston and was of strategic importance during the American Revolution as the only land entrance to New York City.

In the early 1800s the Bowery was predominated by German immigrants, later in the century it became predominantly Jewish, and gradually it became the city's center of theatrical life. However, as a history of Lower Manhattan describes, "After 1870 came the period of the Bowery's celebrated degeneration. Fake auction rooms, saloons specializing in five-cent whiskey and knock-out drops, sensational dime museums, filthy and rat-ridden stale beer dives, together with Charles M. Hoyte's song, 'The Bowery! The Bowery!—I'll Never Go There Any More!' fixed it forever in the nation's consciousness as a place of unspeakable corruption."

The reaction of Prabhupāda's electrician friend was not unusual. The Bowery is still known all over the world as Skid Row, a place of ruined and homeless alcoholics. Perhaps the uptown electrician had done business in the Bowery and had seen the derelicts sitting around passing a bottle or lying unconscious in the gutter, or staggering up to passersby and drunkenly bumping into them to ask for money.

Most of the Bowery's seven or eight thousand homeless men slept in lodging houses that required them to vacate their rooms during the day. Having nowhere else to go and nothing else to do, they would loiter on the street—standing silently on the sidewalks, leaning against a wall, or shuffling slowly along, alone or in groups. In cold weather they would wear two coats and several suits of clothes at once and would sometimes warm themselves around a fire they would keep going in a city garbage can. At night, those without lodging slept on the sidewalks, doorsteps, and street corners, crawled into discarded boxes, or sprawled side by side next to the bars. Thefts were commonplace; a man's pockets might be searched ten or twenty times while he slept. The rates of hospitalization and death in the Bowery were five times higher than the national average, and many of the homeless men bore marks of recent injuries or violence.

Prabhupāda's loft, 94 Bowery, was six blocks south of Houston Street. At Houston and Bowery, derelicts converged in the heavy crosstown traffic. When cars stopped for the light, bums would come up and wash the windshields and ask for money. South of Houston, the first blocks held mostly restaurant supply stores, lamp stores, taverns, and luncheonettes. The buildings were of three and four stories—old, narrow, crowded tenements, their faces covered with heavy fire escapes. Traffic on the Bowery ran uptown and downtown. Cars parked on both sides of the street, and the constant traffic passed tightly. During the business day, working people passed briskly among the slow-moving derelicts. Many of the store windows were covered with protective iron gates, but behind the gates the store-owners lit their varieties of lamps to attract prospective wholesale and retail customers.

Ninety-four Bowery was just two doors north of Hester Street. The corner was occupied by the spacious Half Moon Tavern, which was frequented mostly by neighborhood alcoholics. Above the tavern sat a four-story Bowery flophouse, marked by a neon sign—Palma House—which was covered by a protective metal cage and hung from the second floor on large chains. The hotel's entrance at 92 Bowery (which had no lobby but only a desolate hallway covered with dirty white tiles) was no more than six feet from the entrance to 94.

Ninety-four Bowery was a narrow four-story building. It had long ago been painted gray and bore the usual facing of a massive, black fire escape. A well-worn, black double door, its glass panels reinforced with chicken wire, opened onto the street. The sign above the door read, "A.I.R. 3rd & 4th," indicating that artists-in-residence occupied those floors.

The first floor of the next building north, 96 Bowery, was used for storage, and its front entrance was covered with a rusty iron gate. At 98 Bowery was another tavern—Harold's—smaller and dingier than the Half Moon. Thus the block consisted of two saloons, a flophouse, and two buildings with lofts.

In the 1960s, loft-living was just beginning in that area of New York City. The City had given permission for painters, musicians, sculptors, and other artists (who required more space than available in most apartments) to live in buildings that had been constructed as factories in the nineteenth century. After these abandoned factories had been fitted with fireproof doors, bathtubs, shower stalls, and heating, an artist could inexpensively use a large space. These were the A.I.R. lofts.

Harvey Cohen's loft, on the top floor of 94 Bowery, was an open space almost a hundred feet long (from east to west) and twenty-five feet wide. It received a good amount of sunlight on the east, the Bowery side, and it also had windows at the west end, as well as a skylight. The exposed rafters of the ceiling were twelve feet above the floor.

Harvey Cohen had used the loft as an art studio, and racks for paintings still lined the walls. A kitchen and shower were partitioned off in the northwest corner, and a room divider stood about fifteen feet from the Bowery-side windows. This divider did not run from wall to wall, but was open at both ends, and it was several feet short of the ceiling.

It was behind this partition that Prabhupāda had his personal living area. A bed and a few chairs stood near the window, and Prabhupāda's typewriter sat on his metal trunk next to the small table that held his stacks of *Bhāgavatam* manuscripts. His *dhotīs* hung drying on a clothesline.

On the other side of the partition was a dais, about ten feet wide and five feet deep, on which Prabhupāda sat during his *kīrtanas* and lectures. The dais faced west, toward the loft's large open space—open, that is, except for a couple of rugs and an old-fashioned solid wood table and, on an easel, Harvey's painting of Lord Caitanya dancing with His associates.

The loft was a four-flight walk up, and the only entrance, usually heavily bolted, was a door in the rear, at the west end. From the outside, this door opened into a hallway, lit only by a red EXIT light over the door. The hallway led to the right a few steps and into the open area. If a guest entered during a *kīrtana* or a lecture, he would see the Swami about thirty feet from the entrance, seated on his dais. On other evenings the whole loft would be dark but for the glow of the red EXIT light in the little hallway and a soft illumination radiating from the other side of the partition, where Prabhupāda was working.

Prabhupāda lived on the Bowery, sitting under a small light, while hundreds of derelicts also sat under hundreds of naked lights on the same city block. He had no more fixed income than the derelicts, nor any greater security of a fixed residence, yet his consciousness was different. He was translating *Śrīmad-Bhāgavatam* into English, speaking to the world through his Bhaktivedanta purports. His duty, whether on the fourteenth floor of a Riverside Drive apartment building or in a corner of a Bowery loft, was to establish Kṛṣṇa consciousness as the prime necessity for all humanity. He went on with his translating and with his constant vision of a Kṛṣṇa temple in New York City. Because his consciousness was absorbed in Kṛṣṇa's universal mission, he did not depend on his surroundings for shelter. Home for him was not a matter of bricks and wood, but of taking shelter of Kṛṣṇa in every circumstance. As Prabhupāda had said to his friends uptown, "Everywhere is my home," whereas without Kṛṣṇa's shelter the whole world would be a desolate place.

Often he would refer to a scriptural statement that people live in three different modes: goodness, passion, and ignorance. Life in the forest is in the mode of goodness, life in the city is in passion, and life in a degraded place like a liquor shop, a brothel, or the Bowery is in the mode of ignorance. But to live in a temple of Viṣṇu is to live in the spiritual world, Vaikuṇṭha, which is transcendental to all three material modes.

And this Bowery loft where Prabhupāda was holding his meetings and performing *kīrtana* was also transcendental. When he was behind the partition, working in his corner before the open pages of *Śrīmad-Bhāgavatam,* that room was as good as his room back at the Rādhā-Dāmodara temple in Vṛndāvana.

News of the Swami's move to the Bowery loft spread, mostly by word of mouth at the Paradox restaurant, and people began to come by in the evening to chant with him. The musical *kīrtanas* were especially popular on the Bowery, since the Swami's new congregation consisted mostly of local musicians and artists, who responded more to the transcendental music than to the philosophy. Every morning he would hold a class on *Śrīmad-Bhāgavatam,* attended by David Allen, Robert Nelson, and another boy, and occasionally he would teach cooking to whoever was interested. He was usually available for personal talks with any inquiring visitors or with his new roommate.

Although Prabhupāda and David each had a designated living area in the large loft, the entire place soon became dominated by Prabhupāda's preaching activities. Prabhupāda and David got on well together, and at first Prabhupāda considered David an aspiring disciple.

April 27

He wrote to his friends in India, describing his relationship with David Allen.

> He was attending my class at Seventy-second Street along with others, and when I experienced this theft case in my room, he invited me to his residence. So I am with him and training him. He has good prospect because already he has given up all bad habits. In this country, illicit connection with women, smoking, drinking, and eating of meats are common affairs. Besides that, there are other bad habits, like using [only] toilet paper [and not bathing] after evacuating, etc. But by my request he has given up ninety percent of his old habits, and he is chanting maha mantra regularly. So I am giving him the chance, and I think he is improving. Tomorrow I have arranged for some prasadam distribution, and he has gone to purchase some things from the market.

When David first came to the Bowery, he appeared like a clean-cut college student. He was twenty-one, six feet tall, blue-eyed, handsome, and intelligent-looking. Most of his new friends in New York were older and considered him a kid. David's family lived in East Lansing, Michigan, and his mother was paying one hundred dollars monthly to sublease the loft. Although he did not have much experience, he had read that a new realm of mind expansion was available through psychedelic drugs, and he was heading fast into the hazardous world of LSD. His meeting with the Swami came at a time of radical change and profoundly affected his life.

David: *It was a really good relationship I had with the Swami, but I was overwhelmed by the tremendous energy of being that close to him. It spurred my consciousness very fast. Even my dreams at night would be so vivid of Kṛṣṇa consciousness. I was often sleeping when the Swami was up, because he was up late in the night working on his translations. That's possibly where a lot of the consciousness and dreams just flowed in, because of that deep relationship. It also had to do with studying Sanskrit. There was a lot of immediate impact with the language. The language seemed to have such a strong mystical quality, the way he translated it word for word.*

Prabhupāda's old friend from uptown, Robert Nelson, continued to visit him on the Bowery. He was impressed by Prabhupāda's friendly relationship with David, who he saw was learning many things from the Swami. Mr. Robert bought a small American-made hand organ, similar to an Indian harmonium, and donated it to David for chanting with Prabhupāda. At seven in the morning Mr. Robert would come by, and after *Bhāgavatam* class he would talk informally with Prabhupāda, telling his ideas for making records and selling books. He wanted to continue helping the Swami. They would sit in chairs near the front window, and Mr. Robert would listen while Prabhupāda talked for hours about Kṛṣṇa and Lord Caitanya.

New people began coming to see Prabhupāda on the Bowery. Carl Yeargens, a thirty-year-old black man from the Bronx, had attended Cornell University and was now independently studying Indian religion and Zen Buddhism. He had experimented with drugs as "psychedelic tools," and he had an interest in the music and poetry of India. He was influential among his friends and tried to interest them in meditation. He had even been dabbling in Sanskrit.

Carl: *I had just finished reading a book called* The Wonder That Was India. *I had gotten the definition of a* sannyāsī *and a* brahmacārī *and so forth. There was a vivid description in that particular book of how you could see a* sannyāsī *coming down the road with his saffron robe. It must have made more than just a superficial impression on me, because it came to me this one chilly evening. I was going to visit Michael Grant—probably going to smoke some marijuana and sit around, maybe play some music—and I was coming down Hester Street. If you make a left on Bowery, you can go up to Mike's place on Grand Street. But it's funny that I chose to go that way, because the shorter way would have been to go down Grand Street. But if I had gone that way, I would probably have missed Swamiji.*

So I decided to go down Hester and then make a left. All of a sudden I saw in this dingy alcove a brilliant saffron robe. As I passed, I saw it was Swamiji knocking on the door, trying to gain entrance. There were two bums hunched up against the door. It was like a two-part door—one of them was sealed, and the other was locked. The two bums were lying on either side of Swamiji. One of these men had actually expired—which often happened, and you had to call the police or health department to get them.

I don't think I saw the men lying in the doorway until I walked up to Swamiji and asked him, "Are you a sannyāsī*?" And he answered, "Yes." We started this conversation about how he was starting a temple, and he mentioned Lord Caitanya and the whole thing. He just came out with this flow of strange things to me, right there in the street. But I knew what he was talking about somehow. I had the familiarity of having just read this book and delved into Indian religion. So I knew that this was a momentous occasion for me, and I wanted to help him. We banged on the door, and eventually we got into the loft. He invited me to come to a* kīrtana*, and I came back later that night for my first* kīrtana*. From that point on, it was a fairly regular thing—three times a week. At one point Swamiji asked me to stay with him, and I stayed for about two weeks.*

It was perhaps because of Carl's interest in Sanskrit that Prabhupāda began holding Sanskrit classes. Carl and David and a few others would spend hours learning Sanskrit under Prabhupāda's guidance. Using a chalkboard he found in the loft, Prabhupāda taught the alphabet, and his students wrote their exercises in notebooks. Prabhupāda would look over their shoulders to see if they were writing correctly and would review their pronunciation. His students were learning not simply Sanskrit but the instructions of *Bhagavad-gītā*. Each day he would give them a verse to copy in the Sanskrit alphabet (*devanāgarī*), transliterate into the roman alphabet, and then translate word for word into English. But their interest in Sanskrit waned, and Prabhupāda gradually gave up the daily classes to spend time working on his own translations of the *Śrīmad-Bhāgavatam*.

His new friends may have regarded these lessons as Sanskrit classes, but actually they were *bhakti* classes. He had not come to America as the ambassador of Sanskrit; his Guru Mahārāja had ordered him to teach Kṛṣṇa consciousness. But since he had found in Carl and some of his friends a desire to investigate Sanskrit, he encouraged it. As a youth, Lord Caitanya had also started a Sanskrit school, with the real purpose of teaching love of Kṛṣṇa. He would teach in such a way that every word meant Kṛṣṇa, and when His students objected He closed the school. Similarly, when Prabhupāda found that his students' interest in Sanskrit was transitory—and since he himself had no mission on behalf of Sanskrit linguistics—he gave it up.

By the standard of classical Vedic scholars, it takes ten years for a boy to master Sanskrit grammar. And if one does not start until his late twenties or thirties, it is usually too late. Certainly none of Swamiji's students were thinking of entering a ten-year concentration in Sanskrit grammar, and even if they were, they would not realize spiritual truth simply by becoming grammarians.

Prabhupāda thought it better to utilize his own Sanskrit scholarship in translating the verses of *Śrīmad-Bhāgavatam* into English, following the Sanskrit commentaries of the previous authorities. Otherwise, the secrets of Kṛṣṇa consciousness would remain locked away in the Sanskrit. Teaching Carl Yeargens *devanāgarī, sandhi,* verb conjugations, and noun declensions was not going to give the people of America transcendental Vedic knowledge. Better that he utilize his proficiency in Sanskrit for translating many volumes of the *Bhāgavatam* into English for millions of potential readers.

Carol Bekar came from an immigrant Catholic background, and she immediately associated with Catholicism the Swami's presence as a spiritual authority and his devotional practices of chanting on beads and reciting from Sanskrit scriptures. Sometimes she would accompany Prabhupāda to nearby Chinatown, where he would purchase ingredients for his cooking. He would cook daily, and sometimes Carol and others would come by to learn the secrets of cooking for Lord Kṛṣṇa.

Carol: *He used to cook with us in the kitchen, and he was always aware of everyone else's activities in addition to his own cooking. He knew exactly how things should be. He washed everything and made sure everyone did everything correctly. He was a teacher. We used to make* capātīs *by hand, but then one day he asked me to get him a rolling pin. I brought my rolling pin, and he appropriated it. He put some men on rolling* capāṭis *and supervised them very carefully.*

I made a chutney for him at home. He always accepted our gifts graciously, although I don't think he ever ate them. Perhaps he was worried we might put in something that wasn't allowed in his diet. He used to take things from me and put them in the cupboard. I don't know what he finally did with them, but I am sure he didn't throw them away.

I never saw him eat anything that I had prepared, although he accepted everything.

Prabhupāda held his evening meetings on Mondays, Wednesdays, and Fridays, just as he had uptown. The loft was out of the way for most of his acquaintances and it was on the Bowery. A cluster of sleeping derelicts regularly blocked the street-level entrance, and visitors would find as many as half a dozen bums to step over before climbing the four flights of stairs. But it was something new; you could go and sit with a group of hip people and watch the Swami lead *kīrtana*. The room was dimly lit, and Prabhupāda would burn incense. Many casual visitors came and went. One of them—Gunther—had vivid impressions.

Gunther: *You walked right off the Bowery into a room filled with incense. It was quiet. Everyone was talking in hushed tones, not really talking at all. Swamiji was sitting in the front of the room, and in meditation. There was a tremendous feeling of peace which I have never had before. I'd happened to have studied for two years to become a minister and was into meditation, study, and prayer. But this was my first time to do anything Eastern or Hindu. There were lots of pillows around and mats on the floor for people to sit on. I don't think there were any pictures or statues. It was just Swamiji, incense, and mats, and obviously the respect of the people in the room for him.*

Before we went up, Carl was laughing and saying how Swami wanted everyone to use the hand cymbals just correctly. I had never played the cymbals before, but when it began I just tried to follow Swamiji, who was doing it in a certain way. Things were building up, the sound was building up, but then someone was doing it wrong. And Swamiji just very, very calmly shook a finger at someone and they looked, and then everything stopped. He instructed this person from a distance, and this fellow got the right idea, and they started up again. After a few minutes... the sound of the cymbals and the incense ... we weren't in the Bowery any longer. We started chanting Hare Kṛṣṇa. That was my first experience in chanting—I'd never chanted before. There's nothing in Protestant religion that comes even close to that. Maybe Catholics with their Hail Marys, but it's not quite the same thing. It was relaxing and very interesting to be able to chant, and I found Swamiji very fascinating.

The loft was more open than Prabhupāda's previous place uptown, so there was less privacy. And here some of the visitors were skeptical and even challenging, but everyone found him confident and joyful. He seemed to have far-reaching plans, and he had dedication. He knew what he wanted to do and was single-handedly carrying it out. "It is not one man's job," he had said. But he went on doing all he could, depending on Kṛṣṇa for the results. David was beginning to help, and more people were coming by to visit him.

Almost all of Prabhupāda's Bowery friends were musicians or friends of musicians. They were into music—music, drugs, women, and spiritual meditation. Because Prabhupāda's presentation of the Hare Kṛṣṇa *mantra* was both musical and meditative, they were automatically interested. Prabhupāda stressed that all the Vedic *mantras* (or hymns) were *sung*—in fact, the words *Bhagavad-gītā* meant "The Song of God." But the words of the Vedic hymns were incarnations of God in the form of transcendental sound. The musical accompaniment of hand cymbals, drum, and harmonium was just that—an accompaniment—and had no spiritual purpose independent of the chanting of the name of God. Prabhupāda allowed any instrument to be used, as long as it did not detract from the chanting.

Carol: *It was a very interracial, music-oriented scene. There were a few professional musicians, and a lot of people who enjoyed playing or just listening. Some people were painting in some of the lofts, and that's basically what was going on. We had memorable* kīrtanas. *One time there was a beautiful ceremony. Some of us went over early to prepare for it. There must have been a hundred people who came that day.*

For the Bowery crowd, sound was spirit and spirit was sound, in a merging of music and meditation. But for Prabhupāda, music without the name of God wasn't meditation; it was sense gratification, or at most a kind of stylized impersonal meditation. But he was glad to see the musicians coming to play along in his *kīrtanas,* to hear him, and to chant responsively. Some, having stayed up all night playing somewhere on their instruments, would come by in the morning and sing with the Swami. He did not dissuade them from their focus on sound; rather, he gave them sound. In the *Vedas,* sound is said to be the first element of material creation; the source of sound is God, and God is eternally a person. Prabhupāda's emphasis was on getting people to chant God's personal, transcendental name. Whether they took it as jazz, folk music, rock, or Indian meditation made no difference, as long as they began to chant Hare Kṛṣṇa.

Carol: *Whenever he had the chanting, the people were fairly in awe of the Swami. On the Bowery, a kind of transcendence came out of the ringing of the cymbals. He used the harmonium, and many people played hand cymbals. Sometimes he played the drum. In the very beginning, he stressed the importance of sound and the realization of Godhead through sound. That was, I suppose, the attraction that these musicians found in him—the emphasis on sound as a means to attaining transcendence and the Godhead. But he wanted a serious thing. He was interested in discipleship.*

One serious newcomer was Michael Grant. Mike was twenty-four. His father, who was Jewish, owned a record shop in Portland, Oregon, where Mike grew up. After studying music at Portland's Reed College and at San Francisco State, Mike, who played the piano and many other instruments, moved to New York City, along with his girlfriend, hoping to get into music professionally. But he quickly became disenchanted with the commercial music scene. Playing in nightclubs and pandering to commercial demands seemed particularly unappealing. In New York he joined the musicians' union and worked as a musical arranger and as an agent for several local groups.

Mike lived on the Bowery in an A.I.R. loft on Grand Street. It was a large loft where musicians often congregated for jam sessions. But as he turned more and more to serious composing, he found himself retiring from the social side of the music scene. His interests ran more to the spiritual, quasi-spiritual, and mystical books he had been reading. He had encountered several swamis, *yogīs,* and self-styled spiritualists in the city and had taken up *haṭha-yoga*. From his first meeting with the Swami, Mike was interested and quite open, as he was with all religious persons. He thought all genuinely religious people were good, although he did not care to identify with any particular group.

Mike: *There was a little bit of familiarity because I had seen other swamis. The way he was dressed, the way he looked—older and swarthy—weren't new to me. But at the same time there was an element of novelty. I was very curious. I didn't hear him talk when I first came in—*

he was just chanting—but mainly I was waiting to hear what he was going to say. I had already heard people chant before. I thought, why else would he put himself in such a place, without any comforts, unless the message he's trying to get across is more important than his own comfort? I think the thing that struck me the most was the poverty that was all around him. This was curious, because the places that I had been before had been just the opposite—very opulent. There was a Vedānta *center in upper Manhattan, and others. They were filled with staid, older men with their leather chairs and pipe tobacco—that kind of environment. But this was real poverty. The whole thing was curious.*

The Swami looked very refined, which was also curious—that he was in this place. When he talked, I immediately saw that he was a scholar and that he spoke with great conviction. Some statements he made were very daring. He was talking about God, and this was all new—to hear someone talk about God. I always wanted to hear someone I could respect talk about God. I always liked to hear religious speakers, but I measured them very carefully. When he spoke, I began to think, "Well, here is someone talking about God who may really have some realization of God." He was the first one I had come across who might be a person of God, who could feel really deeply.

* * *

Prabhupāda is lecturing.

Śrī Kṛṣṇa is just trying to place Arjuna on the platform of working in pure consciousness. We have already discussed for so many days that we are not this dull body but we are consciousness. Somehow or other we are in contact with matter. Therefore our freedom is checked.

Attendance is better now than it had been uptown. The loft offers a larger space; in fact, the platform where Prabhupāda sits nearly equals the area of his entire office cubicle on Seventy-second Street. The dingy loft with its unpainted rafters is more like an old warehouse than a temple. The members of his audience, most of them musicians, have come to meditate on the mystical sounds of the Swami's *kīrtana*.

Carl, Carol, Gunther, Mike, David, the crowd from the Paradox, and others join him on Monday, Wednesday and Friday night, when he holds classes beginning punctually at eight o'clock. The program consists of half an hour of chanting Hare Kṛṣṇa, followed by a lecture from

Bhagavad-gītā (usually forty-five minutes long), then a question-and-answer period, and finally another half hour of chanting, everything ending by ten o'clock.

The *kīrtana* has just ended, and Swamiji is speaking.

As spiritual beings we are free to act, free to have anything. Pure, no contamination—no disease, no birth, no death, no old age. And besides that, we have got many, many other qualifications in our spiritual life.

When he speaks he is pure spiritual form. The Vedic scriptures say that a *sādhu,* a saint, is not seen but heard. If the people in the audience want to know Swamiji, they will have to hear him. He is no longer simply the old Indian immigrant who lives on the other side of the partition of this loft, hanging his clothes to dry, barely getting his meals.

But now he is speaking as the emissary of Lord Kṛṣṇa, beyond time and space, and hundreds of spiritual masters in the chain of disciplic succession are speaking through him. He has entered amid New York's Bohemians in 1966 saying that 1966 is temporary and illusory, that he is eternal and they are eternal. This was the meaning of the *kīrtana,* and now he is explaining it philosophically, advocating a total change in consciousness. Yet, knowing that they can't take it all, he urges them to take whatever they can.

You will be glad to hear that this process of spiritual realization, once begun, guarantees one to have his next life as a human being. Once karma-yoga *is begun it will continue. It doesn't matter—even if one fails to complete the course, still he is not loser, he is not loser. Now, if someone begins this* yoga *of self-realization but unfortunately cannot prosecute this task in a nice way—if he falls down from the path—still there is encouragement that you are not a loser. You will be given a chance next life, and the next life is not ordinary next life. And for one who is successful—oh, what to speak of him! The successful goes back to Godhead. So we are holding this class, and although you have multifarious duties, you come here thrice a week and try to understand. And this will not go in vain. Even if you stop coming here, that impression will never go. I tell you, the impression will never go. If you do some practical work, that is very, very nice. But even if you do not do any practical work, simply if you give your submissive aural reception and understand what is the nature of God—if you simply hear and have an idea even—then you will be free from this material bondage.*

He is talking to a crowd who are deeply set in their hip life. He knows that they can't immediately give up taking drugs, and there they sit with their common-law wives. Their path is to play music, live with a woman, and meditate sometimes. And be free. After hearing his lecture they'll stay up all night with their instruments, their women, their drugs, their interracial Bohemian scene. Yet somehow they are drawn to Swamiji. He's got the good vibrations of the *kīrtana,* and they want to help him out. They're glad to help, because he has no one else. So Prabhupāda is saying to them, "That's all right. Even if you can only do a little, it will be good for you. We are all pure spirit souls. But you have forgotten. You have fallen into the cycle of birth and death. Whatever you can do toward reviving your original consciousness is good for you. There is no loss."

The Swami's main stress is on what he calls "dovetailing your consciousness with the Supreme Consciousness." ... *Kṛṣṇa is the Supreme Consciousness. And Arjuna, as the representative individual consciousness, is asked to act intelligently in collaboration with the Supreme Consciousness. Then he will be free from the bondage of birth, death, old age, and disease.*

Consciousness is a popular word in America. There's consciousness expansion, cosmic consciousness, altered states of consciousness, and now—dovetailing the individual consciousness with the Supreme Consciousness. This is the perfection of consciousness, Prabhupāda explains. This is the love and peace that everyone is really after. And yet Prabhupāda talks of it in terms of war.

They are talking on the battlefield, and Arjuna says, "I will not fight. I will not fight with my relatives and brothers for the sake of achieving some kingdom. No, no." Now, to the ordinary man it appears that, "Oh, Arjuna is a very nice man, nonviolent. He has given up everything for the sake of his relatives. Oh, what a nice man he is." This is the ordinary calculation.

But what does Kṛṣṇa say? He says, "You are damned fool number one." Now just see. The things which are estimated in the public eye as very nice, very good, that is here condemned by God. So you have to see whether the Supreme Consciousness is pleased with your actions. And Arjuna's action was not approved by Lord Kṛṣṇa. It was for his own whim, sense gratification, that at first he would not fight—but in the end, for Kṛṣṇa's satisfaction, he did fight. And that is our perfection—when we act for the satisfaction of the Supreme Consciousness.

At this point, some in the audience are filled with reservations. They are all opposed to the role of the United States in Vietnam, and this idea is very difficult for them. Like Arjuna, they want peace. So why is a swami sanctioning war?

He explains: Yes, Arjuna's idea not to fight is good, but then Kṛṣṇa, the Supreme Consciousness, instructs him to fight anyway. Therefore, Arjuna's fighting is above mundane ethics. It is absolute. If we follow Arjuna, give up good and bad, and act for Kṛṣṇa, not for our sense gratification, then that is perfect—because Kṛṣṇa is the Supreme Consciousness.

To some in his audience, although his answer seems philosophically sound, it's not quite what they want to hear. Still, they want to know his political views. Does he support America's involvement in Vietnam? Is he antiwar? But Prabhupāda is neither hawk nor dove. He has no political motive behind his example of Kṛṣṇa and Arjuna. His theme is simple and pure: beyond the good and the bad is the Absolute, and to act in accord with the Absolute is also beyond good and bad.

But what about Vietnam—does Kṛṣṇa say to fight there? No, Swamiji answers. The Vietnam war is different from the Kurukṣetra war. In the Battle of Kurukṣetra, Kṛṣṇa was personally present asking Arjuna to fight. Vietnam is different.

But his audience has yet another objection: If he is not addressing the Vietnamese war, then why not? After all, this is 1966. If he isn't talking about the war, then what is his relevancy? The Swami replies that his message is actually the most urgent and relevant. The Vietnamese war was an inevitable karmic reaction; it was one symptom, not the whole problem. And only *this* philosophy—surrender to the Supreme Consciousness—addresses the real problem.

But for many the reference to fighting is so emotionally charged that they can't go beyond the immediate politics of Vietnam to Prabhupāda's real message of surrender to the Supreme Consciousness. They respect the Swami—they realize he's referring to a deeper philosophy—yet the story of Arjuna and the war makes things difficult. The Swami nonetheless continues to refer to Arjuna's fighting as the classic example of *Bhagavad-gītā's* basic teaching.

It's not the basic teaching his audience is having difficulty with. It's the example. Prabhupāda has deliberately handed his audience a volatile analogy. He hasn't come to join their peace movement, and he doesn't accept their shortsighted concept of peace. He confronts them: It is better to fight in Kṛṣṇa consciousness than to live in a so-called peace devoid of God realization. Yes, the example is hard for them to accept. It makes them think. And if they do accept, then they might come near to understanding the Absolute.

Is it very difficult, dovetailing our consciousness with the Supreme Consciousness? Not at all. Not at all! No sane man will say, "Oh, it is not possible."

He isn't suggesting that to dovetail with the Supreme Consciousness *they* will have to go fight in Vietnam or perform some other horrible act on behalf of God. He knows that spiritual life will have to be more attractive than material life, or his audience will never take to it. He wants to bring the theme of dovetailing with the Supreme Consciousness down to something practical, something all-attractive and beautiful, something anyone could do and would want to do. He wants to encourage them by saying that they can do their own thing—but for Kṛṣṇa. Arjuna, after all, was a lifetime warrior. Kṛṣṇa didn't ask him to give up his work, but to do it for the Supreme. So Prabhupāda is asking the same of his audience. And they can begin with something as simple as offering their food to God.

Because everyone has to eat. So God wants to eat something. Why don't you first offer your food to God? Then you eat. But you may say, "But if God takes it away, then how shall I eat?" No, no. God will not take it. Daily, after preparing our foodstuffs, we are offering to Kṛṣṇa. There is a witness. Mr. David has seen. (Prabhupāda laughs.) *God eats! But His spiritual eating is such that, even after His eating, the whole thing is still there.*

So we shall not suffer a pinch if we dovetail our desires with the Supreme Lord. We simply have to learn the art—how to dovetail. Nothing has to be changed. The fighting man did not change into an artist or a musician. If you are a fighting man, you remain a fighting man. If you are a musician, you remain a musician. If you are a medical man, you remain a medical man. Whatever you are, you remain. But dovetail it. If by my eating the Lord is satisfied, then that is my perfection. If by my fighting the Lord is satisfied, then that is my perfection. So in every sphere of life we have to know whether the Lord is satisfied. That technique we have to learn. Then it is as easy as anything. We have to stop creating our own plans and thoughts and take the perfect plans from the Supreme Lord and execute them. That will become the perfection of our life.

And Lord Caitanya has made acting on the platform of consciousness very easy. Just as there are some note-makers of school books— Easy Study—*so Lord Caitanya has recommended that you be engaged in whatever occupation, but just hear about Kṛṣṇa. Continue to hear the* Bhagavad-gītā *and chant Hare Kṛṣṇa. It is for this that we are trying to organize this institution. So you have come, and whatever work you do, it doesn't matter. Everything will be adjusted by and by, as our mind becomes clear simply by hearing. If you continue this process, chanting the Kṛṣṇa name, you will practically see how much your heart is becoming clear and how much you are making progress toward spiritual realization, the real identity of pure consciousness.*

Prabhupāda is speaking on behalf of the Supreme Consciousness, and he offers his day-to-day activities as an example of dovetailing with the Supreme.

I am here always working at something, reading or writing—something, reading or writing—twenty-four hours. Simply when I feel hungry, I take some food. And simply when I feel sleepy I go to bed. Otherwise, I don't feel fatigued. You can ask Mr. David whether I am not doing this.

Of course, the Swami's daily routine doesn't require certification from David Allen, and any of his regular visitors can see that he is transcendental. His personal life is a perfect example of dovetailing with the Supreme Consciousness. Prabhupāda has always kept himself dovetailed with the Supreme. He had been perfectly dovetailed in Vṛndāvana also and had no personal need or motive to come to America and live on the Bowery. It was for others' sake that he came to the Bowery, and it is for others' benefit that he is speaking tonight. His spiritual master and Lord Kṛṣṇa want the conditioned souls to come out of their illusion before it is too late.

Speaking vigorously, even until he becomes physically exhausted—sometimes shouting, sometimes pleading, sometimes laughing—he gives his audience as much as he feels they can take. As the emissary of Kṛṣṇa and the disciplic succession, he can boldly shout that everyone should dovetail with the Supreme. He can speak as strongly as he likes for as long as they're willing to listen. He is a *sādhu.* (The Sanskrit word means "saint" and "one who cuts.") And he repeats the same message that for thousands of years *sādhus* of the original Vedic culture have spoken. He is reviving the eternal spirit of the Vedic wisdom—to cut the knots of ignorance and illusion.

So everything is illusion. From the beginning of our birth. And that illusion is so strong it is very difficult to get out of. The whole thing is illusion. Birth is illusion. The body is illusion. The bodily relationship and the country are illusion. The father is illusion. The mother is illusion. The wife is illusion. The children are illusion. Everything is illusion. And we are contacting that illusion, thinking we are very learned, advanced. We are imagining so many things. But as soon as death comes—the actual fact—then we forget everything. We forget our country. We forget our relatives. We forget our wife, children, father, mother. Everything is gone.

* * *

Mike Grant: *I went up to him afterward. I had the same feeling I'd had on other occasions when I'd been to hear famous people in concerts. I was always interested in going by after concerts to see musicians and singers just to meet them and see what they were like. I had a similar feeling after Swamiji spoke, so I went up and started talking. But the experience was different from the others in that he wasn't in a hurry. He could talk to me, whereas with others all you could do was get in a few words. They were always more interested in something else. But he was a person who was actually showing some interest in me as a person, and I was so overwhelmed that I ran out of things to say very quickly. I was surprised. Our meeting broke off on the basis of my not having anything further to say. It was just the opposite of so many other experiences, where some performer would be hurrying off to do something else. This time, I was the one who couldn't continue.*

* * *

Prabhupāda liked to take walks. From his doorstep at 94 Bowery, he would see directly across the street the Fulton Hotel, a five-story flophouse. Surrounding him were other lower-Manhattan lodging houses, whose tenants wandered the sidewalks from early morning till dark. An occasional flock of pigeons would stir and fly from one rooftop to the next or descend to the street. Traffic was heavy. The Bowery was part of a truck route to and from Brooklyn by way of the Brooklyn and Manhattan bridges.

The Bowery sloped gently downhill toward the north, and Prabhupāda could see signboards, a few scraggly Manhattan trees, and the street lights and traffic signals as far up as Fourth Street. He could see Con Edison, with its prominent clock tower, and (if there were no clouds) the top of the Empire State Building on Thirty-fourth Street.

He would walk alone in the morning through the Bowery neighborhood. The month of May that year saw more frequent rains than was normal, and Prabhupāda carried an umbrella. Sometimes he walked in the rain. He was not always alone; sometimes he walked with one of his new friends and talked. Sometimes he shopped. Bitter melon, *dāl,* hing, chick-pea flour, and other specialty foods common in Indian vegetarian cuisine were available in Chinatown's nearby markets. On leaving the loft, he would walk south a few steps to the corner of Bowery and Hester Street. Turning right on Hester, he would immediately be in Chinatown, where the shops, markets, and even the Manhattan Savings Bank were identified by signs lettered in Chinese. Sometimes he would walk one block further south to Canal Street, with its Central Asian Food Market and many other streetside fruit and vegetable markets. In the early morning the sidewalks were almost deserted, but as the shops began to open for business, the streets became crowded with local workers, shopkeepers, tourists, and aimless derelicts. The winding side streets of Chinatown were lined with hundreds of small stores, and parked cars lined both sides of the street.

His walks on Hester would sometimes take him into Little Italy, which overlaps Chinatown at Mulberry Street. In this neighborhood, places like Chinese Pork Products and the Mee Jung Mee Supermarket stood alongside Umberto's Clam House and the Puglia Restaurant, advertising *capuccino a la puglia,* coffee from Puglia.

His walks west of Bowery into Chinatown and Little Italy were mainly for shopping. But he also noted prospective sites for a temple; Chatham Tower on Chatham Square particularly drew his attention. Sometimes he would walk in the opposite direction as far as the East River and

Brooklyn Bridge. But when a friend warned him that a sniper had been firing at strollers along the river, he stopped going there.

Despite the bad neighborhood where Prabhupāda lived and walked, he was rarely disturbed. Often he would find several Bowery bums asleep or unconscious at his door, and he would have to step over them. Sometimes a drunk, simply out of his inability to maneuver, would bump into him, or a derelict would mutter something unintelligible or laugh at him. The more sober ones would stand and gesture courteously, ushering the Swami into or out of his door at 94 Bowery. He would pass among them, acknowledging their good manners as they cleared his path.

Certainly few of the Bowery men and others who saw him on his walks knew much about the small, elderly Indian *sādhu,* dressed in saffron and carrying an umbrella and a brown grocery sack.

Sometimes Prabhupāda would meet one of his new friends on the street. Jan, Michael Grant's girlfriend, met him on several occasions as he was out walking.

Jan: *I would see him in the midst of this potpourri of people down there, walking down the street. He always had an umbrella, and he would always have such a serene look on his face. He would just be taking his afternoon jaunts, walking along, sometimes stepping over the drunks. And I would always get sort of nervous when I would meet him on the sidewalk. He would say, "Are you chanting?" and I would say, "Sometimes." And then he would say, "That's a good girl."*

* * *

Sitting cross-legged, his back to the shelf with its assortment of potted plants, a whitish *cādara* wrapped in wide, loose folds across his body, Prabhupāda looked grave, almost sorrowful. The picture and an accompanying article appeared in a June issue of *The Village Voice.* The article read:

> The meeting of the mystical West and practical East comes alive in the curious contrast between A. C. Bhaktivedanta Swami and his American disciples. The swami, a cultivated man of seventy with a distinguished education, is here for a year to preach his gospel of peace, good will, nearness to God, and, more practically, to raise money for his American church. ... Like his teachings, the swami is sensible and direct. His main teaching is that mankind may come closer to God by reciting His holy name.

> Despite the fact that the swami came to America to seek out the root of godless materialism—a disease, he said, that has already enveloped India—he is a realistic man. "If there is any place on earth with money to build a temple, it is here." The swami wishes to found in America an International Society for Krishna Consciousness, which will be open for anyone—including women.

The article had been written by Howard Smith. He had first heard of the Swami by a phone call from a contact who had told him of an interesting holy man from India living in a loft in the Bowery. "Go there any time," Howard's contact had told him. "He's always there. I think you will find it fascinating. I believe he's about to start a major religious movement."

Howard Smith: *So I went down there and went upstairs into this very funky artists' loft. There were carpets all over the place, old and worn out, and a lot of people sitting around in various kinds of hippie garb, plus what I think they must have thought was Indian garb. Most of them were sitting alone around the room facing the wall, like they had nothing to do with each other. They were sitting cross-legged, and each one seemed to be doing something different. Nobody paid any attention to me when I walked in.*

I saw shoes lined up, and I thought, "Maybe I am supposed to take off my shoes," but nobody said anything to me. So I walked around the edge of the carpet, looking for somebody to pay attention to me. I wondered what was going on, and I didn't want to interrupt anybody, because they all seemed deep into whatever kind of prayers they were doing.

In the back of the loft I noticed a little curtain—an Indian madras type of curtain—and so I decided I'd peer into that area. I looked in, and there was Swami Bhaktivedanta sitting there cross-legged in saffron garments, with the markings on his forehead and nose and his hand in the bead bag. Even though he looked like the real thing, he seemed more approachable, and I said, "Hello," and he looked up. I said, "Swami Bhaktivedanta?" and he said, "Yes." I said, "I am Howard Smith." I was expecting to sit down, so I said, "Excuse me, I have to take off my shoes," and he said, "Why do you want to take off your shoes?" I said, "I don't know—I saw all the shoes out there." And he said, "I didn't ask you to take your shoes off." I said, "What are all those people out there doing?" and he said, "I don't know. And they don't know what they're doing. I am trying to teach them, and they seem to be misunderstanding me. They are very confused people."

Then we sat and talked, and I liked him a lot right away. I mean, I'd met a lot of other swamis, and I didn't like them too much. And I don't think it's fair to lump them all together and say, "Those swamis in India." Because he was very, very basic, and that's what I seemed to like about him. He not only made me feel at ease, but he seemed very open and honest—like he asked my advice on things. He was very new in the country.

I thought his ideas stood a good chance of taking hold, because he seemed so practical. His head didn't seem in the clouds. He wasn't talking mysticism every third word. I guess that is where his soul was at, but that isn't where his normal conversational consciousness was at.

Then he said several people had told him that the Voice *would be a very good place to be written up and that basically it would reach the kind of people who already perhaps had a leaning or interest in what he was preaching. And I said that I thought he was correct. He asked me if I had read any books or knew anything about Indian culture, and I said no, I didn't really. We talked a little, and he explained to me that he had these books in English that he had already translated in India. And he handed those to me and said, "If you want more background, you can read these."*

It was obvious to me that I was not talking to some fellow who had just decided that he had seen God and was going to tell people about it. He seemed to be an educated man, much more than myself, actually. And I liked his humbleness. I just plain liked the guy.

He explained everything I wanted to know—the significance of what he was wearing, the mark on his forehead, the bead bag. And I liked all his explanations. Everything was very practical. Then he talked about temples all over the world, and he said, "Well, we have got a long way to go. But I am very patient."

* * *

Prabhupāda had hope for what the *Voice* article had referred to as "his American church." There was life in his lectures and *kīrtanas,* and at least he was acquiring a small, regular following. But from India there was no hope. He had continued corresponding with Sumati Morarji, his Godbrothers, and the Indian Central Government, but their replies had not been encouraging.

In the faith that Padampat Singhania would agree to his plans for a Kṛṣṇa temple in Manhattan and finance its construction, Prabhupāda had petitioned New Delhi to sanction the release of foreign exchange. He had written to the Reserve Bank of India, New Delhi.

> I want to establish this cultural center, and for this I wish to get some exchange from India. I think there are good prospects all over the world for propagating the culture of how to love God in these days of forgetfulness.

A month later the Indian bank had advised him to resubmit his request, through the Indian Embassy in Washington, to the finance minister of the Indian Central Government. Prabhupāda had complied. And another month had passed, with no word from the government.

One of his Godbrothers had written that Swamiji should come back to India and work personally to get the government's sanction. But Prabhupāda didn't want to leave America now. He wrote to Sumati Morarji:

> I am trying to avoid the journey to India and again coming back. Especially for the reason that I am holding at the above address classes thrice a week and training some American youth in the matter of sankirtan and devotional service to the Lord. Some of them are taking the lessons very sincerely and in the future they may be very good Vaiṣṇavas according to the rigid standards.

One day a curious, unsolicited correspondent wrote to Prabhupāda from India. His name was Mukti Brahmacārī. Introducing himself as a disciple of one of Prabhupāda's Godbrothers, and reminding Prabhupāda of their past slight acquaintance, Mukti wrote of his eagerness to join Prabhupāda in America. Certainly Prabhupāda still had hopes for getting assistance from his Godbrothers in India—"This mission is not simply one man's work." Therefore, he invited Mukti to come to America and asked him to request his *guru* to cooperate by working personally to secure government sanction for the release of foreign exchange. Mukti wrote back, reaffirming his eagerness but expressing doubt that his spiritual master would give him permission. Mukti thought he should first come to the United States and *then* request his spiritual master's help. Prabhupāda was annoyed, and he sent an immediate reply:

> Is preaching in America my private business? Srila Prabhupad Bhaktisiddhanta Saraswati wanted to construct some temples in foreign countries as preaching centers of the message of Srila Rupa Raghunath,* and I am trying to do this in this part of the world. The money is ready and the opportunity is open. If by seeing the Finance Minister this work can be facilitated, why should we wait because you cannot talk with your Guru Maharaj about cooperation because you are afraid your journey will be cancelled? Please do not think in that way. Take everything as Srila [Bhaktisiddhanta Sarasvati] Prabhupad's work and try to do the needful. Do not think for a moment that my interest is different from that of your Guru Maharaj. We are executing the will of Srila Prabhupad according to our own capacity. A combined effort would have been far better.

Mukti submitted the entire proposal before his spiritual master, who, as Mukti predicted, canceled the trip. Although Mukti's *guru* was Śrīla Prabhupāda's Godbrother, he did not want to be involved, and he doubted that Prabhupāda would actually get a donation from Padampat Singhania.

And now Mukti Brahmacārī also doubted: "If your program is not bona fide, the approach to a big personality will be a ludicrous one no doubt."

On the same day that Prabhupāda received the "ludicrous" letter, he also received the final blow of noncooperation from the Indian government. Second Secretary Prakash Shah of the Indian Embassy in Washington, D.C., wrote:

> Due to existing conditions of foreign exchange stringency, it is not possible for the government of India to accede to your request for release of foreign exchange. You may perhaps like to raise funds from residents in America.

It was confirmed: Prabhupāda would have to work without outside help. He would continue alone in New York City. His last letter to Mukti Brahmacārī reveals his deep faith and determination.

> So the controversy is now closed, and there is no need of help from anyone else. We are not always successful in our attempts at preaching work but such failures are certainly not ludicrous. In the absolute field both success and failure are glorious. Even Lord Nityananda pretended to be a failure at converting Jagai and Madhai in the first attempt. Rather, He was personally injured in such an attempt. But that was certainly not ludicrous. The whole thing was transcendental, and it was glorious for all parties concerned.

---

* Śrīla Rūpa Gosvāmī and Śrīla Raghunātha dāsa Gosvāmī were two leading disciples of Lord Caitanya in the sixteenth century.

If Kṛṣṇa consciousness were ever to take hold in America, it would have to be without assistance from the Indian government or Indian financiers. Not even a lone Indian *brahmacārī* would join him. Kṛṣṇa was revealing His plan to Prabhupāda in a different way. With the Singhania-sanction schemes finished and behind him, Prabhupāda would turn all his energy toward the young men and women coming to him in his Bowery loft. He wrote to Sumati Morarji:

> I am now trying to incorporate one corporation of the local friends and admirers under the name International Society for Krishna Consciousness, incorporated.

* * *

Of all his friends and admirers, Prabhupāda gave his roommate, David Allen, the most personal attention and training. He felt he was giving David a special chance to become America's first genuine Vaiṣṇava. Prabhupāda would eventually return to India, and he wanted to take David to Vṛndāvana. He would show him temple worship and train him for future preaching in the West. He had requested Sumati Morarji to provide free passage for David as well as for himself.

> You will be pleased to see this American boy. He is coming of a good family and is a sincere soul to this line of culture. There are others also in the class I am holding here, but I wish to take with me only one of them.

I am very glad to say (Prabhupāda said one evening in his lecture) *that our Mr. David says sometimes, "Swamiji, I want to increase my spiritual life* immediately." (Prabhupāda laughed as he imitated David's urgency.) *"Take patience, take patience," I tell him. "It will be done, of course. When you have got such desire, God will help you. He is within you. He is simply trying to see how sincere you are. Then He will give you all opportunities to increase your spiritual life."*

At first David and the Swami lived together peacefully in the large hall, the Swami working concentratedly on his side of the partition, David ranging throughout the large open space. David, however, continued taking marijuana, LSD, and amphetamines, and Prabhupāda had no choice but to tolerate it. Several times he told David that drugs and hallucinations would not help his spiritual life, but David would look distracted. He was becoming estranged from the Swami.

But Prabhupāda had a plan to use the loft as a temple—to transform it into New York's first temple of Rādhā-Kṛṣṇa—and he wanted David's cooperation. Although the neighborhood was one of the most miserable in the world, Prabhupāda talked of bringing Deities from Jaipur or Vṛndāvana and starting temple worship, even on the Bowery. He thought David might help. After all, they were roommates, so there could be no question of David's not cooperating; but he would have to give up his bad habits.

Prabhupāda was trying to help David, but David was too disturbed. He was headed for disaster, and so were Prabhupāda's plans for the loft. Sometimes, even not under the influence of a drug, he would pace around the loft. Other times he appeared to be deep in thought. One day, on a dose of LSD, he went completely crazy. As Carl Yeargens put it, "He just flipped out, and the Swami had to deal with a crazy man." Things had been leading to this—"he was a crazy kid who always took too much"—but the real madness happened suddenly.

Swamiji was working peacefully at his typewriter when David "freaked out." David started moaning and pacing around the large open area of the loft. Then he began yelling, howling, and running all around. He went back to where the Swami was. Suddenly Prabhupāda found himself face to face not with David—nice David, whom he was going to take to India to show the *brāhmaṇas* in Vṛndāvana—but a drugged, wild-eyed stranger, a madman.

Prabhupāda tried to speak to him—"What is the matter?"—but David had nothing to say. There was no particular disagreement. Just madness....

Prabhupāda moved quickly down the four flights of stairs. He had not stopped to gather up any of his belongings or even to decide where he would go or whether he would return. There had been no time to consider anything. He had taken quite a shock, and now he was leaving the arena of David's madness. The usual group of bums were sitting in the doorway, and with their customary flourish of courtesy they allowed him to pass. They were used to the elderly swami's coming in and out, going shopping and returning, and they didn't bother him. But he was not going shopping today. Where was he going? He didn't know. He had come onto the street without knowing where he would go.

He wasn't going back to the loft—that was for sure. But where could he go? The pigeons flew from roof to roof. Traffic rumbled by, and the ever-present bums loitered about, getting drunker on cheap, poisonous alcohol. Although Prabhupāda's home had suddenly become an insane terror, the street at its door was also a hellish, dangerous place. He was shaken. He could call Dr. Mishra's, and they might take him in. But that chapter of his life was over, and he had gone on to something better. He had his own classes, young people chanting and hearing. Was it all over now? After nine months in America, he had finally gotten a good response to his preaching and *kīrtana*. He couldn't just quit now.

A. C. Bhaktivedanta Swami Mahārāja, whom everyone knew and respected in Vṛndāvana as a distinguished scholar and devotee, who had an open invitation to see the vice president of India and many other notables, now had to face starkly that he had not one friend of stature in the United States. Suddenly he was as homeless as any derelict on the street. In fact many of them, with their long-time berths in flophouses, were more secure than he. They were ruined, but settled. The Bowery could be a chaotic hell if you weren't on a very purposeful errand—going directly to the store, or back to your place. It was no place to stand wondering where will you live or is there a friend you can turn to. He wasn't on his way to Chinatown to shop, nor was he taking a little stroll, soon to return to the shelter of the loft. If he couldn't go to the loft, he had no place.

How difficult it was becoming to preach in America amid these crazy people! He had written prophetically in his poem the day he had arrived in Boston Harbor, "My dear Lord, I do not know why You have brought me here. Now You can do with me whatever You like. But I guess You have some business here, otherwise why would You bring me to this terrible place?" What about his scheduled classes? What about David—should he go back and try to talk with the boy? This had been David's first fit of violence, but there had been other tense moments. David had a habit of leaving the soap on the floor of the shower stall, and Prabhupāda had asked him not to, because it was a hazard. But David wouldn't listen. Prabhupāda had continued to remind him, and one day David had gotten angry and shouted at him. But there was no real enmity. Even today's incident had not been a matter of personal differences—the boy was a victim.

Prabhupāda walked quickly. He had free passage on the Scindia Line.

He could go home to Vṛndāvana. But his spiritual master had ordered him to come here. "By the strong desire of Śrī Śrīmad Bhaktisiddhānta Sarasvatī Ṭhākura," he had written while crossing the Atlantic, "the holy name of Lord Gaurāṅga will spread throughout all the countries of the Western world." Before nightfall he would have to find some place to stay, a way to keep up the momentum of his preaching. This is what it meant to be working without government sponsorship, without the support of any religious organization, without a patron. It meant being vulnerable and insecure. Prabhupāda faced the crisis as a test from Kṛṣṇa. The instruction of *Bhagavad-gītā* was to depend on Kṛṣṇa for protection: "In all activities just depend upon Me and work always under My protection. In such devotional service be fully conscious of Me. ... You will pass over all the obstacles of conditional life by My grace."

He decided to phone Carl Yeargens and ask him to help. Hearing the Swami's voice on the phone—it was an emergency!—Carl at once agreed that Prabhupāda could move in with him and his wife, Eva. Their place was close by, on Centre Street, five blocks west of Bowery near Chinatown. Carl would be right over.

After Carl found Prabhupāda, they went straight to Carl's place, an A.I.R. loft, smaller than the one Prabhupāda had been living in. It had a main living area, large and open, with areas for the kitchen and bedroom partitioned off. There were decorative indoor plants and a profusion of throw pillows placed all around. Carl's loft was much brighter than the dingy, factorylike space in the loft on the Bowery. The floor was painted bright orange—Carl used to say it looked like the deck of a ship. The walls and ceiling were white, and light from seven skylights filled the room. Carl and Eva settled the Swami in one corner.

Prabhupāda had left his belongings at David's loft and didn't want to go back, so Carl went over to pick up a few essential items. Prabhupāda asked him to leave most of his things, including his books, suitcases, and reel-to-reel tape recorder, where they were.

Although by this time David had come down from the intense effects of the LSD, he remained crazy. When Carl arrived at the loft, the door was locked and David was inside, afraid to let anyone in, although finally he relented. He had shut and locked all the windows, making the loft oppressively hot and stuffy. Bill Epstein, who also came by that day, analyzed David as having had "a drug-induced nervous breakdown, a narcopsychosis." And although David was sorry he had exploded at the Swami, neither Bill nor Carl thought Prabhupāda should live with David again. Apparently Prabhupāda's chances of making the loft into a Rādhā-Kṛṣṇa temple were finished. Carl and Bill gathered up a few of the Swami's belongings, and David stayed behind in the loft. He wanted to be alone.

Carl Yeargens knew Prabhupāda's living habits and wanted to accommodate him with a suitable place to live and work. In a small alcove at one end of his loft, Carl had a small study, which he allocated for the Swami. Carl also set up a cushioned dais and arranged the living room around it so that guests could sit on the floor in a semicircle. Carl's wife, who didn't really like the idea of a swami moving in, agreed to cover a few cushions with Indian madras material for him anyway.

Things went smoothly for a while. Prabhupāda continued his morning and evening classes, and many of the Bowery hip crowd came by. Three of his regular callers lived right in the same building, and a few others, including Carl's brother, were just around the block. Michael Grant, James Greene—even David Allen came once.

Don Nathanson (an artist): *I was at Carl's loft, and the Swami comes strolling in one day. So I already knew he was on the scene, from David's. Mostly musicians were coming. They were enjoying the private morning session with him. And that's really strange in itself, because these people were up almost all night, and he used to do it at six in the morning, for one hour. He would lead them in chanting with his hand cymbals—dot-dot-dah, dot-dot-dah. It was strange, because that crowd was heavy into drugs and they were well read. But for a short period they used to go every morning, nine or ten of them, and they felt very good about it. They felt very good that they did that in the morning.*

Carl felt that the creative group who came to see the Swami in his studio were all quick to enter into the mood of the *kīrtana,* but they were "using it in their own ways, to supplement their own private visions and ecstasies," with no real intention of adopting the disciplines or the undivided worship of Lord Kṛṣṇa. Prabhupāda was their first real contact with a spiritual person, and yet even without trying to understand, they became absorbed in his *kīrtanas* and in what he had to say. Carl would invite them: "Hey, come on. This is genuine. This is real. You'll like it. It's music. It's dance. It's celebration." Carl saw that "people just felt good being in the Swami's presence and meditating on the chanting and eating the Swami's cooking. It was unlike anything they had experienced before, except maybe for their moments of creative insight."

Yet for Carl and Eva, Prabhupāda's simple presence created difficulty. Never before during his whole stay in America had he been a more inconvenient or unwanted guest. Carl's studio was arranged for him and his wife to live in alone, using the bedroom, kitchen, and living room any way they liked. If they wanted to smoke marijuana or eat meat or whatever, that was their prerogative. This was Carl's home; he lived here with his wife Eva and their dogs and cats. But now they had to share it with the Swami.

Almost at once, the situation became intolerable for Eva. She resented the Swami's presence in her home. She was a feminist, a liberated white woman with a black husband and a good job. She didn't like the Swami's views on women. She hadn't read his books or attended his classes, but she had heard that he was opposed to sexual intercourse except for conceiving children, and that in his view a woman was supposed to be shy and chaste and help her husband in spiritual life. She knew about the Swami's four rules—no meat-eating, illicit sex, intoxication, or gambling—and she definitely did not want Carl's Swami trying to change *their* ways to suit *his*. And he had better not expect her to wait on him as his servant. She sensed the Swami objecting to almost everything she did. If she were to seek his advice, he would probably ask her to stop taking drugs, get rid of the cats and dogs, stop drinking, and stop contraceptive sex. If the Swami had his way, they would probably eat only at certain times and only certain foods. Eva was a heavy smoker, so he probably wouldn't like being around her. She was ready for a confrontation.

But Prabhupāda was not one to make intolerant demands while living in another's home. He kept to his allotted corner of the loft, and he made no demands or criticisms. Hadn't he seen his hosts in Butler eating meat and only remarked, "Think nothing of it"? Nevertheless, his imposing spiritual presence made Eva sorry Carl had ever met him. To Eva the Swami was an inimical force—and she, being candid and independent, let him know. As soon as he asked whether she could bring him something, she replied, "Get it yourself."

Carol Bekar saw the situation as being extremely uncomfortable and tense—"Eva was quite resentful." Eva complained to Carol: here she was paying rent for the loft, working hard, and this man was trying to change their way of life.

Carol: *Eva couldn't handle his teachings, and she couldn't handle his influence over Carl. She didn't feel so constrained, but she felt that Swamiji was making Carl feel constrained.*

This was Eva's main objection—the Swami was influencing Carl. Her relationship with Carl had only recently begun, and Carl was aware that she needed much of his time. He agreed with his wife, yet he couldn't refuse the Swami. He was interested in Indian music, poetry, and religions, and here was a living authority, vastly knowledgeable in all facets of Indian culture, right in his home. Prabhupāda would cook his meals in their kitchen, and right away Carl would be there, eager to learn the art of Indian cuisine. Carl also wanted the Swami to show him how to play the drum. They would have long talks together.

Carol: *Carl was trying to be something he really wasn't, but he would never have suggested that the Swami had to leave. Swami, I am sure, was astute enough to pick up on this tension. As soon as he could, he tried to move to another place.*

Gradually, Carl reached an impasse in his relationship with Prabhupāda. He couldn't share his life with both his wife and the Swami, and ultimately he was more inclined toward his wife.

Carl: *I couldn't see my loft becoming a temple. I was raising cats and dogs, and he wanted them removed. He used to call me a meat-eater. But then he changed our diet. Of course, he was hitting the American culture, which doesn't know what all this business is. I have to put it on myself as much as anyone. I could understand and absorb India through an impersonal agency like a book or a record, but here was the living representative of Godhead, and to me it was as difficult as anything I've ever had to do before or since.*

Prabhupāda was not insensitive to the distress his presence was causing. He didn't want to inconvenience anyone, and of course he could have avoided all inconvenience, both for himself and for people like Eva, if he had never come to America. But he wasn't concerned with convenience or inconvenience, pleasing Eva or displeasing her. He wanted to teach Kṛṣṇa consciousness.

Prabhupāda had a mission, and Carl's loft didn't seem to be the right base for it. Prabhupāda's friends all agreed: he should move more into the center of things. The Bowery and Chinatown were too far out of the way. They would find him a new place.

Forced by conditions he accepted as Kṛṣṇa's mercy, Prabhupāda sat patiently, trying not to disturb anyone, yet speaking about Kṛṣṇa consciousness day and night. Carl assured him that with half a dozen people searching, it wouldn't take long to find a new place, and they would all chip in together and help him with the rent.

* * *

A week passed, and no one had found a suitable place for the Swami. One day Prabhupāda suggested that he and Carl take a walk up to Michael Grant's place and ask him to help.

Mike: *I was awakened one morning very early, and Carl was on the phone saying, "Swamiji and I were just taking a walk, and we thought we'd come up and see you." I said, "But it's too early in the morning." And he said, "Well, Swamiji wants to see you." They were very near by, just down the street, so I had to quickly get dressed, and by the time I got to the door they were there.*

I was totally unprepared, but invited them up. The television had been on from the previous night, and there were some cartoons on. The Swami sat between Carl and me on the couch. I was keeping a pet cat, and the cat jumped up on Swamiji's lap, and he abruptly knocked it off onto the floor. We began to talk, but Swamiji glanced over at the cartoons on the television set and said, "This is nonsense." Suddenly I realized that the television was on and that it was nonsense, and I got up very quickly, saying, "Why, yes, it is *nonsense," and turned it off.*

As Prabhupāda talked, he tried to impress on Mike how difficult it was for him to live with Carl and Eva, and Mike listened. But was the Swami so sure he couldn't go back to the Bowery loft and live with David Allen? Except for that one incident, it had been a nice setup, hadn't it? Prabhupāda explained that David had become a madman from too much LSD. He was dangerous. Mike gave the Swami a half-incredulous look—David Allen, dangerous? Prabhupāda then told a story: "There's an old saying in India that you get yourself a spiritual master, you sit opposite him, you learn everything from him that you can, then you kill him, you move his body to one side, and then you sit in his place, and you become the *guru*." As Prabhupāda spoke, Mike began to feel that David *was* dangerous, so he didn't ask for any more details.

Mike could see that Swamiji was appealing to him for help, and as they all sat together on the couch, Mike and Carl quietly nodded in agreement. The Swami was looking at Mike, and Mike was trying to think.

"So how can we help Swamiji?" Carl interjected.

Mike explained that he was a pianist and he had to practice every day. He had two pianos, two sets of drums, a vibraphone, and other instruments right there in his apartment. Musicians were always coming over to practice, and they all played their instruments for hours. Also, he was living with a girl, and there was a cat in the apartment. But Mike promised that he would help find the Swami a new place. Prabhupāda thanked him and, along with Carl, stood to leave.

Mike felt obligated. He was good at getting things done, and he wanted to do this for the Swami. So the next day he went to *The Village Voice,* got the first newspaper off the press, looked through the classified ads until he found a suitable prospect, and phoned the landlord. It was a storefront on Second Avenue, and an agent, a Mr. Gardiner, agreed to meet Mike there. Carl and the Swami also agreed to come.

Mr. Gardiner and Mike were the first to arrive. Mike noted the unusual hand-painted sign—Matchless Gifts—above the front window. It was a holdover, Mr. Gardiner explained, from when the place had been a nostalgic-gift shop. Mike proceeded to describe the Swami as a spiritual leader from India, an important author, and a Sanskrit scholar. The rental agent seemed receptive. As soon as Prabhupāda and Carl arrived and everyone had been congenially introduced, Mr. Gardiner showed them the small storefront. Prabhupāda, Carl, and Mike carefully considered its possibilities. It was empty, plain and dark—the electricity had not been turned on—and it needed repainting. It would be good for meetings, but not for the Swami's residence. But at $125 a month it seemed promising. Then Mr. Gardiner revealed a small, second-floor apartment just across the rear courtyard, directly behind the storefront. Another $71 a month and the Swami could live there, although first Mr. Gardiner would have to repaint it. The total rent would come to $196, and Carl, Mike, and the others would pitch in.

Prabhupāda had the idea of making Mr. Gardiner the first official trustee of his fledgling Kṛṣṇa consciousness society. During their conversation he presented Mr. Gardiner with a three-volume set of his *Śrīmad-Bhāgavatam,* and inside the front cover he wrote a personal dedication and then signed it, "A. C. Bhaktivedanta Swami." Mr. Gardiner felt flattered and honored to receive these books from their author himself. He agreed to become a trustee of the new society for Kṛṣṇa consciousness, and so pay the Society twenty dollars a month.

Mr. Gardiner took a week to paint the apartment. Meanwhile, Mike arranged for the electricity and water to be turned on and had a phone installed, and he and Carl raised the first month's rent among their friends. When everything was ready, Mike gave Prabhupāda a call at Carl's.

Now it was time to move the Swami into his new place. A few friends who were on hand accompanied the Swami over to the Bowery loft. Maybe they weren't prepared to become his surrendered disciples, but contributing toward the first month's rent and volunteering a few hours of work to help set up his place were exactly the kinds of things they could do very willingly.

At the loft, they all gathered up portions of the Swami's belongings, and then they started out on foot up Bowery. It was like a safari, a caravan of half a dozen men loaded with Prabhupāda's things. Michael carried the heavy Roberts reel-to-reel, and even the Swami carried two suitcases. They did everything so quickly that it wasn't until they were well on their way and Mike's arm began to ache that he realized, "Why didn't we bring a car?"

It was the end of June, and a hazy summer sun poured its heat down into the Bowery jungle. Starting and stopping, the strange safari, stretching for over a block, slowly trekked along. Prabhupāda struggled with his suitcases, past the seemingly unending row of restaurant supply shops and lamp stores between Grand, Broome, and Spring streets. Sometimes he paused and rested, setting his suitcases down. He was finally moving from the Bowery. His electrician friend on Seventy-second Street would have been relieved, although perhaps he would have disapproved of the Second Avenue address also. At least he was finished residing on Skid Row. He walked on, past the homeless men outside the Salvation Army shelter, past the open-door taverns, stopping at streetlights, standing alongside total strangers, keeping an eye on the progress of his procession of friends who struggled along behind him.

The Bowery artists and musicians saw him as "highly evolved." They felt that the spirit was moving him and were eager to help him set up his own place so that he could do his valuable spiritual thing and spread it to others. He was depending on them for help, yet they knew he was "on a higher level"; he was his own protector, or, as he said, God protected him.

The Swami and his young friends reached the corner of Bowery and Houston, turned right, and proceeded east. Gazing steadily ahead as he walked, Prabhupāda saw the southern end of Second Avenue, one block away. At Second Avenue he would turn left, walk just one block north across First Street, and arrive at his new home. As he passed the IND subway entrance, the storefront came into view — "Matchless Gifts." He gripped his suitcases and moved ahead. At Second Avenue and Houston he hurried through a break in the rapid traffic. He could see green trees holding their heads above the high courtyard wall, reaching up like overgrown weeds in the space between the front and rear buildings of his new address.

The streetside building housed his meeting hall, the rear building the apartment where he would live and translate. Adjoining the storefront building on its north side was a massive nine-story warehouse. The storefront structure was only six stories and seemed appended to the larger building like its diminutive child. On its southern side, Prabhupāda's new temple showed a surface of plain cement and was free of any adjoining structure; there was only the spacious lot of the busy Mobil service station that bordered on First Street. As Prabhupāda approached the storefront, he could see two small lanterns decorating the narrow doorway.

There was no certainty of what awaited him here. But already there had been good signs that these American young people, mad though they sometimes were, could actually take part in Lord Caitanya's *saṅkīrtana* movement. Perhaps this new address would be the place where he could actually get a footing with his International Society for Krishna Consciousness.

CHAPTER EIGHTEEN

Breaking Ground

Swami Bhaktivedanta came to USA and went swiftly to the Archetype Spiritual Neighborhood, the New York Lower East Side, and installed intact an ancient perfectly preserved piece of street India. He adorned a storefront as his Ashram and adored Krishna therein and by patience and good humor singing chanting and expounding Sanskrit terminology day by day established Krishna Consciousness in the psychedelic (mind-manifesting) center of America East. ... To choose to attend to the Lower East Side, what kindness and humility and intelligence!

—Allen Ginsberg
from his introduction to
the Macmillan *Bhagavad-gītā As It Is*

PRABHUPĀDA'S NEW NEIGHBORHOOD was not as run-down as the nearby Bowery, though it certainly was less than quaint. Right across from his storefront, a row of tombstones looked out from the somber, dimly lit display windows of Weitzner Brothers and Papper Memorials. North of Weitzner Brothers was Sam's Luncheonette. Next to Sam's stood an ancient four-story building marked A.I.R., then Ben J. Horowitz Monuments (more gravestones), and finally Schwartz's Funeral Home. On the next block at number 43 a worn canvas awning jutted out onto the sidewalk: Provenzano Lanza Funeral Home. Then there was Cosmos Parcels (importers) and a few blocks further uptown the prominent black-and-white signboard of the Village East Theater.

Up a block, but on the same side of the avenue as the storefront, was the Church of the Nativity, an old three-story building with new blue paint and a gold-colored cross on top. The six-story 26 Second Avenue, its face covered by a greenish fire escape, crouched against the massive nine-story Knickerbocker Fireproof Warehouse.

Second Avenue was a main traffic artery for east Manhattan, and the stoplight at the intersection of Houston and Second pumped a stream of delivery trucks, taxis, and private autos past Prabhupāda's door. From early morning until night there would be cars zooming by, followed by the sound of brakes, the competitive tension of waiting bumper to bumper, the impetuous honking, then gears grinding, engines rumbling and revving, and again the zooming by. The traffic was distractingly heavy.

At 26 Second Avenue there were actually two storefronts. The one to the north was a coin laundry, and the one to the south had been a gift shop but was now vacant. Both had narrow entrances, large display windows, and dull paint. Beneath the Matchless Gifts sign was a window, six feet square, that a few weeks before had displayed matchboxes decorated with photos of movie stars of the thirties and forties. The sign—Matchless Gifts—was the only remaining memento of the nostalgic-gift shop that had recently moved out. Below the shop's window, a pair of iron doors in the sidewalk hid stone steps to the cellar and boiler room. The wide sidewalk had been laid down in sections of various shapes and sizes at different times, years past. Certain sections had cracked or caved in, and a fine dust with tiny sparkling shards of glass had collected in the cracks and depressions. A dull black fire hydrant stood on the curb. Midway between the entrances to the two storefronts was the main entrance to number 26. (This door opened into a foyer lined with mailboxes and intercoms, and then a locked inner door opened into a hallway leading to the stairs or back to the courtyard.)

To the left of the gift shop's window was its front door, a dark wooden frame holding a full-length pane of glass. The door opened into the long, narrow storefront, which was now completely bare. Just inside, to the right of the door, a platform extending beneath the display window was just the proper height for a seat. At the far end of the bare, dingy room, two grimy-paned windows covered with bars opened into the courtyard. To the left of the left-hand window was a small sink, fixed to the outside of a very small toilet closet, whose door faced the front of the store. A door on the store's left wall connected to a hallway that led into the courtyard.

The courtyard was paved with concrete geometric sections and encircled with shrub gardens and tall trees. There was a picnic table, a cement birdbath, and a birdhouse on a pole, and near the center of the courtyard were two shrub gardens. The courtyard was bordered north and south by high walls, and front and back by the two tenements. The patch of sky above gave relief.

Overlooking the courtyard from the rear building of 26 Second Avenue was Prabhupāda's second-floor apartment, where he would now live, work, and worship. With help from his Bowery friends, he had cleaned and settled into his new home. In the back room—his office—he had placed against one wall a thin cushion with an elephant-print cover and in front of the cushion his unpainted metal suitcase, which served as a desk. He had set his typewriter on the desk and his papers and books on either side. This became his work area. His manuscripts bundled in saffron cloth, his stock of *Śrīmad-Bhāgavatams,* and his few personal effects he kept in the closet opposite his desk. On the wall above his sitting place he hung an Indian calendar print of Lord Kṛṣṇa. (Kṛṣṇa, as a youth, was playing on His flute with a cow close behind Him. Lord Kṛṣṇa was standing on the planet earth, which curved like the top of a small hill beneath His feet.) There were two windows on the east wall, and the dappled morning sunlight, filtering in through the fire escape, fell across the floor.

The next room was bare except for a fancy coffee table, which became Prabhupāda's altar. Here he placed a framed picture of Lord Caitanya and His associates. On the wall he hung an Indian calendar print of four-armed Lord Viṣṇu and Ananta Śeṣa, the celestial snake. And, as in the Bowery loft, he put up a clothesline.

Both rooms were freshly painted, and the floors were clean hardwood parquet. The bathroom was clean and serviceable, as was the narrow, furnished kitchen. Prabhupāda would sometimes stand by the kitchen window, gazing beyond the courtyard wall. He had moved here without any prospects of paying the next month's rent.

Although Carl, Mike, Carol, James, Bill, and others had encouraged him to move here, some of them now found it a little inconvenient to visit him regularly, but they all wished him well and hoped new people would come here to help him. They felt that this location was the best yet. And he seemed more comfortable here. At the Paradox, Bill would spread the word of Swamiji's new address.

* * *

The Lower East Side has a history of change and human suffering as old as New York. Three hundred years before Prabhupāda's arrival, it had been part of Peter Stuyvesant's estate. Today's landmark of Tompkins Square Park had then been a salt marsh known as Stuyvesant's Swamp.

The Lower East Side first became a slum in the 1840s, when thousands of Irish immigrants, driven by the Irish potato famine, came and settled. Two decades later, the Irish became the image of the American to the next immigrants, the Germans, who gradually grew in numbers to become the largest immigrant group in New York City. Next came East European Jews (Poles and Ukranians), and by 1900 the Lower East Side had become the most densely populated Jewish ghetto in the world. But in the next generation the ghetto began to break up as Jews moved to the suburbs and economic advancement.

Next the Puerto Ricans thronged in—hundreds of thousands in the 1950s—immigrating from their island poverty or moving in from East Harlem. They, and the Negroes from Harlem and Bedford Stuyvesant who arrived next, were the new groups who along with the Poles and Ukranians populated the two square miles of tenements and crowded streets that formed the Lower East Side slums in the 1960s.

Then, only a few years before Prabhupāda's arrival, a different kind of slum-dweller had appeared on the Lower East Side. Although there have been many sociological and cultural analyses of this phenomenon, it remains ultimately inexplicable why they suddenly came, like a vast flock of birds swooping down or like animals in a great instinctual migration, and why after a few years they vanished.

At first the newcomers were mostly young artists, musicians, and intellectuals, similar to the hip crowd of Prabhupāda's Bowery days. Then came the young middle-class dropouts. Because living space was more available and rents were lower than in nearby Greenwich Village, they concentrated here on the Lower East Side, which in the parlance of the renting agents became known as the East Village. Many even came without finding a place to live and camped in the hallways of tenements. Drawn by cheap rent and the promise of Bohemian freedom, these young middle-class dropouts, the avant-garde of a nationwide youth movement soon to be known in the media as "hippies," wandered to the Lower East Side slums in living protest against America's good life of materialism.

As if responding to an instinctual call, younger teenage runaways joined the older hippies, and following the runaways came the police, counselors, social and welfare workers, youth hostels, and drug counseling centers. On St. Mark's Place a new hip commercialism sprang up, with head shops, poster shops, record shops, art galleries, and bookstores that carried everything from cigarette papers to hip clothes and psychedelic lighting.

The hippies journeyed to the Lower East Side in full conviction that this was the place to be, just as their immigrant predecessors had done. For the European immigrants of another age, New York Harbor had been the gateway to a land of riches and opportunity, as they at long last set their eyes on Manhattan's skyline and the Statue of Liberty. Now, in 1966, American youth thronged to New York City with hopes of their own and feasted on the vision of their newfound mystical land—the Lower East Side slums.

It was an uneasy coexistence, with hippies on one side and Puerto Ricans, Poles, and Ukranians on the other. The established ethnic groups resented the newcomers, who didn't really *have* to live in the slums, whereas they themselves did. In fact, many of the young newcomers were from immigrant families that had struggled for generations to establish themselves as middle-class Americans. Nevertheless, the youth migration to the Lower East Side was just as real as the immigration of Puerto Ricans or Poles or Ukranians had been, although the motives of course were quite different.

The hippies had turned from the suburban materialism of their parents, the inane happiness of TV and advertising—the ephemeral goals of middle-class America. They were disillusioned by parents, teachers, clergy, public leaders, and the media, dissatisfied with American policy in Vietnam, and allured by radical political ideologies that exposed America as a cruel, selfish, exploitative giant who must now reform or die. And they were searching for real love, real peace, real existence, and real spiritual consciousness.

By the summer of Śrīla Prabhupāda's arrival at 26 Second Avenue, the first front in the great youth rebellion of the sixties had already entered the Lower East Side. Here they were free—free to live in simple poverty and express themselves through art, music, drugs, and sex. The talk was of spiritual searching. LSD and marijuana were the keys, opening new realms of awareness. Notions about Eastern cultures and Eastern religions were in vogue. Through drugs, *yoga,* brotherhood, or just by being free—somehow they would attain enlightenment. Everyone was supposed to keep an open mind and develop his own cosmic philosophy by direct experience and drug-expanded consciousness, blended with his own eclectic readings. And if their lives appeared aimless, at least they had dropped out of a pointless game where the player sells his soul for material goods and in this way supports a system that is already rotten.

So it was that in 1966, thousands of young people were walking the streets of the Lower East Side, not simply intoxicated or crazy (though they often were), but in search of life's ultimate answers, in complete disregard of "the establishment" and the day-to-day life pursued by millions of "straight" Americans.

That the prosperous land of America could breed so many discontented youths surprised Prabhupāda. Of course, it also further proved that material well-being, the hallmark of American life, couldn't make people happy. Prabhupāda did not see the unhappiness around him in terms of the immediate social, political, economic, and cultural causes. Neither slum conditions nor youth rebellions were the all-important realities. These were mere symptoms of a universal unhappiness to which the only cure was Kṛṣṇa consciousness. He sympathized with the miseries of everyone, but he saw the universal solution.

Prabhupāda had not made a study of the youth movement in America before moving to the Lower East Side. He had never even made specific plans to come here amid so many young people. But in the ten months since Calcutta, he had been moved by force of circumstances, or, as he understood it, "by Kṛṣṇa's will," from one place to another. On the order of his spiritual master he had come to America, and by Kṛṣṇa's will he had come to the Lower East Side. His mission here was the same as it had been on the Bowery or uptown or even in India. He was fixed in the order of his spiritual master and the Vedic view, a view that wasn't going to be influenced by the radical changes of the 1960s. Now if it so happened that these young people, because of some change in the American cultural climate, were to prove more receptive to him, then that would be welcome. And that would also be by Kṛṣṇa's will.

Actually, because of the ominous influence of the Kali millennium, this was historically the worst of times for spiritual cultivation—hippie revolution or not. And Śrīla Prabhupāda was trying to transplant Vedic culture into a more alien ground than had any previous spiritual master. So he expected to find his work extremely difficult. Yet in this generally bad age, just prior to Prabhupāda's arrival on the Lower East Side, tremors of dissatisfaction and revolt against the Kali-yuga culture itself began vibrating through American society, sending waves of young people to wander the streets of New York's Lower East Side in search of something beyond the ordinary life, looking for alternatives, seeking spiritual fulfillment. These young people, broken from their stereotyped materialistic backgrounds and drawn together now on New York's Lower East Side, were the ones who were by chance or choice or destiny to become the congregation for the Swami's storefront offerings of *kīrtana* and spiritual guidance.

The Swami's arrival went unnoticed. The neighbors said someone new had taken the gift shop next to the laundry. There was a strange picture in the window now, but no one knew what to make of it. Some passersby noticed a piece of paper, announcing classes in *Bhagavad-gītā,* taped to the window. A few stopped to read it, but no one knew what to make of it. They didn't know what *Bhagavad-gītā* was, and the few who did thought, "Maybe a *yoga* bookstore or something." The Puerto Ricans in the neighborhood would look in the window at Harvey Cohen's painting and then blankly walk away. The manager of the Mobil gas station next door couldn't care less who had moved in—it just didn't make any difference. The tombstone-sellers and undertakers across the street didn't care. And for the drivers of the countless cars and trucks that passed by, Swamiji's place didn't even exist. But there were young people around who had been intrigued with the painting, who went up to the window to read the little piece of paper. Some of them even knew about the *Bhagavad-gītā,* although the painting of Lord Caitanya and the dancers didn't seem to fit. A few thought maybe they would attend Swami Bhaktivedanta's classes and check out the scene.

* * *

July 1966

Howard Wheeler was hurrying from his apartment on Mott Street to a friend's apartment on Fifth Street, a quiet place where he hoped to find some peace. He walked up Mott Street to Houston, turned right and began to walk east, across Bowery, past the rushing traffic and stumbling derelicts, and toward Second Avenue.

Howard: *After crossing Bowery, just before Second Avenue, I saw Swamiji jauntily strolling down the sidewalk, his head held high in the air, his hand in the bead bag. He struck me like a famous actor in a very familiar movie. He seemed ageless. He was wearing the traditional saffron-colored robes of a* sannyāsī *and quaint white shoes with points. Coming down Houston, he looked like the genie that popped out of Aladdin's lamp.*

Howard, age twenty-six, was a tall, large-bodied man with long, dark hair, a profuse beard, and black-framed eyeglasses. He was an instructor in English at Ohio State University and was fresh from a trip to India, where he had been looking for a true *guru.*

Prabhupāda noticed Howard, and they both stopped simultaneously. Howard asked the first question that popped into his mind: "Are you from India?"

Prabhupāda smiled. "Oh, yes, and you?"

Howard: *I told him no, but that I had just returned from India and was very interested in his country and the Hindu philosophy. He told me he had come from Calcutta and had been in New York almost ten months. His eyes were as fresh and cordial as a child's, and even standing before the trucks that roared and rumbled their way down Houston Street, he emanated a cool tranquillity that was unshakably established in something far beyond the great metropolis that roared around us.*

Howard never made it to his friend's place that day. He went back to his own apartment on Mott Street, to Keith and Wally, his roommates, to tell them and everyone he knew about the *guru* who had inexplicably appeared within their midst.

Keith and Howard had been to India. Now they were involved in various spiritual philosophies, and their friends used to come over and talk about enlightenment. Eighteen-year-old Chuck Barnett was a regular visitor.

Chuck: *You would open the door of the apartment, and thousands of cockroaches would disappear into the woodwork. And the smell was enough to knock you over. So Keith was trying to clean the place up and kick some people out. They were sharing the rent— Wally, Keith, Howard, and several others. Due to a lack of any other process, they were using LSD to try and increase their spiritual life. Actually we were all trying to use drugs to help in meditation. Anyway, Wally, Howard, and Keith were trying to find the perfect spiritual master, as we all were.*

Howard remembers his own spiritual seeking as "reading books on Eastern philosophy and religion, burning lots of candles and incense, and taking *gāñjā* and peyote and LSD as aids to meditation. Actually, it was more intoxication than meditation. 'Meditation' was a euphemism that somehow connected our highs with our readings."

Keith, twenty-nine, the son of a Southern Baptist minister, was a Ph.D. candidate in history at Columbia University. He was preparing his thesis on "The Rise of Revivalism in the Southern United States." Dressed in old denim cutoffs, sandals, and T-shirt, he was something of a *guru* among the Mott Street coterie.

Wally was in his thirties, shabbily dressed, bearded, intellectual, and well read in Buddhist literature. He had been a radio engineer in the army and, like his roommates, was unemployed. He was reading Alan Watts, Hermann Hesse, and others, talking about spiritual enlightenment, and taking LSD.

In India, Howard and Keith had visited Hardwar, Rishikesh, Benares, and other holy cities, experiencing Indian temples, hashish, and dysentery. One evening in Calcutta they had come upon a group of *sādhus* chanting the Hare Kṛṣṇa *mantra* and playing hand cymbals. For Howard and Keith, as for many Westerners, the essence of Indian philosophy was Śaṅkara's doctrine of impersonal oneness: everything is false except the one impersonal spirit. They had bought books that told them, "Whatever way you express your faith, that way is a valid spiritual path."

Now the three roommates—Howard, Keith, and Wally—began to mix various philosophies into a hodgepodge of their own. Howard would mix in a little Whitman, Emerson, Thoreau, or Blake; Keith would cite Biblical references; and Wally would add a bit of Buddhist wisdom. And they all kept up on Timothy Leary, Thomas à Kempis, and many others, the whole mixture being subject to a total reevaluation whenever one of the group experienced a new cosmic insight through LSD.

This was the group that Howard returned to that day in July. Excitedly, he told them about the Swami—how he looked and what he had said. Howard told how after they had stood and talked together the Swami had mentioned his place nearby on Second Avenue, where he was planning to hold some classes.

Howard: *I walked around the corner with him. He pointed out a small storefront building between First and Second streets next door to a Mobil filling station. It had been a curiosity shop, and someone had painted the words Matchless Gifts over the window. At that time, I didn't realize how prophetic those words were. "This is a good area?" he asked me. I told him that I thought it was. I had no idea what he was going to offer at his "classes," but I knew that all my friends would be glad that an Indian swami was moving into the neighborhood.*

The word spread. Although it wasn't so easy now for Carl Yeargens and certain others to come up from the Bowery and Chinatown—they had other things to do—Roy Dubois, a twenty-five-year-old writer for comic books, had visited Prabhupāda on the Bowery, and when he heard about the Swami's new place, he wanted to drop by. James Greene and Bill Epstein had not forgotten the Swami, and they wanted to come. The Paradox restaurant was still a live connection and brought new interested people. And others, like Stephen Guarino, saw the Swami's sign in the window. Steve, age twenty-six, was a caseworker for the city's welfare department, and one day on his lunch break, as he was walking home from the welfare office at Fifth Street and Second Avenue, he saw the Swami's sign taped to the window. He had been reading a paperback *Gītā*, and he promised himself he would attend the Swami's class.

That day as he stood with the Swami before the storefront, Howard had also noticed the little sign in the window:

LECTURES IN BHAGAVAD GITA
A. C. BHAKTIVEDANTA SWAMI
MONDAY, WEDNESDAY, AND FRIDAY
7:00 to 9:00 P.M.

"Will you bring your friends?" Prabhupāda had asked.

"Yes," Howard promised. "Monday evening."

* * *

The summer evening was warm, and in the storefront the back windows and front door were opened wide. Young men, several of them dressed in black denims and button-down sport shirts with broad dull stripes, had left their worn sneakers by the front door and were now sitting on the floor. Most of them were from the Lower East Side; no one had had to go to great trouble to come here. The little room was barren. No pictures, no furniture, no rug, not even a chair. Only a few plain straw mats. A single bulb hung from the ceiling into the center of the room. It was seven o'clock, and about a dozen people had gathered, when the Swami suddenly opened the side door and entered the room.

He wasn't wearing a shirt, and the saffron cloth that draped his torso left his arms and some of his chest bare. His complexion was smooth golden brown, and as they watched him, his head shaven, his ears long-lobed, and his aspect grave, he seemed like pictures they'd seen of the Buddha in meditation. He was old, yet erect in his posture, fresh and radiant. His forehead was decorated with the yellowish clay markings of the Vaiṣṇavas. Prabhupāda recognized big, bearded Howard and smiled. "You have brought your friends?"

"Yes," Howard answered in his loud, resonant voice.

"Ah, very good."

Prabhupāda stepped out of his white shoes, sat down on a thin mat, faced his congregation, and indicated they could all be seated. He distributed several pairs of brass hand cymbals and briefly demonstrated the rhythm: one ... two ... *three*. He began playing—a startling, ringing sound. He began singing: Hare Kṛṣṇa, Hare Kṛṣṇa, Kṛṣṇa Kṛṣṇa, Hare Hare/ Hare Rāma, Hare Rāma, Rāma Rāma, Hare Hare. Now it was the audience's turn. "Chant," he told them. Some already knew, gradually the others caught on, and after a few rounds, all were chanting together.

Most of these young men and the few young women present had at one time or another embarked on the psychedelic voyage in search of a new world of expanded consciousness. Boldly and recklessly, they had entered the turbulent, forbidden waters of LSD, peyote, and magic mushrooms. Heedless of warnings, they had risked everything and done it. Yet there was merit in their valor, their eagerness to find the extra dimensions of the self, to get beyond ordinary existence—even if they didn't know what the beyond was or whether they would ever return to the comfort of the ordinary. Nonetheless, whatever truth they had found, they remained unfulfilled, and whatever worlds they had reached, these young psychedelic voyagers had always returned to the Lower East Side. Now they were sampling the Hare Kṛṣṇa *mantra.*

When the *kīrtana* suddenly sprang up from the Swami's cymbals and sonorous voice, they immediately felt that it was going to be something far out. Here was another chance to "trip out," and willingly they began to flow with it. They would surrender their minds and explore the limits of the chanting for all it was worth. Most of them had already associated the *mantra* with the mystical *Upaniṣads* and *Gītā,* which had called out to them in words of mystery: "Eternal spirit… . Negating illusion." But whatever it is, this Indian *mantra,* let it come, they thought. Let its waves carry us far and high. Let's take it, and let the effects come. Whatever the price, let it come. The chanting seemed simple and natural enough. It was sweet and wasn't going to harm anyone. It was, in its own way, far out.

As Prabhupāda chanted in his own inner ecstasy, he observed his motley congregation. He was breaking ground in a new land now. As the hand cymbals rang, the lead-and-response of the Hare Kṛṣṇa *mantra* swelled, filling the evening. Some neighbors were annoyed. Puerto Rican children, enchanted, appeared at the door and window, looking. Twilight came.

Exotic it was, yet anyone could see that a swami was raising an ancient prayer in praise of God. This wasn't rock or jazz. He was a holy man, a swami, making a public religious demonstration. But the combination was strange: an old Indian swami chanting an ancient *mantra* with a storefront full of young American hippies singing along.

Prabhupāda sang on, his shaven head held high and tilted, his body trembling slightly with emotion. Confidently, he led the *mantra,* absorbed in pure devotion, and they responded. More passersby were drawn to the front window and open door. Some jeered, but the chanting was too strong. Within the sound of the *kīrtana,* even the car horns were a faint staccato. The vibration of auto engines and the rumble of trucks continued, but in the distance now, unnoticed.

Gathered under the dim electric light in the bare room, the group chanted after their leader, growing gradually from a feeble, hesitant chorus to an approximate harmony of voices. They continued clapping and chanting, putting into it whatever they could, in hopes of discovering its secrets. This swami was not simply giving some five-minute sample demonstration. For the moment he was their leader, their guide in an unknown realm. Howard and Keith's little encounter with a *kīrtana* in Calcutta had left them outsiders. The chanting had never before come like this, right in the middle of the Lower East Side with a genuine swami leading them.

In their minds were psychedelic ambitions to see the face of God, fantasies and visions of Hindu teachings, and the presumption that "IT" was all impersonal light. Prabhupāda had encountered a similar group on the Bowery, and he knew this group wasn't experiencing the *mantra* in the proper disciplined reverence and knowledge. But he let them chant in their own way. In time their submission to the spiritual sound, their purification, and their enlightenment and ecstasy in chanting and hearing Hare Kṛṣṇa would come.

He stopped the *kīrtana*. The chanting had swept back the world, but now the Lower East Side rushed in again. The children at the door began to chatter and laugh. Cars and trucks made their rumblings heard once more. And a voice shouted from a nearby apartment, demanding quiet. It was now past 7:30. Half an hour had elapsed.

* * *

Now today, we shall begin the Fourth Chapter—what Lord Kṛṣṇa says to Arjuna.

His lecture is very basic and yet (for restless youth) heavily philosophical. Some can't take it, and they rise rudely upon hearing the Swami's first words, put on their shoes at the front door, and return to the street. Others have left as soon as they saw the singing was over. Still, this is his best group yet. A few of the Bowery congregation are present. The boys from Mott Street are here, and they're specifically looking for a *guru*. Many in the group have already read *Bhagavad-gītā*—and they're not too proud to hear and admit that they didn't understand it.

It's another hot and noisy July evening outside his door. Children are on summer vacation, and they stay out on the street until dark. Nearby, a big dog is barking—"*Row! Row! Row!*"—the traffic creates constant rumbling, just outside the window little girls are shrieking, and all this makes lecturing difficult. Yet despite the distraction of children, traffic, and dogs, he wants the door open. If it is closed, he says, "Why is it closed? People may come in." He continues, undaunted, quoting Sanskrit, holding his audience, and developing his urgent message, while the relentless cacophony rivals his every word....

"*Row! Row! Row!*"

"*Eeeeeeeeek! Yaaaaaaaaa!*" Shrieking like little Spanish witches, the girls disturb the whole block. In the distance, a man shouts from his window: "Get outta here! Get outta here!"

Prabhupāda: *Ask them not to make noise.*

Roy (one of the boys in the temple): *The man is chasing the kids now.*

Prabhupāda: *Yes, yes, these children are making a disturbance. Ask them ...*

Roy: *Yes, that's what ... the man's chasing them right now.*

Prabhupāda: *They are making noises.*

Roy: *Yes, he's chasing them now.*

The man chases the children away, but they'll be back. You can't chase the children off the street—they live there. And the big dog never stops barking. And who can stop the cars? The cars are always there. Prabhupāda uses the cars to give an example: When a car momentarily comes into our vision on Second Avenue, we certainly don't think that it had no existence before we saw it or that it ceases to exist once it has passed from view; similarly, when Kṛṣṇa goes from this planet to another, it doesn't mean He no longer exists, although it may appear that way. Actually, He has only left our sight. Kṛṣṇa and His incarnations constantly appear and disappear on innumerable planets throughout the innumerable universes of the material creation.

The cars are always passing, roaring and rumbling through every word Prabhupāda speaks. The door is open, and he is poised at the edge of a river of carbon monoxide, asphalt, rumbling tires, and constant waves of traffic. He has come a long way from the banks of his Yamunā in Vṛndāvana, where great saints and sages have gathered through the ages to discuss Kṛṣṇa consciousness. But his audience lives *here* amid *this* scene, so he has come here, beside Second Avenue's rushing river of traffic, to speak loudly the ageless message.

He is still stressing the same point: whatever you do in Kṛṣṇa consciousness, however little it may be, is eternally good for you. Yet now, more than uptown or on the Bowery, he is calling his hearers to take to Kṛṣṇa consciousness *fully* and become devotees. He assures them ... .

Anyone can become a devotee and friend of Kṛṣṇa like Arjuna. You will be surprised that Lord Caitanya's principal disciples were all so-called fallen in society. He appointed Haridāsa Ṭhākura to the highest position in His spiritual mission, although he happened to take birth in a Muhammadan family. So there is no bar for anyone. Everyone can become spiritual master, provided he knows the science of Kṛṣṇa. This is the science of Kṛṣṇa, this Bhagavad-gītā. *And if anyone knows it perfectly, then he becomes a spiritual master.*

And this transcendental vibration, Hare Kṛṣṇa, will help us by cleaning the dust from the mirror of our mind. On the mind we have accumulated material dust. Just like on the Second Avenue, due to the constant traffic of motorcars, there's always a creation of dust over everything. Similarly, by our manipulation of materialistic activities, there are some material dusts which are accumulated on the mind, and therefore we are unable to see things in true perspective. So this process, the vibration of the transcendental sound—Hare Kṛṣṇa, Hare Kṛṣṇa, Kṛṣṇa Kṛṣṇa, Hare Hare/ Hare Rāma, Hare Rāma, Rāma Rāma, Hare Hare—will cleanse the dust. And as soon as the dust is cleared, then, as you see your nice face in the mirror, similarly you can see your real constitutional position as spirit soul. In Sanskrit language it is said, bhava-mahā-dāvāgni. *Lord Caitanya said that. Lord Caitanya's picture you have seen in the front window. He is dancing and chanting Hare Kṛṣṇa. So, it doesn't matter what a person was doing before, what sinful activities. A person may not be perfect at first, but if he is engaged in service, then he will be purified.*

Suddenly a Bowery derelict enters, whistling and drunkenly shouting. The audience remains seated, not knowing what to make of it.

Drunk: *How are ya? I'll be right back. I brought another thing.*

Prabhupāda: *Don't disturb. Sit down. We are talking seriously.*

Drunk: *I'll put it up there. In a church? All right. I'll be right back.*

The man is white-haired, with a short grizzly beard and frowsy clothing. His odor reeks through the temple. But then he suddenly careens out the door and is gone. Prabhupāda chuckles softly and returns immediately to his lecture.

So it doesn't matter what a person was doing before, if he engages in Kṛṣṇa consciousness—chanting Hare Kṛṣṇa and Bhagavad-gītā*—it should be concluded that he is a saint. He is a saintly person.* Api cet su-durācāro. *Never mind if he may have some external immoral habit due to his past association. It doesn't matter. Some way or other, one should become Kṛṣṇa conscious, and then gradually he will become a saintly person as he goes on executing this process of Kṛṣṇa consciousness.*

There is a story about how habit is second nature. There was a thief, and he went on pilgrimage with some friends. So at night when the others were sleeping, because his habit was to steal at night, he got up and was taking someone's baggage. But then he was thinking, "Oh, I have come to this holy place of pilgrimage, but still I am committing theft by habit. No, I shall not do it."

So then he took someone's bag and put it in another's place, and for the whole night the poor fellow moved the bags of the pilgrims from here to there. But due to his conscience, because he was on a holy pilgrimage, he did not actually take anything. So in the morning when everyone got up, they looked around and said, "Where is my bag? I don't see it." And another man says, "I don't see my bag." And then someone says, "Oh, there is your bag." So there was some row, so they thought, "What is the matter? How has it so happened?"

Then the thief rose up and told all of the friends, "My dear gentlemen, I am a thief by occupation, and because I have that habit to steal at night, I couldn't stop myself. But I thought, 'I have come to this holy place, so I won't do it.' Therefore I placed one person's bag in another man's place. Please excuse me."

So this is habit. He doesn't want to, but he has a habit of doing it. He has decided not to commit theft anymore, but sometimes he does, habitually. So Kṛṣṇa says that in such conditions, when one who has decided to stop all immoral habits and just take to this process of Kṛṣṇa consciousness, if by chance he does something which is immoral in the face of society, that should not be taken account of. In the next verse Kṛṣṇa says, kṣipraṁ bhavati dharmātmā: *because he has dovetailed himself in Kṛṣṇa consciousness, it is sure that he will be saintly very soon.*

Suddenly the old derelict returns, announcing his entrance: "How are ya?" He is carrying something. He maneuvers his way through the group, straight to the back of the temple, where the Swami is sitting. He opens the toilet room door, puts two rolls of bathroom tissue inside, closes the door, and then turns to the sink, sits some paper towels on top of it and puts two more rolls of bathroom tissue and some more paper towels under the sink. He then stands and turns around toward the Swami and the audience. The Swami is looking at him and asks, "What is this?" The bum is silent now; he has done his work. Prabhupāda begins to laugh, thanking his visitor, who is now moving toward the door: "Thank you. Thank you very much." The bum exits. "Just see," Prabhupāda now addresses his congregation. "It is a natural tendency to give some service. Just see, he is not in order, but he thought that, 'Here is something. Let me give some service.' Just see how automatically it comes. This is natural."

The young men in the audience look at one another. This is really far out—first the chanting with the brass cymbals, the Swami looking like Buddha and talking about Kṛṣṇa and chanting, and now this crazy stuff with the bum. But the Swami stays cool, he's really cool, just sitting on the floor like he's not afraid of anything, just talking his philosophy about the soul and us becoming saints and even the old drunk becoming a saint!

After almost an hour, the dog still barks and the kids still squeal.

Prabhupāda is asking his hearers, who are only beginners in spiritual life, to become totally dedicated preachers of Kṛṣṇa consciousness: "In the *Bhagavad-gītā*, you will find that anyone who preaches the gospel of *Bhagavad-gītā* to the people of the world is the most dear, the dearest person to Kṛṣṇa. Therefore it is our duty to preach the principles of this *Bhagavad-gītā* to make people Kṛṣṇa conscious." Prabhupāda can't wait to tell them—even if they aren't ready. It's too urgent. The world needs Kṛṣṇa conscious preachers.

People are suffering for want of Kṛṣṇa consciousness. Therefore, each and every one of us should be engaged in the preaching work of Kṛṣṇa consciousness for the benefit of the whole world. Lord Caitanya, whose picture is in the front of our store, has very nicely preached the philosophy of Kṛṣṇa consciousness. The Lord says, "Just take My orders, all of you, and become a spiritual master." Lord Caitanya gives the order that in every country you go and preach Kṛṣṇa consciousness. So if we take up this missionary work to preach Bhagavad-gītā *as it is, without interpretation and without any material motives behind it—as it is—then Kṛṣṇa says it shall be done. We should not have any attraction for worldy activities; otherwise we can't have Kṛṣṇa. But it doesn't mean that we should be inimical to the people of the world. No, it is our duty to give them the highest instruction, that you become Kṛṣṇa conscious and—*

A young man in the audience seems unable to contain himself and begins making his own incoherent speech.

Prabhupāda: *No. You cannot disturb just now.*

Man (standing up): *Now wait a minute, man.* (A quarrel begins as others try to quiet him.)

Prabhupāda: *No, no, no. No, no, no, no. Not just now. No, no, you cannot ask just now.*

Man: *Well, I am trying to talk.*

Prabhupāda: *No, just now you cannot ask.*

Man: *But wait a minute, man. Wait.*

Prabhupāda: *Why do you interfere just now? We have a regular question time.*

Others in the audience: *Let the man finish. Yeah, let him talk.* (The man's supporters defend his right to speak, while others try to silence him.)

Second man: *I have just one question, please. How long is an individual allowed or expected to go on without any type of thought? How long?*

Prabhupāda: *I am not finished. We'll give question time after finishing the talk.* (The parties go on quarreling.) *All right, I am very glad you are curious, but please wait. Have some patience, because we have not finished. As soon as we finish, after five minutes, ten minutes, I will tend to your question. Don't be impatient. Sit down.* (The audience quiets down, and the Swami goes on with his talk.)

After five minutes. ...

Prabhupāda: *All right. This gentleman is impatient. We shall stop here. Now what is your question, sir?*

Man: *Practically we tend to place emphasis on those we identify with the fact itself. Many people are meant to explain the whyfores and wherefores of the metaphysical truth, that 'I think, therefore I am.'*

Prabhupāda: *What is your particular question?*

Man: *I have no answer to that question. Rather, but that I attempt, I live, I breathe.*

Prabhupāda: *Yes.*

Man: *So ability—tell me why I have nothing to do with it. May I understand the whyfores and wheres?*

Prabhupāda: *That's all right.*

Man: *I have difficulty in you. I have difficulty in saying.*

Prabhupāda: *So long as we are in this material world there are so many problems.*

Man: *Not many problems. It is not many problems. This is the greatest fact. I have ... I know ...*

Prabhupāda: *Yes.*

Man: *I also know that the whys and wherefores of my particular ...*

Prabhupāda: *Yes.*

Man: *I didn't come here ... But let me explain my position. This isn't necessarily ... I feel I must ... I think the difference is to learn ... You'll find it innumerable times by the same token ... Maybe we are able to reconcile the fact of individual being for a long time to find out why ...*

Prabhupāda (turning to one of the boys): *Roy, can you answer his question? It is a general question. You can answer, yes?*

Roy turns sympathetically to the rambling questioner, and Prabhupāda addresses his audience: "Enough questions." His voice now seems tired and resigned: "Let us have *kīrtana*." And the Lower East Side once again abates. The chanting begins: the brass cymbals, Prabhupāda's voice carrying the melody, and the audience responding. It goes for half an hour and then stops.

It is now 9:00. The audience sits before Swamiji while a boy brings him an apple, a small wooden bowl, and a knife. As most of the audience still sits and watches, gauging the after effects of the chanting as though it had been some new drug, the Swami cuts the apple in half, then in fourths, then in eighths, until there are many pieces. He takes one himself and asks one of the boys to pass the bowl around. Swamiji holds back his head and deftly pops a slice of apple into his mouth, without touching his fingers to his lips. He chews a bit, ruminating, his lips closed.

The members of the congregation munch silently on little pieces of apple. Prabhupāda stands, slips into his shoes, and exits through the side door.

* * *

As Prabhupāda retired to his apartment and his guests disappeared through the front door, back into the city, Don and Raphael would turn out the lights, lock the front door, and go to sleep on the floor in their blankets. Don and Raphael had needed a place to stay when they heard about the Swami's place. Prabhupāda had a policy that any boy who expressed even a little interest in becoming his student could stay in the storefront and make it his home. Of course, Prabhupāda would ask them to contribute toward the rent and meals, but if, like Don and Raphael, they had no money, then it was still all right, provided they helped in other ways. Don and Raphael were the first two boys to take advantage of Prabhupāda's offer. They were attracted to Swamiji and the chanting, but they weren't serious about his philosophy or the disciplines of devotional life. They had no jobs and no money, their hair was long and unkempt, and they lived and slept in the same clothes day after day. Prabhupāda stipulated that at least while they were on the premises they could not break his rules—no intoxication, illicit sex, meat-eating, or gambling. He knew these two boarders weren't serious students, but he allowed them to stay, in hopes that gradually they would become serious.

Often, some wayfaring stranger would stop by, looking for a place to stay the night, and Don and Raphael would welcome him. An old white-bearded Indian-turned-Christian who was on a walking mission proclaiming the end of the world, and whose feet were covered with bandages, once slept for a few nights on a wooden bench in the storefront. Some nights, as many as ten drifters would seek shelter at the storefront, and Don and Raphael would admit them, explaining that the Swami didn't object, as long as they got up early. Even drifters whose only interest was a free meal could stay, and after the morning class and breakfast they would usually drift off again into *māyā*.

Don and Raphael were the Swami's steady boarders, although during the day they also went out, returning only for meals, sleep, and evening chanting. Occasionally they would bathe, and then they would use the Swami's bathroom up in his apartment. Sometimes they would hang out in the storefront during the day, and if someone stopped by, asking about the Swami's classes, they would tell the person all they knew (which wasn't much). They admitted that they weren't really into the Swami's philosophy, and they didn't claim to be his followers. If someone persisted in inquiring about the Swami's teachings, Don and Raphael would suggest, "Why don't you go up and talk to him? The Swami lives in the apartment building out back. Why don't you go up and see him?"

Prabhupāda usually stayed in his apartment. Occasionally he might look out his window and see, through the back windows of the storefront, that the light in the closet-sized bathroom had needlessly been left burning. Coming down to ask the boys to turn it off and not waste electricity, he might find a few boys lying on the floor talking or reading. Prabhupāda would stand gravely, asking them not to leave the light on, stressing the seriousness of wasting Kṛṣṇa's energy and money. He would stand dressed in *khādī,* that coarse handloomed cotton woven from handspun threads, a cloth that to Americans appears somehow exotic. Even the saffron color of Prabhupāda's *dhotī* and *cādara* was exotic; produced from the traditional Indian dye, it was a dull, uneven color, different from anything Western. After Prabhupāda turned off the light, the boys seemed to have nothing to say and nothing more appropriate to do than look with interest at him for a long, awkward moment, and the Swami would leave without saying anything more.

Money was scarce. From his evening meetings he would usually collect about five or six dollars in change and bills. Don talked of going up to New England to pick apples and bring back money for the Swami. Raphael said something about some money coming. Prabhupāda waited, and depended on Kṛṣṇa. Sometimes he would walk back and forth in the courtyard between the buildings. Seeming mysterious to the neighbors, he would chant on his beads, his hand deep in his bead bag.

Mostly he kept to his room, working. As he had said during a lecture when living on the Bowery, "I am here always working at something, reading or writing—something, reading or writing—twenty-four hours." His mission of translating *Śrīmad-Bhāgavatam,* of presenting the complete work in sixty volumes of four hundred pages each, could alone occupy all his days and nights. He worked at it whenever possible, sitting at his portable typewriter or translating the Sanskrit into English. He especially worked in the very early hours of the morning, when he would not be interrupted. He would comb through the Sanskrit and Bengali commentaries of the great *ācāryas,* following their explanations, selecting passages from them, adding his own knowledge and realization, and then laboriously weaving it all together and typing out his Bhaktivedanta purports. He had no means or immediate plans for financing the publishing of further volumes, but he continued in the faith that somehow they would be published.

He had a broad mission, broader even than translating *Śrīmad-Bhāgavatam,* and so he gave much of his time and energy to meeting visitors. Had his only aim been to write, then there would have been no need to have taken the risk and trouble of coming to America. Now many people were coming, and an important part of his mission was to talk to them and convince them of Kṛṣṇa consciousness. His visitors were usually young men who had recently come to live on the Lower East Side. He had no secretary to screen his visitors, nor did he have scheduled visiting hours. Whenever anyone happened by, at any time, from early morning to ten at night, Prabhupāda would stop his typing or translating and speak with them. It was an open neighborhood, and many visitors would come by right off the street. Some were serious, but many were not; some even came intoxicated. Often they came not to inquire submissively but to challenge.

Once a young hippie on an LSD trip found his way upstairs and sat opposite the Swami: "Right now I am higher than you are," he announced. "*I am God.*" Prabhupāda bowed his head slightly, his palms folded: "Please accept my obeisances," he said. Then he asked "God" to please leave. Others admitted frankly that they were crazy or haunted by ghosts and sought relief from their mental suffering.

Lon Solomon: *I was looking for spiritual centers—places where one can go, not like stores where they ask you to leave, but where you can actually talk to people and try to understand the ultimate truth. I would come to the Swami's, knowing it was definitely a spiritual center. There was definitely something there. I was on drugs and disturbed with the notion that I must be God, or some very important personality way out of proportion to my actual situation. I was actually in trouble, mentally deranged because of so much suffering, and I would kind of blow in to see him whenever I felt the whim to do so. I didn't make a point of going to his meetings, but a lot of times I would just come. One time I came and spent the night there. I was always welcome at any time to sleep in the storefront. I wanted to show the Swami what a sad case I was so he should definitely do something for me. He told me to join him and he could solve my problems. But I wasn't ready.*

I was really into sex, and I wanted to know what he meant by illicit sex—what was his definition. He said to me, "This means sex outside of marriage." But I wasn't satisfied with the answer, and I asked him for more details. He told me to first consider the answer he had given me and then come back the next day and he would tell me more.

Then I showed up with a girl. The Swami came to the door and said, "I am very busy. I have my work, I have my translating. I cannot talk with you now." Well, that was the only time he didn't offer me full hospitality and full attention and talk with me as many questions as I had. So I left immediately with the girl. He was correct in his perception that I was simply going to see him just to try to impress the girl. He saw through it right away, and he rejected that type of association. But every time I came I was in trouble, and he always helped me.

Sometimes young men would come with scholarly pretentions to test the Swami's knowledge of *Bhagavad-gītā*. "You have read the *Gītā,*" Prabhupāda would say, "so what is your conclusion? If you claim to know the *Gītā,* then you should know the conclusion that Kṛṣṇa is presenting." But most people didn't think that there was supposed to be a definite conclusion to the *Gītā*. And even if there were such a conclusion, that didn't mean they were supposed to arrange their life around it. The *Gītā* was a *spiritual* book, and you didn't have to follow it.

One young man approached the Swami asking, "What book will you lecture from next week? Will you be teaching the *Tibetan Book of the Dead*?" as if Prabhupāda would teach spirituality like a college survey course in world religions. "Everything is there in *Bhagavad-gītā,*" Prabhupāda replied. "We could study one verse for three months."

And there were other questions: "What about Camus?"

"What is his philosophy?" Prabhupāda would ask.

"He says everything is absurd and the only philosophical question is whether to commit suicide."

"That means everything is absurd for *him*. The material world is absurd, but there is a spiritual world beyond this one. That means he does not know the soul. The soul cannot be killed."

Adherents of various thinkers approached him: "What about Nietzsche? Kafka? Timothy Leary? Bob Dylan?" Prabhupāda would ask what their philosophy was, and the particular follower would have to explain and defend his favorite intellectual hero.

"They are all mental speculators," Prabhupāda would say. "Here in this material world we are all conditioned souls. Your knowledge is imperfect. Your senses are blunt. What good is your *opinion*? We have to hear from the perfect authority, Kṛṣṇa."

"Do you mean to say that none of the great thinkers are God conscious?" a boy asked.

"Their sincerity is their God consciousness. But if we want perfect knowledge of God, then we have to consult *śāstra*."

Often there were challenges, but under the Swami's stare and hard logic, the challenger would usually trail off into thoughtful silence.

"Is the spiritual knowledge of China advanced?"

Prabhupāda would sometimes answer simply by making a sour face.

"Well, I am a follower of *Vedānta* myself."

"Do you know what *Vedānta* means? What is the first aphorism of the *Vedānta-sūtra*? Do you know?"

"No, I ..."

"Then how can you speak of *Vedānta*? *Vedaiś ca sarvair aham eva vedyaḥ:* Kṛṣṇa says that He is the goal of *Vedānta*. So if you are a Vedāntist, then you must become Kṛṣṇa conscious."

"What about the Buddha?"

"Do you follow him?"

"No."

"No, you just talk. Why don't you follow? Follow Kṛṣṇa, follow Christ, follow Buddha. But don't just talk."

"This sounds the same as Christianity. How is it any different?"

"It is the same: love of God. But who is a Christian? Who follows? The Bible teaches, 'Thou shalt not kill,' but all over the world, Christians are expert in killing. Do you know that? I believe the Christians say that Jesus Christ died for our sins—so why are you still sinning?"

Although Prabhupāda was a stranger to America, they were strangers to absolute knowledge. Whenever anyone would come to see him, he wouldn't waste time—he talked philosophy, reason, and argument. He constantly argued against atheism and impersonalism. He spoke strongly, to prove the existence of God and the universality of Kṛṣṇa consciousness. He talked often and vigorously, day and night, meeting all kinds of questions and philosophies.

He would listen also, and he heard a wide range of local testimonies. He heard the dissatisfaction of young Americans with the war and with

American society. One boy told him he didn't want to get married because he couldn't find a chaste girl; it was better to go with prostitutes. Another confided that his mother had planned to abort him, but at the last moment his grandmother had convinced her not to. He heard from homosexuals. Someone told him that a set of New Yorkers considered it chic to eat the flesh of aborted babies. And in every case, he told them the truth.

He talked with Marxists and explained that although Marx says that everything is the property of the State, the fact is that everything is the property of God. Only "spiritual communism," which puts God in the center, can actually be successful. He discounted LSD visions as hallucinations and explained how God can be seen factually and what God looks like.

Although these one-time visitors came and went away, a few new friends began to stay on, watching the Swami deal with different guests. They began to appreciate the Swami's arguments, his concern for people, and his devotion to Kṛṣṇa. He seemed actually to know how to help people, and he invariably offered them Kṛṣṇa consciousness—as much as they could take—as the solution to their problems. A few began to take the Swami's message to heart.

* * *

"We shall call our society ISKCON." Prabhupāda had laughed playfully when he first coined the acronym.

He had initiated the legal work of incorporation that spring, while still living on the Bowery. But even before its legal beginning, he had been talking about his "International Society for Krishna Consciousness," and so it had appeared in letters to India and in *The Village Voice*. A friend had suggested a title that would sound more familiar to Westerners, "International Society for *God* Consciousness," but Prabhupāda had insisted: "*Krishna* Consciousness." "God" was a vague term, whereas "Krishna" was exact and scientific; "God consciousness" was spiritually weaker, less personal. And if Westerners didn't know that Kṛṣṇa was God, then the International Society for *Krishna* Consciousness would tell them, by spreading His glories "in every town and village."

"Kṛṣṇa consciousness" was Prabhupāda's own rendering of a phrase from Śrīla Rūpa Gosvāmī's *Padyāvalī,* written in the sixteenth century. *Kṛṣṇa-bhakti-rasa-bhāvita:* "to be absorbed in the mellow taste of executing devotional service to Kṛṣṇa."

But to register ISKCON legally as a nonprofit, tax-exempt religion required money and a lawyer. Carl Yeargens had already gained some experience in forming religious, political, and social welfare groups, and when he had met Prabhupāda on the Bowery he had agreed to help. He had contacted his lawyer, Stephen Goldsmith.

Stephen Goldsmith, a young Jewish lawyer with a wife and two children and an office on Park Avenue, was interested in spiritual movements. When Carl told him about Prabhupāda's plans, he was immediately fascinated by the idea of setting up a religious corporation for an Indian swami. He visited Prabhupāda at 26 Second Avenue, and they discussed incorporation, tax exemption, Prabhupāda's immigration status, and Kṛṣṇa consciousness. Mr. Goldsmith visited Prabhupāda several times. Once he brought his children, who liked the "soup" the Swami cooked. He began attending the evening lectures, where he was often the only nonhippie member of the congregation. One evening, having completed all the legal groundwork and being ready to complete the procedures for incorporation, Mr. Goldsmith came to Prabhupāda's lecture and *kīrtana* to get signatures from the trustees for the new society.

July 11

Prabhupāda is lecturing.

Mr. Goldsmith, wearing slacks and a shirt and tie, sits on the floor near the door, listening earnestly to the lecture, despite the distracting noises from the neighborhood. Prabhupāda has been explaining how scholars mislead innocent people with nondevotional interpretations of the *Bhagavad-gītā,* and now, in recognition of the attorney's respectable presence, and as if to catch Mr. Goldsmith's attention better, he introduces him into the subject of the talk.

I will give you a practical example of how things are misinterpreted. Just like our president, Mr. Goldsmith, he knows that expert lawyers, by interpretation, can do so many things. When I was in Calcutta, there was a rent tax passed by the government, and some expert lawyer changed the whole thing by his interpretation. The government had to reenact a whole law because their purpose was foiled by the interpretation of this lawyer. So we are not out for foiling the purpose of Kṛṣṇa, for which the Bhagavad-gītā *was spoken. But unauthorized persons are trying to foil the purpose of Kṛṣṇa. Therefore, that is unauthorized.*

All right, Mr. Goldsmith, you can ask anything.

Mr. Goldsmith stands, and to the surprise of the people gathered, he makes a short announcement asking for signers on an incorporation document for the Swami's new religious movement.

Prabhupāda: *They are present here. You can take the addresses now.*

Mr. Goldsmith: *I can take them now, yes.*

Prabhupāda: *Yes, you can. Bill, you can give your address. And Raphael, you can give yours. And Don ... Roy ... Mr. Greene.*

As the meeting breaks up, those called on to sign as trustees come forward, standing around in the little storefront, waiting to leaf cursorily through the pages the lawyer has produced from his thin attaché, and to sign as he directs. Yet not a soul among them is committed to Kṛṣṇa consciousness.

Mr. Goldsmith meets his quota of signers—a handful of sympathizers with enough reverence toward the Swami to want to help him. The first trustees, who will hold office for a year, "until the first annual meeting of the corporation," are Michael Grant (who puts down his name and address without ever reading the document), Mike's girlfriend Jan, and James Greene. No one seriously intends to undertake any formal duties as trustee of the religious society, but they are happy to help the Swami by signing his fledgling society into legal existence.

According to law, a second group of trustees will assume office for the second year. They are Paul Gardiner, Roy, and Don. The trustees for the third year are Carl Yeargens, Bill Epstein, and Raphael.

None of them know exactly what the half a dozen, legal-sized typed pages mean, except that "Swamiji is forming a society."

Why?

For tax exemption, in case someone gives a big donation, and for other benefits an official religious society might receive.

But these purposes hardly seem urgent or even relevant to the present situation. Who's going to make donations? Except maybe for Mr. Goldsmith, who has any money?

But Prabhupāda is planning for the future, and he's planning for much more than just tax exemptions. He is trying to serve his spiritual predecessors and fulfill the scriptural prediction of a spiritual movement that is to flourish for ten thousand years in the midst of the Age of Kali. Within the vast Kali Age (a period which is to last 432,000 years), the 1960s are but an insignificant moment.

The *Vedas* describe that the time of the universe revolves through a cycle of four "seasons," or *yugas,* and Kali-yuga is the worst of times, in which all spiritual qualities of men diminish until humanity is finally reduced to a bestial civilization, devoid of human decency. However, the Vedic literature foretells a golden age of spiritual life, beginning after the advent of Lord Caitanya and lasting for ten thousand years—an eddy that runs against the current of Kali-yuga. With a vision that soars off to the end of the millennium and beyond, yet with his two feet solidly on the ground of Second Avenue, Prabhupāda has begun an International Society for Krishna Consciousness. He has many practical responsibilities: paying the rent, incorporating his society, and paving the way for a thriving worldwide congregation of devotees. Yet he doesn't see his humble beginning as limiting the greater scope of his divine mission. He knows that everything depends on Kṛṣṇa, so whether he succeeds or fails is up to the Supreme. He has only to try.

The purposes stated within ISKCON's articles of incorporation reveal Prabhupāda's thinking. They were seven points, similar to those given in the Prospectus for the League of Devotees he formed in Jhansi, India, in 1953. That attempt had been unsuccessful, yet his purposes remained unchanged.

Seven Purposes of the International Society for Krishna Consciousness:

(a) To systematically propagate spiritual knowledge to society at large and to educate all peoples in the techniques of spiritual life in order to check the imbalance of values in life and to achieve real unity and peace in the world.

(b) To propagate a consciousness of Krishna, as it is revealed in the *Bhagavad Gita* and *Srimad Bhagwatam.*

(c) To bring the members of the Society together with each other and nearer to Krishna, the prime entity, thus to develop the idea within the members, and humanity at large, that each soul is part and parcel of the quality of Godhead (Krishna).

(d) To teach and encourage the sankirtan movement, congregational chanting of the holy name of God as revealed in the teachings of Lord Sri Chaitanya Mahaprabhu.

(e) To erect for the members and for society at large, a holy place of transcendental pastimes, dedicated to the Personality of Krishna.

(f) To bring the members closer together for the purpose of teaching a simpler and more natural way of life.

(g) With a view towards achieving the aforementioned Purposes, to publish and distribute periodicals, magazines, books and other writings.

Regardless of what ISKCON's charter members thought of the society's purposes, Prabhupāda saw them as imminent realities. As Mr. Ruben, the subway conductor who had met Prabhupāda on a Manhattan park bench in 1965, had noted: "He seemed to know that he would have temples filled up with devotees. 'There are temples and books,' he said. 'They are existing, they are there, but the time is separating us from them.'"

The first purpose mentioned in the charter was propagation. "Preaching" was the word Prabhupāda most often used. For him, preaching had a much broader significance than mere sermonizing. Preaching meant glorious, selfless adventures on behalf of the Supreme Lord. Lord Caitanya had preached by walking all over southern India and causing thousands of people to chant and dance with Him in ecstasy. Lord Kṛṣṇa had preached the *Bhagavad-gītā* while standing with Arjuna in his chariot on the Battlefield of Kurukṣetra. Lord Buddha had preached, Lord Jesus had preached, and all pure devotees preach.

ISKCON's preaching would achieve what the League of Nations and the United Nations had failed to achieve—"real unity and peace in the world." ISKCON workers would bring peace to a world deeply afflicted by materialism and strife. They would "systematically propagate spiritual knowledge," knowledge of the nonsectarian science of God. It was not that a new religion was being born in July of 1966; rather, the eternal preaching of Godhead, known as *saṅkīrtana,* was being transplanted from East to West.

The society's members would join together, and by hearing the teachings of *Bhagavad-gītā* and *Śrīmad-Bhāgavatam* and by chanting the Hare Kṛṣṇa *mantra,* they would come to realize that each was a spirit soul, eternally related to Kṛṣṇa, the Supreme Personality of Godhead. They would then preach this to "humanity at large," especially through *saṅkīrtana,* the chanting of the holy name of God.

ISKCON would also erect "a holy place of transcendental pastimes dedicated to the Personality of Krishna." Was this something beyond the storefront? Yes, certainly. He never thought small: "He seemed to know that he would have temples filled up with devotees."

He wanted ISKCON to demonstrate "a simple, more natural way of life." Such a life (Prabhupāda thought of the villages of India, where people lived just as Kṛṣṇa had lived) was most conducive to developing Kṛṣṇa consciousness.

And all six of these purposes would be achieved by the seventh: ISKCON would publish and distribute literature. This was the special instruction Śrīla Bhaktisiddhānta Sarasvatī Ṭhākura had given to Śrīla Prabhupāda. He had specifically told him one day in 1932 at Rādhā-kuṇḍa in Vṛndāvana, "If you ever get any money, publish books."

Certainly none of the signers saw any immediate shape to the Swami's dream, yet these seven purposes were not simply theistic rhetoric invented to convince a few New York State government officials. Prabhupāda meant to enact every item in the charter.

Of course, he was now working in extremely limited circumstances. "The principal place of worship, located at 26 Second Avenue, in the city, county, and state of New York," was the sole headquarters for the International Society for Krishna Consciousness. Yet Prabhupāda insisted that he was not living at 26 Second Avenue, New York City. His vision was transcendental. His Guru Mahārāja had gone out from the traditional holy places of spiritual meditation to preach in cities like Calcutta, Bombay, and Delhi. And yet Prabhupāda would say that his spiritual master had not really been living in any of those cities, but was always in Vaikuṇṭha, the spiritual world, because of his absorption in devotional service.

Similarly, the place of worship, 26 Second Avenue, was not a New York storefront, a former curiosity shop. The storefront and the apartment had been spiritualized and were now a transcendental haven. "Society at large" could come here, the whole world could take shelter here, regardless of race or religion. Plain, small, and impoverished as it was, Prabhupāda regarded the storefront as "a holy place of transcendental pastimes, dedicated to the Personality of Krishna." It was a world headquarters, a publishing house, a sacred place of pilgrimage, and a center from which an army of devotees could issue forth and chant the holy names of God in all the streets in the world. The entire universe could receive Kṛṣṇa consciousness from the International Society for Krishna Consciousness, which was beginning here.

* * *

In Keith, Prabhupāda had a serious follower. Within a week of their meeting, Keith had moved out of the Mott Street apartment and was living with Prabhupāda. He still dressed in his ragged denim shorts and T-shirt, but he began to do all the Swami's shopping and cooking. While in India, Keith had learned some of the etiquette of reverence toward a holy man and the principles of discipleship. His friends watched him curiously as he dedicated himself to the Swami.

Keith: *I saw that he was cooking, so I asked him if I could help. And he was very happy at the suggestion. The first couple of times, he took me shopping, and after that I mostly did it. He showed me how to make* capātīs *without a rolling pin by pressing out the dough with your fingers. Every day we would make* capātīs, *rice,* dāl, *and curries.*

So Keith became the dependable cook and housekeeper in Prabhupāda's apartment. Meanwhile, at the Mott Street apartment, the roommates' favorite topic for discussion was their relationship with the Swami. Everyone thought it was a serious relationship. They knew Swamiji was *guru.* And when they heard that he would be giving daily classes at 6 A.M., up in his apartment, they were eager to attend.

Keith: *I used to walk along the Bowery and look for flowers for him.*

When there were no flowers, I would take a straw or some grass. I loved going over there in the morning.

Howard: *I would walk very briskly over to Swamiji's, chanting Hare Kṛṣṇa, feeling better than ever before. Miraculously, the Lower East Side no longer looked drab. The sidewalks and buildings seemed to sparkle, and in the early morning before the smog set in, the sky was red and golden.*

Chuck: *I brought a few grapes and came to the door of the Swami. This was all new. Previously I would always walk toward McDougall Street, toward Bohemia, aesthetic New York—and now I was walking to the Lower East Side toward the business district, where there were no freaks, artists, or musicians, but simply straight buildings. And somehow, outside the carnival atmosphere, there was the richest attraction for the senses and the heart.*

Howard: *I would sing all the way to the foyer, then ring the buzzer marked "A. C. Bhaktivedanta Swami." And the door would buzz and open and I would walk through the hallway into the small patio and up to his small second-floor apartment, tiptoeing quietly so as not to wake up the neighbors.*

Chuck: *I came into the hall of his building, and there were many, many names printed on plaques over the mailboxes. I immediately found the name, "A. C. Bhaktivedanta Swami," handwritten on a slip of torn paper, slipped into one of the slots. I rang the buzzer and waited. After a few moments, the door buzzed loudly, and I entered through the security lock. I walked through the small garden into the rear building and upstairs.*

Prabhupāda held his classes for almost two months in the privacy of his room, the same room where he typed and talked to guests. To Keith it was not simply a class in philosophy but a mystical experience of sweetness.

Keith: *The sound of his voice, the sun coming up ... we'd chant for a few minutes, softly clapping hands, and Swamiji would speak. The thing that got me most was simply the sound of his voice, especially while he was chanting Sanskrit. It was like music to my ears to hear him speak the raw sound.*

So as not to disturb the neighbors, Prabhupāda would say, "Chant softly," and he asked the boys to clap softly, so softly that their hands barely touched. Then he would chant the prayers to the spiritual master:

saṁsāra-dāvānala-līḍha-loka. "The spiritual master is receiving benediction from the ocean of mercy. Just as a cloud pours water on a forest fire to extinguish it, so the spiritual master extinguishes the blazing fire of material existence." With his eyes closed, he sat singing softly in the dim morning light. The few who attended—Keith, Howard, Chuck, Steve, Wally—sat entranced. Never before had the Swami been so appreciated.

Chuck: *The Swami was sitting there, and in the mornings he would look not shiny and brilliant, but very withdrawn. He looked as if he could sit like a stone maybe forever. His eyes were only two tiny slits of glistening light. He took out his cymbals and played lightly on the edge—one, two,* three—*and he began to sing in a deep voice that was almost atonal in its intervals. It was a melody-monotone that did not express happiness or sadness—a timeless chant that told no story. We chanted along with him as best we could, but several times Swamiji stopped and said, "Softly." After about thirty minutes of chanting, we stopped. Then he opened his eyes wider and said, "We must chant softly, because sometimes the neighbors are complaining."*

After singing, the Swami would give one of the boys a copy of Dr. Radhakrishnan's edition of *Bhagavad-gītā* to read aloud from. He would correct their mispronunciations and then explain each verse. Because there were only a few people present, there was always ample time for everyone to discuss the philosophy. The class would sometimes run an hour and a half and cover three or four verses.

Steve: *Swamiji mentioned that mangoes were the king of all fruits, and he even mentioned that they were not easily available in this country. It occurred to me that I could bring him mangoes. There was a store on First Avenue that always kept a stock of fresh mangoes in the cooler. I began a regular habit. Every day after getting off work, I would purchase one nice mango and bring it to Swamiji.*

Wally: *Some of the boys would say, "I'm doing this for the Swami." So I went to him and said, "Is there something I can do for you?" So he told me I could take notes in his class.*

The boys were sure that their service to Swamiji was spiritual, devotional service. By serving the spiritual master, who was a representative of Kṛṣṇa, you were serving Kṛṣṇa directly.

One morning Prabhupāda told Howard that he needed help in spreading the philosophy of Kṛṣṇa consciousness. Howard wanted to help, so he offered to type the Swami's manuscripts of *Śrīmad-Bhāgavatam.*

Howard: *The first words of the first verse read, "O the King." And naturally I wondered whether "O" was the king's name and "the king" stood in apposition. After some time I figured out that "O king" was intended instead. I didn't make the correction without his permission. "Yes," he said, "change it then." I began to point out a few changes and inform him that if he wanted I could make corrections, that I had a master's in English and taught last year at Ohio State. "Oh, yes," Swamiji said. "Do it. Put it nicely."*

He was giving them the idea of devotional service. "A devotee may not be perfect at first," he said, "but if he is engaged in service, once that service has begun he can be purified. Service is always there, in the material world or the spiritual." But service in the material world could not bring satisfaction to the self—only *bhakti,* purified service, service rendered to Kṛṣṇa, could do that. And the best way to serve Kṛṣṇa was to serve the representative of Kṛṣṇa.

They picked it up quickly. It was something you could do easily; it was not difficult like meditation—it was activity. You did something, but you did it for Kṛṣṇa. They had seen Swamiji respond to the Bowery bum who had come with a gift of toilet paper. "Just see," Swamiji had said, "he is not in order, but he thought, 'Let me give some service.'" But service had to be done voluntarily, out of love, not by force.

Wally: *Swamiji once asked me, "Do you think you could wear the Vaiṣṇava* tilaka *when you are on the streets?" I said, "Well, I would feel funny doing it, but if you want me to I will." And Swamiji said, "No, I don't ask you to do anything you don't want to do."*

Steve: *One day when I brought my daily mango to him he was in his room surrounded by devotees. I gave him my mango and sat down, and he said, "Very good boy." The way he said it, as if I were just a tiny little boy, made everyone in the room laugh, and I felt foolish. Swamiji, however, then changed their mood by saying, "No. This is actually love. This is Kṛṣṇa consciousness." And then they didn't laugh.*

When Howard first volunteered to do editing, he spent the whole morning working in Swamiji's room. "If there is any more typing," Howard said, "let me know. I could take it back to Mott Street and type there."

"More? There's lots more," Swamiji said. He opened the closet and pulled out two large bundles of manuscripts tied in saffron cloth. There were thousands of pages, single-spaced manuscripts of Prabhupāda's translations of the *Śrīmad-Bhāgavatam.* Howard stood before them, astonished. "It's a lifetime of typing," he said. And Prabhupāda smiled and said, "Oh, yes, many lifetimes."

* * *

Because of Prabhupāda's presence and the words that he spoke there and the *kīrtanas,* everyone was already referring to the storefront as "the temple." But still it was just a bare, squalid storefront. The inspiration to decorate the place came from the Mott Street boys.

Howard, Keith, and Wally devised a scheme to surprise the Swami when he came to the evening *kīrtana.* Wally removed the curtains from their apartment, took them to the laundromat (where they turned the water dark brown from filth), and then dyed them purple. The Mott Street apartment was decorated with posters, paintings, and large decorative silk hangings that Howard and Keith had brought back from India. The boys gathered up all their pictures, tapestries, incense burners, and other paraphernalia and took them, along with the purple curtains, to the storefront, where they began their day of decorating.

At the storefront the boys constructed a wooden platform for Prabhupāda to sit on and covered it with old velvet cloth. Behind the platform, on the rear wall between the two windows to the courtyard, they hung the purple curtains, flanked by a pair of orange ones. Against one orange panel, just above Swamiji's sitting place, they hung a large original painting of Rādhā and Kṛṣṇa on a circular canvas that James Greene had done. Prabhupāda had commissioned James, giving him the dust jacket from his *Śrīmad-Bhāgavatam,* with its crude Indian drawing, as a model. The figures of Rādhā and Kṛṣṇa were somewhat abstract, but the Lower East Side critics who frequented the storefront hailed the work as a wonderful achievement.

Keith and Howard were less confident that Prabhupāda would approve of their paintings and prints from India, so they hung them near the street side of the temple, away from Swamiji's seat. One of these prints, well known in India, was of Hanumān carrying a mountain through the sky to Lord Rāmacandra. The boys had no idea what kind of being Hanumān was. They thought perhaps he was a cat, because of the shape of his upper lip. Then there was the picture of a male person with six arms—two arms, painted greenish, held a bow and arrow; another pair, bluish, held a flute; and the third pair, golden, held a stick and bowl.

By late afternoon they had covered the sitting platform, hung the curtains, tacked up the decorative silks and prints and hung the paintings, and were decorating the dais with flowers and candlesticks. Someone brought a pillow for Swamiji to sit on and a faded cushion from an overstuffed chair for a backrest.

In addition to the Mott Street cache, Robert Nelson took one of his grandfather's Belgian-style Oriental rugs from his garage in the suburbs and brought it by subway to 26 Second Avenue. Even Raphael and Don took part in the decorating.

The secret was well kept, and the boys waited to see Swamiji's response. That night, when he walked in to begin the *kīrtana,* he looked at the newly decorated temple (there was even incense burning), and he raised his eyebrows in satisfaction. "You are advancing," he said as he looked around the room, smiling broadly. "Yes," he added, "this is Kṛṣṇa consciousness." His sudden, happy mood seemed almost like their reward for their earnest labors. He then stepped up onto the platform—while the boys held their breaths, hoping it would be sturdy—and he sat, looking out at the devotees and the decorations.

They had pleased him. But he now assumed a feature of extreme gravity, and though they knew he was certainly the same Swamiji, their titterings stuck in their throats, and their happy glances to each other suddenly abated in uncertainty and nervousness. As they regarded Swamiji's gravity, their joy of a few moments before seemed suddenly childish. As a cloud quickly covers the sun like a dark shade, Prabhupāda changed his mood from jolly to grave—and they spontaneously resolved to become equally grave and sober. He picked up the *karatālas* and again smiled a ray of appreciation, and their hearts beamed back.

The temple was still a tiny storefront, with many hidden and unhidden cockroaches, a tilted floor, and poor lighting. But because many of the decorations were from India, it had an authentic atmosphere, especially with Swamiji present on the dais. Now guests who entered were suddenly in a little Indian temple.

Mike Grant: *I came one evening, and all of a sudden there were carpets on the floor, pictures on the wall, and paintings. Just all of a sudden it had blossomed and was full of people. I was amazed how in just a matter of days people had brought so many wonderful things. When I came that evening and saw how it had been decorated, then I wasn't so much worried that he was going to make it. I thought it was really beginning to take hold now.*

Prabhupāda looked at his group of followers. He was moved by their offering him a seat of honor and their attempts at decorating Kṛṣṇa's storefront. To see a devotee make an offering to Kṛṣṇa was not new for him. But *this* was new. In New York, "this horrible place," the seed of *bhakti* was growing, and naturally, as the gardener of that tender sprout, he was touched by Kṛṣṇa's mercy. Glancing at the pictures on the wall he said, "Tomorrow I will come look at the pictures and tell you which are good."

The next day, Prabhupāda came down to appraise the new artwork on display. One framed watercolor painting was of a man playing a drum while a girl danced. "This one is all right," he said. But another painting of a woman was more mundane, and he said, "No, this painting is not so good." He walked to the back of the temple, followed anxiously by Howard, Keith, and Wally. When he came upon the painting of the six-armed person, he said, "Oh, this is very nice."

"Who is it?" Wally asked.

"This is Lord Caitanya," Prabhupāda replied.

"Why does He have six arms?"

"Because He showed Himself to be both Rāma and Kṛṣṇa. These are the arms of Rāma, and these are the arms of Kṛṣṇa."

"What are the other two arms?" Keith asked.

"Those are the arms of a *sannyāsī*."

He went to the next picture. "This is also very nice."

"Who is it?" Howard asked.

"This is Hanumān."

"Is he a cat?"

"No," Prabhupāda replied. "He is a monkey."

Hanumān is glorified in the scripture *Rāmāyaṇa* as the valiant, faithful servant of Lord Rāmacandra. Millions of Indians worship the incarnation of Lord Rāma and His servitor Hanumān, whose exploits are perennially exhibited in theater, cinema, art, and temple worship. In not knowing who Hanumān was, the Mott Street boys were no less ignorant than the old ladies uptown who, when Prabhupāda had asked whether any of them had seen a picture of Kṛṣṇa, had all stared blankly. The Lower East Side mystics didn't know Hanumān from a cat, and they had brought back from their hashish version of India a picture of Lord Caitanya Mahāprabhu without even knowing who He was. Yet there was an important difference between these boys and the ladies uptown: the boys were serving Swamiji and chanting Hare Kṛṣṇa. They were through with material life and the middle-class work-reward syndrome. Their hearts had awakened to Swamiji's promise of expanded Kṛṣṇa consciousness, and they sensed in his personal company something exalted. Like the Bowery bum who had donated toilet paper during Prabhupāda's lecture, the Lower East Side boys did not have their minds quite in order, and yet, as Prabhupāda saw it, Kṛṣṇa was guiding them from within their hearts. Prabhupāda knew they would change for the better by chanting and hearing about Kṛṣṇa.

*   *   *

The summer of 1966 moved into August, and Prabhupāda kept good health. For him these were happy days. New Yorkers complained of the summer heat waves, but this caused no inconvenience to one accustomed to the 100-degree-plus temperatures of Vṛndāvana's blazing summers. "It is like India," he said, as he went without a shirt, seeming relaxed and at home. He had thought that in America he would have to subsist on boiled potatoes (otherwise there would be nothing but meat), but here he was happily eating the same rice, *dāl,* and *capātīs,* and cooking on the same three-stacked cooker as in India. Work on the *Śrīmad-Bhāgavatam* had also gone on regularly since he had moved into the Second Avenue apartment. And now Kṛṣṇa was bringing these sincere young men who were cooking, typing, hearing him regularly, chanting Hare Kṛṣṇa, and asking for more.

Prabhupāda was still a solitary preacher, free to stay or go, writing his books in his own intimate relationship with Kṛṣṇa—quite independent of the boys in the storefront. But now he had taken the International Society for Krishna Consciousness as his spiritual child. The inquiring young men, some of whom had already been chanting steadily for over a month, were like stumbling spiritual infants, and he felt responsible for guiding them. They were beginning to consider him their spiritual master, trusting him to lead them into spiritual life. Although they were unable to immediately follow the multifarious rules that *brāhmaṇas* and Vaiṣṇavas in India followed, he was hopeful. According to Rūpa Gosvāmī the most important principle was that one should "somehow or other" become Kṛṣṇa conscious. People should chant Hare Kṛṣṇa and render devotional service. They should engage whatever they had in the service of Kṛṣṇa. And Prabhupāda was exercising this basic principle of Kṛṣṇa consciousness to the furthest limit the history of Vaiṣṇavism had ever seen.

Although he was engaging the boys in cooking and typing, Prabhupāda was not doing any less himself. Rather, for every sincere soul who came forward to ask for service, a hundred came who wanted not to serve but to challenge. Speaking to them, sometimes shouting and pounding his fists, Prabhupāda defended Kṛṣṇa against the Māyāvāda philosophy. This was also his service to Śrīla Bhaktisiddhānta Sarasvatī Ṭhākura. He had not come to America to retire. So with the passing of each new day came yet another confirmation that his work and his followers and his challengers would only increase.

How much he could do was up to Kṛṣṇa. "I am an old man," he said. "I may go away at any moment." But if he were to "go away" now, certainly Kṛṣṇa consciousness would also go away, because the Kṛṣṇa consciousness society was nothing but him: his figure leading the chanting while his head moved back and forth in small motions of ecstasy, his figure walking in and out of the temple through the courtyard or into the apartment, his person sitting down smilingly to discuss philosophy by the hour—he was the sole bearer and maintainer of the small, fragile, controlled atmosphere of Kṛṣṇa consciousness on New York's Lower East Side.

CHAPTER NINETEEN

Planting the Seed

"Does what you told us this morning," Howard asked, "mean we are supposed to accept the spiritual master to be God?"
"That means he is due the same respect as God, being God's representative," Prabhupāda replied calmly.
"Then he is not God?"
"No," Prabhupāda said, "God is God. The spiritual master is His representative. Therefore, he is as good as God because he can deliver God to the sincere disciple. Is that clear?"

—from dialogue with Hayagrīva

August 1966

IT WAS MAKESHIFT—a storefront-turned-temple and a two-room apartment transformed into the *guru's* residence and study—but it was complete nonetheless. It was a complete monastery amid the city slums. The temple (the storefront) was quickly becoming known among the hip underground of the Lower East Side; the courtyard was a strangely peaceful place for aspiring monks, with its little garden, bird sanctuary, and trees, squeezed in between the front and rear buildings; the Swami's back room was the inner sanctum of the monastery. Each room had a flavor all its own—or rather, it took on its particular character from the Swami's activities there.

The temple room was his *kīrtana* and lecture hall. The lecture was always serious and formal. Even from the beginning, when there was no dais and he had to sit on a straw mat facing a few guests, it was clear he was here to instruct, not to invite casual give-and-take dialogue. Questions had to wait until he finished speaking. The audience would sit on the floor and listen for forty-five minutes as he delivered the Vedic knowledge intact, always speaking on the basis of Vedic authority—quoting Sanskrit, quoting the previous spiritual masters, delivering perfect knowledge supported with reason and argument. While contending with noises of the street, he lectured with exacting scholarship and deeply committed devotion. It appeared that he had long ago mastered all the references and conclusions of his predecessors and had even come to anticipate all intellectual challenges.

He also held *kīrtanas* in the storefront. Like the lectures, the *kīrtanas* were serious, but they were not so formal; Prabhupāda was lenient during *kīrtana.* Visitors would bring harmoniums, wooden flutes, guitars, and they would follow the melody or create their own improvisations. Someone brought an old string bass and bow, and an inspired guest could always pick up the bow and play along. Some of the boys had found the innards of an upright piano, waiting on the curb with someone's garbage, and they had brought it to the temple and placed it near the entrance. During a *kīrtana,* freewheeling guests would run their hands over the wires, creating strange vibrations. Robert Nelson, several weeks back, had brought a large cymbal that now hung from the ceiling, dangling close by the Swami's dais.

But there was a limit to the extravagance. Sometimes when a newcomer picked up the *karatālas* and played them in a beat other than the standard one-two-*three,* Swamiji would ask one of the boys to correct him, even at the risk of offending the guest. Prabhupāda led the chanting and drummed with one hand on a small bongo. Even on this little bongo drum, he played Bengali *mṛdaṅga* rhythms so interesting that a local conga drummer used to come just to hear: "The Swami gets in some good licks."

The Swami's *kīrtanas* were a new high, and the boys would glance at each other with widening eyes and shaking heads as they responded to his chanting, comparing it to their previous drug experiences and signaling each other favorably: "This is great. It's better than LSD!" "Hey, man, I'm really getting high on this." And Prabhupāda encouraged their newfound intoxication.

As maestro of these *kīrtanas,* he was also acting expertly as *guru.* Lord Caitanya had said, "There are no hard-and-fast rules for chanting the holy name," and Prabhupāda brought the chanting to the Lower East Side just that way. "A kindergarten of spiritual life," he once called the temple. Here he taught the ABCs of Kṛṣṇa consciousness, lecturing from *Bhagavad-gītā* and leading the group chanting of Hare Kṛṣṇa. Sometimes, after the final *kīrtana* he would invite those who were interested to join him for further talks in his apartment.

In the back room of his apartment Prabhupāda was usually alone, especially in the early morning hours—two, three, and four A.M.—when almost no one else was awake. In these early hours his room was silent, and he worked alone in the intimacy of his relationship with Kṛṣṇa. He would sit on the floor behind his suitcase-desk, worshiping Kṛṣṇa by typing the translations and purports of his *Śrīmad-Bhāgavatam.*

But this same back room was also used for meetings, and anyone who brought himself to knock on the Swami's door could enter and speak with him at any time, face to face. Prabhupāda would sit back from his typewriter and give his time to talking, listening, answering questions, sometimes arguing or joking. A visitor might sit alone with him for half an hour before someone else would knock and Swamiji would invite the newcomer to join them. New guests would come and others would go, but Swamiji stayed and sat and talked.

Generally, visits were formal—his guests would ask philosophical questions, and he would answer, much the same as after a lecture in the storefront. But occasionally some of the boys who were becoming serious followers would monopolize his time—especially on Tuesday, Thursday, Saturday, and Sunday nights, when there was no evening lecture in the temple. Often they would ask him personal questions: What was it like when he first came to New York? What about India? Did he have followers there? Were his family members devotees of Kṛṣṇa? What was his spiritual master like? And then Prabhupāda would talk in a different way—quieter, more intimate and humorous.

He told how one morning in New York he had first seen snow and thought someone had whitewashed the buildings. He told how he had spoken at several churches in Butler, and when the boys asked what kind of churches they were he smiled and replied, "I don't know," and they laughed with him. He would reminisce freely about the British control of India and about Indian politics. He told them it was not so much Gandhi as Subhas Chandra Bose who had liberated India. Subhas Chandra Bose had gone outside of India and started the Indian National Army; he entered into an agreement with Hitler that Indian soldiers fighting for British India who surrendered to the Germans could be returned to the Indian National Army to fight against the British. And it was this show of force by Bose, more than Gandhi's nonviolence, which led to India's independence.

He talked of his childhood at the turn of the century, when street lamps were gas-lit, and carriages and horse-drawn trams were the only vehicles on Calcutta's dusty streets. These talks charmed the boys even more than the transcendental philosophy of *Bhagavad-gītā* and drew them affectionately to him. He told about his father, Gour Mohan De, a pure Vaiṣṇava. His father had been a cloth merchant, and his family had been intimately related with the aristocratic Mulliks of Calcutta. The Mulliks had a Deity of Kṛṣṇa, and Prabhupāda's father had given him a Deity to worship as a child. He used to imitate the worship of the Govinda Deity in the Mulliks' temple. As a boy, he had held his own Ratha-yātrā festivals each year, imitating in miniature the gigantic festival at Jagannātha Purī, and his father's friends used to joke: "Oh, the Ratha-yātrā ceremony is going on at your home, and you do not invite us? What is this?" His father would reply, "This is a child's play, that's all." But the neighbors said, "Oh, child's play? You are avoiding us by saying it's for children?"

Prabhupāda fondly remembered his father, who had never wanted him to be a worldly man, who had given him lessons in *mṛdaṅga,* and who had prayed to visiting *sādhus* that one day the boy would grow up to be a devotee of Rādhārāṇī.

One night he told how he had met his spiritual master. He told how he had begun his own chemical business but had left home and in 1959 had taken *sannyāsa*. The boys were interested, but so ignorant of the things Prabhupāda was talking about that at the mention of a word like *mṛdaṅga* or *sannyāsa* they would have to ask what it meant, and he would go on conversational tangents describing Indian spices, Indian drums, even

Indian women. And whatever he spoke about, he would eventually shine upon it the light of the *śāstra.* He did not ration out such talk, but gave it out abundantly by the hour, day after day, as long as there was a real, live inquirer.

At noon the front room became a dining hall and in the evenings a place of intimate worship. Prabhupāda had kept the room, with its twelve-foot-square hardwood parquet floor, clean and bare; the solitary coffee table against the wall between the two courtyard windows was the only furniture. Daily at noon a dozen men were now taking lunch here with him. The meal was cooked by Keith, who spent the whole morning in the kitchen.

At first Keith had cooked only for the Swami. He had mastered the art of cooking *dāl,* rice, and *sabjī* in the Swami's three-tiered boiler, and usually there had been enough for one or two guests as well. But soon more guests had begun to gather, and Prabhupāda had told Keith to increase the quantity (abandoning the small three-tiered cooker) until he was cooking for a dozen hungry men. The boarders, Raphael and Don, though not so interested in the Swami's talk, would arrive punctually each day for *prasādam,* usually with a friend or two who had wandered into the storefront. Steve would drop by from his job at the welfare office. The Mott Street group would come. And there were others.

The kitchen was stocked with standard Indian spices: fresh chilies, fresh ginger root, whole cumin seeds, turmeric, and asafetida. Keith mastered the basic cooking techniques and passed them on to Chuck, who became his assistant. Some of the other boys would stand at the doorway of the narrow kitchenette to watch Keith, as one thick, pancakelike *capātī* after another blew up like an inflated football over the open flame and then took its place in the steaming stack.

While the fine basmati rice boiled to a moist, fluffy-white finish and the *sabjī* simmered, the noon cooking would climax with "the *chaunce.*" Keith prepared the *chaunce* exactly as Swamiji had shown him. Over the flame he set a small metal cup, half-filled with clarified butter, and then put in cumin seeds. When the seeds turned almost black he added chilies, and as the chilies blackened, a choking smoke began to pour from the cup. Now the *chaunce* was ready. With his cook's tongs, Keith lifted the cup, its boiling, crackling mixture fuming like a sorcerer's kettle, and brought it to the edge of the pot of boiling *dāl.* He opened the tight cover slightly, dumped the boiling *chaunce* into the *dāl* with a flick of his wrist, and immediately replaced the lid. ... POW! The meeting of the *chaunce* and *dāl* created an explosion, which was then greeted by cheers from the doorway, signifying that the cooking was now complete. This final operation was so volatile that it once blew the top of the pot to the ceiling with a loud smash, causing minor burns to Keith's hand. Some of the neighbors complained of acrid, penetrating fumes. But the devotees loved it.

When lunch was ready, Swamiji would wash his hands and mouth in the bathroom and come out into the front room, his soft, pink-bottomed feet always bare, his saffron *dhotī* reaching down to his ankles. He would stand by the coffee table, which held the picture of Lord Caitanya and His associates, while his own associates stood around him against the walls. Keith would bring in a big tray of *capātīs,* stacked by the dozens, and place it on the floor before the altar table along with pots of rice, *dāl,* and *sabjī.* Swamiji would then recite the Bengali prayer for offering food to the Lord, and all present would follow him by bowing down, knees and head to the floor, and approximating the Bengali prayer one word at a time. While the steam and mixed aromas drifted up like an offering of incense before the picture of Lord Caitanya, the Swami's followers bowed their heads to the wooden floor and mumbled the prayer.

Prabhupāda then sat with his friends, eating the same *prasādam* as they, with the addition of a banana and a metal bowl full of hot milk. He would slice the banana by pushing it downward against the edge of the bowl, letting the slices fall into the hot milk.

Prabhupāda's open decree that everyone should eat as much *prasādam* as possible created a humorous mood and a family feeling. No one was allowed simply to sit, picking at his food, nibbling politely. They ate with a gusto Swamiji almost insisted upon. If he saw someone not eating heartily, he would call the person's name and smilingly protest, "Why are you not eating? Take *prasādam.*" And he would laugh. "When I was coming to your country on the boat," he said, "I thought, 'How will the Americans ever eat this food?' " And as the boys pushed their plates forward for more, Keith would serve seconds—more rice, *dāl, capātīs,* and *sabjī.*

After all, it was spiritual. You were supposed to eat a lot. It would purify you. It would free you from *māyā.* Besides, it was good, delicious, spicy. This was better than American food. It was like chanting. It was far out. You got high from eating this food.

They ate with the right hand, Indian style. Keith and Howard had already learned this and had even tasted similar dishes, but as they told the Swami and a room full of believers, the food in India had never been this good.

One boy, Stanley, was quite young, and Prabhupāda, almost like a doting father, watched over him as he ate. Stanley's mother had personally met Prabhupāda and said that only if he took personal care of her son would she allow him to live in the monastery. Prabhupāda complied. He diligently encouraged the boy until Stanley gradually took on a voracious appetite and began consuming ten *capātīs* at a sitting (and would have taken more had Swamiji not told him to stop). But aside from Swamiji's limiting Stanley to ten *capātīs,* the word was always "More ... take more." When Prabhupāda was finished, he would rise and leave the room, Keith would catch a couple of volunteers to help him clean, and the others would leave.

Occasionally, on a Sunday, Prabhupāda himself would cook a feast with special Indian dishes.

Steve: *Swamiji personally cooked the* prasādam *and then served it to us upstairs in his front room. We all sat in rows, and I remember him walking up and down in between the rows of boys, passing before us with his bare feet and serving us with a spoon from different pots. He would ask what did we want—did we want more of* this? *And he would serve us with pleasure. These dishes were not ordinary, but sweets and savories—like sweet rice and* kacaurīs—*with special tastes. Even after we had all taken a full plate, he would come back and ask us to take more.*

Once he came up to me and asked what I would like more of—would I like some more sweet rice? In my early misconception of spiritual life, I thought I should deny myself what I liked best, so I asked for some more plain rice. But even that "plain" rice was fancy yellow rice with fried cheese balls.

On off nights his apartment was quiet. He might remain alone for the whole evening, typing and translating *Śrīmad-Bhāgavatam,* or talking in a relaxed atmosphere to just one or two guests until ten. But on meeting nights—Monday, Wednesday, and Friday—there was activity in every room of his apartment. He wasn't alone anymore. His new followers were helping him, and they shared in his spirit of trying to get people to chant Hare Kṛṣṇa and hear of Kṛṣṇa consciousness.

In the back room, he worked on his translation of the *Bhāgavatam* or spoke with guests up until six, when he would go to take his bath. Sometimes he would have to wait until the bathroom was free. He had introduced his young followers to the practice of taking two baths a day, and now he was sometimes inconvenienced by having to share his bathroom.

After his bath he would come into the front room, where his assembled followers would sit around him. He would sit on a mat facing his picture of the Pañca-tattva, and after putting a few drops of water in his left palm from a small metal spoon and bowl, he would rub a lump of Vṛndāvana clay in the water, making a wet paste. He would then apply the clay markings of Vaiṣṇava *tilaka,* dipping into the yellowish paste in his left hand with the ring finger of his right. He would scrape wet clay from his palm, and while looking into a small mirror which he held deftly between the thumb and pinkie of his left hand, he would mark a vertical clay strip up his forehead and then trim the clay into two parallel lines by placing the little finger of his right hand between his eyebrows and running it upward past the hairline, clearing a path in the still-moist clay. Then he marked eleven other places on his body, while the boys sat observing, sometimes asking questions or sometimes speaking their own understandings of Kṛṣṇa consciousness.

Prabhupāda: *My Guru Mahārāja used to put on* tilaka *without a mirror.*

Devotee: *Did it come out neat?*

Prabhupāda: *Neat or not neat, that does not matter. Yes, it was also neat.*

Prabhupāda would then silently recite the Gāyatrī *mantra.* Holding his *brāhmaṇa's* sacred thread and looping it around his right thumb, he would sit erect, silently moving his lips. His bare shoulders and arms were quite thin as was his chest, but he had a round, slightly protruding belly. His complexion was as satiny smooth as a young boy's, except for his face, which bore signs of age. The movements of his hands were methodical, aristocratic, yet delicate.

He picked up two brass bells in his left hand and began ringing them. Then, lighting two sticks of incense from the candle near the picture of

Lord Caitanya and His associates, he began waving the incense slowly in small circles before Lord Caitanya, while still ringing the bells. He looked deeply at the picture and continued cutting spirals of fragrant smoke, all the while ringing the bells. None of the boys knew what he was doing, although he did it every evening. But it was a ceremony. It meant something. The boys began to call the ceremony "bells."

After bells Monday, Wednesday, and Friday, it would usually be time for the evening *kīrtana*. Some of the devotees would already be downstairs greeting guests and explaining about the Swami and the chanting. But without the Swami, nothing could begin. No one knew how to sing or drum, and no one dared think of leading the *mantra*-chanting without him. Only when he entered at seven o'clock could they begin.

Freshly showered and dressed in his clean Indian handwoven cloth, his arms and body decorated with the arrowlike Vaiṣṇava markings, Prabhupāda would leave his apartment and go downstairs to face another ecstatic opportunity to glorify Kṛṣṇa. The tiny temple would be crowded with wild, unbrahminical, candid young Americans.

* * *

Don was a test of Swamiji's tolerance. He had lived in the storefront for months, working little and not trying to change his habits. He had a remarkable speech affectation: instead of talking, he *enunciated* his words, as if he were reciting them from a book. And he never used contractions. It wasn't that he was intellectual, just that somehow he had developed a plan to abolish his natural dialect. Don's speech struck people as bizarre, like it might be the result of too many drugs. It gave him the air of being not an ordinary being. And he continuously took marijuana, even after Swamiji had asked those who lived with him not to. Sometimes during the day his girlfriend would join him in the storefront, and they would sit together talking intimately and sometimes kissing. But he liked the Swami. He even gave some money once. He liked living in the storefront, and Swamiji didn't complain.

But others did. One day an interested newcomer dropped by the storefront and found Don alone, surrounded by the sharp aroma of marijuana. "You been smoking pot? But the Swami doesn't want anyone smoking here." Don denied it: "I have not been smoking. You are not speaking the truth." The boy then reached in Don's shirt pocket and pulled out a joint, and Don hit him in the face. Several of the boys found out. They weren't sure what was right: What would the Swami do? What do you do if someone smokes pot? Even though a devotee was not supposed to, could it be allowed sometimes? They put the matter before Swamiji.

Prabhupāda took it very seriously, and he was upset, especially about the violence. "He hit you?" he asked the boy. "I will go down myself and kick him in the head." But then Prabhupāda thought about it and said that Don should be asked to leave. But Don had already left.

The next morning during Swamiji's class, Don appeared at the front door. From his dais, Swamiji looked out at Don with great concern. But his first concern was for ISKCON: "Ask him," Prabhupāda requested Roy, who sat nearby, "if he has marijuana—then he cannot come in. Our society ..." Prabhupāda was like an anxious father, afraid for the life of his infant ISKCON. Roy went to the door and told Don he would have to give up his drugs if he entered. And Don walked away.

Raphael was not interested in spiritual discipline. He was a tall young man with long, straight, brown hair who, like Don, tried to stay aloof and casual toward Swamiji. When Prabhupāda introduced *japa* and encouraged the boys to chant during the day, Raphael didn't go for it. He said he liked a good *kīrtana,* but he wouldn't chant on beads.

One time Swamiji was locked out of his apartment, and the boys had to break the lock. Swamiji asked Raphael to replace it. Days went by. Raphael could sit in the storefront reading Rimbaud, he could wander around town, but he couldn't find time to fix the lock. One evening he dropped by the Swami's apartment, opened the lockless door, and made his way to the back room, where some boys were sitting, listening to Swamiji speak informally about Kṛṣṇa consciousness. Suddenly Raphael spoke up, expressing his doubts and revealing his distracted mind. "As for me," he said, "I don't know what's happening. I don't know whether a brass band is playing or what the heck is going on." Some of the devotees tensed; he had interrupted their devotional mood. "Raphael is very candid," Swamiji replied, smiling, as if to explain his son's behavior to the others.

Raphael finally fixed the lock, but one day after a lecture he approached the Swami, stood beside the dais, and spoke up, exasperated, impatient: "I am not meant to sit in a temple and chant on beads! My father was a boxer. I am meant to run on the beach and breathe in big breaths of air. ..." Raphael went on, gesticulating and voicing his familiar complaints—things he would rather do than take up Kṛṣṇa consciousness. Suddenly Prabhupāda interrupted him in a loud voice: "Then do it! Do it!" Raphael shrank away, but he stayed.

Bill Epstein took pride in his relationship with the Swami—it was honest. Although he helped the Swami by telling people about him and sending them up to see him in his apartment, he felt the Swami knew he'd never become a serious follower. Nor did Bill ever mislead himself into thinking he would ever be serious. But Prabhupāda wasn't content with Bill's take-it-or-leave-it attitude. When Bill would finally show up at the storefront again after spending some days at a friend's place, only to fall asleep with a blanket wrapped over his head during the lecture, Prabhupāda would just start shouting so loud that Bill couldn't sleep. Sometimes Bill would ask a challenging question, and Prabhupāda would answer and then say, "Are you satisfied?" and Bill would look up dreamily and answer, "No!" Then Prabhupāda would answer it again more fully and say louder, "Are you satisfied?" and again Bill would say no. This would go on until Bill would have to give in: "Yes, yes, I am satisfied."

But Bill was the first person to get up and dance during a *kīrtana* in the storefront. Some of the other boys thought he looked like he was dancing in an egotistical, narcissistic way, even though his arms were outstretched in a facsimile of the pictures of Lord Caitanya. But when Swamiji saw Bill dancing like that, he looked at Bill with wide-open eyes and feelingly expressed appreciation: "Bill is dancing just like Lord Caitanya."

Bill sometimes returned from his wanderings with money, and although it was not very much, he would give it to Swamiji. He liked to sleep at the storefront and spend the day on the street, returning for lunch or *kīrtanas* or a place to sleep. He used to leave in the morning and go looking for cigarettes on the ground. To Bill, the Swami was part of the hip movement and had thus earned a place of respect in his eyes as a genuine person. Bill objected when the boys introduced signs of reverential worship toward the Swami (starting with their giving him an elevated seat in the temple), and as the boys who lived with the Swami gradually began to show enthusiasm, competition, and even rivalry among themselves, Bill turned from it in disgust. He allowed that he would go on just helping the Swami in his own way, and he knew that the Swami appreciated whatever he did. So he wanted to leave it at that.

Carl Yeargens had helped Prabhupāda in times of need. He had helped with the legal work of incorporating ISKCON, signed the ISKCON charter as a trustee, and even opened his home to Swamiji when David had driven him from the Bowery loft. But those days when he and Eva had shared their apartment with him had created a tension that had never left. He liked the Swami, he respected him as a genuine *sannyāsī* from India, but he didn't accept the conclusions of the philosophy. The talk about Kṛṣṇa and the soul was fine, but the idea of giving up drugs and sex was carrying it a little too far. Now Prabhupāda was settled in his new place, and Carl decided that he had done his part to help and was no longer needed. Although he had helped Prabhupāda incorporate his International Society for Krishna Consciousness, he didn't want to join it.

Carl found the Second Avenue *kīrtanas* too public, not like the more intimate atmosphere he had enjoyed with the Swami on the Bowery. Now the audiences were larger, and there was an element of wild letting loose that they had never had on the Bowery. Like some of the other old associates, Carl felt sheepish and reluctant to join in. In comparison to the Second Avenue street scene, the old meetings in the fourth-floor Bowery loft had seemed more mystical, like secluded meditations.

Carol Bekar also preferred a more sedate *kīrtana*. She thought people were trying to take out their personal frustrations by the wild singing and dancing. The few times she did attend evening *kīrtanas* on Second Avenue were "tense moments." One time a group of teenagers had come into the storefront mocking and shouting, "Hey! What the hell is this!"

She kept thinking that at any moment a rock was going to come crashing through the big window. And anyway, her boyfriend wasn't interested.

James Greene felt embarrassed. He saw that most of the new men were making a serious commitment to the Swami, whereas he could not. He had no bad feeling toward the Swami and his new movement, but he preferred to live alone.

Robert Nelson, Prabhupāda's old uptown friend, never deviated in his good feelings for Prabhupāda, but he always went along in his own natural way and never adopted any serious disciplines. Somehow, almost all of those who had helped Prabhupāda uptown and on the Bowery did not want to go further once he began a spiritual organization, which happened almost immediately after he moved into 26 Second Avenue. New people were coming forward to assist him, and Carl, James, Carol, and others like them felt that they were being replaced and that their obligation toward the Swami was ending. It was a kind of changing of the guard. Although the members of the old guard were still his well-wishers, they began to drift away.

* * *

Bruce Scharf had just graduated from New York University and was applying for a job. One day an ex-roommate told him about the Swami he had visited down on Second Avenue. "They sing there," his friend said, "and they have this far-out thing where they have some dancing. And Allen Ginsberg was there." The Swami was difficult to understand, his friend explained, and besides that, his followers recorded his talks on a tape recorder. "Why should he have a big tape recorder? That's not very spiritual." But Bruce became interested.

He was already a devotee of Indian culture. Four years ago, when he was barely twenty, Bruce had worked during the summer as a steward aboard an American freighter and gone to India, where he had visited temples, bought pictures of Śiva and Gaṇeśa and books on Gandhi, and felt as if he were part of the culture. When he returned to N.Y.U., he read more about India and wrote a paper on Gandhi for his history course. He would eat in Indian restaurants and attend Indian films and music recitals, and he was reading the *Bhagavad-gītā*. He had even given up eating meat. He had plans of returning to India, taking some advanced college courses, and then coming back to America to teach Eastern religions. But in the meantime he was experimenting with LSD.

Chuck Barnett was eighteen years old. His divorced mother had recently moved to Greenwich Village, where she was studying psychology at N.Y.U. Chuck had moved out of his mother's apartment to one on Twelfth Street on the Lower East Side, in the neighborhood of Allen Ginsberg and other hip poets and musicians. He was a progressive jazz flutist who worked with several professional groups in the city. He had been practicing *haṭha-yoga* for six years and had recently been experimenting with LSD. He would have visions of lotuses and concentric circles, but after coming down, he would become more involved than ever in sensuality. A close friend of Chuck's had suddenly gone homosexual that summer, leaving Chuck disgusted and cynical. Someone told Chuck that an Indian swami was staying downtown on Second Avenue, and so he came one day in August to the window of the former Matchless Gifts store.

Steve Guarino, the son of a New York fireman, had grown up in the city and graduated from Brooklyn College in 1961. Influenced by his father, he had gone into the Navy, where he had tolerated two years of military routine, always waiting for the day he would be free to join his friends on the Lower East Side. Finally, a few months after the death of President Kennedy, he had been honorably discharged. Without so much as paying a visit to his parents, he had headed straight for the Lower East Side, which by then appeared vividly within his mind to be the most mystical place in the world. He was writing stories and short novels under the literary influence of Franz Kafka and others, and he began to take LSD "to search and experiment with consciousness." *A Love Supreme,* a record by John Coltrane, the jazz musician, encouraged Steve to think that God actually existed. Just to make enough money to live, Steve had taken a job with the welfare office. One afternoon during his lunch hour, while walking down Second Avenue, he saw that the Matchless Gifts store had a small piece of paper in the window, announcing, "Lectures in Bhagavad Gita, A. C. Bhaktivedanta Swami."

Chuck: *I finally found Second Avenue and First Street, and I saw through the window that there was some chanting going on inside and some people were sitting up against the wall. Beside me on the sidewalk some middle-class people were looking in and giggling. I turned to them, and with my palms folded I asked, "Is this where a swami is?" They giggled and said, "Pilgrim, your search has ended." I wasn't surprised by this answer, because I felt it was the truth.*

Bruce and Chuck, unknown to one another, lived only two blocks apart. After the suggestion from his friend, Bruce also made his way to the storefront.

Bruce: *I was looking for Hare Kṛṣṇa. I had left my apartment and had walked over to Avenue B when I decided to walk all the way down to Houston Street. When I came to First Street, I turned right and then, walking along First Street, came to Second Avenue. All along First Street I was seeing these Puerto Rican grocery stores, and then there was one of those churches where everyone was standing up, singing loudly, and playing tambourines. Then, as I walked further along First Street, I had the feeling that I was leaving the world, like when you're going to the airport to catch a plane. I thought, "Now I'm leaving a part of me behind, and I'm going to something new."*

But when I got over to Second Avenue, I couldn't find Hare Kṛṣṇa. There was a gas station, and then I walked past a little storefront, but the only sign was one that said Matchless Gifts. Then I walked back again past the store, and in the window I saw a black-and-white sign announcing a Bhagavad-gītā *lecture. I entered the storefront and saw a pile of shoes there, so I took off my shoes and came in and sat down near the back.*

Steve: *I had a feeling that this was a group that was already established and had been meeting for a while. I came in and sat down on the floor, and a boy who said his name was Roy was very courteous and friendly to me. He seemed to be one who had already experienced the meetings. He asked me my name, and I felt at ease.*

Suddenly the Swami entered, coming through the side door. He was wearing a saffron dhotī *but no shirt, just a piece of cloth like a long sash, tied in a knot across his right shoulder and leaving his arms, his left shoulder, and part of his chest bare. When I saw him I thought of the Buddha.*

Bruce: *There were about fifteen people sitting on the floor. One man with a big beard sat up by the front on the right-hand side, leaning up against the wall. After some time the door on the opposite side opened, and in walked the Swami. When he came in, he turned his head to see who was in his audience. And then he stared right at me. Our eyes met. It was as if he were studying me. In my mind it was like a photograph was being taken of Swamiji looking at me for the first time. There was a pause. Then he very gracefully got up on the dais and sat down and took out a pair of hand cymbals and began a* kīrtana. *The* kīrtana *was the thing that most affected me. It was the best music I'd ever heard. And it had meaning. You could actually concentrate on it, and it gave you some joy to repeat the words "Hare Kṛṣṇa." I immediately accepted it as a spiritual practice.*

Chuck: *I entered the storefront, and sitting on a grass mat on the hard floor was a person who seemed at first to be neither male nor female, but when he looked at me I couldn't even look him straight in the eyes, they were so brilliant and glistening. His skin was golden with rosy cheeks, and he had large ears that framed his face. He had three strands of beads—one which was at his neck, one a little longer, and the other down on his chest. He had a long forehead, which rose above his shining eyes, and there were many furrows in his brow. His arms were slender and long. His mouth was rich and full, and very dark and red and smiling, and his teeth were brighter than his eyes. He sat in a cross-legged position that I had never seen before in any* yoga *book and had never seen any* yogī *perform. It was a sitting posture, but his right foot was crossed over the thigh and brought back beside his left hip, and one knee rested on the other directly in front of him. His every expression and gesture was different from those of any other personality I had ever seen, and I sensed that they had meanings that I did not know, from a culture and a mood that were completely beyond this world. There was a mole on his side and a peculiar callus on his ankle, a round callus similar to what a karate expert develops on his knuckle. He was dressed in unhemmed cloth, dyed saffron. Everything about him was exotic, and his whole effulgence made him seem to be not even sitting in the room but projected from some other place. He was so brilliant in color that it was like a technicolor movie, and yet he was right there. I heard him speaking. He was sitting right there before me, yet it seemed that if I reached out to touch him he wouldn't be there. At the same time, seeing him was not an abstract or subtle experience but a most intense presence.*

After their first visit to the storefront, Chuck, Steve, and Bruce each got an opportunity to see the Swami upstairs in his apartment.

Steve: *I was on my lunch hour and had to be back in the office very soon. I was dressed in a summer business suit. I had planned it so that I had just enough time to go to the storefront and buy some books, then go to lunch and return to work. At the storefront, one of the Swami's followers said that I could go up and see the Swami. I went upstairs to his apartment and found him at his sitting place with a few boys. I must have interrupted what he was saying, but I asked him if I could purchase the three volumes of the* Śrīmad-Bhāgavatam. *One of the devotees produced the books from the closet opposite Prabhupāda's seat. I handled the books—they were a very special color not usually seen in America, a reddish natural earth, like a brick—and I asked him how much they cost. Six dollars each, he said. I took twenty dollars out of my wallet and gave it to him. He seemed the only one to ask about the price of the books or give the money to, because none of the others came forward to represent him. They were just sitting back and listening to him speak.*

"These books are commentaries on the scriptures?" I asked, trying to show that I knew something about books. Swamiji said yes, they were his commentaries. Sitting, smiling, at ease, Swamiji was very attractive. He seemed very strong and healthy. When he smiled, all his teeth were beautiful, and his nostrils flared aristocratically. His face was full and powerful. He was wearing an Indian cloth robe, and as he sat cross-legged, his smooth-skinned legs were partly exposed. He wore no shirt, but the upper part of his body was wrapped with an Indian cloth shawl. His limbs were quite slender, but he had a protruding belly.

When I saw that Swamiji was having to personally handle the sale of books, I did not want to bother him. I quickly asked him to please keep the change from my twenty dollars. I took the three volumes without any bag or wrapping and was standing, preparing to leave, when Swamiji said, "Sit down," and gestured that I should sit opposite him like the others. He had said "Sit down" in a different tone of voice. It was a heavy tone and indicated that now the sale of the books was completed and I should sit with the others and listen to him speak. He was offering me an important invitation to become like one of the others, who I knew spent many hours with him during the day when I was usually at my job and not able to come. I envied their leisure in being able to learn so much from him and sit and talk intimately with him. By ending the sales transaction and asking me to sit, he assumed that I was in need of listening to him and that I had nothing better in the world to do than to stop everything else and hear him. But I was expected back at the office. I didn't want to argue, but I couldn't possibly stay. "I'm sorry, I have to go," I said definitely. "I'm only on my lunch hour." As I said this, I had already started to move for the door, and Swamiji responded by suddenly breaking into a wide smile and looking very charming and very happy. He seemed to appreciate that I was a working man, a young man on the go. I had not come by simply because I was unemployed and had nowhere to go and nothing to do. Approving of my energetic demeanor, he allowed me to take my leave.

Chuck: *One of the devotees in the storefront invited me upstairs to see the Swami in private. I was led out of the storefront into a hallway and suddenly into a beautiful little garden with a picnic table, a birdbath, a birdhouse, and flower beds. After we passed through the garden, we came to a middle-class apartment building. We walked up the stairs and entered an apartment which was absolutely bare of any furniture—just white walls and a parquet floor. He led me through the front room and into another room, and there was the Swami, sitting in that same majestic spiritual presence on a thin cotton mat, which was covered by a cloth with little elephants printed on it, and leaning back on a pillow which stood against the wall.*

One night Bruce walked home with Wally, and he told Wally about his interest in going to India and becoming a professor of Oriental literature. "Why go to India?" Wally asked. "India has come here. Swamiji is teaching us these authentic things. Why go to India?" Bruce thought Wally made sense, so he resolved to give up his long-cherished idea of going to India, at least as long as he could go on visiting the Swami.

Bruce: *I decided to go and speak personally to Swamiji, so I went to the storefront. I found out that he lived in an apartment in the rear building. A boy told me the number and said I could just go and speak with the Swami. He said, "Yes, just go." So I walked through the storefront, and there was a little courtyard where some plants were growing. Usually in New York there is no courtyard, nothing green, but this was very attractive. And in that courtyard there was a boy typing at a picnic table, and he looked very spiritual and dedicated. I hurried upstairs and rang the bell for apartment number 2C. After a little while the door opened, and it was the Swami. "Yes," he said. And I said, "I would like to speak with you." He opened the door wider and stepped back and said, "Yes, come." We went inside together into his sitting room and sat down facing each other. He sat behind his metal trunk-desk on a very thin mat which was covered with a woolen blanketlike cover that had frazzled ends and elephants decorating it. He asked me my name and I told him it was Bruce. And then he remarked, "Ah. In India, during the British period, there was one Lord Bruce." And he said something about Lord Bruce being a general and engaging in some campaigns.*

I felt that I had to talk to the Swami—to tell him my story—and I actually found him interested to listen. It was very intimate, sitting with him in his apartment, and he was actually wanting to hear about me.

While we were talking, he looked up past me, high up on the wall behind me, and he was talking about Lord Caitanya. The way he looked up, he was obviously looking at some picture or something, but with an expression of deep love in his eyes. I turned around to see what made him look like that. Then I saw the picture in the brown frame: Lord Caitanya dancing in kīrtana.

Inevitably, meeting with Prabhupāda meant a philosophical discussion.

Chuck: *I asked him, "Can you teach me* rāja-yoga*?" "Oh," he said. "Here is* Bhagavad-gītā.*" He handed me a copy of the* Gītā. *"Turn to the last verse of the Sixth Chapter," he said, "and read." I read the translation out loud. "And of all* yogīs, *he who is worshiping Me with faith and* *devotion I consider to be the best." I could not comprehend what "faith" and "devotion" meant, so I said, "Sometimes I'm getting some light in my forehead." "That is hallucination!" he said. So abruptly he said it—although he did not strain his person, the words came at me so intensely that it completely shocked me. "*Rāja *means 'king'—king* yoga," *he said, "but this is* emperor yoga."

I knew that he had attained such a high state not by using chemicals from a laboratory or by any Western speculative process, and this was certainly what I wanted. "Are you giving classes?" I asked. He said, "Yes, if you come at six in the morning I am giving classes in the Gītā. *And bring some flower or fruit for the Deity." I looked into the adjoining room, which was bare with a wooden parquet floor, bare walls, and a tiny table, and on the table was a picture of five humanlike figures with their arms raised above their heads. Somehow, their arms and faces were not like any mortal that I'd ever seen. I knew that the picture was looking at me.*

When I came out on the street in front of the storefront there were a few people standing around, and I said, "I don't think I'm going to take LSD anymore." I said it out loud to myself, but some other people heard me.

Steve: *I wanted to show my appreciation for spiritual India, so I presented to Swamiji that I had read the autobiography of Gandhi. "It was glorious," I said. "What is glorious about it?" Swamiji challenged.*

When he asked this, there were others present in the room. Although I was a guest, he had no qualms about challenging me for having said something foolish. I searched through my remembrances of Gandhi's autobiography to answer his challenging question, "What is glorious?" I began to relate that one time Gandhi, as a child, although raised as a vegetarian, was induced by some of his friends to eat meat, and that night he felt that a lamb was howling in his belly. Swamiji dismissed this at once, saying, "Most of India is vegetarian. That is not glorious." I couldn't think of anything else glorious to say, and Swamiji said, "His autobiography is called Experiments with Truth. *But that is not the nature of truth. It is not to be found by someone's experimenting. Truth is always truth."*

Although it was a blow to my ego, being exposed and defeated by Swamiji seemed to be a gain for me. I wanted to bring before him many different things for his judgment, just to see what he had to say about them. I showed him the paperback edition of the Bhagavad-gītā *that I was reading and carrying in my back pocket. He perused the back cover. There was a reference to "the eternal faith of the Hindus," and Swamiji began to take the phrase apart. He explained how the word* Hindu *was a misnomer and does not occur anywhere in the Sanskrit literature itself. He also explained that Hinduism and Hindu beliefs were not eternal.*

Bruce: *After I talked about my desire for religious life, I began telling him about a conflict I had had with one of my professors in English literature. He was a Freudian, so he would explain the characters in all the novels and so on in a Freudian context and with Freudian terminology. Everything was sexual—the mother for the son, this one for that one, and so on. But I would always see it in terms of a religious essence. I would see it in terms of a religious impulse, or some desire to understand God. I would write my papers in that context, and he would always say, "The religious can also be interpreted as Freudian." So I didn't do very well in the course. I was mentioning this to the Swami, and he said, "Your professor is correct." I was surprised—I am going to an Indian swami, and he is saying that the professor was correct, that everything is based on sex and not religion! This kind of pulled the rug out from under me when he said that. Then he qualified what he'd said. He explained that in the material world everyone is operating on the basis of sex; everything that everyone is doing is being driven by the sex impulse. "So," he said, "Freud is correct. Everything is on the basis of sex." Then he clarified what material life is and what spiritual life is. In spiritual life, there is a complete absence of sex desire. So this had a profound effect on me.*

He wasn't confirming my old sentimental ideas, but he was giving me new ideas. He was giving me his instructions, and I had to accept them. Talking to the Swami was very nice. I found him completely natural, and I found him to be very artistic. The way he held his head, the way he enunciated his words—very dignified, very gentlemanly.

The boys found Swamiji not only philosophical, but personal also.

Steve: *A few nights later, I went to see the Swami and told him I was reading his book. One thing that had especially caught my attention was a section where the author of* Śrīmad-Bhāgavatam, *Vyāsadeva, was admitting that he was feeling despondent. Then his spiritual master, Nārada, explained that his despondency had come because although he had written so many books, he had neglected to write in such a way as to fully glorify Kṛṣṇa. After hearing this, Vyāsadeva compiled the* Śrīmad-Bhāgavatam.

When I read this, I identified with the fact that Vyāsadeva was a writer, because I considered myself a writer also, and I knew that I was also despondent. "This was very interesting about the author, Vyāsadeva," I said. "He wrote so many books, but still he was not satisfied, because he had not directly praised Kṛṣṇa." Although I had very little understanding of Kṛṣṇa consciousness, Swamiji opened his eyes very wide, surprised that I was speaking on such an elevated subject from the Śrīmad-Bhāgavatam. *He seemed pleased.*

Chuck: *I had come by in the afternoon, and Swamiji had given me a plate of* prasādam. *So I was eating, and a chili burned my mouth. Swamiji said, "Is it too hot?" "Yes," I said. So he brought me a tiny teacup with some milk, and then he took some rice off my plate and took a piece of banana and crushed it all up together with his fingers and said, "Here, eat this. It will kill the action of the chilies."*

Bruce: *There wasn't anything superficial about him, nor was he ever contrived, trying to make some impression. He was just completely himself. In the Swami's room there was no furniture, so we sat on the floor. And I found this to be very attractive and simple. Everything was so authentic about him. Uptown at another swami's place we had sat on big, stuffed living room chairs, and the place had been lavishly furnished. But here was the downtown swami, wearing simple cloth robes. He had no business suit on—he wasn't covering up a business suit with those saffron robes. And he wasn't affected, as the other swami was. So I found myself asking him if I could be his student, and he said yes. I was very happy, because he was so different from the other swami. With the uptown swami I was wanting to become his student because I wanted to get something from him—I wanted to get knowledge. It was selfishly motivated. But here I was actually emotionally involved. I was feeling that I wanted to become the Swami's student. I actually wanted to give myself, because I thought he was great and what he was giving was pure and pristine and wonderful. It was a soothing balm for the horrible city life. Uptown I had felt like a stranger.*

On one occasion, our conversation turned to my previous trip to India in 1962, and I began talking about how much it meant to me, how much it moved me. I even mentioned that I had made a girlfriend there. So we got to talking about that, and I told him that I had her picture—I was carrying the girl's picture in my wallet. So Swamiji asked to see. I took out the picture, and Swamiji looked at it and made a sour face and said, "Oh, she is not pretty. Girls in India are more beautiful than that." Hearing that from the Swami just killed any attachment I had for that girl. I felt ashamed that I had an interest in a girl that the Swami did not consider pretty. I don't think I ever looked at the photograph again, and certainly I never gave her another thought.

* * *

Bruce was a newcomer and had only been to one week of meetings at the storefront, so no one had told him that the members of Ananda Ashram, Dr. Mishra's *yoga* retreat, had invited Swamiji and his followers for a day in the upstate countryside. Bruce had just arrived at the storefront one morning when he heard someone announce, "The Swami is leaving!" And Prabhupāda came out of the building and stepped into a car. In a fit of anxiety, Bruce thought that the Swami was leaving them for good—for India! "No," Howard told him, "we're going to a *yoga-āśrama* in the country." But the other car had already left, and there was no room in Swamiji's car. Just then Steve showed up. He had expected the boys to come by his apartment to pick him up. They both had missed the ride.

Bruce phoned a friend up in the Bronx and convinced him to drive them up to Ananda Ashram. But when they got to Bruce's friend's apartment, the friend had decided he didn't want to go. Finally he lent Bruce his car, and Swamiji's two new followers set out for Ananda Ashram.

By the time they arrived, Prabhupāda and his group were already taking *prasādam*, sitting around a picnic table beneath the trees. Ananda Ashram was a beautiful place, with sloping hills and lots of trees and sky and green grass and a lake. The two latecomers came walking up to Swamiji, who was seated like the father of a family, at the head of the picnic table. Keith was serving from a big wok onto the individual plates. When Prabhupāda saw his two stragglers, he asked them to sit next to him, and Keith served them. Prabhupāda took Steve's *capātī* and heaped it up with a mound of sugar, and Steve munched on the bread and sugar, while everyone laughed.

Prabhupāda began talking somehow about lion tamers, and he recalled that once at a fair he had seen a man wrestling with a tiger, rolling over and over with it down a hill. The boys, who rarely heard Swamiji speak anything but philosophy, were surprised. They were delighted—city kids, taken to the country by their *guru,* and having a good time.

Steve: *I was walking with Swamiji across a long, gentle slope. I wanted him to see and approve a picture of Rādhā and Kṛṣṇa I had found in a small book,* Nārada-bhakti-sūtra. *I had planned to get a color reproduction of it to give to each of his followers. So as we were walking across the grass I showed him the picture and asked him whether it was a nice picture of Rādhā and Kṛṣṇa for reproducing. He looked at the picture, smiled, nodded, and said yes.*

Bruce: *I walked with Swamiji around the grounds. All the others were doing something else, and Swamiji and myself were walking alone. He was talking about building a temple there.*

Prabhupāda walked across the scenic acreage, looking at the distant mountains and forests, and Keith walked beside him. Prabhupāda spoke of how Dr. Mishra had offered him the island in the middle of the *āśrama's* lake to build a temple on. "What kind of temple were you thinking of?" Keith asked. "How big?" Prabhupāda smiled and gestured across the horizon. "As big as the whole horizon?" Keith laughed. "Yes," Prabhupāda replied.

A few Ananda Ashram men and women came by. One woman was wearing a *sārī.* Prabhupāda turned to the other women and said, "A woman who wears a *sārī* looks very feminine."

It was late afternoon when some of Swamiji's followers gathered by the lake and began talking candidly about Swamiji and speculating about his relation to God and their relation to him.

"Well," said Wally, "Swami never claimed to be God or an incarnation, but he says that he is a *servant* of God, teaching *love* of God."

"But he says that the spiritual master is not different from God," said Howard. They stood at the edge of the mirrory calm lake and concluded that it was not necessary to talk about this. The answers would be revealed later. None of them really had much spiritual knowledge, but they wanted their faith to deepen.

Afterward, Keith, Wally, and Howard wandered into the meditation room. There was a seat with a picture of Dr. Mishra, who was away in Europe. But the most remarkable thing was a blinking strobe light. "I feel like I'm in a head shop on St. Mark's Place," said Wally. "What kind of spiritual meditation is this?" Howard asked. A Mishra follower, wearing a white *kurtā* and white bell-bottoms, replied that their *guru* had said they could sit and meditate on this light. "Swamiji says you should meditate on Kṛṣṇa," said Keith.

After sunset, everyone gathered in the large room of the main building to watch a slide show. It was a loose collection, mostly of assorted slides of India and the Ananda Ashram. A record by a popular Indian sitarist was playing in the background. Some of the slides were of Viṣṇu temples, and when one slide passed by quickly, Prabhupāda asked, "Let me see that. Can you go back and let me see that temple again?" This happened several times when he recognized familiar temples in India. Later in the show, there were several slides of a girl, one of the members of Dr. Mishra's *āśrama,* demonstrating Indian dance poses. As one of her pictures passed, an *āśrama* man joked, "Turn back and let me see *that* temple again." The joke seemed at Swamiji's expense and in poor taste. His followers didn't laugh.

Then came Swamiji's lecture. He sat up cross-legged on the couch in the largest room in the mansion. The room was filled with people—the Swami's followers from the Lower East Side as well as the Ananda Ashram *yogīs*—sitting on the floor or standing along the walls and in the doorway. He began his talk by criticizing democracy. He said that because people are attached to sense gratification, they vote for a leader who will fulfill their own lust and greed—and *that* is their only criterion for picking a leader. He went on for forty-five minutes to explain about the importance of Kṛṣṇa consciousness, his reel-to-reel tape recorder moving silently.

Then he led a *kīrtana* that bridged all differences and brought out the best in everyone that night. Several nights before, in his apartment on Second Avenue, Prabhupāda had taught his followers how to dance. They had formed a line behind him while he demonstrated the simple step. Holding his arms above his head, he would first swing his left foot forward across the right foot, and then bring it back again in a sweeping motion. Then he would swing his right foot over the left and bring it back again. With his arms upraised, Prabhupāda would walk forward, swinging his body from side to side, left foot to right side, right foot to left side, in time with the one-two-three rhythm. He had shown them the step in regular time and in a slow, half-time rhythm. Keith had called it "the Swami step," as if it were a new ballroom dance.

Prabhupāda's followers began dancing, and soon the others joined them, moving around the room in a rhythmic circle of ecstasy, dancing, swaying, sometimes leaping and whirling. It was a joyous hour-long *kīrtana,* the Swami encouraging everyone to the fullest extent. A visitor to the *āśrama* happened to have his stringed bass with him, and he began expertly turning out his own swinging bass improvisations beneath the Swami's melody, while another man played the *tablās.*

The Ananda Ashram members had been divided of late into two tense, standoffish groups. There was the elderly crowd, similar to the old ladies who had attended the Swami's uptown lectures, and there was the young crowd, mostly hip couples. But in the *kīrtana* their rifts were forgotten and, as they discovered later, even healed. Whether they liked it or not, almost all of those present were induced to rise and dance.

Then it was late. The Swami took rest in the guest room, and his boys slept outside in their sleeping bags.

Howard: *I awaken three or four times, and each time I am flat on my back looking up at the stars, which are always in different positions. My sense of time is confused. The sidereal shifts dizzy me. Then, just before morning, I dream. I dream of devotees clustered about a beautiful golden youth. To see him is to be captivated. His transcendental body radiates an absolute beauty unseen in the world. Stunned, I inquire, "Who is he?" "Don't you know?" someone says. "That's the Swami." I look carefully, but see no resemblance. The youth appears around eighteen, straight out of Vaikuṇṭha [the spiritual world]. "If that's Swamiji," I wonder to myself, "why doesn't he come to earth like that?" A voice somewhere inside me answers: "People would follow me for my beauty, not for my teachings." And I awake, startled. The dream is clear in my mind—more like a vision than a dream. I feel strangely refreshed, bathed in some unknown balm. Again I see that the constellations have shifted and that the dimmer stars have faded into the encroaching dawn. I remember Swamiji telling me that although most dreams are simply functions of the mind, dreams of the spiritual master are of spiritual significance.*

Keith also had a dream that night.

Keith: *I saw Kṛṣṇa and Arjuna on the Battlefield of Kurukṣetra. Arjuna was inquiring from Kṛṣṇa, and Kṛṣṇa was reciting the* Bhagavad-gītā *to him. Then that picture phased out, and the images changed. And there was Swamiji, and I was kneeling in front of him, and the same dialogue was going on. I had the understanding that now is the time, and Swamiji is presenting the same thing as Kṛṣṇa, and we are all in the position of Arjuna. The dream made it very clear that hearing from Swamiji was as good as hearing from Kṛṣṇa.*

The sun rose over the mountains, streaking the morning sky above the lake with colors. Wally and Keith were walking around the grounds saying to Prabhupāda how beautiful it all was. "We are not so concerned with beautiful scenery," said Prabhupāda. "We are concerned with the beautiful one who has made the beautiful scenery."

Later ... Prabhupāda sat next to Bruce in the Volkswagen returning to the city. The car went winding around on a ribbon of smooth black mountain road, with lush green forests close in and intermittent vistas of mountains and expansive sky. It was a rare occasion for Bruce to be driving Prabhupāda in a car, because none of the Swami's boys had cars. They would always travel by bus or subway. It seemed fitting for the Swami to have a car to ride in, but this was only a little Volkswagen, and Bruce winced whenever they hit a bump and it jostled Prabhupāda. As they wound their way on through the mountains, Bruce recalled something he had read in a book by Aldous Huxley's wife about the best places for meditation. One opinion had been that the best place to meditate was by a large body of water, because of the negative ions in the air, and the other opinion was that it was better to meditate in the mountains, because you are higher up and closer to God. "Is it better for spiritual realization to meditate in the mountains?" Bruce asked. Prabhupāda replied, "This is nonsense. There is no question of 'better place.' Are you thinking that God is up on some planet or something and you have to go up high? No. You can meditate anywhere. Just chant Hare Kṛṣṇa."

After some time the drive became tiring for Prabhupāda, and he dozed, his head resting forward.

Bruce walked with Swamiji up to his apartment, opening the door for him, adjusting the window as he liked it, and preparing things in his room, as if he were the Swami's personal servant. Prabhupāda settled back into his Second Avenue apartment, feeling pleased with the visit to Ananda Ashram. The *kīrtana* had been successful, and one of Dr. Mishra's foremost students had commented that he was impressed by Prabhupāda's followers: simply by chanting they seemed to be achieving an advanced level of *yoga* discipline, whereas "we have more difficulty with all our postures and breath control."

* * *

The United States' recently increased involvement in Vietnam was creating an increase of opposition to the war. On July 29, American planes had bombed North Vietnam's two major population centers, Hanoi and Haiphong—an escalation which brought expressions of regret from several allied countries, including Canada, France, and Japan. United Nations Secretary General U Thant openly criticized America's policy in Vietnam. Further opposition to the war ranged from the U.S. Senate down to newly formed pacifist groups, and dissenters held peace marches, sit-ins, and rallies in protest of the war and draft.

Religious protest was led by Pope Paul VI. And the World Council of Churches decried America's involvement in Vietnam and called for a halt in the fighting as "the most effective step" toward negotiation. On August 6 (the anniversary of the bombing of Hiroshima) there were demonstrations in many major American cities, including a peace vigil at the United Nations Headquarters in New York.

On August 31, there would be another two-week-long peace vigil before the United Nations General Assembly Building, and Mr. Larry Bogart had invited Prabhupāda and his followers to open the vigil of "praying for peace." Larry Bogart, who worked at the United Nations Headquarters, had become friends with the Swami and had volunteered his help by arranging to print stationery for the International Society for Krishna Consciousness. The letterhead was designed by James Greene with a sketch of Rādhā and Kṛṣṇa, and Mr. Bogart's name also appeared on the stationery at the head of the list of ISKCON trustees.

Prabhupāda accepted Mr. Bogart's invitation to the peace vigil. Prabhupāda saw it as an opportunity to publicly chant Hare Kṛṣṇa, so he was glad to attend. He announced to his congregation that Monday the thirty-first, instead of the usual morning class at 6:30, everyone should meet at the United Nations Headquarters for a special *kīrtana.*

August 31

Some met at the storefront and went by bus, carrying *karatālas,* a tambourine, and the Swami's bongo. Swamiji rode with a few of his followers in a taxi. The typical dress of his followers consisted of well-worn sneakers, black pants or blue jeans, and T-shirts or button-down sport shirts. Traveling uptown in the early morning put the boys in a lighthearted spirit, and when they saw Swamiji at the U.N. in his flowing saffron robes they became inspired. Swamiji began the chanting, but right away the peace vigil organizers stepped in and asked him to stop. This was a "silent vigil," they said, and it should have prayerful, nonviolent silence. The boys were crushed, but Swamiji accepted the restriction and began silently chanting on his beads.

A dignitary stood up before the assembly and made a short speech in which he mentioned Gandhi, and then he turned to Prabhupāda and indicated that he could now speak about peace. Standing erectly, the U.N. skyscraper looming behind him, Swamiji spoke in a soft voice. The world must accept that God is the proprietor of everything and the friend of everyone, he said. Only then can we have real peace. Mr. Bogart had scheduled the Swami for two hours of silent prayer. Prabhupāda had the devotees sit together and softly chant *japa* until their two scheduled hours were up. Then they left.

As Prabhupāda rode back downtown in the heavy morning traffic, he said New York reminded him of Calcutta. Amid the start-and-stop motion and noise of the traffic he explained, "We have nothing to do with peace vigils. We simply want to spread this chanting of Hare Kṛṣṇa, that's all. If people take to this chanting, peace will automatically come. Then they won't have to artificially try for peace."

September 1

The New York Post ran a picture of Swamiji's group at the United Nations Building. Steve brought the clipping in to Prabhupāda: "Swamiji, look. They have referred to you here as 'Sami Krishna'!"

Prabhupāda: "'Sami Krishna'? That's all right."

In the picture, some of the boys were sitting with their heads resting on their arms. "Where are you?" Prabhupāda asked. Steve pointed. "Oh, you chant like this, with your head down?"

Prabhupāda had participated in the peace vigil to oblige his contact, Mr. Bogart. Now Mr. Bogart was phoning to offer his appreciation and agreeing to visit the storefront. He wanted to help, and he would discuss how the Swami could work with the U.N. and how he could solicit help from important people for his movement of Indian culture and peace.

Prabhupāda regarded Mr. Bogart's imminent visit as very important, and he wanted to cook for him personally and receive him in his apartment with the best hospitality. When the day arrived, Prabhupāda and Keith cooked together in the small kitchen for several hours, making the best Indian delicacies. Prabhupāda posted Stanley downstairs and told him not to allow anyone to come up while he was cooking the feast for Mr. Bogart. Stanley assented, blinking his eyes with his far-off "saintly" look.

Stanley stationed himself downstairs in the storefront. A few of the boys were there, and he told them, "You can't go up to see the Swami—no one can." About twelve noon, Larry Bogart arrived, pale, elderly, and well dressed, by Lower East Side standards. He said he wanted to see Swami Bhaktivedanta. "Sorry," Stanley informed him, his boyish face trying to impress the stranger with the seriousness of the order, "the Swami is busy now, and he said no one can see him." Mr. Bogart decided he would wait. There was no chair in the storefront, but Stanley brought him a folding chair. It was a hot day. Mr. Bogart looked at his watch several times. A half hour passed. Stanley sat chanting and sometimes staring off blankly. After an hour, Mr. Bogart asked if he could see the Swami now. Stanley assured him that he could not, and Mr. Bogart left in a huff.

Upstairs, Swamiji had become anxious, wondering why Mr. Bogart had not arrived. Finally, he sent Keith downstairs, and Stanley told him about the man whom he had turned away. "What?" Keith exploded. "But that was ..."

Within moments, Swamiji heard what had happened. He became furious. He came down to the storefront: "You fool! You silly fool!" He turned and angrily rebuked everyone in the room, but mostly Stanley. No one had ever seen the Swami so angry. Then Swamiji walked away in disgust and returned to his apartment.

Stanley had been going off the deep end for some time, and now he became even more abstracted in his behavior. Stanley's mother knew her son had been troubled for years, and she had therefore requested Prabhupāda to keep a very close watch on him. But now the boy deteriorated in his responsibilities and stopped cleaning the kitchen and storefront. He would stand alone looking at something. He was gloomy and sometimes spoke of suicide. And he stopped chanting regularly. The boys didn't know what to do, but they thought perhaps he should be sent home to his mother.

One day, Stanley went up to see the Swami. He came in and sat down.

Prabhupāda: "Yes?"

Stanley: "May I have fifty dollars?"

Prabhupāda: "Why?"

Prabhupāda used to handle all the money himself, so when his boys needed something, even if it were only twenty-five cents for the bus, they had to see Swami. He was never wasteful. He was so frugal that whenever he received a letter, he would carefully tear the envelope apart and use the reverse side as writing paper. So he wanted to know why Stanley wanted fifty dollars. Stanley replied in a small voice, "I want to purchase some gasoline and set myself on fire." Prabhupāda saw Chuck at the doorway and told him to call Bruce at once. Bruce quickly came up and sat with Prabhupāda and Stanley. Prabhupāda told Bruce—whom he had recently appointed to handle petty cash—to give Stanley fifty dollars, and he had Stanley repeat why he wanted the money.

"But Swamiji," Bruce protested, "we don't have that much money."

"There, you see, Stanley," Prabhupāda spoke very calmly. "Bruce says we don't have the money." Then they phoned Stanley's mother. Later Prabhupāda said that because Stanley had asked for fifty dollars for gasoline, which cost only thirty-five cents, he could therefore understand Stanley was crazy.

* * *

Keith was cooking lunch in the kitchen as usual, but today Swamiji was standing by the kitchen stove, watching his pupil. Keith paused and looked up from his cooking: "Swamiji, could I become your disciple?"

"Yes," Prabhupāda replied. "Why not? Your name will be Kṛṣṇa dāsa."

This simple exchange was the first request for discipleship and Prabhupāda's first granting of initiation. But there was more to it than that. Prabhupāda announced that he would soon hold an initiation. "What's initiation, Swamiji?" one of the boys asked, and Prabhupāda replied, "I will tell you later."

First they had to have beads. Keith went to Tandy's Leather Company and bought half-inch wooden beads and cord to string them on. It was much better, Swamiji said, to count on beads while chanting—a strand of 108 beads, to be exact. This employed the sense of touch, and like the Vaiṣṇavas of India one could count how many times one chanted the *mantra.* Some devotees in India had a string of more than a thousand beads, he had said, and they would chant through them again and again. He taught the boys how to tie a double knot between each of the 108 beads. The number 108 had a special significance: there were 108 *Upaniṣads,* as well as 108 principal *gopīs,* the chief devotees of Lord Kṛṣṇa.

The initiates would be taking vows, he said, and one vow would be to chant a prescribed number of rounds on the beads each day. About a dozen of Swamiji's boys were eligible, but there was no strict system for their selection: if they wanted to, they could do it.

Steve: *Although I was already doing whatever Swamiji recommended, I sensed that initiation was a heavy commitment. And with my last strong impulses to remain completely independent, I hesitated to take initiation.*

Prabhupāda's friends saw the initiation in different ways. Some saw it as very serious, and some took it to be like a party or a happening. While stringing their beads in the courtyard, Wally and Howard talked a few days before the ceremony.

Wally: *It's just a formality. You accept Swamiji as your spiritual master.*

Howard: *What does that entail?*

Wally: *Nobody's very sure. In India it's a standard practice. Don't you think you want to take him as a spiritual master?*

Howard: *I don't know. He would seem to be a good spiritual master—whatever that is. I mean, I like him and his teachings a lot, so I guess in a way he's already my spiritual master. I just don't understand how it would change the situation.*

Wally: *Neither do I. I guess it doesn't. It's just a formality.*

* * *

September 8

Janmāṣṭamī day, the appearance day of Lord Kṛṣṇa. One year before, Prabhupāda had observed Kṛṣṇa's birthday at sea aboard the *Jaladuta,* just out of Colombo. Now, exactly one year later, he had a small crew of Hare Kṛṣṇa chanters. He would gather them all together, have them observe a day of chanting, reading scripture, fasting, and feasting—and the next day would be initiation.

At six o'clock, Prabhupāda came down and was about to give his morning class as usual, when one of the boys asked if he would read from his own manuscript. Prabhupāda appeared shy, yet he did not hide his pleasure at having been asked to read his own *Bhagavad-gītā* commentary. Usually he would read a verse from Dr. Radhakrishnan's Oxford edition of the *Gītā.* Although the commentary presented impersonalist philosophy, the translations, Prabhupāda said, were ninety-percent accurate. But this morning he sent Roy up to fetch his manuscript, and for an hour he read from its typewritten pages.

For observing Janmāṣṭamī there were special rules: there should be no eating, and the day was to be spent chanting, reading, and discussing Kṛṣṇa consciousness. If anyone became too weak, he said, there was fruit in the kitchen. But better that they fast until the feast at midnight, just like the devotees in India. He said that in India, millions of people—Hindus, Muslims, or whatever—observed the birthday of Lord Kṛṣṇa. And in every temple there were festivities and celebrations of the pastimes of Kṛṣṇa.

"And now," he said at length, "I will tell you what is meant by initiation. Initiation means that the spiritual master accepts the student and agrees to take charge, and the student accepts the spiritual master and agrees to worship him as God." He paused. No one spoke. "Any questions?" And when there were none, he got up and walked out.

The devotees were stunned. What had they just heard him say? For weeks he had stressed that when anyone claims to be God he should be considered a dog.

"My mind's just been blown," said Wally.

"*Everybody's* mind is blown," said Howard. "Swamiji just dropped a bomb."

They thought of Keith. He was wise. Consult Keith. But Keith was in the hospital. Talking among themselves, they became more and more confused. Swamiji's remark had confounded their judgment. Finally, Wally decided to go to the hospital to see Keith.

Keith listened to the whole story: how Swamiji had told them to fast and how he had read from his manuscript and how he had said he would explain initiation and how everybody had leaned forward, all ears ... and Swamiji had dropped a bomb: "The student accepts the spiritual master and agrees to worship him as God." "Any questions?" Swamiji had asked softly. And then he had walked out. "I don't know if I want to be initiated now," Wally confessed. "We have to worship him as God."

"Well, you're already doing that by accepting whatever he tells you," Keith replied, and he advised that they talk it over with Swamiji ... *before* the initiation. So Wally went back to the temple and consulted Howard, and together they went up to Swamiji's apartment. "Does what you told us this morning," Howard asked, "mean we are supposed to accept the spiritual master to be God?"

"That means he is due the same respect as God, being God's representative," Prabhupāda replied, calmly.

"Then he is not God?"

"No," Prabhupāda said, "God is God. The spiritual master is His representative. Therefore, he is as good as God because he can deliver God to the sincere disciple. Is that clear?" It was.

It was a mental and physical strain to go all day without eating. Jan was restless. She complained that she couldn't possibly stay any longer but had to go take care of her cat. Prabhupāda tried to overrule her, but she left anyway.

Most of the prospective initiates spent several hours that day stringing their shiny red wooden beads. Having tied one end of the string to a window bar or a radiator, they would slide one bead at a time up the string and knot it tightly, chanting one *mantra* of Hare Kṛṣṇa for each bead. It was devotional service—chanting and stringing your beads for initiation. Every time they knotted another bead it seemed like a momentous event. Prabhupāda said that devotees in India chanted at least sixty-four rounds of beads a day. Saying the Hare Kṛṣṇa *mantra* once on each of the 108 beads constituted one round. His spiritual master had said that anyone who didn't chant sixty-four rounds a day was fallen. At first some of the boys thought that they would also have to chant sixty-four rounds, and they became perplexed: that would take all day! How could you go to a job if you had to chant sixty-four rounds? How could anyone chant sixty-four rounds? Then someone said Swamiji had told him that thirty-two rounds a day would be a sufficient minimum for the West. Wally said he had heard Swamiji say twenty-five—but even that seemed impossible. Then Prabhupāda offered the rock-bottom minimum: sixteen rounds a day, without fail. Whoever got initiated would have to promise.

The bead-stringing, chanting, reading, and dozing went on until eleven at night, when everyone was invited up to Swamiji's room. As they filed through the courtyard, they sensed an unusual calm in the atmosphere, and Houston Street, just over the wall, was quiet. There was no moon.

As his followers sat on the floor, contentedly eating *prasādam* from paper plates, Swamiji sat among them, telling stories about the birth of Lord Kṛṣṇa. Kṛṣṇa had appeared on this evening five thousand years ago. He was born the son of Vasudeva and Devakī in the prison of King Kaṁsa at midnight, and His father, Vasudeva, immediately took Him to Vṛndāvana, where He was raised as the son of Nanda Mahārāja, a cowherd man.

Prabhupāda also spoke of the necessity of purification for spiritual advancement. "It is not enough merely to chant holy words," he said. "One must be pure inside and out. Chanting in purity brings spiritual advancement. The living entity becomes impure because he wants to enjoy material pleasure. But the impure can become pure by following Kṛṣṇa, by doing all works for Kṛṣṇa. Beginners in Kṛṣṇa consciousness have a tendency to relax their efforts in a short time, but to advance spiritually you must resist this temptation and continually increase your efforts and devotion."

* * *

Michael Grant: *I first heard about the initiation just one day before it was to take place. I had been busy with my music and hadn't been attending. I was walking down Second Avenue with one of the prospective initiates, and he mentioned to me that there was going to be something called an initiation ceremony. I asked what it was about, and he said, "All I know is it means that you accept the spiritual master as God." This was a big surprise to me, and I hardly knew how to take it. But I didn't take it completely seriously, and the way it was mentioned to me in such an offhand way made it seem not very important. He asked me very casually whether I was going to be involved, and I, also being very casual about it, said, "Well, I think I will. Why not? I'll give it a try."*

Jan didn't think she would make an obedient disciple, and initiation sounded frightening. She liked the Swami, especially cooking with him. But it was Mike who convinced her—*he* was going, so she should come along with him.

Carl Yeargens knew something about initiation from his readings, and he, more than the others, knew what a serious commitment it was. He was surprised to hear that Swamiji was offering initiation, and he was cautious about entering into it. He knew that initiation meant no illicit sex, intoxication, or meat-eating, and an initiated disciple would have new responsibilities for spreading the teachings to others. Carl was already feeling less involved since the Swami had moved to Second Avenue, but he decided to attend the initiation anyway.

Bill Epstein had never professed to be a serious disciple. Holding initiation was just another part of the Swami's scene, and you were free to take it seriously or not. He figured it was all right to take initiation, even if you weren't serious. He would try it.

Carol Bekar was surprised to hear that some people would be taking initiation even though they had no intentions of giving up their bad habits. She had stopped coming around regularly ever since the Swami had moved, and she felt no desire to ask for initiation. The Swami probably wouldn't initiate women anyway, she figured.

Robert Nelson hadn't forgotten the Swami and always liked to help whenever he could. But except for an occasional friendly visit, he had stopped coming. He mostly stayed to himself. He still lived uptown and wasn't into the Lower East Side scene.

James Greene thought he wasn't pure enough to be initiated: "Who am I to be initiated?" But the Swami had asked him to bring something over to the storefront. "I came, and it was just understood that I was supposed to be initiated. So, I thought, why not?"

Stanley had been chanting regularly again and had come out of his crazy mood. He was sticking with the Swami and his followers. He asked his mother if he could be initiated, and she said it would be all right.

Steve wanted more time to think about it.

Keith was in the hospital.

Bruce had only been attending for a week or two, and it was too soon.

Chuck was on a week's vacation from the regulated spiritual life at the temple, so he didn't know about the initiation.

No one was asked to shave his head or even cut his hair or change his dress. No one offered Prabhupāda the traditional *guru-dakṣiṇā,* the donation a disciple is supposed to offer as a gesture of his great obligation to his master. Hardly anyone even relieved him of his chores, so Swamiji himself had to do most of the cooking and other preparations for the initiation. He was perfectly aware of the mentality of his boys, and he didn't try to force anything on anyone. Some of the initiates didn't know until after the initiation, when they had inquired, that the four rules—no meat-eating, no illicit sex, no intoxication, and no gambling—were mandatory for all disciples. Prabhupāda's reply then was, "I am very glad that you are finally asking me that."

It was to be a live Vedic sacrifice, with a ceremonial fire right there in the front room of Swamiji's apartment. In the center of the room was the sacrificial arena, a platform of bricks, four inches high and two feet square, covered with a mound of dirt. The dirt was from the courtyard and the bricks were from a nearby gutted building. Around the mound were eleven bananas, clarified butter, sesame seeds, whole barley grains, five colors of powdered dyes, and a supply of kindling. The eleven initiates took up most of the remaining space in the front room as they sat on the floor knee to knee around the sacrificial arena. The guests in the hallway peered curiously through the open door. For everyone except the Swami, this was all new and strange, and every step of the ceremony took place under his direction. When some of the boys had made a mess of trying to apply the Vaiṣṇava *tilaka* to their foreheads, Prabhupāda had patiently guided his finger up their foreheads, making a neat, narrow "V."

He sat before the mound of earth, looking out at his congregation. They appeared not much different from any other group of young hippies from the Lower East Side who might have assembled at any number of happenings—spiritual, cultural, musical, or whatever. Some were just checking out a new scene. Some were deeply devoted to the Swami. But everyone was curious. He had requested them to chant the Hare Kṛṣṇa *mantra* softly throughout the ceremony, and the chanting had now become a continual drone, accompanying his mysterious movements as head priest of the Vedic rite.

He began by lighting a dozen sticks of incense. Then he performed purification with water. Taking a spoon in his left hand, he put three drops of water from a goblet into his right and sipped the water. He repeated the procedure three times. The fourth time he did not sip but flicked the water onto the floor behind him. He then passed the spoon and goblet around for the initiates, who tried to copy what they had seen. When some of them placed the water in the wrong hand or sipped in the wrong way, Swamiji patiently corrected them.

"Now," he said, "repeat after me." And he had them repeat, one word at a time, a Vedic *mantra* of purification:

oṁ apavitraḥ pavitro vā
sarvāvasthāṁ gato 'pi vā
yaḥ smaret puṇḍarīkākṣaṁ
sa bāhyābhyantaraḥ śuciḥ
śrī-viṣṇuḥ śrī-viṣṇuḥ śrī-viṣṇuḥ

The initiates tried falteringly to follow his pronunciation of the words, which they had never heard before. Then he gave the translation: "Unpurified or purified, or even having passed through all situations, one who remembers the lotus-eyed Supreme Personality of Godhead is cleansed within and without." Three times he repeated the sipping of water, the drone of the Hare Kṛṣṇa *mantra* filling the room as the goblet passed from initiate to initiate and back again to him, and three times he led the chanting of the *mantra: oṁ apavitraḥ* ... Then he raised a hand, and as the buzzing of the chanting trailed off into silence, he began his lecture.

After the lecture, he asked the devotees one by one to hand him their beads, and he began chanting on them—Hare Kṛṣṇa, Hare Kṛṣṇa, Kṛṣṇa Kṛṣṇa, Hare Hare/ Hare Rāma, Hare Rāma, Rāma Rāma, Hare Hare. The sound of everyone chanting filled the room. After finishing one strand, he would summon the owner of the beads and hold the beads up while demonstrating how to chant. Then he would announce the initiate's spiritual name, and the disciple would take back the beads, bow to the floor, and recite:

nama oṁ viṣṇu-pādāya kṛṣṇa-preṣṭhāya bhū-tale
śrīmate bhaktivedānta-svāmin iti nāmine

"I offer my respectful obeisances unto His Divine Grace A. C. Bhaktivedanta Swami, who is very dear to Lord Kṛṣṇa, having taken shelter at His lotus feet." There were eleven initiates and so eleven sets of beads, and the chanting lasted for over an hour. Prabhupāda gave each boy a strand of neck beads, which he said were like dog collars, identifying the devotee as Kṛṣṇa's dog.

After Wally received his beads and his new name (Umāpati), he returned to his place beside Howard and said, "That was wonderful. Getting your beads is wonderful." In turn, each initiate received his beads and his spiritual name. Howard became Hayagrīva, Wally became Umāpati, Bill became Ravīndra-svarūpa, Carl became Karlāpati, James became Jagannātha, Mike became Mukunda, Jan became Jānakī, Roy became Rāya Rāma, and Stanley became Stryadhīśa. Another Stanley, a Brooklyn boy with a job, and Janos, a college student from Montreal, both of whom had rather peripheral relationships with the Swami, appeared that night and took initiation with the rest—receiving the names Satyavrata and Janārdana.

Then Swamiji began the fire sacrifice by sprinkling the colored dyes across the mound of earth before him. With fixed attention his congregation watched each mysterious move, as he picked up the twigs and wooden splinters, dipped them into clarified butter, lit them in a candle flame, and built a small fire in the center of the mound. He mixed sesame seeds, barley, and clarified butter in a bowl and then passed the mixture around. Each new disciple took a handful of the mixture to offer into the fire. He then began to recite Sanskrit prayers, asking everyone please to repeat them, each prayer ending with the responsive chanting of the word "*svāhā*" three times. And with *svāhā* the initiates would toss some of the sesame-barley mixture into the fire. Swamiji kept pouring butter, piling up wood, and chanting more prayers, until the mound was blazing. The prayers kept coming and the butter kept pouring and the fire got larger and the room got hotter.

After fifteen or twenty minutes, he asked each of the initiates to place a banana in the fire. With eleven bananas heaped on the fire, the flames began to die, and the smoke thickened. A few of the initiates got up and ran coughing into the other room, and the guests retreated into the hallway. But Swamiji went on pouring the remaining butter and seeds into the fire. "This kind of smoke does not disturb," he said. "Other smoke disturbs, but this kind of smoke does not." Even though everyone's eyes were watering with irritation, he asked that the windows remain closed. So most of the smoke was contained within the apartment, and no neighbors complained.

Swamiji smiled broadly, rose from his seat before the sacrificial fire, the blazing tongue of Viṣṇu, and began clapping his hands and chanting Hare Kṛṣṇa. Placing one foot before the other and swaying from side to side, he began to dance before the fire. His disciples joined him in dancing and chanting, and the smoke abated. He had each disciple touch his beads to the feet of Lord Caitanya in the Pañca-tattva picture on the table, and finally he allowed the windows opened. As the ceremony was finished and the air in the apartment was clearing, Swamiji began to laugh: "There was so much smoke I thought they might have to call the fire brigade."

Prabhupāda was happy. He arranged that *prasādam* be distributed to all the devotees and guests. The fire, the prayers, the vows, and everyone chanting Hare Kṛṣṇa had all created an auspicious atmosphere. Things were going forward. Now there were initiated devotees in the Western world. Finally most of the disciples went home to their apartments, leaving their spiritual master to clean up after the initiation ceremony.

* * *

September 10

The morning after the initiation, Prabhupāda sat in his apartment reading from a commentary on the *Śrīmad-Bhāgavatam*. The large Sanskrit volume lay before him on his desk as he read. He wore horn- rimmed glasses, which changed his demeanor, making him look extremely scholarly. He wore eyeglasses only for reading, and this added to the visual impression that he had now gone into a deep professorial meditation. The room was quiet, and brilliant midmorning sunlight shone warmly through the window.

Suddenly someone knocked on the door. "Yes? Come in." He looked up, removing his glasses, as Mike and Jan, now Mukunda and Jānakī, opened the door, peering in. He had asked to see them. "Yes, yes, come in." He smiled, and they walked in and closed the door behind them, two vivacious young Americans. From his expressive eyes, he seemed to be amused. They sat down before him, and Prabhupāda playfully addressed them by their new initiated names. "So, you are living together, but now you have taken serious vows of initiation. So what will you do about it?"

"Well" — Mukunda seemed puzzled — "isn't there any love in Kṛṣṇa consciousness?"

Swamiji nodded. "Yes, so I am saying why don't you get married?"

They agreed it was a good idea, and Prabhupāda immediately scheduled a wedding date for two days later.

Swamiji said he would cook a big feast and hold the marriage ceremony in his apartment, and he asked Mukunda and Jānakī to invite their relatives. Both Mukunda and Jānakī had grown up in Oregon, and their family members found it impossible to travel such a long distance on such short notice. Only Jānakī's sister, Joan, agreed to come.

Joan: *Little did I know what kind of wedding it would be. All I knew was that they had met a swami and were taking Sanskrit from him as well as attending his small storefront temple on Second Avenue. When I met the Swami he was sitting beside the window in his front room, bathed in sunlight, surrounded by pots of* prasādam, *which he was distributing to the devotees who were sitting around him against the wall. I was a follower of macrobiotics and not so eager for taking this noonday meal. When I entered the room, the Swami said, "Who is this?" and Mukunda said, "This is Jānakī's sister, Joan. She has come from Oregon to attend the wedding." Swamiji said, "Oh? Where is Oregon?" Mukunda said, "It's three thousand miles away, on the other side of the United States." And he asked, "Oh, coming from so far? Very nice. And when will the other members of the family arrive?" Then I said, "I am the only one who is coming for the wedding, Swamiji." He said, "Never mind. It is very nice that you have come. Please sit down and take some* kṛṣṇa-prasādam."

He offered me some dāl, *a rather moist* sabjī, *yogurt, salad, and* capātīs. *But because I was a devotee of macrobiotics, all of this* prasādam *was very unpalatable to me. Practically speaking, it was sticking in my throat the whole time, but I remember looking over at the radiant and beautiful person who was so eager for me to take this* prasādam *that he had prepared. So I took it all, but in my mind I decided this would be the last time I would take this luncheon with the devotees.*

At any rate, somehow I finished the meal, and Swamiji, who had been looking over at me, said, "You want more? You want more?" And I said, "No, thank you. I am so full. It was very nice, but I can't take any more." So finally the prasādam *was finished, and they were all getting up to clean, and Swamiji commented that he wanted to see Mukunda, Jānakī, and myself—for making preparations for the wedding the next day.*

So when we were all there sitting in the room with him, the Swami reached over into the corner, where there was a big pot with crystallized sugar syrup sticking to the outside. I thought, "Oh, this is supposed to be the pièce de résistance, but I can't possibly take any more." But he reached his hand into the pot anyway and pulled up a huge, round, dripping gulābjāmun. *I said, "Oh, no. I am so full I couldn't take any." And he said, "Oh, take, take." And he made me hold out my hand and take it. Well, by the time I finished the* gulābjāmun *I was fully convinced that this would be the last time I would ever come there.*

Then he began explaining how in the Vedic tradition the woman's side of the family made lavish arrangements for the wedding. And since I was the only member of the family who had come to assist, I should come the next day and help him make the wedding feast. So the next morning at nine, while Jānakī was decorating the room for the fire sacrifice, stringing leaves and flower garlands across the top of the room, I went upstairs to meet Swamiji.

When I arrived, he immediately sent me out shopping with a list—five or six items to purchase. One of those items was not available anywhere in the markets, although I spoke to so many shopkeepers. When I came back he asked me, "You have obtained all the items on the list?" And

I said, "Well, everything except for one." He said, "What is that?" I said, "Well, no one knows what tumar is."

He had me wash my hands and sat me down in his front room on the floor with a five-pound bag of flour, a pound of butter, and a pitcher of water. And he looked down at me and said, "Can you make a medium-soft dough?" I replied, "Do you mean a pastry or piecrust or shortcrust dough or pâté brisée *dough? What kind of pastry do you want?" "How old are you?" he said. And I said, "I am twenty-five, Swamiji." "You are twenty-five," he said, "and you can't make a medium-soft dough? It is a custom in India that any young girl from the age of five years is very experienced in making this dough. But never mind, I will show you." So he very deftly emptied the bag of flour and, with his fingertips, cut in the butter until the mixture had a consistency of coarse meal. Then he made a well in the center of the flour, poured in just the right amount of water, and very deftly and expertly kneaded it into a velvety smooth, medium-soft dough. He then brought in a tray of cooked potatoes, mashed them with his fingertips, and began to sprinkle in spices. He showed me how to make and form potato* kacaurīs, *which are fried Indian pastries with spiced potato filling. From eleven until five that afternoon, I sat in this one room, making potato* kacaurīs. *Meanwhile, in the course of the same afternoon, Swamiji brought in fifteen other special vegetarian dishes, each one in a large enough quantity for forty persons. And he had made them singlehandedly in his small, narrow kitchen.*

It was rather hot that afternoon, and I was perspiring. I asked, "Swamiji, may I please have a glass of water?" He peeked his head around the door, and said, "Go wash your hands." I immediately did so, and when I returned Swamiji had a glass of water for me. He explained to me that while preparing this food for offering to the Supreme Lord, one should not think of eating or drinking anything. So after drinking the glass of water, I went in and washed my hands and sat down. About two in the afternoon, I said, "Swamiji, may I have a cigarette?" and he peeked his head around the corner and said, "Go wash your hands." So I did, and when I came back he explained to me the four rules of Kṛṣṇa consciousness. I continued to make the kacaurīs, *and around three-thirty, four o'clock, it was extremely warm in the room, and as Swamiji was bringing in one of his preparations I was wiping my arm and hand across my forehead. He looked down at me and said, "Please go and wash your hands." Again*

I did so, and upon returning he had a moistened paper towel for me. He explained that cooking for Kṛṣṇa required certain standards of cleanliness and purity that were different than the ones I was accustomed to.

About thirty people attended. The decorations were similar to the ones for the initiation a few days before, except that they were more festive and the feast was more lavish. Swamiji's front room was decorated with pine boughs, and leaves and flowers were strung overhead from one side of the room to the other. Some of the new initiates came, their large red beads around their necks. They had taken vows now—sixteen rounds a day—and they chanted on their beads just as Swamiji had shown them, and they happily though self-consciously called one another by their new spiritual names.

Jānakī: *Swamiji said that I should wear a* sārī *at my wedding, and he said it should be made of silk. I asked him what color, and he said red. So Mukunda bought me an absolutely elegant* sārī *and some very nice jewelry.*

The Swami's friends were used to seeing Jānakī, as she always came with Mukunda, but usually she wore no makeup and dressed in very plain clothes. They were astounded and somewhat embarrassed to see her enter wearing jewelry, makeup, and a bright red *sārī.* The bride's hair was up and braided, decorated with an oval silver-filigree hair ornament. She wore heavy silver earrings, which Mukunda had purchased from an expensive Indian import shop on Fifth Avenue, and silver bracelets.

Prabhupāda directed Mukunda and Jānakī to sit opposite him on the other side of the sacrificial fire arena. And just as at the initiation, he lit the incense and instructed them in the purification by water, recited the purification *mantra,* and then began to speak. He explained about the relationship between man and wife in Kṛṣṇa consciousness, and how they should serve each other and how they should serve Kṛṣṇa. Prabhupāda then asked Jānakī's sister to present her formally to Mukunda as his wife. Mukunda then repeated after Swamiji: "I accept Jānakī as my wife, and I shall take charge of her throughout both of our lives. We shall live together peacefully in Kṛṣṇa consciousness, and there will never be any separation." And then Prabhupāda turned to Jānakī: "Will you accept Śrīmān Mukunda dāsa Brahmacārī as your life's companion? Will you serve him always and help him to execute his Kṛṣṇa conscious activities?" And then Jānakī replied, "Yes, I accept Mukunda as my husband throughout my life. There shall never be any separation between us, either in happiness or distress. I shall serve him always, and we shall live together peacefully in Kṛṣṇa consciousness."

No one knew anything of what was going on except Swamiji. He led the chanting, he gave the lines for the bride and groom to exchange, he told them where to sit and what to do—he, in fact, had told them to get married. He had also cooked the elaborate feast that was waiting in the kitchen for the completion of the ceremony.

Prabhupāda asked Mukunda and Jānakī to exchange their flower garlands and after that to exchange sitting places. He then asked Mukunda to rub some vermilion down the part in Jānakī's hair and then to cover her head with her *sārī.* Next came the fire sacrifice, and finally the feast.

The special feature of the wedding was the big feast. It turned out to be quite a social success. The guests ate enthusiastically, asked for more, and raved about the sensational tastes. Prabhupāda's followers, who were accustomed to the simple daily fare of rice, *dāl, sabjī,* and *capātīs,* found the feast intoxicating and ate as much as they could get. Many of Mukunda's friends were macrobiotic followers, and at first they fastidiously avoided all the sweets. But gradually the enthusiasm of the others wore down their resistance, and they became captivated by the Swami's expert cooking. "God, he's a good cook!" said Jānakī. Bruce, who had missed the first initiation, was seeing the Vedic fire sacrifice and tasting the Swami's *kacaurīs* for the first time. He resolved on the spot to dedicate himself to Kṛṣṇa consciousness and become one of the Swamiji's disciples as soon as possible. Almost all the visitors personally approached Swamiji to thank him and congratulate him. He was happy and said it was all Kṛṣṇa's blessings, Kṛṣṇa's grace.

After the ceremony, Mukunda and his wife entertained many of the devotees and guests in their apartment. The evening had put everyone in high spirits, and Hayagrīva was reciting poetry. Then someone turned on the television to catch the scheduled interview with Allen Ginsberg, the poet, and much to everyone's happiness, Allen began playing harmonium and chanting Hare Kṛṣṇa. He even said there was a swami on the Lower East Side who was teaching this *mantra-yoga.* Kṛṣṇa consciousness was new and unheard of, yet now the devotees were seeing a famous celebrity perform *kīrtana* on television. The whole evening seemed auspicious.

Back at his apartment, Prabhupāda, along with a few helpers, cleaned up after the ceremony. He was satisfied. He was introducing some of the major elements of his Kṛṣṇa consciousness mission. He had initiated disciples, he had married them, and he had feasted the public with *kṛṣṇa-prasādam.* "If I had the means," he told his followers, "I could hold a major festival like this every day."

CHAPTER TWENTY

Stay High Forever

But while this was going on, an old man, one year past his allotted three score and ten, wandered into New York's East Village and set about to prove to the world that he knew where God could be found. In only three months, the man, Swami A. C. Bhaktivedanta, succeeded in convincing the world's toughest audience—Bohemians, acidheads, potheads, and hippies—that he knew the way to God: Turn Off, Sing Out, and Fall In. This new brand of holy man, with all due deference to Dr. Leary, has come forth with a brand of "Consciousness Expansion" that's sweeter than acid, cheaper than pot, and nonbustible by fuzz. How is all this possible? "Through Kṛṣṇa," the Swami says.

—from *The East Village Other*
October 1966

PRABHUPĀDA'S HEALTH WAS good that summer and fall, or so it seemed. He worked long and hard, and except for four hours of rest at night, he was always active. He would speak intensively on and on, never tiring, and his voice was strong. His smiles were strong and charming; his singing voice loud and melodious. During *kīrtana* he would thump Bengali *mṛdaṅga* rhythms on his bongo drum, sometimes for an hour. He ate heartily of rice, *dāl, capātīs,* and vegetables with ghee.

His face was full and his belly protuberant. Sometimes, in a light mood, he would drum with two fingers on his belly and say that the resonance affirmed his good health. His golden color had the radiance of youth and well-being preserved by seventy years of healthy, nondestructive habits. When he smiled, virility and vitality came on so strong as to embarrass a faded, dissolute New Yorker. In many ways, he was not at all like an old man. And his new followers completely accepted his active youthfulness as a part of the wonder of Swamiji, just as they had come to accept the wonder of the chanting and the wonder of Kṛṣṇa. Swamiji wasn't an ordinary man. He was spiritual. He could do anything. None of his followers dared advise him to slow down, nor did it ever really occur to them that he needed such protection—they were busy just trying to keep up with him.

During the two months at 26 Second Avenue, he had achieved what had formerly been only a dream. He now had a temple, a duly registered society, full freedom to preach, and a band of initiated disciples. When a Godbrother had written asking him how he would manage a temple in New York, Prabhupāda had said that he would need men from India but that he might find an American or two who could help. That had been last winter. Now Kṛṣṇa had put him in a different situation: he had received no help from his Godbrothers, no big donations from Indian business magnates, and no assistance from the Indian government, but he was finding success in a different way. These were "happy days," he said. He had struggled alone for a year, but then "Kṛṣṇa sent me men and money."

Yes, these were happy days for Prabhupāda, but his happiness was not like the happiness of an old man's "sunset years," as he fades into the dim comforts of retirement. His was the happiness of youth, a time of blossoming, of new powers, a time when future hopes expand without limit. He was seventy-one years old, but in ambition he was a courageous youth. He was like a young giant just beginning to grow. He was happy because his preaching was taking hold, just as Lord Caitanya had been happy when He had traveled alone to South India, spreading the chanting of Hare Kṛṣṇa. Prabhupāda's happiness was that of a selfless servant of Kṛṣṇa to whom Kṛṣṇa was sending candidates for devotional life. He was happy to place the seed of devotion within their hearts and to train them in chanting Hare Kṛṣṇa, hearing about Kṛṣṇa, and working to spread Kṛṣṇa consciousness.

Prabhupāda continued to accelerate. After the first initiations and the first marriage, he was eager for the next step. He was pleased by what he had, but he wanted to do more. It was the greed of the Vaiṣṇava—not a greed to have sense gratification but to take more and more for Kṛṣṇa. He would "go in like a needle and come out like a plow." That is to say, from a small, seemingly insignificant beginning, he would expand his movement to tremendous proportions. At least, that was his desire. He was not content with his newfound success and security at 26 Second Avenue, but was yearning to increase ISKCON as far as possible. This had always been his vision, and he had written it into the ISKCON charter: "to achieve real unity and peace in the world ... within the members, and humanity at large."

* * *

Swamiji gathered his group together. He knew that once they tried it they would love it. But it would only happen if he personally went with them. Washington Square Park was only half a mile away, maybe a little more.

Ravīndra-svarūpa: *He never made a secret of what he was doing. He used to say, "I want* everybody *to know what we are doing." Then one day, D-day came. He said, "We are going to chant in Washington Square Park." Everybody was scared. You just don't go into a park and chant. It seemed like a weird thing to do. But he assured us, saying, "You won't be afraid when you start chanting. Kṛṣṇa will help you." And so we trudged down to Washington Square Park, but we were very upset about it. Up until that time, we weren't exposing ourselves. I was upset about it, and I know that several other people were, to be making a public figure of yourself.*

With Prabhupāda leading they set out on that fair Sunday morning, walking the city blocks from Second Avenue to Washington Square in the heart of Greenwich Village. And the way he looked—just by walking he created a sensation. None of the boys had shaved heads or robes, but because of Swamiji—with his saffron robes, his white pointy shoes, and his shaved head held high—people were astonished. It wasn't like when he would go out alone. That brought nothing more than an occasional second glance. But today, with a group of young men hurrying to keep up with him as he headed through the city streets, obviously about to do *something,* he caused a stir. Tough guys and kids called out names, and others laughed and made sounds. A year ago, in Butler, the Agarwals had been sure that Prabhupāda had not come to America for followers. "He didn't want to make any waves," Sally had thought. But now he was making waves, walking through the New York City streets, headed for the first public chanting in America, followed by his first disciples.

In the park there were hundreds of people milling about—stylish, decadent Greenwich Villagers, visitors from other boroughs, tourists from other states and other lands—an amalgam of faces, nationalities, ages, and interests. As usual, someone was playing his guitar by the fountain, boys and girls were sitting together and kissing, some were throwing Frisbees, some were playing drums or flutes or other instruments, and some were walking their dogs, talking, watching everything, wandering around. It was a typical day in the Village.

Prabhupāda went to a patch of lawn where, despite a small sign that read Keep Off the Grass, many people were lounging. He sat down, and one by one his followers sat beside him. He took out his brass hand cymbals and sang the *mahā-mantra,* and his disciples responded, awkwardly at first, then stronger. It wasn't as bad as they had thought it would be.

Jagannātha: *It was a marvelous thing, a marvelous experience that Swamiji brought upon me. Because it opened me up a great deal, and I overcame a certain shyness—the first time to chant out in the middle of everything.*

A curious crowd gathered to watch, though no one joined in. Within a few minutes, two policemen moved in through the crowd. "Who's in charge here?" an officer asked roughly. The boys looked toward Prabhupāda. "Didn't you see the sign?" an officer asked. Swamiji furrowed his brow and turned his eyes toward the sign. He got up and walked to the uncomfortably warm pavement and sat down again, and his followers straggled after to sit around him. Prabhupāda continued the chanting for half an hour, and the crowd stood listening. A *guru* in America had never gone onto the streets before and sung the names of God.

After *kīrtana,* he asked for a copy of the *Śrīmad-Bhāgavatam* and had Hayagrīva read aloud from the preface. With clear articulation, Hayagrīva read: "Disparity in the human society is due to the basic principle of a godless civilization. There is God, the Almighty One, from whom everything emanates, by whom everything is maintained, and in whom everything is merged to rest. ..." The crowd was still. Afterward, the Swami and his followers walked back to the storefront, feeling elated and victorious. They had broken the American silence.

* * *

Allen Ginsberg lived nearby on East Tenth Street. One day he received a peculiar invitation in the mail:

Practice the transcendental sound vibration,
Hare Krishna, Hare Krishna, Krishna Krishna, Hare Hare
Hare Rama, Hare Rama, Rama Rama, Hare Hare.
This chanting will cleanse the dust from the mirror of the mind.

International Society for Krishna Consciousness
Meetings at 7 A.M. daily
Mondays, Wednesdays, and Fridays at 7:00 P.M.
You are cordially invited to come and
bring your friends.

Swamiji had asked the boys to distribute it around the neighborhood.

One evening, soon after he received the invitation, Allen Ginsberg and his roommate, Peter Orlovsky, arrived at the storefront in a Volkswagen minibus. Allen had been captivated by the Hare Kṛṣṇa *mantra* several years before, when he had first encountered it at the Kumbha-melā festival in Allahabad, India, and he had been chanting it often ever since. The devotees were impressed to see the world-famous author of *Howl* and leading figure of the beat generation enter their humble storefront. His advocation of free sex, marijuana, and LSD, his claims of drug-induced visions of spirituality in everyday sights, his political ideas, his exploration of insanity, revolt, and nakedness, and his attempts to create a harmony of likeminded souls—all were influential on the minds of American young people, especially those living on the Lower East Side. Although by middle-class standards he was scandalous and disheveled, he was, in his own right, a figure of worldly repute, more so than anyone who had ever come to the storefront before.

Allen Ginsberg: *Bhaktivedanta seemed to have no friends in America, but was alone, totally alone, and gone somewhat like a lone hippie to the nearest refuge, the place where it was cheap enough to rent.*

There were a few people sitting cross-legged on the floor. I think most of them were Lower East Side hippies who had just wandered in off the street, with beards and a curiosity and inquisitiveness and a respect for spiritual presentation of some kind. Some of them were sitting there with glazed eyes, but most of them were just like gentle folk—bearded, hip, and curious. They were refugees from the middle class in the Lower East Side, looking exactly like the street sādhus *in India. It was very similar, that phase in American underground history. And I liked immediately the idea that Swami Bhaktivedanta had chosen the Lower East Side of New York for his practice. He'd gone to the lower depths. He'd gone to a spot more like the side streets of Calcutta than any other place.*

Allen and Peter had come for the *kīrtana,* but it wasn't quite time—Prabhupāda hadn't come down. They presented a new harmonium to the devotees. "It's for the *kīrtanas,*" said Allen. "A little donation." Allen stood at the entrance to the storefront, talking with Hayagrīva, telling him how he had been chanting Hare Kṛṣṇa around the world—at peace marches, poetry readings, a procession in Prague, a writers' union in Moscow. "Secular *kīrtana,*" said Allen, "but Hare Kṛṣṇa nonetheless." Then Prabhupāda entered. Allen and Peter sat with the congregation and joined in the *kīrtana.* Allen played harmonium.

Allen: *I was astounded that he'd come with the chanting, because it seemed like a reinforcement from India. I had been running around singing Hare Kṛṣṇa but had never understood exactly why or what it meant. But I was surprised to see that he had a different melody, because I thought the melody I knew was* the *melody, the universal melody. I had gotten so used to my melody that actually the biggest difference I had with him was over the tune—because I'd solidified it in my mind for years, and to hear another tune actually blew my mind.*

After the lecture, Allen came forward to meet Prabhupāda, who was still sitting on his dais. Allen offered his respects with folded palms and touched Prabhupāda's feet, and Prabhupāda reciprocated by nodding his head and folding his palms. They talked together briefly, and then Prabhupāda returned to his apartment. Allen mentioned to Hayagrīva that he would like to come by again and talk more with Prabhupāda, so Hayagrīva invited him to come the next day and stay for lunch *prasādam.*

"Don't you think Swamiji is a little too esoteric for New York?" Allen asked. Hayagrīva thought. "Maybe," he replied.

Hayagrīva then asked Allen to help the Swami, since his visa would soon expire. He had entered the country with a visa for a two-month stay, and he had been extending his visa for two more months again and again. This had gone on for one year, but the last time he had applied for an extension, he had been refused. "We need an immigration lawyer," said Hayagrīva. "I'll donate to that," Allen assured him.

The next morning, Allen Ginsberg came by with a check and another harmonium. Up in Prabhupāda's apartment, he demonstrated *his* melody for chanting Hare Kṛṣṇa, and then he and Prabhupāda talked.

Allen: *I was a little shy with him because I didn't know where he was coming from. I had that harmonium I wanted to donate, and I had a little money. I thought it was great now that he was here to expound on the Hare Kṛṣṇa* mantra*—that would sort of justify my singing. I knew what I was doing, but I didn't have any theological background to satisfy further inquiries, and here was someone who did. So I thought that was absolutely great. Now I could go around singing Hare Kṛṣṇa, and if anybody wanted to know what it was, I could just send them to Swami Bhaktivedanta to find out. If anyone wanted to know the technical intricacies and the ultimate history, I could send them to him.*

He explained to me about his own teacher and about Caitanya and the lineage going back. His head was filled with so many things and what he was doing. He was already working on his translations. He always seemed to be sitting there just day after day and night after night. And I think he had one or two people helping him.

Prabhupāda was very cordial with Allen. Quoting a passage from *Bhagavad-gītā* where Kṛṣṇa says that whatever a great man does, others will follow, he requested Allen to continue chanting Hare Kṛṣṇa at every opportunity, so that others would follow his example. He told about Lord Caitanya's organizing the first civil disobedience movement in India, leading a *saṅkīrtana* protest march against the Muslim ruler. Allen was fascinated. He enjoyed talking with the Swami.

But they had their differences. When Allen expressed his admiration for a well-known Bengali holy man, Prabhupāda said that the holy man was bogus. Allen was shocked. He'd never before heard a swami severely criticize another's practice. Prabhupāda explained, on the basis of Vedic evidence, the reasoning behind his criticism, and Allen admitted that he had naively thought that all holy men were one-hundred-percent holy.

But now he decided that he should not simply accept a *sādhu,* including Prabhupāda, on blind faith. He decided to see Prabhupāda in a more severe, critical light.

Allen: *I had a very superstitious attitude of respect, which probably was an idiot sense of mentality, and so Swami Bhaktivedanta's teaching was very good to make me question that. It also made me question* him *and not take him for granted.*

Allen described a divine vision he'd had in which William Blake had appeared to him in sound, and in which he had understood the oneness of all things. A *sādhu* in Vṛndāvana had told Allen that this meant that William Blake was his *guru.* But to Prabhupāda this made no sense.

Allen: *The main thing, above and beyond all our differences, was an aroma of sweetness that he had, a personal, selfless sweetness like total devotion. And that was what always conquered me, whatever intellectual questions or doubts I had, or even cynical views of ego. In his presence there was a kind of personal charm, coming from dedication, that conquered all our conflicts. Even though I didn't agree with him, I always liked to be with him.*

Allen agreed, at Prabhupāda's request, to chant more and to try to give up smoking.

"Do you really intend to make these American boys into Vaiṣṇavas?" Allen asked.

"Yes," Prabhupāda replied happily, "and I will make them all *brāhmaṇas.*"

Allen left a $200 check to help cover the legal expenses for extending the Swami's visa and wished him good luck. "*Brāhmaṇas!*" Allen didn't see how such a transformation could be possible.

* * *

September 23

It was Rādhāṣṭamī, the appearance day of Śrīmatī Rādhārāṇī, Lord Kṛṣṇa's eternal consort. Prabhupāda held his second initiation. Keith became Kīrtanānanda, Steve became Satsvarūpa, Bruce became Brahmānanda, and Chuck became Acyutānanda. It was another festive day with a fire sacrifice in Prabhupāda's front room and a big feast.

* * *

Prabhupāda lived amid the drug culture, in a neighborhood where the young people were almost desperately attempting to alter their consciousness, whether by drugs or by some other means—whatever was available. Prabhupāda assured them that they could easily achieve the higher consciousness they desired by chanting Hare Kṛṣṇa. It was inevitable that in explaining Kṛṣṇa consciousness he would make allusions to the drug experience, even if only to show that the two were contrary paths. He was familiar already with Indian "*sādhus*" who took *gāñjā* and hashish on the plea of aiding their meditations. And even before he had left India, hippie tourists had become a familiar sight on the streets of Delhi.

The hippies liked India because of the cultural mystique and easy access to drugs. They would meet their Indian counterparts, who assured them that taking hashish was spiritual, and then they would return to America and perpetrate their misconceptions of Indian spiritual culture.

It was the way of life. The local head shops carried a full line of paraphernalia. Marijuana, LSD, peyote, cocaine, and hard drugs like heroin and barbiturates were easily purchased on the streets and in the parks. Underground newspapers reported important news on the drug scene, featured a cartoon character named Captain High, and ran crossword puzzles that only a seasoned "head" could answer.

Prabhupāda had to teach that Kṛṣṇa consciousness was beyond the revered LSD trip. "Do you think taking LSD can produce ecstasy and higher consciousness?" he once asked his storefront audience. "Then just imagine a roomful of LSD. Kṛṣṇa consciousness is like that." People would regularly come in and ask Swamiji's disciples, "Do you get high from this?" And the devotees would answer, "Oh, yes. You can get high just by chanting. Why don't you try it?"

Greg Scharf (Brahmānanda's brother) hadn't tried LSD; but he wanted higher consciousness, so he decided to try the chanting.

Greg: *I was eighteen. Everyone at the storefront had taken LSD, and I thought maybe I should too, because I wanted to feel like part of the crowd. So I asked Umāpati, "Hey, Umāpati, do you think I should try LSD? Because I don't know what you guys are talking about." He said no, that Swamiji said you didn't need LSD. I never did take it, so I guess it was OK.*

Hayagrīva: *Have you ever heard of LSD? It's a psychedelic drug that comes like a pill, and if you take it you can get religious ecstasies. Do you think this can help my spiritual life?*

Prabhupāda: *You don't need to take anything for your spiritual life. Your spiritual life is already here.*

Had anyone else said such a thing, Hayagrīva would never have agreed with him. But because Swamiji seemed "so absolutely positive," therefore "there was no question of not agreeing."

Satsvarūpa: *I knew Swamiji was in a state of exalted consciousness, and I was hoping that somehow he could teach the process to me. In the privacy of his room, I asked him, "Is there spiritual advancement that you can make from which you won't fall back?" By his answer—"Yes"—I was convinced that my own attempts to be spiritual on LSD, only to fall down later, could be replaced by a total spiritual life such as Swamiji had. I could see he was convinced, and then I was convinced.*

Greg: *LSD was like the spiritual drug of the times, and Swamiji was the only one who dared to speak out against it, saying it was nonsense. I think that was the first battle he had to conquer in trying to promote his movement on the Lower East Side. Even those who came regularly to the storefront thought that LSD was good.*

Probably the most famous experiments with LSD in those days were by Timothy Leary and Richard Alpert, Harvard psychology instructors who studied the effects of the drug, published their findings in professional journals, and advocated the use of LSD for self-realization and fulfillment. After being fired from Harvard, Timothy Leary went on to become a national priest of LSD and for some time ran an LSD commune in Millbrook, New York.

When the members of the Millbrook commune heard about the swami on the Lower East Side who led his followers in a chant that got you high, they began visiting the storefront. One night, a group of about ten hippies from Millbrook came to Swamiji's *kīrtana.* They all chanted (not so much in worship of Kṛṣṇa as to see what kind of high the chanting could produce), and after the lecture a Millbrook leader asked about drugs. Prabhupāda replied that drugs were not necessary for spiritual life, that they could not produce spiritual consciousness, and that all drug-induced religious visions were simply hallucinations. To realize God was not so easy or cheap that one could do it just by taking a pill or smoking. Chanting Hare Kṛṣṇa, he explained, was a purifying process to uncover one's pure consciousness. Taking drugs would increase the covering and bar one from self-realization.

"But have *you* ever taken LSD?" The question now became a challenge.

"No," Prabhupāda replied. "I have never taken any of these things, not even cigarettes or tea."

"If you haven't taken it, then how can you say what it is?" The Millbrookers looked around, smiling. Two or three even burst out with laughter, and they snapped their fingers, thinking the Swami had been checkmated.

"I have not taken," Prabhupāda replied regally from his dais. "But my disciples have taken all these things—marijuana, LSD—many times, and they have given them all up. You can hear from them. Hayagrīva, you can speak." And Hayagrīva sat up a little and spoke out in his stentorian best.

"Well, no matter how high you go on LSD, you eventually reach a peak, and then you have to come back down. Just like traveling into outer space in a rocket ship. [He gave one of Swamiji's familiar examples.] Your spacecraft can travel very far away from the earth for thousands of miles, day after day, but it cannot simply go on traveling and traveling. Eventually it must land. On LSD, we experience going up, but we always have to come down again. That's not spiritual consciousness. When you actually attain spiritual or Kṛṣṇa consciousness, you stay high. Because you go to Kṛṣṇa, you don't have to come down. You can stay high forever."

Prabhupāda was sitting in his back room with Hayagrīva and Umāpati and other disciples. The evening meeting had just ended, and the visitors from Millbrook had gone. "Kṛṣṇa consciousness is so nice, Swamiji," Umāpati spoke up. "You just get higher and higher, and you don't come down."

Prabhupāda smiled. "Yes, that's right."

"No more coming down," Umāpati said, laughing, and the others also began to laugh. Some clapped their hands, repeating, "No more coming down."

The conversation inspired Hayagrīva and Umāpati to produce a new handbill:

STAY HIGH FOREVER!
No More Coming Down

Practice Krishna Consciousness
Expand your Consciousness by practicing the

* TRANSCENDENTAL SOUND VIBRATION *

HARE KRISHNA HARE KRISHNA KRISHNA KRISHNA HARE HARE
HARE RAMA HARE RAMA RAMA RAMA HARE HARE

The leaflet went on to extol Kṛṣṇa consciousness over any other high. It included phrases like "end all bringdowns" and "turn on," and it spoke against "employing artificially induced methods of self-realization and expanded consciousness." Someone objected to the flyer's "playing too much off the hippie mentality," but Prabhupāda said it was all right.

Greg: *When these drug people on the Lower East Side came and talked to Swamiji, he was so patient with them. He was speaking on a philosophy which they had never heard before. When someone takes LSD, they're really into themselves, and they don't hear properly when someone talks to them. So Swamiji would make particular points, and they wouldn't understand him. So he would have to make the same point again. He was very patient with these people, but he would not give in to their claim that LSD was a bona fide spiritual aid to self-realization.*

* * *

October 1966

Tompkins Square Park was *the* park on the Lower East Side. On the south, it was bordered by Seventh Street, with its four- and five-storied brownstone tenements. On the north side was Tenth, with more brownstones, but in better condition, and the very old, small building that housed the Tompkins Square branch of the New York Public Library. On Avenue B, the park's east border, stood St. Brigid's Church, built in 1848, when the neighborhood had been entirely Irish. The church, school, and rectory still occupied much of the block. And the west border of the park, Avenue A, was lined with tiny old candy stores selling newspapers, magazines, cigarettes, and egg-creme sodas at the counter. There were also a few bars, several grocery stores, and a couple of Slavic restaurants specializing in inexpensive vegetable broths, which brought Ukranians and hippies side by side for bodily nourishment.

The park's ten acres held many tall trees, but at least half the park was paved. A network of five-foot-high heavy wrought-iron fences weaved through the park, lining the walkways and protecting the grass. The fences and the many walkways and entrances to the park gave it the effect of a maze.

Since the weather was still warm and it was Sunday, the park was crowded with people. Almost all the space on the benches that lined the walkways was occupied. There were old people, mostly Ukranians, dressed in outdated suits and sweaters, even in the warm weather, sitting together in clans, talking. There were many children in the park also, mostly Puerto Ricans and blacks but also fair-haired, hard-faced slum kids racing around on bikes or playing with balls and Frisbees. The basketball and handball courts were mostly taken by the teenagers. And as always, there were plenty of loose, running dogs.

A marble miniature gazebo (four pillars and a roof, with a drinking fountain inside) was a remnant from the old days—1891, according to the inscription. On its four sides were the words *HOPE, FAITH, CHARITY,* and *TEMPERANCE.* But someone had sprayed the whole structure with black paint, making crude designs and illegible names and initials. Today, a bench had been taken over by several conga and bongo drummers, and the whole park pulsed with their demanding rhythms.

And the hippies were there, different from the others. The bearded Bohemian men and their long-haired young girlfriends dressed in old blue jeans were still an unusual sight. Even in the Lower East Side melting pot, their presence created tension. They were from middle-class families, and so they had not been driven to the slums by dire economic necessity. This created conflicts in their dealings with the underprivileged immigrants. And the hippies' well-known proclivity for psychedelic drugs, their revolt against their families and affluence, and their absorption in the avant-garde sometimes made them the jeered minority among their neighbors.

But the hippies just wanted to do their own thing and create their own revolution for "love and peace," so usually they were tolerated, although not appreciated.

There were various groups among the young and hip at Tompkins Square Park. There were friends who had gone to the same school together, who took the same drug together, or who agreed on a particular philosophy of art, literature, politics, or metaphysics. There were lovers. There were groups hanging out together for reasons undecipherable, except for the common purpose of doing their own thing. And there were others, who lived like hermits—a loner would sit on a park bench, analyzing the effects of cocaine, looking up at the strangely rustling green leaves of the trees and the blue sky above the tenements and then down to the garbage at his feet, as he helplessly followed his mind from fear to illumination, to disgust to hallucination, on and on, until after a few hours the drug began to wear off and he was again a common stranger. Sometimes they would sit up all night, "spaced out" in the park, until at last, in the light of morning, they would stretch out on benches to sleep.

Hippies especially took to the park on Sundays. They at least passed through the park on their way to St. Mark's Place, Greenwich Village, or the Lexington Avenue subway at Astor Place, or the IND subway at Houston and Second, or to catch an uptown bus on First Avenue, a downtown bus on Second, or a crosstown on Ninth. Or they went to the park just to get out of their apartments and sit together in the open air—to get high again, to talk, or to walk through the park's maze of pathways.

But whatever the hippies' diverse interests and drives, the Lower East Side was an essential part of the mystique. It was not just a dirty slum; it was the best place in the world to conduct the experiment in consciousness. For all its filth and threat of violence and the confined life of its brownstone tenements, the Lower East Side was still the forefront of the revolution in mind expansion. Unless you were living there and taking psychedelics or marijuana, or at least intellectually pursuing the quest for free personal religion, you weren't enlightened, and you weren't taking part in the most progressive evolution of human consciousness. And it was this searching—a quest beyond the humdrum existence of the ordinary, materialistic, "straight" American—that brought unity to the otherwise eclectic gathering of hippies on the Lower East Side.

Into this chaotic pageant Swamiji entered with his followers and sat down to hold a *kīrtana*. Three or four devotees who arrived ahead of him selected an open area of the park, put out the Oriental carpet Robert Nelson had donated, sat down on it, and began playing *karatālas* and chanting Hare Kṛṣṇa. Immediately some boys rode up on their bicycles, braked just short of the carpet, and stood astride their bikes, curiously and irreverently staring. Other passersby gathered to listen.

Meanwhile Swamiji, accompanied by half a dozen disciples, was walking the eight blocks from the storefront. Brahmānanda carried the harmonium and the Swami's drum. Kīrtanānanda, who was now shaven-headed at Swamiji's request and dressed in loose-flowing canary yellow robes, created an extra sensation. Drivers pulled their cars over to have a look, their passengers leaning forward, agape at the outrageous dress and shaved head. As the group passed a store, people inside would poke each other and indicate the spectacle. People came to the windows of their tenements, taking in the Swami and his group as if a parade were passing. The Puerto Rican tough guys, especially, couldn't restrain themselves from exaggerated reactions. "Hey, Buddha!" they taunted. "Hey, you forgot to change your pajamas!" They made shrill screams as if imitating Indian war whoops they had heard in Hollywood westerns.

"Hey, A-rabs!" exclaimed one heckler, who began imitating what he thought was an Eastern dance. No one on the street knew anything about Kṛṣṇa consciousness, nor even of Hindu culture and customs. To them, the Swami's entourage was just a bunch of crazy hippies showing off. But they didn't quite know what to make of the Swami. He was different. Nevertheless, they were suspicious. Some, however, like Irving Halpern, a veteran Lower East Side resident, felt sympathetic toward this stranger, who was "apparently a very dignified person on a peaceful mission."

Irving Halpern: *A lot of people had spectacularized notions of what a swami was. As though they were going to suddenly see people lying on little mattresses made out of nails—and all kinds of other absurd notions. Yet here came just a very graceful, peaceful, gentle, obviously well-meaning being into a lot of hostility.*

"Hippies!"

"What are they, Communists?"

While the young taunted, the middle-aged and elderly shook their heads or stared, cold and uncomprehending. The way to the park was spotted with blasphemies, ribald jokes, and tension, but no violence. After the successful *kīrtana* in Washington Square Park, Prabhupāda had regularly been sending out "parades" of three or four devotees, chanting and playing hand cymbals through the streets and sidewalks of the Lower East Side. On one occasion, they had been bombarded with water balloons and eggs, and they were sometimes faced with bullies looking for a fight. But they were never attacked—just stared at, laughed at, or shouted after.

Today, the ethnic neighbors just assumed that Prabhupāda and his followers had come onto the streets dressed in outlandish costumes as a joke, just to turn everything topsy-turvy and cause stares and howls. They felt that their responses were only natural for any normal, respectable American slum-dweller.

So it was quite an adventure before the group even reached the park. Swamiji, however, remained unaffected. "What are they saying?" he asked once or twice, and Brahmānanda explained. Prabhupāda had a way of holding his head high, his chin up, as he walked forward. It made him look aristocratic and determined. His vision was spiritual—he saw everyone as a spiritual soul and Kṛṣṇa as the controller of everything. Yet aside from that, even from a worldly point of view he was unafraid of the city's pandemonium. After all, he was an experienced "Calcutta man."

The *kīrtana* had been going for about ten minutes when Swamiji arrived. Stepping out of his white rubber slippers, just as if he were home in the temple, he sat down on the rug with his followers, who had now stopped their singing and were watching him. He wore a pink sweater, and around his shoulders a *khādī* wrapper. He smiled. Looking at his group, he indicated the rhythm by counting, one ... two ... *three*. Then he began clapping his hands heavily as he continued counting, "One ... two ... *three*." The *karatālas* followed, at first with wrong beats, but he kept the rhythm by clapping his hands, and then they got it, clapping hands, clashing cymbals artlessly to a slow, steady beat.

He began singing prayers that no one else knew. *Vande 'haṁ śrī-guroḥ śrī-yuta-pada-kamalaṁ śrī-gurūn vaiṣṇavāṁś ca*. His voice was sweet like the harmonium, rich in the nuances of Bengali melody. Sitting on the rug under a large oak tree, he sang the mysterious Sanskrit prayers. None of his followers knew any *mantra* but Hare Kṛṣṇa, but they knew Swamiji. And they kept the rhythm, listening closely to him while the trucks rumbled on the street and the conga drums pulsed in the distance.

As he sang—*śrī-rūpaṁ sāgrajātaṁ*—the dogs came by, kids stared, a few mockers pointed fingers: "Hey, who is that priest, man?" But his voice was a shelter beyond the clashing dualities. His boys went on ringing cymbals while he sang alone: *śrī-rādhā-kṛṣṇa-pādān.*

Prabhupāda sang prayers in praise of Śrīmatī Rādhārāṇī's pure conjugal love for Kṛṣṇa, the beloved of the *gopīs.* Each word, passed down for hundreds of years by the intimate associates of Kṛṣṇa, was saturated with deep transcendental meaning that only he understood. *Saha-gaṇa-lalitā-śrī-viśākhānvitāṁś ca.* They waited for him to begin Hare Kṛṣṇa, although hearing him chant was exciting enough.

More people came—which was what Prabhupāda wanted. He wanted them chanting and dancing with him, and now his followers wanted that too. They wanted to be with him. They had tried together at the U.N., Ananda Ashram, and Washington Square. It seemed that this would be the thing they would always do—go with Swamiji and sit and chant. He would always be with them, chanting.

Then he began the *mantra*—Hare Kṛṣṇa, Hare Kṛṣṇa, Kṛṣṇa Kṛṣṇa, Hare Hare/ Hare Rāma, Hare Rāma, Rāma Rāma, Hare Hare. They responded, too low and muddled at first, but he returned it to them again, singing it right and triumphant. Again they responded, gaining heart, ringing *karatālas* and clapping hands—one ... two ... *three,* one ... two ... *three.* Again he sang it alone, and they stayed, hanging closely on each word, clapping, beating cymbals, and watching him looking back at them from his inner concentration—his old-age wisdom, his *bhakti*—and out of love for Swamiji, they broke loose from their surroundings and joined him as a chanting congregation. Swamiji played his small drum, holding its strap in his left hand, bracing the drum against his body, and with his right hand playing intricate *mṛdaṅga* rhythms.

Hare Kṛṣṇa, Hare Kṛṣṇa, Kṛṣṇa Kṛṣṇa, Hare Hare/ Hare Rāma, Hare Rāma, Rāma Rāma, Hare Hare. He was going strong after half an hour, repeating the *mantra,* carrying them with him as interested onlookers gathered in greater numbers. A few hippies sat down on the edge of the rug, copying the cross-legged sitting posture, listening, clapping, trying the chanting, and the small inner circle of Prabhupāda and his followers grew, as gradually more people joined.

As always, his *kīrtana* attracted musicians.

Irving Halpern: *I make flutes, and I play musical instruments. There are all kinds of different instruments that I make. When the Swami came,*

I went up and started playing, and he welcomed me. Whenever a new musician would join and play their first note, he would extend his arms. It would be as though he had stepped up to the podium and was going to lead the New York Philharmonic. I mean, there was this gesture that every musician knows. You just know when someone else wants you to play with them and feels good that you are playing with them. And this very basic kind of musician communication was there with him, and I related to it very quickly. And I was happy about it.

Lone musicians were always loitering in different parts of the park, and when they heard they could play with the Swami's chanting and that they were welcome, then they began to come by, one by one. A saxophone player came just because there was such a strong rhythm section to play with. Others, like Irving Halpern, saw it as something spiritual, with good vibrations. As the musicians joined, more passersby were drawn into the *kīrtana*. Prabhupāda had been singing both lead and chorus, and many who had joined now sang the lead part also, so that there was a constant chorus of chanting. During the afternoon, the crowd grew to more than a hundred, with a dozen musicians trying—with their conga and bongo drums, bamboo flutes, metal flutes, mouth organs, wood and metal "clackers," tambourines, and guitars—to stay with the Swami.

Irving Halpern: *The park resounded. The musicians were very careful in listening to the* mantras. *When the Swami sang Hare Kṛṣṇa, Hare Kṛṣṇa, Kṛṣṇa Kṛṣṇa, Hare Hare/ Hare Rāma, Hare Rāma, Rāma Rāma, Hare Hare, there was sometimes a* Kṛ-ṣa-ṇa, *a tripling of what had been a double syllable. It would be usually on the first stanza, and the musicians really picked up on it. The Swami would pronounce it in a particular way, and the musicians were really meticulous and listened very carefully to the way the Swami would sing. And we began to notice that there were different melodies for the same brief sentence, and we got to count on that one regularity, like one would count on the conductor of an orchestra or the lead singer of a madrigal. It was really pleasant, and people would dig one another in their ribs. They would say, "Hey, see!" We would catch and repeat a particular subtle pronunciation of a Sanskrit phrase that the audience, in their enthusiasm, while they would be dancing or playing, had perhaps missed. Or the Swami would add an extra beat, but it meant something, in the way in which the drummer, who at that time was the Swami, the main drummer, would hit the drums.*

I have talked to a couple of musicians about it, and we agreed that in his head this Swami must have had hundreds and hundreds of melodies that had been brought back from the real learning from the other side of the world. So many people came there just to tune in to the musical gift, the transmission of the dharma. *"Hey," they would say, "listen to this holy monk." People were really sure there were going to be unusual feats, grandstanding, flashy levitation, or whatever people* expected *was going to happen. But when the simplicity of what the Swami was really saying, when you began to sense it—whether you were motivated to actually make a lifetime commitment and go this way of life, or whether you merely wanted to appreciate it and place it in a place and give certain due respect to it—it turned you around.*

And that was interesting, too, the different ways in which people regarded the kīrtana. *Some people thought it was a prelude. Some people thought it was a main event. Some people liked the music. Some people liked the poetic sound of it.*

Then Allen Ginsberg and Peter Orlovsky arrived, along with some of their friends. Allen surveyed the scene and found a seat among the chanters. With his black beard, his eyeglasses, his bald spot surrounded by long, black ringlets of hair, Allen Ginsberg, the poet-patriarch come to join the chanting, greatly enhanced the local prestige of the *kīrtana.* Prabhupāda, while continuing his ecstatic chanting and drum-playing, acknowledged Allen and smiled.

A reporter from *The New York Times* dropped by and asked Allen for an interview, but he refused: "A man should not be disturbed while worshiping." The *Times* would have to wait.

Allen: *Tompkins Square Park was a hotbed of spiritual conflict in those days, so it was absolutely great. All of a sudden, in the midst of all the talk and drugs and theory, for some people to put their bodies, their singing, to break through the intellectual ice and come out with total* bhakti—*that was really amazing.*

The blacks and Puerto Ricans were out there with drums too, doing conga. But here was a totally different kind of group, some of them with shaven heads, and it was interesting. It was a repetitious chant, but that was also great. It was an easy chant to get into. It was an open scene. There was no boxed corner there in the actual practice. So, general smiles and approval and encouragement as a beginning of some kind of real communal get-together in the park, with a kind of serious underbase for exchange—instead of just hog-dog on the drums.

Prabhupāda was striking to see. His brow was furrowed in the effort of singing loud, and his visage was strong. The veins in his temples stood out visibly, and his jaw jutted forward as he sang his "Hare Kṛṣṇa! Hare Kṛṣṇa!" for all to hear. Although his demeanor was pleasant, his chanting was intensive, sometimes straining, and everything about him was concentration.

It wasn't someone else's *yoga* retreat or silent peace vigil, but a pure chanting be-in of Prabhupāda's own doing. It was a new wave, something everyone could take part in. The community seemed to be accepting it. It became so popular that the ice cream vendor came over to make sales. Beside Prabhupāda a group of young, blond-haired boys, five or six years old, were just sitting around. A young Polish boy stood staring. Someone began burning frankincense on a glowing coal in a metal strainer, and the sweet fumes billowed among the flutists, drummers, and chanters.

Swamiji motioned to his disciples, and they got up and began dancing. Tall, thin Stryadhīśa, his back pockets stuffed with *Stay High Forever* flyers, raised his hands and began to dance. Beside him, in a black turtleneck, big chanting beads around his neck, danced Acyutānanda, his curly, almost frizzy, hair long and disarrayed. Then Brahmānanda got up. He and Acyutānanda stood facing each other, arms outstretched as in the picture of Lord Caitanya's *kīrtana.* Photographers in the crowd moved forward. The boys danced, shifting their weight from left foot to right foot, striking a series of angelic poses, their large, red chanting beads around their necks. They were doing the Swami step.

Brahmānanda: *Once I got up, I thought I would have to remain standing for as long as Swamiji played the drum. It will be an offense, I thought, if I sit down while he's still playing. So I danced for an hour.*

Prabhupāda gave a gesture of acceptance by a typically Indian movement of his head, and then he raised his arms, inviting more dancers. More of his disciples began dancing, and even a few hippies got up and tried it. Prabhupāda wanted everyone to sing and dance in *saṅkīrtana.* The dance was a sedate swaying and a stepping of bare feet on the rug, and the dancers' arms were raised high, their fingers extended toward the sky above the branches of the autumn trees. Here and there throughout the crowd, chanters were enjoying private ecstasies: a girl with her eyes closed played finger cymbals and shook her head dreamily as she chanted.

A Polish lady with a very old, worn face and a babushka around her head stared incredulously at the girl. Little groups of old women in kerchiefs, some of them wearing sunglasses, stood here and there among the crowd, talking animatedly and pointing out the interesting sights in the *kīrtana.* Kīrtanānanda was the only one in a *dhotī,* looking like a young version of Prabhupāda. The autumn afternoon sunlight fell softly on the group, spotlighting them in a golden glow with long, cool shadows.

The harmonium played a constant drone, and a boy wearing a military fatigue jacket improvised atonal creations on a wooden recorder. Yet the total sound of the instruments blended, and Swamiji's voice emerged above the mulling tones of each chord. And so it went for hours. Prabhupāda held his head and shoulders erect, although at the end of each line of the *mantra,* he would sometimes shrug his shoulders before he started the next line. His disciples stayed close by him, sitting on the same rug, religious ecstasy visible in their eyes. Finally, he stopped.

Immediately he stood up, and they knew he was going to speak. It was four o'clock, and the warm autumn sun was still shining on the park. The atmosphere was peaceful and the audience attentive and mellow from the concentration on the *mantra.* He began to speak to them, thanking everyone for joining in the *kīrtana.* The chanting of Hare Kṛṣṇa, he said, had been introduced five hundred years ago in West Bengal by Caitanya Mahāprabhu. *Hare* means "O energy of the Lord," Kṛṣṇa is the Lord, and Rāma is also a name of the Supreme Lord, meaning "the highest pleasure." His disciples sat at his feet, listening. Rāya Rāma squinted through his shielding hand into the sun to see Swamiji, and Kīrtanānanda's head was cocked to one side, like a bird's who is listening to the ground.

He stood erect by the stout oak, his hands folded loosely before him in a proper speaker's posture, his light saffron robes covering him gracefully. The tree behind him seemed perfectly placed, and the sunshine dappled leafy shadows against the thick trunk. Behind him, through the grove of trees, was the steeple of St. Brigid's. On his right was a dumpy, middle-aged woman wearing a dress and hairdo that had been out of style in the United States for twenty-five years. On his left was a bold looking hippie girl in tight denims and beside her a young black man in a black sweater, his arms folded across his chest. Next was a young father holding an infant, then a bearded young street *sādhu,* his long hair parted in the middle, and two ordinary, short-haired middle-class men and their young female companions. Many in the crowd, although standing close by, became distracted, looking off here and there.

Prabhupāda explained that there are three platforms—sensual, mental, and intellectual—and above them is the spiritual platform. The chanting of Hare Kṛṣṇa is on the spiritual platform, and it is the best process for reviving our eternal, blissful consciousness. He invited everyone to attend the meetings at 26 Second Avenue and concluded his brief speech by saying, "Thank you very much. Please chant with us." Then he sat down, took the drum, and began the *kīrtana* again.

If it were risky for a seventy-one-year-old man to thump a drum and shout so loud, then he would take that risk for Kṛṣṇa. It was too good to stop. He had come far from Vṛndāvana, survived the non-Kṛṣṇa *yoga* society, waited all winter in obscurity. America had waited hundreds of years with no Kṛṣṇa-chanting. No "Hare Kṛṣṇa" had come from Thoreau's or Emerson's appreciations, though they had pored over English translations of the *Gītā* and *Purāṇas.* And no *kīrtana* had come from Vivekananda's famous speech on behalf of Hinduism at the World Parliament of Religions in Chicago in 1893. So now that he finally had *kṛṣṇa-bhakti* going, flowing like the Ganges to the sea, it could not stop. In his heart he felt the infinite will of Lord Caitanya to deliver the fallen souls.

He knew this was the desire of Lord Caitanya Mahāprabhu and his own spiritual master, even though caste-conscious *brāhmaṇas* in India would disapprove of his associating with such untouchables as these drug-mad American meat-eaters and their girlfriends. But Swamiji explained that he was in full accord with the scriptures. The *Bhāgavatam* had clearly stated that Kṛṣṇa consciousness should be delivered to all races. Everyone was a spiritual soul, and regardless of birth they could be brought to the highest spiritual platform by chanting the holy name. Never mind whatever sinful things they were doing, these people were perfect candidates for Kṛṣṇa consciousness. Tompkins Square Park was Kṛṣṇa's plan; it was also part of the earth, and these people were members of the human race. And the chanting of Hare Kṛṣṇa was the *dharma* of the age.

* * *

Walking back home in the early evening, past the shops and crowded tenements, followed by more than a dozen interested new people from the park, the Swami again sustained occasional shouts and taunts. But those who followed him from the park were still feeling the aura of an ecstasy that easily tolerated a few taunts from the street. Prabhupāda, especially, was undisturbed. As he walked with his head high, not speaking, he was gravely absorbed in his thoughts. And yet his eyes actively noticed people and places and exchanged glances with those whom he passed on his way along Seventh Street, past the churches and funeral homes, across First Avenue to the noisy, heavily trafficked Second Avenue, then down Second past liquor stores, coin laundries, delicatessens, past the Iglesia Alianza Cristiana Missionera, the Koh-I-Noor Intercontinental Restaurant Palace, then past the Church of the Nativity, and finally back home to number twenty-six.

There was a crowd of people from the park standing on the sidewalk outside the storefront—young people waiting for him to arrive and unlock the door to Matchless Gifts. They wanted to know more about the dance and the chant and the elderly swami and his disciples who had created such a beautiful scene in the park. They filled the storefront. Outside on the sidewalk, the timid or uncommitted loitered near the door or window, smoking and waiting or peering in and trying to see the paintings on the wall. Swamiji entered and walked directly to his dais and sat down before the largest gathering that had ever graced his temple. He spoke further of Kṛṣṇa consciousness, the words coming as naturally as breathing as he quoted the Sanskrit authority behind what they had all been experiencing in the park. Just as they had all chanted today, he said, so everyone should chant always.

A long-haired girl sitting close to Swamiji's dais raised her hand and asked, seemingly in trance, "When I am chanting, I feel a great concentration of energy on my forehead, and then a buzzing comes and a reddish light."

"Just keep on chanting," Swamiji replied. "It will clear up."

"Well, what does the chanting produce?" She seemed to be coming out of her trance now.

"Chanting produces chanting," he replied. "Just as when you are calling the name of your beloved. If there is someone you love very much, then you want to repeat his name again and again. It is out of love."

A man spoke up without raising his hand. "But isn't it just a kind of hypnotism on sound? Like if I chanted Coca-Cola over and over, wouldn't it be the same?"

"No," Prabhupāda replied, "you take any word, repeat it for ten minutes, and you will feel disgusted. But we chant twenty-four hours, and we don't feel tired. Oh, we feel new energy." The questions seemed more relevant today. The guests had all been chanting in the park, and now they were probing philosophically into what they had experienced. The Swami's followers marked this as a victory. And they felt some responsibility as hosts and guides for the others. Swamiji had asked Kīrtanānanda to prepare some *prasādam* for the guests, and soon Kīrtanānanda appeared with small paper cups of sweet rice for everyone.

"The chanting process is just to cleanse the mind," said Prabhupāda. "We have so many misunderstandings about ourself, about this world, about God, and about the relationships between these things. We have so many misgivings. This chanting will help to cleanse the mind. Then you will understand that this chanting is not different from Kṛṣṇa."

A boy who was accompanying the long-haired girl spoke out incoherently: "*Yes. No. I ... I ... I ...*"

Prabhupāda: *Yes. Yes. Yes. In the beginning we have to chant. We may be in whatever position we are. It doesn't matter. If you begin chanting, the first benefit will be* ceto-darpaṇa-mārjanam: *the mind will be clear of all dirty things, and the next stage will be that the sufferings, the miseries of this material world, will subside.*

Boy: *Well, I don't quite understand what the material world is, because ...*

Prabhupāda: *The material world is full of sufferings and miseries. Don't you understand that? Are you happy?*

Boy: *Sometimes I'm happy, sometimes I'm not.*

Prabhupāda: *No. You are not happy. That "sometimes" is your imagination. Just like a diseased man says, "Oh, yes, I am well." What is that "well"? He is going to die, and he is well?*

Boy: *I don't claim any ultimate happiness.*

Prabhupāda: *No, you do not know what happiness is.*

Boy: *But it's greater or lesser.*

Prabhupāda: *Yes, you do not know what is happiness.*

An older man, standing with his arms folded near the rear of the temple: *Well, of course, that sorrow or that suffering might add the spice to make that suffering that goes in between seem happiness.*

Prabhupāda: *No. The thing is that there are different kinds of miseries.*

That we all understand. It is only due to our ignorance that we don't care for it. Just like a man who is suffering for a long time. He has forgotten what is real happiness. Similarly, the sufferings are there already. For example (and he directed himself to the young man with his girlfriend), *take for example that you are a young man. Now would you like to become an old man?*

Boy: *I will become an old man in the process of—*

Prabhupāda: *"You will become" means you will be forced to become an old man. But you don't like to become an old man.*

Boy: *I am not going to be* forced *to become an old man.*

Prabhupāda: *Yes. Yes. Forced! You will be forced.*

Boy: *I don't see why.*

Prabhupāda: *If you don't want to become an old man, you will be forced to become an old man.*

Boy: *It's one of the conditions of—*

Prabhupāda: *Yes. That condition is miserable.*

Boy: *I find it* not *miserable.*

Prabhupāda: *Because you're a young man. But ask any old man how he is suffering. You see? A diseased man—do you want to be diseased?*

Boy: *I wouldn't search it out.*

Prabhupāda: *Hmm?*

Boy: *I wouldn't search it out.*

Prabhupāda: *No, no. Just answer me. Do you like to be diseased?*

Boy: *What is disease?*

Prabhupāda: *Just answer.*

Boy: *What is disease?*

Prabhupāda: *Oh? You have never suffered from disease? You have never suffered from disease?* (Prabhupāda looks dramatically incredulous.)

Boy: *I have had ... I have had the mumps and the measles and whooping cough, which is what everyone has—and you get over it.* (Some people in the audience laugh.)

Prabhupāda: *Everyone may be suffering, but that does not mean that it is not suffering. We have to admit that we are always in suffering.*

Boy: *If I have never known happiness, I feel sure I have never known suffering either.*

Prabhupāda: *That is due to your ignorance. We are in suffering. We don't want to die, but death is there. We don't want to be diseased, but disease is there. We don't want to become old—old age is there. We don't want so many things, but they are forced upon us, and any sane man will admit that these are sufferings. But if you are accustomed to take these sufferings, then you say it is all right. But any sane man won't like to be diseased. He won't like to be old. And he won't like to die. Why do you have this peace movement? Because if there is war, there will be death. So people are afraid. They are making agitation: "There should be no war." Do you think that death is a very pleasurable thing?*

Boy: *I have never experienced—*

Prabhupāda: *You* have *experienced—and forgotten. Many times you have died. You have experienced, but you have forgotten. Forgetfulness is no excuse. Suppose a child forgot some suffering. That does not mean he did not suffer.*

Boy: *No, I agree. I agree.*

Prabhupāda: *Yes. So suffering is there. You have to take direction from realized souls, from authorities. Just like in the* Bhagavad-gītā *it is said,* duḥkhālayam aśāśvatam: *this world is full of miseries. So one has to realize it. Unless we understand that this place is miserable, there is no question of how to get out of it. A person who doesn't develop this understanding is not fully developed. Just like the animals—they do not understand what misery is. They are satisfied.*

It was late when he finally returned to his apartment. One of the boys brought him a cup of hot milk, and someone remarked they should do the chanting in the park every week. "Every day," he replied. Even while half a dozen people were present, he lay down on his thin mat. He continued to speak for some minutes, and then his voice trailed off, preaching in fragmented words. He appeared to doze. It was ten o'clock. They tiptoed out, softly shutting the door.

* * *

October 10

It was early. Swamiji had not yet come down for class, and the sun had not yet risen. Satsvarūpa and Kīrtanānanda sat on the floor of the storefront, reading a clipping from the morning *Times*.

Satsvarūpa: *Has the Swami seen it?*

Kīrtanānanda: *Yes, just a few minutes ago. He said it's very important. It's historic. He especially liked that it was* The New York Times.

Satsvarūpa (reading aloud): *"SWAMI'S FLOCK CHANTS IN PARK TO FIND ECSTASY."*

> Fifty Followers Clap and Sway to Hypnotic Music at East Side Ceremony. Sitting under a tree in a Lower East Side park and occasionally dancing, fifty followers of a Hindu swami repeated a sixteen-word chant for two hours yesterday ...

It was more *than two hours.*

> ... for two hours yesterday afternoon to the accompaniment of cymbals, tambourines, sticks, drums, bells, and a small reed organ. Repetition of the chant, Swami A. C. Bhaktivedanta says, is the best way to achieve self-realization in this age of destruction. While children played on Hoving's Hill, a pile of dirt in the middle of Tompkins Square Park ...

Hoving's Hill?

Kīrtanānanda: *I think it's a joke named after the Parks Commissioner.*

Satsvarūpa: *Oh.*

> ... Hoving's Hill, a pile of dirt in the middle of Tompkins Square Park, or bicycled along the sunny walks, many in the crowd of about a hundred persons standing around the chanters found themselves swaying to or clapping hands in time to the hypnotic rhythmic music. "It brings a state of ecstasy," said Allen Ginsberg the poet, who was one of the celebrants. "For one thing," Allen Ginsberg said, "the syllables force yoga breath control. That's one physiological explanation.

Satsvarūpa and Kīrtanānanda (laughing): *That's nonsense.*

> "The ecstasy of the chant or mantra Hare Krishna Hare Krishna Krishna Krishna Hare Hare Hare Rama Hare Rama Rama Rama Hare Hare ...

Kīrtanānanda: *The Swami said that's the best part. Because they have printed the* mantra, *it's all-perfect. Whoever reads this can be purified just the same as if they had chanted.*

Satsvarūpa (continuing):

"... has replaced LSD and other drugs for many of the swami's followers," Mr. Ginsberg said. He explained that Hare Krishna, pronounced Hahray, is the name for Vishnu, a Hindu god, as the "bringer of light." Rama, pronounced Rahmah, is the incarnation of Vishnu as "the prince of responsibility."

What? Where did he get that? It sounds like something out of an encyclopedia.

"The chant, therefore, names different aspects of God," Mr. Ginsberg said.

Why so much from Mr. Ginsberg? Why not Swamiji?

Another celebrant, 26-year-old Howard M. Wheeler, who described himself as a former English instructor at Ohio State University, now devoting his full time to the swami, said, "I myself took fifty doses of LSD and a dozen of peyote in two years, and now nothing."

(Laughter.)

The swami orders his followers to give up "all intoxicants, including coffee, tea, and cigarettes," he said in an interview after the ceremony. "In this sense we are helping your government," he added. However, he indicated the government apparently has not appreciated this help sufficiently, for the Department of Immigration recently told Swami Bhaktivedanta that his one-year visitor's visa had expired and that he must leave, he said. The case is being appealed.

The swami, a swarthy man with short-cropped grayish hair and clad in a salmon-colored robe over a pink sweater, said that when he first met his own teacher, or guru, in 1922, he was told to spread the cult of Krishna to the Western countries through the English language. "Therefore in this old age (71) I have taken so much risk."

It says that we're going to come there and chant every Sunday. "His followers include some social workers." I guess that's me.

Kīrtanānanda: *I think this article will bring a lot of new people.*

The Swami came down for class. The morning was chilly, and he wore a peach-colored turtleneck jersey his disciples had bought for him at a shop on Orchard Street. They had also started wearing such jerseys—a kind of unofficial uniform. Swamiji didn't mention the *Times* article. He began singing the Sanskrit prayers. *Vande 'haṁ śrī-guroḥ:* "I offer my obeisances to my spiritual master ..." Then he began singing Hare Kṛṣṇa, and the boys joined in. "Sing softly," Prabhupāda cautioned them.

But no sooner had he spoken than water began pouring down through the cracks in the ceiling. The man upstairs didn't like early-morning *kīrtanas,* and he began stomping his feet to show that this flood was no accident.

"What is this?" Prabhupāda looked up, disturbed, but with a touch of amusement. The boys looked around. Water was pouring down in several places. "Get some pots," he said. A boy ran upstairs to Swamiji's apartment to get pots from the kitchen. Soon three pots were catching the water as it dripped in three separate places.

"How does he do it?" asked Umāpati. "Is he pouring water onto the floor?" Prabhupāda asked Brahmānanda to go up and speak to the man, to tell him that the *kīrtana* would be a quiet one. Then he asked everyone to sit back down amid the dripping and the pots and continue chanting. "Softly," he said. "Softly."

That evening, the temple was filled with guests. "It is so much kindness of the Supreme Lord," Prabhupāda said, "that He wants to associate with you. So you should receive Him. Always chant Hare Kṛṣṇa. Now this language is Sanskrit, and some of you do not know the meaning. Still, it is so attractive that when we chanted Hare Kṛṣṇa in the park, oh, old ladies, gentlemen, boys and girls, all took part. ... But there are also complaints. Just like we are receiving daily reports that our *saṅkīrtana* movement is disturbing some tenants here."

* * *

Ravīndra-svarūpa was walking down Second Avenue, on his way to the Swami's morning class, when an acquaintance came out of the Gems Spa Candy and News Store and said, "Hey, your Swami is in the newspaper. Did you see?" "Yeah," Ravīndra-svarūpa replied, "*The New York Times.*"

"No," his friend said. "Today." And he held up a copy of the latest edition of *The East Village Other.* The front page was filled with a two-color photo of the Swami, his hands folded decorously at his waist, standing in yellow robes in front of the big tree in Tompkins Square Park. He was speaking to a small crowd that had gathered around, and his disciples were at his feet. The big steeple of St. Brigid's formed a silhouette behind him.

Above the photo was the single headline, "SAVE EARTH NOW!!" and beneath was the *mantra:* "HARE KRISHNA HARE KRISHNA KRISHNA KRISHNA HARE HARE HARE RAMA HARE RAMA RAMA RAMA HARE HARE." Below the *mantra* were the words, "See Centerfold." That was the whole front page.

Ravīndra-svarūpa took the newspaper and opened to the center, where he found a long article and a large photo of Swamiji with his left hand on his head, grinning blissfully in an unusual, casual moment. His friend gave him the paper, and Ravīndra-svarūpa hurried to Swamiji. When he reached the storefront, several boys went along with him to show Swamiji the paper.

"Look!" Ravīndra-svarūpa handed it over. "This is the biggest local newspaper! Everybody reads it." Prabhupāda opened his eyes wide. He read aloud, "Save earth now." And he looked up at the faces of the boys. Umāpati and Hayagrīva wondered aloud what it meant—"Save earth now." Was it an ecological pun? Was it a reference to staving off nuclear disaster? Was it poking fun at Swamiji's evangelism?

"Well," said Umāpati, "after all, this is *The East Village Other.* It could mean anything."

"Swamiji *is* saving the earth," Kīrtanānanda said.

"We are trying to," Prabhupāda replied, "by Kṛṣṇa's grace." Methodically, he put on the eyeglasses he usually reserved for reading the *Bhāgavatam* and carefully appraised the page from top to bottom. The newspaper looked incongruous in his hands. Then he began turning the pages. He stopped at the centerfold and looked at the picture of himself and laughed, then paused, studying the article. "So," he said, "read it." He handed the paper to Hayagrīva.

"Once upon a time, ... " Hayagrīva began loudly. It was a fanciful story of a group of theologians who had killed an old man in a church and of the subsequent press report that God was now dead. But, the story went on, some people didn't believe it. They had dug up the body and found it to be "not the body of God, but that of His P.R. man: organized religion. At once the good tidings swept across the wide world. GOD LIVES! ... But where was God?" Hayagrīva read dramatically to an enthralled group. ...

> A full-page ad in *The New York Times,* offering a reward for information leading to the discovery of the whereabouts of God, and signed by Martin Luther King and Ronald Reagan, brought no response. People began to worry and wonder again. "God," said some people, "lives in a sugar cube." Others whispered that the sacred secret was in a cigarette.
>
> But while all this was going on, an old man, one year past his allotted three score and ten, wandered into New York's East Village and set about to prove to the world that he knew where God could be found. In only three months, the man, Swami A. C. Bhaktivedanta, succeeded in convincing the world's toughest audience—Bohemians, acidheads, potheads, and hippies—that he knew the way to God: Turn Off, Sing Out, and Fall In. This new brand of holy man, with all due deference to Dr. Leary, has come forth with a brand of "Consciousness Expansion" that's sweeter than acid, cheaper than pot, and nonbustible by fuzz. How is all this possible? "Through Krishna," the Swami says.

The boys broke into cheers and applause. Acyutānanda apologized to Swamiji for the language of the article: "It's a hippie newspaper."

"That's all right," said Prabhupāda. "He has written it in his own way. But he has said that we are giving God. They are saying that God is dead. But it is false. We are directly presenting, 'Here is God.' Who can deny it? So many theologians and people may say there is no God, but the Vaiṣṇava hands God over to you freely, as a commodity: 'Here is God.' So he has marked this. It is very good. Save this paper. It is very important."

The article was long. "For the cynical New Yorker," it said, "living, visible, tangible proof can be found at 26 Second Avenue, Monday, Wednesday, and Friday between seven and nine." The article described the evening *kīrtanas,* quoted from Prabhupāda's lecture, and mentioned "a rhythmic, hypnotic sixteen-word chant, Hare Krishna Hare Krishna Krishna Krishna Hare Hare Hare Rama Hare Rama Rama Rama Hare Hare, sung for hours on end to the accompaniment of hand clapping, cymbals, and bells." Swamiji said that simply because the *mantra* was there, the article was perfect.

The article also included testimony from the Swami's disciples:

> I started chanting to myself, like the Swami said, when I was walking down the street—Hare Krishna Hare Krishna Krishna Krishna Hare Hare Hare Rama Hare Rama Rama Rama Hare Hare—over and over, and suddenly everything started looking so beautiful, the kids, the old men and women ... even the creeps looked beautiful ... to say nothing of the trees and flowers. It was like I had taken a dozen doses of LSD. But I knew there was a difference. There's no coming down from this. I can always do this any time, anywhere. It is always with you.

Without sarcasm, the article referred to the Swami's discipline forbidding coffee, tea, meat, eggs, and cigarettes, "to say nothing of marijuana, LSD, alcohol, and illicit sex." Obviously the author admired Swamiji: "the energetic old man, a leading exponent of the philosophy of Personalism, which holds that the one God is a person but that His form is spiritual." The article ended with a hint that Tompkins Square Park would see similar spiritual happenings each weekend: "There in the shadow of Hoving's Hill, God lives in a trancelike dance and chant."

* * *

October 12

It was to be a "Love-Pageant-Rally," marking California's new law prohibiting the possession of LSD. The rally's promoters urged everyone to come to Tompkins Square Park in elaborate dress. Although the devotees had nothing to do with LSD laws, they took the rally as another opportunity to popularize the chanting of Hare Kṛṣṇa. So they went, with the Swami's blessings, carrying finger cymbals and a homemade tambourine.

The devotees looked plain in their dark jeans and lightweight zippered jackets. All around them, the dress was extravagant—tie-dyed shirts, tie-bleached jeans, period costumes, painted faces. There was even a circus clown. Tuli Kupferberg of the Fugs rock band carried an American flag with the stars rearranged to spell L-O-V-E. But so far the rally had been a dud—just a strange set of drugged young people milling near the large tree where Swamiji had chanted and spoken just a few days before.

Swamiji's boys made their way through the crowd to a central spot and started chanting Hare Kṛṣṇa. A crowd pressed in close around them.

Everyone seemed to be in friendly spirits—just unorganized, without any purpose. The idea behind the rally had been to show love and a pageant of LSD vision, but not much had been happening. Someone was walking around with a bucket of burning incense. Some hippies sat back on the park benches, watching everything through colored glasses. But the *kīrtana* was attractive, and soon a crowd gathered around the boys as they chanted.

Kīrtanānanda, his shaved head covered with a knit skullcap, stood beside tall Jagannātha, who, with his dark-framed glasses and wavy hair, looked like a great horned owl playing hand cymbals. Umāpati, also playing hand cymbals, looked thoughtful. Brahmānanda sat on the ground in front of them, his eyes closed and his mouth widely open, chanting Hare Kṛṣṇa. Beside him and looking moody sat Raphael, and next to him, ascetically thin-faced Ravīndra-svarūpa. Close by, a policeman stood watching.

The hippies began to pick up the chanting. They had come together, but there had been no center, no lecture, no amplified music. But now they began clapping and swaying, getting into the chanting as if it were their single purpose. The chanting grew stronger, and after an hour the group broke into a spontaneous dance. Joining hands and singing out, "Hare Kṛṣṇa, Hare Kṛṣṇa, Kṛṣṇa Kṛṣṇa, Hare Hare/ Hare Rāma, Hare Rāma, Rāma Rāma, Hare Hare," they skipped and danced together, circling the tree and Swamiji's disciples. To the hippies, it was in fact a Love-Pageant-Rally, and they had found the love and peace they were searching for—it was in this *mantra*. Hare Kṛṣṇa had become their anthem, their reason for coming together, the life of the Love-Pageant-Rally. They didn't know exactly what the *mantra* was, but they accepted it as something deep within the soul, a metaphysical vibration—they tuned in to it. Even the clown began chanting and dancing. Only the policeman remained aloof and sober, though he also could see that the new demonstration would be a peaceful one. The dance continued, and only the impending dusk brought the Love-Pageant-Rally to a close.

The devotees hurried back to Swamiji to tell him all that had happened. He had been sitting at his desk, translating the *Śrīmad-Bhāgavatam*. Although he had not been physically present at the *kīrtana,* his disciples had acted on his instruction. So even without leaving his room, he was spreading the chanting of Hare Kṛṣṇa. Now he sat waiting for the report.

They burst into his room with shining eyes, flushed faces, and hoarse voices, relating the good news. Not only had they dutifully chanted, but hundreds of people had joined them and sung and danced in a big circle, in a spirit of unity. "Swamiji, you should have seen," Brahmānanda exclaimed, his voice now exhausted from chanting. "It was fantastic, fantastic!" Prabhupāda looked from one face to another, and he also became like them, elated and hopeful that the chanting could go on like this. They had proved that their chanting of Hare Kṛṣṇa could lead the love and peace movement. It could grow, and hundreds could take part. "It is up to you to spread this chanting," Swamiji told them. "I am an old man, but you are young, and you can do it."

October 13

The Village Voice ran four large photographs of the Love-Pageant-Rally. The article stated:

> The backbone of the celebration was the mantras, holy chants from the Sanskrit *Bhagavad Gita,* and for three hours it became like a boat on a sea of rhythmic chanting. Led by fifteen disciples of Bhaktivedanta Swami, who operates from a storefront on Second Avenue, the mantras ebbed and flowed with the rhythm of drums, flutes, and soda-cap tambourines.

October 18

It was Sunday. And again they went to Tompkins Square Park. Swamiji played the bongo as before, striking the drumhead deftly as ever, his nimble fingers creating drum rolls, as he sat on the rug in the autumn afternoon. His authentic, melodic voice recited the prayers to the previous spiritual masters: Bhaktivinoda, Gaurakiśora, Bhaktisiddhānta—the centuries-old disciplic succession of which he was the living representative, now in the 1960s, in this remote part of the world. He sang their names in duty, deference, and love, as their servant. He sat surrounded by his American followers under the tall oak tree amid the mazelike fences of the park.

And the same magic occurred. This time the hippies came by with more ease and familiarity. Allen Ginsberg came again, and a hundred others gathered as Prabhupāda loudly sang: Hare Kṛṣṇa, Hare Kṛṣṇa,

Kṛṣṇa Kṛṣṇa, Hare Hare/ Hare Rāma, Hare Rāma, Rāma Rāma, Hare Hare. Of the hundreds who came by, some stayed briefly and then left, some decided to listen and chant for a few minutes or even for the entire afternoon. And a few — very few — marked their encounter with the Swami as an unforgettable change in their lives.

Bob Corens was looking for the Swami. He was walking with his stylishly dressed wife and two-year-old son, Eric. Bob was twenty-six years old and worked as a supervisor in the New York City Welfare Department. He had grown up in Washington, D.C., where he had met his wife. He had a full face and broad forehead, a clear voice and steady eyes.

Bob: *After I graduated from George Washington University, I decided to go straight to what I thought was the heart of the material world, New York City, to seek out whatever was the highest truth. I ended up living around the corner from the first East Village head shop.*

Bob didn't think his job as a social worker really helped anyone — his clients over the years seemed to maintain their same outlook and habits. He and his wife frequented West Village coffee houses, had attended lectures by Leary and Alpert on expanded consciousness, and had taken part in a recent peace march. Bob had come to feel that his aspirations for a master's degree and a better apartment were unfulfilling, and he was looking for something more.

Bob: *I heard about the* I Ching, *a book that was supposed to chart a person's course in life. So I got someone to do a reading for me. The direction was, "Push upward through darkness." I took it as a good sign, a spiritual sign. Then I purchased* The East Village Other, *and I saw the article entitled "Save Earth Now!!" There was a picture of the Swami. I had read in a book by a Sikh teacher that there could be no higher knowledge without a spiritual master.*

Every morning on his way to work, Bob used to pass by the Swami's storefront. Curious, he stopped once and peered in the window, only to find an empty room, with some straw mats on the floor and one of Swamiji's boys. "Oh, these people are Buddhists?" he thought. The door had been open, and the boy came over and invited him in. "No thanks," he said, thinking, "I don't want anything to do with Buddhism." And he went on to his job.

In a head shop one day, he had picked up one of the Swami's *Bhāgavatams* and looked through it, but he thought it was too advanced, so he put it back down. After he read the article in *The East Village Other,* his interest increased. He thought that today might be the last Sunday of chanting in the park before the cold weather came. And so he went to the park hoping to find the Swami and his chanters. His wife was beside him, pushing Eric in a stroller, when he heard the *ching-ching* of the hand cymbals and a chorus of rhythmic chanting from the south side of the park. Thinking it must be the Swami, he followed the sound, while his wife took Eric to play on the swings. Alone now, Bob drew closer, moving into the crowd until he could see the *kīrtana* party and the Swami sitting under the tree. Bob stood among a crowd of hundreds, unnoticed.

"Everything is happening because of me," thought nineteen-year-old Judy Koslofsky. "Everything I see is my own creation, and I am the Supreme. Everything is mine." As the thought of being God obsessed her, Judy forgot her father and everything else. She was confused: "If I am God, why can't I control everything, and why am I so fearful on LSD?"

Judy was a student at the City College of New York, majoring in art and history. She was taking guitar lessons from the Reverend Garry Davis, the blues singer and Christian preacher, who was teaching her the art of sad soul music. Today, however, under the influence of LSD, she had the overwhelming impression that she was God. She'd had a fight with her father, who seemed cold and distant to her and couldn't understand her, and she had left her parents' home in the Bronx and traveled downtown. She was going to visit a girlfriend, and Tompkins Square Park happened to be on the way. When she reached the park the *kīrtana* was going on, but she couldn't see much because of the crowd. She weaved her way in closer until she could see some men—one shavenheaded, several bearded—dancing with upraised hands. And in the center she saw the Swami sitting on the rug, playing his drum.

Dan Clark was twenty-five, thin, intense, horn-rim bespectacled—an avant-garde filmmaker, and his first film was entitled *Rebirth.* He was a conscientious objector to the Vietnam war and was working at a home for children as alternative governmental service. He had been a member of the SDS and the War Resisters League. He had been arrested during a protest demonstration, and he had been suspended one week from his job for wearing a peace button and a black armband. He was into Buddhism, but he had lately been adding "a little psychedelic seasoning." "Everything is nothing, and nothing is everything," was his slogan, and he would go around chanting it like a *mantra*. But he was feeling that, at least psychologically, he needed a devotional tonic; his voidistic meditation was getting stale.

Dan had come to the park today looking for the Swami and the chanting he had read about in *The East Village Other*. He had seen the Swami before, one evening a few months back. He had been waiting for a bus across the street from the Swami's storefront—he was on the way to a rehearsal for a mixed-media show, and his friend had gone into Sam's Luncheonette for a moment—when he noticed that in the storefront an orange-robed Indian man with a shaved head was lecturing to a small group of young people.

Dan: *When I saw him, I imagined myself walking across the street, going into the storefront, sitting down, and renouncing all worldly connections. But I thought to myself, "It's only my imagination. After all, I'm married, and I'm on my way to rehearsal, and I don't know anything about the Swami anyway." So my friend and I got on the bus.*

But Dan lived only a few blocks away from the storefront, and now and then he would pass by. Once, he had stood for several minutes on the sidewalk looking at the cover of the *Śrīmad-Bhāgavatam* taped onto the window.

Dan: *It showed an oval lotus with planets around it, and right then I was introduced to the idea of spiritual sensuality. And when I saw the painting of Lord Caitanya and His associates in the window, that really threw me. I thought, "Yes, this is what I need—juice."*

Dan and his wife walked the paved pathway through the park. He was looking around for the Swami, but he didn't really know what to look for. He expected to see robes and hear Buddhist-style chanting, but he couldn't find anything. He had given up his search and was wandering around to see what musicians were there when he noticed a big crowd gathered around what he figured must have been some musicians.

He was attracted by the beat of their music, a chiming one-two-*three,* one-two-*three,* a simple rhythm with a kind of flamboyance—and very magnetic. He saw an occasional upraised arm above the crowd, and he thought there must be flamenco dancing going on inside the circle. He then got wind of a drifting melody—certainly not flamenco—which accompanied the beat, and this attracted him further. He approached closer and closer, making his way through the crowd. Then he saw people chanting and others dancing and waving their arms in what he took to be a blend of American Indian and Asian dancing. It looked like something from a long-forgotten era. Dan decided that this must be the Hare Kṛṣṇa group. But there were no robes, just the regular dress of the Lower East Side. And where was the Swami? Then he saw him, sitting, inconspicuous, playing a little drum. His eyes were closed, and his brow was knit with concentration.

Dan: *The Swami wasn't calling attention to himself, and at first I didn't attribute any importance to an elderly Indian man's sitting off to one side. He didn't seem to have any special function in the chanting. But it gradually dawned on me who he was. He was the same Swami I had read about in the paper and seen in the storefront.*

After a while he spoke, but I couldn't hear him. Still, I was impressed that he was a very modest person, not interested in getting himself up on a pedestal. He didn't go strutting around, but was still with inner peace, strength, and knowledge.

Bob: *All his disciples were there around his feet. They were chanting, and I tried to chant along and learn the* mantra *too. I had heard the chanting of Hare Kṛṣṇa once before, at a peace march, and I had found it very beautiful. Then the Swami spoke. I had the impression that this person was not earthly, and I thought, "Here is the person I'm looking for." He seemed to be different from anyone else, like he came from some other place or universe. I was attracted.*

After a second *kīrtana,* the Swami and his followers rolled up their rug, picked up their instruments, and began to leave.

Bob walked back to the swings on the other side of the park to find his wife and child, but the image of the Swami stayed with him—"He seemed different from anyone else." His accent had been thick, yet Bob resolved to go to the storefront in a few days to hear him speak. "Here is a leader," thought Bob.

Dan and his wife sauntered off into the park, sampling the various groups of musicians. His wife was surprised that Dan, who was usually shy, had danced at the *kīrtana.* He said he might go over to the storefront one day and hear the Swami speak.

Judy just stood there hallucinating. She held a *Stay High Forever* pamphlet in her hand and read it over and over and over. While she was thinking the whole event must have come from another planet, a man walked up and asked, "Would you like to go to where the Swami is?" She nodded.

At the storefront, one of the devotees offered Judy some *prasādam*—a *capātī*—and then invited her up to the Swami's room. Upstairs, she entered the large front room, which was filled with fragrant smoke. There were tall flower vases, and sesame seeds were on the floor. She saw the Swami bow before the little picture of Lord Caitanya and His associates and then stand and leave the room, closing the door behind him. Judy decided that he must have been bowing to the floor itself. Around her, everyone was softly chanting on beads, and although she couldn't make out the words, it seemed peaceful. One of the Swami's disciples told her she could come into the back room, and she followed, curious. The Swami was sitting there on his mat, looking effulgent. There were about ten other people in the room.

Prabhupāda asked her if she liked the chanting in the park, and she replied, "I loved it."

"Do you live near here?" he asked.

Judy flashed on her idea that she was the all-pervading Truth and answered in a way which she thought must have sounded very mystical. "Oh, I live *veeerrry* near."

"Good," said Swamiji, "then you can come for our morning *kīrtana* and class."

Then she realized that she didn't live so near and that it would mean traveling an hour and a half from the Bronx to visit the Swami. But she decided that since he had asked her, she would come. Then she thought, "I am making this up." But Prabhupāda assured her, as if knowing her thoughts, "This process is nothing you have made up. It is very old, very simple, and sublime." He leaned back. "We are eternal," he said, "and everything around us is temporary." Judy was now coming down from the LSD. By the time she left the Swami it was late. She had wanted to stay overnight, but the boys hadn't allowed her. But she was determined to join.

For Bob, it seemed natural to follow up on what he had seen in the park. He began attending the evening classes, and he started reading the *Bhāgavatam* at home and chanting. He framed the picture from the *Bhāgavatam* dust jacket depicting the spiritual sky and placed it on his small homemade altar. He would offer flowers before the picture and sit before it chanting Hare Kṛṣṇa.

Bob was fascinated by the philosophy and the books and classes, and from the very beginning he was amazed that Swamiji's teachings answered all his questions. He listened carefully and accepted: "It seemed like once I'd decided that he was telling the truth, I just accepted everything he said. Not that part of it was the truth and the rest of it I would have to think about."

October 19

It was Monday evening, after the Sunday *kīrtana* in the park, and Dan arrived at the storefront for *kīrtana.* The *kīrtana* was in full swing, and when he entered, the first thing he noticed was some people playing on the innards of an upright piano leaning against the wall near the door. A boy handed him some wooden sticks, and he sat down and joined in the *kīrtana.* Then came the Swami's lecture, which Dan thought was long and serious, about how sexual desire causes bondage and suffering. The temple was crowded and stuffy, and Dan was shocked by the lecture, but he stayed on because he knew there would be another *kīrtana.* He felt uneasy that the Swami's followers were all celibate, but because he liked the *kīrtanas,* he resolved to keep coming.

The Swami wasn't quite what Dan had expected. He had imagined something of a lighthearted Zen *roshi,* laughing and joking, with sparkling eyes and words filled with paradoxes. But he found the Swami just the opposite—very straightforward and even cutting in his speech and his mouth turned down at the corners, making him look mournful. Dan happily took to the *kīrtanas,* thinking they would aid his impersonal meditation, but the lectures kept stressing that God was a person. Dan resisted. He mentally debated with Prabhupāda. He was partial to Dr. Radhakrishnan's interpretation of the *Gītā,* and yet the Swami often launched ruthless attacks against such impersonal ideas. Gradually, Dan saw his impersonal barrier crumble, and he came to admit that on every count the Swami was right.

Judy began attending both the morning and evening classes. She had to rise by five o'clock to get to the storefront on time, and her mother and father protested. But Judy didn't care. She would ride an hour and a half on the subway, before dawn, downtown to the Swami's meetings, where she would be the only girl present.

When the Swami heard that Judy was an art student, he asked her to paint for Kṛṣṇa. She set up a canvas in the front room of the apartment, and under his guidance she began painting. For her first assignment, he asked her to paint a portrait of his Guru Mahārāja, Śrīla Bhaktisiddhānta Sarasvatī. He gave her a photo and instructed her: There should be a flower garland around Guru Mahārāja's neck, the *tilaka* should be yellowish, not white, and there should be no effulgence or halo around his head.

Bob: *I began chanting and studying the* Śrīmad-Bhāgavatam *at home and attending the* kīrtana *and classes at the storefront. After the last* kīrtana *in the evening, the Swami would take a bowl made of simulated wood and a little paring knife and a couple of apples that had been sitting on the edge of his lectern, and he would cut the apples up in the little bowl and hand the bowl to a disciple. The disciple would then offer him the first piece, and he would pop it into his mouth. The rest of the pieces of apple would be distributed to the crowd. I remember one time when he was chewing on his piece of apple and he spit the seeds out on the floor up against the wall. They bounced off the wall onto the floor next to the dais. And I was thinking, "How wonderful. No one else can do that. No one else would have the nerve to do such a thing."*

With his aesthetic filmmaker's eye, Dan appreciated Swamiji's manner.

Dan: *There was a sink right next to the dais where he sat. It was so close that he could have leaned over and touched it. After cutting up an apple, he would take the scraps and just fling them into the sink. It was very casual. I was very impressed by that.*

And one time Brahmānanda came up and wanted fifty cents for something, and the Swami reached down and picked up his little black purse—the kind that closes by a metal clasp at the top. He snapped it open, looked inside very perspicaciously, and then his hand came up like a bird, like an eagle hovering in flight above its prey. But the hand didn't pounce. It just delicately drifted down, took out a fifty-cent piece, and rose up again as if it were being lifted up on a balloon. It was graceful. It was a dance, a ballet. He just picked up this fifty-cent piece and lifted it into Brahmānanda's hand. I couldn't believe it. Someone asks you for a fifty-cent piece, you just dig in your pockets and throw it at them. But the Swami seemed to treat everything as Kṛṣṇa's property, and this fifty-cent piece was treated with such care.

The weeks went by. Some of the devotees had spoken to Bob about initiation, but he was unsure. He didn't know exactly what initiation was, but it seemed to him that the other devotees were eager to get him initiated because he was working and had a family. To Bob's way of thinking, he represented maturity to them, a middle-class American, and they were eager to land him. Bob's wife wasn't interested, and his friends were downright opposed. He couldn't spend much time with Prabhupāda or the devotees, since he was either at the office or at home with his family.

Bob: *So they were asking me if I was interested in initiation. I said I would think about it. I hadn't stopped smoking. I hadn't made the final decision.*

The first real personal exchange I had with the Swami was when I asked for initiation. The rest of the time I was so much in awe of him that it didn't occur to me to say anything. I always wanted to. I felt puffed up, and I always thought, "Well, I should be able to talk to him. Maybe I should do something." But I was always kind of reluctant to do it. I didn't think it was my place. I guess maybe I was afraid. But I was getting up early and chanting thirty-two rounds a day, many of them on the subway. I was afraid of the material world because I didn't have much association with devotees, and I wanted to insulate myself by chanting more.

Judy was another person who was considering initiation, and I asked her what she was going to do about it, and she said, "I'm thinking about it." And then she told me she had decided she would get initiated and give up all her bad habits. I began to think maybe I could give up these things too, so I asked what to do—how do I approach him? And Kīrtanānanda said, "Well, you go up to his room." I was surprised it was so easy.

I had prepared a little speech in my mind— "My dear Swamiji, would you kindly accept me as your disciple and teach me about Kṛṣṇa consciousness?" I went up to his room, without an appointment, and knocked on the door. I heard him say, "Come in." I entered the room, and he was sitting behind his desk. He was alone. I made obeisances, and he looked at me and said, "Yes?" And I said, "Swamiji, will you make me your disciple?" and that's as far as I got. I was going to say, "and teach me the philosophy of Kṛṣṇa consciousness." But he didn't let me finish my speech. He said, "Yes." It was so simple. I thought, "Well, there's nothing else to say. He has accepted me." So I thanked him and paid my obeisances and left.

"You know you're not supposed to be up here unless you're initiated," Acyutānanda said.

Judy was flustered. She had come upstairs to put some dirty pots in the kitchen. "Oh, yes," she replied, "that's just what I wanted to talk to Swamiji about." And she went into Prabhupāda's room, where he was talking with a few other people.

"Swamiji, could I please get initiated?" she asked.

And he said, "Do you know the four rules?"

"Yes."

"Can you follow them?"

"Yes."

"Then you can be initiated in two weeks."

Dan was also thinking about initiation, but he wanted to wait. He was chanting sixteen rounds and attending all the classes, despite his reluctant wife. He had always had difficulty with authority figures, but he could feel that the Swami was winning him over and wearing down his impersonal barrier.

Two weeks later, Prabhupāda held another initiation ceremony. Bob became Rūpānuga and Judy became Jadurāṇī. Dan needed a little more time.

CHAPTER TWENTY-ONE

Beyond the Lower East Side

But we were shocked that he was going to leave. I never thought that Kṛṣṇa consciousness would go beyond the Lower East Side, what to speak of New York City. I thought that this was it, and it would stay here eternally.

—Brahmānanda

HARE KṚṢṆA WAS becoming popular—regular *kīrtanas* in the park, newspaper coverage. Hayagrīva called it "the Hare Kṛṣṇa explosion." The Lower East Side hippies considered the chanting of Hare Kṛṣṇa "one of the grooviest things happening," and that the Swami's disciples didn't take LSD didn't seem to affect their popularity. The devotees were accepted as angelic people, carrying the peaceful chanting to others and offering free food and a free place to stay. You could get the most interesting vegetarian food free at their place (if you went at the right time). And in their storefront, on the shelf by the door, were books from India.

In the clubs, local musicians played the melody that they had picked up from the Swami when he chanted in the park and at the temple. The Lower East Side was a neighborhood of artists and musicians, and now it was also the neighborhood of Hare Kṛṣṇa.

Burton Green: *Musicians were influenced by it—the Kṛṣṇa chant,*

Govinda jaya jaya, *and other chants. I used some of those chants when I recorded. A lot of musicians reached out for this in different ways. We would explode in a short time and blow off, but then keep the chant underneath as a basis. A lot of people found that spiritual vibration even in the midst of the heavy music they were doing. They were becoming devotee-musicians.*

Evening *kīrtanas* were always big. Brahmānanda used to stand by the back door every night and watch the room fill up until there was no place left to sit. There was a lot of interest in the group chanting and music making, but after the *kīrtana,* when the talk was to begin, people would start to leave. It was not uncommon for half the audience to leave before the talk began, and sometimes people would leave in the middle of the lecture.

One evening, Allen Ginsberg brought Ed Sanders and Tuli Kupferberg of the Fugs to the meeting. The Fugs, a local group that had made a name for themselves, specialized in obscene lyrics. Among the popular songs of Ed Sanders were "Slum Goddess of the Lower East Side," "Group Grope," and "I Can't Get High." Ed had wild red hair and an electric-red beard, and he played a guitar during the *kīrtana.* The devotees were happy to see their prestigious guests. The night of the Fugs, however, Prabhupāda chose to speak on the illusion of sexual pleasure. "Sex pleasure binds us to this material world birth after birth," he said, and he quoted, as he often did, a verse of Yāmunācārya: "Since I have become Kṛṣṇa conscious, whenever I think of sex life with a woman my face at once turns from it, and I spit at the thought." The Fugs never returned.

To speak ill of sexual pleasure was certainly not a strategic move for one who wanted to create followers among the Lower East Side hippies. But Prabhupāda never considered changing his message. In fact, when Umāpati had mentioned that Americans didn't like to hear that sex was only for conceiving children, Prabhupāda had replied, "I cannot change the philosophy to please the Americans."

"What about sex?" asked the ISKCON attorney, Steve Goldsmith, one evening, speaking out from the rear of the crowded temple.

"Sex should only be with one's wife," Prabhupāda said, "and that is also restricted. Sex is for the propagation of Kṛṣṇa conscious children. My spiritual master used to say that to beget Kṛṣṇa conscious children he was prepared to have sex a hundred times. Of course, that is most difficult in this age. Therefore, he remained a *brahmacārī.*"

"But sex is a very strong force," Mr. Goldsmith challenged. "What a man feels for a woman is undeniable."

"Therefore in every culture there is the institution of marriage," Prabhupāda replied. "You can get yourself married and live peacefully with one woman, but the wife should not be used as a machine for sense gratification. Sex should be restricted to once a month and only for the propagation of children."

Hayagrīva, who was seated just to Swamiji's left, beside the large, dangling cymbal, spoke out suddenly. "Only once a month?" And with a touch of facetious humor he added loudly, "Better to forget the whole thing!"

"Yes! That's it! Very good boy." Swamiji laughed, and others joined him. "It is best not to think of it. Best just to chant Hare Kṛṣṇa." And he held up his hands as if he were chanting on a strand of beads. "That way we will be saved from so much botheration. Sex is like the itching sensation, that's all. And as when we scratch, it gets worse, so we should tolerate the itching and ask Kṛṣṇa to help us. It is not easy. Sex is the highest pleasure in the material world, and it is also the greatest bondage."

But Steve Goldsmith was shaking his head. Prabhupāda looked at him, smiling: "There is still a problem?"

"It's just that ... well, it's been proved dangerous to repress the sex drive. There's a theory that we have wars because—"

"People are eating meat," Prabhupāda interrupted. "As long as people eat meat, there will be war. And if a man eats meat, he will be sure to have illicit sex also."

Steve Goldsmith was an influential friend and supporter of ISKCON. But Prabhupāda would not change the philosophy of Kṛṣṇa consciousness "to please the Americans."

* * *

Judson Hall, on West Fifty-seventh Street, cost two hundred dollars to rent for one night. Rāya Rāma thought it was time Swamiji tried reaching some of the more sophisticated New Yorkers, and since Judson Hall was near Carnegie Hall and sometimes had interesting concerts and lectures, he thought it would be a good place to start. Swamiji agreed to the idea, and Rāya Rāma printed an announcement, which he distributed in the midtown bookstores. On the night of the event the devotees paraded through the midtown entertainment areas, beating a bass drum and handing out leaflets. Then they returned to Judson Hall for the program. Only seven people attended.

The devotees felt terrible—they had misled Swamiji and spent the equivalent of a month's rent. "We can cancel the program if you like, Swamiji," Rāya Rāma said. But Prabhupāda replied, "No, let us chant and speak." So the devotees took the stage and chanted with Swamiji and danced, and then sat beside him as he lectured, his voice echoing through the empty hall. Afterward, Swamiji called for questions, and a young man, about fifteen vacant rows back, asked whether he was correct in understanding that the Swami's philosophy was primarily for reforming destitute young people.

"No," Prabhupāda replied. "Everyone in this material world is lost and destitute, even the so-called successful person, because everyone has forgotten Kṛṣṇa."

After the program, Swamiji sat in a chair by the exit as the few members of the audience were leaving. A respectable-looking couple introduced themselves, and Swamiji sat up very straight with folded palms and smiled. Brahmānanda's mother was present, and Swamiji was very cordial toward her. But in general the devotees were depressed at the small turnout. "I'm sorry, Swamiji. We invited you here and almost no one came," Rāya Rāma apologized. But Prabhupāda raised his eyebrows and said, "No one? You did not see Nārada? You did not see Lord Brahmā? When there is chanting of Hare Kṛṣṇa, even the demigods come to participate."

Back at the temple, Prabhupāda chided Rāya Rāma: "I told you we should have charged money. When something is free, people think it is worthless. But just charge three dollars or five dollars, and people will think, 'Oh, you are offering some very valuable thing.' In Bengal there is the story of a man who went house to house offering free mangoes. And no one would take his mangoes, because everyone thought, 'Oh, why is he giving away these mangoes? There must be something wrong with them.' So he charged three rupees, and then they thought, 'These look like good mangoes. The price is only three rupees—all right.' So, when people see that something is free, they think it is worthless. Charge them some money, and they will think it is very nice."

* * *

Burton Green was a musician, fond of the Swami and fond of banging on the innards of the piano in the temple during *kīrtana.*

Burton Green: *We had a really explosive thing to break out of, with this capitalistic, materialistic egg sitting on us. So there was so much ferocity in the music to break out of. But spinning out like that, you could have a nervous breakdown. So it was great to go to the Swami's and chant in his small storefront on Second Avenue. The streets were full of* māyā *and perversion—and his was a place to really mellow out. It was great to chant there, to balance my life. It was great to sit and have* prasādam *with the Swami and get some real authentic Indian cooking and* capātīs *and talk about things, especially when I had very little money in my pocket. It was always nice to go.*

When Burton asked Prabhupāda to attend his piano recital at Town Hall Theater, Prabhupāda agreed.

Brahmānanda: *About seven or eight of us in our sneakers and jeans had ridden on the subway with Swamiji to Town Hall. We went in and took our seats, and the concert began. Burton Green came out, opened the piano top, took a hammer, and began wildly hitting on the strings inside the piano. And it went on for an hour and a half. We were all sitting there with Swamiji, and we all began chanting on our beads. There were only about two dozen people in the whole theater.*

Then the intermission came, and Swamiji wanted to go to the toilet room, and I went along and helped him—turning on the water in the sink, getting a paper towel for him. Doing these little services for Swamiji seemed like the perfection of my life. There was something so great about him that just doing those things was my perfection. And I felt like I was protecting him, like I was his personal bodyguard. Coming up on the subway, I had shown him how the subway worked and answered his questions. It all seemed very intimate.

Anyway, we went back upstairs to our seats, and Burton Green came right up to Swamiji saying, "Swamiji, are you happy? Are you comfortable? Do you like it?" And Swamiji was very polite and said yes. Then Burton said, "Now the second part is coming." I interrupted and tried to say that Swamiji is very tired and he takes rest at ten. It was already after ten, so I said we had to go back. But he pressed Swamiji to stay for the second half, and so we had to stay.

Then the poets came out and recited poetry. We were there until eleven-thirty, and then we had to ride back on the subway. But a few weeks later I learned that Prabhupāda had another reason for going to Town Hall—he was thinking of renting it for a temple, and he wanted to see it.

* * *

The Gate Theater was a small auditorium on Second Avenue about ten blocks north of the storefront.

Satsvarūpa: *We rented the Gate Theater for one night. It was a dark place, painted all black. The theater was almost empty. We had an easel on stage with a painting of the Pañca-tattva. Swamiji spoke, and his talk became very technical. Pointing and referring back to the painting, he described each member of the Pañca-tattva. He first explained that Lord Caitanya is the Supreme Personality of Godhead appearing as a pure devotee. Lord Nityānanda, to the right of Lord Caitanya, is His first expansion, and to the right of Lord Nityānanda is Advaita, who is the incarnation of the Supreme Lord. To the left of Lord Caitanya, he said, is Gadādhara, the internal energy, and Śrīvāsa is the perfect devotee.*

During the talk, I was thinking that this was maybe too elevated for the audience. But I was sitting close beside Swamiji, and like the other devotees I was really enjoying being with him.

After the Gate engagement, Swamiji and his disciples agreed that it was a waste of time trying to rent theaters. It was better to go to Tompkins Square Park. That was the best place for attracting people, and it didn't cost anything.

* * *

It was 11:00 P.M., and only one light was on in Swamiji's apartment—in the kitchenette. Swamiji was staying up, teaching Kīrtanānanda and

Brahmānanda how to cook, because the next day (Sunday) they would be holding a feast for the public. Kīrtanānanda had suggested it be advertised as a "Love Feast," and Swamiji had adopted the name, although some thought it sounded strange at first to hear him say "Love Feast." The devotees had put up posters around the neighborhood and had made a sign for the window of the storefront, and Swamiji had said he would cook enough for at least fifty people. He said the Love Feasts should become an important part of ISKCON. As he had explained many times, food offered to Kṛṣṇa becomes spiritual, and whoever eats the *prasādam* receives great spiritual benefit. *Prasādam* meant "mercy."

His two helpers stood respectfully beside him, sometimes stepping back out of his way as he moved and sometimes looking over his shoulder as he mixed spices or set a pan over the flame or called for another ingredient. He was stirring a big pot of sweet rice with a wooden spoon—it had to be stirred constantly—and slowly adding milk. If the sweet rice burned, it would be ruined, he said, and he handed the spoon to Kīrtanānanda. He next showed them how to make ghee by heating butter in a wok and separating the milk solids from the butterfat. And he simultaneously taught them how to make apple chutney.

Prabhupāda was silent as he cooked. But when Brahmānanda asked him how he had learned so much about cooking, Prabhupāda said that he had learned by watching his mother. He laughed and said it had not been like it is in the West, where you take a lump of flesh from your refrigerator, throw it in a pan, boil it, sprinkle it with salt, and then eat like an animal. And in Korea, he said, they eat dogs. But human beings should eat grains, fruits, vegetables, and milk; and the cow, especially, should not be killed.

While Brahmānanda cut the apples for the chutney and put them in a pot for steaming and Kīrtanānanda stirred the sweet rice, Swamiji prepared *masālā*—the basic mixture of spices—which he would soon add to the steaming apples. The familiar smell of red pepper and cumin seeds entered their nostrils sharply as the *masālā* crackled and smoked in the hot ghee in the tiny frying pan. With three separate operations going at once—sweet rice, steaming apples, and *masālā*—Prabhupāda cautioned Kīrtanānanda to stir the sweet rice steadily and scrape the bottom of the pot, and he took the spoon for a moment from Kīrtanānanda's hand and demonstrated how to stir it properly. Sweet rice, chutney, and certain other dishes could be made in advance of the feast, he explained, but many things would have to be done the next morning.

Prabhupāda rose early, despite having kept late hours the night before, and after the morning class he was back in the kitchen. Now, half a dozen disciples sat in his front room making dough for *purīs* and *samosās.* He had shown them how to make the dough, and Umāpati had kneaded for a while by pounding the soft dough with his fists. But Brahmānanda was better at it, socking the weight of his wrestler's body onto the large lump of dough.

As Swamiji entered the room to examine the quality of the *purīs,* his disciples looked up at him respectfully. They were always serious when he was present. He picked up a *purī* and examined it. "It is not to the standard," he said, "but it will have to do." Then, amid crumpled rejects and oddly shaped pieces of dough, he squatted down beside his helpers, who were trying as best they could, though making a mess. He took a small ball of dough, pressed it flat with his fingers, and then deftly rolled it out until it curled around the wooden pin and then fell off—a perfectly round *purī.* He held it up, displaying a translucent, thin (but not too thin) patty of dough. "Make them like this," he said. "But hurry." On discovering that the dough was too stiff, Swamiji added a little ghee and then a little milk and kneaded the dough to a softer texture. "Everything should be just right," he said, and his disciples took to their menial tasks with concentrated earnestness. Who among them had ever heard of these things before—*purīs* and *samosās*? It was all new, and the challenge something very important; it was a part of devotional service.

Swamiji did much of the cooking as he simultaneously supervised his helpers. He was always near, walking barefoot back to the kitchen, then to the front room, then to his own room in the rear. And even when he went to his back room, his disciples could see him through the window in the wall.

Swamiji saw each of the nearly one dozen dishes through its final stages, and his disciples carried them into the front room in pots, one by one, and placed them before the picture of Lord Caitanya. There was *halavā, dāl,* two *sabjīs,* fancy rice, *purīs, samosās,* sweet rice, apple chutney, and *gulābjāmuns,* or sweetballs—ISKCON bullets. Prabhupāda had personally spent much time slowly deep-frying the sweetballs on a low heat, until they had turned golden brown and full. Then, one by one, he had lifted them out of the ghee with a slotted spoon and put them to soak in sugar syrup. He recognized that these golden, ghee-fried milk balls soaked with sugar water were his disciples' favorite *prasādam* treat. He called them "ISKCON bullets" because they were weapons in the war against *māyā.* He even allowed that a jar of ISKCON bullets, floating in their syrup, be always on hand in the front room, where his disciples could take them without asking permission and without observing any regulated hours. They could take as many as they liked.

Kīrtanānanda brought in the *samosā* filling, which he had prepared from spinach and green peas cooked to a paste and which the Swami had heavily spiced. Stuffing the *samosās* was an art, and Swamiji showed them how to do it. He took a semicircle of dough, shaped it into a cone, stuffed it with a spoonful of filling, and then folded the top over and sealed it—a *samosā,* ready for the hot ghee.

Acyutānanda carried the imperfectly shaped *purīs* into the kitchen, where he and Kīrtanānanda deep-fried them two at a time. If the temperature of the ghee, the consistency of the dough, and the size, shape, and thickness of the *purīs* were all just right, the *purīs* would cook in only a few seconds, rising to the surface of the ghee, where they would inflate like little balloons. The cooks then stood them on edge in a cardboard box to drain off the excess ghee.

As they completed the last preparations for the feast, Swamiji's disciples washed the stiff dough from their hands and went down to the storefront, where they set out the straw mats and awaited the guests and the feast. Upstairs, Swamiji and a couple of his cooks offered all the preparations to Lord Caitanya, reciting the *paramparā* prayer.

The first few Love Feasts were not very well attended, but the devotees were so enthusiastic about the feast *prasādam* that they showed no disappointment over the scarcity of guests. They were prepared to eat everything.

Satsvarūpa: *There was something called* "brāhmaṇa *spaghetti,*" *which was rice-flour noodles cooked in ghee and soaked in sugar water. And there was* halavā, puṣpānna *rice with fried cheese balls,* samosās, *split mung beans fried into crunchy pellets and mixed with salt and spices,* purīs, gulābjāmuns. *And everything was succulent—that was the word Hayagrīva used. "Yes," he would say, expressing it waggishly, "everything was very* succulent."

Eating the feast was an intense experience. We were supposed to be subduing our senses all week, following strict regulations, controlling the tongue. And the feast was a kind of reward. Swamiji and Kṛṣṇa were giving us a taste of full spiritual ecstasy, even though we were still beginners and still in the material world. Before taking my plateful, I would pray, "Please let me remain in Kṛṣṇa consciousness, because it is so nice and I am so fallen. Let me serve Swamiji, and let me now enjoy this feast in transcendental bliss." And I would begin eating, going from one taste sensation to another—the good rice, the favorite vegetable, the bread, and saving the gulābjāmun *for last, thinking, "I can have seconds, and if I like, thirds." We would keep our eyes on the big pots, confident that there was as much as we wanted. It was a time of rededication. We all enjoyed with completely open relish and sense gratification. Eating was very important.*

Gradually, attendance picked up. The feasts were free, and they were reputed to be delicious. Mostly local hippies came, but occasionally a higher class of experimenting New Yorkers or even the parents of one of the devotees would come. When the small temple was filled, guests would sit in the courtyard. They would take their *prasādam*-laden paper plates and their wooden spoons into the backyard garden and sit beneath the fire escape or at the picnic table or anywhere. And after eating, they would go back into the storefront for more. Devotees were stationed behind the pots of *prasādam,* and the guests would come by for seconds. The other tenants were not very happy about seeing the courtyard full of festive guests, and the devotees tried to pacify them by bringing them plates of *prasādam.* Although Swamiji would not go down to the temple, he would take a plate in his room and hear with pleasure about the success of his new program.

One time the devotees were eating so ravenously that they threatened to eat everything available before the guests had all been served, and Kīrtanānanda had to admonish them for their selfish attitude. Gradually, they were understanding that the Sunday feast was not just for their fun and pleasure but to bring people to Kṛṣṇa consciousness.

* * *

Prabhupāda had begun *Back to Godhead* magazine in India. Although he had been writing articles since the 1930s, it was in 1944, in Calcutta, that he had singlehandedly begun the magazine, in response to his spiritual master's request that he preach Kṛṣṇa consciousness in English. It had been with great difficulty that through his pharmaceutical business he had managed to gather the four hundred rupees a month for printing. And he had singlehandedly written, edited, published, financed, and distributed each issue. In those early years, *Back to Godhead* had been Prabhupāda's major literary work and preaching mission. He had envisioned widespread distribution of the magazine, and he had thought of plans for spreading the message of Lord Caitanya all over the world. He had drawn up a list of major countries and the number of copies of *Back to Godhead* he wanted to send to each. He sought donations to finance this project, but help was scarce. Then, in 1959, he had turned his energies toward writing and publishing the *Śrīmad-Bhāgavatam.* But now he wanted to revive *Back to Godhead,* and this time it would not be done singlehandedly. This time he would give the responsibility to his disciples.

Greg Scharf, now Gargamuni since his recent initiation, found a press. A country club in Queens was trying to sell its small A.B. Dick press. Prabhupāda was interested, and he rode out to Queens in a borrowed van with Gargamuni and Kīrtanānanda to see the machine. It was old, but in good condition. The manager of the country club wanted $250 for it. Prabhupāda looked over the machine carefully and talked with the manager, telling him of his spiritual mission. The manager mentioned a second press he had on hand and explained that neither machine was actually of any use to him. So Prabhupāda said he would pay $250 for both machines; the country club did not really need them, and besides, the manager should help out, since Prabhupāda had an important spiritual message to print for the benefit of all humanity. The man agreed. Prabhupāda had Gargamuni and Kīrtanānanda load both machines into the van, and ISKCON had its printing press.

Śrīla Prabhupāda gave over the editorship of *Back to Godhead* magazine to Hayagrīva and Rāya Rāma. For so many years he had taken *Back to Godhead* as his personal service to his spiritual master, but now he would let young men like Hayagrīva, the college English teacher, and Rāya Rāma, the professional writer, take up *Back to Godhead* magazine as their service to *their* spiritual master. In a short time, Hayagrīva and Rāya Rāma had compiled the first issue and were ready to print.

It was an off night—no public *kīrtana* and lecture—and Swamiji was up in his room working on his translation of *Śrīmad-Bhāgavatam.* Downstairs, the printing of the first issue had been going on for hours. Rāya Rāma had typed the stencils, and during the printing he had stood nervously over the machine, examining the printing quality of each page, stroking his beard, and murmuring, "Hmmmmm." Now it was time to collate and staple each magazine. The stencils had lasted for one hundred copies, and one hundred copies of each of the twenty-eight pages and the front and back covers were now lined up along two of the unvarnished benches Raphael had made that summer. A few devotees collated and stapled the magazine in an assembly line, walking along the stacks of pages, taking one page under another until they reached the end of the bench and gave the assembled stack of pages to Gargamuni, who stood brushing his long hair out of his eyes, stapling each magazine with the stapler and staples Brahmānanda had brought from his Board of Education office. Even Hayagrīva, who usually didn't volunteer for menial duties, was there, walking down the line, collating.

Suddenly the side door opened, and to their surprise they saw Swamiji looking in at them. Then he opened the door wide and entered the room. He had never come down like this on an off night before. They felt an unexpected flush of emotion and love for him, and they dropped down on their knees, bowing their heads to the floor. "No, no," he said, raising his hand to stop them as some were still bowing and others already rising to their feet. "Continue what you are doing." When they stood up and saw him standing with them, they weren't sure what to do. But obviously he had come down to see them producing his *Back to Godhead* magazine, so they continued working, silently and efficiently. Prabhupāda walked down the row of pages, his hand and wrist extending gracefully from the folds of his shawl as he touched a stack of pages and then a finished magazine. "ISKCON Press," he said.

Jagannātha had designed the cover, using a pen-and-ink drawing of Rādhā and Kṛṣṇa similar to his painting in the temple. It was a simple drawing set within a pattern of concentric circles. The first page opened with the same motto Prabhupāda had used for years on his *Back to Godhead:* "Godhead is light, nescience is darkness. Where there is Godhead there is no nescience." And on the same page, Hayagrīva had not been able to resist giving a quotation from William Blake, approved by Swamiji, which substantiated the philosophy of Kṛṣṇa consciousness:

> God appears, and God is Light
> To those poor souls who dwell in Night,
> But does a Human Form display
> To those who dwell in realms of Day.

Although the editorial spoke of Blake, Whitman, and Jesus Christ, it stressed:

> ... it is to teach this science [of devotion to God] that Swami Bhaktivedanta has come to America. His message is simple: the chanting of the Holy Name of God: "Hare Krishna, Hare Krishna, Krishna Krishna, Hare Hare ..."
>
> Following the orders of his spiritual master, His Divine Grace Sri Srimad Bhakti Siddhanta Saraswati Goswami Prabhupad, Swami Bhaktivedanta began the initial publication of *Back to Godhead* in 1944. This bi-monthly, published from 1944 to 1956 in Vrindaban, India, ... established Swami Bhaktivedanta as the leading Personalist in India. This issue marks the first publication of *Back to Godhead* in the West.

The main article, a summary of a lecture given by Prabhupāda, was based on notes taken by Umāpati.

> It has been said that when we wake up and when we go to sleep, we should beat our mind a thousand times with a shoe. When the mind says things like, "Why sing 'Hare Krishna'? Why not take LSD?" we should beat it with the same shoe. However, if we always think of Krishna, no beating will be necessary. The mind will be our best friend.

And there was an article by Hayagrīva: "Flip Out and Stay." Hayagrīva had quoted liberally from Hart Crane and Walt Whitman.

> No wonder so many young collegiates are trying to flip out permanently on superdrugs ... Perhaps this is their way of saying, "We don't want any part of this hell you've made for yourselves." So they use psychedelics as a springboard to propel themselves into different realms ... But the drug "flip" is only temporary. It is temporary because it is artificial ... One really begins to wonder where all these "trips" are leading.

Hayagrīva concluded that *kṛṣṇa-kīrtana* is the quickest way to flip out without coming down.

> Your associates will think you mad. That is the first sign of progress. Just let others be mad for *māyā,* the old ephemeral lures of women and gold ... But [you] be mad instead for the Reality.

In the back of the magazine was an ad for Swamiji's essays, *Krishna, the Reservoir of Pleasure* and *Who is Crazy*? and a notice:

> Soon to be printed:
> *Geetopanishad,* or *Bhagavad-gītā As It Is,*
> Translated and with commentaries by Swami Bhaktivedanta.

Prabhupāda's first and main instruction to his editors had been that they should produce the magazine *regularly—every month.* Even if they didn't know how to sell the copies or even if they only turned out two pages, they had to continue bearing the standard.

He called Hayagrīva to his room and presented him a complete three-volume set of his *Śrīmad-Bhāgavatam.* On the front page of each volume he had written, "To Sriman Hayagriva das Brahmacari with my blessings, A. C. Bhaktivedanta Swami." Hayagrīva was grateful and mentioned that he had not been able to afford them. "That's all right," Prabhupāda said. "Now you compile this *Back to Godhead.* Work sincerely, and make it as big as *Time* magazine."

Prabhupāda wanted all his disciples to take part in it. "Don't be dull," he said. "Write something." He wanted to give his disciples *Back to Godhead* for their own preaching. Brahmānanda and Gargamuni took the first issues out that same night on bicycles, riding to every head shop on the Lower East Side, all the way to Fourteenth Street and as far west as the West Village, until they had distributed all one hundred issues. This was an increase in the preaching. Now all his students could take part in the work—typing, editing, writing, assembling, selling. It was *his* preaching, of course, but he wasn't alone anymore.

* * *

"Over a short four months, the society has expanded sufficiently to warrant larger quarters than the small Second Avenue storefront temple," stated the editorial in the second issue of *Back to Godhead.* Prabhupāda had not abandoned his idea for a big building in New York City. Greenwich Village real estate was too expensive, and midtown was out of the question, but Prabhupāda still said he wanted to buy a building. It was difficult for his followers to think of Kṛṣṇa consciousness as anything more than a Lower East Side movement, because who but the people of the Lower East Side would be interested in Kṛṣṇa consciousness? And anyway, who had money to buy a building in Manhattan?

But one day, Ravīndra-svarūpa had happened to meet someone—a wealthy Jewish heir who was sympathetic toward youth movements—who agreed to loan Swamiji five thousand dollars. Ravīndra-svarūpa had arranged the loan, and Swamiji had designated the money as his building fund, to which he had gradually added another five thousand dollars that he had collected through incidental donations. But with suitable buildings starting at one hundred thousand dollars, even this sum seemed petty.

Swamiji went with Brahmānanda to look at a building on Sixth Street that had previously been the Jewish Providential Bank. It had a large lobby with a mezzanine, marble floors, and the atmosphere of a temple. Brahmānanda suggested that the vault area could be remodeled for use as a dormitory, and Swamiji considered the mezzanine for his own apartment. The large lobby, he said, could be used for *kīrtanas* and lectures. On leaving the building, however, Prabhupāda noted that it was located on the corner, by a bus stop. It would not be a good location. The Gaudiya Math branch at Bhag Bazaar in Calcutta, he said, was also located at a bus stop, and the noisy engines of the buses as they started up created a disturbance.

Prabhupāda next looked at the Temple Emanu-El, also on Sixth Street on the Lower East Side. It was even larger than the bank building, and when some of Swamiji's disciples walked through the cavernous, empty rooms, they became bewildered to think how, even if they could get such a place, they would be able to manage or use it.

He visited other places: one so neglected and in such poor repair that it looked as though it had been vandalized, and another, in similar condition, filled with lumber stacked almost to the ceiling. He asked Rūpānuga, who had accompanied him, what he thought, and Rūpānuga said, "Too much time and money to fix it up." So they left. Swamiji returned to his room and went into the bathroom, where he washed his feet in the tub. He said that it was an Indian custom that after walking outside you wash your feet.

Then the devotees met Mr. Price, an elegantly dressed real estate agent. "You have a handful of stars," Mr. Price told Brahmānanda. "You're incorporated as a tax-free religious organization. You have no idea how much money this will save. So many people have to vacate just because they can't pay their taxes. But 'someone up there' is looking after you people, and I have just the place for you and your Swami."

Mr. Price showed Brahmānanda a handsome three-story building near St. Mark's Place. It was a good downtown location, near the young people, yet in an area where the uptown people would feel safe. The floors were polished hardwood, all the doors were ornately hand-carved, and it had a large hall, suitable for a temple. The Marquis de Lafayette had stayed here during his visit in 1824, a fact that added to the building's charm and prestige.

One evening, Mr. Price visited Prabhupāda up in his room, Prabhupāda sitting on the floor behind his desk and Mr. Price sitting on a metal folding chair. Mr. Price wore an elegant suit and a white dress shirt with cuff links and starched cuffs. His expensive dress, meticulously tanned face, and blond hair (which some devotees thought was a wig) contrasted strangely with the Swami's simplicity. Mr. Price kept referring to Swamiji as "Your Excellency," and he expressed much appreciation of Swamiji's work. He spoke optimistically about how, through his connections, he hoped to save Prabhupāda a lot of money and trouble and get him just the place he wanted.

Accompanied by a few disciples, Prabhupāda went with Mr. Price to see the building. While Mr. Price, the devotees, and the custodian of the house were all talking together in a group, Prabhupāda wandered off unnoticed to a corner of the room, where there was an old-fashioned sewing machine. He began pressing the treadle and examining the workings of the machine. As Prabhupāda rejoined the group, Mr. Price said, "If you can just get five thousand dollars down, I can get the owners to draw up a contract. Five thousand dollars down, and another five thousand within two months—that shouldn't be so difficult." Prabhupāda liked the building and told Brahmānanda they should purchase it.

Brahmānanda was inclined to turn the money over right away, but Prabhupāda said that first a suitable contract had to be drawn up. Mr. Price talked to the devotees in private, speaking in the Swami's interest and in the interest of the spiritual movement, and he seemed to be promising them something even *more* than a contract. Perhaps he would *give* them the building. It didn't make sense that he could give the building, but he told them something like that. He wanted the devotees to think of him as their friend, and he invited them over to his house one evening.

When the devotees gathered in his house, sitting stiffly on chairs in his living room, which was lined with bookcases filled not with books, but with two-dimensional designs depicting rows of books, he continued to flatter them. He praised Hayagrīva's writings, and Hayagrīva was obviously embarrassed and flattered. He praised everything about the devotees. He also spoke of how his dog had recently died, and said, "The house seems empty without the little fellow." He was an unusual man, effeminate, and full of flattery and praises. Prabhupāda remained reserved after his first meeting with Mr. Price, though he was interested in getting the building if the proper arrangement could be made.

Brahmānanda continued to negotiate with Mr. Price, and soon, according to Mr. Price, the owners of the building would be expecting the devotees to give proof of their ability to meet the payments. On Prabhupāda's direction, the devotees hired a lawyer to go over the contract. "This Mr. Price is causing us so much pain," Prabhupāda said. "What is the difficulty?" He didn't see the necessity for Mr. Price at all. "Why don't we purchase directly from the owners? Why all these agents?"

"It's just the way it's done here," Brahmānanda said.

* * *

Alan Kallman was a record producer. He had read the article in *The East Village Other* about the swami from India and the *mantra* he had brought with him. When he had read the Hare Kṛṣṇa *mantra* on the front page, he had become attracted. The article gave the idea that one could get a tremendous high or ecstasy from chanting. The Swami's Second Avenue address was given in the article, so one night in November, Alan and his wife visited the storefront.

Alan: *There were about thirty pairs of shoes in the back of the room—people in the front and shoes in the back. We took off our shoes and sat down. Everyone was seated and very quiet. Front and center was a chair, and everyone was staring at this chair. Even then we felt a certain energy in the room. No one was saying anything, and everyone was staring at the chair. The next thing was our first sight of the Swami. He came in and sat down on the chair, and there was a tremendous surge of energy. The Swami began chanting, and it was a very beautiful sound. Swamiji had this little drum he was hitting—very penetrating and exciting. One of the devotees was holding up a sign with the chant written on it so everyone could follow. Then the devotees got up and danced in a circle, a special dance with steps to it. The Swami was looking around the room, and he seemed to smile as he looked at you, as if to encourage you to join.*

The next day, Alan phoned Prabhupāda to propose that he make a record of the chanting. But it was Brahmānanda who answered the phone, and he gave Alan an appointment with the Swami that evening. So again Alan and his wife went down to the East Village, which to them was the neighborhood where things were happening. If you wanted to have some excitement, you went down to the East Village.

When they entered the Swami's room, he was seated at his typewriter, working. As soon as Alan mentioned his idea about making a record, Prabhupāda was interested. "Yes," he said, "we *must* record. If it will help us distribute the chanting of Hare Kṛṣṇa, then it is our duty." They scheduled the recording for two weeks later, in December, at the Adelphi Recording Studio near Times Square. Alan's wife was impressed by how enthusiastically the Swami had gotten to the point of making the record: "He had so much energy and ambition in his plans."

It was the night before the recording date. A boy walked into the storefront for the evening *kīrtana* carrying a large, two-headed Indian drum. This was not unusual, as guests often brought drums, flutes, and other instruments, yet this time Swamiji seemed particularly interested. The boy sat down and was preparing to play when Prabhupāda motioned for the boy to bring him the drum. The boy didn't move—he wanted to play it himself—but Brahmānanda went over and said, "Swamiji wants to play the drum," so the boy gave in.

Brahmānanda: *Swamiji began to play, and his hands were just dancing on the drum. Everyone was stunned that Swamiji knew how to do this. All we had seen was the bongo drum, so I thought it was the proper Indian drum. But when this two-headed drum came out of nowhere and Swamiji started playing it like a master musician, it created an ecstasy a hundred times more than the bongo drum had.*

After the *kīrtana,* Prabhupāda asked the boy if he could borrow the drum for the recording session the next night. The boy at first was reluctant, but the devotees promised to return his drum the next day, so he agreed and said he would bring the drum the next evening. When he left the storefront that night with his drum under his arm, the devotees thought they would never see the boy or his drum again, but the next day, a few hours before Swamiji was to leave for the studio, the boy returned with his drum.

It was a cold December night. The Swami, dressed in his usual saffron *dhotī,* a tweed overcoat, and a pair of gray shoes (which had long since replaced his original white, pointy rubber ones), got into Rūpānuga's VW van with about fifteen of his followers and their instruments and started for the recording studio.

Brahmānanda: *We didn't start recording right away, because there was a group ahead of us. So we went out for a walk in Times Square. We were just standing there with Swamiji, seeing all the flashing lights and all the sense gratification, when a woman came up to Swamiji and said, "Oh, hello. Where do you come from?" in a very loud, matronly way. And Swamiji said, "I am a monk from India." And she said, "Oh, that's wonderful. Glad to meet you." And then she shook Swamiji's hand and left.*

At the studio, everyone accepted the devotees as a regular music group. One of the rock musicians asked them what the name of their group was, and Hayagrīva laughed and replied, "The Hare Kṛṣṇa Chanters." Of course most of the devotees weren't actually musicians, and yet the instruments they brought with them—a tamboura, a large harmonium (loaned by Allen Ginsberg), and rhythm instruments—were ones they had played during *kīrtanas* for months. So as they entered the studio they felt confident that they could produce their own sound. They just followed their Swami. He knew how to play, and they knew how to follow him. They weren't just another music group. It was music, but it was also chanting, meditation, worship.

Prabhupāda sat on a mat in the center of the studio, while the engineers arranged the microphones and assigned each devotee a place to sit according to his particular instrument. They asked for only two pairs of *karatālas* and they approved of the pairs of rhythm sticks, but they wanted several devotees clapping their hands. Rūpānuga's usual instrument was a pair of brass Indian bells with the tongues removed, and when the engineer saw them, he came over and said, "Let me hear that." Rūpānuga played them, and they passed. Since Ravīndra-svarūpa would be playing the drone on the harmonium, he sat apart with his own microphone, and Kīrtanānanda also had a microphone for the tamboura.

When the engineers were satisfied, they cued the devotees, and Swamiji began chanting and playing his drum. The cymbals and sticks and clapping hands joined him, and the chanting went on steadily for about ten minutes, until an engineer came out of the glass studio and stopped them: Brahmānanda was clapping too loudly, creating an imbalance. The engineer went back into his studio, put on his headphones, balanced everyone, and cued them for a second take. This time it was better.

The first sound was the tamboura, with its plucked, reverberating twang. An instant later Swamiji began beating the drum and singing, *Vande 'haṁ śrī-guroḥ* ... Then the whole ensemble put out to sea—the tamboura, the harmonium, the clackers, the cymbals, Rūpānuga's bells, Swamiji's solo singing—pushing off from their moorings, out into a fair-weather sea of chanting ... *lalitā-śrī-viśākhānvitāṁś ca* ...

Swamiji's voice in the studio was very sweet. His boys were feeling love, not just making a record. There was a feeling of success and union, a crowning evening to all their months together.

... *Śrī-kṛṣṇa-caitanya, prabhu-nityānanda* ...

After a few minutes of singing prayers alone, Swamiji paused briefly while the instruments continued pulsing, and then began the *mantra:* Hare Kṛṣṇa, Hare Kṛṣṇa, Kṛṣṇa Kṛṣṇa, Hare Hare. It was pure Bhaktivedanta Swami—expert, just like his cooking in the kitchen, like his lectures. The engineers liked what they heard—it would be a good take if nothing went wrong. The instruments were all right, the drum, the singing. The harmony was rough. But this was a special record—a happening. The Hare Kṛṣṇa Chanters were doing their thing, and they were doing it all right. Alan Kallman was excited. Here was an authentic sound. Maybe it would sell.

After a few rounds of the *mantra,* the devotees began to feel relaxed, as though they were back in the temple, and they were able to forget about making mistakes on the record. They just chanted, and the beat steadied into a slightly faster pace. The word *hare* would come sometimes with a little shout in it, but there were no emotional theatrics in the chorus, just the straight response to the Swami's melody. Ten minutes went by. The chanting went faster, louder and faster—Swamiji doing more fancy things on the drum, until suddenly ... everything stopped, with the droning note of the harmonium lingering.

Alan came out of the studio: "It was great, Swami. Great. Would you like to just go right ahead and read the address now? Or are you too tired?" With polite concern, pale, befreckled Alan Kallman peered through his thick glasses at the Swami. Swamiji appeared tired, but he replied, "No, I am not tired." Then the devotees sat back in the studio to watch and listen as Prabhupāda read his prepared statement.

"As explained on the cover of the record album ..." The sympathetic devotees thought that Swamiji, despite his accent, sounded perfectly clear, reading from his script like an elocutionist. "... this transcendental vibration by chanting of Hare Kṛṣṇa, Hare Kṛṣṇa, Kṛṣṇa Kṛṣṇa, Hare Hare/ Hare Rāma, Hare Rāma, Rāma Rāma, Hare Hare is the sublime method for reviving our Kṛṣṇa consciousness." The language was philosophic, and the kind of people who usually walked out of the temple as soon as the *kīrtanas* ended, before the Swami could even speak a word, would also not appreciate this speech on their record album. "As living spiritual souls," Swamiji preached, "we are all originally Kṛṣṇa conscious entities. But due to our association with matter from time immemorial, our consciousness is now polluted by material atmosphere." The devotees listened submissively to the words of their spiritual master, while at the same time trying to comprehend the effect this would have on the audience. Certainly some people would turn it off at the very mention of a spiritual nature. Swamiji continued reading, explaining that the chanting would deliver one from the sensual, the mental, and the intellectual planes and bring one to the spiritual realm.

"We have seen it practically," he continued. "Even a child can take part in the chanting, or even a dog can take part in it. ... The chanting should be heard, however, from the lips of a pure devotee of the Lord." And he continued reading on to the end. "... No other means, therefore, of spiritual realization is as effective in this age as chanting the *mahā-mantra:* Hare Kṛṣṇa, Hare Kṛṣṇa, Kṛṣṇa Kṛṣṇa, Hare Hare/ Hare Rāma, Hare Rāma, Rāma Rāma, Hare Hare."

Alan again came rushing out of the studio. It was fine, he said. He explained that they had recorded a little echo into the speech, to make it special for the listener. "Now," he pushed back his glasses with his finger. "We've got about ten minutes left on the side with the speech. Would you like to chant again? Or is it too late, Swamiji?" Prabhupāda smiled. No, it was not too late. He would chant the prayers to his spiritual master.

While his disciples lounged around the studio, watching their spiritual master and the technical activity of the engineers behind the glass, Prabhupāda began singing. Again the harmonium's drone began, then the tamboura and drum, but with a much smaller rhythm group than before. He sang through, without any retakes, and then ended the song (and the evening) with a fortissimo drumming as the hand-pumped organ notes faded.

Again, Alan came out and thanked the Swami for being so patient and such a good studio musician. Prabhupāda was still sitting. "Now we are tired," he admitted.

Suddenly, over the studio sound system came a playback of the Hare Kṛṣṇa chanting, complete with echo. When Prabhupāda heard the successful recording of his chanting, he became happy and stood and began dancing, swaying back and forth, dipping slightly from the waist, his arms upraised in the style of Lord Caitanya, dancing in ecstasy. The scheduled performance was over, but now Swamiji was making the best performance of the evening from his spontaneous feelings. As he danced, his half-asleep disciples became startled and also rose to their feet and joined him, dancing in the same style. And in the recording booth behind the glass, the engineers also raised their hands and began dancing and chanting.

"Now you have made your best record," Swamiji told Mr. Kallman as he left the studio for the freezing Manhattan evening. Swamiji got into the front seat of the Volkswagen bus while "The Hare Kṛṣṇa Chanters" climbed into the back with their instruments, and Rūpānuga drove them back home, back to the Lower East Side.

The next morning Prabhupāda didn't get up. He was exhausted. Kīrtanānanda, who was personally serving him, became alarmed when the Swami said something about his heart skipping and about not being able to move. For the first time, it became apparent that he was overexerting himself. Kīrtanānanda thought back through the fall and summer, when the Swami had led them all on hours-long *kīrtanas* in the park or on late-evening ventures—they had come to take it for granted. But now Kīrtanānanda saw that there was cause to be worried for Swamiji's health. Swamiji had no appetite for lunch, although by afternoon he regained his appetite and usual activity.

That same day, a letter arrived from Mukunda in San Francisco. Not long after their wedding, Mukunda and Jānakī had left for the West Coast. Mukunda had told Swamiji that he wanted to go on to India to study Indian music, but after a few weeks in southern Oregon he had ended up in San Francisco. Now he had a better idea. He wanted to rent a place and invite Swamiji to come and start his Hare Kṛṣṇa movement in the Haight-Ashbury district, just as he was doing on the Lower East Side. He said that the prospects there for Kṛṣṇa consciousness were very good. On hearing this, Prabhupāda began unfolding his expansive plans. They should open temples not only in San Francisco but, one by one, all over the world, even in Russia and China, and print the *Bhagavad-gītā* in different languages. And he would translate all the volumes of *Śrīmad-Bhāgavatam* into English and take a party of devotees back to India.

The devotees who heard him were amazed. Kīrtanānanda, who had seen the alarming symptoms of Prabhupāda's ill health, began to forget what he had thought earlier that morning. If Kṛṣṇa desired, Kīrtanānanda thought, Swamiji could do anything.

* * *

When Prabhupāda came down to hold his morning class on November 19, he carried a large red book instead of the usual brown one. But no one noticed the difference. He began as always, softly singing prayers to his spiritual master and accompanying himself with a faint rhythm on his bongo (the neighbors were still asleep).

The weather was cold, but the steam radiators kept the storefront warm. There would be no more outdoor chanting now. In Manhattan, the city opens wide in the summer and shuts tight in the winter, which for the evening classes meant no more noisy children outside the door. And although the morning classes had always been quiet even in the summer, now with winter approaching the group became a tighter, more committed core of sincere students coming together to hear Swamiji speak.

It was now four months since he had begun ISKCON at 26 Second Avenue. He had held three separate initiations and initiated nineteen devotees. Most of them had become serious, although a few remained casual visitors. Now, in these morning classes, Swamiji wanted to instruct them more about how to become devotees.

He led the chanting of Hare Kṛṣṇa for twenty minutes, cautioning them to respond softly, so that the neighbors would not pour water through the ceiling again—although they hadn't done it lately. Prabhupāda always tried to cooperate with the tenants, but occasionally someone would start a petition—which never amounted to much—against the devotees. Sometimes Prabhupāda would help the landlord, Mr. Chutey, by taking out other tenants' garbage or just giving him a hand.

Mr. Chutey was a husky, beer-bellied Polish refugee who lived alone in an apartment on the first floor. Mr. Chutey respected the Swami for his age and scholarship, and Swamiji was always amiable with him. Whenever Mr. Chutey came to the apartment, he would never take his shoes off, and Prabhupāda would always say, "That's all right, that's all right." And one time, when the plumbing didn't work in Prabhupāda's apartment, Prabhupāda went downstairs and took a shower in Mr. Chutey's apartment.

But Swamiji also considered Mr. Chutey a classic example of a foolish materialist, because although he had spent his life's savings to buy this building, he still had to work so hard. Swamiji said he was a fool for having spent his savings to buy such a run-down building. Because the building was in such poor condition, he had to work like an ass to keep it up. "This is how the materialists work," Swamiji would say.

Mr. Chutey, although respectful to the Swami, didn't like the devotees. Prabhupāda told his disciples, "Treat him as if he were your father." So that's what they did. Any time they would have to deal with Mr. Chutey, they would approach him saying, "We are your sons."

Those disciples who lived at the storefront had risen by six-thirty, bathed, and assembled downstairs by seven, while those who lived outside were arriving separately, taking off their coats and piling them on the shelf of the display window. Although women always attended the evening meetings, Jadurāṇī was usually the only girl who came in the morning. After breakfast, she would begin painting upstairs in the Swami's front room. She used a beginner's technique of dividing the canvas into vertical and horizontal grid lines and transposing bit by bit the corresponding sections of a photograph onto the canvas. The process was painstaking, and sometimes her painting was out of proportion. But Jadurāṇī was sincere, and that pleased Prabhupāda. She had completed several paintings of four-armed Viṣṇu, a new painting of Rādhā-Kṛṣṇa, and a painting of Lord Caitanya and His associates. When the painting of Lord Caitanya was finished, Swamiji had it hung in the temple. "Now," he announced, "there should be no more nonsense here. Lord Caitanya is present."

After the morning *kīrtana* Swami said, as usual, "Now chant one round." They chanted together, following him. They all had a vow to chant sixteen rounds daily, but they chanted their first round in the morning in the Swami's presence, so he could see each of them. As Swamiji chanted, he looked out at Second Avenue, which was mostly deserted, or at the pictures on the wall, or, with concerned glances, at the individual devotees. Sometimes he seemed surprised when he saw them chanting so earnestly, giving evidence of the power of the holy name to deliver even the most fallen. Some of the devotees kept their beads in a bead bag like his, but when they chanted the first round together in the morning, they imitated him by holding their beads out in both hands and chanting along with him: Hare Kṛṣṇa, Hare Kṛṣṇa, Kṛṣṇa Kṛṣṇa, Hare Hare, until they finished one round.

Then he held up the unfamiliar red book. "Because you are a little advanced," he said, "I am going to read today from the *Caitanya-caritāmṛta*." Caitanya what? No one was able to pick up the pronunciation. They had heard of Caitanya, certainly, but not of this new book. But in his room the night before, Prabhupāda had informed some of the devotees that he would start reading from a new book, *Caitanya-caritāmṛta.* He said that Lord Caitanya had told one of His disciples that understanding Kṛṣṇa wasn't really possible, but that He would give the disciple just a drop of the ocean of Kṛṣṇa consciousness, so that the disciple could then appreciate what the whole ocean must be like. "Be patient as I present this," he had told them. "It is revolutionary, but you should just be patient."

In the storefront Brahmānanda turned on the reel-to-reel tape recorder as Swamiji began reading the Bengali verses, and both Satsvarūpa and Umāpati opened their notebooks and waited, poised for rapid notetaking. It was almost a college classroom atmosphere as Prabhupāda cleared his throat, put on his eyeglasses, and peered over the large open volume, turning to the correct page. Whenever he wore the glasses, he seemed to reveal a new personality of deep Vaiṣṇava scholarship. This feature of Swamiji emphasized his old age—not that it showed him feeble or invalid, but it emphasized his scholarship and wisdom and his contemplation of the scriptures, in contrast to his vigorous drum-playing in Tompkins Square Park or his alert business dealings while looking for a new building.

Swamiji began reading and translating the story of Sanātana (Satsvarūpa wrote "Suta" and Umāpati wrote "Sonotan") and his brother Rūpa, and how they became intimate associates of Lord Caitanya. It was a historical account. Rūpa and Sanātana had been born as *brāhmaṇas* in India, but they had served in the government under the Muslims, who were in power at that time. The two brothers had even adopted Muslim names. But when Lord Caitanya was touring in their part of the country, they had met Him and had become determined to give up their materialistic ways and follow His path of pure love of God. Rūpa, who was so rich that he had enough gold to fill two boats, left his high government post, divided his wealth, became a mendicant, and joined Lord Caitanya. For Sanātana, however, there were more obstacles.

The Nawab Shah, the chief Muslim ruler of the province of Bengal, was dependent on Sanātana's managerial expertise. But Sanātana began staying home and submitting sick reports, while actually he had employed a dozen *brāhmaṇas,* who were teaching him the *Śrīmad-Bhāgavatam.* The Nawab sent his physician to find out the actual state of Sanātana's health, and when the Nawab heard that Sanātana was not actually ill, he himself arrived one day, surprising Sanātana and the *brāhmaṇas.* The Nawab demanded that Sanātana return to his government work and leave him free to do some hunting and to leave Bengal on a military campaign. But Sanātana said that he could not, that he was now determined to study the scriptures, and that the Nawab could do with him whatever he liked. At this challenge, the Nawab imprisoned Sanātana. ...

Swamiji looked at his watch. Morning classes were shorter than those in the evening—only half an hour—and Rūpānuga, Satsvarūpa, and Brahmānanda had to go to work. He paused in his narration—"So, we will discuss tomorrow." Prabhupāda closed the book, and after a few informal words, he got up and left the storefront, followed by Kīrtanānanda, who carried his book and glasses.

Breakfast was served every morning in the storefront. Either Acyutānanda or Kīrtanānanda would cook an oatmeal cereal for the devotees. Satsvarūpa had read in an English edition of the *Rāmāyaṇa* about some sages preparing a mystical cereal called "Heavenly Porridge." The name had caught on, and the devotees began calling their own cereal Heavenly Porridge. The popular fare would consist of steaming hot Heavenly Porridge (sweetened to taste with sugar syrup from the *gulābjāmun* pot), hot milk, and fruit. And each devotee would get an ISKCON bullet.

At breakfast this morning, the talk was of Rūpa and Sanātana. Umāpati said the *Caitanya-caritāmṛta* was available in an English translation, but maybe the Swami wouldn't want them to read it. "We'll hear it from Swamiji," Kīrtanānanda said. Hayagrīva was amused at the "cliff-hanger" ending of the class. "Tune in tomorrow," he laughed loosely, "and hear what happened to... what's his name?" The devotees responded differently: "Santan" ... "Sonoton" ... "Sanātana." Hayagrīva: "Yeah, tune in tomorrow and hear. Will Sanātana get out of jail?" They were not the most sober group when together, especially after taking the thick, sweet syrup. Acyutānanda spilled some of the syrup on the rug, and Kīrtanānanda admonished him. Jadurāṇī ate silently and hurried to begin a day's painting in Prabhupāda's room. Satsvarūpa adjusted his tie, and he and Rūpānuga and Brahmānanda went to their jobs.

The next morning, the *Caitanya-caritāmṛta* seminar began with Sanātana in jail, planning how to get free to join Lord Caitanya. His brother Rūpa sent him a note saying that he had left a large sum of gold for Sanātana in the care of a grocer, and Sanātana offered the gold to the jailer as a bribe. He told him, "Sir, I know you are a very learned man, and in your Koran it says that if you aid someone in going to spiritual life, then you will be elevated to the highest post. I am going to Lord Caitanya, and if you will assist me in escaping, it will be spiritual gain for you. Also, I will give you five hundred gold coins, so it will be material gain as well." The jail keeper said, "All right. But I am afraid of the king." So Sanātana advised him, "Just say that when I was passing stool by the river, I fell in with my chains and was washed away." For seven hundred gold coins, the jailer agreed to help Sanātana and sawed off the shackles. Sanātana, accompanied by his servant, then fled by the back roads until by nighttime he came upon a hotel.

Now this hotel was kept by thieves, and an astrologer at the hotel read Sanātana's palm and judged by the stars that he had money. When Sanātana asked for assistance in passing over the jungle mountains, the hotel keeper said that he would help Sanātana leave, in the dead of the night. They treated Sanātana with great respect, which made him suspicious, since he hadn't eaten in three days and his clothes were unclean. So he asked his servant if he had any money. The servant said yes, he had seven gold coins, and Sanātana immediately took the money to the hotel keeper, who was already planning to kill him during the night and take his money. ...

Swamiji looked at his watch. Again they had gone overtime. "So we will continue tomorrow," he said, closing the book "—how Sanātana manages to escape the dacoits."

Kīrtanānanda, Brahmānanda, Acyutānanda, Gargamuni, Satsvarūpa, Hayagrīva, Umāpati, Jadurāṇī, Rūpānuga, Dāmodara (Dan Clark)—their lives had all been transformed. Over the months they had transferred the center of their lives to Swamiji, and everything revolved around the routine of classes and *kīrtana* and *prasādam* and coming and going to and from the storefront.

Brahmānanda and Gargamuni had given up their apartment several months ago and moved into the storefront. The ceiling of Acyutānanda's apartment had caved in one day, just minutes after he had left the room, and he had decided to move to the storefront also. Hayagrīva and Umāpati had cleaned up their Mott Street place and were using it only for chanting, sleeping, or reading Swamiji's *Bhāgavatam.* Satsvarūpa had announced one day that the devotees could use his apartment, just around the corner from the temple, for taking showers, and the next day Rāya Rāma had moved in, and the others began using the apartment as a temple annex. Jadurāṇī kept making her early-morning treks from the Bronx. (Swamiji had said that he had no objection to her living in the second room of his apartment, but that people would talk.) Even Rūpānuga and Dāmodara, whose backgrounds and tastes were different, were also positively dependent on the daily morning class and the evening class three nights a week and in knowing that Swamiji was always there in his apartment whenever they needed him.

There were, however, some threats to this security. Prabhupāda would sometimes say that unless he got permanent residency from the government, he would have to leave the country. But he had gone to a lawyer, and after the initial alarm it seemed that Swamiji would stay indefinitely. There was also the threat that he might go to San Francisco. He said he was going, but then sometimes he said he wasn't. If the negotiations through Mr. Price for the building on Tenth Street came through, then, Swamiji said, he would make his headquarters in New York City and not go to San Francisco.

But at least in the morning sessions, as his disciples listened to him speak on *Caitanya-caritāmṛta,* these threats were all put out of mind, and the timeless, intimate teachings took up their full attention. Kṛṣṇa consciousness was a struggle, keeping yourself strictly following Swamiji's code against *māyā*—"No illicit sex, no intoxication, no gambling, no meat-eating." But it was possible as long as they could hear him singing and reading and speaking from *Caitanya-caritāmṛta.* They counted on his presence for their Kṛṣṇa consciousness. He was the center of their newly spiritualized lives, and he was all they knew of Kṛṣṇa consciousness. As long as they could keep coming and seeing him, Kṛṣṇa consciousness was a sure thing—as long as he was there.

Seated on the worn rug, they looked up at him, waiting for him to begin the next installment. Prabhupāda cleared his throat and glanced down at Brahmānanda, who sat beside the silently running tape recorder. Satsvarūpa entered the date in his notebook. Prabhupāda began reading the Bengali verses and paraphrasing. ...

Sanātana took the seven gold coins from his servant and gave them to the hotel keeper. "You have *eight* coins," the astrologer said. And

Sanātana went back and found that his servant was retaining another gold coin. "Why do you carry this death knell on the road?" Sanātana asked. "You are too attached to money." And he took the gold piece from his servant and told him to return home. Sanātana then brought the gold coin to the hotel keeper. But the hotel keeper, who admitted that he had intended to kill Sanātana for his money, now said, "You are a good man, and you may keep your money." But Sanātana refused. Then the hotel keeper provided Sanātana with four assistants. They helped Sanātana through the jungle and then left him alone.

Free from his nuisance servant and from the dacoits, Sanātana felt liberated as he passed along the road alone. Soon he came upon his brother-in-law, who was traveling along the same road. His brother-in-law was a wealthy man carrying a great deal of money to buy horses. "Please stay with me at least a few days," Sanātana's brother-in-law said. "It's really bad how you look." The brother-in-law knew that Sanātana was going to spiritual life, but he requested that he improve his dress by accepting a valuable blanket from him. Sanātana took the blanket and continued on his way.

At last, Sanātana reached Benares, and he went straight to the home of Candraśekhara, where Lord Caitanya was staying, and waited outside the door. Lord Caitanya knew Sanātana had arrived, and He requested Candraśekhara to go to the door and ask the devotee who was waiting there to come in. Candraśekhara went out but saw only the wretched-looking Sanātana, whom he took to be a half-mad Muhammadan fakir. Candraśekhara returned to Lord Caitanya and explained that there was no devotee outside. "Was there anyone at all?" the Lord asked. "Yes," said Candraśekhara, "some wretched fakir." Then Lord Caitanya went to the door and embraced Sanātana. The Lord cried tears of ecstasy, for He had at last found a devotee whom He knew was worthy to receive His entire teachings. And Sanātana cried tears of joy that his life's ambition was being fulfilled; but because he was dirty from his traveling and not worthy, he asked the Lord not to touch him. The Lord replied, "It is I who benefit from touching you; whoever touches a true devotee is blessed."

Prabhupāda closed the book, ending another morning session.

One of Prabhupāda's main concerns was to finish and publish as soon as possible his translation and commentary of *Bhagavad-gītā,* and one day something happened that enabled him to increase his work on the manuscript. Unexpectedly, a boy named Neal arrived. He was a student from Antioch College on a special work-study program, and he had the school's approval to work one term within the *āśrama* of Swami Bhaktivedanta, which he had heard about through the newspapers. Neal mentioned that he was a good typist, if that could be of any help to the Swami. Prabhupāda considered this to be Kṛṣṇa's blessing. Immediately he rented a dictaphone and began dictating tapes, Hayagrīva donated his electric typewriter, and Neal set up his work area in Swamiji's front room and began typing eight hours a day. This inspired Prabhupāda and obliged him to produce more. He worked quickly, sometimes day and night, on his *Bhagavad-gītā As It Is*. He had founded ISKCON five months ago, yet in his classes he was still reading the *Bhagavad-gītā* translation of Dr. Radhakrishnan. But when *Bhagavad-gītā As It Is* would at last be published, he told his disciples, it would be of major importance for the Kṛṣṇa consciousness movement. At last there would be a bona fide edition of the *Gītā*.

Whatever Swamiji said or did, his disciples wanted to hear about it. Gradually, they had increased their faith and devotion to Swamiji, whom they accepted as God's representative, and they took his actions and words to be absolute. After one of the disciples had been alone with him, the others would gather around to find out every detail of what had happened. It was Kṛṣṇa consciousness. Jadurāṇī was especially guileless in relating what Swamiji had said or done. One day, Prabhupāda had stepped on a tack that Jadurāṇī had dropped on the floor, and although she knew it was a serious offense to her spiritual master, the major importance of the event seemed to be how Prabhupāda had displayed his transcendental consciousness. He silently and emotionlessly reached down and pulled the tack from his foot, without so much as a cry. And once, when she was fixing a painting over his head behind the desk, she had accidentally stepped on his sitting mat. "Is that an offense?" she had asked. And Swamiji had replied, "No. For service you could even stand on my head."

Sometimes Brahmānanda would say that Swamiji had told him something very intimate about Kṛṣṇa consciousness in private. But when he would tell what Swamiji had said, someone else would recall that the same thing was in *Śrīmad-Bhāgavatam*. Prabhupāda had said that the spiritual master is present in his instructions and that he had tried to put everything into those three volumes of the *Bhāgavatam*, and the devotees were finding this to be true.

There were no secrets in Swamiji's family of devotees. Everyone knew that Umāpati had left for a few days, disappointed with the Swami's severe criticism of the Buddhists, but had come back, and in a heavy, sincere exchange with Prabhupāda, he had decided to take to Kṛṣṇa consciousness again. And everyone knew that Satsvarūpa had resigned from his job and that when he went to tell Swamiji about it, Swamiji had told him that he could not quit but should go on earning money for Kṛṣṇa and donating it to the Society and that this would be his best service. And everyone knew that Swamiji wanted Gargamuni to cut his hair—Swamiji called it "Gargamuni's Shakespearean locks"—but that he would not do so.

The year ended, and Prabhupāda was still working on his manuscript of *Bhagavad-gītā,* still lecturing in the mornings from *Caitanya-caritāmṛta* and Monday, Wednesday, and Friday evenings from *Bhagavad-gītā,* and still talking of going to San Francisco. Then New Year's Eve came, and the devotees suggested that since this was a holiday when people go out to celebrate, maybe they should hold a Kṛṣṇa conscious festival.

Rūpānuga: *So we had a big feast, and a lot of people came, although it wasn't as crowded as the Sunday feasts. We were all taking* prasādam, *and Swamiji was sitting up on his dais, and he was also taking* prasādam. *He was demanding that we eat lots of* prasādam. *And then he was saying, "Chant! Chant!" So we were eating, and chanting Hare Kṛṣṇa between bites, and he was insisting on more and more* prasādam. *I was amazed. He stayed with us and kept insisting that we eat so much. He stayed until around eleven o'clock, and then he became drowsy. And the party was over.*

Morning after morning, the story of Sanātana Gosvāmī unfolded from the pages of Swamiji's big book, which only he could read and explain. Lord Caitanya told Sanātana that he should be very grateful that Kṛṣṇa had been merciful to him, to which Sanātana replied, "You say that Kṛṣṇa is very merciful, but I do not know who Kṛṣṇa is. *You* have saved me."

Lord Caitanya had many devotees in Benares, and He sent Sanātana to the home of one of His friends where he could get something to eat, take a bath, shave, and dress in new clothing. Sanātana, however, refused the new clothing, and he also refused to become dependent on one place for his meals. Now that he had entered the renounced order, he preferred to go begging his meals at a different place each day. When Lord Caitanya saw all this, He was pleased, but Sanātana sensed that his valuable blanket did not please the Lord, so he traded the new blanket for an old one. This pleased Lord Caitanya, who said, "Now you are completely renounced. Your last attachment is gone, by the mercy of Kṛṣṇa."

Sanātana submitted himself at the lotus feet of Lord Caitanya and said, "I have wasted my time in sense gratification. I am lowborn, and I have low association. I have no qualification for spiritual life. I do not even know what is actually beneficial for me. People say that I am learned, but I am fool number one, because although people say I am learned, and although I accept it, still I do not know who I am." Sanātana presented himself as a blank slate, and he inquired from the Lord, "Who am I? Why am I in this material world? Why am I suffering?" Prabhupāda emphasized that this was the perfect way for a disciple to accept a spiritual master.

After narrating the story of Sanātana's joining Lord Caitanya, Prabhupāda began lecturing on the Lord's teachings to Sanātana. Lord Caitanya first explained that the living being is not the material body but an eternal living soul within the body. Then, for two months, Lord Caitanya instructed Sanātana, revealing to him the deepest and most sublime philosophical truths of Vedic wisdom. He enlightened Sanātana regarding the soul and its relationship with Kṛṣṇa, the nature of the material and spiritual worlds, the characteristics of a fully realized soul, and the transcendental nature of Lord Kṛṣṇa and His unlimited forms, expansions, incarnations, and divine pastimes. He explained the superiority of the path of *bhakti-yoga* over the paths of philosophical speculation and yogic mysticism. And He revealed to Sanātana the esoteric knowledge of spiritual ecstasy experienced by those souls who have achieved pure love for Kṛṣṇa. These teachings of the Lord were like an ocean that overflooded the mind of Sanātana Gosvāmī with its sweetness and grandeur. When Lord Caitanya had finished instructing Sanātana, He gave Sanātana the benediction that all those sublime teachings would be fully manifested within his heart, thus enabling him to compose transcendental literature.

For two months Lord Caitanya had instructed Sanātana Gosvāmī, and for two months, starting in mid-November of 1966, Śrīla Prabhupāda narrated in over fifty lectures the *Caitanya-caritāmṛta's* account of those teachings. Although each of his talks covered the subject matter of the verses, his lectures were never limited to his subject, nor were they prepared talks.

* * *

Sometimes, during the evening gatherings in his room, Swamiji would ask whether Mukunda was ready on the West Coast. For months, Prabhupāda's going to the West Coast had been one of a number of alternatives. But then, during the first week of the New Year, a letter arrived from Mukunda: he had rented a storefront in the heart of the Haight-Ashbury district, on Frederick Street. "We are busy converting it into a temple now," he wrote. And Prabhupāda announced: "I shall go immediately."

Mukunda had told of a "Gathering of the Tribes" in San Francisco's Haight-Ashbury. Thousands of hippies were migrating from all over the country to the very neighborhood where Mukunda had rented the storefront. It was a youth renaissance much bigger than what was going on in New York City. In a scheme to raise funds for the new temple, Mukunda was planning a "Mantra-Rock Dance," and famous rock bands were going to appear. And Swami Bhaktivedanta and the chanting of Hare Kṛṣṇa were to be the center of attraction!

Although in his letter Mukunda had enclosed a plane ticket, some of Swamiji's followers refused to accept that Swamiji would use it. Those who knew they could not leave New York began to criticize the idea of Swamiji's going to San Francisco. They didn't think that people out on the West Coast could take care of Swamiji properly. Swamiji appearing with rock musicians? Those people out there didn't seem to have the proper respect. Anyway, there was no suitable temple there. There was no printing press, no *Back to Godhead* magazine. Why should Swamiji leave New York to attend a function like *that* with strangers in California? How could he leave them behind in New York? How could their spiritual life continue without him? Timidly, one or two dissenters indirectly expressed some of these feelings to Prabhupāda, as if almost wishing to admonish him for thinking of leaving them, and even hinting that things would not go well, either in San Francisco or New York, if he departed. But they found Prabhupāda quite confident and determined. He did not belong to New York, he belonged to Kṛṣṇa, and he had to go wherever Kṛṣṇa desired him to preach. Prabhupāda showed a spirit of complete detachment, eager to travel and expand the chanting of Hare Kṛṣṇa.

Brahmānanda: *But we were shocked that he was going to leave. I never thought that Kṛṣṇa consciousness would go beyond the Lower East Side, what to speak of New York City. I thought that this was it, and it would stay here eternally.*

In the last days of the second week of January, final plane reservations were made, and the devotees began packing Swamiji's manuscripts away in trunks. Ranchor, a new devotee recruited from Tompkins Square Park, had collected enough money for a plane ticket, and the devotees decided that he should accompany Prabhupāda as his personal assistant. Prabhupāda explained that he would only be gone a few weeks, and that he wanted all the programs to go on in his absence.

He waited in his room while the boys arranged for a car to take him to the airport. The day was gray and cold, and steam hissed in the radiators. He would take only a suitcase—mostly clothes and some books. He checked the closet to see that his manuscripts were in order. Kīrtanānanda would take care of his things in his apartment. He sat down at his desk where, for more than six months, he had sat so many times, working for hours at the typewriter preparing his *Bhagavad-gītā* and *Śrīmad-Bhāgavatam,* and where he had sat talking to so many guests and to his followers. But today he would not be talking with friends or typing a manuscript, but waiting a last few minutes alone before his departure.

This was his second winter in New York. He had launched a movement of Kṛṣṇa consciousness. A few sincere boys and girls had joined. They were already well known on the Lower East Side—many notices in the newspapers. And it was only the beginning.

He had left Vṛndāvana for this. At first he had not been certain whether he would stay in America more than two months. In Butler he had presented his books. But then in New York he had seen how Dr. Mishra had developed things, and the Māyāvādīs had a big building. They were taking money and not even delivering the real message of the *Gītā*. But the American people were looking.

It had been a difficult year. His Godbrothers hadn't been interested in helping, although this is what their Guru Mahārāja, Śrīla Bhaktisiddhānta Sarasvatī Ṭhākura, wanted, and what Lord Caitanya wanted. Because Lord Caitanya wanted it, His blessings would come, and it would happen.

This was a nice place, 26 Second Avenue. He had started here. The boys would keep it up. Some of them were donating their salaries. It was a start.

Prabhupāda looked at his watch. He put on his tweed winter coat and his hat and shoes, put his right hand in his bead bag, and continued chanting. He walked out of the apartment, down the stairs, and through the courtyard, which was now frozen and still, its trees starkly bare without a single leaf remaining. And he left the storefront behind.

He left, even while Brahmānanda, Rūpānuga, and Satsvarūpa were at their office jobs. There was not even a farewell scene or a farewell address.

CHAPTER TWENTY-TWO

"Swami Invites the Hippies"

January 16, 1967

AS THE UNITED Airlines jet descended on the San Francisco Bay area, Śrīla Prabhupāda turned to his disciple Ranchor and said, "The buildings look like matchboxes. Just imagine how it looks from Kṛṣṇa's viewpoint."

Śrīla Prabhupāda was seventy-one years old, and this had been his first air trip. Ranchor, nineteen and dressed in a suit and tie, was supposed to be Śrīla Prabhupāda's secretary. He was a new disciple but had raised some money and had asked to fly to San Francisco with Prabhupāda.

During the trip Śrīla Prabhupāda had spoken little. He had been chanting: "Hare Kṛṣṇa, Hare Kṛṣṇa, Kṛṣṇa Kṛṣṇa, Hare Hare/ Hare Rāma, Hare Rāma, Rāma Rāma, Hare Hare." His right hand in his cloth bead bag, he had been fingering one bead after another as he chanted silently to himself. When the plane had first risen over New York City, he had looked out the window at the buildings growing smaller and smaller. Then the plane had entered the clouds, which to Prabhupāda had appeared like an ocean in the sky. He had been bothered by pressure blocking his ears and had mentioned it; otherwise he hadn't said much, but had only chanted Kṛṣṇa's names over and over. Now, as the plane began its descent, he continued to chant, his voice slightly audible—"Kṛṣṇa,

Kṛṣṇa, Kṛṣṇa ..." —and he looked out the window at the vista of thousands of matchbox houses and streets stretching in charted patterns in every direction.

When the announcement for United Airlines Flight 21 from New York came over the public-address system, the group of about fifty hippies gathered closer together in anticipation. For a moment they appeared almost apprehensive, unsure of what to expect or what the Swami would be like.

Roger Segal: *We were quite an assorted lot, even for the San Francisco airport. Mukunda was wearing a Merlin the Magician robe with paisley squares all around, Sam was wearing a Moroccan sheep robe with a hood—he even smelled like a sheep—and I was wearing a sort of blue homemade Japanese samurai robe with small white dots. Long strings of beads were everywhere. Buckskins, boots, army fatigues, people wearing small, round sunglasses—the whole phantasmagoria of San Francisco at its height.*

Only a few people in the crowd knew Swamiji: Mukunda and his wife, Jānakī; Ravīndra-svarūpa; Rāya Rāma—all from New York. And Allen Ginsberg was there. (A few days before, Allen had been one of the leaders of the Human Be-In in Golden Gate Park, where over two hundred thousand had come together—"A Gathering of the Tribes ... for a joyful pow-wow and Peace Dance.") Today Allen was on hand to greet Swami Bhaktivedanta, whom he had met and chanted with several months before on New York's Lower East Side.

Swamiji would be pleased, Mukunda reminded everyone, if they were all chanting Hare Kṛṣṇa when he came through the gate. They were already familiar with the Hare Kṛṣṇa *mantra.* They had heard about the Swami's chanting in the park in New York or they had seen the article about Swamiji and the chanting in the local underground paper, *The Oracle.* Earlier today they had gathered in Golden Gate Park—most of them responding to a flyer Mukunda had distributed—and had chanted there for more than an hour before coming to the airport in a caravan of cars. Now many of them—also in response to Mukunda's flyer—stood with incense and flowers in their hands.

As the disembarking passengers entered the terminal gate and walked up the ramp, they looked in amazement at the reception party of flower-bearing chanters. The chanters, however, gazed past these ordinary, tired-looking travelers, searching for that special person who was supposed to be on the plane. Suddenly, strolling toward them was the Swami, golden-complexioned, dressed in bright saffron robes.

Prabhupāda had heard the chanting even before he had entered the terminal, and he had begun to smile. He was happy and surprised. Glancing over the faces, he recognized only a few. Yet here were fifty people receiving him and chanting Hare Kṛṣṇa without his having said a word!

Mukunda: *We just had a look at Swamiji, and then we bowed down—myself, my wife, and the friends I had brought, Sam and Marjorie. And then all of the young men and women there followed suit and all bowed down to Swamiji, just feeling very confident that it was the right and proper thing to do.*

The crowd of hippies had formed a line on either side of a narrow passage through which Swamiji would walk. As he passed among his new admirers, dozens of hands stretched out to offer him flowers and incense. He smiled, collecting the offerings in his hands while Ranchor looked on. Allen Ginsberg stepped forward with a large bouquet of flowers, and Śrīla Prabhupāda graciously accepted it. Then Prabhupāda began offering the gifts back to all who reached out to receive them. He proceeded through the terminal, the crowd of young people walking beside him, chanting.

At the baggage claim Śrīla Prabhupāda waited for a moment, his eyes taking in everyone around him. Lifting his open palms, he beckoned everyone to chant louder, and the group burst into renewed chanting, with Prabhupāda standing in their midst, softly clapping his hands and singing Hare Kṛṣṇa. Gracefully, he then raised his arms above his head and began to dance, stepping and swaying from side to side.

To the mixed chagrin, amusement, and irresistible joy of the airport workers and passengers, the reception party stayed with Prabhupāda until he got his luggage. Then they escorted him outside into the sunlight and into a waiting car, a black 1949 Cadillac Fleetwood. Prabhupāda got into the back seat with Mukunda and Allen Ginsberg. Until the moment the car pulled away from the curb, Śrīla Prabhupāda, still smiling, continued handing flowers to all those who had come to welcome him as he brought Kṛṣṇa consciousness west.

The Cadillac belonged to Harvey Cohen, who almost a year before had allowed Prabhupāda to stay in his Bowery loft. Harvey was driving, but because of his chauffeur's hat (picked up at a Salvation Army store) and his black suit and his beard, Prabhupāda didn't recognize him.

"Where is Harvey?" Prabhupāda asked.

"He's driving," Mukunda said.

"Oh, is that you? I didn't recognize you."

Harvey smiled. "Welcome to San Francisco, Swamiji."

Śrīla Prabhupāda was happy to be in another big Western city on behalf of his spiritual master, Bhaktisiddhānta Sarasvatī, and Lord Caitanya. The further west one goes, Lord Caitanya had said, the more materialistic the people. Yet, Lord Caitanya had also said that Kṛṣṇa consciousness should spread all over the world. Prabhupāda's Godbrothers had often wondered about Lord Caitanya's statement that one day the name of Kṛṣṇa would be sung in every town and village. Perhaps that verse should be taken symbolically, they said; otherwise, what could it mean—Kṛṣṇa in every town? But Śrīla Prabhupāda had deep faith in that statement by Lord Caitanya and in the instruction of his spiritual master. Here he was in the far-Western city of San Francisco, and already people were chanting. They had enthusiastically received him with flowers and *kīrtana.* And all over the world there were other cities much like this one.

The temple Mukunda and his friends had obtained was on Frederick Street in the Haight-Ashbury district. Like the temple at 26 Second Avenue in New York, it was a small storefront with a display window facing the street. A sign over the window read, SRI SRI RADHA KRISHNA TEMPLE. Mukunda and his friends had also rented a three-room apartment for Swamiji on the third floor of the adjoining building. It was a small, bare, run-down apartment facing the street.

Followed by several carloads of devotees and curious seekers, Śrīla Prabhupāda arrived at 518 Frederick Street and entered the storefront, which was decorated only by a few madras cloths on the wall. Taking his seat on a cushion, he led a *kīrtana* and then spoke, inviting everyone to take up Kṛṣṇa consciousness. After his lecture he left the storefront and walked next door and up the two flights of stairs to his apartment. As he entered his apartment, number 32, he was followed not only by his devotees and admirers but also by reporters from San Francisco's main newspapers: the *Chronicle* and the *Examiner.* While some devotees cooked his lunch and Ranchor unpacked his suitcase, Swamiji talked with the reporters, who sat on the floor, taking notes on their pads.

Reporter: "Downstairs, you said you were inviting everyone to Kṛṣṇa consciousness. Does that include the Haight-Ashbury Bohemians and beatniks?"

Prabhupāda: "Yes, everyone, including you or anybody else, be he or she what is called an 'acidhead' or a hippie or something else. But once he is accepted for training, he becomes something else from what he had been before."

Reporter: "What does one have to do to become a member of your movement?"

Prabhupāda: "There are four prerequisites. I do not allow my students to keep girlfriends. I prohibit all kinds of intoxicants, including coffee, tea and cigarettes. I prohibit meat-eating. And I prohibit my students from taking part in gambling."

Reporter: "Do these shall-not commandments extend to the use of LSD, marijuana, and other narcotics?"

Prabhupāda: "I consider LSD to be an intoxicant. I do not allow any one of my students to use that or any intoxicant. I train my students to rise early in the morning, to take a bath early in the day, and to attend prayer meetings three times a day. Our sect is one of austerity. It is the science of God."

Although Prabhupāda had found that reporters generally did not report his philosophy, he took the opportunity to preach Kṛṣṇa consciousness. Even if the reporters didn't want to delve into the philosophy, his followers did. "The big mistake of modern civilization," Śrīla Prabhupāda continued, "is to encroach upon others' property as though it were one's own. This creates an unnatural disturbance. God is the ultimate proprietor of everything in the universe. When people know that God is the ultimate proprietor, the best friend of all living entities, and the object of all offerings and sacrifices—then there will be peace."

The reporters asked him about his background, and he told briefly about his coming from India and beginning in New York.

After the reporters left, Prabhupāda continued speaking to the young people in his room. Mukunda, who had allowed his hair and beard to grow but who wore around his neck the strand of large red beads Swamiji had given him at initiation, introduced some of his friends and explained that they were all living together and that they wanted to help Swamiji present Kṛṣṇa consciousness to the young people of San Francisco. Mukunda's wife, Jānakī, asked Swamiji about his plane ride. He said it had been pleasant except for some pressure in his ears. "The houses looked like matchboxes," he said, and with his thumb and forefinger he indicated the size of a matchbox.

He leaned back against the wall and took off the garlands he had received that day, until only a beaded necklace—a common, inexpensive item with a small bell on it—remained hanging around his neck. Prabhupāda held it, inspected the workmanship, and toyed with it. "This is special," he said, looking up, "because it was made with devotion." He continued to pay attention to the necklace, as if receiving it had been one of the most important events of the day.

When his lunch arrived, he distributed some to everyone, and then Ranchor efficiently though tactlessly asked everyone to leave and give the Swami a little time to eat and rest.

Outside the apartment and in the storefront below, the talk was of Swamiji. No one had been disappointed. Everything Mukunda had been telling them about him was true. They particularly enjoyed how he had talked about seeing everything from Kṛṣṇa's viewpoint.

That night on television Swamiji's arrival was covered on the eleven o'clock news, and the next day it appeared in the newspapers. The *Examiner's* story was on page two—"Swami Invites the Hippies"—along with a photo of the temple, filled with followers, and some shots of Swamiji, who looked very grave. Prabhupāda had Mukunda read the article aloud.

"The lanky 'Master of the Faith,'" Mukunda read, "attired in a flowing ankle-long robe and sitting cross-legged on a big mattress—"

Swamiji interrupted, "What is this word *lanky*?"

Mukunda explained that it meant tall and slender. "I don't know why they said that," he added. "Maybe it's because you sit so straight and tall, so they think that you are very tall." The article went on to describe many of the airport greeters as being "of the long-haired, bearded and sandaled set."

San Francisco's largest paper, the *Chronicle,* also ran an article: "Swami in Hippie-Land—Holy Man Opens S.F. Temple." The article began, "A holy man from India, described by his friend and beat poet Allen Ginsberg as one of the more conservative leaders of his faith, launched a kind of evangelistic effort yesterday in the heart of San Francisco's hippie haven."

Śrīla Prabhupāda objected to being called conservative. He was indignant: "Conservative? How is that?"

"In respect to sex and drugs," Mukunda suggested.

"Of course, we are conservative in that sense," Prabhupāda said. "That simply means we are following *śāstra*. We cannot depart from *Bhagavad-gītā*. But conservative we are not. Caitanya Mahāprabhu was so strict that He would not even look on a woman, but we are accepting everyone into this movement, regardless of sex, caste, position, or whatever. Everyone is invited to come chant Hare Kṛṣṇa. This is Caitanya Mahāprabhu's munificence, His liberality. No, we are not conservative."

* * *

Śrīla Prabhupāda rose from bed and turned on the light. It was 1 A.M. Although the alarm had not sounded and no one had come to wake him, he had risen on his own. The apartment was cold and quiet. Wrapping his *cādara* around his shoulders, he sat quietly at his makeshift desk (a trunk filled with manuscripts) and in deep concentration chanted the Hare Kṛṣṇa *mantra* on his beads.

After an hour of chanting, Śrīla Prabhupāda turned to his writing. Although two years had passed since he had published a book (the third and final volume of the First Canto of *Śrīmad-Bhāgavatam*), he had daily been working, sometimes on his translation and commentary of the Second Canto but mostly on *Bhagavad-gītā*. In the 1940s in India he had written an entire *Bhagavad-gītā* translation and commentary, but his only copy had mysteriously disappeared. Then in 1965, after a few months in America, he had begun again, starting with the Introduction, which he had composed in his room on Seventy-second Street in New York. Now thousands of manuscript pages filled his trunk, completing his *Bhagavad-gītā*. If his New York disciple Hayagrīva, formerly an English professor, could edit it, and if some of the other disciples could get it published, that would be an important achievement.

But publishing books in America seemed difficult—more difficult than in India. Even though in India he had been alone, he had managed to publish three volumes in three years. Here in America he had many followers; but many followers meant increased responsibilities. And none of his followers as yet seemed seriously inclined to take up typing, editing, and dealing with American businessmen. Yet despite the dim prospects for publishing his *Bhagavad-gītā,* Śrīla Prabhupāda had begun translating another book, *Caitanya-caritāmṛta,* the principal Vaiṣṇava scripture on the life and teachings of Lord Caitanya.

Putting on his reading glasses, Prabhupāda opened his books and turned on the dictating machine. He studied the Bengali and Sanskrit texts, then picked up the microphone, flicked the switch to *record,* flashing on a small red light, and began speaking: "While the Lord was going, chanting and dancing, ..." (he spoke no more than a phrase at a time, flicking the switch, pausing, and then dictating again) "thousands of people were following Him, ... and some of them were laughing, some were dancing, ... and some singing. ... Some of them were falling on the ground offering obeisances to the Lord." Speaking and pausing, clicking the switch on and off, he would sit straight, sometimes gently rocking and nodding his head as he urged forward his words. Or he would bend low over his books, carefully studying them through his reading glasses.

An hour passed, and Prabhupāda worked on. The building was dark except for Prabhupāda's lamp and quiet except for the sound of his voice and the click and hum of the dictating machine. He wore a faded peach turtleneck jersey beneath his gray wool *cādara,* and since he had just risen from bed, his saffron *dhotī* was wrinkled. Without having washed his face or gone to the bathroom he sat, absorbed in his work. At least for these few rare hours, the street and the Rādhā-Kṛṣṇa temple were quiet.

This situation—with the night dark, the surroundings quiet, and him at his transcendental literary work—was not much different from his early-morning hours in his room at the Rādhā-Dāmodara temple in Vṛndāvana, India. There, of course, he had had no dictating machine, but he had worked during the same hours and from the same text, *Caitanya-caritāmṛta.* Once he had begun a verse-by-verse translation with commentary, and another time he had written essays on the text. Now, having just arrived in this corner of the world, so remote from the scenes of Lord Caitanya's pastimes, he was beginning the first chapter of a new English version of *Caitanya-caritāmṛta.* He called it *Teachings of Lord Caitanya.*

He was following what had become a vital routine in his life: rising early and writing the *paramparā* message of Kṛṣṇa consciousness. Putting aside all other considerations, disregarding present circumstances, he would merge into the timeless message of transcendental knowledge. This was his most important service to Bhaktisiddhānta Sarasvatī. The thought of producing more books and distributing them widely inspired him to rise every night and translate.

Prabhupāda worked until dawn. Then he stopped and prepared himself to go down to the temple for the morning meeting.

* * *

Though some of the New York disciples had objected, Śrīla Prabhupāda was still scheduled for the Mantra-Rock Dance at the Avalon Ballroom. It wasn't proper, they had said, for the devotees out in San Francisco to ask their spiritual master to go to such a place. It would mean amplified guitars, pounding drums, wild light shows, and hundreds of drugged hippies. How could his pure message be heard in such a place?

But in San Francisco Mukunda and others had been working on the Mantra-Rock Dance for months. It would draw thousands of young people, and the San Francisco Rādhā-Kṛṣṇa Temple stood to make thousands of dollars. So although among his New York disciples Śrīla Prabhupāda had expressed uncertainty, he now said nothing to deter the enthusiasm of his San Francisco followers.

Sam Speerstra, Mukunda's friend and one of the Mantra-Rock organizers, explained the idea to Hayagrīva, who had just arrived from New York: "There's a whole new school of San Francisco music opening up. The Grateful Dead have already cut their first record. Their offer to do this dance is a great publicity boost just when we need it."

"But Swamiji says that even Ravi Shankar is *māyā,*" Hayagrīva said.

"Oh, it's all been arranged," Sam assured him. "All the bands will be onstage, and Allen Ginsberg will introduce Swamiji to San Francisco. Swamiji will talk and then chant Hare Kṛṣṇa, with the bands joining in. Then he leaves. There should be around four thousand people there."

Śrīla Prabhupāda knew he would not compromise himself; he would go, chant, and then leave. The important thing was to spread the chanting of Hare Kṛṣṇa. If thousands of young people gathering to hear rock music could be engaged in hearing and chanting the names of God, then what was the harm? As a preacher, Prabhupāda was prepared to go anywhere to spread Kṛṣṇa consciousness. Since chanting Hare Kṛṣṇa was absolute, one who heard or chanted the names of Kṛṣṇa—anyone, anywhere, in any condition—could be saved from falling to the lower species in the next life. These young hippies wanted something spiritual, but they had no direction. They were confused, accepting hallucinations as spiritual visions. But they were seeking genuine spiritual life, just like many of the young people on the Lower East Side. Prabhupāda decided he would go; his disciples wanted him to, and he was their servant and the servant of Lord Caitanya.

Mukunda, Sam, and Harvey Cohen had already met with rock entrepreneur Chet Helms, who had agreed that they could use his Avalon Ballroom and that, if they could get the bands to come, everything above the cost for the groups, the security, and a few other basics would go as profit for the San Francisco Rādhā-Kṛṣṇa Temple. Mukunda and Sam had then gone calling on the music groups, most of whom lived in the Bay Area, and one after another the exciting new San Francisco rock bands—the Grateful Dead, Moby Grape, Big Brother and the Holding Company, Jefferson Airplane, Quicksilver Messenger Service—had agreed to appear with Swami Bhaktivedanta for the minimum wage of $250 per group. And Allen Ginsberg had agreed. The lineup was complete.

In San Francisco every rock concert had an art poster, many of them designed by the psychedelic artist called Mouse. One thing about Mouse's posters was that it was difficult to tell where the letters left off and the background began. He used dissonant colors that made his posters seem to flash on and off. Borrowing from this tradition, Harvey Cohen had created a unique poster—KRISHNA CONSCIOUSNESS COMES WEST—using red and blue concentric circles and a candid photo of Swamiji smiling in Tompkins Square Park. The devotees put the posters up all over town.

Hayagrīva and Mukunda went to discuss the program for the Mantra-Rock Dance with Allen Ginsberg. Allen was already well known as an advocate of the Hare Kṛṣṇa *mantra;* in fact, acquaintances would often greet him with "Hare Kṛṣṇa!" when he walked on Haight Street. And he was known to visit and recommend that others visit the Rādhā-Kṛṣṇa Temple. Hayagrīva, whose full beard and long hair rivaled Allen's, was concerned about the melody Allen would use when he chanted with Swamiji. "I think the melody you use," Hayagrīva said, "is too difficult for good chanting."

"Maybe," Allen admitted, "but that's the melody I first heard in India. A wonderful lady saint was chanting it. I'm quite accustomed to it, and it's the only one I can sing convincingly."

With only a few days remaining before the Mantra-Rock Dance, Allen

His Divine Grace
A. C. Bhaktivedanta Swami Prabhupāda
Founder-Ācārya of the International Society for Krishna Consciousness

ABOVE: Beginning from the age of five, Abhay performed a miniature Ratha-yātrā. More than sixty-five years later, he enacted the same festival on a magnificent scale in many Western cities.

ABOVE: The Rādhā-Kṛṣṇa Deities Abhay worshiped in his childhood.

ABOVE: The Rādhā-Govinda Deities have been worshiped in the Mulliks' temple in Calcutta for many generations.

BELOW: From 1916 to 1920, Abhay attended Scottish Churches' College.

BELOW: Abhay Charan first met his spiritual master, Śrīla Bhaktisiddhānta Sarasvatī, in Calcutta in 1922.

ABOVE: Allahabad, circa 1924. Left to right: (sitting) Abhay and his son Prayag Raj; his father, Gour Mohan; his eldest sister, Rajesvari, with his daughter, Sulakshman; (standing) Abhay's wife, Radharani; his nephew Tulasi; his brother Krishna Charan.

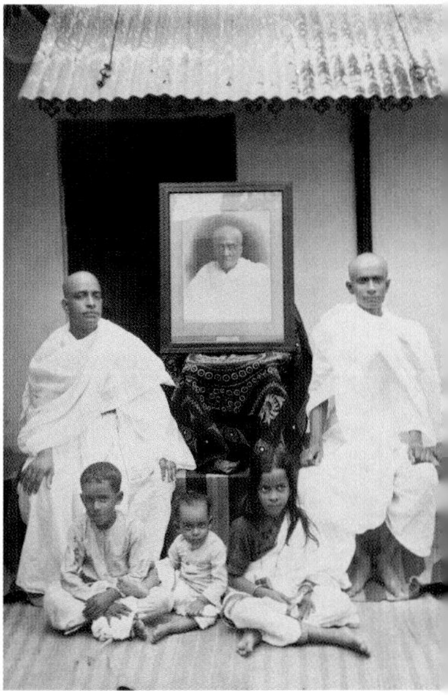

ABOVE: Allahabad, 1930, after the passing away of Gour Mohan De. Left to right: Abhay, Gour Mohan's portrait, Krishna Charan; (on floor) Prayag Raj, Abhay's new son, Sulakshman.

BELOW: His Divine Grace Śrīla Bhaktisiddhānta Sarasvatī initiated Abhay in Allahabad in 1932.

BELOW: An advertisement for one of Abhay's pharmaceutical products.

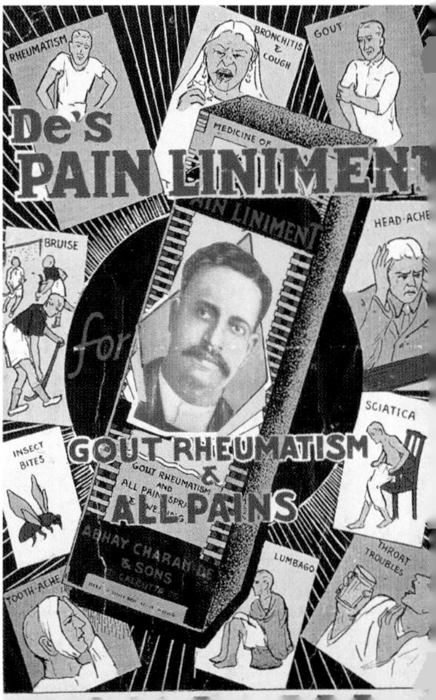

RIGHT: It was at Rādhākuṇḍa, Vṛndāvana, in November 1935, that Śrīla Bhaktisiddhānta Sarasvatī told Abhay, "If you ever get money, print books."

BELOW: His Divine Grace Śrīla Bhaktisiddhānta Sarasvatī Ṭhākura

ABOVE AND BELOW: Abhay used this picture of Śrīla Bhaktisiddhānta Sarasvatī in the logo of *Back to Godhead* magazine.

"Godhead is Light, Nescience is darkness. Where there is Godhead there is no Nescience."

BACK TO GODHEAD

VOL. III | Annual Rs. 2-25, Price 10 nP. a Copy. | Delhi Thursday 20th November 1958 | Fortnightly published. | PART XIV

TRUTH AND BEAUTY

ABOVE: In Jhansi in the early 1950s, Abhay attempted to form a worldwide organization, The League of Devotees.

ABOVE: The buildings for The League of Devotees in Jhansi in 1953.

ABOVE: The altar of the Keśavajī temple in Mathurā. Abhay donated the Lord Caitanya Deity on the left in 1955.

LEFT: Beginning in 1956, Abhay distributed his *Back to Godhead* magazine in New Delhi.

September 17, 1959, the day Abhay took *sannyāsa.* Left to right: Muni Mahārāja, Bhaktiprajñāna Keśava Mahārāja, A. C. Bhaktivedanta Swami.

BELOW: Bhaktivedanta Swami's room at the Rādhā-Kṛṣṇa temple in Chippiwada, New Delhi, which he used as an office during the writing and printing of *Śrīmad-Bhāgavatam.*

ABOVE: A. C. Bhaktivedanta Swami's kitchen at the Rādhā-Dāmodara temple. From this room he could see the *samādhi* of Rūpa Gosvāmī.

ABOVE: A. C. Bhaktivedanta Swami and Prime Minister Lal Bahadur Shastri at the Parliament Building in New Delhi in June 1964.

ABOVE: The press that printed the first volume of *Śrīmad-Bhāgavatam* in 1962.

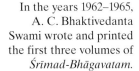

In the years 1962–1965, A. C. Bhaktivedanta Swami wrote and printed the first three volumes of *Śrīmad-Bhāgavatam.*

The cover of the First Canto of *Śrīmad-Bhāgavatam,* published in India in 1962.

BELOW: A. C. Bhaktivedanta Swami completed the three volumes of the First Canto of *Śrīmad-Bhāgavatam* by early 1965.

ABOVE: Photo from the *Butler Eagle,* September 22, 1965. This was the first news coverage of Śrīla Prabhupāda in America.

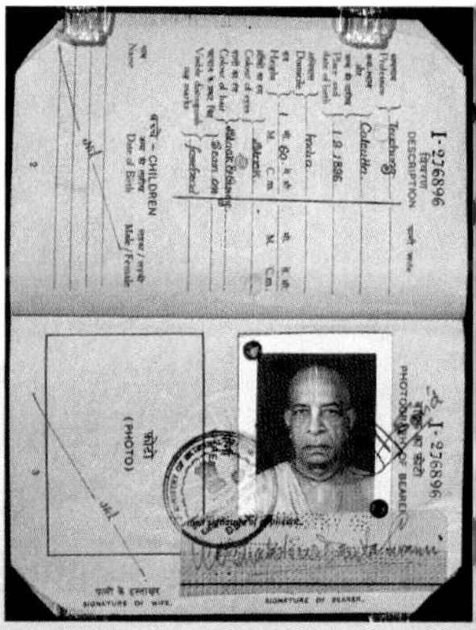

RIGHT: Śrīla Prabhupāda's passport.

BELOW: Śrīla Prabhupāda in his *Jaladuta* diary: "If the Atlantic would have shown its usual face, perhaps I would have died. But Lord Kṛṣṇa has taken charge of the ship."

Cooking lunch in Sally Agarwal's kitchen: "He prepares his meals in a brass pan with separate levels for steaming rice, vegetables, and making 'bread' at the same time."

"He was there when Brij first stood.... It was a celebration."

"SRIMAD BHAGWATAM"
INDIA'S MESSAGE OF PEACE AND GOODWILL

Sixty Volumes of Elaborate English Version by

Tridandi Goswami
A. C. BHAKTIVEDANTA SWAMI

CARRIED BY
THE SCINDIA STEAM NAV. CO., LIMITED
BOMBAY.

All over the world for scientific knowledge of God.

INTERNATIONAL SOCIETY FOR
KRISHNA CONSCIOUSNESS, INC.
26 2nd AVE. N. Y. CITY 10003

ABOVE LEFT: The pamphlet A. C. Bhaktivedanta Swami printed and took with him to America aboard the *Jaladuta*.

ABOVE: The street entrance to 94 Bowery.

LEFT: Śrīla Prabhupāda on the Bowery, photographed by Fred McDarrah of *The Village Voice*, June 1966.

The photo from *The New York Times,* October 10, 1966: *"Swami's Flock Chants in Park to Find Ecstasy."*

In the storefront. From left to right: Jadurāṇī, Gargamuni, and Brahmānanda.

In the storefront, Śrīla Prabhupāda taught the ABCs of Kṛṣṇa consciousness, lecturing from *Bhagavad-gītā* and leading the group chanting of Hare Kṛṣṇa.

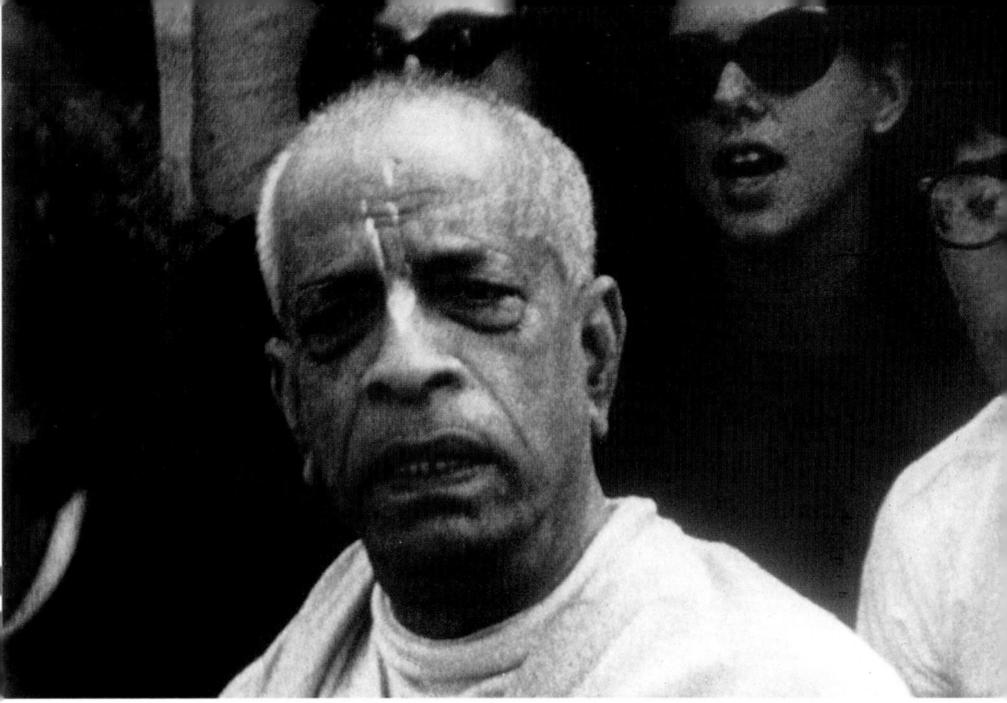

Prabhupāda was striking to see. His brow was furrowed in the effort of singing loud, and his visage was strong. The veins in his temples stood out visibly, and his jaw jutted forward as he sang his "Hare Kṛṣṇa! Hare Kṛṣṇa!" for all to hear. Although his demeanor was pleasant, his chanting was intensive, sometimes straining, and everything about him was concentration.

Chanting in Tompkins Square Park, October 1966: "To choose to attend to the Lower East Side, what kindness and humility and intelligence!"

ABOVE: In the courtyard of 26 Second Avenue. The three windows on the left on the second floor are Śrīla Prabhupāda's rooms.

OPPOSITE PAGE: Śrīla Prabhupāda in the courtyard at 26 Second Avenue.

ABOVE: None of the boys knew what Śrīla Prabhupāda was doing, although he did it every evening. They began to call the ceremony "bells."

BELOW: Guests coming to the evening *kīrtana* at 26 Second Avenue. "It had been a curiosity shop, and someone had painted the words Matchless Gifts over the window."

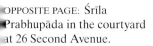

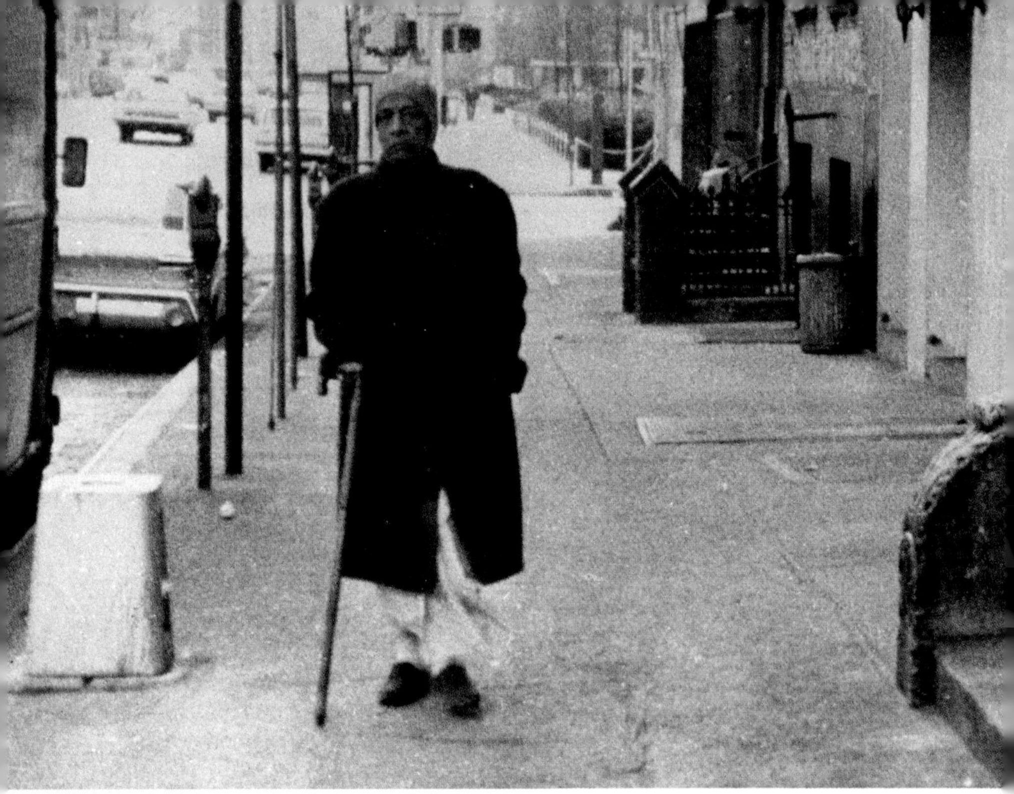

Śrīla Prabhupāda on the Lower East Side, winter 1966.

The East Village Other's coverage of Śrīla Prabhupāda's first *kīrtana* in Tompkins Square Park

THE east village OTHER

VOL. 1 NO. 22 OCTOBER 15-NOVEMBER 1 20¢ outside nyc 15¢

SAVE EARTH NOW !!

HARE KRISHNA HARE KRISHNA KRISHNA KRISHNA HARE HARE
HARE RAMA HARE RAMA RAMA RAMA HARE HARE ...

SEE CENTERFOLD

inner space

Flying Saucers

A FULL LINE OF ORGANIC
GRAINS BEANS AND FLOWERS
TRADITIONAL ORIENTAL FOODS
SEAWEED SEA SALT GREEN TEA
TAHINI AND PURE TAMARI
FINEST AGED MISO
GREENBERG'S FOOD SHOP 125 FIRST AVENUE AL4-2957

came to an early-morning *kīrtana* at the temple and later joined Śrīla Prabhupāda upstairs in his room. A few devotees were sitting with Prabhupāda eating Indian sweets when Allen came to the door. He and Prabhupāda smiled and exchanged greetings, and Prabhupāda offered him a sweet, remarking that Mr. Ginsberg was up very early.

"Yes," Allen replied, "the phone hasn't stopped ringing since I arrived in San Francisco."

"That is what happens when one becomes famous," said Prabhupāda. "That was the tragedy of Mahatma Gandhi also. Wherever he went, thousands of people would crowd about him, chanting, 'Mahatma Gandhi *kī jaya*! Mahatma Gandhi *kī jaya*!' The gentleman could not sleep."

"Well, at least it got me up for *kīrtana* this morning," said Allen.

"Yes, that is good."

The conversation turned to the upcoming program at the Avalon Ballroom. "Don't you think there's a possibility of chanting a tune that would be more appealing to Western ears?" Allen asked.

"Any tune will do," said Prabhupāda. "Melody is not important. What is important is that you will chant Hare Kṛṣṇa. It can be in the tune of your own country. That doesn't matter."

Prabhupāda and Allen also talked about the meaning of the word *hippie*, and Allen mentioned something about taking LSD. Prabhupāda replied that LSD created dependence and was not necessary for a person in Kṛṣṇa consciousness. "Kṛṣṇa consciousness resolves everything," Prabhupāda said. "Nothing else is needed."

At the Mantra-Rock Dance there would be a multimedia light show by the biggest names in the art, Ben Van Meter and Roger Hillyard. Ben and Roger were expert at using simultaneous strobe lights, films, and slide shows to fill an auditorium with optical effects reminiscent of LSD visions. Mukunda had given them many slides of Kṛṣṇa to use during the *kīrtana*. One evening, Ben and Roger came to see Swamiji in his apartment.

Roger Hillyard: *He was great. I was really impressed. It wasn't the way he looked, the way he acted, or the way he dressed, but it was his total being. Swamiji was very serene and very humorous, and at the same time obviously very wise and in tune, enlightened. He had the ability to relate to a lot of different kinds of people. I was thinking, "Some of this must be really strange for this person—to come to the United States and end up in the middle of Haight-Ashbury with a storefront for an* āśrama *and a lot of very strange people around." And yet he was totally right there, right there with everybody.*

On the night of the Mantra-Rock Dance, while the stage crew set up equipment and tested the sound system and Ben and Roger organized their light show upstairs, Mukunda and others collected tickets at the door. People lined up all the way down the street and around the block, waiting for tickets at $2.50 apiece. Attendance would be good, a capacity crowd, and most of the local luminaries were coming. LSD pioneer Timothy Leary arrived and was given a special seat onstage. Swami Kriyananda came, carrying a tamboura. A man wearing a top hat and a suit with a silk sash that said SAN FRANCISCO arrived, claiming to be the mayor. At the door, Mukunda stopped a respectably dressed young man who didn't have a ticket. But then someone tapped Mukunda on the shoulder: "Let him in. It's all right. He's Owsley." Mukunda apologized and submitted, allowing Augustus Owsley Stanley II, folk hero and famous synthesizer of LSD, to enter without a ticket.

Almost everyone who came wore bright or unusual costumes: tribal robes, Mexican ponchos, Indian *kurtās,* "God's-eyes," feathers, and beads. Some hippies brought their own flutes, lutes, gourds, drums, rattles, horns, and guitars. The Hell's Angels, dirty-haired, wearing jeans, boots, and denim jackets and accompanied by their women, made their entrance, carrying chains, smoking cigarettes, and displaying their regalia of German helmets, emblazoned emblems, and so on—everything but their motorcycles, which they had parked outside.

The devotees began a warm-up *kīrtana* onstage, dancing the way Swamiji had shown them. Incense poured from the stage and from the corners of the large ballroom. And although most in the audience were high on drugs, the atmosphere was calm; they had come seeking a spiritual experience. As the chanting began, very melodiously, some of the musicians took part by playing their instruments. The light show began: strobe lights flashed, colored balls bounced back and forth to the beat of the music, large blobs of pulsing color splurted across the floor, walls, and ceiling.

A little after eight o'clock, Moby Grape took the stage. With heavy electric guitars, electric bass, and two drummers, they launched into their first number. The large speakers shook the ballroom with their vibrations, and a roar of approval rose from the audience.

Around nine-thirty, Prabhupāda left his Frederick Street apartment and got into the back seat of Harvey's Cadillac. He was dressed in his usual saffron robes, and around his neck he wore a garland of gardenias, whose sweet aroma filled the car. On the way to the Avalon he talked about the need to open more centers.

At ten o'clock Prabhupāda walked up the stairs of the Avalon, followed by Kīrtanānanda and Ranchor. As he entered the ballroom, devotees blew conchshells, someone began a drum roll, and the crowd parted down the center, all the way from the entrance to the stage, opening a path for him to walk. With his head held high, Prabhupāda seemed to float by as he walked through the strange milieu, making his way across the ballroom floor to the stage.

Suddenly the light show changed. Pictures of Kṛṣṇa and His pastimes flashed onto the wall: Kṛṣṇa and Arjuna riding together on Arjuna's chariot, Kṛṣṇa eating butter, Kṛṣṇa subduing the whirlwind demon, Kṛṣṇa playing the flute. As Prabhupāda walked through the crowd, everyone stood, applauding and cheering. He climbed the stairs and seated himself softly on a waiting cushion. The crowd quieted.

Looking over at Allen Ginsberg, Prabhupāda said, "You can speak something about the *mantra.*"

Allen began to tell of his understanding and experience with the Hare Kṛṣṇa *mantra.* He told how Swamiji had opened a storefront on Second Avenue and had chanted Hare Kṛṣṇa in Tompkins Square Park. And he invited everyone to the Frederick Street temple. "I especially recommend the early-morning *kīrtanas,*" he said, "for those who, coming down from LSD, want to stabilize their consciousness on reentry."

Prabhupāda spoke, giving a brief history of the *mantra.* Then he looked over at Allen again: "You may chant."

Allen began playing his harmonium and chanting into the microphone, singing the tune he had brought from India. Gradually more and more people in the audience caught on and began chanting. As the *kīrtana* continued and the audience got increasingly enthusiastic, musicians from the various bands came onstage to join in. Ranchor, a fair drummer, began playing Moby Grape's drums. Some of the bass and other guitar players joined in as the devotees and a large group of hippies mounted the stage. The multicolored oil slicks pulsed, and the balls bounced back and forth to the beat of the *mantra,* now projected onto the wall: Hare Krishna, Hare Krishna, Krishna Krishna, Hare Hare/ Hare Rama, Hare Rama, Rama Rama, Hare Hare. As the chanting spread throughout the hall, some of the hippies got to their feet, held hands, and danced.

Allen Ginsberg: *We sang Hare Kṛṣṇa all evening. It was absolutely great—an open thing. It was the height of the Haight-Ashbury spiritual enthusiasm. It was the first time that there had been a music scene in San Francisco where everybody could be part of it and participate. Everybody could sing and dance rather than listen to other people sing and dance.*

Jānakī: *People didn't know what they were chanting for. But to see that many people chanting—even though most of them were intoxicated—made Swamiji very happy. He loved to see the people chanting.*

Hayagrīva: *Standing in front of the bands, I could hardly hear. But above all, I could make out the chanting of Hare Kṛṣṇa, building steadily. On the wall behind, a slide projected a huge picture of Kṛṣṇa in a golden helmet with a peacock feather, a flute in His hand.*

Then Śrīla Prabhupāda stood up, lifted his arms, and began to dance. He gestured for everyone to join him, and those who were still seated stood up and began dancing and chanting and swaying back and forth, following Prabhupāda's gentle dance.

Roger Segal: *The ballroom appeared as if it was a human field of wheat blowing in the wind. It produced a calm feeling in contrast to the Avalon Ballroom atmosphere of gyrating energies. The chanting of Hare Kṛṣṇa continued for over an hour, and finally everyone was jumping and yelling, even crying and shouting.*

Someone placed a microphone before Śrīla Prabhupāda, and his voice resounded strongly over the powerful sound system. The tempo quickened. Śrīla Prabhupāda was perspiring profusely. Kīrtanānanda insisted that the *kīrtana* stop. Swamiji was too old for this, he said; it might be harmful. But the chanting continued, faster and faster, until the words of the *mantra* finally became indistinguishable amidst the amplified music and the chorus of thousands of voices.

Then suddenly it ended. And all that could be heard was the loud hum of the amplifiers and Śrīla Prabhupāda's voice, ringing out, offering obeisances to his spiritual master: "Oṁ Viṣṇupāda Paramahaṁsa Parivrājakācārya Aṣṭottara-śata Śrī Śrīmad Bhaktisiddhānta Sarasvatī Goswami Mahārāja *kī jaya!* ... All glories to the assembled devotees!"

Śrīla Prabhupāda made his way offstage, through the heavy smoke and crowds, and down the front stairs, with Kīrtanānanda and Ranchor close behind him. Allen announced the next rock group.

As Swamiji left the ballroom and the appreciative crowd behind, he commented, "This is no place for a *brahmacārī.*"

The next morning the temple was crowded with young people who had seen Swamiji at the Avalon. Most of them had stayed up all night. Śrīla Prabhupāda, having followed his usual morning schedule, came down at seven, held *kīrtana,* and delivered the morning lecture.

Later that morning, while riding to the beach with Kīrtanānanda and Hayagrīva, Swamiji asked how many people had attended last night's *kīrtana.* When they told him, he asked how much money they had made, and they said they weren't sure but it was approximately fifteen hundred dollars.

Half-audibly he chanted in the back seat of the car, looking out the window as quiet and unassuming as a child, with no indication that the night before he had been cheered and applauded by thousands of hippies, who had stood back and made a grand aisle for him to walk in triumph across the strobe-lit floor amid the thunder of the electric basses and pounding drums of the Avalon Ballroom. For all the fanfare of the night before, he remained untouched, the same as ever in personal demeanor: he was aloof, innocent, and humble, while at the same time appearing very grave and ancient. As Kīrtanānanda and Hayagrīva were aware, Swamiji was not of this world. They knew that he, unlike them, was always thinking of Kṛṣṇa.

They walked with him along the boardwalk, near the ocean, with its cool breezes and cresting waves. Kīrtanānanda spread the *cādara* over Prabhupāda's shoulders. "In Bengali there is one nice verse," Prabhupāda remarked, breaking his silence. "I remember. 'Oh, what is that voice across the sea calling, calling: *Come here, come here. ...*' " Speaking little, he walked the boardwalk with his two friends, frequently looking out at the sea and sky. As he walked he softly sang a *mantra* that Kīrtanānanda and Hayagrīva had never heard before: "*Govinda jaya jaya, gopāla jaya jaya, rādhā-ramaṇa hari, govinda jaya jaya.*" He sang slowly, in a deep voice, as they walked along the boardwalk. He looked out at the Pacific Ocean: "Because it is great, it is tranquil."

"The ocean seems to be eternal," Hayagrīva ventured.
"No," Prabhupāda replied. "Nothing in the material world is eternal."

* * *

In New York, since there were so few women present at the temple, people had inquired whether it were possible for a woman to join the Kṛṣṇa consciousness movement. But in San Francisco that question never arose. Most of the men who came to learn from Swamiji came with their girlfriends. To Prabhupāda these boys and girls, eager for chanting and hearing about Kṛṣṇa, were like sparks of faith to be fanned into steady, blazing fires of devotional life. There was no question of his asking the newcomers to give up their girlfriends or boyfriends, and yet he uncompromisingly preached, "no illicit sex." The dilemma, however, seemed to have an obvious solution: marry the couples in Kṛṣṇa consciousness.

Because traditionally a *sannyāsī* would never arrange or perform marriages, by Indian standards someone might criticize Prabhupāda for allowing *any* mingling of the sexes. But Prabhupāda gave priority to spreading Kṛṣṇa consciousness. What Indian, however critical, had ever tried to transplant the essence of India's spiritual culture into the Western culture? Prabhupāda saw that to change the American social system and completely separate the men from the women would not be possible. But to compromise his standard of no illicit sex was also not possible. Therefore, Kṛṣṇa conscious married life, the *gṛhastha-āśrama,* would be the best arrangement for many of his new aspiring disciples. In Kṛṣṇa consciousness husband and wife could live together and help one another in spiritual progress. It was an authorized arrangement for allowing a man and woman to associate. If as spiritual master he found it necessary to perform marriages himself, he would do it. But first these young couples would have to become attracted to Kṛṣṇa consciousness.

Joan Campanella had grown up in a wealthy suburb of Portland, Oregon, where her father was a corporate tax attorney. She and her sister had had their own sports cars and their own boats for sailing on Lake Oswego. Disgusted by the sorority life at the University of Oregon, Joan had dropped out during her first term and enrolled at Reed College, where she had studied ceramics, weaving, and calligraphy. In 1963, she had moved to San Francisco and become the co-owner of a ceramics shop. Although she had then had many friends among fashionable shopkeepers, folksingers, and dancers, she had remained aloof and introspective.

It was through her sister Jan that Joan had first met Śrīla Prabhupāda. Jan had gone with her boyfriend Michael Grant to live in New York City, where Michael had worked as a music arranger. In 1965 they had met Swamiji while he was living alone on the Bowery, and they had become his initiated disciples (Mukunda and Jānakī). Swamiji had asked them to get married, and they had invited Joan to the wedding. As a wedding guest for one day, Joan had then briefly entered Swamiji's transcendental world at 26 Second Avenue, and he had kept her busy all day making dough and filling *kacaurī* pastries for the wedding feast. Joan had worked in one room, and Swamiji had worked in the kitchen, although he had repeatedly come in and guided her in making the *kacaurīs* properly, telling her not to touch her clothes or body while cooking and instructing her not to smoke cigarettes, because the food was to be offered to Lord Kṛṣṇa and therefore had to be prepared purely. Joan had been convinced by this brief association that Swamiji was a great spiritual teacher, but she had returned to San Francisco without pursuing Kṛṣṇa consciousness further.

A few months later, Mukunda and Jānakī had driven to the West Coast with plans of going soon to India but had changed their plans when Mukunda had received a letter from Swamiji asking him to try to start a Kṛṣṇa conscious temple in California. Mukunda had talked about Swamiji to Joan and other friends, and he had found that a lot of young people were interested. Joan had then accompanied Mukunda, Jānakī, and a boy named Roger Segal to the mountains in Oregon, where they had visited their mutual friends Sam and Marjorie, who had been living in a forest lookout tower.

Mukunda had explained what he had known of Kṛṣṇa consciousness, and the six of them had begun chanting Hare Kṛṣṇa together. They had been especially interested in Swamiji's teachings about elevating consciousness without drugs. Mukunda had talked excitedly about Swamiji's having asked him to start a temple in California, and soon he and his wife, Jānakī; Sam and his girlfriend Marjorie; and Roger and Joan, now intimate friends, had moved to an apartment in San Francisco to find a storefront and set the stage for Swamiji.

After Swamiji's arrival, Joan had begun attending the temple *kīrtanas*. She felt drawn to Swamiji and the chanting, and she especially liked the informal visiting hours. Swamiji would sit in his rocking chair with his hand in his bead bag, chanting the holy names, and Joan would sit fascinated, watching his fingers moving within the bag.

One day during Swamiji's visiting hours, while Swamiji was sitting in his rocking chair and Joan and others were sitting at his feet, Jānakī's cat crept in through the hallway door and began slowly coming down the hallway. The cat came closer and closer and slowly meandered right in front of Swamiji's feet. It sat down, looking up intently at Swamiji, and began to meow. None of the devotees knew what to expect. Swamiji began gently stroking the back of the cat with his foot, saying, "Hare Kṛṣṇa, Hare Kṛṣṇa. Are you feeding him *prasādam* milk?"

Joan: *I was touched by Swamiji's activities and his kindness—even to cats—and I longed for more association with him.*

Joan came to understand that serving Swamiji was a serious matter. But she didn't want to jump into initiation until she was one-hundred-percent sure about it. Sometimes she would cry in ecstasy, and sometimes she would fall asleep during Swamiji's lecture. So she remained hesitant and skeptical, wondering, "How can I actually apply Swamiji's teachings to my life?"

One evening Swamiji asked her, "When are you going to be initiated?" Joan said that she didn't know but that she relished reading his books and chanting Hare Kṛṣṇa. She said that because she was attracted to the mountains and to elevated spiritual consciousness, she wanted to travel to Tibet.

Swamiji, sitting in his rocking chair, looked down at Joan as she sat at his feet. She felt he was looking right through her. "I can take you to a higher place than Tibet," he said. "Just see."

Joan suddenly felt that Swamiji knew everything about her, and she understood, "Oh, I have to see through his eyes what Kṛṣṇa consciousness is." He was promising that he would take her to some very elevated realm, but *she would have to see it*. It was then that Joan decided to become Swamiji's disciple.

When she told her boyfriend Roger, he was astounded. He and Joan had been coming to the *kīrtanas* and lectures together, but he still had doubts. Maybe it would be good for him and Joan to get married but not initiated. Joan, however, was more determined. She explained to Roger that Swamiji hadn't come just to perform marriages; you had to get initiated first.

Roger Segal had grown up in New York. He was following a *haṭha-yoga guru,* had experimented with psychedelic chemicals, and had traveled in the Deep South as a civil rights activist, taking part in freedom marches with the blacks. Large-bodied, sociable, and outgoing, he had lots of friends in San Francisco. At the airport, in a merry mood with the Haight-Ashbury crowd, he had seen Swamiji for the first time and been especially struck by Swamiji's regal bearing and absence of self-consciousness. The concept of reincarnation had always intrigued him, but after attending some of Swamiji's lectures and hearing him explain transmigration of the soul, he felt he had found someone who definitely knew the answer to any question about life after death.

One night, after attending the program at the temple, Roger returned to his apartment and sat down on the fire escape to meditate on what Swamiji had said. The world is false, he had said. "But it feels real to me," Roger thought. "If I pinch my arm, I feel pain. So how is that illusion? This fire escape is real; otherwise I would be falling in space. This space is real, isn't it?"

Roger decided he didn't understand what Swamiji meant by *illusion.* "If I try to walk through the wall," he thought, "would that be real or not? Maybe the wall's reality is just in my mind." To test the illusion he went inside his apartment, concentrated his mind, and walked against the wall—smack. He sat down again and thought, "What does Swamiji mean when he says that the world is illusion?" He decided he should ask at the next meeting.

He did. And Śrīla Prabhupāda told him that actually the world is real, because it was created by God, the supreme reality. But it is unreal in the sense that everything material is temporary. When a person takes the temporary world to be permanent and all in all, he is in illusion. Only the spiritual world, Swamiji explained, is eternal and therefore real.

Roger was satisfied by Swamiji's answer. But he had other difficulties: he thought Swamiji too conservative. When Swamiji said that people's dogs must be kept outside the temple, Roger didn't like it. Many visitors brought pet dogs with them to the temple, and now there was a hitching post in front of the building just to accommodate the pets on leashes.

But Swamiji wouldn't allow any pets inside. "This philosophy is for humans," he said. "A cat or dog cannot understand it, although if he hears the chanting of Hare Kṛṣṇa he can receive a higher birth in the future."

Roger also had other points of contention with what he considered Swamiji's conservative philosophy. Swamiji repeatedly spoke against uncontrolled habits like smoking, but Roger couldn't imagine giving up such things. And the instructions about restricting sex life especially bothered him. Yet despite his not following very strictly, Roger felt himself developing a love for Swamiji and Kṛṣṇa. He sensed that Swamiji had much to teach him and that Swamiji was doing it in a certain way and a certain order. Roger knew that Swamiji saw him as a baby in spiritual life who had to be spoon-fed; he knew he had to become submissive and accept whatever Swamiji gave him.

Sam Speerstra, tall and slender with curly reddish-gold hair, was athletic (he had trained as an Olympic skier) yet artistic (he was a writer and wood sculptor). He had graduated from Reed College in Oregon and gone on as a Fulbright scholar to a small college in Switzerland, where he had obtained an M.A. in philosophy. He was popular—as Mukunda saw him, "the epitome of the rugged individualist."

When Mukunda had visited Sam at his mountain lookout tower and told him about Swamiji and Kṛṣṇa consciousness, Sam had been intrigued by the new ideas. Sam's life had nearly reached a dead end, but he had seen hope in what Mukunda and Jānakī had been saying about Swamiji. After spending only a few days with Mukunda, Sam had been eager to help him establish a temple of Kṛṣṇa consciousness in San Francisco.

Sam was the one who knew the local rock stars and had persuaded them to appear at the Avalon with Swami Bhaktivedanta, whom he had never met. Sam had seen Swamiji for the first time when Swamiji had arrived at the San Francisco airport; and Sam had later insisted that he had seen a flash of light come from Swamiji's body.

At first Sam had been afraid to say anything, nor had he known *what* to say—Prabhupāda was completely new to him and seemed so elevated. But the day after the program at the Avalon, when Mukunda told Prabhupāda that Sam had arranged the dance, Prabhupāda sent for him to find out how much money they had made. Sitting across from Prabhupāda, who sat behind his small desk, Sam informed him that they had made about fifteen hundred dollars profit. "Well then," Śrīla Prabhupāda said, "you will be the treasurer." Then Śrīla Prabhupāda asked him, "What is your idea of God?"

"God is one," Sam replied.

Prabhupāda asked, "What is the purpose of worshiping God?"

Sam replied, "To become one with God."

"No," Prabhupāda said. "You cannot become one with God. God and you are always two different individuals. But you can become one in *interest* with Him." And then he told Sam about Kṛṣṇa. After they talked, Prabhupāda said, "You can come up every day, and I will teach you how to do books." So Sam began meeting with Prabhupāda for half an hour a day to learn bookkeeping.

Sam: *I had never been very good at keeping books, and I really didn't want to do it. But it was a good excuse to come and see Swamiji every day. He would chew me out when I would spend too much money or when I couldn't balance the books properly. I really loved the idea that he was so practical that he knew bookkeeping. He became so much more of a friend from the beginning, rather than some idealized person from another sphere of life. I took almost all my practical questions to him. I learned to answer things for myself based on the way Swamiji always answered day-to-day problems. And the first thing he made me do was to get married to my girlfriend.*

Mukunda and his wife, Jānakī, whose apartment was just down the hall from Śrīla Prabhupāda's, were the only couple Śrīla Prabhupāda had already initiated and married. Mukunda, who often wore his strand of large red *japa* beads in two loose loops around his neck, had grown long hair and a short, thick black beard since coming to San Francisco. He had entered the "summer of love" spirit of Haight-Ashbury and was acquainted with many of the popular figures. Although occasionally earning money as a musician, he spent most of his time promoting Prabhupāda's mission, especially by meeting people to arrange gala programs like the one at the Avalon. He was a leader in bringing people to assist Prabhupāda, yet he had no permanent sense of commitment. He was helping because it was fun. Having little desire to be different from his many

San Francisco friends, he did not strictly follow Prabhupāda's principles for regulated spiritual life.

In his exchanges with Śrīla Prabhupāda, Mukunda liked to assume a posture of fraternal camaraderie rather than one of menial servitude, and Śrīla Prabhupāda reciprocated. Sometimes, however, Prabhupāda would assert himself as the teacher. Once when Prabhupāda walked into Mukunda's apartment, he noticed a poster on the wall showing a matador with a cape and sword going after a bull. "This is a horrible picture!" Śrīla Prabhupāda exclaimed, his face showing displeasure. Mukunda looked at the poster, realizing for the first time what it meant. "Yes, it is horrible," he said, and tore it off the wall.

Śrīla Prabhupāda was eager to have someone play the *mṛdaṅga* properly during the *kīrtanas,* and Mukunda, a musician, was a likely candidate.

Mukunda: *The day the drum came I asked Swamiji if I could learn, and he said yes. I asked him when, and he said, "When do you want?" "Now?" I asked. He said, "Yes." I was a little surprised to get such a quick appointment. But I brought the drum to his room, and he began to show me the basic beat. First there was* gee ta ta, gee ta ta, gee ta ta. *And then one slightly more complicated beat,* gee ta ta, gee ta ta, gee ta ta geeeee ta.

*As I began to play the beat, I kept speeding it up, and he kept telling me to slow down. He spent a lot of time just showing me how to strike the heads of the drum. Then I finally began to get it a little. But he had to keep admonishing me to slow down and pronounce the syllables as I hit the drum—*gee ta ta. *The syllables, he said, and the drum should sound the same. I should make it sound like that and always pronounce them.*

I was determined and played very slowly for a long, long time. I was concentrating with great intensity. Then suddenly I was aware of Swamiji standing motionless beside me. I didn't know how long he was going to stand there without saying anything, and I became a little uncomfortable. But I continued playing. When I got up the courage to look up and see his face, to my surprise he was moving his head back and forth in an affirming way with his eyes closed. He seemed to be enjoying the lesson. This came as a complete surprise to me. Although I had taken music lessons before and had spent many years taking piano lessons, I can never remember an instance when the teacher seemed to actually enjoy my playing. I felt very wonderful to see that here was a teacher who was so perfect, who enjoyed what he was teaching so much, not because it was his personal teaching or his personal method, but because he was witnessing Kṛṣṇa's energy pass through him to a conditioned soul like myself. And he was getting great pleasure out of it. I had a deeper realization that Swamiji was a real teacher, although I had no idea what a spiritual master really was.

To Mukunda's wife, Jānakī, Kṛṣṇa consciousness meant dealing in a personal way with Swamiji. As long as he was around she was all right. She enjoyed asking him questions, serving him, and learning from him how to cook. She didn't care much for studying the philosophy of Kṛṣṇa consciousness, but she quickly developed an intense attraction for him.

Jānakī: *There were a group of us sitting around in Swamiji's apartment, and I asked him if he had any children. He looked at me as if I had said something strange, and he said, "You are not my child?" I said, "Well, yes." And he said, "Are not all these my children?" And his answer was so quick that I never doubted that he seriously meant what he said.*

For several hours each morning Prabhupāda showed Jānakī, Joan, and others how to cook. One day in the kitchen he noticed a kind of berry he had never tasted, and he asked Jānakī what they were. She told him strawberries. He immediately popped one into his mouth, saying, "That's very tasty." And he proceeded to eat another and another, exclaiming, "Very tasty!"

One time Jānakī was making whipped cream when Prabhupāda came into the kitchen and asked, "What's that?"

She replied, "It's whipped cream."

"What is whipped cream?" he asked.

"It's cream," she replied, "but when you beat it, it fluffs up into a more solid form."

Although always adamant about kitchen rules (one of the most important being that no one could eat in the kitchen), Śrīla Prabhupāda immediately dipped his finger into the whipped cream and tasted it. "This is yogurt," he said.

In a lighthearted, reprimanding way that was her pleasure, Jānakī replied, "No, Swamiji, it's whipped cream."

Śrīla Prabhupāda corrected her, "No, it is yogurt." And again he put his finger into it and tasted it, saying, "Oh, it tastes very nice."

"Swamiji!" Jānakī accused him. "You're eating in the kitchen!" Śrīla Prabhupāda merely smiled and shook his head back and forth, saying, "That is all right."

Jānakī: *One time I told him, "Swamiji, I had the most exciting dream. We were all on a planet of our very own, and everybody from earth had come there. They had all become pure devotees, and they were all chanting. You were sitting on a very special chair high off the ground, and the whole earth was clapping and chanting Hare Kṛṣṇa." Swamiji smiled and said, "Oh, that's such a lovely dream."*

Bonnie McDonald, age nineteen, and her boyfriend Gary McElroy, twenty, had both come to San Francisco from Austin, where they had been living together as students at the University of Texas. Bonnie was a slight, fair blonde with a sweet southern drawl. She was born and raised in southeast Texas in a Baptist family. In high school she had become agnostic, but later, while traveling in Europe and studying the religious art there and the architecture of the great cathedrals, she had concluded that these great artists couldn't have been completely wrong.

Gary, the son of a U.S. Air Force officer, had been raised in Germany, Okinawa, and other places around the world before his family had settled in Texas. His dark hair and bushy brows gave him a scowling look, except when he smiled. He was one of the first students at the University of Texas to wear long hair and experiment with psychedelic drugs. While taking LSD together, he and Bonnie had become obsessed with the idea of going on a spiritual search, and without notifying their parents or school they had driven to the West Coast "in search of someone who could teach us about spiritual life."

They had spent a few frustrating months searching through spiritual books and amongst spiritual groups in Haight-Ashbury. They had become vegetarians. Gary had started teaching himself to play electric guitar while Bonnie had gone to Golden Gate Park every day to perform a self-styled *haṭha-yoga* meditation. But gradually they had become disillusioned and had felt themselves becoming degraded from drugs.

When the disciple is ready, the *guru* will appear, they had read; and they had waited eagerly for the day when their *guru* would come. Although Bonnie had spent most of her time in the parks of San Francisco, one day she had been looking through a tableful of magazines in a Haight-

Ashbury head shop when she had found a copy of *Back to Godhead,* the mimeographed journal produced by Śrīla Prabhupāda's disciples in New York. She had been particularly attracted to Hayagrīva's article about Swamiji. The descriptions of Swamiji's smile, his bright eyes, his pointy-toed shoes, and the things he said had given her a feeling that this might be the *guru* she had been looking for. And when she had learned that this same Swamiji had opened an *āśrama* in Haight-Ashbury, she had immediately started searching through the neighborhood until she had found the temple on Frederick Street.

Before Bonnie and Gary met Swamiji they had both been troubled. Gary was in anxiety about the threat of being drafted into the Army, and both of them were disillusioned because they had not found the truth they had come to San Francisco to find. So on meeting Śrīla Prabhupāda in his room they began to explain their situation.

Bonnie: *He was sitting in a rocking chair in his little apartment, and he looked at us like we were crazy—because we were—and said, "You come to my classes. Simply come to my classes every morning and every evening, and everything will be all right." That sounded to us like an unbelievable panacea, but because we were so bewildered, we agreed to it.*

I told him I had traveled all over Europe, and he said, "Oh, you have traveled so much." And I said to him, "Yes, I have traveled so much, I have done so many things, but none of it ever made me happy." He was pleased with that statement. He said, "Yes, that is the problem."

We began going to his morning lectures. For us it was a long distance to get there at seven in the morning, but we did it every morning with the conviction that this was what he had said to do and we were going to do it. Then one day he asked us, "What do you do?" When we said that formerly we had been art students at college, he told us to paint pictures of Kṛṣṇa. Shortly after that, we asked to be initiated.

Joan and Roger were soon initiated, receiving the names Yamunā and Gurudāsa. And the very next day they were married. At their wedding ceremony, Swamiji presided, wearing a bulky garland of leaves and rhododendron flowers. He sat on a cushion on the temple floor, surrounded by his followers and paraphernalia for the sacrificial fire. Before him was the small mound of earth where he would later build the fire. He explained the meaning of Kṛṣṇa conscious marriage and how husband

and wife should assist one another and serve Kṛṣṇa, keeping Him in the center. Swamiji had commented that he did not like the Western women's dress, and at his request, Yamunā was dressed in a *sārī*.

Although Swamiji had called for ghee (clarified butter) as one of the sacrificial ingredients, the devotees, thinking ghee too costly, had substituted melted margarine. He had called for firewood also, and the devotees had supplied him the bits of a broken orange crate. Now, with Yamunā and Gurudāsa seated before him on the opposite side of the mound of earth, he picked up a small piece of the splintered orange crate, dipped it into what was supposed to be ghee, and held it in the candle flame to begin the fire. The splinter flamed, sputtered, and went out. He picked up another splinter and moistened it in the melted margarine, but when he touched it to the flame it made the same *svit-svit* sound and sputtered out. After trying unsuccessfully four or five times, Swamiji looked up and said, "This marriage will have a very slow start." Yamunā began to cry.

Bonnie and Gary were initiated just two weeks after they had met Swamiji. Bonnie's initiated name was Govinda dāsī, and Gary's was Gaurasundara. Although still dressed in blue jeans, even at their initiation, and not professing to know much of what was going on, they had confidence in Swamiji. They knew that their minds were still hazy from drugs, but they took their initiation seriously and became strict followers. Gaurasundara threw out whatever marijuana he had, and he and Govinda dāsī began eating only food they had offered to Lord Kṛṣṇa. Two weeks after their initiation, Swamiji conducted their marriage ceremony.

On the evening of the wedding Govinda dāsī's father came from Texas, even though he objected to Kṛṣṇa consciousness as radically un-American. Walking up to Śrīla Prabhupāda's seat in the temple, Govinda dāsī's father asked, "Why do ya have to change my daughter's name? Why does she have to have an Indian name?"

Prabhupāda looked at him and then, with a mischievous gleam, looked at Mr. Patel, an Indian guest standing nearby with his family. "You don't like Indians?" he asked.

Everyone who heard Swamiji laughed—except for Govinda dāsī's father, who replied, "Well, yeah, they're all right. But why does Bonnie have to have a different name?"

"Because she has asked me to give her one," Śrīla Prabhupāda replied. "If you love her, you will like what she likes. Your daughter is happy. Why do you object?" The discussion ended there, and Govinda dāsī's father remained civil. Later he enjoyed taking *prasādam* with his daughter and son-in-law.

Govinda dāsī: *Gaurasundara and I set about reading the three volumes of Swamiji's* Śrīmad-Bhāgavatam. *And at the same time Swamiji had told me to paint a large canvas of Rādhā and Kṛṣṇa and a cow. So every day for the whole day I would paint, and Gaurasundara would read out loud from the* Śrīmad-Bhāgavatam—*one volume after another. We did this continuously for two months. During this time Swamiji also asked me to do a portrait of him standing before a background painting of Lord Caitanya dancing. Swamiji wanted it so that Lord Caitanya's foot would be touching his head. I tried. It was a pretty horrible painting, and yet he was happy with it.*

Prabhupāda's thoughtful followers felt that some of the candidates for initiation did not intend to fulfill the exclusive lifelong commitment a disciple owes to his *guru*. "Swamiji," they would say, "some of these people come only for their initiation. We have never seen them before, and we never see them again." Śrīla Prabhupāda replied that that was the risk he had to take. One day in a lecture in the temple, he explained that although the reactions for a disciple's past sins are removed at initiation, the spiritual master remains responsible until the disciple is delivered from the material world. Therefore, he said, Lord Caitanya warned that a *guru* should not accept many disciples.

One night in the temple during the question-and-answer session, a big, bearded fellow raised his hand and asked Prabhupāda, "Can I become initiated?"

The brash public request annoyed some of Prabhupāda's followers, but Prabhupāda was serene. "Yes," he replied. "But first you must answer two questions. Who is Kṛṣṇa?"

The boy thought for a moment and said, "Kṛṣṇa is God."

"Yes," Prabhupāda replied. "And who are you?"

Again the boy thought for a few moments and then replied, "I am the servant of God."

"Very good," Prabhupāda said. "Yes, you can be initiated tomorrow."

Śrīla Prabhupāda knew that it would be difficult for his Western disciples to stick to Kṛṣṇa consciousness and attain the goal of pure devotional service. All their lives they had had the worst of training, and despite their nominal Christianity and philosophical searching, most of them knew nothing of the science of God. They did not even know that illicit sex and meat-eating were wrong, although when he told them they accepted what he said. And they freely chanted Hare Kṛṣṇa. So how could he refuse them?

Of course, whether they would be able to persevere in Kṛṣṇa consciousness despite the ever-present attractions of *māyā* would be seen in time. Some would fall—that was the human tendency. But some would not. At least those who sincerely followed his instructions to chant Hare Kṛṣṇa and avoid sinful activities would be successful. He gave the example that a person could say that today's fresh food, if not properly used, would spoil in a few days. But if it is fresh now, to say that in the future it will be misused and therefore spoil is only a surmise. Yes, in the future anyone could fall down. But Prabhupāda took it as his responsibility to engage his disciples *now.* And he was giving them the methods which if followed would protect them from ever falling down.

Aside from Vedic standards, even by the standard of Swamiji's New York disciples the devotees in San Francisco were not very strict. Some continued going to the doughnut shop, eating food without offering it to Kṛṣṇa, and eating forbidden things like chocolate and commercial ice cream. Some even indulged in after-*kīrtana* cigarette breaks right outside the temple door. Some got initiated without knowing precisely what they had agreed to practice.

Kīrtanānanda: *The mood in San Francisco was a lot more relaxed. The devotees liked to go to the corner and have their coffee and doughnuts. But Prabhupāda loved the way so many people were coming. And he loved the program at the Avalon Ballroom. But there were two sides: those who strictly followed the rules and regulations and emphasized purity and then those who were not so concerned about strictness but who wanted to spread Kṛṣṇa consciousness as widely as possible. Swamiji was so great that he embraced both groups.*

Michael Wright, twenty-one, had recently gotten out of the Marine Corps, and Nancy Grindle, eighteen, was fresh out of high school. They had met in college in Los Angeles. Feeling frustrated and in need of something tangible to which to dedicate their lives, they had come to San Francisco to join the hippies. But they soon realized that they and the Haight-Ashbury hippies, whom they found dirty, aimless, unproductive, and lost in their search for identity, had little in common. So Nancy took a job as a secretary for the telephone company, and Michael found work as a lineman for the electric company. Then they heard about the Swami in Haight-Ashbury and decided to visit the temple.

It was an evening *kīrtana,* and the irrepressible hippies were twirling, twisting, and wiggling. Michael and Nancy took a seat on the floor off to one side, impressed more by the presence of the Swami than by the *kīrtana.* After the *kīrtana* Prabhupāda lectured, but they found his accent heavy. They wanted to understand—they had an innate feeling that he was saying something valuable—and yet the secrets seemed locked behind a thick accent and within a book written in another language. They decided to come back in the morning and try again.

At the morning program they found a smaller group: a dozen devotees with beads for chanting draped around their necks, a few street people. The *kīrtana* seemed sweeter and more mellow, and Michael and Nancy chanted and danced along with the devotees. Then Prabhupāda spoke, and this time they caught a few of his ideas. They stayed for breakfast and became friends with Mukunda and Jānakī, Sam and Marjorie (now Śyāmasundara and Mālatī), Yamunā and Gurudāsa, and Govinda dāsī and Gaurasundara. They liked the devotees and promised to come again that evening. Soon they were regularly attending the morning and evening programs, and Nancy, along with the other women, was attending Prabhupāda's weekend cooking classes.

Michael was open to Prabhupāda's ideas, but he had difficulty accepting the necessity of surrendering to a spiritual authority. His tendency was to reject authorities. But the more he thought about it, the more he saw that Prabhupāda was right—he had to accept an authority. He reasoned, "Every time I stop at a red light, I'm accepting an authority." And finally he concluded that to progress in spiritual understanding he would have to accept a spiritual authority. Yet because he didn't want to accept it, he was in a dilemma. Finally, after hearing Prabhupāda's lectures for two weeks, Michael decided to surrender to Prabhupāda's authority and try to become Kṛṣṇa conscious.

Michael: *Nancy and I decided to get married and become Swamiji's disciples and members of his Society. We told some of the devotees, "We would like to see Swamiji." They said, "Yes, just go up. He's on the third floor." We were a little surprised that there were no formalities required, and when we got to the door his servant Ranchor let us in. We went in with our shoes on, so Ranchor had to ask us to take them off.*

I didn't know exactly what to say to Swamiji—I was depending on my future wife to make the initial opening—but then I finally said, "We came because we would like to become members of your Kṛṣṇa conscious Society." He said this was very nice. Then I said that actually the main reason we were there was that we wanted to be married. We knew that he performed marriage ceremonies and that it was part of the Society's requirements that couples had to be duly married before they could live together. Swamiji asked me if I liked the philosophy and if I had a job. My answer to both questions was yes. He explained that first of all we would have to be initiated, and then we could be married the next month.

At their initiation Michael received the name Dayānanda, and Nancy received the name Nandarāṇī. Soon Prabhupāda performed their marriage.

Nandarāṇī: *We knew it would be a very big wedding. In Haight-Ashbury, whenever Swamiji would perform a wedding hundreds of people would come, and the temple would be filled. My parents were coming, and Dayānanda's parents were also coming.*

Swamiji said that it was proper that I cook. He said I should come to his apartment on the morning of the wedding and he would help me cook something for the wedding feast. So that morning I put on my best jeans and my best sweatshirt and my boots, and I went off to Swamiji's apartment. When I got upstairs I walked in with my boots on. Swamiji was sitting there in his rocking chair. He smiled at me and said, "Oh, you have come to cook." I said, "Yes." He sat there and looked at me—one of those long silent stares. He said, "First take off the boots."

After I took off my boots and my old leather jacket, Swamiji got up and went into the kitchen. He got a very large pot that had been burned so thick on the bottom that practically there was no metal visible. He handed it to me and said, "We want to boil milk in this pot. It has to be washed."

There wasn't a sink in Swamiji's kitchen, only a teeny round basin. So I went into the bathroom, put the pot in the bathtub, and rinsed it out. I assumed Swamiji didn't want the black off the bottom, because it was burned on. So I brought it back to him, and he said, "Oh, that is very clean, but just take off this little black on the bottom here."

I said okay and got a knife and crawled into the bathtub and started scrubbing the black off. I worked and worked and worked, and I scrubbed and scrubbed. I had cleanser up to my elbows, and I made a mess everywhere. I had gotten about half the black off—the rest seemed to be more or less an integral part of the bottom—so I took the pot back to Swamiji and said, "This is the best I can do. All of this is burned on." He said, "Yes, yes, you've done a wonderful job. Now just take off this black that's left."

So I went back into the bathtub and scrubbed and scrubbed and scrubbed. It was almost midday when I came out of the bathtub with all the black scrubbed off the bottom of that pot. He was so happy when I brought the pot in. It was sparkling. A big smile came on his face, and he said, "Oh, this is perfect." I was exhausted.

Then Swamiji welcomed me into his kitchen and taught me how to make rasagullās. *We boiled the milk, curdled it, and then I sat down and began rolling the curd into balls on a tray. As I rolled the balls I would put them in a little row along the tray. And every single ball had to be exactly the same size. Swamiji would take his thumb and first and second fingers and shoot the balls out of the row when they weren't the right size. And I would have to remake them until they were the right size. This went on until I had a full tray of balls all the same size.*

Then Swamiji showed me how to boil the balls of curd in sugar water. Mālatī, Jānakī, and I were cooking in the kitchen, and Swamiji was singing.

At one point, Swamiji stopped singing and asked me, "Do you know what your name means?" I couldn't even remember what my name was. He had told me at initiation, but because none of us used our devotee names, I couldn't remember what mine was. I said, "No, Swamiji, what does my name mean?" He said, "It means you are the mother of Kṛṣṇa." And he laughed loudly and went back to stirring the rasagullās. *I couldn't understand who Kṛṣṇa was, who in the world His mother would be, or how I was in any way related to her. But I was satisfied that Swamiji felt that I was somebody worth being.*

I finished cooking that afternoon about four o'clock, and then I went home to get dressed for the wedding. Although I had never worn anything but old dresses and jeans, Swamiji had suggested to the other ladies that they find a way to put me into a sārī *for the wedding. So we bought a piece of silk to use for a* sārī. *I went to Mālatī's house. She was going to try to help me put it on. I couldn't keep it on, so she had to sew it on me. Then they decorated me with flowers and took me to Swamiji and showed him. He was very happy. He said, "This is the way our women should always look. No more jeans and dresses. They should always wear* sārīs."

Actually, I looked a fright—I kept stumbling, and they had had to sew the cloth on me—but Swamiji thought it was wonderful. The cloth was all one color, so Swamiji said, "Next time you should buy cloth that has a little border on the bottom, so it's two colors. I like two colors better."

When we went downstairs to the wedding, Swamiji met my relatives. He spoke to them very politely. My mother cried a lot during the ceremony. I was very satisfied that she had been blessed by meeting Swamiji.

Steve Bohlert, age twenty, born and raised in New York and now living the hippie life in San Francisco, had read in *The Oracle* about Swami Bhaktivedanta's coming to San Francisco. The idea of meeting an Indian swami had interested him, and responding to a notice he had seen posted on Haight Street, he had gone along with Carolyn Gold, the woman he was living with, to the airport to meet Swami Bhaktivedanta. He and Carolyn had both gotten a blissful lift by chanting Hare Kṛṣṇa and seeing Prabhupāda, and they began regularly attending the lectures and *kīrtanas* at the temple. Steve decided he wanted to become like the Swami, so he and Carolyn went together to see Prabhupāda and request initiation. Speaking privately with Prabhupāda in his room, they discussed obedience to the spiritual master and becoming vegetarian. When Prabhupāda told them that they should either stop living together or get married, they said they would like to get married. An initiation date was set.

Prabhupāda asked Steve to shave his long hair and beard. "Why do you want me to shave my head?" Steve protested. "Kṛṣṇa had long hair, Rāma had long hair, Lord Caitanya had long hair, and Christ had long hair. Why should I shave my head?"

Prabhupāda smiled and replied, "Because now you are following me." There was a print on the wall of Sūradāsa, a Vaiṣṇava. "You should shave your head like that," Prabhupāda said, pointing to Sūradāsa.

"I don't think I'm ready to do that yet," Steve said.

"All right, you are still a young man. There is still time. But at least you should shave your face clean and cut your hair like a man."

On the morning of the initiation, Steve shaved off his beard and cut his hair around his ears so that it was short in front—but long in the back.

"How's this?" he asked.

"You should cut the back also," Prabhupāda replied. Steve agreed.

To Steve Prabhupāda gave the name Subala and to Carolyn the name Kṛṣṇā-devī. A few days later he performed their wedding.

Since each ceremony was another occasion for *kīrtana* and *prasādam* distribution, onlookers became attracted. And as the spiritual names and married couples increased with each ceremony, Prabhupāda's spiritual family grew. The harmonious atmosphere was like that of a small, loving family, and Prabhupāda dealt with his disciples intimately, without the formalities of an institution or hierarchy.

Disciples would approach him for various reasons, entering the little apartment to be alone with him as he sat on a mat before his makeshift desk in the morning sunlight. With men like Mukunda, Gurudāsa, and Śyāmasundara, Swamiji was a friend. With Jānakī and Govinda dāsī he was sometimes ready to be chided, almost like their naughty son, or he would be their grandfatherly teacher of cooking, the enforcer of the rules of kitchen cleanliness. And to all of them he was the unfathomable pure devotee of Lord Kṛṣṇa who knew the conclusions of all the Vedic scriptures and who knew beyond all doubts the truth of transmigration. He could answer all questions. He could lead them beyond material life, beyond Haight-Ashbury hippiedom and into the spiritual world with Kṛṣṇa.

* * *

It was 7:00 P.M. Śrīla Prabhupāda entered the temple dressed in a saffron *dhotī,* an old turtleneck jersey under a cardigan sweater, and a *cādara* around his shoulders. Walking to the dais in the rear of the room, he took his seat. The dais, a cushion atop a redwood plank two feet off the floor, was supported between two redwood columns. In front of the dais stood a cloth-covered lectern with a bucket of cut flowers on either side. Covering the wall behind the dais was a typical Indian madras, with Haridāsa's crude painting of Lord Caitanya in *kīrtana* hanging against it.

Śrīla Prabhupāda picked up his *karatālas,* wrapped the cloth straps around his forefingers, and looked out at his young followers sitting cross-legged on the burgundy rug. The men were bearded, and almost everyone wore long hair, beads, exotic clothing, and trinkets. The bulbs hanging from the ceiling diffused their light through Japanese paper lanterns, and Navaho "God's-eye" symbols dangled from strings. Prabhupāda began the ringing one-two-*three* rhythm, and Śyāmasundara began pumping the harmonium. Although the harmonium was a simple instrument—a miniature piano keyboard to be played with the right hand and a bellows to be pumped with the left hand—no one in the Frederick Street storefront knew how to play it, so it became simply "the drone." Another important *kīrtana* instrument, the two-headed *mṛdaṅga* from India, was meant for intricate rhythmic accompaniments, but even Mukunda could play it only very simply, matching the one-two-*three* of Prabhupāda's *karatālas.*

There were other instruments on hand: a kettledrum (the pride of the temple), Hayagrīva's old cornet, a few conchshells, and a horn Hayagrīva had made by shellacking a piece of kelp he had found on the beach. Some guests had brought their own flutes, pipes, and bongos. But for now they let their instruments remain still and clapped to Prabhupāda's rhythm as he sang the evening prayers.

Prabhupāda's Sanskrit hymn praised the Vaiṣṇava spiritual masters; for each great devotee in the disciplic succession, he sang a specific prayer. First he chanted the poetic description of the transcendental qualities of Śrīla Bhaktisiddhānta Sarasvatī, then Gaurakiśora dāsa Bābājī, Bhaktivinoda Ṭhākura—one after another. One prayer described Śrīla Bhaktisiddhānta as "the deliverer of the fallen souls," and another praised Gaurakiśora dāsa Bābājī as "renunciation personified, always merged in the feeling of separation and intense love for Kṛṣṇa." Śrīla Prabhupāda sang of Lord Caitanya, the golden-complexioned Supreme Personality of Godhead who distributed pure love of Kṛṣṇa. And he sang of Lord Kṛṣṇa, the ocean of mercy, the friend of the distressed, the source of creation. As Prabhupāda became absorbed in the *bhajana,* his body trembled with ecstatic emotion. The group on the floor sat swaying from side to side, watching him, his eyes closed in meditation, his delicate, practiced fingers expertly playing the cymbals. They heard the heartfelt minor moods and tones of his voice, unlike anything they had heard before.

Then he began the familiar *mantra* they had come to hear—Hare Kṛṣṇa, Hare Kṛṣṇa, Kṛṣṇa Kṛṣṇa, Hare Hare—and immediately they joined him. The horns and drums sounded, and soon all the other instrument players joined in. Gradually, a few at a time, members of the audience rose to their feet and began to dance. Prabhupāda's followers stood and began stepping from side to side as he had shown them, sometimes raising their hands in the air. Others moved as they pleased. Occasionally opening his eyes and glancing around, Prabhupāda sat firmly, chanting, though his head and body were trembling.

After twenty minutes many of the young dancers were leaping, jumping, and perspiring, as Prabhupāda continued to sing, leading the dancers by the beat of his *karatālas.* His eyes were closed, yet he controlled the entire wild congregation, playing his *karatālas* loudly. The chanting and dancing continued, and Prabhupāda approved.

The *kīrtana* of these hippies was different from the chanting of Indian *brāhmaṇas,* but Prabhupāda didn't mind—his standard was devotion. In his Rādhā-Kṛṣṇa temple, whatever *he* accepted, Kṛṣṇa accepted; this was his offering to Kṛṣṇa through his spiritual master, Bhaktisiddhānta Sarasvatī. Prabhupāda was absolutely confident. Even if his young devotees didn't know how to play the harmonium keyboard or the *mṛdaṅga,* even if they didn't know that congregational *kīrtana* should be done not in constant unison (as they were doing) but responsively, and even if they didn't know how to honor the *guru*—still, because they were chanting and dancing, he encouraged them and nodded to them: "Yes."

Wild elements were there, of course—people whose minds and intentions were far away in some chemically induced fantasy—yet the mood was dominated by Śrīla Prabhupāda's followers, who danced with arms upraised and watched their leader carefully. Although in many ways they were still like hippies, they were Swamiji's disciples, and they wanted to please him and follow his instructions; they wanted to attain Kṛṣṇa consciousness. For all the varied punctuation of horns and timpani, the *kīrtana* remained sweet; Hayagrīva even played his cornet in tune, and only during every other *mantra.*

Śrīla Prabhupāda knew that some aspects of the *kīrtana* were wrong or below standard, but he accepted the offering—and not awkwardly, but lovingly. He simply wanted these American boys and girls to chant. That they dressed irregularly, jumped too savagely, or had the wrong philosophy did not overconcern him. These boys and girls were chanting Hare Kṛṣṇa; so at least for the present, they were pure. The hippies knew that, too. And they loved it.

Just as in Jānakī's dream, Śrīla Prabhupāda's pleasure was to see the whole world engaged in *kīrtana.* Somehow or other, he would say, people should be engaged in Kṛṣṇa consciousness. And this was the instruction of Lord Caitanya's chief follower, Rūpa Gosvāmī, who had written, *tasmāt kenāpy upāyena manaḥ kṛṣṇe niveśayet ...:* "Somehow or other, fix the mind on Kṛṣṇa; the rules and regulations can come later."

Inherent in this attitude of Śrīla Prabhupāda's and Śrīla Rūpa Gosvāmī's was a strong conviction about the purifying force of the holy name; if engaged in chanting Hare Kṛṣṇa, even the most fallen person could gradually become a saintly devotee. Śrīla Prabhupāda would often quote a verse from *Śrīmad-Bhāgavatam* affirming that persons addicted to sinful acts could be purified by taking shelter of the devotees of the Lord. He knew that every Haight-Ashbury hippie was eligible to receive the mercy of the holy name, and he saw it as his duty to his spiritual master to distribute the gift of Kṛṣṇa consciousness freely, rejecting no one. Yet while living amongst these *mlecchas,* he required a certain standard of behavior, and he was adamant about preserving the purity of his Kṛṣṇa consciousness Society.

For example, if he were going to distribute free food to the public, it could not be ordinary food but must be *prasādam,* food offered to Kṛṣṇa. Feeding hungry people was futile unless they were given *prasādam* and the chance of liberation from birth and death. And although in the *kīrtanas* he allowed openness and free expression and welcomed the wildest participation, the transcendental sound of the holy name had to dominate. He never allowed the *kīrtana* to degenerate into mere beating on drums or chanting of any old words, nor could anyone in the group become so crazy that others wouldn't be able to hear or take part in congregational chanting.

In his attempts to "somehow or other" get these young people chanting Hare Kṛṣṇa, Prabhupāda instinctively knew what to allow and what not to allow. He was the master, and his new disciples followed him when he permitted an egoistic, sensual dancer to jump around the temple or a drugged madman to argue with him in a question-and-answer period. When a person was too disruptive, Prabhupāda was not afraid to stop him. But stopping was rare. The main thing was giving.

The *kīrtana* lasted more than an hour, as the chanters joined hands and danced around the room and incense poured out the front door.

* * *

The morning and evening *kīrtanas* had already made the Rādhā-Kṛṣṇa temple popular in Haight-Ashbury, but when the devotees began serving a daily free lunch, the temple became an integral part of the community. Prabhupāda told his disciples simply to cook and distribute *prasādam*—that would be their only activity during the day. In the morning they would cook, and at noon they would feed everyone who came—sometimes 150 to 200 hippies from the streets of Haight-Ashbury.

Before the morning *kīrtana,* the girls would put oatmeal on the stove, and by breakfast there would be a roomful of hippies, most of whom had been up all night. The cereal and fruit was for some the first solid food in days.

But the main program was the lunch. Mālatī would go out and shop, getting donations whenever possible, for whole-wheat flour, garbanzo flour, split peas, rice, and whatever vegetables were cheap or free: potatoes, carrots, turnips, rutabagas, beets. Then every day the cooks would prepare spiced mashed potatoes, buttered *capātīs,* split-pea *dāl,* and a vegetable dish—for two hundred people. The lunch program was possible because many merchants were willing to donate to the recognized cause of feeding hippies.

Harṣarāṇī: *The lunch program attracted a lot of the Hippie Hill crowd, who obviously wanted food. They were really hungry. And there were other people who would come also, people who were working with the temple but weren't initiated. The record player would be playing the Swamiji's record. It was a nice, family atmosphere.*

Haridāsa: *It was taken outside too, outside the front. But the main food was served inside. It was amazing. The people would just all huddle together, and we would really line them wall to wall. A lot of them would simply eat and leave. Other stores along Haight-Ashbury were selling everything from beads to rock records, but our store was different, because we weren't selling anything—we were giving it away.*

And we were welcoming everybody. We were providing a kind of refuge from the tumult and madness of the scene. So it was in that sense a hospital, and I think a lot of people were helped and maybe even saved.

I don't mean only their souls—I mean their minds and bodies were saved, because of what was going on in the streets that they just simply couldn't handle. I'm talking about overdoses of drugs, people who were plain lost and needed comforting and who sort of wandered or staggered into the temple.

Some of them stayed and became devotees, and some just took prasādam *and left. Daily we had unusual incidents, and Swamiji witnessed it and took part in it. The lunch program was his idea.*

Mukunda: *The Salvation Army came in one day for lunch. They just unloaded a whole truckload of people on us—about thirty or forty.*

Larry Shippen: *Some of the community of loose people cynically took advantage of the free food. They didn't appreciate the Swami, because they said he was, in his own way, an orthodox minister and they were much more interested in being unorthodox. It was a fairly cynical thing.*

Those who were more interested and had questions—the spiritual seekers—would visit Swamiji in his room. Many of them would come in complete anxiety over the war in Vietnam or whatever was going on—trouble with the law, bad experiences on drugs, a falling out with school or family.

There was much public concern about the huge influx of youth into San Francisco, a situation that was creating an almost uncontrollable social problem. Police and social welfare workers were worried about health problems and poor living conditions, especially in Haight-Ashbury. Some middle-class people feared a complete hippie takeover. The local authorities welcomed the service offered by Swami Bhaktivedanta's temple, and when civic leaders in Haight-Ashbury talked of forming a council to deal with the crisis, they requested Swami Bhaktivedanta to take part. He agreed, but lost interest after the first meeting. No one seemed seriously interested in hearing his solution.

Master Subramuniya: *A lot of responsible citizens in San Francisco were very happy that Swami Bhaktivedanta was working amongst the young people. The young people at that time were searching and needed somebody of a very high caliber who would take an interest in them and who would say, "You should do this, and you should not do that." The consensus was that no one could tell the young people what to do, because they were completely out of hand with drugs and so forth. But Swamiji told them what to do, and they did it. And everyone was appreciative, especially the young people.*

Harṣarāṇī: *Just from a medical standpoint, doctors didn't know what to do with people on LSD. The police and the free clinics in the area couldn't handle the overload of people taking LSD. The police saw Swamiji as a certain refuge.*

Michael Bowen: *Bhaktivedanta had an amazing ability through devotion to get people off drugs, especially speed, heroin, burnt-out LSD cases—all of that.*

Haridāsa: *The police used to come with their paddy wagons through the park in the early hours of the morning and pick up runaway teenagers sleeping in the park. The police would round them up and try to send them back home. The hippies needed all the help they could get, and they knew it. And the Rādhā-Kṛṣṇa temple was certainly a kind of spiritual haven. Kids sensed it. They were running, living on the streets, no place where they could go, where they could rest, where people weren't going to hurt them. A lot of kids would literally fall into the temple. I think it saved a lot of lives; there might have been a lot more casualties if it hadn't been for Hare Kṛṣṇa. It was like opening a temple in a battlefield. It was the hardest place to do it, but it was the place where it was most needed. Although the Swami had no precedents for dealing with any of this, he applied the chanting with miraculous results. The chanting was wonderful. It worked.*

Śrīla Prabhupāda knew that only Kṛṣṇa consciousness could help. Others had their remedies, but Prabhupāda considered them mere patchwork. He knew that ignorantly identifying the self with the body was the real cause of suffering. How could someone help himself, what to speak of others, if he didn't know who he was, if he didn't know that the body was only a covering of the real self, the spirit soul, which could be happy only in his original nature as an eternal servant of Kṛṣṇa?

Understanding that Lord Kṛṣṇa considered anyone who approached Him a virtuous person and that even a little devotional service would never be lost and could save a person at the time of death, Śrīla Prabhupāda had opened his door to everyone, even the most abject runaway. But for a lost soul to fully receive the balm of Kṛṣṇa consciousness, he would first have to stay awhile and chant, inquire, listen, and follow.

As Allen Ginsberg had advised five thousand hippies at the Avalon, the early-morning *kīrtana* at the temple provided a vital community service for those who were coming down from LSD and wanted "to stabilize their consciousness on reentry." Allen himself sometimes dropped by in the morning with acquaintances with whom he had stayed up all night.

Allen Ginsberg: *At six-thirty in the morning we went over to Swami Bhaktivedanta's space station for some chanting and a little Kṛṣṇa consciousness. There were about thirty or forty people there, all chanting Hare Kṛṣṇa to this new tune they've made up, just for mornings. One kid got a little freaked out by the scene at first, but then he relaxed, and afterwards he told me, "You know, at first I thought: What* is *this? But then suddenly I realized I was just not grooving with where I was. I wasn't being where I was."*

On occasion, the "reentries" would come flying in out of control for crash landings in the middle of the night. One morning at 2 A.M. the boys sleeping in the storefront were awakened by a pounding at the door, screaming, and police lights. When they opened the door, a young hippie with wild red hair and beard plunged in, crying, "Oh, Kṛṣṇa, Kṛṣṇa! Oh, help me! Oh, don't let them get me. Oh, for God's sake, help!"

A policeman stuck his head in the door and smiled. "We decided to bring him by here," he said, "because we thought maybe you guys could help him."

"I'm not comfortable in this body!" the boy screamed as the policeman shut the door. The boy began chanting furiously and turned white, sweating profusely in terror. Swamiji's boys spent the rest of the early morning consoling him and chanting with him until the Swami came down for *kīrtana* and class.

The devotees often sent distressed young people to Swamiji with their problems. And they allowed almost anyone to see Swamiji and take up his valuable time. While walking around San Francisco, Ravīndra-svarūpa once met a man who claimed to have seen people from Mars in his tent when he had been stationed in Vietnam. The man, who had just been discharged from an army hospital, said that the Martians had talked to him. Ravīndra-svarūpa told him about Swamiji's book *Easy Journey to Other Planets,* which verified the idea of life on other planets, and he suggested that the Swami could probably tell him more about the people from Mars. So the man visited the Swami up in his apartment. "Yes," Swamiji answered, "there are Martians."

Gradually, Prabhupāda's followers became more considerate of their spiritual master and began protecting him from persons they thought might be undesirable. One such undesirable was Rabbit, perhaps the dirtiest hippie in Haight-Ashbury. Rabbit's hair was always disheveled, dirty, and even filled with lice. His clothes were ragged and filthy, and his dirt-caked body stank. He wanted to meet Prabhupāda, but the devotees refused, not wanting to defile Prabhupāda's room with Rabbit's nasty, stinking presence. One night after the lecture, however, Rabbit waited outside the temple door. As Prabhupāda approached, Rabbit asked, "May I come up and see you?" Prabhupāda agreed.

As for challengers, almost every night someone would come to argue with Prabhupāda. One man came regularly with prepared arguments from a philosophy book, from which he would read aloud. Prabhupāda would defeat him, and the man would go home, prepare another argument, and come back again with his book. One night, after the man had presented his challenge, Prabhupāda simply looked at him without bothering to reply. Prabhupāda's neglect was another defeat for the man, who got up and left.

Israel, like Rabbit, was another well-known Haight-Ashbury character. He had a long ponytail and often played the trumpet during *kīrtana*. After one of Prabhupāda's evening lectures, Israel challenged, "This chanting may be nice, but what will it do for the world? What will it do for humanity?"

Prabhupāda replied, "Are you not in the world? If you like it, why will others not like it? So you chant loudly."

A mustached man standing at the back of the room asked, "Are you Allen Ginsberg's *guru*?" Many of the devotees knew that the question was loaded and that to answer either yes or no would be difficult.

Śrīla Prabhupāda replied, "I am nobody's *guru*. I am everybody's servant." To the devotees, the whole exchange became transcendental due to Swamiji's reply. Swamiji had not simply given a clever response; he had answered out of a deep, natural humility.

One morning a couple attended the lecture, a woman carrying a child and a man wearing a backpack. During the question-and-answer period the man asked, "What about my mind?" Prabhupāda gave him philosophical replies, but the man kept repeating, "What about my mind? What about my mind?"

With a pleading, compassionate look, Prabhupāda said, "I have no other medicine. Please chant this Hare Kṛṣṇa. I have no other explanation. I have no other answer."

But the man kept talking about his mind. Finally, one of the women devotees interrupted and said, "Just do what he says. Just try it." And Prabhupāda picked up his *karatālas* and began *kīrtana.*

One evening a boy burst into a lecture exclaiming that a riot was gathering on Haight Street. The Swami should come immediately, address the crowd, and calm everyone down. Mukunda explained that it wasn't necessary for Swamiji to go; others could help. The boy just stared at Prabhupāda as if giving an ultimatum: unless Swamiji came immediately, there would be a riot, and Swamiji would be to blame. Prabhupāda spoke as if preparing to do what the boy wanted: "Yes, I am prepared." But nobody went, and there was no riot.

Usually during the *kīrtana* at least one dancer would carry on in a narcissistic, egoistic way, occasionally becoming lewd to the point where Prabhupāda would ask the person to stop. One evening, before Śrīla Prabhupāda had come down from his apartment, a girl in a miniskirt began writhing and gyrating in the temple during *kīrtana.* When one of the devotees went upstairs and told Prabhupāda, he replied, "That's all right. Let her use her energy for Kṛṣṇa. I'm coming soon, and I will see for myself." When Prabhupāda arrived and started another *kīrtana,* the girl, who was very skinny, again began to wriggle and gyrate. Prabhupāda opened his eyes and saw her; he frowned and glanced at some of his disciples, indicating his displeasure. Taking the girl aside, one of the women escorted her out. A few minutes later the girl returned, wearing slacks and dancing in a more reserved style.

Prabhupāda was sitting on his dais, lecturing to a full house, when a fat girl who had been sitting on the window seat suddenly stood up and began hollering at him. "Are you just going to sit there?" she yelled. "What are you going to do now? Come on! Aren't you going to say something? What are you going to do? *Who are* you?" Her action was so sudden and her speech so violent that no one in the temple responded. Unangered, Prabhupāda sat very quietly. He appeared hurt. Only the devotees sitting closest to him heard him say softly, as if to himself, "It is the darkest of darkness."

Another night while Prabhupāda was lecturing, a boy came up and sat on the dais beside him. The boy faced out toward the audience and interrupted Prabhupāda: "I would like to say something now."

Prabhupāda politely said, "Wait until after the class. Then we have questions."

The boy waited for a few minutes, still sitting on the dais, and Prabhupāda continued to lecture. But again the boy interrupted: "I got something to say. I want to say what I have to say now." The devotees in the audience looked up, astonished, thinking that Swamiji would handle the matter and not wanting to cause a disturbance. None of them did anything; they simply sat while the boy began talking incoherently.

Then Prabhupāda picked up his *karatālas:* "All right, let us have *kīrtana.*" The boy sat in the same place throughout the *kīrtana,* looking crazily, sometimes menacingly, at Prabhupāda. After half an hour the *kīrtana* stopped.

Prabhupāda cut an apple into small pieces, as was his custom. He then placed the paring knife and a piece of apple in his right hand and held his hand out to the boy. The boy looked at Prabhupāda, then down at the apple and knife. The room became silent. Prabhupāda sat motionless, smiling slightly at the boy. After a long, tense moment, the boy reached out. A sigh rose from the audience as the boy chose the piece of apple from Prabhupāda's open hand.

Haridāsa: *I used to watch how Swamiji would handle things. It wasn't easy. To me, that was a real test of his powers and understanding—how to handle these people, not to alienate or antagonize or stir them up to create more trouble. He would turn their energy so that before they knew it they were calm, like when you pat a baby and it stops crying. Swamiji had a way of doing that with words, with the intonation of his voice, with his patience to let them carry on for a certain period of time, let them work it out, act it out even. I guess he realized that the devotees just couldn't say, "Listen, when you come to the temple you can't behave this way." It was a delicate situation there.*

Often someone would say, "I am God." They would get an insight or hallucination from their drugs. They would try to steal the spotlight. They wanted to be heard, and you could feel an anger against the Swami from people like that. Sometimes they would speak inspired and poetic for a while, but they couldn't sustain it, and their speech would become gibberish. And the Swami was not one to simply pacify people. He wasn't going to coddle them. He would say, "What do you mean? If you are God, then you have to be all-knowing. You have to have the attributes of God. Are you omniscient and omnipotent?" He would then name all the characteristics that one would have to have to be an avatāra, *to be God. He would rationally prove the person wrong. He had superior knowledge, and he would rationally explain to them, "If you are God, can you do this? Do you have this power?"*

Sometimes people would take it as a challenge and would try to have a verbal battle with the Swami. The audience's attention would then swing to the disturbing individual, the person who was grabbing the spotlight. Sometimes it was very difficult. I used to sit there and wonder, "How is he going to handle this guy? This one is really a problem." But Swamiji was hard to defeat. Even if he couldn't convince the person, he convinced the other people in the crowd so that the energy of the room would change and would tend to quiet the person. Swamiji would win the audience by showing them that this person didn't know what he was talking about. And the person would feel the vibrations of the room change, that the audience was no longer listening or believing his spiel, and so the person would shut up.

So Swamiji would remove the audience rather than the person. He would do it without crushing the person. He would do it by superior intelligence, but also with a lot of compassion. When I saw him do these things, then I realized he was a great teacher and a great human being. He had the sensitivity not to injure a person physically or emotionally, so that when the person sat down and shut up, he wouldn't be doing it in defeat or anger—he wouldn't be hurt. He would just be outwitted by the Swami.

Even while translating in the privacy of his room, Śrīla Prabhupāda was interrupted by disturbances. Once police cars and ambulances—sirens screaming, lights flashing—converged beneath his window after the Hell's Angels had started a fight in the Diggers' store, in the next building.

On another occasion, about 1:30 A.M., while Prabhupāda was dictating *Teachings of Lord Caitanya,* a girl repeatedly knocked and called at Prabhupāda's door. At first he ignored the interruption. Since his arrival in San Francisco, he had completed many pages for this important book. Lord Caitanya's discussions with Rūpa Gosvāmī and Sanātana Gosvāmī, Rāmānanda Rāya, and others explored many Kṛṣṇa conscious topics mentioned only briefly in *Bhagavad-gītā.* In the West almost no one knew about these teachings of Lord Caitanya, and now Śrīla Prabhupāda intended to compile these teachings in one volume, providing the most complete presentation of *bhakti-yoga* ever introduced in English. Such a book would give great substance to the Kṛṣṇa consciousness movement. But now his solitary concentration was being interrupted by a knocking at his door and a woman's voice calling.

Getting up from his desk, Prabhupāda went to the front room but did not open the door: "Who is there?"

A young woman answered, "I want to speak to you."

"Come back later in the morning," Prabhupāda told her.

He knew that in San Francisco, just as in New York, he would not always be able to write peacefully. Preaching in America meant having to tolerate just this—a crazy call in the middle of the night, tearing one away from ecstatic concentration on the pastimes of Lord Caitanya. The lost souls of Haight-Ashbury—with their illusions of knowledge, their cries for help, their arrogant challenges—pulled his attention away from his mission of translating and commenting on the scriptures. Now, alone in his apartment, speaking through the locked door, Prabhupāda told his intruder that he had work to do and that she should go away. He promised he would see her later that day.

He was ready to speak with the hippies all day, but the early morning hours were the special time for his literary work. Preaching face to face to the conditioned souls was important; he had come here to preach. But he had picked these early hours to speak intimately to the whole world through his books—without disturbance.

The girl, however, continued pounding and calling, until Prabhupāda finally opened the door. There, standing in the hallway, he saw a teenage hippie with a glassy stare and deranged appearance. He asked her what she wanted. She remained tensely silent. "Speak," he told her. She stepped into his room. He saw her helpless—a victim in the ocean of *māyā*—and he asked her repeatedly what she wanted. Finally, the girl stared at him with widened eyes and exclaimed, *"Looook! Maha ula!"*

Prabhupāda decided to awaken Mukunda, who lived down the hall. He stepped barefoot into the hallway. The girl followed, shutting the self-locking door behind her. Now he was locked out of his apartment. She continued to stare at him defiantly, in the bare, unfriendly surroundings of a corridor of locked doors at one in the morning.

This was why the *bābājīs* of Vṛndāvana stayed in their little cottages chanting the holy name: to avoid being bothered by ungodly people. (The *bābājīs,* of course, never even dreamed of these bizarre intrusions from the psychedelic San Francisco night.)

At Mukunda's door Prabhupāda began pounding and calling loudly, "Mukunda! Mukunda!" Mukunda awoke and opened the door, astonished to see his spiritual master standing barefoot in the hallway, a wild-eyed young girl standing a few feet behind. Yet Prabhupāda remained grave and aloof. "This girl came to my door," he began. He explained briefly what had happened and what should now be done. He did not appear angry or harassed by the girl, and he indicated that Mukunda should deal kindly with her.

Mukunda remembered when Prabhupāda had been driven out of his New York Bowery loft by his roommate David Allen, who had gone mad on LSD. Then also, Prabhupāda had remained coolheaded though caught by a dangerous and awkward circumstance. Mukunda went downstairs and awoke Hayagrīva, who had a key to Prabhupāda's apartment. Śrīla Prabhupāda then returned to his room and to his dictation of *Teachings of Lord Caitanya.*

Mukunda saw the girl down to the street and admonished her not to bother an elderly gentleman like the Swami at such an hour. Staring at Mukunda, she said, "You're not ready," and walked away.

At seven o'clock, when Prabhupāda came down to the temple for the morning class, the girl was sitting in the audience in a calmer state of mind. She apologized. Later in the day, Prabhupāda repeated the story in good humor, recounting how he had several times asked the girl to speak. He opened his eyes wide, imitating her expression, and said, "Look! *Maha ula!*" and laughed.

* * *

"We shall go for a walk at six-thirty," Śrīla Prabhupāda said one morning. "You can drive me to the park."

Several devotees accompanied him to Golden Gate Park's Stowe Lake. They knew the park well and led Śrīla Prabhupāda on a scenic walk around the lake, over a bridge, through forest-enclosed paths, and across a small rivulet, hoping to please him with nature's beauty.

As he walked, striding quickly, he would point to a tree or stop to examine a flower. "What is this tree?" he would ask. "What is this flower?" although his disciples were usually at a loss to answer. "When Caitanya Mahāprabhu passed through the forest of Vṛndāvana," he said, "all the plants, trees, and creepers were delighted to see Him and rejoiced in His presence. The plant life there is like that in the spiritual sky—fully conscious."

"And these trees, Swamiji—how conscious are they?"

"Oh, the spirit soul is there," Prabhupāda said, "but the consciousness has been arrested temporarily. Perception is more limited."

Whatever Prabhupāda saw he saw through the eyes of scripture, and his comments on the most ordinary things were full of transcendental instruction. As he walked, he reflected aloud, "Those who want to see God must first have the qualifications to see God. They must be purified. Just like the cloud is now covering the sun. They say, 'Oh, the sun is not out,' but the sun is there. Only our eyes are covered."

Like tour guides the boys led Prabhupāda to the more picturesque areas. They came upon swans gliding on the lake. "*Śrīmad-Bhāgavatam,*" Prabhupāda said, "compares devotees to swans, and literature about Lord Kṛṣṇa to beautiful, clear lakes." The nondevotees, he said, were like crows attracted by the rubbish of mundane topics. Walking over a gravel path, he stopped and drew their attention: "Look at the pebbles. As many pebbles there are, there are that many universes. And in each universe there are innumerable living entities."

The devotees delighted in bringing Swamiji to a rhododendron glen, its big bushes completely covered with white and pink flowers. And they felt privileged to see Kṛṣṇa through Swamiji's eyes.

The next morning, when Prabhupāda again wanted to go to the park, more devotees accompanied him; they had heard from the others how Swamiji had displayed a different mood while walking. Again the boys were ready to lead him along new trails around the lake; but without announcing a change in plans, he walked up and down the macadam road beside the lake.

Prabhupāda and his followers came upon a flock of sleeping ducks. Awakened by the sound of people walking on the path, the ducks began quacking, moving their wings, and walking away. When a few devotees hurried ahead to shoo the ducks from Prabhupāda's path, the ducks began making sounds of grouching and grumbling. "Move, you ducks," one devotee said. "You're disturbing Swamiji." Prabhupāda said quietly, "As we are thinking they are disturbing us, they are thinking we are disturbing them."

Prabhupāda stopped beneath a large tree and pointed to some bird droppings on the ground. "What does this mean?" he asked, turning to a new boy who stood beside him. Prabhupāda's face was serious. The boy blushed. "I ... *uh* ... I don't know what it means." Prabhupāda remained thoughtful, waiting for an explanation. The devotees gathered around him. Looking intently down at the bird droppings, the boy thought the Swami might be expecting him to decipher some hidden meaning in the pattern of the droppings, the way people read the future in tea leaves. He felt he should say something: "It's the ... *uh* ... excreta, the defecations of ... *uh* ... birds." Prabhupāda smiled and turned toward the others for an answer. They were silent.

"It means," said Prabhupāda, "that these birds [he pronounced the word "*bards*"] have lived in the same tree for more than two weeks." He laughed. "Even the birds are attached to their apartments."

As they passed the shuffleboard courts and the old men playing checkers, Prabhupāda stopped and turned to the boys. "Just see," he said. "Old people in this country do not know what to do. So they play like children, wasting their last days, which should be meant for developing Kṛṣṇa consciousness. Their children are grown and gone away, so this is a natural time for spiritual cultivation. But no. They get some cat or dog, and instead of serving God, they serve dog. It is most unfortunate. But they will not listen. Their ways are set. Therefore we are speaking to the youth, who are searching."

When Prabhupāda and the boys passed a sloping green lawn just off Kezar Drive, the boys pointed out that this was the famous Hippie Hill. In the early morning the gently sloping hill and the big quiet meadow surrounded by eucalyptuses and oaks were silent and still. But in a few hours hundreds of hippies would gather here to lounge on the grass, meet friends, and get high. Prabhupāda advised the boys to come here and hold *kīrtanas.*

CHAPTER TWENTY-THREE

The Price Affair

SWAMIJI'S DISCIPLES IN New York were surprised to find that they could still carry on in his absence. At first, rising early, going to the storefront, and holding the morning *kīrtana* and class had been difficult. Without Swamiji everything had seemed empty. But he had taught them what to do, and gradually they realized that they should simply follow what he had shown them, or even imitate, as a child imitates his parents.

And it worked. At first they had been too shy to speak or lead the *kīrtana,* so they had played tapes of Swamiji's *kīrtanas* and classes. But when the evenings came and guests attended the temple, the devotees felt compelled to give "live" classes. Rāya Rāma, Brahmānanda, Satsvarūpa, and Rūpānuga took turns giving brief talks and even answering challenging questions from the same Lower East Side audiences that Śrīla Prabhupāda had lion-tamed for six months. Things were shaky and lacking without him, and yet in a sense he was still present. And the devotees found that everything—the chanting, the cooking, the taking of *prasādam,* the preaching—could still go on.

On January 19, just three days after his arrival in San Francisco, Prabhupāda had written back to his New York disciples. They were his spiritual children and were very dear to him. Although far from his homeland, India, he hadn't thought first of writing to anyone there. Since he was a *sannyāsī,* he had no interest in writing to any family members or relatives. And as for writing to his Godbrothers, there was not much importance in that, since they had repeatedly shown their reluctance to help. But being in a new city among new faces and having met with an initial fanfare of success, Prabhupāda had wanted to share the news with those most eager to hear from him. He had also wanted to reassure his disciples whom, after only a few months of training, he was expecting to conduct the Kṛṣṇa consciousness movement in New York.

My dear Brahmananda
Hayagriva
Kirtanananda
Satsvarupa
Gargamuni
Acyutananda
Jadurani

Please accept my greetings and blessings of Guru Gouranga Giridhari Gandharvika. You have already got the news of our safe arrival and good reception by the devotees here. Mr. Allen Ginsberg and about fifty or sixty others received us on the air port and when I arrived in my apartment there were some press reporters also who took note of my mission. Two three papers like the Examiner and the Chronicles etc have already published the report. One of the reports is sent herewith please find. I wish that 1,000 copies of this report may be offset printed at once and 100 copies of the same may be sent here as soon as possible.

I understand that you are feeling my absence. Krishna will give you strength. Physical presence is immaterial; presence of the transcendental sound received from the spiritual master should be the guidance of life. That will make our spiritual life successful. If you feel very strongly about my absence you may place my pictures on my sitting places and this will be source of inspiration for you.

I am very much anxious to hear about the final decision of the house. I wish to open the house by the 1st of March 1967 and arrangement may be done dexterously in this connection. I have not as yet received the tapes for Dictaphone and I have sent you tapes yesterday. Please offer my blessings to Sriman Neal.

Sriman Rayarama is cooking well and distributing Prasadam to the devotees numbering sometimes seventy. It is very encouraging. I think this center will be very nice branch without delay. Everything is prospective. Hope you are well and awaiting your early reply.

The letter had helped—especially the second paragraph. Brahmānanda had posted it in the storefront. Now Swamiji had clearly enunciated that they were still with him and he was still in New York with them. It was something special—service to the spiritual master in separation—and even the devotees in San Francisco, who were with Swamiji every day, could not yet know its special taste. While the devotees in New York performed their daily duties, they often quoted from the letter and thought about it: "Krishna will give you strength. Physical presence is immaterial; presence of the transcendental sound received from the spiritual master should be the guidance of life. That will make our spiritual life successful."

Although Prabhupāda had written that they could place his photograph on his seat, no one had a photograph. They had to ask the devotees in San Francisco for one. A boy took some poor color snapshots and sent them to New York, and the devotees placed one at Prabhupāda's sitting place in his apartment. It helped.

For Prabhupāda also, the letter to his disciples in New York marked a milestone. This was the basis on which he hoped to conduct a world movement. He could travel from place to place and yet be simultaneously present in many places by his instructions.

Brahmānanda, as president of the New York temple, frequently phoned San Francisco. "The chanting is the focal point," he told Hayagrīva. "We can always sit and chant. We're beginning to understand what Swamiji meant when he said that worship in separation is more relishable."

And Śrīla Prabhupāda wrote to his New York disciples regularly, at least once a week. Brahmānanda got most of the business instructions: arrange to purchase a new building in New York, see Mr. Kallman and get copies of the *kīrtana* record, get a copy of the movie a filmmaker had made of the devotees, investigate the possibility of publishing *Bhagavad-gītā*. "If I am assisted by one expert type-writer ...," Prabhupāda wrote Brahmānanda, "we can publish every three months a book. And the more we have books the more we become respectable."

Satsvarūpa got a letter from Prabhupāda asking him to type the dictated tapes of the new book, *Teachings of Lord Caitanya*. Although Prabhupāda's typist, Neal, had gone to San Francisco, after a day he had disappeared.

"I think you have five tapes with you because I have got only three with me," Prabhupāda wrote. "See that the tapes do not miss." Satsvarūpa had written inquiring how he would be able to understand transcendental knowledge. "You are a sincere devotee of the Lord," Prabhupāda replied, "and certainly He will bless you with auspicious advancement in the matter of spiritual understanding."

Rāya Rāma got a letter encouraging him to continue publishing the magazine. "*Back to Godhead* will always remain the backbone of the society ... your ambition should always be how to improve the quality. ..."

Acyutānanda, one of the youngest devotees (only eighteen), was now working alone in the kitchen. In a letter Śrīla Prabhupāda wrote to five devotees, signing his name five times, he told Acyutānanda, "Since Kirtanananda is absent certainly you are feeling some strain. But the more you serve Krishna the more you become stronger. I hope you are being properly assisted by your other Godbrothers."

Prabhupāda advised Gargamuni, also eighteen, to cooperate with his older Godbrothers. Asking whether Gargamuni had gone to see his mother, Prabhupāda said he hoped she was all right. Since Gargamuni was the temple treasurer, Śrīla Prabhupāda advised him, "Checks should be drawn with full deliberation."

Prabhupāda wrote Jadurāṇī, "I always remember you as the nicest girl because you are so devoutly engaged in the service of Krishna." She had informed him that she had been cheated by a boyfriend, and Śrīla Prabhupāda replied, "Better you accept Krishna as your Husband, and He will never be unfaithful. ... Devote yourself therefore 24 hours in the service of Krishna and see how you feel happy in all respects."

Rūpānuga had written Prabhupāda that the temperature in New York had dropped below zero and that there had been a two-day blizzard. Śrīla Prabhupāda wrote,

> Certainly this situation would have been a little troublesome for me because I am an old man. I think Krishna wanted to protect me by shifting me here at San Francisco. Here the climate is certainly like India and I am feeling comfortable but uncomfortable also because at New York I felt at Home on account of so many beloved students like you. As you are feeling my absence so I am feeling for you. But we are all happy on account of Krishna Consciousness either here or there. May Krishna join us always in His transcendental service.

The neophyte disciples in New York felt assurance from their spiritual master's words and by their own experience. Service in separation was a transcendental fact. They were improving in chanting on their beads, and the New York center was going on. "So long our *kīrtana* is all right," Prabhupāda wrote, "there is no difficulty at all."

But there was one difficulty. Attempts to purchase a new building, which had gone on smoothly while Prabhupāda had been present, had become a great problem as soon as he had left. Shortly after Śrīla Prabhupāda's departure for San Francisco, Brahmānanda had given Mr. Price a thousand dollars, and Mr. Price had promised to help the devotees get their building. When Prabhupāda heard this, he became perturbed.

> In the opinion of the devotees and the trustees here, $1000.00 has been risked without any understanding. I know that you are doing your best but still there has been an error of judgment. I am not at all displeased with you but they say that Mr. Price will never be able to secure financial help from any other source. He is simply taking time under different pretext, changing constantly. Therefore you should not pay even a farthing more than what you have paid. If he wants any more money you should flatly refuse.

Śrīla Prabhupāda remembered Mr. Price and their first meeting, at which the blond-haired, elegantly dressed businessman, his face tanned even in winter, had addressed him as "Your Excellency." That address alone had made Prabhupāda distrust him. There was a Bengali saying, Too much devotion denotes a thief. Prabhupāda knew that businessmen were prone to cheat and that an American businessman would be particularly difficult to deal with. Prabhupāda's American disciples were innocent children in worldly affairs. He was ready to instruct them step by step, but now, without consulting him, they had become involved in an unbusinesslike transaction, risking a thousand dollars of the Society's money without any written agreement.

Śrīla Prabhupāda had visited the building on Stuyvesant Street, and he wanted it. It was a historical, well-kept, aristocratic building, suitable for his New York headquarters. It was worth the $100,000 price—if they could afford it. But it was difficult for Prabhupāda to know from San Francisco what was going on between Brahmānanda and the businessmen.

And the difficulty increased as letters and phone calls from Brahmānanda introduced other persons involved. Aside from Mr. Price there was Mr. Tyler, the owner, and Mr. Tyler's lawyer, who seemed independent of Mr. Tyler, and finally there was ISKCON's lawyer, who also had a mind of his own.

Although Śrīla Prabhupāda's disciples usually surrendered to his direction, they seemed bent on listening to the businessmen's promises, even though their spiritual master had cautioned them not to. Prabhupāda became disturbed. His preaching in San Francisco was being threatened by fears that the businessmen would cheat his Society of what he had begun in New York.

With no responsible advisors to turn to, Śrīla Prabhupāda sometimes discussed the problem with Mukunda and other devotees in his room. They all agreed that the transaction seemed highly irregular; Brahmānanda was probably being led on by false promises.

Brahmānanda, however, saw Mr. Price as a rare person—a successful man who wanted to help the devotees. Although no other respectable businessman had ever shown interest, Mr. Price listened and sympathized. And he would greet the devotees with "Hare Kṛṣṇa!" Brahmānanda was well aware of the humble economic and social position of the devotees. They were almost all ex-hippies, and they were poor. But here was Mr. Price, a wealthy man with diamond cuff links who was always glad to see him, shake his hand, pat his back, and speak appreciatively of the religion of India and the moral behavior of the small band of devotees.

Mr. Price had received a group of devotees as guests in his apartment and said nice things about each one of them. He had said that Hayagrīva was an excellent writer, and that *Back to Godhead* was the best magazine on the market, and that its mimeographed appearance made it look even better than the slicks. He said he would give the devotees a movie projector. And he came close to saying that if he could liquidate some of his money he would *give* them the building.

Brahmānanda, who saw Mr. Price a few times a week, would come away intoxicated with high hopes. The Kṛṣṇa consciousness movement could rise to success through this wealthy man's patronage. After leaving Mr. Price's office, Brahmānanda would rejoin the devotees in the evening and tell them all that had happened. On nights when there were no public *kīrtanas,* the devotees would hold meetings—Swamiji had named them *iṣṭa-goṣṭhīs*—to discuss the instructions of the spiritual master. And the *iṣṭa-goṣṭhīs* became dominated by talks of Mr. Price and the building.

One night Brahmānanda explained why he had given Mr. Price a thousand dollars: Mr. Price had asked for "something to work with." It was like earnest money, and it was also for a trip Mr. Price had to take to Pittsburgh to see whether he could release some of his wealth to use in Kṛṣṇa's service.

One of the boys asked whether there would be any receipt or written agreement. Swamiji had taught them to use receipts, at least amongst themselves. Gargamuni and Satsvarūpa, as treasurer and secretary, signed each voucher, and Gargamuni kept the vouchers on file. These included requests for items like "fifty cents for a hat" and "three dollars for sneakers." Brahmānanda said he had mentioned a written statement to Mr. Price but hadn't pressed the matter. Anyway, it wasn't necessary, or even desirable, since they were not simply conducting business with Mr. Price but cultivating a relationship. Mr. Price was a well-wisher, a friend, who was helping them as charity. He was going to do big things and use his influence to get the building. This one thousand dollars was just a gesture to show their interest and to show Mr. Price's friends the devotees weren't joking; they had some money.

In fact, the devotees had ten thousand dollars—five thousand in small donations and a five-thousand-dollar donation from a wealthy hippie. In addition to donations, the temple had a regular monthly income of eight hundred dollars—Brahmānanda's four-hundred-dollar paycheck from his job as a substitute teacher for the New York City public school system and the four-hundred-dollar paycheck Satsvarūpa earned as a caseworker for the welfare department.

But the devotees were in no position to buy *any* building, and they knew it—all the more reason, Brahmānanda explained at *iṣṭa-goṣṭhī,* why they had to depend on Mr. Price. After all, he reasoned, Swamiji himself had inspired them to look for a $100,000 building. Swamiji knew they couldn't pay for such a building, except in some extraordinary way. And Mr. Price, Brahmānanda figured, must be the way. Swamiji wanted the building. No sooner had he reached San Francisco than he had written back, "I am very anxious to hear about the final decision of the house. I wish to open the house by the 1st of March 1967 and arrangement may be done dexterously in this connection."

The assembled devotees listened to Brahmānanda's explanations, sympathized, and added their own understanding of how Kṛṣṇa and Swamiji were working. There were a few contrary remarks and opinions, but basically everyone agreed: Brahmānanda's dealings with Mr. Price were all right.

When Kīrtanānanda and Rāya Rāma returned to New York from San Francisco, they consulted with Brahmānanda. Then Brahmānanda went to Mr. Price, who promised that if somehow they couldn't get the building he would return at least $750. (The balance of the money represented travel in the devotees' interest.) But they would get the building, Mr. Price assured him.

Then Mr. Price told Brahmānanda the latest: he had found a wealthy financier, Mr. Hall, who had almost agreed to pay the full $100,000 for the building. Mr. Price was working on Mr. Hall, who happened to be his close friend. Prospects seemed good. But the devotees would also have to do their part, Mr. Price explained, by putting up five thousand dollars. Mr. Price would then arrange everything else.

Mr. Price set up a meeting with an architect on Park Avenue, and soon Brahmānanda and Satsvarūpa were sitting with Mr. Price and his architect friend, reviewing sketches. To give the building that authentic Indian-temple look, the architect proposed a facade with arches and, if they liked, domes. It was wonderful! Of course, they didn't dare ask him how much it would cost. But Mr. Price even hinted that the work might be done free. After Mr. Price served himself and his architect friend some liquor and offered some to the boys (although he knew they wouldn't accept it), the two men held up tinkling glasses, smiled, and politely toasted themselves and the boys, saying, "Hare Kṛṣṇa."

While going down on the elevator, Mr. Price spoke eloquently of the devotees' faith in God. He said that others might argue about the existence of God but the most convincing thing was the devotees' personal experience. "Your personal testimony," Mr. Price assured them, "is the best argument. It is a very powerful thing."

The boys nodded. Later among themselves they laughed about the liquor, but still they figured these men wanted to help.

When Śrīla Prabhupāda heard about the latest developments, he did not share his disciples' optimism. On February 3 he wrote Gargamuni:

> I had a talk with your brother Brahmananda yesterday on the dial. I am glad that Mr. Price has promised to return the amount of $750.00 in case no sale contract is made. But in any case, you should not pay any farthing more than what you have already paid, either to the Lawyer or to Mr. Price, unless there is actual sale contract made. It appears to me very gloomy about the transaction because there was no basic understanding before the payment of $1000.00 either to the Lawyer or to the Real estate. This is not businesslike. Unless there is a basic understanding where is the way of transaction? If there was no basic understanding, why so much waste of time and energy? I

> cannot understand. And if there was basic understanding, why is it changed so quickly? I am therefore perturbed in the mind. When there was no basic understanding, what was the need for appointing Lawyer? Anyway, it is my advice that you should consult me before issuing any further money. But I hope you will make the transaction successful without further delay.

Śrīla Prabhupāda had also instructed Gargamuni to protect the ten thousand dollars in the bank and never withdraw any sum that would leave a balance of less than six thousand. Prabhupāda had left one account for which the devotees were the signers, but he also had an account for which he controlled the funds. He now asked the devotees to put six thousand dollars from their account into his. He wrote Brahmānanda, "This $6000.00 will be transferred forthwith by me as soon as there is a *Sale contract* for purchase of the house."

On February 10 Prabhupāda wrote to Kīrtanānanda,

> Regarding the house, I was correct in my remarks that there was no definite understanding. ... In such negotiations, everything is done in black and white. Nothing is being done in black and white but everything is being done with faith on Mr. Price.
>
> Let this understanding be completed within the 1st of March 1967 and close the chapter. I think this is my last word in this connection. You are all grown up boys and you use your discretion and you can now complete the transaction without prolonging it indefinitely. If, however, we are not able to purchase a house it does not mean closing our activity at 26 Second avenue. So there is no question of packing up and coming to S.F.

Then on February 15 Prabhupāda wrote Satsvarūpa,

> So far I can see from the correspondence of Brahmananda it is not possible for us to get the house for so many reasons. The main reason is that we have no money to pay cash and nobody is going to invest cash in that house because it is neither complete nor has any income. It is simply utopian to think of possessing the house and Mr. Price is simply giving us false hope.
>
> You are all innocent boys without any experience of the world. The cunning world can befool you at any time. So please be careful of the world in Krishna consciousness. When Krishna will desire, the house will come to us automatically.

Śrīla Prabhupāda's doubts were confirmed when Mr. Price wrote to him asking for money. If Mr. Price had so much money, Prabhupāda reasoned, why was Mr. Price asking *him* for money?

On February 17 Śrīla Prabhupāda wrote to Mr. Price to impress upon him that there would have to be a sale contract before ISKCON could actually purchase the building.

> If there is sale contract, my students here and in New York will be able to raise the fund very seriously. In the absence of any sale contract everything appears to be in the air and Mr. Tyler or his lawyer can change his word as he has already done.

Śrīla Prabhupāda's message was clear. Brahmānanda, however, complained of poor communications. Things were always changing, and Brahmānanda wasn't always able to get Swamiji's confirmation on the latest changes. Swamiji would write his instructions in a letter, and although the devotees had to obey whatever he said, the circumstances would often have changed by the time they received the letter. Swamiji would also sometimes change his opinion when he heard new information. Sometimes Brahmānanda would call San Francisco and Swamiji wouldn't be available. Brahmānanda didn't feel right about sending messages through the devotees in San Francisco, because he knew that the devotees there were skeptical about the whole transaction. If New York got the building, San Francisco would have to donate a thousand dollars. And the devotees in San Francisco, of course, had their own plans for how to spend money for Kṛṣṇa.

Mr. Price suggested to the devotees in New York that maybe the Swami didn't understand American business dealings. With all respect, His Excellency couldn't be expected to know all the intricacies of finance in a foreign country. And His Excellency's request for a purchase contract was, as Mr. Price put it, "something that went out with hoop skirts." Brahmānanda and Satsvarūpa didn't know how to reply; the remarks seemed like blasphemy. But Brahmānanda and Satsvarūpa were already entangled in the promises Mr. Price had given and went on meeting with him. They would meet with Mr. Price and then ride back to Second Avenue on the subway, chanting Hare Kṛṣṇa.

Śrīla Prabhupāda wrote almost daily to various devotees in New York. On February 18, he wrote a letter to Brahmānanda with the word CONFIDENTIAL typed at the top of the page.

> Now if you think he is able to secure money for us, if you think that there is something hopeful by this time then you can continue the negotiation as

> he is doing. *But do not for Krishna's sake advance a farthing more on any plea by him.* He may be trying his best, but he is not capable to do this. That is my honest opinion.

While trying to avoid further losses in New York, Prabhupāda continued his active preaching in San Francisco. Mukunda and the others were lining up lots of engagements, and the reception was often enthusiastic. In the same confidential letter to Brahmānanda in which Prabhupāda put forward his strategies for negotiating with Mr. Price and company, he also wrote glowingly of "grand successful" meetings at various Bay Area colleges. The meetings were similar, he said, to the wonderful *kīrtanas* in Tompkins Square Park. This was the way to spread Kṛṣṇa consciousness, not by becoming entangled with treacherous real estate agents.

> I am enclosing herewith a copy of the letter received from Himalayan Academy. See how they are appreciating our method of peace movement. So in this way we have to forward our cause. No businessman will come forward to help us on utopian schemes as contemplated by Mr. Price. We have to try for ourselves. So the summary is to obtain a *hire purchase sale contract* from Mr. Tyler and popularize our movement by outdoor engagements as many as possible.

Śrīla Prabhupāda had done what he could. The boys were foolish, even to the point of not listening to him. But they had raised the money themselves. If despite his instructions they lost it, what further help could he give? So he simply went on with his San Francisco preaching and advised the boys in New York also to become convinced of achieving success through *kīrtana.*

CHAPTER TWENTY-FOUR

New Jagannātha Purī

ŚRĪLA PRABHUPĀDA PUT on a sweater over his turtleneck jersey, wrapped his *cādara* around his shoulders, and left his apartment, accompanied by a few disciples. The weather was beautiful, and the blue, cloudless sky reminded him of India. An hour before, he had sent devotees ahead to start a *kīrtana,* and now one of the girls had come running back to him, excitedly knocking on his door and announcing, "Swamiji, there are so many people!"

The clay *mṛdaṅgas* he had ordered many months ago from Calcutta had recently arrived. Today would be one of the first times he would play a genuine clay *mṛdaṅga* in America. The boys and girls would like it. He had arranged for the drums to be wrapped in cloth and had cautioned the boys to be careful because the clay drums broke easily.

The walk to the park was short, and as usual Prabhupāda walked faster than his young followers. They walked down Frederick Street to Stanyan, where they turned the corner at the doughnut shop (frequented by the Hell's Angels and still sometimes visited by certain devotees). On Stanyan they hurried past the parking lot of Kezar Stadium, the stadium itself looming beyond. At the Wallen Street intersection Prabhupāda continued his rapid stride without stopping or even bothering to look at the light. One of the boys caught his arm: "Wait, Swamiji—the light." But Prabhupāda darted across the street.

As they continued down Stanyan toward Haight Street, the park appeared on the right. They entered, walking past a duck pond with a fountain and a willow tree on its center island. They walked past tall redwoods and eucalyptus trees, which lent fragrance to the surrounding area. There were also maple, oak, and ash trees and flowering shrubs, like azaleas. Prabhupāda said that the park resembled parks in Bombay and that the city was like a holy place because it was named after St. Francis.

They entered a fifty-foot-long tunnel with artificial stalactites hanging from the ceiling and came out onto a path heavily shaded by trees on either side. Just ahead was the meadow, covered with tiny daisies and clover and encircled by redwood and eucalyptus trees. Prabhupāda could hear the chanting, the *karatālas,* and the booming of the timpani. As he entered the meadow, he saw a sloping hill dotted with hundreds of young people—sitting, lying, lounging, smoking, throwing Frisbees, or walking around; and in the meadow below the hill was his *kīrtana.*

The meadow was a popular place. People walked through it on the way to the zoo or the tennis courts. But today many passersby had stopped and were listening in a group, about two hundred feet from the *kīrtana.* Closer in, about fifty feet from the *kīrtana,* was another group, listening more intently. And then there was the *kīrtana* party itself, Prabhupāda's disciples and dozens of young hippies, sitting tightly together and chanting. And others were standing nearby, clapping and swaying to the rhythm of the drum and *karatālas.*

Flags decorated the *kīrtana* area. Three feet by four feet, they had been made by devotees, and each bore the symbol of a different religion. A bright red flag with a yellow star and the crescent moon of Islam flew from a ten-foot bamboo pole stuck into the earth. Beside it waved a pale blue flag with a dark blue Star of David in the center. And beside that, a yellow flag bore the Sanskrit *oṁkāra.*

Prabhupāda's disciples, with their long hair and casual clothes, were indistinguishable from the other young dancers and singers except for the strands of large red chanting beads around their necks. Some of the devotees danced, with arms upraised against the background of uninterrupted blue sky. Others played instruments. The *karatālas* and timpani were there, Hayagrīva had brought his cornet, and there were other instruments brought by devotees and hippies. Little children were taking part. Even a stray dog pranced in the innermost circle of the *kīrtana* party. On Sundays the meadow beneath Hippie Hill was always an open show, and today the *kīrtana* was the featured attraction.

Prabhupāda joined the *kīrtana.* Walking up suddenly, to the surprise and delight of the devotees, he sat down and began playing the *mṛdaṅga* and leading the singing in a loud voice.

Mukunda: *Although we had heard Swamiji play different drums before and some of us had played along with him, when he played the clay* mṛdaṅga *from India it was a completely different feeling. The feeling it created was akin to seeing an old friend after many, many years. It was so right and so natural. It was the very thing our* kīrtanas *had been missing, and it increased our feelings of ecstasy many times over. Obviously Swamiji was in greater ecstasy than ever. You could sense by the way he held the drum, by the ease with which he brought out its intricate rhythms to control the* kīrtana, *that this drum was like a long-lost friend to him. Swamiji playing that drum was the talk of the community. Now we knew what* kīrtana *really was, how it was supposed to sound, what it was really like.*

Prabhupāda was the center of attraction. Even his age and dress made him prominent. Whereas the others in the park were mostly young people dressed in denims or various hippie costumes, Prabhupāda was seventy and distinctly dressed in saffron robes. And the way the devotees had all cheered and bowed before him and were now looking at him so lovingly caused onlookers to regard him with curiosity and respect. As soon as he had sat down, some young children had gathered in close to him. He had smiled at them, deftly playing the *mṛdaṅga,* enthralling and entertaining them with his playing.

Govinda dāsī: *With Swamiji's arrival there was a mastery and an authority about the whole* kīrtana *that was absent before. We were no longer kids in San Francisco chanting Hare Kṛṣṇa. Now we had historical depth and meaning. Now the* kīrtana *had credentials. His presence established the ancient historical quality of the chanting. When Swamiji came, the whole disciplic succession came.*

After an hour of chanting, Prabhupāda stopped the *kīrtana* and addressed the crowd: "Hare Kṛṣṇa, Hare Kṛṣṇa, Kṛṣṇa Kṛṣṇa, Hare Hare/ Hare Rāma, Hare Rāma, Rāma Rāma, Hare Hare. This is the sound vibration, and it is to be understood that the sound vibration is transcendental. And because it is transcendental vibration, therefore it appeals to everyone, even without understanding the language of the sound. This is the beauty. Even children respond to it. ..."

After speaking five minutes, Prabhupāda began the *kīrtana* again. One woman with long, uncombed red hair began dancing back and forth and chanting, her baby in her arms. A man and woman sitting side by side played together on the heads of a pair of bongos. Subala, in tight corduroy pants and a flowing white shirt, danced in a semblance of the step Swamiji had shown him, although Subala looked somewhat like an American Indian dancer. A little girl no more than four years old sat cross-legged, playing *karatālas* and chanting seriously. A suave-looking fellow wearing a vest and round sunglasses played castanets against his palm. Ravīndra-svarūpa sat rocking back and forth as he played the drone on the harmonium. Beside him, Hayagrīva chanted forcefully, his head and upper body lunging forward and back, his long hair and beard jutting out wildly, while nearby a girl stood with her right arm around one boy and her left arm around another, all three of them swaying back and forth, singing with peaceful, blissful smiles, enjoying the chanting and the sunshine. One girl sat silently meditating, while beside her a girl danced provocatively and a five-year-old beside the dancing girl played with two balloons.

Prabhupāda set his *mṛdaṅga* aside and stood, playing *karatālas* and swaying among the dancers, his feet moving in a stately measure. A big black man danced nearby, facing his white girlfriend, both of them moving as if they were at the Avalon. The girl shook her body and head in wild abandon, and her long straight hair completely covered her face. Bright, blonde Nandarāṇī stood on Prabhupāda's right, playing *karatālas.* Sometimes Prabhupāda stopped singing and simply observed the scene, his mouth closed in a stern yet sublimely tolerant expression.

Some of the young people joined hands, forming a circle, and began to dance around and around in front of Swamiji. Then they encircled him, and as he looked on, still swaying and now clapping solemnly, they danced around him hand in hand, jumping and wriggling and chanting Hare Kṛṣṇa. The soft pink hue of his *khādī* robes contrasting with the pied dress of the hippies, Swamiji looked unusual and wonderful, watching and solemnly sanctioning the *kīrtana* performance.

The dancing was free-form and sensuous. But that was the way these young people expressed their feelings—through their bodies. They bounced and bounded into the air. Sometimes the circle of dancers would break and become a single line, weaving in and out among the people sitting on the grass, in and out among the silk flags. A muscular boy held the hand of a girl wearing long dark braids and a black headband in American Indian style. At the end of the line, a boy held a girl's hand with his left hand while with his right he held a wooden recorder to his mouth and tooted as he weaved in and out of the crowd.

Prabhupāda became tired and sat beside the brass-bottomed timpani. Singing and playing *karatālas,* he sat grave and straight like an ancient sage. Nearby, a blonde woman sat in yogic posture, bending her body forward until her forehead touched the ground again and again, in supplication or exhibition. Another girl stretched out her hands imploringly in a mixed expression of inner feelings—physical and spiritual—while her golden earrings jangled. A Mexican in a checkered shirt beat a tom-tom. A white sheep dog wandered from person to person.

Swamiji looked kind and amused. The hippies found him beautiful. He remained gentlemanly, aloof amid the twisting, shaking, rocking, dancing young people. Amid their most sensual movements, he appeared not at all like them, for he moved in a stately, elderly way.

As he surveyed the activities in the meadow, he seemed deeply pleased to see the ring of dancers singing all around him, chanting Hare Kṛṣṇa. Although the enthusiasm of these hippies was often wild and sensual, the gathering assumed a wholesome sweetness due to the chanting of Hare Kṛṣṇa. For Swamiji the main thing was that the chanting was going on and on. Dressed in his saffron cloth that seemed to change colors subtly in the fading afternoon sunlight, he watched in a kindly, fatherly way, not imposing any restraint but simply inviting everyone to chant Hare Kṛṣṇa.

Twenty-five-year-old Linda Katz was walking in the park when she heard the sound of the *kīrtana.* In the crowd of hundreds of people gathered around the scene, Linda found it easy to go close without becoming conspicuous. She felt comfortable watching and even thought of joining the fun. Then she noticed the Swami leading the singing. She was startled, even a little frightened, having never before seen anyone so grave. He was striking.

And the dancers appeared beautiful to her. A girl with arms upraised and eyes closed seemed to be swinging like a tree in the wind. One of the men was tall and attractive, with golden, curly hair. And Linda saw a boy she knew from college in New York, a crazy boy who always wore a shocking-pink wool cap.

Linda had arrived in San Francisco from New York only a few days ago. She had no plans, except to study under a certain dance teacher and maybe get into some of the exciting things she had heard were going on in Haight-Ashbury. As a graduate student in ancient Greek literature at Columbia University, Linda had become attracted to Socrates, who had lived and died for truth. But she hadn't found any of her professors to be at all like Socrates. She had envisioned herself living a life of truth by pursuing scholarship, but it had become dry. The ancient civilization of Greece was a dead idea, not a living truth. It didn't touch the heart.

She had been aching for a new, exciting experience, and she was ready to throw herself into San Francisco's hippie society. She had come here alone, giving up her fashionable clothes and donning bell-bottoms and old shirts. But because she wanted to be serious, she felt awkward trying to fit in with the hippies. She felt that to belong she was supposed to wipe the serious look off her face and just smile mindlessly. So even in the society of San Francisco's hippies, she remained unsatisfied and lost.

The *kīrtana* in the park was the most beautiful sight Linda had ever seen. The dancers were swaying back and forth, their arms raised against the open sky, and in the middle of the dance was a dark, gray-haired wise person sitting and chanting. As she moved in closer, she began to sway with the devotees. Then she sat down and started chanting, wanting to find out what was going on.

After more than an hour of chanting, the elderly leader finally stopped the *kīrtana,* and Linda began talking to some of the devotees. Although the Swami had slipped away, some of his followers had remained, handing out flyers and invitations to the Sunday Love Feast and picking up the timpani and the flags. One of them asked her to come with them to the temple.

Linda found the devotees to be something like hippies, but not scruffy street people like most of the hippies she had met. They were attractive, not repellent. Madrases and plants decorated their little storefront temple. When she stopped before a painting of people singing and dancing, one of the devotees said, "This is Lord Caitanya and His associates." A devotee gave her some *prasādam,* and Linda left that night without meeting the Swami.

The next day, however, at seven in the morning, she returned, eager for another chance to see him. She thought he had noticed her at the park and might remember her. She had made a drawing of him, and she wanted to show him.

That morning, as Prabhupāda chanted prayers and led *kīrtana,* Linda didn't take her eyes off him. And when he asked everyone to chant Hare Kṛṣṇa with him on beads, she excitedly accepted a strand from one of the devotees and tried to chant like him. Then he began reading the Sanskrit verse to begin his lecture, and Linda was captivated by the sound. If she were to continue with her graduate program in Greek, she would study Sanskrit next; so she listened with keen interest, proud that perhaps no one else in the room could understand as well as she.

Later that same morning, she met Śrīla Prabhupāda upstairs in his apartment.

Linda: *In the first conversation I had with him, Swamiji summed up Greek civilization for me in a couple of sentences. He explained that* Śrīmad-Bhāgavatam *was the source of stories like the* Iliad *and the* Odyssey *and was the source of Platonic philosophy. I was thrilled. Of course, I believed him. I knew that whatever he was speaking was the truth. There was no doubt in my mind. And he didn't discourage my love for Socrates. He told me that Socrates was actually a devotee in disguise.*

Then he began telling me the story of Kṛṣṇa as the butter thief, and I said, "Oh, yes, I know that story. I saw a dance about Kṛṣṇa as the butter thief." He was very pleased, and he laughed. He said, "Oh, yes, you know?"

This encounter with Swamiji was like meeting an old friend, because I felt completely at home and protected. And I felt I had found what I was looking for. Here I could use my intelligence and ask the questions I had always wanted to ask in school.

Prabhupāda initiated Linda, giving her the name Līlāvatī. Seeing her eagerness to serve him personally, he decided to teach her to cook by having her prepare his lunch. He already had a little weekend cooking class in which he taught Jānakī, Govinda dāsī, Nandarāṇī, and others the art of cooking for Kṛṣṇa. Now he invited Līlāvatī to come. He would walk back and forth in the small room, showing the girls how to knead dough, cook *capātīs,* measure spices in the right palm, and cut vegetables and cook them in ghee with *masālā.* The foods were basic—rice, *capātīs,* cauliflower with potatoes—but he wanted to teach the girls precisely how to cook.

Mukunda: *One day, just out of curiosity, I went in to witness Swamiji's cooking classes. So I came in and stood at the doorway to Swamiji's kitchen. The women were there learning how to cook, and Swamiji said to me, "What are you doing?"*

"Oh," I said, "I just came to see my wife."

Then Swamiji said, "Are you going back to Godhead or back to wife?" Everyone was amused, and I realized I wasn't welcome, so I left.

The incident made me reflect on Swamiji's seriousness. For one thing, I learned that I should not be so attached to my wife, and secondly I learned that his relationship with the women and what he was teaching them was actually very sacred—not like the sometimes frivolous association between husband and wife. Because he spent many hours in the kitchen teaching them, they were very inspired.

Līlāvatī tended to be proud. Many of the devotees were not college graduates, and none of them were classical scholars. She sometimes typed for Swamiji, did his wash, or brought flowers to his room in the morning. And he had quickly chosen *her* to be his exclusive cook. After only a few days of cooking lessons, Swamiji had told her, "All right, you cook." And now he came in only occasionally to check on her. Once when he saw her rolling *capātīs,* he said, "Oh, you have learned very nicely."

Preparing Swamiji's meals just right—with the proper spicing, without burning anything, and on time—was a challenge. By the time Līlāvatī finished, she would be perspiring and even crying from tension. But when she brought in his lunch he would ask her to bring an empty plate, and he would serve her portions from his own plate and invite her to eat with him. For the first few days, Līlāvatī made remarks about the wonderful tastes of the *prasādam,* and Swamiji would smile or raise his eyebrows. But then she noticed that he never spoke while eating but seemed to be concentrating intensely as he sat, cross-legged, bending his body over the plate of *prasādam* and eating with his right hand.

One day, on Ekādaśī, Līlāvatī arrived late at Swamiji's apartment, thinking there would not be much cooking on a fast day. But when she entered the kitchen she found Swamiji himself busily cooking. He was heating something white in a skillet, vigorously stirring and scraping it from the bottom of the pan. "Oh," he said, "I was just wondering, 'Where is that girl?' "

Līlāvatī was too shy to ask what Swamiji was doing, so she simply busied herself cutting vegetables. "Today is a fast day," she said, as if chiding Swamiji for cooking.

"You have to understand— " he replied, "in Kṛṣṇa consciousness a fast day means a feast day. We are offering this to Kṛṣṇa." Līlāvatī continued to keep her distance from Swamiji's whitish, sticky-looking preparation until he completed it and placed it on the windowsill to cool. "Later it will harden," he said, "and we can cut it and serve it." And with that he turned and walked out of the kitchen.

When Līlāvatī finished cooking and served Swamiji his Ekādaśī lunch, he asked her to bring him some of "that thing" on the windowsill. He took a bite, seemed pleased, and asked Līlāvatī to call Mukunda and Jānakī to taste it.

Jānakī took a bite and exclaimed, "It's wonderful! Simply wonderful! Incredible! What is this?"

Turning to Līlāvatī, Swamiji asked, "What is in this preparation?"

"I don't know, Swamiji," she said.

"You don't know?" he replied. "You were standing right by me in the kitchen, and you don't remember?" Līlāvatī's face turned red.

"Oh, Swamiji," Līlāvatī replied, "I was very busy. I just didn't see."

"Oh, you are busy without intelligence," he replied, and he laughed for a long time, until Mukunda was also laughing. Līlāvatī felt even more humiliated.

Swamiji asked Jānakī if she could tell what was in the preparation. She couldn't, except that it was sweet. He then sent Līlāvatī downstairs to get Govinda dāsī and Gaurasundara. When they entered, Swamiji told Līlāvatī, "Go get some more of that simply wonderful thing."

Again, this time in front of four devotees, Swamiji asked Līlāvatī, "So what is in this preparation?" And again she defended herself; she had been too busy to notice. And again he laughed until everyone was laughing with him. He then asked Govinda dāsī to taste the "simply wonderful" and say what was in it. Immediately she guessed: sugar, butter, and powdered milk.

"Oh," Swamiji looked at Līlāvatī, "she is an artist. She is intelligent."

To Līlāvatī the whole episode was a devastating ordeal. Only later did she understand that Swamiji had been trying to teach her humility.

* * *

It was 7 A.M. Śrīla Prabhupāda sat on his dais in the temple. Beside him, on an altar, stood the recently acquired statue of Kṛṣṇa. The child Kṛṣṇa stood two feet high, with His left hand on His hip, His right hand holding a rod. Gurudāsa had found Him at an import store and had begged the manager to sell Him, and after several visits the man had agreed—for thirty-five dollars. Prabhupāda had given Him the name Kartā Mahāśaya, "the boss." This morning, as Prabhupāda and Kartā Mahāśaya looked out at the devotees in the room, only about six people were present. The night before, the temple had been crowded.

"Where are the others?" Prabhupāda asked. And then he gave the answer himself: "They are sleeping? All this sleeping is not good." He took out his *karatālas* and began playing the one-two-*three* rhythm. Mukunda took up a *mṛdaṅga* and played along, trying to execute the rhythms Śrīla Prabhupāda had recently taught him.

Śrīla Prabhupāda had not even begun singing when the door opened and half a dozen barefoot hippies wandered in, reeking of marijuana. They glanced around, then sat down on the floor with the devotees as Prabhupāda began singing *Gurv-aṣṭakam,* the Vaiṣṇava prayers to the spiritual master.

Although none of his disciples knew the words, they loved to listen to Swamiji sing these morning prayers. Unhurriedly, he sang each verse, several times repeating each line, deliberately developing the mood of unadulterated service to the spiritual master.

Then one of the hippies, a boy with long, straight blonde hair and a red headband, began mumbling, fidgeting, and moaning. Someone softly asked him to be quiet. The boy paused but then moaned again. Swamiji and his followers were used to drugged hippies who stayed up all night and came to the morning program, sometimes disrupting things. Usually the visitors remained submissive. And even if they occasionally called out in a strange mood, they usually found peace in chanting Hare Kṛṣṇa and would try to blend with the energy of the devotees. But today's discordant visitor seemed agitated by the chanting, as if it were challenging him. Rather he sounded like *he* was challenging *it.*

The devotees began clapping in time with Prabhupāda's *karatālas,* and when Prabhupāda began singing Hare Kṛṣṇa, his half-dozen followers immediately joined him, chanting both lead and chorus. Prabhupāda looked at them gravely, encouraging the bedraggled early-morning band of youngsters, and they responded determinedly.

The guests sat in drugged contemplation, although one or two tried singing along. But the blonde boy with the red headband remained adamantly disharmonious, moaning defiantly, as if trying to throw off the effects of the chanting. Nonetheless, despite the boy's moaning, which was sometimes loud and savage, Prabhupāda kept singing, and the devotees kept chanting.

Mukunda and Hayagrīva exchanged anxious glances but tolerated the boy, unsure what else to do. Some of the devotees were disturbed and even frightened, but they had also heard Swamiji say in recent lectures that advanced devotees aren't shaken in any circumstances. Swamiji was their leader, not only in devotional prayers but also in how to respond to this intruder, so they waited and watched him for a sign.

Prabhupāda remained undisturbed. But although after twenty minutes the *kīrtana* was strong and determined, the blonde boy's madness was not going away. As the chanting built up momentum, he became more agitated. He screamed like a lost soul and hollered like a rock singer. He was becoming more and more troubled and angry.

When the devotees rose to their feet and began dancing, the boy began dancing too, but in his own way, crying and pounding his chest. Mukunda played louder on the drum. The sounds were discordant—a clash of individual madness and group chanting—until Prabhupāda finally brought the *kīrtana* to a close.

The devotees bowed their heads to the floor, and Śrīla Prabhupāda intoned the Sanskrit prayers honoring the spiritual masters, the Supreme Lord, and the sacred places. "All glories to the assembled devotees," he said.

They responded, "Hare Kṛṣṇa."

"All glories to the assembled devotees."

"Hare Kṛṣṇa."

"All glories to the assembled devotees."

"Hare Kṛṣṇa."

"Thank you very much," Prabhupāda said. And then, as was his morning custom, he announced, "Chant one round."

Everyone sat down, including the crazy hippie. The devotees put aside the drums and *karatālas,* reached for their large red beads, and began chanting *japa* in unison: "Hare Kṛṣṇa, Hare Kṛṣṇa, Kṛṣṇa Kṛṣṇa, Hare Hare/ Hare Rāma, Hare Rāma, Rāma Rāma, Hare Hare." Fingering one bead at a time, they uttered the *mantra,* then proceeded to the next bead.

Surprised at this turn of events, the blonde boy commented loudly, "Far out!" As rapid chanting filled the room, the boy jumped to his feet and shouted, "Come with me!" He whirled about, faced Śrīla Prabhupāda, and howled, "I AM GOD!" Then he began screaming long, loud, berserk cries: *"OWAHOOOO ... WAHOOOO! AAAA! ... OOOOOOOOOH!"* He sobbed, growled, grumbled, stomped his feet. Like a small child, he explored every sound his voice could make. Beating his fists on his chest again and again, he cried, "I am God!" And one of the boy's friends suddenly played a few notes on a panpipe.

But Śrīla Prabhupāda kept chanting *japa,* and the devotees also tried to continue chanting undaunted, while at the same time keeping an eye on the madman and wondering where it would all end. Then, with a final, violent ejaculation, the boy shrieked, "I AM GOD!" and in anger and disgust strode out of the room, slamming the door behind him, yelling as he ran down the street.

The proper *japa* peacefully engulfed the storefront, and Śrīla Prabhupāda's voice assumed its place more clearly above the voices of all the chanting devotees. After about ten minutes of chanting, Prabhupāda recited, *sarvātma-snapanaṁ paraṁ vijayate śrī-kṛṣṇa-saṅkīrtanam.* "Let there be all glory to the congregational chanting of Hare Kṛṣṇa, which cleanses the dirt from the mirror of the mind and gives a taste of the nectar for which we are always hankering."

As Prabhupāda put on his spectacles and opened the *Bhagavad-gītā* (he had been speaking each morning on the Sixth Chapter), the room settled and became silent for hearing his lecture. His students, some of whom had been imbibing his instructions for more than two months, listened attentively as he spoke the eternal *paramparā* message. It was Kṛṣṇa's timeless message, yet Swamiji was presenting it just for them as they sat on the rug early in the morning in the small storefront, 518 Frederick Street, in Haight-Ashbury.

Prabhupāda lectured on the transmigration of the soul. Foolish people, he said, aspire for material acquisitions. They don't know that these things are finished with the death of the body. Spiritual life, however, is of the utmost importance, because it is never lost. So even if Kṛṣṇa consciousness becomes inconvenient or uncomfortable, one should never give it up.

Śrīla Prabhupāda was again stressing that the devotee is never disturbed, a point that seemed especially relevant in the wake of this morning's interruption. A devotee, Prabhupāda explained, is always tolerant.

Prabhupāda told a story about the great devotee Haridāsa Ṭhākura, a contemporary of Lord Caitanya's, who endured severe beating at the hands of a Muslim magistrate. As Prabhupāda told the story, he improvised dialogue.

"Oh," the magistrate said to Haridāsa, "you are born in such a nice family, and you are chanting Hare Kṛṣṇa?"

And then Prabhupāda spoke for Haridāsa: "Sir, many Hindus also have become Muhammadan, so if some Muhammadan becomes Hindu, what is the harm?"

Prabhupāda didn't change the pitch or accent of his voice while taking different parts of the dialogue. But with a subtle storyteller's art, each voice became a distinct person.

The magistrate spoke threateningly. "Oh, you are arguing?"

Then Prabhupāda became the narrator: "So, it was decided that Haridāsa was to be punished. Give the dog a bad name and hang it."

Then Prabhupāda became Haridāsa's floggers, who despite repeatedly beating Haridāsa were unable to make him cry out in pain. Finally, exhausted, they spoke up. "Sir, the idea was that you would die, but now we see that you do not die. So now punishment is awaiting us."

Haridāsa: "What do you want?"

The floggers: "We want that you should die."

Narrator: "Then he played himself into *samādhi,* and the floggers brought him to the magistrate."

The magistrate: "Throw him in the water. Don't put him in the graveyard. He has become Hindu."

Śrīla Prabhupāda concluded his tale. "The others were flogging him, and he was chanting Hare Kṛṣṇa, Hare Kṛṣṇa, Kṛṣṇa Kṛṣṇa, Hare Hare/ Hare Rāma, Hare Rāma, Rāma Rāma, Hare Hare. He was undisturbed. He was steady. Therefore, Lord Kṛṣṇa says that a person who is spiritually advanced—for him there is no misery, even in this world, and what to speak of the other world."

A devotee suffers no loss, Prabhupāda explained. Even if he doesn't become perfectly Kṛṣṇa conscious, or even if he falls away, his next birth also will be human.

"There was a prince." Prabhupāda began a story to illustrate his point. "His name was Satyavān. But he was to die at a certain age, his horoscope said. But one girl named Sāvitrī—she fell in love with that boy. Now she wanted to marry. Her father told her, 'He'll die at certain age. You don't marry.' But she was bent. She married.

"In course of time, the boy died—say after four or five years—and the girl became widow. But she was so staunch lover that she won't let the dead body go away. And the Yamarāja, the ... what is the English for one who takes away the body or the soul after death? So he came to take the soul away. So this chaste girl would not allow the husband's body to go away."

By Prabhupāda's voice and widening eyes, he appeared as Yamarāja, the lord of death, speaking to the widow Sāvitrī: "'It is my duty that I should take. You give it up. Otherwise, you'll be also punished.' The girl gave up her husband but followed behind Yamarāja." Then Prabhupāda's Yamarāja, by a slight dropping of his voice, became compassionate: "'My dear girl, you go home. I give you benediction that you will have a son. Don't cry for your husband.' But Sāvitrī continued to follow Yamarāja. Yamarāja said, 'Why are you following me?'"

Then Prabhupāda's Sāvitrī spoke—not in a feminine voice, but with the reasoning and heart of Sāvitrī: "'Now you are taking my husband. How can I have my son?'"

Prabhupāda spoke as narrator: "Oh, then he was in dilemma. He returned her husband.

"So, similarly, there is a technique. If you take to Kṛṣṇa consciousness, then your husband, or this human form of life, is guaranteed."

The devotees understood the gist of the story, but they weren't perfectly clear what their lives had to do with the woman in the story. Some, however, understood: if they took to Kṛṣṇa consciousness, their ill-destined lives could become auspicious.

"Yes," Śrīla Prabhupāda continued, "a spiritual life is the most auspicious life." He looked around emphatically at the devotees seated

ABOVE: Śrīla Prabhupāda in the San Francisco Rādhā-Kṛṣṇa temple, early 1967.

ABOVE: This poster advertised Śrīla Prabhupāda's appearance at the Mantra-Rock Dance.

A few days prior to the Mantra-Rock Dance: Allen Ginsberg visiting Śrīla Prabhupāda in his room.

Śrīla Prabhupāda at his desk taking *prasādam.*

Śrīla Prabhupāda entering the Rādhā-Kṛṣṇa temple at 513 Frederick Street.

A *kīrtana* in the Rādhā-Kṛṣṇa temple storefront.

ABOVE: In the early morning Śrīla Prabhupāda would walk with some of his disciples near Golden Gate Park's Stowe Lake.

Śrīla Prabhupāda chants in Golden Gate Park.

Chanting in Golden Gate Park (continued).

ABOVE: In March of 1967 Śrīla Prabhupāda accompanied some of his San Francisco disciples to the beach for *kīrtana.*

LEFT: Śrīla Prabhupāda before the sea wall on a San Francisco beach.

Śrīla Prabhupāda and some of his New York disciples performing *kīrtana* at the Cosmic Love-In at the Village East Theater.

Śrīla Prabhupāda with some of his San Francisco disciples, in 1968.

The deities of Jagannātha, Subhadrā, and Balarāma riding on their cart (a flatbed truck) during the first Ratha-yātrā festival in America, July 9, 1967.

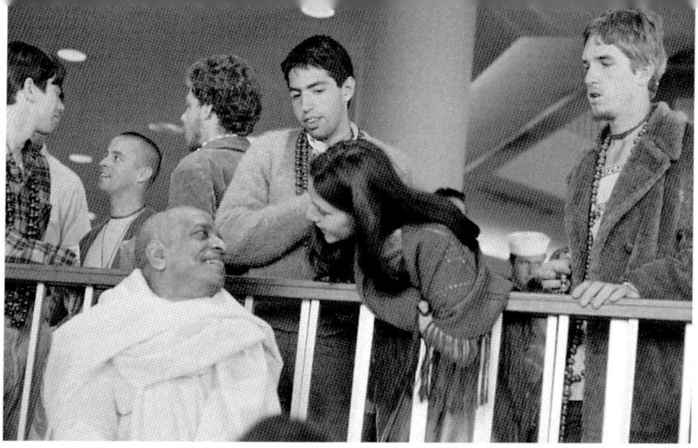

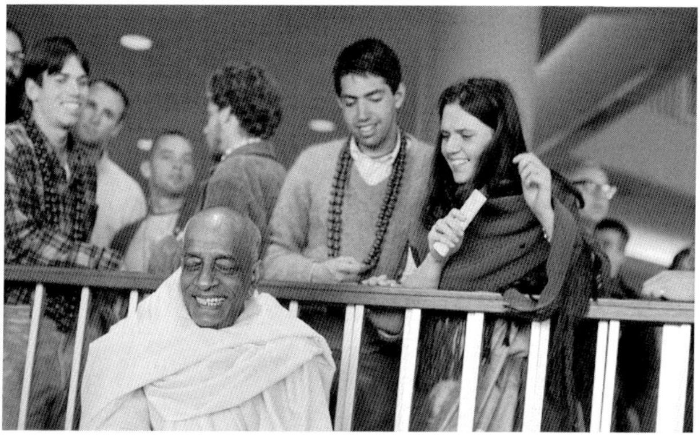

At the San Francisco airport, Jānakī steals Śrīla Prabhupāda's ticket.

Śrīla Prabhupāda performing *kīrtana* with Acyutānanda, Rāmānuja, and members of the Mullik family in the courtyard of the Rādhā-Govinda temple, Calcutta.

Śrīla Prabhupāda at the home of his sister in Calcutta. Sitting to Śrīla Prabhupāda's right is Acyutānanda; Rāmānuja is sitting on his left. Prabhupāda's sister, Bhavatarini, is seated on the floor.

Śrīla Prabhupāda viewing Rādhā-Govinda, the Mullik family's Deities in Calcutta.

ABOVE: Śrīla Prabhupāda at the New Vrindaban farm community, June 1968.

BELOW: George Harrison and Patti Boyd with Śrīla Prabhupāda and Dhanañjaya dāsa at George's home in England, 1969.

BELOW: George Harrison chanting Hare Kṛṣṇa with the devotees in London.

With Sarasvatī outside Śrīla Prabhupāda's quarters.

Śrīla Prabhupāda at Conway Hall, October 1969.

ABOVE: Outside the
elevision studio
n Amsterdam,
November 1969.

Installation of Rādhā-London-Īśvara, London, December 14, 1969.

Gala welcome for Śrīla Prabhupāda in Bombay, September 29, 1970.

Śrīla Prabhupāda with Sumati Morarji, head of the Scindia Steamship Company.

ͨ*īrtana* procession through the streets of Surat.

Ↄevotees lead *kīrtana* offstage at Sadhu-samaj, Bombay.

Pilgrims bathe at the confluence of the Yamunā and Ganges rivers, Prayag.

Śrīla Prabhupāda with Hanuman Prasad Poddar in Gorakhpur, February 1971.

LEFT AND BELOW:
At the Calcutta *paṇḍal*,
April 14–24, 1971.

ABOVE: Śrīla Prabhupāda walks in Red Square, Moscow, June 1971.

BELOW: Śrīla Prabhupāda on Nairobi television.

An initiation ceremony in the Brooklyn temple, July 1971.

before him on the floor. "Anyone who has done something nice, auspicious thing—oh, it will never be vanquished. He will never be put into difficulty. It is such a nice thing."

He ended his lecture and asked for questions. A young woman raised her hand: "You say that people foolishly worship the photograph of someone who has already gone—you gave the example of George Washington or Gandhi. But can't the photo of a spiritual teacher be very helpful to teach others to love him?"

Prabhupāda: "Yes, those who are spiritually advanced—they are not different from their photograph. Just like here is the statue of Kṛṣṇa—He's not different from Kṛṣṇa. The original person Kṛṣṇa and this statue of Kṛṣṇa are the same. Just like we are chanting Hare Kṛṣṇa—Kṛṣṇa and the name of Kṛṣṇa are nondifferent. Do you realize it? If we are not getting some spiritual enlightenment by chanting Hare Kṛṣṇa, then do you think we are simply wasting our time? No. We're not wasting our time. We're actually getting spiritual ecstasy, because there is no difference. Similarly, a spiritually perfect person and his photograph is the same, because it is in the absolute stage. Is that clear?"

Govinda dāsī raised her hand: "You said that after leaving this body a person in Kṛṣṇa consciousness goes to a higher planet?"

Prabhupāda: "No. If you make perfection of Kṛṣṇa consciousness, then after leaving this body you go directly to Kṛṣṇa. But if you are not perfect, if you have simply executed a certain percentage only, then you'll get the chance of another human body. But one who has understood what is Kṛṣṇa—how Kṛṣṇa takes His birth, how Kṛṣṇa acts—he doesn't get any more material birth. Then? Where does he go? *Tyaktvā dehaṁ punar janma naiti mām eti.* 'He comes to Me.' That means in the supreme abode of Kṛṣṇa.

"Therefore, we should be very serious. Why should we wait for another birth, either in very pious family or rich family or in other planet? This human body can give you the highest perfection. But we have to be very serious and try for that perfection. But we are not serious. We are not very serious. Actually, human civilization means that people should be very serious to have perfection of this human body—that is perfect human civilization. That is missing at the present moment."

Śrīla Prabhupāda sat in silence for several minutes, not moving. No one in the audience made a sound. Finally he reached over for his *karatālas* and began loudly ringing them together and singing: *govinda jaya jaya, gopāla jaya jaya.* And the devotees joined him:

govinda jaya jaya
gopāla jaya jaya
rādhā-ramaṇa hari
govinda jaya jaya

It was Prabhupāda's desire to see his disciples raise their Kṛṣṇa consciousness to one hundred percent in their present lifetime. They could do it, too, because the chanting was absolutely potent. If there was something they didn't understand, he would explain it. Govinda dāsī hadn't understood; she had thought that a devotee was meant to go to a higher planet. But now she understood.

And he had told them to become more serious. He knew they sometimes went to the doughnut shop and even smoked cigarettes after *kīrtanas,* and he tolerated it. But he let them know that he really wanted them to be completely serious. Unless they were completely serious, they might have to go to a higher planet within the material universe; and what good was that? To rise to a human birth took many lifetimes. Human life was meant for perfection, so they should be serious. "But," he had said, "we are not serious."

After the *kīrtana,* Śrīla Prabhupāda left the storefront and returned to his apartment. Hayagrīva, turning to Haridāsa, asked why no one had thrown the crazy boy out. "In New York," Hayagrīva said, "Brahmānanda would have removed him at the first outburst."

"You have to be careful with the hippies here," Haridāsa explained. "*Tactful* is the word. In this neighborhood, if someone walks around high on LSD, people automatically assume that he is due all the respect of God and should be tolerated. They come in and jump up and down and scream, but we can't lay a hand on them, because they are LSD saints. If we had touched that boy this morning, the whole neighborhood would be down on us. The Diggers next door are pretty noisy, but they unplug their jukebox during lectures, and they've been very friendly, giving us clothing and helping us decorate the temple. Sometimes the Hell's Angels go over there and raise a lot of noise, and sometimes they even come in here. If they do, best to humor them. They are always trouble."

That very morning some Hell's Angels started a fight in the Diggers' store. The devotees could hear thuds and screams through the walls as a big black beat up three Hell's Angels. The brawl ended only after a police car and an ambulance arrived.

Afterwards, about a dozen people drifted into the temple, talking about the brawl. Harṣarāṇī put out extra plates for the guests.

* * *

One day in March eighteen-year-old Wayne Gunderson was walking down the street when a piece of paper, blowing along the sidewalk, caught on his foot. He tried to kick it off without breaking his stride, but it hung on. Then he stopped and tried to kick it off. He couldn't. He reached down and picked it off and found that it was a flyer—"Stay High Forever"—advertising lectures by Swami Bhaktivedanta at 518 Frederick Street.

Like so many others, Wayne, a mild-mannered young man who worked for the post office, had come to Haight-Ashbury to take part in the revolution. He attended rock concerts and be-ins, browsed through the books and posters in the psychedelic shops, shared an apartment with his girlfriend and another couple, and took drugs. But he was quiet, polite, and solitary. He didn't dress like a hippie, but wore clean, conservative, casual clothes and a whimsical, odd-looking sports cap.

The flyer about the Swami seemed a timely coincidence, because Wayne had been planning to go to India to find a *guru.* He decided to go see Swami Bhaktivedanta on Frederick Street.

Wayne was surprised to find only a storefront. He was startled by the picture of the Swami in the window—no smiling, bearded *yogī,* but a shavenheaded swami with a stern look.

Wayne went in. It was a typical Haight-Ashbury scene, with hippies sitting around. But there were also a few people with big red beads strung like garlands around their necks. And up front he saw the Swami. Wayne was impressed as Prabhupāda began chanting Hare Kṛṣṇa, and he found the lecture firm and authoritative. The Swami stressed, "We are not these bodies." And when he spoke of Kṛṣṇa, he described Kṛṣṇa so personally that it was like being introduced to Kṛṣṇa.

After a few meetings, Wayne got up the nerve to ask a question: "Can one practice *haṭha-yoga* at the same time as Kṛṣṇa consciousness?"

"Oh, why do you want to spend so much time with that body?" Prabhupāda replied, and Wayne felt Prabhupāda's eyes look deep within him. "You are not that body." He said it so strongly that Wayne, who was easily hurt, felt like shrinking into the floor. "This body is not as important as the soul," Śrīla Prabhupāda explained. "So we shouldn't spend so much time with the body, exaggerating its needs." Then he smiled at Wayne. "Besides, all *yogas* culminate in Kṛṣṇa consciousness." And Wayne felt that smile lift him completely out of his diminished and crushed condition.

Several weeks later Wayne asked about initiation. When the devotees told him he should go up and see the Swami, Wayne went home and rehearsed his lines first. Anticipating what Prabhupāda would say, Wayne prepared his own responses and contrived the whole conversation. Then, nervously, he approached Prabhupāda's door.

But before he could even knock, the door opened, and there was Prabhupāda looking at him—not sternly, as in his picture, but kindly, as if expecting him. "Yes," Prabhupāda said, "come in." The incident completely shattered Wayne's planned approach. He concluded that Swamiji could read minds. So, trying to clear his mind of bad thoughts, he entered Prabhupāda's apartment.

Prabhupāda sat in his rocking chair, and Wayne, who usually sat on the floor, sat in the only other chair in the room. Wayne immediately felt uncomfortable, as he realized that it would be more proper to sit at Prabhupāda's feet. But feeling too weakhearted to alter the situation, he kept his seat, nervously fingering his sports cap. "Swamiji," he began, "I would like to be your disciple."

Prabhupāda immediately agreed. He asked whether Wayne could follow the four principles, and Wayne, although not even sure what the four principles were, said he could. Prabhupāda then asked him what principle was the most difficult for him to follow. "Well," he said, "I have difficulty with meat-eating." A lie—he was a vegetarian. But he was too shy to say that his real problem was uncontrolled sexual desire. Prabhupāda laughed, "Oh, that's no problem. We will give you *prasādam.* You can be initiated next week."

Wayne then asked if he would be able to go to India. He felt the Swami would be pleased to hear that his new follower wanted to go to his country. But Prabhupāda seemed displeased: "India? Why India?"

Wayne thought. ... The real reason he had wanted to go to India was to find a *guru.*

"Well," he said, "to learn Sanskrit."

"I will teach you Sanskrit," Prabhupāda replied. So there was no need to go to India. And he would be initiated by a genuine *guru* next week—right here in San Francisco.

Some devotees helped Wayne prepare for his initiation ceremony. Hayagrīva lent Wayne his *dhotī,* a piece of yellow cloth much too large for Wayne. Devotees set up a sacrificial arena in the storefront—a bed of earth, firewood, colored dyes, flowers.

During the ceremony Wayne was nervous. When Prabhupāda chanted the *mantras,* Wayne could not hear them exactly, so he just mimicked as best he could. And when Prabhupāda began the fire sacrifice, Wayne felt a little frightened because the initiation seemed such a serious commitment. He watched Prabhupāda gravely building the fire and saying the *mantras.* When Prabhupāda initiated Wayne with his new name, Upendra, Wayne didn't hear it clearly and began to worry. Then the ceremony ended, and Prabhupāda stood up and abruptly left the storefront.

Upendra: *Someone reminded me that I should go upstairs and give Swamiji an offering. So I decided to give him a baby blanket and a beach towel. It wasn't that I lacked money, but these things had some sentimental value to me, so I wanted to give them to Swamiji. I went upstairs to his room, and he was sitting at the foot of his mattress. I came in and bowed down and presented him with the baby blanket and beach towel. He held them up in his fingers and looked at them both in each of his hands. He said, "These things are useless," and he tossed them down on the floor. I was hurt, and I had nothing to say. I just sat there. After a while, I excused myself and went back to my apartment.*

The next day, I went to see Swamiji during his evening visiting time, and he had the beach towel and baby blanket out on the floor like rugs so that his guests who came to visit could have something to sit on. I felt satisfaction that he had found some use for my offerings.

Prabhupāda said that Upendra was not living up to his vows, since he was still living with his girlfriend. Upendra felt guilty about breaking the principles forbidding illicit sex and intoxication, but he just couldn't follow them. He wanted to tell Swamiji but couldn't bring himself to do it. Besides, he thought, even if he confessed, how could he stop? Upendra's girlfriend didn't like Kṛṣṇa consciousness, didn't want to meet Swamiji, and didn't want to come to the temple. So Prabhupāda decided that instead of marrying Upendra to her, he would save Upendra from her.

Prabhupāda decided to make Upendra a *brahmacārī.* Although Śrīla Prabhupāda had about twenty-five San Francisco disciples, hardly any were *brahmacārīs.* Practically the only solid one was Jayānanda, who was a little older than the rest. Jayānanda worked all day driving a cab, chanting Hare Kṛṣṇa even while driving. And when he was off work he would be at the temple, cooking or doing any service he could find or sitting with Prabhupāda in his apartment with the other devotees. He was known for his serious *japa.* Sitting cross-legged, eyes squeezed tightly shut, he would hold his strand of beads up in both hands and rock forward almost to the floor and back, chanting intensely, oblivious to the outside world. He was serious. And that was the only way one could remain a *brahmacārī.* In New York Prabhupāda had about a dozen *brahmacārīs,* but a more permissive attitude among his followers in San Francisco made *brahmacārī* life more difficult.

In the original Vedic society of ancient India, *brahmacārī* life began at the age of five. Parents would send their son to live with the *guru* at the *gurukula,* where the boy would receive basic education, spiritual instruction, and strict moral discipline under the *guru.* Even Lord Kṛṣṇa, in His transcendental pastimes on earth, had attended a *gurukula* and very humbly served His spiritual master.

The basic principle of *brahmacārī* life was celibacy. By practicing celibacy, the *brahmacārī* would develop great powers of memory and sensory control. And if such a trained *brahmacārī* later decided to take a wife, his sex life would be regulated, not licentious. But although *brahmacārī* life was necessary for a healthy society, Prabhupāda had seen within his own lifetime the rapid deterioration of *brahmacarya* almost to nonexistence.

And in America the situation was of course much worse. *Śrīmad-Bhāgavatam* tells of a young *brāhmaṇa,* Ajāmila, who fell from spiritual life because he had seen a drunken man embracing a half-naked prostitute. In America to see a half-naked prostitute in public was not uncommon. As soon as a *brahmacārī* walked out on the street, he would confront so many allurements. But Prabhupāda was convinced that *brahmacārīs* could protect themselves even in America if they regularly chanted Hare Kṛṣṇa and sincerely tried to follow the rules and regulations. Kṛṣṇa would protect them.

Prabhupāda had decided to ask Upendra to come and live with him as his personal servant. Prabhupāda's former servant, Ranchor, had recently left his position. Although supposedly a *brahmacārī,* he had never been a serious *brahmacārī.* He had even seduced one of the young women devotees in New York. Prabhupāda had found out and had asked the girl why she had indulged in sex with Ranchor if she wasn't planning to marry him. Prabhupāda's "Why?" had so disarmed the girl that she had been unable to answer. Prabhupāda had admonished her, "You girls should not make yourselves so cheap," and had given Ranchor another chance.

But Ranchor never became serious. After playing the drums during the big *kīrtana* at the Avalon Ballroom, Ranchor had become fascinated with the dance hall. He would sneak out from his service, lie to Prabhupāda about his absence, and go looking for girls at the Avalon. One day he never returned. As one of the devotees reported to Prabhupāda, "He just disappeared into the strobe lights." Ranchor did come back once—to ask Prabhupāda for money so that he could return to his home in New York.

Upendra, despite his weaknesses, was spontaneously attracted to Prabhupāda and liked to be with him whenever he could. Sometimes Upendra would go up to the apartment with one or two other devotees and just sit in front of Prabhupāda as Prabhupāda sat on the thin pillow behind his low desk. Sometimes Prabhupāda would continue reading or writing, and Upendra would sit and bask in his presence, simply watching him work. After ten minutes or so, Prabhupāda would look up and say, "All right, that is enough," and the boys would bow and leave. Upendra would also go to see Prabhupāda taking his lunch, and Prabhupāda would take some rice and vegetable from his plate, put them on a *capātī,* and offer them to Upendra. Although the *prasādam* was similar to the *prasādam* the devotees ate downstairs, Upendra thought that it tasted much better.

One day, when Upendra was alone with Prabhupāda in his room, Prabhupāda asked, "You are living with a young girl and people who take intoxicants?" For the second time, Upendra was convinced that Swamiji could read his mind and knew his entire life.

"Yes," Upendra admitted, "but I am not having— "

Prabhupāda interrupted: "That is not good."

"Swamiji, I am not having any sexual connections."

"Where there is a boy and where there is a girl," Prabhupāda said, "there is sex. You must come and live with me."

Upendra was delighted: "Yes, I'll come immediately."

He took a few belongings from his apartment, left everything else with his girlfriend, and moved into the front room of Prabhupāda's apartment. He was now Swamiji's personal servant.

Prabhupāda requested him to keep his job at the post office. Around midnight, as soon as Upendra got off work, he would return to the apartment. (Prabhupāda always left the door unlocked for him.) Usually, soon after Upendra locked the door, crawled into his sleeping bag, and fell asleep, he would be awakened by Prabhupāda speaking into his dictating machine, composing *Teachings of Lord Caitanya*. Upendra would nod off again and sleep until six.

Upendra relished this close association with his spiritual master and became always cheerful. "I just want to be Swamiji's dog," he would often tell the other devotees.

One time Upendra was reading to himself from *Śrīmad-Bhāgavatam:*

> The whole subject matter is so presented through the lips of Srila Sukadeva Goswami that any sincere audience who will lend his ears submissively to this message of the transcendental world, will at once relish the transcendental mellows distinguished from the perverted mellows of the material world. The ripen fruit is not dropped all of a sudden from the highest planet of *Krishna Loka* but it has come down carefully being handled by the chain of disciplic succession without any change or disturbance in the formation of the soft and ripen fruit.

"You don't have any questions?" Prabhupāda asked.

Upendra looked up from the book: "No, Swamiji, I accept everything you say." Prabhupāda began rocking strongly in his rocking chair and smiled as Upendra kept reading. Then Prabhupāda taught Upendra the proper way to hold a book while reading—with the palms of both hands "up and off the lap." This advice gave Upendra greater enthusiasm to please his spiritual master by reading his books.

Upendra was still bothered by sexual desires. He thought that maybe he should get married. But he was confused about what a Kṛṣṇa conscious marriage was supposed to be. How could you be married, he puzzled, if you don't love the girl you want to marry? And how could you love her without having sex with her? He wanted to ask Swamiji about this, but he kept it to himself, waiting for an opportunity and for the courage. Then one day he entered Prabhupāda's room as Prabhupāda paced back and forth from one end of the room, with its three large bay windows overlooking Frederick Street, to the other end, where his rocking chair sat. Now, Upendra decided, he could ask his question.

"Swamiji," he began, "may I ask a question?"

"Yes," Śrīla Prabhupāda replied, stopping his pacing.

"If a boy is separate from a girl, then how can he learn to love her?"

Prabhupāda began to walk back and forth again, chanting on his beads. After a moment he turned and said softly, "Love? Love is for Kṛṣṇa." And he walked toward the window and looked down at the street below. "You want a girl? Pick one." He pointed toward some women passing on the street. "There is no love in this material world," he said. "Love is for Kṛṣṇa."

Gradually, under Śrīla Prabhupāda's pure influence, Upendra began to feel less agitated by sexual demands. He came to understand that he was not a material body but a spiritual soul, that the soul's eternal nature was to love Kṛṣṇa, and that for a pure devotee—for Swamiji—love *was* for Kṛṣṇa.

More and more, Upendra just wanted to be the servant of Swamiji. He thought of what foods to buy for him and how to make things comfortable for him. It was in this mood of wanting to serve Swamiji that Upendra visited the Psychedelic Shop one day. He had heard they had recently received some prints from India, so he went in and browsed through the prints, picked out some pictures of Lord Kṛṣṇa, and took them to Swamiji.

In Prabhupāda's room, along with other devotees, Upendra unrolled the prints one by one on Prabhupāda's desk, waiting to see Prabhupāda's response. As Upendra watched, it seemed to him that Swamiji was looking at photos of his personal friend. He was pleased with the pictures. Hayagrīva commented that the religious art of the Indian prints was a bit garish, but Prabhupāda explained that the technique didn't matter. The important thing was that the pictures were of Kṛṣṇa and were executed according to Vedic descriptions. For the devotee they were beautiful; they were nondifferent from Kṛṣṇa.

Prabhupāda selected as his favorite a picture of Lord Kṛṣṇa standing and playing His flute in the moonlight, the River Yamunā flowing by. In this picture Kṛṣṇa was known as Govinda. Prabhupāda held the picture up and quoted a verse:

smerāṁ bhaṅgī-traya-paricitāṁ sāci-vistīrṇa-dṛṣṭiṁ
vaṁśī-nyastādhara-kiśalayām ujjvalāṁ candrakeṇa
govindākhyāṁ hari-tanum itaḥ keśī-tīrthopakaṇṭhe
mā prekṣiṣṭhās tava yadi sakhe bandhu-saṅge 'sti raṅgaḥ

He then took a sheet of paper and began writing, while the devotees watched him intently, listening to the scratching of the pen on the page. Then he read aloud: "My dear friend, if you still have an inclination to enjoy material life, society, friendship, and love, then please do not see the boy named Govinda, who is standing in a three-curved way, smiling and skillfully playing on His flute, His lips brightened by the full moonshine."

"Yamunā, you can write this nicely?" Prabhupāda knew that Yamunā was a trained calligrapher. He asked her to print the verse and display it, along with the picture, by his sitting place in the temple. He wanted to be able to look at it during *kīrtanas.*

Upendra thought and prayed, "If I can just fix myself steadily in serving Swamiji, who has such love for Kṛṣṇa, then I too will become transcendental." He felt that since it was not possible for him to see Govinda the way Swamiji saw Him, he should serve Swamiji, the pure devotee of Govinda, and in that way become pure. "I just want to become Swamiji's dog," Upendra said as he left the apartment.

* * *

In New York the boys had their orders from Prabhupāda not to give any more money to Mr. Price unless there was a purchase contract. Prabhupāda still wanted the building. He had written to Brahmānanda on March 4, "I hope when I go to New York next I shall enter the new house forthwith." And he had written Rāya Rāma on March 7, "I am very glad to learn that Brahmānanda, yourself and all others have the transcendental courage to take all risks for Krishna and this act will enhance your glory in Krishna consciousness." But he wanted them not to be cheated by false promises.

Meanwhile, Mr. Price was asking the devotees to turn over $5,000 to his financier friend, Mr. Hall, who would then add $20,000 and make the down payment to the owner, Mr. Tyler. Mr. Price wanted Brahmānanda to get the point across to His Excellency that negotiations had to be done in this fashion, and right away, if they seriously wanted to get the house.

Brahmānanda wrote to Prabhupāda, asking him to advise the bank to transfer $5,000 into the account controlled by the boys, the trustees of the International Society for Krishna Consciousness. Prabhupāda gave permission and asked that the check be signed by the president and secretary, because "Brahmananda and Satsvarupa are the main support for purchasing this house, and Kirtanananda is a supplement to this from his kitchen department." But he said that the check should be made to the seller, Mr. Tyler, not to the financier, Mr. Hall. "The money and the society is yours," Śrīla Prabhupāda acknowledged. "You can spend in any way but it is my duty to give you advice as ever well-wisher."

Then Mr. Price invited Brahmānanda to meet Mr. Hall; and he suggested that Brahmānanda come prepared with a check for $5,000. On the way, Mr. Price explained that Mr. Hall was perhaps the biggest real estate dealer in Manhattan—a multi-multimillionaire. He owned skyscrapers. Everything he owned was big. When Brahmānanda entered Mr. Hall's office, he thought it was right out of a Hollywood movie—a conference room ten times bigger than the Second Avenue temple room. And seated at the head of the large oval table was Mr. Hall himself. The room was in semidarkness, with a few spotlights on Mr. Hall, who sat before a battery of telephones. Even as they began to discuss, Mr. Hall paused several times, picking up phones and talking to persons in various places across the country.

"Young man," Mr. Hall said to Brahmānanda, "we are helping you get the house. It is a beautiful house, a New York City landmark." Then Mr. Hall's girlfriend called from a boat in the Caribbean. He talked to her for a while and then returned to Brahmānanda and Mr. Price, who sat in the shadows at his conference table.

Mr. Hall had a big contract he wanted Brahmānanda to sign. Brahmānanda knew that Swamiji wanted a contract—and here it was. He also knew that if he signed over the $5,000 he would have no other money and no extra income; and he knew they knew it. But Swamiji wanted the building. Swamiji himself had looked at $100,000 buildings and had offered to buy them, even though he had very little money to back his offers up. And Brahmānanda always did whatever Swamiji said. To sign this contract, Brahmānanda concluded, was an act of faith in Swamiji and Kṛṣṇa. He didn't analytically ask, "Where will the rest of the money come from?" To do so, he thought, would be like doubting Swamiji.

So here he was in this big-time financier's office. It was awesome. The millionaires were going to help. Mr. Price was at Brahmānanda's elbow. Mr. Hall was telling Brahmānanda that everything was all right: "We are going to get you this house." Now it was actually going to happen. Here was one of the biggest men in Manhattan offering to help. And whereas Brahmānanda had no money, Mr. Hall would be able to pick up the place very easily from the owner. Glancing quickly over the contract, Brahmānanda signed. It was a deal. And he gave them the check for $5,000.

As soon as Brahmānanda and Mr. Price left Mr. Hall's office, there was a distinct change in Mr. Price. Although still acting as Brahmānanda's friend, he now said, "Gee, you know, now you have to get this money." As they walked together on the uptown streets, Mr. Price cheerfully pushed the whole thing onto Brahmānanda. That was the change: before, Mr. Price had been saying that he and Mr. Hall were going to do it, but now he said that it was all up to the devotees. Brahmānanda asked about the legal position. Mr. Price explained that only the Kṛṣṇa Society was bound. But what about the promises? What about Mr. Hall's being so rich and wanting to help them and Mr. Price's wanting to help? Mr. Price assured Brahmānanda that he and Mr. Hall did want to help. They were doing everything they could. But Brahmānanda and the other devotees should also do everything they could and come up with the $20,000 to complete the down payment by the end of the month. And what if they couldn't? Mr. Price made it very clear: "If you don't pay the balance in a month, then you lose your deposit."

By the time Brahmānanda reached 26 Second Avenue he realized he had been cheated. He was crushed. He turned to the other devotees and told them what had happened, but they could only return, "Why did you do it?" Brahmānanda phoned Śrīla Prabhupāda in San Francisco. Now that his eyes had been opened about Mr. Price, Brahmānanda was blunt about his mistake, and he told Prabhupāda that he had given away the $5,000.

"All of it is gone?" Śrīla Prabhupāda asked.

"Yeah," Brahmānanda replied. He heard Prabhupāda hang up the phone. Brahmānanda had been about to explain the whole thing, but Swamiji had just hung up without a word. Brahmānanda placed the receiver back on the hook. He was shaken.

The next day the trustees held a special meeting. The boys sat around in the front room of Prabhupāda's apartment trying to decide what to do. Gargamuni again called Prabhupāda, who advised them to stop the check at the bank. "Swamiji's as smart as a fox," Rāya Rāma smiled. Gargamuni phoned the bank. But it was too late; the check had already been cashed.

They consulted Mr. Goldsmith, their friendly lawyer. He said it sounded like a weak legal case. Price and Hall hadn't legally bound themselves to pay anything if the devotees failed to pay; and if the devotees couldn't pay the $20,000 balance by the end of the month, they would lose their $5,000 deposit. They could sue for fraud, but court fees would be costly.

Then, one by one, Brahmānanda, Satsvarūpa, Kīrtanānanda, Rāya Rāma, Gargamuni, and the others began to look at the letters from Prabhupāda and discuss how he had warned them to avoid being cheated. Their greatest blunder, they began to realize, was disobeying his instructions. He had told them not to trust the promises of these businessmen, and he had told them that the check should be made only to the owner, not to the financier.

Within a few days, further instructions from their spiritual master came in the mail. There were admonishments, but hearing from him, even if he was chastising them, was better than the pain of his hanging up the phone without a word. "But you have not followed my instructions and now you are in trouble," he wrote to the boys.

He wrote Rāya Rāma,

> You are all foolish boys. I repeatedly warned you, even at the last point, that we should not pay the check unless there was agreement between Mr. Tyler and Mr. Hall. The agreement was signed like a marriage ceremony without the presence of the bride-groom. The mistake was there, and now you are repenting.

To Satsvarūpa he wrote,

> You have asked me whether the San Francisco branch will pay some money for purchasing the house. But where is your house and where is the purchase? So far it is talks of Mr. Price and company in which you innocent

> boys have been entrapped. I do not know how I can help you in your great blunder. I can only hope that Krishna will help you.

Unlike the boys and their lawyers, Prabhupāda thought that the legal case against the businessmen would be a strong one.

> I am not a Lawyer but this is common sense affair. Mr. Hall has taken the money, and he must finance to purchase the house. If he has no money to finance then it is a cheating case clear and simple.

The culprits, he said, should be brought to criminal court; their conspiracy and fraud were obvious and could be proven.

> From the telephonic conversation of Brahmananda it appears to be an organised cheating case and you have to face with courage without excusing any one of them. We are not revengeful but we cannot lose Krishna's money for nothing.

The boys had already blundered so much that Prabhupāda doubted whether they could tackle the cheaters. But he said they had to try: "Let us have the house or return back the money. In default, there is clear case of cheating. Now you can do as you like."

Śrīla Prabhupāda wrote the boys' lawyer, relating the history of the case. He also wrote a letter to the financier, the owner, and Mr. Price, threatening to expose everything, including what he alone had seen: that the lawyers involved were also implicated. Brahmānanda could barely understand what was going on, but it appeared that Swamiji was going to get results. The boys were fools, certainly, but the businessmen were certainly cheaters. And Swamiji claimed that he could prove it in court.

While admonishing his blundering disciples and going fiercely after the cheaters, Śrīla Prabhupāda still remained the ultimate shelter for his foolish boys. In a letter to the six trustees of his New York branch, he shed transcendental light into their gloomy minds.

> Forget the chapter. Take it for granted that Krishna has taken away this money from you for your deliberate foolishness. In future be very cautious and abide by the orders of Krishna. If you abide by the orders of Krishna, He can give you things that you may need. Be cheerful and chant Hare Krishna without any lamentation. As I have told you several times, that my Guru-maharaj used to say that this world is not a fit place for a gentleman.

> His version is corroborated by the following verse of Srimad-Bhagavatam. It is said like:
>
> *Yasya asti bhagavati akincana bhakti*
> *Sarvai gunais tatra samasate sura.*
> *Harau abhaktasya kuto mahat guna*
> *Manorathen asato dhavato bahi*
>
> "A person who is not in Krishna consciousness has no good qualifications. However so called gentleman one may be or academically educated he may be he is hovering over the mental plane and therefore he must commit nuisance being influenced by the external energy. A person who has however unflinching faith in the Supreme Personality of Godhead has all the good qualifications of the demigods." In other words you should not keep your trust on so called gentlemen of the world however nicely dressed he may be. In the matter of discharging our mission of Krishna consciousness we have to meet so many so called gentlemen but we must be very cautious for dealing with them as we are cautious in dealing with serpents.

Now, more than ever, the boys in New York wanted Swamiji to come back. Although most of the talk in the temple was still about real estate, they were holding regular *kīrtana* and lecture programs, and two new boys had joined. Jadurāṇī had finished some new paintings of Lord Viṣṇu, which now hung in the temple, and she was waiting anxiously for Swamiji to come and see them. Some devotees had made a new speaker's seat in the temple for Swamiji. They knew they were fools, but they asked him please to come back. He agreed. He set April 9 as the date for his return to New York. But meanwhile he still had much to do in San Francisco.

* * *

One day Mālatī hurried into Śrīla Prabhupāda's apartment, took a small item out of her shopping bag, and placed it on Prabhupāda's desk for his inspection. "What is this, Swamiji?"

Śrīla Prabhupāda looked down and beheld a three-inch wooden doll with a flat head, a black, smiling face, and big, round eyes. The figure had stubby, forward-jutting arms, and a simple green and yellow torso with no visible feet. Śrīla Prabhupāda immediately folded his palms and bowed his head, offering the little figure respects.

"You have brought Lord Jagannātha, the Lord of the universe," he said, smiling and bright-eyed. "He is Kṛṣṇa. Thank you very much." Śrīla Prabhupāda beamed with pleasure, while Mālatī and others sat amazed at their good fortune of seeing Swamiji so pleased. Prabhupāda explained that this was Lord Jagannātha, a Deity of Kṛṣṇa worshiped all over India for thousands of years. Jagannātha, he said, is worshiped along with two other deities: His brother, Balarāma, and His sister, Subhadrā.

Excitedly, Mālatī confirmed that there were other, similar figures at Cost Plus, the import store where she had found the little Jagannātha, and Śrīla Prabhupāda said she should go back and buy them. Mālatī told her husband, Śyāmasundara, and together they hurried back and bought the two other dolls in the set.

Śrīla Prabhupāda placed the black-faced, smiling Jagannātha on the right. In the center he placed the smallest figure, Subhadrā, who had a red, smiling mouth and a rectangular black and yellow torso. The third figure, Balarāma, with a white, round head, red-rimmed eyes, and a happy red smile, had the forward-jutting arms like Jagannātha and a blue and yellow base. Prabhupāda placed Him next to Subhadrā. As Prabhupāda looked at them together on his desk, he asked if anyone knew how to carve. Śyāmasundara said he was a wood sculptor, and Prabhupāda asked him to carve three-foot-high copies of the little Jagannātha, Balarāma, and Subhadrā.

More than two thousand years ago, Śrīla Prabhupāda told them, there was a king named Indradyumna, a devotee of Lord Kṛṣṇa. Mahārāja Indradyumna wanted a statue of the Lord as He had appeared when He and His brother and sister had traveled on chariots to the holy field of Kurukṣetra during a solar eclipse. When the king requested a famous artist from the heavenly planets, Viśvakarmā, to sculpture the forms, Viśvakarmā agreed — on the condition that no one interrupt his work. The king waited for a long time, while Viśvakarmā worked behind locked doors. One day, however, the king felt he could wait no longer, and he broke in to see the work in progress. Viśvakarmā, true to his word, vanished, leaving behind the uncompleted forms of the three deities. The king was nevertheless so pleased with the wonderful forms of Kṛṣṇa, Balarāma, and Subhadrā that he decided to worship them as they were. He installed them in a temple and began worshiping them with great opulence.

Since that time, Śrīla Prabhupāda continued, Lord Jagannātha has been worshiped all over India, especially in the province of Orissa, where there is a great temple of Lord Jagannātha at Purī. Each year at Purī, during the gigantic Ratha-yātrā festival, millions of pilgrims from all over India come to worship Lord Jagannātha, Balarāma, and Subhadrā, as the deities ride in procession on three huge carts. Lord Caitanya, who spent the last eighteen years of His life at Jagannātha Purī, used to dance and chant in ecstasy before the Deity of Lord Jagannātha during the yearly Ratha-yātrā festival.

Seeing this appearance of Lord Jagannātha in San Francisco as the will of Kṛṣṇa, Prabhupāda said that they should be careful to receive and worship Lord Jagannātha properly. If Śyāmasundara could carve the forms, Prabhupāda said, he would personally install them in the temple, and the devotees could then begin worshiping the deities. San Francisco, he said, could be renamed New Jagannātha Purī. He chanted, *jagannāthaḥ svāmī nayana-patha-gāmī bhavatu me.* "This is a *mantra* for Lord Jagannātha," he said. "*Jagannātha* means 'Lord of the universe.' 'O Lord of the universe, kindly be visible unto me.' It is very auspicious that He has chosen to appear here."

Śyāmasundara bought three large blocks of hardwood, and Prabhupāda made a sketch and pointed out a number of details. Using the small statues, Śyāmasundara calculated ratios and new dimensions and began carving on the balcony of his apartment. Meanwhile, the devotees bought the rest of the tiny Jagannāthas from Cost Plus, and it became a fashion to glue a little Jagannātha to a simple necklace and wear Him around the neck. Because Lord Jagannātha was very liberal and merciful to the most fallen, Śrīla Prabhupāda explained, the devotees would soon be able to worship Him in their temple. The worship of the forms of Rādhā and Kṛṣṇa in the temple required very high, strict standards, which the devotees were not yet able to meet. But Lord Jagannātha was so merciful that He could be worshiped in a simple way (mostly by chanting Hare Kṛṣṇa), even if the devotees weren't very much advanced.

Prabhupāda set March 26, the appearance day of Lord Caitanya, as the day for installing the deities. The devotees would have a big feast and begin worshiping Lord Jagannātha. Prabhupāda said they would have to build an altar, and he told them how to prepare it.

While Śyāmasundara hurried to finish his carving, a small splinter lodged itself in his hand, and the wound became infected. Finally

Śyāmasundara got blood poisoning and became so sick that he had to go to the hospital. Lord Jagannātha was taking away the reactions to Śyāmasundara's previous sinful activities, Prabhupāda said.

On March 26, the appearance day of Lord Caitanya, Prabhupāda said that during the morning they would stay together in the temple, read about Lord Caitanya, and hold *kīrtana,* and in the evening they would have a ceremony for installing Lord Jagannātha. Having fasted until moonrise, they would then break fast with a *prasādam* feast.

When Śrīla Prabhupāda entered the temple that morning, he saw the work the devotees had done. The new altar stood in the rear of the room, above where his dais had been, and his dais was now on the right side of the room, against the wall. From his seat he would be able to see the altar very easily. The altar was a simple redwood plank seven feet above the floor and fixed between two thick redwood pillars. A canopy covered the place where the deities would stand. Below the altar hung Haridāsa's painting of Lord Caitanya and His associates dancing during *kīrtana,* and behind the painting was a madras backdrop. About three feet above the floor, a shelf below the painting held candlesticks and would be used for articles to be offered to the deities.

Prabhupāda took his seat. As usual, he led *kīrtana* and then chanted one round of *japa* with the devotees. Then he had Hayagrīva read aloud from the biographical sketch of Lord Caitanya from the first volume of *Śrīmad-Bhāgavatam.* But many devotees were sleepy, despite Hayagrīva's reading loudly with force and elocution. Although Prabhupāda was listening attentively and wanted the others to sit with him and hear about Lord Caitanya, when he saw that so many were dozing he stopped the reading and held another *kīrtana.* Then he chanted *japa* with them for about fifteen minutes.

"All right," he said. "We will read again. Who will read?" Līlāvatī's hand flew up urgently. "All right." He had her sit near his dais, and someone placed a microphone before her. Līlāvatī's reading presented a contrast to the deep tones of Hayagrīva. But she was another scholarly voice. Her careful pronunciation of the Sanskrit words and phrases was pleasing to Śrīla Prabhupāda, and he several times commented, "Oh, very nice." Līlāvatī was thrilled and read on intensely, determined to keep everyone awake.

That evening, devotees and hippie guests filled the room to capacity. Prabhupāda was present, and the mood was reverential and festive. It was a special event. The just-finished deities sat on the altar, and everyone was glancing at them as they stood on their redwood shelf beneath a yellow canopy, their features illumined by spotlights. The deities wore no clothes or ornaments, but were freshly painted in bright black, red, white, green, yellow, and blue. They were smiling. Śrīla Prabhupāda was also glancing at them, looking up to their high altar.

Prabhupāda lectured about the four social and four spiritual orders of life described in the Vedic literatures. According to one's quality and work, he said, each person has a certain occupational duty. "But the ultimate goal of that duty," he explained, "is to satisfy the Supreme Lord." It doesn't matter if one is lowborn or poor. "Material qualification has nothing to do with spiritual evolution. Spiritual evolution is that with your talent, with your capacity, with your work, you have to satisfy the Supreme Lord."

Prabhupāda gave the example of Śrīdhara, an impoverished devotee of Lord Caitanya's who earned the equivalent of less than five cents a day yet offered half his earnings in worship of the Ganges. If one were rich, however, one should still give half his wealth to the service of the Lord. Prabhupāda cited Rūpa Gosvāmī, who had given fifty percent of his wealth for Kṛṣṇa consciousness, given twenty-five percent for his family, and saved twenty-five percent for emergencies. Suddenly Prabhupāda began speaking about the money his disciples in New York had lost: "And twenty-five percent for himself so that in times of emergency ... because as soon as money is gone out of my hand, I have no control. We have recently lost $6,000—not here, in our New York. So as soon as the check is out of hand, now it is gone. It is gone. ..."

Prabhupāda gestured to indicate money flying like a bird out of his hand. At this reference to the troubling, entangling affair with Mr. Price and the foolish boys and their hard-earned money gone, Prabhupāda paused for a moment. Then he continued with the lecture.

"Paying attention to Bhagavān, the Supreme Person, is practical," Śrīla Prabhupāda said. "Here is Kṛṣṇa. Kṛṣṇa's form is there. Kṛṣṇa's color is there. Kṛṣṇa's helmet is there, Kṛṣṇa's advice is there. Kṛṣṇa's instruction is there. Kṛṣṇa's sound is there. Everything Kṛṣṇa. Everything Kṛṣṇa. There is no difficulty.

"But if you turn your attention to the impersonal and to the Supersoul in the heart, as the *yogīs* do, then it is very difficult. It is very difficult. You cannot fix your attention to the impersonal. In the *Bhagavad-gītā* it is said that, *kleśo 'dhikataras teṣām avyaktāsakta-cetasām:* 'Those who are attached to the impersonal feature of the Absolute Truth—their business is very troublesome.' It is not like chanting, dancing, and eating—this is very nice. But *that* is very troublesome. And even if you speculate on the impersonal, the result that is achieved by working hard for many, many lives is that you will have to also eventually come to Kṛṣṇa."

Śrīla Prabhupāda continued describing Kṛṣṇa as the Supreme Personality of Godhead, citing evidence from scriptures like *Bhagavad-gītā* and *Brahma-saṁhitā*. The first step in spiritual life, he explained, was to hear from Kṛṣṇa Himself. But Prabhupāda warned that if one heard the class and then went outside and forgot, he could not improve. "Whatever you are hearing, you should say to others," Prabhupāda said. And he gave the example of how disciples were writing in *Back to Godhead* what they had heard from their spiritual master. And to speak or write what one has heard, a person has to be thoughtful. ...

"You are hearing about Kṛṣṇa, and you have to think. Then you have to speak. Otherwise, it will not work. So, *śrotavyaḥ kīrtitavyaś ca dhyeyaḥ pūjyaś ca*. And you should worship. Therefore, you require this Deity for worshiping. We have to think of, we have to speak, we have to hear, we have to worship (*pūjyaś ca*). And should we do this occasionally? No. *Nityadā:* regularly. Regularly. This is the process. So anyone who adopts this process—he can understand the Absolute Truth. This is the clear declaration of the *Śrīmad-Bhāgavatam*. Thank you very much. Any question?"

A young boy raised his hand and began earnestly: "Well, you mentioned about how we should follow the supreme law, how we should be like what your spirit tells you? Or what you, your supreme, whatever it tells you? I mean ... whatever it tells you? I mean, if you meditate a lot, you feel you should do ... something. ..."

Prabhupāda: "It is not *something*. It must be actual fact."

Boy: "Yeah, I mean like ..."

Prabhupāda: "So, there is no question of *something*."

Boy: "Well, I see ..."

Prabhupāda: "*Something* is vague. You must speak what is that something."

Boy: "Well, let's say, be ... uh ..."

Prabhupāda: "That you cannot express. That means you have no idea. So we have to learn. This is the process. I am speaking of the process. If you want to have knowledge of the Absolute Truth, the first thing is faith. Then you must be thoughtful. Then you must be devoted, and you must hear from authentic sources. These are the different methods. And when you come to the ultimate knowledge—from Brahman platform to Paramātmā platform, then to the Supreme Absolute Personality of Godhead—then your duty shall be to satisfy the Supreme Personality of Godhead. That is the perfection of your active life. These are the processes. And it is concluded that everyone, never mind what he is—his duty is to satisfy the Supreme Personality of Godhead.

"And how can we satisfy? We have to hear about Him, we have to speak about Him, we have to think about Him, we have to worship Him—and that is *regularly*. This will help you. But if you have no worship, if you have no thought, if you have no hearing, if you have no speaking, and you are simply thinking of *something, something, something*—that *something something* is not God."

Boy: "I mean, well, you know, I'm so young. I didn't know what I meant. I don't know what ..."

Prabhupāda: "*Don't know.* That I am speaking—that you have to *know* by these processes. We are all 'don't knows.' So we have to *know*. This is the process."

Young woman: "Since we don't yet understand the supreme law, because we are young and just new to this, then how can we speak about it?"

Prabhupāda: "Therefore you have to hear! The first thing is *śrotavyaḥ:* you have to hear. Unless you hear, how can you speak? We are therefore giving you facility to hear. You hear, and then you can speak. Then you can think. We are giving all facility to hear, to speak, to think, to worship. This is the Society's work. Unless you hear, how can you speak? The first task is given *śrotavyaḥ*. Then *kīrtitavyaś ca dhyeyaḥ pūjyaś ca nityadā*. These are the processes. You have to hear. And hearing, you have to repeat, chant. And then you have to think. You have to worship. These are the processes.

Upendra: "Swamiji ... so we have to hear, I understand. But do we speak, or do we first listen for a long time and then speak?"

Prabhupāda: "No. Why a long time? Suppose you hear two lines. You repeat that two lines. And aside from everything else, you hear Hare Kṛṣṇa. So you can chant Hare Kṛṣṇa. What is the difficulty there? *Śrotavyaḥ kīrtitavyaś ca.* You have to hear and chant. So if you cannot remember all the topics which we are speaking from the *Bhagavad-gītā* or *Śrīmad-Bhāgavatam,* you can at least remember this: Hare Kṛṣṇa. Therefore, it is the easiest process. You hear Hare Kṛṣṇa and chant Hare Kṛṣṇa. The other things will come automatically.

"Now, this is possible for everyone. Even the child can repeat Hare Kṛṣṇa. What is the difficulty? You hear Hare Kṛṣṇa and chant Hare Kṛṣṇa. We are not giving you very difficult or troublesome task. Then everything will follow. We are giving you everything. But if you feel in the beginning it is difficult, then you can do this—this is very nice—chant Hare Kṛṣṇa. You are doing that, actually. Hearing and chanting—this process will help you. It is the basic principle of advancement in spiritual life. Without hearing, we shall simply concoct, waste our time, and mislead people. We have to hear from the authoritative sources."

Śrīla Prabhupāda paused. The philosophical talk had been rigorous, lasting about forty-five minutes. He wasn't tired—he could have gone on—but now he wanted to conduct the deity installation. Everything necessary for spiritual life was here: the temple, the devotees, the books, the Deity, *prasādam.* He wanted these young people to take advantage of it. Why should they remain living like animals and thinking of spiritual life as a vague groping for "something"? They should take advantage of Kṛṣṇa's mercy and be successful and happy. And for this, Prabhupāda was their tireless servant.

Prabhupāda: "So, Hayagrīva? Come here." Prabhupāda had had the devotees arrange for a large candle on a plate. The ceremony he had planned would be a simple one, with devotees and guests one after another coming up and offering the flame in circles before the Jagannātha deities. "This should be lighted up," Śrīla Prabhupāda said, "and when there is *kīrtana,* one must be doing like this before the Deity. [Śrīla Prabhupāda moved his hands around in a circle before the Deity.] You see?"

Hayagrīva: "Yes, yes."

Prabhupāda: "Yes, with the *kīrtana.* And then when one person is tired he should hand it over to another person, devotee. When he is tired he should give to another—as long as the *kīrtana* will go on. This should be done with the *kīrtana* just now. Do you follow? Yes. You begin, and when you are tired you hand over to another. It will go on like that."

Śrīla Prabhupāda, from his seat, guided Hayagrīva in approaching the Deity with the lit candle. Some of the girls tittered with nervous expectation. "Before the Deity," Śrīla Prabhupāda said. "All right. Now better begin *kīrtana*."

Prabhupāda began playing *karatālas* and singing the Hare Kṛṣṇa *mantra* to the popular melody he had introduced in America. "Just in front," he called out, gesturing to Hayagrīva to stand more directly before the deities. Devotees and guests began rising to their feet and dancing, arms raised, bodies swaying rhythmically back and forth as they faced the bright, personal forms of the deities and chanted. Colored lights within the canopy began flashing intermittently blue, red, and yellow, highlighting the extraordinary eyes of Lord Jagannātha, Subhadrā, and Balarāma. Mukunda, who had arranged the lights, smiled and looked to Swamiji, hoping for approval. Prabhupāda nodded and continued forcefully singing Hare Kṛṣṇa.

The young hippies were enthusiastic in singing and dancing, knowing that the *kīrtana* usually lasted an hour. Some had grasped the Swami's words when he had spoken of fixing the mind on the personal form of the Supreme Lord; and they had understood when he had looked up at the deities and said, "Here is Kṛṣṇa." Others hadn't followed, but thought that it was just great and blissful to sing Hare Kṛṣṇa and look at the grinning, big-eyed deities up on the altar, amid the flowers and billowing incense.

Prabhupāda watched with pleasure as one person after another took a turn at offering the candle before Lord Jagannātha. This was a simple procedure for installing the Deity. Although in big temples in India the installation of the Deity was a complex, exact procedure, requiring several days of continuous rituals directed by highly paid priests, in San Francisco there were no *brāhmaṇa* priests to pay, and the many other standards would be impossible to maintain.

For non-Hindus to handle Lord Jagannātha and conduct His worship would be considered heresy by the caste-conscious *brāhmaṇas* of India. Except for Prabhupāda, none of the persons present would have been allowed even to enter the temple at Jagannātha Purī. The white man, the Westerner, was not allowed to see Lord Jagannātha except once a year as He rode in His cart during the Ratha-yātrā festival. But these restrictions were social customs, not the scriptural injunctions. Śrīla Bhaktisiddhānta Sarasvatī had introduced Deity worship and initiation for anyone, regardless of caste, race, or nationality. And Bhaktivinoda Ṭhākura, Śrīla Bhaktisiddhānta Sarasvatī's father, had longed for the day when the people of the West would mingle with their Indian brothers and chant Hare Kṛṣṇa.

Śrīla Prabhupāda had come to the West to fulfill the desires and the vision of his spiritual master and of Bhaktivinoda Ṭhākura by creating Vaiṣṇavas among the Westerners. Now, if the Westerners were to become actual devotees, they would have to be given the Deity worship. Otherwise it would be more difficult for them to become purified. Śrīla Prabhupāda was confident in his spiritual master's direction and in the scriptures. He had faith that Lord Jagannātha was especially merciful to the fallen. He prayed that the Lord of the universe would not be offended by His reception at New Jagannātha Purī.

When the *kīrtana* ended, Prabhupāda asked Haridāsa to bring him the candle. Prabhupāda passed his hands across the flame and touched them to his forehead. "Yes," he said, "show everyone. Each and every one. Whatever they can contribute. Here, take it like this and show everyone." He indicated that Haridāsa should present the candle before each person in the room so that all present could touch their hands to the flame as he had shown and then touch their foreheads. As Haridāsa went from person to person, a few devotees dropped some coins on the plate, and others followed.

Śrīla Prabhupāda explained further: "The *Bhāgavatam* has recommended hearing, chanting, thinking, and worshiping. This process which we just now introduced on the advent of Jagannātha Svāmī means that now this temple is now completely fixed. So this is the worshiping process. This is called *ārati.* So at the end of *kīrtana,* this *ārati* will go on. And the worshiping process is to take the heat of the light and, whatever your condition is, pay something for the worship. So this simple process, if you follow, you just see how you realize the Absolute Truth.

"Another thing I request you: All the devotees—when you come to the temple, you bring one fruit and one flower. If you can bring more fruit, more flower, it is very good. If not, it is not very expensive to bring one fruit and one flower. And offer it to the Deity. So I will request you, when you come to the temple you bring this. Whatever fruit it may be. It does not mean that you have to bring very costly fruit. Any fruit. Whatever you can afford. One fruit and one flower."

He paused, looking around the room: "Yes, now you can distribute *prasādam.*"

The guests sat in rows on the floor, and the devotees began serving *prasādam,* offering the first plate to Prabhupāda. The food preparations were those Prabhupāda had personally taught the devotees in his kitchen: *samosās, halavā, purīs,* rice, several cooked vegetables, fruit chutney, sweets—all the Sunday specials. The guests loved the *prasādam* and ate as much as they could get. While the devotees, especially the expert women, served more and more *prasādam,* the guests relaxed and enjoyed an evening of feasting and convivial conversation. After Prabhupāda tasted all the preparations, he looked up with raised eyebrows: "Very nice preparations. All glories to the cookers."

A few minutes later, as the feasting continued, Śrīla Prabhupāda spoke into the microphone, "*Jagannāthaḥ svāmī nayana-patha-gāmī bhavatu me.* Howard, repeat this."

Hayagrīva swallowed, cleared his throat, and spoke up: "*Jagannāthah svāmī nayana-patha-gāmī bhavatu me.*"

Prabhupāda: "Yes, this should be chanted. *Jagannāthaḥ svāmī nayana-patha-gāmī bhavatu me.*"

A boy asked what it meant. Hayagrīva replied, "Oh ... uh, Lord of the universe, please be present before me."

When Prabhupāda noticed an older, respectably dressed man leaving the room without receiving a feast plate, Prabhupāda became concerned: "Oh, why is he going away? Ask him to come."

A boy ran after him, opening the temple door and calling, "Please don't leave. Swamiji requests ..."

As the man reentered the storefront, Prabhupāda requested, "Please, please, take *prasādam.*" And turning to the servers, he instructed, "Give him *first.*" And so the feasting continued beneath the altar of Lord Jagannātha and under the auspices of His servant, Śrīla Prabhupāda.

The next day, acting on a whim, the devotees took the Jagannātha Deity off the altar and carried Him to Golden Gate Park for a *kīrtana.* Within minutes, hundreds gathered in the meadow below Hippie Hill, dancing and chanting around Lord Jagannātha. After several hours, the devotees returned Him to the altar.

Prabhupāda disapproved: "The Deity should never leave the temple. The deities don't go out to see the people, except on special occasions. They are not for parks for birds to drop stool on. If you want to see the deities, you have to visit *them.*"

Lord Jagannātha's presence quickly beautified the temple. Devotees made garlands for Him daily. Jadurāṇī's paintings of Lord Viṣṇu arrived from New York, and Govinda dāsī had painted a large portrait of Śrīla Prabhupāda, which now hung beside his seat. Devotees also put Indian prints of Kṛṣṇa on the walls. The lights flashing upon Lord Jagannātha made His eyes seem to pulsate and His colors move and jump, and He became a special attraction in the psychedelic neighborhood of Haight-Ashbury.

As Prabhupāda had requested, devotees and guests began bringing offerings before the altar of Lord Jagannātha. Hippies would come by and leave whatever they could: a stalk of wheat, half a loaf of bread, a box of Saltines, a piece of fudge, or candles, flowers, or fruit. Hearing that before using something for yourself you should first offer it to God, some hippies began bringing their new clothes and offering them with a prayer to Lord Jagannātha before wearing them. These hippies didn't follow Lord Jagannātha's instructions, but they wanted His blessings.

Each night, the devotees performed the *ārati* ceremony just as Prabhupāda had taught them, taking turns offering a candle before Lord Jagannātha. When the devotees asked whether they could add anything to the ceremony, Prabhupāda said yes, they could also offer incense. He said there were many more details of Deity worship, numerous enough to keep the devotees busy twenty-four hours a day; but if he were to tell them everything at once, they would faint.

Speaking privately in his room to one of his disciples, Prabhupāda said that during *kīrtana* in the temple he thought of Lord Caitanya dancing before Lord Jagannātha. He told how Lord Caitanya had traveled to Purī and danced before Lord Jagannātha in such ecstasy that He had been unable to say anything more than "Jag—, Jag—." Lord Caitanya had been thinking, "Kṛṣṇa, for so long I wanted to see You. And now I am seeing You." When Lord Caitanya had lived in Purī, as many as five hundred men at a time would visit Him, and every evening there would be a huge *kīrtana* with four parties, each with four *mṛdaṅga* players and eight *karatāla* players. "One party this side, one party this side," Prabhupāda explained. "One party back side, one party front side. And Caitanya Mahāprabhu in the middle. They would all dance, and the four parties would chant, 'Hare Kṛṣṇa, Hare Kṛṣṇa, Kṛṣṇa Kṛṣṇa ...' That was going on every evening so long He stayed at Jagannātha Purī."

The devotees understood that there was a great difference between themselves and Swamiji. He had never been a hippie. He wasn't at home amid the illusion of Haight-Ashbury's LSD, psychedelic posters, rock musicians, hippie jargon, and street people. They knew he was different, though sometimes they forgot. He spent so much time with them every day—eating with them, joking with them, depending on them. But then sometimes they would remember his special identity. When they chanted with him in the temple before Lord Jagannātha, he, unlike them, would be thinking of Lord Caitanya's *kīrtanas* before Lord Jagannātha in Purī. When Lord Caitanya had seen Jagannātha, He had seen Kṛṣṇa, and His love for Kṛṣṇa had been so great that He had gone mad. Prabhupāda thought of these things to a degree far beyond what his disciples could understand—and yet he remained with them as their dear friend and spiritual instructor. He was their servant, teaching them to pray, like him, to be able to serve Kṛṣṇa: "O Lord of the universe, kindly be visible unto me."

* * *

Govinda dāsī had a question for Swamiji. He had mentioned briefly that Lord Caitanya used to cry in separation from Kṛṣṇa and had once even thrown Himself into a river, crying, "Where is Kṛṣṇa?" She was unsure whether her question would be proper, but she waited for an opportunity to ask it.

One evening after the lecture, when Prabhupāda asked for questions and there were none, Govinda dāsī thought, "This is my chance." But she hesitated. Her question wasn't on the subject of his lecture, and besides, she didn't like to ask questions in public.

"No question?" Śrīla Prabhupāda looked around. Govinda dāsī thought Swamiji seemed disappointed that there were no questions. He had said several times that they should ask questions and clear up any doubts. Again he asked, "Have you got any questions?"

Govinda dāsī: "Uh, well, could you tell about Lord Caitanya asking ..."

Prabhupāda: "*Hmm*?"

Govinda dāsī: "... asking where is Kṛṣṇa?"

Prabhupāda: "*Hmm*?"

Govinda dāsī: "Could you tell about Lord Caitanya asking where is Kṛṣṇa and falling in the water? Or would that be not ..."

Prabhupāda smiled. "Yes, yes. Very nice. Your question is very nice. Oh, I am very glad.

"Lord Caitanya—He was the greatest symbol of *kṛṣṇa-bhakti,* a devotee of Kṛṣṇa. So just see from His life. He never said that, 'I have seen Kṛṣṇa.' Never said, 'I have seen Kṛṣṇa.' He was *mad* after Kṛṣṇa. That is the process of Caitanya philosophy. It is called *viraha. Viraha* means 'separation' ... 'separation': 'Kṛṣṇa, You are so good, You are so merciful, You are so nice. But I am so rascal, I am so full of sin, that I cannot see You. I have no qualification to see You.' So in this way, if one feels the separation of Kṛṣṇa—'Kṛṣṇa, I want to see You, but I am so disqualified that I cannot see You'—these feelings of separation will make you enriched in Kṛṣṇa consciousness. Feelings of separation. Not that 'Kṛṣṇa, I have seen You. Finished. All right. I have understood You. Finished. All my business finished.' No! *Perpetually.* Think of yourself that 'I am unfit to see Kṛṣṇa.' That will enrich you in Kṛṣṇa consciousness.

"Caitanya Mahāprabhu displayed this—these feelings of separation. This is Rādhārāṇī's separation. When Kṛṣṇa went from Vṛndāvana to His place, His father's place, Rādhārāṇī was feeling in that way—always mad after Kṛṣṇa. So Kṛṣṇa Caitanya, Caitanya Mahāprabhu, took the separation feeling of Rādhārāṇī. That is the best way of worshiping Kṛṣṇa, becoming Kṛṣṇa conscious. So you know that Lord Caitanya fell on the sea: 'Kṛṣṇa, if You are here. Kṛṣṇa, if You are here.'

"Similarly, the next devotees, Lord Caitanya's direct disciples, the Gosvāmīs—Rūpa Gosvāmī, Sanātana Gosvāmī—they also, the same disciplic succession, they also worship Kṛṣṇa in that separation feeling. There is a nice verse about them."

Śrīla Prabhupāda sang:

he rādhe vraja-devike ca lalite he nanda-sūno kutaḥ
śrī-govardhana-kalpa-pādapa-tale kālindi-vane kutaḥ
ghoṣantav iti sarvato vraja-pure khedair mahā-vihvalau
*vande rūpa-sanātanau raghu-yugau śrī-jīva-gopālakau**

"These Gosvāmīs also, later on when they were very much mature in devotional service—what were they doing? They were *daily* in the Vṛndāvana-dhāma, just like a madman: 'Kṛṣṇa, where You are?' That is the quality.

"It is a very nice question."

Śrīla Prabhupāda paused and uttered a thoughtful "*Mmm.*" He remained silent. They also remained silent, watching him. He sat cross-legged on the black velvet pillow on the redwood dais. His hands were folded, his eyes closed. And he became overpowered by inner feelings of ecstasy. Although the simple devotees present could not know what was happening, they could *see* him enter a deep inward state. They could feel the atmosphere transform into awesome devotional stillness. They kept their eyes fixed on him.

A minute and a half passed. Śrīla Prabhupāda uttered another thoughtful "*Mmm*" and opened his eyes—they were filled with tears. He reached over and grasped his *karatālas,* which rattled in his hand. But he moved no further. Again he withdrew from external consciousness.

Another minute of silence passed. The minute seemed extremely calm, yet intense and long. Another minute passed. After almost four minutes, Prabhupāda cleared his throat and struck the *karatālas* together, beginning the slow rhythm. A devotee began the one-note drone on the harmonium. Prabhupāda sang: *govinda jaya jaya gopāla jaya jaya/ rādhā-ramaṇa hari govinda jaya jaya,* building the chanting to a lively pace. After about ten minutes the *kīrtana* stopped, and Prabhupāda left the room.

---

* "I offer my respectful obeisances to the six Gosvāmīs, namely, Śrī Rūpa Gosvāmī, Śrī Sanātana Gosvāmī, Śrī Raghunātha Bhaṭṭa Gosvāmī, Śrī Raghunātha dāsa Gosvāmī, Śrī Jīva Gosvāmī, and Śrī Gopāla Bhaṭṭa Gosvāmī, who were chanting very loudly everywhere in Vṛndāvana, shouting, 'Queen of Vṛndāvana, Rādhārāṇī! O Lalitā! O son of Nanda Mahārāja! Where are you all now? Are you just on the hill of Govardhana, or are you under the trees on the bank of the Yamunā? Where are you?' These were their moods in executing Kṛṣṇa consciousness."

As the devotees rose and began their various duties—some leaving out the front door behind Prabhupāda and going to the kitchen, others coming together for conversation—they all knew that their spiritual master had been intensely feeling separation from Kṛṣṇa. They had no doubt that it was a deep ecstasy, because just by being in his presence during that long and special stillness they also had felt a glimmer of the same love for Kṛṣṇa.

* * *

On the invitation of his disciples, Śrīla Prabhupāda agreed to hold a *kīrtana* on the beach. On a Tuesday night, with no *kīrtana* or lecture scheduled in the temple, he got into the back seat of one of the devotees' cars. About a dozen initiated followers and a couple of dogs got into other cars, and together they traveled to the beach. When they arrived, some devotees went running across the beach, gathering driftwood and building a fire in the shelter of a sand dune.

The late afternoon air was cool, and there was a seaside wind. Prabhupāda was dressed in a long checkered coat over a hooded sweatshirt. During the *kīrtana* he clapped and danced while the devotees joined hands, forming a circle around him. As the sun was setting, all the devotees faced the ocean, raising their arms and singing as loudly as they could, "*Hariiiiibol*!" But with the surf pounding in on the coast and with the great expanse of windy air around them, their *kīrtana* sounded very small.

Gathering around the fire, the devotees buried foil-wrapped potatoes and foil-wrapped apples filled with raisins and brown sugar under the coals. It was their idea, but Prabhupāda was happy to comply with their ideas of California *kīrtana* fun.

Haridāsa and Hayagrīva had composed a song about the sage Nārada Muni, and they sang it for Prabhupāda.

> Do you know who is the first eternal spaceman of this universe?
> The first to send his wild, wild vibrations
> To all those cosmic superstations?
> For the song he always shouts
> Sends the planets flipping out.
> But I'll tell you before you think me loony

That I'm talking about Narada Muni,
Singing
HARE KRISHNA HARE KRISHNA
KRISHNA KRISHNA HARE HARE
HARE RAMA HARE RAMA
RAMA RAMA HARE HARE

Prabhupāda laughed. He liked anything that had chanting in it. And he asked them to compose more such songs for their countrymen.

Walking together along the beach, they came upon an old, dilapidated Dutch windmill. "Mukunda," Prabhupāda said, "you should approach the government and tell them that we will restore this windmill if they let us build a temple on this site." Mukunda took it as a joke at first, but then he saw that Prabhupāda was completely serious. Mukunda said he would inquire about it.

Prabhupāda, in his oversized checkered coat buttoned up to the neck, was the beloved center of the devotees' outing. After their walk, he sat with them on a big log, eating baked potatoes smeared with melted butter; and when he finished he threw his remnants to the dogs.

As the night grew dark, stars appeared high over the ocean, and the devotees stood close around Prabhupāda for a last *kīrtana*. Then, just as in the temple, they bowed down, and Prabhupāda called out the prayers to the Lord and the disciplic succession. But he ended: "All glories to the assembled devotees! All glories to the assembled devotees! All glories to the Pacific Ocean!"

They all laughed. Swamiji was doing what his disciples wanted: enjoying an evening *kīrtana*-cookout at the beach with them. And they were doing what he wanted: chanting the *mahā-mantra*, becoming devotees of Kṛṣṇa, and becoming happy.

* * *

Hayagrīva sat facing Prabhupāda, alone with Prabhupāda in his room. A few days before, Hayagrīva had shown Prabhupāda a play about Lord Caitanya he had found in the library, and Prabhupāda had said it wasn't bona fide. So Prabhupāda decided to prepare an outline for a bona fide play and have Hayagrīva write it. "I will give you the whole plot complete," Śrīla Prabhupāda said. "Then all you will have to do is execute it."

Prabhupāda was in a relaxed, jolly mood, intent on relating the events of Lord Caitanya's life. He had prepared an outline of twenty-three scenes, and now he wanted to expound each one. Hayagrīva had barely enough time to understand what Prabhupāda was about to do and almost no time to prepare himself for note-taking as Prabhupāda began describing the first scene.

"First scene," he began, "is that people are passing on the road with *saṅkīrtana,* just as we do. There is a very nice procession with *mṛdaṅga* and *karatālas* and that bugle, and all people are doing *saṅkīrtana* in the ordinary way. We have to make a nice procession.

"The second scene shows Kali as decorated blackish with royal dress and very ugly features. And his queen is another ugly-featured lady. So they are disturbed. They will talk amongst themselves that, 'There is the *saṅkīrtana* movement now, so how shall we prosecute our business in this Age of Quarrel, Kali-yuga?' In that scene there will be in one corner two or three people drinking. The scene will be like that. The Age of Quarrel personified and his consort are sitting in the center. In one corner someone is taking part in drinking, and in another part somebody is illicitly talking of lust and love with a woman. In another section there is slaughtering of a cow, and in another section, gambling. In this way, that scene should be adjusted. And in the middle, the ugly man, Kali, and the ugly woman will talk that, 'We are now in danger. The *saṅkīrtana* movement has been started. What to do?' In this way, you have to finish that scene.

"Then the third scene is very nice—*rāsa* dance."

Hayagrīva interrupted. He had some of his own ideas about what he called "the dramatic point of view." "I think," Hayagrīva said, strongly articulating his words, "this can apply for the whole world, in the sense that the names may be Indian but I think the exhibition you described of the assembly of Kali and his consort Sin and the exhibition of illicit sex and the slaughterhouse can all be from Western prototypes."

Śrīla Prabhupāda said that he had no objection to Hayagrīva's suggestion but that he didn't want people to think he was singling out Westerners, as if they were the only ones who committed illicit sex. Hayagrīva was about to reply but decided that this was no time to quibble; Swamiji was eager to go on describing the pastimes of Lord Caitanya.

Prabhupāda: "*Rāsa* dance means Kṛṣṇa and Rādhārāṇī in the center and the *gopīs* are surrounding. You have seen that surrounding scene when they were dancing with us the other day in the park hand to hand?"

Hayagrīva: "Yes, yes."

Prabhupāda: "So one Kṛṣṇa and one *gopī*—they are dancing. That should be the scene. Then the *rāsa* dance should be stopped, and Kṛṣṇa will talk with the *gopīs*. Kṛṣṇa will say to the *gopīs* that, 'My dear friends, you have come to Me in the dead of night. It is not very good, because it is the duty of every woman to please her husband. So what your husband will think if you come in such dead of night? So please go back.'

"So in this way the *gopīs* will reply that, 'You cannot request us to go back, because with great difficulty and with great ecstatic desire we have come to You. And it is not Your duty to ask us to go back.' In this way, you arrange some talking that Kṛṣṇa is asking them to go back but they are insisting, 'No, let us continue our *rāsa* dance.'

"Then when the *rāsa* dance is finished, the *gopīs* will go, and then Kṛṣṇa will say, 'These *gopīs* are My heart and soul. They are so sincere devotees they do not care for family encumbrances or any bad name. They come to Me. So how shall I repay them?' He was thinking, 'How shall I repay their ecstatic love?' So He thought that, 'I cannot repay them unless and until I take up their situation to understand Me. But I Myself cannot understand Me. I have to take the position of the *gopīs*—how they are loving Me.'

"So with that consideration He took the form of Lord Caitanya. Therefore, Kṛṣṇa is blackish, and Lord Caitanya is the color of the *gopīs*. The whole life of Lord Caitanya is the representation of the *gopīs'* love toward Kṛṣṇa. That should be painted in the picture of this scene. Do you have anything to ask?"

Hayagrīva: "This is His determination to incarnate as Lord Caitanya?"

Prabhupāda: "Lord Caitanya, yes."

Hayagrīva: "In order to ...?"

Prabhupāda: "In order to appreciate Kṛṣṇa in the form of a *gopī*. Just like I have got dealings with you. So you have got your individuality, and I have got my individuality. But if I want to study how you are so much obedient and loving to me, then I have to go to your position. It is very natural psychology. You have to paint in that way."

Prabhupāda described and explained one story after another, most of them new to Hayagrīva. Hayagrīva couldn't properly spell or even pronounce the names; he didn't know who Lord Caitanya's mother was or whether Nityānanda was a devotee. And when Prabhupāda told the story of Kṣīra-corā-gopīnātha, the Deity who stole condensed milk for His devotee, Hayagrīva got confused and thought Prabhupāda had said that Lord Caitanya had stolen the condensed milk.

Prabhupāda: "No. Oh. You did not hear? Caitanya, after seeing the Deity, He was sitting and seeing, and meantime Nityānanda Prabhu narrated the story how the Deity's name became Kṣīra-corā-gopīnātha. You do not follow me?"

Hayagrīva groped, "Nityānanda?"

Prabhupāda: "Nityānanda was going with Lord Caitanya ..."

Hayagrīva: "Nityānanda was narrating this to Lord Caitanya?"

Prabhupāda: "Yes, the Deity was known as Kṣīra-corā-gopīnātha. The story"—Prabhupāda repeated for the third time—"was narrated that formerly He stole one pot of condensed milk for His devotee."

Hayagrīva: "Now, what direct relationship does this have to Lord Caitanya?"

Prabhupāda: "Lord Caitanya visited this temple. Anyone in those days going to Jagannātha Purī from Bengal had to pass that way. And on the way, the Kṣīra-corā-gopīnātha temple is there. So everyone used to visit. Formerly, Mādhavendra Purī also visited, and for him the Deity stole the condensed milk. From that time, the Deity is known as Kṣīra-corā-gopīnātha. That story was narrated to Caitanya Mahāprabhu. So while sitting before the Deity, the story was narrated, and Caitanya Mahāprabhu relished that God is so kind that sometimes He steals for His devotee. This is the significance. So here the scene should be arranged that it is a very nice temple, the Deity is within, and Lord Caitanya has entered while chanting Hare Kṛṣṇa. And then He saw the worship, *ārati.* These things are to be shown in this scene. And a little story about Him, that's all."

When Prabhupāda told of Lord Caitanya's visit to the Sākṣi-gopāla temple, Hayagrīva again got lost. "Do you follow?" Prabhupāda asked.

"No," Hayagrīva chuckled. "No."

Eventually, Hayagrīva stopped asking questions and interrupting. Although he had very little knowledge of the identity or meaning of the characters, as soon as he had heard a little about them he had been trying to adjust and rearrange their activities from the "dramatic point of view." Prabhupāda had raised no objections to Hayagrīva's inquiries. In fact, Prabhupāda had invited them, so that Hayagrīva could understand how to present the play. Hayagrīva, however, decided to first try to hear what Prabhupāda was saying.

By the end of the first hour of their talk, Prabhupāda had narrated many scenes from the first half of Lord Caitanya's life: His teasing the *brāhmaṇas* by the Ganges at age five, His civil disobedience movement against the Muhammadan magistrate, His accepting the renounced order at age twenty-four, His last meeting with His beloved mother, His traveling to Purī and touring South India, His meeting and instructing disciples like Sārvabhauma, Rāmānanda Rāya, and Rūpa Gosvāmī and Sanātana Gosvāmī.

Finally Prabhupāda's morning schedule permitted him to go no further. It was time for him to bathe and take lunch. The next day they would meet again.

At the next session Hayagrīva listened more carefully, and the transcendental scenes came quickly, one after another. As Prabhupāda described each scene, speaking the words and thoughts of Lord Caitanya and His associates, Prabhupāda seemed to be seeing the scenes enacted before him. He especially became moved when he spoke of Lord Caitanya and Haridāsa Ṭhākura.

"The life of Haridāsa Ṭhākura," Prabhupāda said, "is that he was born in a Muhammadan family. Some way or other he became a devotee, and he was chanting three hundred thousand times: 'Hare Kṛṣṇa, Hare Kṛṣṇa, Kṛṣṇa Kṛṣṇa, Hare Hare/ Hare Rāma, Hare Rāma, Rāma Rāma, Hare Hare.' And Caitanya Mahāprabhu made him the *ācārya,* the authority of chanting. Therefore, we glorify him—*nāmācārya* Haridāsa Ṭhākura *kī jaya*—because he was made the *ācārya,* the authority of chanting Hare Kṛṣṇa.

"When Lord Caitanya took *sannyāsa,* Haridāsa Ṭhākura decided, 'My dear Lord, You are leaving Navadvīpa. Then what is the use of my life? Either You take me or let me die.'

"So Caitanya Mahāprabhu said, 'No. Why shall you die? You come with Me.' So He took him to Jagannātha Purī. In Jagannātha Purī, because he considered himself born of a Muhammadan family, Haridāsa did not enter the temple. But Caitanya Mahāprabhu gave him a place at

Kāśīnātha Miśra's house. There he was chanting, and Caitanya Mahāprabhu was sending him *prasādam.* In that way he was passing his days. And Caitanya used to come and see him daily."

Śrīla Prabhupāda wanted a scene for the passing away of Haridāsa Ṭhākura.

Hayagrīva: "Is this the same Haridāsa the Muhammadans threw into the river?"

"Yes," Prabhupāda said.

Then very casually Hayagrīva mused aloud, "So he finally met his end there in the fifth scene?"

Prabhupāda hesitated. Here again Hayagrīva revealed his lack of transcendental knowledge, talking as though Haridāsa's passing away was the same as an ordinary man's meeting his end.

"All right," Hayagrīva cued him, "what is this particular incident?"

Prabhupāda: "The particular incident is significant. Caitanya Mahāprabhu was a *brāhmaṇa,* and He was a *sannyāsī.* According to social custom, He should not even touch a Muhammadan. But this Haridāsa Ṭhākura was a Muhammadan, and yet at his death He took the body Himself and danced. And He put him in the graveyard and distributed *prasādam.*

"Because Haridāsa was a Muhammadan, he did not enter the temple of Jagannātha Purī, because the Hindus were very strict. Haridāsa was a devotee, but he thought: 'Why should I create some row?' So Caitanya Mahāprabhu appreciated Haridāsa's humble behavior. Although he had become a devotee, he was not forcibly going to the temple. But then Caitanya Mahāprabhu Himself was daily coming and seeing him. While going to take bath in the sea, He will first of all see Haridāsa: 'Haridāsa, what you are doing?' Haridāsa will offer his respect, and He will sit and talk for some time. Then Caitanya Mahāprabhu will go and take His bath.

"In this way, one day when He came He saw Haridāsa not feeling very well: 'Haridāsa, how is your health?'

" 'Yes, sir, it is not very ... after all, it is the body.'

"Then the third day He saw that Haridāsa is going to leave his body today. So Caitanya Mahāprabhu asked him, 'Haridāsa, what do you desire?' Both of them could understand. Haridāsa said that, 'This is my last stage. If You kindly stand before me.' "

Śrīla Prabhupāda became caught in the intense spiritual emotions of the scene, as if it were happening before him. He closed his eyes: "*Mmm.*" He stopped talking. Then he began again slowly, haltingly. "So Caitanya Mahāprabhu stood before him ... and he left his body." Prabhupāda sighed and became silent. Hayagrīva sat staring at the floor. When he glanced up, he saw that Swamiji was crying.

Prabhupāda quickly summed up a few last scenes and ended his outline. "Now you write," he told Hayagrīva, "and I shall make some addition or alteration. This is the synopsis and framework. Now you can proceed." Hayagrīva left the room. The material was lengthy, and whether he would ever write the play was doubtful. But he was thankful to have received this special discourse.

* * *

Sitting on a bridge table in the student lounge, chanting into a little microphone while his followers played their instruments, Prabhupāda began the *kīrtana* at Stanford University. At first there were about twenty students, but gradually more entered the lounge and gathered around. Everyone was chanting. Then suddenly the lounge became transformed, as more than two hundred Stanford students, most of them completely new to the Hare Kṛṣṇa *mantra,* danced and chanted with as much enthusiasm as the most uninhibited Haight-Ashbury crowd. Prabhupāda led the *kīrtana* for more than an hour.

In his talk afterwards he explained what they had all just experienced: "This Hare Kṛṣṇa dance is the best process for getting out of this illusion that 'I am this body.' Our Society is trying to distribute to the world the priceless gift of the Lord. You did not understand the words, but you still felt the ecstasy to dance."

Prabhupāda took questions from the audience. Everything proceeded in a standard fashion until someone asked whether college students should respond to the military draft. Prabhupāda replied that since they had elected their own government, there was no use complaining if the government told them to go to war. But some of the students—the same students who had chanted and danced only minutes before—began to shout, "No! No!" Prabhupāda tried explaining his point, but they raised their voices in anger until the hall became a bedlam of shouting. Finally

Śrīla Prabhupāda picked up his *karatālas* and began chanting again, and the dissenters left.

The next day, the *Palo Alto Times* ran a front-page story with headlines and a photo of the *kīrtana.*

Ancient trance dance features swami's visit to Stanford

> Hold on there a minute, all you "with it" people. There's a new dance about to sweep the country. It's called "the swami."
>
> It's going to replace the frug, watusi, swim and even the good old barn stomp.
>
> Why? Because you can do any old step to it and at the same time find real happiness. You can rid yourself of the illusion that you and your body are inseparable. ...
>
> The chant started quietly but gained volume as more people joined in.
>
> After half an hour, a long-haired youth with three strings of red beads around his neck stood up and began to dance to the music. He closed his eyes in ecstasy and held his hands palms up shoulder high.
>
> Two girls soon followed him. One had a string of bells around her neck.
>
> A bearded fellow with a fluorescent pink skull cap joined in, still beating on his tambourine.
>
> The Swami cut in a microphone in front of him, and the added volume provoked others to chant and stomp more loudly.
>
> A pretty girl in a sari danced as if in a hypnotic trance.
>
> A short dark man neatly dressed in suit and tie threw off his shoes and joined in. A young math professor did likewise. A pretty, blond, 3-year-old girl rocked and swayed in one corner.
>
> Suddenly most of the audience was dancing and chanting. The pace grew faster and faster. Faces streamed with sweat; the temperature soared.
>
> Then it all stopped.

Śrīla Prabhupāda was pleased with the article and asked for some photocopies of it. "What are they calling the dance?" he laughed. "The Swami?" Across the top of the *kīrtana* photo he typed, "Everyone joins in complete ecstasy when Swami Bhaktivedanta chants his hypnotic Hare Kṛṣṇa."

The devotees got Prabhupāda an engagement at a YMCA, where the audience consisted almost entirely of children. The devotees had decorated the hall with posters of Kṛṣṇa and had hung a big sign with the *mahā-mantra* on it. The children chanted along with Prabhupāda during *kīrtana.* Just before the lecture, Gurudāsa reminded him, "Maybe the talk should be simple, since they are all between nine and fourteen years old." Prabhupāda nodded silently.

"Is there a student here who is intelligent?" Prabhupāda began. No one responded. After a moment a twelve-year-old boy, urged by his teachers and fellow students, raised his hand. Prabhupāda motioned for him to come forward. The boy wore thick glasses, short pants, and a blazer, and his hair was combed back very neatly. Pointing to the boy's head, Prabhupāda asked, "What is that?"

The boy almost scoffed at the simpleness of the question: "My head!"

Prabhupāda then pointed to the boy's arm and said quietly, "What is that?"

"My arm!" the boy said.

Prabhupāda then pointed to the boy's foot: "What is that?"

"My foot," the boy answered, still looking incredulous.

"Yes," Śrīla Prabhupāda said. "You say this is *my* head, *my* arm, *my* foot—*my* body. But where are *you*?" The boy stood perplexed, unable to answer Prabhupāda's simple question.

"We say *my* hand," Śrīla Prabhupāda continued, "but who is the owner of my hand? We say *my* hand, so that means someone owns my hand. But where does the owner live? I do not say '*I* hand,' I say '*my* hand.' So my hand and I are different. I am within my body, and you are within your body. But I am not my body, and you are not your body. We are different from the body. Real intelligence means to know who *I* am."

Haight-Ashbury's Psychedelic Shop, a popular hippie gathering place, had extended to Prabhupāda many invitations to come and speak. After the Mantra-Rock Dance the hippies there had put a sign in the window: A Night of Consciousness. Also in response to the Mantra-Rock Dance, they had opened a meditation room in the rear of their store. But since the hippies at the Psychedelic Shop were almost always intoxicated, Prabhupāda's followers had said that it wouldn't be a good idea for Prabhupāda to go. But the hippies kept entreating. Finally the devotees relented, advising Prabhupāda it might be all right for him to go.

So one Saturday night, Prabhupāda and two devotees walked over to Haight Street, to the Psychedelic Shop. Young people crowded the streets: hippies sitting along the sidewalk selling hashish pipes and other dope paraphernalia; homosexuals; wildly costumed hippies with painted faces; small groups smoking marijuana, drinking, singing, and playing guitars—a typical evening on Haight Street.

At the Psychedelic Shop, marijuana and tobacco smoke hung heavy in the air, mingling with the smell of alcohol and bodies. Prabhupāda entered the meditation room, its ceiling and walls covered with madrases, and sat down. The room was full of hippies, many lying down, heavily intoxicated, looking up at him with half-closed eyes. He spoke in a low voice, but his presence somehow held their attention. Although lethargic, the group was appreciative, and after Prabhupāda had finished, those who were still conscious expressed their approval.

* * *

On Saturday, April 1, near the end of his stay in San Francisco, Prabhupāda accepted an invitation from Lou Gottlieb, head of Morning Star Ranch, a nudist hippie commune. Morning Star was a bunch of young people living in the woods, the devotees explained to Prabhupāda. The hippies there had spiritual aspirations. They grew vegetables and worshiped the sun. They would hold hands and listen to the air. And naturally they were involved in lots of drug-taking and free sex.

When Lou came in the morning to pick up the Swami, they talked, and Prabhupāda gave him a *rasagullā* (a sweet made of bite-sized balls of curd simmered in sugar water). After a few minutes together in Prabhupāda's room, they started for Morning Star, sixty miles north of San Francisco.

Lou Gottlieb: *I told Swamiji to fasten his safety belt. He said no. He said Kṛṣṇa will handle it, or something. So on the way out I was showing off all my vast erudition in having read a biography of Ramakrishna. That's when Bhaktivedanta gave the best advice to the aspirant I ever heard. We were talking about Ramakrishna and Vivekananda and Aurobindo and this and that. So he said, "You know," putting a gentle hand on my knee, "when you have found your true path, all further investigation of comparative religion is merely sense enjoyment."*

Situated in a forest of redwoods more than two hundred feet tall, Morning Star Ranch occupied what had once been an egg farm. Some of the land had been cleared for farming. There were a few tents, some unsubstantial little huts, a couple of tree houses, but the only decent, insulated building was Lou's place, an old chicken house. The commune had about one hundred full-time members, with the number of residents rising to as many as three hundred on the weekends in warm weather, when people would come out to work in the garden or just walk around naked and get high.

Prabhupāda arrived at one in the afternoon on a beautiful sunny day. He first wanted to rest, so Lou offered his own house. Walking to Lou's place, Prabhupāda noticed a few nude men and women hoeing in the garden. One of the workers, a short, stocky young man, Herbie Bressack, stopped his work in the garden and came to greet the Swami.

Herbie: *Lou Gottlieb introduced us. We were planting potatoes at the time. He said, "This is Swami Bhaktivedanta." I came out of the garden and shook Swamiji's hand. I said, "Hello, Swami." He asked me, "What are you doing?" I told him that I was just planting potatoes. He then asked me what I was doing with my life. I didn't answer.*

After resting for a few minutes, Prabhupāda was ready for the *kīrtana.* He and Lou went to a hilly pasture where the hippies had placed a wooden seat for Prabhupāda before a bower of wild flowers arranged like a bandshell. Prabhupāda took his seat and began chanting. The commune members, all of whom had been anticipating the Swami's visit, gathered eagerly for the group meditation.

Mike Morissey: *Some people had clothes on, some people didn't. Some were dancing around. But Swamiji wasn't looking at our bodies, he was looking at our souls and giving us the mercy we needed.*

The *kīrtana* was well received. One of the members of the commune was so enthralled by the *kīrtana* that he decided to put on his clothes and go back to San Francisco with the Swami. Prabhupāda spoke very briefly, and then he prepared to leave, shaking hands and exchanging courtesies as he walked to the car.

Although Śrīla Prabhupāda hadn't spoken much philosophy, his *kīrtana* left a deep impression on the hippies at Morning Star. While leaving he had told one of the young men, "Keep chanting this Hare Kṛṣṇa *mantra* here." And they did.

Lou Gottlieb: *The Swami was an extremely intelligent guy with a job to do. There was no sanctimony or holy pretention, none of that eyes-lifted-silently-to-the-sky. All I remember is just a very pleasant, incredibly safe feeling. There's no doubt that the* mahā-mantra *— once you get the* mantra *into the head, it's there. It never stops. It's in the cells. It awakens the DNA or something. Shortly thereafter, half of the people at Morning*

Star got seriously into chanting. Those that did were extremely sincere God seekers. Their aspiration was a thousand percent sincere, considering the circumstances in which they were found. They were all dopers, that's for sure, but they definitely gave that up once they got in touch with the mahā-mantra.

* * *

His top cloth wrapped loosely around his shoulders, Prabhupāda stood a last moment by the open door of the car and looked back in farewell to the devotees and the storefront temple. It was no longer a mere storefront but had become something worthy: New Jagannātha Purī. Śrīla Bhaktisiddhānta Sarasvatī had asked him to come here. Who among his Godbrothers could imagine how crazy these American hippies were—hallucinating on drugs, crying out, "I am God!" So many girls and boys—unhappy, mad, despite their wealth and education. But now, through Kṛṣṇa consciousness, some were finding happiness.

The first day he had arrived the reporter had asked him why he had come to Haight-Ashbury. "Because the rent is cheap," he had replied. His desire was to spread the movement of Lord Caitanya; why else would he have come to such a dilapidated little storefront to live next to a Chinese laundry and Diggers' Free Store? The reporters had asked if he were inviting the hippies and Bohemians to take to Kṛṣṇa consciousness. "Yes," he had said, "everyone." But he had known that once joining him, his followers would become something different from what they had been before.

Now the devotees were a family. If they followed his instructions they would remain strong. If they were sincere, Kṛṣṇa would help them. Lord Jagannātha was present, and the devotees would have to worship Him faithfully. They would be purified by chanting Hare Kṛṣṇa and following their spiritual master's instructions.

Prabhupāda got into the car, accompanied by some of his disciples, and a devotee drove him to the airport. Several carloads of devotees followed behind.

At the airport the devotees were crying. But Prabhupāda assured them he would return if they would hold a Ratha-yātrā festival. "You must arrange a procession down the main street," he told them. "Do it nicely.

We must attract many people. They have such a procession yearly in Jagannātha Purī. At this time the Deity may leave the temple."

He would have to return, he knew, to tend the delicate devotional plants he had placed in their hearts. Otherwise, how could he expect these neophytes to survive in the ocean of material desires known as Haight-Ashbury? Repeatedly he promised them he would return. He asked them to cooperate among themselves—Mukunda, Śyāmasundara, Gurudāsa, Jayānanda, Subala, Gaurasundara, Hayagrīva, Haridāsa, and the girls.

Only two and a half months ago he had arrived here at this very terminal, greeted by a throng of chanting young people. Many were now his disciples, although just barely assuming their spiritual identities and vows. Yet he felt no compunctions about leaving them. He knew that some of them might fall away, but he couldn't stay with them always. His time was limited.

Śrīla Prabhupāda, the father of two small bands of neophytes, tenderly left one group and headed east, where the other group waited in a different mood, a mood of joyful reception.

CHAPTER TWENTY-FIVE

"Our Master Has Not Finished His Work"

THERE WAS NO warning that Śrīla Prabhupāda's health would break down; or, if there were, no one heeded it. As he moved from his devotees in San Francisco to his devotees in New York, no one passed any words that Swamiji should slow down. After the five-and-a-half hour jet flight, Prabhupāda spoke of a "blockading" in his ears, but he seemed all right. He didn't rest, but went straight through the festive airport reception into three hours of strong lecturing and chanting in the storefront at 26 Second Avenue. To his New York disciples he appeared dazzling and lovable, and by his presence, his glances, and his words, he increased their Kṛṣṇa consciousness. To them his advanced age, now nearing seventy-two years, was but another of his transcendental features. He was their strength, and they never thought to consider *his* strength.

In the temple, speaking from a new dais behind a velvet-covered lectern, Prabhupāda said, "In my absence things have improved." New paintings hung on the freshly painted white walls. Otherwise, it was the same tiny storefront where he had begun his International Society for Krishna Consciousness.

He had written them that he wanted to enter the new building on his return, but they had failed. And they had foolishly lost six thousand dollars. But without dwelling on this, Prabhupāda made a more important observation: his disciples, despite the physical absence of their spiritual master, had made progress by following his instructions.

As he sat looking happily at the freshly painted walls and the bright faces of his disciples, Prabhupāda explained how one obtained expertise in Kṛṣṇa consciousness by submissively following the spiritual master. He gave the example that although an engineer's apprentice may not be expert, if he turns a screw under the direct supervision of the expert engineer *he is acting as an expert.* Many of the devotees were relieved to hear this. They knew that giving up material desires was difficult and that they weren't going to become completely pure devotees overnight. Brahmānanda had even written a poem stating that if, after many lifetimes, he could chant one round of the Hare Kṛṣṇa *mantra, with attention,* he would consider this the greatest success. But Prabhupāda was explaining that even if they weren't expert in love of Kṛṣṇa, if they worked under an expert they were also acting as experts.

The next morning, with the fanfare of Prabhupāda's arrival past, it became apparent just how dependent the devotees were on their spiritual leader. The attendance was down to the dozen or so regulars, and Prabhupāda silently entered the storefront and began to lead the chanting. But when the moment came for the devotees to sing in response and Prabhupāda heard their first chorus, he looked out to them, startled and compassionate. Now he could hear: they were weak—more like croaking than singing. They *had* deteriorated in his absence! The *kīrtanas* had changed while he had been away, and now he was hearing what the devotees were like: helpless souls croaking without joy or verve.

Śrīla Prabhupāda lectured from *Caitanya-caritāmṛta.* "When flying from San Francisco I noticed that the plane was flying above an ocean of clouds. When I came from India by boat I saw an ocean of water, and on the plane I saw an ocean of clouds extending as far as you can see. Above the clouds is the sun, but when we come down through the clouds and land, everything in New York is dim and clouded. But the sun is still shining. Those clouds cannot cover the whole world. They cannot even cover the whole United States, which is no more than a speck in the universe. From an airplane we can see skyscrapers as very tiny. Similarly, from God's position, all this material nonsense is insignificant. As a living entity, I am very insignificant, and my tendency is to come down. But the sun doesn't have the come-down tendency. It is always above the clouds of *māyā. ...*"

A new boy raised his hand: "Why is it that one person, one soul, comes to Kṛṣṇa and another doesn't?"

Prabhupāda replied with another question: "Why is one soul in the Bowery and another has come to the Kṛṣṇa temple?" He paused, but no one could reply. "Because one wants to be here and the other doesn't," he explained. "It is a question of free will. If we use it properly, we can go to Kṛṣṇa. Otherwise we will stay down in the material world."

Everyone had something to ask Swamiji. Throughout the day, devotees would be in and out of his room, asking practical and philosophical questions. And they took up their old ways of reciprocating with him. Once again Prabhupāda was telling Acyutānanda what to cook for lunch and explaining to him that an expert servant learns to anticipate what the master wants even before he asks for it.

Satsvarūpa came in to show Prabhupāda the latest typed manuscripts for *Teachings of Lord Caitanya.* Although there was no difference in Satsvarūpa's assignment, now that he was face to face with Prabhupāda he realized he had to type and edit more seriously. He asked whether he could resign from his job at the welfare office. Prabhupāda said no.

Jadurāṇī continued painting in the outer room of Prabhupāda's apartment. Casting shyness aside, she asked him many questions about how to paint Kṛṣṇa. "How is Lord Viṣṇu situated in the heart?" she asked. "Is He sitting, or standing, or what?"

Prabhupāda replied, "Oh, for that you have to meditate for thousands of years." Jadurāṇī stared at him in dismay. Then Prabhupāda said, "He is standing," and she went off happily to paint.

When Jadurāṇī complained of weak health, Prabhupāda asked Acyutānanda to see that she got milk twice a day. Looking through the window that opened into the outer room, where typing, painting, and sometimes even construction went on, Prabhupāda watched Jadurāṇī one day as she worked on a painting of Lord Caitanya's *saṅkīrtana* party. Just as she started to paint the words of the *mahā-mantra* across the bottom of the painting, Prabhupāda called through the window, "Don't put the *mahā-mantra* there."

"But you told me to put it there," she said.

"I've changed my mind. Hare Kṛṣṇa should not be below Caitanya Mahāprabhu."

One by one, Prabhupāda saw all his old New York followers: Gargamuni, the temple treasurer, who reported good sales of the Hare Kṛṣṇa record and incense; Rāya Rāma, editor of *Back to Godhead,* who talked about his indigestion; and Rūpānuga, who had a good job but was having difficulty convincing his wife about Kṛṣṇa consciousness. Even Mr. Chutey, the landlord, dropped by with complaints about the boys' behavior.

Prabhupāda also met Michael Blumert, a newcomer. Michael had been seeing a psychiatrist as a result of devastating drug experiences. When he had begun coming to the temple, his mother and father had thought the Swami another evil force. On meeting Swamiji, however, Mrs. Blumert accepted his authenticity, although her husband remained doubtful. "Mr. Blumert," Śrīla Prabhupāda said, "your wife is more intelligent." Mr. Blumert said he wanted his son to help the world in a more practical way—by becoming a doctor. Prabhupāda argued that there were already so many doctors but still people were suffering. A Kṛṣṇa conscious person, however, could relieve a person's suffering completely; so the work of Kṛṣṇa consciousness was more valuable. Mr. Blumert was unconvinced, but he agreed to let Michael stay with the devotees and drop going to the psychiatrist. He came to respect the Swami, even though disagreeing with him.

With Brahmānanda, Prabhupāda discussed the urgent problem of obtaining a permanent visa. Prabhupāda had repeatedly extended his visa ever since he had entered the country in 1965. Now immigration officials denied him any further extensions. He didn't want to leave the U.S., but the only way he would be able to stay would be to get permanent residency. He had applied, but so far with no success. "Your government doesn't want me to stay," he had said, "so I may have to go back to India."

Swamiji's going back to India was a frightening prospect. His disciples had barely been able to accept that he could leave them for preaching elsewhere in the U.S. If he were to go back to India! They feared they might fall back into the material world. He was sustaining their spiritual life. How could they go on without him? And Prabhupāda felt the same way.

Brahmānanda managed to find a lawyer to delay the proceedings of the immigration office. The threat of deportation passed. Prabhupāda spoke of going to Montreal and getting permanent residency there, but his main intention was to stay in America and cultivate what he had begun.

Brahmānanda reported to Prabhupāda about printing the *Bhagavad-gītā*. The manuscript was ready, and they were considering the costs and where to print it, even though they didn't have enough money to publish the book themselves. They hadn't seriously attempted the arduous process of finding a publisher, but Prabhupāda pushed Brahmānanda to do so: "The only hope is that I have my books."

Brahmānanda also talked with Prabhupāda about the six thousand dollars he had lost to Mr. Price. Prabhupāda insisted that they prosecute the culprits. He sent Brahmānanda to speak with various lawyers and also to tell Mr. Price and Mr. Tyler that "His Excellency" was back and would take them to court.

At that they relented. Mr. Tyler refunded most of the $5,000 deposit, and Mr. Price returned $750 of the $1,000 he had wheedled out of Brahmānanda. The legal services had cost more than a thousand dollars—so that was lost—but Prabhupāda said that when dealing with a tiger you can expect to get scratched.

In a letter to Kīrtanānanda in Montreal, Prabhupāda described the successful termination of the Price affair: "You will be glad to know that I have been able, by Grace of Krishna, to recover $4227 ... out of the $5000.00 gone in the belly of Sir Conman Fraud (Price). ..."

There were signs that Prabhupāda should be cautious about his health. He had gone through difficulty while appearing on the Allen Burke TV show. Allen Burke was known for sitting back, smoking a cigar, and saying outrageous, even insulting, things to his guests; and if a guest became offended, Mr. Burke would provoke him all the more. It was a popular show.

Before they went on the air, Mr. Burke had asked Prabhupāda's permission to smoke a cigar, and Prabhupāda had graciously consented. Mr. Burke had introduced his guest as "a real swami." When he had asked Prabhupāda why he was against sex, Prabhupāda had said he wasn't; sex should be restricted to marriage for raising Kṛṣṇa conscious children. But Mr. Burke had persisted, wanting to know what was wrong with sex outside of marriage. The real purpose of human life, Śrīla Prabhupāda had replied, was self-realization. When one's mind is preoccupied with capturing new sex partners, keeping the mental peace necessary for self-realization becomes impossible. Mr. Burke had agreed. In fact, his manners had been the best ever. And at the end he had called Prabhupāda "a very charming gentleman."

It was on his way home to the temple that Śrīla Prabhupāda had said that the TV lights had caused him so much pain in his head that at one point he had thought he would not be able to continue.

Then one day Rūpānuga, sitting close to Prabhupāda's dais during a lecture, noticed Prabhupāda's hand shaking as he spoke. Kīrtanānanda had been there when months ago, the morning after they had made the record, Prabhupāda had slept late and complained of his heart skipping and of not being able to move. "If I ever get badly sick," Śrīla Prabhupāda had told Kīrtanānanda, "don't call a doctor. Don't take me to a hospital. Just give me my beads and chant Hare Kṛṣṇa."

Swamiji's disciples were reluctant to restrain him. Kīrtanānanda had tried. At the Avalon, when Swamiji had been dancing and jumping and streaming with perspiration, Kīrtanānanda had insisted that the *kīrtana* stop. But the others had called him paranoid.

Besides, Swamiji didn't like to be restrained. And who were *they* to restrain *him*? He was Kṛṣṇa's empowered representative, able to surmount any difficulty. He was a pure devotee. He could do anything. Hadn't he often described how a pure devotee is transcendental to material pangs?

Swamiji had written a letter consoling a disciple's ailing grandmother.

> All our ailments are due to the external body. Although we have to suffer some time from bodily inconveniences specially in the old age, still if we are God conscious, we shall not feel the pangs. The best thing is therefore to chant the holy Name of the Lord Constantly.

The devotees figured that although Swamiji might give good instructions to someone's old grandmother, nothing like what had befallen her was ever going to affect him. Of course, he referred to himself as an old man, but that was mostly in lectures to show the inevitability of old age.

To the devotees, Prabhupāda's health appeared strong. His eyes shone brightly with spiritual emotions, his complexion was smooth and golden, and his smile was a display of health and well-being. One time, one of the boys said that Swamiji's smile was so virile that it made him think of a bull and iron nails. Swamiji was taking cold showers, going on early-morning walks around the Lower East Side, playing *mṛdaṅga,* eating well. Even if his disciples wanted to slow him down, what could they do?

Some of his disciples had actually tried to prevent him from attending the controversial Cosmic Love-In at the East Village Theater, but not because of his health; they had wanted to protect his U.S. residency case. Śrīla Prabhupāda had been invited to attend the Love-In, a fund-raising show for Louis Abolafia, the "Love and Peace" presidential candidate. Allen Ginsberg, Timothy Leary, and others were attending, along with a full line-up of rock bands. But when Prabhupāda's lawyer heard that he was going, he said it might jeopardize the visa case. Some of the boys took up the lawyer's opinion and opposed Prabhupāda's plan. Prabhupāda agreed that it might be best if he didn't go. But on the day of the Cosmic Love-In he changed his mind and decided to go anyway. "I came to this country to preach Kṛṣṇa consciousness," he declared. Now it was time to speak against these LSD leaders who claimed to be spiritualists. He had been saying that although he wanted to go, he wouldn't go if his disciples forbade him. But in the end he simply said he was going. And that was that.

During the last week of May, Śrīla Prabhupāda began to feel exhausted. He spoke of heart palpitations. Hoping that the symptoms would clear up in a day or two, Kīrtanānanda requested Prabhupāda to rest and see no visitors. But Prabhupāda's condition became worse.

Kīrtanānanda: *Swamiji began to complain that his left arm wasn't functioning properly. And then he began to develop a twitching in his left side, and his left arm would twitch uncontrollably. It seemed to pain him in some mysterious way, internally or psychologically.*

Acyutānanda: *It was Sunday, two days before Memorial Day, and we had arranged a large program in the afternoon in a hall uptown. I went up to get Swamiji, since all the devotees were ready. Swamiji was lying down, and his face was pale. He said, "Feel my heart." And I felt a quivering vibration in his chest.*

I went down, but didn't want to alert everyone and panic them. I went to Kīrtanānanda and quietly said, "The Swami is having some kind of mild heart palpitations." And immediately we both flew back up. Swamiji said, "Just massage here." So I rubbed him on the chest, and he showed me how. He said, "The others go, and Acyutānanda can stay here. If anything happens, he can call you."

So the others went and did the program, and I waited. Once or twice he called me in and had me quickly rub over his chest. Then he looked up, and his color had come back. I was staring with my mouth open, wondering what to do. He looked at me and said, "Why are you sitting idle? Chant Hare Kṛṣṇa." During the evening, palpitations again occurred, so I slept in the room next to his. And late at night he called me in and again had me massage.

Kīrtanānanda: *It was on Tuesday afternoon, Memorial Day, and I was sitting with Swamiji in his room. While* kīrtana *was going on downstairs, the twitching began again. Swamiji's face began to tighten up. His eyes started rolling. Then all of a sudden he threw himself back, and I caught him. He was gasping: "Hare Kṛṣṇa." And then everything stopped. I thought it was the last, until his breathing started again, and with it the chanting. But he didn't regain control over his body.*

Brahmānanda: *I was there along with Kīrtanānanda. It was on Memorial Day weekend. We couldn't understand what was wrong with Swamiji. He couldn't sit up, he was moaning, and nobody knew what was happening. We nursed him—myself and Kīrtanānanda—trying all different things. I had to go out and buy a bedpan for him.*

Prabhupāda's left side was paralyzed. He asked that a picture of his spiritual master be put on the wall in front of him. Thinking that Prabhupāda was preparing to leave his body and wanted to meditate at the last moment on his spiritual master, Acyutānanda taped it to the door facing Prabhupāda.

Devotees entered the front room of the apartment, and Prabhupāda told them to chant Hare Kṛṣṇa. Then he told them to pray to Kṛṣṇa in His form of Nṛsiṁhadeva.

Satsvarūpa: *Swamiji said we should pray to Lord Nṛsiṁha and the prayer should be "My master has not finished his work." At different times he would allow us to take turns and massage different parts of his body. Then he had us go downstairs and hold* kīrtana *through the night.*

Jadurāṇī: *He taught us the prayers to Lord Nṛsiṁhadeva. He said the words one by one, and I wrote them down. I called up the temples in San Francisco and Montreal and told them the prayer. Swamiji said, "You should pray to Kṛṣṇa that, my spiritual master has not yet completed his work, so please let him finish."*

Dāmodara: *I went into the temple. No one was downstairs, so I just sat down to chant some rounds. Then a devotee came down looking very disturbed, so I asked what was going on. When he told me, I rushed upstairs. Everyone was sitting around in the second room, where they could see into Swamiji's room through the window in the wall. They were all chanting on their beads. Jadurāṇī was handing out little slips of paper with writing on them. Swamiji, she explained, wanted us to chant these prayers.*

Brahmānanda: *We brought the painting of Lord Nṛsiṁha into Swamiji's room, and we were all chanting. When Swamiji had to use the bedpan in front of Lord Nṛsiṁha's painting, he begged forgiveness of Lord Nṛsiṁha. He could understand that Lord Nṛsiṁha was sitting right in front of him. I saw it as a painting, but Swamiji saw it as Lord Nṛsiṁha Himself sitting there.*

It was getting worse—total weakness and everything. I couldn't get a doctor, because it was Memorial Day and everything was closed. I even called my family doctor, but he wasn't in. Everyone had gone on vacation, because on Memorial Day everyone leaves the city. I couldn't get anyone. I was calling hospitals, doctors—trying this and that. But I couldn't get anyone. Finally I got a doctor by calling an emergency number for the New York City medical department. The doctor came. He was an old geezer with a real loud voice. When he saw Swamiji he said, "I think the old man is praying too much. I think he should get some exercise. He should go out for a walk in the morning."

Acyutānanda: *The doctor didn't know very much. He said that Swamiji had a cold. I said, "What do you mean? His heart is palpitating."*

"Hmm, *I don't know what to do. Does he take any whiskey?"*

I said, "He doesn't even drink coffee or tea."

"Ohhhh, *very good, very good. Well, I think he has just got a cold."*

Dvārakādhīśa dāsa: *He came and took a look at the place, and you could tell right away he didn't like what he saw. He thought we were just a bunch of hippies. He couldn't wait to get out of the place. But he said, "Oh, he's got influenza." That was a ridiculous diagnosis. And then he said, "Give me my money." We paid him, the doctor left, and Swamiji got worse.*

The devotees called a second doctor, who came and diagnosed Śrīla Prabhupāda as having had a mild heart attack. He said that Prabhupāda should at once go to the hospital.

Max Lerner (a lawyer friend of the devotees): *I got a call one day that the Swami had had a mild heart attack and I could be of some help. At that time they were going to take him to Bellevue Hospital, but I suggested that at least I could try to get him into a private hospital. After several hours of talking and negotiating with people at the hospital, we were able to get Swamiji into Beth Israel Hospital.*

Brahmānanda: *The day after Memorial Day we had to arrange for an ambulance. Beth Israel had no ambulance, so I called a private ambulance company. It was all arranged with the hospital that Swamiji would arrive at nine o'clock that morning. But the ambulance didn't come until about noon. During this time Swamiji kept moaning. Then finally the ambulance came, and they were horrible guys. They treated Swamiji like a bundle of cloth. I thought it would have been better if we had taken Swamiji in a cab.*

Except for Kīrtanānanda, who stayed in Prabhupāda's hospital room as a nurse, no one else was allowed to stay. They all went back to the temple to chant through the night, as Prabhupāda had requested. Kīrtanānanda phoned Hayagrīva in San Francisco and told him what had happened—how Swamiji had suddenly fallen back and cried out, "Hare Kṛṣṇa!" and how there had been nothing for about thirty seconds ... and then a big gasp: "Hare Kṛṣṇa! Hare Kṛṣṇa!" Kīrtanānanda told Hayagrīva that the devotees in San Francisco should chant all night and pray to Lord Nṛsiṁhadeva:

tava kara-kamala-vare nakham adbhūta-śṛṅgaṁ
dalita-hiraṇyakaśipu-tanu-bhṛṅgaṁ
keśava dhṛta-narahari-rūpa jaya jagadīśa hare

Lord Nṛsiṁhadeva, the half-man, half-lion incarnation of Lord Kṛṣṇa, had appeared in another age to save His pure devotee Prahlāda and kill the demon Hiraṇyakaśipu. Prabhupāda had asked his disciples to pray to Lord Nṛsiṁhadeva by chanting the special *mantra* and thinking, "Our master has not finished his work. Please protect him." The boys went back to the temple and chanted together, but after a few hours they fell asleep. They wanted to rest so that they could go to the hospital the next day.

Haridāsa: *When we heard about it in San Francisco, there was grief, and people were crying. There was a tremendous love and thinking about Swamiji and just concentration, a mass concentration of pulling him through, giving him strength and summoning the help of Kṛṣṇa and Lord Caitanya and everybody we could possibly call upon to lend their energies.*

People came into the temple doing rosaries, and whatever faiths or beliefs or trips they were on, they were directing that toward a healing. They were all chanting with us.

Hayagrīva: *It's a night I'll never forget. We turn on the altar lights behind the Jagannāthas, light candles, and chant in the flickering shadows. It is solemn chanting and even more solemn dancing. News quickly spreads down Haight Street, and soon the temple is crowded with others come to chant with us through the night.*

Mukunda and Jānakī phoned New York. But there is no additional information. Kīrtanānanda is spending the night in the hospital beside Swamiji's bed. No one else is being allowed in. Hospital regulations. Yes, everyone in New York is chanting.

We chant past midnight. Most of the guests leave, but none of us yet feel sleepy. The chanting overtakes us in waves. My mind wanders to Swamiji, to New York, to the future, to the past ... I have to yank it back into the room to confront the present, to realize why we are here chanting, to petition Śrī Kṛṣṇa to spare our master a little longer to allow him to spread Lord Caitanya's glorious saṅkīrtana *movement around the world.*

The chanting is always here, insistent.

By 2 A.M. *I begin to tire. I change instruments just to keep awake, sometimes playing* mṛdaṅga, *sometimes cymbals or harmonium. Many dance to stay awake. The girls serve* prasādam*—sliced apples. It is dangerous to sit next to the wall—an invitation to doze off. We are so frail.*

Hare Kṛṣṇa soothes. The chanting releases us from so much needless fretting. Through it we can relieve tensions, grieve, plead, and hope.

It is between 3 and 4 A.M. *The most ecstatic hour, the* brāhma-muhūrta *hour before the dawn. If he is alive at this hour, surely he will live.*

We sing. We chant on beads. Constant Hare Kṛṣṇa. We chant through the usual 7 A.M. kīrtana *hour and into the morning. We chant fourteen hours without cessation. We cleanse the dust from the mind's mirror. We see Kṛṣṇa and Swamiji everywhere. Surely now he is well!*

During the night, Śrīla Prabhupāda's heart pained him. The next day he remained in critical condition. He could speak but softly and was too exhausted to converse. Skeptical of the doctors, he diagnosed himself: a heart attack affecting part of his brain, thus paralyzing the left side of his body. Massage, he said, was the cure.

On the morning of June 1, other disciples joined Kīrtanānanda in Prabhupāda's room and by taking shifts were able to give Prabhupāda a constant massage. They took turns massaging his head, chest, and legs as he directed. This simple act drew each of them into an intimate relationship with him.

When Prabhupāda heard that not only in New York but in San Francisco also the devotees had chanted and prayed all night, he expressed satisfaction, not by his usual hearty smile but by a very slight nodding and an approving sound. Despite his weakness, he was fully conscious.

The doctors, or more often their aides, took blood, gave injections, and investigated. Their diagnosis wasn't conclusive: they had plans for experiments. Then suddenly a doctor came in and announced their next move: a spinal tap. Prabhupāda was too weak to discuss the pros and cons of a spinal tap. He had put himself in the care of his disciples and Kṛṣṇa.

The doctor didn't want to be impeded. He explained why a spinal tap was necessary, but he wasn't asking for consultation or permission. Everyone—except for Kīrtanānanda, who insisted on staying—had to leave the room while the doctor performed the spinal tap. Neither Prabhupāda, who was too weak, nor his boys, who were uncertain how to act on his behalf, opposed the doctor. The devotees filed out of Prabhupāda's room while the doctor readied the largest, most frightening needle they had ever seen.

When they were allowed back, one disciple asked cautiously, "Did it hurt, Swamiji?" Śrīla Prabhupāda, his golden-skinned form wrapped in white hospital garments and lying between the white sheets, turned slightly and said, "We are tolerant."

Rūpānuga: *When Swamiji was first admitted to the hospital, it was very hard for me. I didn't know how I should act. I didn't have much experience with this kind of emergency. I was very uncertain as to what service to do for Swamiji. It was a frightening experience.*

Swamiji's life was at stake, yet his disciples didn't know what to do to save him. He lay on the bed as if at their mercy. But the hospital staff considered him their property—an old man with heart trouble, a subject of investigation. And for Swamiji's disciples this was a hundred times worse than dealing with Mr. Price and company. Now it was not just a matter of risking money but of risking Swamiji! Should they allow the

EEG? What was an EEG? Was an operation necessary? An operation! But Swamiji had said that he should never even be brought to a hospital. "Give me massage," was all he had said, and "Chant Hare Kṛṣṇa."

When Śrīla Prabhupāda mentioned his preference for the Ayurvedic medical treatments available in India, some of the devotees suggested they bring a doctor from India. After considering the expense, Prabhupāda decided to send a letter first. Unable to sit up or write, he slowly dictated a letter to Sri Krishna Pandit, who had given him quarters for several years in his temple in Delhi. Satsvarūpa read it back to Prabhupāda and then typed it right there in Prabhupāda's hospital room.

> I am writing this letter from the hospital. All of a sudden I have developed some headache, as well as throbbing of the chest. When I rub my chest I feel some sensation in my left hand and when I rub my left hand I feel sensation in my chest. My left hand no more works independently. I therefore ask you if there is any good Vedic physician in Mathura who can send me some medicines, that is, you purchase and send them by air mail to our temple: ISKCON, 26 2nd Ave., New York, N.Y. The symptom is predominantly when I get severe pain within my head. And the trembling of the left hand is coming every ten or fifteen minutes. I am afraid if this is not a disease like Lakhya; the boys are taking utmost care of me, there is no scarcity of care. But still after all, this body is subject to death. I came here with a great mission to execute my Spiritual Master's order but my heart is stabbing me. Of course, I'm not afraid of Maya, I know Maya cannot touch me, but still if I die in this condition, my mission will remain unfulfilled. Please therefore pray to Prabhu Lord Chaitanya and Vrindaban Bihar, to rescue me this time, my mission is still not finished. I wish to live for a few more days. They're prepared to call an experienced Ayurvedic physician who treats such diseases but I've not allowed the boys. But if necessary, if you can give me an expert physician who can travel here we can send necessary money for his coming here or arrange for air ticket. You can consult the man in charge of Dacca Shakti.
>
> At last I may inform you that I am inclined toward Ayurvedic treatment. You can consult the Ayurvedic physician in Vrindaban who is a Goudiya Vaishnava. He knows me very well. He sells my books also.
>
> Two things are to be done if it is possible; to send me proper medicines and directions, that will be nice. But if I require to return that also I can do. Please try to reply as soon as possible in English because my students

cannot read Hindi. So long as I'm in bed it's not possible to read letters. You can treat this letter very urgently. Consult necessary physicians and let me know what I am to do. In Mathura there are undoubtedly many Ayurvedic physicians and many quacks also. Try to avoid the quacks. I would have returned to India immediately but the doctors say it is risky. If need be, I shall return as soon as I get strength to take the strain of the journey.

I repeat my symptoms so that you can take necessary care. All of a sudden I developed some throbbing between the heart and stomach about 4 days ago. I was so exhaustive, it was like fainting—then I consulted a doctor who came and gave me medicine but it was of no good effect therefore my students at once transferred me to the hospital where they're spending more or less 400 rupees daily. There is no question of neglect. All scientific treatment is going on. But I think Ayurvedic medicine will be proper. Therefore I request you to take immediate steps and reply me.

I hope this letter will convince you the actual position. While reading this letter you may consult some friend who knows English very well so that he'll read it correctly and reply correctly. There is no scope for corresponding in Bengali or in Hindi.

By Kṛṣṇa's grace, on the afternoon of Śrīla Prabhupāda's second day in the hospital he showed slight improvement. His heart was still causing him pain, his facial expression remained grave, with never a smile, but he was a bit stronger. The interns, nurses, and doctors came and went on schedule, treating him—impersonally. One doctor did seem a little interested in what Prabhupāda was all about, and at Prabhupāda's request, Kīrtanānanda played a taped lecture for the doctor. He listened politely, but then said, "It doesn't ring a bell."

The doctor said that he wanted to run a few more tests and that Swamiji might be able to leave after a few weeks—if all went well. Śrīla Prabhupāda tried speaking to the doctor, wanting to explain about Kṛṣṇa. Jadurāṇī had brought two of her paintings to the hospital room—one of Rādhā and Kṛṣṇa and the other of the fierce half-lion, half-man incarnation, Lord Nṛsiṁha, tearing apart the demon Hiraṇyakaśipu. Speaking in a very low voice, Prabhupāda said that these two pictures show how God is many-sided: "Here He is in His loving exchange, and here also we see that anger comes from Kṛṣṇa, or God."

The doctor politely said that he had his own philosophy and that Swamiji shouldn't be preaching while in such weak health; he should rest. Advising the disciples not to allow their *guru* to speak, the doctor excused himself and continued his rounds.

Śrīla Prabhupāda, with his slight improvement, expressed more disapproval of being in the hands of the hospital personnel. They weren't able to do anything, he said. Kṛṣṇa was in control: "If Kṛṣṇa wants to kill you, then no one can save you. But if Kṛṣṇa wants to save you, then no one can kill you."

Dāmodara: *I was there when a doctor came in to check his reflexes. There was the usual tapping with a little rubber hammer on his knee—that kind of thing. Swamiji was visibly annoyed with this man's coming in and tapping him all over. He was capable of diagnosing and giving the prescription for the cure, and it annoyed him that these men, who obviously didn't know what they were doing, were coming in and interfering with the process of recuperation.*

Acyutānanda: *The nurse would always let the door slam, and every time it slammed Swamiji would wince. He said, "Tell her not to slam the door." She would say, "Okay," and then she would let it slam again.*

Śrīla Prabhupāda began sitting up in bed and taking *prasādam* from the temple, supplemented by some of the vegetarian items on the hospital menu. He would say a prayer and offer the hospital food to the picture of his spiritual master. The devotees would sit at his feet, watching him as he then mixed with his right hand the carrots, peas, and mashed potatoes. And he would always distribute some of his food into the hands of his disciples.

Jadurāṇī: *We brought him many different kinds of fruit. We told him we had brought apples, but he was so tired he only said, "Oh" and seemed disinterested. We told him we had brought oranges, but again—"Oh." He gave so many tired "Oh"s he seemed disinterested. Finally I said, "We brought you watermelons," and immediately his face lit up*—"Ohhh!"

Rotating in four-hour shifts, two devotees at a time were always with Prabhupāda. Although awake, he would remain silent for long intervals; but massaging always continued, except when he was asleep. Gradually, the paralysis on his left side went away.

Once while Śrīla Prabhupāda was sitting up in bed, one boy massaging his leg and another softly, almost consolingly, stroking the back of his neck, Prabhupāda remarked that if he were not sick he would have considered the massaging and rubbing too familiar.

Dāmodara: *I was massaging Swamiji's temples with one hand, my thumb on one temple and other fingers on the other temple. As I was massaging, Swamiji kept saying, "Harder! Harder!" and I would squeeze harder. I thought, "Gee, I don't know if I should squeeze so hard, because he's sick." But he kept insisting: "Harder! Harder!"*

Puruṣottama: *I was massaging Swamiji's head, and I started singing the chant* śrī kṛṣṇa-caitanya. *When I started singing, a very beautiful smile came on his face. Although I did it only briefly, he took pleasure in hearing. He seemed to take it that I was ministering to him just by singing* śrī kṛṣṇa-caitanya.

As Śrīla Prabhupāda gained strength, his disciples were ready with questions. Puruṣottama asked, "Swamiji, in the scriptures when it describes the lotus feet of Kṛṣṇa, what does that mean—lotus feet?"

Prabhupāda then sang a verse:

samāśritā ye pada-pallava-plavaṁ
mahat-padaṁ puṇya-yaśo murāreḥ
bhavāmbudhir vatsa-padaṁ paraṁ padaṁ
padaṁ padaṁ yad vipadāṁ na teṣām

Then he asked the three devotees present to repeat each line after him again and again, until they had learned both the tune and the words. "In this verse from *Śrīmad-Bhāgavatam,*" Śrīla Prabhupāda explained, sitting up in his bed, "the time of death is compared to crossing a vast ocean. It is very fearful. One doesn't know where he will go in the next life. And at every step there is danger in the material world. But for one who has taken shelter at the lotus feet of Lord Kṛṣṇa, that vast, dangerous ocean of birth and death becomes shrunk up to no more than the impression made in mud by a calf's hoofprint. There is danger, but the devotee doesn't care for it. Just like if a gentleman is riding by in a carriage and he passes a small puddle, he considers it insignificant. So do you understand now what 'lotus feet' means?" It was clear.

Then Puruṣottama asked another question: "Why do people say that God has no name?" Śrīla Prabhupāda replied by asking why, since God is everything, He should not have a name. "In fact," he said, "all names are describing Kṛṣṇa." Prabhupāda asked Puruṣottama what his name had been before initiation.

"Paul," he said.

"What does *Paul* mean?" Prabhupāda asked.

"It means 'little.'"

"Yes," Prabhupāda said, "that is Kṛṣṇa. He is the smallest of the small."

Satsvarūpa then volunteered his name, Stephen, which means "crown."

"Yes," Prabhupāda replied, "Kṛṣṇa is the king."

But discussions were rare. Usually the hours were quiet. Prabhupāda rested, and the devotees on watch sat in chairs on opposite sides of his bed, reading or chanting softly on their beads. Late one afternoon, as the Manhattan sky turned to twilight, Prabhupāda sat up after having been silent for an hour and said, "I don't know Kṛṣṇa, but I know my Guru Mahārāja."

One day Brahmānanda began giving Prabhupāda a minute breakdown of the financial condition of the New York temple. In the midst of the detailed report, Brahmānanda suddenly stopped, looked up at Prabhupāda, and said, "Do you want me to tell all the details? I thought you would want me to let you know. I mean, you should know." Prabhupāda replied that if Brahmānanda could take care of everything without his knowing the details, that would be all right.

Suddenly one morning, Swami Satcidananda, the famous *haṭha-yoga guru,* entered Prabhupāda's room, grinning through his big gray beard. He was dressed in a saffron silk *kurtā* and *yogī* pants and accompanied by one of his young American male disciples. Śrīla Prabhupāda sat up in bed, smiling at the pleasant surprise. They had not met before. Śrīla Prabhupāda offered Swami Satcidananda a seat at his bedside and asked Jadurāṇī to stand and give her seat to Swami Satcidananda's disciple.

Prabhupāda and Swami Satcidananda spoke in Hindi, and no one else in the room could follow their conversation. At one point, however, Śrīla Prabhupāda held up his hand and looked at it with indifference and then with disgust. Although his words were Hindi, the gesture and sardonic expression conveyed his meaning: the body was material and therefore could not be expected to be well.

Prabhupāda asked Acyutānanda to read aloud from a particular purport of the *Śrīmad-Bhāgavatam.*

> If there is enough milk, enough grains, enough fruit, enough cotton, enough silk and enough jewels then why the people need for economic development in the shape of machine and tools? Can the machine and tools supply vigour and vitality to the man and animals? Can the machinery produce grains, fruits and milk or jewellery or silk? Is not jewellery and silk, varieties of food stuff prepared with ghee and grains or milk and fruits sufficient for man's pure luxurious and healthy life? Then why there is artificial luxurious life of cinema, cars, radio, flesh and hotels? Has this civilisation produced any good result more than the dog's mentality of quarreling with one another individually and nationally? Has this civilisation enhanced the cause of equality and fraternity by sending thousands of men in the hellish factory and the war fields at the whims of a particular man?

When Prabhupāda offered to play the record he and his disciples had made, Swami Satcidananda politely agreed. But when Prabhupāda offered to play the other side of the record, Swami Satcidananda said he had to leave. He offered Prabhupāda some fruits, and Prabhupāda, after accepting them, told his disciples, "Distribute these, and give him some of our fruit in exchange."

As Swami Satcidananda rose to leave, Śrīla Prabhupāda suddenly got out of bed and stood shakily. "No, no, no." Swami Satcidananda protested. "Don't disturb yourself." And then he was gone, escorted by Acyutānanda. Śrīla Prabhupāda lay back in bed.

"Is he a swami?" Jadurāṇī asked.

"Why not?" Prabhupāda replied. But after a few moments he added, "*Swami* means one who knows Kṛṣṇa." There was no more talk about it, but Prabhupāda was pleased by the unexpected visit.

The constant coming and going of Śrīla Prabhupāda's young followers, wearing *tilaka* on their foreheads and carrying watermelons, special food, flowers, and paintings of Kṛṣṇa, created a special interest among the hospital staff. Sometimes workers would ask questions, and sometimes the devotees would talk with them about the Hare Kṛṣṇa movement. Once a nurse came by Prabhupāda's room and asked, "In the caste system in India, what is the name of the highest caste? What are they called?"

"Kṛṣṇa conscious," Prabhupāda firmly replied. He asked a disciple to give the nurse *prasādam.*

On June 5 Prabhupāda received an affectionate letter signed by all his disciples in San Francisco. After reading how they had stayed up all night chanting and praying for his recovery, he dictated a short letter.

> My dear boys and girls,
> I am so much obliged to you for your prayers to Krishna to save my life. Due to your sincere and ardent prayer, Krishna has saved my life. I was to die on Tuesday certainly but because you prayed sincerely I am saved. Now I am improving gradually and coming to original condition. Now I can hope to meet you again and chant with you Hare Krishna. I am so glad to receive the report of your progressive march and hope there will be no difficulty in your understanding Krishna consciousness. My blessings are always with you and with confidence you go on with your chanting Hare Krishna Hare Krishna Krishna Krishna Hare Hare Hare Rama Hare Rama Rama Rama Hare Hare.

The following day a tape arrived from Mukunda: a recording of the San Francisco devotees singing *śrī rāma jaya rāma jaya jaya rāma* and other *bhajanas.* Prabhupāda dictated another letter, saying that as soon as he got strength for traveling he would come again to San Francisco. "In the meantime," he wrote, "I shall be very glad to know what arrangements you are going to do for the Ratha-yātrā festival. Make it a grand procession and unique introduction in the United States."

Some of Swamiji's disciples gathered in the storefront at 26 Second Avenue one night. Sitting around on the faded rug, they discussed the meaning of Swamiji's illness. He had said that when the heart attack had come, it had been meant for his death; therefore he had called out loudly, "Hare Kṛṣṇa!" thinking that the moment of death had come. Kīrtanānanda remembered that Swamiji had once told him that when he was on the boat coming to America the captain's wife had read his palm and said that if he survived his seventy-first year he would live to be a hundred.

Madhusūdana asked, "How could a pure devotee be subject to a death blow?" Kīrtanānanda replied that it was impersonal to think that because Swamiji was a pure devotee nothing could happen to him and that they should not even worry about him. Of course, the apparent suffering or even the passing away of a pure devotee wasn't the same as an ordinary man's. Swamiji had given the example of the cat: sometimes she carries her kittens in her mouth, and sometimes she catches a mouse in the same jaws. The mouse feels the jaws of death, but the kitten feels safety and affection. So although Swamiji's death call might have appeared similar to an ordinary man's, for Swamiji there had been no fear or danger.

As the disciples discussed their realizations, they began to clear away their doubts about why such an apparent setback had come upon their spiritual master. Satsvarūpa mentioned the letter he had typed for Swamiji at the hospital. In the letter Swamiji had said he was not afraid of *māyā* and could not be touched by *māyā*. But he had also referred to being stabbed by his heart. Brahmānanda said that Swamiji had once told him that a spiritual master may suffer for the sins of his disciples, because he has to take their *karma*. Swamiji now had about fifty disciples, so maybe that had been the cause of his heart attack. They talked about the importance of being very strict and not committing any sins with which to burden their spiritual master.

Another reason for Swamiji's illness, Kīrtanānanda said, was that Kṛṣṇa had arranged it to engage them all in intimate service to Swamiji. By serving a pure devotee, one gains the favor of Kṛṣṇa, and Kṛṣṇa was letting them all become purified by massaging and serving Swamiji so intimately.

Satsvarūpa recalled that Swamiji had said in a letter to the devotees in San Francisco that he was supposed to have died but their prayers had saved him. Swamiji had told Kīrtanānanda that Kṛṣṇa had heard the devotees' prayers and had granted their wishes. Kṛṣṇa was allowing Swamiji to go on with his mission of spreading Kṛṣṇa consciousness in the West. It wasn't on his own behalf that Swamiji wanted to live, but to continue his mission.

Everyone agreed with Kīrtanānanda that it was a form of impersonalism for them to think that because Swamiji was a pure devotee he didn't need their loving care. They should continue to care for Swamiji even after he got better. He had put himself in their care, and they had to reciprocate accordingly. Swamiji had said they were like fathers to him; so they should not allow him to play the drum long and vigorously, to sing in the park for hours, to stay up talking late at night, or to do anything that might endanger his health.

Rāya Rāma said that Swamiji had asked him to reply to several letters from devotees on the West Coast and explain that he would probably never again be able to take on the strain of public lectures; the *saṅkīrtana* movement now rested on their shoulders. Rāya Rāma had explained in his letters that it was Kṛṣṇa's grace that Swamiji was still with them and able to advise them when things got rough; but now they must increase their efforts to distribute Kṛṣṇa consciousness to the world.

The talk turned to the need for them to realize Swamiji's instructions and become strong devotees. Everyone agreed that they could do this by studying Swamiji's books more carefully and always acting according to his instructions.

When they told Prabhupāda about their philosophical discussions, he replied only briefly: "Kṛṣṇa heard all your sincere prayers, and He thought, 'All right, let him stay and do his nonsense—so many devotees are praying on his behalf.'"

* * *

Before Prabhupāda's illness, the devotees had planned a big event in Tompkins Square Park for Sunday, June 4. The parks department had given them the use of a loudspeaker system and the stage in the band shell. Mr. Kallman, producer of the Hare Kṛṣṇa record, had encouraged them to advertise and had gotten in touch with the TV stations. The devotees had begun making Hare Kṛṣṇa *mantra* signs so that everyone, even the TV viewer, could chant.

Although now unable to go, Śrīla Prabhupāda said they should still have their festival; he would compose a special address for Kīrtanānanda to read to the public. From his hospital bed he dictated the short speech: "An Address to American Youth," by A. C. Bhaktivedanta Swami.

On June 4, several hundred people gathered around the band shell in Tompkins Square Park, while the devotees played harmonium, *karatālas,* and *mṛdaṅgas* and chanted Hare Kṛṣṇa over the P.A. system. Many people in the crowd chanted along, playing their own instruments and even joining the devotees onstage.

Kīrtanānanda stood before the microphone and announced that Bhaktivedanta Swami, although ill at Beth Israel Hospital, had prepared a message for everyone. Many among the Lower East Side crowd were acquainted with Bhaktivedanta Swami and his chanting of Hare Kṛṣṇa. They listened as Kīrtanānanda read.

My dear young beautiful boys and girls of America,

I have come to your country with great hope and a great mission. My Spiritual Master, Om Vishnupad Paramahansa Paribrajaka Acharya Sri Srimad Bhaktisiddhanta Saraswati Goswami Maharaja, asked me to preach this cult of Lord Sri Chaitanya Mahaprabhu in the Western world. That was the seed-giving incident. Gradually the seed fructified, and I was prepared to come to the Western world. Still, I do not know why I was so much attracted by the land of America. But from within Krishna dictated that instead of going to Europe I should better go to America. So you can see that I have come to your country under order of superior authority. And even after arriving here, when I perceived that some of the youngsters are being misled, confused and frustrated—this is not the condition of your country only, but in every country, the young people are neglected, although it is they who are the flower and future hope of everyone—so I thought to myself that if I go to the American youth with my message and they join with me in this movement, then it will spread all over the world, and then *all* the problems of the world will be solved. How I would like to be with you in person today, but Krishna has prevented that, so please pardon me and accept my blessings in this written form.

This process of samkirtan—this singing and dancing—is so nice because from the very beginning it places everyone on the spiritual platform. There are different platforms or levels to our existence: the bodily platform, the mental platform, the intellectual platform, and the spiritual platform. When you stand on the spiritual platform, then all the problems created by the necessities of the body, mind, intellect, and ego become solved. Therefore I appeal to you to join this movement most seriously. The process is very simple: we ask everyone to come join with us in chanting, hear something of the philosophy of life taught by Lord Krishna, take a little prasadam (foodstuff that is prepared and offered to the Lord), and peacefully, with refreshed mind, go home. That is our mission.

We do have certain restrictions; practically, they are not restrictions, but something better in place of something inferior. The other day, Mr. Alan Burke questioned me on his television program, "Swamiji, why do you insist on marriage?" And I answered him, "Unless one becomes peaceful in home life, how can he make any advance in any other area of life or knowledge? Therefore everyone should get married—just to be happy and peaceful." You are all beautiful, nice, educated boys and girls—why shouldn't you get married and live happily? If you live peacefully regulated lives, eating nothing but Krishna prasadam, then the tissues in your brain will develop for spiritual consciousness and understanding.

However, if you are not agreeable to these simple restrictions, still I request you to join the chanting with us. Everybody can do that, and that will gradually clarify everything, and all problems will be solved, and you will find a new chapter of your life. Just this week I have received a letter from a girl in New Jersey who has had such an experience. She writes:

"Dear Swamiji,
"You don't know me by name, but I am the girl who joined your parade in Washington Square this past Saturday.

"When I first saw your group I thought you were all crazy. Either that or on dope of some kind. After listening and talking with some of you I realized that it was neither of those. You people plainly believed in what you were doing and I admired you for that much; but my curiosity drove me further and I had to find out why. So I followed you, and as I did, the chant you sang began to take hold. The next thing I knew I felt free of myself and I was singing too. I didn't know where I was or where I was going but I was too elated to care. It wasn't until we stopped that I learned where I was.

"By that time I had picked up bits and pieces of what Krishna Consciousness was about. One of your members asked me to visit your temple and I followed you still further, hoping to discover just what it was that made you feel so strong about something I'd never heard of.

"After having taken a meal with you and reading your literature I left; but not alone. I took with me a new awareness of life. It occurred to me how futile my desires for the material things in life were: that a new dress, or big house, or color television were not important. If only people would open their eyes to the endless number of pleasures God has already given us, there would be no need for looking any further.

"You people are truly lucky. You may have had to do without many things, but because of this you are able to enjoy the simple God-given treasures of the world. Because of your beliefs, you are the wealthy; and I thank you for sharing a bit of that wealth with me."

So we invite you to please chant with us—it is such a nice thing. Come to our temple if you like, take a little prasadam, and be happy. It is not very difficult if you just chant this HARE KRISHNA, HARE KRISHNA, KRISHNA KRISHNA, HARE HARE, HARE RAMA, HARE RAMA, RAMA RAMA, HARE HARE. That will save you. Thank you very much, and God bless you.

* * *

Śrīla Prabhupāda was eager to leave the hospital. For several days he had wanted to go. "They are simply sticking needles," he complained. And each day was putting his Society into further debt. The devotees had rented a small seaside house in Long Branch, New Jersey, where Prabhupāda could go to recuperate. Kīrtanānanda, they decided, would be Prabhupāda's cook, and Gaurasundara and his wife, Govinda dāsī, were arriving from San Francisco to do the housekeeping and help. But the doctor wanted Prabhupāda to stay for another brain wave test and more observation.

One day while Brahmānanda and Gargamuni were visiting Prabhupāda, the doctor entered and announced that the Swami would have to go downstairs for an X ray.

"No needle?" Prabhupāda asked.

"Yes," the doctor replied, "it's all right."

When the nurse brought in a bed on wheels, Prabhupāda said he wanted Gargamuni to push it. He then sat on it cross-legged and put his hand in his bead bag, and Gargamuni, following the nurse, wheeled him out the door, down the hall, and onto the elevator. They went down to the third floor and entered a room. The nurse left them alone. Gargamuni could sense Prabhupāda's uneasiness. He was also nervous. It was such an unlikely place for him to be with his spiritual master. Then a different nurse entered, with a needle: "Time to give the Swami a little injection."

"No." Prabhupāda shook his head.

"I'm sorry," Gargamuni said flatly. "We're not going to do it."

The nurse was exasperated but smiled: "It won't hurt."

"Take me back," Prabhupāda ordered Gargamuni. When the nurse insisted, Gargamuni acted rashly—his usual tendency—and stepped between the nurse and Śrīla Prabhupāda.

"I'm ready to fight if I have to," Gargamuni thought. "I won't let you do it," he said and wheeled the bed out of the room, leaving the nurse behind.

Gargamuni was lost. He was somewhere on the third or fourth floor, faced with corridors and doors. And Prabhupāda's room was on the sixth floor. Unsure where he was going, Gargamuni wheeled through the corridors with Prabhupāda sitting cross-legged, chanting on his beads.

Brahmānanda arrived at the X-ray lab seconds after Gargamuni's escape. The nurse and an intern complained to him about what had happened.

Brahmānanda: *They considered this a theft. Swamiji was their prop-*

erty. As long as he was in the hospital, he was theirs to do whatever they pleased with. Gargamuni had stolen Swamiji away from them.

Gargamuni got to the elevator. He had difficulty maneuvering the bed and in his haste bumped into the wall. He forgot what floor Swamiji was on. He only knew that he was protecting Swamiji, who wanted to be taken away.

When Gargamuni finally reached Prabhupāda's room, 607, an intern was there and spoke angrily. "I don't care," Gargamuni said. "He doesn't want any more needles or tests. We want to leave." Brahmānanda arrived, calmed his younger brother, and helped Prabhupāda back into bed.

Prabhupāda said he wanted to leave. When the doctor came in, Prabhupāda sat up and spoke decisively. "Doctor, I am all right. I can go." And he shook the doctor's hand to show him he was hale and hearty. The doctor chuckled. He said that although Swamiji was getting stronger, he would have to stay a few more days. He was by no means out of danger yet. He required careful medical surveillance. They needed to run another electroencephalogram.

Śrīla Prabhupāda still had pains around his heart, but he told the doctor his boys had a place for him to rest by the seaside. This was very good, the doctor said, but he couldn't let his patient go just yet.

But Prabhupāda had made up his mind. Brahmānanda and Gargamuni arranged for a rented car. They gathered Prabhupāda's things and helped him dress. As they escorted him out of his room and the hospital staff saw that the boys were actually taking the old man away, some of the doctors and nurses tried to stop them. Brahmānanda told them not to worry: Swamiji was very dear to them, and they would take good care of him. He would get regular massages and plenty of rest, and they would get him whatever medicines the doctors prescribed. After a rest by the seaside he could come back for a checkup.

Brahmānanda: *Then the doctors became fed up. They threatened us: "This man is going to die." They really scared us. They said, "This man is going to die, and it is going to be your fault." Even as we left they said, "This man is condemned to death." It was horrible.*

At 10 A.M. on June 8 they left the hospital. Prabhupāda wanted to stop briefly at the temple at 26 Second Avenue before going to the house in Long Branch. Entering the storefront, walking shakily, he came before the portraits of his spiritual master, Bhaktisiddhānta Sarasvatī, and his spiritual master's father, Bhaktivinoda Ṭhākura. For the first time, Prabhupāda's disciples saw him offer fully prostrated obeisances. As he prostrated himself before his Guru Mahārāja, his disciples also paid obeisances and felt their devotion increase.

When Prabhupāda arrived at his cottage in Long Branch at one o'clock, he had Kīrtanānanda immediately begin cooking lunch. It would be Prabhupāda's first regular hot meal—rice, *dāl, capātīs, sabjī*—since his stroke nine days ago.

Prabhupāda went to bed but soon got up and came into the kitchen, asking, "Is it ready?" Kīrtanānanda made a few excuses and said he would hurry. After a few minutes, Prabhupāda returned. He seemed furious: "Why are you taking so long?" Kīrtanānanda moved as quickly as he could, but he couldn't make the *dāl* boil any faster. "Whatever you have," Prabhupāda said, "let me eat it. I don't care if it is raw." Kīrtanānanda served lunch, and Prabhupāda ate with the relish of a person in good health. Kīrtanānanda telephoned his pal Hayagrīva in San Francisco: "He ate like anything. It was wonderful to see."

The small one-story cottage was situated in a quiet suburb a short walk from the beach. The back yard was enclosed by trees and shrubs, and the neighborhood bloomed with fragrant roses.

But the weather was often blustery and the sky gray. Prabhupāda spoke of returning to India to recuperate. In Delhi, Sri Krishna Pandit had refused Prabhupāda's urgent request for Ayurvedic medicine: "You are in such a long place—if the medicine gives some bad reaction, then how to arrange for the good?" Prabhupāda had written back asking if an Ayurvedic physician could be sent to America, but the proposal seemed impractical. It would be better for Prabhupāda to go to India. He received Swami Nārāyaṇa Mahārāja's reply that since no Ayurvedic doctor would go to America, Swamiji should come and be treated in Calcutta. Nārāyaṇa Mahārāja also enclosed a letter to Prabhupāda's secretary, Rāya Rāma: "There is no need for anxiety. Always utter hari nama (Hare Krishna Hare Krishna Krishna Krishna Hare Hare, Hare Rama Hare Rama Rama Rama Hare Hare) near his ears. God will do for the best."

Śrīla Prabhupāda talked of going to India not only for his health; he told Kīrtanānanda and Gaurasundara he wanted to start in Vṛndāvana an "American House," a place where his American disciples could learn Vedic culture to help them preach all over the world. He also said he wanted to make some of his disciples—Kīrtanānanda, Brahmānanda, Hayagrīva—into *sannyāsīs* and he would do that also in India. His real work, however, was in America—if he could just regain his health. But where was the sunshine?

Govinda dāsī had cherished the desire to serve Swamiji personally ever since she had first met him in San Francisco. She saw that he was selfless, and his love for his disciples was unlike anything she had ever known before. She didn't mention her cherished desire to anyone, even to Gaurasundara. But now Kṛṣṇa was fulfilling her desire by allowing her and Gaurasundara to come to New Jersey to serve Swamiji. To the devotees in New York, having a married couple take care of Swamiji seemed the best arrangement, and Govinda dāsī and Gaurasundara had been available. These were external reasons, but Govinda dāsī understood that Kṛṣṇa was fulfilling her desire.

Serving Swamiji, Govinda dāsī felt completely satisfied. Now that she was actually dedicating herself to Swamiji as she had always wanted, nothing else was on her mind. Despite the problems of working with Kīrtanānanda—who seemed to think she was less intelligent because she was a woman and who sometimes corrected her—she was happy.

Govinda dāsī: *Swamiji would sit on a little couch with a table before him, and Gaurasundara and Kīrtanānanda and I would sit on the floor, and we would all eat together, like a family. We would talk, and one time the subject was rice. Kīrtanānanda said, "White rice is for human beings, and brown rice is for animals." So I said, "I must be an animal, then, because I really like brown rice better." And Swamiji just laughed and laughed and laughed. He thought it was so funny. I guess it did sound pretty simple. But he laughed and laughed.*

Prabhupāda was sitting in the back yard when Govinda dāsī saw a large slug climbing on a wall. She showed it to Prabhupāda. "Chant to the poor thing," he said, and she began to chant Hare Kṛṣṇa.

Govinda dāsī would take walks daily and, with the neighbors' permission, pick dozens of roses. On returning she would arrange them in vases and place them all around in Prabhupāda's room. One time when

Prabhupāda heard her loudly singing Hare Kṛṣṇa as she returned from the neighborhood, he remarked to Gaurasundara, "She is very simple-hearted."

Govinda dāsī: *Swamiji talked about Kṛṣṇa in such a way that Kṛṣṇa was present in the room. This was so striking to me. He would talk about Kṛṣṇa's activities—about how Kṛṣṇa is doing this and that and how Kṛṣṇa is so wonderful and mother Yaśodā is thinking like this. He would talk, and he would get into such a beautiful state that the whole room would glow golden. I would feel as if I were being transported to some other realm, and it was all very new to me. I didn't have any great understanding of what was going on, but it was all very new to me, and it was an actual transcendental experience of feeling Kṛṣṇa's presence and almost glimpsing within the heart the memory of His pastimes.*

Swamiji playing *karatālas,* Swamiji walking on the beach, Swamiji sitting in his room or taking a nap—everything he did seemed wonderful to Govinda dāsī. And everything he did or said seemed to endear him more and more to her.

Devotees would travel—no more than two at a time and only once a week—from Manhattan to Long Branch to visit Swamiji. Mostly they would see him sitting on his bed, but sometimes they would walk with him on the beach. The morning sunshine, he said, would help him. But the gray skies persisted.

As Prabhupāda sat one morning with Kīrtanānanda, Gaurasundara, Satsvarūpa, Govinda dāsī, and Jadurāṇī on a blanket spread on the sand, he noticed some boys with surfboards trying to ride the waves. "They think this is bliss, playing in the water," he said. "Actually there is some bliss there, but it is not *ānanda,* the bliss of the spiritual world. On Kṛṣṇaloka everything is conscious. The water is conscious, the land is conscious. And everything is blissful. Here that is not so." Devotees looked with him at the surfers bobbing in the sea. "Yes," Kīrtanānanda said, "and also here it is dangerous. At any moment one of the surfboards could jump up and hit them on the head."

"Yes," Śrīla Prabhupāda said, "this is not real *ānanda.* Prahlāda Mahārāja has said that this material world is crushing him like a grinding wheel of repeated birth and death. He says that in material life he experiences either separation from what is beloved to him or meeting up with an obstacle he doesn't want. And in order to combat this condition, the remedy he takes is even worse than the disease. LSD is like that, a remedy worse than the disease."

Except that Prabhupāda's face looked thin, his appearance was the same as before his illness. He sat among them, wrapped in a gray wool *cādar.* They knew he must be very careful about how much he did. They would never forget, as they had forgotten before, that he was seventy-two years old. Perhaps never again would they be able to enjoy spending as much time with him as before. Certainly for now his intimate association had become a rare treasure.

Sitting inches away from Prabhupāda on the beach blanket, Satsvarūpa asked a question on behalf of the devotees in New York. "Swamiji, is wearing of leather shoes permissible?"

"No."

"What if someone has given us some leather shoes?"

"Leather means violence," Prabhupāda said. He pointed to Satsvarūpa's shoes of inexpensive man-made material. "Your country is very nice. By your technology you can get these shoes easily without wearing leather." For Satsvarūpa and the others the question was answered for a lifetime; and the time and place became a reference, like a chapter and verse number in the scriptures.

As Jadurāṇī helped Govinda dāsī gather flowers, the two girls talked together. Both had heard the men say that women were less intelligent, and they felt discouraged. Later Govinda dāsī told Prabhupāda about the problem. "Is it true," she asked, "that because we are women we won't make advancement as quickly as the *brahmacārīs*?"

"Yes," Prabhupāda answered. "If you think of yourselves as women, how will you make any advancement? You must see yourself as spirit soul, eternal servant of Kṛṣṇa."

Śrīla Prabhupāda gave Jadurāṇī a photograph of himself to paint from. Taken in India, before he had come to America, it showed him grave and standing very straight against a blank white wall. "Oh, Swamiji," Jadurāṇī remarked, "you look so unhappy here."

"*Noooo,*" he said thoughtfully, stretching out the sound of the word. "No. That is not unhappy. That was a moment of ecstasy."

Prabhupāda drew Jadurāṇī's attention to a picture on his wall. Mother

Yaśodā was rebuking her son, Kṛṣṇa, for stealing butter, while in the distance two of Kṛṣṇa's friends were hiding behind a tree, laughing. Prabhupāda asked, "Do you think that Kṛṣṇa would let Himself get caught and His friends get away?" She looked at the picture again. By the light of Swamiji's words she could see that Kṛṣṇa's friends would also soon be caught. She suddenly felt she was there in Vṛndāvana. They both laughed.

After staying with Prabhupāda for two days, Satsvarūpa and Jadurāṇī, the devotees visiting from New York, had to return to their duties. Although Prabhupāda had been resting, he awoke just as they were about to depart, so they came into his room. In a faint voice Prabhupāda spoke a few words from his bed. Then he sat up and Gaurasundara began to massage him. People who think God is dead are crazy, Prabhupāda said. Although no one had introduced the subject, for Prabhupāda, preaching about Kṛṣṇa was always apropos. His voice picked up volume as he denounced the atheists: "Just like if I go to the doctor. If he checks my heart and it is beating well and if he checks my blood pressure and it is going on and my breathing is there, and after observing all these symptoms of life if I ask him, 'So, doctor, what is the condition?' if the doctor says, 'My dear sir, you are dead'—is this not a crazy diagnosis?"

Gaurasundara, still massaging, glanced wide-eyed at the others. Prabhupāda was now speaking in a loud, forceful voice, as if addressing a large audience instead of a few visitors in his sickroom. "Similarly, just see the signs of life in this universe! The sun is rising just on time, the planets are all moving in their orbits, there are so many signs of life. And the universe is God's body. And yet they are seeing all these symptoms and declaring God is dead? Is it not foolishness? They are rascals! I challenge them. Simply rascals!"

A few soft words had become half an hour of strong, emphatic speech meant to move the audience against all kinds of atheistic theorists. Although Kīrtanānanda had at first cautioned Swamiji, reminding him about his health, Swamiji had dismissed the caution by saying, "That's all right." But now he was exhausted and had to lie back down.

The devotees had just seen Swamiji immediately use up whatever energy he had gained from his afternoon's rest. Although they admired how he was using everything for Kṛṣṇa, they were also fearful. But they were helpless to restrain him. They were even implicated—they wanted to hear him.

When Satsvarūpa and Jadurāṇī returned to New York, Brahmānanda had them tell the others about Swamiji. Satsvarūpa told how he had slept in the room with Swamiji and had felt that this nearness to Swamiji was very auspicious. He had felt light and peaceful and close to Kṛṣṇa all night. Satsvarūpa and Jadurāṇī told about sitting on the beach with Swamiji and his talking about everything's being conscious in Kṛṣṇaloka. And they told how Swamiji had sat up in bed and had used his energy preaching, showing them that they should also use everything in the service of Kṛṣṇa. Brahmānanda beamed at the other devotees. "Just look! By your *talking* about Swamiji, everyone is feeling blissful."

Prabhupāda stayed in Long Branch for three weeks. But when Sri Krishna Pandit wrote saying that he couldn't arrange for an Ayurvedic doctor to come to America, Prabhupāda began to think more seriously about going back to India. In India he could get sunshine and Ayurvedic treatment. But his plans would vary from one day to another — San Francisco, Montreal, India, New York. He told Kīrtanānanda to inform the devotees in San Francisco that if they held a Ratha-yātrā festival he would come.

At the end of June, he returned to 26 Second Avenue and to the hospital for a checkup. The doctor was surprised at Swamiji's recovery and had no objection to his flying to San Francisco. So in search of sunny skies, and eager to guide his followers in performing the first Ratha-yātrā, Prabhupāda had airline tickets booked for himself and Kīrtanānanda to San Francisco, New Jagannātha Purī.

CHAPTER TWENTY-SIX

Swamiji's Departure

AT THE SAN Francisco airport Prabhupāda smiled but said little as the devotees greeted him with flowers and *kīrtana*. It was different this time. He walked straight ahead, with the aid of a cane.

Jayānanda was waiting with his station wagon to drive Prabhupāda to the private house they had rented north of the city, at Stinson Beach. But first, Prabhupāda said, he wanted to visit the San Francisco Rādhā-Kṛṣṇa temple. Jayānanda drove to 518 Frederick Street. Prabhupāda got out of the car and entered the small storefront, which was filled with waiting devotees and guests. He bowed before the smiling Jagannātha deities and, without speaking a word, left the room, returned to the car, and departed for Stinson Beach.

The ride up through the seaside cliffs was so winding and climbing that Prabhupāda became nauseated. And even lying down in the back seat and having Jayānanda drive slower didn't help much. Kīrtanānanda realized that it would be too difficult for Prabhupāda to visit the San Francisco temple from Stinson Beach. But maybe that would be just as well; he could spend all of his time recuperating.

It was a modern single-story six-room house with a Japanese roof. A sign out front read Paradisio. Śrīla Prabhupāda noticed in the front yard, amidst fashionable lawn furniture, a statue of Lord Buddha—

a garden ornament. When Prabhupāda entered the house, he found Mukunda and his wife, Jānakī, waiting for him. They bowed down, and Jānakī wept in happiness. Prabhupāda smiled but kept walking, slowly and silently, through the house. The large living room overlooking the Pacific Ocean was decorated with some of Jadurāṇī's paintings of Lord Viṣṇu, Rādhā and Kṛṣṇa, and Lord Caitanya, as well as with Indian prints of Jagannātha Purī. Prabhupāda's bedroom, also facing the ocean, had sliding windows. On the wall was a portrait of Śrīla Bhaktisiddhānta Sarasvatī and a painting of Rādhā and Kṛṣṇa. Prabhupāda smiled and said the paintings were very nice.

The devotees agreed that only Kīrtanānanda and Upendra would stay and serve Swamiji. They wanted Swamiji's stay to be peaceful, so that his health could improve.

That night Śrīla Prabhupāda felt pain in his heart and couldn't sleep. And he didn't rise early for translating. At 5 A.M. Kīrtanānanda came in and opened the window slightly so that Prabhupāda could receive the soft ocean breeze. Prabhupāda sat up in his bed chanting his *japa* and gazing at the feet of Lord Kṛṣṇa and Śrīmatī Rādhārāṇī. A mountain range to the east blocked the morning sun.

Ever since Prabhupāda's stroke, Kīrtanānanda had been regularly massaging Prabhupāda morning and evening. Kīrtanānanda would rub Prabhupāda's head vigorously and then sit behind him and massage his back; next he would massage Prabhupāda's chest, his arms, and his legs, the complete massage lasting sometimes more than an hour. Since leaving the hospital, Prabhupāda had also been taking daily morning walks, even while on the Lower East Side. And this morning he went down for a walk on the beach, accompanied by Kīrtanānanda and Upendra.

As Prabhupāda walked on the beach, he pointed his cane towards some bubbles in the sand. "Just see," he said. "There are living entities everywhere. There is no place without living entities. And yet they say there is no life on the moon!" The beach was rocky, and there were cliffs where the waves crashed powerfully like thunder. "You hear this sound?" Śrīla Prabhupāda asked. "This is an echo of the *gopīs*' heartbeats when they are feeling separation from Kṛṣṇa."

He walked for an hour, until his two young servants were both tired. "Do I tire you walking?" he laughed. "This walking and massaging are saving my life from day to day." Then he continued walking.

By eleven o'clock the sun finally appeared over the mountains and through the clouds. Śrīla Prabhupāda, his head wrapped with a towel, sat in a folding chair on the beach, taking in the sunshine. He kept saying he needed more sun. After lunch the sky was again overcast.

In the evening Prabhupāda called Kīrtanānanda and Upendra into the large living room and led them in a subdued *kīrtana,* singing Hare Kṛṣṇa and *Govinda Jaya Jaya.* He stood and led them in a large circle around the room. He would stop before the picture of Kṛṣṇa, bow slightly with folded palms, turn around, and then continue in the circle.

On July 8, after Prabhupāda had been at Paradisio for two days, Śyāmasundara and Mukunda drove up from San Francisco. The next day was to be Ratha-yātrā, and Śyāmasundara and Mukunda, the first devotees to visit Prabhupāda since his arrival at Stinson Beach, told Prabhupāda all about the festival preparations. Of course, the whole festival had been Prabhupāda's idea, but the devotees in San Francisco were trying to do exactly as he had asked.

Śrīla Prabhupāda had first gotten the idea for the festival while looking out the window of his room above Frederick Street. Noticing flatbed trucks passing below, he thought of putting Jagannātha deities on the back of such a truck and conducting an American-style Ratha-yātrā festival. He had even sketched a truck with a four-pillared canopy on the back and decorated with flags, bells, and flower garlands. And he had called in Śyāmasundara: "Make me this cart for Ratha-yātrā." Now, ready and sitting outside the temple on Frederick Street, was the cart—a yellow Hertz rental truck, compliments of the Diggers and complete with five-foot columns and a pyramidal cloth canopy.

Sitting with Prabhupāda on the beach, Mukunda told how all the devotees were working with great enthusiasm and how the hippies in Haight-Ashbury were talking about the Jagannātha parade that would take place the next day. The devotees had tried to route the parade through Golden Gate Park, but the police department would only give permission for them to go south down Frederick Street to the sea. Mukunda said the devotees planned to have Jagannātha under the canopy, facing the right side of the truck, Subhadrā facing the rear, and Balarāma facing the left side; he wanted to know if that was all right. Actually, Prabhupāda said, the deities should ride in separate carts, pulled with ropes by the crowd through the streets; maybe that could happen in future years.

"Do it nicely," he cautioned them. "And don't hurry it up." The devotees should drive the truck slowly through the streets down to the beach, and there should be constant *kīrtana.*

Mukunda and Śyāmasundara glorified Jayānanda: he drove all around San Francisco getting donations of fruits and flowers, found people to help decorate the cart, installed the sound system on the truck, and distributed posters in the stores. He was tireless, and his enthusiasm was inspiring everyone else to take part. The women had been cooking *capātīs* all day, so there should be thousands to give away to the crowd. The devotees had prepared hundreds of Hare Kṛṣṇa Ratha-yātrā festival balloons to release on the streets as the parade began.

When the devotees asked what else they should do, Prabhupāda said that this was all—a procession, *prasādam* distribution, *kīrtana.* The people should get a chance to see Lord Jagannātha and chant Hare Kṛṣṇa. There should be chanting and dancing in front of the cart throughout the procession. "But do everything nicely," Prabhupāda said. "Do it as well as you can, and Lord Jagannātha will be satisfied."

The next day, in the quiet afternoon, Prabhupāda was sitting in the living room, chanting on his beads. Upendra was with him, and Kīrtanānanda was in the kitchen cooking a feast. Suddenly Prabhupāda heard the familiar ringing of cymbals, and he became very happy, his eyes widening. Looking outside he saw the Ratha-yātrā truck, with Lord Jagannātha, Subhadrā, and Balarāma and dozens of devotees and hippies eager to see him. He went out to greet them and had them bring the deities inside and set them on top of the upright piano. Devotees and guests followed, filling the large living room. Smiling, Prabhupāda embraced some of the men while others made obeisances at his feet. Some devotees helped Kīrtanānanda in the kitchen get ready to distribute the large feast he had prepared. Others reported on the success of the Ratha-yātrā festival.

It was great! It was wonderful! It was a beautiful day, they said. And Prabhupāda listened, moved by his disciples' description of the celebration. Many hippies had joined the large procession. Mukunda, Haridāsa, Hayagrīva, and some of the women had been on the cart, and the instruments, including Yamunā's playing on the harmonium, had all been amplified. Everyone in the streets had liked it. The police motor escorts had tried to hurry the devotees, but so many people had crowded in front that the parade had been obliged to go slowly, just as Swamiji had asked. Subala had danced wildly the whole time, and Jayānanda had been jumping up and down, playing *karatālas*. From the truck some of the women had handed out cut oranges, apples, and bananas, and others had thrown flowers. The crowds had loved it.

Śyāmasundara told how they had been going up a steep hill—Śyāmasundara had been driving, with his dog Ralph beside him on the front seat—when the truck had stalled. He had tried to start the engine but couldn't. Then the brakes wouldn't hold. The truck began rolling backward downhill! Finally he had managed to stop. But when he had tried to go forward the engine had stalled and the truck had rolled backwards again! He would get it started, the truck would go forward, then stall, then roll backwards. Everyone had been in anxiety. At last the truck had started forward, and the procession had continued all the way to the beach.

Śrīla Prabhupāda smiled. It was a pastime of Lord Jagannātha's, he said. The same thing had happened when Lord Caitanya had attended Ratha-yātrā in Jagannātha Purī. Then also the cart had gotten stuck, and no one had been able to move it. The king of Orissa had brought forward the most powerful wrestlers to push the cart and pull on the ropes. But it wouldn't go. Even the elephants couldn't move it. Lord Caitanya Mahāprabhu had then put His head against the cart and pushed, and only then did the cart begin to move. Now Ratha-yātrā had come to the West, and with it this pastime of Lord Jagannātha's.

Prabhupāda noticed some devotees were missing. "Where are Yamunā and Jānakī?" he asked. The devotees told him that some hippies had handed out candy spiked with LSD and that a few of the devotees had unwittingly accepted it and were just now recovering.

Subala related how, after the festival, they had traveled out on the freeway in their flower-bedecked, canopy-covered truck carrying thirty devotees and the deities of Jagannātha, Subhadrā, and Balarāma. They had driven up through the mountains in what must have been one of the most unusual vehicles ever seen.

After all the visitors departed, the deities remained in the house with Prabhupāda and his servants. Prabhupāda felt satisfied that his disciples had successfully held a Ratha-yātrā festival. Although untrained, they were sincere. Bhaktisiddhānta Sarasvatī and Bhaktivinoda Ṭhākura would have been pleased to see the first American Ratha-yātrā.

The whole world was in anxiety, Prabhupāda explained to the devotees gathered in his room that evening. Only in the spiritual world was there freedom from anxiety. Becoming free from all anxiety and returning to the spiritual world was the purpose of Kṛṣṇa consciousness. And festivals like Ratha-yātrā made people Kṛṣṇa conscious. Prabhupāda had many, many ideas for festivals. If he had the money and the manpower, he said, he could have a festival every day. There was no limit to Kṛṣṇa consciousness. This Ratha-yātrā festival was another sign of the good reception for Kṛṣṇa consciousness in the West.

He wrote Brahmānanda in New York:

> The house is situated in an exceptionally nice spot and the house itself is aristocratic. So there is nothing to complain about the house and place. The only difficulty is that I cannot go to the temple on account of the zigzag course of the road and crossing the mountains. Anyway, the devotees are coming here, and the Ratha-yatra festival was just performed with great pomp. More than five hundred people followed the procession to the beach, and there were about two dozen cars. They distributed thousands of chopaties, and at last Sri Jagannatha, Subhadra and Baladeva kindly came here in our house and will stay here for one week and then return.

* * *

Śrīla Prabhupāda still talked of going to India. He had virtually made up his mind to go; the question now was when, and whether by the western route, via Japan, or the eastern route, via New York. The gray skies and unseasonably cool temperatures of Stinson Beach were a disappointment. His health was still poor. He even spoke of dying. It didn't matter whether he died in America or in Vṛndāvana, he said. If a Vaiṣṇava dies in Vṛndāvana, the land where Kṛṣṇa appeared, he is assured of joining Kṛṣṇa in the spiritual world. Yet when Lord Caitanya had traveled outside Vṛndāvana, His devotee Advaita had assured Him, "Wherever You are is Vṛndāvana." To be always absorbed in thinking of Kṛṣṇa was also Vṛndāvana. So if he were to pass away while preaching Kṛṣṇa consciousness—anywhere in the world—certainly he would still attain to the eternal Vṛndāvana in the spiritual sky.

Nevertheless, Prabhupāda wanted to go to Vṛndāvana. It was the best place—to die or to recuperate. Besides, he had a plan for bringing his disciples to Vṛndāvana for training. He expressed this plan in a letter to Sumati Morarji, the owner of the Scindia Steamship Company.

> I am thinking of going back to India as soon as I get sufficient strength. I am now considerably old; I will be 72 years next September. But the work which I have begun in the western world is not yet finished, and I require to train some of the American boys to preach this cult all over the western world. So if I return to India I will have to take with me some of the boys for training. They are all nice boys to take up the training. So your cooperation in this connection is greatly needed. You have already allowed my men from India free passage; similarly if you allow free passage for some of my American disciples they can come to India and taking training from me at Vrindaban. The idea is that in this old age I do not know when death will overcome me. And I wish to die in the last days of my life at Vrindaban.

Prabhupāda told Kīrtanānanda, Hayagrīva, and others that he would take them with him and show them the sacred places of Kṛṣṇa's pastimes. With the New York temple's building fund, he would start his American House in Vṛndāvana.

> I may come to Montreal, perform the opening ceremony of installation of Radha-Krishna Vigraha. Then I may go back to India for six months, as there is a program for construction of an American house for training preachers at Vrindaban. Vrindaban is the only solitary transcendental abode within this universe where Krishna consciousness automatically reveals. Therefore I have a great hope to train some of my disciples for preaching work, even in my absence. I am now old man, and attacked with serious disease; I may be overcome by death at any moment. Therefore I wish to leave some trained preachers so that they can do the work of Krishna consciousness in the Western world. That is my ambition. I hope you all pray to Krishna so that I may be able to execute my duty properly.

When Govinda dāsī wrote Prabhupāda that she was anxious to serve him again as she had in New Jersey, he replied that he would be going to India to try to construct an American House "where you will be invited to come and live for all the days. Both your husband and yourself, you will find a very peaceful atmosphere in Vrindaban to worship Krishna."

Waiting for sufficient strength to travel, Prabhupāda continued his daily routine at Stinson Beach. One or two at a time, devotees would visit him from San Francisco. His morning walks on the beach, his sitting to take in the sunshine whenever it peeked through the clouds, and his evenings of *kīrtana* or reading in the living room remained undisturbed and peaceful.

Upendra: *He would sit in his chair on the beach side of the house. He liked to see us go in the water and play. At first I felt a bit strange going in the water and knowing that Swamiji was watching me. But I went in and began washing my body. When I looked back at Swamiji he was motioning from his chair, throwing his arms up like he was splashing in the water. He kept doing it until finally I understood that he wanted me to splash and play in the water. As I began to splash and jump around in the water, he nodded his head and smiled broadly.*

Mukunda: *I went on a walk on the beach with Swamiji, and when he sat down, I sat down opposite him. Then he asked me, "What is your definition of Kṛṣṇa?" I said, "Kṛṣṇa is God. He is the Supreme Being. Our duty is to worship and serve Him." Swamiji seemed fairly satisfied, and then he said, "You must chant sixty-four rounds per day on your beads." I was shocked at this and could not answer. I did not know if there was any need to answer. I just kept looking at Swamiji, and he looked at me. After some time he said, "Or at least you can chant thirty-two rounds a day." Still silence. I considered it to be very difficult to chant even sixteen rounds. I was wondering how I could possibly chant thirty-two rounds. After some time, Swamiji said, "At the very least you must chant sixteen rounds every day." I said, "Yes, Swamiji." I knew that I could at least try to handle that much.*

Prabhupāda told Kīrtanānanda that he wanted to play the piano. (The Jagannātha deities, who had sat atop the piano for a week, were now back in San Francisco at the temple.) But when Kīrtanānanda and Upendra moved the piano away from the wall, they heard the thud of a falling object. "What is that?" Prabhupāda asked. Kīrtanānanda reached behind the piano and produced a framed canvas wrapped in a madras. He uncovered it and revealed a painting of Lord Nṛsiṁhadeva. "Why is this being hidden behind the piano?" Prabhupāda asked. Jānakī happened to be visiting at the time, and she confessed. While she had been arranging the house for Prabhupāda's arrival, someone had sent the painting out to the house. She had found it and hidden it. It was ghastly, she explained. Lord Nṛsiṁha was tearing open Hiraṇyakaśipu's abdomen, and there was blood everywhere.

Patiently Prabhupāda explained that although materialistic people feel sorry for Hiraṇyakaśipu, devotees become ecstatic when they see Nṛsiṁhadeva tearing him apart. Hiraṇyakaśipu, he said, had terrorized the whole universe and had usurped the throne of Indra, the king of heaven. Hiraṇyakaśipu had even tortured his own five-year-old son, Prahlāda, a pure devotee of Lord Kṛṣṇa. So there was nothing wrong in Lord Nṛsiṁha's pastime. In fact, Hiraṇyakaśipu, having been killed by the Lord, had been liberated.

After directing the devotees to hang the picture on the wall, Śrīla Prabhupāda sat down and played the piano. The devotees had seen Prabhupāda beautifully play the Indian harmonium—his left hand pumping the bellows, his right hand fingering the keyboard—but never a piano. They weren't aware he knew how. But he expertly played the melodies of Indian *bhajanas.* After about five minutes he stopped.

Some evenings Prabhupāda would speak or arrange debates, although Kīrtanānanda was constantly cautioning. When Prabhupāda wanted to speak, it was impossible for any of his disciples to stop him. Sometimes he would ask Kīrtanānanda to debate with one of the visiting devotees. One devotee would argue for the impersonalist's or atheist's position, and the other would argue for the Kṛṣṇa conscious position. Prabhupāda would judge. But no sooner would the argument begin than Prabhupāda would interrupt, take the position of the devotee, and defeat the atheistic or impersonalistic argument. The devotees loved it. Prabhupāda was unable to confine himself either to the role of a silent judge or to that of a recuperating patient.

"Why do we concentrate on the impersonalists?" Kīrtanānanda asked. "Why do we attack them so much? Why don't we concentrate our attack on the atheists?"

"You say that because you are an impersonalist," Prabhupāda answered angrily.

On another occasion, Prabhupāda explained that nondevotees who mislead the innocent public are demons and should be exposed. Kīrtanānanda objected. "If we call them demons, they'll never come around."

"But they are demons," Prabhupāda replied.

"But we can't call them demons, Swamiji."

"Yes, they are demons! Unless you understand this point, you will not make any advancement in Kṛṣṇa consciousness."

"Can demons become devotees?" Kīrtanānanda asked.

"Oh, yes," Prabhupāda answered. "If they chant Hare Kṛṣṇa and render service, even demons become devotees."

Most of the devotees had to remain in San Francisco, hoping for a chance to visit Swamiji. From the few who knew firsthand, they heard about Swamiji's plans to leave for India, perhaps never to return. It was painful to hear. His going almost to death but then returning by Kṛṣṇa's grace and rejoining them in San Francisco, yet being unable to stay with them as before, and now his plans of going to India, maybe forever—these activities intensified their concern and love for him.

Devotees worried, speculating on whether they could carry on without Swamiji. One devotee suggested that perhaps one of Swamiji's Godbrothers should come to America and fill in for Swamiji and, if the worst happened, take over the leadership of the International Society for Krishna Consciousness. When the suggestion reached Prabhupāda, he considered it without immediately replying.

Mukunda: *I was sitting alone with Swamiji in his room, and he was very grave and silent. His eyes were closed. Then, suddenly, tears began flowing from his eyes. And he said in a choked voice, "My spiritual master was no ordinary spiritual master." Then he paused for some time, and wiping the tears from his cheeks, he said in an even more choked voice, "He saved me." At that point I began to understand the meaning of "spiritual master" and dropped all consideration of ever replacing Swamiji.*

After two days Prabhupāda said he would not call any of his Godbrothers to come and take care of his disciples. He said, "If this person speaks just one word different from what I am speaking, there will be great confusion among you." Actually, he said, the idea was an insult to the spiritual master.

Prabhupāda said that he would initiate the new followers in San Francisco and asked that they come one at a time and stay overnight. Without performing any fire ceremonies, he simply talked with each new person, asking him to follow the four rules and chant sixteen rounds a day. When the follower promised, Prabhupāda initiated him, sitting on the bed while the disciple sat before him on the floor. Prabhupāda would chant quietly on the disciple's beads and then give him or her a spiritual name.

One day one of the new candidates for initiation came in very nervously and bowed down before Prabhupāda. The boy didn't get up. "You can get up now," Prabhupāda said. "So you want to be initiated?" The boy said yes and began chanting, not knowing what else to say. "I'll chant on your beads," Prabhupāda said. After chanting for ten minutes he returned them, saying, "Your name is Aniruddha."

"What does that mean?" the boy asked.

"He's the grandson of Kṛṣṇa. Do you have any questions?" Aniruddha couldn't think of anything—he had already forgotten his name—and Prabhupāda said he could go.

Later, Prabhupāda called for Aniruddha, but Aniruddha didn't know that it was his name being called. "Aniruddha," Kīrtanānanda said and looked at him. "Swamiji is calling you."

Another boy who came out received the name Uddhava. The next day, as Prabhupāda was sitting in the yard, he called, "Kīrtanānanda, Upendra, Uddhava." He wanted to read them a verse he had encountered while studying *Śrīmad-Bhāgavatam*. Kīrtanānanda and Upendra came and sat at Prabhupāda's feet. "Oh, where is Uddhava?" Prabhupāda asked. Upendra told him that Uddhava had gone up to the hills to look at the cows and chant to them. Upendra thought that Swamiji would be pleased to hear that his new disciple had climbed the hills just to chant to the cows. But Prabhupāda shook his head unhappily: "Restlessness!" He had wanted the new boy to hear the verse.

jayati jayati devo devakī-nandano 'sau
jayati jayati kṛṣṇo vṛṣṇi-vaṁśa-pradīpaḥ
jayati jayati megha-śyāmalaḥ komalāṅgo
jayati jayati pṛthvī-bhāra-nāśo mukundaḥ

Prabhupāda gave the translation: "All glories to the Supreme Personality of Godhead, who is known as the son of Devakī. All glories to the Supreme Personality of Godhead, the light of the Vṛṣṇi dynasty. All glories to the Supreme Personality of Godhead, whose bodily luster is like that of a new cloud and whose body is as soft as lotus flowers. All glories to the Supreme Personality of Godhead, who walks on the planet earth to deliver the world from the scorn of demons and who can offer liberation to everyone." After repeating the Sanskrit and the translation, he told them they could return to their duties.

* * *

Prabhupāda told Kīrtanānanda he had definitely decided to go to India, via New York, as soon as possible. Kīrtanānanda packed Swamiji's things and drove Swamiji down to San Francisco to spend the night at the temple. They would leave the next morning.

The temple and even Prabhupāda's apartment were very hectic that night, with many devotees and guests wanting to see Prabhupāda and dozens of people wanting initiation. When Kīrtanānanda advised Prabhupāda not to exert himself by going down for the evening program, Prabhupāda insisted on at least going and sitting during the *kīrtana.*

When he entered the storefront, the devotees immediately stopped their *kīrtana,* dropping down to offer obeisances. There was a hush. He commanded a new reverence. This might be the last time they would see him. They watched him during the *kīrtana* as he played his *karatālas,* singing with them for the last time. The uninitiated wanted to accept him as their spiritual master—tonight, before it was too late.

Śrīla Prabhupāda asked for the microphone. No one had expected him to speak. Kīrtanānanda, the only person in a position to restrain him, said nothing and sat before him like the others, submissive and expectant. Prabhupāda spoke quietly about his mission: under the order of his spiritual master he was bringing Lord Caitanya's movement to America, and Kṛṣṇa had kindly sent him so many sincere souls. "I have a few children in India from my family days," he said, "but you are my real children. Now I am going to India for a little while."

Everyone fixed his attention on Swamiji as he sat before them, leaning against the madras-covered wall, speaking softly. Suddenly the door opened, and Ravīndra-svarūpa unhappily entered. Everyone knew that Ravīndra-svarūpa wanted to leave Kṛṣṇa consciousness. He hadn't taken his initiation vows seriously. He wanted to move on. He didn't want a spiritual master any more. The other devotees had discouraged him, but he had persisted. They were incredulous. How could he do such a thing on the night before Swamiji's departure!

Ravīndra-svarūpa fell to the floor to offer obeisances. But he didn't rise up. Instead, he began crawling on his hands and knees towards Prabhupāda. Ravīndra usually had a cavalier manner, enhanced by a handsome face, long tousled hair, and a beard. But now he was wretched and sobbing and crazy. He crawled towards Prabhupāda, who sat but two steps off the floor on the simple redwood dais. Prabhupāda looked at him with compassion: "Come here, my boy." Ravīndra crawled up the steps and placed his bushy head on Prabhupāda's lap. Moved, the devotees watched as Prabhupāda stroked Ravīndra's head and the boy cried and cried.

"What's wrong, my son? You don't have to be so unhappy."

Ravīndra bawled out, "I want ...," he sobbed, "*aah* ... to ... *aah* ... reach God directly! Without anyone in between!"

Prabhupāda continued to pat and stroke the boy's head: "No, you continue to stay with us if possible. Don't be a crazy fellow." Ravīndra's weeping subsided, and Prabhupāda continued, speaking both to Ravīndra and to the emotion-struck group in the room. "I am an old man," he said. "I may die at any moment. But please, you all carry on this *saṅkīrtana* movement. You have to become humble and tolerant. As Lord Caitanya says, be as humble as a blade of grass and more tolerant than a tree. You must have enthusiasm and patience to push on this Kṛṣṇa conscious philosophy."

Suddenly Ravīndra's tears were gone. He jumped up, dejectedly stood, hesitating for a moment, and then hurried out the door, banging it behind him.

Ravīndra-svarūpa's dramatic exit from Kṛṣṇa consciousness shocked the devotees. Prabhupāda sat still and continued speaking to them gravely, asking them to stick together and push on the movement, for their own benefit and for others. Whatever they had learned, he said, they should repeat.

They realized, perhaps for the first time, that they were part of a preaching mission, a movement. They were together not just for good times and good vibrations; they had a loving obligation to Swamiji and Kṛṣṇa.

Prabhupāda returned to his apartment, which soon became chaotic. It was late. Many people wanted initiation. Mukunda, Jayānanda, and other temple leaders tried to determine which candidates were sincere.

They selected candidates, half a dozen at a time, and allowed them into Prabhupāda's room.

Prabhupāda sat behind his little desk, chanted on each person's beads, and returned them, giving each person a spiritual name. Kīrtanānanda requested him to stop; further initiations could be done through the mail. But Prabhupāda said he would continue initiating whoever was present.

Mukunda and Jayānanda set priorities. Some persons had been waiting months to be initiated and were obviously sincere. Others would have to be turned away.

John Carter: *At the end of the lecture I was sure that I wanted to be initiated. And even though there was some talk of being initiated by mail, I knew I wanted to have that personal connection with my spiritual master and be personally initiated by him, personally accepted. I ran up to Mukunda and said, "How many are on the list? I would like to get on the list."*

He said, "Well, Swamiji isn't really taking them in any particular order. We are just going to try to pick out the most sincere people."

"Please put my name on the list," I said. "I am really sincere, I really want to get initiated."

So he put me down and took the list up to Swamiji, and Swamiji began calling for people one by one. After the third person, when my name wasn't called, I became a little worried. Then after the fourth person, I was really sitting on edge. Then when they called the fifth person and it wasn't me, I was totally destroyed. I felt, "Oh, he's going to India, and then he's going back to Kṛṣṇa. I just lost my chance. This is it. There's no use in me living anymore."

I was trying to make it to the coat rack and get my coat and get out before anybody could see me crying. I hadn't started crying, but I could tell it was coming. A couple of people patted me on the back and said, "It's all right. He can write you a letter and tell you your name." All I could think was, "Yeah, the way he was talking tonight, it may never happen." I could barely stand up. I went outside and started walking across the parking lot towards Golden Gate Park. I was kind of heading towards the Golden Gate Bridge. I thought, "I'll just jump off." I hadn't been there long enough to understand that if you commit suicide you have to become a ghost. I just figured my life was useless.

I got about halfway across the parking lot when the idea struck me:

"What if he decided to take one more and I was out here somewhere?" The thought filled me with so much hope that I turned around and ran back to the temple. And just as I walked in the front of the temple Jānakī ran down and said, "He will take one more." And she grabbed somebody else and ran up the stairs. I felt my knees start to collapse and tears came jutting out of my eyes. Harṣarāṇī was standing there, and she grabbed me by the arm and said, "Come with me." She raced up the stairs, pulling me to the top, and burst into Swamiji's room without even knocking.

Swamiji looked up with amazement. She said, "Swamiji, you have to initiate this boy." I was just bawling, and Swamiji began to laugh. He said, "It's all right. Don't cry. Everything will be all right." He chanted on my beads and gave me the name Jīvānanda.

*　　*　　*

The next morning, Prabhupāda had to leave his affectionate followers. Several cars filled with devotees accompanied him to the San Francisco airport.

Nandarāṇī: *Some were sincere, and some were crying because it was appropriate to cry when the spiritual master leaves. Actually, none of us really knew much about what the spiritual master was.*

Jānakī mischievously stole the ticket and passport from Prabhupāda's hand. "Now you can't go," she said.

"That's all right," he smiled. "I already have my boarding ticket. I am Indian. They will let me into my own country."

Prabhupāda turned to his adoring followers gathered close around him at the boarding gate: "Actually I have only one desire, and whoever does this will please me very much. Now I have a temple in New York, in Montreal, and a temple in San Francisco. But I do not have any temple in Los Angeles." He told them to remain in Kṛṣṇa consciousness and to please preach.

They watched as he turned and walked through the gate, his cane in one hand, boarding pass in the other.

*　　*　　*

In New York there was hardly time for sadness. Śrīla Prabhupāda telegraphed Sri Krishna Pandit that his arrival in Delhi would be on July 24 at

7:30 A.M. and that Sri Krishna Pandit should prepare Prabhupāda's quarters at the Chippiwada temple. In the telegram Prabhupāda mentioned his intention to consult a physician in Delhi and then go to Vṛndāvana. He was anxious to return to Vṛndāvana.

The day before his departure, Prabhupāda wrote to Sumati Morarji. In reply to his last letter she had agreed to provide free steamship passage to India for him, but not for his disciples. "As I had arranged for your passage to America," she had written, "I think it is my duty to see that you return back to India safely, more so due to your indifferent health." But she would not allow free passage for any disciples.

On July 20, Prabhupāda wrote:

> I am feeling too much to return to Vrindabana to the lotus feet of Vrindabana Behary Lord Krishna; and therefore I have decided to return to India immediately. I would have liked to return via sea, as you have so kindly offered me passage in your letter, but in my precarious state of health that is not possible. So by the mercy of Krishna and through one friend here, somehow or other, I have received air passage, and I am expecting to leave here for New Delhi on Saturday next, reaching the Palam airport on the 24th instant at 7:30 a.m. From there I shall proceed to Vrindabana after a few days rest in Delhi.
>
> I can understand that at present you cannot allow free passage to my disciples. But if you don't do so, at least in the near future, then my mission will be half finished or failure. I am just enclosing one letter of appreciation for one of my principal students (Bruce Scharf) from Professor Davis Herron, and another from Professor Roberts of New York University. I think these letters will convince you how much my movement of Krishna consciousness is taking ground in the western world. The holy name of Hare Krishna is now being chanted not only in this country but also in England, Holland, and Mexico, that *I know* of. It may be even more widespread. I have sent you one gramophone record which I hope you may have received by this time. You will enjoy to learn how Krishna's Holy Name is being appreciated by the Western World.

Acyutānanda told Prabhupāda he wanted to go to India to study intensively, gather experiences, and become attached to Kṛṣṇa. He had heard Prabhupāda say that one could become more Kṛṣṇa conscious in two days in Vṛndāvana than in ten years in America. "Do you think I'll be able to go?" Acyutānanda asked.

"Rest assured," Prabhupāda told him, "we will meet again in Vraja."

Devotees had been asking Satsvarūpa to transfer his civil service job to Boston and open a Kṛṣṇa conscious center there. They had also asked Rūpānuga to do the same in Buffalo. Satsvarūpa and Rūpānuga approached Prabhupāda to find out what he wanted. He became very pleased. Subala was going to open a center in Santa Fe, he said, and Dayānanda was going to Los Angeles. "Hare Kṛṣṇa *mantra* is like a big cannon," he told them. "Go and sound this cannon so everyone can hear it, and it will drive away *māyā*."

The devotees wanted to ask, "But what if you don't return?" They were fearful. What if Kṛṣṇa kept Swamiji in Vṛndāvana? What if Swamiji never returned? How could they survive against *māyā*? But Swamiji had already assured them that whatever Kṛṣṇa consciousness he had given them would be enough, even if he never returned.

Just thirty minutes before he had to leave for the airport, Prabhupāda sat in his room chanting on the beads of a girl who had asked to be initiated. Then, as he had done many times before, he left his apartment, went downstairs, crossed the courtyard, and entered the storefront.

Sitting on the old carpet, he spoke quietly and personally. "I may be going, but Guru Mahārāja and Bhaktivinoda are here." He looked toward the paintings of his spiritual master and Bhaktivinoda Ṭhākura. "I have asked them to kindly take care of all of you, my spiritual children. The grandfather always takes care of the children much better than the father. So do not fear. There is no question of separation. The sound vibration fixes us up together, even though the material body may not be there. What do we care for this material body? Just go on chanting Hare Kṛṣṇa, and we will be packed up together. You will be chanting here, and I will be chanting there, and this vibration will circulate around this planet."

Several devotees rode with Prabhupāda in the taxi—Brahmānanda in the front with the driver, Rāya Rāma and Kīrtanānanda in the back beside their spiritual master. "When Kīrtanānanda sees Vṛndāvana," Prabhupāda said, "he will not be able to understand how I could have left that place and come to this place. It is so nice. There are no motorcars there like here, rushing whoosh! whoosh! and smelling. Only there is Hare Kṛṣṇa. Everybody always chanting. Thousands and thousands of temples. I will show you, Kīrtanānanda. We will walk all about there, and I will show you."

Brahmānanda began to cry, and Prabhupāda patted him on the back. "I can understand that you are feeling separation," he said. "I am feeling for my Guru Mahārāja. I think this is what Kṛṣṇa desires. You may be coming there to me and be training up, and we will spread this movement all over the world. Rāya Rāma—you will go to England. Brahmānanda—you want to go to Japan or Russia? That's all right."

The devotees converged on the Air-India waiting room, near a crowded cocktail lounge. Wearing a sweater, his *cādara* folded neatly over one shoulder, Prabhupāda sat in a chair. His disciples sat as closely as possible around his feet. He held an umbrella, just as when he had first come alone to New York, almost two years ago. Although exhausted, he was smiling.

Prabhupāda noted a mural of Indian women carrying large jars on their heads, and he called the name of a young girl who had recently gone with her husband, Haṁsadūta, to join the ISKCON center in Montreal. "Himavatī, would you like to go to India and learn to carry this waterpot like the Indian women?"

"Yes, yes," she said. "I'll go."

"Yes," Śrīla Prabhupāda said, "some day we will all go."

Kīrtanānanda was carrying a portable battery-operated phonograph and two copies of the Hare Kṛṣṇa *mantra* record. "Kīrtanānanda," Prabhupāda asked, "why not play the record? They will enjoy." Kīrtanānanda played the record very softly, its sound catching the attention of people in the cocktail lounge. "Make it a little louder," Prabhupāda asked, and Kīrtanānanda increased the volume. Prabhupāda began nodding his head, keeping time.

Soon the devotees began humming along with the record, and then quietly singing, until gradually they were singing loudly. Kīrtanānanda, Brahmānanda, and other devotees began to cry.

Haṁsadūta: *I was sitting right next to Swamiji, and all the time I was thinking, "Oh, my spiritual master is going to India." And he said, "I want to die in Vṛndāvana." We all* knew *Swamiji was going, but now it was the last moment. I was also seeing that I hadn't done anything for my spiritual master. "He doesn't even know who I am," I thought. "There's no relationship. I must do something. I must do something* now. *I must serve him in some way which will establish some place in his heart. Something." I was thinking, "What can I do?" I was crying, and he didn't even look at me. It was like I wasn't even there, just like a chair or something. He was just always looking around and everything, and I was trying to catch his eye: if all of a sudden he would say something.*

The kīrtana *was getting heavier and heavier, and so was the crying. And the people in the waiting room were just looking at Swamiji like he was someone very special. And in the middle of it all, Swamiji was completely relaxed, as if this were his place and this was just a normal thing to do.*

When the record ended, Haṁsadūta asked, "Swamiji, can I take a collection?" Prabhupāda nodded. Haṁsadūta stood and made a little speech: "Our mission is to spread Kṛṣṇa consciousness. We have a temple in New York. We are always badly in need of money. Please help us." Borrowing a hat from a soldier, Haṁsadūta went around taking a collection.

"Our traveling is very auspiciously beginning," Prabhupāda said. "We had a nice *kīrtana,* and we had a nice collection. It is all Kṛṣṇa's mercy."

Then it was time to board the plane. Prabhupāda embraced each of his men. They stood in a line, and one after another approached him and embraced him. He patted a few of the women on the head.

Rūpānuga: *Swamiji was embracing the men: Kīrtanānanda, Brahmānanda, Gargamuni. I never expected that he would ask* me *to step forward. I didn't consider myself in the same category with the other devotees, so I was very much surprised when Swamiji motioned to me and spoke my name, "Rūpānuga." I got up and walked to Swamiji. It might have been ten feet, but it seemed like a long distance. I embraced him, and that embrace was the most memorable embrace of my life. Right away I noticed Śrīla Prabhupāda's strength. He was so strong it was like embracing a young man—a man my age. I was twenty-seven, and he seemed even stronger and younger than I. And he hugged me tightly, and I also embraced him very firmly. He was smaller than me in stature, so I instinctively buried my chin in the hollow of his left shoulder. While I was embracing him I felt very blissful, and I felt a light. I felt there was a light, something bright and pure, some kind of energy emanating from my face. I opened my eyes and I saw Kīrtanānanda watching. He was standing behind Swamiji, a few feet away, and I looked right into his eyes. And I was so happy and blissful that it reflected in him somehow. He broke into a big smile, smiled at me. And his eyes were very bright. It was as if some spiritual energy was actually emanating from me.*

That airport scene was a very important part of my life. Because for me, a person who always had difficulty in loving another person, Swamiji's leaving forced out a lot of love from my heart I didn't even know was there. It's like becoming a spiritual person when you feel love really developing for the spiritual master. I was becoming a spiritual person. It was a tremendous outpouring of feelings of separation and grief at his departure, because we all knew he was our life and soul. And to a person, none of us were sure we would ever see him again.

Accompanied by Kīrtanānanda, whose head was shaven and who wore an incongruous black woolen suit, Prabhupāda walked slowly toward the gate. As he disappeared from view, the devotees ran for the observation deck to get a last look at his departing plane.

A gentle rain was washing the airfield as the devotees raced across the wet observation deck. There below were Prabhupāda and Kīrtanānanda, walking towards their plane. Abandoning decorum, the devotees began to shout. Prabhupāda turned and waved. He climbed the movable stairway, turning again at the top and raising his arms, and then entered the plane. The devotees chanted wildly while the boarding steps moved away, the door closed, and the plane began to turn. The devotees had pressed close to the rail, but they pulled back as the jet exhaust blasted them with heat. With a great roar the Air-India jet, lights blinking, taxied out to the runway. The devotees continued to chant Hare Kṛṣṇa until the plane left the ground, became a speck in the sky, and then disappeared.

CHAPTER TWENTY-SEVEN

India Revisited: Part 1

THE PLANE FLEW during the night and arrived in London by morning. Śrīla Prabhupāda had planned a stopover. He checked into an airport hotel, took his massage, and rested. In the afternoon he rose and bathed, and then he and Kīrtanānanda boarded their plane, bound for New Delhi via Moscow. While the plane was still on the ground, however, a crew member announced "a short delay due to health regulations." A passenger who had disembarked earlier that day was now sick, apparently with smallpox, so the plane would have to be thoroughly fumigated. Prabhupāda and Kīrtanānanda stayed in a room at the Excelsior Hotel for the night.

Early the next morning, July 24, seated in his hotel room, complete with air conditioning and television, neither of which he had used, Śrīla Prabhupāda wrote a letter to Brahmānanda in New York.

> Accept my blessings. I am always thinking of your separation feelings. Please do your duty nicely and Krishna will help you in all respects. We were delayed here for 16 hours. Starting this morning at nine for Delhi. The attention of Mr. B. K. Nehru the Ambassador of India was drawn to me the other day. I have told him about my Permanent Visa and He has promised to help me when I come back. Please make an appointment with him informing that I wish to present him our set of Bhagavatam and our other literatures. Then go to him and personally present the books etc. at Washington D.C. It may be that as soon as I feel some strength I shall be coming back. Up to

> now there was no disturbance about my health and I hope to reach Delhi this night. I shall write you again after reaching Vrindaban. Convey my ardent affection and blessings for all the boys and girls. I am very much hopeful of my movement. Please keep steady, follow all my instructions scrupulously, chant Hare Krishna and Krishna will give you all strength.

Prabhupāda and Kīrtanānanda flew to Moscow. There they walked around the terminal, observing what Prabhupāda called "propaganda pictures." After a one-hour stopover they reboarded and flew another eight hours, arriving in Delhi around midnight.

The wall of heat that greeted them felt good to Prabhupāda. He had come for this. Inside the airport terminal, overhead fans stirred the muggy air as Prabhupāda and Kīrtanānanda stood in slow-moving lines while uniformed clerks checked passports and customs forms, without Western-style computers or efficiency. Just beyond the areas for immigration and customs, people waiting for arriving passengers were waving, calling, and coming together with friends and family members.

After Prabhupāda and Kīrtanānanda claimed their luggage and cleared customs, they stood on the sidewalk outside the terminal. Although Prabhupāda had removed his sweater, Kīrtanānanda stood sweltering in his black wool suit. It was 2 A.M. All around, passengers were meeting loved ones, who embraced them—sometimes even garlanded them—and helped them into cars or taxis. But no one was there for Prabhupāda. It was certainly different from the recent tearful airport scenes, where Prabhupāda had been with *his* loved ones. Now, instead of being surrounded by loving disciples, Prabhupāda was besieged by taxi drivers and porters wanting to carry his luggage for a fee. In Hindi Prabhupāda asked one of the drivers to take them to Chippiwada, in Old Delhi. The driver put their luggage in the trunk, and Prabhupāda and his disciple climbed into the back seat.

The small Ambassador taxi drove through streets well known to Śrīla Prabhupāda. Nighttime traffic was light—an occasional taxi or motor ricksha. Mostly the streets were empty and quiet, the shops closed, an occasional person or cow sleeping outdoors.

Just a few years before, Prabhupāda had sold *Back to Godhead* magazines, solicited donations, and printed his *Śrīmad-Bhāgavatams* here. In those days he had been alone, practically without money or residence. Yet he had been happy, completely dependent on Kṛṣṇa.

But India's leaders were rejecting Vedic culture and imitating the West. Although some Indians still professed to follow Vedic culture, mostly they were victims of hodgepodge teachers who didn't accept Kṛṣṇa as the Supreme Personality of Godhead. So he had felt obliged to leave—to go and transplant the Vedic culture in the West. He had held strictly to the vision of his predecessor spiritual masters, and he had been proven right: the West was a very good field for Kṛṣṇa consciousness.

As the taxi drove through Old Delhi and approached Chawri Bazaar, Prabhupāda saw the printing and paper shops, now closed for the night. And the usual dense traffic of human-hauled carts was now absent, though some laborers were sleeping on their carts till the morning, when they would bathe in an outdoor well and begin another day's hauling. When Śrīla Prabhupāda had been overseeing the publishing of his first volumes of *Śrīmad-Bhāgavatam,* he had daily walked these streets, buying paper, picking up proofs from the printer, returning with the corrected proofs. His First Canto had been a triumph.

Chawri Bazaar led to side streets that led to the narrow lanes of Chippiwada, where upright metal posts blocked autos and rickshas from entering. The driver stopped the taxi on an empty road and turned for his payment. Prabhupāda took from his billfold forty rupees (the same forty rupees he had carried with him on the boat to America in 1965). But the driver took the entire forty rupees and said he would keep it all as the just fare. Prabhupāda protested; the fare should not be even half that! Loudly they argued back and forth in Hindi. The driver had pocketed the money and would give no change. Prabhupāda knew that to get a policeman at this hour would be very difficult. Finally, although this had been nothing less than a robbery, Prabhupāda let the man go. "He cheated me," Prabhupāda said. He and Kīrtanānanda took their luggage and walked the last block, up to the door of the Chippiwada Rādhā-Kṛṣṇa temple.

It was locked. As they pounded loudly, Prabhupāda called out for Sri Krishna Pandit until a man came to the door, recognized Prabhupāda, and let them in. The man showed them upstairs and unlocked the door to Prabhupāda's room. Prabhupāda turned on the light.

The room was bare and dusty, and the bulb hanging from the ceiling created stark light and shadows. On the floor was the three-foot-high cement dome indicating that directly below were the altar and the Deities of Rādhā and Kṛṣṇa. (The dome prevented anyone from accidentally committing the offense of walking directly above the Deities.) The closet was stacked with printed *Śrīmad-Bhāgavatam* pages, *Śrīmad-Bhāgavatam* dust jackets, and form letters to prospective members of the League of Devotees. Everything was just as Prabhupāda had left it.

"This is the room where I compiled *Śrīmad-Bhāgavatam,*" Śrīla Prabhupāda told Kīrtanānanda. "I slept here. And over here was my cooker and my typewriter. I would sleep and type and cook and type and sleep and type." Kīrtanānanda was shocked to think of Swamiji living here in such a poor, humble place. It wasn't even clean.

Although Kīrtanānanda was uncomfortable in his suit and wondered when he would be able to get rid of it, he managed to get a thin mattress for Swamiji. Two Ayurvedic doctors came. They both agreed that the trouble was Swamiji's heart but that the danger was now past. They gave him medicines and advised him to keep to a regulated schedule of eating, resting, and working. Sri Krishna Pandit came by to sit and converse, and Prabhupāda told him of his success in America and of all the young devotees in New York and San Francisco. Prabhupāda played his record for Sri Krishna Pandit, and this drew a crowd of curious persons from other rooms in the temple.

In the afternoon Prabhupāda developed a cough. It didn't seem serious, and he said he wanted to travel the next day to Vṛndāvana. But by evening the cough had become persistent; he couldn't rest. Kīrtanānanda tried massages and the pills the Ayurvedic doctors had prescribed, but nothing worked; Prabhupāda remained awake all night, and when Kīrtanānanda touched him in the morning he was feverish.

The doctors came again. Prabhupāda's temperature was over 104. They gave teas and Ayurvedic powders while Kīrtanānanda looked on skeptically. Because Prabhupāda was having a lot of difficulty breathing when he lay down, Kīrtanānanda thought it might be pneumonia. So Kīrtanānanda gave him penicillin, of which he had brought a supply. In the afternoon an elderly Sikh doctor who practiced Western medicine came by and gave Prabhupāda a penicillin injection. Prabhupāda then fell asleep and rested quietly for the first time in twenty-four hours.

While Prabhupāda slept, Kīrtanānanda wrote a letter to his Godbrothers in New York.

> I know you would like me to say straight out my opinion as to how He is, and that is not good. The outcome—as always, but now very apparently—is only in Krishna's hands. Please chant HARE KRISHNA for that is the only thing that can save Him. That is what saved Him before, and that can do it again. I know that His task is not yet complete, and by Krishna's Mercy He can again be spared.

Kīrtanānanda also asked the New York devotees to call the devotees in San Francisco, Santa Fe, and Boston and have them continue chanting for Swamiji's health. He reminded them to strictly follow all of Swamiji's instructions.

The next day Śrīla Prabhupāda's fever was down to 100.6. He was still sick, but he talked again of going to Vṛndāvana. He dictated a letter to his bookselling agents in Delhi, Atmarama & Sons, asking them for an up-to-date account of their sales of his *Śrīmad-Bhāgavatam.* Old acquaintances came by and were disappointed to find Swamiji unable to accept their invitations. Prabhupāda asked that they invite Kīrtanānanda in his stead.

For several days Kīrtanānanda visited the homes of these pious Hindus. He played the record on his portable phonograph, chanting along and dancing with his arms upraised. Then he would give a short speech. His hosts accepted him as a *sādhu,* fascinated that an American had taken so seriously to Kṛṣṇa consciousness.

* * *

On August 1, after six days in Delhi, Prabhupāda went to Vṛndāvana. Kīrtanānanda wrote back to New York:

> My dear brothers and sisters,
>
> Greetings in the NAME of KRISHNA from VRINDABAN.
>
> Obviously Swamiji is much better—especially after reaching Vrindaban—His eyes now have a special glow. We left Delhi yesterday (31st) morning on the Taj Express, and in two hours were at Mathura. We rode "special third class" and it was quite satisfactory, not at all crowded like the usual third class. Anyway, we are now here and are in the process of settling down. Swamiji has two very nice rooms—quite cool—just off the porch where the Bhagavatam is read. How appropriate! The only difficulty on His behalf is that these Indians all want to see Him—and they are very persistent, and I am not very successful in keeping them out. ...
>
> Vrindaban, seen materially, is a very beautiful place. The country is very flat, and there are many trees, monkeys, peacocks, and of course temples.

> It is also very poor. Both the people and the temples are in a bad state of disrepair. But spiritually considered there are many great devotees here, and it is wonderful to walk down the streets and see teeloks all over the place, and people chanting on their beads. If I can develop a fraction of their devotion for Krishna, my life will be successful. It is also thrilling to hear the temple bells ringing so many times throughout the day. Last night I played our record for Lord Damodar here in the temple and then performed kirtan with some of the local devotees. It was very nice. But you will be surprised, I think, when I say that I prefer your kirtan in N.Y.

After Prabhupāda had been in Vṛndāvana only one day and his health had only slightly improved, he began planning his return to America. "I am always thinking of you," he wrote to the devotees, whom he addressed as his "dear students."

> I cannot stop my western world activities and I have taken leave from you only for six months; and it may be that on or before I will come to you again. Kirtanananda says from my bodily feature that I am improving. I am also feeling like that.

In Delhi Prabhupāda had received a letter from Brahmānanda saying that the Macmillan Company was definitely interested in publishing the *Bhagavad-gītā*. In Vṛndāvana Prabhupāda wrote Brahmānanda to sign a contract at once on his behalf. Prabhupāda had been considering whether to print privately in Japan or India or to wait for Macmillan. He wasn't concerned with the prestige and financial advantages of publishing through Macmillan; his first concern was to *print as quickly as possible.*

> I shall be satisfied with the commission and shall only be glad to see that the books are being read by hundreds and thousands of men. Whatever profit may be derived from it will be utilized for the development of an American House here.

Prabhupāda stayed in his old rooms at the Rādhā-Dāmodara temple. Still incapacitated, he was being massaged and cared for by Kīrtanānanda, who himself was listless and tired from the heat. But Prabhupāda continued to range from one active and ambitious vision for his youthful Kṛṣṇa consciousness movement to another. He would think aloud about the volumes of *Śrīmad-Bhāgavatam* ready to be published—if Macmillan would take them and the boys could act on his behalf. There was so much to do. He wanted to return by October and oversee things personally.

Temperatures rose to more than 110 degrees, and Prabhupāda and Kīrtanānanda had to stay inside with the doors shut and the overhead fan on. Although Kīrtanānanda could barely perform his duties, Prabhupāda found the heat bracing and said that it was restoring his health. Then, after the first week, the monsoon rains began, and the heat broke.

On August 10 Kīrtanānanda wrote home again.

> God is it a hot place! But at last the rains have started again and there is some relief—from the heat. You can believe me when I say it was hot. But now it is raining a great deal of the time, and that has made the weather quite comfortable for me—but unfortunately not for Swamiji. Also I have developed the inevitable case of dysentery, which has been persisting for about a week now.
>
> Yesterday began the festival of *Jhulan,* in which Radha and Krishna come out and swing for about five days, so I made the rounds of about a half dozen temples here. Some of them are extremely beautiful inside, although most are small. Still I can say this with all truthfulness and sincerity that none are so transcendentally beautiful and spiritual as *3720 Park Avenue Montreal*—and I think even Swamiji would agree with me there.

Kīrtanānanda's letter gave heart to the devotees back home and confirmed their suspicion: it was not Hinduism, not India—it was Swamiji and chanting Hare Kṛṣṇa that was sustaining their spiritual life.

As Prabhupāda's spiritual children wrote from the fledgling centers in half a dozen cities in North America, he would reply.

> Vrindaban is an inspiration only but our real field work is all over the world. Even if I die you are my future hopes & you will do it. I am feeling very much for you all. Please let the ball roll on just as it is set.

Brahmānanda wrote from New York asking for an explanation of why Swamiji, a pure devotee, was suffering serious illness. Swamiji had explained that conditioned souls and even beginning devotees are "attacked by *māyā.*" But was Swamiji also being attacked by *māyā*? On August 14 Śrīla Prabhupāda replied.

> Don't be afraid of my being attacked by maya. When there is fight between two belligerent parties, it is always expected that there will sometimes be reverses. Your country and the western world is mostly under the grip of Maya and the modes of nature in passion and ignorance, and my declaration of war against the maya is certainly a great battle. Maya saw me very successful within one year, so that I got so many sincere young followers like yourself and others, so it was a great defeat to the activities of maya: western country youngsters giving up illicit sex, intoxication, meat-eating and gambling is certainly a great reverse in the activities of maya. Therefore she took advantage of my old age weakness and gave me a death dash. But Krishna saved me; therefore we should thank more Krishna than eulogize maya. So far as my present health is concerned I think I am improving: at least I am taking lunch better than in N.Y. So, as soon as I am a little fit to return to the field of battle I shall again be in your midst.

* * *

Śrīla Prabhupāda envisioned an American House, a place where resident disciples could study Sanskrit and Vaiṣṇava literature in Vṛndāvana. When he had suffered his stroke he had said that Rāya Rāma should finish the translation of the *Bhāgavatams.* He had also requested Acyutānanda, Gaurasundara, and others to learn Sanskrit, Bengali, and Hindi so that if he did not recover they could carry on his work. And he hoped that some of his leading men, like Brahmānanda, Hayagrīva, and Rāya Rāma, would come to India, obtain property, and establish his American House. "Even if I am well," he wrote on September 9, "it is not possible for me to look after the affairs of the American House."

Prabhupāda decided to ask one of his Godbrothers, Swami B. H. Bon Mahārāja, to accommodate some students from America at his Institute of Oriental Philosophy. Swami Bon Mahārāja's institute was a provincial college of about three hundred students, located in Vṛndāvana and affiliated with Agra University. It was what is known in India as a "degree college," an institution geared toward improving the economic condition of its graduates by making them eligible for better jobs.

When Śrīla Prabhupāda and Kīrtanānanda visited Swami Bon Mahārāja at the Institute of Oriental Philosophy, Swami Bon received them in a clean parlor furnished with chairs, couches, and a radio. Swami Bon, wearing leather slippers, shorts visible through his thin *dhotī,* and an ironed shirt with brass studs, appeared suave and sophisticated—an educated man with straight, neatly parted graying hair. Although a resident of Vṛndāvana, in the 1930s he had spent several years in England, where he had been received by members of the royal family and had lectured at a number of colleges. But he had aroused no lasting interest. When Prabhupāda had been struggling alone in New York in 1965, he had written to Swami Bon asking for help. But Swami Bon had not responded. Even now, as Prabhupāda told him of the work in America, Bon Mahārāja didn't have much to say. But he *was* interested in the prospect of Americans coming to live and study at his institute; foreign students would enhance the prestige of the institute in the eyes of the government. He said the students could possibly be accommodated free of charge.

Encouraged by the meeting with Bon Mahārāja, Prabhupāda wrote several letters to his disciples, inviting them to come and study Sanskrit.

> If you want to learn Sanskrit, there is ample opportunity in this institute. We had some preliminary talks, and it is hopeful that Swami Bon can give us some land for our own building; but even so, arrangements can be made with the existing facilities so that there would be no difficulty for the students who come here to study Sanskrit and the Goswami literature. ... It is a good opportunity for our students, and I shall be very glad to learn how many of you desire to come.

* * *

On Janmāṣṭamī day, August 28, Śrīla Prabhupāda awarded the order of *sannyāsa* to Kīrtanānanda in a ceremony in the Rādhā-Dāmodara temple. Kīrtanānanda thus became Śrīla Prabhupāda's first disciple to become a *sannyāsī:* Kīrtanānanda Swami. During the initiation hundreds of visitors were present observing the birthday of Lord Kṛṣṇa, and many of them came by to congratulate the young *sannyāsī.* Someone said he looked like Lord Caitanya. Śrīla Prabhupāda wrote,

> He will be going back to the States very soon to begin preaching work with greater vigor and success. In the meantime, I shall try to utilize this "white sannyasi" for recruiting some members in India.

Early in September, Acyutānanda arrived in Delhi. A Hindu lady gave him five rupees, and he took the train to Mathurā, where he got directions to the Keśavajī Gaudiya Math. Nārāyaṇa Mahārāja, a friend of Prabhupāda's, took Acyutānanda under his care and, after showing him the hall where Prabhupāda had taken *sannyāsa* in 1959, put him on a bus to Vṛndāvana with an old gentleman for an escort. Accompanied by this escort, Acyutānanda arrived by ricksha before the Rādhā-Dāmodara temple.

Acyutānanda walked into Prabhupāda's room and fell prostrate at his feet. "Oh," Prabhupāda said, "you are here." When Acyutānanda looked up he saw that Swamiji had a five-day beard and was wearing only one piece of cloth, wrapped around his waist from behind, crossed over his chest, and tied behind his neck. Prabhupāda smiled, apparently in good health.

Kīrtanānanda Swami also greeted Acyutānanda and showed him his new *daṇḍa.*

For Acyutānanda, the most wonderful thing about Swamiji in Vṛndāvana was the simplicity of his life. Although in New York Swamiji had worn simple robes, he had always been regal, a *guru.* But here he lived very simply and humbly. Once when he sat down on the veranda outside his room to wash his hands, his body instantly became covered with flies. Kīrtanānanda and Acyutānanda were always being bothered by the flies—this was the rainy season—but Prabhupāda scarcely noticed them and sat quietly washing his hands.

Kīrtanānanda and Acyutānanda agreed that Swamiji wasn't just another Vṛndāvana *bābājī.* There was no one else like him. Certainly Gaurachand Goswami, proprietor of the Rādhā-Dāmodara temple, wasn't like Swamiji. He wore thick glasses and could barely see, and when Kīrtanānanda and Acyutānanda went before the Deities in the temple, Gaurachand Goswami asked them loudly, "So how do you like 'em? Which one do you like the best?"

"I like them all," said Acyutānanda.

"I like that big one on the end there," said the priest, pointing in an offhand manner at the Deity of Kṛṣṇa. "It looks a bit like General Choudry." The Swami's boys exchanged looks—what kind of guys are these?—and went back to Swamiji for an explanation.

"They are caste *gosvāmīs,*" Prabhupāda explained. The original *gosvāmīs,* such as Jīva Gosvāmī, who established the Rādhā-Dāmodara temple, had engaged householders to worship the Deities. And these caste *gosvā-*

mīs were descendants of those first householder *pūjārīs.* Prabhupāda explained that the caste *gosvāmīs* were the proprietors of the temples and that they maintained the temples and ran the Deity worship as a business to support their families. Several years ago each of the Deities now on the altar had had His own temple, land, income, and priests. But for economy the *gosvāmīs* had sold the property, reduced the opulence of the worship, and amalgamated the Deities.

There were many other interesting characters: the old widow Sarajini, with bald head and *śikhā* and callused bare feet, who slept in a room by the gate of the temple and swept Swamiji's kitchen and washed his clothes; Pancudas Goswami, the temple proprietor's son, who always chewed *pān* and went around sleepy-eyed in a silk *dhotī* with a red-embroidered border; the dark old *bābājī* who came at night, who was constantly laughing, and who made sandalwood paste for Swamiji; the local herbal doctor, Vanamali Kaviraja, who presided, brightly smiling, from behind a desk in a tiny chamber filled from ceiling to floor with little bottles; and a famous *paṇḍita* who visited Swamiji and wore a gold linked *tulasī* necklace and diamond rings. All of these persons were devotees, residents of holy Vṛndāvana. But no one was like Swamiji.

Kīrtanānanda Swami even became disappointed that no one else in Vṛndāvana was like Swamiji. In the land where everyone was an Indian and everyone was a devotee, Swamiji was still unique. No one else was so simple, so grave, so able to penetrate through falsity, so attractive to the heart, or so absolutely attached to Kṛṣṇa. No one else could lead them.

If Kīrtanānanda Swami and Acyutānanda were doubtful about some of the residents of Vṛndāvana, some of the residents of Vṛndāvana were also doubtful of them. When a European hippie couple wandered into Vṛndāvana one day, Acyutānanda accompanied them to some of the temples. But at the Raṅganātha temple they were refused entry. Acyutānanda told Prabhupāda, who replied, "That's because you went with those fools." When Prabhupāda walked in the streets, people regularly nodded to him with respect, saying, "Daṇḍavat, Mahārāja." But they were cautious about accepting his American followers as Vaiṣṇavas.

* * *

Śrīla Prabhupāda, accompanied by his two disciples, again visited Swami Bon. Riding to Swami Bon's institute by ricksha, Prabhupāda told Acyutānanda that Swami Bon had started the institute as an academy of Vaiṣṇava studies but had affiliated with Agra University because the institute had not been bringing in any money. Now Swami Bon had money, but the institute had become an ordinary school, devoid of spiritual value.

As Śrīla Prabhupāda and his disciples sat in Swami Bon's parlor, Bon Mahārāja made it clear that although he would not donate land for Prabhupāda's American House, Prabhupāda's students could come and study at his institution. Acyutānanda, he suggested, could be the first one.

Swami Bon then took them to the main building to visit a class in session. Instead of seeing *paṇḍitas* and *brahmacārīs* studying Sanskrit, as they had expected, Prabhupāda's disciples saw boys with thin mustaches and giggling girls. Prabhupāda lectured and then asked Kīrtanānanda to play the Hare Kṛṣṇa record. After a few minutes, Bon Mahārāja told Kīrtanānanda to stop the record, but Kīrtanānanda, seeing Swamiji enjoying the record, let it play.

Acyutānanda: *We walked around the place, and I thought, "This is just a mundane school. I don't want to go here. If I could learn Sanskrit and live at the Rādhā-Dāmodara temple, then I could have a nice time in India."*

They continued their tour of the facilities, and after seeing the dormitory Prabhupāda doubted whether his American disciples could endure the austerity and the academic studies. It seemed that one of the two boys was always sick. First Kīrtanānanda Swami had gotten dysentery, then something had been wrong with Acyutānanda's stomach, then they had both been exhausted from the heat. "On the whole," Śrīla Prabhupāda wrote to Rūpānuga in New York, "the American boys who come here become first depressed, so I do not know how far our American House in Vrindaban will be successful." His boys were not particularly studious or austere. Besides, both Kīrtanānanda Swami and Acyutānanda had developed a definite dislike for the rector of the Institute of Oriental Philosophy. And Śrīla Prabhupāda obviously had reservations about the place. "You can go and study there," Prabhupāda told them, "but don't live there. Live at the Rādhā-Dāmodara temple and go. You can get a bicycle and go there."

Gradually, the idea of immediately acquiring an American House in

Vṛndāvana began to dwindle. Prabhupāda needed his own place for his disciples, and that would take time.

* * *

With regular medication, massages, rest, and the heat of Vṛndāvana, Prabhupāda felt himself recovering. By mid-September he declared himself ninety percent fit to return to the United States. He predicted that he would be back there by the end of October.

B. R. Śrīdhara Mahārāja, Prabhupāda's Godbrother, whose *āśrama* was in Navadvīpa, West Bengal, wrote to invite Prabhupāda to spend the month of Kārttika with him at the *āśrama* and join him for his Vyāsa-pūjā celebration. Śrīla Prabhupāda liked the idea of going to the holy land of Navadvīpa, where Lord Caitanya had spent His early years, and seeing his Godbrother. He also wanted to visit Delhi again and inquire about printing his books.

"Swamiji," Acyutānanda asked, "when you go to Navadvīpa am I supposed to stay here in Vṛndāvana and study?"

"Don't you want to see the birthplace of Lord Caitanya?" Prabhupāda asked.

Acyutānanda did, and Prabhupāda, Kīrtanānanda Swami, and Acyutānanda left Vṛndāvana together and returned to the Chippiwada temple in Delhi.

For Prabhupāda's two disciples, life at the Chippiwada temple was hard. Delhi was blazing hot and lacked the charm of Vṛndāvana. There was water for only two hours a day, early in the morning, and that only a slow trickle. They would fill two clay jugs for Prabhupāda's room and several buckets for his bath and their own, and then there would be no more water for the rest of the day. A mongoose ran freely through the building.

"Do they eat snakes?" Acyutānanda asked.

"They eat snakes," said Śrīla Prabhupāda, "they eat garbage, they eat anything." Prabhupāda, who regarded the heat, the lack of water, and even the mongoose as normal, was undisturbed. Several young Indian musicians in the adjacent room regularly played cinema music on their electric organ, bongo drums, and electric guitars, rehearsing for a dance. Prabhupāda tolerated it.

Sri Krishna Pandit praised Prabhupāda's work in America and his English translation of *Śrīmad-Bhāgavatam.* As manager of the Chippiwada Rādhā-Kṛṣṇa temple and secretary of an active Hinduism society, Sri Krishna Pandit was interested in spreading Hindu *dharma,* and therefore he wanted Prabhupāda to speak at the nearby Gaurī-Śaṅkara temple, one of Delhi's most popular Hindu temples. Prabhupāda agreed to go and take with him Acyutānanda (Kīrtanānanda Swami had already left for the West on August 22).

The Gaurī-Śaṅkara temple was on Chandi Chowk. After a short walk through some of the busiest, most congested streets of Old Delhi, Prabhupāda and Acyutānanda removed their shoes at the door and entered the temple. The main deity was Lord Śiva, but there were many others: Rāma, Durgā, Kālī, Rādhā-Kṛṣṇa, Hanumān. The crowds stood before the elaborate altars, viewing and petitioning the various deities.

Acyutānanda had learned about demigod worship from Prabhupāda at 26 Second Avenue. According to *Bhagavad-gītā,* demigods fulfill only material desires and are therefore worshiped by the less intelligent. A Vaiṣṇava, Prabhupāda had said, respects the demigods—in fact, he respects all living beings, even the ant—but he worships only the Supreme Personality of Godhead, Kṛṣṇa, or Viṣṇu.

Acyutānanda had already seen firsthand that impersonalists were misleading Indians to disavow the personal form of God and accept all methods of worship as equal. Most Indians had no clear understanding of *Bhagavad-gītā* or Kṛṣṇa. Acyutānanda kept this in mind as Prabhupāda led him in bowing down before a few of the demigods' altars. Then Prabhupāda brought him before the Deity of Rādhā-Kṛṣṇa. "Just see," Prabhupāda said, "Kṛṣṇa is just playing His flute. As for the demigods, someone is holding bows and arrows, someone is holding clubs, someone is holding weapons, but Rādhā and Kṛṣṇa are just dancing, and Kṛṣṇa is holding a flute. So He is the Supreme Lord."

In one large room a heavyset man with a great white beard and wearing flower garlands sat on several pillows. Many people stood staring at him. He reminded Acyutānanda of Santa Claus. "Swamiji, who is that?" Acyutānanda asked.

"Some *yogī,*" Prabhupāda replied indifferently.

The main lecture hall had a large painting of Lord Śiva on the wall and was crowded with people—women in colored *sārīs* and many of the men in bright turbans. Amid such a welter of rituals and worshipers, Acyutānanda felt protected by Swamiji. They sat on the dais, and Sri Krishna Pandit introduced his friend Bhaktivedanta Swami to the crowd. Śrīla Prabhupāda spoke in Hindi for about an hour.

Walking back to Chippiwada, Acyutānanda wondered why Swamiji had gone to speak at a place with such hodgepodge worship. But without his asking, it occurred to him that Swamiji was willing to speak about Kṛṣṇa *anywhere* to *anyone.* Hadn't he come to New York City? And what could be a more hodgepodge place than New York's Lower East Side?

Sitting on the veranda outside his room, Prabhupāda could see the huge domes of the Jama Mosque in the early evening sky. One evening, as Prabhupāda sat softly chanting *japa* and as Acyutānanda, who had not yet memorized the Gāyatrī *mantra,* sat nearby reading it to himself, a Hindu gentleman came and conversed with Prabhupāda. Acyutānanda soon finished the Gāyatrī *mantra* and sat listening to his spiritual master talk in Hindi to the unknown gentleman. Acyutānanda could catch only a word here or there—some mention of Ayurvedic medicine, addresses, Indian names, cities. They talked for hours, and Acyutānanda wondered who this man was who could speak so long with Swamiji. When the man left, Acyutānanda asked, "Swamiji, was he your Godbrother?"

Prabhupāda said, "No."

"Is he a *swami?*"

Prabhupāda said, "No."

"Is he one of your relatives?"

"No."

"Well, who was he?"

"He's my friend!" Prabhupāda answered emphatically.

Sometimes Prabhupāda's visitors would bring donations of cloth or fruits or even complete cooked meals in metal *tiffins.* One visitor—a middle-aged woman who had heard Prabhupāda speak at the Gaurī-Śaṅkara temple—came to Prabhupāda's office in Chippiwada requesting initiation. Prabhupāda spoke with her, agreed, and had Acyutānanda prepare a small fire sacrifice. At her initiation he gave her the name Mukunda dāsī. She came daily to clean Prabhupāda's room, and when she saw that his wooden-peg sandals were broken, she bought him new ones.

Chandrashekhar had known Prabhupāda for several years and was supposed to have been his secretary. But he was a drunkard. Prabhupāda suspected him of having stolen from his mailbox more than two thousand rupees during the past two years. Prabhupāda's Chippiwada address was listed in his magazines and books, and people had been sending money for books and *Back to Godhead* subscriptions. Even in the past two months, Prabhupāda's disciples had written that they were enclosing money in their letters, but Prabhupāda never found any. One day he caught sight of Chandrashekhar in the building and asked him, "Where is my mailbox key?"

"I believe you have it," Chandrashekhar replied. "Or maybe Sri Krishna Pandit has it." Chandrashekhar was drunk.

"Swamiji," Acyutānanda said angrily, "maybe we should make a police case."

Prabhupāda shook his head, "No."

"Well," Acyutānanda said, "if he's not punished by the law, then in his next birth Kṛṣṇa will punish him."

"That's true," Prabhupāda agreed. Chandrashekhar looked fearfully from Prabhupāda to his American disciple.

"Then there's only one thing to do," Acyutānanda said. "Shall I call the police?"

"No," said Prabhupāda, "I forgive him." Yet only a few days later Prabhupāda's record player disappeared, and Prabhupāda suspected the drunkard, Chandrashekhar.

Prabhupāda brought Acyutānanda with him to his bank, the Bank of Baroda, to exchange some American currency. As they were about to enter the door, the guard refused them entry, thinking they were *sādhus* come to beg. Prabhupāda was angry. He spoke loudly in Hindi to the guard, an old man with a shotgun, a big strap of bullets, and a shabby semi-official uniform. "I have an account here," Prabhupāda protested. Finally the guard allowed them to enter.

Prabhupāda went straight to the manager and complained. "Do you think," Prabhupāda said, "because I am a *sādhu* I am to be regarded as a beggar?" Prabhupāda told the man of his organization in America and his account in the Bank of Baroda. The manager apologized and reprimanded the guard.

One day Prabhupāda sent Acyutānanda to a certain restaurant. "If you want to see varieties of Indian food," Prabhupāda said, "tell the man you want ten rupees of sweets and ten rupees of salty preparations—that is called *miṣṭi* and *nimaka*. And just see the varieties." Acyutānanda was sick and couldn't imagine eating a lot of sweets. But he stopped by the restaurant and looked. When he returned to the temple at Chippiwada he told Prabhupāda that he had seen the food, although he couldn't eat it. "Yes, but just see the varieties," Prabhupāda concluded. And he explained how Kṛṣṇa consciousness was personal and full of varieties, not dry.

Another American disciple joined Prabhupāda—Rāmānuja, from Haight-Ashbury. He had been initiated just before Swamiji had left San Francisco, and he sported a full black beard. Prabhupāda didn't like the beard. Cautiously and indirectly he mentioned it; but Rāmānuja's beard stayed. Rāmānuja carried a book about Tibetan Buddhism, and he didn't seem fixed in Kṛṣṇa consciousness philosophy. But here he was, one of the looser, sentimental San Francisco devotees, ready for Indian adventures with Swamiji.

* * *

Śrīla Prabhupāda visited the wealthy Delhi industrialist Mr. Seth Dalmia to discuss plans for printing some of his books in India. Mr. Dalmia received him well but gave only vague promises of help. Prabhupāda also met with Hitsaran Sharma, Mr. Dalmia's secretary, who worked closely with Hanuman Prasad Poddar of the popular religious publishing company Gita Press. Śrīla Prabhupāda was already acquainted with all three gentlemen, since they had all donated toward his first volume of *Śrīmad-Bhāgavatam.* Prabhupāda wanted Gita Press to publish his *Gītopaniṣad* and *Śrīmad-Bhāgavatam.* Hitsaran Sharma showed him an illustrated *Gītā* in Hindi poetry that he had recently published. "But my *Gītā,* my *Bhāgavatam,*" said Śrīla Prabhupāda, appearing disgusted, "is the description of God. It is the description of Kṛṣṇa." Mr. Sharma said he couldn't see how Gita Press could print Prabhupāda's voluminous writings. Nevertheless, Prabhupāda still considered privately printing *Gītopaniṣad,* with Mr. Sharma as his agent.

On October 11, Prabhupāda wrote to Brahmānanda,

> We must have our books printed; we have wasted much time in the matter of editing and finding out a suitable publisher. When I was alone there was three volumes published but during the last two years I could not publish a single volume more. It is a great defeat. If I have one or two sincere souls like you and if we can make more publications, then our mission will be a great success. I am prepared to sit down underneath a tree with one sincere soul and in such activity I shall be freed of all diseases.

* * *

Devotees from America were regularly writing Swamiji, anxious to see him again in good health. But he didn't want to leave India, he explained, until he personally saw that the printing of his *Gītopaniṣad* was under way. Printing *Gītopaniṣad* and obtaining approval for permanent residency in the U.S. were the two short-term goals he wished to achieve before returning. But he thought often of his return to America.

> As you are all feeling my separation, similarly I'm also anxious to return as soon as possible. I think I'm fit to go back to your country at present and as scheduled previously I'm sure by the end of October. I must be fit to return, but before this there are many things to be done. I'm not yet assured of the permanent visa. The best thing will be that from each center an invitation should be sent that my presence is urgently required. ... Presently I'm very much anxious to begin printing here if Macmillan company does not take up the work. Please, therefore, let me know yes or no from Macmillan. If he is not serious, then immediately send the manuscripts finished or not to the following address: Pundit Hitsaran Sharma c/o Dalmia Enterprises, Scindia House, New Delhi. After dispatching let me know and I shall do the needful.

Indian friends who visited Prabhupāda's room listened eagerly as he told them about America—the millions of cars and the superhighways and thousands of young people rejecting their fathers' wealth. But Prabhupāda's visitors weren't fully able to understand his visit to America. Not that they were too simple to understand and not just that they had never traveled in the West. Prabhupāda's experience in America consisted of intimate spiritual relationships with his disciples. How could an outsider understand the dynamics of his temples and his disciples in the West? How could anyone except Prabhupāda and his disciples understand these things?

> My mind is always with you. Practically your country is my home now. India is a foreign country for me. The reason is that my spiritual family is there and my material relationships are in India; therefore factually where my spiritual family exists, there is my home.

Śrīla Prabhupāda's vision of a worldwide society of devotees preaching in temples and publishing books—a vision he had had even before he had gone to America—was now becoming manifest. But it was dependent on him. In his absence his disciples were sustained only by carrying out his orders and receiving his letters. When Dayānanda and Nandarāṇī had gone from the San Francisco temple to start a temple in Los Angeles, it had been Śwamiji's instructions that had sustained and guided them: "Wherever there is a new branch of our society for Krishna Consciousness I become very very happy. And my blessings in heart and soul are with you." On receipt of Swamiji's letter, they knew they had done the right thing. No matter that husband and wife sometimes quarreled and that there wasn't enough money—the main thing was that Swamiji was pleased.

From Boston, Satsvarūpa wrote that he and the other devotees there were moving from an apartment to a rented storefront near Boston University. The first time Satsvarūpa entered the new storefront, he found on the floor an aerogram from Swamiji, dated October 6 from Delhi.

> I can understand that you have secured a very nice place in Boston and there is a very good possibility of pushing our movement amongst the student community there. Our movement is certainly very much appealing to the younger section of your country and if we are successful in the matter of attracting the student community in your country certainly this movement will scatter all over the world and fullfill the foretelling of Lord Caitanya that in every village and every town of the world the Lord will be famous for His glorious sankirtana movement. Please try for this with your heart and soul and your life will be a successful mission.

The letter was as good as Swamiji coming personally to open the storefront and begin the preaching. It gave Satsvarūpa full direction and inspiration. And it was personal. In that same letter, Prabhupāda had written:

> I am always aspiring after returning to your care and overload you with typewriting tasks. ... I hope we shall very soon meet again and help each other in the matter of discharging Krishna conscious engagements. I am now 90% alright and I think I can return safely. This typewriting work is done by me. For two days I am alone and doing everything myself as experiment. This proves that I am now well. Please offer my blessings to all the boys and girls there.

In New Mexico, Subala was trying to arrange public speaking engagements for Prabhupāda's return, and Prabhupāda was encouraging him: "If you think I can be on television by the first week in December, then you can arrange for it because I must be in your country by the middle of November."

Śrīla Prabhupāda wrote to Janārdana in Montreal answering his philosophical doubts and encouraging him to be patient with his spiritually reluctant wife. And to Rāya Rāma, who was editing *Back to Godhead* magazine in New York, he gave another kind of thoughtful assurance.

> I am very happy that since it [BTG] is entrusted to you the things are improving. This means that Krishna is giving you more & more facilities. Krishna is such a nice boss that he gives more facilities & improvement to the sincere servant.

On October 9, the day Prabhupāda started for Calcutta, he left behind a different kind of letter for Sri Krishna Pandit. Prabhupāda had been negotiating with Sri Krishna Pandit to purchase the Chippiwada temple for ISKCON or at least to rent the single room through a formal contract. Prabhupāda wanted the room as a Delhi headquarters for printing his books. On the day of his departure, however, Sri Krishna Pandit was unavailable, and Prabhupāda left him a short handwritten note.

> If you are not settling anything with the room, then I may not come back to Delhi any more. I will go to U.S.A. directly from Calcutta via the Pacific route for which Sri Dalmia Seth has already promised for the ticket.

CHAPTER TWENTY-EIGHT

India Revisited: Part 2

PRABHUPĀDA'S TRAIN, THE Kalka Mail, pulled into Delhi Station. Prabhupāda and his two disciples had tickets with reserved seat numbers— but no car number. So while Prabhupāda waited with the baggage, Acyutānanda and Rāmānuja ran from one end of the train to the other looking for their car.

After they had found their seats and boarded, Acyutānanda untied Prabhupāda's bedding and spread it open on the upper tier. Prabhupāda climbed the little ladder, sat comfortably on his cotton-stuffed quilt, and opened his Sanskrit *Śrīmad-Bhāgavatam,* while Acyutānanda and Rāmānuja took their seats. It would take around twenty-four hours to reach Calcutta.

Near the end of the journey, a group of educated Bengali gentlemen struck up a philosophical conversation with the Swami. "We do not worship any form," said one, speaking fluent English in a loud, deep voice. "We have a marble *oṁkāra* that we worship, and we sit and pray to that."

"That is also a form," said Prabhupāda. He was reluctant to attack their philosophical position directly.

"We practice *karma-yoga,*" the gentleman went on, not heeding Prabhupāda's previous point. "Because in *karma-yoga* you can stay within your position."

"But *karma-yoga* is not full surrender of the soul," said Prabhupāda. "One must come to the stage of *bhakti.*"

"Oh, no," the man protested, "emotionalism is very harmful. *Karma-yoga*— "

Śrīla Prabhupāda exploded: "*Karma-yoga* is for the fools!" Silence.

Another man, not with the Bengalis but seated beside them, spoke up. "Obviously Swamiji is a learned scholar," he said. "You shouldn't argue like that." The Bengali that Prabhupāda had shouted at got up and moved to another seat. Later, he came back.

"Are you insulted?" Prabhupāda asked him.

"No, no, no," he replied. "But I have never heard anyone say that about the teachings of the *Gītā*."

The Bengalis then talked with Acyutānanda, lighting their cigarettes and smoking freely before him, although they had not dared to do so before Prabhupāda (it wasn't proper to smoke in front of a *sādhu*). Bengalis, Acyutānanda told them, citing one of Prabhupāda's examples, were very sorry that East Pakistan had been cut off from the rest of Bengal. But Kṛṣṇa consciousness could elevate people to international, universal consciousness. Then there wouldn't be any such division. The Bengalis appreciated Acyutānanda's remark, though they continued to blow smoke in his face as the train rattled over the last miles to Calcutta.

Prabhupāda was greeted at Calcutta's Howrah Station by relatives, mostly from his sister's family, and by devotees of the Goswami Math. About fifty people were on hand. They offered Prabhupāda flower garlands and sandalwood paste and then escorted him and his disciples into a car. Acyutānanda and Rāmānuja noticed that although Swamiji's sister was shorter and more rotund than Prabhupāda, her facial features were strikingly similar. Her name was Bhavatarini, but Prabhupāda told them to call her Pisimā, "aunt."

As Prabhupāda rode through the streets he saw many images of goddess Kālī, ten-armed, riding a lion. Calcutta was observing the biggest religious celebration in Bengal, Kālī-pūjā, a month of festivities in honor of the goddess Kālī. Throughout the city, brass bands and radio music blared, and there were decorative lights, stages, and tents.

When Prabhupāda arrived at Pisimā's house in south Calcutta, his relatives seated him and performed an *ārati* ceremony in his honor, reverently offering him the traditional items: incense, a flaming lamp, flowers. They also bathed his feet. He sat smiling within the crowded room of relatives, who were proud of his having journeyed to America on behalf of Lord Kṛṣṇa.

As Prabhupāda's family members sang Hare Kṛṣṇa *kīrtana,* from outside the room the ladies of the house began singing a high, shrill whooping sound. Acyutānanda and Rāmānuja were startled.

Pisimā had prepared a large feast, much of it cooked in mustard seed oil, for the homecoming celebration. And Prabhupāda satisfied her by honoring the *prasādam,* even though he wasn't feeling well and was tired from the train ride.

Soon after the festivities Prabhupāda and his disciples retired. Again his health wavered—this time because of his sister's heavy cooking—and he felt a strain on his heart. He sent for an Ayurvedic doctor, who taught Acyutānanda how to do a very gentle massage to help circulation and restricted Prabhupāda from sweets.

As Prabhupāda recovered he began regularly lecturing in his room during the evening. Although he spoke in English (for his disciples), the room would soon fill to capacity with relatives and friends. There were generally disturbances from outside due to the noises of Kālī-pūjā. Nearby Pisimā's house was a large tent, a center for evening street parties, which included a sweets counter, fireworks, and an excessively loud public address system that incongruously blared Julie Andrews singing songs from *The Sound of Music.*

One evening as Prabhupāda spoke—"My only qualification is that I have unflinching faith in my spiritual master"—a large firecracker exploded right outside the door. The audience smiled tolerantly. "Yes," Prabhupāda said, taking the explosion as confirmation of his words, "it is glorious."

One night Prabhupāda explained that according to *Bhagavad-gītā,* demigod worshipers are less intelligent. People worship Kālī for material rewards, he said, but since all material things are temporary, such worship is inferior to the worship of Kṛṣṇa. Kālī is not able to grant the worshiper liberation from birth and death.

"Which is better?" Acyutānanda asked, "the worship of the Christians and Jews, which is mostly impersonal, or the worship of the non-Absolute by the worshipers of Kālī?"

"Worship of Kālī is better," Prabhupāda said, "because the worshipers are in the Vedic system. They are more likely to bow down to Rādhā-Kṛṣṇa or chant Hare Kṛṣṇa than a Christian or Jew. There is a chance that they will become Kṛṣṇa devotees in the future, if they lose their material attachments."

Prabhupāda regularly invited his Godbrothers and their disciples to join him in America. Sometimes he seemed to do it just to get them at least to think more of preaching. Bhaktisiddhānta Sarasvatī had once chided that the Gaudiya Math *āśrama* was no more than a "joint mess," the members going out each day and collecting enough alms so that they could eat together, but with no dynamic vision for preaching. So Prabhupāda's frequent invitations—"You should go to America. Come back with me"—would stir them, even if they couldn't actually come. On visiting the *āśrama* of Bhaktisāraṅga Goswami, Prabhupāda saw that the audience consisted almost entirely of old widows. But he spoke as usual.

One day, Prabhupāda's Godbrother Haridāsa Swami came by. He was heavyset and loud, and he spoke very rapidly: "Very happy to see you coming here from America. This is wonderful—Kṛṣṇa is the summum bonum, the cause of all causes—I want you to come to my temple. ..."

When Haridāsa Mahārāja went into a separate room, Prabhupāda turned to Acyutānanda: "He wants us to go to his temple. But to go there I will have to go onto a ricksha and then onto a tramcar and then onto a train and then another ricksha." Aware of Prabhupāda's weak condition, Acyutānanda began shaking his head negatively.

When Haridāsa Mahārāja returned, Acyutānanda said that Swamiji couldn't come to his *maṭha*. "Who are you?" Haridāsa Mahārāja said angrily. "You are just a *brahmacārī*! You should risk your life!"

Acyutānanda replied, "I will risk *my* life, but I can't risk my spiritual master's life."

Haridāsa Mahārāja left insulted. "Don't worry," Prabhupāda said. "He is just very talkative."

Prabhupāda paid a visit to B. P. Keśava Mahārāja, the Godbrother who had awarded him the *sannyāsa* order in 1959. Prabhupāda sat on the floor and spoke in Bengali to his Godbrother, who was very old and apparently on his deathbed. Prabhupāda had Acyutānanda sing for Keśava

Mahārāja. Keśava Mahārāja requested Prabhupāda to visit his *āśrama,* Devananda Math, in Navadvīpa.

* * *

Śrīla Prabhupāda had wanted to return to the U.S. as a permanent resident, but his students in America hadn't been able to get the necessary clearance from the U.S. immigration department. The devotees in Boston had gotten in touch with a few Harvard Indology professors but had obtained no signed statements about Prabhupāda's importance. All the ISKCON centers had written formal letters inviting A. C. Bhaktivedanta Swami and had presented copies to the U.S. immigration office. But unless the devotees could produce something more impressive, like a government recommendation or a university's offer for him to join their faculty, Prabhupāda could not become a U.S. resident.

On October 13 Prabhupāda wrote to his disciples in Montreal:

> I am very anxious to go to Montreal. Therefore you must try your best to get my immigration visa on the basis of my being an authorized Vaishnava minister, based on Srimad Bhagawatam and Srimad Bhagavad Gita.

Rather than wait indefinitely for permanent residency, Prabhupāda decided to apply for a visitor's visa. He went with Acyutānanda to the U.S. Consulate on Harrington Road. There, in the middle of Calcutta, they entered a small piece of America, with everything shiny, new, and efficient: air conditioners, stainless steel water coolers, electric security doors, U.S. Marines, and American flags. Sitting before the secretary of the Consulate, Prabhupāda looked small and humble. "I want a visa to see my students in America," he said softly.

"Do you have any letters?" the secretary asked. Acyutānanda handed over the letters from the temples. The secretary reviewed them and quickly gave Prabhupāda a four-month visa. While leaving the building Prabhupāda remarked, "I will just get anything, and then it can be extended."

On October 19, Prabhupāda wrote Hayagrīva regarding his imminent return:

> I am already preparing for returning to U.S.A. & I have obtained a visitor's visa the day before yesterday. Most probably I shall take the first chance to return to U.S.A. upon my return from Navadwipa.

And on October 22 he wrote Umāpati:

> You will be glad to know that I have already secured a visitor's visa to your country and have asked my travel agent to book my seat on the earliest possible date. I think I shall be in your midst by the middle of Nov.

* * *

On October 24 Prabhupāda traveled with Acyutānanda and Rāmānuja to Navadvīpa. Although the local train took four hours, the lush Bengal countryside gradually revealed its heavenly beauty, and Prabhupāda's health seemed to improve just from the pleasant journey. By the time they arrived at Navadvīpa, Acyutānanda and Rāmānuja were also feeling relief from the rigors of Calcutta; for the first time in weeks they could open their eyes without blinking through drops of perspiration.

A large *kīrtana* party of *brahmacārīs,* mostly members of Keśava Mahārāja's Devananda Gaudiya Math, met Śrīla Prabhupāda at the Navadvīpa train station. The *brahmacārīs* were meticulously neat, with their robes all dyed the same shade of saffron, their Vaiṣṇava *tilaka* markings bold and distinct, their heads smoothly shaved, their *śikhās* precise. They offered Prabhupāda and his party aromatic garlands made from flowers resembling lotuses and gathered around Śrīla Prabhupāda with worshipful enthusiasm. Also present were a few of Śrīdhara Mahārāja's disciples, waiting with rickshas to take Prabhupāda and his disciples to their *guru's āśrama.* Although between the two groups there was an unspoken competition for Prabhupāda's presence, he had previously agreed to go to Śrīdhara Mahārāja's place. He promised the members of Devananda Math that he would visit them next.

Soon after leaving the station the rickshas turned onto a road lined with lush tropical vegetation: banana trees, tall bamboos, exotic blossoming flowers. Prabhupāda saw simple villagers working near their straw-and-mud huts and, in the distance, the spire of Śrīdhara Mahārāja's temple.

A kīrtana party greeted Prabhupāda at the outer gates of Śrīdhara Mahārāja's *āśrama,* chanting Hare Kṛṣṇa and playing *karatālas* and clay *mṛdaṅgas.* Prabhupāda entered the temple, offered obeisances before the Deities of Rādhā and Kṛṣṇa, and then went to see his Godbrother.

Śrīdhara Mahārāja was very old, his sight failing, his joints stiff with arthritis. He stayed mostly in his room or sometimes on his veranda and moved only with slow, rickety motions. He was an austere and kindly Vaiṣṇava and smiled heartily on seeing Prabhupāda and his disciples. In fluent English he began praising Prabhupāda's preaching in America, repeatedly using Prabhupāda's phrase "Kṛṣṇa consciousness." Swamiji's work, he said, was the fulfillment of Lord Caitanya's prophecy that Kṛṣṇa consciousness would one day spread all over the world. He laughed and smiled and praised the Kṛṣṇa consciousness movement with no trace of jealousy.

"So you appreciate this phrase, 'Kṛṣṇa consciousness.'" Prabhupāda smiled.

"Yes," Śrīdhara Mahārāja replied, "and the disciples of Swami Mahārāja also." And he turned towards Acyutānanda and Rāmānuja. "With very little effort your preaching will go far."

The boys were astonished. This was really something to write home about: sitting on the roof of a temple in this jungle paradise with old Śrīdhara Mahārāja appreciating Swamiji's work as the greatest work on behalf of Lord Caitanya, and Swamiji sitting relaxed, grinning, and making humble replies! It was the high point of the trip.

> My dear Satsvarupa,
>
> Please accept my blessings. I have already duly received the invitation from Harvard University. It is understood that they are scheduling me for 20 Nov. between 6 and 10 p.m. I can start immediately on the strength of my visitor's visa, but I am awaiting for Mukunda's reply for his trying for my permanent visa. Yesterday we have all come to Navadvipa. This place is another establishment of one of my Godbrothers. It is very nice and extensive place and my Godbrother, B. R. Sridhar Maharaj, has spared one entire nice house for our stay. He has also agreed to cooperate with our society. We shall observe his birthday ceremony tomorrow and the brahmacaris shall learn how to celebrate the spiritual master's birthday.

Vyāsa-pūjā day, the observance of B. R. Śrīdhara Mahārāja's birthday, was October 27. His disciples had erected a *paṇḍāl* on the temple road, and about a hundred people attended. Śrīdhara Mahārāja sat on his *vyāsāsana,* and Prabhupāda and other *sannyāsīs,* all wearing flower garlands, sat in chairs next to Śrīdhara Mahārāja. Prabhupāda spoke in Bengali. Some of Śrīdhara Mahārāja's disciples, inspired by Prabhupāda's preaching about the glories of spreading Kṛṣṇa consciousness in the West, delivered speeches in English as Vyāsa-pūjā homages to their spiritual master. Śrīdhara Mahārāja, also speaking in English, gave a very scientific lecture on Kṛṣṇa consciousness and the senses. Afterwards Prabhupāda told his disciples, "He has very high realizations, but he is keeping them to himself."

Every morning before dawn Śrīdhara Mahārāja sent out a party of *brahmacārīs* to perform *kīrtana* in the villages. On Prabhupāda's request, Acyutānanda and Rāmānuja joined them, leaving before sunrise and returning at dusk. Although Prabhupāda and Śrīdhara Mahārāja usually remained at the temple, one day they got into a ricksha and accompanied the chanting party through the streets of Navadvīpa.

The festival at the Devananda Math was a big affair. In contrast to Bhaktisāraṅga Goswami's *āśrama* in Calcutta, where only widows had attended, B. P. Keśava Mahārāja's Devananda Math had about two hundred *brahmacārīs* and twenty *sannyāsīs*. Some of the *brahmacārīs*, however, were not full-time but were attending school outside; so the *āśrama's* atmosphere was a little like that of a social club. But when the *kīrtana* and the circumambulation of the temple began, seven hundred people took part. The impeccably dressed *sannyāsīs*—whose every piece of saffron cloth, including their cloth-wrapped *daṇḍas,* was dyed exactly the same shade—danced back and forth before the Deities. A dozen *sannyāsīs* danced in a group, their *daṇḍas* moving together, dipping and rising, forward and back, to the delight of the *brahmacārīs*.

Prabhupāda sat on a dais with other dignitaries and spoke to the festival audience. Acyutānanda, on Prabhupāda's request, spoke a few words in Bengali, bringing laughs and applause. Śrīdhara Mahārāja spoke gravely in Bengali. A *sannyāsī* from the Devananda Math, speaking for their absent leader, B. P. Keśava Mahārāja, proclaimed in empassioned tones that although Lord Caitanya Mahāprabhu's movement had been predicted to spread throughout the world, no one had known how it could be possible. Now, thanks to the work of Bhaktivedanta Swami, it was happening.

After a large feast in the evening, Prabhupāda's party returned to Śrīdhara Mahārāja's *āśrama*. Śrīdhara Mahārāja intimated to Prabhupāda that the Devananda Math emphasized quantity whereas his own *āśrama* emphasized quality. Curious as to what this meant, Acyutānanda wanted to ask Prabhupāda. But the time didn't seem appropriate.

After nine days in Navadvīpa Prabhupāda was ready to return to Calcutta and prepare for his trip back to the United States. He and his two disciples took rickshas to Navadvīpa and caught a morning train to Calcutta.

On the train, Acyutānanda timidly put forward the question that had been on his mind: "Swamiji, what did you and Śrīdhara Mahārāja discuss?"

"Oh, many, many things," Prabhupāda replied. "But if I were to tell you now, you would faint." After a silence Prabhupāda added, "Still, I offered him to be president of our Society. I knew he would not accept. He is keeping things within him. Anyway, this is all beyond you. Do not have any ill feelings towards any of my Godbrothers. They are all great souls. There are just some differences on preaching and spreading. Even in your mind do not feel any ill will towards them. At the same time, do not mix very thickly with them."

Acyutānanda suggested, "Maybe if these two *sannyāsīs* had each other's qualities combined ..."

"Ah, yes," Prabhupāda said, "now you have understood me."

* * *

Śrīla Prabhupāda's intention in coming to Calcutta was simply to prepare to leave for America. He had his visitor's visa already, but he thought that if he stayed in India a little longer, in San Francisco Mukunda might be able to secure permanent American residency for him. He went to his sister's house to spend his last days in Calcutta there, but after only a few days he felt that the Rādhā-Govinda Deity—the Deity he had worshiped in his childhood—was calling him.

When Prabhupāda had been no more than an infant, his servant used to take him and his cousin Subuddhi Mullik on a perambulator, wheel them into the temple courtyard, and take them before the altar of Rādhā-Govinda. And as soon as Prabhupāda could walk, his father would hold his hand and take him before the Deity every day. Sometimes Prabhupāda would go alone and stand for hours gazing upon Rādhā and Kṛṣṇa, who appeared very beautiful to him with Their slanted eyes and fine dress and ornaments. It had been for the pleasure of Rādhā-Govinda that as a child, beginning at the age of five, he had performed his miniature Ratha-yātrā festival.

Just two weeks ago, when Prabhupāda had been staying at his sister's house, his health had prevented him from going to north Calcutta to see the Deity; so he had gone to Navadvīpa without taking Their blessings. But now, although still weak and although preoccupied with traveling to the U.S., he felt that the Deity was calling him.

For the past 150 years, the Rādhā-Govinda temple had been maintained by the aristocratic Mulliks, a branch of Prabhupāda's own family. The Mulliks had owned the entire block on Harrison Road (now Mahatma Gandhi Road), and rents from the block-long building opposite the temple had financed the opulent worship of Rādhā-Govinda. In those days the Deities had been worshiped on a gorgeous altar in the large *kīrtana* hall, and They had been dressed in silks and ornamented with gilded and bejeweled crowns and necklaces. All the pious Vaiṣṇava families of the neighborhood would visit; and on Janmāṣṭamī, Kṛṣṇa's birthday, even British gentlemen and ladies would come.

But today the Mullik family possessed only remnants of the European art and furnishings that had once filled their homes and temple—relics from an age of former grandeur. And the worship of Rādhā-Govinda had pitifully deteriorated.

Śrīla Prabhupāda was pained to see the neglect. No longer were Rādhā and Govinda the center of the Mulliks' lives. The Deity worship still continued—conducted by paid *brāhmaṇas*—but few people came to see. The main attraction now was the golden deity of the goddess Kālī on the large altar in the *kīrtana* hall. Rādhā and Govinda, "in the family" for many generations, had been relegated to a small upstairs room in the Mullik compound. Their dress was no longer elegant, Their valuable crowns and ornaments had disappeared, and there were no large *kīrtanas* as before. Only a paid *brāhmaṇa* came in the morning to rub sandalwood pulp on Their shining bodies, dress Them carefully in whatever simple clothes remained, and place jasmine garlands around Their necks while a widow or two watched the silent proceedings.

Kṛṣṇa consciousness was dying in India, dying from neglect. At least it was dying here in Calcutta. And in many other places in India, even in

Vṛndāvana, the impersonal philosophy prevailed, and grand old temples had become residences for pigeons, monkeys, and dogs. Sad as it was, it only reinforced Prabhupāda's conviction of the need to return to the fertile ground in the West. Although here in India the spirit of devotion was dying, in the West it was just beginning to grow—in New York, San Francisco, Montreal, Boston.

If pure Kṛṣṇa consciousness were dying in India, then why shouldn't it be transplanted in the fertile West? There it would flourish. It would spread worldwide and even back to India again. When India, bent on following the West, saw the materially advanced Americans taking to Kṛṣṇa consciousness, she would reevaluate her own culture.

Prabhupāda saw a Kṛṣṇa conscious revolution beginning in the United States. He didn't consider himself its creator; he was the servant of Kṛṣṇa consciousness. Lord Caitanya's desire was that every Indian help to spread Kṛṣṇa consciousness worldwide. Unfortunately, the very verses in the scriptures that prophesied a worldwide Kṛṣṇa consciousness movement were a puzzle even to most of Śrīla Prabhupāda's Godbrothers. They admitted it.

But soon they would see. There was great potential in the West. Prabhupāda had shown many of his Godbrothers the newspaper articles—"Swami's Flock" chanting in Tompkins Square Park, "Ancient Trance Dance" at Stanford University—and he had brought some disciples with him. These were only beginnings. Much more had to be done.

And who would help? B. P. Keśava Mahārāja was dying. Śrīdhara Mahārāja couldn't come out. Who else? Most Indians were impersonalists, nondevotional *yogīs,* or demigod worshipers. As Śrīla Prabhupāda stood before the Rādhā-Govinda Deity, explaining to Acyutānanda and Rāmānuja how he had worshiped Them in his childhood and how They had been his first inspiration in Kṛṣṇa consciousness, he understood deeply that he must take Kṛṣṇa consciousness all over the world, even if singlehandedly. Of course, he was not alone; he had disciples. And they were opening new centers even in his absence. He would have to return to them very soon and supervise his growing movement.

The Mulliks regarded Prabhupāda more as a relative than as a spiritual leader. To them he was a hometown cousin who had done something successful in America. Narendranath Mullik, a childhood friend of

Prabhupāda's, called Prabhupāda Dādā, "brother," and regularly joked with him.

The Mulliks were glad to give Prabhupāda and his two followers a large room in the temple compound for as long as they wanted to stay in Calcutta. Prabhupāda set up his usual arrangement: a mat on the floor, a low table for a desk, and beside the desk his few possessions. Here he could study and write, receive guests, or rest. Daily some local women brought Prabhupāda and his disciples simple *prasādam* in a *tiffin.*

The Kālī-pūjā celebrations drew large crowds into the main hall before the Kālī deity, and Prabhupāda gave regular lectures there from *Śrīmad-Bhāgavatam.* He also spoke in the homes of various Mullik families. The hosts, members of the dwindling Bengali aristocracy, would offer Prabhupāda and his disciples Rādhā-Govinda *prasādam:* cut fruits, water chestnuts, minced ginger, and soaked, salted mung beans.

Most of those who came to visit Prabhupāda in his room were not really interested in spiritual life, but they wanted his blessings. There was a local *brāhmaṇa* whose occupation was to go from shop to shop carrying a few flowers, a cup of water, and a brass container with sandalwood paste and *kuṅkuma* powder. Using this paraphernalia, he would offer a blessing to the shopkeepers every day and receive a few *paisā* in payment. Knowing Prabhupāda to be a Vaiṣṇava, the *brāhmaṇa* came to see him to receive a spiritual benediction. The man's forehead was decorated with both Vaiṣṇava *tilaka* (two vertical lines) and Śaivite *tilaka* (three horizontal lines). After the man left, Acyutānanda asked, "Swamiji, who was that?"

"He is a hired *brāhmaṇa,*" Prabhupāda said. "When he goes to the Vaiṣṇavas he gives them blessings, and when he goes to the Śaivites he gets money. He has to make a living."

Another man came, asserting that he wanted to teach Prabhupāda's disciples Hindi. He asked Prabhupāda to help him get to America, but Prabhupāda told him, "You must take *sannyāsa.* Then I will bring you to America." After two visits, the man stopped coming.

A Mullik relation, a small, bald, bright-eyed man, came by one day carrying a book entitled *Interesting Studies.* He posed philosophical questions—simple queries about *karma, jñāna,* and *bhakti*—but then would interrupt Prabhupāda and answer them himself. Finally when the man asked one of his questions, Prabhupāda replied, "So what is *your* answer?" The man gave a general answer. But later, when Prabhupāda began explaining that Lord Kṛṣṇa, the speaker of *Bhagavad-gītā,* is the Supreme Personality of Godhead, the man interrupted: "You may call God 'Kṛṣṇa,' call Him 'Śiva,' call Him — "

"No," Prabhupāda said. "Kṛṣṇa is the Supreme Lord, and all others are demigods." The man became a little nervous and quoted a popular Bengali impersonalist who taught that all gods and all methods of worship are the same.

"He's an upstart," Prabhupāda said. "That is not the teaching of the *Gītā.* What is this other teaching? It is all utter confusion."

"If you go on speaking like this," the man said angrily, "I'll have to leave this place. Please don't criticize this *paramahaṁsa.*"

"Why not?" Prabhupāda said. "He is a concocter." The man got up and left, calling out, "You don't know Kṛṣṇa!" as he left the room.

Prabhupāda turned to Acyutānanda and Rāmānuja and smiled: "Every time you introduce Kṛṣṇa they say, 'Why only Kṛṣṇa?' But that is what Kṛṣṇa says. *Mattaḥ parataraṁ nānyat:* 'There is no truth superior to Me.' These rascal impersonalists have ruined Bengal."

One day a man gave Prabhupāda a two-hundred-rupee donation, and Prabhupāda immediately asked the *pūjārī* for an old set of Rādhā-Govinda's clothes, gave the clothes to some of the temple ladies along with the two hundred rupees, and asked that the ladies make gold embroidered dresses for Rādhā-Govinda. "Rādhā-Govinda are taking care of us," he said, "so we can take care of Them also."

Rāmānuja's beard was huge. Looking like an ordinary hippie, he misrepresented Śrīla Prabhupāda wherever they went. Prabhupāda told Acyutānanda, "Tell your friend to shave." Acyutānanda and Rāmānuja talked, but Rāmānuja wouldn't shave. Wanting Rāmānuja to agree on his own, Prabhupāda didn't ask him again, but when a copy of the latest *Back to Godhead* magazine arrived from the States, Prabhupāda got an idea. Two illustrations in the magazine showed Haridāsa Ṭhākura converting a prostitute. After her conversion the prostitute had shaved her head. Showing the pictures to Rāmānuja, Prabhupāda asked, "What is the difference between this picture and that picture?"

"I don't know, Swamiji," Rāmānuja replied.

"No," Prabhupāda said, pointing to the pictures. "What is the difference in this picture?"

"Oh, she's a devotee."

"Yes," Prabhupāda said, "but what else?"

"Oh, she has a shaved head."

"Yes." Prabhupāda smiled. "A devotee has a shaved head."

"Do you want me to shave my head?"

"Yes."

Rāmānuja shaved. But within a few days he began growing his beard and hair back. "From now on," Prabhupāda told Acyutānanda, "no more cheap initiations. They have to know something."

Rāmānuja hung on. Prabhupāda wanted Rāmānuja and Acyutānanda to remain in India after his departure and continue to try for the American House in Vṛndāvana. Rāmānuja wrote his own impressions to his friend Mukunda in San Francisco.

> Please be advised that we're doing all we can to get him off as soon as possible but this primitive Indian government is putting obstacles in our way. The man who could have given Swamiji clearance for his P-form has just drowned, so the clearance has to be made in Bombay. This is the delay. Here in Calcutta we are having lots of fun addressing different people. Swamiji makes Acyutānanda and myself give a short speech. I am becoming more and more expert at this. I think that he makes us speak in order to show the audience that we American Vaiṣṇavas are for real. And also he wants everyone to preach Krishna Consciousness. ... It is very difficult to take care properly of Swamiji's health here. For one thing it is a big thing to serve sweets in India and it is impolite to decline. Also we get all kinds of visitors. We have not been able to go to bed before 11 o'clock and Swamiji automatically wakes at 3. In this respect the people here are very inconsiderate but if Acyutānanda and I ask them to leave they will ask Swamiji if they should and Swamiji of course says no. Anyway his heart beat is a little fast and sometimes it is alarmingly fast, so I suggest that you get a good heart specialist to see him. ... Please arrange for this doctor and above all make sure that Swamiji gets plenty of rest. You need not restrict visitors too strictly because if the company is good Swamiji seems to enjoy visitors. Please do all you can to get Swamiji's beat to normal again. His chariot needs to be fixed up so that he can remain on this earth for at least another ten years.

* * *

Knowing that Swamiji would soon be returning, the devotees in America began to increase their entreaties, each group asking him to come to their particular city. On November 4 Prabhupāda wrote Mukunda, "As you say that my absence is being felt now surely more deeply than ever, so I also feel to start immediately without waiting." And to Mukunda's wife, Jānakī, he wrote, "Every minute I think of you and as you asked me to go to San Francisco while returning from India, I am trying to fulfill my promise. I am thinking of going directly to San Francisco." At the bottom of the same letter to Mukunda and Jānakī, Acyutānanda added a health report:

> Swamiji is looking healthy and living and working regularly, but his pulse rate is generally too fast. Last night it was 95—unusually fast even for him as it generally hovers between 83 and 86.

Prabhupāda decided not to wait any longer on the chance that Mukunda might secure him permanent residency. "I want to return to your country, where there is good air and good water," he told Acyutānanda one day. "Every day we are receiving letters that the devotees want me there. I thought that in my absence they might deteriorate, and I was reluctant to even come to India. But now I see that it is growing. There is need for me to go and supervise the expansion. So I want to go back."

The only impediment now seemed to be a delayed P-form, a clearance from the Bank of India required for an Indian citizen traveling abroad.

> I am just ready for starting for America but as you know our competent government is very slow in action. The P-form was submitted almost a month ago, but still it is undergoing red tapism. The visa was granted to me within half an hour. The passage money was deposited within two days but unfortunately the Reserve Bank of India is delaying the matter unnecessarily. I expect the P-form at any moment and as soon as I get it I shall start for your country.

Just to make certain that Swamiji would come first to San Francisco, Mukunda sent a telegram to Calcutta: "SWAMIJI. BRAHMANANDA AND I AGREE YOU START IMMEDIATELY. ADVISE EXACT ARRIVAL DATE. MUKUNDA."

Prabhupāda had planned his route through Tokyo, intending to stop for a day "to probe if there is any possibility of starting a center." In Tokyo he would let Mukunda know by telephone his arrival time in San Francisco. But three weeks passed while Prabhupāda continued to wait for his P-form.

Meanwhile, he received good news from New York. The Macmillan

Company's interest in *Bhagavad-gītā* was real; the contract was being drawn. Pleased with Brahmānanda, he wrote to him on November 11 explaining his visions for distributing Kṛṣṇa conscious literature.

> If publications are there we can work from one center only like New York or San Francisco for propagating our cult all over the world. Let us stick to the publication of BTG more and more nicely and publish some Vedic literatures like Srimad Bhagavatam, Chaitanya Charitamrita, etc. ...

As Prabhupāda's mind turned more to the preaching that awaited him in America, he assessed what he had done so far, what he would do, and the process by which he would do it.

> I am not in agreement with Mr. Altman that we are expanding very thinly. In my opinion, a single sincere soul can maintain a center. You know I started the center at 26 2nd Ave. alone. I took the risk of 200.00 dollars per month for Rent. At that time there were no assistants. Mukunda was at that time a friend but there was no responsibility for him for maintaining the center. Gradually Kirtanananda and Hayagriva joined but they did not take any responsibility. Still I was maintaining the establishment simply depending on Krishna and then Krishna sent me everything—men and money. Similarly, if a sincere soul goes out and opens a center in any part of the world Krishna will help him in all respects. Without being empowered by Krishna, nobody can preach Krishna Consciousness. It is not academic qualification or financial strength which helps in these matters, but it is sincerity of purpose which helps us always. Therefore I wish that you [Brahmānanda] will remain in charge of New York, let Satsvarupa be in charge of Boston, Let Mukunda be in charge of San Francisco, Let Janardan be in charge of Montreal. Let Nandarani and Dayananda be in charge of Los Angeles. And let Subal das be in charge of Santa Fe. In this way you will follow my example as I did in the beginning at 26 2nd Ave. That is Preaching, cooking, writing, talking, chanting everything one man's work. I never thought about the audience. I was prepared to chant if there were no man to hear me. The principle of chanting is to glorify the Lord and not to attract a crowd. If Krishna hears nicely then he will ask some sincere devotee to gather in such place. Therefore be advised that thousands of centers may be started if we find out a sincere soul for each and every center. We do not require more men to start. If there is one sincere soul that is sufficient to start a new center.

On November 12 Śrīla Prabhupāda wrote to Kṛṣṇā-devī,

> I am coming soon to San Francisco. I shall let you know the exact date some time next week. I am coming over very soon to see you when everything will be adjusted. Hope you are well.

And the health notes from Acyutānanda continued to arrive.

> Please tell the devotees out there to take good care of him. It is a very hard task trying to restrain him from overworking himself, but they must be strict. He still has to take his medicines and get his massage every day.

On November 20 Prabhupāda dispatched by boat to New York more than eight hundred copies of the first three volumes of his *Śrīmad-Bhāgavatam.* And on the next day his P-form finally cleared. Immediately he booked passage on Pan American Airlines and sent a cable informing Mukunda that he would arrive in San Francisco on November 24 at 12:45 P.M.

But again his departure was delayed—this time by a strike by the Communist Party in Calcutta. Businesses closed. Cars, buses, rickshas, and trains stopped running. Riots broke out. There were murders and assassinations. Meanwhile, Prabhupāda remained at the Rādhā-Govinda temple.

> My return to your country is already settled. But due to a petty revolution in Calcutta I am not able to leave. ... Our San Francisco friends may be very anxious because I sent them two telegrams, one informing them of my arrival and the other canceling it. Future arrangements are pending.

Two weeks passed. While waiting in his room for the political strike to end, Prabhupāda received a letter from Umāpati, one of the devotees he had initiated at the first initiation in New York, in September of 1966. Umāpati had given up practicing Kṛṣṇa consciousness for half a year, but now he wrote to say he was back. Prabhupāda replied:

> It is my duty to deliver you the right thing in right earnestness and it is the duty of the receiver to act in the standard spiritual regulation. When you left us I simply prayed to Krishna for your return to Krishna Consciousness because that was my duty. Any good soul who approaches me once for spiritual enlightenment is supposed to be depending on my responsibility to get him back to Krishna, back to home. The disciple may misunderstand a bona fide spiritual master being obliged to do so under the pressure of Maya's influence. But a bona fide spiritual master never lets go a devotee once accepted. When a disciple misunderstands a bona fide spiritual master, the master regrets for his inability to protect the disciple and sometimes he cries with tears in the eyes. We had an experience while my Guru Maharaja was alive. One of His disciples who accepted sannyas was one

> day forcibly dragged by his wife. My Guru Maharaj lamented with tears in His eyes saying that He could not save the soul. We should always therefore be careful of being attacked by Maya's influence and the only means of guarantee is to chant Hare Krishna offenselessly.

When Prabhupāda received news of quarreling in the Los Angeles temple he replied to Nandarāṇī:

> I know that my presence is very urgently required. Arrangement is already completed and circumstances alone have checked my departure. Please therefore don't be worried. I am coming to your place within a fortnight.

At the end of the first week of December the strike ended, and Śrīla Prabhupāda again booked passage.

> You will be pleased to know that I have purchased my ticket for New York via Tokyo and San Francisco. I am starting tomorrow morning at nine thirty. By evening reaching Tokyo via Bangkok and Hong Kong. I shall rest 24 hours in Tokyo and on the 14th at night, I am starting for San Francisco. By local time I am reaching San Francisco on the same day, the 14th at 12:45 p.m. by P.A.A. 846. Yesterday I have sent one telegram to this effect, and I hope I shall reach there safely as scheduled. I am so glad to learn that Satyabrata and yourself are trying to get the teachings of Lord Caitanya published. You do not know how pleased I am to hear this news. When one book is published I think I have conquered an empire. So try to publish as many books as possible and that will enhance the beauty and prestige of our society. The impersonalist mission has nothing to say substantial but because they have money and have published so many rubbish literatures they have become very cheaply popular. You can just imagine how much powerful our society will become when we have as many substantial literatures published. We should not only publish in English but also in other important languages such as French and German.

When the day for Prabhupāda's departure finally arrived he gave last instructions to Acyutānanda and Rāmānuja.

"Just pray to Lord Kṛṣṇa that I can go to America," he requested Acyutānanda.

"How can I?" Acyutānanda replied. "You'll be leaving me."

"No," Śrīla Prabhupāda replied, "we'll always remain packed up together if you remember my teachings. If you preach you will become strong, and all these teachings will be in the proper perspective. When we stop our preaching, then everything becomes stagnated, and we lose our life. Even here in India people think that they know everything, but they are wrong. There is no end to hearing about Kṛṣṇa. God is unlimited. So no one can say, 'I know everything about God.' Those who say they know everything about God do not know. So everyone will appreciate you. Do not fear."

Acyutānanda: *When I returned to the room after sending off Swamiji and paying my obeisances at the airport, I felt a void. I felt very lonely and rather weak. I returned to the room in front of Śrī Śrī Rādhā-Govinda, and chanting on my beads I started pacing back and forth. "What will I preach?" The black and white marble floor passed under me. I stepped on the cracks, in between the cracks, and on the black and white marble again and again. Then I realized I wasn't seeing Rādhā-Kṛṣṇa. So I sat down directly in front and saw the brilliant form of Rādhā-Govindajī, and my eyes filled with tears.*

* * *

Śrīla Prabhupāda spent his stopover in Tokyo mostly in going to his hotel and checking into a room, bathing, resting, eating, and returning to the airport the next day in time for his flight to San Francisco. But he did speak with a government secretary, explaining that Kṛṣṇa consciousness was a universal philosophy for reviving a person's original, eternal consciousness. And he explained the crucial need for Kṛṣṇa consciousness in human society. The secretary, however, said he felt certain that the Japanese government wouldn't be able to help a religious movement.

Prabhupāda was annoyed. This supposedly educated man was so ignorant as to mistake Kṛṣṇa consciousness for merely another sectarian religion. Prabhupāda wanted intelligent men to try to understand Kṛṣṇa consciousness and understand that the *Gītā* was actual knowledge, transcendental knowledge, beyond the inferior knowledge of the senses and the mind. But he had his plane to catch. Japan would have to wait.

The passengers and flight crew saw Prabhupāda as an elderly Indian man dressed in saffron robes. The stewardesses weren't sure at first whether he spoke English, but when he asked them for fruits they saw that he could and that he was a kind gentleman. He was quiet, putting on his glasses and reading from an old book of Indian scripture for hours at a time, or moving his lips in prayer while fingering Indian prayer beads in a cloth pouch, or sometimes resting beneath a blanket, his eyes shut.

No one knew or bothered to inquire into what he was doing. They didn't know that anxious young hearts were awaiting him in San Francisco, or that the Macmillan Company in New York wanted to publish his English translation of *Bhagavad-gītā,* or that he had spiritual centers in two countries, with plans for expansion all over the world. Prabhupāda sat patiently, chanting often, his hand in his bead bag, depending on Kṛṣṇa as the hours passed.

After a ten-hour flight the plane landed in San Francisco. Standing with hundreds of other passengers, Prabhupāda gradually made his way to the exit. Down the long attached tunnel, even before he reached the terminal building, he could see Govinda dāsī and a few other disciples smiling and waving on the other side of a glass partition. As he entered the terminal building he moved towards the glass, and his disciples dropped to their knees, offering obeisances. As they raised their heads he smiled and continued walking down the corridor while they walked alongside, only the glass partition separating them. Then they disappeared from his view as he walked down the stairway towards immigration and customs.

The downstairs area was also glassed in, and Prabhupāda could see more than fifty devotees and friends waiting eagerly. As they again caught sight of him, they cried out as a group, "Hare Kṛṣṇa!"

Swamiji looked wonderful to them, tanned from his six months in India, younger, and more spritely. He smiled and triumphantly held up his hands in greeting. Devotees were crying in happiness.

As Prabhupāda stood in line at the customs inspection point, he could hear the devotees' *kīrtana,* the glass walls only partially masking the sound. The customs officials ignored the chanting, although the connection between the saffron-robed passenger and the joyful chanters was not hard to see.

Śrīla Prabhupāda waited in line, glancing now and then at his chanting disciples. Since he had already sent ahead the eight hundred books and several crates of musical instruments, he had only one suitcase to place on the table before the inspector. Methodically the inspector went through the contents: cotton *sārīs* for the girls, silk garlands for the Jagannātha deities, *karatālas,* saffron *dhotīs* and *kurtās,* a coconut grater, and little bottles of Ayurvedic medicine.

"What are these?" the inspector probed. The little bottles looked strange, and he called for another inspector. A delay. Swamiji's disciples became perturbed by the petty-minded customs inspectors' poking through Swamiji's things, now opening the tightly corked bottles, sniffing and checking the contents.

The inspectors seemed satisfied. Prabhupāda tried to close his suitcase, but he couldn't work the zipper. Another delay. The devotees, still anxiously chanting, watched as Swamiji, with the help of the gentleman behind him, managed to zip his suitcase closed.

Swamiji walked towards the glass doors. The devotees began chanting madly. As he stepped through the door a devotee blew a conchshell that resounded loudly throughout the hall. Devotees garlanded him, and everyone pressed in, handing him flowers. He entered their midst as a beloved father enters and reciprocates the embrace of his loving children.

CHAPTER TWENTY-NINE

Unlimited Opportunity, Limited Time

Montreal
August 1968

ŚRĪLA PRABHUPĀDA WAS in his room, speaking with several disciples. "So, Annapūrṇā, you have got some news?" he asked. Annapūrṇā was a young British girl. A few months ago her father had written from England that he might be able to provide a house if some devotees came there.

"Yes," she replied.

"So, what is our next program?" She was reticent. "That letter from your father is encouraging?"

"Yes, he encourages me. But he says he can't provide any place if we come there."

Prabhupāda looked disappointed. "That's all right. It is up to Kṛṣṇa. When we go to someone to preach, we have to stand before them with folded hands, with all humility: 'My dear sir, please take to Kṛṣṇa consciousness.' "

"Prabhupāda?" Pradyumna spoke up. "I was reading a book by this big atheist swami."

"Hmm?"

"There are some letters in the back of the book, and I was looking at them ..."

"Atheist swami's book," Prabhupāda said, "we have nothing to do with."

"I wasn't looking at his philosophy," Pradyumna explained. "I was just looking at the techniques he used when he was in America. He wanted to go to Europe, so he had a man, a rich benefactor, who went on a six-week tour of France, England, Germany, Switzerland, Holland, and then back, arranging lectures. That's how he did most of his tour. He had one or two influential people, and they arranged everything. And the lectures were arranged, and the society ..."

"So, you can arrange like that?" Prabhupāda asked.

"I was thinking that there would be a Royal Asiatic Society in London. I think Ṭhākura Bhaktivinoda was a member of that."

"But where is Ṭhākura Bhaktivinoda's *saṅga* [association]?" Prabhupāda asked.

"Well," Pradyumna continued, "still there may be some people you could open correspondence with. They might be interested in sponsoring you."

"Is there anything about Kṛṣṇa in that swami's speech?" Prabhupāda asked.

"No."

Prabhupāda sat thoughtfully. In England he would have no place to stay. Pradyumna might talk of influential persons traveling ahead and making all the arrangements, but where were such persons? Here was a shy girl who could barely speak up, whose father would not help, and Pradyumna reading an atheist swami and talking of a Royal Asiatic Society—but nothing practical. Prabhupāda had plans, though. He had asked Mukunda and Śyāmasundara to go to London and try to establish an ISKCON center. They had agreed and would be arriving in Montreal from San Francisco in a few days.

Śrīla Bhaktisiddhānta Sarasvatī, Prabhupāda's own spiritual master, had wanted Kṛṣṇa consciousness in Europe. During the 1930s he had sent his most experienced *sannyāsīs* to London, but they had returned, nothing accomplished. It wasn't possible to teach Kṛṣṇa consciousness to the *mlecchas,* they had complained. Europeans couldn't sit long enough to hear the Vaiṣṇava philosophy. One of the *sannyāsīs* had met Lord Zetland, who had inquired curiously, "Swamiji, can you make me a *brāhmaṇa*?" The *sannyāsī* had assured Lord Zetland he could, certainly, if Zetland would give up meat-eating, intoxication, gambling, and illicit sex. "Impossible!"

Lord Zetland had replied. And the *sannyāsīs* had accepted this response as the standard for all Europeans. The *sannyāsīs* had returned to India; Vaiṣṇavism could never take hold in the West. Prabhupāda had faith that his disciples would succeed; they would help him establish ISKCON centers in Europe, just as they had in North America. Certainly such success would greatly please Śrīla Bhaktisiddhānta Sarasvatī. Prabhupāda told of a man who found a gourd lying on the road and picked it up and then found a stick and a wire and picked them up. In themselves, the three parts were useless. But by putting the gourd, the stick, and the wire together, the man made a *vīṇā* and began to play beautiful music. Similarly, Prabhupāda had come to the West and found some rejected youths lying here and there, and he himself had been rejected by the people of New York City; but by Kṛṣṇa's grace the combination had become successful. If his disciples remained sincere and followed his orders, they would succeed in Europe.

Three married couples—Mukunda and Jānakī, Śyāmasundara and Mālatī (with their infant daughter, Sarasvatī), and Gurudāsa and Yamunā—arrived in Montreal, eager to travel to London. These three couples had begun the temple in San Francisco, where they had had close association with Śrīla Prabhupāda. They had helped Prabhupāda introduce *kīrtana, prasādam,* and Ratha-yātrā among the hippies of Haight-Ashbury. Now they were eager to help him introduce Kṛṣṇa consciousness in London.

Prabhupāda asked the three couples to remain with him in Montreal for a week or two, so that he could train them to perform *kīrtana* expertly. Chanting Hare Kṛṣṇa was not a theatrical performance but an act of devotion, properly conducted only by pure devotees—not by professional musicians. Yet if Prabhupāda's disciples became proficient in their singing, Londoners would better appreciate Kṛṣṇa consciousness.

The thought of these devotees preaching in England made Prabhupāda ecstatic. With their *kīrtana* they would become more popular than the *yogīs,* with their gymnastics and impersonal meditation. As the London program became a tangible fact, Prabhupāda began to reveal more plans. Prabhupāda already seemed to have hundreds of detailed plans for implementing Kṛṣṇa consciousness around the world—he only needed willing helpers.

In the daily *kīrtana* rehearsals, Prabhupāda taught the devotees to chant Hare Kṛṣṇa and other devotional songs, beginning with a slow tempo and building gradually. He would regularly interrupt and have them begin again. Listening carefully as Yamunā led the chanting, Prabhupāda would stop her at times to correct her Sanskrit pronunciation.

After two weeks in Montreal, the London party came together for a final meeting with Prabhupāda. He was sending them to start a center in London to fulfill his spiritual master's dream. The *sannyāsīs* Śrīla Bhaktisiddhānta Sarasvatī had sent to London, Prabhupāda told them, had lectured in a few places, posed for photos with lords and ladies, and then returned to India. But Prabhupāda wanted his disciples to go out boldly, chant the holy name, and attract others to chant.

Lord Caitanya had personally used this method while touring South India. *Caitanya-caritāmṛta* describes that whoever saw Lord Caitanya became ecstatic in love of God; then that ecstatic person would chant the holy name and ask others to chant; and when they saw that person, they too would become ecstatic. Thus the waves of ecstatic love of Kṛṣṇa would increase.

Prabhupāda predicted that when the devotees chanted Hare Kṛṣṇa, the people of London would hear the *mantra,* become devotees, and then enlighten others. Kṛṣṇa consciousness would grow. The only requirement was that the chanting be done purely, without any material motivation. Prabhupāda's enthusiasm was contagious, and as he spoke he filled his disciples with the same contagious enthusiasm.

When Mukunda asked Prabhupāda if he had any specific instructions, Prabhupāda replied with a story. In his youth, he had once seen a movie of Charlie Chaplin. The setting was a formal ball held outdoors, and off from the main dance arena were lanes with benches where couples sat. Some mischievous boys had plastered glue on one of the benches, and a young man and his girlfriend came and sat down. "When the young man got up"—Prabhupāda laughed as he told the story—"his tails tore up the middle."

Prabhupāda told how the couple had returned to the dance, unaware of what had happened. But now they drew stares from the other dancers. Wondering why he was suddenly attracting so much attention, the young man went into the dressing room and saw in the mirror his ripped coattails. Deliberately, he then tore his coat all the way up to the collar, returned to his partner, and began dancing exuberantly.

Then another man joined, ripping his own coattails and dancing with his partner, as if to compete with the first couple. One by one, the other dancers followed, ripping their coattails and dancing with abandon.

By the conclusion of the story, the devotees in Prabhupāda's room were all laughing uproariously. But finally their laughter subsided and the meeting ended. Not until the devotees were already at the airport did Mukunda, talking with Śyāmasundara, begin to appreciate and marvel at how expertly Prabhupāda had answered his question. By their bold, enthusiastic, confident preaching, they would attract people. Not everyone would immediately "join in the dancing," as had the people in the Charlie Chaplin film; the devotees might even be considered crazy at first. But they would be offering Kṛṣṇa consciousness, the highest and rarest gift, and intelligent people would gradually appreciate this, even if at first they scoffed.

By Śrīla Prabhupāda's order, his London-bound disciples, holding *kīrtana* in public, would present a profile quite different from the reserved profile of his *sannyāsī* Godbrothers. His Godbrothers had imitated the British ways; but Prabhupāda wanted the British to imitate the Vaiṣṇavas. To appear in the streets of London with shaven heads and *dhotīs* would require boldness. But it would be exciting to chant, carrying out the order of Lord Caitanya. And the people would follow—gradually, but definitely. It was the will of Lord Caitanya.

* * *

Śrīla Prabhupāda's visit to Montreal took place early in the summer of 1968, six months after his return to America. In India, from July to December of 1967, he had recovered his health, and on December 14 he had returned to San Francisco. After a few weeks he had gone to Los Angeles, where a small group of disciples had opened a storefront temple in a middle-class black and Hispanic neighborhood. The storefront was bare and the location secluded. Prabhupāda had stayed there two months, delivering lectures, holding *kīrtanas,* and giving strength and inspiration to his disciples. Although a buzzing in his head had made working difficult, he had found the warm climate and sunshine agreeable and had continued to translate *Śrīmad-Bhāgavatam,* dictating tapes and sending them to Boston for typing.

A reporter from *Life* had come to Śrīla Prabhupāda's apartment and interviewed him for an upcoming *Life* feature, "The Year of the Guru." When the story had appeared it had mixed Śrīla Prabhupāda and his movement with coverage of other *gurus.* Although the article had carried a large color photo of Śrīla Prabhupāda and favorably described a reporter's visit to the New York ISKCON center, Prabhupāda had said that being grouped with *gurus* who taught concoctions of *yoga* and meditation was not good.

In May, a few months after leaving Los Angeles, Prabhupāda had paid a first visit to his ISKCON center in Boston. There also he had found a few disciples based in a small storefront. He had lectured at many of the local universities, including Harvard and M.I.T. At M.I.T., addressing a gathering of students and faculty, he had challenged, "Where in this university is there a department to teach scientifically the difference between a living body and a dead body?" The most fundamental science, the science of the living soul, was not being taught.

After Boston, Śrīla Prabhupāda had come to Montreal. And after three months in Montreal, Prabhupāda flew to Seattle, where he stayed for one month. Then he briefly visited Santa Fe, New Mexico, where the ISKCON center was a tiny, isolated storefront.

Prabhupāda's reasons for traveling from center to center were to train and convince each disciple and to speak with newcomers. Many young people came to hear, but Prabhupāda found the majority already ruined by illicit sex and drugs. They were "rich men's sons," but they had become hippies, wandering the streets. By Kṛṣṇa's grace, now some of them were being saved.

Even while recuperating in India, Prabhupāda had always thought of returning to America to continue his movement. The Indians had seemed interested only in sense gratification, like that of the Americans. But many American youths, disillusioned with their fathers' wealth, were not going to the skyscrapers or to their fathers' businesses. As Prabhupāda had seen from his stay in New York City and San Francisco, thousands of youths were seeking an alternative to materialism. Frustrated, they were ripe for spiritual knowledge.

The devotees, still neophytes, knew nothing of spiritual life and in most cases very little of material life. But because they were sincerely taking to

Kṛṣṇa consciousness, Prabhupāda was confident that their shortcomings would not prevent their spiritual progress. Although naturally beautiful, these Western youths were now dirty and morose; their beauty had become covered. But the chanting of Hare Kṛṣṇa was reviving them, Prabhupāda said, just as the monsoon revives the land of Vṛndāvana, making it fresh and verdant. And as the Vṛndāvana peacocks sometimes dance jubilantly, so the devotees, having shed their material bonds, were now ecstatically dancing and chanting the holy names. When a reporter asked Prabhupāda if his disciples were hippies, Prabhupāda replied, "No, we are not hippies. We are happies."

More than being a visiting lecturer or a formal guide, Śrīla Prabhupāda was the spiritual father of his disciples. They accepted him as their real father, and he found them devoted and affectionate, far more than his own family had been. These young American boys and girls—"the flower of your country," Prabhupāda called them—had received the blessing of Lord Caitanya and were delivering that blessing to their countrymen. Prabhupāda said it was up to his American disciples to save their country. He was giving them the method, but they would have to implement it.

Śrīla Prabhupāda loved his disciples, and they loved him. Out of love, he was giving them the greatest treasure, and out of love they were following his instructions. This was the essence of spiritual life. On the basis of this love, the Kṛṣṇa consciousness movement would grow. Not surprisingly, some disciples had fallen away to their former, materialistic way of living. But Prabhupāda sought those sincere souls who would stay. That was the important thing, he said. One moon is more valuable than many stars; so even a few sincere workers would accomplish wonderful things. The sincere and intelligent would stay, and Lord Caitanya Mahāprabhu would empower them to carry out His desires for distributing love of Kṛṣṇa. In this way, the devotees' lives would become perfect. Many disciples, in fact, already felt this happening. Kṛṣṇa consciousness worked because they sincerely practiced it and because Śrīla Prabhupāda carefully and patiently tended the growing plants of transcendental loving service he had planted in their hearts.

Los Angeles
October 1968

Śrīla Prabhupāda returned to find the devotees living and worshiping in an exciting location on Hollywood Boulevard. A large *saṅkīrtana* party, organized by his disciple Tamāla Kṛṣṇa, would chant Hare Kṛṣṇa on the streets all day and sell *Back to Godhead* magazines in larger quantities than ever before—as many as two hundred magazines a day, with a collection of over one hundred dollars.

Then one day, shortly after Prabhupāda's arrival, the landlord evicted the devotees from their place on Hollywood Boulevard. With no temple the devotees moved to scattered locations throughout the city. As many evenings as possible, however, they would all gather in someone's garage, lent to them for the evening, and Śrīla Prabhupāda would chant Hare Kṛṣṇa with them and lecture.

Then Prabhupāda rented a former Christian church on La Cienega Boulevard. He introduced a more regulated Deity worship and an increased Sunday love feast. Each week would bring a new, specially planned festival with a big feast and hundreds of guests. These new programs in Los Angeles encouraged Prabhupāda, and he wanted to see them introduced in ISKCON centers throughout the world.

* * *

Śrīla Prabhupāda was planning to go to England. But first he wanted to visit his farm project in West Virginia, and he had also been promising the devotees in San Francisco he would attend their Ratha-yātrā festival in July. This traveling to establish and expand his ISKCON was alone enough to keep him busy; yet he was also always meditating on his work of translating and commenting on Vedic literatures.

In L.A. during December, Śrīla Prabhupāda had begun *The Nectar of Devotion,* a summary study of Rūpa Gosvāmī's *Bhakti-rasāmṛta-sindhu. The Nectar of Devotion* would be a handbook for his disciples, elaborately explaining the science and practice of *bhakti-yoga.* Simultaneous with *The Nectar of Devotion,* he had also begun *Kṛṣṇa, the Supreme Personality of Godhead,* a summary study of *Śrīmad-Bhāgavatam's* Tenth Canto. Visiting the temple only on Sundays, he had spent most of his time at his small rented house on the outskirts of Beverly Hills, where he worked intensely on his two major literary projects.

Prabhupāda's most ambitious literary undertaking, the completion of *Śrīmad-Bhāgavatam,* was to be no less than sixty volumes. He had begun in India in 1959, and all along he had been aware that he was attempting a gigantic task at an advanced age. Now Kṛṣṇa was giving him opportunities both for writing Vedic literatures and for traveling, and he was working at an amazing pace.

The force driving Prabhupāda was the desire of his spiritual master, Śrīla Bhaktisiddhānta Sarasvatī. As for how much time he had remaining to execute his mission—that was in Kṛṣṇa's hands. Everything was up to Kṛṣṇa: "If Kṛṣṇa wants to kill you, no one can save you; and if Kṛṣṇa wants to save you, no one can kill you." Yet although Prabhupāda was always in transcendental consciousness, beyond the effects of old age, he was aware that he didn't have many more years left. All along he had had the vision of a spiritual movement for all nations and cultures, and to establish this he was racing against time.

Śrīla Prabhupāda's mood of urgency was the natural mood of the Vaiṣṇava preacher—an ambition to engage everyone in loving service to Kṛṣṇa. Without Kṛṣṇa consciousness the bewildered, conditioned souls of Kali-yuga were all heading for the horrible consequences of their sinful lives. Prabhupāda's sense of urgency, therefore, was an expression of his compassion. He wanted to save the gross materialists, who were blind to the existence of the soul. If they wasted their human life, they would suffer millions of years before getting another chance to awaken their Kṛṣṇa consciousness and go back to Godhead.

The heart attack Prabhupāda had endured in 1967 had accelerated his mood of urgency. Although before the heart attack he had often worked like a young man and played the drum for hours, now Kṛṣṇa's warning was clear. The heart attack was to have been the time of his death, Prabhupāda had said, but because his disciples had prayed, "Our master has not finished his work. Please protect him," Kṛṣṇa had spared him. Similarly, on the boat to America in 1965 his heart had almost failed. But then also Kṛṣṇa had saved his life.

The scope of Prabhupāda's work was enormous; even with many years and good health he could never finish. Prabhupāda saw that in future generations many people would come forward to help, and thus, by a combined effort, the Kṛṣṇa consciousness movement would continue to check the forces of Kali-yuga and save the entire world. Caitanya Mahāprabhu had predicted this, and Prabhupāda knew that it must come to pass. But the task of erecting the framework for this universal effort rested on Prabhupāda alone. And he worked tirelessly, knowing that unless he established a complete foundation the entire mission might later collapse.

Beginning with Prabhupāda's first success in New York City in 1966, Kṛṣṇa had shown unlimited opportunities for spreading Kṛṣṇa consciousness. But how much time was there? Only Kṛṣṇa could say; it was up to Him. Prabhupāda remained ever mindful of the vast scope of his mission and the ever-narrowing span of time he had in which to complete it. "I am an old man," he often told his disciples. "I could pass away at any moment."

* * *

Śrīla Prabhupāda would receive several letters a week from the devotees in London. It was now December 1968—the devotees had been in London four months—and still they had no temple, nor even a place where they could live and worship together. Mostly they had been visiting Hindu families, holding *kīrtana* and sharing *prasādam*. Śrīla Prabhupāda had encouraged this, but after hearing a few reports he decided the program was stagnant. The devotees should not expect much from the Hindus, he said. "They have become hodgepodge due to so many years of subjugation by foreigners and have lost their own culture. ... I am concerned to preach this gospel amongst the Europeans and Americans."

The devotees were jolted, but they knew Prabhupāda was right. Determined to change their tactics, they immediately began lecturing at colleges and universities and chanting in the streets. They were preaching to the British, and it felt right. When they wrote to Prabhupāda that although they had accomplished little they were "planting seeds," Prabhupāda replied:

> Regarding your analogy of sowing Krishna Consciousness seeds, I may inform you that there is a Bengali proverb—Sa bure Meoya Phale. This means that fruits like chestnuts and pomegranates, or similar other valuable fruits and nuts take some time to be fructified. So any good thing comes into our possession after hard struggle and endeavor. So Krishna Consciousness is the greatest of all good fruits. We must therefore have necessary endurance and enthusiasm to get the result. We shall never be disappointed when things are presented in reversed order. Anyway, your honest labor is now

coming to be fructified. Always depend upon Krishna and go on working with enthusiasm, patience and conviction.

* * *

Through the spring and summer of 1969, Prabhupāda continued touring his American ISKCON centers. From Los Angeles he had sent Gaurasundara and Govinda dāsī, a young married couple, to Hawaii; and on their invitation that he come during the mango season, he joined them. But when he got there in March he found that it was not mango season and that his disciples had accomplished little. They had taken jobs and were working full time just to support themselves.

New York City
April 9, 1969

Prabhupāda traveled to New York City, the birthplace of his Kṛṣṇa consciousness society, where his movement had been growing for nearly three years. Although the center was established and his books were being distributed, he still had to visit to strengthen the devotees. His presence gave them determination and courage. For seven months they had carried on without his personal touch, but his visits—when he would sit in his room and reciprocate warmly with them—were vital. Nothing could equal these intimate meetings.

Many devotees, new and old, crowded into Prabhupāda's apartment at 26 Second Avenue. "There was one reporter for the *Honolulu Advertiser,*" Prabhupāda said, "—he was putting questions to me. And then he wrote an article: 'The swami is a small man, but he is delivering a great message.' That is true. I am small. But the message—that is not small."

Brahmānanda showed Prabhupāda a globe with markers representing ISKCON centers. "Now there is one in North Carolina," Brahmānanda said.

"Then it becomes fifteen?" Prabhupāda asked. He was smiling and looking directly from one devotee to another. "I want each of you to go and start a center. What is the difficulty? Take one *mṛdaṅga.* Then another person will come and join you—he will take *karatālas.* When I came here, Brahmānanda and Acyutānanda were dancing. And after chanting, hundreds of men will come to your storefront and enjoy chanting and dancing."

"The girls also?" Rukmiṇī asked.

"There is no harm," Prabhupāda said. "Kṛṣṇa does not make distinction—female dress or male dress. I mean to say, the female body is weaker, but spiritually the body does not matter. In the absence of Lord Nityānanda, His wife, Jāhnavā-devī, was preaching. First you must understand the philosophy. You must be prepared to answer questions. Kṛṣṇa will give you intelligence. Just like I was not prepared to answer all these questions, but Kṛṣṇa gives intelligence."

After eight days in his New York City home, Prabhupāda went to Buffalo. At State University of New York at Buffalo, Rūpānuga was teaching an accredited course in Kṛṣṇa *yoga* with some sixty students enrolled, regularly chanting the Hare Kṛṣṇa *mantra* on beads. Prabhupāda stayed for a few days, lecturing and initiating disciples. Then he went to Boston for more initiations and several marriages.

Columbus, Ohio
May 9, 1969

The devotees had arranged for Prabhupāda and Allen Ginsberg to chant onstage at Ohio State University.

Allen had been a friend of the Kṛṣṇa consciousness movement from its first days on the Lower East Side. Shortly after Prabhupāda's arrival in Columbus, he stopped by Prabhupāda's house and discussed philosophy with Prabhupāda for several hours. Allen was friendly with Prabhupāda, as always. But he doubted whether Kṛṣṇa consciousness could become popular in America. "The need," he said, "is for a large, single, unifying religious movement in America."

"So here is Kṛṣṇa," Prabhupāda replied, "—all-attractive. Now you can say, 'Why shall I accept Kṛṣṇa?' But since you ask for a unifying element, then I say, 'Here is Kṛṣṇa.' Now you can analyze: Why should you accept Kṛṣṇa? And I shall reply, 'Why you shall not?' Whatever you want or expect from the Supreme or Unifying, everything is there in Kṛṣṇa."

If Prabhupāda wanted his movement popularized, Allen suggested, he should consider omitting many of the sectarian Hindu aspects, such as the dress, the food, and the Sanskrit.

Kṛṣṇa consciousness, Prabhupāda replied, was not sectarian or Hindu.

Lord Caitanya had said that a person could chant *any* name of God—but one must chant. As for the food, Prabhupāda explained that any food was acceptable as long as it was purely vegetarian. And dress—there was no stricture that Americans wear robes and shave their heads. The Hare Kṛṣṇa *mantra,* Prabhupāda added, was a natural sound, not foreign.

Allen objected. The Hare Kṛṣṇa *mantra* sounded foreign; perhaps they should think of an alternative, more American *mantra.*

"This is going on," Prabhupāda replied. "Some people are inclined to one thing and some to others. And it will go on until the end of creation. But our position is that we are searching after the center. And here is the center."

At Ohio State's Hitchcock Hall a thousand students occupied the seats, and a thousand more crowded the aisles and stage. The program began with a *kīrtana* led by Allen Ginsberg. Allen then introduced Prabhupāda, and Prabhupāda lectured. When Prabhupāda began the second and final *kīrtana* of the evening, the students responded wildly. Those seated stood and danced, some jumping in their seats, and those in the aisles and on the stage also joined in. Amid the thunderous *kīrtana* of nearly two thousand voices, Prabhupāda began to dance, jumping up and down on the speaker's dais, his hands raised high. He threw flowers from his garland, and the students scrambled for them. The wildly ecstatic *kīrtana* continued for almost an hour, and then Prabhupāda brought it to a close.

Afterward hundreds of students crowded close around Prabhupāda, asking him questions. Many students continued to chant as they left the hall, and some left crying from the new sensations of spiritual happiness. The next day the ecstatic night of chanting at Hitchcock Hall was the talk of the campus. Prabhupāda was pleased with the evening, and he described the event in a letter to devotees in Los Angeles:

> Yesterday, at the Ohio State University we had a tremendous meeting, and nearly two thousand students were dancing, clapping and chanting along with us. So it is clear that the student community has a nice potential for accepting this philosophy.

* * *

New Vrindaban
May 21, 1969

Accompanied by Kīrtanānanda Swami and Hayagrīva, Prabhupāda then traveled from Columbus to the New Vrindaban farm project in the hills of West Virginia. When their car got stuck in a neighbor's garden near the entrance to the property, Prabhupāda decided to walk the final two miles along the muddy access road that led to the farm. The road soon ended, however, and Prabhupāda and his two guides picked up a footpath, entering the dense forest.

The mid-May trees were still coming into foliage, and the sunlight broke through the branches to a carpet of brilliant purple phlox. Prabhupāda walked quickly ahead of Kīrtanānanda Swami and Hayagrīva, who hurried to keep up. A winding creek repeatedly crossed the path, and Prabhupāda would cross by stepping from stone to stone. The road, he said, would not be difficult to travel by ox cart; the forest was like a jungle, just as he had expected and wanted.

For the past year, Prabhupāda had corresponded with Kīrtanānanda Swami and Hayagrīva concerning New Vrindaban, and this correspondence had established the direction for Kṛṣṇa conscious country living. Prabhupāda had said he wanted the community based on Vedic ideals, everyone living simply, keeping cows, and working the land. The devotees would have to develop these ideas gradually; it would take time. But even in the beginning the keynote should be "simple living and high thinking." Because the community would remain completely aloof from the city, it would at first appear inconvenient and austere. But life would be peaceful, free from the anxieties of the artificial urban society based on hard work for sense gratification. And most important, the members of such a community would be serving Kṛṣṇa and chanting His name.

Prabhupāda spoke little, making his way along the path as if at his own home. They stopped beside the creek, and Prabhupāda sat down on a blanket Kīrtanānanda Swami and Hayagrīva spread for him on the grass. "We are stopping for Kīrtanānanda," Prabhupāda said. "He is tired." Prabhupāda and his party drank water from the creek, rested briefly, and then continued.

As they rounded a curve in the road, Prabhupāda could see a clearing on the ridge ahead. A small frame house and a barn stood at the lower end of the ridge. These two ancient structures, Hayagrīva explained, were the only buildings on New Vrindaban's 120 acres. As no vehicles traveled here, the paths were overrun with high grass. A willow spread its branches close by the old house. The settlement was the picture of undisturbed primitive life.

Prabhupāda liked the simple life at New Vrindaban, and whatever simple thing the devotees offered him he accepted with satisfaction. They served him freshly ground wheat cereal cooked in milk, and he said it was wonderful. When he saw the kitchen's dirt floor covered with cow dung, he approved, saying it was just like in an Indian village.

Prabhupāda also liked his room in the attic, directly above the temple room. He brought out the small Rādhā-Kṛṣṇa Deities he had been traveling with for the last month and a half and had his servant, Devānanda, improvise an altar on a small table to one side of the room. Arranging his two trunks as a desk and placing a picture of his spiritual master on one of the trunks, Prabhupāda immediately resumed his usual schedule.

He would take his late-morning massage sitting outside and then bathe with warm water in an improvised outdoor shower stall. Kīrtanānanda Swami prepared Prabhupāda's usual lunch of *dāl,* rice, and *capātīs*— plus some local pokeweed. The previous summer, Kīrtanānanda Swami and Hayagrīva had picked and canned blackberries, which they now served Prabhupāda as blackberry chutney. The *capātīs* were from freshly milled whole wheat, and everything was cooked over a wood fire. The best fuel for cooking, Prabhupāda said, was cow dung; wood was second, gas third, and electricity last.

Prabhupāda spent much of the day out of doors, under a persimmon tree about a hundred feet from the house. There he would sit and read at a low table one of the men had built. Often he would look up from his reading and gaze across the deep valley to the distant ridge, where the forest met the sky.

In the late afternoon, devotees would gather under the persimmon tree with Prabhupāda, sitting and talking with him until after sunset. They saw Prabhupāda's living with them as a practical demonstration of New Vrindaban's importance; if he, the greatest devotee, could be satisfied living simply and chanting Hare Kṛṣṇa in this backwoods setting, then they should follow his example.

Comparing New Vrindaban to the Vṛndāvana in India, Prabhupāda said that New Vrindaban was in some ways better, since Vṛndāvana,

India, was now congested with worldly men. Five hundred years ago the Gosvāmī followers of Lord Caitanya had excavated the sites of Kṛṣṇa's pastimes in Vṛndāvana, and only pure devotees had lived there. But in recent years Vṛndāvana had become a place for materialists and impersonalists. New Vrindaban, however, should admit only the spiritually inclined. In Vedic society, Prabhupāda said, everyone had been satisfied to live like this, in a small village beside a river. Factories were unnecessary. Prabhupāda wanted this Vedic way of life for the entire world, and New Vrindaban could serve as a model for the benefit of the masses.

New Vrindaban had no phone, and mail had to be fetched by a two-mile walk. In this, Prabhupāda said, New Vrindaban was like Vṛndāvana, India—both Vṛndāvanas lacked in modern amenities. This "difficulty," however, coupled well with the Vaiṣṇava philosophy that modern amenities were not worth the trouble required to get them. A devotee, accepting whatever nature provides, spends his time and energy in spiritual life.

New Vrindaban's only cow was a black and white crossbreed named Kāliya, and Prabhupāda would drink a little of her milk morning, noon, and night. "I haven't tasted milk like this in sixty-five years," he said. One day, he predicted, New Vrindaban would have many cows, and their udders would be so full that the dripping milk would muddy the pastures. Although people in the West were blind to their great sin of cow slaughter and its grievous karmic reactions, he said, New Vrindaban would demonstrate to the world the social, moral, and economic advantages of protecting the cow and utilizing her milk, rather than killing her and eating her flesh.

Prabhupāda wanted the New Vrindaban devotees to build cottages. He wanted many buildings, even if at first they were primitive, and he gave a plan for a simple structure of baked mud. He also wanted a Kṛṣṇa conscious school, and the country, he said, would be the best place for it. "The city is made by man, and the country is made by God," Prabhupāda said, paraphrasing the British poet Cowper. The young students should learn reading, writing, and arithmetic, and at the same time they should become pure devotees. In their play they could imitate the pastimes of Kṛṣṇa and His cowherd boyfriends, with one child massaging Kṛṣṇa, another wrestling with Kṛṣṇa—just as in the spiritual world. The women in New Vrindaban, Prabhupāda said, should care for the children, clean the temple, cook for the Deities, and churn butter.

He had many plans for New Vrindaban, and he was giving only idea seeds, with few details. "You develop it to your heart's content," he told Kīrtanānanda Swami. An ideal Vedic community with the members producing all their own food and necessities was what Prabhupāda wanted. Unless the devotees at New Vrindaban could become self-sufficient, he said, there was no use in their occupying such a big piece of land.

Even before Prabhupāda's visit to New Vrindaban, he had requested Kīrtanānanda Swami and Hayagrīva to plan for seven temples on the property. These seven temples should be named after the major temples of old Vṛndāvana: Madana-mohana, Govindajī, Gopīnātha, Rādhā-Dāmodara, Rādhā-ramaṇa, Śyāmasundara, and Rādhā-Gokulānanda. Prabhupāda said he would personally secure Rādhā-Kṛṣṇa Deities for each temple.

It was inevitable that Prabhupāda leave New Vrindaban; letters from London, Los Angeles, and San Francisco compelled him to travel. On the day of his departure, the New Vrindaban devotees teased him, saying he couldn't go. Kīrtanānanda Swami went so far as to say they would block his way on the road. But Prabhupāda corrected him, "You can't do that to the spiritual master."

Accompanied by Kīrtanānanda Swami and the New Vrindaban devotees, Prabhupāda walked along the forest path. The New Vrindaban countryside was verdant, the summer air hot and moist. Prabhupāda was silent. He had come here to encourage his disciples, and he himself had also become encouraged. Here was simple village life as Kṛṣṇa Himself had lived it, depending on the land and the cow. That cow Kāliya had given such nice milk. New Vrindaban's cows were not ordinary; they knew they would not be killed. So far only a few devotees were here, but by Kṛṣṇa's grace more would come.

Prabhupāda and Kīrtanānanda Swami walked together along the forest path, saying little, but their mutual understanding was deep. Prabhupāda hadn't given him many specific instructions: a few words while sitting or walking together outdoors, a gesture, a facial expression of pleasure or concern. Kīrtanānanda Swami could understand, however, that New Vrindaban was very dear to his spiritual master and should become dear to him also. Prabhupāda assured him that because the devotees of New Vrindaban were centered on chanting Hare Kṛṣṇa, serving the Deities, and protecting the cows, Kṛṣṇa would bless them with success. The community was already successful, and Kṛṣṇa would continue to protect the devotees against all impediments and difficulties.

At the end of the two-mile walk, Prabhupāda, surrounded by his followers, stood beside the car that was to take him to the airport in Pittsburgh, from where he would fly to Los Angeles. His suitcases, which had come out on a horse-drawn cart, were loaded into the car's luggage compartment, and Prabhupāda got in the back seat. Amid cries of "Hare Kṛṣṇa!" and "Prabhupāda!" the car pulled out onto the country highway, and Prabhupāda continued chanting Hare Kṛṣṇa on his beads.

* * *

Prabhupāda had been hearing regularly from his six disciples in London. Having little money and living as separate couples in different parts of the city, they found their greatest inspiration in Prabhupāda's letters. They would repeatedly read his instructions and dream of when he would one day visit them in London. Although in San Francisco Kṛṣṇa consciousness had been fun for the three couples, in England it was becoming more and more difficult. The devotees, being foreigners, were not allowed to earn a salary, and except for a few contacts they knew no one. Although unable to live together, they were trying to maintain their morale and Kṛṣṇa consciousness.

Yamunā: *I had to move to a Jamaican ghetto, the top floor of one of the buildings. It was awful. Day after day after day I would sit and listen to a tape of Prabhupāda singing. It was a beautiful tape he had just done in Los Angeles. And I would pray to him, "Please come. Please come."*

Mukunda: *Letters—that's what kept us alive. Prabhupāda would write and say, "I am coming." Two or three times he wrote to say, "I am coming by March." And we would write back and say we wanted to get a place first. We really felt it wouldn't be right for him to come unless we had a place first. He wrote a letter to my wife: "I was planning to come by March, but your husband is not allowing me. What can I do?"*

The devotees in London had not seen Prabhupāda in four months, and still there was no date set for his visit. Although they sometimes became discouraged and talked of going back to America, they persevered. Prabhupāda had promised he would come when they got a temple, and that promise helped them remember that they were personally serving him. They felt that *he* was doing the work and they were his assistants. His absence was only external. By his instructions, whether written, spoken, or remembered in the heart, he was always with them. He was constantly directing them.

While trying out various schemes to popularize Kṛṣṇa consciousness in London, Śyāmasundara arranged for a program to which he invited many of London's prominent citizens. About one hundred people responded to Śyāmasundara's formal invitation—one member of Parliament, a few government officials, but mostly young people.

The devotees served a feast and showed a film of Śrīla Prabhupāda walking by Stowe Lake in Golden Gate Park. Prabhupāda had sent a tape recording specifically for the evening, and the devotees highlighted it as the evening's special attraction, even though they hadn't had time to hear it in advance. Gurudāsa started the tape, and suddenly there was Prabhupāda's voice.

"Ladies and gentlemen, please accept my greetings in the happy year of 1969, and blessings of Śrī Kṛṣṇa, the Supreme Personality of Godhead, for your kindly participating in this happy meeting of Kṛṣṇa consciousness."

Although Prabhupāda had recorded the tape in the quiet of his room in Los Angeles, the devotees were astonished to feel Prabhupāda's direct presence, preaching Kṛṣṇa consciousness to the English.

"Lord Caitanya informed us that the absolute Supreme Personality of Godhead can descend in transcendental sound vibration, and thus when we chant Hare Kṛṣṇa *mantra* offenselessly we immediately contact Kṛṣṇa and His internal energy. Thus we become immediately purified from all dirty things in our heart."

The guests sat listening politely as Prabhupāda described the soul's travail of transmigrating from body to body and the path of the soul's liberation through chanting Hare Kṛṣṇa, Hare Kṛṣṇa, Kṛṣṇa Kṛṣṇa, Hare Hare/ Hare Rāma, Hare Rāma, Rāma Rāma, Hare Hare. Kṛṣṇa consciousness was "transcendentally colorful and full of transcendental pleasure." Chanting could be done anywhere—on the street, in the park, or at home. Prabhupāda concluded his talk.

"But to assemble and sit together we require a place for congregation. Therefore a temple of the Kṛṣṇa consciousness movement is required to be established in various centers in the world, irrespective of the particular country's culture, philosophy, and religion. Kṛṣṇa consciousness is so universal and perfect that it can appeal to everyone, irrespective of his position. Therefore I fervently appeal to you all present in this meeting to extend your cooperation for successful execution of this great movement. Thanking you once more."

There was a pause, and then Prabhupāda began playing the harmonium and singing Hare Kṛṣṇa. Afterward he again spoke.

"My disciples in London have very eagerly asked me to visit there, and I am also very anxious to see you all. So as soon as there is opportunity, I shall go with my *saṅkīrtana* party, who are now engaged in Los Angeles. And that will be a great pleasure, for you all to meet together. That is all."

Only a few weeks after this meeting the group received their first important publicity: a photo of the six devotees and little Sarasvatī appeared with an article by the famous columnist Atticus in the *Sunday Times.* Gurudāsa was quoted as saying, "Hare Kṛṣṇa is a chant which sets God dancing on your tongue. Try chanting 'Queen Elizabeth' and see the difference." The article described the missionary group from America as "very gentle people, a bit unworldly, but not at all ingenuous." Citing their renunciation of illicit sex and intoxication, the article commented, "Tame you might think, but they look very well on it. And what's likely to earn them a public is their chanting." Within a few days the same article appeared in the *San Francisco Chronicle,* but with a new headline: "Krishna Chants Startle London." Prabhupāda was pleased when he saw the headline. Indeed, his *gṛhastha* disciples had succeeded where his *sannyāsī* Godbrothers had failed. Although several of Prabhupāda's scholarly Godbrothers had lectured around England over the last thirty-five years, only one person, an elderly English lady named Elizabeth Bowtell, had shown interest.

Yamunā had written Prabhupāda to find out if they should visit Mrs. Bowtell (she had received the name Vinoda-vāṇī dāsī), and Prabhupāda had replied, "The history of this Vani dasi is that she is an old lady, and has a house and has hung a sign, Gaudiya Math, but that is all." If they liked, Prabhupāda had said, they could pay her a courtesy call and see if she would let them use her place for *kīrtanas.* One of the men had gone to see her at her home, several hours out of the city. But from behind her closed door she had refused to meet with him unless he brought an introductory letter from the Gaudiya Math in New Delhi. Vinoda-vāṇī dāsī was the fruit of thirty-five years of *sannyāsīs'* preaching in England, whereas in four months Prabhupāda's young American missionaries were "startling London."

After months of living scattered throughout the city, the devotees met a landlord who allowed them to stay together rent-free in a vacant warehouse at Covent Garden. The devotees improvised a temporary temple and soon recruited their first three British devotees. The newcomers at once took to the full Kṛṣṇa conscious regimen, including the *dhotī* and shaved head—and loved it.

The devotees, thrilled to see their group expanding and Prabhupāda's potency working, decided to phone Prabhupāda from their landlord's office. The telephone was a conference phone, and Prabhupāda's voice came over the little loudspeaker on the desk. The devotees sat around the desk, listening tensely.

"Prabhupāda," Mukunda said, "we have some new *brahmacārīs* here."

"Oh, are they cooking *capātīs?*" Prabhupāda asked from across the ocean. The devotees laughed uncontrollably, then hushed to hear more.

"No," said Mukunda. "But they will be now." The devotees each told Prabhupāda how they missed him, and he said he missed them too and would come as soon as they could get a place.

After allowing the devotees three months in the warehouse at Covent Garden, the landlord announced that he needed to use the space and the devotees would have to move. The couples moved to three separate locations, and again their strong group spirit dissipated.

Prabhupāda began sending two or three letters a week to the scattered couples, praising them for their sincere determination. The devotees would gather regularly, if only to show one another their latest letters. Prabhupāda wrote to Mukunda of his desire to preach Kṛṣṇa consciousness in the West, specifically London:

> So far as I am concerned, I always wish only to expedite my mission of life to spread Krishna Consciousness in the Western part of the world. I am still firmly convinced that if I can establish this movement through the help of all the boys and girls who have now joined with me, then it will be a great achievement. I am old man, and there has already been warning, but before I leave this body, I wish to see some of you very strong in Krishna Consciousness understanding. I am very glad and proud also that you six boys and girls, although you have not been able to establish a nice center in London, still you have done your best. And the news has reached far away in India that my disciples are doing very nice work in Krishna Consciousness. So that is my pride. I have received a letter from my Godbrother informing

> me that it has been advertised in India that in Vietnam also somebody is spreading Hare Krishna Movement. So there is no need to be disappointed. You go on with your work as best as Krishna gives you the opportunity, and there is no cause of your anxiety. Everything is going smoothly. But since you are now separated, the strength of your activities appears to be a little disturbed. Now you try to assemble together in the same spirit as you were doing, and in that case, temple or no temple, your movement will go on progressively. We are not much concerned about the temple because temple worship is not primary factor in this age. Primary factor is Sankirtan. But sometimes we want a center where people may gather and see, so a temple is required secondarily. So try your best immediately to live together. I am very much eager to see that you are again living together.

For Śrīla Prabhupāda's disciples, his instruction that they preach in London was much more binding than any other obligation. He was in their hearts, and they thought of him constantly. In carrying out his orders and trying to please him, they were constrained not by force or law but by love. To please the spiritual master is to please the Supreme Personality of Godhead; and for Prabhupāda's sincere disciples, to please him seemed the end in itself.

* * *

Los Angeles
June 23, 1969

After leaving New Vrindaban, Śrīla Prabhupāda visited his center in Los Angeles, where he installed Deities of Rādhā and Kṛṣṇa. Although, as he had told his disciples in London, the "primary factor" was *saṅkīrtana,* Deity worship was also necessary. In his writings Prabhupāda had discussed the need for Deity worship, and he had gradually introduced higher and higher standards of Deity worship in each of his ISKCON centers. Los Angeles, having become the model ISKCON center, was the natural place for him to introduce a more opulent and demanding standard for worshiping Rādhā and Kṛṣṇa.

While more than a hundred devotees and guests sat in the spacious hall, Prabhupāda bathed and dressed the little forms of Rādhā and Kṛṣṇa, then placed Them on the altar. He was inviting Rādhā and Kṛṣṇa to descend, to give his disciples the opportunity to serve Them. He was offering his disciples Rādhā and Kṛṣṇa, with faith that his disciples would not neglect Them. If the devotees somehow lost their enthusiasm, Prabhupāda explained in his lecture, then the worship would become like idol worship.

"If there is no life, then it is idol worship. Where there is life, feeling, then you think, 'Where is Kṛṣṇa? Here is Kṛṣṇa. Oh, I have to serve Him. I have to dress Him. I have to serve Rādhārāṇī. She is here. Oh, I just have to do it very nicely and, as far as possible, decorate Her to the best capacity.' If you think like this, then you are Kṛṣṇa conscious. But if you think that it is a brass-made doll or idol, then Kṛṣṇa will reciprocate with you accordingly. If you think that this is a brass-made idol, then it will remain brass-made idol to you forever. But if you elevate yourself to a higher platform of Kṛṣṇa consciousness, then Kṛṣṇa — this very Kṛṣṇa — will talk with you. This Kṛṣṇa will talk with you."

With each visit to each center, Prabhupāda gave the devotees more service, deepening their commitment to Kṛṣṇa. All the various services were actually the spiritual master's responsibility, he said, and when a disciple cleaned the temple or performed any service, he did so as the spiritual master's assistant. And any job done improperly was the spiritual master's anxiety. If the devotees whimsically changed the Deity worship or neglected the temple, then Prabhupāda, more than any disciple, would feel distress.

Whenever Prabhupāda saw a disciple eager to take on more of the anxiety of preaching Kṛṣṇa consciousness, he would assign that devotee greater responsibility. Anxiety for serving Kṛṣṇa, Prabhupāda said, was the greatest satisfaction. As Bhaktivinoda Ṭhākura had stated, "The trouble I encounter in Your devotional service I will consider the greatest happiness."

Satisfaction for the devotee, Prabhupāda explained, lay in pleasing the previous spiritual masters, and that was best accomplished by preaching to the fallen souls. To the degree that the devotees carried out that order, they would satisfy their spiritual master and subsequently feel satisfaction themselves. Prabhupāda gave the example of Kṛṣṇa and the *gopīs*. When the *gopīs* pleased Kṛṣṇa in the *rāsa* dance, Kṛṣṇa smiled, and when the *gopīs* saw Kṛṣṇa's smile their happiness and beauty increased a million times. When Kṛṣṇa saw the newly increased beauty of the *gopīs* He became more pleased, and thus the happiness and beauty of the *gopīs* increased even more. This loving competition increased on and on unlimitedly.

Even in dealings between spiritual master and disciple a sense of loving competition prevailed, each wanting to serve the other, neither seeking service for himself. Prabhupāda was increasing the duties and responsibilities in each of his ISKCON centers, and sincere disciples were coming forward to accept those responsibilities; thus everyone was feeling satisfaction. This was pure devotional service—to be free from all material desires and to serve Kṛṣṇa as directed by the spiritual master and the scriptures.

When Prabhupāda said that his disciples would become happy by serving Kṛṣṇa, he spoke from his own deep realization of that ecstasy. Whenever he installed a Deity in one of the temples, his ecstasy was greater than that of any of his disciples. At the Ratha-yātrā festivals in Golden Gate Park or any public preaching function, he was the most enlivened. He, more than any of his disciples, wanted the public to come and chant and dance in the temple and see the Deity of Kṛṣṇa, and when they did, he was the most pleased. And if a disciple fell away, Prabhupāda was the most displeased.

Nor was Prabhupāda aloof from the details of temple management: the cost of things, how the devotees were being received in public, how each disciple was advancing. Although his disciples saw him as the most exalted Vaiṣṇava and intimate associate of Lord Kṛṣṇa, they knew he was always available to guide them in their services. He was their leader, but he was with them. He was far above them, but he remained close to them. Only rarely did he leave them behind—as at the Los Angeles Deity installation, when he began to cry, speaking directly to Kṛṣṇa: "Kṛṣṇa, I am most rotten and fallen, but I have brought this thing for You. Please take it." Except for such rare moments, Prabhupāda's disciples saw him preaching and serving along with them.

* * *

San Francisco
July 25, 1969

The day before the Ratha-yātrā festival, Prabhupāda arrived at the San Francisco airport, where a crowd of fifty chanting devotees greeted him. Reporters stepped forward with what to them was an important, relevant question: "Swami, what is your opinion on the recent manned U.S. moon landing?"

"Shall I flatter you or tell the truth?" Prabhupāda asked.

The truth, they said.

"It is a waste of time because it does not benefit you if you cannot live there. The time could have been better spent in Kṛṣṇa consciousness. We must go beyond this universe to the spiritual sky, which is eternal, beyond birth, death, old age, and disease." The *San Francisco Chronicle* printed a picture and story: "Ecstasy in Concourse B."

On the day of the Ratha-yātrā parade, a hundred devotees and a crowd of one thousand gathered on Haight Street before the tall cart. The deities of Jagannātha, Subhadrā, and Balarāma, from their elevated platform within the cart, smiled down upon the crowd. A group of devotee-musicians seated themselves within the cart, made last-minute checks of their loudspeaker system, and began *kīrtana.* In the center of the cart, just beneath the deity platform, a red upholstered *vyāsāsana* awaited Prabhupāda's arrival.

As Prabhupāda's car approached he could hear the cries of the devotees, and as he stepped from the car he saw them all bow down in obeisances. Folding his hands and smiling, he acknowledged his enthusiastic disciples, and he looked around with pleasure at the large crowd that had already gathered. Turning toward the cart, he beheld the deities on their throne, the same deities who had inaugurated Ratha-yātrā in America two years before. They were beautifully dressed and garlanded, and multicolored pennants and thick garlands of carnations decorated their cart. Ratha-yātrā was becoming more wonderful each year. Prabhupāda bowed down before Jagannātha, Subhadrā, and Balarāma, and his disciples all bowed with him.

As Prabhupāda took his seat on the cart the *kīrtana* began again, and the cart, pulled with two long ropes by dozens of men and women, slowly began to move forward. Buckets of burning frankincense poured aromatic clouds from the deities' platform above Prabhupāda's head, as slowly the cart moved along the road to the park.

"How many people are behind us?" Prabhupāda asked, turning to Tamāla Kṛṣṇa, who rode beside him on the cart and had been leading the *kīrtana*. Tamāla Kṛṣṇa climbed back and surveyed the crowd as far as he could see.

"Five thousand!"

"Sing '*Jaya* Jagannātha,'" Prabhupāda said, and Tamāla Kṛṣṇa then changed the chant from Hare Kṛṣṇa to "*Jaya* Jagannātha! *Jaya* Jagannātha!"

Throughout the parade Prabhupāda sat serenely watching, his right hand in his bead bag. The large crowd consisted mostly of young hippies but also included businessmen dressed in suits and ties, elderly persons with their grandchildren and families, and a few stray dogs. A mixed Sunday crowd.

Suddenly devotees in front began shouting, "Stop the cart! Stop the cart!" Ahead, the low arch of a park bridge spanned the roadway. The devotees managed to stop the 35-foot-high cart just before it reached the bridge. Although the parade appeared to have reached an unforeseen impasse, the chanting continued unabated. The previous year the procession had taken this same route—with a smaller cart—and even then Śyāmasundara had had to climb up and saw off the spire. This year, however, Nara-Nārāyaṇa had devised a collapsible dome with a crank to lower the canopy and superstructure. When Prabhupāda had heard of these plans, he had asked, "Are you sure you want to depend on mechanical means? It could be a disaster." Now the time to lower the canopy had come, and the crank wouldn't work.

With the cart stopped before the bridge, the chanters gathered in greater numbers, facing Prabhupāda and Lord Jagannātha. Under the bridge at least a thousand voices sang together, creating an incredible echo. Then Prabhupāda stood, raised his arms to the crowd, and began dancing.

Bhavānanda: *Everyone went wild. The sound was so uproarious you were deafened under that bridge. Prabhupāda was dancing, jumping on the cart.*

Nara-Nārāyaṇa: *He was dancing, and as he danced his feet crushed the flowers. His garland broke and flowers began cascading everywhere as he danced up and down. He was leaping very deliberately, almost like slow motion.*

Tamāla Kṛṣṇa: *Prabhupāda was jumping up and down, and the people went crazy seeing him in complete ecstasy. He kept jumping and slowly turned around until he was face to face with Lord Jagannātha.*

Prabhupāda sat down and still the car didn't go, and the people were roaring.

"What do they want?" Prabhupāda asked Tamāla Kṛṣṇa.

"I think they want to see you dance again, Śrīla Prabhupāda," Tamāla Kṛṣṇa replied.

"Do you think so?"

"Yes." He then got up and started dancing again. The white wool cap pushed to the back of his head, his arms extended, with the right hand still clutching the *japa* bead bag, his right forefinger extended, and long robes flowing.

The ecstatic chanting and dancing continued. After about fifteen minutes, Nara-Nārāyaṇa finally got the crank to work, and down came the canopy. Again the cart moved forward, under the bridge and on through the park. The crowd had grown now to ten thousand. This was much bigger than any Kṛṣṇa conscious festival ever held before.

Bhavānanda: *Many of these people who attended Ratha-yātrā were intoxicated. We were not intoxicated, of course, but we were higher than they. That we could understand. Everyone was smiling, everyone was laughing, everyone was in ecstasy, everyone was dancing, everyone was chanting. And we were doing it more than anyone. We were doing more chanting, more laughing and smiling, and feeling more freedom. We were free to have a shaved head, free to wear a* dhotī, *free to blow a conchshell, free to spin around on the street and jump up. Even if you were a hippie you couldn't be more far out than the* ratha *cart and Jagannātha, because no one looks more far out than Him. The hippies had come dressed up in outfits with big feathers in their hair and everything, but they were dim compared to Jagannātha.*

The parade route ended at an oceanside dance hall, The Family Dog Auditorium, where the devotees had prepared ten thousand feast plates of *prasādam*—fruit salad, apple chutney, *halavā,* and watermelon slices. Although the cart had stopped, the chanting continued, as Prabhupāda led the crowd inside the auditorium to a temporary stage and altar the devotees had erected among the bizarre trappings of the dance hall. A giant silk screen of Lord Caitanya covered the hall's Tibetan *maṇḍala,* and pictures of Lord Viṣṇu and Śrīla Bhaktisiddhānta Sarasvatī were on the stage. The Jagannātha deities now looked down from their high platform above Prabhupāda's seat, and a garlanded statue of Lord Kṛṣṇa stood on a marble pillar.

Prabhupāda began speaking, and the crowd quieted. He quoted a song by Narottama dāsa Ṭhākura: "My dear Lord Caitanya, please be merciful upon me. I do not find anyone as merciful as You." Drawing the audience's attention to the large silkscreen of Lord Caitanya, Prabhupāda described the Lord's merciful distribution of the holy name of God. Lord Caitanya, he said, was teaching the same thing Lord Kṛṣṇa had taught in *Bhagavad-gītā:* "My dear sons, do not suffer in this abominable condition of material existence. Come back to Me. Come back to home. Enjoy eternal, blissful life, a life of knowledge."

Prabhupāda explained the simplicity of Kṛṣṇa consciousness:

"Lord Caitanya appeared five hundred years ago to establish the direct principles of *Bhagavad-gītā.* He showed that even if you do not understand the process of religion, then simply chant Hare Kṛṣṇa, Hare Kṛṣṇa, Kṛṣṇa Kṛṣṇa, Hare Hare/ Hare Rāma, Hare Rāma, Rāma Rāma, Hare Hare. The results are practical. For example, when we were chanting Hare Kṛṣṇa all the members who are assembled here were joining in, but now when I am talking about philosophy some are leaving. It is very practical. You can see. The Hare Kṛṣṇa *mantra* is so enchanting that anyone in any condition can take part. And if he continues to chant, gradually he will develop his dormant love of God. It is very simple.

"We are requesting everyone to chant the Hare Kṛṣṇa *mantra* and take *prasādam.* When you are tired of chanting, the *prasādam* is ready; you can immediately take *prasādam.* And if you dance, then all bodily exercise is Kṛṣṇa-ized. And all of the attempts of the *yoga* processes are attained by this simple process.

"So chant, dance, take *prasādam.* Even if you do not at first hear this philosophy, it will act, and you will be elevated to the highest platform of perfection."

* * *

In the middle of a winter of struggle came a fortunate break for the London devotees: a meeting with George Harrison of the Beatles. For a long time the devotees had been thinking of ways to get the Beatles to chant Hare Kṛṣṇa. To the Beatles' Apple Records Studio they had once sent an apple pie with *Hare Krishna* lettered on it. Another time they had sent a wind-up walking apple with the Hare Kṛṣṇa *mantra* printed on it. They had even sent a tape of one of their *kīrtanas* and had received a standard rejection letter from Apple Records. So it seemed to be Kṛṣṇa's special arrangement when Śyāmasundara suddenly met one of the most sought-after celebrities in the world, George Harrison.

In a crowded room at Apple Records, Śyāmasundara, shavenheaded and wearing robes, sat hoping for a chance to have a few words with someone connected with the Beatles. Then George came down the stairs from a conference. As he entered the room, he saw Śyāmasundara. Walking over and sitting down beside Śyāmasundara, he asked, "Where have you been? I've been trying to meet the Hare Kṛṣṇa people for the last couple of years." Śyāmasundara and George talked together for an hour, while everyone else hovered around. "I've really been trying to meet you people," George said. "Why don't you come to my place tomorrow?"

The next day Śyāmasundara went to George's for lunch, where he met the other Beatles: Ringo Starr, John Lennon, and Paul McCartney. They all had questions, but George was especially interested.

George: *I had a copy of the Hare Kṛṣṇa album with Śrīla Prabhupāda singing Hare Kṛṣṇa with the devotees. I'd had the record at least two years. But I got it the week it was pressed. I was open to it. You attract those things. So I used to play that a lot of the time. I was chanting the Hare Kṛṣṇa* mantra *long before I met Śyāmasundara, Gurudāsa, and Mukunda. I was just pleased to hear the Hare Kṛṣṇa* mantra *and have a copy of the record.*

And I knew about Prabhupāda because I had read all the liner notes on that album. Having been to India I could tell where the devotees were all coming from, with the style of dress and shaved heads. I had seen them on the streets of Los Angeles and New York. Having read so many books and looking for yogīs, *my concept of the devotees wasn't like the other people, who think the devotees have all escaped from a lunatic asylum in their pajamas. No, I was aware of the thing and that it was a pretty heavy one, much more austerities than other groups—like no coffee, chocolate, or tea.*

Śyāmasundara continued to see George regularly, and they soon became friends. George, who had been practicing a *mantra* given him by Maharishi Mahesh Yogi, began to hear for the first time about *bhakti-yoga* and the Vedic philosophy. He talked openly to Śyāmasundara, Gurudāsa, and Mukunda of his spiritual quest and his realizations of *karma*.

George: *A* yogī *I met in India said, "You are really lucky. You have youth, fame, fortune, health, but at the same time that's not enough for you. You want to know about something else." Most people don't even get to the point where they realize there's something beyond that wall. They are just trying to get up on top of that wall, to be able to eat and have a nice house and be comfortable and all that. But I was fortunate enough to get all that in time to realize there's something else to life, whereas most people get worn out just trying to attain material things.*

After a visit to Haight-Ashbury in 1967 George had begun to feel guilty for his role in promulgating the LSD culture. He had had the impression that the hippies of Haight-Ashbury were creative craftsmen, but when he saw them drugged, dirty, and hopeless—"a West Coast extension of the Bowery"—he felt partly responsible. He decided to use his influential position by writing and singing songs about something more than psychedelics and sex. He was also feeling an increasing interest in Indian spirituality, due, he felt, to *karma* from his previous lives.

George: *I feel at home with Kṛṣṇa. I think that's something that has been there from a previous birth. So it was like the door was opening to me at that time, but it was also like a jigsaw puzzle and I needed all these little pieces to make a complete picture. And that is what has been happening by the devotees and Swami Bhaktivedanta coming along, or some devotee giving me a book or my hearing that album. It's all been slowly fitting together.*

And these are some of the reasons why I responded to Śyāmasundara and Gurudāsa when they first came to London. Let's face it, if I'm going to have to stand up and be counted, then I'll be with these guys rather than with those over there. It's like that. I'll be with the devotees rather than with the straight people who are the so-called saints.

George offered to help the devotees get a building in London, and he and Śyāmasundara spoke of making a Hare Kṛṣṇa record. But Śyāmasundara never pressed him.

George was the glamorous superstar, the "quiet, serious Beatle," the fabulous guitarist and singer who had access to all the greats, to presidents and queens, wherever he went. And Śyāmasundara had a glamor of his own. He was tall, six feet two, and although shavenheaded, strikingly handsome. And he was a Vaiṣṇava, fully dedicated to the Indian spirituality George was so fond of.

When Prabhupāda heard about George, he took seriously the possibility that George might fully take up Kṛṣṇa consciousness. Carrying this to its logical conclusion, Prabhupāda envisioned a world revolution in consciousness—spearheaded by the Kṛṣṇa conscious Beatles:

> It is understood from your letter that Mr. George Harrison has a little sympathy for our movement, and if Krishna is actually satisfied on him surely he will be able to join with us in pushing on the Samkirtan movement throughout the world. Somehow or other the Beatles have become the cynosure of the neighboring European countries and America also. He is attracted by our Samkirtan Party and if Mr. George Harrison takes the leading part in organizing a huge Samkirtan Party consisting of the Beatles and our ISKCON boys, surely we shall change the face of the world so much politically harassed by the maneuvers of the politicians.

For the London devotees, George's friendship heightened the excitement of Prabhupāda's coming to London. Now that a world-famous personality was waiting to meet Prabhupāda, they felt perhaps they had another way to please him and to make preaching in London a success.

George, by his association with Kṛṣṇa consciousness and by dint of his own spiritual evolution, began to express his devotion to Lord Kṛṣṇa in his songs. Reading Prabhupāda's *Bhagavad-gītā As It Is,* he could appreciate the superiority of the personal conception of God over the impersonal. Gurudāsa showed George the verse in the *Gīta* where Kṛṣṇa says that He is the basis of the impersonal Brahman. George liked the concepts of Kṛṣṇa consciousness, but he was wary of showing exclusive devotion to Prabhupāda and Kṛṣṇa. The devotees, therefore, dealt with him accordingly, so as not to disturb him.

On January 11 Śrīla Prabhupāda wrote another letter to the devotees in London, expressing more ideas of how George could best serve Kṛṣṇa:

> I am so glad that Mr. Harrison is composing songs like "Lord whom we so long ignored." He is very thoughtful. When we actually meet, I shall be able to give him thoughts about separation from Krishna, and they will be able to compose very attractive songs for public reception. The public is in need of such songs, and if they are administered through nice agents like the Beatles, it will surely be a great success.

Prabhupāda cautioned the devotees not to simply depend on George for help but to try to find a building themselves and rent it. George did want to help, however, and again he suggested the devotees make a record on the Apple label. An old favorite idea of the London devotees had been to get the Beatles to make a record chanting Hare Kṛṣṇa; if the Beatles did it, the *mantra* would certainly become world-famous. George liked the idea, but he preferred that the devotees sing it and he produce it on the Apple label. "You guys make the money, rather than we get it," he said. "Let's make a record."

So the devotees went over to George's house for a chanting session. George dubbed in his guitar, and a few weeks later the devotees returned and heard their tape. George was ready to try a session at the studio, so the devotees agreed to meet him and his musician friend Billy Preston at Trident Studios on St. Anne's Alley. They recorded for a few hours; the tape sounded good. George and Śyāmasundara agreed on a date for the actual recording.

On the day of the recording about a dozen devotees, including some newly recruited Britishers, assembled at E.M.I. recording studios on Abbey Road. When the first group of devotees arrived in George's Mercedes, a crowd of teenagers began singing Hare Kṛṣṇa to the tune popularized by the rock musical *Hair.* While Yamunā applied Vaiṣṇava *tilaka* to the foreheads of the recording technicians, Mālatī began unpacking the picnic baskets of *prasādam* she had brought, and some of the other devotees put up pictures of Kṛṣṇa and lit incense. The studio was Kṛṣṇa-ized.

With Paul McCartney and his wife, Linda, operating the control console, the recording session began. Everyone worked quickly, making Side One of the 45 rpm record in about an hour. George played organ, and Mukunda played *mṛdaṅga.* Yamunā sang the lead with Śyāmasundara backing her, and the other voices blended in a chorus. And to make it come out exactly right, everyone concentrated on Prabhupāda and prayed for spiritual strength.

On the fourth take, everything went smoothly, with Mālatī spontaneously hitting a brass gong at the end. Then they recorded the flip side of the record: prayers to Śrīla Prabhupāda, Lord Caitanya and His associates, and the six Gosvāmīs. Afterward, George dubbed in the bass guitar and other voices. The devotees, engineers—everyone—felt good about it. "This is going to be big," George promised.

As the record went into production the devotees returned to their regular work, still living separately. Prabhupāda set the time of his arrival for early September. He would go to Hamburg and then come to London, he said—even if there was no temple. Miraculously, only two months before Prabhupāda's arrival, things began to come together.

Gurudāsa met a real estate agent with a building on Bury Place, near the British Museum; the devotees could move in immediately. An ideal location, forty-one pounds a week, and immediate occupancy—it was wonderful. Mukunda wrote Prabhupāda asking him for money for the down payment. Prabhupāda agreed. Śyāmasundara got a letter from George on Apple Corporation Ltd. stationery stating that Apple would guarantee payments if the devotees defaulted. Within a week, the devotees had a five-story building in central London.

But when the devotees went to live at their new center on Bury Place, city officials said they did not have the proper housing permits. The red tape could take weeks, even months. Again the devotees were without a place to live and worship together. Śyāmasundara, however, on faith that everything would work out, began constructing a temple room of California redwood in the building.

John Lennon then suggested to Śyāmasundara that the devotees come and live with him at Tittenhurst, a large estate he had recently purchased near Ascot. He needed some renovation done, and if the devotees would help he would give them a place to live. "Can our *guru* also stay there?" Śyāmasundara asked. John agreed, and the devotees moved into the former servants' quarters at John's estate.

Only a few weeks before Prabhupāda's arrival the record, "Hare Krishna Mantra," was released. Apple Records staged a promotion and brought press reporters and photographers in a multicolored bus to a blue and white pavilion where the devotees had gathered with George.

The first day the record sold seventy thousand copies. Within a few weeks the devotees appeared on the popular TV show *Top of the Pops,* singing "their song."

John Lennon's estate, formerly owned by the Cadbury family, consisted of seventy-six acres of lawn and forest, with a large manor and many smaller buildings. John and his wife, Yoko, lived in the manor. The servants' quarters, where Prabhupāda and the devotees were to live, were four separate apartments in a single narrow building near the manor. About fifteen devotees moved in, reserving one apartment for Prabhupāda and his servant.

John wanted the devotees to tear out the hardwood walls and floors in the main house and replace them with new walls and black and white marble tile floors. While this renovation was beginning, Īśāna, who had recently arrived from Canada, began with a few helpers to convert the old music recital hall into a temple, complete with *vyāsāsana* for Śrīla Prabhupāda. The devotees worked day and night on Prabhupāda's quarters, the temple room, and Prabhupāda's *vyāsāsana*. With such energy did they work that John and Yoko could see that the devotees were obviously in love with their spiritual master. When the devotees were making a tape to send to Prabhupāda in Germany, Īśāna asked John if he had anything he wanted to say to their *guru*. John smiled and said he would like to know Prabhupāda's secret that made his followers so devoted.

The stage was set. The time had come for the principal character to enter. Lord Kṛṣṇa's pure devotee was at last coming to England. For the six devotees who had pioneered Kṛṣṇa consciousness in London, it had been a long struggle. But now it seemed that all their once-impossible dreams were coming true. They had found a place for Prabhupāda to live in, and they had obtained a temple in the center of London. This was Kṛṣṇa's blessing.

CHAPTER THIRTY

London: A Dream Fulfilled

London
September 11, 1969

WITH THE COOPERATION of Apple Records and Lufthansa German Airlines, the devotees arranged a reception for Prabhupāda at London's Heathrow Airport. As soon as Prabhupāda descended the stairs of the airplane, he was escorted to a car and driven to a V.I.P. lounge, bypassing the formalities of immigration and customs. As Prabhupāda stepped from the car, the devotees ran out of the terminal and offered obeisances on the wet pavement, while Śrīla Prabhupāda looked down on them, smiling. The devotees rose, brushing wet macadam from their *dhotīs* and *sārīs,* and joyfully surrounded Prabhupāda as he entered the lounge.

Inside the terminal Prabhupāda confronted a mass of reporters and cameramen and several dozen friends of the devotees. A clean cloth covered one of the lounge sofas, and vases with yellow gladioluses sat on either side. Prabhupāda walked over to the sofa and sat down, and Śyāmasundara garlanded him with red and white carnations. Prabhupāda began leading *kīrtana.*

The devotees were oblivious to all but Prabhupāda, and the reporters resigned themselves to simply standing and observing while the devotees sang and danced ecstatically. The eager devotees were unabashed during the *kīrtana,* and their shouts of "*Haribol*!" and "*Jaya* Prabhupāda!" as well as blasts from a conchshell, punctuated the regular chanting of Hare Kṛṣṇa.

After the *kīrtana* the reporters remained at a distance as Prabhupāda spoke affectionately to almost each devotee seated before him. "Where is Jānakī?" he asked. "Oh, yes, how are you? Vibhāvatī, how is your daughter? Actually, you are all my fathers and mothers. You are taking such care ..."

For the devotees, only they and Prabhupāda were present in the lounge, and they strained to catch everything he did or said. They couldn't have cared less about any outsider's reaction. Finally, Mukunda invited the reporters to come forward: "If any of you gentlemen have any questions, you can ask them of Prabhupāda."

The reporters, moving in: "What do you think of this reception?"

Prabhupāda: "I am not very much fond of reception. I want to know how people give reception to this movement. That is my concern."

Devotees in unison: "*Haribol!*"

Reporter: "Is this a very special welcome for you, or is this a performance you go through each day?"

Prabhupāda: "No, wherever I go, I have got my disciples. In Western countries I have got now about twenty centers, especially in America. So the American boys are very enthusiastic. I think in Los Angeles and San Francisco I got a very great reception. In the Ratha-yātrā festival about ten thousand boys and girls followed me for seven miles."

Devotees: "*Haribol*!"

Sun reporter: "What do you try to teach, sir?"

Prabhupāda: "I am trying to teach what you have forgotten."

Devotees (laughing): "*Haribol*! Hare Kṛṣṇa!"

Sun reporter: "Which is what?"

Prabhupāda: "That is God. Some of you are saying there is no God. Some of you are saying God is dead. And some of you are saying God is impersonal or void. These are all nonsense. I want to teach all the nonsense people that there is God. That is my mission. Any nonsense can come to me—I shall prove that there is God. That is my Kṛṣṇa consciousness movement. It is a challenge to the atheistic people: This is God. As we are sitting here face to face, you can see God face to face, if you are sincere and if you are serious. That is possible. Unfortunately, you are trying to forget God. Therefore you are embracing so many miseries of life. So I am simply preaching that you become Kṛṣṇa conscious and be happy. Don't be swayed by these nonsense waves of *māyā,* or illusion."

When a reporter asked if the singing was "essential to the sustenance of your faith," Prabhupāda answered at length, describing the cleansing effect of chanting Hare Kṛṣṇa. He quoted *Śrīmad-Bhāgavatam's* declaration that anyone without God consciousness has no good qualities. "Test any of our students," Prabhupāda said, "—how they are good, how they are advanced. Test it. Bring anyone in the world and compare with any one of our boys. You will find how much difference there is in their character and their feeling and their consciousness. If you want a peaceful society, then you must make people God conscious, Kṛṣṇa conscious. Everything will be automatically resolved. Otherwise your so-called United Nations will not help."

The reporters asked about Billy Graham, the moon landing, the war in Ireland, and the whereabouts of Prabhupāda's wife and children. They asked him to turn his head toward them, and they clicked away with their cameras. They thanked him, and the reception dispersed.

Prabhupāda went from the building to the gleaming white Rolls Royce awaiting him outside, courtesy of John Lennon. Prabhupāda entered the back seat and sat cross-legged. The limousine was equipped with darkened windows and a lavish interior, including a television. The devotees had become so confused in their excitement that none of them had thought to join Prabhupāda, and the chauffeur whisked him away to Tittenhurst. Prabhupāda sat silently, except for his occasionally audible chanting, as the chauffeur headed through the winding roads leading away from the airport.

He was in England. His father, Gour Mohan, had never wanted him to come to England. Once an uncle had told Gour Mohan that his son should go to England to become a barrister. But Gour Mohan had said no; if his son went there the meat-eaters, drinkers, and sex-mongers might influence him. But now, seventy years later, Prabhupāda had indeed come to London—not to be influenced by the Englishmen but to influence them. He had come to teach them what they had forgotten.

And he was off to a good start, under Kṛṣṇa's special care. When he had had to live alone in New York City without any money, that had been Kṛṣṇa's mercy. And now he was entering England in a chauffeured limousine, also Kṛṣṇa's mercy. Accepting the ride as part of Kṛṣṇa's plan, Prabhupāda remained deeply fixed in his purpose of carrying out the order of his spiritual master, whatever circumstances awaited.

As they turned onto Route 4, proceeding toward Slough, Prabhupāda saw factories and warehouses and then the flat countryside, with orchards, fields, and grazing horses. The grey, chilly weather hinted of winter ahead. After about twenty minutes Prabhupāda reached the wealthy neighborhood of Ascot and soon, appearing on the left, the high redwood fence surrounding the Lennon estate.

Prabhupāda had arrived before his disciples. But those who had remained at the manor excitedly received him and showed him to his room on the second floor of the servants' quarters. The small room was chilly and damp, with a low table for a desk and wall-to-wall carpeting made from pieces of rug taken from the other rooms. The adjoining room was bare and even smaller. Prabhupāda sat down at his low desk. "Where is everyone?" he asked. As he leaned back and gazed out the window he saw rain just beginning to fall.

When George, John, and Yoko dropped by after Prabhupāda's lunch, Śyāmasundara invited them to come up and meet Prabhupāda. George turned to John and asked, "Do you want to go up?" The bearded, bespectacled master of Tittenhurst, hair down to his shoulders, assented. Yoko also was curious. So up they all went to Prabhupāda's little room.

Smiling graciously from behind his desk, Prabhupāda asked his guests to enter and be seated. Here were two of the most famous people in England, and Kṛṣṇa wanted him to speak to them. Prabhupāda removed his garland and handed it to Śyāmasundara, indicating that he should put it around George's neck.

"Thank you," said George. "Hare Kṛṣṇa."

Prabhupāda smiled. "This is Kṛṣṇa's blessing."

"Hare Kṛṣṇa," George replied again.

"Yes," Prabhupāda said, "there is a verse in *Bhagavad-gītā: yad yad ācarati śreṣṭhas tat tad evetaro janaḥ/ sa yat pramāṇaṁ kurute lokas tad anuvartate*. The idea is that anything which is accepted by the leading persons, ordinary persons follow them. *Yad yad ācarati śreṣṭhaḥ. Śreṣṭhaḥ* means 'leading persons.' *Ācarati* means 'act.' Whatever leading persons act, people in general follow them. If the leading person says it is nice, then it is all right—the others also accept it. So by the grace of God, Kṛṣṇa, you are leaders. Thousands of young men follow you. They like you. So if you give them something actually nice, the face of the world will change."

Although George and John were about the same age as most of Prabhupāda's disciples, Prabhupāda considered them *śreṣṭhas,* respected leaders. "You are also anxious to bring some peace in the world," Prabhupāda continued. "I have read sometimes your statement. You are anxious also. Everyone is. Every saintly person should be anxious to bring in peace in the world. But we must know the process." He explained the "peace formula" according to *Bhagavad-gītā:* only those who recognize the Supreme Personality of Godhead as the proprietor of everything, the object of all sacrifices, and the friend of everyone can find peace.

Prabhupāda then told the two Beatles even more directly what he had already hinted at: they should learn Kṛṣṇa consciousness and help teach it to the world. "I request you to at least understand this philosophy to your best knowledge," he said. "If you think it is nice, pick it up. You are also willing to give something to the world. So try this. You have read our books, this *Bhagavad-gītā As It Is?*"

John: "I've read bits of the *Bhagavad-gītā.* I don't know which version it was. There's so many different translations."

Prabhupāda: "There are different translations. Therefore I have given this edition, *Bhagavad-gītā As It Is.*"

Prabhupāda explained that the material world is a place of misery. Nature is cruel. In America President Kennedy was thought to be the most fortunate, happy man, honored throughout the world. "But within a second"—Prabhupāda loudly snapped his fingers—"he was finished. Temporary. Now what is his position? Where is he? If life is eternal, if the living entity is eternal, where he has gone? What he is doing? Is he happy, or is he distressed? He is born in America, or China? Nobody can say. But it is a fact that, as living entity, he is eternal. He is existing."

Prabhupāda explained the transmigration of the soul. Then again he requested, "Try to understand it, and if it is nice you take it up. You are after something very nice. Is my proposal unreasonable?" The two Beatles glanced at one another but didn't answer. Prabhupāda gave a soft, amused laugh. "You are all intelligent boys. Try to understand it."

Prabhupāda spoke of the importance of music in the *Vedas*. "The *Sāma Veda*," he said, "is *full* of music. Followers of the *Sāma Veda* are always in music. Through musical vibration they are approaching the Supreme." He then sang slowly three verses from *Śrīmad-Bhāgavatam:*

matir na kṛṣṇe parataḥ svato vā
mitho 'bhipadyeta gṛha-vratānām
adānta-gobhir viśatāṁ tamisraṁ
punaḥ punaś carvita-carvaṇānām

na te viduḥ svārtha-gatiṁ hi viṣṇuṁ
durāśayā ye bahir-artha-māninaḥ
andhā yathāndhair upanīyamānās
te 'pīśa-tantryām uru-dāmni baddhāḥ

naiṣāṁ matis tāvad urukramāṅghriṁ
spṛśaty anarthāpagamo yad-arthaḥ
mahīyasāṁ pāda-rajo-'bhiṣekaṁ
*niṣkiñcanānāṁ na vṛṇīta yāvat**

Then Prabhupāda asked his guests what philosophy they were following. "Following?" John asked.

---

* "Because of their uncontrolled senses, persons too addicted to materialistic life make progress toward hellish conditions and repeatedly chew that which has already been chewed. Their inclinations toward Kṛṣṇa are never aroused, either by the instructions of others, by their own efforts, or by a combination of both.

"Persons who are strongly entrapped by the consciousness of enjoying material life, and who have therefore accepted as their leaders or *guru* a similar blind man attached to external sense objects, cannot understand that the goal of life is to return home, back to Godhead, and engage in the service of Lord Viṣṇu. As blind men guided by another blind man miss the right path and fall into a ditch, materially attached men led by another materially attached man are bound by the ropes of fruitive labor, which are made of very strong cords, and they continue again and again in materialistic life, suffering the threefold miseries.

"Unless they smear upon their bodies the dust of the lotus feet of a Vaiṣṇava completely freed from material contamination, persons very much inclined toward materialistic life cannot be attached to the lotus feet of the Lord, who is glorified for his uncommon activities. Only by becoming Kṛṣṇa conscious and taking shelter at the lotus feet of the Lord in this way can one be freed from material contamination." (*Śrīmad-Bhāgavatam,* 7.5.30–32)

"We don't follow anything," Yoko said. "We are just living."

"We've done meditation," said George. "Or I do my meditation, *mantra* meditation."

They began to ask questions—the same questions Prabhupāda had heard so many times before. After hearing Prabhupāda's explanation of Brahman, the all-pervading spiritual energy of the Supreme Personality of Godhead, Yoko doubted whether Brahman could remain pure and not deteriorate in time. Prabhupāda advised that she would have to become a serious student before she could actually understand spiritual philosophy.

John and Yoko, being devoted eclectics, had difficulty accepting Prabhupāda's concept of Vedic authority.

John: "We still have to keep sifting through, like through sand, to see who's got the best."

Prabhupāda: "No. One thing you try to understand. Why these people—if Kṛṣṇa is not the supreme authority—why they are taking Kṛṣṇa's book and translating? Why don't you try to understand?"

George: "I'm not saying Kṛṣṇa isn't the Supreme. I believe that. There is a misunderstanding about the translation of the Sanskrit *Gītā* into English. And I was saying that there are many versions, and I think we thought you were trying to say your version, your translation, was the authority and that the other translations were not. But we didn't really have misunderstanding as to the identity of Kṛṣṇa."

Prabhupāda: "That's all right. If you believe Kṛṣṇa is the Supreme Lord, if that is your version, then you have to see who is most addicted to Kṛṣṇa. These people are twenty-four hours chanting *Kṛṣṇa.* And another person, who has not a single word *Kṛṣṇa*—how can he become a devotee of Kṛṣṇa? How can he, who does not utter even the name of Kṛṣṇa, become a representative of Kṛṣṇa? If Kṛṣṇa is authority—and that is accepted—therefore those who are directly addicted to Kṛṣṇa, they are authorities."

After more than an hour of conversation, Prabhupāda distributed some *prasādam* to John, George, Yoko, and the few disciples in his room. If these *śreṣṭhas* were to take up Kṛṣṇa consciousness, that would be good for them and many others also. He had done his duty and provided them the opportunity. It was Kṛṣṇa's message, and to accept it or not was now up to them.

John said he had something to do, and he excused himself. As everyone was leaving, Yoko, walking down the stairs, turned to John and said, "Look at how simply he's living. Could you live like that?"

In the evening Prabhupāda sat with the three couples—Śyāmasundara and Mālatī, Gurudāsa and Yamunā, and Mukunda and Jānakī. After a year's separation they were happily with Prabhupāda, and he was happy to be with them. The love they shared and their mutual satisfaction at being together was based on a unifying desire to establish Lord Caitanya's *saṅkīrtana* movement in this important city. Now that Prabhupāda had come to London, work would not slacken; it would increase under his expert guidance. Prabhupāda could daily instruct the men on organizing more London preaching, and they could report to him as necessary.

The women could also directly serve him, cleaning his quarters, washing and ironing his laundry, and cooking his meals.

"No one can afford a house like this in England anymore," Prabhupāda said. "England has gone down. Now these young boys own a place like this. And we are here."

"Prabhupāda," Śyāmasundara spoke up, "our record sold fifty thousand copies yesterday."

"Oh!" Prabhupāda's eyes widened. "Very big business!"

Prabhupāda said that their money and energy should go toward opening the temple in the city. Now they were living comfortably on this aristocratic estate in the suburbs, and certainly they should try to involve these important celebrities in Kṛṣṇa consciousness as far as possible. But the main business should be to open a temple in the city. Bhaktisiddhānta Sarasvatī had preferred to establish temples in the cities, where the people were. Of course, if John could give this place to Kṛṣṇa and if the devotees could maintain cows and cultivate the land, as in New Vrindaban, then that would be a different matter. They would have to see what Kṛṣṇa desired.

Prabhupāda was sorry that some of his disciples were obliged to work full time renovating the estate in exchange for their stay. *Brāhmaṇas* and Vaiṣṇavas, he said, had the serious work of cultivating spiritual knowledge and teaching it to others, and they deserved the respect and support of the rest of society. The arrangement at Tittenhurst seemed more business than charity. But they should tolerate it as a temporary situation.

Prabhupāda talked with Śyāmasundara, Mukunda, and Gurudāsa

about their struggle to get housing permits and renovate the temple downtown. Śyāmasundara had been right, Prabhupāda said, to begin renovating the temple; Kṛṣṇa would protect their investment. When Prabhupāda learned they had secured a series of public lectures that would commit him to three months in London, he smiled. He would be glad to stay and preach in England, he said, for as long as it took to open the London center.

Prabhupāda commended his six London pioneers on succeeding where his *sannyāsī* Godbrothers had failed. He told them that because they had chanted Hare Kṛṣṇa with faith, they had succeeded. They were not great scholars or renunciants, yet they had faith in the holy name and the order of their spiritual master. Prabhupāda said that he also was not a great scholar, but that he had staunch faith, the real requirement for spiritual success.

A devotee could go to many places and accomplish many things, Prabhupāda said, but unless he was free of material motives he would not be able to implant the seed of *bhakti* into the hearts of others. Prabhupāda cited Śivānanda, who had gone alone to Hamburg and tried his best, with faith in his spiritual master. Now Kṛṣṇa was blessing Śivānanda with a little success: a storefront temple, newly recruited devotees, an interested professor, and other guests coming and chanting. Even one lone preacher could accomplish many things for Kṛṣṇa, provided the preacher was free from sense gratification and the desire for profit, adoration, and distinction.

Śrīla Prabhupāda rose early, about 1 A.M., and began dictating his latest book, *Kṛṣṇa, the Supreme Personality of Godhead. Kṛṣṇa,* begun in Los Angeles eight months before, was a summary of *Śrīmad-Bhāgavatam's* Tenth Canto. Starting in 1959 with the First Canto, Prabhupāda had been translating each successive verse, giving a roman transliteration, Sanskrit-English synonyms, the English translation, and then his commentary. *Kṛṣṇa,* however, was all in English, with translation and commentary blended together as transcendental stories.

In his verse-by-verse translation of the *Bhāgavatam,* Prabhupāda was still working on the Third Canto, so to reach the Tenth Canto could take many years. But he was uncertain how many years longer he would live, and the thought of passing away without giving the world an authorized, readable account of the Tenth Canto had been unbearable. Being the account of Lord Kṛṣṇa's earthly pastimes, the Tenth Canto was the climax of *Śrīmad-Bhāgavatam* and the richest nectar of transcendental literature. Now Prabhupāda had enough manuscript pages to print a first volume, complete with the many color illustrations he had commissioned his artists to paint. To print such a book would be expensive, and Prabhupāda had no money. But he depended fully on Kṛṣṇa and translated quickly in the quiet of early morning.

At 4:30 Prabhupāda's secretary, Puruṣottama, entered, followed by Yamunā dāsī. Puruṣottama offered *ārati* to Prabhupāda's small Rādhā-Kṛṣṇa Deities while Yamunā watched, eager to learn. Prabhupāda sang prayers, accompanying himself on the harmonium.

During Prabhupāda's *maṅgala-ārati* ceremony, the other dozen or so disciples assembled for their own *maṅgala-ārati* at the temple. As they walked the damp pathway to the temple they felt the cold air and heard the bell and Prabhupāda's singing. They could see through the predawn mist the light coming from Prabhupāda's window on the second floor, and the building looked like a lantern in the dark. The sound of the harmonium drifted mystically through the trees.

Later that morning some of the devotees brought Prabhupāda several news articles about his London arrival. The *Daily Sketch,* with its headline "Enter His Divine Grace Abhaya Charan Bhaktivedanta Swami," carried a foot-high photo of Prabhupāda playing *karatālas.* The *Sun's* story, "Happiness is Hare Krishna," appeared with a photo of Prabhupāda and the devotees. And the *Daily Mirror* showed Sarasvatī and one of the adult devotees.

The Daily Telegraph, however, carried a different kind of article: "Hindu Temple Protests." "Conversion of office premises in Bloomsbury into a Hindu temple is being investigated by the Ministry of Public Buildings and Works," the article began. The devotees' neighbors at Bury Place had apparently complained about the renovation that had been going on for the past two weeks. The article quoted a Camden council member: "If their planning application is not granted, it will cost them a lot of money."

Prabhupāda said the devotees should do everything they could to prevent delays or obstacles to their establishing the temple and installing Deities of Rādhā and Kṛṣṇa. He suggested they go daily into the city, work carefully and persistently with the officials, and secure the authorization. Meanwhile, Śyāmasundara should continue his remodeling work at Bury Place.

For Prabhupāda, such diplomatic and legal strategy was as spiritual as translating *Kṛṣṇa* or singing before his Deities. He was serious, heavy; and his disciples sensed this as he looked at them with full concentration, his intelligent gaze penetrating to see if they understood his directions. This heaviness of the *guru* was an essential part of their relationship with him. They were young men, inexperienced, and he was sending them on a mature assignment that required both transcendental and worldly expertise.

Serving as Prabhupāda's menial messengers and workers, his disciples imbibed his gravity. And they too became heavy. They too became dedicated servants of their *guru*. To bungle an important order because of naiveté or carelessness would be a spiritual disqualification. Prabhupāda had often told them a Vaiṣṇava is not a retired person who only sleeps and eats and chants Hare Kṛṣṇa. Rather, a Vaiṣṇava fights for Kṛṣṇa, as did Arjuna and Hanumān. And as the devotee tries his best, working in full surrender, Kṛṣṇa supports and protects him.

Dawn arrived, and time for Prabhupāda's morning walk. The cold September night shrouded the morning in heavy fog. Some of the low-lying grounds were waterlogged this time of year, and even in the higher plots the long grass would remain wet until mid-morning. "This climate," Prabhupāda admitted, "is not at all suitable for me." But having heard of the beauty of the grounds, he insisted on taking his usual morning walk.

Tittenhurst dated back to the 1770s, when the estate had been renowned for its many varieties of trees and shrubs—one of the most unusual collections in England. Even now, cypresses, weeping beech, austin poplars, royal palms, redwoods, varieties of pines, monkey puzzle trees, and orchards of cherry and apple graced the stately grounds. One cypress stood more than 125 feet tall, and the redwoods grew even taller. Bushes and vines grew in dense thickets. Close by the main house were hundreds of rhododendrons, a formal rose garden, and several fountains. The estate had its own lake, stocked with goldfish and perch, and at a far end of the property stood a row of greenhouses for grapes and peaches. Designed so as to be abloom in every season, the grounds had been carefully kept for generations, a recent owner having employed more than twenty gardeners. John, however, was deliberately allowing the grass to go uncut.

Prabhupāda walked out into the morning mist, onto the long, wet grass. Dressed almost entirely in black, he wore a Russian hat with earmuffs and black rubber Wellington boots. A black, full-length overcoat, given him by the devotees in Germany, covered his robes and sweater, leaving only glimpses of saffron cloth.

As Prabhupāda walked, accompanied by several of his disciples, he passed a fountain near the main house and entered a grove. The path narrowed, with vines and bushes close in, and led them into an open meadow, once a well-tended lawn but now a field of high grass. Bulldozers had excavated an area which according to rumor would soon be a helicopter landing field.

At the bottom of the sloping meadow, Prabhupāda entered an orchard. Many leaves had fallen from the trees, and the sun's first rays now revealed shavings of autumn gold at Prabhupāda's feet. He stood under one of the trees, and the diffused sunlight made the sky beyond the branches glow golden. "In my childhood," he said, "there were so many names given to me. My maternal uncle called me Nandu, because I appeared the day after Kṛṣṇa appeared and there was a great celebration on that day. I was called Nandu because I was born the day after Kṛṣṇa. And I was also called Govardhana. One of my sisters used to call me Kacha. I've been called so many names. As children we were all very beautiful. There are always so many names given to them. But all these names—they are all dead and gone." He turned and began to walk again, saying nothing more on the subject.

Prabhupāda mentioned the British economy, which he said was sinking into the sea because of the pound's devaluation. So many British lords had gained their wealth by exploiting other nations; now, having exhausted their good *karma,* they were suffering the results of their sins. They were too poor to maintain their great estates. "They used to have seventeen men working full time just on the garden," Prabhupāda exclaimed, "and now they cannot even pay the taxes. So they have to give the whole thing up. And it is falling into the hands of the *śūdras.*"

Īśāna asked Prabhupāda, "How is it that a person like me, from such a degraded background, can come to Kṛṣṇa consciousness?"

"Because you are intelligent," Prabhupāda replied.

"I don't understand."

"Because you are intelligent," Prabhupāda repeated.

Īśāna's wife, Vibhāvatī, asked, "What is the meaning of *spiritual master*?"

"Actually I am not your spiritual master," Prabhupāda replied. "That title is simply a formality. You should think of me as your spiritual father, your eternal father."

As they walked past a tractor, Kulaśekhara remarked, "The tractor is a very wonderful invention, isn't it?"

Prabhupāda turned to Kulaśekhara. "This tractor is the downfall of the Indian village system."

"Why is that? It does the work of ten men."

"Yes," Prabhupāda said. "Previously, the young men of the village would be engaged in plowing the field. Then this tractor came along and did the work of all those young men, and they had nothing to do. So they went to the cities to try to find work, and they fell into illusion."

Stopping beside a clump of yellowed grass, Prabhupāda asked, "Why is this yellow grass different?" No one answered. "The other grass is green," he said, "but this is yellow. What is the reason?" Still no one answered. "This yellow grass is drying up," Prabhupāda explained, "because the roots are not attached. Therefore it is yellow. Similarly, when we detach ourselves from Kṛṣṇa, then we will dry up."

They walked to a spot where the grass grew almost six feet high. Stopping at a path the tractor had cut, Prabhupāda smiled. "Oh, we can go through there?" And he strode ahead with his cane into the head-high jungle of grass and weeds. He walked until he came to a low hill that had been cleared, and he stopped. As he stood there, surrounded by the sea of grass and a few disciples, Kulaśekhara asked about the song Prabhupāda had been singing earlier that morning.

"The song," Prabhupāda said, "is about Lord Caitanya Mahāprabhu. He would rise, and He would go out at this time of morning, when the sun has risen but is not yet in the sky." As Prabhupāda spoke, the mist was already dissipating, and the golden glow in the sky had moved higher above the horizon. Prabhupāda raised his hands and swayed from side to side. "In this way," he said, "Caitanya Mahāprabhu would dance in the morning."

As they returned by the main house John Lennon stood gazing out through the glass doors, watching. Prabhupāda, walking with a cane, dressed in his black coat and his Wellingtons, looked like the gentleman of the estate out for his morning walk. Stopping now and then, he would look at certain trees, touching their bark, rubbing their leaves, inspecting them closely. At the beginning of the walk, a devotee had picked a rose and handed it to him, and he still held it in his hand with care. He had walked for an hour. Everywhere the scenery had been beautiful, and everywhere he had instructed his followers in Kṛṣṇa consciousness.

As Prabhupāda approached the building where he lived, he met little Sarasvatī. Taking her hand, he walked along with her to the foot of the stairs, where they stopped. Prabhupāda was halfway up the stairs when he turned and saw Sarasvatī standing in the doorway, watching. He beckoned and called to her, "Come on," and she crawled up the stairs after him.

When Sarasvatī came into Prabhupāda's room, he asked her, "So, are you old enough to go to *gurukula*?"

"No," she said, shaking her head.

"Come here, I am going to put a stamp on your forehead, and then we are going to put you in a red mailbox and send you to *gurukula*."

Sarasvatī began to cry, "Mālatī! Mālatī! I don't want to go!" and ran and hid behind her mother.

"Come on, Sarasvatī," Prabhupāda coaxed. "Come sit on my lap, and I will give you some *prasādam*." She came and sat on Prabhupāda's knee. "Now get me the stamps, Puruṣottama," he teased. "We are going to send her to *gurukula*." Sarasvatī shrieked and ran to Mālatī.

To Śrīla Prabhupāda, Sarasvatī was a pure spirit soul, but because she was in a small child's body he didn't teach her philosophy; he teased her, gave her *prasādam*, and treated her with the affection of a grandfather. But through her attachment to him, she would become attached to Kṛṣṇa.

After breakfast, when the sun had warmed the air, Prabhupāda opened his windows, sat down at his harmonium, and sang *bhajanas*. As he sang with closed eyes, his head shaking, he played the harmonium, and Yamunā sat at the bottom of the stairs, crying tears of appreciation. Prabhupāda had been singing for a while when he stopped and called for Yamunā. "Do you enjoy my *kīrtana*?" he asked.

"Yes," she nodded, "very much."

"The prayers of Narottama dāsa Ṭhākura," he said. "This sound is above the material platform. It is directly from the spiritual platform.

And there is no need of understanding the language. It is just like a thunderburst. Everyone can hear the sound of thunder—there is no misunderstanding. Similarly, these songs are above the material platform, and they crack like thunder within your heart. Why don't you come here every day during my chanting?"

"That would be wonderful!"

"Yes," said Prabhupāda, "from now on we will record." And every morning after that, Prabhupāda sang, and Puruṣottama and Yamunā would come to his room and record.

"What is your favorite *bhajana*?" Yamunā asked.

"What's yours?" Prabhupāda returned.

"Lord Caitanya's *Śikṣāṣṭakam* prayers."

"My favorite," said Prabhupāda, "is *Hari hari viphale.*" He recited the gist of the prayer in English: "'O Lord Hari, I have spent my life uselessly. Although I have taken this rare human birth, I have not worshiped Rādhā and Kṛṣṇa, and so I have knowingly drunk poison.' There is so much depth of meaning in Narottama dāsa Ṭhākura's prayers."

Puruṣottama: *Once Prabhupāda was sitting alone in his room. I walked by, and I heard him singing a prayer I'd never heard before. And I went in. Of course everyone knows he sings—he can sing very beautifully, very greatly inspired—but I'd never heard him sing as beautifully as he did that one time. I'd heard him sing many, many times in many temples, but I'd never heard him sing as beautifully as this. I felt very honored to hear it, very privileged. It was beautiful. When he was done, he just got up and said, "Let's go now."*

Prabhupāda also chanted one chapter of *Bhagavad-gītā* daily for eighteen days. "Anywhere *Bhagavad-gītā* is chanted," he said, "that place becomes a *tīrtha* [a holy place]."

Puruṣottama reported to the devotees in the United States these activities of Śrīla Prabhupāda:

> He is singing prayers a lot, and much of it is being recorded. I must admit that the tapes of songs and prayers he is making now are the best ones I have ever heard. Wait until you hear them when we get back. As the *Bhāgavatam* says, "Drink deep this nectar, O man of piety, and you shall be taken from this mortal frame!"

The women cooking for Prabhupāda were serving him American desserts: apple pie, doughnuts, glazed cookies. Prabhupāda would smile, but he would only nibble at his dessert. One afternoon he said, "These sweets are very nice, but no one has made me *sandeśa.*" None of the devotees knew how to make Bengali sweets, so Prabhupāda took them into the kitchen and taught them to make *sandeśa.* Although they had watched carefully, their first attempts produced *sandeśa* that was dry and grainy. But Prabhupāda accepted it, preferring the *sandeśa* —which Kṛṣṇa Himself used to eat—to the Western confections.

For the devotees at Tittenhurst, to have Prabhupāda living among them was again to witness Kṛṣṇa's pure devotee as he engaged constantly in ecstatic devotional service with his body, mind, and words. They could see how Prabhupāda was speaking and acting in Kṛṣṇa consciousness at every moment, and his presence confirmed that the most exalted platform of pure devotional service was a reality. His disciples felt bliss and renewed determination just being with him.

Prabhupāda's hosts, John and Yoko, also had the valuable opportunity to be near Prabhupāda, although they chose to keep apart. Remaining together in their own world, they mingled but rarely with the devotees. Prabhupāda's men continued to work under John's managers, and John was content to let the Swami and his entourage stay. When the head gardener asked John how to treat the devotees, he said, "Let them please themselves." On hearing of certain activities in the main house, Prabhupāda commented about the bad influence women sometimes have on men, but he kept out of John and Yoko's affairs. He had his own affairs in Kṛṣṇa consciousness.

* * *

Having been whisked from the airport to Tittenhurst, Prabhupāda had seen little of London, and one day he asked Śyāmasundara to take him on a tour of the city. Prabhupāda had grown up in British Calcutta hearing London praised as the seat of Britain's world empire, so when he saw how small many of London's historic landmarks were he was particularly surprised. At Buckingham Palace he remarked, "We have many houses in Calcutta bigger than this." The Thames, celebrated in the writings of British authors he had studied in college, was a disappointment also. "It's a canal" he said. "It's only a canal. In my mind I thought it was bigger than the Ganges."

But the most interesting sight was the building at 7 Bury Place. City officials had recently granted the devotees permission to occupy the temple. That part of the battle was won. Now Śyāmasundara and his few helpers had to finish the remodeling. On seeing the temple's location near the British Museum and Madame Tussauds Wax Museum, Śrīla Prabhupāda became even more anxious that Śyāmasundara fix an opening date as soon as possible.

* * *

In September Śrīla Prabhupāda wrote to Satsvarūpa about his stay at Tittenhurst Park.

> Here there is a nice big hall, exactly suitable for a temple. I have begun to give lectures here on specific days, but there are no outsiders coming.

Prabhupāda wanted to preach to the "outsiders," and if they wouldn't come to him, he would go to them. His first outside meeting, arranged by the devotees, was at Camden Town Hall, in the heart of London, and was well attended both by Britishers and by Indians. After Prabhupāda's brief lecture—only about fifteen minutes—a lively question-and-answer session began.

Woman: "Would you say Kṛṣṇa is God or Kṛṣṇa is love?"

Prabhupāda: "Without love, how can Kṛṣṇa be God?"

Woman: "No, I asked *you*."

Prabhupāda: "Yes. That is the real position. *Kṛṣṇa* means 'all-attractive.' Anything which is all-attractive you generally love."

Man: "Then the particle of the Supreme Being, man, is also all-love?"

Prabhupāda: "Yes, you are part and parcel of Kṛṣṇa. You want to love somebody, and Kṛṣṇa wants to love you. This is loving exchange. But instead of loving Kṛṣṇa, you are trying to love something else. That is your trouble. The love is there in you and Kṛṣṇa, and when the love will be exchanged between you and Kṛṣṇa, that will be your perfection of life."

Man: "Thank you."

Indian woman: "Would it matter if I worshiped any other? Would it matter whether I worshiped Kṛṣṇa or Śiva or Christ or Buddha? Would it matter?"

Prabhupāda: "If you worship Śiva, you'll get Śiva. If you worship Kṛṣṇa, you'll get Kṛṣṇa. Why do you expect Kṛṣṇa by worshiping Śiva? What is your idea?"

Indian woman: "My idea is, would it matter?"

Prabhupāda: "Don't you suppose if you purchase a ticket for India you'll go to India? How can you go to America?"

Indian woman: "This is not the point."

Prabhupāda: "This *is* the point. That is explained in *Bhagavad-gītā: yānti deva-vratā devān pitṝn yānti pitṛ-vratāḥ.*"

Indian woman: "But my point is ..."

Prabhupāda: "Your point, you understand. Why don't you understand the description of *Bhagavad-gītā*? If you worship demigods like Śiva and others, you will go there. If you worship Kṛṣṇa, you'll go to Kṛṣṇa. What is the difficulty to understand?"

Indian woman: "Do you think that Śiva is a demigod?"

Prabhupāda: "Yes, why not?"

Indian woman: "But Kṛṣṇa says that it doesn't matter the way you worship. All means have the same goal, and you will reach the same goal. 'You can take the different paths, but you will come to Me eventually.'"

Prabhupāda: "Try to understand. Suppose you have to go to the forty-second floor of a building. And you are going up one after another. So the goal is the forty-second story, but you cannot claim that after going a few steps, 'I have come to the goal, the forty-second story.' The path is one—that's all right—but you have to reach the ultimate goal. You do not know what is the ultimate goal. You simply say all paths reach to this goal. But you do not know what is the ultimate goal."

A young hippie stood up and shouted, "Hey, Swamiji!" People in the audience turned around and looked. "You said if we're not careful, in the next life we'll become a dog. But I want to tell you that I don't mind if I become a dog in my next life."

"You have my blessings," said Prabhupāda, and the young man sat down.

One-night lectures in scattered places around the city proved further the need of a temple. Prabhupāda had experienced a similar situation in New York City in 1965. At that time also he had had no temple. His audiences would listen respectfully and then disperse, and he would never see them again. To become Kṛṣṇa conscious, however, a person needed to hear about Kṛṣṇa repeatedly, and for that a temple was required. Once Prabhupāda had his temple established in London, thousands would be able to come and hear about Kṛṣṇa, take *prasādam,* and appreciate the lovely Deity form of the Lord. A temple would provide guests with regular, intimate contact with the devotees of the Lord, and this was essential. In the absence of a temple, however, Prabhupāda was prepared to go on lecturing all over London. Kṛṣṇa's teachings, Kṛṣṇa's *kīrtana,* and Kṛṣṇa's *prasādam* were absolute good; they would act regardless of the external situation.

Conway Hall was a five-hundred-seat auditorium in Red Lion Square in central London. By arranging a series of twelve lectures over the next three months, the devotees hoped to oblige Prabhupāda to stay in England at least that long. Gurudāsa had drawn up a list of lecture titles and printed fifty thousand handbills. Admission would be two shillings and sixpence.

The first night at Conway Hall about a hundred people attended. Prabhupāda sat on a cushion atop a table, leading *kīrtana,* while his disciples sat on the floor. Yamunā played harmonium, and Mukunda and Kulaśekhara played *mṛdaṅgas.* Prabhupāda's Rādhā-Kṛṣṇa Deities stood on Their altar on a separate table beside Prabhupāda. A Hare Kṛṣṇa *mantra* banner hung against the back wall.

Gurudāsa had billed tonight's lecture "Teachings of the *Vedas,*" and Prabhupāda explained that Vedic teachings can be understood only by hearing them from self-realized saints. After Prabhupāda's lecture the audience gave a sustained round of applause. Prabhupāda answered questions and had Yamunā lead a final *kīrtana.* The next day Prabhupāda wrote to a Dr. Shyam Sundar das Brahmacari in India: "I spoke for about one hour, and after that they continued clapping, which confirms their appreciation."

At the second Conway Hall engagement, when Prabhupāda stood during the *kīrtana* and began to dance, the devotees onstage joined him, dancing in a circle. Īśāna played his trumpet, and even Sarasvatī, her diapers showing beneath her short dress, jumped up and down in ecstasy. Each week would bring another Conway Hall meeting, and Prabhupāda's dancing became a regular feature.

One night at Conway Hall an Englishman stood and asked, "Why is it you don't try to help the people of your own country? Why did you come so far? Why don't you simply approach the big politicians? There are big politicians to try to help *there.*"

Prabhupāda: "You are a great politician. Therefore, I am approaching you. Is that all right?"

Another man asked: "If this is the absolute truth, how come there's so many people in London but not so many people are in attendance here?"

Prabhupāda: "When you are selling diamonds, you don't expect many customers. But if you are giving cut glass, the fools will come. We have a very precious thing—this Kṛṣṇa consciousness movement. Don't expect that all the foolish people will take to it. Some sincere souls have come. You please also take it."

Prabhupāda felt encouraged by the response of the English. Regularly the audiences would join in the chanting and dancing.

> In London things are going on nicely, and last evening we had a meeting in Conway Hall and several hundred persons were joining us in chanting and dancing. After the meeting one reporter from the biggest London newspaper came behind the stage to get further information about our movement for publication in his paper. So I am very encouraged to see the nice reception that the people and the news medias are giving to our activities in London.

Late in October Prabhupāda spoke at the English Speakers Union to a predominantly Indian audience.

He began his talk, "Although we are a small gathering today, this is a very important meeting. India has got a message. You are all respectable Indians present here in an important city of the world, London, and I have come here with an important mission. It is not the same mission as Indians generally have who come here and to other foreign countries—to beg something. I have come here to *give* something. So you please try to cooperate with me."

On October 30 Prabhupāda lectured at Oxford Town Hall. His talk was basic, although embellished with more Sanskrit quotes than usual. His disciples had not expected much of a response from the Oxford students, yet the hall was filled. And when Prabhupāda stood and gestured for everyone to raise their hands and dance, practically the entire audience responded. While Mukunda played the huge pipe organ and hundreds joined the chanting, Prabhupāda held his arms high and began powerfully jumping up and down.

> Yesterday we had a very successful meeting at Oxford at the Town Hall. About 350 boys, girls, old men, ladies and gentlemen participated and we made them all dance and chant with us, every one. After the meeting, many boys and gentlemen came to congratulate me.

Prabhupāda received an invitation to appear on Britain's most popular TV talk show, "Late Night Line-Up." The interviewer, accustomed to snappy repartee, tried to engage Prabhupāda in his style of conversing, avoiding long, philosophical answers.

"Swamiji," he asked, "do you have a concept of hell in your religion?"

"Yes," Prabhupāda replied. "London is hell."

The host appeared stunned, as if beaten at his own game from the start. Prabhupāda continued, "It is always damp, cloudy, and raining. In India the sun is always shining."

The interviewer was still at a loss for words, and Prabhupāda, perhaps sensing the man's embarrassment, added, "Of course, it is a very great credit to the English people to have established such a great civilization in such a climate."

There were other questions, and Prabhupāda talked for an hour, explaining the Kṛṣṇa consciousness movement and philosophy. The next day a London newspaper announced, "Swami Calls London Hell."

The "Hare Krishna Mantra" record was still high on the charts in England and throughout the continent, and this fame led a Dutch television company to invite Prabhupāda's disciples to Amsterdam, all expenses paid, to do a show. They would have only five minutes of air time, but Prabhupāda accepted it. "Five minutes," he said, "is sufficient. We will preach the whole philosophy of Kṛṣṇa consciousness in five minutes."

Prabhupāda and his party took the ferry from Dover across the English Channel to France and then traveled by train to Amsterdam. The television studio, located outside the city, was in a modern, air-conditioned building, with constant loudspeaker announcements, artificial plants, a TV in every room—but no windows.

The receptionist brought Prabhupāda and his disciples to a windowless room with painted concrete walls. "In India," Prabhupāda said, "we wouldn't consider living in a place without windows and fresh air. I want to sit by a window." So the devotees checked through the entire building until finally, in the third-floor hallway, they found a window. Moving their chairs with them, they went with Prabhupāda and sat by the window.

"By the year 2000, no one will see the light of day," Prabhupāda said. "Cities will be forced to live underground. They will have artificial light and food, but no sunlight."

The producer of the program arrived, surprised to find that "the Swami" was also going to be part of the act. The surprise was a pleasant one, and he welcomed Prabhupāda to his show. "Now, what I want you and your group to do," he explained, "is to sing your record, 'Hare Krishna Mantra.' You don't have to actually sing out loud. We're going to play your record, and you mime. Pretend you're playing those instruments. Pretend you're singing." He allowed that afterward Prabhupāda could speak—for two minutes.

Just before Prabhupāda and the devotees went onstage, they had to wait in the wings while a local Dutch group danced around, pretending to play their saxophones, trumpets, and drums. Then the producer brought in a table with a cushion on it for Prabhupāda and seated the devotees around Prabhupāda on the floor.

The cameras began, the record played, and the devotees started to mime. Suddenly clouds, produced by dry ice, rolled in on the set—a "mystical" effect. As the devotees disappeared under clouds of carbon dioxide, only Prabhupāda remained clearly visible. Seeing the special effect unsuccessful, the producer motioned the devotees to stand and dance beside the Swami.

The song ended, and a camera closed in on Prabhupāda. "Now you have two minutes, Swamiji," the producer said. Prabhupāda began.

"We have been chanting this Hare Kṛṣṇa *mantra.* This is a transcendental sound vibration, nondifferent from the Lord. The Lord's name and His form are the same. Please chant this sublime sound, and your life will become perfect. You'll become happy, and you'll realize your true nature—that you are an eternal servant of God, Kṛṣṇa. This process is called *bhakti-yoga,* and we request everyone to take to this chanting. Thank you very much."

Prabhupāda was pleased as his disciples' record continued to be a hit in Europe.

> The Hare Krishna record is selling very nicely. Yesterday, it sold 5,000 copies, and this week it is on the chronological list as 20. They say next week it will come to be 3, and after that it may come to 1. So they are very much hopeful of this record.

To Satsvarūpa in Boston Prabhupāda wrote:

> The Hare Krishna record is going on in England nicely, and I heard that in Australia it stands 4th on the list of 50 important records.

"Hare Krishna Mantra" became the number one song in West Germany, number one in Czechoslovakia, and among the top ten all over Europe and even in Japan. With the income from the record, the devotees began paying their bills and financing the renovations of the Bury Place temple.

Sometimes the devotees would perform at concerts with professional groups, and sometimes they would receive invitations to appear in nightclubs. After one particularly late and nasty nightclub engagement, Yamunā went to Prabhupāda and told him what the place had been like. Prabhupāda called for all the devotees. "These places," he explained, "are not good for *brahmacārīs.* The principle is that we have to make devotees. So we have to think where we are going. If we are going somewhere to preach but we can't make any devotees there, what is the use? So we have to think like that." He said he wasn't forbidding them to preach in the nightclubs, but he told them to be careful.

One of the devotees asked if showing slides of Kṛṣṇa mixed in with psychedelic slides was permissible. Prabhupāda said no. Kṛṣṇa should be on a throne or an altar. If they watered Kṛṣṇa consciousness down, it would become idol worship.

Not since Prabhupāda had first left India in 1965 had he preached to Indians as extensively as now. Indians would always attend his lectures, and even if they didn't dance and chant they appreciated Kṛṣṇa consciousness. Even before Prabhupāda's arrival in England, a few Indians had stepped forward to help the devotees, and now the majority of Prabhupāda's occasional guests at Tittenhurst were Indians. Bringing their families, they would sit and chat with Prabhupāda, often inviting him to their homes for dinner.

Kedar Nath Gupta: *Prabhupāda agreed to come to our house. We received him with a warm welcome, and many other people also came to hear him. He was very much pleased to see that we had our family Deities of Rādhā and Kṛṣṇa, given by my mother. And he commented, "I am very much pleased to come to this place and see that Rādhā and Kṛṣṇa are here."*

He gave a very nice lecture and told that the purpose of the human form of life is self-realization. He said one should be inquisitive to know who he is. All those assembled who had come to hear him were very much pleased and impressed by his lecture. After his lecture, I did the ārati, *and we offered the foodstuffs to the Deity. And then we distributed* prasādam *to everyone. Prabhupāda took the* prasādam, *and he was very much pleased to take* prasādam *in our house. As he was leaving I requested him, "When can I see you next?" He said, "You can see me any time you want."*

Sometimes there would be disagreements over philosophy, but Prabhupāda's arguments were always convincing. The Indians were respectful to Prabhupāda and repeatedly invited him to their homes. One of Britain's most prominent and respected Indians visited, Praful Patel, as did many businessmen with the means to help Prabhupāda's mission. But few were willing to sacrifice.

* * *

The second moon landing by American astronauts was scheduled for mid-November, only a few weeks away. For months the moon shots had received much press coverage, and Prabhupāda would speak of them often. Almost a year ago in Los Angeles he had answered a reporter's queries on the possibility of man's landing on the moon: "Just like we are going from one place to another by motorcar or by airplane, this mechanical process will not help us go to the moon planet. The process is different, as described in the Vedic literature. One has to qualify. According to our literature, our information, it is not possible. In this body we cannot go there."

At Tittenhurst Prabhupāda often brought up the moon landing while talking with his disciples. "The moon landing was a hoax," he said one evening in his room, "for they cannot go to the moon. The moon planet, Candraloka, is a residence of the demigods, higher beings than these drunkards and cow-eating slaughterers who are trying to inhabit it. You cannot think this travel is allowed—like when I migrated from India to the U.S. The moon planet cannot be visited so quickly. It is not possible."

Śrīla Prabhupāda's disciples accepted his statements. He was giving not simply his opinion but the verdict of the Vedic scriptures. Because he accepted Vedic authority over modern science, so did his disciples—but not Puruṣottama.

Detecting Puruṣottama's dubious mentality, Prabhupāda would often joke lightly in Puruṣottama's presence. Someone would ask a question—"Where is Jānakī?"—and Prabhupāda would reply, "Oh, Jānakī has gone to the moon." Then everyone, except Puruṣottama, would laugh.

The devotees knew of Puruṣottama's difficulty—he was an American, and proud that the Americans were conquering space—and they knew that Prabhupāda was joking about it. Puruṣottama was up on the latest scientific advancements. He was impressed by NASA's achievements and astronaut Neil Armstrong's "giant step for mankind."

Although Puruṣottama went on with his duties, he became sullen, and Prabhupāda noted his lack of enthusiasm. One morning Puruṣottama and Yamunā were together with Prabhupāda in his room. Puruṣottama had several day's growth of beard and was wearing the same orange sweater he had slept in, whereas Yamunā was neat and clean. Although she had only two simple cotton *sārīs,* she would always put on a freshly washed and ironed one before going to see Prabhupāda. Looking at his two servants, Prabhupāda said, "Yamunā, you have so many *sārīs.* They are all so beautiful."

Yamunā looked up at Prabhupāda in surprise. "I don't have so many, Śrīla Prabhupāda."

"No," he said, "you are wearing a new piece of cloth every day. It's so nice. You're always looking so neat and clean—and your *tilaka.* Puruṣottama, what do you think? Who do you think has the best *tilaka*?" Puruṣottama didn't answer. "Beautiful *tilaka,*" Prabhupāda said, "means beautiful person."

About six o'clock that same evening, Yamunā was cooking *purīs* and potatoes for Prabhupāda when she heard him ring the servant's bell. Leaving the ghee on the fire, she ran up to Prabhupāda's quarters. He talked with her about the lecture he would give that evening and eventually asked, "When will *prasādam* be ready—before the discourse?"

"Yes, Śrīla Prabhupāda. I'm ..." Yamunā smelled smoke. "Oh!" she gasped. "Please excuse me, Prabhupāda! I've left some ghee on the fire!" Rushing downstairs, she found the kitchen filled with black smoke. She couldn't see the stove. "Puruṣottama! Puruṣottama!" she cried. Puruṣottama arrived, and together they groped through the smoke. Somehow Puruṣottama extinguished the fire before it caused serious damage.

Puruṣottama and Yamunā were covered with soot. Their faces were black, and Puruṣottama's orange sweater, his robes, and Yamunā's *sārī* were all blackened. Suddenly Prabhupāda rang the servant's bell, and they both hurried upstairs to tell him about the fire. When Jānakī returned downstairs and saw the mess, she ran upstairs to Prabhupāda's room, where Yamunā and Puruṣottama stood, still covered with soot, before Prabhupāda.

"What has happened here?" Jānakī burst out.

Prabhupāda looked at her soberly and said, "Today Puruṣottama has gone to the moon."

"What?" Jānakī asked.

Prabhupāda repeated, "Yes, our Puruṣottama has gone to the moon."

"Prabhupāda," Puruṣottama said, "I am a *brahmacārī*. Why are you saying these things?"

"Being a *brahmacārī* is no restriction from going to the moon. Anyone can go," Prabhupāda said, winking.

* * *

The devotees regularly encountered John and Yoko. Although originally interested in a business relationship, John was inclined toward the devotees, but his friends advised him not to get involved with the Swami and his group. So he remained aloof.

Īśāna dāsa: *I was in the kitchen working, and John was sitting at the piano. He had a piano in the kitchen, a great upright piano with all the varnish removed—bare wood. And in this way he was sitting at the piano, playing Hare Kṛṣṇa. The man was actually a great musician, and he played Hare Kṛṣṇa in every musical idiom you could think of—bluegrass music or classical music or rock-and-roll or whatever. He would go at will from one idiom to another, always singing Hare Kṛṣṇa. It was so natural for him, and one could see that he was a musical genius. And in this way he was entertaining me, and he was obviously really enjoying it. So anyway, while this piano-playing was going on with great vigor and enthusiasm, this chanting Hare Kṛṣṇa, his wife, Yoko Ono, appeared in a nightgown or what have you and said, in a very distressed tone, "Please, John, I have a* terrible *headache. Can't you stop that sort of thing and come upstairs with me?"*

George was different. He was drawn to Prabhupāda. When one of the devotees had asked, "Why out of all the Beatles are only you interested?" George had replied, "It's my *karma.* One of the things in my sign is the spiritual side."

George Harrison: *Prabhupāda just looked like I thought he would. I had like a mixed feeling of fear and awe about meeting him. That's what I liked about later on after meeting him more—I felt that he was just more like a friend. I felt relaxed. It was much better than at first, because I hadn't been able to tell what he was saying and I wasn't sure if I was too worldly to even be there. But later I relaxed and felt much more at ease with him, and he was very warm towards me. He wouldn't talk differently to me than to anybody else. He was always just speaking about Kṛṣṇa, and it was coincidental who happened to be there. Whenever you saw him, he would always be the same. It wasn't like one time he would tell you to chant the Hare Kṛṣṇa* mantra *and then the next time say, "Oh, no, I made a mistake." He was always the same.*

Seeing him was always a pleasure. Sometimes I would drop by, thinking I wasn't planning to go but I better go because I ought to, and I would always come away just feeling so good. I was conscious that he was taking a personal interest in me. It was always a pleasure.

George was attracted to Kṛṣṇa, and he liked to chant. Even before meeting Prabhupāda, he had learned something of Kṛṣṇa from Maharishi Mahesh Yogi, from the autobiography of Paramahansa Yogananda, and from traveling in India. But Prabhupāda's instructions in particular impressed upon him that Lord Kṛṣṇa was the Absolute Truth, the origin of everything.

George: *Prabhupāda helped me to realize the multifaceted way to approach Kṛṣṇa. Like the* prasādam, *for example. I think it is a very important thing,* prasādam, *even if it's only a trick. Like they say, the way to a man's heart is through his stomach. Well, even if it's a way to a man's spirit soul, it works. Because there is nothing better than having been dancing and singing or just sitting and talking and then suddenly they give you some food. It's like it's a blessing. And then when you learn to touch Him or taste Him, it's important.*

Kṛṣṇa is not limited. And just by Prabhupāda's being there and pouring out all this information, I was moved. It's like the mind is stubborn, but it's all Kṛṣṇa. That's all you need to know—it's all Kṛṣṇa. This world is His material energy too—the universal form. And in Prabhupāda's books there are these pictures showing Kṛṣṇa in the heart of a dog and a cow and a human being. It helps you to realize that Kṛṣṇa is within everybody.

Although Prabhupāda might have been teaching some higher aspect, what came through to me a lot was a greater understanding of how Kṛṣṇa is everywhere and in everything. Prabhupāda explained about the different aspects of Kṛṣṇa, and he provided a meditation where you could see Kṛṣṇa as a person everywhere. I mean, there isn't anything that isn't Kṛṣṇa.

Prabhupāda saw George as a "nice young boy," and a devotee of Kṛṣṇa. According to the *Bhāgavatam,* no matter what a person may be materially, if he is a nondevotee and never utters the holy name of God he cannot possess *any* good qualities. Many swamis and *yogīs* in India, even some who considered themselves Vaiṣṇavas, had no faith in or understanding of the holy names of Kṛṣṇa. But George liked to chant Hare Kṛṣṇa, and he had put the holy name of Kṛṣṇa in his songs, which were tremendously popular all over the world. So he was serving Kṛṣṇa through his music, and that made all the difference.

> Mr. George Harrison appears to be a very intelligent boy, and he is, by the Grace of Krishna fortunate also. On the first day, he came to see me along with John Lennon, and we had talks about 2 hours. He wanted to talk with me more, but he has now gone to his sick mother in Liverpool.

Prabhupāda also saw George as a rich man, and Lord Caitanya had strictly instructed devotees in the renounced order not to mix with worldly men. But Lord Caitanya had also taught that a devotee should accept any favorable opportunity for propagating Kṛṣṇa consciousness.

> If this boy cooperates with our movement, it will be very nice impetus for after all, he is a monied man. These monied men have to be very cautiously dealt with in spiritual life. We have to sometimes deal with them on account of preaching work; otherwise, Lord Chaitanya Mahaprabhu has strictly restricted to mix with them for Krishna Conscious people. But we

> get instruction from Rupa Goswami that whatever opportunity is favorable for pushing on Krishna Consciousness we should accept.

Prabhupāda dealt with George cautiously, but encouraged him to chant the Lord's name, take His *prasādam,* and surrender all his works to Him.

When the devotees in the U.S. heard of Prabhupāda's dealings with the Beatles, some of them exaggerated the closeness of the relationship, especially in the case of John Lennon. Prabhupāda heard of this and immediately stopped it.

> Regarding the booklet you and Gargamuni are sending, in the introductory portion signed by you and Gargamuni you have said that I am "personally instructing John Lennon and George Harrison in the yoga of ecstasy." This is not very satisfactory. Of course, George Harrison sometimes comes to see me and naturally I instruct him on the bhakti yoga. But the statement in the letter gives hint as if I have been invited by them for this. If this comes to their notice, they may take some objection which will not go to our credit. These things should not be publicly advertised, and I do not know why this has been done. Anyway, if you have not distributed many of them, you just try to take out the portion which is not a fact.

George: *Prabhupāda never really suggested that I shouldn't do what I was doing. I heard that at different times he would say to the devotees that I was a better devotee because of my songs and the other things I was doing. He never actually said that to me, but I always heard that. And the good thing for me was that I didn't have a feeling that I needed to join full time. I think it would have spoiled it if he had always been on at me, saying, "Why don't you pack in doing what you are doing and go and live in a temple somewhere?" He never made me feel any different, like I wasn't quite in the club. He was never like that.*

I'm a plainclothes devotee. It's like that. I saw my relationship—that I should help when and where I could, because I know people in society. It's like any half-decent person; you just try and help each other a little bit.

He was always pleased with me, because anything I did was a help. I mean not just to the Kṛṣṇa temple as such, but just to anything spiritual that I did, either through songs or whatever—it pleased him. He was just always very friendly. He was always chanting, and at times he said that to me—just to keep chanting all the time, or as much as possible. I think once you do that, you realize the chanting is of benefit.

There are some gurus *who go around making out that they are "it," but*

Prabhupāda was saying, "I am the servant of the servant of the servant of Kṛṣṇa," which is really what it is, you know. He wasn't saying, "I am the greatest," and "I am God," and all that. With him it was only in the context of being a servant, and I liked that a lot. I think it's part of the spiritual thing. The more they know, then the more they actually know that they are the servant. And the less they know, the more they think they are actually God's gift to mankind.

So although he was obviously a very powerful individual, very spiritually advanced, he always retained that humbleness. And I think that is one of the most important things, because you learn—more than all the words he says—you learn really from the example of how he lives and what he does.

* * *

The *Daily Sketch* reported, "Krishna people dine out at John and Yoko's place." A photograph showed the devotees seated out of doors, taking *prasādam.*

> Lunch time at Tittenhurst Park, stately home of John Lennon and Yoko Ono—and some of the Lennon's house guests take their places in yesterday's sunshine.
>
> The picnickers are followers of the Indian Swami, His Divine Grace Abhay Charan Bhaktivedanta.
>
> They have adopted the ways of the East, from their clothes and shaven heads right down to the Indian curry they eat with their fingers.
>
> Which is all rather out of character for a place like Tittenhurst Park, which cost John £ 150,000 and covers sixty acres of most exclusive Sunninghill near Royal Ascot race course.

Prabhupāda and his people and John and Yoko and theirs made an odd combination. Two days after Prabhupāda's arrival at Tittenhurst, John and Yoko had flown to Canada to perform with the Plastic Ono Band at Toronto's Rock-N-Roll Revival at Varsity Stadium. In October John and Yoko had recorded *Wedding Album* and begun work on a film, *Rock-and-Roll Circus,* and John had recorded "Cold Turkey." Although John was usually shy, the devotees working at the main house found him openhearted and generous with his possessions. He invited the devotees to stay permanently at Tittenhurst and farm. Whatever he had, he said, he would share with them.

One day Yoko asked Yamunā if a devotee couple could stand in for her and John onstage at a London theater. She and John had previously appeared there dressed in only a burlap bag and were supposed to make another appearance, but Yoko thought perhaps a devotee couple could take their place. The crowd, she said, might never know the difference, and even if they did, it would be a hilarious publicity stunt for the devotees. Politely declining, Yamunā explained why devotees could never do such a thing. When she told Prabhupāda, he was adamant: none of his disciples would go. For days afterward, he condemned this sensuality.

John invited Prabhupāda to the manor to hear his recent recording of "Cold Turkey." Although such a song held little interest for Prabhupāda, John whimsically wanted him to hear it. Taking the opportunity to preach to the great man of the world, Prabhupāda went. Within John's main sitting room, Prabhupāda sat on the couch before the fireplace. The tape was ready on the large sixteen-track machine that had recorded it, and as Prabhupāda sat patiently, John began to work the controls.

But the machine wouldn't play. John began cursing under his breath, turning knobs and pushing buttons. Although only Puruṣottama had accompanied Prabhupāda, two other devotees hid outside beneath the windows, listening. When they peeked in and saw John struggling with the machine, they began giggling in the shadows.

"Oh," Prabhupāda said, "so your machine is not working. Well, never mind. We have also made some recording, and we would like to play this music for your pleasure." John resigned himself to listening to Prabhupāda's singing, and Prabhupāda was saved from the "Cold Turkey."

Prabhupāda kept his visit short. As he was leaving, he saw on the wall framed, life-size photos of John and Yoko naked. He also saw black and white silhouettes of a man and woman in various positions of sexual intercourse. On returning to his room, he commented, "It is not good for us to continue staying here." He asked Mukunda to find him an apartment in London. The Bury Place renovations were still incomplete, and Prabhupāda said he preferred to be in the city so that he could oversee the work. The natural setting of Tittenhurst was pleasant, but Prabhupāda's hosts' way of life and his were incompatible.

One day John and Yoko, dressed in black, came to visit Prabhupāda. Acknowledging him to be a great *yogī* with mystic power, they asked him to use his powers to arrange with Kṛṣṇa that they be reunited after death. Prabhupāda was disappointed.

"This is not my business," he said. "Kṛṣṇa provides you with life, and He takes it away in the form of death. It is impossible that you can be united after death. When you go back home, back to Godhead, you can be united with Kṛṣṇa. But husband and wife—this is simply a mundane relationship. It ends with the body at the time of death. You cannot pick up this kind of relationship again after death."

* * *

At one end of the estate lived a bricklayer and his wife in a small, neglected Georgian house. Hired by John to build a recording studio on the property, the bricklayer had only recently moved to Tittenhurst. A tough, burly man, he never spoke to the devotees, until one day he asked several of them if they believed in ghosts.

"Oh, yes," Kulaśekhara said. "Prabhupāda says there are ghosts."

"I don't believe," the bricklayer said. "My wife is having dreams, but I don't believe in ghosts."

The bricklayer's wife revealed that both she and her husband had been hearing "something" at night. Last night they had gone running to John Lennon's house, terrified, complaining of sounds: chains rattling, boot heels pounding, and the noise of something "like a body being dragged across the floor." The bricklayer had seen his wife violently shaken by the shoulders, although no one else was there.

When the devotees told Prabhupāda, he said, "You tell John Lennon that if he wants we can get rid of these ghosts." Mukunda relayed the message, but John had already invited his friend, a white witch, to come and exorcise the ghost.

The warlock visited the bricklayer's cottage, and a few devotees tagged along. Over the fireplace in the main room they found a carving of a person with a ghost coming out of his forehead, and on the opposite wall, mahogany runes. "These are ancient witch runes," the warlock said, shaking his head. "I can't do anything here."

When John asked the devotees to try their method, Prabhupāda directed them. At the bricklayer's cottage they should sprinkle water offered to Kṛṣṇa in the doorways, blow conchshells, and then have *kīrtana*. A group of devotees went, and Kulaśekhara led the *kīrtana*. After half an hour of chanting, Kulaśekhara felt a great release of pressure within the room, and the *kīrtana* became ecstatic. The devotees returned to their engagements, assuring John that the ghosts would not return, and the bricklayer and his wife moved in again.

The next morning Prabhupāda passed the old cottage on his walk. "So, how is the ghost?" he asked.

"No news, Prabhupāda," Kulaśekhara replied.

The following morning Prabhupāda again asked, "How is the ghost? Would they like to have him back?"

Years ago in India, Prabhupāda said, when he was running his chemical business, he had detected ghosts in the building at night.

"What did you do?" one of the devotees asked.

"I simply chanted Hare Kṛṣṇa, and the ghosts would go away." Prabhupāda then opened his eyes wide and gestured with both hands, mimicking the frightened workers in the plant who had come running to him: "Bābājī! Bābājī! There is ghost! There is ghost!" The devotees laughed.

"Actually," Prabhupāda said, "there are many ghosts here. Especially over by the stable areas. They are attached to this place. But they will not harm you if you just chant Hare Kṛṣṇa."

* * *

Prabhupāda was anxious to leave Tittenhurst, and by late October some of the devotees had moved to Bury Place. Prabhupāda no longer had any business at Tittenhurst. Mr. Lennon was an influential person who had seemed interested in Kṛṣṇa, but now there was no point in Prabhupāda's staying on at the estate.

Yoko and her ex-husband, Dan, now John's manager, were also pressing John to be rid of the devotees. Dan complained that the devotees were trying to take over the place. The devotees, on the other hand, complained to John that Dan and Yoko were misrepresenting them. On one side were Dan and Yoko, on the other the devotees. John was in the middle; he had to choose.

John told Mukunda that as far as he was concerned he got along fine with the devotees, but the people around him were having difficulty. He would give the devotees a couple more weeks to move to their new temple in the city. The devotees were already in the process of moving to Bury Place, and Mukunda had found an apartment for Prabhupāda a short drive from the temple. In a few days everything would be ready for Prabhupāda to move.

On the day Prabhupāda left Tittenhurst, he stopped at his car and said, "I want to say good-bye to a few friends first." He then took a last walk through the grounds, giving careful attention to the trees, sometimes touching their leaves, just as on his morning walks. Then he left. The next day a severe storm swept through the Tittenhurst estate, breaking windows and uprooting trees.

* * *

November 3, 1969

Prabhupāda moved into his furnished apartment on Baker Street, a ten-minute drive from the Bury Place temple. After two months in London, he was anxious to see his temple open, and Śyāmasundara was working hard, although progressing slowly.

For the temple's interior Śyāmasundara had an artistic concept taken from photographs he had seen of the Ajanta Caves, South Indian temples with walls and ceilings of carved stone. His inspiration was to produce a similar effect using California redwood he and Mukunda had shipped to England a year ago. On first hearing the plans, Prabhupāda had asked, "Why make it so artistic?" But Śyāmasundara had been so set on the idea that Prabhupāda had permitted him. With the ceiling partly finished, there was no turning back.

Śyāmasundara toiled day and night, yet each day the temple design seemed to grow more elaborate, with the walls and floor fashioned of solid redwood and the ceiling lined with redwood arches. Śyāmasundara took great care to see that each piece fit exactly into place. As Śyāmasundara inched along, devotees joked that the room looked like an upside-down boat. But Prabhupāda encouraged him, telling him it was very beautiful.

Prabhupāda often allowed his disciples to work as they liked. He reasoned that they were raising the money and could spend it in Kṛṣṇa's service as they pleased. He also did not care to interfere in every detail of a disciple's service, especially when that disciple was strongheaded and had ideas that were not harmful or obstructive. All Prabhupāda's disciples were ultimately under his absolute decision, but he was often lenient—"eighty-percent lenient," he would sometimes say.

Śyāmasundara particularly thrived on having his own big projects. He had arranged for the Mantra-Rock Dance in San Francisco, built the first Ratha-yātrā carts, established a friendship with George Harrison, and now he was designing a temple. Prabhupāda allowed it—watchfully, like a father.

Consulting the Vedic calendar, Prabhupāda chose December 14 for the temple-opening celebration. And despite predictions from Śyāmasundara and others that the deadline would be impossible to meet, Prabhupāda ordered invitations printed immediately. The devotees had tremendous work to do, and little time. Not only did they have the temple to complete, but also Prabhupāda's quarters on the second floor and the kitchen in the basement. Faced with their tight deadline, they worked harder.

As Prabhupāda was anxious about the temple opening, he was also anxious about publishing the first volume of *Kṛṣṇa*. But he had no money.

According to printers' estimates, the book would cost about $19,000. Prabhupāda told Śyāmasundara to ask his friend George for a donation. Śyāmasundara, who had always been careful not to ask George for money, was hesitant. But Prabhupāda insisted, and Śyāmasundara gave in.

George agreed, but regretted it afterward. Then Śyāmasundara began to feel sorry. After all, he hadn't really wanted to ask George, and George hadn't really wanted to be asked. When Prabhupāda heard of this, he invited George to see him.

George told Prabhupāda that every day people were asking him for his money. But when Prabhupāda explained the importance of the *Kṛṣṇa* book and how George's donation would be devotional service to Kṛṣṇa, George dismissed his regrets. He also agreed to write a foreword to the volume.

George: *I didn't really think I was qualified to write the foreword to Prabhupāda's book. But one way of looking at it is, because I am known, it would help. But from the other point of view, it could really hinder, because not everyone wants to listen or to believe what I say. There are a lot of people who would be put off just because I'm saying it. I mean, if I picked up a book on Kṛṣṇa and the foreword was written by Frank Zappa or somebody like that, I would think, "God, maybe I don't want to know about it."*

So I thought that although he asked me, maybe Prabhupāda didn't really want me to write the foreword. But it was one of those things I couldn't get out of: Everybody had their minds made up, "You're writing the foreword, and that's it." So I just did it.

When Śrīla Prabhupāda asked to watch the moon landing, the devotees rented a television and placed it in Prabhupāda's living room. Prabhupāda took his massage as usual, sitting in a chair before the television.

Puruṣottama announced, "Well, Prabhupāda, it's about time, so I'll turn on the television, and soon we'll be getting some pictures from the astronauts out in space."

A reporter was speaking from Cape Canaveral, Florida: "We are just about to get the first pictures of this historic occasion." The picture appeared fuzzy, then cleared. The spacecraft had landed on the moon. As the astronauts emerged from the ship, they slowly eased themselves down onto the moon's surface. Puruṣottama was in ecstasy.

Dhanañjaya: *I was attempting to massage Prabhupāda's head and at the same time watch the program. All of a sudden, as the men were landing, Prabhupāda motioned for me to sit in front of him, so I came around. As soon as I sat down, Prabhupāda started to massage my head. I was quite embarrassed. "You have forgotten how to massage properly?" he asked. "This is how you do it." He massaged my head for about two minutes.*

Then I stood behind Prabhupāda and again began massaging his head. By this time, the astronauts were moving across the landscape. They had gotten out their little American flag and were sticking it in the ground and were jumping up and down. Apparently they were defying gravity, because every time they jumped up they would float through the air and then gently land again. There was a lot of jubilation and sounds from them.

"So, Puruṣottama," Prabhupāda asked, "they have come to the moon?"

"Yes, Prabhupāda," Puruṣottama said excitedly. "They've landed on the moon!"

Prabhupāda smiled.

Dhanañjaya: *Again, Prabhupāda motioned me to the front. I moved around and sat down. I thought he wanted me to massage him from the front. But again he put his hands on my head and massaged. He said, "Can't you learn this simple thing, massaging my head?" I had been watching the television and not giving my full attention to my service.*

I tried again, but again Prabhupāda said, "You still don't know how to do this." I said, "Well, Prabhupāda, I am trying my hardest." He laughed and said, "That is all right. Continue."

Prabhupāda asked Puruṣottama, "So, what can you see?"

"They're exploring the moon's surface," he said.

"So, what is there?"

"Well, it looks like they have landed inside a crater somewhere, and the ground is sandy with some rocks. Oh, look, they're showing some shadows from some of the rocks that are lying around!"

"That's all you can see? There are no people? There are no trees? There are no rivers? There are no buildings?"

"No," Puruṣottama replied. "The moon is barren."

"They have not landed on the moon," Prabhupāda said emphatically. "This is not the moon."

Later when Mālatī brought in Prabhupāda's lunch, he said, "What Mālatī has done, she has made this little *kicharī* for Kṛṣṇa, and that is far greater than what they have done."

Even though Prabhupāda's quarters were incomplete and temple renovation made 7 Bury Place noisy and hectic, Prabhupāda decided to move in. "I am not attached to a comfortable apartment," he said. "My attachment is to living in the association of devotees." He was moving into the temple at a time when the record sales were low and the devotees were having to purchase supplies piecemeal, whenever they got money. Yet with Prabhupāda living with them and supervising their work, they were satisfied.

Tamāla Kṛṣṇa arrived from Los Angeles, and in addition to supervising much of the construction, he began taking the devotees out daily to chant on the streets and sell *Back to Godhead* magazines. Yamunā was sewing curtains from morning until night. Īśāna, Śyāmasundara, and others were working every possible hour on the renovation. And every day Prabhupāda would walk through the building to see the progress.

With only one week left until the opening, Śyāmasundara still labored on the temple ceiling. He had not even begun the altar. Again the other devotees complained to Prabhupāda that Śyāmasundara was too slow, but Prabhupāda replied, "He wants to make it artistic. Let him do it."

Śyāmasundara, this time on his own, asked George for a donation for an altar. George gave two thousand pounds, and Śyāmasundara picked out a slab of golden sienna marble and two slabs of red marble. Although Prabhupāda had a pair of seventeen-inch carved wood Deities of Rādhā and Kṛṣṇa, he didn't plan to use Them. And the size of the altar Śyāmasundara was building clearly required larger Deities.

One day a Mr. Doyal phoned, representing a large London Hindu society. He had heard the devotees wanted Rādhā-Kṛṣṇa Deities, and he had a pair he would donate. When Prabhupāda heard the news, he sent Tamāla Kṛṣṇa, Mukunda, and Śyāmasundara to Mr. Doyal's home to see the Deities.

Rādhā and Kṛṣṇa were white marble and stood about three feet high. Never before had the devotees seen such large Deities, and they offered obeisances. When they returned to the temple and told Prabhupāda, he said, "Take me there at once!"

Śrīla Prabhupāda, accompanied by Śyāmasundara, Mukunda, and Tamāla Kṛṣṇa, arrived by van at Mr. Doyal's home. Prabhupāda entered the living room and sat down. The Deities, covered by a cloth, stood on a table in the corner. Tamāla Kṛṣṇa was about to unveil Them when Prabhupāda checked him: "No. That's all right." Prabhupāda sat and spoke with Mr. Doyal, asking him about his work and where he had come from in India, and he met Mr. Doyal's family. Prabhupāda and his host chatted while the devotees listened.

"Swamiji," Mr. Doyal said at length, "I want to show you my Deities."

"Yes," Prabhupāda replied, "I will see Them after some time."

Prabhupāda began to speak about his Kṛṣṇa consciousness mission, and after a while Mr. Doyal again requested, "Please take a look at these Deities." And with that he walked over and unveiled Rādhā and Kṛṣṇa.

"Oh, yes," Prabhupāda said, folding his hands respectfully. Mr. Doyal explained that he had ordered the Deities from India for his own use, but in transit a tiny piece of Rādhārāṇī's finger had chipped off; therefore, according to Hindu tradition, the Deities could not be installed.

"Tamāla Kṛṣṇa," Prabhupāda said. "See how heavy these Deities are."

Tamāla Kṛṣṇa, placing one hand at Rādhārāṇī's base and the other around Her shoulder, lifted Her. "Not so heavy," he said.

"Śyāmasundara," Prabhupāda said. "See how heavy is Kṛṣṇa." The Deities were actually heavy for one man to carry, but the devotees understood Prabhupāda's intention.

"Not bad," Śyāmasundara said, holding Kṛṣṇa a few inches off the table.

"Yes," Prabhupāda said conclusively, "I think They're all right. Let us take Them. We have our van." And suddenly Prabhupāda was leaving, with his disciples following, carefully carrying Rādhā and Kṛṣṇa. Prabhupāda thanked Mr. Doyal.

"But Swamiji! Swamiji!" protested Mr. Doyal, who was not prepared for this sudden exit. "Please, we will arrange to bring Them. Our society will bring Them." But Prabhupāda was already out the door and leading his men to the van.

"Please wait," Mr. Doyal persisted. "We have to fix Them first, then you can take Them."

"We have an expert man," Prabhupāda said. "He can fix these things." Prabhupāda was assuring Mr. Doyal and at the same time directing his disciples. He opened the door of the van, and Śyāmasundara and Tamāla Kṛṣṇa slowly entered, cautiously setting Rādhā and Kṛṣṇa within. Tamāla Kṛṣṇa knelt in the back to hold the Deities secure, while Śyāmasundara got into the driver's seat.

"Now drive," Prabhupāda said. And off they went, with Prabhupāda smiling from the window to Mr. Doyal and his family, who stood together on the curb.

Śyāmasundara had driven but a few blocks when Prabhupāda asked him to stop the van. Turning around in his seat, Prabhupāda began offering prayers: *Govindam ādi-puruṣaṁ tam ahaṁ bhajāmi* ... He looked long at Kṛṣṇa, who was white with a slight bluish cast, and at the exquisite white Rādhārāṇī by His side. "Kṛṣṇa is so kind," he said. "He has come like this." Then he had Śyāmasundara continue driving slowly back to the temple.

Carefully, Prabhupāda supervised his disciples' carrying the Deities up to the second floor. The devotees were astounded and delighted to see Prabhupāda in such an animated and intense state, bringing Rādhā and Kṛṣṇa into Their temple. He had the Deities placed in a curtained-off section of his own room, and then he sat at his desk.

Prabhupāda smiled. "Kṛṣṇa has played a great trick." In the *Mahābhārata* also, he said, there are incidents where Kṛṣṇa plays tricks. One such trick was Kṛṣṇa's agreeing to be on the side of the general He saw first in the morning. The two opposing generals, Arjuna and Duryodhana, had both come to Kṛṣṇa's tent early in the morning as Kṛṣṇa slept. They had agreed that one of them would stand at Kṛṣṇa's head and the other at Kṛṣṇa's feet and that they would wait until Kṛṣṇa awoke. Duryodhana chose to stand by Kṛṣṇa's head, while Arjuna chose His feet. Kṛṣṇa awoke and saw Arjuna.

"That was one great trick that was played by Kṛṣṇa," Prabhupāda said. "Similarly, this is a great trick." He told how Kṛṣṇa had also tricked Mother Yaśodā when she had tried to discipline Kṛṣṇa. He had run away, and she had run after Him, caught Him, and tried to tie Him with ropes. "But every time she came with more rope," Prabhupāda said, "it was just a little too short. Kṛṣṇa can play any kind of trick. Another such trick has been played. They made so much effort to bring these Deities here, thinking They will be for their Hindu Centre. But all the time Kṛṣṇa wanted to come here. So this chip on the Deity's hand is just Kṛṣṇa's trick. And we have caught Them."

"Prabhupāda," Mukunda said, "you kidnapped Kṛṣṇa."

"Yes," Prabhupāda said. "Once I was in the bank, and the manager had some scheme. But I foiled his scheme. So he said to me, 'Mr. De, you should have been a politician.'" Prabhupāda laughed. Then he became grave and asked the devotees not to talk about the incident. Many people would not understand how he could install a chipped Deity. The devotees agreed to keep the secret, but they had no doubt that Prabhupāda's love for Kṛṣṇa was transcendental to Hindu customs; Rādhā and Kṛṣṇa had come to London on Prabhupāda's desire.

"How do you dress big Deities like this?" Yamunā asked. "They already have clothes on."

Prabhupāda said, "You bring me some cloth."

"What kind of cloth, Prabhupāda? What should the clothes look like?"

"Like in the pictures," he replied.

"Well, there are so many different pictures," she said. "Sometimes Kṛṣṇa has a ruffled skirt on, and sometimes He has a *dhotī* on, and sometimes He has a big crown on."

"Kṛṣṇa looks very beautiful in saffron," Prabhupāda said. "So you bring me some silk *dhotīs* in yellow and saffron color."

Yamunā collected six silk *sārīs* with silver and gold borders, and Prabhupāda indicated the design he wanted and told Yamunā how to arrange the crowns. With only a few days remaining before the installation ceremony, Yamunā began working almost continuously at her sewing machine. Several times a day Prabhupāda would come to see her progress.

Śyāmasundara had completed most of the altar, except for Lord Jagannātha's altar and the canopy over Rādhā and Kṛṣṇa's throne. Both the canopy and Lord Jagannātha's altar would be supported by four heavy wooden columns more than six feet high. Two rear columns would hold a marble slab for the Jagannātha deities to stand on, and two front columns were now supporting Rādhā and Kṛṣṇa's large velvet canopy. The columns were big and heavy; Śyāmasundara called them "elephant-leg columns." The columns now stood in place on the altar, although Śyāmasundara hadn't had a chance to secure them. The day before the installation Śyāmasundara collapsed upstairs in exhaustion.

On opening day many guests, Indians especially, crowded the temple, responding to flyers and advertisements. Apple Records had supplied a professional florist, who had decorated the room with floral arrangements. A BBC television crew was on hand to videotape the ceremony. While most of the devotees held *kīrtana,* Prabhupāda, behind a curtain at the other end of the temple, bathed Rādhā and Kṛṣṇa.

The plan was that after the bathing ceremony the Deities would be placed on the altar and Yamunā would dress Them. Once they were dressed and enthroned, the curtain would open for all the guests to behold Śrī Śrī Rādhā and Kṛṣṇa. Prabhupāda would lecture, and then everyone would feast. But because of Śyāmasundara's oversight, the installation almost became a disaster.

Prabhupāda had finished bathing the Deities and They had been placed on the marble altar, when suddenly the "elephant-leg columns" tottered. The canopy above the Deities began to collapse. Prabhupāda, seeing the danger, jumped onto the altar and seized the heavy columns in a split second. With great strength he held the two front pillars in place. "Get this out of here!" he shouted. While Prabhupāda's arms protected the Deities, the men removed the canopy, and then two men at a time carried each of the pillars away. The Deities remained unharmed.

While Prabhupāda was behind the curtain rescuing Rādhā and Kṛṣṇa, on the other side of the curtain guests and reporters awaited the unveiling of the Deities. Unaware of the mishap, the guests saw only men emerging from behind the curtain carrying large pillars and a canopy. The BBC camera crew began filming the canopy and pillars as they appeared from behind the curtain, taking them to be part of a ceremonial procession.

The few devotees behind the curtain with Prabhupāda were amazed. But there was no time now for apologies or appreciations. Yamunā dressed the Deities, Prabhupāda hurrying her. When at last everything was ready, Prabhupāda opened the main curtain, revealing the graceful forms of Lord Kṛṣṇa and Rādhārāṇī to the temple full of guests. A devotee began to offer *ārati,* while Prabhupāda, wearing a saffron *cādara* and a garland of carnations, stood to one side, reverentially looking upon Rādhā and Kṛṣṇa as their worshiper and protector.

This was the culmination of months of effort. Actually, years of planning had preceded this auspicious occasion. One hundred years before, Bhaktivinoda Ṭhākura had hoped for the day when Kṛṣṇa consciousness would come to England, and Śrīla Bhaktisiddhānta Sarasvatī had also desired it. Now that an authorized temple of Rādhā and Kṛṣṇa was preaching Kṛṣṇa consciousness in London, it was a historic occasion for Gauḍīya Vaiṣṇavism; a long-standing order of the previous *ācāryas* had been fulfilled. Prabhupāda had sent invitations to several of his Godbrothers in India. None of them had been able to come, of course, but at least they should have been pleased to learn that this dream of Śrīla Bhaktisiddhānta Sarasvatī's had been fulfilled.

Prabhupāda was seventy-three. He had now opened twenty-one temples in three years. Recently he had told some of his disciples that they should try to form a governing body for ISKCON, to relieve him of the management and allow him to concentrate fully on presenting Kṛṣṇa conscious literature. This literature could be introduced all over the world into homes, schools, and colleges for the benefit of everyone. It would be in such literature that he would live on. How much time he had left in this world he didn't know, he said, but he wanted to go on serving and trying to please his Guru Mahārāja, life after life.

Nevertheless, despite Prabhupāda's desire to retire from active work and absorb himself in writing books, here he was installing Deities in a new temple and protecting Them from his disciples' carelessness. Had he not been present, the celebration would have been a disaster. So many hardworking disciples, and they still needed his personal guidance.

ISKCON was just beginning to grow. Prabhupāda wanted to open not just twenty-one temples, but at least 108. His world traveling and book printing were just beginning, and, like everything else, the number of disciples would increase. The prestige of his movement would increase, and with it opposition from the atheists. Kṛṣṇa consciousness was growing, and Prabhupāda was in the forefront. "All around I see bright," he said. "That is the glory of Kṛṣṇa." He saw himself as a servant of his spiritual master; the bright future was in Kṛṣṇa's hands.

Prabhupāda called for Śyāmasundara. Although Prabhupāda was angry at first because of the near-disaster on the altar, he admitted that his disciples had done their best. The temple was beautiful, he told Śyāmasundara; he liked it. He then asked that a sign be placed out front with gold letters on a blue background:

RADHA-KRISHNA TEMPLE

This temple was constructed with great labor and effort
by Shyamasundar das Adhikary

On the day of Prabhupāda's departure from London, he distributed some of his personal effects, such as sweaters and scarves, to his disciples. He then went downstairs alone into the temple to see the Deities. He offered fully prostrated obeisances on the floor for a long time and then stood, looking at Rādhā and Kṛṣṇa.

Yamunā: *Prabhupāda was looking at the Deities with complete devotion. He loved those Deities. He had commented about Their exquisite beauty and how They complemented each other—how sometimes Rādhārāṇī looked more beautiful but how Kṛṣṇa's moonlike face and eyes were shining. Prabhupāda saw me and matter-of-factly said, "If you practice what I have taught you and follow the instructions of how I have taught you to worship the Deity, and if you read the books that we have printed, it is sufficient for you to go back to Godhead. You need not learn anything new. Simply practice what I have taught you, and your life will be perfect." Then he left—just left.*

CHAPTER THIRTY-ONE

A Threat Against ISKCON

Boston
December 21, 1969

MORE THAN ONE hundred of Prabhupāda's disciples and followers are in the lobby of the International Terminal of Boston's Logan Airport. Kīrtanānanda Swami has come from New Vrindaban with a truckload of devotees. The devotees from New York are here with a large banner: NEW YORK ISKCON WELCOMES SRILA PRABHUPADA. Most of the devotees wear heavy coats over their *dhotīs* and *sārīs* and are chanting Hare Kṛṣṇa; some play drums and cymbals. A few babies and children are present. Waiting passengers can only watch, startled.

Prabhupāda's plane is late, and the devotees continue chanting, often leaping into the air with outstretched arms. They haven't seen Prabhupāda in a long time, and they are waiting, expecting to see him at any moment. Oblivious of the proprieties of being in public, the devotees chant emotionally, building almost to uncontrolled ecstasy. The state police step in to tell the biggest devotee, Brahmānanda, "Cool it!" The chanting falls away to a murmur of *japa:* Hare Kṛṣṇa, Hare Kṛṣṇa, Kṛṣṇa Kṛṣṇa, Hare Hare/ Hare Rāma, Hare Rāma, Rāma Rāma, Hare Hare.

The plane from London arrives! The devotees are unable to see the passengers entering in the glassed-in immigration and customs area because the bottom six feet of the glass wall is painted black. Straining to see over the top, the devotees press forward, chanting, feverish, some almost hysterical. Suddenly they see Prabhupāda's raised hand with bead bag on the other side of the wall! They can see only his raised hand and bead bag. They go wild.

Fearlessly, with drums and *karatālas,* the *kīrtana* explodes again: Hare Kṛṣṇa, Hare Kṛṣṇa, Kṛṣṇa Kṛṣṇa, Hare Hare/ Hare Rāma, Hare Rāma, Rāma Rāma, Hare Hare. Advaita is tearfully smashing the *karatālas* together and chanting. Brahmānanda, jumping up and down, trying to glimpse into the customs room, is crying uncontrollably and yelling, "Prabhupāda! Prabhupāda!"

Śrīla Prabhupāda, free of customs, suddenly appears before them. Kīrtanānanda Swami, reserved until now, leaps around airport chairs and runs to him. Everyone is pushing and running, trying to be where Prabhupāda is.

Prabhupāda's saffron robes are wrinkled from the long flight, and he wears a knit sweater. He holds his white plastic attaché case in his left hand and again raises his right arm with forefinger and thumb extended from the bead bag. He smiles wonderfully, beaming to his children. Devotees cheer and cry: "All glories to Prabhupāda!"

As he walks toward a saffron-covered sofa in the airport lounge, the devotees move with him in an ecstatic wave, pressing in close. He sits down. Paramānanda, from New Vrindaban, comes forward with his infant son, the first boy born in ISKCON, and holds him forward to Prabhupāda for blessings. Prabhupāda is smiling, and the devotees are completely, unabashedly blissful.

"Where is Hayagrīva?" Prabhupāda asks. The question is repeated by the devotees, and big Hayagrīva lurches through the crowd, grumbling and falling flat at Prabhupāda's feet in obeisance. One by one, the leaders of the various ISKCON centers come forward and place garland after garland around Prabhupāda.

Prabhupāda looks beyond the wall of devotees at the newsmen with their cameras and at the baffled, curious, and disdainful onlookers. A bystander says, "I think he must be some kind of politician."

"So"—Prabhupāda begins speaking—"the spiritual master is to be worshiped as God. But if he is thinking that he is God, then he is useless. My request is, please don't take Kṛṣṇa consciousness as a sectarian religion. ..." Prabhupāda explains that Kṛṣṇa consciousness is a great science, culminating in pure love of God. "These boys and girls had never heard of Kṛṣṇa before," Prabhupāda continues, "but now they have taken it up so naturally—because it is natural." Prabhupāda says that he is an old man yet he is sure that even if he passes away his students will continue the Kṛṣṇa consciousness movement. The potency of this movement is such that it can awaken awareness of God within anyone's heart. After the lecture Prabhupāda stands and is escorted outside, where a limousine waits to drive him off through the newly fallen snow.

Riding joyfully in the car with Prabhupāda were Kīrtanānanda Swami, Brahmānanda, Satsvarūpa, and Puruṣottama. A professional chauffeur drove. Prabhupāda talked of London. It was an old, aristocratic city, he said, and the temple was in a very influential area near the British Museum. "The location is—what it is called—downtown?"

They passed a large billboard advertising a restaurant and lounge: CONTINENTAL. On seeing the billboard, Prabhupāda said, "*Cintāmaṇi*—what is that? Oh, no, Continental."

The devotees looked at one another: "*Cintāmaṇi*." Prabhupāda had thought that the sign had read *Cintāmaṇi,* meaning the spiritual gems that make up the transcendental land of Kṛṣṇaloka. But Prabhupāda himself was *cintāmaṇi,* pure and innocent, coming to the cold, dirty city of Boston yet always thinking of Kṛṣṇa wherever he was. How fortunate to be with him! Satsvarūpa glanced at the professional chauffeur. "Drive carefully," he said.

Prabhupāda spoke softly from the back seat, while the devotees in front peered back, barely able to see him in the darkness and completely awed by his friendly yet inconceivable presence. "The other day," he said, "I told George Harrison that if he thought his money belonged to him, that was *māyā*."

At the Sumner Tunnel the limousine pulled up at an automatic toll booth. The driver threw a coin into the chute, and the red light turned green. Prabhupāda asked if sometimes people drove through without paying, and Brahmānanda replied that an alarm would go off. They moved ahead into the Sumner Tunnel, usually an eerie, nerve-racking place—but not when riding with Prabhupāda.

"I told George to give his money to Kṛṣṇa," Prabhupāda said, "not that he had to give it to Kṛṣṇa by giving it to me, necessarily, but that somehow or other he must spend all of his money for Kṛṣṇa."

"But you are the only way to Kṛṣṇa," Brahmānanda said.

Prabhupāda laughed lightly. "Yes," he admitted, "at least in the West."

This was the great privilege of being able to ride with Prabhupāda: to hear him say little things or serious things and to see his fathomless expression or his kind smiling. It was a rare opportunity.

"I am representing unadulterated teachings," Prabhupāda continued. "Kṛṣṇa says in *Bhagavad-gītā,* 'Surrender to Me,' and I say, 'Surrender to Kṛṣṇa.' It is very simple. So many swamis come and present themselves as Kṛṣṇa, and it is all spoiled. But I say, 'Surrender to Kṛṣṇa.' I do not say anything new or adulterated. Kṛṣṇa says, 'Surrender to Me,' and I say, 'Surrender to Kṛṣṇa.'"

Prabhupāda asked Brahmānanda if fifty thousand copies of *Back to Godhead* magazine were being printed. Brahmānanda answered that they were. "Good," Prabhupāda replied. Turning his attention to Satsvarūpa, Prabhupāda asked how the composing machine was working, and Satsvarūpa said that hundreds of pages were being composed each month. Prabhupāda asked Kīrtanānanda Swami about New Vrindaban. New Vrindaban would improve, Prabhupāda said; the only thing wrong was that it got "blocked up" in the winter.

Each devotee in the car felt completely satisfied by his brief exchange with Prabhupāda, and they rode with him intoxicated in spiritual bliss.

Most of the devotees had raced ahead to the temple on Beacon Street and were waiting excitedly. The limousine pulled up, and again the devotees were unrestrained in their adoration of their spiritual master. Regally Prabhupāda walked up the walkway, onto the porch steps, through the front door, and into the vestibule, where he gazed around at the purple walls and the pink and green doorways. Surrounded by cheers and loving looks, he smiled.

The second-floor parlor, now the temple room, was filled with more than 150 disciples and guests, and they could see Prabhupāda's form rise into view as he came up the stairs. He still carried his white attaché case in his left hand and his bead bag in his right. And although he had just come out of the winter's night, he wore no coat, only cotton robes and a sweater. He appeared radiant.

Prabhupāda approached the altar. He seemed to notice everything: the small Rādhā-Kṛṣṇa Deities enthroned beneath a red velvet canopy, the larger deities of Jagannātha, Subhadrā, and Balarāma on a raised shelf above the picture of Lord Caitanya and His *saṅkīrtana* party, even the brass *ārati* paraphernalia, brightly shining on the small table near the altar. Turning to his secretary and traveling companion, Puruṣottama, he asked, "What do you think, Puruṣottama? Isn't this very nice?"

Crossing the room, Prabhupāda sat on the red velvet *vyāsāsana*. He spoke, and the audience was attentive. After praising the London center, the Deity worship there, the expertly made *purīs* for Rādhā and Kṛṣṇa, he turned toward the altar and said, "If you clean the Deities' utensils, your heart will become cleansed." By polishing the Deities' paraphernalia, he said, the devotees were cleaning their spiritual master's heart also. As he spoke, focusing simply and purely on devotion to the Deity, the devotees suddenly realized the importance of this aspect of their Kṛṣṇa consciousness. "Who has made these clothes?" Prabhupāda asked, glancing at Rādhā and Kṛṣṇa's little flounced dresses.

"Śāradīyā," a few devotees called out.

Prabhupāda smiled. "Thank you very much." Then he threw back his head and laughed. "Is Śāradīyā still fighting with her husband?"

The devotees and guests laughed, while Śāradīyā covered her face with her hands. "Don't fight with your husband," Prabhupāda said. "He is a good boy. Anybody that comes to Kṛṣṇa consciousness is good." He then asked to see the rest of the house.

A hundred devotees, straining to see and hear Prabhupāda's responses, followed him as he went downstairs. Although the crowd surrounded him, he remained relaxed and unhurried. He entered the press room, a long hall directly beneath the temple room. A large old offset press, a paper cutter, a folder, and flats of paper stock filled the room, which smelled like a print shop. Advaita, the press manager, bowed down in his green khakis before Prabhupāda. He rose up smiling, and Prabhupāda stepped forward and embraced him, putting his arm around Advaita's head. "Very good," he said.

Standing before the printing press, Prabhupāda folded his palms together and offered a prayer to his spiritual master: "*Jaya* Oṁ Viṣṇupāda Paramahaṁsa Śrī Śrīmad Bhaktisiddhānta Sarasvatī Gosvāmī Mahārāja Prabhupāda *kī jaya*!" Advaita asked Prabhupāda to give the press a transcendental name. "ISKCON Press," Prabhupāda said matter-of-factly, as if it had already been named.

"Keep all the machines very clean," Prabhupāda said, "and they will last a long time. This is the heart of ISKCON."

"You are the heart of ISKCON, Prabhupāda," a devotee said.

"And this is *my* heart," said Prabhupāda.

Leaving the main press room, Prabhupāda toured the other press facilities. Squeezing in, ducking under, standing on tiptoe, the crowd of devotees followed him step by step. He peeked into a little cubbyhole where a devotee was composing type. The typesetters, he said, should proceed very slowly at first, and in that way they would become expert. Turning to Advaita, he said, "Everyone in India who speaks Hindi has a Gita Press publication. So everyone who speaks English should have an ISKCON Press publication."

Compared to most authors, Prabhupāda's literary contribution was already substantial. But he wasn't just "an author." His mission was to flood the world with literature glorifying Lord Kṛṣṇa. Prabhupāda's ISKCON was now three years old, yet his disciples were only beginning to execute his plans for printing and distributing transcendental literature.

Printing was an important step—the first step. Months ago Prabhupāda had written:

> The press must work on continuously, and we shall produce immense volumes of literature. If the press goes on nicely, I shall be able to give you material for publishing a book every two months. We have got so much material for the Krishna consciousness movement.

And just prior to coming to Boston he had written:

> *Samkirtan* and distributing *Back to Godhead* and our other literatures is the fieldwork of this movement. Temple worship is secondary.

Now ISKCON was printing fifty thousand copies of *Back to Godhead* per month, and Prabhupāda hoped to increase the sales more and more.

Standing in the crowded, chilly basement, surrounded by devotees, press machines, and transcendental literature, Prabhupāda described how he wanted ISKCON Press to operate. He said that after dictating a tape he would mail it to Boston to be transcribed. The transcription should take no more than two days. During the next two days, someone would edit the transcribed manuscript. Then another editor would take two days to edit the transcript a second time. A Sanskrit editor would add diacritical markings, and the manuscript would be ready for composing.

Prabhupāda said he could produce fifteen tapes—three hundred manuscript pages—every month. At that rate, ISKCON Press should produce a book every two months, or six books in a year. Prabhupāda wanted to print at least sixty books. Therefore his press workers would have plenty to do for the next ten years. If the devotees simply printed his books incessantly, he said, even if they had to work twenty-four hours a day in shifts, it would give him "great delight." He was ready, if necessary, to drop all his activities except for publishing books.

This was the special nectar the press devotees were hankering to hear. Printing books was Prabhupāda's heart; it was the thing most dear to him.

During Prabhupāda's week in Boston, Puruṣottama continued as secretary and servant, out of duty. His difficulties in London had increased. Doubtful and morose, he came before Prabhupāda two days before their departure.

Puruṣottama: *I had decided to leave in London. I just felt like there were different things I wanted to do. But I felt obligated to stay with him because he needed me there. It was my job to at least get him back to the States. I felt that he needed someone to travel with him. And I just felt that I should complete that, have everything in order, so I couldn't say to myself that I had just quit when he needed me like that in a foreign country.*

I didn't tell anybody. I didn't speak against him or anything. I performed my duties, but in my attitude I let him know I was really getting kind of distant the last few days. I didn't bow down to him. I would come in, but I just wouldn't bow down to him.

He entered Prabhupāda's room. He didn't bow down. He stood. He was too uncomfortable to sit, because of the gravity of what he would say. Prabhupāda looked up from his desk. "Yes, Puruṣottama?"

Puruṣottama: *I went in to see him. I knew I was going to leave, and it kind of made me sick to do it. Anyway, I told him I have a lot of questions about the movement, the moon, and everything. I just don't believe all of this. He was very congenial about the whole thing. He took it nicely.*

He said to me, "If you have questions, why don't you ask me?" And I said, "You yourself have said that we should only ask questions to somebody we feel we can believe or trust." He looked very hurt. He knew what I was saying. I felt like I really hurt him. I didn't mean it to be so defiant, but there I was.

He said, "I've noticed that you haven't been well lately. You've had some problems?"

I said, "Well, I haven't been trying to hide it." I guess I was trying to prepare him for what was coming. I wanted to leave that night. So I said, "I want to leave." But he said to me, "You've been with me so long, and now you're so anxious to go? You can't even stay a night?" He said, "Why don't you stay at least till my plane leaves." That was two days later. I said, "O.K., I'll do that then."

I was going to go back to New York. Actually I didn't have the money for the ticket, and he gave me the money, he gave me the bus fare. I really appreciated that. I could have borrowed some money from someone else, but he said, "Well, you take it, and you can pay me back later." And I did. I gave it back the next week.

He was very gracious about the whole thing. Actually I could see that he had a very special loving way of looking at the world. I felt that sometimes I could see things in a loving way, like he did, and I realized that I got that viewpoint from him—you know, that little loving spirit. He had that, and I kind of caught some of that from him. And that's one of the things I always remember about him. And I know that through his movement I came to believe in God. Before I met him, I didn't believe in God.

After Puruṣottama left, Prabhupāda spoke with Bhavānanda about Puruṣottama's doubts concerning the moon landing and his consequent doubts of Kṛṣṇa consciousness. "I can understand that he might not accept it because I said it, but how could he disbelieve the Vedic *śāstras*?"

Boston's weather was miserable. When the rain stopped, the snow fell, and when the snow stopped, the rain came again. Prabhupāda tried taking a walk in the front yard, Bhavānanda beside him with the umbrella, watching cautiously to guard him from falling on the ice. But after a week of Boston's nasty December weather, Prabhupāda's cold was getting worse. He would go to Los Angeles.

* * *

Los Angeles
February 25, 1970

On the auspicious occasion of Bhaktisiddhānta Sarasvatī Ṭhākura's appearance day anniversary, the Los Angeles devotees received permission to enter their new temple on Watseka Avenue. The rooms had not even been cleaned, and the large hall was bare; but the devotees brought in Prabhupāda's *vyāsāsana* from the old temple on La Cienega, and Prabhupāda had them place on it a large picture of his spiritual master. Standing before his spiritual master, Prabhupāda offered *ārati* while some fifty disciples gathered around him, chanting Hare Kṛṣṇa and dancing in the otherwise empty hall.

After the *ārati,* Prabhupāda directed his disciples in offering flowers to the picture of Bhaktisiddhānta Sarasvatī. Then, still standing before the *vyāsāsana,* he said he had nothing to offer his spiritual master on this day except his own disciples. He then read aloud the names of all his disciples.

Taking his seat on a low *vyāsāsana* beside the large *vyāsāsana* of Bhaktisiddhānta Sarasvatī Ṭhākura, Prabhupāda gave a short history of his Guru Mahārāja, son of Bhaktivinoda Ṭhākura and powerful *ācārya* of the mission of Caitanya Mahāprabhu. As Prabhupāda recalled his first meeting with his spiritual master, he told how Bhaktisiddhānta Sarasvatī had told him to teach Kṛṣṇa consciousness to the English-speaking world. This large new temple, Prabhupāda said, had been provided by Bhaktisiddhānta Sarasvatī as a gift for the devotees to use in Kṛṣṇa's service. They should not become attached to the opulence, Prabhupāda said, but they should use this wonderful place for preaching. As he spoke, he wept.

"Now bring them *prasādam!*" Prabhupāda called. And the feast began. While devotees sat on the floor in rows, Prabhupāda from his *vyāsāsana* directed the servers, having them bring another *samosā* to one devotee, more chutney to another, and so on. He watched over all of them, encouraging them to take Kṛṣṇa's *prasādam.*

That afternoon Prabhupāda toured the buildings. In addition to the main hall, which he would have the devotees convert into a temple, he saw the equally large lecture hall. These rooms, plus a three-room apartment, ample separate quarters for male and female devotees, a parking lot, and a front lawn, made this the finest physical facility in all of ISKCON. "We don't require such a nice place for ourselves," Prabhupāda told the temple president, Gargamuni. "We are prepared to live anywhere. But such a nice place will give us opportunity to invite gentlemen to come and learn about this Kṛṣṇa consciousness."

The cost of the building had been $225,000, with a $50,000 down payment. Prabhupāda had had more than $10,000 in his book fund, but that was exclusively for printing books. So although he usually didn't like to deal personally in such negotiations, he had made an exception in this case and had asked the other temples to donate to the new "world headquarters" in Los Angeles. He had even mailed snapshots of the buildings to various temple presidents around the world. Thus he had collected the down payment, and on Śrīla Bhaktisiddhānta Sarasvatī's appearance day ISKCON became the legal owner.

This was the only temple ISKCON actually owned—all the other buildings were leased or rented—and Prabhupāda wanted to design everything himself. Hiring professionals would be too expensive, but Prabhupāda had plenty of disciples eager to do the renovation. Karandhara knew a little carpentry, plumbing, and general construction, and he could learn more by experience. Bhavānanda had been a professional designer, and he was filled with Prabhupāda's enthusiasm to transform the plain church into a dazzling palace for the Supreme Personality of Godhead. "First you make my apartment," Prabhupāda told Bhavānanda. "Let me move in, and then we will work on the temple room."

Bhavānanda: *We picked out a part of the Los Angeles temple for Prabhupāda's quarters, and Karandhara built a bathroom. When Prabhupāda came up to the rooms, he said, "This will be my sitting room. This will be my bedroom." And when he came to a third room, with a skylight, he said, "This will be my library."*

Prabhupāda had told me once in Boston that as a child he had lived in a palace with blue walls, red marble floors, and orange and gold trim—the Mulliks' house in Calcutta. So we painted the walls of his sitting room blue, and I put in a white tile floor. The drapes were burnt-orange satin with gold cords and gold fringe. Prabhupāda liked this color scheme very much.

In the bedroom I asked Prabhupāda where he wanted his bed, and he said, "Put the bed in the middle of the room." We had put down a rug, and Prabhupāda said, "Now you should get sheets and cover the rug with them. In India they have rugs like this, nice rugs, and they cover them with sheets. And on special days they take the sheets off. Otherwise they would become ruined." So I went out and bought sheets.

Prabhupāda was in his sitting room when I came in and started putting the sheet over the rug in the bedroom. Prabhupāda came in and said, "Yes, this is very nice. Again I have introduced something new. This is something new for all of you—sheets on rugs." Then he told me, "Now make sure there are no wrinkles in the sheet." I was on my hands and knees on the rug, and Prabhupāda also got down on his hands and knees right next to me. We were both pressing out the wrinkles from the sheet, and when we got to the end, Prabhupāda folded the sheet under the rug.

He was very happy there, because it was our own place. We had never had our own place before.

In the temple room Prabhupāda showed Karandhara where to build the three altars. He indicated the measurements and instructed that before each altar should be a pair of doors and over them the symbols of Viṣṇu: a conchshell over the altar for Guru and Gaurāṅga; a wheel and club over Rādhā and Kṛṣṇa's altar in the center; and a lotus over Lord Jagannātha's. The spiritual master's *vyāsāsana* was to go at the opposite end of the temple, facing Rādhā and Kṛṣṇa. The walls should be yellow, which Prabhupāda said was in the mode of goodness. The ceiling should be covered with a canopy, and there should be chandeliers.

Once the altars were completed, Prabhupāda wanted to bring the Deities, even though much of the renovation was yet unfinished. After constructing an umbrella-covered cart and decorating it with flowers, the devotees brought the Deities in procession from the old temple on La Cienega Boulevard to Their new home.

Bhavānanda: *The first time he came into the temple room after his morning walk, he went to the Guru-Gaurāṅga altar and paid his obeisances. We all paid our obeisances. Then he stood up, and he went to Rādhā and Kṛṣṇa, and then paid obeisances, then to Jagannātha, and we all followed. Then we walked back and he sat on his* vyāsāsana, *and he told us, "Now you line up facing each other from the* vyāsāsana *to Rādhā and Kṛṣṇa, face each other. This way, that way, one way you look is* guru, *and the other way God. And then back and forth that way. Always leave this aisle," he said, "so I can see."*

The Deity was the king, Prabhupāda said, and all the temple residents were His personal servants. The temple, therefore, should be like a palace. An elaborate temple was important for preaching, Prabhupāda explained, because most people, especially Westerners, were not inclined to undergo any austerities for obtaining spiritual life. There was an Indian saying, No one listens to a poor man. Were the devotees to advertise classes on *bhakti-yoga* in such-and-such empty field under a certain tree, Prabhupāda said, no one would come. But a clean, beautiful building with chandeliers and comfortable rooms would attract many people to visit and become purified.

The temple was also for those who wanted to live there as Kṛṣṇa conscious devotees. Devotees, Prabhupāda said, should be willing to live and sleep anywhere. But as the loving, protecting father of his disciples, Prabhupāda took great care to establish a large temple and an adequate dormitory facility. He was making a home for his family. To see that his spiritual children had a place to live and practice their devotional service was just another aspect of his mission.

A special feature of the new temple was Śrīla Prabhupāda's garden. The devotees had excavated a large patch of concrete behind the temple, filled it in with earth, surrounded it with a cinder-block wall, and planted a lawn with flower gardens all around.

Karandhara: *I had dug some beds along the inside perimeter and planted a plant here and a plant there. But Prabhupāda said, "No, plant something everywhere. Everywhere there should be something growing. Everywhere there is a place, you plant something. Let there be growing everywhere." He wanted it overgrown like a jungle, a tropical area where plants just grow luxuriantly everywhere.*

Śrīla Prabhupāda always enjoyed sitting in the garden in the evening with the fresh, cool evening air and the fragrance of the flowers. The topics of conversation in the garden were as varied as Śrīmad-Bhāgavatam*— all different subjects. Sometimes there would be lively conversations with guests or devotees, and sometimes Prabhupāda would spend the entire time just chanting, with very little conversation. Sometimes Prabhupāda would just have somebody read from the* Kṛṣṇa *book.*

Prabhupāda said that his mother maintained a garden on the roof of their house when he was young and that he would go up there in the evenings and play. He remembered that. He always remembered what he liked to do as a child. You would hear him reminisce with pleasure about it. Many times he would comment, "My mother maintained a garden on the roof of our residence, and as a child I would go there in the evening and play. Now I also have such a nice place to come."

Under Prabhupāda's personal direction, the Los Angeles center became a model for the rest of ISKCON. At the morning *Bhāgavatam* class, for example, he had the devotees responsively chant the Sanskrit *mantras* after him, and he asked that this become the standard program in all his temples. In May 1970, he wrote to each of his twenty-six temple presidents throughout North America and Europe, inviting them to visit him at Los Angeles:

> Now at the present moment, I am concentrating my energy in this Los Angeles Center as ideal for all other centers in respect of Deity worship, Arotrik, Kirtan and other necessary paraphernalia. As I have curtailed my moving program, I wish that you may come here at your convenience and stay here for a few days and see personally how things are going on; and by meeting with me personally for necessary instruction, I hope simultaneously in all Centers the activities will be of the same standard.

The temple presidents who visited Prabhupāda, most of them young men in their twenties, came with practical as well as philosophical questions. They came with their notebooks, writing down everything from the temple schedule to color schemes, noting the tunes used in the *kīrtanas,* learning how to manage a *saṅkīrtana* party. And perhaps most important of all, they would note the things Prabhupāda did and the words he spoke personally to them. The temple presidents would then return to their own centers—in Berkeley or Hamburg or Toronto or Sydney—glowing with ecstasy and ready to implement dozens of new standards they had imbibed from Prabhupāda at the Los Angeles world headquarters.

Although Prabhupāda still spoke of expanding his movement more and more, he seemed content to stay in Los Angeles, reaching the rest of the world through his temple presidents, his *saṅkīrtana* parties, and his books. New plans were unfolding, however, and Prabhupāda again spoke of a governing body, twelve hand-picked disciples to manage all of ISKCON's affairs. He also spoke of initiating more *sannyāsīs* and taking them with him to India to train as itinerant preachers. And to insure that his books were regularly and properly printed, he wanted to form a special committee in charge of book publication.

Sometimes managing his worldwide religious movement, sometimes leading the growing group of devotees in chanting Sanskrit *mantras* in the Los Angeles temple, and sometimes sitting alone and translating in the pre-dawn hours, Prabhupāda lived happily in Los Angeles.

One day a record arrived from London. The London devotees, who with George Harrison's help had already produced an album, had now also released a new single, "Govinda." The song consisted of verses Prabhupāda had taught them from *Brahma-saṁhitā,* each verse ending with the refrain *govindam ādi-puruṣaṁ tam ahaṁ bhajāmi.* Prabhupāda asked that the record be played during the morning program in the temple. The next morning, after he had entered the temple room, bowed down before the Deity, and taken his seat on the *vyāsāsana* to begin the class, the record began.

Suddenly, Prabhupāda became stunned with ecstasy. His body shivered, and tears streamed from his eyes. The devotees, feeling a glimmer of their spiritual master's emotion, began to chant Hare Kṛṣṇa as if chanting *japa.* The moments seemed to pass slowly. Finally Prabhupāda spoke: "*Govindam ādi-puruṣaṁ tam ahaṁ bhajāmi.*" He was again silent. Then he asked, "Is everyone all right?" The response was a huge roar: "*Jaya* Prabhupāda!" And he began the *Śrīmad-Bhāgavatam* class.

* * *

Vaiṣṇavera kriyā-mudrā vijñe nā bujhāya. "No one can understand the mind of a Vaiṣṇava." Only a pure devotee can understand another pure devotee perfectly. But by observing the main activities of Prabhupāda's life, we can see that whatever he did was pure service to Lord Kṛṣṇa and was a perfect example of how to surrender to Kṛṣṇa. He taught by precept and by example. Often encouraging, even praising his disciples, he always pushed them into more and more participation in the blissful *saṅkīrtana* movement of Lord Caitanya. But he also exposed the faults of his disciples, and these faults were sometimes great and painful to see, both for him and for his disciples.

One day, as Prabhupāda came into his quarters at the Los Angeles temple, he saw that one of the devotees cleaning his room had placed his picture upside down. A simple mistake. But it indicated something wrong in the disciple's mentality. Every morning the devotees sing prayers to the spiritual master honoring him as the direct representative of God. How could any sincere disciple not notice that he is standing God's representative upside down?

Then a more serious discrepancy. Prabhupāda went to the temple, greeted the Deities, and went to take *caraṇāmṛta,* the scented water from the bathing of the Deities. It was part of his daily schedule. After his morning walk, he would return to the temple and offer obeisances to the Deities while the "Govinda" record was being played. A devotee would then offer him a few drops of *caraṇāmṛta* in his right palm, and he would sip it. He had mentioned this item of devotional service in *The Nectar of Devotion.* "Scented with perfumes and flowers, the water comes gliding down through His lotus feet and is collected and mixed with yogurt. In this way this *caraṇāmṛta* not only becomes very tastefully flavored, but also has tremendous spiritual value. ... The devotees who come to visit and offer respects to the Deity take three drops of *caraṇāmṛta* very submissively and feel themselves happy in transcendental bliss."

On this particular morning, however, as Śrīla Prabhupāda took *caraṇāmṛta,* he frowned. Someone had put salt in it! He walked the length of the temple room, took his seat on the *vyāsāsana,* and before a room full of a hundred devotees, asked, "Who has put salt in the *caraṇāmṛta?*" A young girl in a *sārī* stood and with a nervous smile said she had done it.

"Why have you done it?" Prabhupāda asked gravely.

"I don't know," she giggled.

Prabhupāda turned to Gargamuni: "Get someone responsible."

Everyone present felt Prabhupāda's anger. The unpleasant moment marred the pure temple atmosphere. A disciple worships Kṛṣṇa by pleasing Kṛṣṇa's representative, the spiritual master; therefore to displease the spiritual master was a spiritual disqualification. The spiritual master was not merely a principle; he was a person—Śrīla Prabhupāda.

When ISKCON Press in Boston misprinted Prabhupāda's name on a new book, he became deeply disturbed. The small paperback chapter from the Second Canto of *Śrīmad-Bhāgavatam* bore his name on the cover as simply A. C. Bhaktivedanta. Omitted was the customary "His Divine Grace" as well as "Swami Prabhupāda." Śrīla Prabhupāda's name stood almost divested of spiritual significance. Another ISKCON Press publication described Prabhupāda as "*ācārya*" of ISKCON, although Prabhupāda had repeatedly emphasized that he was the founder-*ācārya.* There had been many *ācāryas,* or spiritual masters, and there would be many more; but His Divine Grace A. C. Bhaktivedanta Swami Prabhupāda was the sole founder-*ācārya* of the International Society for Krishna Consciousness.

To make matters worse, when Prabhupāda first opened the new *Bhāgavatam* chapter, the binding cracked and the pages fell out. Prabhupāda glowered.

The devotees in Boston, hearing of Prabhupāda's anger, knew at once that their mistake in misprinting Śrīla Prabhupāda's name was a serious oversight. Minimizing the spiritual master's position was a grave offense, and they had even published the offense. The serious implications were difficult for the devotees to face, and they knew they would have to rectify their mentality before they could make spiritual progress. Prabhupāda criticized the mentality behind these mistakes, and his criticisms were instructive to his disciples. Unless *he* instructed them about the absolute position of the spiritual master, how would they learn?

At the beginning of the *Śrīmad-Bhāgavatam* class one morning, Prabhupāda called on one of the women devotees: "Nandarāṇī." She stood respectfully. "Do you chant sixteen rounds every day?"

"Well, I try to, Prabhupāda."

"This is the problem," Prabhupāda said, turning to the temple president. If Nandarāṇī, one of the senior, responsible women, wasn't chanting regularly, then certainly the new women under her weren't either. This was the managers' fault. Prabhupāda had praised and encouraged his disciples for laboring hard to renovate the temple and for going out daily into the streets to chant and distribute magazines. But for a devotee to not chant the prescribed rounds was to neglect the most important instruction.

What Nandarāṇī hadn't said was that the temple authorities had told her that chanting all her sixteen rounds wasn't necessary, as long as she worked. They had told her this, even though Prabhupāda clearly instructed his disciples at initiation to always chant at least sixteen rounds daily.

Then another incident. During the morning class, Prabhupāda was discussing Sārvabhauma Bhaṭṭācārya, an associate of Lord Caitanya.

Looking among the devotees, he asked, "Who can tell me who is Sārvabhauma Bhaṭṭācārya?" No one spoke. Prabhupāda waited. "*None* of you can tell me who is Sārvabhauma Bhaṭṭācārya?" he asked. One girl raised her hand; she had "read something about him"—that was all.

"Aren't you ashamed?" Prabhupāda looked at the men. "You should be the leaders. If the men cannot advance, then the women cannot advance. You must be *brāhmaṇas.* Then your wives will be *brāhmaṇas.* But if you are not *brāhmaṇas,* then what can *they* do?" Without improving their chanting and without reading Kṛṣṇa conscious literature, Prabhupāda said, they would never attain the purity necessary for preaching Lord Caitanya's message.

While the local anomalies were weighing heavily on Śrīla Prabhupāda, he learned of strange things his disciples in India had written in their letters, and he became more disturbed. One letter to devotees in America reported that Prabhupāda's Godbrothers in India objected to his title Prabhupāda. According to them, only Bhaktisiddhānta Sarasvatī should be called Prabhupāda, and they referred to Prabhupāda as "Swami Mahārāja." Prabhupāda also learned that some of his disciples were saying he was not the only spiritual master. They were interested in reading Bhaktisiddhānta Sarasvatī's books—as if to discover some new teaching Prabhupāda had not yet revealed.

Prabhupāda regarded these remarks as dangerous for ISKCON. Advancement in spiritual life was based on implicit faith in the spiritual master, and to Prabhupāda these new ideas indicated a relative conception, as opposed to the absolute conception, of the spiritual master. Such a conception could destroy all he had established; at least, it could destroy the spiritual life of anyone who held it.

Though sometimes ignorant, his disciples, he knew, were not malicious. Yet these letters from India carried a spiritual disease transmitted by several of Prabhupāda's Godbrothers to his disciples there. Prabhupāda had already been troubled when some of his Godbrothers had refused to help him secure land in Māyāpur, the birthplace of Lord Caitanya. Although he had asked them to help his inexperienced disciples purchase land, they had not complied. In fact, some of them had worked against him. Prabhupāda had written to one of his Godbrothers, "I am so sorry to learn that there is a sort of conspiracy by some of our Godbrothers as not to give me a place at Māyāpur."

Prabhupāda was sensitive to any threat to ISKCON. His accepting the name Prabhupāda, his teaching that the disciple must approach the spiritual master as the direct representative of Kṛṣṇa, without attempting to jump over him to the previous spiritual masters—these things he had carefully explained to his disciples. But now a few irresponsibly spoken remarks in India were weakening the faith of some of his disciples. Perhaps this insidious contamination that was now spreading had precipitated the blunders at ISKCON Press and even the discrepancies in Los Angeles. Talks about the relative position of the spiritual master could only be the workings of *māyā,* the Lord's illusory energy. *Māyā* was attempting to bewilder the devotees of ISKCON. That was her job: to lead the conditioned souls away from Kṛṣṇa's service.

The recent events began to hamper Prabhupāda's writing. He had been working quickly in Los Angeles and had recently finished the second and final volume of *Kṛṣṇa.* And on the very tape on which he had dictated the last chapter of *Kṛṣṇa,* he had immediately begun a summary of the Eleventh Canto of *Śrīmad-Bhāgavatam.* Gradually, however, his writing stopped.

Karandhara: *Prabhupāda's translating would require a great deal of concentration. He would have two or three of his big* Bhāgavatam *volumes opened up and sometimes a number of other small books, which he would refer to for something or other. He would sit, wearing his glasses and speaking into his dictating machine, and he would be completely absorbed in reading. Sometimes he would make a brief note, then look into one of his books, then open another book, turn back to another page, make a note, and then dictate. It required a great deal of concentration. I think that's why Prabhupāda did most of it at night, after he would rise from his late evening nap. From one or two in the morning until six or seven in the morning he would be absorbed. It was quiet at that time, and he could become absorbed.*

But when Prabhupāda became disturbed about the problems in ISKCON, it inhibited his work. He was spending his time discussing with visiting devotees or myself or whoever was there. Then he would spend more time thinking matters over or pondering the problem, and he wouldn't be able to concentrate on his translating. These difficulties disturbed him, and he would think about them and say, "I have not been able to concentrate. I have been thinking about this problem."

Although the spiritual master suffers for his disciples' mistakes,

Prabhupāda's perspective was not simply negative. He continued chanting and lecturing in the temple and inviting the leaders of his movement to visit him in the ideal center of Los Angeles; but he also corrected the diseased mentality wherever it appeared. When, for example, Gurudāsa wrote from London to say that they had allowed an Indian guest to lecture in the temple while sitting on Prabhupāda's *vyāsāsana,* Prabhupāda immediately wrote back, correcting him:

> I am surprised how you allowed Mr. Parikh to sit on the Vyasasana. You know that Vyasasana is meant for the representative of Vyasadeva, the Spiritual Master, but Mr. Parikh does not come in the Parampara to become the representative of Vyas, neither does he have any sound knowledge of Vaisnava principles. I understand from your letter that sometimes discussions on Aurobindo philosophy are done by Mr. Parikh from the Vyasasana, so I am a little surprised how did you allow like this. I think you should rectify immediately all these mistakes as stated by you in the last two lines of your letter, "I think the best thing to do is to stop his class. Nonsense ought not to be tolerated."

In a letter from Paris, Tamāla Kṛṣṇa asked Prabhupāda philosophical questions about the perfection of the spiritual master, and Prabhupāda answered fully, but sternly:

> A Spiritual Master is always liberated. In any condition of His life He should not be mistaken as an ordinary human being. This position of the Spiritual Master is achieved by three processes. One is called *sadhan siddha.* That means one who is liberated by executing the regulative principles of devotional service. Another is *kripa siddha,* one who is liberated by the mercy of Krishna or His devotee. And another is *nitya siddha* who is never forgetful of Krishna throughout his whole life. These are the three features of the perfection of life.
>
> So far Narada Muni is concerned, in His previous life He was a maidservant's son, but by the mercy of the devotees He later on became *siddha* and next life He appeared as Narada with complete freedom to move anywhere by the grace of the Lord. So even though he was in His previous life a maidservant's son there was no impediment in the achievement of His perfect spiritual life. Similarly any living entity who is conditioned can achieve the perfectional stage of life by the above mentioned processes and the vivid example is Narada Muni.
>
> So I do not know why you have asked about my previous life. Whether I was subjected to the laws of material nature? So, even though accepting that I was subjected to the laws of material nature, does it hamper in my

> becoming Spiritual Master? What is your opinion? From the life of Narada Muni it is distinct that although He was a conditioned soul in His previous life, there was no impediment of His becoming the Spiritual Master. This law is applicable not only to the Spiritual Master, but to every living entity.
>
> So far I am concerned, I cannot say what I was in my previous life, but one great astrologer calculated that I was previously a physician and my life was sinless. Besides that, to corroborate the statement of *Bhagavad-gita* "sucinam srimatam gehe yogabhrasta 'bhijayate," which means an unfinished yogi takes birth in rich family or born of a *suci* or pious father. By the grace of Krishna I got these two opportunities in the present life to be born of a pious father and brought up in one of the richest, aristocratic families of Calcutta (Kasinatha Mullik). The Radha Krishna Deity in this family called me to meet Him, and therefore last time when I was in Calcutta, I stayed in that temple along with my American disciples. Although I had immense opportunities to indulge in the four principles of sinful life because I was connected with a very aristocratic family, Krishna always saved me, and throughout my whole life I do not know what is illicit sex, intoxication, meat-eating or gambling. So far my present life is concerned, I do not remember any part of my life when I was forgetful of Krishna.

Prabhupāda thought some of his leaders had become entangled in ISKCON management and were trying to gain control for themselves. In the classes he would speak of this only indirectly, as he had when he had exposed that the devotees weren't chanting and reading enough. Consequently, most devotees were unaware of Prabhupāda's anxiety. But occasionally, while sitting in his room or in the garden, Prabhupāda would express his concern. He wanted his disciples to manage ISKCON, but to do so they must be pure. Only then would he be able to concentrate on writing books. In June he wrote to Brahmānanda:

> Now my desire is that I completely devote my time in the matter of writing and translating books, and arrangement should now be done that our Society be managed automatically. I think we should have a central governing body for dealing with important matters. I have already talked with Gargamuni about this. So if you come back by the Rathayatra festival, we can have a preliminary meeting at San Francisco in this connection.

* * *

In July Prabhupāda visited San Francisco for the fourth annual ISKCON Ratha-yātrā. It was the biggest festival ever, with ten thousand people joining in the procession through Golden Gate Park to the beach. Prabhupāda felt ill and didn't join the parade until about midway. He danced in the road before the carts, as a hundred disciples encircled him, chanting and playing *karatālas* and *mṛdaṅgas.*

Afterward, Prabhupāda wanted to ride in the cart, just as he had done the year before, but some of his disciples restrained him. A gang of hoodlums, they said, had caused trouble earlier, and for Prabhupāda to ride on the cart might be dangerous. He disagreed, but finally relented and rode in his car to the beach.

At The Family Dog Auditorium on the beach Prabhupāda began his lecture. "I want to thank you all for coming. Although I am not well, I felt it my responsibility to come, as you have so kindly attended Lord Jagannātha's Ratha-yātrā festival. I felt it my duty to come and see you and address you." His voice was frail.

Later in his apartment in San Francisco, Prabhupāda complained that he had not been allowed to ride in the cart. As leader of the Hare Kṛṣṇa movement, he should have ridden on the cart. Not only had his disciples refused him, but several disciples had prominently ridden on the cart—as if in his place.

Prabhupāda asked the many temple presidents assembled for the Ratha-yātrā to meet and discuss forming a governing body to manage ISKCON. The devotees met and then reported that they thought only one of them should be elected the chief representative.

They hadn't understood. The strength should be in a group, Prabhupāda said, not in a single individual. Since he was ISKCON's founder-*ācārya,* what need was there for another single leader? He asked them to meet again.

* * *

Returning to Los Angeles, Prabhupāda announced he would award several of his disciples the *sannyāsa* order. The devotee community excitedly prepared for the festival. The *sannyāsīs,* Prabhupāda said, would leave their temples to travel and preach. It was an unprecedented change for ISKCON, a sensation, and the devotees loved it.

Although Prabhupāda was awarding *sannyāsa* to some of his most advanced disciples, he also said the *sannyāsa* initiation was to purify these disciples and to rid them of their entanglement in material desires. He set the initiation for the end of July, two weeks later.

One day in Los Angeles, a visiting devotee speaking with Prabhupāda in his room humbly asked why Prabhupāda hadn't answered his questions in a recent letter. Prabhupāda remembered no such letter. Inquiring from his secretary, Prabhupāda discovered that his secretary often showed incoming letters to certain temple leaders, who at their discretion would sometimes withhold letters they considered petty or too disturbing.

Prabhupāda was outraged. How dare they come between him and his other disciples? How could they presume to make such decisions on their own? How could a disciple censor his spiritual master's mail?

Although Prabhupāda reprimanded the devotees involved, the incident only increased the already heavy burden on his mind. Again the thought of spiritual disease transmitted in letters from India disturbed him. He found no one close to him in Los Angeles with whom he could speak confidentially about this serious minimization of the spiritual master. As his anxiety affected him bodily, he fell ill and stopped eating.

Karandhara: *I'd heard some things, but in the spirit of "going on" it had all been glossed over. And Prabhupāda didn't talk much about it either. One time, though, I was in his room, right after the* sannyāsīs *had left Los Angeles, and he asked me if I understood what had gone on. I said, "Well, I think so." But I didn't really know very much.*

At that time the devotees who were going out on saṅkīrtana *were in the alleyway chanting, and Prabhupāda was at his desk. Hearing the* kīrtana, *he turned back, looking in the direction of the devotees below his window, and smiled. Then he turned to me. "They're innocent," he said. "Do not involve them in this business."*

Karandhara still didn't understand, and he wondered what not to involve them in. He did know, however, that a shadow was hanging over the heads of the *sannyāsīs.*

Prabhupāda requested three trusted disciples to come be with him in Los Angeles.

Rūpānuga: *I was in Buffalo and the phone rang. Someone said, "Śrīla Prabhupāda is on the telephone." I said, "What? You're kidding!" It wasn't Śrīla Prabhupāda, but it was his servant, Devānanda. Devānanda said, "Śrīla Prabhupāda wants you to come to Los Angeles." I said, "What's wrong?" He said, "Well, he doesn't want ..." Then he said, "Śrīla Prabhupāda wants to talk about it now."*

So Śrīla Prabhupāda got on the phone, and as soon as I heard him on the line, I paid my obeisances. Then I said, "Śrīla Prabhupāda, what's wrong?" He said, "You didn't know I was ill?" I said, "No!" He said, "You should come immediately."

Then I said, "Uh ... uh ... Śrīla Prabhupāda, let me speak to Devānanda." I didn't know what was going on, so I asked Devānanda, "Tell me what's going on." Then he said, "Śrīla Prabhupāda said he will talk with you when you come. He will explain everything."

Bhagavān dāsa: *One day after coming back from* saṅkīrtana, *I received a call from Rūpānuga, who told me he was on his way to Los Angeles, having received a call from Prabhupāda that there was some disturbance there. He couldn't tell me more, but he said he would call me when he returned.*

This set my mind reeling. I sat in the chair, hot and sweaty after coming back from saṅkīrtana, *my mind absorbed in thinking of Prabhupāda and what could be going on. I called Los Angeles to talk to Prabhupāda's secretary, Devānanda, who told me he couldn't really say anything at that point. I was hoping somehow or other I would get more information of the situation, but after waiting some time, I went in to take my shower.*

I was in the shower when all of a sudden someone banged on the door. "Prabhupāda is on the telephone. He wants to speak with you." I was sure there was some misunderstanding—how is it possible that the spiritual master could be on the telephone? Anyway, I ran out of the shower, all wet, and picked up the telephone and said, "Hello?"

There was a long pause. Then all of a sudden I heard Śrīla Prabhupāda's voice on the other end: "Bhagavān dāsa?"

"Yes," I said. "Śrīla Prabhupāda, please accept my humble obeisances. How can I serve you?" I was completely stunned. Then Prabhupāda's voice came slowly on the phone, "There are many things that you will do, but the first thing is that you must come here immediately." I said, "Of course, Śrīla Prabhupāda, I will be there right away." And with that we both hung up.

I managed to gather the money together to take the flight to Los Angeles. And when I got on the plane in Detroit, it just so happened that Rūpānuga was also on the same plane. We sat together and discussed what could possibly be happening in Los Angeles to cause Śrīla Prabhupāda so much distress.

When we arrived at the airport, Karandhara picked us up and told us that some of the older devotees had been plotting against Prabhupāda and that that day Prabhupāda had given several of the men sannyāsa *and sent them away to preach. This was all quite amazing to me, and I didn't really know what to make of it.*

When we came into Prabhupāda's room, he looked distressed and was rubbing his head, complaining of the blood pressure that was caused by the conspiracy.

Tamāla Kṛṣṇa: *I had written Śrīla Prabhupāda a lengthy letter from Paris, describing how we wanted to expand our preaching efforts in Europe, and suddenly I received a telegram from His Divine Grace that said, "Received your letter 26 July. Come Los Angeles immediately." I was quite surprised, and I remember disentangling myself that very day and leaving that night, even though I was in charge of the activities there.*

When I arrived in Los Angeles, I found Rūpānuga, Bhagavān, Kīrtanānanda Swami, and Karandhara. I was in a very enthusiastic, blissful mood from having done so much saṅkīrtana, *and I had no idea of any difficulty. But these devotees were all in a heavy, sober, somber mood, and they tried to explain to me what was going on. But actually I could not get a very clear understanding. I had arrived in the late afternoon, and I could not see Śrīla Prabhupāda.*

Early the next morning, when Prabhupāda was informed that I had arrived, he called for me before maṅgala-ārati. *I went up to his quarters, and when I came through the door, Prabhupāda was sitting in his room with his head downward. He looked up, and he appeared to be almost ill. He was gaunt and looked very sorrowful. He said meekly, just as I was bowing down, "Have they told you?"*

Of course, I hadn't really understood everything, but in reply to his question I said, "Yes, they have told me some things." And Prabhupāda said, "Can you help me?" So I answered, "Yes, Śrīla Prabhupāda." He said, "Can you take me out of here?" I said, "Yes, Śrīla Prabhupāda."

Of course, I didn't feel that I could help Śrīla Prabhupāda, but I could understand that I had to say yes. How can you say, "No, I won't"? But how far could I help? It's like lifting the heaviest object in the world. The guru *is so heavy, and yet I had to say yes.*

So Prabhupāda asked me next, "Where will you take me?" And I said,

"Well, we can go to Florida." He said, "No, that is not far enough." I said, "I could take you to Europe." He said, "No, that also will not be good. The problem may be there also." So anyway, we didn't conclude where to go at that time. But Prabhupāda said, "It is like a fire here. I must leave at once. It has become like a fire."

Prabhupāda confided in Rūpānuga, Tamāla Kṛṣṇa, and Bhagavān about the various incidents: his mail withheld, his name misprinted, his riding in the Ratha-yātrā parade restricted. He mentioned these and other indications that certain persons wanted to move him into the background, out of the reach of his disciples. He didn't want to stay in Los Angeles, he didn't want to stay in the United States, he didn't even want to go to Europe. He wanted to leave the arena of his disciples' offenses. But before leaving, he wanted to complete his plans for establishing a governing body to manage ISKCON. To this end he dictated the following on July 28:

> I, the undersigned, *A. C. Bhaktivedanta Swami,* disciple of Om Visnupad Paramhansa 108 Sri Srimad Bhaktisiddhanta Sarasvati Gosvami Maharaj Prabhupada, came in the United States in 1965 on September 18th for the purpose of starting Krishna Consciousness Movement. For one year I had no shelter. I was travelling in many parts of this country. Then in 1966, July, I incorporated this Society under the name and style the International Society for Krishna Consciousness, briefly ISKCON. ... Gradually the Society increased, and one after another branches were opened. Now we have got thirty-four (34) branches enlisted herewith. As we have increased our volume of activities, now I think a Governing Body Commission (hereinafter referred to as the GBC) should be established. I am getting old, 75 years old, therefore at any time I may be out of the scene, therefore I think it is necessary to give instruction to my disciples how they shall manage the whole institution. They are already managing individual centers represented by one president, one secretary and one treasurer, and in my opinion they are doing nice. But we want still more improvement in the standard of Temple management, propaganda for Krishna consciousness, distribution of books and literatures, opening of new centers and educating devotees to the right standard. Therefore, I have decided to adopt the following principles and I hope my beloved disciples will kindly accept them.

Prabhupāda then listed the names of the twelve persons who would form the G.B.C.:

1. Sriman Rupanuga Das Adhikary
2. Sriman Bhagavandas Adhikary

3. Sriman Syamsundar Das Adhikary
4. Sriman Satsvarupa Das Adhikary
5. Sriman Karandhar Das Adhikary
6. Sriman Hansadutta Das Adhikary
7. Sriman Tamala Krishna Das Adhikary
8. Sriman Sudama Das Adhikary
9. Sriman Bali Mardan Das Brahmacary
10. Sriman Jagadisa Das Adhikary
11. Sriman Hayagriva Das Adhikary
12. Sriman Krishnadas Adhikary

> These personalities are now considered as my direct representatives. While I am living they will act as my zonal secretaries and after my demise they will be know as Executors.

Prabhupāda further described the role of the *sannyāsīs:*

> I have already awarded Sannyas or the renounced order of life to some of my students and they have also got very important duties to perform in this connection. The Sannyasis will travel to our different centers for preaching purpose as well as enlightening the members of the center for spiritual advancement.

Prabhupāda's legal document went on to set forth general directions for the G.B.C. secretaries. They should travel regularly to the temples in their respective zones to insure that each devotee chanted sixteen rounds and followed a regulated schedule and that the temples were clean. His twelve G.B.C. secretaries would relieve him of management, and they would rectify present and future difficulties within the society. That rectification, Prabhupāda's document explained, would be possible only when the devotees in each temple engaged fully in regulated devotional service: rising early for *maṅgala-ārati* at four-thirty, attending *Śrīmad-Bhāgavatam* class and reciting the Sanskrit verses, and chanting in the streets and distributing *Back to Godhead* magazines and other Kṛṣṇa conscious literature. This emphasis on strictly following Kṛṣṇa conscious principles would supersede all material formulas for management. The G.B.C. would insure that in their appointed zones all the devotees were properly engaged. There would be no *māyā*.

The next day Prabhupāda drafted another significant statement, naming Bhagavān, Rūpānuga, and Karandhara trustees of his Bhaktivedanta Book Trust.

> The Bhaktivedanta Book Trust account will be used to publish my books and literature and to establish Temples throughout the world, specifically three temples are to be established, one each in Mayapur, Vrndavana, and Jagannath Puri.

Since returning to America in 1967, Prabhupāda had often said he would stay permanently in America as the adopted son of his disciples. Now he revealed new plans. He spoke of going to India to preach and to establish large ISKCON temples. For the devotees, who based their activities mostly in small rented houses, Prabhupāda's constructing cathedrallike buildings in India was inconceivable. In India, Prabhupāda said, he would teach his disciples how to preach and how to establish temples.

Prabhupāda picked a team, including two newly initiated *sannyāsīs,* to accompany him to India. In the future, he said, more disciples could join him, for India would become an important field for Kṛṣṇa consciousness. Prabhupāda wrote Satsvarūpa and Uddhava in Boston:

> You are all my children, and I love my American boys and girls who are sent to me by my spiritual master and I have accepted them as my disciples. Before coming to your country I took sannyas in 1959. I was publishing B.T.G. since 1944. After taking sannyas I was more engaged in writing my books without any attempt to construct temples or to make disciples like my other God-brothers in India.
>
> I was not very much interested in these matters because my Guru Maharaj liked very much publication of books than constructing big, big temples and creating some neophyte disciples. As soon as He saw that His neophyte disciples were increasing in number, He immediately decided to leave this world. To accept disciples means to take up the responsibility of absorbing the sinful reaction of life of the disciple.
>
> At the present moment in our ISKCON campus politics and diplomacy has entered. Some of my beloved students on whom I counted very, very much have been involved in this matter influenced by Maya. As such there has been some activity which I consider as disrespectful. So I have decided to retire and divert attention to book writing and nothing more.

On July 31 Prabhupāda wrote Brahmānanda and Gargamuni, explaining why he was leaving for India:

> In order to set example to my other Sannyasi students I am personally going to Japan with a party of three other Sannyasi students. Although it is beyond my physical condition, still I am going out so that you may learn the responsibility of Sannyas. ...

> I am fervently appealing to you all not to create fracture in the solid body of the Society. Please work conjointly, without any personal ambition. That will help the cause.
>
> It is the injunction of the Vedas that the Spiritual Master should not be treated as ordinary man even sometimes the Spiritual Master behaves like ordinary man. It is the duty of the disciple to accept Him as a Superhuman Man. In the beginning of your letter your comparison of the soldier and the commander is very appropriate. We are on the Battlefield of Kurukshetra—one side Maya, the other side Krishna. So the regulative principles of a battlefield, namely to abide by the order of the commander, must be followed. Otherwise it is impossible to direct the fighting capacity of the soldiers and thus defeat the opposing elements. Kindly therefore take courage. Let things be rightly done so that our mission may be correctly pushed forward to come out victorious.

Prabhupāda wrote other letters revealing his plans to travel to India:

> Our life is very short. The Krishna consciousness movement is not meant for fulfilling one's personal ambition, but it is a serious movement for the whole world. I am therefore going to the Eastern hemisphere, beginning from Japan. We are going four in a party and all of us are Sannyasis. In this old age I am going with this party just to set an example to my disciples who have taken recently the Sannyas order.

In preparation for Prabhupāda's trip to India, Prabhupāda's secretary, Devānanda, now Devānanda Swami, asked him questions from the immigration form, mechanically reading the questions and filling in the answers as Prabhupāda replied. "Have you ever committed any criminal acts?" Devānanda asked, reading from the form.

Prabhupāda's eyes widened: "You are asking your spiritual master if he did anything criminal?" And he turned to Bhagavān: "You see, I am simply surrounded by people I cannot trust. It is a dangerous situation."

Prabhupāda sat in his garden the night before his departure. "Don't be disturbed," he told the disciples with him. "We are not going backward. We are going forward. I will reveal everything to you. I will rectify." His strong words and criticisms, he said, had been to enlighten his disciples, to warn them and show them the subtleties of *māyā*.

Karandhara mentioned that the temple leaders had arranged that only a few devotees go with Prabhupāda the next day to the airport. "Where did this idea come from?" Prabhupāda asked. "*Śrīmad-Bhāgavatam* instructs that when a saintly person leaves your company, all present should follow the departing vehicle as far as possible, until it is out of sight."

So the next day the devotees all accompanied Prabhupāda, chanting and dancing behind him through the long corridors of Los Angeles International Airport. After many months with them, he was now leaving. Devotees cried.

Prabhupāda, dressed in new garments, his head freshly shaven, looked effulgent. He sat in the departure lounge, head held high, as grave and unfathomable as ever. He was embarking on a new adventure for Lord Caitanya. He was old and might not return, he said, but his disciples should continue the Kṛṣṇa consciousness movement seriously. "If you follow this new schedule," he said, "you will keep *māyā* from attacking." And then he left them.

* * *

En route to Japan Prabhupāda stopped overnight in Hawaii. He stayed in a motel, and Gaurasundara and Govinda dāsī came to talk with him. Govinda dāsī wanted Prabhupāda to stay and install their Deities of Rādhā and Kṛṣṇa in the temple. If Gaurasundara agreed, Prabhupāda said, he would stay a few days longer to perform the Deity installation. "Let me consult," Gaurasundara replied. And the next day Prabhupāda flew on to Japan. From Japan Prabhupāda wrote Govinda dāsī:

> It is very encouraging to learn that people inquired about me and were eager to hear my speaking. I could have stayed one or two more days, there was no hurry, but you did not make any arrangement. I personally proposed to Gaurasundara that I shall install the Deities, and he replied that, "Let me consult." But he never informed me of the result of that consultation and with whom he had to consult. So this is the present situation in our ISKCON Society. It is clear that a great mischievous propaganda was lightly made and the effect has created a very unfavorable situation and I am very much afflicted in this connection. Still there is time to save the Society out of this mischievous propaganda and I hope all of you combine together to do the needful.

At the Tokyo airport Prabhupāda was greeted by executives of Dai Nippon Printing Company, the printers of *Kṛṣṇa, the Supreme Personality of Godhead* and the twenty thousand monthly copies of *Back to Godhead*. Prabhupāda and his entourage rode in a limousine, courtesy of Dai Nippon, to a small private apartment about forty-five minutes from the temple.

Prabhupāda had developed a severe cough and several other symptoms of ill health, due, he said, to his disciples' behavior. Yet despite his illness he would talk for hours of his concern for ISKCON, especially with his traveling G.B.C. secretary, Tamāla Kṛṣṇa.

Soon after their arrival in Japan, Prabhupāda's secretary received a disturbing call from a devotee attending the society-wide Janmāṣṭamī celebration at New Vrindaban. Four of the newly initiated *sannyāsīs* had arrived, the devotee said, and were teaching a strange philosophy. Devotees were confused. Prabhupāda had left America, the *sannyāsīs* were saying, because he had rejected his disciples. The *sannyāsīs* were blaming themselves and other disciples for not realizing that *Prabhupāda was actually Kṛṣṇa*!

When Prabhupāda heard this, he said, "That is why I did not go. I knew this would happen. This is impersonalism." He defined the Māyāvāda (impersonal) misconception of the *guru* and Kṛṣṇa. If one says that the *guru* is God, or if the *guru* himself says that he is God, that is Māyāvāda philosophy.

For the Māyāvādīs, spiritual realization is realization of one's identity with Brahman, the all-pervading spirit. Despite their austerities and their detachment from materialistic society, and despite their study of *Vedānta-sūtra* and the commentaries of Śaṅkara, they mistakenly think that Kṛṣṇa's body, name, pastimes, service, and devotees are all facets of *māyā*, or illusion; therefore they are called *Māyāvādīs.* A Māyāvāda spiritual master does not reveal to his disciple the holy name of Kṛṣṇa, the holy pastimes of Kṛṣṇa, or the transcendental form of Kṛṣṇa, since the Māyāvādī considers all these *māyā.* Instead, the *guru* explains the oneness of all things, teaching the disciple that the concept of separate existence and ego is illusion. The Māyāvādīs sometimes compare the *guru* to a ladder. One uses the ladder to reach a higher position, but if the ladder is no longer needed one kicks it away.

Coughing intermittently and speaking with physical discomfort, Prabhupāda explained the Māyāvādīs' dangerous misconceptions. The impersonalists held a cheap, mundane view of the *guru,* the *guru's* worship, and the *guru's* instructions. If one says that the *guru* is God and God is not a person, then it follows logically that the *guru* has no eternal personal relationship with his disciples. Ultimately the disciple will become equal to the *guru,* or in other words he will realize that he, too, is God.

Arguing from the Vedic scripture, Prabhupāda refuted the Māyāvādīs' claims. The individual souls, he said, are Kṛṣṇa's eternal servants, and this master-servant relationship is eternal. Service to Kṛṣṇa, therefore, is spiritual activity. Only by serving the *guru,* however, can a disciple fully revive his eternal relationship with Kṛṣṇa. The Vedic literature gives paramount importance to serving the spiritual master. He is the representative of God, the direct, manifest link to God. No one can approach God but through him. Lord Kṛṣṇa says, "Those who are directly My devotees are actually not My devotees. But those who are devotees of My servant (the spiritual master) are factually My devotees."

For hours Prabhupāda drilled his disciples. He would pose a Māyāvāda argument, then ask his disciples to defeat it. If they failed, he would defeat it himself. He stressed that the relationship between the spiritual master and disciple was eternal—not because the *guru* was Kṛṣṇa, but because he was the confidential *servant* of Kṛṣṇa, eternally. A bona fide spiritual master never says that he is Kṛṣṇa or that Kṛṣṇa is impersonal.

The devotees began to understand how the offenses of minimizing Śrīla Prabhupāda's position were products of Māyāvāda philosophy. For the Māyāvādī, to increase devotion to the *guru* is unnecessary; if individual relationships are all ultimately illusion, why increase the illusion? If the master-servant relationship is ultimately illusion, then the less the disciple sees his *guru* as master and himself as servant, the more he is advancing. The Māyāvāda philosophy was a subtle and insidious poison.

At least Prabhupāda had been spared the pain of being personally present in New Vrindaban to witness the Māyāvāda rantings of certain of his disciples and the appalling display of ignorance of most of the others. He had his small entourage and was on his way to preach in India. While here in Tokyo, he would try to obtain many *Back to Godhead* magazines and *Kṛṣṇa* books to take with him.

Prabhupāda observed Janmāṣṭamī at his apartment by having disciples read aloud to him from *Kṛṣṇa, the Supreme Personality of Godhead* throughout the day. If they kept reading, he said, they might be able to finish the book in one day. The devotees had decorated Prabhupāda's room with leaves and flowers strung from the ceiling and along the walls, and Prabhupāda sat on a thin mattress behind his low desk, hearing the pastimes of Kṛṣṇa. At 9 P.M., after fasting all day, the devotees were still reading to him when he asked if they would be able to finish the book by midnight. The devotees replied that they would not.

"Then you stop, and I will read." Prabhupāda opened a Sanskrit volume of the Tenth Canto of *Śrīmad-Bhāgavatam* and, for the next two hours, chanted the Sanskrit verses. "You cannot understand the Sanskrit," he said, "but I know you can feel. The verses are so potent that just by hearing one can be purified."

During the reading, Kīrtanānanda Swami and Kārttikeya Swami cooked a feast in the kitchen. At midnight the devotees served Śrīla Prabhupāda the Janmāṣṭamī feast. Taking only a few bites, he watched his disciples eat heartily.

The next day was Vyāsa-pūjā, Prabhupāda's seventy-fourth birthday, and he went to the Tokyo ISKCON temple. The temple was only two rooms—one for living, one for worshiping—with Japanese grass mats on the floor. Prabhupāda sat to the right of the altar, looking at Lord Jagannātha, while his disciples sat on the floor before him, singing *Gurv-aṣṭaka* prayers glorifying the spiritual master. None of them, however, knew exactly how to conduct the Vyāsa-pūjā ceremony, and after a while they ended the *kīrtana.* In the painfully awkward moments that followed, the devotees realized they were supposed to do something special. But what?

Prabhupāda appeared angry: "Don't you have *puṣpa-yātrā*? Isn't *prasādam* ready?" The devotees looked at one another. "This is not Vyāsa-pūjā," Prabhupāda said. "You have not been to Vyāsa-pūjā before? Don't you know how to celebrate the Vyāsa-pūjā, how to honor the spiritual master?" One of the *sannyāsīs* began to cry. "Tamāla Kṛṣṇa," Prabhupāda said, "didn't you see how I observed my Guru Mahārāja's birthday? Where is *puṣpa*?" (*Puṣpa* is Sanskrit for "flowers.")

Puṣpa? *Puṣpa*? Tamāla Kṛṣṇa decided Prabhupāda must mean *puṣpānna,* a fancy rice dish. "I'm not sure," he said.

"What kind of Vyāsa-pūjā is this with no *puṣpa*?" Prabhupāda asked.

"We can get some, Prabhupāda," Tamāla Kṛṣṇa offered.

Tamāla Kṛṣṇa grabbed Sudāmā. "Prabhupāda wants *prasādam.* He wants *puṣpānna* rice." They ran into the kitchen and hurriedly started the rice.

Meanwhile, in the temple the devotees struggled through their version of a Vyāsa-pūjā ceremony. Kīrtanānanda Swami stood and began to read aloud from the introduction of *Kṛṣṇa, the Reservoir of Pleasure,* which included a short biography of Prabhupāda. But Prabhupāda interrupted, scolding his disciples for concocting and for acting improperly. "If you don't know," he said, "then why didn't you ask me how to do this properly?"

The Japanese guests present didn't understand English, but they could see the spiritual master was disturbed. Prabhupāda explained that in devotional service everything must be done properly, according to the *paramparā* method, without concocting. "We will observe Vyāsa-pūjā again tomorrow," he said. "Come to my room. I will tell you what to do."

The next day, after a simple, traditional ceremony, the devotees felt ecstatic. Afterward they agreed: when one displeases his spiritual master, there is no happiness; but as soon as the spiritual master is pleased, the disciple becomes blissful.

The Janmāṣṭamī–Vyāsa-pūjā festival in New Vrindaban had become a nightmare. Hundreds of devotees had converged there from the East Coast, with many others from California and even Europe. They had come for a blissful festival but instead had found Śrīla Prabhupāda's newly initiated *sannyāsīs* expounding a devastating philosophy.

The *sannyāsīs,* speaking informally to groups here and there, would explain how the devotees had offended Prabhupāda and how he had subsequently withdrawn his mercy. The *sannyāsīs* revealed their special insights that Prabhupāda was actually God, that none of his disciples had recognized him as such, and that all of them, therefore, beginning with the *sannyāsīs,* were guilty of minimizing his position. And that was why Prabhupāda had left for India; he had "withdrawn his mercy" from his disciples.

The devotees were devastated. None of them knew what to say in reply. The *sannyāsīs,* by their preaching, had projected gloom everywhere, which was proper, they said; everyone should feel guilty and realize that they had lost the grace of their spiritual master. No use trying to cheer one another up by chanting Hare Kṛṣṇa or eating a feast; everyone should accept the bitter medicine.

Although Prabhupāda had given his disciples three volumes of *Śrīmad-Bhāgavatam,* as well as *Bhagavad-gītā As It Is, The Nectar of Devotion,*

Teachings of Lord Caitanya, and other literature, none of the devotees were well-versed in them. Many devotees wondered if the philosophy the *sannyāsīs* were preaching was correct, but none of them knew enough of the scriptures to immediately refute it. The devotees turned to the new G.B.C. men, Prabhupāda's appointed leaders and guardians of ISKCON. The G.B.C., along with other senior devotees, began carefully searching through Prabhupāda's books to ascertain exactly what he had said about the position of the spiritual master.

Then Hayagrīva announced that a letter had just arrived from Śrīla Prabhupāda in Tokyo. As soon as the devotees all gathered under the pavilion roof to hear, Hayagrīva read aloud: "My dear Sons and Daughters ..." and then Prabhupāda listed almost all the New Vrindaban residents. The devotees immediately felt a wave of hope. Just to hear Prabhupāda say "My dear Sons and Daughters" was a great relief.

Hayagrīva continued to read: "Please accept my blessings."

Prabhupāda hadn't rejected them!

The letter went on to say that Śrīla Prabhupāda was pleased with the work of the New Vrindaban devotees, and he promised to come and visit them. Soon he would send for other devotees to join him in India, he said. As he described what preaching in India would be like, the devotees became caught up in the momentum of Śrīla Prabhupāda's preaching spirit. They cheered. They felt blissful.

Then Prabhupāda specifically referred to the difficulty facing ISKCON: "Purge out of New Vrindaban the non-Vrindaban atmosphere that has entered." His letter turned the tide against the Māyāvāda teachings.

The G.B.C. then called a meeting of all disciples in the temple room. Reading selections from *The Nectar of Devotion,* they established that the spiritual master, although not God, should be honored as much as God because he is the confidential servant of God. Several senior devotees spoke their heart's convictions, citing examples from their association with Prabhupāda to prove that he had not rejected them—he was too kind. The *sannyāsīs* might *feel* rejected because of their own guilt, someone said, but they should not project their guilt on others.

The false teachings, however, had dealt a blow from which many devotees would need time to recover. Newcomers at the festival were especially unsettled. But the cloud of gloom that had hung over New Vrindaban now lifted, thanks to Śrīla Prabhupāda's timely letter.

The *sannyāsīs* admitted their confusion. The G.B.C. then phoned Kīrtanānanda Swami in Tokyo and told him that Prabhupāda's letter had resolved most of the problems, but that the *sannyāsīs* still held their misconceptions. Hearing this, Prabhupāda felt his suspicions confirmed.

Certain disciples had been contaminated by the poisonous philosophy from India. Consequently, material desires for power and control had overwhelmed them, even in Prabhupāda's presence.

Turning to Tamāla Kṛṣṇa, Sudāmā, and the three *sannyāsīs* with him, Prabhupāda asked what they thought should be done. With the previous day's philosophic drilling still sharp in their minds, they suggested that anyone teaching Māyāvāda philosophy should not be allowed to stay within ISKCON. Prabhupāda agreed. If these *sannyāsīs* continued to preach Māyāvāda philosophy, he said, they should not be allowed to stay in his temples but should go out and "preach" on their own. Tamāla Kṛṣṇa conveyed this message to the G.B.C. in the U.S., and Prabhupāda was satisfied that the problem would be adjusted. He had created his G.B.C. to handle such matters.

On September 2 Prabhupāda wrote Haṁsadūta in Germany:

> Regarding the poisonous effect in our Society, it is a fact and I know where from this poison tree has sprung up and how it affected practically the whole Society in a very dangerous form. But it does not matter. Prahlad Maharaj was administered poison, but it did not act. Similarly Lord Krishna and the Pandavas were administered poison and it did not act. I think in the same parampara system that the poison administered to our Society will not act if some of our students are as good as Prahlad Maharaj. I have therefore given the administrative power to the Governing Body Commission.

To Hayagrīva in New Vrindaban Prabhupāda wrote:

> I am very glad to know that the GBC is actively working to rectify the subversive situation which has been weakening the very foundation of our Society. All you members of the GBC please always remain very vigilant in this connection so that our Society's growth may go on unimpeded by such poisonous elements. Your preaching in New Vrindaban as well as intensified study of our literatures with seriousness is very much encouraging. Please continue this program with vigour and reestablish the solidity of our movement.
>
> From the beginning I was strongly against the impersonalists, and all my books stressed on this point. So my oral instruction as well as my books are

> all at your service. Now you GBC consult them and get a clear and strong idea. Then there will be no more disturbance. The four Sannyasis may bark, but still the caravan will pass.

Prabhupāda wrote Satsvarūpa in Boston:

> I am very glad to know that you are not affected by the propaganda of the Sannyasis that I am displeased with all the members of the Society—I am never displeased with any member.

The worst was over, Prabhupāda thought. For months this problem had upset him and his writing. Relentlessly he had instructed his disciples, for their own benefit and for the benefit of his movement. The disease had taken its toll, and that was unfortunate. But the devotees were being forced to turn to Prabhupāda's books and apply their teachings, and that was the positive outcome. Now they should clearly understand the position of the spiritual master and never again be led astray by false philosophies or sentiment.

Prabhupāda's main business in Tokyo was with Dai Nippon. Considering him an important author and a venerable religious monk, they had provided him a car and apartment. Each morning they sent a private car to drive Prabhupāda to Imperial Palace Park, where he could take his morning walk. Prabhupāda liked the neatly planted trees and gravel walks, and he appreciated the habits of the Japanese people. As he would pass, elderly ladies would bow to him from the waist, and others would fold their hands respectfully, acknowledging his being a holy man.

On the morning of Prabhupāda's meeting with Dai Nippon, he came out of his apartment with Tamāla Kṛṣṇa and Devānanda Mahārāja and got into the back seat of a Dai Nippon company car. The car proceeded through the early-morning streets, and Prabhupāda chanted his Gāyatrī *mantra* silently.

A Dai Nippon junior executive escorted Prabhupāda and his two disciples into an elevator and up to a spacious room with a long conference table. Prabhupāda's guide cordially offered him a seat at the table, and Prabhupāda sat down, with Tamāla Kṛṣṇa and Devānanda Mahārāja on either side. Soon there entered Dai Nippon's six top executives, including the corporation president. Each stood behind his respective chair, and each in turn, beginning with the president, bowed slightly from the waist and presented his calling card. Addressing Prabhupāda as "Your Divine Grace," they introduced themselves, announced their posts, and took their seats.

"We are very honored to have you here," the president began. "You are a great religious author, and it is our great privilege to be publishing your books." After the president had spoken briefly, tea was served. Prabhupāda requested hot milk. Conversation was informal, and Prabhupāda spoke of the importance of his mission and his Kṛṣṇa conscious literature. No one discussed business, however, and the Dai Nippon executives soon excused themselves. They would meet again the next morning.

When Prabhupāda was again alone in the room with his disciples and the junior executive who had escorted him, he asked the young Japanese, "So what is your goal in life?" By way of answer, the man gathered up all the business cards that lay scattered before Prabhupāda on the table and stacked them, with the president's on top, then the first vice-president's, and so on, putting his own card in its place on the bottom. He then dramatically removed his card from the bottom of the stack and slapped it on top—a graphic answer to Prabhupāda's question.

Prabhupāda smiled. To become president of the company, he said, was temporary. All material life was temporary. He explained on the basis of *Bhagavad-gītā* that the body was temporary and that the self was eternal. All the identities and positions people hankered after were based on the bodily conception of life and would one day be frustrated. The purpose of life, therefore, was not to become the temporary president of a temporary corporation within the temporary material world, but to realize the eternal soul's relationship with the Supreme Personality of Godhead and gain eternal life. Prabhupāda spoke for almost half an hour while the man listened politely.

At the next day's meeting, negotiations began. The conference room was different, the table smaller, and three of Dai Nippon's international sales representatives sat opposite Prabhupāda. Prabhupāda presented his price: $1.35 per book.

"Oh, Your Divine Grace," one of the salesmen exclaimed, "it is not possible for us to give this price. We will lose too heavily. We cannot afford it." They explained their position, quoting paper costs and other expenses.

Prabhupāda began to speak about his mission. ISKCON's book distribution, he said, was a charitable work for the benefit of all humanity. ISKCON distributed these books for whatever donations people were able to make, and he received no profit or royalties. It was spiritual education, the most valuable literature. "In any case," Prabhupāda said in closing, "you deal with my secretary in this regard." And he sat back in his chair. The burden was on Tamāla Kṛṣṇa.

Tamāla Kṛṣṇa began by saying that Prabhupāda had been too kind, because ISKCON could actually never pay such a high price. He then quoted a price forty cents lower per book than Prabhupāda's quote. "Mr. Tamāla,"—the salesmen were again upset—"please reconsider your point." A polite argument ensued.

Suddenly Prabhupāda interrupted, presenting himself as an impartial third party. He said he would settle the difference that had arisen between his secretary and the salesmen. "I have heard both sides," he said, "and I feel that the price should be $1.25 per book. That's all."

"Yes, Your Divine Grace," the salesmen agreed, "that is right."

After further negotiations, Prabhupāda agreed on a contract that included a reprint of Volume One and a first printing of Volume Two of *Kṛṣṇa, the Supreme Personality of Godhead,* two issues of *Back to Godhead,* a Hindi issue of *Back to Godhead,* and a new book, *Śrī Īśopaniṣad.* ISKCON had to pay only $5,000 cash, and Dai Nippon would deliver everything on credit.

Prabhupāda held a feast at his apartment for the Dai Nippon executives, who especially liked the *samosās* and *pakorās.* They presented Prabhupāda with a watch and continued to see to his comfort during his stay in Tokyo. Prabhupāda also met a Canadian-born Japanese boy, Bruce, who was seriously interested in Kṛṣṇa consciousness. Prabhupāda invited him to come and join him in India, and the boy eagerly agreed.

CHAPTER THIRTY-TWO

India: Dancing White Elephants

Calcutta
August 29, 1970

FOR THE FIRST time in almost three years, Prabhupāda returned to India—to Calcutta, his hometown. Although it was late and the journey from Tokyo had been twelve hours, Prabhupāda felt happy as he descended the stairway from the airplane. Acyutānanda and Jayapatāka, his only American disciples in India, were standing on the airfield, and as they saw him approaching in his saffron silk robes, they bowed down. Prabhupāda smiled and embraced them. They ushered him to a flower-bedecked car and accompanied him to the terminal building, where he entered the V.I.P. lounge.

Some of Prabhupāda's Godbrothers and old Calcutta friends were present to receive him, and a *kīrtana* party from the Chaitanya Math was chanting. The reception was large and festive. As the room resounded with Hare Kṛṣṇa, Prabhupāda took his seat. The sound of the *kīrtana,* the many pictures of Kṛṣṇa, and the smell of incense and jasmine flowers combined with Prabhupāda's transcendental presence to transform the drab airport into a heavenly scene.

Indians crowded forward to place flower garlands around Prabhupāda's neck, and as the garlands piled higher, Prabhupāda removed them. But the garlands kept coming, and again they piled up, almost covering

Prabhupāda's face. The American devotees watched in fascination as the Bengali *brahmacārīs* played their *mṛdaṅgas* with exotic rhythms. The people in the crowd pressed in closer to touch Prabhupāda's feet and ask his blessings, and Prabhupāda smiled, seeming quite at home. When the *kīrtana* ended, he began to speak.

"I am coming back to the city after three years. Hare Kṛṣṇa. I have been around the world and have found that happiness and peace cannot be established in this world by materialistic advancement. I have seen Japan, which is highly advanced in machines and technology. Yet there is no real happiness there. But the people of India, even if they do not understand the significance of *saṅkīrtana,* they enjoy listening to it. My advice to the Indians is that if you advance only in science and technology, without paying attention to *hari-nāma,* then you will remain forever backward. There is tremendous strength in *hari-nāma. ...*"

Reporter: "You have said, and I quote, 'Even communism, if it is without *kṛṣṇa-nāma,* is void.' Why do you say that?"

Prabhupāda: "Why do you refer to communism in particular? Without Kṛṣṇa consciousness, everything is void. Whatever you do, Kṛṣṇa must remain in the center. Whether you are communist or capitalist or anything else—it doesn't matter. We want to see whether your activities are centered around Kṛṣṇa."

Reporter: "Right now there is too much turmoil in Bengal. What is your advice to us at this time?"

Prabhupāda: "My advice is to chant Hare Kṛṣṇa. This is the piece of advice to both the capitalists and the communists. All animosity between them will cease completely, and all their problems will be solved, if they take this advice."

The crowd, affirming Prabhupāda's words, began to shout, "*Sādhu*! *Sādhu*!"

Prabhupāda sat in the back seat, on his way from the airport to the home of Mr. Das Gupta on Hindustan Road. Outside the car window the familiar scenes of Calcutta passed by. For the newcomers riding with him, however, Calcutta was foreign and unfamiliar. Gaunt, loitering cows and street dogs, small horses pulling huge loads, barefoot ricksha-wālās, open shops with exotic foods, dense crowds of pedestrians, the sultry heat, and the incredible traffic—these, although familiar to Prabhupāda, plunged the disciples who had flown with him into culture shock. Tamāla Kṛṣṇa looked nervously at the driver, who swerved in and out of traffic, honking his horn. Prabhupāda laughed softly. "Tamāla Kṛṣṇa, how do you like this driving?"

Acyutānanda and Jayapatāka, however, were acclimatized to Calcutta and had learned to appreciate its culture. They had met high-class, cultured Bengalis who accepted them as *sādhus* despite their American birth. They had preached in many homes and had attracted curious crowds by chanting in public. They had not, however, achieved a solid foothold for ISKCON. But now Prabhupāda had come to change that. He would preach wonderfully, just as he had done in America, and his disciples were eager to serve as his instruments. He would be their vital force, their inspiration, for he was empowered by Lord Caitanya.

Prabhupāda reached the home of Mr. Das Gupta at almost midnight. Many people wanted to see him, and when Devānanda Mahārāja tried to turn them away Prabhupāda said, "No, no, let them come in." Prabhupāda's sister, Bhavatarini, arrived with an array of special dishes she had cooked.

"We can't eat now," one of the *sannyāsīs* protested. "It's late at night."

"No," Prabhupāda said, "we must eat everything. Whatever my sister cooks, we have to eat. This is her favorite activity. She likes to cook for me and feed me. Everyone must take *prasādam*." The devotees at the Chaitanya Math had also cooked a feast, and as Prabhupāda was honoring the *prasādam* prepared by his sister the *prasādam* from the Chaitanya Math arrived. He took a little and induced his followers to eat sumptuously.

It was 1:00 A.M. Prabhupāda sat in his room with Acyutānanda, Jayapatāka, and Devānanda Mahārāja. He explained how irresponsible letters from his disciples in India had perpetrated within ISKCON a deep misunderstanding of the spiritual master's position. He quoted the verse *sākṣād-dharitvena samasta-śāstraiḥ* and explained it: "The *guru* is on an equal level with Hari, the Supreme Personality of Godhead. He is not God, but he is the dearmost servant of God."

Prabhupāda continued preaching to his disciples, clearing away any misconceptions about the spiritual master's position. All the past unpleasant events, he said, were now being rectified. The devotees should continue working together with new life and vigor.

Acyutānanda asked Prabhupāda if he could take *sannyāsa.* The Indians, he said, would respect a *sannyāsī* more. Prabhupāda agreed that *sannyāsa* would help Acyutānanda's preaching, and he said that Jayapatāka should also take *sannyāsa.* The ceremony would be in a week, on Rādhāṣṭamī.

The *Amrita Bazar Patrika* carried a front-page news story of Prabhupāda's arrival. A photo showed Prabhupāda walking, with his hand in his bead bag, surrounded by young *sannyāsīs* carrying *daṇḍas.*

> Many VIP's have come to Dumdum Airport before but never have we seen gaiety and celebrations of this magnitude. ... It was difficult to imagine that he was 75 years old because he was completely fresh after this long journey. With a little smile on his face, he blessed one and all with the word, "Hari Bol!"

Prabhupāda wrote to the devotees in Japan:

> In India, from the very moment we stepped down from the airplane, there is good propaganda work going on. ... The boy Bruce is improving and becoming more interested. He has now sacrificed his hairs for Kṛṣṇa—that is a good sign.

Calcutta was in political turmoil. A group of Communist terrorists, the Naxalites, had been rioting, murdering prominent businessmen and threatening the lives of many others. Many wealthy Marwari industrialists were leaving the city for Delhi and Bombay. Aside from the terrorists, Bengali college students were growing unruly. But the older people of West Bengal, comprising most of Prabhupāda's visitors, were alarmed by the violence and unrest. The only shelter, Prabhupāda told them, was Kṛṣṇa.

> People are in very much perturbed condition. All of them are expecting me to do something for ameliorating the situation, but I am simply advising them to chant Hare Kṛṣṇa because this transcendental sound is the only panacea for all material diseases.

Prabhupāda saw no need to fabricate a special program for the social problems of Calcutta. Chanting Hare Kṛṣṇa was "the only panacea for all material diseases." The question was how best to use his American disciples to give this panacea to the Indians. Prabhupāda had his party of ten devotees, and he had asked his leaders in the West for twenty more within the month. He had ordered $60,000 worth of books and magazines from Dai Nippon, and his *sannyāsīs* were going daily into the streets to perform *kīrtana.*

The *saṅkīrtana* party was getting a good response. Shavenheaded Westerners, wearing *śikhās,* Vaiṣṇava *tilaka,* and saffron robes, playing *karatālas* and *mṛdaṅgas,* chanting Hare Kṛṣṇa with heart and soul, quoting Sanskrit verses from *Bhagavad-gītā,* affirming Lord Kṛṣṇa to be the Supreme Personality of Godhead—for the Bengalis this was sensational, and hundreds would gather to watch. Prabhupāda knew the great appeal his disciples would have; everyone would want to see them. He therefore affectionately called them his "dancing white elephants."

These same devotees, who had grown to love chanting Hare Kṛṣṇa in the streets of San Francisco, Los Angeles, and New York, were now going into an exhausting heat never encountered in America and chanting on Dalhousie Square for several hours daily. Crowds would press in closely, sometimes teasing, laughing, or scoffing, but more often looking on with deep amazement.

Prabhupāda's idea was that when Indians saw young Western people adopting the principles of Kṛṣṇa consciousness the faith of the Indians in their own culture would increase. Prabhupāda explained to his disciples how formerly, during the time of Mahārāja Yudhiṣṭhira, India had been a Kṛṣṇa conscious state. For the last thousand years, however, India had been under foreign subjugation, first under the Moguls and then under the British. As a result, the intelligentsia and, to a lesser degree, the masses of India had lost respect for their own culture. They were now pursuing the materialistic goals of the West, and they saw this as more productive and more practical than religion, which was only sentimental.

Westerners living as renounced Vaiṣṇavas could, as Prabhupāda was well aware, turn the heads and hearts of the Indians and help them regain faith in their own lost culture. It was not a material tactic, however, but a spiritual strength. Prabhupāda stressed that the devotees must be pure in their actions; this purity would be their force.

The chanting in Dalhousie Square and along Chowranghee had gone on for about ten days when Prabhupāda decided to stop it. The street *kīrtana,* although an excellent method of preaching, was not the most effective method for India, he said. There were many professional *kīrtana* groups in Bengal, and Prabhupāda didn't want his disciples to be seen like that—as professional performers or beggars. He wanted them to preach in a way that would bring them closer to the more intelligent, respectable Indians, and he unfolded his new plan.

He called it "Life Membership." His disciples would invite Indians interested in supporting and associating with ISKCON to become members. A membership fee of 1,111 rupees would entitle the member to many benefits, such as copies of Śrīla Prabhupāda's books and free accommodation in ISKCON centers around the world.

Speaking one evening in a private home before a group of wealthy businessmen, Prabhupāda initiated his life membership program. After lecturing, he invited his audience to become ISKCON life members, and several Calcutta merchants immediately signed.

B. L. Jaju: *I was really overwhelmed by the simplicity of Prabhupāda's nature. He told me how he had been carrying on his regular business when his* guru *had told him that four hundred years back Caitanya Mahāprabhu had said that Hare Rāma, Hare Kṛṣṇa would be chanted all throughout the world. He said that that was the job given to him by his spiritual master and that he would have to go to America and do it.*

I found no snobbery in him. He was very simple. And he was telling, as if my brother was telling to me, simply how he went to U.S.A., how he started, and how gradually he planned to have this Kṛṣṇa consciousness throughout the world.

Seeing his disciples who had changed their lives, I began to think, "Why not I? In my humble way, I should do something, without worrying what other people are doing." I found that imperceptibly he was affecting my life. My wife and even my son were really surprised when they found that these white people, whom we thought could never turn to Kṛṣṇa consciousness, had changed so much. So we thought we also must try to follow better the teaching of the Gītā.

Whether at a life member's home, at a formal lecture before a large audience, or in his own room, Prabhupāda continued speaking from *Bhagavad-gītā* and *Śrīmad-Bhāgavatam* about Kṛṣṇa and Kṛṣṇa consciousness. Of this he never tired. A guest would ask a question, and

Prabhupāda would begin his answer by having one of his disciples read a relevant verse from the *Gītā.* Then he would explain it. If the guest was unsubmissive and wanted to challenge, Prabhupāda would argue.

Sitting at his low desk, occasionally drinking water from his *loṭā,* Prabhupāda would talk hour after hour. The temperature rose to 100 degrees, and as Prabhupāda sat in his room preaching, he wore no shirt, only a simple top cloth, which left his arms, shoulders, and part of his chest bare. Sometimes the devotees sitting with him would be sick or sleepy or otherwise inattentive, and sometimes they would excuse themselves, returning hours later to find him still preaching. Guests also came and went. Yet except for a nap after lunch, Prabhupāda kept preaching, often throughout the day and into the night. Never bored with his subject matter, he would speak as long as there was an interested hearer.

His audiences varied. Sometimes he would speak to a room of husbands and wives, all cultured and well dressed, and sometimes he would speak to one lone old man. Sometimes his audience listened quietly, or argued, or even when appreciating showed their misunderstanding. Sometimes a guest would ask him why he criticized Bengal's reputed saints and politicians, and he would explain on the basis of *Bhagavad-gītā* that the real *sādhu* always glorifies Kṛṣṇa.

Prabhupāda often related his preaching to events of particular interest to his audience, such as Calcutta's political unrest or the downfall of Vedic culture. Yet his concern for local affairs was only the practical necessity of the moment, for he was beyond India. He was thinking of people, places, and activities all around the world. In answering his letters, he would deeply ponder matters in England, Australia, Hawaii, or New Vrindaban. And beyond this, he would always be thinking of Kṛṣṇa. He wanted to glorify Kṛṣṇa throughout the world; India happened to be his present field.

The devotees in India had the privilege of closely observing Prabhupāda in his preaching. His superior tolerance and kindness both inspired them and, by contrast, exposed to them their own inadequacies. As newcomers to India, the devotees were still greatly involved with the practical affairs of living in Calcutta. Weather, disease, and culture shock distracted their minds from Kṛṣṇa consciousness. But Prabhupāda's presence, his preaching, and his example reminded them that reality was beyond the body.

Sometimes the devotees criticized certain of Prabhupāda's visitors.

They met Indians who sat with Prabhupāda and presented a facade of godliness but who later smoked cigarettes and showed other signs of low character. Once a group of devotees complained to Prabhupāda about these hypocritical Indians, but Prabhupāda told them the story of the bee and the fly. The bee, he explained, always looks for honey, and the fly for a nasty sore or infection. The devotee should be like the honeybee and see the good in others, not like the fly, looking for the faults.

Prabhupāda's disciples discovered that the best way to learn to live in India was to follow exactly what Prabhupāda did. When taking *prasādam* with him at someone's home, they would eat the same foods as he, and in the same order. When he would finish, they would finish; and when he would wash his hands, they would wash. Life in India was strange, even bewildering, and Prabhupāda's disciples did not have Prabhupāda's vision of his mission in India. But they were following him, like little ducks, wherever he went.

As the devotees came closer to Prabhupāda and witnessed more of his unique qualities, they came to love him more than ever. Sitting in his room on a white cushion and leaning back on the white bolster, Prabhupāda appeared golden-hued and regal, despite his simple surroundings. The devotees could see that he was unaffected by his surroundings, whether in Los Angeles, where he had lived comfortably amid opulence, or in Calcutta. He was at home in India, but he was not just another Indian, not even just another Indian *sādhu*. He was unique. And he was theirs.

* * *

From Prabhupāda's first day in Calcutta he had thought of going to Māyāpur, the sacred birthplace of Lord Caitanya. Bhaktivinoda Ṭhākura, father of Śrīla Prabhupāda's spiritual master and pioneer in spreading Lord Caitanya's teachings beyond India, had longed for the day when Americans and Europeans would join with their Bengali brothers in Māyāpur, chanting the holy names. Prabhupāda wanted to purchase land, establish a Māyāpur center for his Western disciples, and fulfill the dream of his spiritual predecessors. He had written to one of his Godbrothers,

> I wish to go to Mayapur to pay my respects to our Beloved Spiritual Master His Divine Grace Sri Srila Prabhupada as well as to complete the purchase

> of the land. So if Jagmohan Prabhu will accompany us to finish this transaction it will be very kind of him and I hope you will kindly request him to accompany us.

The followers of Lord Caitanya accept Māyāpur, one hundred and ten miles north of Calcutta, to be identical with Vṛndāvana. Five thousand years ago Lord Kṛṣṇa lived in Vṛndāvana, performing His childhood pastimes, and five hundred years ago Lord Kṛṣṇa appeared in Māyāpur as Lord Caitanya. For the Gauḍīya Vaiṣṇavas, therefore, Māyāpur and Vṛndāvana are the two most dear and sacred places on earth. What better place for ISKCON to have its world headquarters than in Māyāpur! But despite various attempts over the past several years, Śrīla Prabhupāda had still not acquired property there.

He had gone to Māyāpur with Acyutānanda in 1967, seen a plot of land, and asked Acyutānanda to try and get it. But Acyutānanda and the Muhammadan owner had never reached an agreement. Some of Prabhupāda's Godbrothers had temples and property in Māyāpur, but they wouldn't help. Some even seemed to be working against him. When Prabhupāda had written one of his Godbrothers in Māyāpur asking him to help Acyutānanda secure land, the Godbrother's secretary had replied that he was unable to do so. The secretary had remarked, "One must be very fortunate to get land in Māyāpur."

Prabhupāda criticized his Godbrothers' uncooperative spirit. He was becoming impatient. "Why are we not able to get the land in Māyāpur?" he asked his disciples. "This is dragging on for three hundred years!" Again he wrote one of his Godbrothers.

> Regarding propagating the Name of Sri Mayapur as Birthplace of Lord Caitanya, it is going on regularly in our different literatures and books. If you kindly take the trouble of coming here conveniently, I can show you how we are giving publicity to the Birthsite of Lord Caitanya. Perhaps you know that I begged from His Holiness Sripad Tirtha Maharaj a little piece of land at Mayapur for constructing a home for my Western disciples, but he refused the proposal. Srila Bhaktivinode Thakur wanted that the American and European devotees would come to Mayapur, and the prophecy is now fulfilled. Unfortunately they are loitering in the streets of Calcutta without having a suitable place at Mayapur. Do you think it is all right?

Accompanied by a small party of men, Prabhupāda took the train to Navadvīpa, just across the Ganges from Māyāpur. There they were met by members of the Devananda Math. Riding in rickshas to the Devananda Math, the devotees were charmed by the rural atmosphere of Navadvīpa. Everything was lush from the rainy season, and the devotees found their romantic expectations of India now being fulfilled as they proceeded along roads lined with tropical vegetation. At the Devananda Math Prabhupāda and his disciples were given special *prasādam* and good accommodations.

Then the rains returned. Day after day the rains came, and the Ganges rose higher and higher, until crossing the swift river into Māyāpur became impossible. Since the rains were not likely to abate soon, Prabhupāda decided to leave. He and his disciples boarded an early-morning train to Calcutta.

The tracks were flooded. Repeatedly the train had to stop—once for more than eight hours. The heat and the crowds of passengers constantly passing through the car made the wait torturous for the devotees. Prabhupāda asked one of his disciples to take a ricksha and try to arrange better transportation. Nothing was available. At last the train continued toward Calcutta, only to stop at the next station, where all the passengers changed to another train. Finally Prabhupāda reached Calcutta and Mr. Das Gupta's home.

"Maybe Lord Caitanya does not want us to establish our headquarters in Māyāpur," Prabhupāda said. The two purposes in his mind—establishing a place in Calcutta and purchasing land in Māyāpur—he had not accomplished.

Prabhupāda continued holding programs in people's homes and talking with guests in his room. One day a Mr. Dandharia visited Prabhupāda and mentioned Bombay's upcoming Sadhu Samaj, a gathering of the most important *sādhus* in India. It was to be held at Chowpatti Beach and promised to be a big affair. Mr. Dandharia requested Prabhupāda to attend, and Prabhupāda accepted.

* * *

Bombay
October 1970

Responding to Śrīla Prabhupāda's request for more disciples to join him in India, a group of twenty American devotees traveled to Brussels and took an inexpensive flight aboard a propeller-driven craft to Bombay. At the airport, while the devotees were wondering where they should go, Mr. Kailash Seksaria, a wealthy Bombay businessman and nephew of Mr. Dandharia, approached them with a letter from Prabhupāda. Mr. Seksaria had arranged for several cars, and he escorted the devotees to his home in an affluent Bombay residential area on Marine Drive. He fed them and provided them with living quarters.

Two days later a telegram arrived informing the devotees and their host that Prabhupāda would be arriving the next day. Prabhupāda arrived at the Bombay airport and, after an enthusiastic reception, rode with Mr. Seksaria to his home.

Marine Drive runs along the seashore, and the houses lining it belong to the very rich. Mr. Seksaria's residence was seven stories, and he offered Śrīla Prabhupāda the first floor, with its large rooms overlooking the Arabian Sea.

Bombay, Prabhupāda said, was India's most materialistic city. It was the nation's movie capital and the city where, more than in any other Indian city, the people wore Western dress. The "gateway to India," it boasted the most industries, the most businesses, and the most billboards. It was a cosmopolitan melting pot of cultures and religions but had none of the Naxalite terrorism of Calcutta or the heavy political atmosphere of New Delhi. Nor did it have the aristocratic families who worshiped Lord Caitanya and His *saṅkīrtana* movement. But it had its own advantages for preaching, Prabhupāda said. It was a city of wealth, with many pious citizens who were intelligent and quick to adopt a good idea. He predicted Bombay would be a favorable city for Kṛṣṇa consciousness.

Prabhupāda's first Bombay preaching engagement was at a gathering of *sādhus,* a *paṇḍāl* in an open field just a few blocks from Mr. Seksaria's home. Prabhupāda's disciples had also been invited, and they arrived several hours before Prabhupāda. The array of Indian *sādhus,* sitting onstage in long rows, startled the devotees. Some of the *sādhus* were bearded, some shavenheaded, some with long matted hair and holding tridents, some covered with ashes, some adorned with beads and clay markings. The devotees were amazed, and many of the *sādhus,* on seeing the white-skinned Vaiṣṇavas, were also amazed.

When the devotees came onstage and began their *kīrtana,* the audience responded by clapping in rhythm and chanting. Afterward, on the advice of Mr. Seksaria, the devotees took their *kīrtana* out into the streets, and many in the audience followed.

That evening the devotees returned to the *paṇḍāl* with Prabhupāda. Prabhupāda sat on a raised platform, and his disciples sat at his feet. After having three of his disciples speak in English, Prabhupāda spoke in Hindi, while the audience of more than five hundred listened silently. After his lecture he came down from the platform, and a crowd gathered around him, touching his feet and following him to his car.

When Prabhupāda heard from his disciples of their spontaneous *kīrtana* through the streets of Bombay, he said they should go to the busiest bazaars and chant daily. So they did. Wherever large numbers of people gathered, the devotees would go and chant. They were strong, youthful, exuberant, and faithful, and they would chant in the streets for three or four hours each day.

Although Prabhupāda did not physically go into the streets chanting with his disciples, he was with them by his instructions and by his presence before they went out in the morning and when they returned in the evening. They were chanting because he had told them to. And they knew that chanting was the natural activity of the soul; everyone should chant. The devotees knew that at the end of life they would go back home, back to Godhead. And better than that, at the end of the day they would go back to Marine Drive to Prabhupāda, who would smile and encourage them.

Radio stations and newspapers took note of the Western devotees chanting in the city. One article appeared in the October 10 edition of the *Times of India:*

> A group of Americans, including women with babes in arms, belonging to the International Society for Krishna Consciousness (ISKCON) has been moving around Bombay during the past few days chanting Hare Krishna Hare Krishna, Krishna Krishna Hare Hare, or Hare Rama Hare Rama, Rama Rama Hare Hare, to the accompaniment of cymbals, castanets, and drums (mridangams).
>
> ... Can the materialistic West, or at any rate, a microscopic part of it, have turned at last to embrace the spiritualism of the east? I met several of the Kirtan-chanting Americans (who have come here to attend the seventh

All-India Conference at the Bharat Sadhu Samaj which begins here today) and was at once struck by their sincerity and utter surrender to the cult they have adopted. The Vaishnavas of Mathura could not be so guileless I thought, as this band of Bhakti enthusiasts.

* * *

The sand of Chowpatti Beach was fine and clean. The audience numbered in the thousands. *Sādhus* sat onstage, Prabhupāda and his followers among them. It was twilight. The sky above the Arabian Sea was cloudy, and a pleasant breeze was stirring.

There had already been two lectures expounding the Māyāvāda philosophy, and now it was time for Prabhupāda to speak—the last scheduled speaker of the evening. The audience was eager to hear him; his accomplishments in the West had caused great curiosity, especially now that he had arrived in Bombay and his devotees were chanting daily in public. Prabhupāda's disciples, bored and exasperated by the preceding two hours of Hindi oratory, could scarcely wait any longer for Prabhupāda to speak. But Prabhupāda, instead of addressing the audience, turned to his disciples and said, "Begin chanting."

As soon as the devotees began the *kīrtana,* little Sarasvatī stood and began to dance. Following her, the other devotees rose and began to dance. As the *kīrtana* came alive with *mṛdaṅgas* and *karatālas,* the dancing and chanting of the devotees seemed to disturb some of the *sādhus* onstage, who rose one by one and left. The audience, however, responded enthusiastically, many of them standing and clapping. After five minutes of ecstatic *kīrtana,* the devotees spontaneously jumped down onto the sand and headed toward the audience. Thousands in the crowd rose to their feet and began to move along with the devotees in a dance, backward and forward.

Indians began crying in uncontrolled happiness, overwhelmed by the genuine *kṛṣṇa-bhakti* of these foreigners. Never before had such a thing happened. Policemen and press reporters joined in the chanting and dancing. Chowpatti Beach was in an uproar of Hare Kṛṣṇa *kīrtana,* as Prabhupāda and his disciples showed the potency of Lord Caitanya's *saṅkīrtana* movement.

After about ten minutes the *kīrtana* ended, though a tumultuous unrest pervaded the talkative crowd. Fifteen minutes elapsed before all the people returned to their seats and the program could continue. The devotees had left the stage and taken their seats on the ground level, leaving Prabhupāda alone onstage. Prabhupāda's voice echoed over the public-address system.

"Ladies and gentlemen, I was requested to speak in Hindi, but I am not very much accustomed to speak in Hindi. Therefore, the authorities in this meeting have allowed me to speak in English. I hope you will follow me, because it is Bombay and most people will be speaking English. The problem is, as this evening's speaker, His Holiness Swami Akhandanandaji spoke to you, how we can make everyone accustomed to take up good habits—*sad-ācāra*? I think in this age, Kali-yuga, there are many faults." Prabhupāda went on to explain the power of Lord Caitanya's movement to clean the hearts of everyone. He referred to the two great rogues whom Lord Caitanya had delivered, Jagāi and Mādhāi.

"Now we are saving, wholesale, Jagāis and Mādhāis. Therefore, if we want peace, if we want to be situated on the *sad-ācāra* platform, then we must spread the *hari-nāma mahā-mantra* all over the world. And it has been practically proven. The American and European Vaiṣṇavas who have come here, who have chanted Hare Kṛṣṇa *mantra*—they were cowflesh eaters, they were drunkards, they were illicit sex mongers, they were all kinds of gamblers. But having taken to this Kṛṣṇa consciousness movement, they have given up everything abominable. *Sad-ācāra* has come automatically. They are no more meat-eaters, they are no more gamblers, they are no more illicit sex mongers, they are no more intoxicators. They do not even take tea, they do not even take coffee, they do not even smoke, which I think is very rare to be found in India. But they have given up. Why? Because they have taken to this Kṛṣṇa consciousness."

Prabhupāda ended his talk after about five minutes.

"I do not feel that I have to say very much. You can see what is the result of Kṛṣṇa consciousness. It is not something artificial. It is there in everyone. I have not done anything magical. But this Kṛṣṇa consciousness is present in all of us. We simply have to revive it."

The audience responded with cheers and a great round of applause. Prabhupāda, with greater force and eloquence than the long-winded Māyāvādīs, had shown the essence of spiritual life—ecstatic chanting of the holy names. And he had offered the living testimony of his American disciples.

For the next week, Prabhupāda and his disciples were the talk of Bombay, and they began receiving many invitations to speak and perform *kīrtana* throughout the city. The *Times Weekly's* coverage of the Sadhu Samaj spotlighted the memorable presence of Śrīla Prabhupāda and his disciples.

> A group of twenty Americans, members of the Hare Krishna delegation, took over the dais. The air was filled with the beating of mridangas, the clash of cymbals and the music of the maha-mantra. Swaying from side to side, their tufts of hair tossing in the breeze they chanted: Hare Krishna ...
>
> One greying reporter whom I had always regarded as a particularly unsentimental person said to me in an emotion-choked voice: "Do you realize what is happening? Very soon Hinduism is going to sweep the West. The Hare Krishna movement will compensate for all our loss at the hands of padres through the centuries."

About twenty-five newsmen came to a press conference on the fifth floor of Mr. Seksaria's residence. Prabhupāda sat with his disciples on a large mattress and answered questions, and the devotees showed a film of the San Francisco Ratha-yātrā. The reporters asked about New Vrindaban. They questioned the devotees: Why had they become *sādhus*? Why had they left their country?

The next day the press was full of stories of Prabhupāda and his movement. The *Times of India* picked up on a particular angle: "U.S. MILLIONAIRE'S SON SEEKS SOLACE IN KRISHNA SOCIETY." The article told of Girirāja's renouncing his father's wealth to join Prabhupāda's movement. One newspaper quoted Girirāja: "My father works hard and earns fabulous money. He also fights with my mother. My sisters ran away from the house. Thus, in spite of material comforts, nobody is happy." Quoting Śyāmasundara: "My father is very rich, but he has to take sleeping tablets every night." And there were other articles.

Soon letters appeared in the letters column of the *Times of India.*

> As far as my knowledge goes, these foreign Hindus of the Hare Krishna movement cannot be equal to the native original brahmanas and Hindus. They will have to be relegated to the lower castes. It is significant to see one of the newly converted sadhus, Sri Gopal dasa, formerly Charles Poland of Chicago, stated that he was a construction worker formerly. Doing sudra's

work, it would thus become necessary to allot the three lower castes to these foreign converts according to their profession.

Another letter stated, "The Hare Krishna movement is just a sporadic fad of sentimentalists."

Prabhupāda said these letters should be answered, and he personally outlined replies, delegating their writing to specific disciples. Within a few days, Prabhupāda's replies appeared in the press.

In India even amongst the brahmanas in different provinces there is no social intercourse. So if they are socially accepted or not doesn't matter. For example, amongst the qualified legal practitioners in different provinces there may not be social intercourse, but that does not mean they are not qualified lawyers. This is a cultural movement, and if the whole world accepts this cult, even though Indian brahmanas do not accept it will do no harm at all. ... We are not striving for social or political unity, but if Krishna consciousness is accepted there will automatically be political, social and religious unity. ...

The fact that one of our boys was a construction worker does not mean that he belongs to the sudra community. The sudra community is the less intelligent class or illiterate class who have no information of the value of life. In America even the highest cultured and educated person can go to work as an ordinary construction worker because they accept the dignity of labor. So although a boy was working as a construction worker in America, he is not a sudra.

But even if he is accepted as a sudra, Lord Krishna says that anyone who comes to Him is eligible to be elevated to the highest position of going back to home, back to Godhead.

In a letter signed by Girirāja, Prabhupāda refuted the charge that his movement was a "sporadic fad of sentimentalists."

... How can our movement be sporadic when this science was taught in the Gita five thousand years ago and instructed to the sun-god millions of years before that? How can it be called sporadic when our activity is sanatana-dharma, the eternal occupation of the living entity? Would faddists give up all meat-eating, intoxicants, illicit sex, and gambling for over five years now? Would faddists give up friends, family, and money and get up at 4:00 A.M. daily, ready to go to any country in the world and preach in any conditions immediately on the request of their spiritual master?

Prabhupāda saw all news coverage of the Kṛṣṇa consciousness movement as an aid to propagating Kṛṣṇa consciousness. Even by criticizing the Kṛṣṇa consciousness movement, he said, the papers were broadcasting the holy name of Kṛṣṇa. And Kṛṣṇa's name was absolute.

Mr. Seksaria held a special program for many important dignitaries of Bombay. Although he had expected no more than two hundred persons, many more came. They were Bombay's elite—the women dressed in expensive silk *sārīs* and wearing gold and jewels, the men in silk Nehru-collared suits or white starched *dhotīs* and *kurtās*.

Prabhupāda held *kīrtana* with his disciples, and then he spoke, briefly and gravely. "You are all very intelligent persons," he said. "You are all very learned and educated. You are all very great persons. I beg you—I take the straw of the street between my teeth, and I beg you—just chant Hare Kṛṣṇa. Please chant Hare Kṛṣṇa."

After his talk, Prabhupāda left, and the devotees showed slides of the Hare Kṛṣṇa movement's activities around the world. They also made their first public life membership appeal, and Mr. G. D. Somani, one of India's leading industrialists, as well as Mr. Seksaria, signed on as members.

Although Prabhupāda was happy to see the number of ISKCON's life members increasing, that his shipment of books from Dai Nippon had not yet arrived made him anxious. The devotees were promising life members books, but where were these books? Every day the problem became more and more pronounced.

Prabhupāda learned of a Calcutta port strike. His books had apparently arrived, but the ship, unable to unload cargo in Calcutta, had left port. He worried that the ship would unload the books in some other Indian port. The exact whereabouts and condition of the books, however, remained unknown. Prabhupāda was greatly concerned. He decided to send a competent disciple, Tamāla Kṛṣṇa, to Calcutta to try and retrieve the books. Meanwhile he would continue preaching, depending on Kṛṣṇa.

* * *

Amritsar
October 21, 1970

Accompanied by a group of disciples (seven men and two women), Prabhupāda began the two-day train ride from Bombay to Amritsar. Years ago Prabhupāda had traveled as a preacher in India alone, riding the trains to Jhansi, Delhi, Kanpur, Calcutta, and Bombay to publish *Back to Godhead* and solicit support. After only five years in the West, he now had the great advantage of sincere disciples, and now the Indians were taking notice.

He had stationed Acyutānanda Swami, Jayapatāka Swami, Haṁsadūta, and others in Calcutta; Tamāla Kṛṣṇa, Śyāmasundara, and others in Bombay. His disciples would make life members and try to establish permanent ISKCON centers in two of India's major cities. His Kṛṣṇa consciousness movement was beginning in India, and he wanted to travel with his disciples wherever there was an opportunity to preach. Just as he had worked in America—never settling comfortably in one place, but always traveling, speaking about Kṛṣṇa, meeting new people and offering them devotional service—so he would also work in India.

The train arrived at Kurukṣetra station. "Near here," said Prabhupāda, "Lord Kṛṣṇa spoke *Bhagavad-gītā* five thousand years ago. They say it does not exist—a mythological place. It is a symbol of the field of the body and the senses, they say. It is an allegorical place. But here we are at the station." As he spoke, the sun was setting, and a bright, orange sky shone over the flat land. "How can they say Kurukṣetra is not a real place?" he continued. "Here it is before us. And it has been a historical place for a long, long time."

When the train arrived at Amritsar station, members of the Vedanta Sammelan committee received Prabhupāda and escorted him and his disciples to a park on the outskirts of the city. They showed him the large *paṇḍāl* the Niketan Ashram had erected for the Vedanta Sammelan and assigned him and his disciples their quarters—three small rooms. Prabhupāda took one room, the two women the second room, and four of the men crowded into the third, leaving three men to sleep outdoors on cots. The first night in the northern climate was cold. Available bedding was meager, and none of the devotees had brought warm clothing.

At four the next morning the devotees congregated in Śrīla Prabhupāda's room for *maṅgala-ārati* and *kīrtana* before the Deities of Rādhā and Kṛṣṇa—the same Deities who had been traveling with Prabhupāda for the past one and a half years. Despite the austere conditions, the devotees felt fortunate to have such intimate contact with Prabhupāda and Rādhā-Kṛṣṇa. Prabhupāda played *mṛdaṅga,* leading the chanting of prayers to the spiritual master. Afterward, he had the *pūjārī* distribute to each devotee a bit of the fruit and sweetmeats that had just been offered to the Deities. It was still before sunrise, and the room was chilly. As the devotees sat huddled beneath a naked bulb, Prabhupāda had them read aloud from *Śrīmad-Bhāgavatam.*

That same morning Prabhupāda attended the Vedanta Sammelan. There were thousands of people in the audience, and since most of them did not understand English, Prabhupāda spoke in Hindi. His presentation pleased everyone, and the committee members honored him by making him president of the Vedanta Sammelan.

Although the program was scheduled only for several hours in the morning and evening, Prabhupāda did not limit his preaching to these times; he preached every hour of the day. While he sat in his room, a constant stream of guests came to him, hundreds of pious Hindus seeking his blessings. Recognizing this vestige of Vedic culture, he pointed it out to his disciples. "Just see," he said, "how they treat a saintly person."

Prabhupāda also began receiving the usual flood of invitations to visit the homes of Hindu families. He accepted as many invitations as possible—more than possible, it seemed to his disciples.

Prabhupāda moved quickly. When the cars were ready, he would come out of his room and go, leaving behind anyone who wasn't ready. After each engagement, he would get into his car and go directly to the next. Latecomers would sometimes find he had already left. They would then jump into bicycle rickshas and try to catch him. A wrong direction or a missed turn might make them miss the next engagement. And when at last they would catch up, they would find Prabhupāda coolly, gravely in the midst of a lecture on *Bhagavad-gītā* or laughing and taking *prasādam* with his host.

Every day brought at least a half-dozen engagements—"Come to our temple for *darśana,*" "Come to our house for *prasādam.*" And whenever Prabhupāda would return to his *āśrama,* he would find a long line of guests waiting to spend a few moments with him.

None of the devotees could match Prabhupāda's pace and enthusiasm. His energy seemed never to wane. For his disciples, being invited insistently to take a full meal at half a dozen homes in one day was too much. They tended to overeat, and some of them got sick. But Prabhupāda knew how to handle the situation expertly. He would fully satisfy each host, speak about Kṛṣṇa consciousness, hold *kīrtana,* take a little *prasādam,* and move on.

One evening, in response to an invitation, Prabhupāda visited the home of Baladeva Indra Singh, a descendant of one of ancient Punjab's ruling families. Although nearing sixty, Mr. Singh was still a robust Punjabi *kṣatriya,* handsome, tall, and sporting a big black mustache. He showed Prabhupāda and his disciples through his elegant home, with its large portraits of ancestors, uniformed *kṣatriyas* with their helmets and swords. In the trophy room, which had many animal skins and stuffed heads mounted on the wall, Mr. Singh brought Prabhupāda and his disciples before his prize trophy, a large tiger's head. Prabhupāda approached closely. "You have killed this?" he asked.

"Yes," Mr. Singh replied. And he described the details of the hunt. The man-eater had killed many people in a nearby village, Mr. Singh explained. "So I went and shot it."

Prabhupāda's eyes widened, and he turned to his disciples. "Oh, very nice!"

Later, Prabhupāda sat in a chair, and Mr. Singh sat before him on the floor. He said something was troubling him. An astrologer had told him that in a previous lifetime, thousands of years ago, he had fought in the Battle of Kurukṣetra—but on the side *against* Kṛṣṇa!

"That's not possible," Prabhupāda said. "Everyone present at the Battle of Kurukṣetra was liberated. If you had actually been at the Battle of Kurukṣetra, you would not still be within this material world." Mr. Singh wasn't certain whether to feel relieved or disappointed. But Prabhupāda assured him, "That's all right. Don't worry. Now you are a devotee of Kṛṣṇa."

When Prabhupāda asked Mr. Singh to become a life member of ISKCON, he agreed immediately. He confessed that when he had first invited Prabhupāda and his disciples he had actually been skeptical, but after being with Śrīla Prabhupāda for a few minutes, he said, all his doubts and suspicions had vanished. He would be happy to become ISKCON's first life member in Amritsar.

Although the devotees requested Prabhupāda to take fewer engagements, he would not slow down. It was his disciples, he said, who were finding the pace difficult. One night, after the eighth and final engagement of the day, Prabhupāda returned to his room just a little before midnight. For the devotees the day had been exhausting, and they were eager to get to bed as soon as possible. Noticing Prabhupāda's light still on, one of them went to his window. Prabhupāda was sitting at his desk, leaning back against the wall, listening to a tape recording of one of the talks he had given that day.

* * *

One afternoon Prabhupāda and his disciples went to see the famous Golden Temple of the Sikhs. A guide took them around and answered Prabhupāda's questions. Sikh businessmen, the guide explained, maintained the temple and its expenses. The Sikhs pride themselves in the assertion that no one in Amritsar goes hungry, and they daily feed *dāl* and *capātīs* to ten thousand people. This interested Prabhupāda, and he observed their massive operation. He watched the group of men rolling *capātīs,* flipping them deftly through the air onto a giant griddle while other men, using long paddles, turned the *capātīs,* held them briefly over the hot coals, and then placed them in stacks. "This is how to distribute *prasādam,*" Prabhupāda said.

Prabhupāda signed the guest book "A. C. Bhaktivedanta Swami." Under *Religion* he wrote "Kṛṣṇaite." And under *Comments* he wrote "very spiritual."

Prabhupāda and his disciples visited Rāma-tīrtha-sarovara, the lake where in a bygone age the great sage Vālmīki had his *āśrama.* The terrain surrounding Rāma-tīrtha-sarovara was dry and rocky, and vegetation was sparse. As they stopped at the beautiful bathing *ghāṭa,* its steps leading down into the lake, the devotees were in a jubilant mood, happy to be on a field trip with their transcendental father and teacher. The peaceful lake and the beautiful *ghāṭa* seemed an ideal setting for being with Prabhupāda.

The devotees, who knew little of Lord Rāma, listened intently as Prabhupāda began to tell some of the pastimes of the Supreme Personality of Godhead in His incarnation of Lord Rāmacandra. During the last days of His earthly pastimes, Prabhupāda said, Rāma banished Sītā, His wife and eternal consort. Pregnant and alone, Sītā sought shelter at the *āśrama* of Vālmīki, where she soon gave birth to a son, Lava. Vālmīki created another son for Sītā from straw and named him Kuśa.

When Sītā learned that Rāma was sending a challenge horse throughout the world, she instructed her sons to catch the horse. In this way, she concluded, they would capture their father and bring Him before her. Unfortunately, while the boys were away on their mission, they learned that Lord Rāmacandra had departed from the world. Grief-stricken, they returned to Vālmīki. To mitigate the boys' anguish of separation, Vālmīki sang to them *Rāmāyaṇa,* the transcendental narrative of Lord Rāma's activities. One day, as Sītā was out walking, the ground opened before her, and she returned into the earth from which she had appeared.

These events, Prabhupāda explained as he stood with his followers by Rāma-tīrtha-sarovara, had happened no less than eight hundred thousand years ago. For the devotees, it was as if Prabhupāda had opened a new door to the spiritual world.

* * *

The organizers of the Vedanta Sammelan repeatedly asked Prabhupāda and his party to play a larger part in the *paṇḍāl* program. The scheduled discourses were mostly on Māyāvāda philosophy: God is impersonal, all religious paths are equal and lead to the Supreme One, all is one, we are all God. Such dry speculations could not hold the public's attention, and the Sammelan organizers daily requested the devotees to hold *kīrtana* in the *paṇḍāl.* But with so much other preaching, Prabhupāda preferred holding programs of his own in private homes around the city.

A devotee asked Prabhupāda about a Māyāvāda slogan he saw posted: *Tat Tvam Asi,* with the English translation underneath: "You are that too." This was a favorite saying of the impersonalists, who imagine that the living entity is God, Prabhupāda said. He explained elaborately the distinction between God and the living entity and told how God, when He appears, displays certain unmistakable characteristics that identify Him as the Supreme Personality of Godhead. "These *yogīs* will just talk and talk *Vedānta,*" Prabhupāda said. "It is simply mental speculation, and they never come to any conclusion. They will go on speculating for years and lifetimes, but we will realize God simply by eating." And from the plate of *prasādam* before him he took a sweet and popped it into his mouth.

In the midst of his activities in Amritsar, Prabhupāda continued to think of his spiritual children in various places throughout the world, and he regularly wrote them. To the devotees in Calcutta he wrote, "I am very much anxious to hear what you are doing there and if you have made any life members by this time." He asked them to register ISKCON with the government and try to establish a permanent center there.

To his disciples in Bombay he wrote, "I am very anxious to know your situation; whether you have removed to the Rāma Temple or where you are stationed now." To Karandhara in Los Angeles he wrote:

> I hope everything is going on well with you in our Los Angeles World Headquarters.
>
> Please send me a report of your general activities. ... and also your Governing Body Commission activities. Please offer my blessings to all the members of our Temples. How is the Deity worship being carried on?

Replying to Upendra in the Fiji Islands:

> Regarding worship of demigods, the whole Hindu society is absorbed in this business, so unless our preaching work is very vigorous it is very difficult to stop them.

And to Bhavānanda in New York:

> Please conduct the Samkirtan program regularly and that will give me great pleasure. Regarding our new temple in Brooklyn, Kṛṣṇa has given you very good chance to serve Him.

* * *

October 30, 1970

After ten days in Amritsar, Prabhupāda was on the train heading back to Bombay. He rode in a small first-class compartment with Gurudāsa, while the rest of his disciples rode in another part of the train.

Prabhupāda's car, being close to the locomotive, caught soot from the engine's smoke stack, until he was soon flecked from head to foot with small black particles.

Yamunā: *We were traveling between Amritsar and Delhi, and I decided to go see how Śrīla Prabhupāda was doing, if there was anything he wanted (because sometimes when the train stopped he would ask for a devotee to purchase fresh fruit and other things from the vendors on the train platform). So Kauśalyā and I made our way through several cars to Prabhupāda's first-class compartment. He was lying back on several pillows with one knee up, looking like a monarch. He had a beautiful smile on his face.*

We paid our obeisances, and Śrīla Prabhupāda looked at us with a twinkle in his eye. "Is there anything hot to eat?" he asked. "What do you mean?" I said. "Do you want me to get your lunch, Śrīla Prabhupāda?" "No," he said, "not that. Some rice, some hot rice." I said, "What do you mean, Śrīla Prabhupāda—from the train?" He said, "Well, no. If you can make me some hot rice." I said I would.

I had no idea how I was going to prepare hot rice for Śrīla Prabhupāda, but Kauśalyā and I found our way to the kitchen. Nobody was there, only two men dressed in black, turmeric-stained shorts, standing over the coal stove smoking cigarettes. I didn't know how to speak Hindi, but I said the best I could, "My Guru Mahārāja wants some cāval, *some hot rice."*

The men laughed at us as if we were crazy, and so I thought we had better find someone who would give us permission. But when we found the manager of the restaurant, he said, "No. Impossible. You can't cook in the kitchen." I said, "I'm sorry, this is for my Guru Mahārāja. There is no question of choice. I have said to him that I will fix rice, and I have to fulfill this." But again he said, "No, it is impossible."

I went and found the conductor of the train and explained the situation to him. "If I can't do this for my spiritual master," I said, "then I might as well jump off the train." The conductor took us very seriously and said, "Of course, of course, you can fix whatever you like in the kitchen."

So he brought us back to the kitchen and told the head of the kitchen as well as the head of the restaurant that he was giving us permission. The coal stove was gigantic, and I was completely unfamiliar with it. All sorts of aluminum pots and dishes were hanging around the kitchen. We cleaned out one of the pots as best we could, boiled the water, and put in the cāvāl. *We prepared a gigantic platter of very hot rice with butter, fresh lemon, salt, and pepper and carried it through the train to Prabhupāda's compartment.*

"Here's your rice, Śrīla Prabhupāda," I said as we entered. And his eyes lit up and opened wide. He gave a huge grin. "Oh, my goddesses of fortune have come," he said. "They have brought me my rice. Thank you very much. This is just what I wanted." He ate so much *from this huge plate. He took a little* kacaurī *and* purī *with it, and a little pickle. He was very pleased.*

That night the train pulled into the New Delhi station, with its scurrying crowds of passengers, hawking vendors, refreshment counters, newsstands, beggars, and coolies in their dingy red jackets. The stopover would be twenty minutes.

Suddenly a man appeared in Prabhupāda's compartment, identifying himself as D. D. Gupta. Although Prabhupāda had not met him before, they had corresponded. He was a Delhi man, not especially influential or wealthy, but he wanted to help. Offering Prabhupāda a box of sweets, he invited him to stay in Delhi. Prabhupāda, however, already had other plans and had even wired ahead to notify the devotees in Bombay of his arrival.

Prabhupāda looked over at Gurudāsa, who was feeling happy and especially blessed to have this intimate contact with his spiritual master. Twelve hours they had spent in the same compartment, eating together, talking together. Just minutes before, Prabhupāda had been stressing the importance of farming and explaining how the scarcity of food was due to mismanagement, not to lack of rain or arable land. Gurudāsa was happy, and he was looking forward to the next leg of the journey with Prabhupāda, anticipating the scenery and his return to Bombay.

"This man is inviting us," Prabhupāda said. "Get down and see what you can do."

"*Get down*?" There was hardly time to ask questions or discuss what to do in Delhi; the train would be leaving immediately. Gurudāsa said he would stay, but he would need help. He and Prabhupāda agreed on a team: Yamunā (Gurudāsa's wife), Girirāja, Durlabha, Bruce, and Gopāla. Gurudāsa ran to tell his wife and the *brahmacārīs* the news.

The devotees had little trouble picking up their light bags and getting off the train, but they felt sad to be leaving Śrīla Prabhupāda. As the train pulled away they offered obeisances outside Prabhupāda's window and waved to him, praying for his mercy. This was an austerity—perhaps a tiny drop of what Prabhupāda had gone through when he had first arrived in America.

* * *

Bombay
November 1970

For the next month, Prabhupāda and his disciples stayed at Manoharlal Agarwal's Sītā-Rāma temple in Chembur. Actually it was Mr. Agarwal's residence, but since he maintained the worship of Sītā-Rāma Deities he called his home Ram Sharanam, "under the shelter of Lord Rāma." Prabhupāda occupied one room, and his disciples two other rooms, with access to a kitchen and bath. The Sītā-Rāma temple and suburban neighborhood provided a peaceful atmosphere, and Prabhupāda returned to concentrated work on *Śrīmad-Bhāgavatam,* corresponding with ISKCON centers around the world and looking after the small group of disciples who were with him. He had great hope Kṛṣṇa would provide a way for ISKCON to become well established in India.

> We are just now receiving great publicity and it is reported that Bombay has now got its atmosphere filled with Krishna Consciousness. It is a fact, and the important members of the Bombay community are appreciating our Movement. ...
>
> For the present I am more prominent than all swamis. People are appreciating—What are these swamis? They cannot go outside. There is a Bengali saying that a jackal is king in a small forest. The story is that a jackal became king in the forest by fooling the other animals for some time, but he remained always a jackal and his ruse was at last exposed.

Although Mr. Agarwal was honored that Prabhupāda had accepted his invitation and was now living as his guest, Prabhupāda knew that the situation would ultimately prove inconvenient for everyone involved. To open one's home to a dozen guests and feed them daily was a strain, even for a wealthy man; and for the devotees to live in those tiny quarters under the already trying conditions of irregular hours, frequent sickness, and tropical heat was not easy.

The solution, of course, was for the devotees to get their own place, an ISKCON center in Bombay. As a *sannyāsī,* Prabhupāda was prepared to stay anywhere, moving as often as necessary, accepting alms. He had lived that way for years before going to America. But now he had twenty spiritual children to support in India, and more on the way. They were not mature. He wanted them near him so that they could observe how he did things and imbibe the spirit of preaching in India.

When a Hindu organization in downtown Bombay requested a few devotees to attend a three-day program, Prabhupāda approved. But when the program was over and the leaders of the organization invited the devotees to stay on indefinitely, Prabhupāda said, "No. They will simply eat and sleep." Better for them to stay with him at crowded Ram Sharanam.

Mrs. Sumati Morarji, the wealthy director of Scindia Steamship Lines, had financed the printing of the third volume of Prabhupāda's *Śrīmad-Bhāgavatam* in 1964, and in 1965 she had provided him free passage to America. Now she invited Prabhupāda to speak at Scindia House, near Juhu Beach. Seated onstage, Prabhupāda and Sumati Morarji reminisced, celebrating Prabhupāda's success.

"I did not think you would come back alive," Mrs. Morarji said. "But I am so much pleased to see you." No longer was Prabhupāda the poor *sādhu* Mrs. Morarji had met six years ago. He was a success, and Sumati Morarji and her staff and friends were happy to hear about the Kṛṣṇa consciousness movement in the West.

Before Prabhupāda's lecture, Tamāla Kṛṣṇa formally introduced him to the audience. "Śrīla Prabhupāda left for the West five years ago from this city. He had almost no money. He went to New York, where he chanted Hare Kṛṣṇa in a park, underneath a tree. Soon he opened a temple, where he continued his chanting and held classes on Vedic philosophy. Many people came, and gradually he opened new centers: San Francisco, Montreal, Boston, and so on. Now he has many devotees and over forty temples. In each temple there is a full-scale program of *saṅkīrtana,* Deity worship, and *prasādam* distribution. India has sent many ambassadors and ministers to the West, but none of them can say that he made the Americans give up eating meat, fish, and eggs and got them to chant Hare Kṛṣṇa. Everyone is indebted to Śrīla Prabhupāda, because he came to relieve the suffering of all the fallen souls. ..."

Prabhupāda sang three verses from the *Brahma-saṁhitā* and invited the audience to join in the chorus: *Govindam ādi-puruṣaṁ tam ahaṁ bhajāmi.* After speaking for half an hour, he accepted *prasādam* with Sumati Morarji and honored guests and dignitaries. He met Dr. C. Bali and his wife, the famous dancer and movie actress Vaijayanti Mala. He spoke only briefly with them, and they became life members of ISKCON.

Vaijayanti Mala: *Swami Prabhupāda made his preaching so simple that even a layperson would understand what our great philosophy and our great teachings meant. Not only was he propagating the great culture of our Lord Kṛṣṇa, but he was making the people of other parts of the world really understand its meaning and its significance. By his simple and yet very great teachings of Kṛṣṇa, he took this message so far and so wide that it's really a marvel that a person single-handedly could do so much. He not only preached and, you know, just talked about the whole thing, but he also established so many centers in so many parts of the world. This is really amazing that he could do it in spite of all difficulties. But his perseverance and his persistence, I think, kept him on.*

The public sensation of Prabhupāda's disciples chanting in the streets of Bombay and at the Sadhu Samaj had died down; the regular news coverage had stopped. Still Prabhupāda was sought after by many important people in Bombay. His accomplishments after five years in America commanded the esteem and attention of intelligent Indians, and daily he received respectable visitors who accepted him as the authority on Kṛṣṇa consciousness.

The Indians regarded Prabhupāda as unique. Even in a culture where *swamis* and holy men are commonly treated with respect, he was regarded as special. His visitors would beg him to come to their homes and sanctify them. And this was also in line with Prabhupāda's desire; he wanted to engage the Indians in chanting Hare Kṛṣṇa, hearing the philosophy of *Bhagavad-gītā,* and honoring the Lord's *prasādam.* He wanted them to appreciate the purity of the Kṛṣṇa consciousness movement, enlist as life members of ISKCON, and help him establish a large center in Bombay.

In preaching to Indians, Prabhupāda would often urge them to return to their all-but-forgotten spiritual culture. "Our culture is Kṛṣṇa consciousness," he said before a group of Bombay citizens. "But we are forgetting and becoming too materially absorbed. Lord Ṛṣabhadeva says that this is not good, because according to the law of *karma* you will have to take another body. But you don't have to give up your hard struggle for material life. Arjuna was not advised to do this. He remained in his position and executed Kṛṣṇa consciousness." Prabhupāda concluded, "I am begging. I have forty-two temples in the West, and in each one there are fifty to one hundred disciples. Thousands of books have to be printed. Please help me with this movement."

Manoharlal Agarwal, Prabhupāda's host at Ram Sharanam, would often sit with him for hours, inquiring about spiritual life. Mr. Agarwal was particularly interested in hearing of Prabhupāda's work in America: How had he transformed so many Christians into *rāma-bhaktas*? Had he been alone, or had there been helpers? How did he dress in America? What was his approach? Prabhupāda recounted his early preaching on the Lower East Side of New York, and he explained how everything had happened by Kṛṣṇa's desire.

Mr. Agarwal doubted whether Westerners would be able to stay with Kṛṣṇa consciousness for very long. "Now in the radiance of your company," he said, "as long as you are here bodily and physically, they may continue to observe all these restrictions. But when your physical influence will not be there, one day when you will have to leave this world, then all these people that have come in contact with you, will they go bad?"

"No," Prabhupāda said firmly.

"Your claim is very tall," replied Mr. Agarwal. "Can you tell me what is the basic foundation of your claim?"

Prabhupāda reminded him that all his disciples had been initiated into the chanting of the Hare Kṛṣṇa *mantra* and that according to the Vedic scriptures the constant chanting of the Lord's holy name will save even the most fallen souls and protect them from falling again. Even after his passing away, Prabhupāda predicted, his disciples would not fall victim to *māyā,* as long as they continued their prescribed chanting.

One day Mr. Agarwal asked how long Prabhupāda and his disciples were planning to stay. Prabhupāda said that he was very happy staying where he was but would try to find a new place immediately. Mr. Agarwal insisted that he had no intention of asking Prabhupāda to leave; his home belonged to Prabhupāda, not to himself. He begged him to kindly continue to stay.

Prabhupāda said this reminded him of an incident from the *Caitanya-caritāmṛta,* and he told a story about Haridāsa Ṭhākura, the great devotee of Lord Caitanya. Haridāsa Ṭhākura used to live alone in a cave, where he chanted Hare Kṛṣṇa day and night. Many pilgrims would visit him, but when they learned that a python was also living within the cave, they became afraid. Although Haridāsa Ṭhākura was satisfied with his cave, he didn't want to inconvenience his visitors, so he said he would leave the cave that very day and not return again. Yet even as he spoke, the huge python came winding out from the back of the cave into the presence of all. Passing near Haridāsa Ṭhākura, the snake bowed his head to the ground and slithered away. The Supersoul within the heart of the python had impelled him to leave the cave so that Haridāsa Ṭhākura could remain.

Prabhupāda laughed as he told the story. "Agarwalji," he said, "you have said the same thing. You have said that you will go away and that we will stay. But no, no, we will go. We will go."

CHAPTER THIRTY-THREE

A Lot of Ground to Be Covered

Indore
December 3, 1970

INDIA CONTINUED TO be like a dream for Prabhupāda's disciples, who gazed out the windows as the train moved them through India's unfamiliar rural world. The trackside bushes blossomed in yellow. Mile after mile of irrigated agricultural fields passed by—wheat, rice, sugarcane, and varieties of *dāl*. Small villages—mud-walled houses with straw roofs, or thatched walls with tile roofs—drifted peacefully by. An occasional village temple made of stone would rise above the surrounding simple structures. Cowherd boys with sticks tended their herds on the grassy banks of meandering streams. And the grazing cows, the oxen plowing in the ancient fields, the dung patties drying in the sun for fuel, the smoke rising from the cooking fires, and the smell of the warm earth—all were part of a peaceful, simple way of life the devotees were coming to appreciate through Prabhupāda's association.

Prabhupāda and his disciples were en route to Indore, a city of 475,000 in the central Indian province of Madhya Pradesh, thirteen hours northeast of Bombay. The directors of the Gita Jayanti Mahotsava, a festival to celebrate the teachings of *Bhagavad-gītā,* had invited Prabhupāda and his disciples to attend their convention and public meeting.

In Indore Śrīla Prabhupāda and his disciples settled into their quarters near the Gita Bhavan, the site of the Gita Jayanti Mahotsava. The directors of the convention had assigned Prabhupāda a bungalow with a lawn and garden and had provided nearby facilities for his disciples.

The devotees toured the grounds of the Gita Bhavan, noting the many swamis and *sādhus* who had arrived from various parts of India for the Mahotsava. They saw the large *paṇḍāl* and stage, the eye hospital run by the Gita Bhavan, and the diorama exhibit. The diorama exhibit they regarded as the kind of eclectic mixing of spiritual paths that Prabhupāda often referred to as "hodgepodge." Kṛṣṇa, Buddha, Jesus, Vivekananda, Ramakrishna, and demigods and animals were all on display. While admiring the energy and imagination that had produced such an exhibit, the devotees questioned the benefit of such a conglomeration.

On the first night of the festival Prabhupāda was scheduled as the last speaker. His disciples, who sat with him onstage, grew bored and restless from the ordeal of so many hours of Hindi speeches. And knowing that these speakers were presenting Māyāvāda misconceptions made the evening especially painful. Śrīla Prabhupāda sat sternly and waited, his hand in his bead bag, his head held high, his lips murmuring the Hare Kṛṣṇa *mantra.*

When Prabhupāda finally spoke, he began by explaining that in the West he was spreading the teachings of the *Gītā* as it is. *Bhagavad-gītā,* he said, could be properly understood only in disciplic succession, just as Arjuna, the original student of the *Bhagavad-gītā,* had understood it. The *Gītā* was for the devotee of Kṛṣṇa and should not be misinterpreted by nondevotees. To misinterpret the *Gītā,* he said, was to cheat in the name of religion. He also spoke strongly against pseudoincarnations.

Prabhupāda concluded his talk and asked his disciples to begin *kīrtana.* It was an ecstatic, spontaneous event, and Prabhupāda began dancing onstage along with his disciples. The crowd came to life and began clapping rhythmically. Haṁsadūta jumped down from the stage, still playing *mṛdaṅga,* and began inducing members of the audience to join in chanting and dancing. Several other devotees also jumped down, and soon hundreds of people had risen to their feet, swaying, clapping, and singing: Hare Kṛṣṇa, Hare Kṛṣṇa, Kṛṣṇa Kṛṣṇa, Hare Hare/ Hare Rāma, Hare Rāma, Rāma Rāma, Hare Hare. This was the real Gita Jayanti Mahotsava. The holy name of Kṛṣṇa was being sung, and everyone was happily united in the *kīrtana*.

Greatly pleased by the performance of Prabhupāda and his disciples, the *paṇḍāl* directors visited Prabhupāda the next day in his bungalow. Prabhupāda complained at having to wait so long before he could speak; his disciples shouldn't be required to sit through hours of speeches in a language they couldn't understand. When Prabhupāda intimated that the speeches seriously deviated from the teachings of the *Gītā*, the director of the Gita Bhavan replied, "We do not favor any particular way. Followers of the Śaṅkara school and others also come to our institution. We do not subscribe wholly that Śrī Kṛṣṇa is the sole God or anything of the sort. There is a power behind Him ..."

This remark drew fire from Śrīla Prabhupāda. What kind of glorification of the *Gītā* was this if the speakers did not accept Kṛṣṇa as He is explained in the *Gītā*? The *Gītā* declares Kṛṣṇa to be the highest truth: *mattaḥ paratarań nānyat*. Prabhupāda advised the directors of the Gita Bhavan to try to understand the meaning of *Bhagavad-gītā*. The directors did not change their opinion, but they were intelligent enough to see that Prabhupāda was a great *paṇḍita* and saint, and they listened respectfully. Nodding, they said they accepted his point of view.

After the men left, Prabhupāda continued, "They are thinking that there is something beyond Kṛṣṇa or that it is the spirit within Kṛṣṇa that we have to surrender to. But they do not know that the within and the without of Kṛṣṇa are all absolute, eternal, and full of bliss."

Prabhupāda said he could see that the organizers of the Gita Jayanti Mahotsava had invited him to draw larger crowds. But they would not make him sit again through all the Māyāvādī nonsense, he said. From now on, he would go with his disciples, speak, chant, and then leave.

The next night, however, despite promises by the *paṇḍāl* directors, Śrīla Prabhupāda again had to wait until the end of the program before he could speak and hold *kīrtana*. This night, the crowd was larger than before, and they were clearly waiting for Śrīla Prabhupāda and the foreign *sādhus*. When Prabhupāda's turn came at last, he spoke and then asked his disciples to begin *kīrtana*.

During the *kīrtana* one of the members of the Gita Bhavan gestured to the devotees to jump down into the crowd as they had done on the preceding night. But what had been a spontaneous event the night before could not be artificially staged simply as a crowd pleaser. The man, however, was insistent. He came forward to the edge of the stage, reached up, and began grabbing at the feet of the dancing devotees, trying to pull them into the audience. The devotees became annoyed. Grabbing indiscriminately, the man pulled at one of the women's *sārīs*. Śrīla Prabhupāda was also dancing, but when he saw this he rushed to the edge of the stage, swinging his *karatālas* toward the man's face and shouting, "Stop this!" The man retreated, and Prabhupāda and his disciples continued their *kīrtana*. Although little-noticed by the crowd, Prabhupāda's burst of lionlike ferocity had amazed his disciples.

The festival directors were once again pleased with Prabhupāda's lecture and *kīrtana*. But Prabhupāda sent them word that he would not again sit through the other lectures, waiting his turn to speak. He had wearied of hearing opinions on *Bhagavad-gītā* that avoided the conclusion of *Bhagavad-gītā*—surrender to Śrī Kṛṣṇa, the Absolute Truth. Some speakers made the *Gītā* an allegory, some said Kṛṣṇa was not an actual historical personality, and some simply took advantage of the *Gītā's* popularity to put forward their own political or social philosophies. A person with his own philosophy should write his own book, Prabhupāda said, not use as a vehicle for his own ideas the *Bhagavad-gītā*, a scripture worshiped by millions and respected throughout the world. Why should a conference under the name Gita Jayanti become a forum for speculative philosophies? *Bhagavad-gītā* states that the *Gītā* itself is the essence of knowledge, meant to benefit the entire world. To misrepresent the *Gītā*, therefore, was the greatest disservice. Prabhupāda felt that by sitting through such a program, he and his disciples were tacitly approving the blasphemous speeches.

On the third night of the festival, Prabhupāda and his disciples came early to the stage, having been promised by the festival directors that they would be first on the program. But when another speaker stood and began his discourse, Prabhupāda, followed by his disciples, stood and walked off the stage. The festival director was quite disturbed by this, since most of the audience had come especially for the *kīrtana*. He pleaded with Prabhupāda to return, but Prabhupāda refused. He did agree, however, to send his disciples every night; they would speak and hold *kīrtana.*

* * *

Śrīla Prabhupāda's disciples found the morning *Bhāgavatam* classes in Indore especially relishable. Not only was the setting intimate—ten devotees sitting with Prabhupāda in his room—but the *Bhāgavatam* story was intriguing, one they had never before heard.

"We are talking of Ajāmila, a *brāhmaṇa* residing in Kanyākubjā, presently known as Kanpur," Prabhupāda began, and he narrated the story of Ajāmila's life, pausing from time to time to read the Sanskrit text or to elaborate on the story and its lessons. Ajāmila, a young *brāhmaṇa,* had strictly followed the religious principles, until he became infatuated with a prostitute. As Prabhupāda lectured he focused on the bogus speakers at the Gita Jayanti Mahotsava.

"There are so many things to know, but these things are not being discussed here. It is very cheap to do whatever you like—you simply meditate and you become God. So much cheating is going on all over the world. The so-called *yogīs* say, 'You meditate, and as soon as you are realized, you become God.'

"The *Bhagavad-gītā* is being interpreted in so many different ways. And these so-called explanations are being accepted by the innocent public as authoritative knowledge. Someone is explaining that *kurukṣetra* means this body, and *pañca-pāṇḍava** means the senses. But this is not explaining. How can you explain the *Bhagavad-gītā* as it is when you do not understand it? Such an attempt is nonsense."

In his second lecture Prabhupāda narrated more of Ajāmila's life: his leaving his chaste wife and going to live with the prostitute, his adopting illegal means for supporting her, his having ten children by her and living sinfully until his eightieth year. This story took place, Śrīla Prabhupāda said, thousands of years ago. "At that time there was only one Ajāmila, but you will find many Ajāmilas like that at the present moment, because it is the Age of Kali."

* The five Pāṇḍava brothers, pure devotees of Lord Kṛṣṇa, are referred to in *Bhagavad-gītā.* They were the victors of the Battle of Kurukṣetra.

Ajāmila had great affection for his youngest son, Nārāyaṇa. And as Ajāmila lay on his deathbed and saw the agents of death approaching, he cried out for his son—"Nārāyaṇa!" Prabhupāda continued his story.

"He was just on the point of death, so—naturally he had affection for his son—so he was calling, 'Nārāyaṇa! Nārāyaṇa! Nārāyaṇa! Please come here! Please come here!' That is natural. I know my father—when he was dying, I was not at home. So he was living for one day to see me. He was always inquiring whether Abhay has come back. Like that. So father's paternal affection is like that, and similarly Ajāmila was calling, 'Nārāyaṇa! Nārāyaṇa!'"

Nārāyaṇa is also a name of Kṛṣṇa. And Prabhupāda said that, according to *Bhagavad-gītā,* if a person remembers Nārāyaṇa, or Kṛṣṇa, at the time of death, he becomes liberated. One's mentality at death determines one's next birth. Because the devotee is Kṛṣṇa conscious, he enters the spiritual world at death; and because the materialist is absorbed in sense pleasure and mental speculation, he has to take birth after birth in the material world. Prabhupāda gave an example.

"One gentleman in Calcutta was a fairly big businessman. He was dealing in shares, stocks. So at the time of death he was crying, 'Kamarhati! Kamarhati!' So the result might be that he might have taken his birth as a rat in the Kamarhati mill. It is possible. At the time of death, whatever you think, that will carry you to your next type of body."

Because Ajāmila had called on the name of the Lord, even though referring to his son, he became purified of all sins. Yet because of his sinful life, the messengers of Yamarāja, the lord of death, also appeared, to take him for punishment.

"When Ajāmila was dying, he saw that there were three ferocious persons, very fearful persons, with ropes in their hands. Sometimes a dying man cries, because he sees somebody has come to take him to Yamarāja. He sees, and he is very fearful. So Ajāmila also became fearful. The assistants of Yamarāja have hair very curled, and the hairs on their bodies are standing. Now at the time of Ajāmila's death, the assistants of Yamarāja came to take him."

Prabhupāda paused. "We shall discuss sometime again." And he ended his lecture.

* * *

Prabhupāda began making life members in Indore by sending Haṁsadūta out alone. Haṁsadūta was inexperienced and even skeptical that anyone would pay the 1,111 rupees.

Haṁsadūta: *One day Prabhupāda told me to go to the market with a neighbor and take these books—he had three* Kṛṣṇa *books—and try to make some life members. Just show them the books, he said, and tell them this is a token of our work. Then ask them to please help our mission by becoming a life member for 1,111 rupees. I was thinking that no one was going to give one thousand rupees for two or three books, so I just didn't do anything about it. I just avoided the issue. The next day Prabhupāda gave me the same instruction, but again I didn't do anything. On the third day he said I had to go, so I went next door and got a man who took me to the cloth merchants.*

We went to the shop of the biggest cloth merchant in Indore. The man didn't speak English, so the neighbor who had accompanied me translated. I would say, "Tell him this. Tell him that." And the man would translate everything. After I had exhausted my presentation, I said, "Now ask him to give a check for 1,111 rupees." My translator relayed the message, and the merchant immediately took out his checkbook and wrote the check.

Then we visited another merchant, and the same thing happened—he immediately wrote a check. We went to another merchant, and he also became a life member. So I made three life members on the first day, and when I came back and told Prabhupāda, he was in ecstasy.

By sending disciples and by sometimes going out himself, Śrīla Prabhupāda soon had a dozen ISKCON life members in Indore. Prabhupāda, Haṁsadūta, and Girirāja visited the king of Indore and invited him to become a life member, but the king declined. The devotees were disappointed, and in the car on the way back to Gita Bhavan, Haṁsadūta asked Prabhupāda, "Did I say the right thing about the books?"

"My books are like gold," Prabhupāda replied. "It doesn't matter what you say about them. One who knows the value, he will purchase."

* * *

Because visitors often asked Prabhupāda and his disciples what they thought of various popular spiritual teachers, Prabhupāda gave his disciples hints on answering such questions. If the teacher was not a bona fide follower of Vedic scripture, Prabhupāda said, the devotee should reply, "Swami *who*?" By thus indicating that he had not heard of the particular teacher, he would minimize the teacher's importance. Then the devotee should ask, "What is this swami's philosophy?" When the person explained, the devotee could defeat the particular philosophy, without attacking the person.

India had many Māyāvādī *gurus,* Prabhupāda explained, and they often traveled in groups from one convention to another. Although each had his particular style, primarily they were interested in *capātīs.* "And for every *capātī,*" he said, "there are many Māyāvādīs. So there is competition."

* * *

One of Prabhupāda's frequent visitors was Vairaghi Baba, an educated man who had visited America and who spoke fluent English. He regularly joined in the *kīrtana* with the devotees, chanting and dancing with them onstage, and when he visited Prabhupāda in his room he behaved with Prabhupāda in a familiar way—too familiar, Prabhupāda's disciples thought. But Prabhupāda tolerated him.

One day some devotees met Vairaghi Baba at a lunch engagement, and they noticed he was drinking tea. Almost naively, and yet with an air of challenge, one of the devotees asked why he was drinking tea. "Oh, I am an *avadhūta,*" Vairaghi Baba replied. The devotees, who had never heard this word before, reported the incident to Prabhupāda. "*Avadhūta,*" Prabhupāda explained, "means one who is beyond the regulative principles. Generally this refers to Nityānanda Prabhu."* Prabhupāda disapproved of Vairaghi Baba's tea-drinking and especially of his calling himself an *avadhūta*.

A small group of devotees were sitting with Prabhupāda in his room one afternoon. "Śrīmatī Rādhārāṇī's excellence was Her cooking,"

---

* An incarnation of Lord Kṛṣṇa who descended along with Lord Caitanya to spread the chanting of Hare Kṛṣṇa and deliver the fallen souls of this age. His supremely independent activities, without regard of rules and regulations that apply to human beings, made Him famous as an *avadhūta.* His unusual pastimes are relished by devotees and are not to be imitated.

Prabhupāda said. "She could also sing and dance, but Her great service was Her cooking for Kṛṣṇa. Mother Yaśodā would ask Her personally to come and cook for Kṛṣṇa and the cowherd boys. So, all in a line, She would feed them *prasādam.*"

An Indian lady came to the door, bringing an offering of *chidwa*—fried cashews, potatoes, and raisins with spices. Śrīla Prabhupāda took some, then distributed the rest to the other devotees. "Do you like this?" he asked, turning to Yamunā.

"Oh, it is very, very tasty," she replied.

"Yes," he said, "you should learn to prepare this. I like it very much. My Guru Mahārāja was also fond of potato *chidwa,* and he would sometimes request it late in the afternoon. He was very fond of it."

"Śrīla Prabhupāda," a devotee asked, "may we publish pictures of you without *tilaka?*"

"Yes," he replied, "my Guru Mahārāja has been recorded without *tilaka.* You have seen that picture where he is looking up from his books at his working table?"

"Yes," the devotee replied, "I have seen that picture. I have seen you look in that very same way, with the very same expression as in the picture of your Guru Mahārāja."

"You have only seen the glitter," Prabhupāda corrected. "He is the gold. I am only iron. Iron can never be gold. But you have seen the glitter of real gold."

One afternoon a renowned astrologer visited Prabhupāda and offered to read his palm. "No," Prabhupāda replied, "I am finished with that. But you may read my disciples' palms." The astrologer read the palms of the several devotees present, made his predictions, and then left. The devotees turned to Prabhupāda, wondering what to make of it. "As soon as you clap your hands in front of the Deities during *ārati,*" Prabhupāda said, smiling, "all the lines of your palm are changed."

Śrīla Prabhupāda told his disciples a story about when he had lived in Vṛndāvana. A Bengali widow walked to the Yamunā River to take her bath every morning. And every morning without fail she would return with a pot of water for the Rādhā-Dāmodara *pūjārīs* to use in bathing the Deities. Prabhupāda said he would sometimes open the gate for the woman, since he also rose very early, and she would enter and wake the *pūjārī*.

"Although the Vṛndāvana nights are cold in the winter," Prabhupāda said, "the woman never once failed to come with the water. For this activity she will return back to Godhead. One who cannot rise early in the morning is not very serious about spiritual life. One must rise before the *brāhma-muhūrta* hour—that is very auspicious. And one will take the trouble to do so if he is serious about spiritual life."

One day Prabhupāda was sitting outside near his bungalow, chanting on his beads, when an unknown man approached, calling out the names of Kṛṣṇa. Suddenly the man fell to the ground, rolling and crying, appearing to be in great ecstasy. Prabhupāda remained seated and observed the exhibition but made no response. The man continued his crying and rolling and chanting; Prabhupāda now ignored him completely. After several minutes, the man got up and walked away, obviously disappointed.

Early one morning as Prabhupāda sat in his room with his disciples, a gentleman entered and tearfully announced that his mother was dying. The devotees, watching for Prabhupāda's reaction, saw him remain grave. He didn't try to reassure the man or preach to him, but made only a very mild comment. Prabhupāda was unpredictable. He was always Kṛṣṇa conscious, and he always acted in accord with *guru* and *śāstra.* But exactly how he would act in a given situation was unpredictable. Whatever he did, however, was Kṛṣṇa conscious and correct, and he was always instructing them by his example.

* * *

On Prabhupāda's last morning in Indore he continued the story of Ajāmila. He explained that because Ajāmila had uttered the holy name, he had immediately obtained salvation, even though he had been so sinful.

"So Ajāmila, at the time of his death, just remembered his youngest son, whose name was Nārāyaṇa. The very name of Nārāyaṇa has got the full potency of the Supreme Personality of Godhead, Nārāyaṇa. That is the secret of this *nāma-saṅkīrtana* movement. By chanting the holy name of Nārāyaṇa, you immediately contact with the Supreme Personality of Godhead. *Nāma,* the Lord's name, is not material—it is spiritual. Kṛṣṇa and Kṛṣṇa's name, there is no difference. ...

"In a very appealing voice Ajāmila began to ask his son Nārāyaṇa, 'Please come here. I am dying.' He was very afraid of the Yamadūtas.

"Kṛṣṇa sent the Viṣṇudūtas to give Ajāmila shelter. The Viṣṇudūtas looked just like Lord Nārāyaṇa, with four hands. With a grave voice, they said to the Yamadūtas, 'What are you doing? Stop! You cannot take this man to Yamarāja.'"

Prabhupāda ended his lecture—and his stay in Indore. Having accepted an invitation to travel to Surat in the state of Gujarat and hold Kṛṣṇa conscious programs, he and his disciples would be leaving shortly. Devotees from Bombay would also join them. Prabhupāda had come to Indore for the Gita Jayanti Mahotsava, but actually the Mahotsava was but a small part of his preaching in Indore. He had met hundreds of people, made life members and friends. He had touched their lives. His presence in Indore would leave a lasting impression.

Baba Balmukund: *I've seen many* sādhus *and great saints in this Gita Bhavan. I saw Śrīla Prabhupāda also in the same place. I was very much impressed by Śrīla Prabhupāda and his preaching. It was because Prabhupāda had revealed the reality about* bhakti, *because he was a pure* bhakta, *that he could change the people of the West and give them another dress, he could give them another diet, he could entirely change their culture and give them true* bhakti. *And this was the greatest thing Prabhupāda has done. Let the world say as it likes, but he has done a marvelous thing regarding Lord Kṛṣṇa's* bhakti. *What Swami Vivekananda, Swami Ram Tirtha, and others could not do, Śrīla Prabhupāda has done. It is a marvelous thing.*

* * *

Surat
December 17, 1970

It was like a dream come true. Thousands lined the street for many blocks, while the devotees, playing *karatālas* and *mṛdaṅgas* and chanting

Hare Kṛṣṇa, made their way along. Spectators stood on rooftops or clustered at windows and doorways, while others joined the procession. The police had stopped traffic at the intersections, allowing only the *kīrtana* procession to pass. The earthen road, freshly swept and sprinkled with water, had been decorated with rice flour designs of auspicious Vedic symbols. Green, freshly cut banana trees adorned either side of the way. Overhead, women's *sārīs* strung like bunting across the narrow roadway formed a brightly colored canopy over the *kīrtana* party.

Mr. Bhagubhai Jariwala, Prabhupāda's host in Surat, had advertised the daily parade routes in the local newspapers, and now, day after day, the devotees were holding a *kīrtana* procession through various sections of the city. While more than twenty of Prabhupāda's disciples led the daily procession, thousands of Indians chanted, cheered, and clamored to see, and women threw flower petals from the rooftops.

Often the procession would have to stop as families came forward to garland the devotees. Sometimes the devotees would receive so many garlands that their blissful faces would be scarcely visible, and they would distribute the garlands to the people in the crowd. Never before had the devotees met with such a reception.

"It is a city of devotees," Prabhupāda said. He compared the people of Surat to dry grass catching fire. By nature they were Kṛṣṇa conscious, but the arrival of Śrīla Prabhupāda and his *saṅkīrtana* party had been like a torch, setting the city spiritually ablaze.

The entire population of Surat seemed to turn out every morning, as tens of thousands flocked at 7 A.M. to the designated neighborhood. Men, women, laborers, merchants, professionals, the young, the old, and all the children—everyone seemed to be taking part. Cramming the streets and buildings, they would wait for the *kīrtana* party, and when the devotees arrived, everyone became joyous.

Prabhupāda attended only a couple of the morning processions, preferring to stay in his quarters at Mr. Jariwala's home. Each morning Prabhupāda would come out onto his second-floor balcony, just as the devotees were leaving. Although the mornings were cold and many of the devotees sick, seeing Prabhupāda on the balcony offering them his blessings eased their troubles. Prabhupāda would wave, and the devotees would set off down the street, chanting.

The devotees had no special paraphernalia other than *mṛdaṅgas* and *karatālas*—no flags, no marching band, no *ratha* (cart), just an enthusiastic *kīrtana* party. And there was no official *paṇḍāl,* no Sadhu Samaj, no Vedanta Sammelan, no Gita Jayanti Mahotsava—just an entire city of *kṛṣṇa-bhaktas* waiting eagerly for the American Hare Kṛṣṇa chanters.

To be worshiped for chanting Hare Kṛṣṇa was just the opposite of what the devotees had experienced in the West. In Hamburg, Chicago, New York, London, Los Angeles, the devotees had been insulted, threatened with arrests, assaulted, and ignored. Of course, sometimes they had been tolerated and even appreciated, but never honored.

The daily *saṅkīrtana* outing was exhausting, since the route was long and the stops frequent. Many of the devotees had sore throats from singing, and the usual digestive upsets persisted. But the devotees took everything as the mercy of Lord Caitanya, who was allowing them to engage a whole city in His *saṅkīrtana* movement.

Twenty devotees from the West had just arrived in Surat, as had an American photographer, John Griesser, on assignment for *Asia Magazine.* John went out every day to shoot the *kīrtana* processions, and as he did he felt himself becoming caught up in something much greater than a mere photo assignment.

The people of Surat, who considered themselves *kṛṣṇa-bhaktas* at heart, saw Prabhupāda as a great saint. And they saw his disciples, in whom they found the true Vaiṣṇava qualities, as saints also. The devotees' dress, behavior, and way of life showed pure *bhakti-yoga,* and their *kīrtana* was genuine worship of the holy name. By honoring the Lord's devotees, the people of Surat knew they were honoring Lord Kṛṣṇa Himself. Devotion to Kṛṣṇa was the heart of their own culture, yet they had never expressed it to such a degree as now.

After several days of *kīrtana* processions, the mayor of Surat, Mr. Vaikuntha Sastri, closed all schools and proclaimed a holiday throughout the city. Everyone was now free to celebrate the mercy of Lord Caitanya and chant Hare Kṛṣṇa. Signs throughout the city read, in Gujarati, "Welcome to the American and European Devotees of Krishna," and "Welcome to Members of the Hare Krishna Movement."

The devotees felt tired and blissful as they returned to Mr. Jariwala's home, and Prabhupāda was waiting for them. As soon as they saw him, they all bowed down.

Cidānanda: *Prabhupāda was at the foot of the stairs, greeting us. We were in complete bliss, with flower garlands all over us, big smiles on our faces. We were very happy that we had been so well received. It was as if Prabhupāda was standing there saying, "Just see how wonderful this Kṛṣṇa consciousness is! Just see how happy you are!" He was standing there smiling. He was so happy that we were happy.*

The devotees were not alone, however, as they returned to Mr. Jariwala's home, for hundreds of Indians thronged behind them, eager to see Śrīla Prabhupāda. Śrīla Prabhupāda, his disciples, and a clamoring crowd of Surat devotees squeezed tightly into Prabhupāda's room. The guests—those who got in—inquired about ISKCON and its activities, while those outside pushed to get inside. The crowd around the house grew so great that traffic couldn't pass. While Prabhupāda continued to answer questions inside, the crowd outside grew larger and more restless. By their good fortune, they had realized Prabhupāda's greatness, and they wanted to be with him. As their desire became stronger, their eagerness more intense, Prabhupāda got up from his seat and walked out to the balcony. The crowd roared, "Hare Kṛṣṇa!" their arms upraised.

When Prabhupāda returned inside, the crowd remained unsatisfied, and he asked some of his disciples to try and pacify them. Several devotees went out to the people, answering their questions and telling them Prabhupāda would come out to see them again.

Bhagubhai Jariwala had come in touch with Prabhupāda's movement several years before in San Francisco, when he had donated a silver *mūrti* of Kṛṣṇa to the San Francisco temple. Now the Jariwala family, to accommodate their guests, had moved into modest quarters on the roof of their home and offered the rest of the house to Prabhupāda and his disciples. Hospitable hosts, they made the devotees feel welcome to stay forever.

At lunch and again in the evening, Prabhupāda would take *prasādam* with the devotees and guests, the devotees sitting in rows on the floor and Prabhupāda sitting at the head, in a chair at a table. Mr. Jariwala and his family would serve everyone. Often respectable citizens would also attend the lunches. Mr. Chandra Desai, the chief minister of Gujarat; Mr. Vaikuntha Sastri, Surat's mayor; the state education minister; and others attended.

The *prasādam* was the finest Gujarati cooking, and when a dish was particularly to Prabhupāda's liking he would ask one of his women disciples to learn from Mrs. Jariwala how to cook it. Honoring *prasādam* twice a day with Prabhupāda was another intimacy the devotees shared with their spiritual master in India. Had they been with him in any other part of the world, such intimacy would probably have been impossible.

Beginning at 4:30 A.M. Prabhupāda would hold *kīrtana* and *ārati* before Rādhā and Kṛṣṇa and lecture from *Śrīmad-Bhāgavatam*. His room would be filled with guests, including the members of the Jariwala family. Although at outside engagements Prabhupāda usually spoke Hindi, in these morning meetings he always spoke English, for his disciples. He continued lecturing on Ajāmila, focusing on Ajāmila's degradation due to bad association and on his deliverance by chanting of the holy name. To Śrīla Prabhupāda's disciples, who were all aspiring to chant Hare Kṛṣṇa purely and go back to Godhead, these topics were urgently relevant. He was speaking of them.

"Anyone who utters the name of Kṛṣṇa is immediately freed from all sinful activities. That is the power of Kṛṣṇa's name. The difficulty is that after being freed we again commit mistakes. Kṛṣṇa's name has got the power—as soon as you utter the name you immediately become freed from all contaminations. But if one thinks, 'I am chanting Hare Kṛṣṇa, so even if I commit sinful activities it will be counteracted by my chanting,' that is the greatest offense. Just like sometimes in Christian churches they go on Sundays and confess and they are supposed to be excused from sinful reaction. But again, after coming back from the church, they commit the same sin with the expectation that 'Next week when I go to the church I shall confess, and it will be counteracted.' This kind of understanding is prohibited. ... If you accept spiritual life and at the same time go on committing sinful activities, then you will never be able to progress."

Prabhupāda's outdoor evening engagements were well attended. The city officials made one of Surat's main intersections a festival site, rerouted all traffic, and set up a stage and sound system. Thousands would gather nightly. The crowd was sometimes so large and excited that Prabhupāda would have difficulty speaking above the noise, so he would hold a *kīrtana*. In the quiet that followed, he would have one or two of his disciples speak. Then he would speak. If the audience again became noisy, he would again say, "All right, let us have *kīrtana*." Or sometimes he would simply sit and distribute bits of crystalized sugar candy to the thousands who approached him to touch his lotus feet and take a piece of *prasādam*.

Girirāja: *All the area around this block was completely packed with people. They were all mad after Śrīla Prabhupāda and Kṛṣṇa consciousness. Although a very big area, still people were occupying every space available, perching on rooftops, looking out windows, sitting on odd cement boulders or blocks scattered here and there.*

Everything about Prabhupāda's program was completely satisfying to everyone. The old people liked it because there was the saintly figure of Śrīla Prabhupāda with his young foreign disciples. And the intellectuals liked it because Śrīla Prabhupāda was giving such sound philosophy. And the children liked it because they could run and dance and join in the kīrtana.

Mādrī dāsī: *At one program they mobbed us so, we couldn't even get out of the cars, they were so eager to see Śrīla Prabhupāda. There were so many people. Prabhupāda said, "All right, the next night will be a night for ladies only." So the next night only ladies came, but still it was just as packed, and Prabhupāda gave a wonderful lecture.*

Bruce: *One program was so noisy that no one stopped talking, so Prabhupāda just started chanting the* Brahma-saṁhitā. *That was the whole program. He just chanted the* Brahma-saṁhitā. *Then he gave up and went out.*

Cidānanda: *Before going out to attend these programs, Prabhupāda looked like a general getting ready to go out for battle. He would come out of his room, beautifully dressed and effulgent, ready to go out and fight* māyā. *There were thousands and thousands of people waiting. I didn't know what to make of it. I couldn't handle so many people. But Prabhupāda was waging war on* māyā. *He was there to convince all these people, and the more people would come, the stronger he would get.*

Prabhupāda preached in the outlying villages also. He would ride in a car with Mr. Jariwala, several disciples, and his Rādhā-Kṛṣṇa Deities to Bardoli or Meol. The village dwellings were made of baked mud, with straw roofs and cow dung walls and floors. For Prabhupāda's visit the villagers drew rice flour designs on the ground outside their houses and lined their lanes with clay pots, plantain leaves, and coconuts.

Mr. N. D. Patel: *The people in my village were much impressed by the presence of Prabhupāda. They used to say that he has done miracles by chanting. "He is a miracle saint, no doubt," people were saying. "So many Western people have become devotees, just by chanting the name of the Lord." The people were very much impressed by Prabhupāda's practical way of* bhakti. *In his lecture Śrīla Prabhupāda created such a good impression, not only on Vaiṣṇavas but so many Christians, Parsis. Even some Muhammadan friends started believing in Lord Kṛṣṇa as the universal Godhead.*

With regards to all the saints, nobody has been able to spread this philosophy like this in the past. In our village we are already Vaiṣṇavas, of course, but we used to believe in Sūryajī, Durgā, Ṭhākurajī, and all these things. But after Prabhupāda's explanation of what is Gītā, *what is Lord Kṛṣṇa, we are chanting Hare Kṛṣṇa, Hare Kṛṣṇa, Kṛṣṇa Kṛṣṇa, Hare Hare/ Hare Rāma, Hare Rāma, Rāma Rāma, Hare Hare. After Prabhupāda conducted his discourse here in the village, the people were so impressed that even in his absence they chant the* mahā-mantra *loudly and they greet people with the words "Hare Kṛṣṇa, Hare Kṛṣṇa." At the time of departure the people wished every devotee and Prabhupāda with the words "Hare Kṛṣṇa!"*

When there were no outside engagements, Prabhupāda would sit in his room and receive visitors. To a member of Parliament who came to visit, Prabhupāda said that wherever he traveled he encountered the concept of India as a beggar, backward and poverty-stricken. Ambassadors from India, he said, had only reinforced that image by going to Western countries and begging, "Give me rice, give me money, give me alms." India, Prabhupāda explained, had the greatest wealth of spiritual culture and the knowledge of *Bhagavad-gītā*. Prabhupāda had taken this wealth to the West and given it away freely. He was not a beggar.

Yamunā: *During visiting hours, riding in the car, walking, standing, or sitting, Prabhupāda was chanting* japa *all the time in Surat. His fingers were always moving within his saffron bead bag. He was always a Vaiṣṇava—the pure devotee of Kṛṣṇa, well groomed, with beautiful, neat* tilaka *on, and his hand was always in his bead bag. As he was sitting to greet people, one would be struck by his inconceivable beauty. Śrīla Prabhupāda said persons who give themselves to others are called magnanimous. And this was how Śrīla Prabhupāda was during his pastimes in Surat. He was always delivering Kṛṣṇa to everyone he met. He affected people's hearts by his great potency.*

Every morning in *Śrīmad-Bhāgavatam* class Prabhupāda added another installment of the Ajāmila story. Sometimes he would refer to the degradation of Indian culture, citing specific examples he had seen during his India tour.

"Now I am very sorry to inform you that in your city I have seen two temples—they are known as Rama Mandir. But there is no Rāma. This cheating is going on, and you are accepting. There is no Rāma Deity worship, but a man's photo is there, Sri Rama. And people are so foolish they do not question why this is going on. In Indore I have been in the Gita Bhavan, and so many nonsense things are there. Another place I saw Gita Samiti, and there was not a single photograph of Kṛṣṇa, but a lamp is there. And this is in the name of *dharma.*

"Last night this boy informed me that *Bhagavad-gītā* is going to be distributed by some swami, but according to *Bhagavad-gītā* that swami is fool number one. He is distributing *Bhagavad-gītā,* and people are accepting and paying for it. This is going on. It is a very serious situation all over the world. In the name of *dharma* [religion], *adharma* [irreligion] is going on."

Just as Ajāmila had become degraded, Prabhupāda explained, Indian culture had also become degraded. The only hope was for people to return to their rightful position of Kṛṣṇa consciousness.

"So all over the world—not only in India—there cannot be peace unless you reform the whole social structure. And that can be done only by this movement, Kṛṣṇa consciousness. Now see how this man fell down. Lusty people—they don't care for society, they don't care for elderly persons, they do it in the road, in the street, on the sea beach, anywhere, in the cinema. These things are going on. It is advertised also in the cinema nowadays to attract people. Formerly in India it was not so. But they are introducing all of this nonsense to make people more lusty. To become lusty means he is going to hell. If you want to open the door to your liberation, then you should engage yourself in serving the *mahat,* the pure devotees. If you want to open the door to the hellish condition of life, then you mix with those who are too much attached to women."

He spoke of the slaughterhouse and continued to decry the public display of illicit sex. Regarding illicit sex, he said that what had been a rare incident in the time of Ajāmila was now a common affair.

"How can young people protect themselves? They are not trained up. This Ajāmila was trained up, and yet he fell down. I saw in many parks, such as Golden Gate Park, within the cars the young boys and girls .... Now here it is said that this behavior is expected of the *śūdra,* not from the higher castes. So just try to understand. They are thinking that they are becoming advanced. But they are not becoming advanced. They are becoming degraded. The whole world is degraded, and India is also imitating their degradation. How, by degraded association, one becomes himself degraded—that this story will reveal."

Prabhupāda had accomplished in Surat what he had intended. He had given the holy name, and the people had embraced it. The people of Surat, though not prepared to alter their lives radically and live as ISKCON devotees, appreciated that Prabhupāda had turned Westerners into devotees of Lord Kṛṣṇa and that he was teaching the pure message of the scriptures and chanting Hare Kṛṣṇa. They had responded to Prabhupāda not out of a dogma or ritual but out of an appreciation of the importance of spiritual life and a recognition that Prabhupāda and ISKCON were genuine.

For Prabhupāda's disciples, the visit to Surat had given them a glimpse of what the world would be like if everyone was a devotee.

* * *

Allahabad
January 1971

Kumbha-melā is the greatest congregation of human beings on earth. Every twelve years in Allahabad, *sādhus* and pilgrims from all over India gather at the Triveṇī, the confluence of the three holy rivers Ganges, Yamunā, and Sarasvatī. And at an auspicious time that assures the worshiper liberation from the cycle of birth and death, as many as fifteen million people enter the sacred waters. A smaller version, the Māgha-melā, takes place annually during the month of Māgha (December–January). January of 1971, however, happened to fall halfway through the twelve-year cycle from one Kumbha-melā to the next, and the Melā was known as Ardha-kumbha-melā. Millions would attend, and Śrīla Prabhupāda decided to take advantage of the opportunity and attend the Melā with his disciples to preach.

While his disciples took the train from Surat to Allahabad, Prabhupāda, accompanied by Tamāla Kṛṣṇa, Haṁsadūta, Nanda Kumāra, and others, went briefly to Bombay and then to Calcutta, where he satisfied himself that his shipment of books from Dai Nippon was safely stored at a Scindia warehouse. He also purchased twenty-four-inch brass Rādhā-Kṛṣṇa Deities to take with him to Allahabad. On January 11 he wrote:

> ... tomorrow morning we are going to Allahabad to attend the Ardha Kumbha Mela festival. We shall be going all 40 strong devotees and there are an expected 7,000,000 going by there also for the month of Magh.

About twenty-five devotees had taken the train from Surat to Allahabad, and others, newcomers from the U.S. and England, would soon be arriving. After a twenty-three-hour train ride, the first group arrived. As they disembarked, they could see only fog. With the address of a *brahmacārī-āśrama* where they were to stay until they could pitch their tents at the Melā site, they started forward.

The devotees knew little of what to expect as they crowded into several one-horse *ṭāṅgās* and proceeded toward the appointed *brahmacārī-āśrama.* They had heard that the Kumbha-melā was the most auspicious time to bathe at the Triveṇī and that the water was icy cold. In the foggy morning, they saw pilgrims along the road, riders on camels, and guards carrying rifles. Reaching the *āśrama* at sunrise, they could see the sacred Ganges before them.

The next morning the devotees started for the pilgrimage site, joining the stream of pilgrims funneling toward the Triveṇī. As they passed the Ram Bhag train station, a sign read, "From this point the confluence of the holy rivers Ganges and Yamunā and the forts are five kilometers." Riding in bicycle rickshas, the devotees merged with the moving tide of pilgrims, and soon they saw before them, on what one week before had been an empty plain, a city of tents. From the small tents, big tents, and giant *paṇḍāls* with flags flying rose a dissonance of sounds—music, loudspeaker announcements in different languages, *bhajanas,* and the hum of prayers.

The devotees got down from their rickshas, paid their drivers, and proceeded ahead, moving with the flow of pilgrims. As they walked, the ground transformed from grass to sand to mud, and the amplified music and the din of *mantras* and chants increased. The entire way was lined by beggars with leprosy, elephantiasis, and deformities.

The Melā committee had given ISKCON a good location near one of the entrance gates, and a few of the experienced devotees engaged workers in setting up the tents. ISKCON's *paṇḍāl* was large and brightly colored, with three smaller tents close by—one for the men, one for the women, and one for Śrīla Prabhupāda. A flimsy shack of corrugated tin served as a kitchen. Prabhupāda was to arrive the next day, and the devotees worked quickly putting down hay and rolling out *darīs* (large carpets of coarse cotton fabric). The devotees would have to build their own fires, gather their own vegetables, wash their own clothes, and do everything for themselves—all in the middle of a cold, barren sand flat. It was a far cry from being served like princes at a life member's home.

The devotees were in the midst of a great religious festival and human spectacle, and without Prabhupāda most of them were bewildered by the strange sights and sounds. *Yogīs* sat all day in the same posture, while crowds stood watching. Trident-carrying Śaivites, with simple red cloth, *rudrākṣa* beads, and matted hair, sat smoking *gāñjā*. A procession of elephants, followed by two long files of naked *sādhus,* strode by. An ascetic lay on a bed of thorns. And there were still others, extreme renunciants rarely seen by the rest of civilization. And of course the various Hindu sects abounded, their chants and prayers rising into the air to mingle with the morning mist and the smoke from the ten thousand campfires that clouded the sky above the city of tents.

When Prabhupāda arrived at the ISKCON camp the next day, the devotees were ecstatic. Eagerly they began to tell him of the bizarre sights of the Melā. One of them mentioned a *guru* riding on an elephant and added, "Actually, *you* should ride on the elephant."

"No," Prabhupāda replied, "I would put Rādhā and Kṛṣṇa there."

Prabhupāda's presence reassured his disciples, reminding them that spiritual life was neither exotic nor bewildering, but simple and practical. In Prabhupāda's presence the devotees' attractions to mystic *yoga,* Vedic rituals, and material blessings and benedictions vanished. They accepted that great spiritual benefit awaited the pilgrims at the Melā, but as Prabhupāda had said, "To go to a holy place means to find a holy person and hear from him. A place is holy because of the presence of the saintly persons." The devotees understood, therefore, that the greatest spiritual benefit lay in hearing from Śrīla Prabhupāda.

Sitting in his tent with his disciples, Prabhupāda explained the significance of Ardha-kumbha-melā. For millions of years, he said, this had been among the most sacred places in India. During the appearance of the tortoise *avatāra,* when the demons and demigods had been churning immortal nectar, a drop of that nectar had fallen here. Since then, every six and twelve years certain auspicious planets form a jug, and this jug, filled with immortal nectar, is said to pour that nectar upon the Triveṇī. Lord Rāmacandra and Hanumān appeared here in Allahabad, and here Lord Caitanya taught Rūpa Gosvāmī the science of devotional service. Prabhupāda said he had also lived in Allahabad with his wife and family, and Śrīla Bhaktisiddhānta Sarasvatī had initiated him at Allahabad's Rūpa Gosvāmī Gaudiya Math in 1932. As for the Melās, anyone who came and bathed at the auspicious times when the *prāṇa* was pouring down from the heavens was guaranteed either promotion to the heavenly planets or liberation.

John Griesser: *I talked with other so-called* gurus, *and they were very impersonal. They didn't seem to care so much for persons, especially Westerners. They had a dislike, sort of a disdain, even though occasionally some of them would have a Western disciple. Prabhupāda was completely different. He didn't seem so much concerned about externals but was very concerned about a person's philosophy, his consciousness. And of course he always tried to inject Kṛṣṇa consciousness into everyone he met.*

Prabhupāda said that although most of the saints and *sādhus* present were inauthentic, many were perfect *yogīs,* some of them three and four hundred years old. These *yogīs,* from remote parts of India, would come out for the Melā and then return to seclusion. "I have personally seen," he said, "that they take bath in the Ganges and come up in the seven sacred rivers. They go down in the Ganges and come up in the Godāvarī River. Then they go down and come up in the Kṛṣṇā River, and go down, like that." The devotees, therefore, should respect everyone who attended the Melā.

"So actually it's true," one of the devotees inquired, "that just by bathing here they are liberated?"

"Yes," Prabhupāda said, "it's true. They come here for liberation. But we have not come for liberation. We have come to preach. Being engaged in Kṛṣṇa's unalloyed devotional service, we are already liberated. We are not interested in liberation. We have come to preach devotional service."

When Prabhupāda rose early the next morning, the temperature was near freezing. His tent had no heat. He walked to the *paṇḍāl* to lead the *kīrtana* at *maṅgala-ārati,* and as he sat on his *vyāsāsana* a disciple handed him his quilt, which he wrapped around himself. To rise and bathe in such cold was difficult for most of the devotees. A few went to the Ganges, others bathed at a nearby pump, and some refused to get up at all.

Girirāja: *The program was very rigorous, because it was bitterly cold at night and we were expected to get up at four o'clock in the morning and bathe and attend* maṅgala-ārati. *So a few staunch devotees like Tamāla Kṛṣṇa and Haṁsadūta got up early—by three or three-thirty—and walked all the way from our camp to the Ganges to take an early-morning bath. But those of us staying in the brahmacārī tent were not so staunch, and generally when it was time to get up at four o'clock it was so cold out that we preferred to remain in our sleeping bags.*

Śrīla Prabhupāda also started to notice that some of us were coming late to maṅgala-ārati *and that some of us were not coming at all. Prabhupāda became very upset about this, because he knew how important* maṅgala-ārati *was for us. So one morning, although he was a little frail in health, he got up at four o 'clock and came out in his* gamchā, *sat down under the pump, and took that ice-cold bath early in the morning—just to encourage us to get up, bathe, and come to* maṅgala-ārati. *That had a very profound effect on all of us, and we felt so ashamed that we just couldn't sleep late anymore.*

After *kīrtana* Prabhupāda lectured on *Śrīmad-Bhāgavatam,* resuming the story of Ajāmila. This particular story, with its glorification of the Lord's holy name, seemed especially relevant. The holy name was so powerful that by chanting only once Ajāmila had been saved. Chanting, therefore, was far more beneficial than the *prāṇa* coming down from the constellations.

Dawn came and the sky lightened—but only barely. A damp, heavy fog from the river, mingling with the smoke from the campfires, clung to everything. Rain began to fall. The devotees were unprepared for this weather. With food hard to get and cook and toilet facilities the crudest, the devotees wondered how they would last for the scheduled two weeks.

Prabhupāda, however, who shared with his disciples all these austerities, remained transcendental and apparently unaffected. If the sun peeked through the clouds, he would sit outside and take his massage. Then he would bathe himself, sitting in his *gamchā,* dipping his *loṭā* into warmed Ganges water, and pouring it over his body. He seemed so content, the devotees took heart. He wasn't complaining, so why should they?

Early in the morning, Prabhupāda took the devotees out chanting. He wore his gray woollen *cādara* and his swami hat strapped under his chin, and his disciples dressed in the warmest clothes they had—sweaters, hats, *cādaras.* Prabhupāda led the party as they weaved and wandered through the densely populated tent city. The *kīrtana* was a joy to the other pilgrims. Ironically, amid such an exotic gathering of *yogīs,* renunciants, naked *sādhus,* and the like, Prabhupāda and his disciples created the greatest stir.

And they were preaching. Although other groups were uttering *mantras* or lecturing in their tents, there was nothing else like this. This was the only *saṅkīrtana,* and everyone welcomed it. With Prabhupāda stately but joyful at the head, the procession grew, and Indians joined the Western *sādhus* in chanting Hare Kṛṣṇa.

Prabhupāda sent the devotees out on *saṅkīrtana* each morning. As the *kīrtana* party roamed from camp to camp, many pilgrims would run up, offering prostrated obeisances, money, and respect. With strong, experienced street *kīrtana* drummers and chanters like Madhudviṣa, Dīnanātha, and Haṁsadūta leading the chanting party, the devotees would forget the cold and the austerity.

Prabhupāda stressed the importance of chanting; always there must be *kīrtana,* he said. Philosophy and lectures would not be as effective at such gatherings, because the common people would not understand. Lord Caitanya had never lectured in public, but always He had held *kīrtana.*

As a result of the devotees' *kīrtana,* thousands would stream into ISKCON's large *paṇḍāl* to see the Rādhā-Kṛṣṇa Deities and take *prasādam.* ISKCON had the only Kṛṣṇa Deity at the whole Melā, and thousands would line up to see Him. Prabhupāda would speak in English in the morning and in Hindi at night, and his evening *kīrtanas* in the *paṇ-*

ḍāl became a great success. The Western *sādhus* with the women and the little child were a great curiosity to behold.

Prabhupāda also arranged for mass *prasādam* distribution, and he assigned Revatīnandana and a few helpers to cook almost nonstop over two small wood fires in the kitchen shed. Some nights the devotees would cook vegetables and *halavā* or vegetables and *purīs* for as many as seven hundred people. ISKCON's impact on the Melā pleased Prabhupāda.

> In the meantime our program for touring India has been going with all success in every place we are invited. Now we have come to the Ardha Kumbha Mela at Prayag (Allahabad) and we have got undisputed prominence amongst all groups here in the large gathering.

Śrīla Prabhupāda's lectures on Ajāmila gave life to the cold and sometimes sick devotees. This opportunity to hear from Prabhupāda was the reward for all their austerities. In each morning class, Prabhupāda continued to stress the importance of chanting the holy names purely.

"The purification of one's chanting *hari-nāma* means as soon as you chant the holy name of Kṛṣṇa you will see the form of Kṛṣṇa, realize the qualities of Kṛṣṇa, remember the pastimes of Kṛṣṇa. That is pure chanting of Hare Kṛṣṇa *mantra.* That is stated in the commentary of Śrīla Jīva Gosvāmī—that a pure devotee who chants Hare Kṛṣṇa *mantra* immediately realizes the *nāma, rūpa, guṇa, līlā,** everything about Kṛṣṇa, simply by chanting the names. You will feel the form of Kṛṣṇa. You will remember all His qualities—'Oh, Kṛṣṇa is so qualified; He is so magnanimous.' Then you will remember His *līlā,* pastimes—'Oh, Kṛṣṇa instructed Arjuna. Kṛṣṇa played with His cowherd boys. Kṛṣṇa had very nice talks with the *gopīs,* with His mother, Yaśodā.' These things you will remember. That is the actual perfection of chanting."

Prabhupāda reiterated that the only reason he had come with his disciples to the Melā was to glorify Lord Kṛṣṇa so that others could understand the importance of the Kṛṣṇa consciousness movement. But if the devotees were to successfully give Kṛṣṇa consciousness to others, they must first realize Kṛṣṇa themselves. It was possible, he said, to think of Kṛṣṇa always. He gave the example of the Indian women carrying big waterpots on their heads. Just as they have learned to keep their balance, in spite of all other movements, so a devotee, despite his activities and

* Name, form, qualities, and pastimes, respectively.

despite any mental agitation, should always remember Kṛṣṇa. And the best way to remember Kṛṣṇa is to practice always chanting the holy name.

"I remember one of our teachers in our school life instructed that if you always think, 'I shall pass my examination with distinction,' then you will pass in the first division. If you think, 'I shall pass my examination in the first division,' then you will probably pass in the third division. And if you think, 'I will somehow or other pass my examination in the third division,' then you will fail. This means that if you expect more than your capacity, then it may be possible that at the time of examination you will pass. So when chanting the Hare Kṛṣṇa *mantra,* Caitanya Mahāprabhu has said not that you chant only one hour—no. One should *practice,* and that practice was shown by Haridāsa Ṭhākura (who chanted almost twenty-four hours daily). But because we cannot, therefore we have to engage always in the service of Kṛṣṇa. That will make you remember Kṛṣṇa."

Prabhupāda said that the chanting of Hare Kṛṣṇa is exactly like a lion's roar. As a lion's roar frightens all small creatures, the chanting of Hare Kṛṣṇa ends all one's sinful reactions. He repeatedly warned the devotees, however, to avoid the most dangerous offense, that of committing sins on the strength of the holy name.

"But even if you fall down, there is no loss. That is the statement of Nārada. If one takes to Kṛṣṇa sincerely and executes devotional service but then again falls down, still he will come back. Just like we have practical experience. Some of our students have fallen down. But whatever sincere service he has rendered, that is his permanent credit. And one day he will be saved, just like Ajāmila."

On Prabhupāda's last day in Allahabad a Mr. Gourkishore visited him in his tent, inviting him to Benares. As chairman of the 45th annual festival commemorating Lord Caitanya's visit to Benares, Mr. Gourkishore wanted Prabhupāda to attend the festival as the honored guest. When Prabhupāda said he felt ill and that perhaps some of his disciples could go in his stead, Mr. Gourkishore persisted until Prabhupāda finally agreed. But first Prabhupāda wanted to visit Gorakhpur.

* * *

Gorakhpur
February 3, 1971

The Ardha-kumbha-melā over, some devotees went to Delhi, some to Bombay, and others to Calcutta. Prabhupāda and the remaining devotees went to Gorakhpur—a ten-hour journey on the antiquated meter-gauge railway. Prabhupāda had been invited by his only disciple in Gorakhpur, Dr. R. P. Rao (now Rāmānanda), a research chemist who had met Prabhupāda in San Francisco, taken initiation in 1967, and since returned to his family and four children to teach chemistry at Gorakhpur University.

Prabhupāda and his disciples moved into crowded quarters at Rāmānanda's modest home, and about one hundred people attended Prabhupāda's lecture that evening. Prabhupāda already had plans for a Rādhā-Kṛṣṇa temple on the Gorakhpur University campus as well as accredited courses and degrees in Kṛṣṇa consciousness—B.A., M.A., and Ph.D. He envisioned graduates going out to teach Kṛṣṇa consciousness in schools, colleges, and temples all over the world. He inspired Rāmānanda and a group of his friends to form a committee to introduce Kṛṣṇa consciousness within the university, and he initiated about one dozen disciples. Since they all professed to be following the rules against illicit sex, intoxication, and gambling and had been lifelong vegetarians, he waived the usual six-month trial period. He asked them to chant sixteen rounds daily and to make their city Kṛṣṇa conscious. In his absence they should maintain Rāmānanda's home as an active ISKCON center and try to establish courses in Kṛṣṇa consciousness at the university.

* * *

Benares
February 6, 1971

Mr. Gourkishore was counting heavily on Prabhupāda's participation in the upcoming celebration. The climax of the week-long observance of Lord Caitanya's visit to Benares would be a parade, Mr. Gourkishore said, and Prabhupāda and his disciples had an important part in it. Newspaper articles, handbills, and loudspeaker carts had announced throughout the city the presence of Śrīla Prabhupāda and his "foreign disciples." The devotees sensed they were being treated like entertainers, expected to perform as if under contract—but without salary.

On the day of the procession Prabhupāda rode in a silver chariot, the kind customarily used in extravagant wedding processions. The chariot was pulled by a pair of white horses, wearing silver crowns and decorative blankets. The leading float in the parade bore a six-foot statue of Lord Caitanya in yellow *nim* wood. Next followed a file of decorated elephants. One elephant carried a banner reading *Harer Nama Eva Kevalam,* one carried actors dressed as Lord Rāma and Sītā, another carried two actors dressed as Rādhā and Kṛṣṇa, who waved to the crowds, and another a picture of Lord Caitanya and His associates performing *saṅkīrtana.* Next came a decorated flatbed truck with children portraying Lord Caitanya and Lord Nityānanda, chanting and dancing. Then followed a series of professional *kīrtana* groups and Prabhupāda's "foreign disciples" dancing and performing *kīrtana.*

Behind the devotees, Śrīla Prabhupāda rode in his chariot. On either side of the chariot walked a devotee fanning Prabhupāda with a *cāmara* whisk, while Prabhupāda sat with his right hand in his bead bag, his left hand on his cane. He was dressed in silk, with pearl buttons on his *kurtā.* A wide patch of sandalwood paste covered his forehead. He didn't wave or smile or turn to see the crowds, but sat calmly, chanting Hare Kṛṣṇa on his beads.

Following Prabhupāda's chariot was a *śāhnāī* group, several more *kīrtana* parties, and finally another statue of Lord Caitanya, carried by eight men.

The festival committee said three hundred thousand attended, double what they would have had without Prabhupāda and his foreign disciples. The procession was over, however, and as the star attraction, Prabhupāda had made his appearance and drawn a large crowd, and now nothing more was required. He felt tired. He and his disciples were taken to a nearby *dharmaśālā* and served a feast. Prabhupāda remained grave and as soon as possible returned to his quarters and his regular schedule.

A student at the University of Benares who had met Prabhupāda at the Allahabad Melā stopped by to visit. The boy's father had given him a biography of Lord Caitanya as a gift for Prabhupāda, and when the boy showed Prabhupāda a picture of his father, Prabhupāda said, "Yes, your father is a devotee. So why don't you also take initiation?"

The boy was hesitant. As he walked with Prabhupāda in the garden,

Prabhupāda said, "You have got the seed of devotional service from your father, so you must now cultivate."

"But how can I shave my head?" the boy inquired. "I am a university student."

"No, it is a custom. You should shave once, and then you can keep short hair."

"But how can I wear *tilaka*? They will laugh at me."

Prabhupāda said the boy should not fear criticism. He should become a soldier of Kṛṣṇa. Just as the government honors its valiant soldiers, Kṛṣṇa rewards a devotee who accepts difficulties and criticism on His behalf.

"What about *guru-dakṣiṇā*?" the boy asked.

"*Guru-dakṣiṇā* is just a formality," Prabhupāda said. "It was a custom in olden days that when someone gets initiation, he goes to the various homes. It is a sign that you have become a servant of your *guru*, you are prepared to beg alms for your *guru*. It is whatever you give."

The boy returned home and told his father. The next day was an auspicious day, his father said—the appearance day of Lord Nityānanda. A good day to receive spiritual initiation.

So the next day, on Nityānanda Trayodaśī, Śrīla Prabhupāda initiated the boy, giving him the name Nirañjana dāsa. When Prabhupāda asked Nirañjana if he had any questions, Nirañjana said he wanted to know his eternal relationship with Kṛṣṇa; was it as servant, as friend, as parent?

Prabhupāda replied that servitude was the common ground in all transcendental relationships with Lord Kṛṣṇa. By chanting Hare Kṛṣṇa, Nirañjana would become more and more purified and realize more and more his relationship with Kṛṣṇa. Nirañjana asked how he would understand his relationship.

"No, don't jump," Prabhupāda said. "You have some *śraddhā* [faith] from your father, and now you are associating with devotees and chanting. Gradually you will realize."

Nirañjana agreed to be patient.

Prabhupāda asked Nirañjana to arrange a lecture for him on campus, and Nirañjana, with the help of his uncle, a philosophy professor, got Prabhupāda a speaking engagement for his last morning in Benares.

On the day Prabhupāda was to leave, he met with John Griesser, the American photographer traveling with him and his party since Surat. John, who had shaved his mustache and thought a lot about his future, came to say good-bye—until Bombay, where they would meet again in a few weeks.

John found Prabhupāda in the courtyard, enjoying the sunshine and eating *gur* (date sugar) from a clay pot. Prabhupāda asked that the pot be broken and distributed to John and the other devotees present, and while John sat licking *gur* from a piece of clay pot, Prabhupāda talked about his boyhood in Calcutta.

John: *Prabhupāda was talking in his accented, rhythmic English about his boyhood days in Calcutta, and he described a gracious city, before the crowding and squalor of today. As a schoolboy he had seen splendid Victorian buildings of white marble, surrounded by stately lawns and trees.*

Suddenly Prabhupāda looked over at me and laughed. "So, John," he said, "I think Kṛṣṇa has captured you." I agreed I had known it for quite a while, but now Śrīla Prabhupāda confirmed it.

When Prabhupāda was leaving Benares to return to Gorakhpur, many of his disciples went to the wrong train station. While Prabhupāda and a few followers waited at the correct train station, Kauśalyā asked him, "How did you like it here in Benares, Śrīla Prabhupāda?"

"It is all right," he said, indifferently.

"Did you have a nice rest?" she asked, trying to think of some positive aspect of the visit.

"Rest I can have any time," said Prabhupāda. "But I like to be with my devotees."

Surrounded by luggage, Prabhupāda sat on the bench, while Tamāla Kṛṣṇa and Śyāmasundara ran from the ticket office to the train and back. The train would leave soon. But where were the other devotees? Prabhupāda watched as his spiritual sons argued with the conductor, telling him the train couldn't go until the other devotees arrived. "They do not know what they are doing," Prabhupāda said, and he smiled.

* * *

Gorakhpur
February 10, 1971

On hearing that Prabhupāda wanted to preach in Gorakhpur, Hanuman Prasad Poddar, eminent head of the Gita Press publishing company, offered one of his properties, a two-story house (his former residence), known as Krishna Niketan. Mr. Poddar, who was bedridden in another house in Gorakhpur, had first met Prabhupāda in 1962, and he appreciated Prabhupāda's mission.

When Prabhupāda received permission to use the Krishna Niketan, he acted quickly. It was not proper, he said, that the Deities of Rādhā and Kṛṣṇa he had brought from Calcutta had been packed away in a trunk after the Ardha-kumbha-melā. They had already been worshiped, so Their worship should not be stopped. "The Deities have to be installed tomorrow," he said, and he put Kauśalyā and Nanda Kumāra in charge of the preparations.

Seeing that Nanda Kumāra and Kauśalyā needed more help, Prabhupāda called for all his disciples, and soon twenty American devotees were scurrying about, preparing for the next day's festival. Prabhupāda directed the devotees in cleaning the temple room from ceiling to floor and in building the altar. He asked Himavatī to donate her fanciest *sārī,* which he hung like a curtain before the table that was to be the Deities' altar. The altar needed a backdrop, he said, and while Kauśalyā stood on the table he handed her pieces of colored fabric to arrange against the wall. The backdrop completed, Prabhupāda took a rug a devotee had bought in Allahabad and placed it over the table-altar.

That night Prabhupāda surveyed the temple room. "Oh, it is very nice," he said. He retired to his room, and two devotees stayed up all night sewing clothes for Rādhā and Kṛṣṇa. The next morning the Deities were placed on the altar, and the devotees resumed Their worship, offering Them *prasādam* and *ārati* six times a day.

The devotees were living in an ISKCON temple atmosphere for the first time since they had arrived in India, and their lives became regulated and secure. The weather warmed, and the devotees—many of whom had exhausted their health in Allahabad—felt relief. The Gorakhpur temple was situated on several acres of agricultural land outside the city; it was a peaceful place. During the day Prabhupāda would rest, as the sunshine came through the window and warmed his body.

In the evenings guests would come for *kīrtana* and Prabhupāda's lecture. Speaking on the Sixth Canto of *Śrīmad-Bhāgavatam,* Prabhupāda referred repeatedly to Śrīdhara Svāmī's commentary, from the fourteenth century.

Śrīdhara Svāmī said that simply by chanting—without any regulative principles—one becomes liberated. So how is that? Śrīdhara Svāmī replies, also, that there are regulative principles. The idea is that chanting of the holy name is so powerful that it can immediately liberate the chanter. But because we are prone to fall down again, therefore there are regulative principles. ...

"Morning, noon, and evening, we should daily chant Hare Kṛṣṇa *mantra* with devotion and faith. By doing this, one can avoid volumes of miserable conditions of life—simply by chanting. So one should be so much careful and faithful. You should know that as soon as you are chanting, Kṛṣṇa is dancing on your tongue. Therefore, how much careful and respectful we should be."

Each night Prabhupāda would take the commentaries of Śrīdhara Svāmī as his text.

"So Śrīdhara Svāmī gives this example, that without knowing that there is a very nice medicine a man takes so many thousands of medicines. Similarly, the great stalwart leaders of religious principles, without knowing this Hare Kṛṣṇa *mantra,* take so many troublesome ritualistic ceremonies. Actually, there is no need. The whole thing is—Śrīdhara Svāmī is giving the stress very strongly—that you can simply chant Hare Kṛṣṇa *mantra* without understanding any ritualistic ceremonies. ..."

Śrīdhara Svāmī's commentary was filled with quotations from various scriptures about the supreme benefit of chanting the holy names of Kṛṣṇa.

"Then Śrīdhara Svāmī says, *akhila-ceṣṭitam.* That means that any endeavor for pushing on Kṛṣṇa's glories, that is as good as chanting the holy name. When you go out for canvassing, for pushing on this movement, people might think that you are not chanting. But suppose you are canvassing for a life member—that topic is also as good as chanting Hare Kṛṣṇa *mantra,* because it is *akhila-ceṣṭitam.* One's life must be dedicated simply for Kṛṣṇa's service."

Speaking before his Indian audiences, Śrīla Prabhupāda also told about his preaching in the West. One evening he gave a personal history, describing how his spiritual master, on their first meeting, had immediately told him to preach Lord Caitanya's message to the English-speaking world.

"At that time I argued with him that we are a dependent nation, and who is going to hear about our message? So he defeated my argument. Yes. He was a learned scholar. So what I was? I was a tiny boy. So I agreed that I was defeated." Prabhupāda laughed softly.

Prabhupāda told about his business years in Allahabad and how he again met his spiritual master and became initiated. He told of starting *Back to Godhead* in 1944, of taking *sannyāsa,* and of finally traveling to America in 1965. He mentioned his struggles in New York City and how the first boys had joined him when he started his movement in a storefront on Second Avenue.

"So practically we began work from 1968. In 1966 I started, but in '67 I became very much sick, so I came back to India. And again I went there in 1968. Practically this propaganda work began vigorously from 1968. From '68, '69, '70, and this is '71. So three, four years, all these branches have grown up, and now practically throughout the whole continent of Europe and throughout America they know what is Hare Kṛṣṇa movement, due to our propaganda."

Early each morning before sunrise, Prabhupāda would sit in the temple room before his disciples and lecture from *Śrīmad-Bhāgavatam.* And each morning the lights would go out, leaving everyone in darkness. It was a typical Indian power failure, and Prabhupāda would stop lecturing while a devotee lit two candles by his *vyāsāsana* and two candles on the altar. Long shadows would mix with the luminous gold of the Rādhā-Kṛṣṇa Deities, and Prabhupāda, wearing spectacles and holding open the *Śrīmad-Bhāgavatam* in his hand, would appear wonderfully mysterious.

One morning Śrīla Prabhupāda sang a new song, *Jaya Rādhā-Mādhava.*

"I will teach you this song," he said. Reciting the first line, he had the devotees repeat it again and again. One line at a time, he went through the song.

jaya rādhā-mādhava kuñja-bihārī
gopī-jana-vallabha giri-vara-dhārī
yaśodā-nandana braja-jana-rañjana
yāmuna-tīra-vana-cārī

They should know it, he told them, by the next morning.

Only a few devotees managed to memorize the song, so the next morning Prabhupāda went through it again, line by line. During the evening lecture he explained the meaning of the song.

"*Jaya rādhā-mādhava kuñja-bihārī.* Kṛṣṇa is enjoying in Vṛndāvana. That is the real picture of God—simply enjoying. The *vṛndāvana-līlā* of Kṛṣṇa is the perfect presentation of the Supreme Personality of Godhead—He is simply enjoying.

"All the inhabitants of Vṛndāvana—the *gopīs,* the cowherd boys, Mahārāja Nanda, Yaśodā—*everyone* is simply anxious how to make Kṛṣṇa happy. They have no other business. The residents of Vṛndāvana have no other business than to satisfy Kṛṣṇa, and Kṛṣṇa has no other business. *Yaśodā-nandana braja-jana-rañjana yāmuna-tīra-vana-cārī.* He is acting as the little son of Yaśodā. And His only business is how to please the residents of Vṛndāvana.

"*Yaśodā-nandana braja-jana-rañjana yāmuna-tīra-vana-cārī.* He is wandering in the forest of Vṛndāvana on the bank of the Yamunā. This is the actual picture of the Supreme Personality of Godhead.

"But Brahmā, Indra, big, big demigods, they are also bewildered. They are sometimes mistaken how this cowherd boy can be the Supreme Personality of Godhead. Just like some of us think like that. But those who are thinking like that, for them also there is manifestation of Kṛṣṇa's supremacy. *Gopī-jana-vallabha giri-vara-dhārī.* Although He is engaged in pleasing the residents of Vraja, when there is need He can lift up the Govardhana Hill at the age of seven years. Or He can kill the Pūtanā at the age of three months.

"So many demons used to visit daily. Kṛṣṇa used to go with the calves and cows, with His friends in the forest, and every day Kaṁsa used to send a demon to kill Him. Aghāsura, Bakāsura, Dhenukāsura—so many.

"So also, Kṛṣṇa is playing just like a cowherd boy. His supreme mercy as the Supreme Personality of Godhead is never absent there. That is God. God is not created by meditation. God is God. God is never manufactured. We should know this."

On the third morning after introducing *Jaya Rādhā-Mādhava,* Prabhupāda again sang it with the devotees responding. Then he began to explain it further. Rādhā-Mādhava, he said, have Their eternal loving pastimes in the groves of Vṛndāvana.

He stopped speaking. His closed eyes flooded with tears, and he began gently rocking his head. His body trembled. Several minutes passed, and everyone in the room remained completely silent. Finally, he returned to external consciousness and said, "Now, just chant Hare Kṛṣṇa."

After this, the Rādhā-Kṛṣṇa Deities of Gorakhpur became known as Śrī Śrī Rādhā-Mādhava.

Kauśalyā would regularly wash the temple floor while Prabhupāda gave his *Śrīmad-Bhāgavatam* lecture. One morning Prabhupāda interrupted his lecture. "Just see this girl," he said—Kauśalyā was down at the other end of the room, scrubbing. "This is first-class service."

The next day Prabhupāda called Kauśalyā forward. "Every morning you are washing the floor so nicely," he said, "but this morning you are washing the floor like a crow takes a bath." Prabhupāda shook his hand, as if flicking water about. "You do not know how to wash the floor. I am going to show you." Prabhupāda came down from his *vyāsāsana* and walked to the other end of the room, followed by all the devotees.

"Where is your bucket?" Kauśalyā brought over her bucket. Prabhupāda asked for a rag. She gave him hers. He then crouched down and started scrubbing. "This is how you wash the floor," he said, "—with lots of water. And you do it a section at a time." It should be done in two stages: first with a wet rag, and then with a wrung rag.

The devotees stood in amazement, watching. Several times Prabhupāda repeated the procedure, washing a section of the floor and then drying it, careful not to touch the clean area with his feet. "See?" he said. "That is expert."

When Tamāla Kṛṣṇa requested Prabhupāda to move on to Bombay and bigger preaching, Prabhupāda replied, "Let us see if Kṛṣṇa wants us to have this place." Haṁsadūta also became restless to preach, and Prabhupāda sent him with a group of *brahmacārīs* to Aligarh and Agra.

Little appeared to be happening in Gorakhpur, but Prabhupāda had plans. He was still negotiating with the university authorities for land for constructing a temple.

> If we are successful in our attempt, it will be unique in all the world and soon more and more college campuses will follow. ... And if we can establish a seat of Krishna Consciousness then students may take their doctorate degree in Krishna Consciousness and go out and preach all over the world.

Prabhupāda had three goals: to reach the Gorakhpur university students, to introduce *kīrtana* into the factories, and to introduce *kīrtana* into the homes. The main obstacle was lack of commitment from the local people. Many were willing to attend his evening lectures, but to actually surrender time, money, and energy in the service of Kṛṣṇa was more difficult. At least the Rādhā-Kṛṣṇa temple was lively, and Prabhupāda hoped the directors of Gita Press would turn the Krishna Niketan building over to ISKCON permanently.

Prabhupāda continued lecturing, morning and evening. For three consecutive evenings he spoke on a single verse of *Caitanya-caritāmṛta,* defeating the Māyāvāda arguments that the Absolute Truth is ultimately impersonal Brahman.

"The Māyāvādī philosophers say that the Absolute is impersonal and that there is no different energy. So Caitanya Mahāprabhu's challenge is that the Absolute Truth has got multienergies. Suppose someone has a big business, a big factory. So if the proprietor says, 'I am all-pervading over this factory,' that is correct. Take, for example, Birla. They say, 'Birla's factory.' Birla's name is there. Although Birla is a person and he is not personally present in that factory, everyone says, 'Birla's factory.' That means Birla's money, Birla's energy, is there. If there is any loss in that factory, the suffering goes to Birla. Or if there is any gain in the factory, the profit goes to Birla. Therefore Birla's energy is there in the factory. Similarly, the whole creation is a manifestation of Kṛṣṇa. Everything there is Kṛṣṇa, His energy. He is represented by His energy. That is called simultaneously one and different, *acintya-bhedābheda-tattva.*"

Discussing preaching in America, Prabhupāda said the Western world was ninety-nine percent in the modes of ignorance and passion. Although America was the richest nation on earth, its youth were becoming hippies, much to the dismay of parents and government leaders. So despite their wealth, they were unhappy. They were ripe, however, for understanding spiritual knowledge.

"This is the causeless mercy of Lord Caitanya. Now you can see that these boys, when they are chanting—how they are in ecstasy. They are immediately on the transcendental platform. Not only here, everywhere they are chanting—in every temple. The advantage of these boys and girls is that they have no hodgepodge in their head. They directly accept Kṛṣṇa as the Supreme Personality of Godhead, and they directly accept the instruction of Lord Caitanya. Therefore they are making advancement. Their fortune is that their brain is not congested with hodgepodge ideas. They have given up all other occupations and accepted Kṛṣṇa as the Supreme Personality of Godhead. So in India we can also do that. What is the difficulty? We must do this. Just accept this: *kṛṣṇas tu bhagavān svayam.** And surrender unto Him."

Prabhupāda celebrated the appearance day of Śrīla Bhaktisiddhānta Sarasvatī in Gorakhpur. At the morning gathering he said, "We should honor this day and very respectfully pray to Bhaktisiddhānta Sarasvatī Gosvāmī that 'We are engaged in your service, so give us strength. Give us intelligence. We are being guided by your servant.' So in this way we have to pray. And I think in the evening we shall distribute *prasādam.* There will be so many guests coming, so they can be distributed *prasādam.*"

Prabhupāda said life members and other friends should be invited for the flower offering at noon. One of the devotees asked about the feast.

Prabhupāda: "Feasting means *purī* and *halavā* and a vegetable and chutney. That's all—four things. Make it simple."

Tamāla Kṛṣṇa: "Prabhupāda? You want us to offer a feast to your Guru Mahārāja at noontime? A special plate of feast?"

Prabhupāda: "Not a special plate. The process is that whatever we offer to the Deity, that is offered to *guru.* And *guru* offers to his *guru.* In this way, it goes to Kṛṣṇa. We don't directly offer to Rādhā-Kṛṣṇa. No. We have no right. Nor does Kṛṣṇa accept in that way. The pictures of the *ācāryas*—why are they there? Actually you have to offer the plate to your *guru,* and he will offer to his *guru,* he offers to his *guru,* his *guru.* In this way, it will go to Kṛṣṇa. That is the process. You cannot directly approach Kṛṣṇa or predecessor *ācāryas.* That is not possible."

One day Prabhupāda visited Hanuman Prasad Poddar. Mr. Poddar had been gravely ill for some time, but he was able to sit up and speak briefly with Prabhupāda. As the pioneer of the *Kalyana* magazine, which printed installments of the *Mahābhārata* and other Vedic classics, Hanuman Prasad Poddar was a world-famous patron of Indian religious thought.

* "Kṛṣṇa is the Supreme Personality of Godhead." (*Bhāg.* 1.3.28)

His inexpensive Hindi *Bhagavad-gītā* translation had been distributed by the millions, so that even a poor man could have a copy of *Bhagavad-gītā.* Mr. Poddar had been a friend to Prabhupāda when in 1962 Prabhupāda had come to him in Gorakhpur and shown him his manuscript for the first volume of the *Śrīmad-Bhāgavatam.* Appreciating the importance of the work, Mr. Poddar, by his word of approval, had helped Prabhupāda get a donation for its printing from the Delhi industrialist Mr. Dalmia. Now, almost ten years later, Prabhupāda was showing Mr. Poddar his recently published books *Kṛṣṇa, the Supreme Personality of Godhead, Teachings of Lord Caitanya, The Nectar of Devotion,* and his magazine *Back to Godhead.* Mr. Poddar was impressed, and he and Prabhupāda exchanged their sincere appreciation of each other's work.

Mr. Suryakant Fogla: *Hanuman Prasad Poddar was my grandfather. He was very much ill at the time Prabhupāda came here to meet him in his bedroom upstairs. There are certain things which cannot be explained, but they were talking in the language of their eyes. My grandfather expressed some gratitude, some affection, some regard by his eyes, and Prabhupāda's reply was also in the same way. The appreciation from both sides could easily be seen and appreciated by the persons who were present. A lot of Prabhupāda's disciples were there, and everyone was almost in tears when those two saints, great people, met and talked to each other.*

They were talking about the spiritual world, and they were praising each other for their deeds. My grandfather also was saying that what Prabhupāda has done, it is unforgettable for anyone of the world. Because to take our Indian culture to Western countries—the credit entirely goes to our beloved Prabhupāda. And he was the only person who took Rādhā-Kṛṣṇa and the holy name outside—in such a way that nobody else could and will be able to in the future.

Since Mr. Poddar was ill and weak, Prabhupāda left after about half an hour. Prabhupāda had spent two weeks in Gorakhpur, and now he was eager to go to Bombay. Leaving two disciples behind to attend to the Deity worship and continue preaching in Gorakhpur, he left.

* * *

ISKCON's Bombay headquarters was a four-room flat on the seventh floor of the Akash-Ganga Building. Rent was nearly three thousand rupees a month, and the devotees had no guaranteed monthly income.

Yet because the building was in a vital, prestigious location, Prabhupāda had taken the risk. Such a headquarters would be a necessary base for the preaching he wanted to do in Bombay, and his next preaching would be a grand eleven-day *paṇḍāl* program. "If you are going to hunt," Prabhupāda said, "then you should hunt for a rhinoceros. In that way, if you don't succeed, everyone will simply say, 'Oh, it couldn't be done anyway.' But if you do succeed, then everyone will be surprised. Everyone will be amazed."

As Prabhupāda revealed his plans for a gigantic *paṇḍāl* festival, the devotees became keenly aware that Prabhupāda's inspiration was motivating all their preaching; without him they could never attempt anything so bold and ambitious as a giant *paṇḍāl* festival in Bombay. Often "the American and European disciples" had been billed along with him, as if of equal importance, but the devotees saw themselves as only foolish servants trying to help the genuine pure devotee of the Lord. Although Prabhupāda credited his disciples, his disciples knew that Prabhupāda was Kṛṣṇa's empowered representative. He was their authority and personal link to Kṛṣṇa; his words and actions evinced full transcendental potency. As Kṛṣṇa was unlimited, Śrīla Prabhupāda, Kṛṣṇa's dearmost friend, was entitled to demand unlimited service on Kṛṣṇa's behalf. In the service of Kṛṣṇa, no project was impossible. *Impossible,* Prabhupāda said, was a word in a fool's dictionary.

But as Prabhupāda unfolded his plans for the *paṇḍāl* festival, the devotees doubted: How could they ever raise the money? How could they erect such a huge tent? Where would they get so much food? And who would cook it? Prabhupāda seemed amused at their doubts. "You are all Americans," he said. "So what is the use of being American unless you do something wonderful?"

A Bombay *paṇḍāl,* Prabhupāda said, would be the perfect way to link America's ingenuity with India's spirituality. He gave the example of a blind man and a lame man. Although separately they are helpless, by cooperating—the blind man carrying the lame man on his shoulders, and the lame man giving directions—the two can work successfully. America, because of materialism and ignorance of God, was blind. And India, because of foreign invasions, poverty, and misinterpretations of Vedic knowledge, was lame. America had technological advancement and wealth, and India had spiritual knowledge. The job of the Kṛṣṇa consciousness movement was to combine the two strengths and uplift the world. And one practical application would be the Bombay *paṇḍāl* festival.

Prabhupāda divided the work, assigning Śyāmasundara to publicity, Tamāla Kṛṣṇa to the *paṇḍāl* arrangements, Girirāja to fund-raising, and Madhudviṣa to the scheduled programs onstage. Catching Prabhupāda's spirit of "shooting the rhinoceros," Śyāmasundara organized a massive publicity campaign, with giant posters and banners strung across the streets, announcing "His Divine Grace A. C. Bhaktivedanta Swami Prabhupāda will speak in English language about the science of God. Prasadam distribution and bhajan singing will be led by his American and European bhaktas—Hare Krishna Festival at Cross Maidan—March 25 to April 4."

Girirāja: *Śrīla Prabhupāda took Bombay by storm. The whole city was alive with excitement about the Hare Krishna Festival. We had banners at all the major intersections in Bombay. We had posters up on all the walls, many posters on every wall, and we had very big advertisements in the newspaper, with a beautiful picture of Śrīla Prabhupāda superimposed over a globe, and the words* Bhagavat Dharma Discourses: A Hare Krishna Festival. World Preacher of Bhakti Cult, His Divine Grace A. C. Bhaktivedanta Swami.

Day by day the momentum grew more and more, and every day something new was happening. Finally, in the last two days, we got a huge billboard at Victoria Train Station, the busiest intersection of downtown Bombay. By then everyone knew so much about the festival and where it was going to be and everything that all this billboard said was Hare Krishna *in huge letters. By then everyone knew, so just these two huge words* Hare Krishna *was enough.*

Then Śyāmasundara had arranged for a big helium-filled balloon that was attached to a very long rope at the Cross Maidan site. That balloon just hovered over the city, and there was a streamer attached to the balloon, saying Hare Krishna Festival. *It was real American ingenuity, flair, and dynamism.*

Inspired by Śyāmasundara's lead and taking up a spirit of competition, the other devotees worked at their projects with great enthusiasm. When Prabhupāda called a meeting of the local ISKCON life members and supporters, the turnout was disappointing—only about a dozen. And even those, on hearing the proportions of Prabhupāda's plan, became hesitant. The festival would cost more than one hundred thousand rupees! Although some life members doubted whether the devotees could actually execute such a large production, a handful of stalwarts—Sadajiwatlal, Chandulal Bahl, Kartikeya Mahadevia, Kailash Seksaria, Ramchand Chabria, G. D. Somani, and others—vowed they would do their best to help raise the funds.

Prabhupāda remained actively involved, and he warned his disciples to be wary of cheaters during their business transactions. Every night the devotees would report to him, and he would ask about many details. He wanted the best location, the best work, and the best price. He wanted to know everything: What about the cooking area? Are all the devotees working to their full capacity? Is the mailing list complete? Have the invitations been sent? What about the latrines? What was the cost for the sound system? He scrutinized every detail with sharp, critical intelligence.

Girirāja's fund-raising work was going well. He had donations solicited from businessmen and had printed a souvenir pamphlet. But he was feeling a strain, and he came to Prabhupāda for solace. "Can we use force in Kṛṣṇa consciousness?" he asked.

Prabhupāda frowned. "No. We cannot use force."

"But what if we see one of the workers is lazy on the job and not doing what he is supposed to?"

"No," Prabhupāda replied. "We can never use force."

"Well, what about in making life members?"

"Force we cannot use," Prabhupāda repeated. "But we can trick them." He told a story about a boy who didn't want to do arithmetic; as soon as the teacher wrote *one plus one* on the board, the boy would balk. So the teacher drew a picture of a cow on the board and asked the boy, "If a man has one cow and then he buys another cow, how many cows will he have?" The boy answered, "Two." Thus the teacher began teaching him arithmetic, even though he was unwilling to learn.

"So people may be averse to serving Kṛṣṇa," Prabhupāda explained, "but we can trick them and get them to serve without their knowing it. But we can never use force. These people are all businessmen. They are always calculating profit and loss. But they are also pious, and they want to go to Kṛṣṇa. So you have to convince them that by giving this money they will gain so much by coming closer to Kṛṣṇa. And that is the truth. When they are convinced, then they will give."

Prabhupāda had ordered from Jaipur two sets of large white marble

Deities (paid for by a donation from R. D. Birla). One set was to be installed in the Bombay temple and the other worshiped at the *paṇḍāl* and later sent to one of the temples in the West. But the devotees were anxious that the Deities be finished and shipped on time. And there were other sources of anxiety, right up until the very day of the festival. *Paṇḍāl* construction, *prasādam* distribution, seating arrangements, sound systems—whether these things would be ready on time and whether there would be enough money remained uncertain. But under Prabhupāda's direction the devotees worked steadily, with firm faith in Kṛṣṇa.

And all turned out successful, with ten thousand people attending the first day and twenty thousand that night. The devotees, including those just arrived from the West, numbered about a hundred, and the large stage easily accommodated them, with ample space for dancing *kīrtanas.* Onstage, within a gorgeous, golden-domed altar, surrounded by profuse flower arrangements, stood Rādhā and Kṛṣṇa. Prabhupāda's large red *vyāsāsana,* covered by a canopy, stood at stage center. Also onstage was a display of Prabhupāda's books. The tall and spacious *paṇḍāl,* built to hold more than thirty thousand, was lined with fluorescent bulbs, and the stage glowed with colorful flashing lights.

The program was *kīrtana, prasādam,* a lecture, and slides, more *kīrtana,* and more *prasādam.* And the Bombayites—devotees at heart, despite their sophistication and Westernization—loved these very things: Rādhā and Kṛṣṇa, *kīrtana,* and *prasādam.* And that all this was being presented by Westerners made the *paṇḍāl* especially attractive.

The cooks prepared *prasādam* at the *paṇḍāl* site, cooking over a hard coal fire and using big paddles to stir *kicharī* and *halavā* in woks eight feet across. Each night the devotees would serve thousands of plates.

Prabhupāda's appearance in the evening was always the high point. He would sit on his *vyāsāsana,* little Sarasvatī would walk out and garland him, and the crowd would cheer. He would wait for the crowd to quieten, which never happened. So he would just begin speaking, his voice ringing over the powerful sound system. He titled his first lecture "Modern Civilization Is a Failure, and the Only Hope Is Krishna Consciousness."

Prabhupāda sat, eyes half closed in concentration, addressing the largest audience that had ever assembled to hear him. His speaking was particularly forceful, as he glorified Kṛṣṇa and criticized the enemies of Kṛṣṇa. He spoke against governments that were not Kṛṣṇa conscious and against *gurus* who neglected the worship of Kṛṣṇa. He stressed the necessity of teaching Kṛṣṇa's message to the whole world, while his Godbrothers from the Bombay Gaudiya Math sat in the audience, listening respectfully.

"And you are practically seeing that all over the world these *Bhagavad-gītā* principles — Kṛṣṇa, the Supreme Lord — is being accepted. All these boys and girls who are dancing in Kṛṣṇa consciousness — four years ago, four years back, they never heard of Kṛṣṇa. Of course, some of them knew *Bhagavad-gītā,* because *Bhagavad-gītā* is very widely read. But because *Bhagavad-gītā* was not properly presented, although for the last hundred or two hundred or more than that years *Bhagavad-gītā* is widely read all over the world, there was not a single *kṛṣṇa-bhakta.* But since *Bhagavad-gītā* is being presented as it is, within four years there are hundreds and thousands of *kṛṣṇa-bhaktas.* That is our point, that you present the thing as it is, without any adulteration... .

"So it is our mission. It is India's culture. People are hankering after this culture, Kṛṣṇa culture. So you should prepare yourself to present *Bhagavad-gītā* as it is. Then India will conquer all over the world by this Kṛṣṇa culture. Rest assured. But we are hankering after help from others. Our government men go there in America: 'Please give us wheat. Please give us money. Please give us soldiers.' Simply begging business. But here is a thing which you can give to them. Simply begging does not glorify your country."

Girirāja: *Prabhupāda was preaching forcefully to the people of Bombay, and every evening the* paṇḍāl *was packed with at least twenty thousand people. Śrīla Prabhupāda would preach so strongly, emphasizing following religious principles. He knew that these people are Hindus but they are not following these principles. Prabhupāda was speaking so powerfully that I knew that what he was saying would be hard for many of the audience to accept.*

"We have something to give to the whole world. That is Kṛṣṇa consciousness. ... Why you neglect this treasure of Vedic knowledge? And the summarized knowledge is *Bhagavad-gītā.* So if we simply try to understand *Bhagavad-gītā* as it is, we understand immediately the science of God. And because we are all parts and parcels of God, we are actually hankering after uniting with God. That is our seeking. *Ānandamayo 'bhyāsāt.* God is *ānandamaya* [by nature, full of pleasure], and we, being part and parcel of God, or Kṛṣṇa, we are also *ānandamaya.* But we are seeking *ānanda* [pleasure] in a different atmosphere, in the material atmosphere. Therefore we are being baffled. The only remedy is that you take to Kṛṣṇa consciousness and you will be happy. So it is the duty of every Indian to understand this science."

Girirāja: *At that time I was thinking that if Prabhupāda had wanted to flatter the audience or compromise his philosophy, he could have attracted millions of followers. But because he was preaching so boldly and forcefully without compromise, many of the audience did not like it, because it was a challenge to their sense gratification and to their sentiment.*

"This is a science. It is not a dogmatic, bluffing thing. It is a science, and spoken by the Lord Himself, and understood by all the *ācāryas.* Kṛṣṇa says, *ācāryopasanam:* we have to understand things through the *ācāryas. Ācāryavān puruṣo veda:* one who is not following the footsteps of the *ācāryas,* he cannot understand anything. Kṛṣṇa also says, *tad-vijñānārtham.* That is said in the *Kaṭhopaniṣad: tad-vijñānārthaṁ sa gurum evābhigacchet.* Kṛṣṇa says, *tad viddhi praṇipātena paripraśnena sevayā.* So everywhere the same instruction is there, 'You approach a person who is coming in disciplic succession—*evaṁ paramparā-prāptam*—and try to learn *Bhagavad-gītā* as it is.' Your life will be sublime. Your life will be successful. That is our mission."

Girirāja: *The fact is that people were wild about Prabhupāda and ISKCON. One night we showed slides of the Ratha-yātrā in San Francisco, and the audience was going wild. In front of ten thousand people Prabhupāda announced that we will hold Jagannātha Ratha-yātrā in Bombay, and everyone started to cheer and applaud.*

Day after day, the *paṇḍāl* festival was a success. Bombay's most important citizens came and were impressed. White-shirted businessmen and their well-groomed wives joined in the chanting. For hundreds of thousands of Bombay citizens, coming to the Cross Maidan to attend an evening *paṇḍāl* program was easy enough. Some were intent on listening to the lecture and inquiring deeply into devotional service, others came mostly to see the Deity, take *prasādam,* or appreciate the *kīrtana.* In any case, A. C. Bhaktivedanta Swami Prabhupāda and the Hare Kṛṣṇa devotees were a refreshing addition to the life of the city. It was the biggest public event in Bombay.

One evening Prabhupāda conducted a Vedic marriage ceremony and an initiation before thousands of people. The marriage was arranged between Vegavān who was Swedish, and Padmavatī dāsī, who was Australian. They completely enchanted the whole audience—she with her ornate red *sārī* and Indian jewelry, including a nose ring, and he with his nice white *dhotī* and *kurtā* and clean-shaven head. Six *brahmacārīs* were initiated at that time also.

Girirāja: *The audience was impressed. First of all they were amazed just to see foreign devotees, foreign* sādhus. *Then, on top of that, to see them being initiated, and even more than that, being married in front of ten thousand people—it was overwhelming. So during the ceremony, as Śrīla Prabhupāda made the boy and girl husband and wife, he mentioned that she was from Australia and he was from Sweden. Then Śrīla Prabhupāda said, "This is the real United Nations," and everyone burst into applause. It was the most glamorous, wonderful program.*

The final night of the festival, the devotees carried the Deities of Rādhā and Kṛṣṇa in a palanquin to the seaside. Prabhupāda spoke and held *kīrtana* before a crowd of twenty-five thousand.

The next day, the *Indian Express* reported, "FITTING FINALE TO HARE KRISHNA FESTIVAL."

> It was a grand, fitting finale to the 11-day Hare Krishna festival which attracted thousands of devotees at Cross Maidan in South Bombay.
>
> The decorated murtis of Radha and Krishna were taken in procession on a regal ratha from the venue through Dirgaum Road to Chaoupatty in the evening.
>
> Dozens of nama-sankirtana mandalas from all over the city spearheaded the procession with loud and ecstatic chanting of the Hare Krishna maha-mantra, followed by His Divine Grace A. C. Bhaktivedanta Swami Prabhupada in an elegant horse-drawn coach chanting. Crowds chanted Hare Krishna on the road sides as the ratha was pulled by devotees along the route.
>
> At Chaoupatty the four-foot-tall Deities, splendidly dressed and decorated with jewels and garlands, were displayed on Their magnificent "simhasana" (throne) donated to the Hare Krishna movement by Madhav Baug and Mumba devi temples.
>
> During the celebrations Prabhupada spoke from the Gita and Srimad-Bhagavatam daily, morning and evening. More than thirty of his foreign disciples conducted kirtana, aratika, and film shows in the specially erected pandals.
>
> Prabhupada will deliver his final public message to the citizens before leaving in a few weeks on a preaching tour of the major cities of Russia.

Bombayites would not soon forget the Hare Kṛṣṇa festival, and a letter from Prabhupāda to the ISKCON life members pledged that it had been only the beginning:

> By the Grace of Their Lordships Sri Sri Radha and Krishna our recent festival in Cross Maidan Exhibition Ground has been counted a grand success, and quite noticeably the spirit of bhakti has been actively revived in Bombay. My blessings go especially to all of you who have joined with us in service.
>
> As you may know, my plan is to establish in this most auspicious city a unique International Krishna Conscious Training Centre, where hundreds of persons from abroad may be educated in the Vedic way of life, while at the same time Indian boys and girls may be trained up for *prachar* (preaching) work in foreign countries. We will construct classrooms, workrooms, dormitories, kitchen for large-scale public *prasad* distribution, a lecture hall, library, and a beautiful temple for the glorification of Radha and Krishna.
>
> We are on the threshold of bringing this important project to fruition, and we are very excited to inform you the progress made in this respect.
>
> You will agree with me that your active participation and your direct involvement in this is most essential, and hence I appeal to you to spare your valuable time for Krishna and make it a point, inspite of your extremely busy life, to extend your unstinted co-operation. It is proposed to hold a meeting on Monday, the 26th April 1971, at 6:30 p.m., "Akash Ganga," 7th floor, 89 Bhulabhai Desai Road, Bombay-26, to discuss and to finalise plans to channel our united energies to achieve the goal. It will also be a great opportunity for like-minded Krishna devotees to meet, to have darshan of the deities, and to exchange views and suggestions to make rapid progress in spiritual life.
>
> I very much want to meet you again, so kindly make it a "*must*" to attend our meeting; there is a lot of ground to be covered to spread Krishna Consciousness to millions and millions of our slumbering brothers and sisters!

That so many were accepting ISKCON and the *saṅkīrtana* movement as bona fide testified to the purity of Śrīla Prabhupāda's presentation of Lord Kṛṣṇa's teachings. His teachings were not sectarian; they were meant for everyone all over the world. He was teaching love of Kṛṣṇa, the universal principle for all humanity. In his lectures at the *paṇḍāl* he had lamented that although India was known as the land of religion, where God consciousness had traditionally permeated society, India's leaders were becoming atheists and communists. Whether Indians, polluted by the madness for sense gratification and confused by a hodgepodge of pseudoreligious teachings, could still recognize and adopt the real thing remained to be seen. But at least in Bombay, the *paṇḍāl* program had had a great effect—of that Prabhupāda felt satisfied.

The program had been the same program he had introduced everywhere: chanting, dancing, taking *prasādam,* worshiping the Deity, hearing about Kṛṣṇa. It was Lord Caitanya's program, adapted slightly according to the particular circumstances—but Lord Caitanya's program nonetheless. This *saṅkīrtana* was the only possible remedy for the disease of modern society. Yet people were reluctant to take the remedy. Prabhupāda, therefore, had "labeled the bottle." The medicine was unchanged, but he had labeled it attractively: a gala evening of entertainment, music, and refreshments, featuring the youth of America and Europe transformed into Vaiṣṇavas.

The labeling was simple, nondeceptive; everyone in Bombay knew well that the Hare Kṛṣṇa *paṇḍāl* festival was a product of their own Vedic heritage. They were fully aware that the Hare Kṛṣṇa leader was a great *ācārya* in the ancient tradition. But it had come to them in such a spectacular and attractive way that they had become caught up in it.

Madhudviṣa: *No one really thought Prabhupāda was leaving India. In India Prabhupāda was the cutting edge of the whole movement. He was the force. Things were moving because of Prabhupāda. In the Western world Prabhupāda would give the idea, and the devotees would expand on it; Prabhupāda was the overseer, but he didn't have such an integral, active part in the West. But in India Prabhupāda was right in the thick of it. He was checking the accounts. He was so much involved in the Indian scene that Ṛṣi Kumāra, the Bombay treasurer, would have to go to Prabhupāda every other day and show him the accounts. He was very much involved in everything. The whole movement in India depended on Prabhupāda. Because of this, no one thought that Prabhupāda would really leave us.*

CHAPTER THIRTY-FOUR

Jet-Age Parivrājakācārya

May 1971

ŚRĪLA PRABHUPĀDA PREPARED for extensive world travel. Although his itinerary was indefinite, his general plan was to travel widely for a few months, then tour the U.S., visit London, and then return to India. He had sent disciples to Australia and Malaysia, and he wanted to visit them. He also wanted to go to Moscow and was awaiting a letter of permission from the Soviet government. As he had spread his movement in America, visiting major cities and preaching and then stationing a few faithful disciples there to carry on, he now expanded his field to include the whole world.

Śrīla Prabhupāda's traveling was in the mood of Nārada Muni, the eternally wandering devotee. In the First Canto of *Śrīmad-Bhāgavatam,* Śrīla Prabhupāda had translated Nārada Muni's words:

> I travelled all over the earth fully satisfied and without being proud or envious. ... I do travel everywhere, by the Grace of the Almighty Vishnu either in the transcendental world or in the three divisions of the material world without any restriction because I am fixed up unbroken in the devotional service of the Lord. I do travel as abovementioned by constantly singing the glories of the Lord in transcendental message by vibrating this instrument of Vina charged with transcendental sound and given to me by Lord Krishna.

And in his *Bhāgavatam* purports, Śrīla Prabhupāda had explained:

> It is the duty of a mendicant to have experience of all varieties of God's creation as *Paribrajakacharya* or travelling alone through all forests, hills, towns, villages etc. to gain faith in God and strength of mind as well as to enlighten the inhabitants of the message of God. A Sannyasi is duty bound to take all these risks without any fear and the most typical Sannyasi of the present age is Lord Chaitanya Who travelled in the same manner through the central India jungles enlightening even the tigers, bears, snakes, deers, elephants and many other jungle animals.

In the Age of Kali, Prabhupāda had explained, *sannyāsa* is especially difficult. If, however, one did take *sannyāsa,*

> One who may take the vow of renunciation of family life may not imitate the *Paribrajakacharyas* like Narada or Lord Chaitanya but may sit down at some holy place and devote the whole time and energy in hearing and repeatedly chanting the holy scriptures left by the great Acharyas like the six Gosvamins of Vrindaban.

Yet Prabhupāda was traveling as a mendicant missionary, *parivrājakācārya.* Having already attained the advanced stage wherein the pure devotee resides in Vṛndāvana and chants Hare Kṛṣṇa incessantly, he was now traveling for the good of the whole world. He, like Nārada, was traveling to all parts of the world. As a news writer in India had appropriately titled him, he was "a jet-age *parivrājakācārya.*"

A few *brahmacārīs,* each only recently initiated by Śrīla Prabhupāda, had been preaching alone on the tropical peninsula of Malaysia for several months. With nearly a million Indians in Malaysia, many of them wealthy and influential, the *brahmacārīs* were meeting with success. During one program at a Hindu temple in Kuala Lumpur, a South Indian doctor and his lawyer wife expressed their appreciation of the devotees and offered to donate a house and some land to ISKCON. When the devotees visited the property and found that the offer was serious, they informed Prabhupāda, who decided to visit.

Prabhupāda, accompanied by his disciple Vegavān, flew from Bombay to Kuala Lumpur. Since he planned to go next to Sydney and install Rādhā-Kṛṣṇa Deities in the new temple there, he carried the Deities with him, the same Rādhā and Kṛṣṇa who had presided at the Bombay *paṇ-*

ḍāl. Lord Kṛṣṇa rode in a wooden box in the plane's luggage compartment, and Śrīmatī Rādhārāṇī, wrapped in cloth, rested on Vegavān's lap. Within a brief time after Prabhupāda's arrival at Kuala Lumpur, he was lecturing before a large audience at his host's home.

> I'm very glad to inform you that we have reached Malaysia very shortly, that on my arrival there was a nice meeting, and then we have come outside the city. Yesterday I was very busy all day.

For two days Prabhupāda stayed in the home of a wealthy Sindhi merchant of Kuala Lumpur. The house was large and luxurious, with thick carpets and large mirrors. But when Prabhupāda learned that his hosts were meat-eaters, he refused to eat anything except fruit and milk, even though his disciples offered to cook for him. His disciples, having traveled throughout Malaysia, considered eating at the homes of meat-eaters permissible, as long as the devotees could prepare their *prasādam* in pots not used for cooking meat. But Prabhupāda's standard was higher.

One room in the house held a large collection of marble Deities, about fifty sets of Lakṣmī-Nārāyaṇa and Rādhā-Kṛṣṇa Deities in rows. It appeared to be more of a collector's display than worship, however, and Prabhupāda was unimpressed.

Prabhupāda lectured at the Kuala Lumpur town hall and the Lakṣmī-Nārāyaṇa temple, mostly to Indians. He explained that people could be united only on the spiritual platform. "Look at the United Nations," he said. "They are adding more and more flags. And there are only more and more wars. This Kṛṣṇa consciousness movement will be the real United Nations." Prabhupāda had brought with him slides of ISKCON's activities, and he had one of his disciples narrate a slide show, coaching him on what to say. When a slide appeared of Ratha-yātrā in London's Trafalgar Square, Prabhupāda prompted the devotee, "Now it's no more Lord Nelson. Now it's Lord Jagannātha."

When Prabhupāda met the couple offering the land, he discovered that the agreement had certain important conditions. The doctor and his wife said that they would give ISKCON a large piece of land near the main highway and that their own construction company would build the temple. Within two years, however, if the company hadn't completed the building, the doctor and his wife would reclaim the property. Always eager to consider any serious donation of land, Prabhupāda accepted the conditional offer. But he knew that such offers were usually too conditional. Already the doctor and his wife had hinted of "Indian *brāhmaṇas*" running the temple and of ISKCON's having only a side altar.

One evening as Prabhupāda talked with the doctor, a gynecologist, the talk turned to birth control. Prabhupāda explained its sinfulness, and he gave an example. If someone poisoned the air in the room he and the doctor were sitting in, then they would have to leave the room or die. Similarly, Prabhupāda explained, contraception meant to poison the womb, denying a soul its rightful shelter.

Like Prabhupāda's previous host, the doctor ate meat, although the devotees had been pushing him to give it up. Prabhupāda was gentle. "Try to stop eating meat," he urged. It was Ekādaśī, and Prabhupāda decided to fast from all food, again showing extreme reluctance to eat in the home of a meat-eater.

* * *

Sydney
May 9, 1971

The Sydney devotees weren't ready for Prabhupāda. An early telegram had informed them he was coming, but a later telegram had said, "Prabhupāda not coming now." A third telegram had come, announcing that Bali-mardana, the Australian G.B.C. secretary, was coming. When a fourth telegram had stated only "Arriving" and the date and flight number, the devotees had presumed this referred to Bali-mardana, not to Prabhupāda. The devotees had taken a small garland and had gone to meet the plane, and when the doors to the customs area opened and Prabhupāda himself walked out, they were flabbergasted.

A white attaché case in his left hand, a cane in his right, a lightweight *cādara* around his shoulders, Śrīla Prabhupāda entered the airport. Reporters, on hand to interview Bali-mardana, came eagerly forward, one of them inquiring why Prabhupāda had come to Australia.

Replying softly, Prabhupāda said he traveled everywhere, just as a salesman travels everywhere. A salesman looks for customers wherever he can find them, and Prabhupāda was traveling, searching for anyone intelligent enough to accept his message. "There is no difference in coming to Australia," he said. "The governments have made a demarcation—'This is Australia'—but we see everywhere as the land of Kṛṣṇa."

One of the devotees hurried to phone the temple—Prabhupāda was coming!

Like Prabhupāda's original temple at 26 Second Avenue in New York, the Sydney temple was a one-room storefront on a main business thoroughfare. On the storefront's plate glass window, one of the devotees had painted a picture of Rādhā and Kṛṣṇa. Prabhupāda entered the room and found it bare, except for a simple wooden altar with three-inch Jagannātha deities, and a big cloth-covered *vyāsāsana.* An old rug hid the floor. The blue haze hanging in the air was smoke from the downstairs kitchen, where a devotee was frantically burning cumin seeds to spice Prabhupāda's lunch.

Prabhupāda remained grave as he walked deliberately to the rear door and looked outside. But when he saw garbage and boards stacked high against the building, his gravity turned to sternness. "What is all this?" he asked. Someone tried an explanation. Unsatisfactory. A devotee brought a glass of milk. "Too hot," Prabhupāda said, and the devotee took it away.

Prabhupāda sat on the large *vyāsāsana.* He looked around the room at each face. None of the fifteen or so devotees had ever seen him before, and only a handful had been initiated (by mail). They were untrained. The carpet was dirty, he said; it should be replaced. And why were there no flowers on the altar? He had brought Rādhā and Kṛṣṇa Deities, but before the devotees could begin Their worship, everything must be very clean. The devotees would have to become *brāhmaṇas* before they could worship Rādhā and Kṛṣṇa.

These devotees, Prabhupāda saw, knew little of Kṛṣṇa consciousness. The devotees who had come to Australia originally, Upendra and Balimardana, had opened the center and left, returning but rarely. Thus an entire temple of inexperienced devotees had been virtually left on its own. Since none of the Sydney devotees could lecture well, the daily classes had consisted of readings from Prabhupāda's abridged *Bhagavad-gītā As It Is,* the only book they had. Yet their firm faith in Prabhupāda compensated for their lack of training. They accepted him as a pure devotee directly in touch with God, and they accepted his books as truth and Kṛṣṇa as the Supreme Personality of Godhead. But many practical things they didn't know, such as how to cook, lecture, and worship the Deities. They knew Prabhupāda wanted them to chant Hare Kṛṣṇa publicly and distribute *Back to Godhead* magazines to the people of Sydney, and this they did daily. Despite frequent arrests, they continued with their *saṅkīrtana.* Sincerity they had. They only lacked training.

A devotee brought Prabhupāda his lunch, poorly cooked—the *capātīs* half burned, half raw, the vegetables wrongly spiced. Prabhupāda rebuked the cook, "If you didn't know how to cook, why didn't you tell me? I can show you." And he went into the kitchen. One of the cooks had tried to make *kacaurīs* and had failed. Although she knew that the dough had to be rolled thin, the filling put in just right, and then the edges folded over precisely, neither she nor any of the other devotees had been able to do it. Prabhupāda, using the same dough and filling, demonstrated the art and made perfect *kacaurīs.*

The devotees explained their difficulty in making *capātīs.* There was no flame on their electric stove. The *capātīs* always came out dry or raw or burned and never puffed up. The excuse only annoyed Prabhupāda, however, who showed exactly how to make *capātīs* that puffed up every time—even on an electric burner. Then he taught the cooks a simple vegetable dish, advising as he cooked. After he left the kitchen, the devotees tried the *capātīs* again. They wouldn't puff. It seemed a magical art only Prabhupāda knew.

Śrīla Prabhupāda had his reasons for bringing Rādhā and Kṛṣṇa to Australia—some of them apparent, others so deep that only he and Rādhā and Kṛṣṇa could understand them. Of course, he was always expanding his movement, of which Deity worship was an important part. So that was one reason for bringing Rādhā and Kṛṣṇa to Australia: to strengthen the devotees and establish more solidly his movement there.

And Prabhupāda loved these Deities. They had presided over the Bombay *paṇḍāl,* and when They hadn't been onstage he had kept Them in his room, where he could look at Them during the day. He had brought Them from Bombay to Malaysia to Sydney, and now he proposed to install Them in this fledgling ISKCON center. But the infinite purity of his heart and the depth of his determination to risk anything for Their Lordships Śrī Śrī Rādhā and Kṛṣṇa are unfathomable. Śrīla Prabhupāda's activities are most grave, and their deeper meaning eludes an observer. Of Lord Caitanya, Kṛṣṇadāsa Kavirāja wrote, "I do not know the deep meaning of Śrī Caitanya Mahāprabhu's activities. I am just trying to describe them externally."

When Prabhupāda came to the temple to perform the initiation ceremony and Deity installation, the devotees weren't ready. Only one small vase of flowers decorated the almost bare altar, and the devotees had not made garlands for the Deities. Prabhupāda was displeased. The small temple was packed, however, and guests and devotees crowded the open doorway and peered through the front window. TV crews filmed the action under hot lamps.

While devotees hurriedly strung garlands for the Deities, Prabhupāda performed the initiation ceremony. There were fifteen initiates in all. To some devotees he gave first initiation, to some second initiation, and to others both first and second. Then he lovingly bathed the forms of Rādhā and Kṛṣṇa and performed the fire sacrifice. While dressing the Deities, he remarked that Their clothes had been poorly made and that the devotees should make new ones immediately. He named the Deities Śrī Śrī Rādhā-Gopīnātha.

Vaibhavī: *He initiated everyone in the temple, anyone who was there—even one boy who had just joined that week and had only come across Kṛṣṇa consciousness the week before, and people who weren't living in the temple, just anyone who was there and somehow serving. He wanted Kṛṣṇa consciousness to be established in Australia, so he just initiated everybody. He gave first and second initiations at the same time, because, having installed the Deities, there had to be some* brāhmaṇas.

But we didn't know anything. We weren't even ready. The altar wasn't finished. Prabhupāda explained to me that we had to string flowers for a garland—the Deity was supposed to wear one. I was running up and down the street trying to find some flowers and get some thread and make a garland.

Same with the sacred thread. There were no sacred threads. Prabhupāda gave the men a sacred thread at brāhmaṇa *initiation, but no one really knew what it was. So I had to run and buy some string. And while Prabhupāda was initiating people, I was sitting there in the arena making sacred threads, copying the one that Bali-mardana had taken off himself.*

I made five of them, and then I was next. After the sacrifice, and after I came out of Prabhupāda's room, where he'd given me the Gāyatrī mantra, *the other devotees said, "You're a* brāhmaṇa *now. So you have to have a sacred thread, too." They told me to make one for myself which I didn't, because someone told me later a woman wasn't supposed to wear one. We just didn't know much.*

At Sydney Grammar School, an elite school for boys, Prabhupāda led his disciples and a group of students in a *kīrtana* procession through the schoolyard. About two hundred boys and several teachers took part, some children frolicking and laughing, some singing the *mantra,* some soberly following the procession, as the teachers smiled and watched. The procession ended in a large room with a row of chairs in the front. Prabhupāda sat in the headmaster's elaborately carved thronelike seat in the center and began playing *karatālas,* continuing the chanting of Hare Kṛṣṇa. Seeing only a few students responding, he stopped and looked around at the children sitting before him.

"So you are all beautiful boys. Why you do not join us in chanting Hare Kṛṣṇa? Is it very difficult? Will you not try to chant? Hare. Say *Ha-re.*"

A few children: "Hare."

Prabhupāda: "All of you chant, Hare."

The children, weakly: "Hare." Some giggled.

Prabhupāda led them through the *mantra,* one word at a time. Still some children were reticent.

Prabhupāda: "There are only three words: *Hare, Kṛṣṇa,* and *Rāma*. Is it very difficult? Chant again—Hare."

Children: "Hare."

Teasing and prodding, Prabhupāda coaxed them. "Oh, you cannot chant? You are all dumb?" The children broke into laughter. "How is that? Three words you cannot chant? Oh, that is very astonishing. Chant! *Hare*!"

"Hare."

"*Kṛṣṇa*!"

"*Kṛṣṇa*!"

Prabhupāda began rhythmically ringing his *karatālas,* the children following him as he sang: Hare Kṛṣṇa, Hare Kṛṣṇa, Kṛṣṇa Kṛṣṇa, Hare Hare/ Hare Rāma, Hare Rāma, Rāma Rāma, Hare Hare.

After a short time Prabhupāda brought the *kīrtana* to a close. Sitting in the beautiful ornate chair, he smiled at the children. "Three words: *Hare, Kṛṣṇa,* and *Rāma*. Do you know what is God? Can any of you stand up and tell me what is God?"

There was silence, then whispering. Finally, one twelve-year-old boy stood. His schoolmates applauded and laughed.

"Oh, thank you," Prabhupāda said. "Come here."

The boy approached.

"Do you know what is God?" Prabhupāda asked.

"Yes," the boy replied. "God is self-realization, and God is found in the unconscious mind."

"Thank you."

Again the children applauded.

"No, wait. Don't go away," Prabhupāda said. "Now you must explain what you mean. What is self-realization?"

Boy: "It is tapping the powers of the unconscious mind and seeing yourself..."

Prabhupāda: "Do you think the mind is unconscious?"

Boy: "The mind is unconscious."

Prabhupāda: "To understand the unconscious, you have to find out what is consciousness."

Boy: "I'm not talking about consciousness—the *un*consciousness."

Prabhupāda: "Unless you know consciousness, how can you describe unconsciousness?"

Boy: "The unconsciousness. The id."

Prabhupāda: "Unconsciousness is the negative side of consciousness. So you should explain what is consciousness. Then we can understand unconsciousness."

Boy: "Consciousness?"

Prabhupāda: "Yes. Try to understand what is consciousness. Then you will understand what is unconsciousness. Consciousness is spread all over the body. Suppose I pinch any part of your body. You feel some pain. That is consciousness. This feeling of pain and pleasure is consciousness. But that consciousness is individual. I cannot feel the pains and pleasures of your body, neither you can feel the pains and pleasures of my body. Therefore, your consciousness is individual and my consciousness is individual. But there is another consciousness, who can feel the pains and pleasures of your body and who can feel the pains and pleasures of my body. That is stated in the *Bhagavad-gītā.*

"You have heard the name of *Bhagavad-gītā*? You? Any of you?"

Another boy: "Yes."

Prabhupāda: "Who says yes? Please come here. Thank you. Very good.

At least one of you knows what is *Bhagavad-gītā*. In the *Bhagavad-gītā* it is stated that..." And Śrīla Prabhupāda proceeded to explain the difference between the material body and the soul and between the individual souls and the Supreme Soul, Kṛṣṇa.

"You are individual knower of your body. I am knower individually of my body. So everyone is knower of his own body. But there is another person, who says, 'I know everything of everyone's body.' Just like I know something of my body, or I know something of this world. Similarly, there is another *ātmā* (soul), supreme *ātmā*, who knows everything of this universe. He is sometimes called God or the Paramātmā or Kṛṣṇa, whatever, according to different language."

After describing the soul's intimate relationship as an eternal servant of Kṛṣṇa and the soul's suffering caused by forgetting that relationship, Prabhupāda concluded his lecture.

"These teachings should be introduced in every school and college so that from the very beginning children understand what is God, how great He is, how we are related with God, and how we have to live.

"So our movement, Kṛṣṇa consciousness, is teaching that thing. Don't think that it is a sectarian religion. We are making people God conscious. It doesn't matter to what religion you may belong. If by following the principles of religion one becomes advanced in God consciousness, that is first-class religion. That is our motto, and we are preaching all over the world.

"Therefore, I request your teachers here to make the students from the beginning God conscious. Then their future life will be very peaceful, prosperous, and hopeful. Thank you very much. Hare Kṛṣṇa."

Prabhupāda also agreed to speak at Wayside Chapel, a center in downtown Sydney ministering to drug addicts and prostitutes. A Wayside sponsor met Prabhupāda at the temple and accompanied him to the Chapel. The sponsor, a long-haired young man in hippie dress, boasted of how Wayside Chapel helped drug addicts. Prabhupāda, however, took it that he was saying the Chapel supplied drugs to the addicts.

At Wayside Chapel a skeptic in the audience challenged Prabhupāda. Prabhupāda had explained that the chanting of the holy names of God was the only way to actually help people, but the cynic challenged, "What good actually is this chanting of Hare Kṛṣṇa?"

"It saves you from death!" Prabhupāda answered forcibly.

May 12, 1971

In his quarters in Sydney, Prabhupāda wrote the Preface to the upcoming edition of *Bhagavad-gītā As It Is.* The Macmillan Company had now agreed to print the unabridged manuscript. The contract was signed, the book was being readied for printing; only the Preface remained to be written.

Prabhupāda wrote in his Preface that although he was known for starting the Kṛṣṇa consciousness movement in America, actually "the original father of this movement is Lord Kṛṣṇa Himself." Giving all credit for his own achievements to his spiritual master, Prabhupāda said that the only qualification he himself had was that he had tried to present *Bhagavad-gītā* as it is, without adulteration.

> Instead of satisfying his own personal material senses, he [a person] has to satisfy the senses of the Lord. That is the highest perfection of life. The Lord wants this, and He demands it. One has to understand this central point of *Bhagavad-gītā.* Our Kṛṣṇa consciousness movement is teaching the whole world this central point, and because we are not polluting the theme of *Bhagavad-gītā As It Is,* anyone seriously interested in deriving benefit by studying the *Bhagavad-gītā* must take help from the Kṛṣṇa consciousness movement for practical understanding of *Bhagavad-gītā* under the direct guidance of the Lord. We hope, therefore, that people will derive the greatest benefit by studying *Bhagavad-gītā As It Is* as we have presented it here, and if even one man becomes a pure devotee of the Lord we shall consider our attempt a success.

As Prabhupāda explained in his Preface, he was publishing the full *Gītā* manuscript "to establish the Kṛṣṇa consciousness movement more soundly and progressively." He would do this by presenting transcendental literature like *Bhagavad-gītā.* But he would also have to go, as Lord Caitanya has said, "to every town and village"—either personally or through his agents, his disciples. And wherever he went, he would preach *Bhagavad-gītā* to whoever would listen.

Tomorrow Prabhupāda would leave Australia for a big *paṇḍāl* festival in Calcutta, then on to Moscow, Paris, Los Angeles...

Lord Kṛṣṇa states in *Bhagavad-gītā* that no servant is more dear to Him than one who teaches *Bhagavad-gītā* to the devotees. And

Prabhupāda, in all his activities—whether writing a Preface, lecturing to the prostitutes and drug addicts, teaching a disciple to cook *capātīs* without burning them, or planning grand projects yet to come—was always teaching *Bhagavad-gītā* and therefore was always the dearest servant of Lord Kṛṣṇa.

Prabhupāda stood before the Deities of Rādhā-Gopīnātha with folded hands. After less than a week in Sydney, he was leaving. He knew that the devotees here were not up to the standard required for worshiping Rādhā and Kṛṣṇa. And he knew he was taking a risk, entrusting Their worship to neophyte disciples. Yet as an empowered *ācārya* and as the representative of Lord Caitanya, he had to implant Kṛṣṇa consciousness anywhere it might take root. The world was in desperate need. If his disciples followed the process he had given them—chanting, hearing, observing regulative principles—he knew they would quickly become purified.

He had given an analogy: Although in material life a man must first become a highly qualified lawyer before sitting on the judge's bench, in Kṛṣṇa consciousness a sincere devotee is first allowed to "sit on the bench," to become a *brāhmaṇa,* and later, by the mercy of the holy name and the spiritual master, he becomes qualified. The devotees in Sydney, however, were particularly immature, and Prabhupāda made an extraordinary request of Rādhā-Gopīnātha: "Now I am leaving You in the hands of the *mlecchas.* I cannot take the responsibility. You please guide these boys and girls and give them the intelligence to worship You very nicely."

* * *

Calcutta
May 13, 1971

Prabhupāda arrived just in time for the ten-day Calcutta *paṇḍāl* festival. On his orders, Girirāja and Tamāla Kṛṣṇa had come to organize the festival, just as they had the one in Bombay. Prabhupāda had written to Jayapatāka Swami, president of ISKCON Calcutta:

> In the San Kirtan festival pandel if a very big kitchen arrangement can be made, then we shall distribute prasadam daily. Try to make this arrange-

> ment. Puri, halevah, kitrie—whatever can be arranged as much as possible. Tamal Krishna and Giriraj have all the ideas.

Attendance surpassed that of the Bombay *paṇḍāl,* with twenty to thirty thousand people attending daily, including ministers of Parliament and other distinguished speakers. It was one of the biggest religious functions Calcutta had ever seen; the whole city became aware of the strength of the Hare Kṛṣṇa movement.

In the early afternoon the devotees would begin selling Prabhupāda's books from a booth, performing *kīrtana* onstage, and distributing *prasādam* to the masses. Around 6:30 the evening program would begin with a long, intense *kīrtana,* which would increase in its fervor as Prabhupāda arrived for the evening *ārati* before the Deities of Rādhā and Kṛṣṇa. Prabhupāda would lecture, sometimes in Bengali and sometimes in English. Afterward the devotees would show slides of the Kṛṣṇa consciousness movement around the world, and Prabhupāda would answer questions from the audience. After the program, people would push forward to receive a morsel of the *prasādam* that had been offered to the Deity.

Naxalite terrorists threatened Prabhupāda's life. These young Communist terrorists, who had been active in Calcutta during Prabhupāda's visit of 1970, had never disturbed him until now. Their tactic was to approach prominent businessmen in their homes or on the street and coerce them into cooperation with Naxalite political objectives. If a businessman refused, the Naxalites would burn his home or place of business or even assassinate him. The Naxalites, who were eager for all of Bengal to turn from their religious traditions and embrace Communism, saw Prabhupāda rekindling the religious spirit in Calcutta. Prabhupāda's tremendous crowd-gathering *paṇḍāl,* they concluded, was undermining the principles of Communism.

"Fly or Die," read the note Prabhupāda received. He informed the police, who regretted their inability to help. The whole of Calcutta, they said, was in terror of the Naxalites. Prabhupāda, however, refused to be intimidated; he would not fly. Even if they were to attack him, he said, what better way for a Vaiṣṇava to leave his body than while preaching the glories of the Lord?

The next night as Prabhupāda came before the crowd to speak, he noticed a group of rowdy young men, Naxalites, near the stage. They were protesting the preferential seating of certain dignitaries onstage. When one young radical shouted that the radicals themselves wanted to dance onstage, the devotees invited them to join in a *kīrtana.* The Naxalites backed down, but continued shouting and disrupting the meeting. They began banging the seats of the wooden folding chairs, calling out Naxalite slogans, and threatening to burn the place down. Others in the audience began talking nervously among themselves, increasing the commotion. In a vain attempt to bring order, some of the devotees threatened the dissenters. Pushing and scuffling broke out in the audience.

"*Cintāmaṇi-prakara-sadmasu kalpa-vṛkṣa-/ lakṣāvṛteṣu surabhīr abhipālayantam ...*" Prabhupāda's voice rang over the powerful loudspeaker system. Appearing uninterested in the crowd, depending only on Kṛṣṇa, he began singing prayers from *Brahma-saṁhitā,* and within minutes everyone quieted. Those who wanted to leave left, and those who wanted to stay sat down. The crowd subdued, Prabhupāda lectured.

Several more "fly or die" notes came, and the Naxalites returned the next night, threatening again to burn the *paṇḍāl.* "Call them," Prabhupāda said. "I will meet with them." The devotees thought it unsafe, but Prabhupāda insisted. In a small room behind the *paṇḍāl,* Prabhupāda spoke with the hostile youths. They were angry and disrespectful at first, but as Prabhupāda explained to them the Vedic concept of communism—with Kṛṣṇa at the center—he caught their interest. They agreed to allow Prabhupāda's meetings to continue without any further disruptions.

Acyutānanda Swami: *The last night of the ten-day* paṇḍāl *program was a grand finale, with over forty thousand people attending. I had just stepped out to get sugarcane juice. The* paṇḍāl *was completely packed when I left, but when I got outside, I saw rivers of people flowing through the four main gates into the* paṇḍāl *tent. I thought this must be Kṛṣṇa's mystic power, because the tent was already packed and still thousands of people were entering it. I thought that Kṛṣṇa must be unlimitedly expanding the dimensions of space.*

The climax of the evening was a big procession, beginning at the *paṇḍāl* and going up Park Street to the ISKCON temple on Albert Road. The Deities of Rādhā-Govinda rode on a palanquin to the temple, where They were placed on the altar. After an *ārati* in the temple, the remaining crowd dispersed.

Acyutānanda Swami was standing next to Prabhupāda that night in the Calcutta temple. "Prabhupāda," he said, "someone put Kṛṣṇa's flute in backward." Prabhupāda looked. It *was* backward. "Kṛṣṇa is all-powerful" he said, turning to Acyutānanda Swami. "He can play from the back end also."

Śrīla Prabhupāda was still striving for a plot of land in Māyāpur. Having abandoned the idea that his Godbrothers in Māyāpur might help, he had been working through Bengali friends in negotiating with Muslim farmers in Māyāpur. On returning from Australia, Prabhupāda had sent Tamāla Kṛṣṇa to Māyāpur with orders not to come back until he had purchased land. Tamāla Kṛṣṇa's mission was successful, and after six days he returned to Prabhupāda in Calcutta, having purchased nine *bighas,* three acres, in Māyāpur.

Conceiving the value of Māyāpur was difficult for the devotees, however. One devotee journeyed from Calcutta to see the new ISKCON property and on returning asked Prabhupāda, "What are we going to do there? It's just a big empty field. Nothing is there."

"Because there are no factories and cars," Prabhupāda replied, "therefore you think there is nothing to do. But we are going to chant Hare Kṛṣṇa in Māyāpur. We will build a big temple there, and all the devotees in the world can go out and chant Hare Kṛṣṇa in the place of Lord Caitanya's birth." On May 28 Prabhupāda wrote:

> You will be glad to learn that we have purchased about five acres of land in Mayapur, the birthsite of Lord Chaitanya, and we have proposed to hold a nice festival there from Janmastami day for two weeks. At that time the foundation stone will be set down. I wish that all our leading disciples come to India at that time. There are 50 branches, so at least one from each branch should attend the function.

* * *

June 1971

For months Prabhupāda had been planning to visit Moscow. Aside from his desire to preach to the Russian people, he had a specific meeting in mind with a Russian Indology professor, G. G. Kotovsky. Professor Kotovsky headed the department of Indian and South Asian studies at

Moscow's U.S.S.R. Academy of Sciences, and Prabhupāda had been corresponding with him for a year.

Kṛṣṇadāsa in West Germany, with the help of a Dr. Bernhardt of the University of Hamburg, had obtained the names of other Russian scholars of Indology. A letter to Kṛṣṇadāsa in December of 1970 had revealed Prabhupāda's plans for preaching in Russia.

> I am very encouraged to see your enthusiasm for preaching this message to the Russian people, and your idea to send letters with the help of Dr. Bernhardt is very good. He is a big scholar and he also appreciates our movement. So if you arrange a tour of Russia for me, I am prepared to accept. Let us see what Krishna desires. ... If we can go to Russia with our World Sankirtan Party, I am certain that it will be very much appreciated and people will see the real peace movement is chanting process—chanting the Holy Names Hare Krishna, Hare Krishna, Krishna Krishna, Hare Hare/ Hare Rama, Hare Rama, Rama Rama, Hare Hare. So try for it.

Śrīla Prabhupāda had coached Kṛṣṇadāsa on how to best cultivate the Russian Indologists.

> You can ask them some questions like: What is the ultimate goal of life? What is your ideal ultimate goal of life? What is the difference between animal and human life? Why is religion accepted by all kinds of civilized societies? What is your conception of the original creation? In this way questions may be put to find out what is their standing. We do not grudge an atheist provided he has got some philosophical standing. In this way try to elicit some answers from the Professors. If you can finally establish one Moscow center, it will be a great credit to you. So far studying Russian language, it is not necessary, but if you do so it is all right. I want very much a center in Russia, so for the time being I shall desire that Moscow Center.

In March 1971, Professor G. G. Kotovsky had replied to Kṛṣṇadāsa's letter.

> I thank you for your information about Swami Bhaktivedanta's lecturing tour. If he would come to Moscow, the Soviet scholars doing research in ancient Indian culture would be very happy to meet him in the Institute of Oriental Studies, USSR Academy of Sciences. I would be thankful to you for your information on the dates of Swami Bhaktivedanta's arrival and stay in the USSR.

Śrīla Prabhupāda had personally replied to Professor Kotovsky.

> ... it was understood that you and your university are interested in hearing about Krishna culture and philosophy. This ancient Krishna culture and philosophy is the oldest in the world or in the universe. At least from a historical point of view it is not less than 5,000 years old.
>
> Perhaps you may know that I have started this cultural movement since 1966 and it is already spreading all over the world. Krishna culture is so popular in India that even the government attracts many foreigners by Air India time table to visit Vrindavan, the land of Krishna culture. Enclosed please find one page from the latest Air India time table (April 1971) wherein the Krishna culture is depicted for general attraction.
>
> My life is dedicated to spreading this Krishna culture all over the world. I think if you give me a chance to speak about the great Krishna culture and philosophy in your country, you will very much appreciate this simple programme with great profit. This culture is so well planned that it would be acceptable by any thoughtful man throughout the whole world.

Having preached a year in the Eastern Hemisphere, Prabhupāda was eager to return to the West, and he planned to fly to Moscow and on to Europe. For Prabhupāda and his traveling companions, Śyāmasundara and Aravinda, getting tourist visas for Russia was simple. They would take a five-day, government-controlled tour, with every activity planned by the Soviet Tourist Bureau and everything paid for in advance.

Captain Lal, the pilot of the flight to Moscow, considered Prabhupāda an important passenger and came back to visit him during the flight. They spoke of Prabhupāda's movement, his chances for lecturing in Moscow, and of Bombay, where Prabhupāda was trying to purchase land. Captain Lal invited Prabhupāda to the cockpit, and Prabhupāda came and sat behind the captain, asking technical questions about the equipment and the flight. Prabhupāda and Captain Lal agreed to meet again in Moscow.

Prabhupāda, his secretary, and his servant cleared Soviet customs and immigration quickly and smoothly, and a government tourist guide escorted them by limousine to the Hotel National. The hotel, near Red Square, Lenin's Tomb, and the Kremlin, was expensive but plain. Prabhupāda found his room dingy and cramped, with barely space for a bed and two chairs. The room for Śyāmasundara and Aravinda was far away, and Prabhupāda decided that Aravinda should share the room with him instead, crowding Prabhupāda's room all the more.

Aravinda told the hotel manager that they would not eat the hotel fare, but would have to cook their own meals. The manager refused at first, but finally allowed them use of the maid's kitchen.

That problem solved, the next was getting food. Prabhupāda sent Śyāmasundara out. Across the street, Śyāmasundara found a milk and yogurt store, but he returned to Prabhupāda's room without any fruit, vegetables, or rice. Prabhupāda sent him out again, and this time Śyāmasundara was gone practically all day, returning with only a couple of cabbages. Prabhupāda sent him out the next day for rice. When Śyāmasundara returned with rice after several hours, Prabhupāda saw that it was a poor North Korean variety, very hard. Prabhupāda asked for fruit, but Śyāmasundara had to hike for miles through the city to find anything fresh—a few red cherries.

Prabhupāda remained peaceful and regulated, keeping to his daily schedule. He would rise early and translate, and in the cool of early morning he would go out for a walk through the all-but-deserted streets. Prabhupāda, wearing a saffron *cādara,* strode quickly, Śyāmasundara sometimes running ahead to photograph him.

As they would pass Lenin's Mausoleum a queue would already be forming. "Just see," Prabhupāda commented one morning, "that is their God. The people don't understand the difference between the body and the spirit. They accept the body as the real person."

Prabhupāda appreciated the sparseness of the traffic—some trolleys and bicycles, but mostly pedestrians. As he walked among the old, ornate buildings, he saw elderly women hosing the wide streets—a good practice, he said. The Russian people appeared to live structured, regulated lives, much more so than the Americans. These simple, austere people, unspoiled by the rampant hedonism so common in America, were fertile for Kṛṣṇa consciousness. But devoid of spiritual sustenance, they appeared morose.

Prabhupāda had Śyāmasundara arrange a meeting with Professor Kotovsky and invite Captain Lal to come along. The tourist bureau provided a car and guide, and Prabhupāda and his party rode outside the city to Professor Kotovsky's office in an old white brick building at the Academy of Sciences.

When Prabhupāda arrived, the middle-aged Russian professor, dressed in a gray suit, got up from his cluttered desk and welcomed Prabhupāda into his small office. Professor Kotovsky appeared a bit hesitant, however, more cautious than in his letters. When Śyāmasundara mentioned Prabhupāda's eagerness to lecture before interested scholars at the Academy, Professor Kotovsky flatly refused—it would never be allowed. Prabhupāda was disappointed.

The next moment, however, Prabhupāda seemed unaffected and began speaking in his humble, genteel manner, sitting in a straight-backed office chair beside Professor Kotovsky, who sat at his desk. Śyāmasundara turned on the tape recorder, which the professor eyed cautiously but didn't object to.

Prabhupāda: "The other day I was reading in the paper, *Moscow News*. There was a Communist congress, and the president declared that, 'We are ready to get others' experiences to improve.' So I think the Vedic concept of socialism or communism will much improve the idea of Communism."

Professor Kotovsky listened intently and politely as his foreign visitor explained how the *gṛhastha* in Vedic culture provides for everyone living in his house—even for the lizards—and how, before taking his meal, he calls in the road to invite any hungry person to come and eat. "In this way," Prabhupāda explained, "there are so many good concepts about the socialist idea of communism. So I thought that these ideas might have been distributed to some of your thoughtful men. Therefore I was anxious to speak."

Professor Kotovsky's academic interest was piqued. "You know, it is interesting," he said, his articulate English heavily accented. "As it is here in our country, there is now great interest in the history of old, old thought." He described the accomplishments of his colleagues and himself, particularly a booklet they had recently prepared highlighting Soviet studies in Indology. He said he would like to give a copy to Prabhupāda.

Professor Kotovsky: "You will be interested to discover that we published not all but some *Purāṇas,* then some parts of the *Rāmāyaṇa,* eight volumes in Russian of the *Mahābhārata,* and also a second edition of the *Mahābhārata,* translated by different people in full and published. *Manu-smṛti* is also translated in full and published with Sanskrit commentaries. And such was the great interest that all of these publications were sold in a week. They are now completely out of stock. It is impossible to get them in the book market after a month. Such a great interest among reading people here in Moscow and the U.S.S.R. towards ancient Vedic culture."

Prabhupāda: "Among these *Purāṇas,* the *Śrīmad-Bhāgavatam* is called the *Mahā-purāṇa.*" And he told of his own translation of *Śrīmad-Bhāgavatam,* "the ripened fruit of the Vedic desire tree." He would show some volumes to the professor if he was interested.

Professor Kotovsky said the Moscow and Leningrad libraries had nearly all the major texts of Indian culture in Sanskrit. These libraries housed not only ancient texts but more recent literature as well, comprising an up-to-date study of Hinduism.

"Hinduism," Prabhupāda interrupted, "is a very complex topic." And they both laughed. Professor Kotovsky acknowledged that Hinduism was more than a religion; it was a way of life. But Prabhupāda explained that the name Hindu was actually a misnomer. The real term to explain Vedic culture was *varṇāśrama.* Briefly Prabhupāda described the four orders: *brāhmaṇa, kṣatriya, vaiśya,* and *śūdra.*

Professor Kotovsky: "You have told that in any society there are four divisions, but it is not so easy to distinguish. For instance, one can group together different social classes and professional groups into four divisions in any society. There is no difficulty. The only difficulty is, for instance, in socialist society, in our country and other socialist societies, how can you distinguish productive group and workers?"

Prabhupāda welcomed the professor's questions, although grounded in Soviet socialist vested interests. Prabhupāda considered the professor not so much an academician as a pawn of the Soviet university system; much as one political power tries to understand its adversary, the professor was inquiring into Indian culture so that his government might penetrate it with their own ideology. Behind Professor Kotovsky's apparent interest in Vedic culture, Prabhupāda could see the view of the Communist party, a view diametrically opposed to Vedic philosophy. Nevertheless, Prabhupāda tactfully continued to present Kṛṣṇa consciousness in accord with *paramparā,* and he tried to convince Professor Kotovsky through scripture and logic.

Quoting *Bhagavad-gītā,* a *śāstra* with which the professor was familiar (in his own way), Prabhupāda described Lord Kṛṣṇa as the creator of the four divisions of society. Professor Kotovsky immediately countered with the theory of the Soviet scholars that the *varṇāśrama* divisions were a recent addition to Vedic culture. He also again registered his opinion that the divisions of *varṇāśrama* had no meaning within socialism.

Professor Kotovsky: "There is a great distinction between socialist society and all societies preceding socialism, because in modern Western society you can group all social and professional classes in the particular class divisions—*brāhmaṇas, kṣatriyas, vaiśyas* (or factory owners), and *śūdras,* or menial workers. But here we have no *vaiśyas.* Because we have administrative staff in factories, managerial staff—you can call them *kṣatriyas*—and then *śūdras,* the workers themselves, but not this intermediate class."

Prabhupāda: "That is stated, *kalau śūdra-sambhavaḥ.* 'In this age, practically all men are *śūdras.*' That is stated. But if there are simply *śūdras,* then the social order will be disturbed. In spite of your state of *śūdras,* the *brāhmaṇas* are there. That is necessary. So if you do not divide the social order in such a way, then it will be chaos. That is the scientific estimation of the *Vedas.* You may belong to the *śūdra* class, but to maintain the social order you have to train some of the *śūdras* to become *brāhmaṇas.* It cannot depend on the *śūdras.*"

Prabhupāda gave his standard analogy, comparing the social body to the human body. All the parts are necessary, not only the legs but the belly, the arms, and the head. "Otherwise," he said, "it will not work properly. As long as this is going on, there will be some disturbance."

Modern society's missing point, Prabhupāda said, was an understanding of the purpose of human life. "They do not know what is the next life," he said. "There is no department of knowledge or scientific department to study what is there after finishing this body."

Professor Kotovsky objected—politely, completely. "Swamiji," he said, "when the body dies, the owner also dies." Prabhupāda marked his reply.

"No," Prabhupāda quickly replied. "This fact you must know. Why is there no department of knowledge in the university to study this fact scientifically? That is my proposition. That department is lacking. It may be as you say, it may be as I say, but there must be a department of knowledge. Now recently a cardiologist, a doctor in Montreal and Toronto, has accepted that there is a soul. I had some correspondence with him. He strongly believes that there is a soul."

Prabhupāda continued to build his argument: "We accept knowledge from authority." The professor countered that everything had to be accepted on the basis of empirical evidence. But then, in midsentence, he stopped arguing and inquired, "Have you many branches of your society in the world?"

Prabhupāda began speaking about ISKCON, with its sixty-five branches all around the world, and of how he was going next to Paris, where his disciples had recently acquired a new center, and of how the American boys and girls especially were joining his movement. He told of the four prohibitive rules (no meat-eating, no illicit sex, no intoxication, and no gambling) and of the books he had published. As Prabhupāda described the workings of his movement, Professor Kotovsky nodded approvingly.

When Prabhupāda returned to comparing Kṛṣṇa consciousness to Communism, he concluded that the two philosophies were in agreement. And both stressed surrender to an authority. The devotee surrenders to Kṛṣṇa, the Communist to Lenin.

Prabhupāda: "Our life is by surrender, is it not? Do you disagree with this point?"

Kotovsky: "To some extent you surrender."

Prabhupāda: "Yes. To the full extent."

Kotovsky: "You have to surrender to the society, for instance—the whole people."

Prabhupāda: "Yes, to the whole people or to the state or king or government or whatever you say. The surrender must be there. It may be different."

Kotovsky: "The only difficulty is we cannot have surrender to government or to a king. The principal difference is of surrender to a king, who is a single person, or to the whole society."

Prabhupāda: "No, that is a change of color only. But the surrender is there. The principle of surrender is there. Whether you surrender to monarchy, democracy, aristocracy, or dictatorship, you have to surrender. That is a fact. Without surrender there is no life. It is not possible. So we are educating persons to surrender to the Supreme, wherefrom you get all protection. Just like Kṛṣṇa says, *sarva-dharmān parityajya.* So surrender is there. No one can say, 'No, I am not surrendered to anyone.' The difference is *where* he surrenders. And the ultimate surrendering object is Kṛṣṇa. Therefore in *Bhagavad-gītā* it is said, *bahūnāṁ janmanām ante jñānavān māṁ prapadyate:* 'After surrendering to so many things, birth after birth, when one is factually wise he surrenders unto Me.'"

Professor Kotovsky agreed. But surrender had to be accompanied by revolution, he said. The French Revolution, for example, was a revolt against one kind of surrender, and yet the revolution itself was another surrender, surrender to the people. "So it is not enough to come full stop," the Professor argued. "Surrender is to be accompanied with revolt against surrender to other people."

Prabhupāda: "Yes, the surrender will be full stopped when it is surrender to Kṛṣṇa. That is full stop: no more surrender. Other surrender you have to change by revolution. But when you come to Kṛṣṇa, then it is sufficient—you are satisfied. Just like—I give you one example. A child is crying and people change laps: 'Oh, it has not stopped.' But as soon as the baby comes to the lap of its mother..."

Kotovsky: "It stops."

Prabhupāda: "Yes, full satisfaction. So this surrender, the changes will go on in different categories. The sum total of all these surrenders is surrender to *māyā* (material illusion). But the final surrender is to Kṛṣṇa, and then you will be happy."

After only three days, Prabhupāda's mission in Moscow seemed finished. The meeting with Professor Kotovsky over, what was left? The government would allow nothing else. It had not allowed him to bring in books, and now he had been refused the opportunity to speak publicly. Foreigners were not to talk with the Russians. He could go nowhere, unless on an accompanied tour. So with no preaching and no prospects, he stayed in his cramped room, taking his massage, bathing, accepting whatever food Śyāmasundara could gather and cook, dictating a few letters, chanting Hare Kṛṣṇa, and translating *Śrīmad-Bhāgavatam.*

Prabhupāda took a guided tour of Moscow, riding with other tourists on a crowded bus. He saw elderly Russians going to church, armed guards stationed at the door. He soon tired of the tour, however, and the tour guide got him a taxi and instructed the driver to return him to the Hotel National.

Śyāmasundara continued to spend most of his day looking for fresh food. Hearing that oranges were available at a certain market across town, he set out across the city. With his shaved head and his white *dhotī* and *kurtā* he drew stares from everyone he passed, and as he was returning after dark, uniformed men wearing red armbands accosted him, taking him to be a local deviant. Grabbing him, they pinned his arms behind his back and shouted at him in Russian. Śyāmasundara caught the word *dakumyent* ("document, passport"). He replied, "*Dakumyent*, hotel! Hotel!" Realizing Śyāmasundara was a tourist, the officers released him, and he returned to the hotel and informed Prabhupāda of what had taken place. "There is no hope in Russia without Kṛṣṇa consciousness," Prabhupāda said.

Once Śyāmasundara was standing in line at the yogurt store when a man behind him asked him about *yoga*. "I really want to talk with you," the man said, and he gave Śyāmasundara his name and address and a time they could safely meet. When Śyāmasundara told Prabhupāda, Prabhupāda said, "No, he is a policeman. Don't go."

One day two young men, one the son of an Indian diplomat stationed in Moscow, the other a young Muscovite, were loitering near Red Square when they saw an amazing sight. Out of the usual regimented routine of city traffic, a tall young man with a shaved head, a long reddish ponytail, and flowing white robes approached. It was Śyāmasundara. Familiar with Śyāmasundara's dress, the son of the Indian diplomat stopped him. Śyāmasundara smiled, "Hare Kṛṣṇa, brother." And he began talking with the Indian, whose name was Nārāyaṇa. The Russian, Ivan, knew a little English and followed the conversation as closely as he could. The talk grew serious.

"Why don't you come up and meet my spiritual master?" Śyāmasundara asked. Honored, the boys immediately accompanied Śyāmasundara to the Hotel National. When they arrived, they found Prabhupāda seated on his bed, aglow and smiling, Aravinda massaging his feet. Śyāmasundara entered, offering obeisances before Prabhupāda. Ivan was completely fascinated.

"Come on," Prabhupāda said, and the three of them sat at Prabhupāda's feet. Turning first to Nārāyaṇa, Prabhupāda asked his name and his father's occupation. Nārāyaṇa liked Prabhupāda and offered to bring him green vegetables; his father, being highly placed at the Indian Embassy, had produce flown in from India.

Ivan was interested even more than his Indian friend, and Prabhupāda began explaining to him the philosophy of Kṛṣṇa consciousness, while

Nārāyaṇa helped by translating. Ivan inquired with respect and awe, and Prabhupāda answered his questions, teaching as much basic information about Kṛṣṇa consciousness as was possible in one sitting. Prabhupāda explained the difference between the spirit soul and the body and described the soul's eternal relationship with Kṛṣṇa, the Supreme Personality of Godhead. He spoke of *Bhagavad-gītā,* of his network of temples around the world, and of his young men and women disciples all practicing *bhakti-yoga.*

Prabhupāda mentioned his desire to preach in Russia, which was a great field for Kṛṣṇa consciousness because the people were openminded and hadn't been polluted by sense gratification. He wanted to introduce Kṛṣṇa conscious literature in Russia through a library or a reading room or in whatever way possible. Kṛṣṇa conscious philosophy, he said, should be taught to Russia's most intelligent people, but because of government restrictions it would have to be done discreetly. Devotees would not be able to sing and dance in the streets, but they could chant quietly together in someone's home. Prabhupāda then began singing very quietly, leading the boys in *kīrtana.*

Ivan's taking to Kṛṣṇa was like a hungry man's eating a meal. After several hours, however, he and his friend had to go. They would return the next day.

Śyāmasundara began spending time with Ivan and Nārāyaṇa. Ivan, a student of Oriental philosophies, was very intelligent and eager to know what was going on in the outside world. He was fond of the Beatles, and Prabhupāda told him of his association with George Harrison and John Lennon. Ivan and Śyāmasundara had long talks about the ambitions and hopes of young people outside Russia, and Śyāmasundara explained to him how Kṛṣṇa consciousness was the topmost of all spiritual paths. Śyāmasundara also taught him basic principles of *bhakti-yoga,* such as chanting the prescribed sixteen rounds of *japa* daily, and gave him his own copy of *Bhagavad-gītā As It Is.*

Prabhupāda showed Ivan how to prepare *capātīs* and rice and asked him to give up eating meat. Joyfully, Ivan accepted the chanting, the new way of eating—everything. Ivan was being trained so that after Prabhupāda left, Ivan could continue on his own. Ivan would be able to feel himself changing and advancing in spiritual life, and after practicing for some time he could be initiated. Ivan said he would tell his friends about

Kṛṣṇa consciousness. With only two days left in Moscow, Prabhupāda taught Ivan as much as he could. In this young Russian's eagerness and intelligence, Prabhupāda found the real purpose of his visit to Russia.

Prabhupāda gave the analogy that when cooking rice the cook need test only one grain to determine whether the whole pot of rice is done. Similarly, by talking with this one Russian youth, Prabhupāda could tell that the Russian people were not satisfied in their so-called ideal land of Marxism. Just as Ivan was keenly receptive to Kṛṣṇa consciousness, millions of other Russians would be also.

Cāṇakya Paṇḍita says that one blooming flower can refresh a whole forest and that a fire in a single tree can burn the whole forest. From the Marxist point of view, Ivan was the fire that would spread Kṛṣṇa consciousness to others, thus defeating the communist ideology. And from Prabhupāda's point of view, he was the aromatic flower that would lend its fragrance to many others. Prabhupāda's visit to Russia was no obscure interlude, but had become an occasion for planting the seed of Kṛṣṇa consciousness in a destitute land.

Śrīla Prabhupāda had brought the movement of Lord Caitanya to yet another country. Caitanya Mahāprabhu Himself had predicted that the *saṅkīrtana* movement would go to every town and village, yet for hundreds of years that prediction had remained unfulfilled. Prabhupāda, however, in the few years since his first trip to America in 1965, had again and again planted Lord Caitanya's message in one unlikely place after another. And of all places, this was perhaps the most unlikely; during a brief, government-supervised visit to Moscow, he had planted the seed of Kṛṣṇa consciousness within the Soviet Union. He was like the needle, and everyone and everything connected with him was like the thread that would follow.

Professor Kotovsky had remarked that Prabhupāda's stay in an old-fashioned hotel would not prove very interesting. But Prabhupāda, unknown to Professor Kotovsky, was transcendental to Moscow or any other place in the material world. Prabhupāda had come to this place, and Kṛṣṇa had sent a sincere soul to him to receive the gift of Kṛṣṇa consciousness. This had happened not by devious espionage against the Soviet government but by the presence of Kṛṣṇa's pure devotee and his natural desire to satisfy Kṛṣṇa by preaching. In response to Prabhupāda's pure desire, Kṛṣṇa had sent one boy, and from that one boy the desire would spread to others. Nothing, not even an Iron Curtain, could stop Kṛṣṇa consciousness. The soul's natural function was to serve Kṛṣṇa. And Kṛṣṇa's natural will was to satisfy the pure desires of His devotee.

In a farewell letter to Professor Kotovsky, Prabhupāda tried to encourage further correspondence.

> You wanted to see the manuscripts of my lectures, therefore I am sending herewith an *Introduction* to the lectures, and if you so desire I shall be glad to send essays on these subjects:
>
> 1. Vedic Conceptions of Socialism and Communism
> 2. Scientific Values of Classless Society
> 3. Knowledge by Authoritative Tradition

In a letter to Tamāla Kṛṣṇa, Prabhupāda summed up his Moscow visit.

> The city is well-planned. There are big, big houses and roads and at day time the streets are busy with buses, cars, and underground trains which are far better than American or English. The underground streets are very neat and clean. The surface streets are also daily washed. But there is some difficulty in collecting vegetarian foodstuffs; still we are cooking our meals by the cooker which has saved our lives. We talked with one big professor Mr. Kotovsky, and Shyamsundar talked with many great writers and musicians. Two boys are working with us; one Indian and one Russian. So there is good prospect for opening a center, although the atmosphere is not very good. The embassy was no help. So our visit to Moscow was not so successful, but for the future, it is hopeful. Tomorrow I go to Paris for one day, then to S.F. Ratha-yātrā and then I shall come back to London.

* * *

Paris
June 25, 1971

Śrīla Prabhupāda was lying on the couch in the conference room of the Indian Tourist Office, having just come from Orly Airport. Two disciples, Ārādhana and his wife, Śantanu, had come with him in the taxi and were the only others in the room. Since there was to be a press conference later, Prabhupāda said he wanted to rest, and he closed his eyes.

At the airport, Paris immigration officials had detained Prabhupāda while some thirty European devotees, none of whom had ever met him, had waited anxiously. They had glimpsed him as he had walked from the plane to the terminal building, and they had watched him carrying his *sannyāsa-daṇḍa* with umbrella strapped to it. He had waved to them, holding up his bead bag. But then he had been kept from them, just beyond a thin wall, until finally, after two hours, Paris immigration had allowed him through.

The Paris devotees had not arranged a car for Prabhupāda, so when he had asked for one, several devotees had run off to hail a taxi. When the taxi had arrived, Prabhupāda, along with Ārādhana and Śantanu, had started for the Indian Tourist Office, leaving the others to join him later.

After a brief rest, Prabhupāda opened his eyes and saw Ārādhana, Śantanu, and Śyāmasundara in the room. The other devotees and the press would be arriving soon. As Prabhupāda sat up, Śantanu offered him some mango, and Śrīla Prabhupāda smiled.

Yogeśvara: *I sat outside the door to Prabhupāda's room, eating the peel of the mango Prabhupāda had eaten. My heart was pounding, and I had no idea what it was going to be like after having been initiated for a year and a half and having never met my spiritual master personally—but now knowing that he was just behind that door!*

Then Śyāmasundara opened the door and peered out and saw me sitting there. He stuck his head back inside the door and said, "There's a devotee here. Shall I let him in now, Śrīla Prabhupāda?" I peeked around the door, and Śrīla Prabhupāda, who had been lying down on the couch, was now sitting up with his hand on his knee very solidly, with a royal, majestic look. He responded to Śyāmasundara's question by motioning with his hand that we could all come in. It was the first perfect thing I had ever seen in my life—that one gesture. So I came in and immediately fell flat on the floor. And then I understood that "Now I am with my spiritual master."

Gradually the devotees began arriving from the airport, and they came into Prabhupāda's room. The press also arrived, as Prabhupāda spoke warmly and pleasantly with his followers, encouraging them in their preaching and telling them of his own recent preaching in Moscow. Hardly any of the devotees had ever been with their spiritual master before, and Locanānanda began introducing them to Śrīla Prabhupāda.

Hari-vilāsa: *I arrived late, and when I came in I was mixed up with surprise, with elation, with egotistical pride, and with amazement that the Lord's pure devotee was there. I walked in with Ghanaśyāma, the boy who had started translating some of Prabhupāda's books into French. The room was almost filled, and Ghanaśyāma immediately sat down in the back. I was the president of the temple, and I was very proud and puffed up about it. So I made my way all the way up to the front, where Śrīla Prabhupāda was, and I sat down right next to him. I looked at him, expecting him to look at me and smile or something, some recognition. But he didn't look at me at all.*

Locanānanda was introducing all the devotees to Prabhupāda. Locanānanda said, "This is Ghanaśyāma. He is the translator." Prabhupāda said, "Where is he?" And everyone looked around to Ghanaśyāma in the back. Prabhupāda said, "Let him stand up, please." Ghanaśyāma stood, and Prabhupāda looked at him and smiled and said, "Oh, thank you very much."

Right then I felt a little funny. I sat there wondering, "What have I done? I've walked all the way up to the front, and I'm expecting so much recognition."

Then Locanānanda said, "This is Hari-vilāsa. He is the president of the temple." Prabhupāda didn't even look at me. And I knew, yes, I had made a big mistake. I began to realize, "This is my spiritual master." Because immediately he had acted in such a way as to point out a great fault in me.

Reporters began their questioning, and Prabhupāda patiently answered them, taking advantage of their sometimes superficial questions to elaborate on the philosophy of Kṛṣṇa consciousness and explain the Kṛṣṇa consciousness movement. The conference ran one hour.

As Prabhupāda left the Indian Tourist Office he found that there was no car to take him to the temple. While several devotees ran around trying to find a taxi, Prabhupāda waited, standing before a sidewalk café.

Thinking that Prabhupāda must be tired from the rigorous press conference and his long flight from Moscow, one of the devotees asked, "Śrīla Prabhupāda, would you like to sit here for a minute?" And the devotee pulled one of the café chairs out away from its table.

"What is this place?" Prabhupāda asked.

"This is a sidewalk café," the devotee replied.

"What do people do here? Do they smoke and drink?"

"Yes, Śrīla Prabhupāda, it's a café. They serve alcoholic beverages."

"No," Prabhupāda replied. "*Guru* cannot sit in such a place."

When Prabhupāda reached the temple, he bathed and took *prasādam*. The next day he was scheduled to leave for Los Angeles, and his one day in Paris was filled with outside engagements. He rested and again went out to preach.

The devotees had rented the Olympia Theater, a large auditorium meant to seat more than two thousand. But because the devotees had advertised Prabhupāda's lecture only two days in advance, only forty people attended. Prabhupāda was undaunted, and he lectured and held *kīrtana*. Afterward he went to a television studio for an interview.

By the time Prabhupāda returned to the temple, it was one in the morning. Śyāmasundara told the devotees, who had all accompanied Prabhupāda during the day, that they should rest a full six hours before rising. But the next morning Prabhupāda rose as usual, and at five o'clock he was demanding to know why there was no *maṅgala-ārati*. He sent his servant to wake the devotees, and as the devotees were hurrying to the temple room to begin their morning worship Prabhupāda was going out on his morning walk.

Accompanying Prabhupāda on his walk were Śyāmasundara, Aravinda, and the Paris temple president, Hari-vilāsa. The spring morning was sunny, and Prabhupāda, walking with his cane, appeared noble. "Śyāmasundara," Prabhupāda asked, "Why are all the householders in *māyā*?" When Śyāmasundara couldn't reply, Prabhupāda said, "That's all right. That is their position—to be in *māyā*."

He said that when he had gone to America his plans had been to make *sannyāsīs*, but when he saw the free mixing of the sexes in the West he had decided to let his disciples first get married and have a child, and then the wife could go to Vṛndāvana with the child, and the husband could take *sannyāsa*. Prabhupāda laughed. Man becomes entangled by his family, he said—by his home, his bank account, his animals, and so many other attachments.

Near the end of his walk, Prabhupāda spoke specifically of Paris. "Three things are prominent here," he said, "wine, women, and money. What do you think, Hari-vilāsa? Is this a fact?"

Hari-vilāsa replied, "Yes, Prabhupāda, this is definitely a fact—wine, women, and money."

Prabhupāda said that although these attachments were very strong, the Kṛṣṇa consciousness movement could overcome their influence.

Prabhupāda said that the houses in the Paris suburb, with their attractive fenced-in yards, were excellent. But everything was being wasted for sense gratification. Although a French gentleman may have such a first-class house, garden, wife, bank account, and car, he has no spiritual knowledge. Therefore, he would always remain attached to his first-class possessions, and at the end of his life his great attachment would lead him to take birth as a cockroach or rat or dog within that same house.

As Prabhupāda and the devotees continued walking, Prabhupāda asked Hari-vilāsa how he thought the temple's preaching was faring. Hari-vilāsa said he thought it would be successful but that it might be a good idea to make extra income by starting a business.

"Your business is preaching," Prabhupāda said. "If there are some householders, they can do business."

When Prabhupāda and his party arrived at the temple, they found the devotees eagerly waiting for Prabhupāda's morning *Bhāgavatam* lecture. But there was no time. Prabhupāda had to leave at once for the airport. He was returning to America.

CHAPTER THIRTY-FIVE

"This Remote Corner of the World"

ALTHOUGH ŚRĪLA PRABHUPĀDA had been away from America for a year, his Kṛṣṇa consciousness movement had flourished, by Kṛṣṇa's grace, and the devotees' attachment for him had grown. His disciples, having heard reports and seen photos of his triumphant tour of India, had felt inspired to increase their own preaching. In each American center new devotees had been joining and were learning Prabhupāda's teachings from the senior devotees. Already accepting Śrīla Prabhupāda as their spiritual master, hundreds of newcomers were eagerly awaiting initiation.

How different from Prabhupāda's first arrival in America, alone in 1965. Walking the cold streets with no money and no temple, he had been ignored. Sometimes he had thought of quitting, taking a boat back to India. But he had maintained absolute faith. And now, less than six years later, in dozens of ISKCON centers throughout America, hundreds of disciples worshiped him and would throng ecstatically to receive him.

Los Angeles
June 26, 1971

When Prabhupāda had left Los Angeles a year ago, the political turmoil there had troubled his mind, but on returning he found the devotees recovered. Faithfully they were executing his orders to chant publicly, distribute *Back to Godhead* magazine, and worship the Deity of Rukmiṇī-Dvārakādhīśa. In the gorgeously decorated Los Angeles temple, Prabhupāda performed a large initiation ceremony, accepting dozens of new disciples.

On June 27 Śrīla Prabhupāda traveled from Los Angeles to San Francisco for the fifth annual Ratha-yātrā. Two hundred followers met him at the airport.

"How many devotees do you have?" a reporter asked.

"Unlimited," Prabhupāda said. "Some admit and some don't admit. Admit you are a servant of Lord Kṛṣṇa, and your life will be a success."

After two days in San Francisco, Prabhupāda returned to Los Angeles and on July 16 flew to Detroit. Bhagavān dāsa, Prabhupāda's Governing Body secretary for the Midwest, had preached vigorously in his zone, opening centers in St. Louis, Chicago, and other cities. Almost three hundred devotees, most of whom had never seen Prabhupāda, assembled at the Detroit airport to receive him.

Sureśvara: *Devotees had come from all over the midwestern U.S. and eastern Canada to greet Śrīla Prabhupāda at Detroit's Metro Airport. A red and gold throne stood in the center of the reception room, and the devotees were chanting Hare Kṛṣṇa and dancing, awaiting Prabhupāda's arrival. When the plane finally landed, all bliss broke loose. The disembarkation dolly joined the plane, but we couldn't see Śrīla Prabhupāda. I became anxious—when would he enter the room? Suddenly a cry went up, and I looked around. Devotees were bowing down.*

Urukrama: *Śrīla Prabhupāda entered the room as bright as the sun, and everyone immediately prostrated themselves on the floor. Not like the other times when we bowed down together, but this was like an overwhelming force hit us and we were being thrown to our knees. When I stood up, I couldn't believe my eyes. There was Prabhupāda! Almost everyone in the room was crying.*

Indradyumna: *My first glimpse of Prabhupāda was through the lens of my camera, and I thought he looked just like he did in his pictures. I had only seen him in pictures, and now he looked just like the pictures, only moving. All the devotees began to cry and fall to the ground. It was a transcendental, emotional thing. I was looking, watching all the older devotees—how much love they had for Śrīla Prabhupāda. And I was feeling unqualified and sinful.*

Urukrama: *Prabhupāda appeared powerful, yet at the same time delicate and soft, like a very wonderful flower. As he moved along very slowly, the devotees lined up and made an aisle for him to walk. He walked up to Kīrtanānanda Mahārāja, put a garland around him, and embraced him. Kīrtanānanda Mahārāja was crying tears of ecstasy, and he looked like a little boy next to his father. Then Prabhupāda went to Bhagavān and patted him on the head. Then he embraced Bhagavān, who also began to weep like a little boy who has just seen his father after a very long time.*

Viśvakarmā: *I arrived late. When I got there, I was afraid to look at Śrīla Prabhupāda, because I felt too fallen to look upon the pure representative of the Lord. So I stayed behind a wall of devotees, afraid to look. Finally, I realized this is ridiculous, as the perfection of the eyes is to behold the form of Kṛṣṇa's pure devotee. I raised my head, and I saw him sitting on his* vyāsāsana, *drinking a cup of water. Never had I seen anyone drink water like that—without touching the goblet to their mouth. The water poured from the cup like a shining silver stream, straight into Śrīla Prabhupāda's mouth and throat, and he finished the water in a few swallows. He appeared to be a grand sage from the spiritual realm, and as everyone chanted, he looked around at the devotees, smiling with great pleasure. Everyone was overwhelmed with transcendental joy, and I joined with over half the devotees in weeping.*

Prabhupāda began speaking.

"This is very satisfactory that so many devotees, boys and girls, are taking part in this great movement, Kṛṣṇa consciousness movement. It is a very important movement, because it is correcting the human civilization. It is a great defect in the modern civilization—people are accepting this body as self. And based on this mistake in the foundation, everything is going wrong. Accepting this body as the self is the beginning of all problems. The great philosophers, scientists, theologians, and thoughtful men do not know what is the defect.

"Recently I was in Moscow. So I had a nice talk with a professor of Indology, Professor Kotovsky. He was speaking that, 'Swamiji, after this annihilation of this body, everything is finished.' So I was astonished that a learned professor, posing himself in a very responsible post, had no idea about the soul and the body—how they are different, how the soul is migrating from one body to another. ..."

As Prabhupāda spoke, a voice announced over the public address system that the departure lounge had to be cleared for the next flight. "They are speaking about ourselves?" Prabhupāda asked. "We shall stop? All right. Let us go."

That evening, in the temple room of Detroit's ISKCON center, Śrīla Prabhupāda sat on his *vyāsāsana* before the deities of Lord Jagannātha, Subhadrā, and Balarāma. While a devotee led the *kīrtana,* Prabhupāda played his *karatālas,* looking around the room at his disciples. He was nodding his head, pleased to see them dancing and chanting. After the *kīrtana,* he lectured.

"Just see how their characters are being formed, how they are becoming purified, how their faces are becoming brighter. It is practical. So our request is, take full advantage of the center—you come here. It is being guided by one of my best disciples, Bhagavān dāsa. So he and others will help you. Please come regularly to this temple and take advantage of it."

After his lecture, Prabhupāda asked for questions. Bahulāśva raised his hand. "Śrīla Prabhupāda, what is the thing that will please you the most?"

"Chant Hare Kṛṣṇa," Prabhupāda replied, and the devotees spontaneously cried out, "*Jaya*! *Jaya*!"

Prabhupāda: "That is the simplest thing. You are chanting. I am very much pleased. That's all. I came to your country to chant that you would chant also along with me. You are helping me by chanting, so I am pleased.

"But this tendency is very nice, that you want to please me. That is very good. And to please me is not very difficult. Caitanya Mahāprabhu said that 'Under My order, every one of you go preach and become spiritual master.' And what is that order? The order is, 'Whomever you meet, you talk to him about Kṛṣṇa.'"

Prabhupāda emphasized that if one wanted to preach and represent Kṛṣṇa, then he could not change the message of Kṛṣṇa but must repeat what Kṛṣṇa says. "I have come here for the first time," Prabhupāda continued, "but before me, Bhagavān dāsa, he has organized. And what is his credit? He has presented things as I told him. That's all. This is wonderful. In Los Angeles also a program is going on very nicely. My disciple in charge there is Karandhara. He is present here. He is simply doing what I instruct, and he is doing very nicely—first class. Everyone who comes, they come and are enchanted by the temple, with the activities, with the disciples. So this is the way. This is called *paramparā* system. Don't concoct."

As Prabhupāda was leaving the temple that evening, the mother of one of his disciples approached him. "You know," she said, "these boys actually *worship* you!"

"Yes," Prabhupāda said, "that is our system. I am also worshiping my Guru Mahārāja." The devotees around Prabhupāda looked at one another and smiled. Although the woman had tried to make it appear extraordinary that Prabhupāda's disciples worshiped him, Prabhupāda had taken it casually. One *must* worship the *guru*. It was the Vaiṣṇava standard and nothing to wonder at.

* * *

Śrīla Prabhupāda had so many centers in the U.S. that to visit each one was not practical. During his year in India, many new centers had opened—on the West Coast, in Florida, Texas, the Midwest, the East. Prabhupāda said he had more establishments than a wealthy businessman, and more residences. Were he to stay at each of his "houses," he quipped, he couldn't visit them all in a year. And especially to Indian audiences he would cite the monthly expenditures for his centers.

Though proud of ISKCON's growth, Prabhupāda was never proud on his own account; he never considered using ISKCON for his own enjoyment. Whenever he visited a center, his quarters were usually an apartment arranged at the last minute, often fraught with annoyances like noisy neighbors and incompetent cooks. At seventy-five years, his constant traveling was hardly an arrangement for his health and comfort.

Prabhupāda never felt complacent over the small success his society enjoyed, nor would he claim the credit for that success. Rather, he said, it was due to the mercy of his spiritual master and the previous spiritual masters. ISKCON still had but little influence in the world; people considered it a small, exotic religious sect. But by the blessings of the previous *ācāryas,* it was growing. Prabhupāda was initiating more and more disciples, and the potential was unlimited.

One of Lord Caitanya's chief followers, Jīva Gosvāmī, had warned that a spiritual master should not accept many disciples; many neophyte disciples would bring suffering to the spiritual master. Yet on Prabhupāda's

U.S. tour during the summer of 1971, he initiated more disciples than ever before. As Lord Caitanya's empowered representative, he wanted to increase the number of devotees more and more. He was aware of the risk, but he was also aware of the great need. As he had written in *The Nectar of Devotion:*

> The one point is that without increasing the number of disciples, there is no propagation of the cult of Kṛṣṇa consciousness. Therefore, sometimes even at a risk, a *sannyāsi* in the line of Lord Caitanya Mahāprabhu may accept even a person who is not thoroughly fit to become a disciple. Later on, by the mercy of such a bona fide spiritual master, the disciple is gradually elevated. However, if one increases the number of disciples simply for some prestige or false honor, he will surely fall down in the matter of executing Kṛṣṇa consciousness.

Śrīla Prabhupāda's test of a prospective disciple's readiness for initiation was standard: the candidate must have followed the four rules and chanted sixteen rounds daily for at least six months and have the recommendation of the temple president and local G.B.C. secretary. Prabhupāda accepted anyone who fulfilled these conditions, and he expected the disciple to remain sincere and true to the vows of initiation.

Despite Prabhupāda's growing number of disciples, he intimately touched each of their hearts. Although a few disciples enjoyed extended association with him, most of his hundreds of disciples saw him only from afar. Yet each of them was certain that Prabhupāda was his own. Each could say "my spiritual master." Each could say "Prabhupāda" and feel close to their dearest friend and well-wisher, the one who was saving them from death. They knew that Prabhupāda was the direct representative of Kṛṣṇa and the most empowered *ācārya* of Lord Caitanya's message. Those who were sincere knew without doubt that their connection with Prabhupāda was transcendental, not to be interrupted or limited by physical or geographical considerations. If they surrendered to Prabhupāda's orders, Kṛṣṇa within their hearts would help them advance. If they were sincere, Kṛṣṇa would help them become better disciples of Śrīla Prabhupāda.

The devotees' love for Prabhupāda was not a vague sentiment. He was engaging them in Kṛṣṇa's service, and they were directly experiencing the transcendental results. Only a devotee, however, could understand Śrīla Prabhupāda's personality or the depth of his disciples' attraction for him or the debt they owed him. No wonder onlookers at the Detroit airport had not understood the apparently delirious devotees in their blissful reception of Śrīla Prabhupāda.

* * *

New York City
July 19, 1971

After Detroit, Prabhupāda visited Boston and then flew to New York, where another large group of devotees had gathered. The *New York Daily News* covered his airport arrival with photos and an article: "Swami, How They Love You."

Bhavānanda, the New York temple president, had decorated the temple room of the Brooklyn center with bright colors. Prabhupāda's *vyāsāsana* was a special creation of plaids, stripes, and checks in fuchsia, lime, black, white, and red. Prabhupāda liked it very much.

Two hundred devotees—many having waited for more than a year to be initiated—converged on the Brooklyn temple, and Prabhupāda held initiations for five consecutive days, initiating around two dozen disciples each day. One after another, the young men and women would approach Prabhupāda on his multicolored *vyāsāsana* to receive their initiation beads and spiritual names. Those receiving the *brāhmaṇa* initiation went one by one to see Prabhupāda in his room and receive the Gāyatrī *mantra.*

Madhumaṅgala: *I went to Prabhupāda's room and offered obeisances. "Come here," he said. So I went and sat close to him. He began teaching me the Gāyatrī* mantra, *and I was looking up at him. The sun was right behind his head. He looked like a mountain, like the Himalayas, and I was like a mole, a stone. He was very big, and I seemed very insignificant.*

Rikthānanda: *Prabhupāda turned to face me, and his eyes seemed like limitless pools of an entrancing liquid. I knew he was focused always on Kṛṣṇa, and his eyes were a reflection of that happiness. He said something to me, and I said, "No, sir." Saying "sir" to him seemed natural, and he seemed to be happy that I had said it. Then in a very clear, soft, steady voice, he began to teach me the Gāyatrī* mantra. *Then he took the sacred thread and put it around my neck and across my shoulder, very gracefully and with such precision in his movements. "Now," he said, "you are a* brāhmaṇa."

Daivī-śakti: *Prabhupāda had the Gāyatrī* mantra *written on a small piece of paper, and as he was teaching it to me he had his eyes closed. I would repeat it word for word after him. When he got to the third line, however, instead of saying* gurudevāya *he said the word from the fifth line. I didn't know whether to follow what he had said or just say what was on the paper. So I said what was on the paper, and then Prabhupāda immediately realized what he had done and changed it. But I suddenly realized that the perfect chanting of* mantras *was not so significant. Prabhupāda was fully absorbed in thinking of Kṛṣṇa, and although there may have been some apparent flaw in his pronunciation, he was perfect, regardless. I saw that the real perfection of devotional service was to follow Prabhupāda.*

After I received my Gāyatrī mantra, *I asked Prabhupāda if I could ask him some questions, and he said yes. "Śrīla Prabhupāda," I said, "I haven't been able to serve you in rapt attention. What can I do to serve you?" I was praying he would give me a special service to do for him personally. "Chant Hare Kṛṣṇa," was all he said.*

"Is there anything more?" I asked. He said, "Are you married?" I said, "Yes." So he said, "Serve your husband."

I said, "My husband and I don't get along." So he said, "Be a pūjārī*—there are so many things."*

His answer seemed to solve all my difficulty. First and foremost was to chant Hare Kṛṣṇa. And in addition to that, there are so many other services. If you don't do one of them, then go on to the next one—"There are so many things." When he said those words, it relieved all my anxiety.

In New York Prabhupāda lectured gravely and authoritatively from *Śrīmad-Bhāgavatam,* stressing surrender to Kṛṣṇa through surrendering to the Kṛṣṇa consciousness movement. Unlike any other *Bhāgavatam* lecturer, Prabhupāda was able to offer a movement, a society, and a way of life that were fully Kṛṣṇa conscious and that gave any interested person practical entrance into the devotional service of the Lord.

Someone asked how a person who had been very sinful could be relieved of his *karma,* and Prabhupāda replied simply, "Come and live with us. That's all. Is it very difficult? Our students—they are living with us. You simply come and live with us, and you are free from all *karma.* Is it difficult? Then do that. We shall give you food, we shall give you shelter, we shall give you nice philosophy. If you want to marry, we shall give you a good wife. What do you want more? So come and live with us. That's all."

Prabhupāda stressed this same point in his lectures: if a person seeking spiritual fulfillment lived and served with the ISKCON devotees, even material fulfillment would come.

"These Kṛṣṇa conscious boys and girls—in sixty centers—they are living in the best houses. They are eating the best food. They are in the best consciousness. They have got the best hope. Everything best. Their feature of body is best. What material happiness do you want more than this? They have got wife, children, happiness, home—everything full. So material happiness is nothing to a Kṛṣṇa conscious person. Material happiness will roll at his feet, saying, 'Please take me, please take me.' There is no need of asking for it. Simply be steady and ask Kṛṣṇa, 'Please engage me in Your service.' Then your satisfaction will automatically come. Don't bother for material happiness."

Nanda-kiśora asked, "What happens to a person out on the street if we just give him one Simply Wonderful* or some *prasādam*?"

Prabhupāda: "Then it is wonderful—simply wonderful. (The devotees laughed.) He has not tasted such wonderful sweet in his life. Therefore, you give him wonderful, and because he is eating that wonderful sweet, one day he will come to your temple and become wonderful. Therefore it is simply wonderful. So go on distributing this simply wonderful. Your philosophy is simply wonderful, your *prasādam* is simply wonderful, you are simply wonderful. And your Kṛṣṇa is simply wonderful. The whole process is simply wonderful. Kṛṣṇa acts wonderfully, and it is acting wonderfully. Who can deny it?"

Kīrtanānanda Mahārāja: "Prabhupāda is simply wonderful."

While Prabhupāda continued in New York, poised to leave for London in a few days, his secretary mentioned that many U.S. centers were still vying for his presence. Prabhupāda casually remarked that if any center could arrange a good lecture program and pay his travel expenses plus one thousand dollars, then he would go there before leaving for London.

---

* A sweet made from powdered milk, butter, and sugar and offered to Lord Kṛṣṇa.

Hearing this, the devotees in Gainesville, Florida, determined to meet Prabhupāda's transcendental challenge. The temple president, Hṛdayānanda, assigned an uninitiated devotee, David Liberman, to find a sponsor at the University of Florida willing to pay one thousand dollars for Prabhupāda to come and speak. David visited every student organization on campus until he found a donor.

Prabhupāda agreed to come, even though his secretary informed him that the flight would lay over two hours in Atlanta and then continue to Jacksonville, a one-and-a-half-hour car ride from Gainesville.

* * *

Atlanta
July 29, 1971

The ten residents of the recently opened Atlanta temple arranged to receive Prabhupāda during his layover at the Atlanta airport. They prepared a large feast and decorated the Eastern Airlines V.I.P. lounge with fruits, flowers, and garlands.

Bill Ogle: *Although Śrīla Prabhupāda was not big physically, he immediately captured the consciousness of the entire Atlanta airport when he entered. Everyone was watching as he walked, with his head held high, his cane moving gracefully with every step. The airport is one of the busiest in the country, but everyone who saw Prabhupāda looked at him in amazement. Airport officials voluntarily began clearing a path for Prabhupāda to walk. But what was even more amazing was that he was so submissive to such insignificant disciples as we.*

Prabhupāda entered the V.I.P. lounge with his disciples and about twenty Indian guests. Confronting the portable *vyāsāsana* atop a marble table, Prabhupāda declined; the seat seemed unsteady. But the devotees assured him that it was sturdy, so Prabhupāda climbed up, sat down, and began leading a *kīrtana.* After speaking for about fifteen minutes, Prabhupāda concluded his lecture.

"This is not sentimental chanting, but it is based on the soundest philosophy, Vedic literatures. We have got so many books, and you can buy them in our bookstore. Where is the bookstore?"

There was a long pause. The devotees had remembered fruits, flowers, the chair, the feast, invitations to the Indians—but they had forgotten Prabhupāda's books. Prabhupāda continued to wait for an answer to his question, until finally the senior disciple, Janamejaya, replied, "Prabhupāda, we usually have a book store."

"Hmm" was all Prabhupāda said. Again a long silence. "So," Prabhupāda said, looking to the audience, "any questions?"

Prabhupāda chatted with the Indians, asking their names and where they were from in India. Most of them were young men with families and treated him respectfully, like a grandfather or a revered swami. One Indian man, about thirty-five, mentioned that he was getting his Ph.D. in biology.

"Oh, biology," Prabhupāda said. "Hmm, poor frogs." Everyone in the lounge—except the biologist—burst into laughter.

"No, no," the biologist protested, embarrassed. "Why 'poor frogs'?"

"Because you are killing," Prabhupāda said.

"But it is for the advancement of knowledge," said the biologist. "So it is worthwhile. It is for the advancement of knowledge."

"All right," said Prabhupāda, "if I ask you now, will you give your body for the advancement of knowledge?" Everyone in the room began to laugh.

"Yes! Yes, I would!" the man replied. But the more he protested, repeating, "Yes, I would!" the more ridiculous he seemed, and the harder everyone laughed.

"How many species of life are there?" Prabhupāda asked.

"Fifty million," the biologist replied.

"Oh?" said Prabhupāda. "You have seen them all?"

"No."

"How many have you seen?"

"Perhaps five thousand."

"And you are wrong," Prabhupāda said. "There are 8,400,000 species of life. We have scientific knowledge from the *Vedas.*"

Bill Ogle: *After Prabhupāda took* prasāda, *we performed a play for him. The play was "The* Brāhmaṇa *and the Cobbler." I played Viṣṇu. It was terrible. I had to be Viṣṇu, and my wife had to be Lakṣmī. I was lying down as Lord Viṣṇu, and my wife was massaging my feet. Prabhupāda kept looking at me, and I thought he must be thinking, "Who is this rascal playing Viṣṇu?" My feeling was, "This is not very good. I shouldn't be doing this." I was very embarrassed to be in front of Prabhupāda like that.*

Jayasena was Nārada Muni, and he offered obeisances about a hundred times throughout the play. Because Prabhupāda was there, Jayasena was constantly offering obeisances to everyone and anything. So although he was playing Nārada Muni, he offered obeisances to the cobbler. But some of the Indians spoke up. They were a little taken aback that Nārada Muni, such a great saint, was offering obeisances to a cobbler, who is ordinarily a very low-class person.

So at this point Prabhupāda interrupted and began to explain. "Actually," he said, "it is all right that Nārada Muni has offered obeisances to the cobbler, because the cobbler is a Vaiṣṇava. Any Vaiṣṇava can receive obeisances, more than a brāhmaṇa.*" He continued, narrating the play. He told the story, and we continued acting. It was ecstatic.*

As Prabhupāda was leaving the lounge to board his flight for Jacksonville, a lady in a wheelchair, the mother of one of the devotees in Atlanta, raised herself up and threw herself at Prabhupāda's feet. With tears in her eyes, she cried out, "I am dying of cancer. Save me! Save me!" Śrīla Prabhupāda bent down and put his hand on her head. "That is all right," he said comfortingly. "That is all right."

As Prabhupāda, garlanded with red roses and magnolias, walked down the corridor toward his plane, the devotees thought that Prabhupāda appeared majestic, like a king. He emanated a golden effulgence, and he seemed powerful, yet humble. The devotees felt spiritual strength and pledged to follow Prabhupāda's teachings. They last glimpsed him walking across the airfield toward the small plane that would take him to Jacksonville. His saffron silk *dhotī* and *kurtā* blowing in the breeze, he turned to them and waved.

* * *

Gainesville
July 29, 1971

Śrīla Prabhupāda asked how fast the car was going and how long it would take them to get to Gainesville. Sixty-five miles per hour, the driver said; it would take an hour and a half. Prabhupāda observed the scenery along the highway—pine forests, marshes, exotic birds, an occasional armadillo foraging near the highway. Lotuses and lilies grew wild in the canals along the roadside, and bright sunshine warmed the clear air.

Gainesville was a side trip for Prabhupāda, a special day of preaching. He had left Śyāmasundara, his secretary, in New York and brought with him only Aravinda, his servant. He had come for a day to bring the mercy of Lord Caitanya to yet another city. When the devotees had picked him up at the airport, he had appeared grave. But on catching sight of the devotees he had smiled wonderfully, and then, turning to Hṛdayānanda, he had asked, "Which way?" He was like a transcendental fighter, asking to be pointed toward the battle.

Prabhupāda walked along a flower-sprinkled pathway and into the temple, a rented house near the University of Florida campus. In the temple room he stood a moment, studying a crude but sincerely executed painting of Lord Caitanya and His associates. Hṛdayānanda asked Prabhupāda if he would like to rest, and he nodded. While the devotees performed *kīrtana,* Prabhupāda retired to his room, returning later to sit on the large blue velvet *vyāsāsana* in the small temple room. In addition to Prabhupāda's disciples from Gainesville, Miami, Tallahassee, and New Orleans, many university students and other guests were also present.

"It is so nice to see so many young boys and girls here," Śrīla Prabhupāda began, "in this remote corner of the world, so far away from the birthplace of Lord Caitanya."

Prabhupāda lectured about the saving grace of chanting the holy name of the Lord. One of his disciples, he said, had been present when his mother was dying. "Because he had been telling her about Kṛṣṇa and Hare Kṛṣṇa, she said to her son in her last words, 'Where is your Kṛṣṇa? Is He here now?' And then she died." For her uttering the holy name and thinking of Kṛṣṇa, Prabhupāda said, she would go to the spiritual world.

After Prabhupāda finished his talk, a girl reporter from the university newspaper raised her hand. "I see almost all young people here," she said. "Why is that?"

Prabhupāda replied with a question: "Why are there so many young people in the university?"

The girl reflected a moment, "Well ... I guess that's the age for education."

"Yes," Prabhupāda said, "so this is the age for Kṛṣṇa consciousness. You cannot teach an old dog new tricks."

The engagement for which Prabhupāda had come, and for which the University of Florida was paying a thousand dollars, was to be that afternoon on campus at the Plaza of the Americas. When Prabhupāda arrived, several hundred students were gathered near the temporary stage, sitting casually on the grass, lounging beneath the fragrant magnolia trees. The sky was overcast, and rain threatened.

As more students gathered, the crowd grew to five hundred. Then just as Prabhupāda was about to speak, a light drizzle began to fall, and Hṛdayānanda came onstage to hold an umbrella over Śrīla Prabhupāda.

Prabhupāda, sitting on his *vyāsāsana,* said softly into the microphone, "Someone is smoking," and the students politely extinguished their cigarettes. No sooner did Prabhupāda begin his lecture, however, than a dog started yapping. Prabhupāda paused. "Who is that dog?" he asked. When the dog persisted, Śrīla Prabhupāda said, "He also wants to talk." Finally the barking stopped, and so did the rain. But Hṛdayānanda continued to hold the umbrella over Prabhupāda's head.

While riding in the car back to the temple, Prabhupāda asked to hear the tape recording of his lecture. When he heard the dog barking at the beginning of his talk, he laughed.

"Prabhupāda," Hṛdayānanda said, "your lecture was wonderful. Everyone liked it. The students liked it, the devotees liked it, the professors liked it."

"All right," Prabhupāda said. "Hare Kṛṣṇa."

Śrīla Prabhupāda's day of preaching was not over yet. Next was an evening television interview.

The interviewer had done some preparatory reading, and he introduced Śrīla Prabhupāda by first describing who Kṛṣṇa was, according to Vedic literature, and how Śrīla Prabhupāda was in the disciplic succession from

Lord Caitanya. When the interviewer asked Prabhupāda for an introductory statement, Prabhupāda explained, "The Kṛṣṇa consciousness movement is trying to invoke in all people the original consciousness that we are a part and parcel of Kṛṣṇa."

When the interviewer asked Prabhupāda, "Who is your spiritual master?" Prabhupāda lowered his head humbly and stated the full name of his Guru Mahārāja, "Oṁ Viṣṇupāda Paramahaṁsa Parivrājakācārya Bhaktisiddhānta Sarasvatī Gosvāmī Mahārāja Prabhupāda."

The interviewer, however, seemed bent on controversy. "In what way, sir, may I ask, did you think and do you think right now that the teaching of love of God that you are preaching is different and perhaps better than the teachings of love of God that were being conducted in this country and have been conducted in the rest of the world for centuries?"

Śrīla Prabhupāda: "This teaching is the most authorized. That is a fact. We are following in the footsteps of Lord Caitanya. He is accepted by us, according to the authority of Vedic religion, to be personally Kṛṣṇa Himself. For example, you are the expert in this establishment. If someone is doing something under your guidance and if you personally teach him, 'Do like this,' that is very authorized. So when Lord Caitanya taught God consciousness, God Himself was teaching."

Prabhupāda had answered positively, avoiding the sectarian dispute the interviewer had invited. Yet repeatedly the interviewer tried to involve him in a controversy. He seemed to want Prabhupāda to appear arrogant, sectarian, and anti-American. Prabhupāda, however, insisted he was not opposed to any other religion and that anyone in the world could chant the name of God as it appeared in his religion.

Interviewer: "But there must have been an element of dissatisfaction on your part with the way Godhead was being professed in this part of the world before you came. Otherwise, there would have been no sense in your being here."

Śrīla Prabhupāda: "It is not just this part of the world. Practically every part of the world has very little interest in God. They have more interest in dog."

Prabhupāda's answers were strong and philosophically strong. The interviewer, trying his professional best, again attempted to find some fault.

Interviewer: "It seems to me, sir, as interpreted in your writings, that there is a very high emphasis placed on the relationship between the individual and God."

Śrīla Prabhupāda: "Yes. That is found everywhere."

Interviewer: "Yes, but you place more emphasis on that relationship than on the relationship between one individual and another. Am I right in that?"

Śrīla Prabhupāda: "We have to establish, first of all, our lost relationship with God. Then we can understand what is our relationship between one individual and another. If the central point is missing, then there is practically no relation. You are an American, and another is an American, and both of you feel American nationality because the center is America. So unless you understand God, you cannot understand who I am, nor can I understand who you are."

Interviewer: "I think that in this part of the world, in the Western world, we place a great deal of emphasis on religion in the ways it gets one man to deal with another man—the ethic of religion. Now in the Kṛṣṇa consciousness movement ..."

Śrīla Prabhupāda: "We are not concerned how one man deals with another man."

Interviewer: "Isn't that part of your Kṛṣṇa consciousness movement?"

Śrīla Prabhupāda: "No, this is not important. Because we know as soon as one knows how to deal with God, he will automatically deal very nicely with others."

Interviewer: "But let's take the Christian religion for an example. You know the Ten Commandments? There is a heavy emphasis in the ten commandments on the relationships between one human being and another: 'Thou shalt not steal. Thou shalt not kill.' You know, that sort of thing."

Śrīla Prabhupāda: "But I say that Jesus Christ never said and never meant that 'Thou shalt not kill' refers to only human beings. Where is that evidence? Jesus Christ never said that 'Thou shalt not kill' refers only to human beings. Thou shalt not kill any animal."

Interviewer: "Any life?"

Śrīla Prabhupāda: "Any life. That is religion."

Interviewer: "It has never been interpreted that way."

Śrīla Prabhupāda: "You have interpreted it differently, but he said, 'Thou shalt not kill.' He never said, 'Thou shalt not kill amongst human beings.' Why do you interpret it that way?"

Prabhupāda had given the TV interviewer the very thing he was after, controversy, but because it was not desirable controversy the interviewer promptly dropped it. Instead, he asked Prabhupāda how one could recognize a true follower of Kṛṣṇa consciousness by his behavior.

"He'd be a perfect gentleman," Prabhupāda said, "that's all. ... Therefore, I prohibit my disciples to eat meat."

Interviewer: "To eat meat?"

Śrīla Prabhupāda: "Yes. And therefore I prohibit illicit sex life. Therefore I prohibit intoxication. They do not even smoke, what to speak of other intoxication."

When Prabhupāda said that whoever observed these four rules would become a perfect gentleman, the interviewer asked whether there was a place for women in the religion. Prabhupāda replied that women and men had the same rights and followed the same principles. The interviewer asked whether Prabhupāda was encouraged or discouraged, and Prabhupāda said he was encouraged because so many devotees were joining. The interviewer doubted that many were joining, since out of two hundred million Americans, only two dozen devotees were present in the TV studio. "When you sell diamonds," Prabhupāda replied, "you cannot expect that everyone will purchase."

As a final question, the interviewer asked if Prabhupāda had any major complaints about American society.

Śrīla Prabhupāda: "I have no complaint. These boys and girls are very nice. I am, rather, encouraged that these boys and girls are hankering after something nice. They are frustrated. So now, since they have the best thing, they are coming."

The interviewer asked Śrīla Prabhupāda and his followers to chant Hare Kṛṣṇa, and within half a minute they were off the air. The hot studio lights went out, and the engineers started talking among themselves. The interviewer bid Śrīla Prabhupāda a polite farewell—he had no intention of continuing their talk—but Śrīla Prabhupāda continued preaching. On-camera or off-camera made no difference to him. He saw the interviewer not merely as a television personality but as someone to receive Kṛṣṇa's mercy.

The two had been sitting very closely for the interview, and Prabhupāda now leaned toward the interviewer and said, "Let me ask you one question. If you have some disease and you want to cure this disease, what is the best way to go about it? By asking a friend or by going to a medical doctor and asking how to cure this disease? Would you go to a friend?"

The man replied, "Yes." Prabhupāda shook his head, "You would go to a friend?" Again the man said, "Yes."

The interviewer was not concentrating, so Prabhupāda patiently repeated his example. "Try to understand," he said. "If you have some disease, then would you go to a medical doctor or would you go to a friend?" The man could not grasp the point, so Prabhupāda answered, "No, you would not go to a friend. You would go to a physician—one who knows the answer. That is the spiritual master." They talked a while longer, and finally Prabhupāda and the devotees left.

It was almost midnight, and Prabhupāda went to his room. When he had first arrived in Gainesville he had agreed to initiate the five eligible candidates and had even taken their *japa* beads. But now the day had passed, there had been no initiation, and Prabhupāda still had five strands of beads. Joseph and Sam, who had come all the way from New Orleans, and David Liberman and his wife, Adrienne, and a Gainesville boy named Gary were all in anxiety. They had stayed up, talking among themselves, wondering whether Śrīla Prabhupāda would hold an initiation ceremony in the morning, before he left.

Aravinda told them there would be no time for a ceremony in the morning, but that he would ask Śrīla Prabhupāda when they could have their beads back. He went to Prabhupāda's room, leaving the devotees to sit and talk about Śrīla Prabhupāda. When Aravinda returned, he surprised everyone by announcing, "Prabhupāda is going to give you your beads now. He is going to give you your initiation in his room." The devotees excitedly hurried to Śrīla Prabhupāda's room.

Prabhupāda sat on his bed. He wore no shirt, only his *dhotī,* which he had pushed up high on his thighs and tucked under himself, like a loincloth or *gamchā.* His body was smooth and glowing. The devotees sat on the floor around his bed while he held their beads in his hands and chanted.

Prabhupāda handed Gary his beads. "So your name is now Dharma dāsa. This means 'one who is a strict follower of all religious principles.'"

Dharma: *I was actually very nervous, and I was practically shaking, because I was afraid I would do something wrong in front of Śrīla Prabhupāda. I was so nervous practically I couldn't even hear properly. But I was very happy to have been accepted by Śrīla Prabhupāda. I knew, of course, there was no question of ever leaving the movement now. I never wanted to leave anyway, but now this was official. Even if I had considered it before, now there was no question of it.*

Then there was Joseph from New Orleans. "What is his name?" Prabhupāda asked Aravinda. Aravinda read from a sheet, "Bhāgavata dāsa." Prabhupāda smiled and said, "Oh, Bhāgavata dāsa. Very good. There are two things. There is the book *bhāgavata*—*Śrīmad-Bhāgavatam* and *Bhagavad-gītā*—and the person *bhāgavata,* who follows perfectly those teachings. He is a living manifestation of the book *bhāgavata.* And you are Bhāgavata dāsa. That means you are the servant of the book *bhāgavata* and the person *bhāgavata.*

Bhāgavata: *I always wanted a name that meant I was the servant of the* guru. *So when I heard this, I was very happy. Prabhupāda started to hand me my beads, but then he pulled them back and asked, "And what are the four regulative principles?" So I told him, and he said, "Very good."*

Then he went to hand me my beads again, but again he pulled them back. He asked, "How many rounds do you chant?" I was very proud, because I had been chanting twenty rounds a day for about five months, so I sat up real straight and said, "You're supposed to chant sixteen rounds a day, Śrīla Prabhupāda. But I chant twenty."

Śrīla Prabhupāda just turned away from me and said, "That's all right." It was like he was saying, "Don't get puffed up." Then he turned to me and said, "Here are your beads."

Handing Dave his beads, Prabhupāda said, "Your name is Amarendra. This means 'the best of the immortals.'" He named Adrienne "Gāyatrī dāsī" and Sam "Suvrata."

When Suvrata stood and Prabhupāda noticed he was not wearing neck beads, he withheld the chanting beads and said, "You have no neck beads? Where are your neck beads?" Prabhupāda turned to Bhāgavata dāsa. "You also have no neck beads?" Bhāgavata thought that Prabhupāda was going to take his chanting beads back, so he hid them against his stomach. Then Prabhupāda turned to the senior devotees in the room, criticizing. "What is the matter with you?" he said sternly. "You are leaders, and you don't know these things? Don't you know that you must put neck beads in giving initiation?"

The senior devotees were frightened by Prabhupāda's anger. "We are sorry, Prabhupāda," someone said. "Tomorrow for the fire *yajña* they will have neck beads."

"Yes," Prabhupāda said, "you cannot do the fire *yajña* without neck beads. They must have neck beads."

Although it was midnight, Prabhupāda asked if the devotees had any questions. Bhāgavata dāsa raised his hand. "How is it that we are on a transcendental platform but sometimes we are affected by the three modes of nature?"

"It is just like you are on a boat," Prabhupāda replied. "If you are on the boat, then I cannot say you are not on the boat. Is it not? So you are on the transcendental boat. Therefore, you are on the transcendental platform. You cannot say that you are not. But the waves are coming, and they are rocking the boat." Prabhupāda gestured with his hands like a boat rocking. "So the waves of the material nature are coming," he continued, "and they are rocking the boat. But when you become an expert boatman, then even in the greatest storm you can stay steady and steer the boat, and it will not rock."

"Well, how does one become an expert boatman?" Bhāgavata asked.

"You become expert," Prabhupāda replied, "by becoming enthusiastic, sincere, confident, determined, and patient." Seeing Bhāgavata's anxious face, Prabhupāda added, "And you must be patient. Everything will come in due course."

Sitting informally on the bed, in his abbreviated *dhotī,* Prabhupāda had answered Bhāgavata's questions in such a way as to fully satisfy all the devotees. The devotees were already satisfied just to be with Prabhupāda, but by his answers to their questions not only they but all devotees could take encouragement and be satisfied. They would tell the others what he had said, and everyone would cherish these instructions of Śrīla Prabhupāda.

Amarendra also had a question. Amarendra was intense and impassioned, and so was his inquiry. Before becoming a devotee, he had been a leader of campus radicals. Now he wanted to bring that same intensity to bear in spreading Kṛṣṇa consciousness. "Śrīla Prabhupāda," Amarendra asked, "how can we make them take to this Kṛṣṇa consciousness? What can we say when we go to preach to people? What can we say that will make them take it?" His voice was heavy and forceful, demanding action.

"You simply ask them to please chant Hare Kṛṣṇa," Prabhupāda replied. "Whether they take or not, that is their business. That is between them and Kṛṣṇa. But you have done your business. You have done your duty for Kṛṣṇa by simply asking them, 'Please chant Hare Kṛṣṇa.' "

"How do we take our minds away from *māyā* and bring them to Kṛṣṇa?" Rādhāvallabha asked.

"You must *drag* the mind," Prabhupāda said. "You must *drag* the mind back to the sound vibration of Hare Kṛṣṇa, Hare Kṛṣṇa, Kṛṣṇa Kṛṣṇa, Hare Hare." And again he repeated, "You must *drag* the mind back to the sound vibration."

"All right." Prabhupāda looked around. "You are satisfied now?"

The devotees responded, "Yes, Śrīla Prabhupāda. Thank you very much." Then they all left. It had been the greatest day and night of their lives, they all agreed, and they would never forget it.

While Prabhupāda rode to the Jacksonville airport in a car with a few disciples, the other devotees followed in their van, bringing the *vyāsāsana* from the temple for Prabhupāda to use at the airport. Śrīla Prabhupāda closed his eyes and rested as he rode, and the devotees in the back seat of his car ate the remnants of his *prasādam.*

Hṛdayānanda: *It was my idea to bring Prabhupāda's* vyāsāsana *to the airport. I was thinking, "How can my spiritual master sit in the same seats that* karmīs *sit on?" It just seemed impossible. How could Prabhupāda put his lotus body, how could he sit, on the same seats as the* karmīs? *I was very agitated by that. Amarendra had built the* vyāsāsana, *and he used to build everything like a tank. The* vyāsāsana *must have weighed several hundred pounds. It took four or five devotees to carry it.*

So Prabhupāda arrived first, and the vyāsāsana *wasn't there. By the time he got to his boarding gate and the* vyāsāsana *still wasn't there, I was in anxiety, because I didn't want him to sit in a regular seat. I thought it would be a great offense on my part. Then as I looked down the long, long airport corridor, I saw six* brahmacārīs, *half of them without their shoes on, lugging Prabhupāda's* vyāsāsana *down the corridor. It was such an absurd scene. Prabhupāda just stood there looking in disbelief and disgust, and finally several sweating, groaning* brahmacārīs *came and dropped the* vyāsāsana *down in front of Prabhupāda. Prabhupāda just looked at it with disdain, walked past it, and sat down in the ordinary seat.*

While most of the devotees sat at Prabhupāda's feet, chanting the

Gurv-aṣṭaka prayers to the spiritual master, Hṛdayānanda was preaching to the people who were standing and watching the spectacle. He had some of Śrīla Prabhupāda's books, and he was trying to distribute them. Prabhupāda gave more attention to this preaching than to the devotees seated at his feet.

* * *

Having visited half a dozen cities in a little more than a month's time, Śrīla Prabhupāda was planning next to visit London. Clearly, his field had become the entire world. And his traveling was the practical enactment of his conviction that Kṛṣṇa consciousness should be given to people everywhere.

By Prabhupāda's wide traveling and bold preaching, the old idea that the *Bhagavad-gītā* and Kṛṣṇa were only for the Hindus had become an anachronism, a prejudice. Barriers of race, religion, nation, sex, class—all were now down. The Hindu saying that a swami should not cross the ocean had become a superstition, intended perhaps to protect lesser swamis but certainly never to restrict the message of the Absolute Truth from being spread.

Caitanya Mahāprabhu's express desire was that in every town and village of the world His name be heard, and no Vedic injunction could prohibit that. Of course, the Vedic literatures advised a devotee to live in a secluded place and avoid worldly men and women, and they advised a devotee not to disturb the minds of innocent persons or preach to the faithless. According to one Vedic injunction, a devotee should not even see the face of a nonbeliever. Such rules and regulations, however, intended mainly for the protection and purification of the neophytes, were superseded by a stalwart *ācārya* acting on the higher principle of compassion.

And in support of that higher principle Lord Kṛṣṇa had promised, "My devotee shall never be vanquished." The surrendered preacher, taking up Lord Caitanya's highest order, would be immunized against contamination, despite regular contact with worldly persons. Even at the risk of his own spiritual life, the preacher approached worldly people, and in return Kṛṣṇa protected him.

Prabhupāda was merciful to everyone, everywhere. Therefore he was *jagad-guru,* the spiritual master for the entire world. To become *jagad-guru* didn't mean to claim that one was better than everyone else or that he was the best *guru* in the world. *Jagad-guru* meant that, like Nārada Muni, a preacher of Kṛṣṇa consciousness went everywhere, preached everywhere, and had disciples everywhere. And Śrīla Prabhupāda did that.

On arriving at one U.S. airport, Śrīla Prabhupāda had mentioned that *yogīs* had formerly traveled in three different ways: by flying carpet, by pigeons, and by *mantra.* "Then why have you come today on American Airlines?" the reporter had challenged. "Just to be one with you," Śrīla Prabhupāda had said, smiling.

But that Prabhupāda had come by jet instead of by some extraordinary mystic power was actually no less miraculous. The miracle was that he was always traveling and that wherever he went he spoke the message of Kṛṣṇa consciousness, created faith in the faithless, and transformed the low-grade persons of Kali-yuga into pure Vaiṣṇavas.

Śrīla Prabhupāda, in addition to his selfless, compassionate traveling, was also offering volumes of transcendental literature. His disciples in sixty-five centers around the world were gratefully accepting their role of assisting him, assuring him that they were able to preach to the people in their areas and that he should feel confident to go on opening new frontiers of Kṛṣṇa consciousness and presenting more and more transcendental literature. His disciples especially wanted him to have time for translating *Śrīmad-Bhāgavatam,* because he had told them that that was his desire. Often he said that if he could simply spend time translating *Śrīmad-Bhāgavatam* he would stop traveling. He could not stop traveling for very long, however. Even if he found enough peace and a suitable place for concentrating on the *Bhāgavatam,* duty would call; again he would have to travel—to see new people, to introduce *saṅkīrtana* in a new place, to insure that his movement was progressing smoothly.

Prabhupāda, therefore, had developed a routine of translating *Śrīmad-Bhāgavatam* anywhere he went, for at least a few hours a day. He had a briefcase with Sanskrit *Bhāgavatams* and commentaries and a suitcase with a dictating machine. Wherever he was, he would rise in the middle of the night, sit at his desk with his dictating machine and Sanskrit and Bengali volumes, and take up where he had left off, translating the verses into English and composing his Bhaktivedanta purports. Thus his busy traveling and his translating were able to go on simultaneously.

CHAPTER THIRTY-SIX

In Every Town and Village

London
August 1971

FROM FLORIDA, "THIS remote corner of the world," Prabhupāda returned to New York and after three days flew to London. There he became ill. On August 14 he wrote to Tamāla Kṛṣṇa:

> I am sick here since the last four days. There is no sunshine. Almost always there is darkness and rain. So it has affected my health, because I am already rheumatic.

Prabhupāda said he wanted to retire from traveling and management: "This body is old, it is giving warning." But he didn't have sufficient confidence that his leading managers could push on—without his pushing them.

Prabhupāda complained to his secretary, Śyāmasundara, criticizing him and the other zonal secretaries for not producing and distributing his books on a large scale. "Why are there no books?" Prabhupāda demanded, and Śyāmasundara cringed, unable to give a satisfactory answer. Śyāmasundara said he would immediately write to his Godbrothers on the Bhaktivedanta Book Trust.

"Why have a book trust?" Prabhupāda argued. "What have they done?

There is no stock of big books.* There are no literatures in foreign languages after years of promises and plans. Why hasn't the unabridged *Bhagavad-gītā As It Is* been printed yet?"

"Well," Śyāmasundara replied, "because they ..."

"No! It's *your* responsibility," Prabhupāda yelled. "Why haven't *you* done it?" Prabhupāda chastised his G.B.C. secretaries around the world through the one secretary before him. The G.B.C.'s duties were to see that Prabhupāda's books were always in stock, that *Back to Godhead* magazine was being published regularly, that accounts were being paid regularly, and that the devotional life in the temples was healthy.

"Our business is how to expand," said Prabhupāda, "—how to introduce Kṛṣṇa consciousness into educational circles. Let any philosopher, scientist, or educationist come—we have got enough stock. But this sleeping, this leisurely work will not do. They can learn activity from an old man like me, because my determination is like this: If I die working, it is a great credit. Just like a marshal, if he dies on the battlefield, it is his credit. Arjuna was told, 'Even if you die, you are still the gainer.'

"This slow process of printing is the most condemned position. Why should I go on translating when you cannot print? You say, 'Retire and translate.' But why should I translate? No one will ever see it! I can give you volumes. There is Dai Nippon, who will print in Japan on credit, so why don't you print? Always, 'It is to be done. It is to be done.' That's all. And big men complaining, 'Either he goes or I go.'

"This restlessness, this diversion has to stop. When the father is providing, it is the duty of the son to serve. I am the father. I am giving you everything. Why don't you serve me by printing these books? If one book only is read and understood, that is sufficient to make him Kṛṣṇa conscious. Don't you see how important it is?

"They are always asking me, 'Is such-and-such book bona fide?' They can't even take the time to read one of my books, and still they ask for one of my Godbrothers' books. How will things go on? First Canto of *Śrīmad-Bhāgavatam* is not even edited or corrected, what to speak of printed. So many books unprinted. So tell them: From the book fund not a farthing should be for eating."

---

* *Teachings of Lord Caitanya; The Nectar of Devotion; Śrīmad-Bhāgavatam; Kṛṣṇa, the Supreme Personality of Godhead.*

One day Advaita, the manager of ISKCON Press, called from New York with some good news: in a week they would be sending Dai Nippon the negatives for five big books. ISKCON Press had also sent a shipment of the German *Īśopaniṣad* to Europe. And other foreign-language books were forthcoming. Prabhupāda was pleased, and Śyāmasundara informed his G.B.C. Godbrothers.

> Needless to say, this was just the medicine required to treat Prabhupāda's slackening faith in us. Things are looking up, but still Prabhupāda encourages us all to write up these reports and get a clear all-around picture of the total book situation.

Although Prabhupāda's health was still weak, he felt heartened to hear that his books were being printed, and he continued with his translation and commentary of *Śrīmad-Bhāgavatam.*

Ranchor: *One night I was up very late, one o'clock in the morning. As I came in I saw that Prabhupāda's lights were on in his front room, and I could hear his voice speaking into the dictating machine. I came up the stairs, being as quiet as I possibly could so Prabhupāda wouldn't know that I was up so late. But as I passed his door I couldn't resist the temptation to just stop and listen for a while. I tried looking through the keyhole, but I couldn't see anything. So I just listened to Prabhupāda's voice as he was dictating* Śrīmad-Bhāgavatam.

Then all of a sudden he stopped. I supposed he was just thinking about what he was going to say next. But then I got the feeling that he knew I was out there, listening through the door. I became frightened and went up the stairs as quietly as I could, although the stairs creaked. Everyone was asleep—not only the temple, but practically the whole city of London—at one o'clock in the morning. But Prabhupāda was awake and translating. He had been speaking quietly, but with a voice of great strength and determination. All during the day he was under pressure to organize things and see people, and yet at night, the one time when he could have some peace and quiet, he was up dictating.

In London Prabhupāda began a book on the Western philosophers, beginning with Socrates. Every morning Śyāmasundara would present a synopsis of a major philosophy to Prabhupāda, and for several hours Prabhupāda would discuss the philosopher's major points from the light of Kṛṣṇa consciousness. Daily Śyāmasundara was busy transcribing the morning discussions and preparing the next philosopher.

On August 14 Śrīla Prabhupāda observed Janmāṣṭamī, the birthday of Lord Kṛṣṇa. On the next day, Prabhupāda's own seventy-fifth birthday, a paperback book of collected homages by his disciples arrived. Many of the Vyāsa-pūjā homages praised Śrīla Prabhupāda for his extensive traveling to deliver fallen souls all over the world and for the vast scope of his merciful preaching.

> This year you have been traveling to India personally speaking and managing ISKCON and showing us the meaning of *ācārya* by example. And now you are traveling and inspiring the devotees and centers in the U.S. and Europe.
>
> At Vyās Pūjā time we, your intimate children, are gathered at your feet to tell you our feelings as best we can. By your blessing, we can go forth from this Vyās Pūjā gathering of 1971 and, all devotees together as one great ISKCON, without faction, truly perform the work with our thoughts, words, and deeds. Let us go and distribute this literature of Śrīla Prabhupāda's—Kṛṣṇa's message—kindly delivered to the Western countries. Let us cooperate without ill feelings among ourselves. Let us very strictly observe all the regulative principles and stay as pure representatives. Let us celebrate pure *saṅkīrtana* and magazine distribution to please you. All glories to Śrīla Prabhupāda!
>
> All your disciples pray that you will remain in our presence for many years to come, and by our cooperation you will be able to spend time writing volumes of *Bhāgavatam* while we carry on the program and mission of your Guru Mahārāja.

Prabhupāda's ill health continued.

> I was sick for four or five days; now I am a little better but the disease is prolonging in a different way. I cannot sleep at night more than 2 hours and during the day sometimes I am feeling some dizziness. Otherwise everything is all right. I am chanting Hare Krishna as usual and writing my books regularly.

Śyāmasundara: *Aravinda and I were sleeping right outside of Prabhupāda's room. I was on a lower bunk bed, and I heard "Śyāmasundara." It was a really urgent sound, and I woke up so hard that I hit my head on the bunk above. I ran into Prabhupāda's room. As I was opening the door, he collapsed in the doorway. I caught him. He felt so light, like a little doll, and his face was gray. I took him over to his bed and thought, "Oh, my God, what's going on?"*

He was shivering. I turned the electric heater way up and put it next to his bed. I covered him with a lot of blankets and waited. He was just still. His eyes were closed.

Finally he said, "Śyāmasundara, go get me some black pepper." He described how to make a black pepper paste. "Rub it on my forehead," he said. So I ran down to the kitchen and prepared it and came up and put it on his head. I asked him, "Are you ... what's wrong?" I don't believe he made a response. He closed his eyes and appeared to be asleep.

I slept there by him on the floor for a while. At some point in the night, he said, "You may go back to your room. I'll be all right." He stayed in bed until about eight or nine o'clock the next morning. And then he was just completely well, like nothing had happened. His spirit was so strong that although he had encountered devastating blows to his body, he had come right out of it. I could tell it wasn't a physical event. He had made a full recovery from what must have been something close to death.

* * *

One day while meeting with an Indian man, a Mr. R. B. Pandya from Mombassa, East Africa, Prabhupāda mentioned his illness. Mr. Pandya said he owned a house on the ocean at Mombassa, where it was always sunny and warm, with pleasant sea breezes—a perfect place for Prabhupāda to recover his health. Mr. Pandya invited Prabhupāda to go and live there as long as he liked. Taking the offer seriously, Prabhupāda began to think of going to Africa—not only for health, but for preaching. Three months ago he had sent Brahmānanda Swami and Jagannivāsa to East Africa, so a visit there would encourage them as well as enable Prabhupāda to work personally at expanding the Kṛṣṇa consciousness movement on the African continent. Prabhupāda sent Bhavānanda and Nara-Nārāyaṇa from London to Mombassa to see if it would really be possible for him to stay there as Mr. Pandya had suggested.

When Bhavānanda and Nara-Nārāyaṇa arrived, Brahmānanda Swami, who had been struggling in East Africa with only one assistant, was delighted to see them and to hear that Prabhupāda was coming soon. Previously, Brahmānanda Swami had been preaching in Florida, and Prabhupāda had written him to go to Pakistan. Immediately he had gone, along with one assistant, Jagannivāsa, flying to Paris and then taking the Orient Express through Eastern Europe. On hearing that war fever was building in Pakistan, Prabhupāda had sent a second letter to Brahmānanda Swami in Florida, advising him not to go to Pakistan. But Brahmānanda Swami had never received the letter. En route to Pakistan, while holding public *kīrtana* in Turkey, Brahmānanda and Jagannivāsa had been arrested and detained for several days on suspicion of being Christian missionaries.

Finally, Brahmānanda and Jagannivāsa had arrived in Pakistan, where students had spit at them, accused them of being spies, threatened them, and called them names. Several times people on the street had rubbed the Vaiṣṇava *tilaka* off the devotees' foreheads and warned them not to show themselves in public or they would be stabbed. Local Hindus had warned the devotees to leave as soon as possible, and so they had reluctantly decided to go to Bombay to see Prabhupāda.

Meanwhile, in Bombay Prabhupāda had read in an Indian newspaper that Pakistani soldiers in Dacca had killed four Hare Kṛṣṇa missionaries. "I am very much anxious to know about Brahmānanda," Prabhupāda had written. "The day has been full of anxiety with this bad news, and still it is going on."

When Śrīla Prabhupāda had heard that Brahmānanda Swami had actually arrived in Bombay, he had asked to see him at once. Like a father recovering his lost child, Prabhupāda had embraced him. "You risked your life just on my order," Prabhupāda had said. After some days Prabhupāda had told Brahmānanda Swami, "You should go to Africa. If you go, then we will be on all the continents."

Now, after preaching in Africa, Brahmānanda Swami eagerly awaited the visit of his beloved spiritual master.

* * *

Nairobi
September 9, 1971

As Śrīla Prabhupāda disembarked in Nairobi from the East African Airlines 747 jet, he wore a wool *cādara* over his shoulders and carried the same white vinyl attaché case he had taken with him all over the world. Flanked by his secretary and servant, he walked with his cane across the airfield toward the terminal building. Inside, he sat on a cloth-covered chair and joined in the *kīrtana,* while Indians and Africans gathered around to watch.

Kul Bhusana, a journalist and friend of Brahmānanda Swami's, approached Prabhupāda with questions. He asked Prabhupāda what he had come to teach, and Prabhupāda answered, "Modern civilized man has forgotten his relationship with Kṛṣṇa, or God, and is therefore suffering. Whether you are Hindu, Muslim, or Buddhist, that doesn't matter. Unless you reestablish your relationship with God, you cannot be happy."

"Have you come only for Hindus?" asked Mr. Bhusana.

"No," Prabhupāda replied, "for everyone."

Mr. Bhusana: "East Africa, especially Kenya, is one of those countries which enjoys a great amount of racial harmony in brotherhood of man. What is your special message you can bring to Kenya?"

Śrīla Prabhupāda: "That brotherhood of man can be complete when they are in God consciousness. Otherwise, it will again break."

Mr. Bhusana: "So your disciples will be making special efforts to reach the Africans rather than confine themselves to the Hindus? That is very important here in this country."

Śrīla Prabhupāda: "Our method is the same. But the method is so powerful that it appeals to everyone. We do not have to convey a new method for a new place. The method is the same—universal. It will appeal to everyone."

After spending one night in Nairobi, Prabhupāda and his party flew the next day in a small propeller aircraft to Mombassa. Mr. Pandya was away, and his family, although not very enthusiastic, opened their home to Śrīla Prabhupāda. The large house was of contemporary design, with rounded corners, porthole windows, and a spacious living room with a veranda facing the ocean.

Prabhupāda, standing by the window in his room, beheld an aquamarine sea, a cloudless blue sky, and a white sandy beach fringed with palms. Turning back toward Brahmānanda Swami and the others, he said, "Brahmānanda told me that this was one of the most beautiful places in the world. Now I see he is correct."

Prabhupāda had come with a chronic cough, but walking on the beach and relaxing in the Mombassa sunshine, he soon recovered his health. Prabhupāda maintained his program begun in London of daily dialogues with Śyāmasundara concerning the Western philosophers. Chronologically he had proceeded from Socrates to Descartes.

Śyāmasundara: "He is saying, 'I think, therefore I am.' First of all, he has discovered that 'I am.' This was his innate basis for truth. In his time there was no real authority."

Prabhupāda: "But this is not big knowledge. Long, long ago there were many who could understand 'I am.' This is called *ātmānaṁ manyate jagat:* a fool thinks all others are fools. He is not the first man to realize the identification of the self. Kṛṣṇa says *aham. Aham evāsam evāgre:* 'I existed in the beginning, and when everything is finished, I shall continue to exist.' This we also say. 'I existed before this body was created, and I shall exist when the body is annihilated.' This conception of I is there in God; it is in me. Then where is the new thing?"

As soon as he felt better, he was ready to preach. Mombassa, he said, was a small place, and Nairobi, the capital, would be better for preaching. So he returned to Nairobi.

Nairobi
September 18, 1971

In Nairobi Śrīla Prabhupāda demonstrated how a *sannyāsī* should preach. For one month he strictly followed Vedic tradition by staying only three days or less in the home of each of his Indian hosts. Then, although his hosts always provided him good food and comfortable accommodations, he would move on to the next place. This was the rule for *sannyāsīs,* Prabhupāda said; it kept them from becoming attached to bodily comforts and from inconveniencing their hosts.

For Śrīla Prabhupāda to practice these rudimentary lessons of *sannyāsa* was, of course, unnecessary, for he was a *paramahaṁsa,* a *sannyāsī* in the highest order of Kṛṣṇa consciousness. His body, mind, and words being totally engaged in Kṛṣṇa's transcendental service, he was automatically detached from material comforts. Nevertheless, he followed the Vedic system, just to instruct his disciples by his example. He was following the system of *madhukarī*—named for the bee, which takes only a little pollen from a flower and then goes on to the next. This system of brief visits also enabled Prabhupāda to involve more families in Kṛṣṇa consciousness and to honor the abundance of invitations.

Wherever Prabhupāda went, he was undisputably the *guru,* the venerable *sādhu.* Yet he would deal intimately with his hosts, developing friendships and behaving practically like an elder member of the family. His hosts would offer him the best room in their home, usually their own bedroom, and the lady of the house, along with her assistants, would cook elaborate meals. Prabhupāda's natural Kṛṣṇa conscious bearing was commanding, and his behavior was always aristocratic; yet his hosts were charmed by his humility. Quickly he was becoming the friend and Vaiṣṇava *guru* of many families in Nairobi.

Prabhupāda's behavior in Nairobi was instructive for the few Western disciples who accompanied him. On one occasion a Mr. Devaji Dhamji invited Prabhupāda to bless the temple room in his home. Prabhupāda entered, and Mr. Dhamji offered him a deerskin to sit on. "We do not sit on deerskin," Prabhupāda said. "It is pure, but our Vaiṣṇavas don't wear them or sit on them. That is for the *yogīs.*"

Bhavānanda: *Mr. Dhamji invited Prabhupāda to sit on a sofa, which had been covered by a clean white cloth. Prabhupāda sat down, and they bathed his feet. This was the first time I ever saw anyone bathe Prabhupāda's feet. They bathed his feet with milk and then with water and rose petals. Then they put* candana *on his feet, then red* kuṅkuma *powder, rice powder, and jasmine flowers. His toes were red from* kuṅkuma, *and grains of rice and little white jasmine flowers just stayed on his feet. And then he gave a talk. I had never noticed the* guru's *feet up until that time. That was the first time I realized that the feet of the* guru *are special. And they are astoundingly beautiful.*

Prabhupāda wasn't satisfied preaching only to the Indians. He wanted to preach to the Africans. Indians and Africans were completely segregated. But since a Kṛṣṇa conscious person does not make distinctions based on the body, Prabhupāda said the Indians had a duty to share their spiritual culture with the Africans.

Prabhupāda impressed on Brahmānanda Swami that his first duty in Africa was to give Kṛṣṇa consciousness to the Africans. Because of bad experience in Turkey and Pakistan, Brahmānanda Swami had been reluctant to hold public *kīrtanas* in Nairobi. Besides, the Africans spoke mostly Swahili; they were culturally different and usually too poor to buy books, so Brahmānanda Swami didn't know how to preach to them effectively. Going to the Indians had been easy and natural.

But Prabhupāda wanted the Africans. "It is an African country," he said simply. "They are the proprietors. We should be preaching to them."

As with everything else in Kṛṣṇa consciousness, Prabhupāda demonstrated how to do this also. He got the use of a Rādhā-Kṛṣṇa temple in a predominantly African downtown area. The temple had a hall with doors opening onto the busy street, and Prabhupāda instructed the devotees to hold *kīrtana* in the hall, keeping the doors open. The devotees did as he asked, and in five minutes the hall began filling up with people. It was a shabby area of town, and the people who entered were illiterate and dirty. But they were curious, and they happily joined in the *kīrtana,* smiling, clapping, and dancing.

Brahmānanda Swami left the hall and went to the nearby house where Prabhupāda was staying. "The place is filled with people," Brahmānanda Swami said, "but it's not necessary for you to come. We can carry on and do the program ourselves."

"No," Prabhupāda said, "I must go."

Brahmānanda Swami tried to discourage him.

"No, I must go," Prabhupāda repeated. "Are you going to take me?"

When Brahmānanda Swami arrived with Śrīla Prabhupāda, the hall was even more crowded than it had been a few minutes before. Prabhupāda, in his silken saffron robes, appeared effulgent as he entered the dingy, poorly lit auditorium. As he walked the crowd parted, leaving an aisle for him to pass among them, and they watched him curiously. Onstage Prabhupāda led a *kīrtana* and lectured. Although the Swahili-speaking audience was unable to understand Prabhupāda's lecture, the people were respectful. And the *kīrtana* they loved.

Members of the Indian community had been apprehensive of Prabhupāda's opening their hall to the Africans, and some of them had attended to see what would happen. Observing Prabhupāda's compassionate program, however, the Indians were impressed. Such an apparently simple program had the spiritual potency to erase cultural boundaries.

This should be Brahmānanda Swami's mission in Africa, Prabhupāda insisted—offering Kṛṣṇa consciousness to the Africans. And the program should be simple: distributing *prasādam,* distributing free books, and chanting Hare Kṛṣṇa with drums and *karatālas.* Kṛṣṇa consciousness should not be just another Nairobi Hindu religious society. The Hindus should take part by donating money, but Brahmānanda Swami's preaching and recruiting should be among the Africans.

When several black American disciples joined Prabhupāda in Nairobi, Prabhupāda told them, "Four hundred years ago your ancestors were taken away from here as slaves. But ah, just see how you have returned as masters!"

Prabhupāda also organized Nairobi's first outdoor *kīrtana* performance. The devotees went to Kamakunji Park's largest tree, a historical landmark connected with Kenyan independence. As they stood chanting beneath the tree, a large crowd gathered, and many began chanting. Some even danced in a sort of tribal shuffle. One young man stepped forward and offered to translate Brahmānanda Swami's speech into Swahili. The devotees distributed sweet *bundi,* and the people in the crowd really enjoyed themselves. The whole affair was a great success.

Rushing back to Prabhupāda, Brahmānanda Swami reported on the wonderful *kīrtana* in the park. Brahmānanda felt the same emotion as in 1966 when he had reported to Prabhupāda the success of the first *kīrtana* at Washington Square Park in New York City. Now, as then, Brahmānanda Swami had followed Prabhupāda's instructions, and the results had been successful. Prabhupāda, by his personal example and by his pushing Brahmānanda Swami, had within a few days changed the emphasis of preaching in Africa—from Indians to Africans.

The night of Śrīla Prabhupāda's lecture at the University of Nairobi, two thousand African students filled the auditorium, with hundreds more standing outside to look in through the doors and windows. First Prabhupāda had Bhūta-bhāvana, a black American disciple, deliver a short introduction, using some borrowed Swahili phrases. "*Harambay,*" he began—which means "Welcome, brothers. Let us work together." Then Prabhupāda spoke.

"The whole world is simply hankering and lamenting. You African people are now hankering to be like the Europeans and Americans. But the Europeans have lost their empire. They are now lamenting. So one party is hankering, and one party is lamenting. ...

"We have come to these African countries to invite all intelligent Africans to come and understand this philosophy and distribute it. You are trying to develop yourselves, so develop very soundly. But don't imitate the Americans and Europeans, who are living like cats and dogs. Such civilization will not stand. The atom bomb is already there. As soon as the next war breaks out, all the skyscraper buildings and everything else will be finished. Try to understand from the real standpoint, the real view of human life. That is the Kṛṣṇa consciousness movement, and we request you to come and try to understand this philosophy. Thank you very much."

The audience burst into applause, giving Prabhupāda a standing ovation. This response proved once again that Kṛṣṇa's message spoke to the heart; it was for all people, regardless of their political, geographic, or social predicament. When Prabhupāda had first landed at the Nairobi airport, he had assured the reporter that he would be preaching to the Africans. And now he was. He was delivering to the Africans the same message and the same process of devotional service he had delivered to the Americans. What the Americans wanted and what the Africans wanted could be realized only in Kṛṣṇa consciousness. Kṛṣṇa consciousness would work anywhere, if sincere and intelligent persons would only come forward and help distribute it.

Prabhupāda continued with outside speaking engagements. While appearing on the popular TV show *Mambo Leo,* Prabhupāda displayed a painting of Lord Caitanya dancing and chanting with His devotees. The interviewer asked Prabhupāda why only Caucasians appeared to be in the picture. "Well, there are many colors in India," Prabhupāda replied.

"And who is the central figure here?" the interviewer asked.

"This is Śrī Caitanya Mahāprabhu," Prabhupāda replied. "He is God."

"He cannot be God!" the large, burly interviewer retorted. "What do you mean He is God? This is a human being."

But Prabhupāda became even more aggressive than the interviewer. "Why do you say He cannot come as a human being? Why God cannot come as a human being?"

In another of his many Nairobi lectures, Prabhupāda stressed that peace was possible only on the spiritual platform. Kṛṣṇa consciousness alone would unite the present factions.

"For instance, in Africa the Indians may be satisfied with their own methods, but the Africans are not satisfied. So if one is dissatisfied in material life, then another is satisfied—and there will be disturbance. But if you come to the Kṛṣṇa conscious platform, if you engage yourself in the transcendental loving service of the Supreme Personality of Godhead, then your mind and soul will be fully satisfied."

Prabhupāda went on to explain his plans for helping Africans.

"We have come to Africa to educate the people—not only Indians or the Hindus, but also the native people, the local population. I am glad that our people are going to *saṅkīrtana* party in the streets, as we go everywhere—in London, in New York, and all the big cities of the world. We are trying to lead our *saṅkīrtana* parties through the streets, and the local African boys and girls and gentlemen are gathering. They are receiving this movement.

"So there is every possibility of spreading Kṛṣṇa consciousness everywhere. This movement has come here, so I request that those who are present try to cooperate with the Kṛṣṇa consciousness movement. And I am sure that the African boys and girls will take part in it, as you have experienced. We have a great many African boys and girls as our students in America, so there is no difficulty.

"It is not that because one is very busy, therefore he cannot serve God. Or that because one is poor, or black, or white, that he cannot serve God. No. Anyone who takes to the process of pure devotional service will never be checked."

Prabhupāda also asked his audience to help the devotees establish a center in Nairobi.

"We must have a place to stay. Unless we stay, how can we prosecute the movement? Therefore, help us immediately. Give us a place and see how things improve. You have already tested this movement and found that it has been successful all over the world. Why not in Africa? We are not a sectarian group. We don't consider whether one is African or American."

In Nairobi Prabhupāda heard of a new law in Tanzania that after ten years all private property would automatically become the property of the state and that the owner would be entitled to only a ten-percent reimbursement. This was a typical Kali-yuga law, Prabhupāda remarked. The state passes a law with no reasoning and no benefit for the people. The state should protect the people, Prabhupāda said. In Vedic history, during the misrule of the demoniac king Vena, the sages and *brāhmaṇas* had become very disturbed and had punished him; the *sādhus'* duty was to make sure the kings ruled justly. But today, nowhere in the world were political affairs in order. There was no sane philosophy to guide society.

"We must begin to interfere," Prabhupāda urged his disciples. "Now we are five hundred men, and we each have fifty years. So think of what we can do. But you must become dedicated as I am. Sometimes a Vaiṣṇava is criticized as doing nothing. But Arjuna and Hanumān were Vaiṣṇava warriors. When the high-court judges wear *tilaka,* then we are successful—my Guru Mahārāja said that. My Godbrothers were for getting temples, some rice, eating a little, chanting. But for us—first we work, then *samādhi.*"

The word *samādhi* technically refers to a state of trance, in which one is completely absorbed in Kṛṣṇa and forgets the material world and all material desires. Generally, *samādhi* is thought of in terms of secluded meditation; a highly advanced *yogī* goes to a solitary, peaceful place and meditates or chants constantly. But Prabhupāda demonstrated by his life's example that the world situation was too urgent for a devotee to retire and meditate. Rather, a devotee should labor hard to increase the Kṛṣṇa consciousness movement. This would benefit both the devotee and the masses. Prabhupāda's disciples, therefore, as servants of their spiritual master, should work now; and later, perhaps in old age and spiritual maturity, they could retire to a holy place to constantly chant and hear about Kṛṣṇa.

Prabhupāda emphasized work. Yet what was that work? At least for Śrīla Prabhupāda, propagating Kṛṣṇa consciousness was *samādhi* itself. *Samādhi* didn't have to be limited to sitting in a solitary place. The full meaning of *samādhi* implied complete absorption in the loving service of Kṛṣṇa, with the senses, mind, and intelligence fixed in trance. Thus in *samādhi* one could be active—traveling, preaching, distributing *Back to Godhead* magazines, chanting in the streets. If a devotee always thought of Kṛṣṇa and worked on behalf of Kṛṣṇa, then he was the topmost *yogī.* This had also been Lord Kṛṣṇa's advice to Arjuna: "Remember Me, and at the same time fight." Śrīla Prabhupāda was the emblem of active *samādhi*—always hearing about, glorifying, and remembering Kṛṣṇa, and always fighting as a soldier on behalf of Lord Caitanya.

Prabhupāda's preaching in Nairobi had been especially active. He had established Kṛṣṇa consciousness in a new city, setting the example for Brahmānanda Swami to emulate, showing the standard for spreading Kṛṣṇa consciousness throughout the continent. And Śyāmasundara was keeping his G.B.C. Godbrothers informed of Prabhupāda's amazing activities.

> The pace has been lightning fast, and His Divine Grace is opening up yet another vast theater of operations. The people are thronging with curiosity and serious questions. ...
>
> Prabhupāda, after finishing one late-night preaching marathon, asked for food and remarked, "You see, I am hungry. Keep me talking—that is my life. Don't let me stop talking. ..."

But Nairobi was only one city in one country on one continent, and Prabhupāda's desire was to see Kṛṣṇa consciousness in every city, town, and village in the world. How could he do it in one lifetime—traveling to every city in the world, printing and distributing books in every language, constructing fabulous temples? He couldn't. But he wanted to do as much as possible in whatever time Kṛṣṇa allotted to him, to insure that the Kṛṣṇa consciousness movement would survive. He criticized the politicians' typical attitude that unless they themselves remained active everything they had worked for would crumble. Such politicians were always reluctant to retire, preferring to remain in office until their last breath. Prabhupāda, however, had no personal ambition, and he knew that results were awarded by Kṛṣṇa. As a true *sannyāsī,* he had renounced the world and worldly ambition. But he had not become lazy.

He was executing his mission at an advanced age, and Lord Kṛṣṇa was rewarding his attempts. Prabhupāda, therefore, in a mood of reciprocating with Kṛṣṇa, kept working to expand the Kṛṣṇa consciousness movement. Knowing that Lord Kṛṣṇa wanted the world flooded with love of God, Śrīla Prabhupāda had earnestly tried to do it, beginning in a storefront in New York City. And Kṛṣṇa had responded, sending him a few men and enough money to pay the rent. Then Śrīla Prabhupāda had attempted to do more, and again Kṛṣṇa had responded. Thus a second ISKCON center and a third and a fourth and more had sprung up, and book printing had begun. Śrīla Prabhupāda, in his mood of loving reciprocation with Kṛṣṇa, just kept attempting more and more.

Now it was no longer simply one person's work; Śrīla Prabhupāda was entrusting the work to his disciples. And those disciples, if they were actually to help, would have to adopt Prabhupāda's selfless dedication.

As they tried to follow him in his expansive plans, however, their minds faltered. For a handful of devotees to maintain even one temple in one city was a big job, yet Prabhupāda was doing this a hundred times over. He wanted the movement he had started to continue for thousands of years, and he was confident that as long as his followers remained pure, working within the guidelines he had given, they would be successful.

Although the present Age of Kali was the worst of all ages, in which people had little or no interest in spiritual life, Prabhupāda had faith in the past *ācāryas'* predictions that Kṛṣṇa consciousness was destined to enter a golden age of worldwide influence. True, it was the worst of times; yet by the influence of the holy name of Kṛṣṇa it would become the best of times. The chanting of the holy name was the religion of the age; the people of Kali-yuga could find deliverance simply in chanting Hare Kṛṣṇa.

Śrīla Prabhupāda's activities show he was empowered by Kṛṣṇa. This is evident from his childhood, when at the age of five he held a Ratha-yātrā festival, and it is certainly evident from these years, 1968 to 1971, when he actively expanded his Kṛṣṇa consciousness movement. Prabhupāda compared ISKCON to the Varāha incarnation of Kṛṣṇa, who at first had been no bigger than a thumb but had quickly expanded to half the size of the universe.

ISKCON's rapid growth was not simply due to rapid communications and modern travel, nor to its founder-*ācārya's* material organizational abilities. Prabhupāda, judged materially, was not a likely person to conduct a worldwide movement, to travel vigorously, to write volumes of books, and to train thousands of disciples on every continent. He was satisfied with a simple, regulated life, and he disdained all such cultural items as music, fashion, sports, politics, art, food—anything not related to Kṛṣṇa. He worked and traveled out of an intense desire to benefit the world with real culture, to implant spiritual culture in what to him was the desert of a materialistic society.

Therefore, accepting that Prabhupāda was not materialistically ambitious, we can understand his proclivity for worldwide propaganda and dissemination of a spiritual movement as entirely transcendental. He was acting solely to carry out the desires of Lord Kṛṣṇa, the Supreme Personality of Godhead.

Śrīla Prabhupāda saw himself as a servant of his spiritual master, Śrīla Bhaktisiddhānta Sarasvatī, whose message he was carrying. That message, which was also the message of Lord Kṛṣṇa, had come down through disciplic succession: "We are all spiritual souls, eternal servants of the Supreme Personality of Godhead, Kṛṣṇa. We have now fallen into forgetfulness and are suffering birth after birth in this material world. By chanting Hare Kṛṣṇa, we can revive our lost relationship with God."

With Prabhupāda's first success in America, a few of his Godbrothers in India had minimized his work. Bhaktivedanta Swami, they had said, happened to have a temperament suited to mixing with lower-class Western youth. The fact, however, as Prabhupāda's own experience testified, was that the young people among whom he preached were not particularly receptive, nor had he arrived timely and welcomed, simply to discourse on *Śrīmad-Bhāgavatam* to throngs of submissive disciples. He had been successful because of his great patience, tolerance, and compassion.

It was not, therefore, the advent of the jet plane (although Prabhupāda gladly took advantage of it), nor was it happenstance, nor luck, nor even a social or historical phenomenon that enabled Śrīla Prabhupāda to spread Vedic culture from East to West and back again. No. It was the will of Kṛṣṇa and the sincerity of His servant.

Caitanya-caritāmṛta states that unless one is possessed of *kṛṣṇa-śakti,* special power from God, one cannot propagate the chanting of the holy name:

kali-kālera dharma—kṛṣṇa-nāma saṅkīrtana
kṛṣṇa-śakti vinā nahe tāra pravartana

"The fundamental religious system in the Age of Kali is the chanting of the holy name of Kṛṣṇa. Unless empowered by Kṛṣṇa, one cannot propagate the *saṅkīrtana* movement." (*Cc. Antya* 7.11) This verse describing Lord Caitanya Mahāprabhu also describes Lord Caitanya's servant, Śrīla Prabhupāda. Had Śrīla Prabhupāda not been empowered by Kṛṣṇa, he could not have inspired so many people to accept the chanting of Hare Kṛṣṇa.

According to Vedic literature, when a person has extraordinary spiritual endowment, *kṛṣṇa-śakti,* he is known as a *śaktyāveśa-avatāra.* Although the word *avatāra* generally refers to incarnations of God Himself, the term *śaktyāveśa-avatāra* refers to an individual empowered by God to enact the mission of God in this world.

Śaktyāveśa-avatāras and their particular functions are mentioned in the Vedic literature. For example, the emperor Pṛthu possessed the *śakti* for God conscious administration; the four Kumāras possessed the *śakti* of transcendental knowledge; and Nārada Muni possessed the *śakti* of devotional service. Lord Buddha, whose name and activities are described in *Śrīmad-Bhāgavatam,* is also a *śaktyāveśa-avatāra,* and even other divinely empowered personalities outside the Vedic culture, such as Jesus Christ and Muhammad, are accepted by Vaiṣṇava *ācāryas* as *śaktyāveśa-avatāras.*

Śrīla Prabhupāda's activities during the years 1968 through 1971 establish him as a *śaktyāveśa-avatāra,* and he fulfills the predictions of the scriptures.

pṛthivīte āche yata nagarādi grāma
sarvatra pracāra haibe mora nāma

"In all the villages and towns all over the world, everywhere, the *saṅkīrtana* movement of Lord Caitanya will be preached."

Even from the viewpoint of religious history, Prabhupāda's preaching was a fulfillment of the mission of Lord Caitanya, who had appeared in West Bengal about five hundred years before Kṛṣṇa consciousness came West. The Vedic literature and the Vaiṣṇava *ācāryas* concur that Lord Caitanya is the original Supreme Personality of Godhead, Kṛṣṇa Himself, appearing in this age as a pure devotee of the Lord. And just as Lord Kṛṣṇa appeared with His plenary expansion Lord Balarāma, Lord Caitanya appeared with Lord Balarāma's incarnation for Kali-yuga, Lord Nityānanda.

Śrīla Prabhupāda can be appreciated not only generally, as the empowered representative of God, but specifically, as the manifestation of Lord Nityānanda. According to Gauḍīya Vaiṣṇava philosophy, Lord Kṛṣṇa manifests Himself to the souls of ordinary men through Lord Nityānanda. The individual soul requires the help of God to realize God. This help comes by the causeless mercy of Lord Nityānanda, who is therefore known as the original *guru.* Although Lord Nityānanda is the direct expansion of Lord Caitanya, His pastime is to serve Lord Caitanya by redeeming the fallen souls.

Lord Nityānanda and His representative, the spiritual master, do not alter the scriptures or the teachings of Lord Kṛṣṇa but make them more accessible and understandable. Lord Caitanya commissioned Lord Nityānanda to preach the holy name at everyone's door, and Lord Nityānanda's exemplary mood of vigorous, compassionate preaching was also the mood of Śrīla Prabhupāda. As Śrīla Prabhupāda imparted this mood to his disciples, they in turn went out into the streets of cities around the world to distribute to everyone the mercy of the holy name of God.

Lord Nityānanda is especially renowned for saving two drunkard brothers, Jagāi and Mādhāi, even though they had assaulted Him when He had attempted to bless them with the holy name. In Lord Nityānanda's time, Prabhupāda on several occasions explained, there were only one Jagāi and Mādhāi, but now the whole world is filled with Jagāis and Mādhāis. And Prabhupāda was recruiting his disciples from these Jagāis and Mādhāis. Śrīla Prabhupāda fully displayed Lord Nityānanda's compassion in taking all risks and freely giving the holy name.

Even Lord Nityānanda Himself, during His appearance in India, did not approach as many fallen souls as Śrīla Prabhupāda, nor did He approach souls in such degraded conditions of life or in so many rejected parts of the world. But He has done so now, through His representative Śrīla Prabhupāda. As the recipient of the combined mercy of Gaura-Nitāi (Lord Caitanya and Lord Nityānanda), Śrīla Prabhupāda blessed the world with love of God.

Śrīla Prabhupāda, however, never described himself as a great empowered personality, either in public or among his disciples. But he stressed that he was in disciplic succession, carrying the authorized knowledge. And he encouraged his disciples to take the same position: "We want to create many pure devotees, so that other people will benefit by their association. In this way, the number of pure devotees increases."

Prabhupāda knew well that propagating Kṛṣṇa consciousness was not a professional business. Although in India many professionals spoke or wrote on *Śrīmad-Bhāgavatam* to earn their livelihood, they could not convert materialistic people to devotional service. Only a pure devotee could change the materialistic heart.

Prabhupāda did not even conclude that *he* was a pure devotee, only that he was the servant of a pure devotee, Śrīla Bhaktisiddhānta Sarasvatī, his Guru Mahārāja.

Prabhupāda prayed that before he left the world he could create a living family of pure devotees to spread the *paramparā* teachings of

Kṛṣṇa consciousness and protect them from being changed or obscured. He emphasized that all the preachers of the Kṛṣṇa consciousness movement could become pure devotees by following the regulative principles, avoiding sinful life, and regularly chanting Hare Kṛṣṇa. Only in this way, he said, could the devotees have an effect on others.

October 18, 1971

Having spent a busy five weeks in Africa, Prabhupāda was ready to travel on to India. His plan was to visit Bombay, Calcutta, and Delhi. He had made a strong beginning for ISKCON in India—with land in Māyāpur and centers in Bombay, Calcutta, and New Delhi, and he had groups of disciples strategically located in other parts of India. Indians were recognizing ISKCON and appreciating its festivals, *kīrtanas,* and *prasādam.* Life members were offering service and being benefited, they were receiving and reading ISKCON publications, and they were helping support the ISKCON centers.

And this was only a start. To get a foothold—anywhere, whether in India, Africa, America, or Russia—was certainly a great accomplishment. But a foothold was not enough. Although much had been done to establish the mission of Lord Caitanya, much more remained to be done. Preaching Kṛṣṇa consciousness was not a job that at some point would be completed.

Of course in one sense it was already complete and perfect. Prabhupāda's preaching had always been successful, even when he had struggled alone in India to make his message heard through *Back to Godhead* magazine, the League of Devotees, and his translations of *Śrīmad-Bhāgavatam.* He had always remained fixed in the transcendental order of his spiritual master and Kṛṣṇa; therefore, he had been successful. The Kṛṣṇa consciousness movement was already complete, and now, by the will of its author, Lord Caitanya Mahāprabhu, this completeness was becoming manifest. But the work, the ecstasy, the *samādhi* of selflessly and single-pointedly serving that mission was unending and ever unfolding. Now there was a foothold in Africa. Tomorrow he would fly to Bombay, where Kṛṣṇa had already allowed him a foothold. And, as Kṛṣṇa desired, he would continue to travel and to send his devotees and his books and his message until he reached every town and village in the world.

Appendixes

Foreword to the First Printing of Śrīla Prabhupāda-līlāmṛta — Volume One (Chapters 1–11)

It is a distinct and unusual honor for me to be asked to write a foreword to this eloquent and informative biography of His Divine Grace A.C. Bhaktivedanta Swami Prabhupāda. To my great regret, I never met him during his sojourn here in America. But I feel that I have met him. The spiritual reality of a great teacher lives on in many ways, not the least in the lives of those he has touched. Since I have come to know many of Śrīla Prabhupāda's disciples over the past years, as well as many devotees who were influenced by him without knowing him personally, I sense a certain acquaintanceship. To write this foreword seems, then, in some measure, like introducing a friend.

Although it is not true to say in all cases that a religious movement is the shadow of a great teacher, still there is some measure of truth even in that familiar statement. It will surely help readers of this book understand ISKCON better to know the man who founded it and to be aware of the soil from which he comes. The patience and care with which the author of this volume has reconstructed the long life Śrīla Prabhupāda had already lived even before he set forth for America makes for absorbing and inspiring reading. I read it, I confess, not just because of my own interest in Śrīla Prabhupāda but because the milieu the author recreates tells us so much more than a mere life story could. It reminds us of how very ensconced Śrīla Prabhupāda was in one of the oldest religious traditions in the world. It recalls how very much went on in the generations, centuries, and even millenia before him that seems to be gathered and focused in his life and in his teaching. In one sense Śrīla Prabhupāda was not at all "original," and reading the story of his life raises questions about our typical Western proclivity to attach such value to originality. What the book makes clear, on the contrary, is that Śrīla Prabhupāda is a man who incarnates an ancient tradition. The opening verses of the fourth chapter of *Bhagavad-gītā,* the Indian text most precious to ISKCON, teach that the ageless science of *bhakti-yoga* (what Christians might call the "devotional path" to God) is always received by what the Indians call *paramparā,* that is, it is passed from one teacher to the next in a living chain, from ancient times to the present. Śrīla Prabhupāda is best understood, as this book presents him, as one particularly effective link in this chain.

Yet, it must be added, Śrīla Prabhupāda was also a unique person. To say that the teachings of the ancient ones come to us through a series of teachers does not mean that the teachers themselves are interchangeable. If they were so faceless, there would be little point in writing a biography of any of them. But this life of Śrīla Prabhupāda is pointed proof that one can be a transmitter of truth and still be a vital and singular person, even—in a sense I now feel safe to use—in some ways "original." Śrīla Prabhupāda lived during a particularly critical period in Indian history, that of British colonial rule and its aftermath. He worked with and among dozens of people who befriended, opposed, supported, or ignored him. He initiated *Back to Godhead* magazine. At what almost anyone would consider a very advanced age, when most people would be resting on their laurels, he harkened to the mandate of his own spiritual teacher and set out on the difficult and demanding voyage to America. Śrīla Prabhupāda is, of course, only one of thousands of teachers. But in another sense, he is one in a thousand, maybe one in a million.

As a Christian, it is very important and impressive to me that Śrīla Prabhupāda took it upon himself to bring the teaching he so well represents to America. This sentence I am sure requires some explanation. First of all, as a Christian I come from a tradition in which God's sending of someone to bring a vital message to those who desperately need it is held in very high esteem. Throughout the Hebrew scriptures, Yahweh sends prophets to remind the people how far they have strayed from His will, to expose the way they have misused the poor and failed to defend the widow and the fatherless. In the New Testament, Jesus sends forth his disciples two by two, asking them to take along only the scantiest clothing and equipment, telling them to bear the message of peace and salvation to the uttermost parts of the earth. God Himself is depicted as sending His only son into the world on a mission that would ultimately cost him his life. Christians are taught to respect and admire those who are willing to pay the heavy price of leaving comfort and security behind to go somewhere else to carry a message of liberation.

Today, however, many Christians have become comfortable and complacent, not only unwilling themselves to engage in such hardship but often unable even to understand or appreciate those who do. It is a great loss. Even though some people claim it is a good thing that many Christians are no longer as interested in carrying their message to other parts of the world, that they have become less presumptuous or arrogant, I personally believe it has more to do with sloth and the satiety of consumer society than with humility. I have little patience with zealous proselytizing no matter who inflicts it on whom. I do believe, however, that any spiritual teaching worth following is also worth sharing. When I visited India, living in fact in the very place where Śrīla Prabhupāda's tradition is centered, Vṛndāvana, I was thankfully received by everyone there, including the sages and holy men, and was asked to share my tradition with them. I spoke to them as a Christian about what Jesus Christ means to me and about what his teaching has to offer to the world. They listened attentively and gratefully. Their only complaint, as I recall, was that I had not spoken long enough! Indians, unlike Americans, seem in no hurry to rush off to something else if there is a serious spiritual discussion to be followed. Given the fact that I was so well received in Śrīla Prabhupāda's own land, I am sorry that he and his students still often find it so difficult to be heard or to be taken seriously here in America.

I am grateful for this book for two additional reasons that its writer could not have known. First, the author uses, among other methods, the growingly important method we in the West call "oral history." He incorporates the fruits of many interviews with the people who knew Śrīla Prabhupāda or who encountered him, who contribute some little bit of information, however tiny or fleeting, to make up the whole picture. In a few years all these people will have passed on. Those sources will be lost, at least to our mortal ears, forever. It is extremely important that the writer used this method and used it so very skillfully. I hope others will use it as effectively.

Also, perhaps without fully intending to, the author is giving us a portrait of an age the apex and the nadir of the passing epoch of which might be called "Western dominance." He shows us the devastation wreaked by "cultural imperialism" and demonstrates how stubbornly its destructive residues remain in the mental habits—and even in the eating patterns—of a previously colonized people long after the actual political rule of the outsider has been thrown off. Especially since this volume covers that period of Śrīla Prabhupāda's life before he came to America, it is vital to see that he was also instrumental in leading a revival of traditional Indian spiritual and cultural values in India itself before he came to our shores. Since that selfsame phenomenon is now underway wherever the long arm of European dominance once reached, the book can also be read as an integral part of the growing literature of "Third World cultural renaissance."

Obviously this volume can be appreciated in many ways. It can also be read, I should add, as the very fascinating story of a very fascinating man. In any case, however the present reader wishes to approach it, I am glad now to terminate this foreword and allow him or her to get on with the joy of reading.

Harvey Cox
Professor of Divinity
Harvard University

Foreword to the First Printing of Śrīla Prabhupāda-līlāmṛta — Volume Two (Chapters 12–21)

The story you are about to read is, like many true stories, highly improbable. An elderly Indian swami comes to New York City in the mid-1960s on a vaguely defined mission. Charged by his teacher in India to bring his spiritual message to the West, he arrives in New York with no prior knowledge of America, no base of support, almost no money, and no clear plan of action. He moves about the city somewhat aimlessly, lives for a while in an artist's loft on the Bowery, and finally—with help from a few early followers—rents a storefront building in the area known as East Village, the heart of the 1960s' drug and counterculture movement. There he begins to preach an unlikely message of sexual restraint, abstention from drugs, and purity of mind and body—and in behalf of devotion to the Hindu God Kṛṣṇa.

What follows is a remarkable tale of faith, determination, and success beyond anyone's expectation. The present volume gives only the beginnings of the story, but it tells us in fascinating detail how the first seeds of success were planted in what seemed such unpromising ground. It is a very human story, with a very human A. C. Bhaktivedanta Swami at the center.

Religions are a composite of many factors, some of which are largely collective products such as social movements, institutions, and systems of belief and practice. The history of religions is often put in terms of these relatively objective factors, so that religious history becomes part of the more general history of various times and places. The story of Bhaktivedanta Swami reminds us forcefully that there are other factors, more personal and elusive, which also shape the history of world religion. Social and cultural factors make a difference, but so also do individuals: holy men, saints, religious leaders, and their often flawed but faithful followers. The value of this book is the way in which it brings together these two dimensions—social history and individuals—to describe the founding of a major religious movement.

The temporal setting of the story is important. The 1960s was a unique period in American history, a time when major changes were taking place in our society. The place is important also, since New York City in general and East Village in particular were on the leading edge of these changes. The author of this biography was very much a part of this time and place as one of Bhaktivedanta Swami's earliest disciples in New York. From his own recollections, from recordings and writings of the time, and from extensive interviews with other participants, he has put together a series of striking vignettes of the 1960s that have independent historical value. Threading through these scenes, however, and binding the individuals together in collective effort, is the dominant figure of A. C. Bhaktivedanta Swami. Bhaktivedanta Swami seems curiously out of place in this setting. Born in the late nineteenth century, he had spent his whole career in India and for many years had lived the life of a celibate Hindu monk. What relevance could he have in the center of American youth culture, where "do your own thing" was the die for action, and "don't trust anyone over thirty" was the watchword against authority? The answer to this can best be conveyed in the book which follows. Since spiritual power can never be precisely pinned down, this book will not give a complete answer–nor will all of the massive evidence on which it is based. It is to Bhaktivedanta's credit that he believed in keeping nothing secret, and it is to Satsvarūpa's credit that he has presented the events of this critical period as objectively as possible. Seldom before have we had such an intimate and detailed account of a spiritual master bringing forth a new religious movement, and probably never has there been such a wealth of contemporary data to back it up. Those of us who are historians of religion will be working this rich vein for years to come.

Some who read this book will simply enjoy an absorbing story. Others, perhaps more appropriately, will respond in faith or greater commitment to their own religious quest. Whatever your response, this first published volume of a great religious biography will be a rare treat.

Dr. Thomas J. Hopkins
Chairman
Department of Religious Studies
Franklin and Marshall College
Lancaster, Pennsylvania

Foreword to the First Printing of Śrīla Prabhupāda-līlāmṛta — Volume Three (chapters 22–28)

In the course of doing research for my book on the Hare Kṛṣṇa movement and afterwards—during the late sixties and seventies—I had the good fortune, on several occasions, to meet and speak with A. C. Bhaktivedanta Swami Prabhupāda. I feel honored, therefore, to write the Foreword to this volume.

This work by Satsvarūpa dāsa Goswami is an eloquent tribute to the memory of a man who played a central role in American religious history during the countercultural sixties and seventies. It will provide a mine of information to scholars and to anyone else interested in the movement Prabhupāda brought to America from India, and in the counterculture itself, the social milieu in which the movement took root and flourished in its early years.

In this volume we encounter one of the most important periods in Śrīla Prabhupāda's life, as he courageously establishes and develops his movement in San Francisco's Haight-Ashbury district, the counterculture capital of the West Coast. That he, an elderly foreigner with a thick Bengali accent and a relative stranger to Western (what to speak of countercultural) ways could minister so effectively to the hippies of the Haight-Ashbury—where sexual promiscuity and drug abuse were blended into a "do-your-own-thing" ethic and where bowing to any sort of authority was rejected on principle—gives some indication of his extraordinary ability and fortitude. The author presents a number of brief case histories of some of Śrīla Prabhupada's early followers, personal accounts that illuminate the struggle of many youths to find meaning and an alternative way of life within a counterculture lacking cohesion and direction. Unable to identify with the religious institutions of the establishment, these young people found truth in the message of Śrīla Prabhupāda and experiential validation of that truth in the chanting of the *mahā-mantra,* the divine names of Kṛṣṇa. In reading these accounts, the reader will be struck with Śrīla Prabhupāda's personal qualities—his strength of purpose, his genuine humility, and his deep spirituality—by which he gently led his erring disciples from hedonism to Kṛṣṇa. He was a practical man. He knew that not all who attended his sessions would become converts. But he believed that even a little contact with Kṛṣṇa consciousness would bring them tangible spiritual benefit.

In this volume we have, in effect, a fascinating close-up study of the process of religious conversion, about which psychologists and sociologists are so intrigued. We witness how Śrīla Prabhupāda's disciples gradually changed their ways, accepting moral and spiritual discipline under his compassionate guidance, and we learn of backsliders whose conversions were insufficient to keep them from giving in to sensual temptations. For some of his followers, those with doubts and inner struggles, conversion was a slow or vascillating process. This compelling story reveals much of the process and degrees of conversion. The incidents themselves clearly contradict the loosely made claims of some uninformed critics that the Hare Kṛṣṇa movement employs some kind of occult "mind-control." These examples make it sufficiently clear that conversion to Kṛṣṇa consciousness is a process that engages the full range of intellectual, emotional, and volitional faculties.

Although never compromising his lofty principles, Śrīla Prabhupāda mobilized existing resources of the contemporary subculture to make the Vaiṣṇava faith better known. Without endorsing the drug abuse of the hippies to whom he was ministering, he dared to have set up and then appear at a "Mantra-Rock Dance" featuring such attractions as Janis Joplin and the Grateful Dead. What a contrast! Amid the intermingling of incense and marijuana smoke and pulsating strobe lights illuminating depictions of Kṛṣṇ's life, Śrīla Prabhupāda delivered his timeless message of Kṛṣṇa consciousness. Then, with the aid of poet Allen Ginsberg, he soon had the entire crowd dancing and swaying like grain in the wind as they chanted the *mahā-mantra:* Hare Kṛṣṇa, Hare Kṛṣṇa, Kṛṣṇa Kṛṣṇa, Hare Hare/ Hare Rāma, Hare Rāma, Rāma Rāma, Hare Hare.

This is also the story of Śrīla Prabhupāda's sacrificial life. He brought his message to America at an advanced age when most elderly gentlemen in India are content to retire in comfort in the bosom of their families. As might be expected, the accumulative strain of traveling, lecturing, and sleeping little while spending his early morning hours translating and commenting on religious texts he was preparing for publication brought illness. His weak health led him to return to India and to his Vedic doctors, in whom he showed considerably more faith than in Western medicine. Still, he was not content to remain in India, and this volume closes with his return to America and to his anxiously waiting disciples.

Perhaps more than anything else, this volume reveals those extraordinary personal attributes of Śrīla Prabhupāda that elicited such deep reverence and affection from his disciples. Besides being a man of deep moral strength, humility, and holiness, he was genuinely renounced. Unlike many modern *gurus,* he was content to live as his disciples did. Even when his health failed and he returned to the blazing heat of Delhi for his recovery, he sought nothing better than a poorly furnished room, without air-conditioning, in a Hindu temple where he had resided before coming to America. Śrīla Prabhupāda's life, as it is revealed here, is the epitome of his ideal, an ideal that he set forth for others to follow. In an age of pervasive hypocrisy and cynicism, it is this kind of rare model that we need.

Dr. J. Stillson Judah
Professor Emeritus, History of Religions
Graduate Theological Union and Pacific
School of Religion
Berkeley, California

Foreword to the First Printing of Śrīla Prabhupāda-līlāmṛta — Volume Four (Chapters 29–36)

Though I have been a student of the Kṛṣṇa devotional traditions in India for fifteen years, in the late sixties I was influenced by the then common notion among academicians (not to mention the general public) that the movement begun by Bhaktivedanta Swami was simply another watered-down product of an Indian *guru's* attempt to make Hindu teachings attractive to Western youth. The anticult campaigns of the midseventies highlighted ISKCON (International Society for Krishna Consciousness) as one of the spurious "cults." However, my research into the validity of such attitudes led me to conclude that the Kṛṣṇa movement in America was more authentically Indian than I had first imagined. When the opportunity presented itself, in 1980, for me to live in Kṛṣṇa temples in California for three weeks, I began an intensive study of ISKCON that has since taken me to fourteen temples throughout America and India. Through living in the temples and speaking at length with ISKCON leaders and devotees, I have come to regard many members of the movement as good friends and their *guru,* Bhaktivedanta Swami, as a man worthy of the attention and acclaim this biographical series affords.

In this volume of Bhaktivedanta Swami's biography, one of the central lessons taught the astute reader is the complexity and depth of the *guru*–disciple relationship. Much of the criticism from parents and anticult groups centers on the authoritarian demand of "cult" leaders for absolute submission from their followers. It is assumed that the leader has personal motives (e.g. power or monetary gain) that drive him to control others, while the surrendered disciples are manipulated, in an unthinking state, by the capricious whim of the spiritual master. In this volume of the life of Bhaktivedanta Swami, we see the foolishness of such an analysis. What springs from page after page is the willing devotion of young men and women to a man whom they admire for his deep faith and humility, not his autocratic or forceful demands. Early in ISKCON's life in America, the very fabric of this fledgling institution was threatened by schismatic teachings of newly ordained ascetics on the *relative* place of the *guru* in the life of faith and in the institution. Bhaktivedanta Swami had to state forcefully the Indian tradition that the *guru's* position is absolute—that of the eternal spiritual father—not simply one of convenience, to be overshadowed by time.

Yet we can see why some of the young devotees were confused as Bhaktivedanta Swami prostrated himself before the images of Kṛṣṇa and of his *guru* in the line of spiritual teachers before him. Such, however, is the character of *paramparā,* or *guru* succession. One's *guru* is the *only* channel through which one's devotion is transmitted faithfully to God, and such is also the case for one's *guru* (though some, like Bhaktivedanta Swami, seem also to have direct access as well). Thus to a mother who exclaims, "You know, these boys actually *worship* you!" Bhaktivedanta Swami responds, "Yes, that is our system. I am also worshiping my Guru Mahārāja." (p. 981)

This volume of Bhaktivedanta Swami's biography reveals the religious dimensions of the *guru*–disciple relationship in the varied attempts this remarkable Vaiṣṇava ascetic made to nurture the deepening faith of his new American children in a God and a spiritual tradition foreign to their native soil. From loosely performed rituals to standardized *pūjās* (Deity worship) done according to classic Bengali texts, we see the old master encourage greater attention to the details of worship. From spontaneous but uninformed attempts to celebrate their *guru's* birthday to formal Vyāsa-pūjās set in traditional Bengali songs and prayer, Bhaktivedanta Swami's disciples are led into old Indian traditions of honoring one's spiritual master as a part of the act of worshiping God. But what struck me as I read the pages that follow is the model of piety set by Bhaktivedanta Swami himself as he became deeply immersed in the praises of God while singing, or chanting, or dancing. It becomes quite clear that the lesson of the master is not merely what he says, but what he does. And it is also clear that the followers of Bhaktivedanta Swami struggled—not always successfully—to match up to the high standard of living and devotion the mature Bhaktivedanta Swami set.

The reader will marvel at the persistence, ingenuity, and faithfulness to Bhaktivedanta Swami's vision his disciples evidence in their attempt to spread Kṛṣṇa consciousness to every town and village. From the married couples who pioneered the movement in England and accomplished with the aid of the Beatles' Harrison and Lennon (!) what renowned sages from India before them could not, to the disciples who endured the worst that India's climate and cuisine could produce to work long days and nights bringing faith in Kṛṣṇa back to India's own people, the contagious devotion of the master lives on in his spiritual children. Thus the success of ISKCON in these formative years (1969–1971) can be understood only when both partners in the *guru*–disciple relationship are given due attention. Nonetheless, it is Bhaktivedanta Swami, with his deep faith, energetic preaching, and persistent ideals, who forms the nucleus of the fledgling community of faith we observe in the early years of ISKCON.

What begins to happen before the careful readers' eyes in this volume is the institutionalization or routinization of ISKCON's dress, ritual behavior, and administrative structure. With the formation of the Governing Body Commission (G.B.C.) to run the practical affairs of the institution (book publication, temple economics, etc.), Bhaktivedanta Swami accomplished something his own master had envisioned but had not accomplished before his death, namely, to provide an administrative structure that could hold together disparate temples in varied locations with their separate leaderships. It is clear after Bhaktivedanta Swami's death in 1977 that the G.B.C. has enabled ISKCON to weather storms from within (including the defection of one of Bhaktivedanta Swami's eleven appointed successors) and from without (e.g. the tax and legal challenges to ISKCON's religious status in California) that would have been impossible without central leadership. We see in this volume the beginnings of that leadership core and the freedom from administrative detail the G.B.C. afforded Bhaktivedanta Swami.

Having interviewed Satsvarūpa dāsa Goswami and visited a farm under his management, I have seen the same devotion expressed for him by his disciples that he expresses here for Bhaktivedanta Swami. That is not surprising when one realizes that even with effective institutional structures like the G.B.C. in place, communities of faith remain vital only so long as there are living models to give expression to ideals and beliefs that can otherwise seem quite remote. Critics of ISKCON who see only the outward trappings of surrender to the *guru* miss the humility before God and *guru* that is demanded of each *guru* as well. This volume is a success not because of some academic standard of objectivity (which few biographers meet in any case), but because of the skillful blend of oral history, documented reminiscences, and transparent admiration, all of which bring Bhaktivedanta Swami to life for the reader as a real (and exceptional) person. We not only sense, but observe that it is complete devotion to God through the person of one's spiritual master that animated ISKCON in its early years and continues to do so now, as evidenced by the author himself. Thus this book reads like a personal yet precise diary relating the formative years of ISKCON and its founder-teacher. And just as in reading a diary, we learn as much from reading between the lines as we do from the events and persons described. This is a fascinating chronicle I urge you to read.

Dr. Larry D. Shinn
Danforth Professor of Religion
Oberlin College
Oberlin, Ohio

Significant Events in the Life of Śrīla Prabhupāda

September 1, 1896	Abhay Charan De was born in the Calcutta suburb of Tollygunge.
circa 1901	Began his own Ratha-yātrā.
circa 1902	Began his own Deity worship.
1904	Entered Mutty Lall Seal Free School.
circa 1912	Mother, Rajani, died.
1916	Entered Scottish Churches' College.
1918	Married Radharani Datta.
1920	Rejected college diploma and began dressing as a Gandhian.
1921	Began working as a department manager in Dr. Kartick Chandra Bose's pharmaceutical company.
1922	Met Śrīla Bhaktisiddhānta Sarasvatī for the first time.

1923	Moved with his family to Allahabad and started the Prayag Pharmacy.
1925	Visited Vṛndāvana for the first time.
1928	Encountered disciples of Śrīla Bhakti-siddhānta Sarasvatī at Allahabad and helped them start an Allahabad branch of the Gaudiya Math.
1930	Father, Gour Mohan, died.
October 28, 1932	Traveled to Kosi where he heard Śrīla Bhaktisiddhānta Sarasvatī speak for the second time.
November 1932	Received initiation from Śrīla Bhakti-siddhānta Sarasvatī at Allahabad.
1933–34	Went to Bombay to start a pharmaceutical business. There he met some of his Godbrothers and helped them establish a Bombay branch of the Gaudiya Math.
February 25, 1935	Presented his Vyāsa-pūjā homage before the members and guests of the Bombay Gaudiya Math on the appearance day of Śrīla Bhakti-siddhānta Sarasvatī.
November 1935	Met Śrīla Bhaktisiddhānta Sarasvatī at Rādhā-kuṇḍa.
December 13, 1936	Śrīla Bhaktisiddhānta Sarasvatī wrote to Abhay asking him to preach the message of Lord Caitanya in English.
January 1, 1937	Śrīla Bhaktisiddhānta Sarasvatī passed away at Purī.
1938	Abhay moved his family and business back to Calcutta to 6 Sita Kanta Banerjee Lane.

1939	His Godbrothers honored him with the title Bhaktivedanta.
February 1944	Began *Back to Godhead* magazine in Calcutta.
1945	Opened a pharmaceutical factory in Lucknow, Abhay Charan De & Sons.
December 7, 1947	Wrote to Mahatma Gandhi.
1948	*Geetopanishad* manuscript stolen. Lost Lucknow factory.
1949	Began writing for *Gauḍīya Patrikā* magazine.
February 1952	Revived *Back to Godhead* from Allahabad.
October 1952	Began his Jhansi preaching.
1953	Initiated his first disciple, Ācārya Prabhākar, in Jhansi.
May 16, 1953	Grand opening day of the League of Devotees in Jhansi.
1953	His Allahabad business burglarized.
1954	Left family.
1955	Left Jhansi for Mathurā.
July 1955	Began editing *Sajjana-toṣaṇī* from Gaudiya Sangha in Delhi.
October 1955	Relieved of duties with *Sajjana-toṣaṇī*. Alone in Delhi trying to preach.
February 1956	Began *Back to Godhead* again, from Delhi.
September 1956	Moved to the Vaṁśī-gopālajī temple in Vṛndāvana.

January 1957	Visited Bombay to preach, on Ācārya Prabhākar's invitation.
Spring, 1957	Solicited members for the League of Devotees in Kanpur.
1958	Returned to Bombay for preaching.
Fall, 1958	Wrote "Vṛndāvana-bhajana" at Vaṁśī-gopālajī temple.
October 20, 1958	Revived *Back to Godhead* from Delhi, after two years.
December 1958	Wrote "Viraha-aṣṭaka" for Śrīla Bhaktisiddhānta Sarasvatī's disappearance day.
September 17, 1959	Accepted *sannyāsa* from Keśava Mahārāja in Mathurā.
early 1960	Acquired quarters in Chippiwada temple, Delhi.
Fall, 1960	Published *Easy Journey to Other Planets* (his first book) in Delhi.
February 1961	(on Śrīla Bhaktisiddhānta Sarasvatī's appearance day) Submitted an offering sharply criticizing his Godbrothers for not following their spiritual master's orders.
July 1962	Moved from Vaṁśī-gopālajī temple to Rādhā-Dāmodara temple in Vṛndāvana for writing *Śrīmad-Bhāgavatam,* late 1962. Published *Śrīmad-Bhāgavatam,* Canto One, Volume One, in Delhi.
early 1964	Published *Śrīmad-Bhāgavatam,* Canto One, Volume Two.

June 1964	Met Prime Minister Shastri and gave him a copy of *Śrīmad-Bhāgavatam,* Canto One, Volume One.
August 31, 1964	(on Janmāṣṭamī day) Held festival at Rādhā-Dāmodara temple for promoting his *Bhāgavatam* volumes and his mission of preaching abroad.
January 1965	Published *Śrīmad-Bhāgavatam,* Canto One, Volume Three.
May 1965	Received No Objection Certificate from Indian government.
June 10, 1965	Received his passport.
Summer, 1965	Sumati Morarji agreed to send Bhaktivedanta Swami to America.
July 28, 1965	Obtained visa.
August 13, 1965	Set sail from Calcutta for the United States.
September 17, 1965	Arrived at Boston's Commonwealth Pier.
September 19, 1965	Arrived in Butler, Pennsylvania.
October 18, 1965	Left Butler for New York city. Stayed at Dr. Mishra's *haṭha-yoga* studio on 72nd Street.
February 15, 1966	Moved out of Dr. Mishra's studio and began his own classes.
April 1966	Typewriter and tape recorder stolen. Moved to the Bowery. The first serious newcomer, Michael Grant, helps.
end June 1966	Moved to 26 Second Avenue. Storefront lectures began to draw a steady crowd.

July 11, 1966	ISKCON incorporated.
September 9, 1966	First disciples in the United States initiated.
September 13, 1966	First ISKCON wedding.
October 1966	Regular *kīrtanas* in Washington Square Park started. *Back to Godhead* restarted and distribution begun.
January 16, 1967	Arrived in San Francisco.
March 1967	Lord Jagannātha arrived.
March 26, 1967	Lord Jagannātha, Baladeva and Lady Subhadrā, the first deities in ISKCON, installed at the San Francisco temple.
May–June 1967	Heart attack and recuperation.
end June 1967	Stayed in beach cottage near San Francisco.
July 1967	Traveled to Vṛndāvana for health.
December 14, 1967	San Francisco temple on Frederick St. Returned to America from India after four and a half months of preaching and recuperating from heart attack.
January 1968	Los Angeles temple on West Pico Blvd. Interviewed by *Life* magazine.
May 1968	Boston, temple on Glenville Ave. Lectured at Harvard and M.I.T.
June–Aug. 1968	Montreal temple on Park Ave. Sent six disciples (three married couples) to preach in London.

Sept.–Oct. 1968	Visited ISKCON centers in Seattle and Santa Fe.
October 1968	Los Angeles temple on La Cienega Blvd.
December 1968	Began work on *The Nectar of Devotion* and *Kṛṣṇa, the Supreme Personality of Godhead.*
March 1969	Introduced more regulated Deity worship and weekly festivals.
May 1969	Columbus, Ohio. Appeared on stage with Allen Ginsberg at Ohio State University and led 2,000 students in ecstatic *kīrtana.*
May–June 1969	First visit to the New Vrindaban farm community in West Virginia.
June 23, 1969	Los Angeles temple on La Cienega Blvd. Installed Deities of Rādhā-Kṛṣṇa.
July 26, 1969	Presided over San Francisco Ratha-yātrā.
August 1969	Visited ISKCON center in Hamburg, Germany.
September 11, 1969	London arrival. Resided at Tittenhurst, John Lennon's Ascot country estate.
Sept.–Oct. 1969	Lectured at Camden Town Hall. Gave a series of lectures at Conway Hall. Lectured at English Speakers Union. Appeared on TV talk show "Late Night Line-Up." Traveled to Amsterdam for TV appearance.
October 30, 1969	Oxford Town Hall lecture.
November 3, 1969	Moved from Tittenhurst to an apartment on Baker Street, near the Bury Place temple.

December 1969	Moved into Bury Place temple. Received $19,000 donation from George Harrison for publishing Vol. I of *Kṛṣṇa, the Supreme Personality of Godhead.* Acquired Rādhā-Kṛṣṇa Deities for Bury Place temple.
December 14, 1969	Inaugurated first Gauḍīya Vaiṣṇava temple in London and installed Deities of Rādhā and Kṛṣṇa.
December 21, 1969	Boston temple on Beacon St. Visited ISKCON Press.
Jan.–July 1970	Resided at Los Angeles temple on La Cienega Blvd.
February 25, 1970	Los Angeles. Appearance day of Śrīla Bhaktisiddhānta. Moved into temple on Watseka Ave., ISKCON world headquarters and model for all ISKCON temples.
July 5, 1970	San Francisco Ratha-yātrā.
July 28, 1970	Awarded *sannyāsa* order to several disciples.
July 29, 1970	Formed the Governing Body Commission (G.B.C.) of ISKCON.
29 July 1970	Formed the Bhaktivedanta Book Trust (BBT).
August 1970	Hawaii, enroute to India. Tokyo. Instructed disciples on proper observance of Vyāsa-pūjā. Wrote letter to New Vrindaban, resolving the growing misconception of the spiritual master's position. Made contract with Dai Nippon Printing Company.
August 29, 1970	Calcutta. Instituted ISKCON Life Membership program.

October 1970	Bombay. Home of Mr. Kailash Seksaria on Marine Dr. Chowpatti Beach *paṇḍāl,* Sadhu Samaj. Developed Bombay Life Membership.
late October 1970	Amritsar. Preached at the Vedanta Sammelan. Daily accepted numerous invitations. Enlisted life members. Visited Golden Temple of the Sikhs. Visited Rāma-tīrtha-sarovara, *āśrama* of Vālmīki Muni.
November 20, 1970	Bombay. Resided at Sītā-Rāma temple in Chembur. Invited by Sumati Morarji to speak at Scindia House.
December 3, 1970	Indore. Gita Jayanti Mahotsava. Established Life Membership.
December 17, 1970	Surat. Resided at home of Mr. Bhagubhai Jariwala. Daily *kīrtana* processions through city. Citywide holiday proclaimed. Preached in outlying villages.
January 1971	Bombay and Calcutta.
Jan.–Feb. 1971	Allahabad. Attended Ardha-kumbha-melā.
February 1971	Gorakhpur. Resided at home of disciple Dr. R. P. Rao. Formed committee to introduce Kṛṣṇa consciousness within Gorakhpur University.
February 1971	Benares. Attended festival of Lord Caitanya's visit to Benares and rode in the procession in a silver chariot.
Feb.–Mar. 1971	Gorakhpur. Resided at second home of Hanuman Prasad Poddar. Introduced the song *Jaya Rādhā-Mādhava.* Negotiated with university authorities for land for

	constructing an ISKCON temple. Met with Hanuman Prasad Poddar, head of Gita Press.
March–April 1971	ISKCON center at the Akash-Ganga Building. *Paṇḍāl* at Cross Maidan with nightly attendance of 20,000. Revealed plan for Bombay center in letter to life members.
May 4, 1971	Visited Kuala Lumpur, Malaysia, and lectured at the Town Hall. Lectured at Lakṣmī-Nārāyaṇa temple.
May 9, 1971	Sydney. Brought and installed Śrī Śrī Rādhā-Gopīnātha. Performed initiations.
May 1971	Sydney Grammar School engagement. Lectured at Wayside Chapel, a rehabilitation center in downtown Sydney.
May 12, 1971	Wrote Preface to *Bhagavad-gītā As It Is.*
May 13, 1971	Arrived in Calcutta for a ten-day *paṇḍāl.* Naxalite youths threatened his life. Lectured to more than 40,000 at *paṇḍāl's* grand finale and led a procession to ISKCON temple on Albert Road, where he placed Rādhā-Govinda on the altar.
May 1971	Purchased land in Māyāpur through disciple Tamāla Kṛṣṇa.
June 1971	Moscow. Met with Indologist Professor G.G. Kotovsky. Instructed a Russian youth, Anatoly, in Kṛṣṇa consciousness.
June 25, 1971	Paris press conference. Olympia Theater television interview.
June 26, 1971	Los Angeles initiations.

June 27, 1971	San Francisco. Fifth annual Ratha-yātrā festival.
Summer 1971	Initiated several hundred disciples in Los Angeles, Detroit, and Brooklyn. Gainesville. Lectured at University of Florida. Television interview.
August 1971	London. Serious illness. Stressed displeasure at delayed book publication.
September 1971	Nairobi. Interviewed by reporters. Mombassa. Recovered health in home of Mr. Pandya.
Sept.–Oct. 1971	Nairobi. Set example for *sannyāsī* by staying three days or less in the home of each host. Stressed preaching to the Africans. Organized Nairobi's first outdoor *kīrtana* at Kamakunji Park. Lectured at University of Nairobi to 2,000 students. Appeared on TV show *Mambo Leo.*
October 19, 1971	Departure for Bombay.

Śrīla Prabhupāda's Writings in India

BACK TO GODHEAD

Parts I, II, III, & IV (1944) "First Appearance on the Vyasa Puja Day 1944" (a special 44-page booklet)

"Message of His Divine Grace" (translated from Bengali)
"Message of Thakur Bhakti Vinode" (translated from Bengali)
"Back to Godhead" (editorial)
"Godhead and His Potentialities"
"Theosophy Ends in Vaishnavism"
"The Science of Congregational Chanting of the Name of the Lord"

Volume I, Part II (October 1944)

"Thanks to the Government of India"
"Gandhi–Jinnah Talks"
"Mr. Churchill's 'Humane World'"
"Mr. Bernard Shaw's Wishful Desire"
"Spontaneous Love of Godhead"

Volume I, Part IX (16 February 1952) "First Appearance on the Vyasa Puja Day 1944... Reappearance on the 16th Feb. 1952"
"Paramahansa Sri Srimad Bhaktisiddhanta Saraswati Goswami Maharaja"
"Karma Yoga of Bhagwat Gita"
"Theosophy Concluded" (continued)

Volume III, Part I (1 March 1956)
"The S.R.C. Catastrophe"
"Decoration of the Dead Body"

Volume III, Part II (16 March 1956)
"Who Is a 'Sadhu'?"

Volume III, Part III (5 April 1956)
"The Lowest of the Mankind"
"Lord Shri Chaitanya: His welfare activities"

Volume III, Part IV (20 April 1956)
"Philosophical Problems Within Social Awareness"
"Godless Creation: An atheistic and dangerous theory"
"Human Welfare Activities"

Volume III, Part V (5 May 1956)
"Sufferings of Humanity: Is Providence responsible for it?"
"Conception of Universal Brotherhood"
"Lord Buddha: The emblem of Theism"

Volume III, Part VI (20 May l956)
"'Yajna' or Sacrifice for the Supreme: Conception of Classless Society"
"How to Broadcast the Teachings of Bhagwat Geeta"
"Grow More Food"

Volume III, Part VII (5 June 1956)
"Religion Pretentious and Religion Real"
"The Eight Stanzas of His Lordship Shri Chaitanya Mahaprabhu
"Purity of Conduct: Basic Principle of Human Civilization"
"How to Broadcast the Teachings of Bhagwat Geeta" (Part 2)

Volume III, Part XIX (5 May 1960)
"Chaitanya Charitamrita, Essays and Text" (continued from Part XVI)
"Bhakti Rasamrita Sindhu"

Volume III, Part XX (20 May 1960)
"Bhakti Rasamrita Sindhu" (continued)
"Chaitanya Charitamrita" (continued)

Volume III, Part XXI (5 June 1960)
"Bhakti Rasamrita Sindhu" (continued)
"Chaitanya Charitamrita, Essays and Text" (continued)

Volume III, Part XXII (5 July 1960)
"Bhakti Rasamrita Sindhu" (continued)
"Chaitanya Charitamrita, Essays and Text" (continued)

Volume III, Part XXIII (20 July 1960)
"Sanatan Dharma is the Religion of All Living Entities"
"Sri Ishopanishad"

Volume III, Part XXIV (5 August 1960)
"Sri Ishopanishad" (continued)

Volume IV, Part I (5 September 1960)
"Sri Ishopanishad" (continued)

EASY JOURNEY TO OTHER PLANETS

Delhi, League of Devotees (1960)

GAUḌĪYA PATRIKĀ (in Bengali)

Volume I, Number 2 (April 1949)
"Letter of Appreciation to Keśava Mahārāja for having received first edition of Gauḍīya magazine"

Volume I, Number 5 (July 1949)
"Reply to Sriyukta Jitendra Narayana Vasu's Questions"

Volume I, Number 6 through Volume II, Number 8 (Aug. 1949–Oct. 1950)
"Topics of the Supreme Lord"

Volume III, Number 1 through Volume IV, Number 8 (March 1951–October 1952)
"Topics of Bhakti-yoga"

Volume IV, Number 9 and Number 10 (November & December 1952)
"Topics of Jñāna-yoga" (continued in Volume VI, Number 10)

Volume V, Number 1 (February 1953)
"Play of Renunciation"

Volume V, Number 2 (April 1953)
"Review of Various Books"
"Criticism of Līlā-kīrtana"

Volume V, Number 4 (June 1953)
Article announcing the start of the League of Devotees—16 May 1953

Volume V, Number 7 (September 1953)
"The Magnanimity of Lord Caitanya"

Volume VI, Number 10 through Number 12 (Dec. 1954–Feb. 1955)
"Topics of Jñāna-yoga" (continued from Volume IV, Number 10)

Volume VII, Number 6 and Number 7 (August & September 1955)
"Life of the Bhāgavata"

Volume VII, Number 8 (October 1955)
"Material Life"

Volume VII, Number 11 (January 1956)
"The Devotion of Gopannara (A Great Devotee of Lord Rāmacandra)"

Volume IX, Number 1 and Number 2 (March & April 1957)
"Śrī Kṛṣṇa, The Knower of the Vedas"

Volume IX, Number 3 (May 1957)
"The Error of the Gita Press"

Volume IX, Number 6 through Number 8 (August–October 1957)
"The Identity and Extent of Sin"

Volume IX, Number 12 (February 1958) plus Volume X, numbers 3, 4, 5, 8 & 12 (May 1958–February 1959)
"The Error of the Sages (Critical review of Dr. Radhakrishnan's *Gītā* commentary)"

Volume X, Number 9 and Number 10 (November & December 1958)
"Poem on Vṛndāvana Worship (Bhajana)"

Volume X, Number 11 (February 1959)
"Eight Stanzas on Separation from Bhaktisiddhānta Sarasvatī"

Volume XI, Number 1 and Number 2 (March & April 1959)
The Fallen Brāhmaṇa or 'Poor Nārāyaṇa'; In Opposition to an Article by Dr. Sri Naliniranjana Sena"

Volume XI, Number 3 (May 1959)
"The Atomic Living Entity and the Supreme Lord"

Volume XI, Number 4 and Number 5 (June & July 1959)
"The Spiritual Sky"

Volume XI, Number 8 (October 1959)
"The Prayer of Emperor Kulaśekhara"
Article on acceptance of *sannyāsa*

Volume XI, Number 9 (November 1959)
"The Prayer of Emperor Kulaśekhara" (continued)

Volume XI, Number 12 (February 1960)
"The Modern Scientists' Discovery of the Supreme Lord's Abode (Dhāma)"

Volume XIV, numbers 4, 7, & 8 (June, September, & October 1962)
"Śrī Gīta-gāna"

SRIMAD BHAGWATAM, Volume 1

Delhi, The League of Devotees (1962)

SRIMAD BHAGWATAM, Volume 2

Delhi, The League of Devotees (1964)

SRIMAD BHAGWATAM, Volume 3

Delhi, The League of Devotees (1965)

MISCELLANY (published)

1936
"Sree Vyas Puja Homage" (published in *The Harmonist*)

1949
Essay, "The Preaching of Gaudiya Vaishnava Dharma Outside Bengal"

16 March 1953
Essay, "The Preaching of Gaudiya Vaishnava Dharma Outside Bengal" (different from the above)

7 July 1953

Letter, "Hindu Missionaries" (published in the *Amrita Bazar Patrika* at Allahabad)

1964

Essay, "Re-creation of Man" (printed in *Indian Philosophy and Culture,* Vol. IX)

Undated essays

"The Cure for the Material Disease"
"A Glorification of Devotional Service"
"God is Alive"
"The True Identity of the Living Being"

MISCELLANY (unpublished essays)

21 April 1939

"Introduction to Geetopanishad"

1950

Man is the Architect of His Own Fortune ... " (essay fragment followed by a list of twenty-four current world crises)

5 February 1950

"Love Affairs of Śrī Kṛṣṇa—the Supreme Lord"
"Science of Devotion (Bhakti Rasamrita Sindhu)" (thirty-three numbered sections comprising a summary study of the first chapter of *Bhakti-rasāmṛta-sindhu*)
"Secretary—Ministry of Education"

10 September 1959

"Solution of Present Crisis by *Bhagavad-gītā:* Twenty-Eight Points"

5 March 1952

"Contribution of Lord Caitanya to the People of the World"

8 June 1952

Untitled essay

1955

"Divine Relation"
"Light of the Bhagwat" (fifty illustrations with purports)
"Man Made Planet?"
"Message of Godhead"

6 December 1955

"Rai Bahudar"
"Temple Entry Movement"

1957

Essay on black marketers (handwritten)
Untitled essay (handwritten)
"What is the Matter with the World?"

1958–1959 (approximately)

"An Analysis of *Bhagavad-gītā*"
"Conception of Gītā-nāgarī on the Principles of Gandhi"
"Interpretations of *Bhagavad-gītā*"
"Knowledge Transcendental"
"Liberation in Practice"
"Misuse of Public Funds in the Name of Religion"
"Obstacles in the Devotional Path" (fragment)
"Perfection at Home—A novel contribution to the fallen humanity"
"A Study of *Bhagavad-gītā*—Means to Learn the *ABCD* of Spiritual Science"
Untitled fragment on the goal of human life as discussed by Lord Caitanya and Rāmānanda Rāya
Untitled fragment on morality and social organization "World Pacifist and the *Bhagavad-gītā*"

1961

Vaiśiṣṭyāṣṭakam" (eight prayers glorifying Bhaktisiddhānta Sarasvatī)

21 January 1961

Bhagavad-gītā facts and figures (seventeen short paragraphs with verse references)

Undated

"Devotee and the Divinity"
"Divinity of Lord Caitanya" (fragment)
"Human Welfare Activities"
"Shaktipujah" (handwritten review)

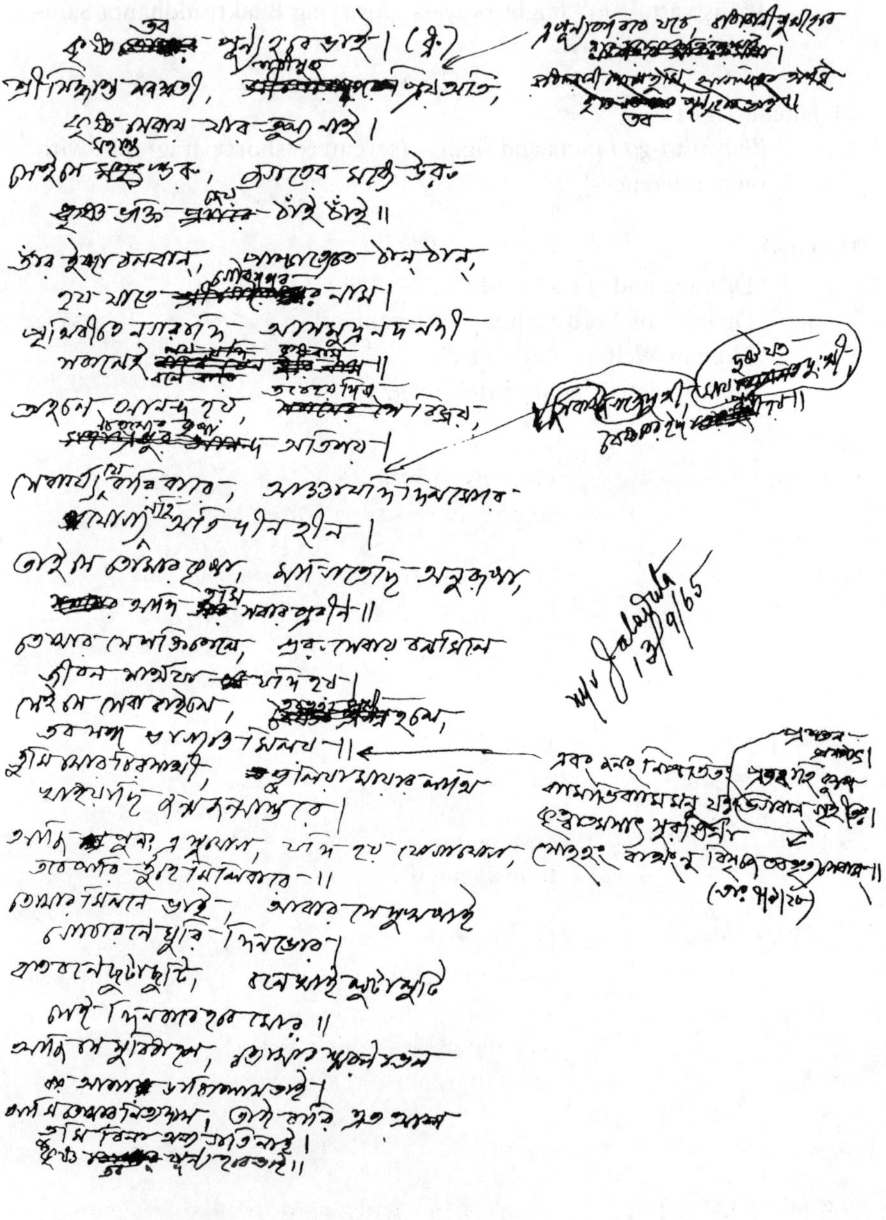

Prayer to the Lotus Feet of Kṛṣṇa

(refrain)
kṛṣṇa taba puṇya habe bhāi
e-puṇya koribe jabe rādhārāṇī khusī habe
dhruva ati boli tomā tāi

Translation: I emphatically say to you, O brothers, you will obtain your good fortune from the Supreme Lord Kṛṣṇa only when Śrīmatī Rādhārāṇī becomes pleased with you.

śrī-siddhānta saraswatī, śacī-suta priya ati,
kṛṣṇa-sebāya jāra tula nāi
sei se mohānta-guru, jagater madhe uru,
kṛṣṇa-bhakti dey ṭhāi ṭhāi

Translation: Śrī Śrīmad Bhaktisiddhānta Sarasvatī Ṭhākura, who is very dear to Lord Gaurāṅga, the son of mother Śacī, is unparalleled in his service to the Supreme Lord Śrī Kṛṣṇa. He is that great, saintly spiritual master who bestows intense devotion to Kṛṣṇa at different places throughout the world.

tāra icchā balavān, pāścātyete ṭhān ṭhān,
hoy jāte gaurāṅger nām
pṛthivīte nagarādi, āsamudra nada nadī,
sakalei loy kṛṣṇa nām

Translation: By his strong desire, the holy name of Lord Gaurāṅga will spread throughout all the countries of the Western world. In all the cities, towns, and villages on the earth, from all the oceans, seas, rivers, and streams, everyone will chant the holy name of Kṛṣṇa.

tāhale ānanda hoy, tabe hoy dig-vijay,
caitanyer kṛpā atiśay
māyā duṣṭa jata duḥkhī, jagate sabāi sukhī,
vaiṣṇaver icchā pūrṇa hoy

Translation: As the vast mercy of Śrī Caitanya Mahāprabhu conquers all directions, a flood of transcendental ecstasy will certainly cover the land. When all the sinful, miserable living entities become happy, the Vaiṣṇavas' desire is then fulfilled.

se kārja je koribāre, ājñā jadi dilo more,
jogya nahi ati dīna hīna
tāi se tomāra kṛpā, māgitechi anurūpā,
āji tumi sabār pravīṇa

Translation: Although my Guru Mahārāja ordered me to accomplish this mission, I am not worthy or fit to do it. I am very fallen and insignificant. Therefore, O Lord, now I am begging for Your mercy so that I may become worthy, for You are the wisest and most experienced of all.

tomāra se śakti pele, guru-sebāya bastu mile,
jībana sārthak jadi hoy
sei se sevā pāile, tāhale sukhī hale,
taba saṅga bhāgyate miloy

Translation: If You bestow Your power, by serving the spiritual master one attains the Absolute Truth—one's life becomes successful. If that service is obtained, then one becomes happy and gets Your association due to good fortune.

evaṁ janaṁ nipatitaṁ prabhavāhi-kūpe
kāmābhi kāmam anu yaḥ prapatan prasaṅgāt
kṛtvātmasāt surarṣiṇā bhagavan gṛhītaḥ
so 'haṁ kathaṁ nu visṛje tava bhṛtya-sevām

Translation: "My dear Lord, O Supreme Personality of Godhead, because of my association with material desires, one after another, I was gradually falling into a blind well full of snakes, following the general populace. But Your servant Nārada Muni kindly accepted me as his disciple and instructed me how to achieve this transcendental position. Therefore, my first duty is to serve him. How could I leave his service?" [Prahlāda Maharāja to Lord Nṛsiṁhadeva, *Śrīmad-Bhāgavatam* 7.9.28]

tumi mor cira sāthī, bhuliyā māyār lāthi,
khāiyāchi janma-janmāntare
āji punaḥ e sujoga, jadi hoy jogājoga,
tube pāri tuhe milibāre

Translation: O Lord Kṛṣṇa, You are my eternal companion. Forgetting You, I have suffered the kicks of *māyā* birth after birth. If today the chance to meet You occurs again, then I will surely be able to rejoin You.

tomāra milane bhāi, ābār se sukha pāi,
gocārane ghuri din bhor
kata bane chuṭāchuṭi, bane khāi luṭāpuṭi,
sei din kabe babe mor

Translation: O dear friend, in Your company I will experience great joy once again. In the early morning I will wander about the cowherd pastures and fields. Running and frolicking in the many forests of Vraja, I will roll on the ground in spiritual ecstasy. Oh, when will that day be mine?

āji se subidhāne, tomāra smaraṇa bhela,
baro āśā ḍākilām tāi
āmi tomāra nitya-dāsa, tāi kori eta āśa,
tumi binā anya gati nāi

Translation: Today that remembrance of You came to me in a very nice way. Because I have a great longing I called to You. I am Your eternal servant, and therefore I desire Your association so much. O Lord Kṛṣṇa, except for You there is no other means of success.

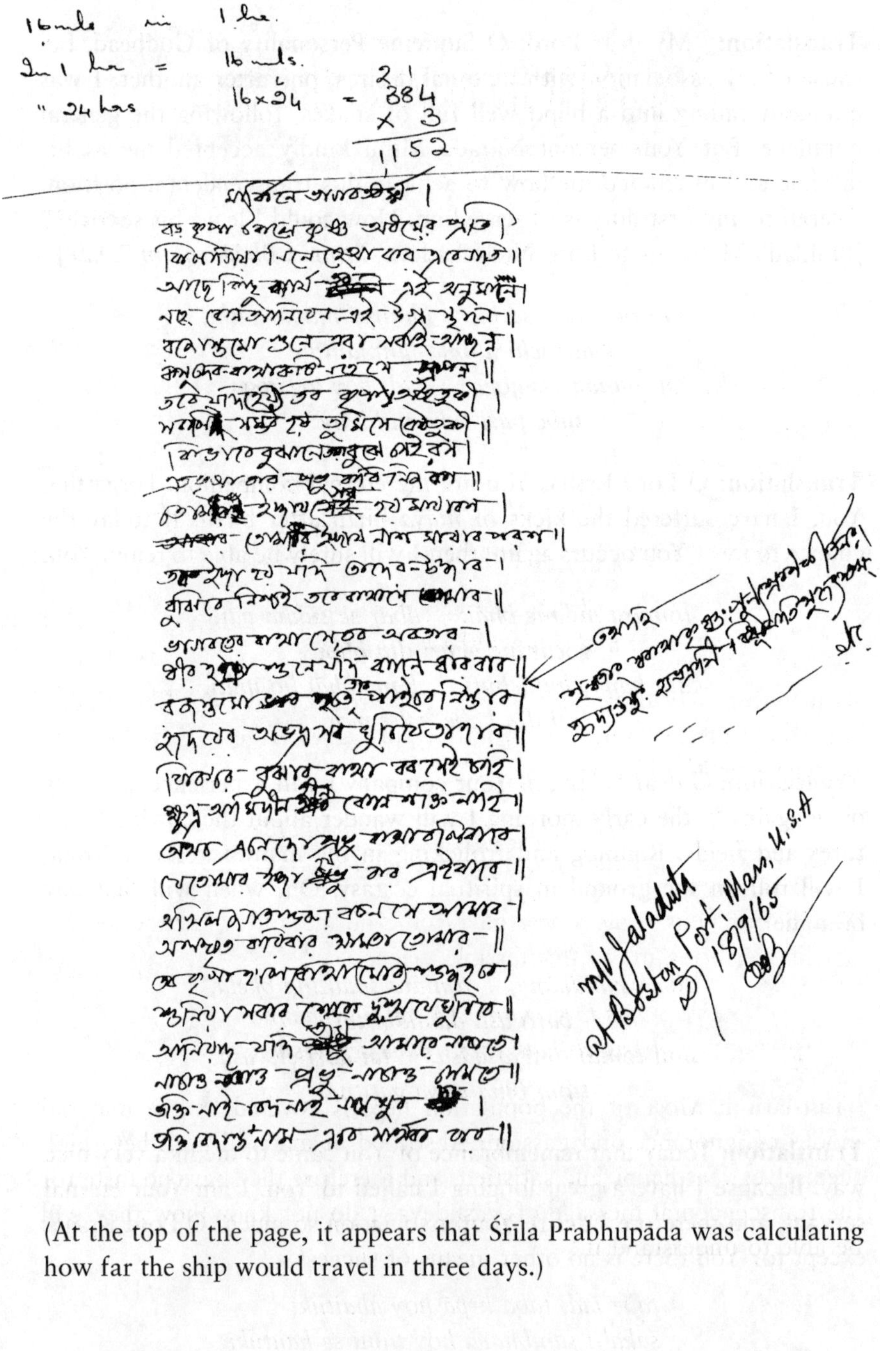
16 miles in 1 hr.
In 1 hr = 16 mils.
" 24 hrs 16×24 = 384
× 3
1152
M/V Jaladuta
at Boston Port, Mass, U.S.A
18/9/65

(At the top of the page, it appears that Śrīla Prabhupāda was calculating how far the ship would travel in three days.)

Mārkine Bhāgavata-dharma

(written at Boston Harbor, September 18, 1965)

baro-kṛpā kaile kṛṣṇa adhamer prati
ki lāgiyānile hethā koro ebe gati

Translation: My dear Lord Kṛṣṇa, You are so kind upon this useless soul, but I do not know why You have brought me here. Now You can do whatever You like with me.

āche kichu kārja taba ei anumāne
nahe keno āniben ei ugra-sthāne

Translation: But I guess You have some business here, otherwise why would You bring me to this terrible place?

rajas tamo guṇe erā sabāi ācchanna
bāsudeb-kathā ruci nahe se prasanna

Translation: Most of the population here is covered by the material modes of ignorance and passion. Absorbed in material life, they think themselves very happy and satisfied, and therefore they have no taste for the transcendental message of Vāsudeva. I do not know how they will be able to understand it.

tabe jadi taba kṛpā hoy ahaitukī
sakal-i sambhava hoy tumi se kautukī

Translation: But I know Your causeless mercy can make everything possible, because You are the most expert mystic.

ki bhāve bujhāle tārā bujhe sei rasa
eta kṛpā koro prabhu kori nija-baśa

Translation: How will they understand the mellows of devotional service? O Lord, I am simply praying for Your mercy so that I will be able to convince them about Your message.

tomāra icchāya saba hoy māyā-baśa
tomāra icchāya nāśa māyār paraśa

Translation: All living entities have come under the control of the illusory energy by Your will, and therefore, if You like, by Your will they can also be released from the clutches of illusion.

taba icchā hoy jadi tādera uddhār
bujhibe niścai tabe kathā se tomār

Translation: I wish that You may deliver them. Therefore if You so desire their deliverance, then only will they be able to understand Your message.

bhāgavater kathā se taba avatār
dhīra haiyā śune jadi kāne bār bār

Translation: The words of *Śrīmad-Bhāgavatam* are Your incarnation, and if a sober person repeatedly receives it with submissive aural reception, then he will be able to understand Your message.

śṛṇvatāṁ sva-kathāḥ kṛṣṇaḥ
puṇya-śravaṇa-kīrtanaḥ
hṛdy antaḥ-stho hy abhadrāṇi
vidhunoti suhṛt satām

naṣṭa-prāyeṣv abhadreṣu
nityaṁ bhāgavata-sevayā
bhagavaty uttama-śloke
bhaktir bhavati naiṣṭhikī

tadā rajas-tamo-bhāvāḥ
kāma-lobhādayaś ca ye
ceta etair anāviddhaṁ
sthitaṁ sattve prasīdati

evaṁ prasanna-manaso
bhagavad-bhakti-yogataḥ
bhagavat-tattva-vijñānaṁ
mukta-saṅgasya jāyate

bhidyate hṛdaya-granthiś
chidyante sarva-saṁśayāḥ
kṣīyante cāsya karmāṇi
dṛṣṭa evātmanīśvare

Translation: It is said in the *Śrīmad-Bhāgavatam* (1.2.17–21): "Śrī Kṛṣṇa, the Personality of Godhead, who is the Paramātmā [Supersoul] in everyone's heart and the benefactor of the truthful devotee, cleanses desire for material enjoyment from the heart of the devotee who relishes His messages, which are in themselves virtuous when properly heard and chanted. By regularly hearing the *Bhāgavatam* and rendering service unto the pure devotee, all that is troublesome to the heart is practically destroyed, and loving service unto the glorious Lord, who is praised with transcendental songs, is established as an irrevocable fact. At the time loving service is established in the heart, the modes of passion [*rajas*] and ignorance [*tamas*] and lust and desire [*kāma*] disappear from the heart. Then the devotee is established in goodness and he becomes happy. Thus established in the mode of goodness, the man rejuvenated by loving service to the Lord gains liberation from material association [*mukti*] and comes to know scientifically of the Personality of Godhead. Thus the knots of the heart and all misgivings are cut to pieces. The chain of fruitive actions [*karma*] is terminated when one sees the Self as master."

rajas tamo hate tabe pāibe nistār
hṛdayer abhadra sab ghucibe tāhār

Translation: He will become liberated from the influence of the modes of ignorance and passion and thus all inauspicious things accumulated in the core of the heart will disappear.

ki ko're bujhābo kathā baro sei cāhi
khudra āmi dīna hīna kono śakti nāhi

Translation: How will I make them understand this message of Kṛṣṇa consciousness? I am very unfortunate, unqualified, and the most fallen. Therefore I am seeking Your benediction so that I can convince them, for I am powerless to do so on my own.

athaca enecho prabhu kathā bolibāre
je tomār icchā prabhu koro ei bāre

Translation: Somehow or other, O Lord, You have brought me here to speak about You. Now, my Lord, it is up to You to make me a success or failure, as You like.

akhila jagat-guru! bacana se āmār
alaṅkṛta koribār khamatā tomār

Translation: O spiritual master of all the worlds! I can simply repeat Your message, so if You like You can make my power of speaking suitable for their understanding.

taba kṛpā ha'le mor kathā śuddha habe
śuniyā sabāra śoka duḥkha je ghucibe

Translation: Only by Your causeless mercy will my words become pure. I am sure that when this transcendental message penetrates their hearts, they will certainly feel engladdened and thus become liberated from all unhappy conditions of life.

āniyācho jadi prabhu āmāre nācāte
nācāo nācāo prabhu nacāo se-mate
kāṣṭhera puttali jathā nācāo se-mate

Translation: O Lord, I am just like a puppet in Your hands. So if You have brought me here to dance, then make me dance, make me dance, O Lord, make me dance as You like.

bhakti nāi beda nāi nāme khub daro
"bhaktivedānta" nām ebe sārthak koro

Translation: I have no devotion, nor do I have any knowledge, but I have strong faith in the holy name of Kṛṣṇa. I have been designated as Bhaktivedanta, and now, if You like, You can fulfill the real purport of Bhaktivedanta.

Signed—the most unfortunate,
insignificant beggar
A. C. Bhaktivedanta Swami,
on board the ship Jaladuta,
Commonwealth Pier,
Boston, Massachusetts, U.S.A.
dated 18th of September, 1965

Sanskrit Pronunciation Guide

The system of transliteration used in this book conforms to a system which scholars have accepted to indicate the pronunciation of each sound in the Sanskrit language.

The short vowel **a** is pronounced like the **u** in b**u**t, long **ā** like the **a** in f**a**r. Short **i** is pronounced as **i** in p**i**n, long **ī** as in piq**ue**, short **u** as in p**u**ll and long **ū** as in r**u**le. The vowel **ṛ** is pronounced like **ri** in **ri**m, **e** like the **ey** in th**ey**, **o** like the **o** in g**o**, **ai** like the **ai** in **ai**sle and **au** like the **ow** in h**ow**. The *anusvāra* (**ṁ**) is pronounced like the **n** in the French word *bo***n**, and *visarga* (**ḥ**) is pronounced as a final **h** sound. At the end of a couplet, **aḥ** is pronounced **aha** and **iḥ** is pronounced **ihi**.

The guttural consonants—**k, kh, g, gh** and **ṅ**—are pronounced from the throat in much the same manner as in English. **K** is pronounced as in **k**ite, **kh** as in Ec**kh**art, **g** as in **g**ive, **gh** as in di**g-h**ard and **ṅ** as in si**ng**.

The palatal consonants—**c, ch, j, jh** and **ñ**—are pronounced with the tongue touching the firm ridge behind the teeth. **C** is pronounced as in **ch**air, **ch** as in staun**ch-h**eart, **j** as in **j**oy, **jh** as in he**dgeh**og and **ñ** as in ca**ny**on.

The cerebral consonants—**ṭ, ṭh, ḍ, ḍh** and **ṇ**—are pronounced with the tip of the tongue turned up and drawn back against the dome of the palate. **Ṭ** is pronounced as in **t**ub, **ṭh** as in ligh**t-h**eart, **ḍ** as in **d**ove, **ḍh** as in re**d-h**ot and **ṇ** as in **n**ut.

The dental consonants—**t, th, d, dh** and **n**—are pronounced in the same manner as the cerebrals, but with the forepart of the tongue against the teeth.

The labial consonants—**p, ph, b, bh** and **m**—are pronounced with the lips. **P** is pronounced as in **p**ine, **ph** as in u**ph**ill, **b** as in **b**ird, **bh** as in ru**b-h**ard and **m** as in **m**other.

The semivowels—**y, r, l** and **v**—are pronounced as in **y**es, **r**un, **l**ight and **v**ine respectively. The sibilants—**ś, ṣ** and **s**—are pronounced, respectively, as in the German word **s***prechen* and the English words **sh**ine and **s**un. The letter **h** is pronounced as in **h**ome.

Glossary

A

Ācārya—one who teaches by example.

Ādi Gaṅgā—the original course of the Ganges, passing through Calcutta.

Advaita Ācārya—the older associate of Lord Caitanya Mahāprabhu who prayed that the Lord appear on earth.

Age of Kali—*See:* Kali-yuga.

Ajñānīs—persons in ignorance.

Ārati—a ceremony for worshiping the Deity of the Lord with offerings of lamps, fans, flowers, and incense.

Arjuna—the intimate devotee of Lord Kṛṣṇa who heard the teachings of *Bhagavad-gītā* from Him on the Battlefield of Kurukṣetra.

Ārya Samāj—a recent sect whose teachings are based exclusively on the four *Vedas,* rejecting all other Vedic scriptures.

Āśrama—a place of shelter conducive to the practice of spiritual life.

Aurobindo—a popular teacher who misled his followers with false interpretations of the *Vedas.*

Avatāra—an appearance of the Supreme Lord within this material world.

Ayurvedic medicine—a system of medicine based on the *Vedas.*

B

Bābājī—a renounced devotee who practices chanting Hare Kṛṣṇa in solitude.

Bābū—a respectable gentleman.

Baladeva—the first expansion of Lord Kṛṣṇa, appearing as His elder brother.

Balarāma—*See:* Baladeva.

Bastī—a slum.

Bhagavad-gītā—"Song of God"; the essential summary of spiritual knowledge spoken to Arjuna by the Supreme Lord, Śrī Kṛṣṇa.

Bhāgavata-dharma—the science of devotional service to the Supreme Lord (Bhagavān).

Bhāgavatam—*See: Śrīmad-Bhāgavatam.*

Bhāgavata-prasādam—*See: Prasādam.*

Bhajana-kuṭīr—a small hut in which a renounced devotee lives and practices his worship of the Lord.

Bhajanas—worship of God by the chanting of His holy names.

Bhakti—devotion to the Supreme Personality of Godhead.

Bhaktisiddhānta Sarasvatī Ṭhākura—the spiritual master of A.C. Bhaktivedanta Swami, Śrīla Prabhupāda.

Bhaktivedanta Swami—Śrīla Prabhupāda's title as a member of the renounced order of spiritual life.

Bhaktivinoda Ṭhākura—a great Kṛṣṇa conscious spiritual master in the chain of disciplic succession from Lord Caitanya.

Bhakti-yoga—devotional service as the means of linking up with the Supreme.

Bhubaneswar—a city sacred to Lord Śiva, near Jagannātha Purī.

Brahmacārī—a celibate monk; the first of the four *āśramas,* or spiritual orders of life.

Brāhma-muhūrta hour—an auspicious hour before sunrise.

Brahman—the Absolute Truth, the Supreme Spirit; especially the impersonal aspect of the Absolute.

Brāhmaṇa—an intelligent man who understands the spiritual purpose of life and can instruct others; the first Vedic social order, or *varṇa.*

Brahma-saṁhitā—a Vedic scripture describing Lord Kṛṣṇa, the Supreme Personality of Godhead.

Brahmin—*See: Brāhmaṇa.*

Braja Mandal—the sacred district that includes Vṛndāvana.

Buddha—an incarnation of the Supreme Lord who taught nonviolence.

C

Cādara—a blanket or cloth used to cover the upper part of the body.

Caitanya-bhāgavata—the authorized account of Lord Caitanya Mahāprabhu's early life, written by Vṛndāvana dāsa Ṭhākura.

Caitanya-caritāmṛta—the standard biography of Lord Caitanya Mahāprabhu, written by Kṛṣṇadāsa Kavirāja Gosvāmī.

Caitanya-līlā—the pastimes of Lord Caitanya Mahāprabhu.

Caitanya Mahāprabhu—the *avatāra* of Lord Kṛṣṇa in this age whose mission is to teach love of God through the chanting of His holy names.

Cakra—the wheel weapon of Lord Viṣṇu.

Capātīs—whole wheat flat breads.

Caste Gosvāmīs—those who presume the status of *gosvāmī* by birthright.

Chaitanya-bhagavata—*See: Caitanya-bhāgavata*

Chaitanya Mahaprabhu—*See:* Caitanya Mahāprabhu

Chandi Chowk—a street in Old Delhi.

Chawri Bazaar—a shopping street in Old Delhi.

Chāy—tea.

Chippiwada temple—a temple of Lord Kṛṣṇa in Old Delhi where Śrīla Prabhupāda maintained an office before coming to America.

Chutney—a spicy relish made of fruits, spices, and herbs.

D

Dacca—the present capital of Bangladesh, formerly part of Bengal.

Dāl—a spicy soup made from *dāl* beans.

Dāmodara—a name of Lord Kṛṣṇa.

Daṇḍa—the sacred staff carried by a person in the renounced order of life.

Daṇḍavats—prostrate obeisances.

Darśana—audience with a revered personality or a Deity.

Deity—the authorized form of the Lord worshiped in temples.

Delhi—the capital of India.

Demigods—powerful living beings who control natural forces under the direction of the Supreme Lord.

Devakī—the mother of Lord Kṛṣṇa.

Devanāgarī—the sacred script with which Sanskrit (as well as Hindi) is written.

Dhāma—an eternal abode of the Supreme Lord.

Dharma—eternal occupational duty; religious principles.

Dharmaśālā—an inexpensive residence set up especially for pilgrims.

Dhotī—the standard Indian men's garment, a simple piece of cloth wrapped around the lower body.

Dīkṣā—formal initiation into devotional life.

Durgā—the demigoddess who predominates over the Lord's material energy.

Dvārakā—the capital city of Lord Kṛṣṇa in His later pastimes as a great prince.

E

Ekādaśī—the eleventh day of the waning or waxing moon.

G

Gamchā—a short cloth wrapped around the lower part of the body.

Gāndharvikā—another name for Rādhā, Lord Kṛṣṇa's eternal consort.

Gaṇeśa—the son of Lord Śiva who is worshiped to remove material impediments.

Ganges—a sacred river in northern India.

Gañjā—marijuana.

Gaudiya Math—the mission established in India by Śrīla Bhaktisiddhānta Sarasvatī Ṭhākura for spreading Kṛṣṇa consciousness.

Gauḍīya Vaiṣṇava—a follower of Lord Kṛṣṇa (Viṣṇu) in the line of Lord Caitanya Mahāprabhu.

Gaurakiśora dāsa Bābājī—the initiating spiritual master of Śrīla Bhaktisiddhānta Sarasvatī Ṭhākura.

Gaurāṅga—a name for Lord Caitanya.

Gaurī-śaṅkara—a temple of Lord Śiva and his consort, Gaurī, in Old Delhi.

Gāyatrī—a *mantra* chanted three times daily by the *brāhmaṇas*.

Geetopanishad—*See: Bhagavad-gītā.*

Ghāṭas—bathing places on a holy river.

Ghee—clarified butter used as oil in cooking.

Giridhārī—a name for Lord Kṛṣṇa glorifying His pastime of lifting Govardhana Hill.

Gītā—*See: Bhagavad-gītā.*

Gītopaniṣad—*See: Bhagavad-gītā.*

Godbrother—a fellow disciple of the same spiritual master.

Gokula—the village in which Lord Kṛṣṇa spent part of His early childhood.

Goloka Vṛndāvana—the topmost planet in the spiritual sky; residence of Lord Kṛṣṇa.

Gopīs—the cowherd girls of Vṛndāvana, who are the most advanced and intimate devotees of Lord Kṛṣṇa.

Gosvāmī—one who has mastered his senses. *See also:* Six Gosvāmīs.

Goudiya Vaishnava—*See:* Gauḍīya Vaiṣṇava.

Gouranga—*See:* Gaurāṅga.

Govardhana—the sacred hill in the region of Vṛndāvana lifted by Lord Kṛṣṇa as a child.

Govinda—the Supreme Lord, Kṛṣṇa, proprietor of the senses of all living beings.

Gṛhastha—one who is practicing spiritual life while living with wife and children; the second *āśrama,* or spiritual order.

Gujarati—inhabitants of Gujarat, presently the westernmost province of India.

Guru—spiritual master.

Gurukula—the school of the spiritual master.

Guru Mahārāja—a form of respectful address to the *guru,* or spiritual master.

Gurv-aṣṭakam—the standard prayer to the Vaiṣṇava spiritual master, written by Viśvanātha Cakravartī Ṭhākura.

H

Haight-Ashbury—the hippie district of San Francisco in the late 1960s.

Halavā—a dessert made from toasted grains, butter, and sugar.

Hanumān—the monkey chieftain who became a great devotee of Lord Rāma.

Hare Kṛṣṇa—the holy names of the Lord. *See also: Mahā-mantra.*

Hari-bhakti-vilāsa—the Vaiṣṇava guide, written by Sanātana Gosvāmī.

Hari Bol—"Chant the names of Lord Hari!"

Haridāsa Ṭhākura—the great devotee of Lord Caitanya Mahāprabhu who, although born a Muhammadan, was designated *ācārya* of the holy name.

Hari-kathā—*See: Kṛṣṇa-kathā.*

Hari-kīrtana—glorification of Lord Hari (Kṛṣṇa) by chanting His names.

Hari-nāma—the holy name of the Supreme Lord.

Haṭha-yoga—the physical practice of postures and breathing exercises as a means toward controlling the senses.

I

Indraprastha—the ancient capital of the Pāṇḍavas, presently Old Delhi.

Initiation—the formal establishing of the connection between the spiritual master and disciple.

ISKCON—the International Society for Krishna Consciousness.

Iṣṭa-goṣṭhī—a meeting of devotees to discuss the instructions of their spiritual master.

J

Jagannātha—"Lord of the universe"; a special Deity of Lord Kṛṣṇa, originating in Orissa on the east coast of India at Purī.

Janmāṣṭamī—the birthday of Lord Kṛṣṇa.

Japa—measured chanting of the Lord's holy names.

Jāti-gosāi—*See:* Caste Gosvāmīs.

Jaya Rādhe—"Glories to Śrīmatī Rādhārāṇī!"

Jīva—the individual spirit soul, in contrast to the Supreme Soul, God.

Jñāna—the path of knowledge.

K

Kacaurī—a fried pastry.

Kali—the being who introduces the principles of sinful life in the Age of Quarrel.

Kālī—*See:* Durgā.

Kālī-pūjā—the worship of Kālī, or Durgā.

Kali-yuga—the present age of confusion and quarrel, which began five thousand years ago.

Kaṁsa—the demoniac king who made great efforts to kill young Lord Kṛṣṇa.

Kaṇṭhi-mālā—sacred beads worn around the neck of a devotee of Lord Kṛṣṇa.

Karatālas—sacred hand-cymbals.

Karma—fruitive action, for which there is always a reaction, good or bad.

Karma-yoga—the process of linking up with the Supreme by selflessly offering the fruits of one's work.

Kārttika—a lunar month of the autumn season.

Kasbā—the Muhammadan section of a village.

Kāśīnātha Miśra—an associate of Lord Caitanya.

Keśavajī Gaudiya Math—the temple in Mathurā where Śrīla Prabhupāda accepted the renounced order of spiritual life.

Keśī—a demon who took the form of a horse and was killed by Lord Kṛṣṇa in Vṛndāvana.

Keśī-ghāṭa—the sacred bathing place commemorating the killing of Keśī.

Khādī—homespun cotton.

Kicharī—a cooked preparation made from rice and lentils.

Kī jaya—an expression of acclaim.

Kīrtana—glorification of God, especially by the chanting of His holy names.

Krishna Loka—*See:* Kṛṣṇaloka.

Kṛṣṇa—the Supreme Personality of Godhead.

Kṛṣṇa-bhaktas—devotees of Lord Kṛṣṇa.

Kṛṣṇa-bhakti—*See: Bhakti.*

Kṛṣṇa-kathā—discussion of topics about the Supreme Lord.

Kṛṣṇa-līlā—the pastimes of Lord Kṛṣṇa.

Kṛṣṇa-nāma—the holy name of Lord Kṛṣṇa.

Kṣatriya—the administrative and protective occupation according to the system of social and spiritual orders.

Kumbha-melā—a sacred fair held once every twelve years at Prayāga.

Kurtā—an Indian men's shirt.

Kuśa grass—special grass used for making sanctified sitting mats.

L

Lakṣmī—the goddess of fortune and eternal consort of the Supreme Lord, Viṣṇu.

Lalitā—one of the female associates of Lord Kṛṣṇa's eternal consort, Rādhārāṇī.

Leela—*See: Līlā.*

Līlā—pastimes of the Supreme Lord.

Loṭā—a waterpot.

M

Mādhavendra Purī—the grand-spiritual-master of Lord Caitanya Mahāprabhu.

Madhva—the fifth *ācārya* in the Vaiṣṇava disciplic succession, who taught the philosophy of pure dualism.

Madhva-Gauḍīya Vaiṣṇava—*See:* Gauḍīya Vaiṣṇava.

Māgha-melā—a minor version of Kumbha-melā, held every year.

Mahābhārata—the great epic of ancient India that tells the story of the conflict between the Pāṇḍavas and Kurus and that includes the *Bhagavad-gītā.*

Mahā-mantra—the great chanting for deliverance: Hare Kṛṣṇa, Hare Kṛṣṇa, Kṛṣṇa Kṛṣṇa, Hare Hare/ Hare Rāma, Hare Rāma, Rāma Rāma, Hare Hare.

Mandira—a temple of the Supreme Lord.

Maṅgala-ārati—the first worship ceremony of the day, observed before sunrise.

Mantra—a sound vibration that liberates the mind.

Mantra-yoga—the process of self-realization by hearing and chanting the holy names of God.

Masālā—a standard mixture of spices, which can be of several varieties, used in Vedic cooking.

Maṭha—monastery.

Mathurā—the city where Lord Kṛṣṇa took birth, eight miles from Vṛndāvana.

Māyā—the illusory energy of the Supreme Personality of Godhead.

Māyāpur—the holy birthplace of Lord Caitanya Mahāprabhu, in Bengal.

Māyā-saṁsāra—*See: Saṁsāra.*

Māyāvāda—the impersonal philosophy of Śaṅkarācārya and his followers.

Māyāvādī—a follower of Māyāvāda philosophy.

Māyāvādīs—impersonalist philosophers who maintain that there is no difference between God and the living entity.

Miṣṭi—Indian sweets.

Mleccha—meat-eater.

Mound—an Indian weight approximately equal to six pounds.

Mṛdaṅga—a sacred drum, made of clay, used in *kīrtana.*

Mūrti—a cast or sculpted Deity form.

N

Naimiṣāraṇya—the holy forest, located at the exact center of the universe, where the assembly of sages headed by Śaunaka heard *Śrīmad-Bhāgavatam* from Sūta Gosvāmī.

Nāma—name.

Nāmācārya—Haridāsa Ṭhākura, the foremost teacher of the chanting of the holy names of the Lord.

Nanda Mahārāja—Kṛṣṇa's father in the village of Vṛndāvana.

Nārada Muni—the sage among the demigods, who is the son of Lord Brahmā and the spiritual master of Vyāsadeva.

Nārāyaṇa—the Supreme Lord in His majestic feature as Lord of the spiritual world.

Navadvīpa—the holy birthplace of Lord Caitanya Mahāprabhu, in Bengal.

Nimaka—a type of salty food.

Nityānanda—the chief associate of Lord Caitanya.

Nṛsiṁha(deva)—an incarnation of Kṛṣṇa as half-man, half-lion.

O

Oṁkara—the syllable *oṁ.*

P

Pān—an intoxicant.

Pañca-tattva—the Supreme Truth appearing as Lord Caitanya Mahāprabhu together with His four principal associates.

Paṇḍāl—a tent.

Pāṇḍavas—the five brothers—Yudhiṣṭhira, Bhīma, Arjuna, Nakula, and Sahadeva—who were opposed by Duryodhana in the Kurukṣetra war.

Paṇḍita—a scholar.

Paramahaṁsa—"the topmost swanlike person"; a self-realized personality.

Paramparā—the authorized line of disciplic succession.

Prabhu—master.

Prabhupāda—"the spiritual master at whose feet all others take shelter."

Prāṇa—the life air within the body.

Prasādam—food spiritualized by first being offered to the Supreme Lord for His enjoyment.

Pūjā—worship according to authorized ceremony.

Pūjārī—priest.

Purāṇas—historical Vedic literatures.

Purī—the abode of Lord Jagannātha in Orissa (on the east coast of India).

Purīs—puffy wheat breads fried in ghee.

R

Rādhā-Dāmodara—Jīva Gosvāmī's worshipable Deities, still present in Vṛndāvana.

Rādhā-Govinda—a Deity of Kṛṣṇa and His eternal consort, Rādhā.

Rādhā-kuṇḍa—"Rādhā's pond," the most holy place for Gauḍīya Vaiṣṇavas, located in the region of Vṛndāvana.

Rādhā-Mādhava—Rādhā and Kṛṣṇa.

Rādhā(rāṇī)—the eternal consort of Lord Kṛṣṇa and manifestation of His internal pleasure potency.

Rādhāṣṭamī—the appearance day of Rādhārāṇī, Kṛṣṇa's eternal consort.

Rāma(candra)—the incarnation of the Supreme Lord as the ideal king.

Ramakrishna—a teacher of impersonalist philosophy.

Rāmānanda Rāya—one of Lord Caitanya's intimate associates.

Rāmāyaṇa—the epic history of Lord Rāmacandra written by the sage Vālmīki.

Rāsa dance—Kṛṣṇa's pastime of dancing with the *gopīs*.

Rasagullā—a milk sweet made from curd soaked in sweet water.

Rasaleela—*See: Rāsa-līlā.*
Rāsa-līlā—Kṛṣṇa's pastime of dancing with the *gopīs.*
Ratha-yātrā—the annual cart festival of Lord Jagannātha.
Ricksha—a cart pulled by a man.
Rudra—Lord Śiva.
Rudrākṣa beads—chanting beads used by devotees of Rudra (Lord Śiva).
Rūpa Gosvāmī—*See:* Six Gosvāmīs.

S

Sabjī—cooked vegetables.
Sādhu—a saintly person.
Saffron robes—orange-colored robes worn by celibate men in the spiritual orders of life.
Śahnāī—an oboelike musical instrument.
Śaivite—a worshiper of the demigod Śiva.
Śālagrāma—a special Deity of the Supreme Lord in the form of a round stone.
Samādhi—yogic trance.
Samosā—a fried pastry, stuffed with spiced vegetables.
Sampradāya—*See: Paramparā*
Saṁsāra—the cycle of repeated birth and death.
Sanātana-dharma—the eternal religion, to render service to the Supreme Lord.
Sanātana Gosvāmī—*See: Six Gosvāmīs.*
Sandeśa—a sweet prepared from milk curd.
Sandhyā-ārati—the evening worship ceremony.
Śaṅkarācārya—the influential ninth century teacher of monism, a philosophy which maintains that there is no distinction between God and the living entities.
Saṅkīrtana—congregational chanting of the holy names of the Lord, the recommended process of *yoga* for this age.
Sannyāsa—the renounced order of life; the fourth *āśrama,* or spiritual order, of Vedic society.
Sannyāsa-daṇḍa—the sacred staff carried by a person in the renounced order of life.
Sannyāsa-guru—the spiritual master who initiates a devotee into the renounced order of life.

Sannyāsī—one in the *sannyāsa* order.
Sari—the standard woman's garment in Indian society.
Sārvabhauma—an associate of Lord Caitanya.
Śāstra—scripture.
Śāstrī—an authority on Vedic scriptures.
Ṣaṭ-sandarbha—an authoritative, topically arranged commentary on *Śrīmad-Bhāgavatam* by Jīva Gosvāmī.
Śeṣaśāyī Viṣṇu—a Deity form of Lord Viṣṇu lying on the many-headed serpent Ananta Śeṣa.
Śikhā—the tuft of hair remaining on the back of the shaven head of a Vaiṣṇava.
Six Gosvāmīs—Rūpa, Sanātana, Raghunātha dāsa, Raghunātha Bhaṭṭa, Gopāla Bhaṭṭa, and Jīva Gosvāmī; the followers of Lord Caitanya Mahāprabhu who established devotional service as a scientific process for God realization in the modern age.
Smārta—a ritualistic follower of the *Vedas.*
Śrāddha—the Vedic sacrifice performed for departed parents to ensure their good fortune in the next life.
Śrī—a form of respectful address indicating great beauty and opulence.
Śrīla—a form of respectful address.
Śrīla Bhaktisiddhānta Sarasvatī—the spiritual master of His Divine Grace A.C. Bhaktivedanta Swami Prabhupāda.
Śrīmad-Bhāgavatam—a scripture of eighteen thousand verses in twelve cantos which is one of the eighteen *Purāṇas* (Vedic histories) and advocates and establishes pure devotional service to the Supreme Lord exclusively.
Subhadrā—the younger sister of Lord Kṛṣṇa and personification of His spiritual potency.
Śūdra—a laborer; the fourth *varṇa,* or social order, which is compared to the legs of society.
Śukadeva Gosvāmī—the great sage who originally spoke the *Śrīmad-Bhāgavatam.*
Suvarṇa-vaṇik—a gold merchant.
Swami—*See: Gosvāmī.*
Swamiji—familiar form of *swami.*
Syāma-kuṇḍa—"Lord Kṛṣṇa's pond," a very sacred place next to Rādhā-kuṇḍa.

T

Taj Express—train running from Delhi to Agra.

Tāṅgā—a horse-drawn cart.

Tiffin—a stacked set of metal food containers.

Tilaka—sacred clay marking the body of a devotee as a temple of God.

Tompkins Square Park—a park on Manhattan's Lower East Side.

Tridaṇḍi-sannyāsa—the renounced order of life as practiced by Vaiṣṇavas, contrasted to the *ekadaṇḍa-sannyāsa* of the impersonalists.

Tulasī—the plant most sacred to Lord Viṣṇu.

Tulasī-mālā—chanting beads made of sacred *tulasī* wood.

V

Vaikuṇṭha—"place of no anxiety"; the spiritual sky, the eternal abode of Lord Viṣṇu.

Vaiṣṇava(s)—a devotee of the Supreme Lord Viṣṇu (Kṛṣṇa).

Vānaprastha—retirement from active family life, the third spiritual order, wherein one makes pilgrimage to holy places, prior to *sannyāsa.*

Vedāṅgas—supplements to the original *Vedas.*

Vedānta-sūtra—the summary of all Vedic conclusions, written in short aphorisms by Vyāsadeva.

Vedas—the four original texts first spoken by the Lord Himself and their supplements, compiled by Śrīla Vyāsadeva.

Vedic—based on the *Vedas.*

Vigraha—the authorized Deity form of the Lord.

Vishnu—*See:* Viṣṇu.

Viṣṇu—the Supreme Lord, Kṛṣṇa, appearing in His majestic four-armed form.

Viśvarūpa—the older brother of Lord Caitanya Mahāprabhu.

Vivekananda—a teacher of impersonalist philosophy.

Vraja—*See:* Vṛndāvana.

Vrindaban Behary—a name of Kṛṣṇa as the enjoyer of pastimes in Vṛndāvana.

Vrindaban Bihar—*See:* Vrindaban Behary.

Vṛndāvana—the personal abode of Lord Kṛṣṇa, the inhabitants of which are all His intimate servants.

Vṛndāvana-candra—the "moon of Vṛndāvana," Lord Kṛṣṇa.
Vṛṣṇi—the family in which Lord Kṛṣṇa appeared.
Vyāsadeva—the great sage who compiled all the Vedic literatures at the beginning of this age, five thousand years ago.
Vyāsa-pūjā—the observance of the appearance day of one's spiritual master, who is worshiped as the representative of Vyāsadeva.
Vyāsāsana—the honored seat of the spiritual master.

Y

Yadu—the ancient king in whose family Lord Kṛṣṇa appeared.
Yamunā River—sacred river flowing through Vṛndāvana.
Yaśodā—the mother of Lord Kṛṣṇa in Vṛndāvana.
Yoga—any of various spiritual disciplines meant for purification and ultimate realization of one's position as servant of God.
Yogī—a *yoga* practitioner.

General Index

References to Śrila Prabhupāda in this volume can be found under three headings: "Abhay Charan De," for references to him as a child and a young man, "Bhaktivedanta Swami," for references to him later in life, after he entered the renounced order, and "Prabhupada, Srila," for references to him after he arrived in America.

References to initiated devotees may also appear under multiple headings, one referring to them by their legal name, before initiation, and another bytheir post-initiation name.

A

Abbey Road, recording studios on, 790
Abhay Charan De
  See also: Abhay Charan De cited; ... quoted; Bhaktivedanta Swami; Prabhupāda, Śrīla
  Abdullah &, 94
  Ācārya Prabhākar &, 151–54, 164, 200–202
  as Advaita Ācārya in play, 21
  advertisement by, for *Gītā* classes, 175
  Agarwal (R. N.) &, 174
  agnosticism challenged by, 97–98
  in Agra, 51
  in Allahabad, 47–49, 52, 77, 133, 151
  Amrita Bazar quoted by, 130–31
  Amritlal Bose &, 20–21
  Anandesvar Satsang Mandal &, 203
  Anthony Eden quoted by, on war, 106
  "An Appeal to the Generous Public" by, 202
  aravinda added to name of, 70
  Archbishop of India quoted by, 105
  articles by. *See: Back to Godhead,* articles in
  astrology of, 2, 27, 47, 76
  atheists opposed by, 184–86
  Atulānanda Brahmacārī &, 53–54, 67
  as author (books listed), 172
    See also: Abhay, *Back to Godhead...*
  Baba, Hari, &, 173
  Back to Godhead
    in New Delhi, 176, 180, 181, 183, 184, 185–86, 187
    in tea stalls, 181, 183
    in Vṛndāvana, 197
    founded by, 104
    mailed by, 183, 186, 204
    printed by, 104, 113, 137, 138, 175–87, 200, 211
    written by. *See: Back to Godhead,* articles in
  Badshahi Mundi residence of, 48
  Bahadur (Narain Dass Rai) endorses, 173
  Bengal Chemical offers position to, 76
  Bengal Company as agent of, 93

Abhay Charan De (*continued*)
  beriberi contracted by, 18
  Bhagavad-gītā classes advertised by, 175
  Bhagavad-gītā commentary by. *See:* Abhay, *Geetopanishad* by; *Geetopanishad*; *Bhagavad-gītā As It Is*
  Bhagavad-gītā recited by, in school, 20
  Bhagwat Week opposed by, 205–6
  Bhaktipradīpa Swami &, 53, 83
  Bhakti-rasāmṛta-sindhu, ordered to study, 70
  in Bhaktisāraṅga *āśrama,* 166–72
  Bhaktisāraṅga meets, for first time, 78
  Bhaktisāraṅga's letters to, 167–68, 170
  Bhaktisiddhānta
    affectionate to, 72
    chastises, 72
    debates with, 37–38, 129
    dreamt of by, 113, 134, 216
    encourages separateness from *maṭha* for, 86, 97
    gives gift to son of, 87
    initiates, 69–70
    instructs, 37, 88, 89, 134, 216
    meets, 37–41
    orders *sannyāsa* initiation for, 134, 189, 219
    praises, 69, 83, 190
    predicts activities of, 86
    remembered by, during business life, 49
    visited by, in Vṛndāvana, 86–88
    warns, of trouble in Gaudiya Math, 88
    writes to, 59, 89
    written to by, 89
  Bhaktisiddhānta's appearance day observed by, 79–83
  Bhaktisiddhānta's disappearance day observed by, 212–15
  Bhaktisiddhānta's disappearance, reaction to, 90
  in Bhaktisiddhānta's *parikrama,* 62–64
  "Bhaktivedanta" added to name of, 99, 103
  as Bhaktivedanta Swami. *See:* Bhaktivedanta Swami

C

D

G

H

I

J

Kīrtanānanda dāsa (*continued*)
letters to, by Prabhupāda. *See:* Prabhupāda, letters by ...
in London, 717
in Long Branch, 688, 690, 691
"Love Feast" named by, 517
at Love-Pageant-Rally *kīrtana,* 499
at Mantra-Rock Dance, 559, 560–61
in Montreal, 669
in Moscow, 718
in New York, 670, 671, 672, 674–75, 683–84
Prabhupāda &. *See:* Prabhupāda, Kīrtanānanda dāsa &
prasādam served by, 490
quoted. *See:* Kīrtanānanda dāsa quoted
robes worn by, 481, 487
sannyāsa awarded to, 725
shaven-headed, 481, 499
at Stinson Beach house, 698–99, 704, 705–6
tamboura played by, at recording studio, 530
in Tompkins Square Park, 487
in Vṛndāvana, 721–29
See also: Keith; Kīrtanānanda Swami
Kīrtanānanda dāsa cited
See also: Kīrtanānanda dāsa quoted
on devotee & suffering, 684
on serving Prabhupāda, 684
Kīrtanānanda dāsa quoted
See also: Kīrtanānanda dāsa cited
on hearing *Caitanya-caritāmṛta,* 537
on Prabhupāda, 496
on Prabhupāda's illness, 671, 672
on strictness, 574
Kīrtanānanda Swami
at Boston arrival of Prabhupāda, 837–40
in Calcutta, 892
as cook for Prabhupāda, 773, 868
in Detroit, 987
at Logan Airport, 837
in Los Angeles, 860
in New Vrindaban, 772–75
in New York, 993
Prabhupāda &. *See:* Prabhupāda, Kīrtanānanda Swami &
in Tokyo, 868–69
See also: Keith; Kīrtanānanda dāsa
Kittapur port, 102
Kleśo 'dhikataras teṣām
verse quoted, 640
Knowledge
biologist &, 995
transcendental, 333, 361, 423, 501
Koran, 123, 310, 538
Korea, eating habits in, 517
Koslofsky, Judy. *See:* Judy Koslofsky
Kotovsky, Professor
bodily concept of life &, 973, 987
cited on revolution, 975
position of, at U.S.S.R. Academy of Sciences, 968
Kotovsky, Professor (*continued*)
Prabhupāda's conversation with, 970–75, 978
quoted. *See:* Kotovsky, Professor, quoted
socialist views of, 972–73
Kotovsky, Professor, quoted
on body & death, 973
on surrender, 974
on Vedic literature in Russia, 971
Kripalini, Acharya, 124
"Krishna Chants Startle London" article, 778
Krishna Charan, 49
Krishna Niketan, as Prabhupāda's residence, 935
Krishna Pandit, Sri
as Chippiwada temple's manager, 730–31
letter to Prabhupāda by, 690
Prabhupāda &. *See:* Prabhupāda, Krishna Pandit &
quoted on Prabhupāda's daily routine, 233
Kṛpā-siddha defined, 855
Kṛpāsindhu, 208
Kṛṣṇa, Lord
Abhay never forgetful of, 40
abode of
Vṛndāvana as, 191, 195
See also: Vṛndāvana
as Absolute Truth, 819
activity done for, 414
advent of, 1
as all-attractive, 809
Aniruddha &, 707
appearance day of. *See:* Janmāṣṭamī
Arjuna &, 329, 332, 358, 359, 393, 395, 409, 559
as authority, 404, 799
Balarāma expansion of, 1026
as basis of impersonal Brahman, 789
Bhagavad-gītā's description of, 907
as *Bhagavad-gītā's* speaker, 97, 201, 749
Bhāgavatam incarnation of, 205
birthplace of, 193
blasphemy against, 908
boar incarnation of, 1024
Brahmā bewildered by, 938
as butter thief, 613, 694
as Caitanya. *See:* Caitanya Mahāprabhu
Caitanya teaches love for, 351, 536, 543
chanting name of. *See:* Chanting Hare Kṛṣṇa
cited. *See:* Kṛṣṇa, Lord, cited
consciousness expansion via, 467, 497
as cowherd boy, 938
as dancing on tongue of chanter, 936
Deity of. *See:* Deities of Supreme Lord
demons killed by, 938
depending on, 372
Devakī mother of, 707
devotees of. *See:* Devotees; *specific devotees*
devotional service to. *See: Bhakti;* Devotional service; Kṛṣṇa consciousness; *specific services*

L

M

N

O

P

T

U

V

Y

Z

Books by His Divine Grace A.C. Bhaktivedanta Swami Prabhupāda

Bhagavad-gītā As It Is
Śrīmad-Bhāgavatam (multiple volumes; with disciples)
Śrī Caitanya-caritāmṛta
Kṛṣṇa, The Supreme Personality of Godhead
Teachings of Lord Caitanya
The Nectar of Devotion
The Nectar of Instruction
Śrī Īśopaniṣad
The Light of the Bhāgavata
Easy Journey to Other Planets
Teachings of Lord Kapila, the Son of Devahūti
Teachings of Queen Kuntī
Message of Godhead
The Science of Self-Realization
The Perfection of Yoga
Beyond Birth and Death
On the Way to Kṛṣṇa
Rāja-vidyā: The King of Knowledge
Elevation to Kṛṣṇa Consciousness
Kṛṣṇa Consciousness: The Matchless Gift
Kṛṣṇa Consciousness: The Topmost Yoga System
Perfect Questions, Perfect Answers
Life Comes From Life
Geetar-gan (Bengali)
Buddhi-yoga (Bengali)
Bhakti-ratna-boli (Bengali)
Back to Godhead magazine (founder)

Books compiled and edited after Śrīla Prabhupāda's lifetime

The Journey of Self-Discovery
Civilization and Transcendence
The Laws of Nature
Renunciation Through Wisdom
Beyond Illusion and Doubt
Dharma, The Way of Transcendence
The Quest for Enlightenment

ONE WAY